The University of Chicago Spanish Dictionary
Student Edition

Universidad de Chicago Diccionario Español–Inglés,
Inglés–Español
Edición Escolar

Universidad de Chicago Diccionario Español–Inglés, Inglés–Español
Edición Escolar

Compilación original de Carlos Castillo y Otto F. Bond

QUINTA EDICIÓN

David Pharies
Director

María Irene Moyna
Redactora Adjunta

Gary K. Baker
Asistente de Dirección

Erica Fischer Dorantes
Ayudante de Dirección

POCKET BOOKS
NEW YORK   LONDON   TORONTO   SYDNEY

The University of Chicago Spanish Dictionary
Spanish–English • English–Spanish
Student Edition

Originally Compiled by Carlos Castillo and Otto F. Bond

FIFTH EDITION

David Pharies
Editor in Chief

María Irene Moyna
Associate Editor

Gary K. Baker
Assistant Editor

Erica Fischer Dorantes
Editorial Assistant

POCKET BOOKS
NEW YORK   LONDON   TORONTO   SYDNEY

POCKET BOOKS, a division of Simon & Schuster, Inc.
1230 Avenue of the Americas, New York, NY 10020

ISBN-13: 978-0-7434-9252-2
ISBN-10:   0-7434-9252-8

First Pocket Books printing December 2003

10   9   8   7   6   5

POCKET and colophon are registered trademarks of
Simon & Schuster, Inc.

Manufactured in the United States of America

For information regarding special discounts for bulk purchases,
please contact Simon & Schuster Special Sales at 1-800-456-6798
or business@simonandschuster.com.

Contents

Preface to the Fifth Edition   vi

Preámbulo a la quinta edición   viii

How to Use *The University of Chicago Spanish Dictionary*   x

Cómo usar el *Universidad de Chicago Diccionario Español–Inglés, Inglés–Español*   xiv

Spanish–English · Español–Inglés

List of Abbreviations   1

Spanish Pronunciation   2

Notes on Spanish Grammar   6

Common Spanish Suffixes   8

Spanish Regular Verbs   10

Spanish Irregular and Orthographic Changing Verbs   11

Spanish–English Dictionary, A–Z   23

Inglés–Español · English–Spanish

Lista de abreviaturas   273

Pronunciación inglesa   274

Notas sobre gramática inglesa   275

Sufijos comunes del inglés   277

Verbos irregulares de la lengua inglesa   280

Diccionario inglés–español, A–Z   285

Preface to the Fifth Edition

The University of Chicago Spanish Dictionary has been compiled for the general use of the American English-speaking learner of Spanish and the Spanish-speaking learner of American English.

With this purpose in mind, the editors of the fifth edition have introduced a number of significant improvements. One of the most important changes is the addition of many new words and meanings in order to bring the dictionary up to date with the latest technical advancements and cultural changes. Especially significant are additions in the fields of medicine (*anorexia, antioxidant, clone, defibrillate, gene splicing, HIV, hypoglycemia, liposuction, mammography, melanoma, metastasis, progesterone, scoliosis*), electronics (*CD, fax, magnetic resonance imaging, microwave, satellite dish*), computers (*browser, cache, chat room, megabyte, on-line, scanner, search engine, URL, website*), and science and technology (*entropy, genome, nanosecond, polyurethane, pulsar, smart bomb*). Recent cultural phenomena are captured in items such as *bungee jumping, e-commerce, mountain bike, politically correct, pro-life, sexual harassment*, and *surrogate mother*, as well as in slang terms such as *bigtime, ditsy, hype*, and *no-brainer*. In order to provide the most up-to-date picture of the language, many obsolescent or obsolete terms have been eliminated, such as *aught, ere, forenoon, fortnight, kerchief, knave, morrow*, and *o'er*.

Another significant improvement in the fifth edition is the consistent use of parenthetical words meant to guide the choice of equivalents from a series. For example, among the various equivalents of *soft*, the user is advised to choose *blando* to apply to butter, *suave* to apply to skin, and *tenue* to apply to light. Similarly, users are enabled by these parenthetical words to choose appropriate equivalents for *sheet* according to whether reference is being made to a sheet of paper (*hoja*), of ice (*capa*), of glass (*lámina*), or to a bed covering (*sábana*).

A change that will enhance the usability of the dictionary is the integration into the entries themselves of material that was formerly presented in charts and lists, such as idioms, proverbs, names of nations, and cardinal and ordinal numbers.

The amount and quality of grammatical information has been expanded. For the first time, gender markings for Spanish noun equivalents are provided on the English–Spanish side, thus freeing users from having to seek this information on the Spanish–English side. Additionally, transitive and intransitive verbal meanings are distinguished.

The frequent references to regional usage characteristic of the fourth edition have been de-emphasized here, partly for reasons of space, partly because of the notorious unreliability of the available information on regional dialects. In the present edition, such information is provided only where a word of more general currency might not be understood (see the various equivalents of Eng. *bean*) or where the word is universally recognized as being characteristic of a given dialect (see Sp. *che, cuate*).

Acknowledgments

The Editor in Chief and the University of Chicago Press wish to acknowledge with thanks the contributions to early project planning made by the following Advisory Board, all from the University of Chicago: Paolo Cherchi, Gene B. Gragg, Eric P. Hamp, Salikoko Mufwene, and Michael Silverstein.

Preámbulo a la quinta edición

Este libro se ha compilado para el uso general del anglohablante estadounidense que estudia español y para el hispanohablante que estudia el inglés americano.

Con este propósito, los editores de la presente edición han incorporado una cantidad sustancial de mejoras. Uno de los cambios más importantes es la adición de muchos términos y significados nuevos que han puesto el diccionario al día con los avances tecnológicos y las transformaciones culturales. De especial importancia son las incorporaciones en los campos de la medicina (*anorexia, antioxidante, clon, desfibrilar, empalme genético, escoliosis, hipoglucemia, VIH, liposucción, mamografía, melanoma, metástasis, progesterona*), la electrónica (*CD, fax, imagen por resonancia magnética, microondas, parabólica, píxel*), la informática (*bit, caché, en línea, escáner, megabyte, motor de búsqueda, navegador, protector de tensión, sitio web, URL*) y la ciencia y la tecnología (*bomba inteligente, entropía, genoma, nanosegundo, púlsar, poliuretano*). Los recientes fenómenos culturales se ven reflejados en términos tales como *antiaborto, bicicleta de montaña, lifting, limpieza étnica, madre de alquiler, políticamente correcto,* y *puénting* además de palabras familiares, tales como *chute, coca, curro, mala leche, truja*. Al mismo tiempo, para captar la lengua en su forma más actualizada se han eliminado muchas palabras arcaicas o caídas en desuso como *acullá, albéitar, asaz, luengo* y *postrer*.

Otra mejora considerable de la quinta edición es el uso sistemático de indicadores semánticos, que van entre paréntesis y cuyo objetivo es guiar en la elección del equivalente apropiado a partir de una serie de posibilidades. Por ejemplo, entre los diferentes equivalentes de *destino*, se advierte al usuario que opte por *fate* cuando significa 'hado', por *destination* cuando significa 'lugar adonde se viaja' y por *use* cuando significa 'uso'. Del mismo modo, la presencia de estos indicadores semánticos posibilita al usuario elegir con certeza entre los equivalentes de *calmar* según se hable de los nervios (*to calm*), dolor (*to soothe*), miedo (*to allay, to quell*) o sed (*to quench*).

Otro cambio que sin duda facilitará el empleo del diccionario es la integración, en el cuerpo del mismo, de material que en ediciones anteriores se presentaba en forma de cuadros y listas, tal como expresiones idiomáticas, refranes, nombres de países y números cardinales y ordinales.

También se ha incrementado la cantidad y calidad de la información gramatical. Por primera vez se proporcionan las marcas de género gramatical para los sustantivos en la sección inglés–español, lo cual elimina la necesidad de consultar la sección español–inglés para obtener esta información. Además, se distinguen los significados verbales transitivos e intransitivos.

En comparación con la edición anterior, la nueva insiste mucho menos en las diferencias dialectales en el vocabulario del español, en parte por razones de espacio y en parte porque la información disponible sobre este aspecto del vocabulario es incompleta y poco fidedigna. En la presente edición las referencias al léxico regional se limitan a unos cuantos tipos de términos, concretamente, aquellos que pueden resultar desconocidos en una determinada comunidad lingüística (como los muchos equivalentes españoles del ingl. *bean*) y aquellos que son universalmente reconocidos como típicos de un dialecto dado (ver *che*, *cuate*).

Agradecimiento

El Director y la Editorial de la Universidad de Chicago desean expresar su gratitud por las contribuciones a la planificación de la obra hechas por los miembros del Consejo Editorial, concretamente por Paolo Cherchi, Gene B. Gragg, Eric P. Hamp, Salikoko Mufwene y Michael Silverstein.

How to Use *The University of Chicago Spanish Dictionary*

Order of Entries

Alphabetical order is observed irrespective of hyphens or spaces, such that *air conditioner* precedes *aircraft* and *middle school* precedes *middle-sized*. Homographs are placed under a single entry (*lie* 'to prevaricate', *lie* 'to recline', both pronounced [laɪ]), with different pronunciations if applicable (e.g., *bow* [baʊ] 'forward end of a vessel', *bow* [bo] 'bend, curve'). Regarding Spanish, according to the current policy of the Spanish Royal Academy,[1] *ch* and *ll* are no longer recognized as separate letters, such that *ch* now follows *ce* and precedes *ci*, and *ll* follows *li* and precedes *lo* in alphabetization.

Compounds listed within entries are also alphabetized. However, the need to list compounds under their first element sometimes interferes with alphabetization, as when *slumlord*, a compound listed under *slum*, comes before the next headword, *slumber*, even though strict alphabetization would require the reverse.

Spelling

Spelling of English words reflects common American usage, variants being noted where applicable (*ax, axe; sulphur, sulfur; stymie, stymy*). The spelling of Spanish words, where possible, follows the conventions of the Spanish Royal Academy. For the orthography of problematic Spanish words such as recent borrowings (*escáner, scooter*), country names (*Malí, Irak*) and adjectives of nationality (*zimbabuo*), a variety of authorities were consulted, including the *Diccionario del español actual*, the *Diccionario de dudas*, the *Libro de estilo* published by the Madrid newspaper *El País*, and various Internet sources.[2] It should be noted that there is vacillation in some cases, cf. *Bahrain*, which is listed as *Bahrein* in the *Libro de estilo* and as *Bahráin* or *Bahréin* in the *Diccionario de dudas*. In these cases, we either opt for the form that appears to be most generally accepted or provide multiple equivalents.

---

1. Real Academia Española, *Ortografía de la lengua española* (Madrid: Espasa-Calpe, 1999), p. 2.

2. Manuel Seco, Olimpia Andrés, and Gabino Ramos, *Diccionario del español actual* (Madrid: Aguilar, 1999); Manuel Seco, *Diccionario de dudas y dificultades de la lengua española*, 10th ed. (Madrid: Espasa-Calpe, 1998), *El País: Libro de estilo*, 9th ed. (Madrid: Ediciones El País, 1990).

Omissions

Some categories of words are systematically omitted from the vocabulary entries. First, irregular English past tense and participial forms (e.g., *drunk*, *smitten*), formerly included among the entries, have been removed and are presented instead in a verb table (p. 282). Second, adverbial forms in *-ly* (English) and *-mente* (Spanish) are included only when their usage and meaning are not transparently derivable from their adjectival bases. Thus, *clearly* is omitted, as its usage is predictable from its adjectival base ('in a clear way'), while *surely* is included, since it means, in addition to 'in a sure way', also 'undoubtedly' or 'without fail'. Similarly, *claramente* 'clearly' is omitted, while *atentamente* is retained, since the latter, in addition to meaning 'in an attentive manner', is also used as a farewell, equivalent to 'yours truly'. Third, English nouns in *-ing* and adjectives in *-ed*, which may appear as glosses of Spanish words, are not always accorded separate entries on the English–Spanish side, due to their derivational regularity and to considerations of space.

Structure of Entries

1. HEADWORD. Spelling variants, if any, follow the most frequent form, which appears first. In Spanish, occupational designations, titles, and kinship terms are shown in both masculine and feminine forms, as in *abogado -da*.
2. PRONUNCIATION. Pronunciation of English words is indicated through a modified version of the International Phonetic Alphabet, whose conventions are explained on p. 276. No individual transcription of Spanish words is required, given the simplicity and consistency of the Spanish orthographic system. See "The Spanish Spelling System and the Sounds Represented" (p. 2) for an explanation.
3. GRAMMATICAL CATEGORY. Meanings are marked according to whether they reflect usage as a noun (*n*), adjective (*adj*), adverb (*adv*), conjunction (*conj*), preposition (*prep*), pronoun (*pron*), interjection (*interj*), transitive verb (*vt*), or intransitive verb (*vi*). The exception to this rule is that nouns on the Spanish–English side are marked only by gender, i.e., *m* (masculine noun) or *f* (feminine noun).

    Order of meanings within an entry reflects frequency of usage. Where more than one grammatical category can be rendered by the same gloss, the two are listed together, cf. Eng. *red*, which can be glossed as Sp. *rojo* in both its adjective and noun meanings.

    Traditionally, Spanish adjectives are listed in their masculine form only. However, where the adjective normally functions as a noun as well, it is shown with both masculine and feminine forms if both are possible, cf. the case of *africano -na*, which can mean *African* in the adjectival sense as well as *African (man)* and *African (woman)*.

    Special mention must be made of the combination "vi/vt." Occasionally, a single verb form may function both transitively and intransitively, e.g., both *to eat* and its Spanish equivalent *comer*. Not infrequently, however, Spanish glosses of English intransitives require the addition of the pronominal particle *-se*. Thus, in cases such as *to bathe*, marked "vi/vt" and glossed *bañar(se)*, it should be understood that the bare form is transitive, and the *-se* form intransitive. Finally, where transitivity differs between a headword and its equivalent in the second language, particles must be added to reflect this, as in the case of the transitive English verb *to regret*, which is glossed in Spanish as *arrepentirse de*, since *arrepentirse* alone is intransitive. Where an English verb can be used both transitively and intransitively and its Spanish equivalent is only intransitive, the latter may sometimes be made transitive through the addition of a preposition, which appears in parentheses. Thus, English *fight* is glossed as *pelear (con)* to show that its intransitive equivalent is *pelear*, whereas its transitive equivalent is *pelear con*.

Again for reasons of economy, pronominal forms of Spanish verbs are omitted in two cases: First, when the particle *-se* functions as a direct object, either reflexive or reciprocal, cf. *mirarse*, which can mean both *to look at oneself*, and *to look at each other*, and second, when the addition of *-se* does not affect the English translation, cf. *bañar(se)*, glossed in both meanings as *to bathe*. In contrast, pronominal forms of verbs are included when they differ substantially in meaning from the bare forms, cf. *ir*, glossed as *to go*, vs. *irse*, which means *to leave*.

4.   DELIMITERS.   Whenever a word, within a grammatical category, is considered to have two or more meanings, these are differentiated by means of delimiters, that is, explanatory markers. Most commonly, synonyms are used, cf. *retort*, which in the meaning 'reply' is glossed as *réplica* and in the meaning 'vessel' as *retorta*, though on occasion other strategies may be adopted. Thus, transitive verbs are sometimes best differentiated according to the objects they take, cf. *to negotiate* (a contract), which is glossed *negociar*, while *to negotiate* (an obstacle) is glossed *salvar*. Similarly, adjectives may be most easily distinguished by showing the referents to which they regularly apply, cf. *refreshing*, which applied to drink is *refrescante*, to sleep is *reparador*, and to honesty is *amable*. Not infrequently, a single equivalent covers almost all meanings of a headword in a single grammatical category. In such cases, only the "exceptional" meaning, placed second, is delimited. For example, the equivalent of Eng. *net* in almost all its meanings is Sp. *red*, though when it refers specifically to a hairnet it is *redecilla*. Although delimiters typically precede the gloss they are meant to distinguish, occasionally they are placed afterward. In these cases they are meant to erase doubts about the applicability of a given gloss in a specific secondary context, cf. *site*, whose gloss *sitio* is followed by the delimiter "also Internet."

5.   GLOSSES.   Insofar as is possible, glosses are intended to match the headword in terms of meaning, register, and frequency. Thus, *cop* is glossed as *poli* rather than the more formal *policía*. Similarly, *orinar* is glossed as *to urinate* rather than the informal *to pee*. Glosses separated by a comma are to be considered interchangeable, if not perfectly synonymous. Semicolons, on the other hand, indicate separate meanings.

6.   REGIONAL USAGE.   No systematic attempt has been made to reflect regional usage in either English or Spanish, since in the great majority of cases a word of more general currency is available as a gloss. Thus, among the many Spanish equivalents of Eng. *peasant*, Sp. *campesino* is understood everywhere, even where a local term also exists, such as Puerto Rican *jíbaro*, Cuban *guajiro*, and Chilean *guaso*. However, Spanish regional usage is marked where either of the following conditions are met: (1) there is no term of international currency, or it might not be understood in a given location (cf. the various regional Spanish equivalents of Eng. *bean*), or (2) a specific regionalism is known throughout the Spanish-

speaking world to be typical of a given dialect, cf. River Plate *che*, Mexican *ándale*, *cuate*.

7. STYLISTIC MARKERS. Because, as mentioned earlier, equivalents are chosen in order to match headwords in all aspects of their meaning, including register and frequency, stylistic markers are only infrequently employed. For example, there is no need to mark the Spanish gloss *tonto* as familiar, since it is meant to be equivalent to the equally familiar Eng. *fool*. Only five register markers are employed: literary (*lit*), which also includes poetic and formal language, familiar (*fam*), which designates words used among family and friends, vulgar (*vulg*), for words whose use is socially censured, pejorative (*pej*), which implies a negative evaluation, and *offensive* (not abbreviated), for words meant to insult people.

8. COMPOUNDS. Ease of usage would dictate that each lexical item receive its own entry, but for reasons of economy this is not possible in a concise dictionary. This explains why compound words, which are composed of two or more preexisting words, are listed in almost all cases under the entry of their initial constituent, at the end of the corresponding grammatical category. Thus, *doghouse* is listed as —*house*, under *dog*. There are certain exceptions to this convention, however. First, compounds are listed under the headword of their second constituent when the first is extremely frequent, as are the so-called empty verbs such as Eng. *keep*, *take*, *turn*, Sp. *hacer*, *tener*, *tomar*. Thus, *to have a good time*, glossed *divertirse*, is listed under *time* rather than *have*, and *tener paciencia*, glossed *to be patient*, is under *paciencia* rather than *tener*. Second, English compounds whose first element is a preposition (*offsides*, *outcast*, *overcome*) are listed as separate headwords, chiefly because of their frequent grammatical complexity, cf. *overhead*, which can be an adverb (*it flew overhead*), an adjective (*overhead projector*), or a noun (*overhead from grant money*). Conversely, derived words, that is, words that contain one or more affixes (e.g., *antiabortion*, composed of the prefix *anti-* plus *abortion*, and *kingdom*, composed of *king* plus the suffix *-dom*), are listed as separate headwords.

9. ILLUSTRATIVE PHRASES. Appearing together with the compound words pertinent to any given grammatical category are illustrative phrases, a category defined so as to include idioms, collocations, proverbs, and, especially, sentences required to clarify usage in some way, as when the usage of *gustarle a uno* as a gloss of *to like* is illustrated by the phrase *he likes dogs*, with the translation *le gustan los perros*.

Cómo usar el *Universidad de Chicago Diccionario Español–Inglés, Inglés–Español*

Orden de las entradas

Se respeta el orden alfabético, independientemente de la presencia de guiones o espacios, de tal manera que *air conditioning* precede a *aircraft* y *middle school* precede a *middle-sized*. Los homógrafos se ubican en una sola entrada (*lie* 'mentir' y *lie* 'yacer', ambos con la pronunciación [laɪ]), y se indican sus distintas pronunciaciones si corresponde (e.g., *bow* [baʊ] 'proa' y *bow* [bo] 'curva'). En cuanto al español y siguiendo la política oficial de la Real Academia Española,[1] *ch* y *ll* ya no se reconocen como letras independientes, de tal manera que *ch* ahora sigue a *ce* y precede a *ci*, y *ll* sigue a *li* y precede a *lo* en el orden alfabético.

Asimismo, los compuestos incluidos dentro de una entrada determinada aparecen en orden alfabético a continuación de su primer elemento, lo cual a veces interfiere con el orden alfabético general. Así, por ejemplo, *rompeolas* aparece a continuación de *romper*, porque se trata de un compuesto de dicho verbo, si bien el orden alfabético requeriría lo contrario.

Ortografía

La ortografía de los vocablos ingleses refleja el uso general en inglés americano, y las variantes se incluyen en los casos pertinentes (*ax, axe; sulphur, sulfur; stymie, stymy*). La ortografía española sigue las convenciones de la Real Academia Española. Para la grafía española de palabras problemáticas, tales como préstamos recientes (*escáner, scooter*), nombres de países (*Malí, Irak*) y gentilicios (*zimbabuo*), se consultaron fuentes tales como el *Diccionario del español actual*, el *Diccionario de dudas*, el *Libro de estilo* de *El País* de Madrid y varios sitios en el Internet.[2] Corresponde hacer notar que la grafía de algunos términos vacila entre varias posibles, cf. la versión española de *Bahrain*, que aparece como *Bahrein* en el *Libro de estilo* y como *Bahráin* o *Bahréin* en el *Diccionario de dudas*, en cuyo caso damos la forma que parece más generalmente aceptada u ofrecemos varias.

---

1. Real Academia Española, *Ortografía de la lengua española* (Madrid: Espasa-Calpé, 1999), p. 2.
2. Manuel Seco, Olimpia Andrés y Gabino Ramos, *Diccionario del español actual* (Madrid: Aguilar, 1999); Manuel Seco, *Diccionario de dudas y dificultades de la lengua española*, 10ª ed. (Madrid: Espasa-Calpe, 1998), *El País: Libro de estilo*, 9ª ed. (Madrid: Ediciones El País, 1990).

Omisiones

Algunas categorías de palabras se omiten sistemáticamente de las entradas del diccionario. En primer lugar, las formas irregulares de los pretéritos y participios pasados del inglés (e.g., *drunk*, *smitten*), que en ediciones anteriores aparecían incluidas en el cuerpo del diccionario, se han eliminado y se presentan ahora tabuladas (p. 282). En segundo lugar, las formas adverbiales en *-mente* (español) y en *-ly* (inglés), se incluyen solamente cuando su uso y significado no pueden deducirse claramente de sus bases adjetivas. De esta forma, *claramente* se omite, ya que su significado es predecible a partir de su base adjetiva ('de manera clara'), mientras que *atentamente* se incluye, ya que además de significar 'de manera atenta', también se usa como fórmula de despedida epistolar. Del mismo modo, se omite *clearly*, porque su equivalente, *de manera clara*, se deduce de su base adjetiva, mientras que se incluye *surely* porque además de significar *de forma segura* también quiere decir *sin duda*. Finalmente, debe notarse que los sustantivos ingleses terminados en *-ing* y los adjetivos en *-ed*, que pueden aparecer como traducción de palabras españolas en la parte español–inglés, no figuran siempre como cabezas de artículo en la parte inglés–español debido a la total regularidad de su formación y a consideraciones de espacio.

Estructura de las entradas

1. PALABRAS CABEZA DE ARTÍCULO. Las variantes ortográficas, si las hay, siguen a la forma más frecuente, que aparece en primer término. En español, las designaciones de profesiones y oficios, los títulos y las relaciones de parentesco aparecen tanto en la forma masculina como en la femenina, como por ejemplo, *abogado -da*.

2. PRONUNCIACIÓN. La pronunciación de las palabras inglesas se indica mediante una versión modificada del Alfabético Fonético Internacional, cuyas convenciones se explican en la p. 276. No se requiere transcripción individual de las palabras españolas, gracias a la simplicidad y sistematicidad de la ortografía española. Para detalles, ver la sección titulada "The Spanish Spelling System" en la p. 2.

3. CATEGORÍA GRAMATICAL. Los significados se marcan según reflejen el uso de la palabra como sustantivo masculino (*m*), sustantivo femenino (*f*), adjetivo (*adj*), adverbio (*adv*), conjunción (*conj*), preposición (*prep*), pronombre (*pron*), interjección (*interj*), verbo transitivo (*vt*) o verbo intransitivo (*vi*). En inglés, en cambio, los sustantivos se marcan con *n*, abreviación de *noun*.

   Los significados dentro de una entrada aparecen ordenados de manera que el más frecuente figure primero. Cuando la misma traducción cubre el significado de dos categorías gramaticales, ambas aparecen juntas, cf. el inglés *red*, que puede traducirse como *rojo* tanto en su significado sustantivo como en el adjetivo.

   Siguiendo la tradición, los adjetivos españoles aparecen exclusivamente en su forma masculina. Sin embargo, cuando el adjetivo frecuentemente funciona además como sustantivo, se muestra tanto en la forma masculina como en la femenina si ambas son posibles, cf. el caso de *africano -na*, traducido al inglés como *African*, forma adecuada para todos sus usos.

   La combinación "vi/vt" merece mención especial. En ocasiones, una única forma verbal funciona tanto transitiva como intransitivamente, v.g., tanto *comer* como su equivalente inglés *to eat*. Sin embargo, es también frecuente que las traducciones españolas de verbos intransitivos ingleses requieran el agregado de una partícula pronominal *-se*. Así, en casos tales como *to bathe* que se marca "vi/ vt," y se traduce como *bañar(se)*, debe entenderse que la forma no pronominalizada es transitiva y la forma con *-se* es intransitiva. En aquellos casos en los que la palabra cabeza de artículo y su equivalente en la otra lengua difieren en transitividad, se deben agregar partículas para reflejar esta diferencia. Tal es el caso del verbo *aprobar*, que se traduce al inglés como *to approve of* en algunos de sus significados, ya que *to approve* es intransitivo si no va acompañado de preposición. Finalmente, en los casos en los que un verbo español puede usarse tanto intransitiva como transitivamente y su equivalente inglés es exclusivamente intransitivo, este último puede a veces volverse transitivo mediante el agregado de una preposición entre paréntesis. Así, el esp. *chivar* se traduce como *to snitch (on)* para mostrar que su forma intransitiva en inglés es *to snitch* mientras que el equivalente transitivo es *to snitch on*.

Por razones de espacio se omiten las formas pronominales de los verbos españoles en dos casos. En primer lugar, se omiten si la partícula pronominal hace las veces de complemento directo reflexivo o recíproco, cf. *mirarse* (a sí mismo o el uno al otro). En segundo lugar no se incluyen tampoco si la partícula pronominal no afecta la traducción al inglés, como en el caso de *bañar* y *bañarse*, ambos *to bathe*. Sí se incluyen aquellas formas pronominales que difieren semánticamente de sus verbos de base, cf. *ir* vs. *irse*.

4. INDICADORES SEMÁNTICOS. En aquellos casos en los que una palabra, dentro de una misma categoría gramatical, tiene dos o más acepciones, estas se distinguen por medio de indicadores semánticos, o sea, explicaciones parentéticas. Lo más frecuente es que se empleen sinónimos, cf. *arco*, que se traduce *arc* cuando se trata de una curva, como *arch* cuando se refiere a una estructura arquitectónica, y como *bow* cuando se trata de un arma, aunque en otras ocasiones se adoptan otras estrategias. Así, los verbos transitivos a veces se distinguen con mayor facilidad mediante los tipos de complementos directos que los acompañan, cf. *acordonar* (un zapato) *to lace*, (un lugar) *to rope off*, (una moneda) *to mill*, mientras que la forma más sencilla de distinguir adjetivos es mostrar los tipos de referentes a los cuales se aplican con mayor frecuencia, cf. *inseguro*, que aplicado a una personalidad se traduce por *insecure*, a un vehículo por *unsafe*, y al andar por *unsteady*. Es frecuente que un único equivalente abarque casi todas las acepciones de una palabra cabeza de artículo dentro de una categoría gramatical determinada. En esos casos, solamente el significado "excepcional," que aparece en segundo lugar, se acompaña de un indicador semántico. Por ejemplo, el equivalente de *acceso* en casi todas sus acepciones es *access*, excepto cuando se refiere a un ataque de tos o rabia, en cuyo caso se traduce como *fit*. Aunque los indicadores semánticos normalmente preceden a la traducción que les corresponde, en ocasiones se ubican después. En estos casos tienen como objetivo eliminar dudas acerca del empleo de una traducción determinada en un contexto secundario específico, cf. *acompañar*, cuya traducción *to accompany* va seguida de un indicador semántico "también en música" para confirmar al lector su aplicación a ese contexto.

5. TRADUCCIONES. En la medida de lo posible, se ha tratado de que las traducciones sean equivalentes a la palabra cabeza de artículo en cuanto a su significado,

registro y frecuencia. Así, *poli* se traduce como *cop* y no como *policeman*, palabra más formal. De la misma forma, *to urinate* se traduce como *orinar* y no como *hacer pipí*, expresión más familiar. Las traducciones separadas por una coma deben considerarse equivalentes, aunque no sean exactamente sinónimas. El uso del punto y coma indica acepciones distintas.

6. USO REGIONAL. No se ha hecho ningún esfuerzo sistemático por reflejar usos regionales, ni en inglés ni en español, ya que en la gran mayoría de los casos existe una palabra de uso general. Así, entre los muchos equivalentes españoles de la palabra inglesa *peasant*, su equivalente español *campesino* se entiende en todo el mundo de habla hispana, aun cuando existan términos locales, tales como *jíbaro* en Puerto Rico, *guajiro* en Cuba y *guaso* en Chile. Sin embargo, el uso regional se indica para el español en dos casos específicos. En primer lugar se encuentran los casos en los que una palabra determinada podría resultar desconocida en una región dada, como los varios equivalentes españoles del ingl. *bean*. Segundo, se han incluido regionalismos que se reconocen en todo el mundo de habla hispana como típicos de un dialecto determinado, cf. español rioplatense *che*, mexicano *ándale, cuate*.

7. INDICADORES DE ESTILO. Ya que, como se mencionó anteriormente, los equivalentes se eligen para que correspondan a las palabras cabeza de artículo en todos los aspectos de su significado, incluyendo nivel de lengua y frecuencia, los indicadores de estilo se usan poco. Por ejemplo, no hay necesidad de indicar que la palabra inglesa *fool* es familiar, ya que figura como equivalente del español *tonto*. Se han empleado cinco indicadores de estilo: literario (*lit*), que incluye lenguaje poético y formal, familiar (*fam*), que designa palabras que se usan en situaciones de intimidad, vulgar (*vulg*), que designa términos cuyo uso está censurado socialmente, peyorativo (*pey*), que designa palabras que tienen una carga connotativa negativa hacia el referente y *ofensivo* (sin abreviar), que designa insultos.

8. COMPUESTOS. El criterio de facilidad de uso requeriría que cada palabra recibiera su propia entrada, pero por razones de economía de espacio esto no es posible en un diccionario conciso. Por lo tanto, las palabras compuestas, que están formadas por dos o más vocablos preexistentes, aparecen en casi todos los casos en la entrada de su primer constituyente, al final de la categoría gramatical correspondiente. De tal forma, *hombre rana* aparece como — *rana*, en la entrada de *hombre*. Hay ciertas excepciones a esta regla, sin embargo. En primer lugar, los compuestos aparecen bajo la cabeza de artículo de su segundo constituyente cuando el primero es extremadamente frecuente, tal como lo son los verbos semánticamente "vacíos" como el español *hacer, tener, tomar* y el inglés *keep, take, turn*. De este modo, *tener paciencia* aparece en la entrada de *paciencia* y no en la de *tener*, y *to have a good time* figura bajo *time* y no bajo *to have*. En segundo lugar, los compuestos ingleses cuyo primer elemento es una preposición (*offsides, overcome, outcast*), aparecen como cabezas de artículo independientes, sobre todo debido a su complejidad gramatical, cf. *overhead*, que puede ser adverbio (*it flew overhead*, que equivale a *voló en lo alto*), adjetivo (*overhead projector*, es decir, *retroproyector*) y sustantivo (*overhead from grant money*, o sea, *gastos generales de una subvención*). No obstante, las palabras derivadas, i.e., aquellas que contienen uno o más afijos (e.g., *anticuerpo*, compuesta del prefijo *anti-* y *cuerpo*, y *cabezón*, compuesta por *cabeza* y el sufijo *-ón*), figuran como cabezas de artículo independientes.

9. FRASES ILUSTRATIVAS. Junto con las palabras compuestas de una determinada categoría gramatical figuran las frases ilustrativas, una categoría que incluye expresiones idiomáticas, colocaciones típicas, refranes y especialmente, oraciones necesarias para aclarar el uso de alguna palabra, como cuando el uso de *like* como traducción de *gustar* se ilustra con la frase *he likes dogs*, que se traduce *le gustan los perros*.

Spanish–English · Español–Inglés

List of Abbreviations / Lista de abreviaturas

adj	adjetivo	adjective
adv	adverbio, adverbial	adverb, adverbial
Am	América	America
art	artículo	article
conj	conjunción	conjunction
def	definido	definite
dem	demostrativo	demonstrative
Esp	España	Spain, Spanish
f	femenino	feminine
fam	familiar	familiar
indef	indefinido	indefinite
interj	interjección	interjection
interr	interrogativo	interrogative
inv	invariable	invariable
lit	literario	literary
loc	locución	locution
m	masculino	masculine
Méx	México	Mexico
num	numeral	numeral
pej	peyorativo	pejorative
pers	personal	personal
pl	plural	plural
pos	posesivo	possessive
prep	preposición, preposicional	preposition, prepositional
pron	pronombre	pronoun
rel	relativo	relative
RP	Río de la Plata	River Plate
sg	singular	singular
v aux	verbo auxiliar	auxiliary verb
vi	verbo intransitivo	intransitive verb
vt	verbo transitivo	transitive verb
vulg	vulgar	vulgar

Spanish Pronunciation

Spanish orthography very closely mirrors Spanish pronunciation, much more so than is the case in English. This explains why, in bilingual dictionaries such as this, each English entry must be accompanied by a phonetic representation, while Spanish pronunciation may be presented in synoptic form.

This synopsis is only meant as an introduction, however. In spite of the clarity of the orthographical system of Spanish, the individual sounds of the language are difficult for adult native speakers of English to pronounce, and this difficulty is compounded by the syllabic structure of the language. For these reasons, readers who wish to perfect their pronunciation of Spanish are strongly advised to seek the help of a competent teacher.

To say that orthography mirrors pronunciation means that there is a close correlation between letters and sounds. Thus, most Spanish letters correspond to a single sound, or to a single family of closely related sounds, as is the case for all vowels, and the consonants *f*, *l*, *m*, *n*, *p*, *t*, and *s*. In a few cases a single letter represents two very different sounds, as *c*, which is pronounced as *k* before *a*, *o*, and *u*, but *th* (as in *thin*, or as *s* in America) before *e* or *i*. Rarely, two letters represent a single sound, as in the case of *ch*.

The overarching differences between Spanish and English pronunciation are tenseness of articulation and syllabification within the breath group. Due to the tenseness of their articulation, for example, all Spanish vowels have a clear nondiphthongal character, unlike English long vowels, which tend to be bipartite (e.g., *late*, pronounced [leʰt]). Syllabification is a problem for English speakers because in Spanish, syllables are formed without respect to word boundaries, such that *el hado* 'fate' and *helado* 'ice cream' are both pronounced as e-la-do, and the phrase *tus otras hermanas* 'your other sisters' is syllabified as tu-so-tra-ser-ma-nas. In fast speech, vowels may combine, as in *lo ofendiste* 'you offended him', pronounced lo-fen-dis-te. Finally, when Spanish consonants occur in clusters, very often the articulation of the second influences that of the first, as when *un peso* 'one peso' is pronounced um-pe-so, and *en que* 'in which' is pronounced eŋ ke, where ŋ represents the sound of the letters *ng* in English.

The Spanish Spelling System and the Sounds Represented

I. VOWELS

i as a single vowel always represents a sound similar to the second vowel of *police*. Examples: **hilo, camino, piso.** As a part of a diphthong, it sounds like the *y* of English *yes, year.* Examples: **bien, baile, reina.**

e is similar to the vowel of *late* ([leʰt]), but without the diphthong. Examples: **mesa, hablé, tres.**

a is similar to the vowel of *pod.* Examples: **casa, mala, América.** Notably, **a** is always pronounced this way, even when not stressed. This contrasts with the English tendency to reduce unstressed vowels to schwa ([ə]), as in *America*, pronounced in English as [ə-mé-rɪ-kə].

o has a value similar to that of the vowel in Eng. *coat* [ko^wt], but without the diphthong. Examples: **no, modo, amó.**

u has a value similar to that of English *oo*, as in *boot* [bu^wt], but without the diphthong. Examples: **cura, agudo, uno.** Note that the letter **u** is not pronounced in the syllables **qui, que, gui,** and **gue** (unless spelled with dieresis, as in *bilingüe*). When **u** occurs in diphthongs such as those of **cuida, cuento, deuda,** it has the sound of *w* (as in *way*).

II. CONSONANTS

b and **v** represent the same sounds in Spanish. At the beginning of a breath group or when preceded by the *m* sound (which may be spelled *n*), they are both pronounced like English *b*. Examples: **bomba, en vez de, vine, invierno.** In other environments, especially between vowels, both letters are pronounced as a very relaxed *b*, in which the lips do not completely touch and the air is not completely stopped. This sound has no equivalent in English. Examples: **haba, uva, la vaca, la banda.**

c represents a *k* sound before **a, o, u, l,** and **r.** However, this sound is not accompanied by a puff of air as it is in Eng. *can* and *coat* (compare the *c* in *scan*, which is more similar to the Spanish sound). Examples: **casa, cosa, cuna, quinto, queso, crudo, aclamar.** (Note that, as mentioned above, the vowel **u** is not pronounced in **quinto** and **queso.**) In contrast, when appearing before the vowels **e** and **i, c** is pronounced as *s* in Spanish America and the southwest of Spain, and as *th* (as in *thin*) in other parts of Spain (see **s** for more information).

ch is no longer considered to be a separate letter in the Spanish alphabet. However, it represents a single sound, which is similar to the English *ch* in *church* and *cheek*. Examples: **chato, chaleco, mucho.**

d is phonetically complex in Spanish. In terms of articulation, it is pronounced by the tongue striking the teeth rather than the alveolar ridge as in English. Second, it is represented by two variants. The first of these, which is similar to that of English *dame* and *did*, occurs at the beginning of breath groups or after **n** and **l.** Examples: **donde, falda, conde.** In all other situations the letter represents a sound similar to the *th* of English *then.* Examples: **hado, cuerda, cuadro, usted.** This sound tends to be very relaxed, to the point of disappearing in certain environments, such as word-final and intervocalic.

f is very similar to the English *f* sound. Examples: **faro, elefante, alfalfa.**

g is phonetically complex. Before the vowels **e** and **i,** it is pronounced as *h* in most American dialects, while in northern Spain it is realized like the *ch* in the German word *Bach*. Examples: **gente, giro.** At the beginning of breath groups before the vowels **a, o, u,** and before the consonants **l** and **r,** it is pronounced like the **g** of English *go.* Examples: **ganga, globo, grada.** In all other environments it is pronounced as a very relaxed *g.* Examples: **lago, la goma, agrado.**

3

h is silent. Examples: **hoja, humo, harto.**

j is realized in most American dialects as *h*, while in northern Spain it is pronounced like the *ch* in the German word *Bach*. Examples: **jamás, jugo, jota.**

k sounds like Eng. *k*, but without the accompanying puff of air. Examples: **kilo, keroseno.**

l is pronounced forward in the mouth, as the *l* in *leaf, leak*, never in the back, as in *bell, full*. Examples: **lado, ala, sol.**

ll is no longer considered to be a separate letter in the Spanish alphabet. However, it does represent a single sound, which differs widely in pronunciation throughout the Spanish-speaking world. In most areas, it is pronounced like the *y* of Eng. *yes*, though with greater tension. In extreme northern Spain and in parts of the Andes, it sounds like the *lli* in Eng. *million*. In the River Plate area it is pronounced like the *g* in *beige* or the *sh* in *ship*. Examples: **calle, llano, olla.**

m is essentially the same as in English. Examples: **madre, mano, cama.** However, in final position, as in **álbum** 'album', it is pronounced *n*.

n is normally pronounced like Eng. *n*. Examples: **no, mano, hablan.** There are exceptions, however. For example, before **b, v, p,** and **m,** it is pronounced *m*, as in **en Barcelona, en vez de, un peso,** while before **k, g, j, ge-,** and **gi-,** it is realized as [ŋ], the final sound of Eng. *sing*, as in **anca, tengo, naranja, engendrar.**

ñ is similar to but more tense than the *ny* of Eng. *canyon*. Examples: **cañón, año, ñato.**

p is like English *p* except that it is not accompanied by a puff of air, as it is in Eng. *pill* and *papa* (compare the *p* in *spot*, which is more similar to the Spanish sound). Examples: **padre, capa, apuro.**

q combined with **u** has the sound of *k*. Examples: **queso, aquí, quien.**

r usually represents a sound similar to that of the *tt* in Eng. *kitty*, and the *dd* in *ladder*. Examples: **caro, tren, comer.** In contrast, at the beginning of words, and after **n, l, s,** the letter **r** is realized as a trill, as in **rosa, Enrique, alrededor, Israel.** The double letter **rr** always represents a trill, as in **carro, correr, guerrero.**

s is pronounced the same as in standard American English in most parts of Spanish America and in parts of southern Spain. In most of Spain, in contrast, it is realized with the tip of the tongue against the alveolar ridge, producing a whistling sound that is also common in southern dialects of American English. Examples: **solo, casa, es.** In the Caribbean and in coastal Spanish generally, there is a strong tendency to pronounce **s** in certain environments (usually preconsonantal) as *h*, or to eliminate it entirely. In these dialects, *esta* may be pronounced as *ehta* or *eta*.

t differs from English *t* in two respects: first, it is articulated by the tongue touching the teeth rather than the alveolar ridge, and second, it is not accompanied by a puff of air, as it is in English *too* and *titillate* (compare the *t* in *stop*, which is more similar to the Spanish sound). Examples: **tela, tino, tinta.**

x has a wide range of phonetic realizations. Between vowels, it is usually pronounced *ks* or *gs* (but never *gz*), as in **examen, próximo,** though in a few words it is pronounced as *s*, e.g., *exacto, auxilio.* Before a consonant, **x** is almost always pronounced *s*, as in **extranjero, experiencia.** In many Mexican and Central American words of indigenous origin, **x** represents *h*, as in **México.**

y varies regionally in its pronunciation. In most areas it is pronounced like the *y* of Eng. *yes*, though with greater tension. In the River Plate area it is pronounced like the *g* in *beige* or the *sh* in *ship*. Examples: **yo, ayer.**

z is subject to dialectal variation as well. In most parts of Spain, except the southwest, it is pronounced as the *th* in Eng. *thin, cloth.* In southwestern Spain and all of Spanish America, in contrast, it is pronounced *s*. Examples: **zagal, hallazgo, luz.**

Stress Assignment in Spanish and the Use of the Written Accent

Spanish words are normally stressed on the next-to-last syllable when they end in a vowel or the consonants **n** or **s**. Examples: **mesa, zapato, acontecimiento, hablan, mujeres.** Words whose pronunciation does not conform to this rule are considered exceptions, and their stressed syllable is indicated with an accent mark. Examples: **lámpara, estómago, género, acá, varón, además.**

Conversely, Spanish words are normally stressed on the final syllable when they end in a consonant other than **n** or **s**. Examples: **mujer, actualidad, pedal, voraz.** Words whose pronunciation does not conform to this rule are considered exceptions, and their stressed syllable is indicated with an accent mark. Examples: **nácar, volátil, lápiz.**

For the purposes of stress assignment, diphthongs are considered the same as simple vowels. Thus, **arduo** and **industria** are considered to have two and three syllables respectively, with regular stress on the penultimate syllable. However, some sequences of vowels are not considered diphthongs. For example, **alegría** and **continúo** are both considered to have four syllables, with the stress mark indicating the absence of a diphthong.

Until recently certain words received written accents in order to differentiate functions, even though they are pronounced identically (this is still true in certain cases, such as **de** 'of', **dé** 'give'). Thus, the orthography **esta** was assigned to the demonstrative adjective ('this', fem.), while the demonstrative pronoun ('this one', fem.) was written **ésta.** This convention is no longer observed by most writers.

Notes on Spanish Grammar

The Noun

Gender. All Spanish nouns, not just those that denote male or female beings, are assigned either masculine or feminine gender. As a general rule, male beings (**muchacho** 'boy', **toro** 'bull') and all nouns ending in **-o** (**lodo** 'mud') are assigned masculine gender (exceptions: **mano** 'hand', **radio** 'radio', **foto** 'photo', all feminine). Similarly, female beings (**mujer** 'woman', **vaca** 'cow') and nouns ending in **-a** (**envidia** 'envy') tend to be assigned feminine gender (exceptions: **mapa** 'map', **drama** 'drama', **día** 'day', all masculine). In addition, nouns ending in **-ción**, **-tad**, **-dad**, **-tud**, and **-umbre** are always feminine: **canción** 'song', **facultad** 'college', **ciudad** 'city', **virtud** 'virtue', and **muchedumbre** 'crowd'. Otherwise, nouns ending in consonants and vowels other than **-o** and **-a** are of unpredictable gender. Some are feminine (**barbarie** 'savagery', **clase** 'class', **nariz** 'nose', **tribu** 'tribe'), while others are masculine (**antílope** 'antelope', **corte** 'cut', **mesón** 'lodge', **nácar** 'mother of pearl').

Nouns in **-o** that denote human beings (and to some extent, animals) form the feminine by replacing **-o** with **-a**, as in **tío** 'uncle' / **tía** 'aunt', **niño** 'boy' / **niña** 'girl', **oso** 'bear' / **osa** 'she-bear'. Where the masculine noun does not end in **-o**, the rules of formation are more complex. For example, nouns ending in **-ón**, **-or**, and **-án** require the addition of **-a**, as in the pairs **patrón** / **patrona** 'patron', **pastor** / **pastora** 'shepherd', **holgazán** / **holgazana** 'lazy person'. In other cases the difference is more unpredictable: **poeta** / **poetisa** 'poet', **emperador** / **emperatriz** 'empress', **abad** / **abadesa** 'abbess'.

Some nouns have different genders according to their meanings: **corte** (m) 'cut', (f) 'court', **capital** (m) 'money capital', (f) 'capital city', while others have invariable endings which are used for both the masculine and the feminine: **artista** 'artist' (and all nouns ending in **-ista**), **amante** 'lover', **aristócrata** 'aristocrat', **homicida** 'murderer', **cliente** 'customer'. Finally, some words vacillate as to gender, e.g., **mar** 'sea', which is normally masculine but is feminine in certain expressions (**en alta mar** 'on the high seas') and in poetic contexts, and **arte,** which is masculine in the singular but feminine in the plural. Some words, such as **armazón** and **esperma,** can be both masculine and feminine.

Pluralization. Nouns ending in an unaccented vowel and **-é** add **-s** to form the plural: **libro** / **libros**, **casa** / **casas**, **café** / **cafés**, while nouns ending in a consonant, in **-y**, or in an accented vowel other than **-é** add **-es**: **papel** / **papeles**, **canción** / **canciones**, **ley** / **leyes**, **rubí** / **rubíes**. Exceptions to this rule include the words **papá** / **papás**, **mamá** / **mamás**, and the small group of nouns ending in unaccented **-es** and **-is**, which do not change in the plural: **lunes** 'Monday', 'Mondays', **tesis** 'thesis', 'theses'.

Articles

Definite Article. The equivalent of English **the** is as follows: masculine singular, **el;** feminine singular, **la;** masculine plural, **los;** feminine plural, **las.** Feminine words beginning with stressed **a** or **ha** take **el** in the singular and **las** in the plural: **el alma** 'the soul' / **las almas** 'the souls', **el hacha** 'the hatchet' / **las hachas** 'the hatchets'. In spite of this, these nouns remain feminine in the singular, as shown by adjective agreement: **el alma bendita** 'the blessed soul'. When preceded by the prepositions **a** and **de,** the masculine singular article **el** forms the contractions **al** and **del.**

Indefinite Article. The equivalent of English **a, an** is as follows: masculine singular, **un;** feminine singular, **una.** In the plural, masculine **unos** and feminine **unas** are equivalent to English **some.** Feminine words beginning with stressed **a** or **ha** take **un** in the singular and **unas** in the plural: **un alma** 'a soul' / **unas almas** 'some souls', **un hacha** 'a hatchet' / **unas hachas** 'some hatchets'.

Adjectives

Agreement. The adjective in Spanish agrees in gender and number with the noun it modifies: **el lápiz rojo** 'the red pencil', **la casa blanca** 'the white house', **los libros interesantes** 'the interesting books', **las flores hermosas** 'the beautiful flowers'.

Formation of the Plural. Adjectives follow the same rules as nouns for the formation of the plural: **pálido, pálidos** 'pale', **fácil, fáciles** 'easy', **cortés, corteses** 'courteous', **capaz, capaces** 'capable'.

Formation of the Feminine. Adjectives ending in **-o** change to **-a: blanco, blanca** 'white'. Adjectives ending in other vowels are invariable: **verde** 'green', **fuerte** 'strong', **indígena** 'indigenous, native', **pesimista** 'pessimistic', **baladí** 'trivial', as are adjectives ending in a consonant: **fácil** 'easy', **cortés** 'courteous', **mayor** 'older', 'larger'. Some cases are more complex: (a) adjectives ending in **-ón, -án, -or** (except comparatives like **mayor**) add **-a** to form the feminine: **holgazán, holgazana** 'lazy', **preguntón, preguntona** 'inquisitive', **hablador, habladora** 'talkative', (b) adjectives of nationality ending in a consonant add **-a** to form the feminine: **francés, francesa** 'French', **español, española** 'Spanish', **alemán, alemana** 'German'.

Adverbs

Most adverbs are formed by adding **-mente** to the feminine form of the adjective: **clara** 'clear' / **claramente** 'clearly', **fácil** 'easy' / **fácilmente** 'easily'.

Comparison of Inequality in Adjectives and Adverbs

The comparative of inequality is formed by placing **más** or **menos** before the positive form of the adjective or adverb: **más rico que** 'richer than', **menos rico que** 'less rich than', **más tarde** 'later', **menos tarde** 'less late'. The superlative is formed by placing the definite article **el** before the comparative: **el más rico** 'the richest', **el menos rico** 'the least rich'.

The following adjectives and adverbs have irregular forms of comparison:

Positive	Comparative	Superlative
bueno	mejor	el (la) mejor
malo	peor	el (la) peor
grande	mayor	el (la) mayor
pequeño	menor	el (la) menor

Common Spanish Suffixes

-aco   is a pejorative suffix: **pajarraco** 'ugly bird' (from **pájaro** 'bird'), **libraco** 'large, bulky book' (**libro** 'book')

-ada *a.* attaches to verbal stems to indicate an action: **mirada** 'look' (**mirar** 'to look'), **empujada** 'push' (**empujar** 'to push')

 b. attaches to noun stems to indicate a blow: **cachetada** 'blow on the cheek' (**cachete** 'cheek'), **puñalada** 'stab with a dagger' (**puñal** 'dagger')

 c. attaches to nominal stems to indicate an action characteristic of a person or group: **bobada** 'foolish act' (**bobo** 'fool'), **niñada** 'childish act' (**niño** 'child')

-al, -ar   attach to nouns indicating trees to form nouns that denote a grove: **naranjal** 'orange grove' (from **naranjo** 'orange tree'), **pinar** 'pine grove' (**pino** 'pine tree')

-azo   attaches to noun stems, forming nouns that indicate
 a. augmentation: **hombrazo** 'big man' (**hombre** 'man'), **marranazo** 'large hog' (**marrano** 'hog')

 b. a blow or explosion: **porrazo** 'blow with a club' (**porra** 'club'), **cañonazo** 'cannon shot' (**cañón** 'cannon')

-cito   is a diminutive suffix: **cochecito** 'a little car' (**coche** 'car'), **mujercita** 'little woman' (**mujer** 'woman')

-dor   forms agent nouns from verbs: **hablador** 'talker' (**hablar** 'to talk'), **regulador** 'regulator' (**regular** 'to regulate'), which are sometimes used as adjectives: **hablador** 'talkative', **regulador** 'regulating'

-ejo   is a pejorative suffix: **librejo** 'worthless book' (**libro** 'book'), **lugarejo** 'Podunk' (**lugar** 'place')

-ería   attaches to noun stems to denote
 a. a place where something is made or sold: **zapatería** 'shoestore' (**zapato** 'shoe'), **pastelería** 'pastry shop' (**pastel** 'pastry')

 b. a profession, business, or occupation: **carpintería** 'carpentry' (**carpintero** 'carpenter'), **ingeniería** 'engineering' (**ingeniero** 'engineer')

 c. a group: **chiquillería** 'bunch of children' (**chiquillo** 'little kid')

-ero *a.* attaches to nouns to indicate a person who makes, sells, or is in charge of something: **librero** 'bookseller' (**libro** 'book'), **zapatero** 'shoemaker' (**zapato** 'shoe'), **carcelero** 'jailer' (**cárcel** 'jail')

 b. attaches to nominal stems to form adjectives: **guerrero** 'warlike' (**guerra** 'war'), **conejero** 'for hunting rabbits' (**conejo** 'rabbit')

-ez, -eza   are used to make abstract nouns from adjectival bases: **vejez** 'old age' (**viejo** 'old'), **niñez** 'childhood' (**niño** 'child'), **grandeza** 'greatness' (**grande** 'large, great'), **rareza** 'rarity' (**raro** 'rare')

-ía   forms adjective abstracts: **valentía** 'courage' (**valiente** 'brave'), **cobardía** 'cowardice' (**cobarde** 'coward')

-ico   is a diminutive suffix: **ratico** 'little while' (**rato** 'while'), **momentico** 'brief moment' (**momento** 'moment')

-(i)ento   attaches to adjectives to indicate attenuation, as in **amarillento** 'yellowish' (**amarillo** 'yellow'), or an undesirable quality, as in **hambriento** 'hungry' (**hambre** 'hunger')

-illo   is sometimes a diminutive suffix: **politiquillo** 'insignificant politician' (**político** 'politician'), **chiquillo** 'little kid' (**chico** 'child')

-ísimo   attaches to adjectives to indicate an extreme degree of a quality: **hermosísimo** 'very beautiful' (**hermoso** 'beautiful')

-ito   is a diminutive suffix: **librito** 'small book' (**libro** 'book'), **casita** 'little house' (**casa** 'house')

-izo   forms adjectives from nominal stems, indicating a tendency or attenuation: **rojizo** 'reddish' (**rojo** 'red'), **olvidadizo** 'forgetful' (**olvidar** 'to forget')

-mente   is the adverbial ending attached to the feminine form of the adjective: **generosamente** 'generously' (**generoso** 'generous'), **claramente** 'clearly' (**claro** 'clear')

-ón   *a.*   is an augmentative adjectival suffix: **barrigón** 'pot-bellied' (**barriga** 'belly'), **cabezón** 'large-headed' (**cabeza** 'head')
        b.   attaches to verb stems to denote sudden actions: **tirón** 'pull, jerk' (**tirar** 'to pull'), **apretón** 'push' (**apretar** 'to push')

-oso   forms adjectives from nouns, indicating abundance or character: **rocoso** 'rocky' (**roca** 'rock'), **tormentoso** 'stormy' (**tormenta** 'storm')

-ote, -ota   is an augmentative and pejorative suffix attached to nouns: **discursote** 'long, boring speech' (**discurso** 'speech'), **narizota** 'big ugly nose' (**nariz** 'nose')

-udo   forms adjectives from nouns, indicating an excess: **peludo** 'hairy' (**pelo** 'hair'), **panzudo** 'big-bellied' (**panza** 'belly')

-ura	forms abstract nouns from adjectives: **negrura** 'blackness' (**negro** 'black'), **altura** 'height' (**alto** 'high')

-uzco	forms adjectives from other adjectives, indicating attenuation: **blancuzco** 'whitish' (**blanco** 'white'), **negruzco** 'blackish' (**negro** 'black')

Spanish Regular Verbs

First Conjugation

Infinitive	**hablar**
Pres. Indic.	hablo, hablas, habla, hablamos, habláis, hablan
Pres. Subj.	hable, hables, hable, hablemos, habléis, hablen
Pret. Indic.	hablé, hablaste, habló, hablamos, hablasteis, hablaron
Imp. Indic.	hablaba, hablabas, hablaba, hablábamos, hablabais, hablaban
Imp. Subj.	hablara, hablaras, hablara, habláramos, hablarais, hablaran, *or* hablase, hablases, hablase, hablásemos, hablaseis, hablasen
Fut. Indic.	hablaré, hablarás, hablará, hablaremos, hablaréis, hablarán
Cond.	hablaría, hablarías, hablaría, hablaríamos, hablaríais, hablarían
Imperatives	habla (tú), hable (usted), hablad (vosotros), hablen (ustedes)
Pres. Part.	hablando
Past Part.	hablado

Second Conjugation

Infinitive	**comer**
Pres. Indic.	como, comes, come, comemos, coméis, comen
Pres. Subj.	coma, comas, coma, comamos, comáis, coman
Pret. Indic.	comí, comiste, comió, comimos, comisteis, comieron
Imp. Indic.	comía, comías, comía, comíamos, comíais, comían
Imp. Subj.	comiera, comieras, comiera, comiéramos, comierais, comieran, *or* comiese, comieses, comiese, comiésemos, comieseis, comiesen
Fut. Indic.	comeré, comerás, comerá, comeremos, comeréis, comerán
Cond.	comería, comerías, comería, comeríamos, comeríais, comerían
Imperatives	come (tú), coma (usted), comed (vosotros), coman (ustedes)
Pres. Part.	comiendo
Past Part.	comido

Third Conjugation

Infinitive	**vivir**
Pres. Indic.	vivo, vives, vive, vivimos, vivís, viven
Pres. Subj.	viva, vivas, viva, vivamos, viváis, vivan
Pret. Indic.	viví, viviste, vivió, vivimos, vivisteis, vivieron
Imp. Indic.	vivía, vivías, vivía, vivíamos, vivíais, vivían

Imp. Subj.	viviera, vivieras, viviera, viviéramos, vivierais, vivieran, *or*
	viviese, vivieses, viviese, viviésemos, vivieseis, viviesen
Fut. Indic.	viviré, vivirás, vivirá, viviremos, viviréis, vivirán
Cond.	viviría, vivirías, viviría, viviríamos, viviríais, vivirían
Imperative	vive (tú), viva (usted), vivid (vosotros), vivan (ustedes)
Pres. Part.	viviendo
Past Part.	vivido

Spanish Irregular and Orthographic Changing Verbs

The superscript number or numbers listed as part of a verb entry indicate that the verb is to be conjugated like the model verb in this section that has the corresponding number. Only the tenses that have irregular forms or spelling changes are given, wherein irregular forms and spelling changes are shown in boldface type.

1. **pensar**
Pres. Indic.	**pienso, piensas, piensa,** pensamos, pensáis, **piensan**
Pres. Subj.	**piense, pienses, piense,** pensemos, penséis, **piensen**
Imper.	**piensa** (tú), **piense** (usted), pensad (vosotros), **piensen** (ustedes)

2. **contar**
Pres. Indic.	**cuento, cuentas, cuenta,** contamos, contáis, **cuentan**
Pres. Subj.	**cuente, cuentes, cuente,** contemos, contéis, **cuenten**
Imper.	**cuenta** (tú), **cuente** (usted), contad (vosotros), **cuenten** (ustedes)

3. *a.* **sentir**
Pres. Indic.	**siento, sientes, siente,** sentimos, sentís, **sienten**
Pres. Subj.	**sienta, sientas, sienta, sintamos, sintáis,** sientan
Pret. Indic.	sentí, sentiste, **sintió,** sentimos, sentisteis, **sintieron**
Imp. Subj.	**sintiera, sintieras, sintiera, sintiéramos, sintierais, sintieran,** or **sintiese, sintieses, sintiese, sintiésemos, sintieseis, sintiesen**
Imperative	**siente** (tú), **sienta** (usted), sentid (vosotros), **sientan** (ustedes)
Pres. Part.	**sintiendo**

   b. **erguir**
Pres. Indic.	**yergo, yergues, yergue,** erguimos, erguís, **yerguen**
Pres. Subj.	**yerga, yergas, yerga, irgamos, irgáis, yergan**
Pret. Indic.	erguí, erguiste, **irguió,** erguimos, erguisteis, **irguieron**
Imp. Subj.	**irguiera, irguieras, irguiera, irguiéramos, irguierais, irguieran,** or **irguiese, irguieses, irguiésemos, irguieseis, irguiesen**
Imperative	**yergue** (tú), **yerga** (usted), erguid (vosotros), **yergan** (ustedes)
Pres. Part.	**irguiendo**

4.   **dormir**
        Pres. Indic.   **duermo, duermes, duerme**, dormimos, dormís, **duermen**
        Pres. Subj.   **duerma, duermas, duerma, durmamos, durmáis, duerman**
        Pret. Indic.   dormí, dormiste, **durmió**, dormimos, dormisteis, **durmieron**
        Imp. Subj.   **durmiera, durmieras, durmiera, durmiéramos, durmierais, durmieran**, or **durmiese, durmieses, durmiese, durmiésemos, durmieseis, durmiesen**
        Imperative   **duerme** (tú), **duerma** (usted), dormid (vosotros), **duerman** (ustedes)
        Pres. Part.   **durmiendo**

5.   **pedir**
        Pres. Indic.   **pido, pides, pide**, pedimos, pedís, **piden**
        Pres. Subj.   **pida, pidas, pida, pidamos, pidáis, pidan**
        Pret. Indic.   **pedí**, pediste, **pidió**, pedimos, pedisteis, **pidieron**
        Imp. Subj.   **pidiera, pidieras, pidiera, pidiéramos, pidierais, pidieran**, or **pidiese, pidieses, pidiese, pidiésemos, pidieseis, pidiesen**
        Imperative   **pide** (tú), **pida** (usted), pedid (vosotros), **pidan** (ustedes)
        Pres. Part.   **pidiendo**

6.   **buscar**
        Pres. Subj.   **busque, busques, busque, busquemos, busquéis, busquen**
        Pret. Indic.   **busqué**, buscaste, buscó, buscamos, buscasteis, buscaron
        Imperative   busca (tú), **busque** (usted), buscad (vosotros), **busquen** (ustedes)

7.   **llegar**
        Pres. Subj.   **llegue, llegues, llegue, lleguemos, lleguéis, lleguen**
        Pret. Indic.   **llegué**, llegaste, llegó, llegamos, llegasteis, llegaron
        Imperative   llega (tú), **llegue** (usted), llegad (vosotros), **lleguen** (ustedes)

8.   **averiguar**
        Pres. Subj.   **averigüe, averigües, averigüe, averigüemos, averigüéis, averigüen**
        Pret. Indic.   **averigüé**, averiguaste, averiguó, averiguamos, averiguasteis, averiguaron
        Imperative   averigua (tú), **averigüe** (usted), averiguad (vosotros), **averigüen** (ustedes)

9.   **abrazar**
        Pres. Subj.   **abrace, abraces, abrace, abracemos, abracéis, abracen**

Pret. Indic.	**abracé,** abrazaste, abrazó, abrazamos, abrazasteis, abrazaron
Imperative	abraza (tú), **abrace** (usted), abrazad (vosotros), **abracen** (ustedes)

10. *a.* **convencer**

Pres. Indic.	**convenzo,** convences, convence, convencemos, convencéis, convencen
Pres. Subj.	**convenza, convenzas, convenza, convenzamos, convenzáis, convenzan**
Imperative	convence (tú), **convenza** (usted), convenced (vosotros), **convenzan** (ustedes)

b. **esparcir**

Pres. Indic.	**esparzo,** esparces, esparce, esparcimos, esparcís, esparcen
Pres. Subj.	**esparza, esparzas, esparza, esparzamos, esparzáis, esparzan**
Imperative	esparce (tú), **esparza** (usted), esparcid (vosotros), **esparzan** (ustedes)

c. **cocer**

Pres. Indic.	**cuezo,** cueces, cuece, cocemos, cocéis, cuecen
Pres. Subj.	**cueza, cuezas, cueza, cozamos, cozáis, cuezan**
Imperative	cuece (tú), **cueza** (usted), coced (vosotros), **cuezan** (ustedes)

11. *a.* **dirigir**

Pres. Indic.	**dirijo,** diriges, dirige, dirigimos, dirigís, dirigen
Pres. Subj.	**dirija, dirijas, dirija, dirijamos, dirijáis, dirijan**
Imper.	dirige (tú), **dirija** (usted), dirigid (vosotros), **dirijan** (ustedes)

b. **coger**

Pres. Indic.	**cojo,** coges, coge, cogemos, cogéis, cogen
Pres. Subj.	**coja, cojas, coja, cojamos, cojáis, cojan**
Imperative	coge (tú), **coja** (usted), coged (vosotros), **cojan** (ustedes)

12. **distinguir**

Pres. Indic.	**distingo,** distingues, distingue, distinguimos, distinguís, distinguen
Pres. Subj.	**distinga, distingas, distinga, distingamos, distingáis, distingan**
Imperative	distingue (tú), **distinga** (usted), distinguid (vosotros), **distingan** (ustedes)

13. *a.* **conocer**

Pres. Indic.	**conozco,** conoces, conoce, conocemos, conocéis, conocen
Pres. Subj.	**conozca, conozcas, conozca, conozcamos, conozcáis, conozcan**
Imperative	conoce (tú), **conozca** (usted), conoced (vosotros), **conozcan** (ustedes)

b. **lucir**

Pres. Indic.	**luzco,** luces, luce, lucimos, lucís, lucen
Pres. Subj.	**luzca, luzcas, luzca, luzcamos, luzcáis, luzcan**
Imperative	luce (tú), **luzca** (usted), lucid (vosotros), **luzcan** (ustedes)

14. **creer**

Pret. Indic.	creí, creíste, **creyó,** creímos, creísteis, **creyeron**
Imp. Subj.	**creyera, creyeras, creyera, creyéramos, creyerais, creyeran,** or **creyese, creyeses, creyese, creyésemos, creyeseis, creyesen**
Pret. Part.	**creyendo**

15. **reír**

Pres. Indic.	**río, ríes, ríe,** reímos, reís, **ríen**
Pres. Subj.	**ría, rías, ría, riamos, riáis, rían**
Pret. Indic.	reí, reíste, **rió,** reímos, reísteis, **rieron**
Imp. Subj.	**riera, rieras, riera, riéramos, rierais, rieran,** or **riese, rieses, riese, riésemos, rieseis, riesen**
Imperative	**ríe** (tú), **ría** (usted), reíd (vosotros), **rían** (ustedes)
Pres. Part.	**riendo**

16. **enviar**

Pres. Indic.	envío, envías, envía, enviamos, enviáis, envían
Pres. Subj.	envíe, envíes, enviemos, enviéis, envíen
Imperative	envía (tú), envíe (usted), enviad (vosotros), envíen (ustedes)

17. **continuar**

Pres. Indic.	continúo, continúas, continúa, continuamos, continuáis, continúan
Pres. Subj.	continúe, continúes, continúe, continuemos, continuéis, continúen
Imperative	continúa (tú), continúe (usted), continuad (vosotros), continúen (ustedes)

18. **gruñir**

Pret. Indic.	gruñí, gruñiste, **gruñó,** gruñisteis, **gruñeron**
Imp. Subj.	**gruñera, gruñeras, gruñera, gruñéramos, gruñerais, gruñeran,** or **gruñese, gruñeses, gruñese, gruñésemos, gruñeseis, gruñesen**
Pres. Part.	**gruñendo**

19. **bullir**

Pret. Indic.	bullí, bulliste, **bulló,** bullimos, bullisteis, **bulleron**
Imp. Subj.	**bullera, bulleras, bullera, bulléramos, bullerais, bulleran,** or **bullese, bulleses, bullese, bullésemos, bulleseis, bullesen**
Pres. Part.	**bullendo**

20. **andar**

Pret. Indic.	**anduve, anduviste, anduvo, anduvimos, anduvisteis, anduvieron**
Imp. Subj.	**anduviera, anduvieras, anduviera, anduviéramos, anduvierais, anduvieran,** or
	anduviese, anduvieses, anduviese, anduviésemos, anduvieseis, anduviesen

21. **asir**

Pres. Indic.	**asgo,** ases, ase, asimos, asís, asen
Pres. Subj.	**asga, asgas, asga, asgamos, asgáis, asgan**
Imperative	ase (tú), **asga** (usted), asid (vosotros), **asgan** (ustedes)

22. **caber**

Pres. Indic.	**quepo,** cabes, cabe, cabemos, cabéis, caben
Pres. Subj.	**quepa, quepas, quepa, quepamos, quepáis, quepan**
Pret. Indic.	**cupe, cupiste, cupo, cupimos, cupisteis, cupieron**
Imp. Subj.	**cupiera, cupieras, cupiera, cupiéramos, cupierais, cupieran,** or **cupiese, cupieses, cupiese, cupiésemos, cupieseis, cupiesen**
Fut. Indic.	**cabré, cabrás, cabrá, cabremos, cabréis, cabrán**
Cond.	**cabría, cabrías, cabría, cabríamos, cabríais, cabrían**
Imperative	cabe (tú), **quepa** (usted), cabed (vosotros), **quepan** (ustedes)

23. **caer**

Pres. Indic.	**caigo,** caes, cae, caemos, caéis, caen
Pres. Subj.	**caiga, caigas, caiga, caigamos, caigáis, caigan**
Pret. Indic.	caí, caiste, **cayó,** caímõs, caísteis, **cayeron**
Imp. Subj.	**cayera, cayeras, cayera, cayéramos, cayerais, cayeran,** or **cayese, cayeses, cayese, cayésemos, cayeseis, cayesen**
Imperative	cae (tú), **caiga** (usted), caed (vosotros), **caigan** (ustedes)
Pres. Part.	**cayendo**

24. **conducir**

Pres. Indic.	**conduzco,** conduces, conduce, conducimos, conducís, conducen
Pres. Subj.	**conduzca, conduzcas, conduzca, conduzcamos, conduzcáis, conduzcan**
Pret. Indic.	**conduje, condujiste, condujo, condujimos, condujisteis, condujeron**
Imp. Subj.	**condujera, condujeras, condujera, condujéramos, condujerais, condujeran,** or **condujese, condujeses, condujese, condujésemos, condujeseis, condujesen**
Imperative	conduce (tú), **conduzca** (usted), conducid (vosotros), **conduzcan** (ustedes)

25. **dar**

Pres. Indic.	**doy,** das, da, damos, dais, dan
Pres. Subj.	**dé,** des, **dé,** demos, deis, den
Pret. Indic.	**di, diste, dio, dimos, disteis, dieron**
Imp. Subj.	**diera, dieras, diera, diéramos, dierais, dieran,** or **diese, dieses, diese, diésemos, dieseis, diesen**

26. **decir**[1]

Pres. Indic.	**digo, dices, dice,** decimos, decís, **dicen**
Pres. Subj.	**diga, digas, diga, digamos, digáis, digan**
Pret. Indic.	**dije, dijiste, dijo, dijimos, dijisteis, dijeron**
Imp. Subj.	**dijera, dijeras, dijera, dijéramos, dijerais, dijeran,** or **dijese, dijeses, dijese, dijésemos, dijeseis, dijesen**
Fut. Indic.	**diré, dirás, dirá, diremos, diréis, dirán**
Cond.	**diría, dirías, diría, diríamos, diríais, dirían**
Imperative	**di** (tú), **diga** (usted), decid (vosotros), **digan** (ustedes)
Pres. Part.	**diciendo**
Past Part.	**dicho**

27. **errar**

Pres. Indic.	**yerro, yerras, yerra,** erramos, erráis, **yerran**
Pres. Subj.	**yerre, yerres, yerre,** erremos, erréis, **yerren**
Imperative	**yerra** (tú), **yerre** (usted), errad (vosotros), **yerren** (ustedes)

28. **estar**

Pres. Indic.	**estoy, estás, está,** estamos, estáis, **están**
Pres. Subj.	**esté, estés, esté,** estemos, estéis, **estén**
Pret. Indic.	**estuve, estuviste, estuvo, estuvimos, estuvisteis, estuvieron**
Imp. Subj.	**estuviera, estuvieras, estuviera, estuviéramos, estuvierais, estuvieran,** or **estuviese, estuvieses, estuviese, estuviésemos, estuvieseis, estuviesen**
Imperative	**está** (tú), **esté** (usted), estad (vosotros), **estén** (ustedes)

29. **haber**

Pres. Indic.	**he, has, ha, hemos,** habéis, **han**
Pres. Subj.	**haya, hayas, haya, hayamos, hayáis, hayan**
Pret. Indic.	**hube, hubiste, hubo, hubimos, hubisteis, hubieron**
Imp. Subj.	**hubiera, hubieras, hubiera, hubiéramos, hubierais, hubieran,** or **hubiese, hubieses, hubiese, hubiésemos, hubieseis, hubiesen**
Fut. Indic.	**habré, habrás, habrá, habremos, habréis, habrán**

1. The compound verbs of *decir* have the same irregularities with the exception of the following: The future and conditional of the compound verbs *bendecir* and *maldecir* are regular: *bendeciré, maldeciré,* etc.; *bendeciría, maldeciría,* etc. The familiar imperative is regular: *bendice tu, maldice tu, contradice tu,* etc. The past participles of *bendecir* and *maldecir* are regular when used with haber or in the passive with ser: *bendecido, maldecido.*

	Cond.	**habría, habrías, habría, habríamos, habríais, habrían**

30. **hacer**

Pres. Indic.	**hago,** haces, hace, hacemos, hacéis, hacen
Pres. Subj.	**haga, hagas, haga, hagamos, hagáis, hagan**
Pret. Indic.	**hice, hiciste, hizo, hicimos, hicisteis, hicieron**
Imp. Subj.	**hiciera, hicieras, hiciera, hiciéramos, hicierais, hicieran,** or **hiciese, hicieses, hiciese, hiciésemos, hicieseis, hiciesen**
Fut. Indic.	**haré, harás, hará, haremos, haréis, harán**
Cond.	**haría, harías, haría, haríamos, haríais, harían**
Imperative	**haz** (tú), **haga** (usted), haced (vosotros), **hagan** (ustedes)
Past Part.	**hecho**

31. *a.* **huir**

Pres. Indic.	**huyo, huyes, huye,** huimos, huís, **huyen**
Pres. Subj.	**huya, huyas, huya, huyamos, huyáis, huyan**
Pret. Indic.	huí, huiste, **huyó,** huimos, huisteis, **huyeron**
Imp. Subj.	**huyera, huyeras, huyera, huyéramos, huyerais, huyeran,** or **huyese, huyeses, huyese, huyésemos, huyeseis, huyesen**
Imperative	**huye** (tú), **huya** (usted), huid (vosotros), **huyan** (ustedes)
Pres. Part.	**huyendo**

    b. **argüir**

Pres. Indic.	**arguyo, arguyes, arguye,** argüimos, argüís, **arguyen**
Pres. Subj.	**arguya, arguyas, arguya, arguyamos, arguyáis, arguyan**
Pret. Indic.	argüí, argüiste, **arguyó,** argüimos, argüisteis, **arguyeron**
Imp. Subj.	**arguyera, arguyeras, arguyera, arguyéramos, arguyerais, arguyeran,** or **arguyese, arguyeses, arguyese, arguyésemos, arguyeseis, arguyesen**
Imperative	**arguye** (tú), **arguya** (usted), argüid (vosotros), **arguyan** (ustedes)
Pres. Part.	**arguyendo**

32. **ir**

Pres. Indic.	**voy, vas, va, vamos, vais, van**
Pres. Subj.	**vaya, vayas, vaya, vayamos, vayáis, vayan**
Imp. Indic.	**iba, ibas, iba, íbamos, ibais, iban**
Pret. Indic.	**fui, fuiste, fue, fuimos, fuisteis, fueron**
Imp. Subj.	**fuera, fueras, fuera, fuéramos, fuerais, fueran,** or **fuese, fueses, fuese, fuésemos, fueseis, fuesen**
Imperative	**ve** (tú), **vaya** (usted), id (vosotros), **vayan** (ustedes)
Pres. Part.	**yendo**

33. **jugar**

Pres. Indic.	**juego, juegas, juega,** jugamos, jugáis, **juegan**
Pres. Subj.	**juegue, juegues, juegue,** juguemos, juguéis, **jueguen**
Pret. Indic.	**jugué,** jugaste, jugó, jugamos, jugasteis, jugaron
Imperative	**juega** (tú), **juegue** (usted), jugad (vosotros), **jueguen** (ustedes)

34. **adquirir**

Pres. Indic.	**adquiero, adquieres, adquiere,** adquirimos, adquirís, **adquieren**
Pres. Subj.	**adquiera, adquieras, adquiera,** adquiramos, adquiráis, **adquieran**
Imperative	**adquiere** (tú), **adquiera** (usted), adquirid (vosotros), **adquieran** (ustedes)

35. **oír**

Pres. Indic.	**oigo, oyes, oye,** oímos, oís, **oyen**
Pres. Subj.	**oiga, oigas, oiga, oigamos, oigáis, oigan**
Pret. Indic.	oí, oíste, **oyó,** oímos, oísteis, **oyeron**
Imp. Subj.	**oyera, oyeras, oyera, oyéramos, oyerais, oyeran,** or **oyese, oyeses, oyese, oyésemos, oyeseis, oyesen**
Imperative	**oye** (tú), **oiga** (usted), oíd (vosotros), **oigan** (ustedes)
Pres. Part.	**oyendo**

36. **oler**

Pres. Indic.	**huelo, hueles, huele,** olemos, oléis, **huelen**
Pres. Subj.	**huela, huelas, huela,** olamos, oláis, **huelan**
Imperative	**huele** (tú), **huela** (usted), oled (vosotros), **huelan** (ustedes)

37. **placer**

Pres. Indic.	**plazco,** places, place, placemos, placéis, placen
Pres. Subj.	**plazca, plazcas, plazca, plazcamos, plazcáis, plazcan**

38. **poder**

Pres. Indic.	**puedo, puedes, puede,** podemos, podéis, **pueden**
Pres. Subj.	**pueda, puedas, pueda,** podamos, podáis, **puedan**
Pret. Indic.	**pude, pudiste, pudo, pudimos, pudisteis, pudieron**
Imp. Subj.	**pudiera, pudieras, pudiera, pudiéramos, pudierais, pudieran,** or **pudiese, pudieses, pudiese, pudiésemos, pudieseis, pudiesen**
Fut. Indic.	**podré, podrás, podrá, podremos, podréis, podrán**
Cond.	**podría, podrías, podría, podríamos, podríais, podrían**
Pres. Part.	**pudiendo**

39. **poner**

Pres. Indic.	**pongo,** pones, pone, ponemos, ponéis, ponen

Pres. Subj.	**ponga, pongas, ponga, pongamos, pongáis, pongan**
Pret. Indic.	**puse, pusiste, puso, pusimos, pusisteis, pusieron**
Imp. Subj.	**pusiera, pusieras, pusiera, pusiéramos, pusierais, pusieran,** or **pusiese, pusieses, pusiese, pusiésemos, pusieseis, pusiesen**
Fut. Indic.	**pondré, pondrás, pondrá, pondremos, pondréis, pondrán**
Cond.	**pondría, pondrías, pondría, pondríamos, pondríais, pondrían**
Imperative	**pon** (tú), **ponga** (usted), poned (vosotros), **pongan** (ustedes)
Past Part.	**puesto**

40. **querer**

Pres. Indic.	**quiero, quieres, quiere,** queremos, queréis, **quieren**
Pres. Subj.	**quiera, quieras, quiera,** queramos, queráis, **quieran**
Pret. Indic.	**quise, quisiste, quiso, quisimos, quisisteis, quisieron**
Imp. Subj.	**quisiera, quisieras, quisiera, quisiéramos, quisierais, quisieran,** or **quisiese, quisieses, quisiese, quisiémos, quisieseis, quisiesen**
Fut. Indic.	**querré, querrás, querrá, querremos, querréis, querrán**
Cond.	**querría, querrías, querría, querríamos, querríais, querrían**
Imperative	**quiere** (tú), **quiera** (usted), quered (vosotros), **quieran** (ustedes)

41. **saber**

Pres. Indic.	**sé,** sabes, sabe, sabemos, sabéis, saben
Pres. Subj.	**sepa, sepas, sepa, sepamos, sepáis, sepan**
Pret. Indic.	**supe, supiste, supo, supimos, supisteis, supieron**
Imp. Subj.	**supiera, supieras, supiera, supiéramos, supierais, supieran,** or **supiese, supieses, supiese, supiésemos, supieseis, supiesen**
Fut. Indic.	**sabré, sabrás, sabrá, sabremos, sabréis, sabrán**
Cond.	**sabría, sabrías, sabría, sabríamos, sabríais, sabrían**
Imperative	sabe (tú), **sepa** (usted), sabed (vosotros), **sepan** (ustedes)

42. **salir**

Pres. Indic.	**salgo,** sales, sale, salimos, salís, salen
Pres. Subj.	**salga, salgas, salga, salgamos, salgáis, salgan**
Fut. Indic.	**saldré, saldrás, saldrá, saldremos, saldréis, saldrán**
Cond.	**saldría, saldrías, saldría, saldríamos, saldríais, saldrían**
Imperative	**sal** (tú),[2] **salga** (usted), salid (vosotros), **salgan** (ustedes)

---

2. The compound *sobresalir* is regular in the familiar imperative: **sobresale tú.**

43.   **ser**
        Pres. Indic.   **soy, eres, es, somos, sois, son**
        Pres. Subj.   **sea, seas, sea, seamos, seáis, sean**
        Imp. Indic.   **era, eras, era, éramos, erais, eran**
        Pret. Indic.   **fui, fuiste, fue, fuimos, fuisteis, fueron**
        Imp. Subj.   **fuera, fueras, fuera, fuéramos, fuerais, fueran,** or
                           fuese, fueses, fuese, fuésemos, fueseis, fuesen
        Imperative   **sé** (tú), **sea** (usted), sed (vosotros), **sean** (ustedes)

44.   **tener**
        Pres. Indic.   **tengo, tienes, tiene,** tenemos, tenéis, **tienen**
        Pres. Subj.   **tenga, tengas, tenga, tengamos, tengáis, tengan**
        Pret. Indic.   **tuve, tuviste, tuvo, tuvimos, tuvisteis, tuvieron**
        Imp. Subj.   **tuviera, tuvieras, tuviera, tuviéramos, tuvierais,**
                           tuvieran, or **tuviese, tuvieses, tuviese, tuviésemos,**
                           tuvieseis, tuviesen
        Fut. Indic.   **tendré, tendrás, tendrá, tendremos, tendréis,**
                           tendrán
        Cond.   **tendría, tendrías, tendría, tendríamos, tendríais,**
                           tendrían
        Imperative   **ten** (tú), **tenga** (usted), tened (vosotros), **tengan** (ustedes)

45.   **traer**
        Pres. Indic.   **traigo,** traes, trae, traemos, traéis, traen
        Pres. Subj.   **traiga, traigas, traiga, traigamos, traigáis, traigan**
        Pret. Indic.   **traje, trajiste, trajo, trajimos, trajisteis, trajeron**
        Imp. Subj.   **trajera, trajeras, trajera, trajéramos, trajerais,**
                           trajeran, or **trajese, trajeses, trajese, trajésemos,**
                           trajeseis, trajesen
        Imperative   trae (tú), **traiga** (usted), traed (vosotros), **traigan** (ustedes)
        Pres. Part.   **trayendo**

46.   **valer**
        Pres. Indic.   **valgo,** vales, vale, valemos, valéis, valen
        Pres. Subj.   **valga, valgas, valga, valgamos, valgáis, valgan**
        Fut. Indic.   **valdré, valdrás, valdrá, valdremos, valdréis, valdrán**
        Cond.   **valdría, valdrías, valdría, valdríamos, valdríais,**
                           valdrían
        Imperative   **val** or vale (tú), **valga** (usted), valed (vosotros), **valgan**
                           (ustedes)

47.   **venir**
        Pres. Indic.   **vengo, vienes, viene,** venimos, venís, **vienen**
        Pres. Subj.   **venga, vengas, venga, vengamos, vangáis, vengan**
        Pret. Indic.   **vine, viniste, vino, vinimos, vinisteis, vinieron**
        Imp. Subj.   **viniera, vinieras, viniera, viniéramos, vinierais,**
                           vinieran, or **viniese, vinieses, viniese, viniésemos,**
                           vinieseis, viniesen

Fut. Indic.	**vendré, vendrás, vendrá, vendremos, vendréis, vendrán**
Cond.	**vendría, vendrías, vendría, vendríamos, vendríais, vendrían**
Imperative	**ven** (tú), **venga** (usted), venid (vosotros), **vengan** (ustedes)
Pres. Part.	**viniendo**

48. **ver**

Pres. Indic.	**veo**, ves, ve, vemos, veis, ven
Pres. Subj.	**vea, veas, vea, veamos, veáis, vean**
Imp. Indic.	**veía, veías, veía, veíamos, veíais, veían**
Imperative	ve (tú), **vea** (usted), ved (vosotros), **vean** (ustedes)
Past Part.	**visto**

49. **yacer**

Pres. Indic.	**yazco** or **yazgo,** yaces, yace, yacemos, yacéis, yacen
Pres. Subj.	**yazca, yazcas, yazca, yazcamos, yazcáis, yazcan,** or **yazga, yazgas, yazga, yazgamos, yazgáis, yazgan**
Imperative	yace (tú), **yazca** or **yazga** (usted), yaced (vosotros), **yazcan** or **yazgan** (ustedes)

50. Defective Verbs

The following verbs are used only in the forms that have an **i** in the ending: **abolir, agredir, aterirse, empedernirse, transgredir.**

The verb **atañer** is used only in the third person, most frequently in the present indicative: atañe, atañen.

The verb **concernir** is used only in the third person of the following tenses:

Pres. Indic.	**concierne, conciernen**
Pres. Subj.	**concierna, conciernan**
Imp. Indic.	concernía, concernían
Imp. Subj.	concerniera *or* concerniese, concernieran *or* concerniesen
Pres. Part.	concerniendo

The verb **roer** (also **corroer**) has three forms in the first person of the present indicative: **roo, royo, roigo,** all of which are infrequently used. In the present subjunctive the preferable form is **roa, roas, roa,** etc., although the forms **roya** and **roiga** are found.

The verb **soler** is used most frequently in the present and imperfect indicative. It is less frequently used in the present subjunctive.

Pres. Indic.	**suelo, sueles, suele,** solemos, soléis, **suelen**
Pres. Subj.	**suela, suelas, suela,** solamos, soláis, **suelan**
Imp. Indic.	solía, solías, solía, solíamos, solíais, solían

51.   Additional Irregular Past Participles
        absolver—**absuelto**
        abrir—**abierto**
        circunscribir—**circunscrito**
        componer—**compuesto**
        cubrir—**cubierto**
        decir—**dicho**
        deponer—**depuesto**
        descomponer—**descompuesto**
        describir—**descrito**
        descubrir—**descubierto**
        desenvolver—**desenvuelto**
        deshacer—**deshecho**
        devolver—**devuelto**
        disolver—**disuelto**
        encubrir—**encubierto**
        entreabrir—**entreabierto**
        entrever—**entrevisto**
        envolver—**envuelto**
        escribir—**escrito**
        hacer—**hecho**
        imprimir—**impreso** (often regular, **imprimido**)
        inscribir—**inscrito**
        morir—**muerto**
        poner—**puesto**
        prescribir—**prescrito**
        proscribir—**proscrito**
        proveer—**provisto** (often regular, **proveído**)
        pudrir—**podrido**
        reabrir—**reabierto**
        reescribir—**reescrito**
        resolver—**resuelto**
        revolver—**revuelto**
        romper—**roto**
        satisfacer—**satisfecho**
        subscribir—**subscrito**
        transcribir—**transcrito**
        ver—**visto**
        volver—**vuelto**

Aa

a PREP voy — **Londres** I'm going to London; **te lo doy — ti** I'm giving it to you; **se sentó — la sombra** she sat down in the shade; **tumbarse —l sol** to lie down in the sun; **una soga —l cuello** a rope around his neck; **lo miraba — la luz de una vela** she looked at him by the light of a candle; — **dos pesetas cada uno** at two pesetas each; — **las tres y media** at three-thirty; **sentarse — la mesa** to sit down at the table; **prestar dinero —l 15%** to lend money at 15%; **en grupos de — cinco** in groups of five; **cocina — gas** gas cooker; **fotos — todo color** full-color photos; **nadie le gana — testaruda** no one touches her for stubbornness; **terminaron — puñetazos** they ended up fighting; **¡— jugar!** let's play! **¿— qué vienen?** what are they coming for? **veo — mi mamá** I see my mother

abacá M manila

abad -esa M abbot; F abbess

abadejo M cod

abadía F abbey

abajo ADV (dirección) down; (posición relativa) below; **mirar para —** to look down; **el piso de —** the apartment below; **véase —** see below; **— de** under, underneath; **Stefan está — del coche** Stefan is under / underneath the car; **¡— el rey!** down with the king! **firmante** undersigned; **echar —** to knock down; **río —** downstream; **venirse —** to go to ruin

abalanzarse[9] VI to lunge at, to swoop down upon

abanderado -da MF standard-bearer

abandonado ADJ abandoned; **es una persona muy abandonada** she's very unkempt

abandonar VT (a una persona, a una familia) to leave, to desert; (el hogar, un partido) to abandon; (una carrera, el poder) to give up; (una carrera, a un enamorado, el hábito de fumar) to quit; (en los naipes) to fold; (un curso) to drop out of

abandono M (acción de descuidar) neglect; (acción de abandonar, condición de abandonado) abandonment; **por —** by default

abanicar[6] VT to fan

abanico M (utensilio) fan; (de posibilidades) array; **abrirse en —** to fan out

abaratar VT (bajar el precio) to lower the price of; (desprestigiar) to cheapen

abarcar[6] VT (categorías) to embrace, to encompass; (un período de tiempo) to span

abarrotería F Méx grocery store

abarrotero -ra MF Méx grocer

abarrotes M PL Méx groceries; **tienda de —** Méx grocery store

abastecer[13] VT (un ejército, una ciudad) to supply; (una tienda) to stock

abastecimiento M supply

abasto M supply; **mercado de —s** farmers' market; **yo sola no doy —** I can't cope alone

abatido ADJ dejected, despondent, downcast

abatimiento M dejection, despondency

abatir VT (bajar) to lower; (derribar) to knock down; (desanimar) to depress; (matar a tiros) to shoot; **—se** to swoop down

abdicar[6] VI/VT to abdicate

abdomen M abdomen

abdominal ADJ abdominal; M sit-up

abecedario M alphabet

abedul M birch

abeja F bee; **— asesina** killer bee

abejón M bumblebee

abejorro M bumblebee

aberración F aberration

abertura F (acción) opening; (de una cueva) mouth

abeto M fir

abierto ADJ (no cerrado, no cubierta) open; (franco) frank; **— de par en par** wide open

abigarrado ADJ motley

abigeato M cattle rustling

abismal ADJ abysmal

abismo M abyss, chasm; **— generacional** generation gap

ablandar VT to soften

abnegación F self-denial

abobado ADJ silly

abocar[6] VI to turn onto; **—se a** to devote oneself to

abochornar VT (calentar) to make too hot; (avergonzar) to embarrass; **—se** to get embarrassed

abocinar VT to flare

abofetear VT to slap

abogacía F legal profession; **ejercer la —** to practice law

abogado -da MF lawyer, attorney

abogar[7] VI **— por** to advocate, to plead for

abolengo M ancestry
abolición F abolition
abolir[50] VT to abolish
abollado ADJ dented
abolladura F dent
abollar VT to dent; **—se** to get dented
abolsarse VI to sag
abombar VT to make bulge
abominable ADJ abominable, loathsome
abominación F abomination
abominar VI to detest
abonado -da MF subscriber
abonar VT (suscribir) to subscribe; (pagar) to make a payment; (poner abono) to fertilize; **—se** to subscribe
abono M (a una revista) subscription; (para una temporada deportiva) season ticket; (para el autobús) pass; (para la tierra) fertilizer
abordar VT (un avión, un buque) to board; (un problema) to tackle, to approach; (a una persona en la calle) to accost
aborigen ADJ aboriginal; M primitive inhabitant; **— australiano** Australian aborigine
aborrascarse[6] VI to become stormy
aborrecer[13] VT to abhor, to loathe
aborrecible ADJ hateful, abhorrent
aborrecimiento M abhorrence
abortador -ora MF abortionist
abortar VI to miscarry, to have a miscarriage; VI/VT to abort
abortero -ra MF abortionist
aborto M (espontáneo) miscarriage; (provocado) abortion
abotargarse[7] VI to bloat
abotonar VT to button; **—se** to button up
abovedar VT (una iglesia) to vault, to cover with a vault; (una calle) to arch, to cover as a vault
abozalar VT to muzzle
abracadabra M abracadabra
abrasador ADJ burning
abrasar VT to burn; **—se** to be consumed
abrasión F abrasion
abrasivo ADJ abrasive
abrazadera F clamp
abrazar[9] VT (rodear con los brazos) to hug, to embrace; (rodear una cosa sujetando) to clasp; (una opinión) to espouse
abrazo M hug, embrace
abrevadero M trough
abrevar VT (dar de beber) to water; (beber) to drink
abreviación F abbreviation
abreviar VT to abbreviate, to abridge
abreviatura F abbreviation

abridor M opener
abrigado ADJ (ropa) warm; (lugar) sheltered
abrigar[7] VT to shelter; (emociones) to harbor; **—se** to bundle up
abrigo M (refugio) shelter; (prenda de vestir) coat, wrap
abril M April
abrillantar VT to make shiny
abrir[51] VI/VT to open; VT (con llave) to unlock; (un grifo) to turn on; **— el apetito** to whet one's appetite; **— paso** to make way; M SG **abrebotellas** bottle opener; **abrelatas** can opener; VI (el cielo) to clear up; **—se** to open up; **—se paso** to press through; **en un — y cerrar de ojos** in the twinkle of an eye
abrochar VT to fasten; **—se** to buckle (up)
abrogación F repeal
abrogar[7] VT to repeal
abrojo M bur, sticker
abrumador ADJ overwhelming
abrumar VT to overwhelm, to weigh down; **—se** to become foggy
abrupto ADJ abrupt
absceso M abscess
absolución F acquittal
absoluto ADJ absolute; **en —** absolutely not
absolver[2,51] VT to absolve, to acquit
absorbente ADJ absorbent
absorber VT to absorb
absorción F absorption
absorto ADJ absorbed, engrossed
abstemio -mia ADJ abstemious; MF teetotaler
abstenerse[44] VI to abstain; **— de** to abstain from, to refrain from
abstinencia F abstinence
abstracción F abstraction
abstracto ADJ abstract
abstraer[45] VT to abstract; **—se de** to shut out
abstraído ADJ lost in thought
absurdo ADJ absurd, preposterous; M absurdity
abuchear VI/VT to boo, to jeer
abucheo M boo, jeer
abuelo -la M grandfather; F grandmother; **—s** grandparents
abulia F apathy
abultado ADJ bulgy
abultar VI to bulge
abundancia F abundance, plenty
abundante ADJ abundant, plentiful
abundar VI to abound; **— en** to abound in
aburrido ADJ (sin entretenimiento) bored; (pesado) boring, tiresome
aburrimiento M boredom
aburrir VT to bore; **—se** to become bored

abusar VT — **de** to abuse; (sexualmente) to molest

abuso M abuse; — **de confianza** breach of trust; — **de sustancias** substance abuse

abyecto ADJ abject

acá ADV (en este lugar) here; (a este lugar) over here, *lit* hither; — **y allá** here and there

acabado ADJ finished; M finish

acabar VT to finish; VI to end; — **de** to have just; — **por** to end up by; — **con** (la corrupción) to put an end to; (las cucarachas) to get rid of; **él y yo hemos acabado** he and I are through; **se acabaron los dulces** the candy is all gone; **se nos acabaron las ideas** we ran out of ideas; **y se acabó** and that's that

academia F (corporación, escuela militar) academy; (centro privado de enseñanza) private school

académico ADJ academic

acallar VT to silence, to quiet

acalorado ADJ heated

acaloramiento M **sufrió un —** he got too hot

acalorarse VI/VT (sofocarse) to overheat; (emocionarse) to get excited

acampada F camping

acampante MF camper

acampar VT to camp

acanalar VT to groove

acantilado ADJ sheer, steep; M bluff, cliff

acantonar VT to quarter

acaparar VT (productos) to hoard; (atención) to capture; (monopolizar) *fam* to hog

acaramelar VT to candy

acariciar VT to caress; — **una esperanza** to harbor a hope

ácaro M mite

acarrear VT (transportar) to cart, to transport; (ocasionar) to bring about

acarreo M cartage, carriage, transport

acaso ADV perhaps; **por si —** just in case

acatamiento M compliance

acatar VT to abide by, to comply with

acatarrar VI to chill; **—se** to catch cold

acaudalado ADJ wealthy

acceder VI — **a** to accede to

accesible ADJ accessible, convenient

acceso M access; (de ira) fit

accesorio ADJ & M accessory

accidentado -da ADJ (viaje) eventful; (terreno) uneven; MF accident victim

accidental ADJ accidental

accidentarse VI to have an accident

accidente M (suceso imprevisto) accident; (del terreno) feature; (automovilístico) wreck; **por —** by accident

acción F (acto) action; (valor de bolsa) share of stock; — **de gracias** thanksgiving; **las buenas acciones** good deeds; **acciones preferenciales** preferred stock; **acciones ordinarias** common stock

accionar VT to operate

accionista MF shareholder, stockholder

acebo M holly

acechar VT (emboscar) to lie in ambush; (amenazar) to stalk

acecho M **rondar en —** to prowl; **estar al — ** to lie in wait

aceitar VT to oil

aceite M oil; — **de linaza** linseed oil; — **de oliva** olive oil; — **de ricino** castor oil; — **vegetal** vegetable oil

aceitera F oilcan

aceitoso ADJ oily

aceituna F olive

aceleración F acceleration

acelerador M accelerator

acelerar VT to accelerate, to speed up; VI to accelerate, to step on the gas; — **en vacío** to rev, to race; **—se** to get nervous

acémila F pack animal

acento M (rasgos fonéticos, signo) accent; (especial intensidad) stress

acentuar[17] VT (la hermosura) to accentuate; (ortográficamente) to accent; (oralmente) to stress; **—se** to accentuate

acepción F gloss, meaning

aceptable ADJ acceptable

aceptación F acceptance

aceptar VT to accept

acequia F irrigation ditch

acera F sidewalk

acerado ADJ made of steel

acerar VT to steel

acerca PREP — **de** about, concerning

acercamiento M approach

acercar[6] VT to bring near; **os acerco a la estación** I'll give you a ride to the station; **—se** to come near, to approach

acería F steel mill

acero M steel; — **inoxidable** stainless steel

acérrimo ADJ bitter

acertado ADJ right

acertar[1] VT to hit; VI to be right; — **con** to hit upon; — **a** to happen to; **no —** to miss the mark

acertijo M riddle, conundrum

acervo M heritage

acetona F acetone

achacar[6] VI to blame

achacoso ADJ infirm

achaparrado ADJ (planta) stunted; (persona)

squat
achaque M affliction, ailment; **—s** aches and pains
achicado ADJ weak-kneed
achicar[6] VT (empequeñecer) to make small; (un vestido) to take in; (agua) to bail; **—se** (acobardarse) to feel intimidated; (empequeñecerse) to get smaller
achicoria F chicory
aciago ADJ unlucky
acicalado ADJ clean-cut
acicalarse VI to dress up
acicate M incentive
acidez F (de un ácido) acidity; (del vinagre) sourness; **— de estómago** heartburn
ácido M acid; ADJ (como el ácido) acidic; (fruta) sour, tart
acierto M (contestación correcta) right answer; (buena elección) felicitous choice
aclamación F acclamation, acclaim; **por —** by acclamation
aclamar VT to acclaim, to hail
aclaración F clarification
aclarar VT (con explicaciones) to clarify; (con agua) to rinse; (la voz) to clear; VI to dawn; **aclaró después de la tormenta** it cleared up after the storm; **—se** to lighten
aclimatar VT to acclimate
acné M acne
acobardar VT to intimidate
acogedor ADJ (persona) hospitable; (cuarto) cozy
acoger[11b] VT (una sugerencia) to receive; (a un refugiado) to shelter; **—se** to take refuge; **—se a la ley** to have recourse to the law
acogida F reception
acogimiento M reception
acolchar VT (pespuntear) to quilt; (rellenar) to pad
acollarar VT to collar
acometer VT (atacar) to attack; (emprender) to undertake
acometida F attack
acomodado ADJ well-off
acomodador -ora MF usher
acomodar VT (arreglar) to arrange; (ajustar) to adjust; (adaptar) to adapt; **—se** (ponerse cómodo) to make oneself comfortable; (adaptarse) to adapt oneself
acomodo M position
acompañamiento M (acción, música) accompaniment; (grupo de personas que acompaña) retinue; (comida) side dish
acompañante ADJ accompanying; MF (compañero) companion; (en música) accompanist
acompañar VI/VT to accompany (también en música); (escoltar) to escort; (en una carta) to enclose; **—se de** to be accompanied by; **esperemos que el tiempo acompañe** we hope the weather cooperates; **te acompaño en el sentimiento** my thoughts are with you
acompasado ADJ rhythmical, measured
acomplejado ADJ self-conscious
acondicionar VT to prepare
acongojar VT to distress; **—se** to become distressed
aconsejable ADJ advisable
aconsejar VT to advise, to counsel
acontecer[13] VI to take place
acontecimiento M event; **todo un —** quite a happening; **a esta altura de los —s** at this point in the proceedings
acopiar VT to stockpile
acopio M (acción de guardar) storing; (cosas guardadas) stockpile
acoplamiento M coupling; **— universal de cardán** universal joint
acoplar VT to couple; **—se** (juntarse) to couple, to join; (parlantes) to have feedback
acople M coupling, connection
acorazado ADJ armored; M battleship, warship
acorazar[9] VT to armor
acordar[2] VI **— en** to arrange to; **—se (de)** to remember
acorde ADJ in agreement; **— con** in agreement with; M chord
acordeón M accordion
acordonar VT (un zapato) to tie with a lace; (un lugar) to rope off, to seal off; (una moneda) to mill
acorralar VT (meter en un corral) to corral; (impedir la salida) to corner
acortamiento M shortening
acortar VT to shorten
acosar VT (perseguir) to harry; (atacar) to beset; (atormentar) to badger; (solicitar sexualmente) to harass
acostar[2] VT to put to bed; **—se** to go to bed; **—se con** to sleep with
acostumbrado ADJ accustomed; (habitual) customary; **estar — a** to be used / accustomed to
acostumbrar VT to accustom; (soler) to be accustomed to; **—se (a)** to get accustomed (to)
acotación F (anotación) marginal note; (en una obra de teatro) stage directions
acotar VT (un terreno) to mark off; (un

texto) to make marginal notes on
acre ADJ acrid, pungent, sharp; M acre
acrecentamiento M growth, increase
acrecentar[1] VI to grow
acreditar VT (una cuenta) to credit; (a un
profesional) to accredit; **a quien pueda
— ser el dueño de** to whoever can prove
he is the owner of
acreedor -ora ADJ deserving; **saldo —**
positive balance; MF creditor
acribillar VI (a balazos) to riddle; (a
pedradas) to pelt
acrílico ADJ & M acrylic
acritud F acrimony
acrobacia F (arte) acrobatics; (ejercicio de
acróbata) stunt
acróbata MF INV acrobat
acrobático ADJ acrobatic
acrofobia F acrophobia
acrónimo M acronym
acta F (de nacimiento) certificate; (de una
reunión) minutes; (de un congreso)
proceedings
actitud F attitude
activar VT to activate
actividad F activity
activismo M activism
activista MF activist
activo ADJ active; **en —** working; M assets; **—
líquido** liquid assets
acto M (solemne, de una obra de teatro) act;
(acción) action; **— seguido** immediately
after; **— fallido** Freudian slip; **en el —**
on the spot; **hacer — de presencia** to
show up
actor -triz M actor; F actress; **— de carácter**
character actor
actuación F (acción de actuar) acting; (modo
de actuar) performance
actual ADJ current, present
actualidad F present time; **—es** latest news;
de — up-to-date
actualización F (de información) update;
(de ordenador) upgrade
actualizado ADJ up-to-date
actualizar[9] VT to update; (ordenador) to
upgrade
actualmente ADV presently
actuar[17] VI to act; (ante el público) to
perform
actuario -ria MF (judicial) clerk; (de seguros)
actuary
acuarela F watercolor
acuario M aquarium
acuartelar VT to quarter
acuático ADJ aquatic
acuchillar VT to stab, to slash

acuclillado ADJ squatting
acuclillarse VI to squat
acudir VI (ir) to go; (asistir) to attend; **— a** to
turn to; **— al llamado** to respond to the
call; **— al socorro de** to go to the rescue
of; **— en masa** to flock
acueducto M aqueduct
acuerdo M agreement; **estar de —** to be in
agreement; **ponerse de —** to come to an
agreement; **de — con** in accordance with
acumulación F accumulation, build-up
acumulador M storage battery
acumular VT to accumulate; (una fortuna) to
amass; **—se** to collect
acumulativo ADJ cumulative
acuñación F coinage, minting
acuñar VT (hacer monedas, una expresión) to
coin; (meter cuñas) to wedge
acuoso ADJ watery
acupuntor -ora MF acupuncturist
acupuntura F acupuncture
acurrucarse[6] VI to nestle, to huddle
acusación F accusation, charge
acusado -da MF accused; (en un juicio)
defendant
acusador -ora MF accuser
acusar VT (señalar como culpable) to accuse;
(detectar) to detect; (revelar) to betray;
(entre niños) to tattle, to tell; **— el golpe**
to feel the blow; **— recibo** to
acknowledge receipt
acuse M acknowledgment
acusetas MF SG tattletale
acusica MF INV tattletale
acústica F acoustics
acústico ADJ acoustic
adagio M adage
adaptabilidad F resilience
adaptación F adaptation
adaptar VT to adapt
adecuado ADJ appropriate
adecuar VT to adapt; **—se a** to be suitable
for
adefesio M sight, hideous thing
adelantado ADJ (economía, alumno)
advanced; (reloj) fast; (tren) ahead of time,
ahead of schedule; **por —** in advance
adelantamiento M (de una fecha) bringing
forward; (de un coche) overtaking
adelantar VT (una fecha, dinero) to advance;
(la mano) to move forward; (un coche) to
pass; (una noticia) to tell before; VI (un
reloj) to gain; **— en** to make progress in;
—se (sacar ventaja) to get ahead; (actuar
antes) to go ahead; (innovar) to be ahead;
(hablar antes) to get ahead of oneself
adelante ADV forward; **— con los faroles**

let's get started; **— de mí** in front of me;
de aquí en — from now on; **hacia —**
forward; **ir —** to go ahead; **más —** later;
sacar — to make prosper; **seguir —** to go
on

adelanto M (de la ciencia) advance,
breakthrough; (de un coche) passing;
(pago) advance; **el — de los relojes**
setting the clocks forward

adelfa F oleander

adelgazar[9] VI to lose weight; VT to lose;
(hacer perder peso) to make one lose
weight; (hacer menos espeso) to thin;
(hacer parecer delgado) to make one look
thinner; **—se** to get thinner

ademán M gesture; **hacer un — a alguien**
to motion to someone

además ADV moreover, besides, in addition;
— de deberme dinero besides/in
addition to owing me money

adentro ADV inside; **ir para/hacia —** to go
inside; **hablar para sus —s** to talk to
oneself; **con lo de — para afuera** inside
out

aderezar[9] VT (embellecer) to adorn;
(condimentar) to season, to garnish

aderezo M (adorno) adornment; (de un
alimento) seasoning; (de una ensalada)
salad dressing

adeudar VT (deber) to owe; (cargar en
cuenta) to debit

adeudo M (endeudamiento) indebtedness; (a
una cuenta) debit

adherencia F adhesion

adherir[3] VI to adhere; **—se a** (una cosa) to
stick to; (una huelga) to join; (una idea) to
subscribe to

adhesión F (a una cosa) adhesion; (a una
doctrina) adherence

adhesivo ADJ adhesive; M (pegamento)
cement, adhesive; (calcomanía) sticker

adicción F addiction

adición F addition

adicional ADJ additional

adictivo ADJ addictive

adicto -ta ADJ addicted; MF addict

adiestramiento M training

adiestrar VT to train

adinerado ADJ wealthy, well-to-do

adiós INTERJ goodbye; **hacer — con la
mano** to wave goodbye

adiposo ADJ fatty

aditivo M additive

adivinanza F riddle

adivinar VT to guess

adivino -na MF fortune teller

adjetivo ADJ & M adjective

adjudicación F award

adjudicar[6] VT to award; **—se** to be awarded

adjuntar VT (incluir en una carta) to enclose;
(añadir) to add

adjunto ADJ (unido) attached; (en un mismo
envío) enclosed; (asistente) adjunct; ADV
herewith

adminículo M gadget

administración F administration; **—
pública** civil service

administrador -ora MF administrator

administrar VT (una empresa, un
medicamento) to administer; (justicia) to
dispense; **—se** to budget

administrativo ADJ administrative

admirable ADJ admirable

admiración F admiration

admirador -ora MF admirer; (de una estrella
de cine) fan

admirar VT to admire; **—se** to be amazed;
—se de to wonder at

admisible ADJ admissible, allowable

admisión F (aceptación) admission;
(reconocimiento) acknowledgment

admitir VT (dejar entrar, reconocer) to admit;
(aceptar) to accept; (permitir) to allow

ADN (ácido desoxirribonucleico) M DNA

adobar VT (aderezar una comida) to fix;
(curtir una piel) to tan; (encurtir) to pickle

adobe M adobe

adobo M sauce for seasoning

adoctrinar VT to indoctrinate

adolecer[13] VI **— de** to suffer from

adolescencia F adolescence

adolescente ADJ adolescent; MF adolescent,
teenager

adonde ADV REL **esa es la casa — vamos**
that's the house (where) we're going to

adónde ADV INTERR & PRON where

adopción F adoption

adoptar VT to adopt

adoptivo ADJ adoptive

adoquín M cobblestone

adorable ADJ adorable

adoración F (a un ser amado) adoration; (a
un dios) worship

adorador -ora MF worshiper

adorar VT (a una persona) to adore; (a un
dios) to worship

adormecer[13] VT (dar sueño) to make drowsy;
(entumecer) to numb; **—se** (de sueño) to
become drowsy; (de frío) to go numb

adormilado ADJ sleepy

adornar VT to adorn, to embellish

adorno M adornment, ornament, decoration

adquirir[34] VT to acquire; (una característica)
to take on

adquisición F acquisition; (a una colección, al personal) addition; (de una compañía) takeover

adrede ADV on purpose

adrenalina F adrenaline

aduana F customs; (edificio) customshouse

aduanero -ra MF customs officer

aducir[24] VT to offer as proof

adueñarse VI to take possession

adulación F flattery

adulador -ora ADJ flattering; MF flatterer

adular VI/VT to flatter

adulón -ona ADJ flattering

adulterar VT to adulterate

adulterio M adultery

adúltero -ra MF adulterer

adulto -ta ADJ & MF adult

adusto ADJ stern

advenedizo ADJ upstart

advenimiento M advent

adverbio MF adverb

adversario -ria MF adversary, opponent

adversidad F adversity

adverso ADJ adverse

advertencia F (aviso) notice; (amonestación) warning, admonition

advertir[3] VT (avisar) to warn; (notar) to notice; (notificar) to advise, to tip off

Adviento M Advent

adyacente ADJ adjacent

aéreo ADJ aerial; **correo —** air mail

aeróbic M aerobics

aeróbico ADJ aerobic

aerobio ADJ aerobic

aerodeslizador M hovercraft

aerodinámica F aerodynamics

aerodinámico ADJ aerodynamic, streamlined

aeródromo M airport

aeroespacial ADJ aerospace

aeronáutica F aeronautics

aeronave F aircraft

aeropuerto M airport

aerosol M (suspensión) aerosol; (aparato) spray can

aerotransportado ADJ airborne

aerotransportar VT to airlift

afabilidad F affability, friendliness

afable ADJ affable, friendly

afamado ADJ famed

afán M eagerness

afanar VT *fam* to swipe; **—se** to work hard

afanoso ADJ hardworking

afasia F aphasia

afear VT to make ugly; **—se** to become ugly

afección F condition

afectación F affectation

afectado ADJ (por un desastre) affected,

stricken; (modales) affected, unnatural

afectar VT to affect

afecto M affection, fondness; **— a** fond of

afectuoso ADJ affectionate, loving

afeitado ADJ clean-shaven; M shave

afeitadora F shaver

afeitar VT to shave

afelpado ADJ & M plush

afeminado ADJ effeminate, sissy

aferrado ADJ stubborn, obstinate

aferrar VT (agarrar) to grasp; (atar) to grapple; **—se** to cling

affaire M affair

Afganistán M Afghanistan

afgano -na ADJ & MF Afghan, Afghani

afianzar[9] VT to secure; (un préstamo) to guarantee

afiche M poster

afición F (inclinación) inclination; (afecto) fondness; (conjunto de aficionados) fans

aficionado -da ADJ **— a** fond of; MF (no profesional) amateur; (hincha) fan

aficionarse VI **— a** to become fond of

afilado ADJ sharp; M sharpening

afilador -ora MF grinder, sharpener

afilar VT to sharpen, to grind

afiliarse VI **— con** to affiliate oneself with

afín ADJ kindred, related

afinación F tune-up

afinado ADJ in tune

afinador -ora MF tuner

afinar VT (una destreza) to perfect; (un plan) to fine-tune; (un piano) to tune; **—se** to become thinner

afinidad F (afecto) affinity; (parentesco) kinship

afirmación F (aseveración) assertion; (aseveración positiva) affirmation

afirmar VT (decir) to assert, to declare; (decir que algo es cierto) to affirm; (sujetar) to secure; **—se** to steady oneself

afirmativa F affirmative answer

afirmativo ADJ affirmative

aflicción F affliction, woe

afligir[11] VT (dar dolor) to afflict; (entristecer) to distress

aflojar VT (una soga) to slacken, to loosen; (la vigilancia) to relax; **— el dinero** to hand over the money; VI to ease up, to slack off; **—se** to work loose

afluencia F influx

afluente M tributary

afluir[31] VI (ríos) to flow (into); (turistas) to flock

afortunado ADJ fortunate, lucky

afrecho M bran

afrenta F affront

afrentar VT to offend

África F Africa

africano -na ADJ & MF African

afroamericano -na ADJ & MF African-American

afrontar VT to face

afuera ADV outdoors, outside; F PL **—s** outskirts

agachar VT to lower; **—se** to crouch, to stoop

agalla F (de pez) gill; (de roble) gallnut; **tener —s** to have guts / spunk

agarrado ADJ tight-fisted

agarrar VT (sujetar) to seize, to grasp, to grab; (capturar) to catch; (adherirse a) to grip; **— por sorpresa** to catch by surprise; **—le la onda a algo** to get the swing of something; **—se** to hold on; **—se de** to latch onto; **agarré por la calle ocho** I took eighth street; **agarró y se fue** he up and went

agarre M grip

agarrón M grab

agarrotarse VI (el cuerpo) to stiffen up; (un motor) to seize (up)

agasajar VT to entertain

agasajo M entertainment

agazaparse VI to crouch

agencia F agency, bureau; **— de viajes** travel agency

agenciar VT to wrangle

agente MF agent; (espía) operative; **— de policía** police officer

ágil ADJ agile, nimble

agilidad F agility

agitación F (acción de agitar, nerviosismo) agitation; (protesta) turmoil, unrest

agitado ADJ (estado) agitated; (vida) eventful, hectic; (mar) choppy; (sueño) uneasy

agitador -ora M (aparato) agitator; MF agitator, troublemaker

agitar VT (sacudir) to agitate, to shake up; (incitar a la protesta) to agitate; **—se** (ponerse nervioso) to get worked up; (moverse) to thrash around

aglomeración F crowd

aglomerado M particle board

aglomerarse VI to crowd together

agnóstico -ca ADJ & MF agnostic

agobiado ADJ (por los enemigos) embattled; (por el trabajo) overwhelmed

agobiante ADJ overwhelming

agobiar VT (con una carga excesiva) to weigh down; (con el trabajo) to overwhelm; (con impuestos) to burden

agolparse VI to crowd together

agonía F throes of death; **ser un —s** to be a whiner

agonizante ADJ dying

agonizar[9] VI to be in the throes of death

agorafobia F agoraphobia

agorero -ra ADJ ominous; MF soothsayer

agosto M August; **hacer su —** to make hay while the sun shines

agotado ADJ (una persona) worn-out; (un libro) out-of-print; (una mercancía) out-of-stock

agotamiento M (de una persona) exhaustion; (de un recurso) depletion

agotar VT (un recurso) to exhaust, to use up, to deplete; (la energía) to sap; (un libro) to go out of print; (a una persona) to wear down; **—se** (acabarse) to be all gone; (venderse) to sell out; (secarse) to dry up

agraciado ADJ attractive

agraciar VT to grace

agradable ADJ (persona) agreeable, pleasant, congenial; (situación) pleasant, enjoyable

agradar VT to please

agradecer[13] VT (dar las gracias) to thank; (sentir gratitud) to be grateful for; **se agradece** thank you

agradecido ADJ thankful, grateful

agradecimiento M thankfulness, appreciation; (en un libro) acknowledgment

agrado M pleasure; **de su —** to his liking

agrandamiento M enlargement

agrandar VT to enlarge

agrario ADJ agrarian

agravar VT to aggravate, to make worse; **—se** to get worse

agraviar VT to outrage

agravio M outrage

agredir[50] VT to assault

agregado -da MF (funcionario de embajada) attaché; (profesor asociado) adjunct; M (mezcla) aggregate

agregar[7] VT to add

agresión F (violencia) aggression; (ataque) assault; **— con lesiones** assault and battery

agresivo ADJ aggressive

agresor -ora MF aggressor, assailant

agreste ADJ rough

agriar[16] VT to make sour; **—se** to go sour

agrícola ADJ INV agricultural

agricultor -ora MF agriculturist, farmer

agricultura F agriculture, farming

agridulce ADJ (sabor) sweet-and-sour; (memoria) bittersweet

agrietarse VI to crack; (los labios) to chap

agrimensor -ora MF surveyor

agrimensura F surveying

agrio ADJ sour

agrisarse VI to gray

agropecuario ADJ agricultural

agrumarse VI to lump

agrupación F group

agrupar VT to group

agua F water; — **con gas** sparkling water; — **corriente** running water; — **de colonia** cologne; — **de grifo** tap water; — **de manantial** spring water; — **dulce** fresh water; —**marina** aquamarine; — **mineral** mineral water; — **oxigenada** hydrogen peroxide; — **salada** salt water; —**s abajo** downstream; —**s arriba** upstream; —**s negras** sewer water; **hacer** — **fam** to take a leak; **se me hace** — **la boca** my mouth is watering

aguacate M avocado

aguacero M shower, cloudburst, downpour

aguada F watering hole

aguadero M watering hole

aguado ADJ (fruta) watery; (vino, sopa) watered-down

aguantar VT (miserias) to endure; (a una persona molesta) to bear, to stand; (un peso) to bear; (la respiración) to hold; VI (mantenerse) to stand; (durar) to last; (esperar) to wait; (no pudrirse) to keep; **aguántate** grin and bear it

aguante M (para el trabajo) endurance, stamina; (para el vino) tolerance

aguar[8] VT (añadir agua, despojar de fuerza) to water down; (estropear) to spoil; —**se** to become diluted; MF SG **aguafiestas** killjoy, wet blanket

aguardar VI to wait; VT to wait for, to await

aguardentoso ADJ hoarse

aguardiente M brandy

aguarrás M turpentine

agudeza F (visual) sharpness, keenness; (del ingenio) quickness; (para los negocios) acumen; (dicho agudo) witticism

agudo ADJ (dolor, enfermedad, ángulo) acute; (vista, mente) sharp, keen; (mentón) pointed; (voz) high-pitched; (chiste) witty

agüero M portent, omen; **de mal** — portentous

aguijada F goad

aguijar VT to goad

aguijón M (de planta) spur; (de insecto) sting, stinger

aguijonear VT (a un animal) to goad, to prod; (insecto) to sting

águila F eagle; **es un** — he is sharp

aguilucho M eaglet

aguinaldo M Christmas bonus

aguja F (para coser, tejer, de tocadiscos, de pino, de velocímetro) needle; (de reloj) hand; (riel móvil) railroad switch; (chapitel) steeple, spire; — **de croché** crochet hook; — **de punto** knitting needle; — **de zurcir** darning needle; **como una** — **en un pajar** like a needle in a haystack

agujerear VT to pierce

agujero M hole; (de una ley) loophole; (déficit) shortfall; — **negro** black hole; **tapar** —**s** to pay debts

aguzar[9] VT to sharpen; — **el oído** to prick up one's ears

ahechaduras F PL chaff

ahí ADV there; **por** — over there, thereabouts; **de** — hence; — **te quiero ver** I want to see you in that situation

ahijado -a M godson; F goddaughter

ahínco trabajar con — to work hard

ahogar[7] VT (asfixiar en agua) to drown; (inundar un motor con combustible) to flood; (asfixiar por falta de aire) to smother; (reprimir un grito) to stifle; (asfixiar por presión al cuello) to throttle, to strangle, to choke; — **las penas bebiendo** to drown one's sorrows in drink; —**se** (en agua) to drown

ahogo M (por calor, falta de aire) suffocation; (por un esfuerzo) breathlessness; **vivir sin** —**s** to live a comfortable life

ahondar VT (un hoyo) to deepen; (un asunto) to dig deeper into; —**se** to become deeper

ahora ADV now; — **bien** now then; — **mismo** right now; **por** — for the present, for now; **hasta** — to date, up to now, so far

ahorcar[6] VT to hang, **fam** to string up

ahorrar VT to save; (librar de una molestia) to spare

ahorrativo ADJ frugal, thrifty

ahorro M thriftiness; —**s** savings

ahuecar[6] VT to hollow out; — **la voz** to speak in a hollow voice

ahumado ADJ smoked; M smoking

ahumar VT to smoke

ahuyentar VT to drive away, to scare away; —**se** to get scared

airado ADJ irate

airarse VI to get angry

airbag M airbag

aire M air; (melodía) tune; (manera de ser) manner; — **acondicionado** air conditioning; — **libre** outdoors; **al** — **libre** outdoors; **cambiar de** —**s** to change surroundings; **darse** —**s** to posture; **en el** — up in the air; **estar en**

el — to be on the air; **tener — de** to look like; **tomar —** to breathe in; **tomar el —** to get some air

airear VT to air out

airoso ADJ graceful

aislacionismo M isolationism

aislado ADJ (persona) isolated; (lugar) secluded

aislador M insulator; ADJ insulating

aislamiento M (acción de aislarse) isolation; (cosa que aísla) insulation; (soledad) seclusion

aislante M insulator

aislar VT (dejar separado, separar) to isolate; (poner fuera de contacto) to insulate; (rechazar socialmente) to ostracize

ajar VT (una planta) to wither; (las manos) to make rough; (la piel) to age

ajedrez M chess

ajeno ADJ (de otro) belonging to someone else; (extraño) alien; **— a un peligro** oblivious to a danger; **— a mi voluntad** beyond my control; **— a mi experiencia** foreign to my experience

ajetrearse VI to bustle about

ajetreo M bustle, hustle and bustle

ají M chili

ajo M garlic

ajuar M (de novia) trousseau; (mobiliario) furnishings

ajustado ADJ tight, snug; **— a la ley** in accordance with the law

ajustar VT (hacer corresponder, retocar una prenda) to adjust; (retocar un contrato) to tweak; (apretar) to tighten; VI to fit tight; **— cuentas** to settle accounts; **—se a derecho** to be in accordance with the law

ajuste M (acción de ajustar) adjustment; (del cinturón) tightening; (de una máquina) fine-tuning; (de cuentas) settlement; (de una prenda) alteration; **hacer —s** to tinker with

ala F (de ave) wing; (de sombrero) brim; **cortarle las —s a alguien** to clip someone's wings

alabanza F praise

alabar VT to praise

alabeo M warp

alacena F pantry

alacrán M scorpion

alamar M (adorno con flecos) frog; (presilla) clasp

alambique M still

alambrada F wire fence

alambrado M (barrera) wire fence; (acción de alambrar) wiring

alambrar VT to wire

alambre M wire; **— de púas** barbed wire

alameda F poplar grove

álamo M poplar (tree)

alancear VT to wound with a lance, to spear

alano M mastiff

alarde M show; **hacer — de** to boast of, to show off

alardear VI **— de** to boast about

alargar[7] VT (hacer más largo) to lengthen; (un brazo, un guiso) to stretch (out); **— la vista** to peer into the distance; **—se** to go on (longer than expected)

alarido M scream, howl

alarma F alarm; **— antirrobo** burglar alarm; **— contra incendios** fire alarm

alarmar VT to alarm

alba F dawn

albacea MF INV executor

albanés -esa ADJ & MF Albanian

Albania F Albania

albañal M sewer

albañil M mason, bricklayer

albañilería F masonry

albaricoque M apricot

albatros M albatross

alberca F (depósito) reservoir; (piscina) *Méx* swimming pool

albergar[7] VT (dar refugio) to shelter; (hospedar) to lodge; (ser sede de) to house; (guardar rencor, un secreto) to harbor; **—se** to take shelter

albino -na MF albino

albóndiga F meatball

albor M dawn

alborada F dawn; reveille

albornoz M bathrobe

alborotador -ora ADJ rowdy; MF troublemaker

alborotar VT (el pelo) to muss; (la casa) to mess up; (la calle) to cause trouble in; (a los niños) to excite; **—se** to get excited

alboroto M hubbub, fuss

alborozado ADJ joyful

alborozar[9] VT to gladden; **—se** to rejoice

alborozo M joy

albricias F PL & INTERJ congratulations

álbum M album

alcachofa F artichoke

alcahuete -ta MF (soplón) tattletale; (mediador, encubridor) procurer

alcaide M warden

alcalde -esa MF mayor

álcali M alkali

alcalino ADJ alkaline

alcance M (de una persona) reach; (de los deseos) attainment; (de un misil) range; (de una ley) scope; **de corto(s) —(s)**

meager intellect; **al** — at hand, within reach; **a su** — within his reach; **al** — **del oído** within hearing; **dar** — **a** to catch up with; **de gran** — far-reaching; **de largo** — long-range

alcancía F piggybank

alcanfor M camphor

alcantarilla F (para agua sucia) sewer; (para lluvias) gully, gutter

alcantarillado M sewage system

alcanzar[9] VT (llegar a un punto, cumplir un deseo) to reach; (igualar) to catch up with; (pasar, poner en la mano) to pass; (herir a balazos) to get; **no alcanzo a verlo** I can't quite see it; **no me alcanza el dinero** I don't have enough money; **alcancé a conocer a mi abuela** I was born soon enough to meet my grandmother

alcaparra F caper

alcaucil M artichoke

alcázar M fortress

alce M elk; (norteamericano) moose

alcoba F bedroom

alcohol M alcohol; — **etílico** ethyl alcohol

alcohólico -ca ADJ & MF alcoholic

alcoholismo M alcoholism

alcornoque M (árbol) cork tree; (persona) blockhead

alcuza F oilcan

aldaba F (para llamar) knocker; (para cerrar) bolt

aldabón M large knocker

aldea F village, hamlet

aldeano -na MF villager; **joven aldeana** village girl

aleación F alloy

alear VT (metales) to alloy; (alas) to flap

aleatorio ADJ random

aleccionar VT to teach a lesson

aledaños M PL vicinity

alegar[7] VT (aducir) to adduce; (pretender) to claim

alegato M (a favor de) plea; (en contra de) allegation

alegoría F allegory

alegrar VT (a una persona) to gladden; (una fiesta) to brighten up; **—se** to be glad; (por efecto del alcohol) to get tipsy

alegre ADJ joyful, cheerful, lighthearted; (ebrio) tipsy, lit

alegría F joy, merriment, cheer

alejamiento M withdrawal

alejar VT (distanciar) to move away; (ahuyentar) to scare off; **—se** (físicamente) to move away; (emocionalmente) to withdraw

alelar VT to stupefy

alemán -ana ADJ & MF German; M (lengua) German

Alemania F Germany

alentar[1] VT (animar) to encourage, to cheer up; VI to breathe

alergia F allergy

alérgico ADJ allergic

alergólogo -ga MF allergist

alero M eaves

alerón M (de avión) aileron, flap; (de coche) spoiler

alerta ADJ INV, ADV & F alert

alertar VT to alert

aleta F (de pez) fin; (de ballena) fluke; (de buceador) flipper

aletargado ADJ sluggish

aletargarse[7] VI to fall into a lethargy

aletazo M flap of a wing

aletear VI to flap, to flutter

aleteo M flapping, flutter

alevín M small fry

alevosía F treachery

alevoso ADJ treacherous

alfabetismo M literacy

alfabetización F literacy

alfabetizar[9] VI (enseñar a leer y a escribir) to teach to read and write; VT (disponer en orden alfabético) to alphabetize

alfabeto M alphabet

alfalfa F alfalfa

alfanumérico ADJ alphanumeric

alfarería F pottery

alfarero -ra MF potter

alféizar M windowsill

alfeñique M (golosina) sugar paste; (persona) weakling

alférez MF second lieutenant; — **de fragata** ensign

alfil M bishop

alfiler M pin; — **de corbata** tiepin; **no cabe un** — it's totally full

alfiletero M pincushion

alfombra F carpet; (suelta) rug

alfombrar VT to carpet

alfombrilla F mat

alforja F saddlebag

alga F seaweed; — s algae

algarabía F uproar

algarrobo M locust tree

algazara F merriment

álgebra F algebra

algo PRON something, anything; ADV somewhat; — **es** — something is better than nothing; **por** — **será** there must be reason

algodón M cotton; — **de azúcar** cotton

candy; **se crió entre algodones** he had
a protected childhood

algoritmo M algorithm

alguacil M sheriff, marshal; (en un tribunal)
bailiff

alguien PRON INDEF somebody, someone;
vino — a hablarte someone came to
talk to you; (en preguntas) anybody,
anyone; **¿— lo vio?** did anyone see him?

alguno ADJ some; **—s** some, a few; **sin
ruido —** without a sound; **en alguna
parte** somewhere; **de alguna manera**
somehow; **en algún momento**
sometime; **¿lo has visto alguna vez?**
have you ever seen him? **¿hay alguna
forma de hacer esto?** is there any way
to do this?

alhaja F jewel (también persona); **—s** jewelry

alhajero M jewelry box

alharaca F fuss

alhelí M wallflower

aliado -da ADJ allied; MF ally

alianza F alliance; (de Dios) covenant

aliar[16] VT to ally

alias M alias

alicaído ADJ crestfallen

alicates M PL pliers

aliciente M inducement

aliento M (aire respirado) breath; (ánimo)
encouragement; **cobrar —** to catch one's
breath; **contener el —** to hold one's
breath; **sin —** out of breath, breathless

aligerar VT to lighten; **— el paso** to quicken
one's pace

alijo M cache, stash

alimentación F (de una persona)
nourishment, food; (de una máquina)
feeding

alimentar VT (a una persona) to feed, to
nourish; (un fuego) to stoke

alimenticio ADJ nutritious, nourishing;
industria alimenticia food industry;
pensión alimenticia alimony

alimento M food, nourishment

alineación F (de un equipo deportivo)
lineup; (de un coche) alignment

alinear VT (un grupo de cosas) to line up; (a
un deportista) to put in the lineup; **—se
con** to align oneself with

aliño M condiment, seasoning

alisar VT to smooth; (pelo) to straighten

alistamiento M enlistment

alistar VT to enlist

aliviar VT (hacer menos pesado) to lighten;
(mitigar) to alleviate, to relieve;
(tranquilizar) to relieve; **—se** (mejorarse)
to get better; (hacer sus necesidades) to

relieve oneself

alivio M relief

aljaba F quiver

aljibe M cistern

allá ADV there, over there; **más —** farther,
beyond; **el más —** the hereafter; **— tú**
that's your problem

allanamiento M raid; **— de morada**
forcible entry

allanar VT (la tierra) to level, to smooth;
(una dificultad) to iron out; (una casa) to
raid; **— el camino** to smooth the way

allegado -da ADJ close to; MF relative

allegar[7] VT to gather; **—se** to arrive

allí ADV (punto en el espacio) there; (punto
en el tiempo) then; **por —** through there

alma F soul; **con toda el —** from the
bottom of one's heart; **hasta el —** to the
bone; **ni un —** not a soul; **no me cabía
el — en el cuerpo** I was overjoyed; **se
me fue el — al piso** my heart sank

almacén M (depósito) warehouse, storehouse,
depot; (tienda) department store;
almacenes department store

almacenaje M storage

almacenamiento M storage

almacenar VT to store, to stock up on

almacenista MF wholesaler

almáciga F nursery

almádena F sledgehammer

almanaque M (publicación anual) almanac;
(calendario) calendar

almeja F clam

almendra F almond

almendro M almond tree

almiar M haystack

almíbar M syrup

almidón M starch

almidonado ADJ stiff

almidonar VT to starch

almirante M admiral

almohada F pillow; **consultarlo con la —**
to sleep on it

almohadilla F (para sentarse) cushion; (en
las patas de los perros) pad

almohadón M cushion

almohaza F currycomb

almohazar[9] VT to groom

almorranas F PL piles, hemorrhoids

almorzar[2,9] VT to lunch, to eat lunch

almuerzo M lunch

alocado ADJ wild

áloe M aloe vera

alojamiento M lodging, accommodations;
(militar) quarters

alojar VT (a un invitado) to lodge, to
accommodate; (a unos huérfanos) to

house; (a las tropas) to quarter; **—se** (una bala) to lodge; (una persona) to board, to room

alondra F lark

alpaca F alpaca

alpinismo M mountain climbing

alpinista MF mountain climber, mountaineer

alpino ADJ alpine

alpiste M birdseed

alquería F farmhouse

alquilar VT to rent; **se alquila** for rent

alquiler M (pago mensual) rent; (acción de alquilar) renting; **coche de —** rental car; **dar en —** to hire out

alquitrán M tar

alquitranar VT to tar

alrededor ADV around; **— de la casa** around the house; **—es** (de un área) surroundings; (de una ciudad) outskirts

alta F discharge; **dar de —** to discharge

altanería F haughtiness

altanero ADJ haughty

altar M altar

alteración F alteration; **alteraciones al orden público** public disturbances

alterar VT to alter; **— el ánimo** to upset; **—se** to get upset

altercado M altercation

altercar[6] VT **— con** to quarrel with

alternador M alternator

alternar VT to alternate; **— con** to rub elbows with

alternativa F alternative

alternativo ADJ (cambiante) alternating; (optativo) alternative

alterno ADJ alternate; **alterna y continua** AC/DC

alteza F highness

altibajos M PL ups and downs

altillo M attic

altímetro M altimeter

altiplano M high plateau

altisonante ADJ high-sounding

altitud F altitude

altivez F haughtiness

altivo ADJ haughty

alto ADJ (que está arriba) high; (que tiene mayor altura vertical) tall; **de alta fidelidad** high fidelity; **de alta potencia** high-powered; **de alta velocidad** high-speed; **en — grado** to a great extent; **en alta mar** on the high seas; M **altavoz** loudspeaker; **altoparlante** loudspeaker; M (altura) height; (piso) upper story; **— el fuego** cease-fire; ADV loud; **hablar —** to talk loud; **cotizarse —** to be set high; INTERJ

halt!

altruismo M altruism

altura F (de persona, edificio, ola, epidemia) height; (de avión) altitude; (del suelo sobre el mar, lugar alto) elevation; **a estas —s** at this stage; **a la — de la calle ocho** at eighth street; **a la — de las circunstancias** equal to the circumstances

alubia F bean

alucinar VT (causar alucinaciones) to hallucinate; (fascinar) to fascinate; (deslumbrar) to bowl over; VI (sufrir alucinaciones) to hallucinate

alud M avalanche

aludir VI **— a** to allude to, to refer to

alumbrado M lighting; ADJ lit

alumbramiento M childbirth

alumbrar VT to light up; (dar a luz) to give birth

aluminio M aluminum

alumnado M student body

alumno -na MF (de enseñanza primaria) pupil; (de enseñanza secundaria) student

alusión F allusion

aluvión M (de preguntas, pedidos) barrage; (de personas) flood

alza F appreciation; **— de precios** boost in prices

alzamiento M (acción de alzar) raising; (insurrección) uprising

alzaprima F crowbar

alzar[9] VT (la mano, la voz, una casa) to raise; (a un niño) to lift up; **— la vista** to look up; **—se** to rise up in rebellion; **—se con** to make off with

amabilidad F kindness; **¿tendría la — de…?** would you mind…?

amable ADJ kind, nice

amado -da MF beloved

amaestrador -ora MF trainer

amaestramiento M training

amaestrar VT to train

amagar[7] VI/VT **amagó que iba a llover** it looked like it was going to rain; **amagó con llover** it threatened to rain

amago M **hacer —** to make as if

amalgamar VT to amalgamate

amamantar VT to nurse, to breast-feed

amanecer[13] VI to dawn; **— enfermo** to wake up ill; **amanecí en Londres** I woke up in London; M dawn, sunrise, daybreak

amanerado ADJ effete

amansar VT to tame

amante MF lover; ADJ **— de** fond of

amañar VT (una elección) to rig; (un documento) to tamper with

amapola F poppy

amar VT to love

amargar[7] VT to embitter

amargo ADJ bitter

amargor M bitterness

amargura F bitterness

amarillear VI/VT to yellow, to turn yellow

amarillento ADJ yellowish

amarillo -lla ADJ yellow; MF (esquirol) scab

amarra F cable, rope; **—s** moorings; **soltar —s** to cast off

amarrar VT (un barco) to moor; (una cosa) to secure, to tie down

amartillar VT (pegar con martillo) to hammer; (un arma) to cock

amasar VT (masa) to knead; (una fortuna) to amass

amateur ADJ & MF amateur

amatista F amethyst

Amazonas M Amazon River

ambages M **hablar sin —** to not mince words, to speak plainly

ámbar M amber

ambición F ambition

ambicionar VT to have the ambition of

ambicioso ADJ ambitious; (codicioso) overambitious

ambidiestro ADJ ambidextrous

ambiental ADJ environmental; (temperatura) ambient

ambiente ADJ ambient; M (condiciones biológicas) environment; (atmósfera) atmosphere, ambiance; (sector social) milieu

ambigüedad F ambiguity

ambiguo ADJ ambiguous

ámbito M (ambiente) scene; (alcance) scope; (esfera) sphere

ambivalente ADJ ambivalent

ambos ADJ & PRON both

ambulancia F ambulance

ambulante ADJ itinerant

ameba F ameba

amedrentar VT to scare

amén INTERJ amen; **decir —** to approve without discussion; **— de** besides

amenaza F threat, menace

amenazador ADJ threatening

amenazar[9] VT to threaten; **— con** to threaten to

amenidad F (cualidad de ameno) pleasantness; (placer) pleasure

amenizar[9] VI to make entertaining

ameno ADJ enjoyable, entertainment

América F America

americano -na ADJ & MF American; F sport coat

ametrallador -ora MF gunner; F (arma) machine gun

ametrallar VT to strafe

amianto M asbestos

amigable ADJ friendly

amígdala F tonsil

amigdalitis F tonsillitis

amigo -ga ADJ friendly; **— de** fond of; **— de lo ajeno** thieving; MF friend

aminoácido M amino acid

aminorar VT to lessen

amistad F (relación) friendship; (amigo) friend; **trabar —** to strike up a friendship

amistoso ADJ friendly, amicable

amnesia F amnesia

amniocentesis F amniocentesis

amnistía F amnesty

amo -ma M (de esclavo, sirviente) master; (de animal) owner; F (de esclavo, de sirviente) mistress; (de animal) owner; **ama de leche** wet nurse; **ama de llaves** housekeeper; **ama de casa** homemaker

amodorrado ADJ drowsy

amodorrar VI to make drowsy; **—se** to become drowsy

amolar[2] VT to annoy

amoldar VT to mold

amonestación F admonition, warning

amonestar VT to admonish, to warn

amoníaco M ammonia

amontonamiento M pile

amontonar VT to pile up

amor M love; **— propio** self-esteem; **de mil —es** gladly; **hacerle el — a** to make love to; **por el — de Dios** for God's sake; **por — al arte** unremunerated

amoral ADJ amoral

amoratado ADJ (de golpes) black-and-blue; (de frío, por falta de oxígeno) blue

amordazar[9] VT (a una persona) to gag; (a un perro, a los críticos) to muzzle

amorfo ADJ amorphous

amorío M love affair

amoroso ADJ loving, amorous

amortajar VT to shroud

amortiguador M shock absorber

amortiguar[8] VT (un sonido) to muffle, to absorb; (un golpe) to cushion, to absorb; (un dolor) to deaden, to dull

amortizar[9] VT (recuperar a plazos) to amortize; (depreciar) to depreciate

amoscarse[6] VI to get peeved

amostazarse[9] VI to get peeved

amotinarse VI (en un barco) to mutiny; (en una ciudad) to riot

amparar VT (proteger) to protect; (refugiar) to shelter; **—se** to protect oneself

amparo M (protección) protection; (refugio) shelter; **al — de** under the protection of

amperio M ampere

ampicilina F ampicillin

ampliación F (de una foto) enlargement; (de una casa) extension

ampliar[16] VT (una foto) to enlarge; (una calle) to extend; (una explicación) to expand; (un volumen) to amplify

amplificador M amplifier

amplificar[6] VT (un sonido) to amplify; (una imagen) to magnify

amplio ADJ (información, tiempo) ample; (piso) spacious, roomy; (región, resonancia, sonrisa) broad; (vestido) full; **de amplias miras** open-minded

amplitud F (de comprensión) breadth; (de onda) amplitude

ampolla F (de la epidermis) blister; (vasija) vial

ampollar VT to blister

ampuloso ADJ bombastic

amputar VT to amputate

amueblar VT to furnish

amuleto M amulet, charm

anacronismo M anachronism

ánade M duck

anadear VI to waddle

anadeo M waddle

anaerobio ADJ anaerobic

anal ADJ anal

anales M PL annals

analfabetismo M illiteracy

analfabeto -ta ADJ & MF illiterate

analgésico ADJ & M analgesic

análisis M analysis

analítico ADJ analytical, analytic

analizar[9] VT to analyze

analogía F analogy

analógico ADJ (relativo a la analogía) analogical; (no digital) analog

análogo ADJ analogous

ananás M pineapple

anaquel M shelf

anaranjado ADJ & M (color) orange

anarquía F anarchy

anarquista MF anarchist

anatema M anathema

anatomía F anatomy

anatómico ADJ anatomical

anca F haunch, rump

ancho ADJ wide, broad; **a sus anchas** at his ease; **me viene —** it's too wide for me; M width, breadth; **a lo —** widthwise; **tiene un metro de —** it's one meter wide

anchoa F anchovy

anchura F width, breadth

ancianidad F old age

anciano -na ADJ elderly, aged; MF old person

ancla F anchor

anclar VI/VT to anchor

andada F **volver a las —s** to backslide

andador -ora MF walker

Andalucía F Andalusia

andaluz -za ADJ & MF Andalusian

andamiaje M (para construcción) scaffolding; (fundamento) framework

andamio M scaffold

andanada F broadside

andante ADJ walking

andanzas F PL adventures

andar[20] VI to walk; (coche, motor, reloj) to run; (el tiempo) to pass; (un aparato) to work; **— con cuidado** to be careful; **— en coche** to travel by car, to ride in a car; **— mal** to be in bad shape, to be a mess; **— mal del corazón** to have heart trouble; **—se por las ramas / con vueltas** to beat around the bush; **no —se con rodeos** to make no bones about it; **en eso ando** that's what I'm up to; **¡andando!** move on! **¿dónde anda a estas horas?** where is he at this hour? **¡ándale!** _Méx_ (apresúrate) come on! (de acuerdo) OK; M gait

andariego ADJ fond of walking

andas F **llevar en —** _RP_ to carry on one's shoulders

andén M platform

Andes M PL Andes

andino ADJ Andean

Andorra F Andorra

andorrano -na ADJ & MF Andorran

andrajo M rag, tatter

andrajoso ADJ ragged, tattered

andrógino ADJ androgynous

anécdota F anecdote

anegar[7] VT to flood

anejo ADJ attached; M accompanying volume

anemia F anemia; **— falciforme** sickle cell anemia

anémico ADJ anemic

anestesia F (acción de anestesiar) anesthesia; (sustancia) anesthetic

anestésico ADJ & M anesthetic

anestesiología F anesthesiology

aneurisma M aneurysm

anexar VT to annex; (con una carta) to enclose

anexión F annexation

anexo ADJ attached; M (de un edificio) annex, extension; (a una ley) rider

anfeta F _fam_ speed

anfetamina F amphetamine

anfibio ADJ & M amphibian
anfiteatro M amphitheater
anfitrión -ona M host; F hostess
ángel M angel; **— de la guarda** guardian angel
angelical ADJ angelic
angélico ADJ angelic
angina F **—s** tonsillitis; **— del pecho** angina pectoris
angioplastia F angioplasty
anglosajón -ona ADJ & MF Anglo-Saxon
Angola F Angola
angolano -na, angoleño -ña, angolés -esa ADJ & MF Angolan
angostar VT to narrow, to contract
angosto ADJ narrow
angostura F (cualidad de angosto) narrowness; (desfiladero) narrows
anguila F eel; **— eléctrica** electric eel
angular ADJ angular
ángulo M (figura geométrica, enfoque) angle; (rincón, esquina) corner; **— muerto** blind spot; **— recto** right angle
anguloso ADJ angular
angustia F (desasosiego) anguish, anxiety, distress; (congoja) heartache; (desazón existencial) angst
angustiado ADJ distraught
angustiante ADJ nerve-wracking
angustiar VT to distress; **—se** to feel distressed
angustioso ADJ distressing
anhelante ADJ longing
anhelar VT to long for, to yearn for
anhelo M longing, yearning
anidar VI to nest
anillas F PL gymnastics rings
anillo M ring; **— de boda** wedding ring; **me queda como — al dedo** it fits me like a glove
ánima F soul of the departed
animación F (viveza) animation, liveliness; (en películas) animation
animado ADJ (vivo) animate; (bullicioso) lively
animador -ora MF (de un espectáculo) host; (de un equipo) cheerleader
animal ADJ & M animal
animar VT (dar vida) to animate, to enliven; (incitar) to encourage, to urge on; (dar aliento) to cheer up; **—se** (alegrarse) to cheer up; (atreverse) to gather courage
ánimo M (espíritu) spirit; (aliento) encouragement; (humor) mood; (intención) intention; **no estoy de — para eso** I'm not in the mood for that; INTERJ hang in there!

animosidad F animosity
animoso ADJ spirited
aniñado ADJ childlike
aniquilar VT to annihilate, to wipe out
anís M anise
aniversario M anniversary
anoche ADV last night
anochecer[13] VI to get dark; **anochecimos en París** night found us in Paris; M nightfall, dusk
anomalía F anomaly
anómalo ADJ anomalous
anonadado ADJ dumbfounded
anonadar VT (aniquilar) to annihilate; (desconcertar) to dumbfound; **—se** to become dumbfounded
anónimo ADJ anonymous; M anonymous letter
anorak M anorak
anorexia F anorexia
anoréxico ADJ anorexic
anormal ADJ abnormal; MF freak
anotación F (nota) annotation, notation; (en fútbol) goal
anotar VT (apuntar) to note; (marcar un tanto) to score; **—se** to sign up
anquilosarse VT (las articulaciones) to become stiff; (una institución) to become stagnant
ansia F (deseo) eagerness; (congoja) anguish
ansiar[16] VT to covet
ansiedad F anxiety
ansioso ADJ anxious, eager
antagonismo M antagonism
antagonista MF antagonist
antagonizar[9] VT to antagonize
antaño ADV in the old days
antártico ADJ antarctic
Antártida F Antarctica
ante PREP before; **— este problema** in the face of this problem; **— todo** above all; M suede
anteanoche ADV night before last
anteayer ADV day before yesterday
antebrazo M forearm
antecedente ADJ & M antecedent; **—s** (profesionales) background; (criminales) record
antecesor -ora MF (antepasado) ancestor; (predecesor) predecessor
antedicho ADJ aforesaid
antelación LOC ADV **con —** beforehand
antemano LOC ADV **de —** beforehand
antena F (de radio) antenna, aerial; (de insecto) antenna, feeler
anteojera F blinder
anteojos M PL glasses, spectacles; **— de sol**

sunglasses; — **bifocales** bifocals

antepasado -da MF ancestor, forebear

antepecho M sill

anteponer[39] VT (poner delante, poner antes) to place before; (dar preferencia) to give priority to

anterior ADJ (en el tiempo) previous; (en el espacio) anterior, front; — **a** prior to

antes ADV before; — **de** before; — **la muerte** I'd rather die; — **bien** rather

antiaborto ADJ antiabortion, right-to-life

antiácido ADJ & M antacid

antiaéreo ADJ antiaircraft

antibacteriano ADJ antibacterial

antibalas ADJ INV bulletproof

antibalístico ADJ antiballistic

antibiótico ADJ & M antibiotic

antibloqueo ADJ INV antilock

anticipación LOC ADV **con** — in advance

anticipado LOC ADV **por** — in advance

anticipar VT (una fecha) to move up; (dinero) to advance; (el porvenir) to anticipate; —**se a los acontecimientos** to jump the gun

anticipo M advance, deposit

anticoncepción F contraception

anticonceptivo ADJ & M contraceptive

anticongelante M antifreeze

anticuado ADJ antiquated, out-of-date, outdated

anticuerpo M antibody

antidepresivo ADJ & M antidepressant

antídoto M antidote

antieconómico ADJ wasteful

antiestético ADJ unsightly

antígeno M antigen

antigualla F old piece of junk

antiguano -na ADJ & MF Antiguan

Antigua y Barbuda F Antigua and Barbuda

antigüedad F (cualidad de antiguo) antiquity; (objeto) antique; (tiempo en un cargo) seniority

antiguo ADJ (era, historia) ancient; (ropa) old; (mueble) antique; **a la antigua** in the old style; **la antigua capital** the former capital; **más** — with more seniority

antihistamínico M antihistamine

antiinflamatorio ADJ & M anti-inflammatory

Antillas F PL West Indies

antílope M antelope

antimonio M antimony

antimonopolio ADJ antitrust

antioxidante ADJ & M antioxidant

antiparras F PL goggles

antipatía F antipathy

antipático ADJ unfriendly, unkind

antipoliomielítico ADJ antipolio

antisemitismo M anti-Semitism

antiséptico ADJ & M antiseptic

antisocial ADJ antisocial

antítesis F antithesis

antitranspirante M antiperspirant

antitrust ADJ antitrust

antojadizo ADJ whimsical

antojarse VI **se le antojó comer salchicha** he took a notion to eat sausage; **esa tarea se me antoja difícil** that task seems hard to me

antojo M (deseo) whim, craving; (mancha de nacimiento) birthmark

antología F anthology, reader

antónimo M antonym

antorcha F torch

antracita F anthracite

ántrax M anthrax

antro M (bar) dive, joint; — **de perdición** den of iniquity

antropología F anthropology

antropólogo -ga MF anthropologist

anual ADJ annual, yearly

anualidad F annuity

anuario M annual, yearbook

anudar VT to knot; **se le anudó la garganta** he got all choked up

anulación F (de un contrato) cancellation; (de un matrimonio) annulment

anular VT (un matrimonio) to annul; (un contrato, un evento) to cancel; (una sentencia) to overrule, to overturn; (un talón) to void; M ring finger

anunciador -ora MF announcer

anunciante MF advertiser

anunciar VT (información) to announce; (un producto) to advertise

anuncio M (de información) announcement; (de un producto) advertisement; — **clasificado** classified advertisement; — **publicitario** advertisement; **poner un** — to place an ad

anzuelo M fishhook; **morder / picar el** — to take the bait

añadidura F addition; **por** — in addition

añadir VT to add

añejo ADJ aged, vintage

añicos M **hacerse** — to break into a thousand pieces

añil M indigo, bluing

año M year; (de la escuela) grade; (de vino) vintage; — **bisiesto** leap year; — **luz** light-year; **de cuarenta** —**s** aged forty; **el** — **pasado** last year; **en los** —**s veinte** in the 1920s; **entrado en** —**s** getting on in years; **¿cuántos —s tienes?** how old are you?

añojo -ja MF yearling

añoranza F longing; (del hogar) homesickness

añorar VT to long for, to be homesick for

añoso ADJ old

añublo M blight

aorta F aorta

apabullar VT (impresionar) to bowl over; (derrotar) to crush

apacentar[1] VI to graze, to pasture

apacible ADJ good-natured

apaciguar[8] VT (pacificar) to pacify; (aplacar) to mollify, to appease; **—se** to calm down

apadrinar VT to sponsor; (en un bautismo) to act as godfather to; (en una boda) to act as best man for; (en un duelo) to second

apagado ADJ (no llamativo) flat; (no intenso) dull

apagar[7] VT (un fuego) to put out, to extinguish; (una luz) to turn off, to turn out; (motor) to turn off, to kill; (una vida) to kill, to snuff out; (la sed) to quench; **—se** (luz) to go out; (un color) to fade; (una voz) to trail off; (un volcán) to become extinct

apagón M blackout, outage

apalabrarse VI **— con** to make a verbal agreement with

apalear VT to thrash

aparador M sideboard, buffet, cupboard

aparato M (de gimnasia) apparatus; (de cocina) appliance; (teléfono) telephone; (máquina, dirigencia política) machine; (boato) pomp; **— circulatorio** circulatory system; **— de televisión** television set; **— ortodóntico** braces; **— ortopédico** leg brace

aparatoso ADJ pompous

aparcamiento M (lugar para aparcar) parking lot; (acción de aparcar) parking

aparcar[6] VI/VT to park; MF SG **aparcacoches** valet

aparcero -ra MF sharecropper

aparear VT (animales) to mate; (calcetines) to match, to pair; **—se** (animales) to mate; (en un baile) to pair off

aparecer[13] VI (ponerse a la vista, publicarse) to appear; (hacer acto de presencia) to show up; **se me apareció un ángel** an angel appeared to me

aparejar VT (un cuarto, un ejército) to prepare; (problemas) to entail; (una embarcación) to rig

aparejo M (de caballo) harness; (de buque) rigging; (para pescar) tackle; **—s** equipment

aparentar VT to feign; VI to show off; **aparenta la edad que tiene** she looks her age

aparente ADJ apparent; **un precio —** an acceptable price

aparición F (fantasma) apparition; (acción de aparecer) appearance

apariencia F (aspecto) appearance; (fingimiento) pretense, semblance; **las —s engañan** appearances are deceiving; **guardar las —s** to keep up appearances

apartado M section; **— postal** post office box; ADJ (recóndito) secluded; (distante) distant; **muy —** far apart

apartamento M apartment

apartamiento M separation

apartar VT **aparta las monedas de veinticinco centavos** set aside / sort out the quarters; **apartó la silla de la pared** he moved the chair away from the wall; **lo aparté para hablarle** I took him aside to talk to him; **apartó la cacerola del fuego** she took the pan off the fire; **lo apartó de un empujón** she pushed him away; **apartaron al ministro de su cargo** they removed the minister from his post; **apartó la vista** he looked away; VI **se apartaron del buen camino** they strayed from the straight and narrow; **los resultados se apartan de lo esperado** the results depart / deviate from the norm; **se apartó para que no lo atropellara el coche** he got out of the way so the car wouldn't hit him

aparte ADJ separate; ADV **bromas —** kidding aside; **dejar —** to exclude; **punto y —** new paragraph; M aside; PREP **— de** (además de) besides; (salvo) except for

apasionado ADJ (amor, hombre) passionate; (defensa, comentario) impassioned

apasionar VT **eso me apasiona** I love that; **—se por** to be passionate about

apatía F apathy

apático ADJ apathetic

apear VT to get down; **—se** to dismount

apechugar[7] VI **— con** to put up with

apedrear VT to stone

apegado ADJ attached

apegarse[7] VI to become attached

apego M attachment

apelación F appeal

apelar VI/VT to appeal

apellidarse VI to have the surname of

apellido M surname, last name

apelotonarse VI (una almohada) to ball up; (gente) to bunch together

apenado ADJ grieved

apenar VT to grieve, to pain; **—se** to be grieved

apenas ADV hardly, scarcely, barely; **— llegó, se desmayó** no sooner had he arrived than he fainted

apéndice M (órgano, parte de un libro) appendix; (añadido) appendage

apendicectomía F appendectomy

apendicitis F appendicitis

apercibir VT to warn; **—se de** to notice

aperitivo M appetizer

apero M farm implement

apertura F opening

apesadumbrado ADJ doleful

apestar VT (hacer heder) to stink up; (causar la peste) to plague; VI to stink, to reek

apestoso ADJ smelly

apetecer[13] VI **no me apetece ir contigo** I don't feel like going with you

apetecible ADJ appetizing

apetito M appetite

apetitoso ADJ appetizing

apiadarse VI **— de** to pity, to take pity on

ápice M apex; (de la lengua) tip; **no apartarse ni un —** not to diverge a jot

apio M celery

apisonadora F steamroller

apisonar VT to pack down

aplacamiento M appeasement

aplacar[6] VT (a una persona) to appease, to mollify; (miedo) to allay; (sed, pasión) to quench; **—se** to relent

aplanadora F steamroller

aplanamiento M flattening, leveling

aplanar VT (un terreno) to level, to flatten; (con una aplanadora) to roll

aplastado ADJ flattened

aplastamiento M crushing

aplastante ADJ (derrota) crushing; (victoria) sweeping

aplastar VT (achatar) to squash, to crush; (derrotar) to plaster, to stomp; (una revolución) to squelch, to smash, to crush; **—se** to crumple

aplaudir VI/VT to applaud

aplauso, aplausos M (PL) applause

aplazamiento M postponement; (de un proceso legal) continuance

aplazar[9] VT to postpone, to put off

aplicable ADJ applicable

aplicación F (acción de aplicarse) application; (de un castigo) administration

aplicado ADJ industrious

aplicar[6] VT to apply; **—se** to work hard, to apply oneself

aplomado ADJ (equilibrado) poised; (vertical) plumb

aplomar VT to plumb

aplomo M poise

apnea M apnea

apocado ADJ timid

apocalipsis MF apocalypse

apocamiento M timidity

apocarse[6] VT to become intimidated

apodar VT to nickname

apoderado -da MF proxy, agent

apoderarse VI **— de** to take possession of, to seize

apodo M nickname

apogeo M apogee; **en su —** (una fiesta) in full swing; (un estilo) in its heyday, at its peak

apolillado ADJ (comido por las polillas) moth-eaten; (anticuado) antiquated

apología F apology

aporrear VT to club, to cudgel

aportación F contribution

aportar VT (posibilidades, evidencia) to provide; (dinero) to contribute

aporte M contribution

aposento M chamber

apostador -ora MF bettor

apostar[2] VI/VT to bet, to wager; (a un centinela) to station, to post; **— por** (caballo) to bet on; (cambio) to commit to

apóstol M apostle

apóstrofe MF apostrophe, invocation

apóstrofo M apostrophe

apostura F bearing

apoyar VT (sostener) to rest; (respaldar) to support, to back; (votar por) to second; (respaldar un argumento) to buttress; **—se en** (recostarse contra) to lean on, to prop against; (basarse en) to be based on; M SG **apoyabrazos** armrest

apoyo M support

apreciable ADJ (digno de aprecio) esteemed; (perceptible) noticeable; (registrable) appreciable

apreciación F appreciation

apreciado ADJ dear

apreciar VT (reconocer la valía) to appreciate; (percibir) to notice; (registrar) to measure; (considerar) to take into consideration; (sentir afecto) to cherish; **—se** (un fenómeno) to be noticeable; (moneda) to appreciate

aprecio M appreciation

aprehender VT (a un delincuente) to apprehend; (contrabando) to seize; (una idea) to grasp

aprehensión F (arresto) apprehension; (incautación) seizure

apremiante ADJ pressing

apremiar VT to pressure

apremio M pressure

aprender VI/VT to learn; **— de memoria** to memorize, to learn by heart

aprendiz -za MF (de un oficio) apprentice, trainee; (de una lengua, canto) learner

aprendizaje M (de un oficio) apprenticeship; (acto de aprender) learning

aprensión F apprehension, misgivings

aprensivo ADJ apprehensive

apresar VT (aprisionar) to imprison; (incautar) to seize

aprestar VT to prepare; **—se a** to get ready to

apresurado ADJ hasty, hurried

apresurar VT to hurry, to hasten

apretado ADJ (zapato) tight; (beso) hard; (racimo) compact; (síntesis) succinct; (jornada) busy; (situación) difficult, dangerous

apretar[1] VT (un botón) to press; (un gatillo) to squeeze; (un tornillo) to tighten; (los dientes, puños) to clench; (a un bebé) to clasp; **me apretó para que le diera dinero** he pressured me to give him money; **ese profesor nos aprieta mucho** that teacher demands a lot of us; VI (zapatos) to be tight, to pinch; (sol) to be intense; (esforzarse) to try hard, to bear down; **—se** to crowd together

apretón M squeeze; **— de manos** handshake

aprieto M jam, fix, predicament; **en —s** need, hard-pressed, in dire straits; **estar en un —** to be in a tight spot, to be in trouble, to be in a pickle; **poner en —s** to embarrass

aprisa ADV quickly

aprisco M (para el ganado) fold

aprisionar VT to trap

aprobación F (aceptación) approval; (de una ley) passage, adoption; (nota) passing grade

aprobar[2] VT (una medida, una opinión) to approve of; (una ley) to pass, to approve; (un examen) to pass; VI to pass

aprontar VT to ready

apropiación F appropriation; **— indebida** embezzlement

apropiado ADJ appropriate, suitable

apropiarse VT to appropriate

aprovechable ADJ usable

aprovechado ADJ opportunistic

aprovechamiento M use

aprovechar VT (una ocasión) to take advantage of; (el espacio) to utilize; (la enseñanza) to profit from; vi to be useful; **—se de** to take advantage of; **¡que aproveche!** enjoy your meal!

aproximación F approach

aproximado ADJ approximate

aproximar VT to bring near; **—se** to approach; **— a** to approximate

aptitud F aptitude; **—es musicales** musical aptitude

apto ADJ apt, suitable; **— para menores** for general audiences

apuesta F bet, wager

apuesto ADJ good-looking

apuntalar VT to prop up, to shore up

apuntar VT (señalar) to point out; (dirigir a un blanco) to aim; (matricular) to enroll; (escribir) to write down, to note; (ayudar a un actor) to prompt; vi (una flecha) to point; (canas) to sprout; **—se** to score; **— a un blanco** to aim at a target; **me apunto para ir con vosotros** I'm game to go with you

apunte M notation; **—s** notes; **tomar —s** to take notes; **llevar el — a alguien** to pay attention to someone

apuñalar VT to stab

apurado ADJ (situación) difficult; (persona) in dire straits; Am (apresurado) in a hurry

apurar VT (consumir) to drink up; (apremiar) to put under pressure

apuro M predicament, fix; Am (prisa) hurry; **estar en —s** to be in distress

aquejado ADJ stricken

aquejar VT to afflict, to trouble

aquel ADJ that; **aquella chica se llama María** that girl is named María; **aquellas ciudades son antiguas** those cities are old; PRON that one; **— es el mayor** that one is the oldest; **aquellos son mis hijos** those are my children; **de mis dos hijos, Juan y Pedro, este es gordo y — es flaco** of my two sons, Juan and Pedro, the latter is fat and the former is thin; **en / por — entonces** back then

aquí ADV here; **está por —** it is around here; **ven por —** come this way; **hasta —** this far; **de — a cuatro horas** four hours from now; **de — en adelante** from now on; **de — para allá** to and fro, back and forth; **— y ahora** here and now

aquietar VT to quiet; **—se** (los nervios) to calm down; (una tormenta) to subside

ara LOC ADV **en —s** for the sake of

árabe MF (persona) Arab; (caballo) Arabian; (lengua) Arabic; ADJ Arabian; (costumbre, arte) Arab

Arabia Saudí, Arabia Saudita F Saudi
Arabia
arácnido M arachnid
arado M plow
Aragón M Aragon
aragonés -esa ADJ Aragonese; MF (persona)
Aragonese; M (dialecto) Aragonese
arancel M (impuesto) tariff; (lista de
honorarios) list of fees
arancelario ADJ **acuerdo —** tariff agreement
arándano M cranberry
arandela F washer
araña F (arácnido) spider; (candelabro)
chandelier
arañar VT (rayar) to scratch; (herir con
garras) to claw, to scratch; (raspar) to
scrape, to score
arañazo M scratch
arañero M warbler
arar VI/VT to plow, to till
arbitraje M arbitration
arbitrar VT (un desacuerdo) to arbitrate; (un
partido) to referee, to officiate; (un partido
de béisbol) to umpire
arbitrario ADJ arbitrary
arbitrio M (libre albedrío) free will;
(capricho) whim; (decisión) discretion;
(deseos) wishes
árbitro -tra MF (del buen gusto) arbiter; (de
conflictos) arbitrator; (de encuentros
deportivos) referee
árbol M tree; (mástil) mast; **— de Navidad**
Christmas tree; **— de levas** camshaft; **—
genealógico** family tree
arbolado ADJ woody, wooded
arboleda F grove, clump
arbóreo ADJ arboreal
arbusto M shrub, bush
arca F ark; **— de Noé** Noah's ark; **las —s
municipales** municipal coffers
arcada F arcade, archway; **tener / dar —s** to
gag
arcaico ADJ archaic
arcaísmo M archaism
arcano ADJ arcane
arce M maple (tree)
arcén M shoulder of a road
archienemigo -ga MF archenemy
archipiélago M archipelago
archisabido ADJ very well-known
archivador M filing cabinet
archivar VT (guardar en un archivo) to file;
(arrinconar) to shelve
archivo M (lugar) archive; (fichero de
ordenador) file; (acción de archivar) filing
arcilla F clay
arco M (curva, eléctrico) arc; (estructura

arquitectónica) arch; (arma, varilla de
violín) bow; **— iris** rainbow
arder VT to burn; **la cosa está que arde**
things are really getting hot; **el trigo se
ardió** the wheat spoiled
ardid M scheme, artifice
ardiente ADJ (de deseo) ardent; (de calor,
fuego, deseo) burning
ardilla F squirrel; **— de tierra** gopher; **—
listada** chipmunk
ardite M **no valer un —** not to be worth a
penny
ardor M (de pasión) ardor; (de fuego) heat; **—
de estómago** heartburn
arduo ADJ arduous, grueling
área F area
arena F (tierra) sand; (plaza) arena; **—
movediza** quicksand
arenero M sandbox
arenga F harangue
arengar[7] VT to harangue
arenisca F sandstone
arenisco ADJ sandy
arenoso ADJ sandy
arenque M herring
arete M earring
argamasa F mortar
Argelia F Algeria
argelino -na ADJ & MF Algerian
Argentina F Argentina
argentino -na ADJ Argentine, Argentinian;
(propio de la plata) silvery; MF Argentine,
Argentinian
argolla F iron ring
argón M argon
argot M slang
argucias F PL trickery
argüir[31] VT to argue
argumentar VT to argue
argumento M (razonamiento) argument;
(conjunto de sucesos) plot
aridez F dryness
árido ADJ (seco) arid, dry, barren; (aburrido)
dry; **—s** dry goods
ariete M battering ram
arisco ADJ surly
arista F (borde) edge; (de trigo) beard; **limar
—s** to overcome difficulties
aristocracia F aristocracy
aristócrata MF INV aristocrat
aristocrático ADJ aristocratic
aritmética F arithmetic
aritmético ADJ arithmetical
arma F (instrumento bélico) arm, weapon;
(división del ejército) branch; **— blanca**
sharp weapon; **— de fuego** firearm; **a las
—** to arms; **de —s tomar** resolute;

tomar las —s to take up arms
armada F armada, fleet
armado ADJ armed; **a mano armada** at gunpoint; M assembly, putting together
armador -ora MF shipowner
armadura F (piezas de hierro) armor; (de un edificio) framework; (de gafas) frame; (de música) key signature
armamento M armament
armar VT (proveer de armas) to arm; (abastecer una embarcación) to equip; (reforzar) to reinforce; (ensamblar) to assemble, to put together; (levantar una tienda de campaña) to pitch; **— jaleo** to whoop it up; **— relajo** to make a mess; **—se de** to arm oneself with; **— una pendencia** to pick a fight, to start a quarrel
armario M (de ropa) wardrobe, closet; (de cocina) cabinet, armoire
armatoste M unwieldy object
armazón MF framework, skeleton
Armenia F Armenia
armenio -nia ADJ & MF Armenian
armería F (depósito de armas) armory; (tienda de armas) gun shop
armiño M ermine
armisticio M armistice
armonía F harmony
armónico ADJ & M harmonic
armonioso ADJ harmonious
armonizar[9] VI/VT to harmonize, to blend
ARN (ácido ribonucleico) M RNA
arnés M harness
aro M (de baloncesto) hoop; (de rueda) rim
aroma M (olor agradable) aroma; (del vino) bouquet
aromático ADJ aromatic
arpa F harp
arpía F shrew
arpillera F burlap
arpón M harpoon
arponear VT to harpoon
arqueado ADJ arched
arquear VT to arch
arqueología F archaeology
arquetipo M archetype
arquitecto -ta MF architect
arquitectónico ADJ architectural
arquitectura F architecture
arrabal M outlying slum
arraigar[7] VT to take root
arrancar[6] VT (una planta) to uproot; (el pelo) to tear out; (un diente) to pull; (un vicio) to eradicate; (una flor) to pick; (una confesión) to extract; **— de** to wrest from; VI/VT (un vehículo) to start; **arrancó**

para el valle he took off for the valley; **arrancó a sudar** he began to sweat; **sus problemas arrancan de su niñez** his problems are rooted in his childhood; **—se los cabellos** to tear one's hair (out)
arranque M (proceso de arrancar un coche) starting; (dispositivo para arrancar un coche) starter; (decisión, empuje) gumption; **— de ira** fit of rage
arrasar VT (destruir) to level, to raze; (derrotar) to crush; **— con** to obliterate; VI to win
arrastrado ADJ wretched
arrastrar VT (mover por el suelo) to drag; (llevarse consigo) to sweep away; (atraer) to draw; (soportar) to bear; (pronunciar lentamente) to draw out; **— los pies** (moverse con dificultades) to shuffle; (ser renuente) to stall; VI to hang down to the floor; **—se** (una serpiente) to slither; (una lagartija, un insecto) to crawl; (una persona) to grovel; M SG **arrastrapiés** shuffle
arrayán M myrtle
arrear VT to drive, to herd
arrebatar VT (quitar) to snatch away, to wrest away; (quemar) to burn on the outside; **—se** to have a fit
arrebatiña F mad scramble
arrebato M fit, outburst
arreciar VI to increase in intensity
arrecife M reef
arreglar VT (poner en orden, concertar, adaptar música) to arrange; (ordenar) to tidy up; (reparar) to fix, to repair; (resolver) to settle; **— cuentas** to settle accounts; **ya te arreglo** I'll fix you; **—se** (embellecerse) to fix oneself up; (llevarse bien con) to get along with; (entablar relaciones amorosas) to start dating; (reconciliarse) to make up; (conformarse) to make do; (despejarse) to clear up; **—se en** to agree on; **arreglárselas** to cope, to manage
arreglo M arrangement; **con — a** in accordance with; **no tiene —** it can't be helped; **llegar a un —** to settle; **—s** alterations
arrellanarse VI to lounge, to loll
arremangado ADJ turned up
arremangar[7] VT to roll up; **—se** to roll up one's sleeves, to knuckle down
arremeter VI to attack; **— contra** to lunge at
arremetida F thrust, lunge
arremolinarse VT (viento) to whirl around; (agua) to eddy

arrendajo M bluejay
arrendamiento M rental
arrendar VI/VT to rent, to lease
arrendatario -ria MF tenant
arreo M adornment; **—s** tack, harness
arrepentido ADJ repentant, rueful
arrepentimiento M (contrición) repentance;
  (disgusto) regret
arrepentirse³ VI (de los pecados) to repent;
  (de los errores) to regret
arrestar VT to arrest
arresto M arrest
arriar¹⁶ VT (la bandera) to lower; (un cabo)
  to slacken
arriate M flower bed
arriba ADV above; **¡—!** get up! **¡— las
  manos!** stick 'em up! **¡— Juan!** long live
  Juan! **de — abajo** from top to bottom;
  lleno hasta — full to the brim; **te vas
  para —** you are doing well; **viven —**
  they live upstairs
arribar VI LIT to arrive; (buque) to put into
  port
arribista MF social climber
arribo M LIT arrival
arriendo M leasing, rental
arriero -ra MF animal driver
arriesgado ADJ (peligroso) risky; (valiente)
  daring
arriesgar⁷ VT to risk; **—se** to take a chance
arrimar VT (acercar) to bring near; (golpear)
  to strike; **—se a** (apoyarse) to lean on;
  (acercarse) to get near
arrinconar VT (acorralar) to corner; (poner
  en un rincón) to put in a corner;
  (abandonar) to abandon
arritmia F arrhythmia
arrobamiento M rapture
arrobarse VI to be enraptured
arrodillarse VI to kneel
arrogancia F arrogance
arrogante ADJ arrogant
arrogarse⁷ VT to assume
arrojadizo ADJ projectile
arrojar VT (lanzar) to throw, to hurl;
  (expulsar) to throw out; (botar) to throw
  away; (vomitar) to throw up, to vomit;
  (proyectar una luz) to shed, to throw; **—
  un saldo de** to show a balance of; **—se**
  to hurl oneself
arrojo M boldness, daring
arrollador ADJ overwhelming
arrollar VT (poner en forma de rollo) to roll
  up; (arrastrar) to run over; (derrotar) to
  defeat
arropar VT to wrap up; (en la cama) to tuck
  in; **—se** to pull up the covers

arroyo M stream, creek
arroz M rice; **— integral** brown rice
arrozal M rice field
arruga F wrinkle
arrugar⁷ VT to wrinkle; **— el ceño** to knit
  one's brow; **—se** (pasar a tener arrugas) to
  get wrinkles; (asustarse) to be afraid
arruinar VT (estropear) to ruin; (destruir) to
  destroy, to ravage; (aguar) to spoil; (dejar
  en la quiebra) to bankrupt, to ruin; **—se**
  to go to ruin
arrullar VI (una paloma) to coo; VT (a un
  enamorado) to whisper sweet nothings to;
  (a un niño) to rock to sleep, to lull to
  sleep
arrullo M (de la tórtola) cooing; (del agua)
  babbling
arrumbar VT (arrinconar) to put aside;
  (marginalizar) to marginalize
arsenal M (depósito) arsenal; (astillero) navy
  yard
arsénico M arsenic
arte M SG art; F PL arts; M (destreza) skill,
  ability; (actividad técnica) craft; **bellas —s**
  fine arts; **el — por el —** art for art's sake;
  malas —s wiles; **no tener ni — ni
  parte en algo** to have nothing to do
  with something; **por — de** by means of
artefacto M (aparato útil) contrivance,
  device; (bomba) bomb
arteria F artery
arteriosclerosis F arteriosclerosis
artero ADJ artful, wily
artesanía F (trabajo, obra) craft; (habilidad)
  craftsmanship
artesano -na MF artisan, craftsman
ártico ADJ arctic
articulación F (acción de articular)
  articulation; (juntura) joint
articular VT (pronunciar) to articulate, to
  enunciate; (unir) to join
artículo M article; (entrada en un
  diccionario) article, entry; **— de fondo**
  editorial; **— definido** definite article;
  hacer el — to give a sales pitch
artífice MF (autor) architect; M (artesano)
  craftsman; F craftswoman
artificial ADJ artificial
artificio M artifice
artificioso ADJ affected, contrived
artillería F artillery
artillero -ra MF gunner
artimaña F trick, wile
artista MF artist
artístico ADJ artistic
artritis F arthritis
artroscópico ADJ arthroscopic

Aruba F Aruba

arveja F pea

arzobispo M archbishop

arzón M saddletree

as M ace (también atleta)

asa F handle

asado ADJ roasted; M (carne asada) roast; (acción de asar) roasting

asador -ora M spit; MF barbecue cook

asalariado -da MF wage-earner

asaltante MF mugger

asaltar VT (a una persona) to assault, to assail; (un banco) to hold up; (con preguntas) to assail; **—le a uno una idea** to be struck by an idea

asalto M (ataque) assault; (de un banco) holdup, stickup; **tomar por —** to storm

asamblea F assembly, gathering

asar VT to roast; **— a la parrilla** to grill; **— con adobo** to barbecue

asbesto M asbestos

ascendencia F ancestry

ascendente ADJ (que incrementa) ascending, rising; (hacia arriba) upward

ascender[1] VT (a un empleado) to promote; (una montaña) to climb; VI to ascend; **— a** to amount to

ascendiente MF ancestor

ascenso M (acción de ascender) ascent; (en el trabajo) promotion

ascensor M elevator

asceta MF INV ascetic

ascético ADJ ascetic

asco M disgust, revulsion; **hacer —s a** to reject; **me da —** it makes me sick, it disgusts me; **ese hombre está hecho un —** that man is a mess

ascórbico ADJ ascorbic

ascua F ember; **estar en —s** to be on pins and needles; **tener en —s** to string along

aseado ADJ well-groomed

asear VT to clean up

asediar VT to besiege

asedio M siege

asegurar VT (una victoria) to assure; (una frontera, una cerradura) to secure; (con un contrato de seguro) to insure; **—se (de)** to make sure (of); **te lo aseguro** I assure you

asemejarse VI **— a** to resemble

asentaderas F PL buttocks

asentar VT (datos) to enter; (una población) to establish; **—se** (posarse) to settle; (madurar) to settle down

asentimiento M assent, acquiescence

asentir[3] VI to assent, to acquiesce; **— con la cabeza** to nod

aseo M (acción de asearse) cleaning; (cualidad de aseado) cleanliness; (cuarto de baño) bathroom; (servicio) toilet, restroom

asequible ADJ (que se puede obtener) available; (que se puede pagar) affordable

aserción F assertion

aserradero M sawmill, lumber mill

aserrado ADJ serrated; M sawing

aserrar[1] VT to saw

aserrín M sawdust

aserto M assertion

asesinar VT to murder; (a una figura pública) to assassinate

asesinato M murder, killing; (de una figura pública) assassination

asesino -na ADJ murderous; MF killer, murderer; (de una figura pública) assassin

asesor -ora MF consultant, advisor

asesoramiento M consulting, advising

asesorar VT to advise

asestar VT **— un golpe** to inflict / deal a blow

aseveración F assertion

aseverar VT to assert

asexual ADJ asexual

asfalto M asphalt

asfixia F suffocation, asphyxiation

asfixiar VT to suffocate, to smother

así ADV so, thus, like this; **— —** so-so; **— como** in the same way that; **— de grande** that big; **— que** so that; **¿— que no vienes?** so you're not coming?

Asia F Asia

asiático -ca ADJ & MF Asian

asidero M hold; **eso no tiene — en la realidad** that has no basis in reality

asiduo ADJ (lector) assiduous; (cliente) steady

asiento M (lugar donde sentarse, parte de una silla, de válvula) seat; (de nóminas) entry, record; **tomar —** to take a seat

asignación F (acción de asignar) assignment; (acción de dar fondos) appropriation; (pago) allowance

asignar VT (una tarea) to assign; (fondos) to allot, to allocate

asignatura F subject

asilado -da MF inmate

asilar VT (a un político) to give asylum to; (un animal) to shelter

asilo M (para los perseguidos) asylum; (para huérfanos, ancianos) home

asimétrico ADJ asymmetric

asimilar VT (vitaminas, un grupo étnico) to assimilate; (información) to absorb

asimismo ADV likewise

asir[21] VT to grasp, to grip; **—se a** to hold onto

asistencia F (presencia, personas presentes) attendance; (ayuda) assistance, aid; (servicio para averías) roadside assistance; **— médica** health care; **— social** (ayuda) welfare; (profesión) social work

asistente -ta ADJ assistant; MF assistant, helper; **— social** social worker

asistir VT **— a** (estar presente) to attend; (ayudar) to help, to assist

asma F asthma

asmático ADJ asthmatic

asno M ass, donkey

asociación F association

asociado -da MF associate

asociar VT to associate; **—se** to join

asolamiento M desolation

asolar VT to desolate, to devastate

asomar VI to show; VT to poke out, to stick out; **—se a** to look out

asombrar VT to astonish, to amaze, to astound; **—se** to be astonished

asombro M astonishment, amazement

asombroso ADJ astonishing, amazing

asomo LOC ADV **ni por —** by no means

asonancia F assonance

aspa F (de hélice) blade; (de ventilador) vane

aspecto M (faceta) aspect, feature; (apariencia) looks

aspereza F roughness, harshness; **limar —s** to smooth over disagreements

áspero ADJ (terreno, mano) rough; (lucha) bitter; (tiempo, voz) harsh

aspiración F (ambición) aspiration, ambition; (respiración) breathing in; (succión) suction

aspiradora F vacuum cleaner

aspirante MF applicant, candidate

aspirar VT to breathe in, to inhale; **— a** to aspire to

aspirina F aspirin

asqueado ADJ disgusted

asquear VT to disgust

asquerosidad F nastiness; **¡estás hecho una —!** you're gross!

asqueroso ADJ nasty, disgusting, gross

asta F (de toro) horn; (de ciervo) antler; (de bandera) flagpole; (de lanza) shaft; **a media —** at half mast

asterisco M asterisk, star

asteroide M asteroid

astigmatismo M astigmatism

astilla F (de madera) chip, splinter; (de vidrio) sliver; **—s** kindling

astillar VT to chip, to splinter

astillero M shipyard

astringente ADJ & M astringent

astro M (del cielo) celestial body; (de cine)

movie star

astrofísica F astrophysics

astrología F astrology

astronauta MF astronaut

astronáutica F astronautics

astronomía F astronomy

astrónomo -ma MF astronomer

astucia F (listeza) cunning, guile; (treta) trick

asturiano -na ADJ & MF Asturian

Asturias F SG Asturias

astuto ADJ shrewd, wily, cunning

asueto M time off

asumir VT (una responsabilidad) to assume, to shoulder; (una mala noticia) to accept; **— un cargo** to take office

asunto M (cuestión) matter; (de una obra artística) theme

asustadizo ADJ easily frightened, jumpy

asustado ADJ frightened

asustar VT to frighten, to scare; **—se** to become frightened

atacante ADJ attacking; MF assailant

atacar[6] VT to attack, to assault; **—se de risa** to have a laughing fit

atado M bundle

atadura F **sin —s** with no strings attached

atajador M tackle

atajar VT (interrumpir) to cut off; VI (tomar un atajo) to take a shortcut

atajo M shortcut

atalaya F watchtower

atañer[18,50] VI to concern, to pertain to

ataque M (violento, de asma) attack; (de rabia, de tos) fit; (de epilepsia) seizure; **— cardíaco** heart attack; **— de nervios** nervous breakdown; **— relámpago** blitz

atar VT (sujetar) to tie, to bind; **— cabos** to make sense of something; **—se los zapatos** to tie one's shoes

atardecer[13] VI to get dark; M late afternoon, dusk, evening; **al —** at dusk

atareado ADJ busy

atarearse VI to busy oneself

atascadero M (lodazal) quagmire; (de tránsito) bottleneck

atascado ADJ stuck

atascar[6] VT (un tubo) to stop up; (una máquina) to jam; (el tráfico) to obstruct; **—se** (un vehículo) to get stuck; (una máquina) to get jammed

ataúd M coffin, casket

ataviar[16] VT to attire, to array; **—se** to dress up

atavío M attire, garb

ateísmo M atheism

atemorizar[9] VT to frighten

atención F attention; (médica) care; (acto de

cortesía) courtesy; **a la — de** to the attention of; **llamar la —** (hacer notar) to call attention; (ser llamativo) to attract attention; (interesar) to interest; INTERJ watch out!

atender[1] VI **— a** to pay attention to; (el trabajo) to attend to, to take care of; VT (a un enfermo) to take care of, to look after; (una súplica) to heed; (a un cliente) to serve

atenerse[44] VI **— a los hechos** to bear the facts in mind; **— a la ley** to abide by the law

atentado M assassination; assassination attempt; **un — contra** an affront to

atentamente ADV (con atención) attentively; (despedida en cartas) yours truly / sincerely

atentar[1] VI **— contra la vida de alguien** to make an attempt on someone's life

atento ADJ (que presta atención) attentive; (amable) thoughtful

atenuar[17] VT (la violencia) to attenuate; (una luz) to dim; **—se** to abate

ateo -a MF atheist

aterciopelado ADJ velvety

aterido ADJ stiff with cold

aterirse[50] VI to become stiff with cold

aterrador ADJ terrifying

aterrar VT to terrify

aterrizaje M landing; **— forzoso** crash landing

aterrizar[9] VI/VT to land

aterrorizar[9] VT to terrify

atesorar VT (memorias) to treasure; (dinero) to hoard

atestado ADJ crowded, crammed

atestar VT (certificar) to attest to; (llenar) to jam, to pack

atestiguar[8] VT to bear witness, to testify

atiborrar VT to stuff; **—se** to stuff one's face

atiesar VT to stiffen

atildado ADJ spruced up

atinar VT (dar en el blanco) to hit the mark; (adivinar) to guess right; **no — a decir palabra** not to manage to get a word out

atisbar VT (mirar con disimulo) to peek at, to peep at; (vislumbrar) to catch a glimpse of; VI to peek

atisbo M glimpse, hint

atizar[9] VT (un fuego) to poke, to stake; (las pasiones) to stir up, to stoke

atlántico ADJ Atlantic; M **Océano Atlántico** Atlantic Ocean

atlas M atlas

atleta MF athlete

atlético ADJ athletic

atletismo M track and field

atmósfera F atmosphere

atmosférico ADJ atmospheric

atolladero M quagmire

atolondrado ADJ scatterbrained; (muchacha) ditsy

atómico ADJ atomic

atomizar[9] VT to atomize

átomo M atom

atónito ADJ dumbfounded

atontado ADJ stupefied

atontar VT to stupefy

atorar VT to jam; **—se** to choke

atormentar VT to torment; **—se por** to agonize over

atornillar VT to bolt

atracadero M dock

atracar[6] VT (amarrar) to dock; (robar) to hold up, to mug; **—se** to gorge oneself

atracción F attraction

atraco M holdup, stickup

atracón M **darse un —** to gorge

atractivo ADJ (capacidad de atraer) attractiveness, appeal; M (cosa que atrae) attraction; **— sexual** sex appeal

atraer[45] VT to attract

atragantarse VI to choke

atrancar[6] VT to bolt, to bar

atrapada F catch

atrapar VT (en una trampa) to trap, to ensnare, to catch; (una pelota, el interés) to catch

atrás ADV **— de la casa** behind the house; **cuatro años —** four years back; **hacia —** backward; **para —** back / backwards; **quedarse —** to fall behind

atrasado ADJ (pasado) late; (en el pago) in arrears, behind; (país) backward; (un libro de biblioteca) overdue; **tengo sueño —** I'm behind in my sleep; **el reloj anda —** the clock is slow; **feliz cumpleaños —** happy belated birthday

atrasar VT (un plazo) to delay; (una mesa) to push back; (un reloj) to turn back; VI (un reloj) to run slow; **—se** to fall behind, to lag

atraso M (condición de atrasado) backwardness; (pago) back payment; (de trabajo) backlog; **con dos meses de —** two months in arrears

atravesar[1] VT (cruzar) to cross; (ir de lado a lado) to span; (penetrar) to impale, to run through; **— un momento difícil** to go through a difficult moment; **se me atravesó un caballo** a horse crossed in front of me; **—se en la cama** to lie crossways in bed

atreverse VI to dare

atrevido ADJ (audaz) bold, daring; (insolente) insolent

atrevimiento M (cualidad de atrevido) boldness, daring, audacity; (acción atrevida) daring act

atribución F attribution; **atribuciones** powers

atribuir[31] VT to attribute, to ascribe

atribular VT to distress; **—se** to be distressed

atributo M attribute

atril M stand

atrincherar VT to entrench

atrio M atrium

atrocidad F atrocity

atrofia F atrophy

atrofiar VT to atrophy, to stunt

atronador ADJ thunderous, deafening

atronar[2] VI to make a racket

atropellar VT (a un peatón) to run over, to run down; (los derechos de alguien) to trample upon

atropello M (de un peatón) running over; (ultraje) outrage; (de derechos) trampling

atroz ADJ (modales, crimen) atrocious; (dolor) excruciating; (ofensa) grievous

atuendo M getup

atún M tuna

aturdido ADJ bewildered; **estar —** to be in a daze

aturdimiento M bewilderment

aturdir VT to bewilder, to daze

atusar VT to smooth, to fix

audacia F audacity, boldness

audaz ADJ audacious, bold

audible ADJ audible

audición F audition

audiencia F (tribunal) court; (reunión, conjunto de oyentes) audience; (hecho de oír un pleito) hearing

audífono M (para los sordos) earphone; (para música) headphones

audio M audio; **—libro** book on tape; **—visual** audiovisual

audiología F audiology

auditar VI/VT to audit

auditivo ADJ auditory

auditor -ora MF auditor

auditoría F audit

auditorio M (público) audience; (local) auditorium

auge M (del mercado) boom; (de una moda) heyday; (de una carrera) peak

augurar VT to foretell; **no — nada bueno** not to bode well

aula F (de clase) classroom; (de conferencia) lecture hall

aullar VI to howl

aullido M howl

aumentar VT to augment, to increase; VI (los precios) to rise, to escalate; (población) to swell; (violencia) to escalate

aumento M increase; (de expectativas) buildup; (de población) growth; (de precios) rise, upturn; (de peso) gain

aun ADV even; **— así** even so; **— cuando** even though / if

aún ADV still

aunque CONJ though, although

aura F aura

áureo ADJ golden

aureola F halo

auricular M (de teléfono) receiver; **—es** headphones, earphones

aurora F dawn, aurora; **— boreal** aurora borealis, northern lights

auscultar VT to listen to with a stethoscope

ausencia F absence

ausentarse VT to absent oneself

ausente ADJ absent, missing

ausentismo M absenteeism

auspicios M PL auspices

austeridad F austerity

austero ADJ austere, stern

Australia F Australia

australiano -na ADJ & MF Australian

Austria F Austria

austríaco -ca ADJ & MF Austrian

autenticar[6] VT to authenticate

auténtico ADJ authentic

autismo M autism

auto M (coche) auto; (orden judicial) writ; **— de choques** bumper car

autoadhesivo M decal; (para el parachoques) bumper sticker

autoayuda F self-help

autobiografía F autobiography

autobomba M fire engine

autobús M bus

autocine M drive-in movie theater

autocompasión F self-pity

autocontrol M self-control

autócrata MF INV autocrat

autóctono ADJ indigenous

autodestructivo ADJ self-destructive

autodisciplina F self-discipline

autoestima F self-esteem

autogobierno M self-government

autógrafo M autograph

autoimagen F self-image

automático ADJ automatic

automatización F automation

automatizar[9] ADJ (mecanizar) to automate; (hacer automáticamente) to do automatically

automóvil M automobile
automovilista MF motorist
automovilístico ADJ automotive
autonomía F autonomy; (de un vehículo) range
autopista F freeway, turnpike
autopropulsado ADJ self-propelled
autopsia F autopsy
autor -ora MF author
autoridad F authority
autoritario ADJ (tiránico) authoritarian; (respetado) authoritative
autorización F authorization
autorizar[9] VT to authorize; (dar propiedad intelectual) to license
autosatisfacción F self-satisfaction
autoservicio M (sistema de venta) self-service; (tienda) convenience store
autosuficiente ADJ self-sufficient; (presumido) smug
autovía F freeway
auxiliar VT to help; ADJ auxiliary; MF assistant; — **de vuelo** (hombre) steward; (mujer) stewardess
auxilio M help
avalancha F avalanche
avalar VT to guarantee, to co-sign
avaluar[17] VT to appraise
avalúo M appraisal
avance M (acción de avanzar, adelanto) advance, headway; (sinopsis de película) trailer
avanzada F scouting party
avanzado ADJ advanced
avanzar[9] VI (ir hacia adelante) to advance; (progresar) to make headway; **a medida que avanzaba la mañana** as the morning progressed; VT to move forward; (una cinta) to fast-forward
avaricia F avarice
avariento ADJ avaricious, miserly
avaro ADJ miserly, avaricious
avasallar VT to subjugate
ave F bird; — **de corral** poultry; — **de rapiña** bird of prey; — **canora** songbird; — **zancuda** wading bird
avecindarse VI to take up residence
avellana F hazelnut
avellano M hazel
avena F oats
avenencia F agreement
avenida F avenue
avenir[47] VI to reconcile; —**se a** to come around; —**se bien** to get along
aventadora F fan, blower
aventajar VT (ser mejor) to be superior to; (sobrepasar) to get ahead of

aventón M **dar un** — *Méx* to give a lift
aventura F (suceso que implica riesgo) adventure; (relación amorosa) fling, affair
aventurado ADJ (arriesgado) risky; (atrevido) daring
aventurar VT (arriesgar) to risk; (sugerir) to venture; —**se a** to dare to
aventurero -ra ADJ adventurous; MF adventurer
avergonzado ADJ (tímido) abashed; (arrepentido) ashamed
avergonzar[2,9] VT to shame, to embarrass; —**se** to be ashamed / embarrassed
avería F (de frutas) damage; (de coche) breakdown, mechanical trouble
averiado ADJ (un coche) broken-down; (un televisor) on the blink
averiarse[16] VI (fruta) to become damaged; (un coche) to break down
averiguar[8] VT to find out, to ascertain
aversión F aversion, dislike
avestruz MF ostrich
avezado ADJ seasoned
aviación F aviation
aviador -ora MF aviator
aviar[16] VT to fix
avidez F eagerness
ávido ADJ eager, avid
avinagrado ADJ sour
avinagrar VT to sour; —**se** to become sour
avío M tidying up; —**s de pescar** fishing tackle
avión M (máquina) airplane; (ave) martin; — **comercial** airliner; — **a reacción** jet airplane; — **caza** fighter airplane
avisar VT (notificar) to advise; (a la policía) to alert
aviso M notice; — **publicitario** advertisement; **estar sobre** — to be forewarned; **poner sobre** — to forewarn; **sin previo** — without warning
avispa F wasp
avispado ADJ lively
avisparse VI to wise up
avispero M wasp's nest; **alborotar el** — to stir up a wasp's nest
avispón M hornet
avistar VT to catch sight of
avivar VT (una fiesta) to enliven; (un fuego, un debate) to fuel; (una llama) to fan
avizorar VT to spy on
axila F underarm
ay INTERJ (de dolor) ouch; (de decepción) oh, no; (de sorpresa desagradable) oh; — **de mí** poor me
ayer ADV yesterday
ayuda F help; (después de un desastre) relief

ayudante -ta MF assistant, helper; — **de médico** physician's assistant
ayudantía F assistantship
ayudar VT to help, to aid
ayunar VI to fast
ayunas F PL **en —** (antes de comer) without having eaten; (despistado) clueless; **estoy en —** I am fasting
ayuno M fast
ayuntamiento M (gobierno) municipal government; (edificio) city hall
azabache M jet; ADJ jet-black, raven
azada F hoe
azadón M hoe
azafato -ta MF (en aviones) flight attendant; (en ferias) host
azafrán M saffron
azahar M orange blossom
azar M chance; **al —** by chance, at random
azaroso ADJ (arriesgado) risky; (aleatorio) random
azerbaijano -na, azerbaiyano -na ADJ & MF Azerbaijani, Azerbaijanian
Azerbaiyán F Azerbaijan
azogar[7] VT to silver
azogue M (sustancia) quicksilver, mercury; (niño inquieto) restless child; **tener — en el cuerpo** to be restless
azorar VT to embarrass
azotaina F flogging
azotar VT (con azote) to whip, to lash, to flog; VI/VT (el viento) to whip, to buffet; (el sol) to beat down; (la lluvia) to sting
azote M (instrumento) whip; (golpe) lash; (aflicción) scourge; (golpe de viento) buffet
azotea F flat roof
azúcar MF sugar; **— moreno -na** brown sugar
azucarar VT to sugar
azucarera F (fábrica) sugar mill; (recipiente) sugar bowl
azucarero M sugar bowl
azucena F white lily
azufre M sulfur / sulphur
azul ADJ blue; **— acero** steel blue; **— celeste** sky-blue; **— claro** light blue; **— marino** navy blue
azulado ADJ bluish
azular VT to color blue
azulear VI (tener color azul) to be blue; (ponerse azul) to become blue; VT (dar color azul) to color blue
azulejar VT to tile
azulejo M tile
azuzar[9] VT (a un perro) to sic; (a una persona) to egg on

Bb

baba F drivel, drool, slobber; (de un caracol, de agua estancada) slime; **se le cae la baba por el coche nuevo** he's drooling over the new car
babear VI to drivel, to drool
babero M bib
babor M portside
babosa F slug
babosear VI/VT to slobber (on)
baboso ADJ (caracol) slimy; (persona que babea) driveling; (persona tonta) idiotic; (adulador) fawning
babuino M baboon
baca F luggage rack
bacalao M cod
bache M pothole; (momento) bad time; (de aire) air pocket
bacheado ADJ bumpy
bachiller -ra M (graduado) high school graduate; (alumno) high school student
bachillerato M baccalaureate
bacilo M bacillus
backgammon M backgammon
bacteria F bacteria
bacteriología F bacteriology
badajo M bell clapper
badana F sheepskin
bagaje M baggage
bagatela F trifle
bagazo M pulp
Bahamas F PL Bahamas
bahameño -ña ADJ & MF Bahamian
bahía F bay
Bahrein M Bahrain
bahreiní ADJ & MF Bahraini
bailador -ora MF folk dancer; ADJ dancing
bailar VI/VT to dance; **me bailan los pantalones** my pants are falling off; **me tocó — con la más fea** I was left holding the bag; **que me quiten lo bailado** I enjoyed it anyway
bailarín -ina MF dancer
baile M (movimiento rítmico) dance; (fiesta) dance, ball; **— aeróbico** aerobic dance; **— de máscaras** masked ball; **— folklórico** folk dance; **— zapateado** clog dance
bailongo M hop
bailotear VI to jig
baivel M bevel
baja F (caída barométrica) drop; (de precios) decline; (víctima de guerra) casualty; (del

ejército) discharge, dismissal; (licencia) leave; **dar de** — to discharge; **darse de** — to call in sick

bajada F (acción de bajar, pendiente) descent; (de un caballo) dismount; — **contra-reloj** downhill ski race

bajar VI to go down; (corriendo) to run down; (de un árbol) to climb down; (de un caballo) to get down; (de un ómnibus) to step off, to get off; (empeorar) to worsen; (alcanzar) to reach down; (la marea) to ebb; (una creciente) to subside; VT (las escaleras) to go down; (un avión de un tiro) to shoot down; (comida con agua) to wash down; (la cabeza) to lower; (un cargamento) to let down; (el volumen) to turn down; (focos) to dim; (la voz) to lower, to soften; — **de categoría** to demote; — **el cursor** to scroll down; — **en picada** to dive; —**se los pantalones** to pull down one's pants

bajeza F (cualidad) baseness; (acción) vile act

bajío M shoal

bajista ADJ (bolsa) bearish

bajo ADJ (nubes, estante, precio, voz grave) low; (persona) short; (voz débil) soft; (río) lower; (vista, persianas) lowered; (acto) base; **baja espalda** small of the back; **de baja ley** base; PREP under; — **control** under control; — **cuerda** under-the-table; — **fianza** on bail; — **fuego** under fire; — **sospecha** under a cloud; — **tierra** underground; **poner** — **llave** to lock up; **por lo** — under one's breath; M (voz grave) bass; (de pantalón) cuff; **hacer los** —**s** to cuff; ADV low

bala F (de pistola) bullet; (de prueba olímpica) shot; (de cañón) ball

balada F ballad

baladí ADJ trivial

balance M (cálculo) balance; (documento) balance sheet; (de víctimas) toll; (movimiento) sway; **hacer un** — to take stock

balancear VT to swing; VI to sway; —**se** to sway

balanceo M (de un cuerpo) swinging, swing; (de un barco) rolling, roll

balancín M seesaw

balanza F scale; — **comercial** balance of trade; — **de pagos** balance of payments

balar VI to bleat

balasto M ballast

balaustrada F banister

balazo M (disparo) shot; (herida) bullet wound

balbucear VI to stammer; (un bebé) to babble

balbuceo M stammer; stammering; (de bebé) babble, babbling

balcón M balcony

balde M pail, bucket; **de** — gratis; **en** — in vain

baldear VT to flush

baldío ADJ (terreno) fallow; (acción) useless

baldosa F (en una casa) floor tile; (en una calle) flagstone

balido M bleat, bleating

balística F ballistics

balístico ADJ ballistic

ballena F whale; (hueso) whalebone

ballenato M whale calf

ballet M ballet

balneario M summer resort; (con aguas medicinales) spa

balón M ball; **baloncesto** basketball; **balonmano** European handball; F **balonvolea** volleyball

balsa F raft, balsa; (lago) pond

bálsamo M balsam, balm

baluarte M bulwark, stronghold

bambolear VT to sway, to swing; —**se** to sway, to swing

bamboleo M swinging, swaying

bambú M bamboo

banal ADJ banal; **una respuesta** — a pat answer

banana F banana

banano M banana tree

banca F (industria) banking; (en el juego) bank

bancario -ria ADJ bank, banking; MF banker

bancarrota F bankruptcy

banco M (establecimiento) bank; (asiento) bench; (de peces) school; (de arena) shoal, spit; — **de datos** data bank; — **de niebla** fog bank

banda F (musical) band; (cinta ancha) band, sash; (grupo) gang, band, ring; (dibujo) stripe; (de un neumático) tread; (lindero) side, edge, border; (de un barco) side; — **de frecuencia** frequency band; — **horaria** time slot; — **magnética** magnetic strip; — **sonora** sound track

bandada F (de aves) flock, flight; (de peces) school

bandeja F tray; **me lo sirvieron en** — **(de plata)** they served it to me on a silver platter

bandera F flag; **jurar la** — to pledge allegiance to the flag

banderín M pennant

banderola F pennant

bandido -da MF bandit, outlaw; (como

epíteto) rascal
bando M (decreto) edict; (partido) camp
bandolero -ra MF bandit
Bangladesh M Bangladesh
banjo M banjo
banquero -ra MF banker
banqueta F (taburete) stool; (acera) *Méx*
  sidewalk
banquete M banquet
banquetearse VI to feast
banquillo M bench
bañar VT to bathe; (una torta) to ice, to frost;
  —se to take a bath, to bathe
bañera F bathtub
bañista MF bather
baño M (acción) bath; (cuarto) bathroom,
  lavatory; (de torta) icing, frosting; **darse**
  un — (bañarse) to take a bath; (nadar) to
  take a swim; **— (de) María** double boiler;
  — de sangre bloodbath
bar M bar
barahúnda F ruckus, racket
baraja F pack/deck of cards
barajada F shuffle
barajar VI/VT (naipes) to shuffle;
  (alternativas) to weigh
baranda F railing, guard rail
barandal M banister
barandilla F rail, railing
barata F *Méx* sale
baratear VT to sell cheap
baratija F trinket, knickknack
barato ADJ cheap
baratura F cheapness
barba F beard; **—s** whiskers; **hacer algo en**
  las —s de alguien to do something right
  under someone's nose
barbacoa F barbecue
barbadense ADJ & MF Barbadian
barbado ADJ bearded
Barbados M Barbados
barbaridad F atrocity; **una —** de a lot of;
  ¡qué —! what nonsense!
barbarie F savagery
bárbaro -ra ADJ (salvaje) barbarous, barbaric;
  (estupendo) cool, super; MF barbarian
barbecho M fallow land
barbería F barbershop
barbero -ra MF barber
barbilla F chin
barbitúrico M barbiturate
barbudo ADJ bearded
barca F rowboat
barcaza F barge
barco M boat
bardo M bard
bario M barium

barítono ADJ & M baritone
barlovento M windward
barniz M (para madera) varnish; (para
  cerámica) glaze; (de cultura) veneer
barnizar[9] VT (madera) to varnish; (cerámica)
  to glaze
barómetro M barometer
barón M baron
barquero -era M boatman; F boatwoman
barquillo M rolled wafer
barquinazo M **dar —s** to lurch
barra F (de hierro, arena, chocolate, en un
  bar) bar; (en gimnasia) crossbar; (signo
  ortográfico) slash; **— de jabón** bar of
  soap; **— espaciadora** space bar
barrabasada F mischief
barraca F (en las fiestas) stall, stand;
  (casucha) hovel
barracuda F barracuda
barranca M ravine
barranco M gully, ravine
barrena F (de un taladro) bit; (de un avión)
  tailspin; **entrar en —** to go into a
  tailspin
barrenar VT to drill
barrendero -ra MF street sweeper
barrer VI/VT to sweep; (derrotar) to defeat
  decisively; M SG **barreminas** minesweeper
barrera F barrier; (valla) barrier, bar; **—**
  arancelaria tariff barrier; **— de coral**
  barrier reef; **— del sonido** sound barrier
barrica F vat
barricada F barricade
barrida F sweep
barrido M (acción de barrer) sweeping;
  (movimiento) sweep
barriga F belly; (gorda) paunch; **rascarse la**
  — to do nothing
barrigón ADJ pot-bellied
barril M barrel, keg, drum
barrio M neighborhood, quarter; **—**
  residencial residential neighborhood; **—s**
  bajos slums
barritar VI to trumpet
barro M (lodo) mud; (arcilla) clay; (acné)
  pimple; **de —** earthen
barroco ADJ & M baroque
barroso ADJ muddy
barrote M bar
barruntar VT to suspect
barrunto M suspicion
bártulos M PL stuff
barullo M hubbub
basal ADJ basal
basalto M basalt
basar VT to base; **—se en** (depender de) to

rely on; (fundamentar en) to be based on

basca F nausea

báscula F scale

base F (apoyo, área militar, química) base; (punto de partida) basis; (de maquillaje) foundation; (de una campaña) plank; — **de concurso** contest rules; — **de datos** database; — **de lanzamiento** launching pad; **con** — **en** on the basis of; **en** — **a** on the basis of; **las** —**s** (de un partido) grass roots; (de un sindicato) rank and file; **salario** — base salary; **tener una** — **sólida** to be on a strong footing

basic M (lenguaje de programación) basic

básico ADJ basic; (comida) staple

bastante ADJ & PRON enough, sufficient; ADV (suficientemente) enough; (mucho) quite a lot; (algo) quite, pretty

bastar VI to be enough, to suffice; **¡basta!** enough!

bastardilla F italics

bastardo -da ADJ & MF *ofensivo* bastard

bastedad F coarseness

bastidor M (de un teatro) wing; (para bordado) frame; (de un coche) chassis; (de una ventana) sash; **entre** —**es** (en teatro) offstage; (en privado) behind the scenes

bastimentos M PL provisions

basto ADJ coarse, crude; M suit in the Spanish deck of cards

bastón M (para andar) cane, walking stick; — **de esquí** ski pole

basura F rubbish, garbage, trash

basural M *Am* dump

basurero -ra MF (persona) garbage collector; M (lugar) dump

bata F (para llevar en casa) robe, housecoat; (de laboratorio) lab coat; (de pacientes) hospital gown; — **de baño** bathrobe

batahola F racket

batalla F battle; (de coches) wheelbase; — **naval** sea battle; **ropa de** — everyday clothing; **trabar** — to engage in battle

batallar VI to battle

batallón M battalion

batata F sweet potato

bate M baseball bat

batea F tray

bateador -ora MF batter

batear VI to bat

batería F (de coche, artillería) battery; (de cocina) pots and pans; (musical) drums

baterista MF drummer

batiburrillo M hodgepodge

batido M shake, milk shake

batidor M whisk, beater

batidora M mixer

batintín M gong

batir VT (una alfombra) to beat; (un terreno) to comb; (mantequilla) to cream, to churn; (un récord) to break; (huevos) to beat; (crema) to whip; (alas) to flap, to beat; —**se en duelo** to duel; —**se en retirada** to retreat; — **palmas** to clap, to applaud

batuta F baton; **llevar la** — to call the shots

baudio M baud

baúl M trunk

bautismo M baptism, christening; — **de fuego** baptism of fire

bautizar[9] VT to baptize, to christen

bautizo M christening, baptism

baya F berry

bayeta F cleaning cloth

bayo ADJ bay

bayoneta F bayonet

baza F card trick; **meter** — **en una conversación** to participate in a conversation

bazar M bazaar

bazo M spleen

bazofia F slop

bazuca F bazooka

beagle M beagle

beato ADJ (bendito) blessed; (piadoso) beatified; (santurrón) overly pious

bebé M baby, infant

bebedero M (recipiente) drinking trough; (lugar) watering hole

bebedor -ora MF drinker

beber VI/VT to drink

bebercio M *fam* booze

bebida F drink, beverage

beca F scholarship, fellowship

becario -ria MF scholar, fellow

becerro M calf; (piel) calfskin

becuadro M natural sign

befa F jeer

befar VT to jeer at

beicon M *Esp* bacon

beige ADJ INV & M beige

beldad F beauty

belga ADJ & MF Belgian

Bélgica F Belgium

Belice M Belize

beliceño -ña ADJ & MF Belizean

bélico ADJ warlike

belicoso ADJ (guerrero) bellicose; (agresivo) feisty

beligerante ADJ & MF belligerent

bellaco M rascal, scoundrel

bellaquería F mischief

belleza F beauty

bello ADJ beautiful

bellota F acorn
bemol ADJ & M flat; **tener —es** to be tricky
bencina F benzine
bendecir[26b] VT to bless
bendición F (parte de la misa) benediction; (acción y efecto de bendecir) blessing; (cosa excelente) boon, blessing
bendito ADJ (agua) holy; (alma) blessed; **— sea** may he be blessed; **dormir como un —** to sleep like a log; **es un —** he is a saint
benefactor -ora M benefactor, patron; F benefactress, patroness
beneficencia F charity; **— pública** welfare
beneficiar VT to benefit; **—se de** to benefit from
beneficiario -ria MF (de una herencia, perdón, acto de bondad) beneficiary; (de un cheque) payee
beneficio M benefit (también espectáculo)
beneficioso ADJ beneficial
benéfico ADJ beneficent
benemérito ADJ worthy of esteem
benevolencia F benevolence
benévolo ADJ benevolent
bengala F flare
benigno ADJ benign
Benín M Benin
beninés -esa ADJ & MF Beninese
benjamín -ina MF youngest child
beodo ADJ drunk
berbiquí M carpenter's brace
berenjena F eggplant
bermejo ADJ reddish
bermellón ADJ vermilion
berrear VI (animal) to bellow, to bawl; (bebé) to squall
berrido M (de animal) bellowing, bawling; (de bebé) squall, squalling
berrinche M tantrum
berro M watercress
berza F cabbage
besar VT to kiss
beso M kiss
bestia F beast
bestial ADJ bestial
best-seller ADV best seller
besuquear VT to kiss repeatedly; **—se** to make out
betabel M *Méx* beet
betún M shoe polish
Biblia F Bible
bíblico ADJ biblical
bibliografía F bibliography
biblioteca F library; (estante) bookcase
bibliotecario -ria MF librarian
bicarbonato M bicarbonate; **— de sosa**
bicarbonate of soda
bíceps M SG bicep(s)
bicho M (insecto) bug (también en informática); (animal) *fam* critter; **— raro** odd bird; **mal —** creep; **¿qué — te ha picado?** what's gotten into you? **—s** vermin
bici F bike
bicicleta F bicycle; **— de montaña** mountain bike; **— estática** stationary bike
biela F connecting rod
Bielorrusia F Belarus
bien ADV well; **—aventurado** blessed; **— arreglado** well groomed; **— hecho** well-made, well-done; **— poco** very little; **agarrarse —** to hold on tight; **ahora —** now then; **apretar —** to press hard; **está — —** she is fine; **más —** rather; **me doy — cuenta** I'm perfectly aware; **pues —** now; **qué —** how wonderful; **si —** although; **ya está —** that's enough; M good; **—es** property, assets; **—es inmuebles** real estate; **—es muebles** personal property; **—es raíces** real estate; **—estar** well-being, welfare; **—hechor** benefactor; **persona de —** a good person
bienio M biennium
bienvenida F welcome
bienvenido ADJ welcome
bifurcación F fork, forking; (en un programa de computadora) branch
bifurcarse[6] VI to fork, to branch off
bigamia F bigamy
bigote M mustache; (de animal) whisker
bikini M bikini
bilateral ADJ bilateral
bilingüe ADJ & MF bilingual
bilingüismo M bilingualism
bilis F bile
billar M billiards, pool; (mesa) pool table
billete M (de viaje, para espectáculos) ticket; (de banco) bill, banknote
billetera F billfold
billón M trillion
bimestral ADJ bimonthly
bimestre M two-month period
binario ADJ binary
bingo M bingo
binomial ADJ binomial
binomio M binomial
biodegradable ADJ biodegradable
biofeedback M biofeedback
biografía F biography
bioingeniería F bioengineering
biología F biology
biombo M folding screen

biopsia F biopsy
bioquímica F biochemistry
biorritmo M biorhythm
biotecnología F biotechnology
bipartidista ADJ bipartisan
bipolar ADJ bipolar
birlar VT *fam* to pinch, to swipe
Birmania F Burma
birmano -na ADJ & MF Burmese, from Myanmar
birrete M mortarboard
bis M encore
bisabuelo -la M great-grandfather; F great-grandmother
bisagra F hinge
bisecar⁶ VT to bisect
bisel M bevel
biselar VT to bevel
bisiesto ADJ **año —** leap year
bisnieto -ta M great-grandson; F great-granddaughter
bisonte M bison, buffalo
bistec M beefsteak
bisturí M scalpel
bisutería F costume jewelry
bit M bit
bizarría F gallantry
bizarro ADJ gallant
bizco ADJ cross-eyed
bizcocho M sponge cake
bizcochuelo M sponge cake
bizquear VI to be cross-eyed
black-jack M black-jack
blanca ADJ half note
blanco ADJ (color) white; (tez) fair; M (color) white (también de huevos, ojos); (de tiro) target; (de una burla) butt; **— fácil** sitting duck; **dar en el —** to hit the target; **en —** (hoja de papel, mente) blank; (sin dormir) sleepless; **en — y negro** in black and white
blancura F whiteness; (de tez) fairness
blancuzco ADJ whitish
blandir VT to brandish, to wield
blando ADJ soft; (sensiblero) mushy
blandura F softness
blanqueador M bleach
blanquear VT (una pared) to whitewash; (dinero) to launder; (verduras) to blanch; **—se** to whiten
blanquecino ADJ whitish
blanqueo M whitening
blasfemar VI/VT to blaspheme
blasfemia F blasphemy
blasón M coat of arms
blasonar VI to boast
blazer M blazer

blindado ADJ armored
blindaje M armor
blindar VT to armor
bloc M writing tablet, pad of paper
bloque M block (también de motor, político); (edificio) building; **en —** together
bloquear VT (una carretera, un asalto, un pase) to block; (un puerto) to blockade; (cuentas bancarias) to freeze; **—se** to choke
bloqueo M block; (militar) blockade
blues M PL. blues
bluff M bluff
blusa F blouse, top
boa F boa constrictor
boato M pomp
bobada F foolish act; (fruslería) trifle
bobalicón -ona ADJ goofy; MF nincompoop
bobear VI to fool around, to monkey around
bobería F (cualidad) foolishness; (dicho) foolish remark; (hecho) foolish act
bobina F (de hilo) bobbin; (de alambre, de coche) coil; (de película) reel
bobinar VT to reel
bobo -ba ADJ (tonto) dumb, dimwit, silly; (estupefacto) flabbergasted; MF booby, fool
boca F mouth; (de un arma de fuego) muzzle; (del estómago) pit; (de una cueva) opening; **— a —** mouth-to-mouth; **— abajo** face down; **— arriba** face up; **—calle** intersection; **a — de jarro** at close range; **callarse la —** to shut up
bocadillo M snack; *Esp* sandwich
bocado M bite, morsel, mouthful; (de una brida) bit
bocanada F (de líquido) mouthful; (de humo) puff; (de aire) sniff
bocazas MF SG loudmouth
boceto M sketch
bochorno M (calor) oppressive heat; (vergüenza) embarrassment
bochornoso ADJ (caluroso) sultry, oppressive, muggy; (vergonzoso) embarrassing
bocina F (de coche) horn; (megáfono) megaphone
bocinazo M honk, toot
boda F wedding; **— de oro** golden anniversary; **— de plata** silver anniversary
bodega F (despensa subterránea) cellar; (para vinos) wine cellar; (vinería) winery; (espacio en un barco, avión) hold; (tienda de comestibles) *Caribbean, Central America* grocery store
bodeguero -ra MF wine producer; *Caribbean, Central America* grocer

bofe M (de animal) lung; **echar los — s** to tire oneself out
bofetada F slap
boga LOC ADV **en —** in vogue, fashion
bogar[7] VI/VT to row
bohemio -mia ADJ & MF Bohemian
boicot M boycott
boicotear VT to boycott
boicoteo M boycott
boina F beret
bol M bowl
bola F (pelota) ball; (canica) marble; (de helado) dip; **— blanca** cue ball; **en —s** in the buff; **no dar pie con —** to be lost; **no dar ni —** not to pay attention
bolera F bowling alley
boleta F (de lotería) ticket; (de votación) *Méx* ballot
boletín M bulletin
boleto M ticket
boliche M (juego) bowling; (bolera) bowling alley
bolígrafo M ballpoint pen
bolita F pellet
Bolivia F Bolivia
boliviano -na ADJ & MF Bolivian
bollo M bun, roll
bolo M bowling pin; **jugar a los —s** to bowl
bolsa F bag, purse; (de canguro) pouch; (de valores) stock market; **— de aire** airbag; **— de estudio** scholarship; **— de miseria** pocket of poverty; **hace —s** it pooches out
bolsillo M pocket; **de —** pocket-sized
bolsista MF stockbroker
bolso M (grande) bag; (pequeño) purse
bomba F (para agua, gasolina) pump; (noticia, mujer) *fam* bombshell; (artefacto explosivo) bomb; **— atómica** atomic bomb; **— de hidrógeno** hydrogen bomb; **— de neutrones** neutron bomb; **— de tiempo** time bomb; **— fétida** stink bomb; **— incendiaria** incendiary bomb; **— inteligente** smart bomb; **lo pasamos — we** had a blast
bombacha F *RP* panties, underpants
bombardear VT to bombard
bombardeo M bombardment, bombing
bombardero -era MF (tripulante) bombardier; M (avión) bomber
bombear VT to pump
bombero -era MF firefighter
bombilla F lightbulb
bombo M bass drum; **dar —** to extol; **con — y platillo** with great fanfare
bombón M (dulce de chocolate) bonbon, candy; (mujer atractiva) *fam* dish

bombonería F candy store
bonachón ADJ (amable) good-natured; (inocente) naïve
bonanza F (buen tiempo) fair weather; (prosperidad) prosperity
bondad F goodness, kindness; **—es** virtues; **tenga la — de** would you please
bondadoso ADJ kind, kindly
boniato M sweet potato
bonito ADJ pretty; M tuna
bono M (financiero) bond; (vale) voucher
boñiga F dung
boqueada F gasp
boquear VI to gasp
boquete M opening
boquiabierto ADJ openmouthed, astonished
boquilla F (para cigarros) cigarette holder; (para una trompeta) mouthpiece; **defender de —** to pay lip-service to
bórax M borax
borbollar VI to bubble
borbollón M bubbling; (alboroto) *Am* commotion; **a borbollones** bubbling over
borbotar VI to bubble, to gurgle
borboteo M bubbling, gurgling
bordado M embroidery, needlework
bordar VI/VT to embroider
borde M edge, border; (de un vaso) rim, brim; (de un desastre) brink; (de una calle) *Méx* curb
bordear VT (rodear) to skirt, go along the edge of; (adornar) to trim
bordillo M curb
bordo LOC ADV **a —** on board
bordó, bordeaux ADJ & M maroon
borla F (de birrete) tassel; (algodón) powder puff
boro M boron
borra F dregs
borrachera F (estado) drunkenness; (juerga) drunken spree
borrachín -ina M drunkard
borracho -cha ADJ drunk, wasted; **no lo hago ni —** I would never do such a thing; MF drunkard, wino
borrador M (bosquejo) rough draft; (goma) eraser
borrar VT to erase; **—se de un club** to withdraw from a club
borrasca F squall
borrego M lamb
borrico M donkey
borrón M blot, blotch, smudge; **hacer — y cuenta nueva** to start over at square one
borronear VT to smudge
borroso ADJ blurry, fuzzy

boscaje M thicket
Bosnia-Herzegovina F Bosnia and Herzegovina
bosnio -nia ADJ & MF Bosnian
bosque M forest, woods
bosquecillo M grove
bosquejar VT to sketch, to outline
bosquejo M sketch, outline
bosta F dung
bostezar[9] VI to yawn
bostezo M yawn
bota F (calzado) boot; (bolsa) leather wine bag
botadura F launch
botánica F botany
botánico ADJ botanical
botar VT (una pelota) to bounce; (un buque) to launch; (a un borracho) to throw out
botarate M fool
bote M (jarro) can; (embarcación) boat; (rebote) bounce; — **de basura** garbage can; — **de remos** rowboat; — **de salvamento** lifeboat; **de** — **en** — filled to overflowing
botella F bottle
botero M boatman
botija F earthen jug
botijo M earthen jar
botín M (de guerra) booty, plunder; (de ladrón) loot, haul
botiquín M (en el baño) medicine cabinet; (de primeros auxilios) first-aid kit
botón M (de planta) bud; (de aparato, de camisa) button; (remache) stud; **botones** bellboy, page
Botsuana F Botswana
bouquet M bouquet
boutique F boutique
bóveda F (techo) arched roof, vault; — **celeste** the vault of heaven
bowling M bowling
box M pit
boxeador -ora MF boxer, prizefighter
boxear VI/VT to box
boxeo M boxing
bóxer M boxer
boya F (en el mar) buoy; (corcho) float
boyante ADJ buoyant
boyar VI to buoy
bozal M muzzle
bozo M fuzz on the lip
bracear VI to move one's arms
bracero -ra MF migrant worker
bragas F PL underpants, panties
bragueta F fly
brainstorming M brainstorming
bramar VI (ciervo, cochino) to bellow; (león,

viento) to roar
bramido M (de ciervo, cochino) bellow; (de león, viento) roar
brandy M brandy
brasa F ember
brasero M brazier
Brasil M Brazil
brasileño -ña ADJ & MF Brazilian
brasilero -ra ADJ & MF Brazilian
bravata F act of bravado
bravío ADJ wild
bravo ADJ (animal, río) wild; (terreno) rugged; (persona) brave; (barrio) tough; INTERJ bravo!
bravucón -ona ADJ bullying; MF bully
bravuconería F bullying
bravura F (de bestia) fierceness; (de persona) courage
braza F fathom
brazada F (cantidad) armful; (en natación) stroke
brazalete M bracelet
brazo M arm (también de silla); (de cornamenta) branch; (de balanza) beam; — **de mar** sound; — **derecho** right-hand man; —**s** day laborers; **con los** —**s abiertos** with open arms; **con los** —**s cruzados** with crossed arms; **ir del** — to go arm in arm; **luchar a** — **partido** to fight to the end
brea F pitch, tar
brecha F breach, gap
brécol M broccoli
bregar[7] VI to struggle, to toil
breña F scrubland
breve ADJ brief, short; (bikini) scanty; **en** — shortly
brevedad F brevity, shortness; **a la** — as soon as possible
bribón -ona ADJ roguish; MF rascal, rogue, scoundrel
brida F bridle
brigada F brigade
brillante ADJ brilliant, bright; M brilliant, gem
brillantez F brilliance
brillantina F glitter
brillar VI to shine; (los ojos) to sparkle, to twinkle; (nieve) to glisten; — **por su ausencia** to be conspicuous by its absence
brillo M shine, luster, sparkle; (de los ojos) twinkle; (de nieve) glistening; (del pelo, plumas) sheen; (de diamantes) sparkle; **dar** — to give luster; **sacar** — to polish
brilloso ADJ shiny
brincar[6] VI to hop, to skip

brinco M hop, skip

brindar VI to toast; **— por alguien** to toast someone; **—se a hacer algo** to volunteer to do something

brindis M toast

brío M spirit

brioso ADJ spirited

brisa F breeze

británico ADJ British

brizna F blade of grass

broca F drill bit

brocado M brocade

brocal M curb

brocha F paint brush; **de — gorda** coarse

broche M (alhaja) brooch; (sujetador) clasp, clip; (para el pelo) barrette; **— de oro** grand finale

brocheta F skewer

brócoli, bróculi M broccoli

broma F (chiste) joke; (réplica) jest, wisecrack; **— pesada** practical joke; **—s aparte** kidding aside; **en —** in jest; **gastar una —** to play a joke; **ni en —** no way; **no estoy para —s** I'm not in the mood for kidding

bromear VI to joke, to kid

bromista MF wag, joker

bromo M bromine

bromuro M bromide

bronca F row; **armar una —** to cause a disturbance, to raise a rumpus; **echarle — a alguien** to bawl someone out

bronce M bronze

bronceado ADJ (cubierto de bronce) bronzed; (piel) tanned; (de color bronce) bronze; M suntan

broncear VT (un objeto) to bronze; (a una persona) to tan; **—se** to get a tan

bronco ADJ (voz) gruff; (terreno) rough; (caballo) wild

bronquio M bronchial tube

bronquitis F bronchitis

brotar VI (planta) to sprout; (enfermedad eruptiva) to break out; (agua) to gush, to flow, to issue

brote M (de una enfermedad) outbreak; (retoño) sprout, spear

broza F brushwood

bruces LOC ADV **de —** face down

brujería F deviltry, witchcraft

brujo -ja M wizard, sorcerer; F witch

brújula F compass

bruma F mist

brumoso ADJ misty

brunch M brunch

bruneano -na ADJ & MF Bruneian

Brunéi M Brunei

bruñir[18] VT to burnish

brusco ADJ (descortés) brusque, curt; (repentino) sudden

brusquedad F (descortesía) brusqueness; (lo repentino) suddenness

brutal ADJ brutal

brutalidad F brutality

bruto -ta ADJ (ignorante) ignorant; (maleducado, burdo) uncouth; (violento) brutish; (no neto) gross; **a lo —** roughly; **en —** in the rough; **recaudar en —** to gross; MF (ignorante) blockhead; (persona violenta) brute; (mal educado) lout, brute

bucal ADJ oral

bucear VI to scuba-dive; (indagar) to explore

buceo M scuba diving

buche M (en las aves) crop; (bocado) mouthful

bucle M curl, ringlet; (en informática) loop

budín M pudding

bueno ADJ good; **buena voluntad** willingness; **a la buena de Dios** haphazardly; **de buenas a primeras** out of the blue; **estar —** to be sexy; **hace buen tiempo** it is fine weather; **lo —** the good thing; **por las buenas o por las malas** by hook or by crook; **ser — con los números** to be good at figures; INTERJ OK! **—s días** good day/morning; **buenas noches** good night/evening; **buenas tardes** good afternoon

buey M ox, steer

búfalo M buffalo, bison

bufanda F scarf, muffler

bufar VI to snort; **está que bufa** he is incensed

bufete M (despacho) lawyer's office; (negocio) practice

buffet M buffet

bufido M snort

bufón -ona MF buffoon, jester

bufonear VI to clown

buhardilla F (desván) attic, garret; (ventana) dormer

búho M owl

buhonero -ra MF peddler

buitre M vulture, buzzard

buje M bushing

bujía F spark plug

bulbo M bulb

buldog M bulldog

bulevar M boulevard

Bulgaria F Bulgaria

búlgaro -ra ADJ & MF Bulgarian

bulla F uproar, fuss, bustle

bulldozer M bulldozer

bullicio M uproar, racket, bustle

bullicioso ADJ boisterous, rowdy
bullir[19] VI (hervir) to boil; (hacer burbujas) to bubble; (ajetrearse) to bustle; (moverse) to stir
bullón M puff
bulto M (paquete) bundle; (tumor) lump, growth; (silueta) shape; (saliente) bulge; **a —** approximately; **escurrir el —** to slack off
bungaló M bungalow
bungee M bungee jumping
búnker M bunker
buñuelo M fritter
buque M ship
burbuja F bubble
burdel M brothel
burdo ADJ coarse
burgués ADJ bourgeois
burla F ridicule, mockery; **hacer — a alguien** to mock someone
burlar VT to mock; **—se de** to scoff at, to make fun of
burlesco -esa ADJ burlesque
burlón ADJ mocking
burocracia F bureaucracy
burócrata MF INV bureaucrat
burrez F stupidity
burro M (animal) donkey, ass; (persona) dunce; ADJ dense
burundés -esa ADJ & MF Burundian
Burundi M Burundi
bus M bus
busca LOC ADV **en — de** in search of
buscar[6] VT to seek, to look for, to search for; (datos, palabras) to look up; (provocar) to provoke; (la verdad) to seek after; (minerales) to prospect for; (talento) to scout for; **—se problemas** to invite trouble; **tú te lo buscaste** you asked for it; **ir a —** to fetch; M SG **buscapersonas** beeper
búsqueda F search; **— del tesoro** treasure hunt
busto M bust
butaca F armchair; (en el teatro) orchestra seat
Bután M Bhutan
butanés -esa ADJ & MF Bhutanese
butano M butane
buzo M diver
buzón M mailbox; **— de sugerencias** suggestion box
bypass M bypass operation
byte M byte

Cc

cabal ADJ (completo) complete; (exacto) exact; (honrado) upright; **estar uno en sus —es** to be in one's right mind
cabalgar[7] VI to ride horseback
caballa F mackerel
caballada F herd of horses
caballejo M nag
caballeresco ADJ chivalrous
caballería F (tropas a caballo) cavalry; (equino) equine; (condición de caballero) knighthood
caballeriza F stable
caballerizo M groom
caballero M (señor) gentleman; (hidalgo) knight, cavalier; **— andante** knight errant; ADJ gentlemanly
caballerosidad F chivalry
caballeroso ADJ chivalrous, gentlemanly
caballete M (soporte de madera) sawhorse; (de la nariz) bridge; (de pintor) easel; (de tejado) ridge
caballo M (animal) horse; (en ajedrez) knight; (heroína) *fam* smack; **a —** on horseback; **— de carreras** racehorse; **— de batalla** hobbyhorse; **— de fuerza** horsepower; **— de Troya** Trojan horse
cabaña F (casa tosca) hovel; (casa de campo) cabin, cottage; (conjunto de ganado) livestock
cabaret M cabaret
cabecear VI (con la cabeza) to nod; (dormirse) to nod off; (un barco) to bob, to pitch
cabeceo M (de la cabeza) nodding; (de un barco) pitching
cabecera F (de cama) headboard; (de mesa) head
cabecilla MF INV ringleader
cabellera F head of hair
cabello M hair; **traido por los —s** far-fetched
caber[22] VI to fit; **no cabe duda** there is no doubt; **no cabe nadie más** there is no room for anybody else; **no — uno en sí** to be puffed up with pride; **no cabe en lo posible** it is absolutely impossible; **¿en qué cabeza cabe?** who would believe that?
cabestrillo M sling
cabestro M halter
cabeza F head; **— de chorlito** scatterbrain,

airhead; **— de playa** beachhead; **— de puente** bridgehead; **— de turco** scapegoat, fall guy; **— rapada** skinhead; **a la —** at the forefront; **caerse de —** to fall headfirst; **echarse de —** to plunge headlong; **ir a la —** to lead the way; **por —** each; **romperse la —** to rack one's brains; **se le fue la —** it went to his head; **sentar —** to settle down; **tiene la — cuadrada** she's a square

cabezada F nod; **dar —s** to nod off

cabezal M magnetic head

cabezazo M butt (with the head)

cabezón ADJ (de cabeza grande) big-headed; (testarudo) pig-headed; (fuerte) strong

cabezudo ADJ (de cabeza grande) big-headed; (testarudo) pig-headed

cabida F capacity; **dar —** to include; **tener — en** to fit in

cabina F (de pasajeros) cabin; (de piloto) cockpit; (de camión) cab; (de teléfono, control) booth

cabizbajo ADJ crestfallen, downcast

cable M cable

cableado M wiring

cablevisión F cable television

cabo M (parte extrema) end; (hilo) thread; (cuerda) rope; (saliente de la costa) cape; (rango militar) corporal; **— suelto** loose end; **al — de** at the end of; **atar —s** to make sense of; **de — a rabo** from beginning to end; **llevar a —** to carry out

cabotaje M coastal trade

Cabo Verde M Cape Verde

caboverdiano -na ADJ & MF Cape Verdean

cabra F goat; **— montés** mountain goat; **como una —** completely crazy

cabrearse VI to get mad

cabrestante M winch

cabrillas F PL whitecaps

cabrio M rafter

cabrío ADJ **macho —** he-goat

cabriola F caper

cabriolar VI to cavort

cabritilla F kid (leather)

cabrito M kid (goat)

cabrón -ona M (macho de cabra) he-goat; (hombre cuya mujer le engaña) cuckold; MF (cobarde) wimp

caca F poop; **hacer —** to poop

cacahuate M *Méx* peanut

cacahuete M *Esp* peanut

cacao M cocoa

cacarear VI to cackle, to squawk

cacareo M cackling, squawking

cacatúa F cockatoo

cacería F hunt; **— de brujas** witch hunt

cacerola F saucepan

cacha F (de navaja) handle; (nalga) hip; **hasta la —** completely

cachalote M sperm whale

cacharro M (vasija) earthen pot; (coche viejo) clunker, jalopy

cachaza F slowness

cachazudo ADJ slow

caché M (en informática) cache; (distinción) cachet

cachear VT to body-search, to frisk

cachet M artist's fee

cachetada F slap

cachete M cheek

cachiporra F blackjack

cachivaches M PL stuff, odds and ends

cacho M hunk

cachorro M (de oso, lobo, tigre, león) cub; (de perro) puppy

cacique -ca M (de indios) chief, chieftain; MF (caudillo) political boss

cacofonía F cacophony

cacto M cactus

cactus M cactus

cada ADJ each; **— uno** each one; **— vez más** more and more; **— vez menos gente** fewer and fewer people; **— vez menos harina** less and less flour; **— vez peor** worse and worse; **doscientas pesetas — una** two hundred pesetas each/apiece

cadalso M gallows

cadáver M corpse; (para disecar) cadaver

cadavérico ADJ ghastly

caddie, caddy MF caddie

cadena F (serie de piezas) chain; (de televisión) network; (cordillera) mountain range; **— de montaje** assembly line; **— perpetua** life sentence; **—s** shackles; **tirar la —** to flush

cadencia F cadence

cadera F hip

cadete MF cadet

cadmio M cadmium

caducar[6] VI to lapse, to expire

caducidad F expiration

caduco ADJ (destinado a caer) deciduous; (decrépito) decrepit

caer[23] VI to fall; (perder el equilibrio) to fall down; (colgar) to hang; (ir a parar) to end up; **al — la noche** at nightfall; **— en desgracia** to fall into disfavor; **— en desuso** to fall into disuse; **— en cama** to fall ill; **— en cuenta** to catch on; **— en ruina** to fall into disrepair; **—le bien/mal a uno** (una persona) to make a good/bad impression; (una comida) to agree with; **—le en suerte a uno** to fall

to one's lot; — **muy bajo** to fall so low;
caiga quien caiga let fall who may;
dejar — to drop; **está al** — he's about to
show up; **—se** to fall down; **—se de culo**
to fall on one's bottom

café M (bebida) coffee; (color) brown;
(establecimiento público) coffee shop

cafeína F caffeine

cafetal M coffee plantation

cafetera F coffeepot

cafetería F snack bar, cafeteria, diner

cafetero -ra MF coffee dealer; ADJ **industria
cafetera** coffee industry

cafeto M coffee bush

caída F (acción de caer) fall, tumble, spill; (de
presión arterial) drop; (de un ordenador)
crash; (de una cortina) hang; — **libre** free
fall; — **del sol** sunset

caído ADJ (orejas) floppy; (arco del pie) fallen;
los —s the fallen

caimán M alligator

caja F box; — **chica** petty cash; — **de
ahorros** savings bank; — **de cambios**
transmission; — **de escalera** stairwell; —
de fusibles fuse box; — **de
herramientas** tool kit; — **de
jubilaciones** pension fund; — **de
música** music box; — **de reloj**
watchcase; — **fuerte** safe; —
registradora (aparato) cash register, till;
(lugar) checkout counter; — **tonta** idiot
box; — **torácica** rib cage; **entrar en** —
to get going

cajero -ra MF cashier; (en un banco) teller; —
automático ATM

cajetilla F pack (of cigarettes)

cajilla F pack (of cigarettes)

cajón M (para transportes) crate; (parte de un
mueble) drawer; **eso es de** — that's a
foregone conclusion

cajuela F *Méx* car trunk

cal F lime; **cerrar a** — **y canto** to close
hermetically

calabacín M zucchini

calabaza F (grande y redonda) pumpkin;
(pequeña y/o alargada) squash; (vaciado)
gourd; **dar —s** to turn down

calabozo M dungeon

calado M draft

calamar M squid

calambre M cramp

calamidad F calamity

calamina F calamine

calandria F lark

calar VT (agujerear) to perforate; (empapar)
to soak, to drench; — **a alguien** to see
through someone; — **hondo** to resonate;

—**se** to get drenched

calavera F skull; M libertine

calcar[6] VT (sobre papel) to trace; (imitar) to
copy

calcetería F hosiery

calcetín M sock

calcinar VT to bake

calcio M calcium

calco M (acción de calcar) tracing; **es el** — **de
su padre** he's the spitting image of his
father

calcomanía F decal

calculador ADJ calculating

calculadora F calculator

calcular VT (averiguar una cantidad) to
calculate, to figure; (sopesar) to weigh;
(prever) to reckon

cálculo M (acción de calcular) calculation;
(aritmética) arithmetic; (integral,
diferencial) calculus; — **biliar** gallstone;
— **renal** kidney stone

caldear VT to warm up; — **los ánimos** to
get everyone upset

caldera F (en una máquina de vapor) boiler;
(recipiente con asas) kettle; (de la
calefacción) furnace

calderón M hold

caldo M broth, stock; — **de cultivo** culture
medium

calefacción F heat, heating; — **central**
central heating

calendario M calendar

caléndula F marigold

calentador M heater; — **de agua** water
heater

calentamiento M warming; (en deportes)
warm-up; — **global** global warming

calentar[1] VI/VT (poner caliente) to warm, to
heat; —**se** (ponerse caliente, prepararse
para un partido) to warm up, to heat up

calentura F (fiebre) fever

calesa F buggy

caletre M **no tener** — to have no brains

calibrador M caliper

calibrar VT to gauge, to calibrate

calibre M (de pistola, tubo) caliber; (de
alambre) gauge; (instrumento para medir)
caliper

calicó M calico

calidad F quality; **de** — of good quality;
estoy aquí en — **de representante** I'm
here in my capacity as representative

cálido ADJ warm

caliente ADJ (agradable) warm; (excesivo) hot

calificación F (nota) grade, mark; (acción de
asignar notas) grading; (juicio) rating; **le
dieron la** — **de genio** they called him a

genius

calificar[6] VT (expresar la calidad) to rate, to adjudge; (asignar nota) to grade; **—se como** to be characterized as

caligrafía F (calidad de letra) penmanship; (arte) calligraphy

calina F haze

callado ADJ silent, quiet; **estarse —** to keep quiet

callar VT (no manifestar, hacer que calle) to quiet; (no hablar) to remain silent; (dejar de hablar) to shut up; **—se la boca** to shut up, to pipe down

calle F street; (en un campo de golf) fairway; **— abajo** down the street; **— arriba** up the street; **— de sentido único** one-way street; **hacer la —** *fam* to cruise for Johns; **no pisar la —** to stay home

calleja F narrow street

callejear VI to walk the streets

callejero ADJ **perro —** stray dog; **caos —** chaos in the streets

callejón M alley; **— sin salida** blind alley, dead end

callo M callus, corn

calloso ADJ callous

calma F calm; **— chicha** absolute calm; **mantener la —** to keep one's temper; **tomar las cosas con —** to take things easy

calmante ADJ & M sedative

calmar VT (los nervios) to calm; (dolor) to sooth; (miedo) to allay, to quell; (sed) to quench; **—se** (una persona) to calm down; (una tormenta, la ira) to subside, to abate

calmo ADJ calm

calmoso ADJ easygoing

calor M heat, warmth; (actitud acogedora) warmth; **hace — hoy** it's hot today; **los —es** hot flashes; **tengo —** I'm hot

caloría F calorie

calumnia F calumny, slander

calumniar VT to slander, to malign

calumnioso ADJ slanderous

caluroso ADJ (día) hot; (recepción) warm

calva F bald spot

calvario M **mi vida es un —** *fam* my life is hell

calvo ADJ bald, baldheaded; **ni tanto ni tan — ** *fam* it ain't necessarily so; **quedarse —** to go bald

calza F long sock

calzada F pavement

calzado M footwear

calzador M shoehorn

calzar[9] VT (poner zapatos) to shoe; (hacer zapatos para) to make shoes for; **— a la**

familia to buy shoes for the family; **calzo 42** I take size 10; **—se** to put on shoes

calzones M PL (de mujer) panties; (de hombre) shorts

calzoncillos M PL underpants, briefs; **— largos** long johns

cama F bed; **— de agua** waterbed; **— doble** double bed; **— elástica** trampoline; **— individual** twin bed; **guardar —** to be confined to bed; **meterse en la — con** to sleep with

camada F litter

camafeo M cameo

camaleón M chameleon

cámara F (espacio) chamber; (de neumático) inner tube; (fotográfica) camera; **— de comercio** chamber of commerce; **— de diputados** lower house; **— de gas** gas chamber; **— de oxígeno** oxygen tent; **— frigorífica** locker; **— legislativa** legislature; **en — lenta** in slow motion; MF INV (persona que maneja una cámara) camera operator

camarada MF INV comrade

camarero -ra M (en un restaurante) waiter, server; (en un coche cama) steward; F (en un restaurante) waitress, server; (en un coche cama) stewardess; (en un hotel) maid

camarilla F clique

camarógrafo -fa M cameraman; F camerawoman

camarón M shrimp

camarote M cabin, stateroom

cambalache M fraudulent swap

cambalachear VI/VT to swap fraudulently

cambiante ADJ (que cambia) changing; (propenso a cambiar) changeable; (temperamento) volatile

cambiar VI/VT to change; VT (una cosa por otra) to exchange, to swap, to trade; **— de marcha** to shift gears; **— de opinión / parecer** to change one's mind; **— de sitio** to move

cambio M (acción de cambiar) change; (marcha) gear; (cotización) exchange rate; (de ferrocarril) railway switch; **— de divisas** foreign exchange; **— para peor** a turn for the worse; **— y fuera** over and out; **a — (de)** in return (for); **en —** on the other hand

cambista MF money changer

Camboya F Cambodia

camboyano -na ADJ & MF Cambodian

camellear VT to push (drugs)

camello -lla M (animal) camel; (vendedor de

droga) pusher; F (animal) female camel;
(vendedora de droga) pusher
camerino M dressing room
Camerún M Cameroon
camerunés -esa ADJ & MF Cameroonian
camilla F stretcher, litter
camillero -ra MF hospital orderly
caminante MF walker, wayfarer
caminar VI/VT to walk
caminata F long walk; (por un lugar agreste)
hike
camino M (carretera) road; (itinerario,
dirección que hay que seguir) way; **— de**
on the way to; **— de mesa** table runner;
— de rosas bed of roses; **abrirse —** to
make way; **a medio —** halfway; **en — (a)**
on the way (to); **llevar por mal —** to
lead astray; **mostrar el —** to lead the
way; **ponerse en —** to set out; **señalar
el —** to show the way
camión M truck; *Méx* bus; **— de la basura**
garbage truck; **— de mudanzas** moving
van; **— de remolque** tow truck, wrecker;
— de reparto delivery truck; **—
volteador** dump truck
camionero -ra MF truck driver; *Méx* bus
driver
camioneta F (furgoneta) van, minivan;
(camioncito) pickup truck; (coche sin
maletero) station wagon
camisa F shirt; **— de fuerza** straitjacket;
meterse en — de once varas to get into
a jam
camiseta F (exterior) T-shirt; (interior)
undershirt
camisón M nightgown
camorrista MF rowdy
campamento M (de refugiados,
exploradores) camp; (recreativo)
campground
campana F bell; **tocar una —** to ring a bell
campanario M belfry, bell tower
campanilla F (campana pequeña) small bell;
(flor) bluebell; (órgano en la boca) uvula
campanilleo M ringing
campánula F bellflower
campaña F campaign; **de —** on the front;
hacer — to campaign
campechano ADJ straightforward
campeón -ona MF champion
campeonato M championship
campero ADJ **hombre —** a man from the
country
campesino -na MF peasant; ADJ **casa —**
peasant house
campestre ADJ rural
camping M (lugar) campground; (actividad)

camping
campiña F open country
campista MF camper
campo M (fuera de la ciudad) country,
countryside; (para cultivos, deportes,
ámbito) field; (grupo en un conflicto)
camp; **— abierto** range; **— de acción**
field of action; **— de batalla** battlefield;
— de concentración concentration
camp; **— de golf** golf course; **— de tiro**
shooting range; **— libre** free rein; **—
magnético** magnetic field; **— minado**
minefield; **—santo** churchyard; **— visual**
visual field; **a — traviesa** cross-country
campus M campus
camuflaje M camouflage
camuflar VT to camouflage
can M dog
cana F white hair; **echar una — al aire** to
go out for a good time
Canadá M Canada
canadiense ADJ & MF Canadian
canal M (cauce artificial de agua) canal;
(estrecho marítimo, banda de frecuencia)
channel; (emisora) station
canalé M ribbed fabric
canalizar[9] VT to channel
canalla MF *ofensivo* scum, lowlife
canalón M spout
canana F cartridge belt
canapé M divan
canario -ria M canary; ADJ of / from the
Canary Islands; MF Canary Islander
canasta F basket
canasto M hamper
cancelación F cancellation
cancelar VT (un contrato, un sello) to cancel;
(una deuda) to pay off; (una actividad) to
call off
cáncer M cancer; **— de mama** breast cancer
cancerígeno ADJ carcinogen
canceroso -sa MF cancer patient
cancha F (de baloncesto, tenis) court; (de
fútbol) field; **¡abran —!** gangway! **falta
—** there's no room
canciller MF (de Alemania, de universidades)
chancellor; (de EEUU) Secretary of State
canción F song; **— de cuna** lullaby
candado M padlock
candela F candle
candelabro M candelabrum
candelero M candlestick; **en —** in the
limelight
candente ADJ red-hot
candidato -ta MF candidate
candidatura F (hecho de ser candidato)
candidacy; (conjunto de candidatos en

equipo) ticket
candidez F innocence
cándido ADJ naïve
candil M oil lamp
candilejas F PL footlights
candor M innocence
canela F (especia) cinnamon; (árbol) cinnamon tree
canesú M yoke of a shirt
cangrejo M crab
canguro M kangaroo; MF INV *Esp* baby-sitter
caníbal ADJ & MF cannibal
canica F toy marble
caniche M poodle; — **enano** toy poodle
canilla F (espinilla) shin; (pantorrilla) calf; (grifo) faucet
canino ADJ canine; **tener un hambre canina** to be ravenous; M canine (tooth)
canje M exchange
canjear VT (prisioneros, libros) to exchange; (un cupón) to redeem
cano ADJ gray-haired
canoa F canoe
canon M (regla, modelo) canon; (canción) round
canónigo M canon
canoso ADJ gray-haired
cansado ADJ (fatigado) tired, weary; (fatigoso) wearing, tiring
cansancio M weariness
cansar VT (fatigar) to tire, to tire out; (aburrir) to bore; —**se** to get tired
cantante MF singer
cantar VI/VT to sing; VT (anunciar) to call out; (confesar) to confess; — **a tono** to sing on key; —**le a alguien las cuarenta** to give someone a piece of one's mind; — **victoria** to declare victory; **en menos que cante un gallo** before you can say Jack Robinson; M epic poem; **eso es otro** — that's another story
cántaro M pitcher; **llover a** —**s** to rain cats and dogs
cantera F quarry
cantero M *RP* flowerbed
cántico M chant
cantidad F quantity, amount; (de dinero) amount, sum; — **de gente** a lot of people
cantimplora F canteen
cantina F (lugar donde comer) mess hall, mess, canteen; (bar) tavern
cantinela F chant
cantinero -ra MF bartender
canto M (cosa cantada) song; (piedra) pebble; — **de cisne** swan song; — **llano** chant; — **rodado** rounded pebble; **de** — on edge

cantor -ora MF singer
canturrear VI to hum
canturreo M hum, humming
caña F (planta gramínea) reed; (de azúcar) cane; (cerveza) *Esp* beer; (vaso para cerveza) *Esp* beer glass; — **de pescar** fishing pole; **dale** — floor it
cañada F (barranco) ravine; (arroyo) brook
cáñamo M hemp
cañaveral M reed patch
cañería F (en la calle) piping; (en la casa) plumbing
caño M (tubo) pipe; (grifo) spout; (de arma) barrel; **de doble** — double-barreled
cañón M (arma) cannon; (pieza hueca) barrel; (cañada profunda) canyon; (de pluma, bolígrafo) shaft
cañonero M gunboat
caoba F mahogany
caos M chaos
caótico ADJ chaotic
capa F (prenda) cape, cloak; (de pintura, animal) coat; (de tierra) layer; (de hielo) sheet; — **de ozono** ozone layer; — **freática** water table; **de** — **y espada** cloak and dagger
capacidad F capacity; —**es** aptitude, ability, capability
capacitar VT (entrenar) to train; (habilitar) to qualify
capar VT to castrate
caparazón M shell
capataz -za MF boss, overseer
capaz ADJ (que puede hacer algo) capable, able; (apto) apt; (espacioso) spacious, roomy; (competente) competent
capear VT to ride out; — **un temporal** to weather a storm
capellán M chaplain
caperuza F pointed hood
capilar ADJ & M capillary
capilla F chapel; **estar en** — (castigado) to be in the doghouse; (esperando una noticia) to be on pins and needles
capital M (dinero) capital; (de préstamo) principal; — **de riesgo** venture capital; **el gran** — big business; F capital (city); ADJ main
capitalino ADJ **atmósfera capitalina** capital city atmosphere
capitalismo M capitalism
capitalista MF capitalist; ADJ capitalistic
capitalización F capitalization
capitalizar[9] VT (aportar capital) to capitalize; (aprovechar) to capitalize on
capitán -ana MF captain
capitanear VT to captain

capitel M capital
capitolio M capitol
capitular VI to capitulate
capítulo M chapter
capó M hood (of a car)
capo M mafia boss
capota F top
capote M cloak; (de coche) *Méx* hood; **decir para su —** to say under one's breath
capricho M caprice, whim, notion
caprichoso ADJ (impredecible) capricious; (impulsivo) whimsical, fanciful; (malcriado) willful
cápsula F capsule
captar VT (un concepto) to grasp; (atención, interés) to capture; (una emisión) to receive; (una indirecta) to get; **— la onda** to get the drift
captor -ora MF captor
captura F (acción de capturar) capture; (pesca capturada) catch
capturar VT to capture; (pescado) to catch
capucha F (de cabeza) hood, cowl; (de lapicero) cap
capuchina F nasturtium
capuchino M cappuccino
capullo M (de insecto) cocoon; (de flor) bud
caqui M khaki
cara F (rostro) face; (de cubo) surface; (de papel, moneda) side; (morro) nerve; **— a —** face to face; **— o cruz** heads or tails; **dar la —** to face up to things; **de — al sur** facing south; **decir en la —** to tell to one's face; **de dos —s** two-sided; **la otra — de la moneda** the other side of the coin; **poner buena —** to put on a good face; **se le ve en la —** it's written all over his face; **tener — (dura)** to have a lot of nerve; **un ojo de la —** an arm and a leg; **volverle la — a** to snub
caracol M (molusco) snail; (concha) snail shell; **¡—es!** *fam* darn!
carácter M (temperamento, signo) character; (rasgo) characteristic; (índole) kind
característica F characteristic, feature
característico ADJ characteristic
caracterizar[9] VT to characterize
caramba INTERJ *fam* darn! good grief! heck!
carámbano M icicle
carambola F carom; **por —** indirectly
caramelo M (azúcar fundido) caramel; (dulce pequeño) bonbon
caramillo M reed pipe
carátula F (máscara) mask; (portada) title page
caravana F (en el desierto, convoy) caravan; (remolque) trailer

caray INTERJ *fam* shoot!
carbohidrato M carbohydrate
carbón M (sustancia sólida) coal; (pedazo) piece of coal; **— de leña** charcoal
carboncillo M charcoal drawing
carbonera F coal bin
carbono M carbon
carburador M carburetor
carca MF INV *fam* fossil, old fogey
carcaj M quiver
carcajada F burst of laughter, guffaw
carcamal MF INV *fam* fossil, old fogey
cárcel F jail, prison
carcelero -ra MF jailer
carcinógeno M carcinogen
carcinoma M carcinoma; **— de célula basal** basal cell carcinoma
carcomido ADJ worm-eaten
carda F card, comb
cardán M universal joint
cardar VT (lana) to card, to comb; (pelo) to rat, to tease
cardenal M (pájaro, prelado) cardinal; (moretón) bruise
cardíaco -ca ADJ cardiac; MF heart patient
cardinal ADJ cardinal
cardiología F cardiology
cardiovascular ADJ cardiovascular
cardo M thistle
cardumen M school of fish
carear VT to bring face to face; **—se** to meet face to face
carecer[13] VI to lack
carencia F lack; (en la dieta) deficiency
carenciado ADJ disadvantaged
carente ADJ lacking; **— de** lacking in
carero ADJ expensive
carestía F (escasez) scarcity; (costo alto) high cost
careta F mask
carga F (cosa cargada) load, freight; (de la prueba, impuesto) burden; (hipoteca) lien; (de encendedor) refill; (de explosivo, electricidad) charge; **— de municiones** round of ammunition; **— útil** payload; **volver a la —** to insist
cargado ADJ (bebida) stiff; (pausa) pregnant; (cartucho) live; **— de deudas** deep in debt; **— de espaldas** stooping
cargador M (de batería) charger; (de arma de fuego) clip, magazine
cargamento M cargo, load, shipment
cargar[7] VT (cargamentos, dados, un arma, un programa de ordenador) to load; (una batería, a una cuenta) to charge; (de obligaciones) to burden with; (a un niño) to carry; (a un estudiante) *Esp* to flunk;

(molestar) to bother; **— a alguien de
responsabilidades** to saddle someone
with responsibilities; **— al hombro** to
shoulder; **— con la culpa** to saddle with
blame; **— de combustible** to fuel; VI to
charge; **— sobre** to charge, to attack

cargo M (función en una empresa) position;
(en una factura, a una cuenta) charge;
(acusación) count, charge; **— de
conciencia** guilt feelings; **a mi —** under
my charge; **hacerse — de**
(responsabilizarse de) to take charge of;
(ser consciente de) to understand;
investir de un — to induct into office;
los niños están a — de la maestra the
children are under the care of the teacher;
la maestra está a(l) — de los niños
the teacher is in charge of the children

cargoso ADJ fussy

carguero ADJ freight-carrying

caribeño ADJ Caribbean

caricatura F (retrato) caricature; (con texto)
cartoon

caricaturista MF cartoonist

caricaturizar⁹ VT to caricature

caricia F caress

caridad F charity

caries F cavity, tooth decay

carillón M chimes

cariño M (amor) affection, fondness; (apodo)
honey; **darle —s a alguien** to send love
to someone; **ella y el perro se hacen
—s** she and the dog nuzzle each other;
hacer con — to do with great care;
tenerle — a alguien to be fond of
someone

cariñoso ADJ affectionate, loving

carisma M charisma

caritativo ADJ charitable

cariz M complexion

carmesí ADJ & M crimson

carmín M (carmesí) crimson; (lápiz de labios)
lip gloss

carnal ADJ carnal

carnaval M carnival

carne F (para comer) meat; (de animal vivo,
de persona, de tomate) flesh; **— de
cañón** cannon fodder; **— de cerdo** pork;
— de cordero mutton; **— de gallina**
goose bumps; **— de res** beef; **— de
venado** venison; **— y hueso** flesh and
blood; **como — y uña** *fam* thick as
thieves; **en — viva** raw; **metido en —s**
overweight

carnear VT to butcher

carnero M ram

carnet M **— de conducir** driver's license; **—**

de identidad identification card

carnicería F (tienda) butcher's shop;
(matanza) carnage, bloodbath

carnicero -ra MF butcher; ADJ (carnívoro)
carnivorous; (cruel) cruel

carnívoro ADJ carnivorous

carnoso ADJ fleshy

caro ADJ expensive, costly, high-priced; ADV
at a high price

carona F saddle pad

carótida F carotid artery

carozo M *RP* pit

carpa F (pez) carp; (tienda de circo) circus
tent

carpeta F (para documentos, también en
ordenador) folder; (cartera) portfolio

carpintería F (oficio) carpentry; (taller)
carpenter's shop

carpintero -ra MF carpenter

carraspear VI to clear one's throat

carraspera F scratchy throat

carrera F (conjunto de estudios, trayectoria
profesional) career; (competición) race; (en
las medias) run; (recorrido corto) run,
dash; (de pistón) stroke; **— a pie** footrace;
— de caballos horse race; **— de relevos**
relay race; **a la —** running; **hacer —** to
succeed in a profession; **tomar —** to get a
running start

carreta F wagon

carrete M (de película) reel; (de hilo) bobbin;
(de alambre) spool

carretera F highway; **— de circunvalación**
bypass; **— de peaje** toll road

carretero ADJ **sistema —** highway system

carretilla F (de una rueda) wheelbarrow; (de
más de una rueda) dolly; **de — by**
memory

carretón M large wagon

carril M (de ferrocarril) rail; (de calle) lane

carrillo M cheek; **a dos / cuatro —s**
voraciously

carrillón M chimes

carrizo M reed

carro M (vehículo de dos ruedas) cart;
(automóvil) car; (de máquina de escribir)
roll; **— alegórico** parade float; **—
blindado** armored car; **— de guerra**
chariot; **poner el — delante de los
bueyes** to put the cart before the horse;
subirse al — to get on the bandwagon

carrocería F auto body

carroña F carrion

carroza F (coche de caballos) coach; (de
desfile) parade float; (fúnebre) hearse

carruaje M carriage, coach

carta F (misiva) letter; (naipe) card; (de

restaurante) menu; (constitución) charter;
(mapa) chart; — **blanca** free hand; **a la**
— à la carte; **echarle las —s a alguien**
to do a card-reading for someone; **tomar**
—s en la situación to take charge of a
situation

cartearse VI to correspond

cartel M poster, placard; **en —** showing

cartelera F (de periódico) entertainment
section; (publicitaria) billboard; (tablón
para anuncios) bulletin board

cárter M oil pan

cartera F (para dinero) wallet, billfold; (para
papeles) briefcase; (de alumnos) satchel;
(bolsa) handbag; (de valores) portfolio

carterista MF pickpocket

cartero -ra MF letter carrier; M mailman,
postman

cartílago M cartilage

cartilla F (libro para aprender a leer) reader;
(librito de información) booklet; **— de**
racionamiento ration book

cartografiar[16] VT to chart

cartón M cardboard, pasteboard; **— de**
cigarrillos carton of cigarettes

cartuchera F cartridge belt

cartucho M (de arma de fuego) cartridge,
shell; (de monedas) roll; (de dinamita)
stick; **— de fogueo** blank cartridge;
quemar el último — to exhaust one's
resources

cartulina F thin cardboard

casa F (edificio) house; (hogar) home;
(negocio) business firm; **— de ancianos**
old folks' home; **— de citas** cheap motel
for rendezvous; **— de empeños**
pawnshop; **— de la moneda** mint; **— de**
muñecas dollhouse; **— de pompas**
fúnebres funeral home; **— de reposo**
rest home; **— embrujada** haunted
house; **— rodante** house trailer; **—**
solariega manor house; **de — en —**
from house to house; **en —** at home;
entró como Perico por su — he made
himself right at home; **estás en tu —**
make yourself at home; **ir a —** to go
home; **la — paga** on the house; **poner**
una — to set up a household; **quedarse**
en — to stay home; **tirar la — por la**
ventana to live it up

casaca F riding jacket

casadero ADJ marriageable

casado ADJ married

casamentero -ra MF matchmaker

casamiento M wedding, marriage ceremony

casar VT to marry off; **—se** to get married, to
wed; **—se con** to get married to; **no —se**

con nadie to remain independent

cascabel M (cosa que tintinea) jingle bell; (de
víbora) rattle; **ser un —** to be lively;
poner el — al gato to stick one's neck
out

cascada F cascade, waterfall

cascajo M old wreck

cascar[6] VT (quebrar) to crack; (dar bofetadas)
to slap around; **—se** to crack open; M SG
cascanueces nutcracker

cáscara F (de huevo, fruto seco) shell; (de
granos, arvejas) husk; (de fruto seco) hull;
(de fruta) rind; (de naranja, manzana) peel

cascarrabias MF SG crab, grouch; ADJ INV
grouchy

casco M (de ciclista, militar) helmet; (de
obrero) hard hat; (de barco) hull; (de
naranja) shell; (uña del pie de caballería)
hoof; **— urbano** limits of the city

cascote M rubble

caserío M (aldea) hamlet; (casa) *Esp*
farmhouse

casero -ra ADJ (doméstico) domestic; (hecho
en casa) homemade; MF caretaker; M
landlord; F landlady

caseta F (en un mercado) booth, stall; (de
guardia) guardhouse; (de perro) doghouse

casete MF cassette

casi ADV almost, nearly; **— diez mil** almost /
nearly ten thousand; **— lo hago** I almost
did it; **— siempre** almost always; **—**
nadie hardly anyone; **— nunca** hardly
ever

casilla F (en el tablero de ajedrez) square; (en
una tabla) box; (en un casillero)
pigeonhole, cubbyhole; **— de perro**
doghouse; **sacarle a alguien de sus —s**
to drive someone up the wall

casino M (club) men's club; (lugar de recreo)
casino

caso M case; **en — de** in the event of; **en —**
de que in case that; **el — es que** the deal
is that; **en todo —** in any case, at any
rate; **en último —** as a last resort; **eso no**
viene al — that is beside the point;
hacer — (de) to pay attention (to);
hacer — omiso de to disregard; **no hay**
— there's no point; **pongamos por —**
let's suppose that; **venir al —** to come to
the point

caspa F dandruff

casquillo M (de bala) case; (de lámpara)
socket

cassette MF cassette

casta F caste

castaña F chestnut; **— de cajú** cashew

castañetear VI to chatter; **— con los dedos**

to snap one's fingers

castañeteo M (de dientes) chattering; (de dedos) snapping

castaño M (árbol) chestnut tree; (color, madera) chestnut; ADJ chestnut-colored, brown

castañuela F castanet

castellano ADJ & MF Castilian; M (lengua) Castilian

castidad F chastity

castigar[7] VT to chastise, to punish

castigo M chastisement, punishment; **¡qué —!** what a nuisance!

Castilla F Castile

castillo M castle; **— de arena** sand castle; **—s en el aire** *fam* pie in the sky

casting M casting

castizo ADJ traditional

casto ADJ chaste

castor M beaver

castrar VT (a un hombre, animal) to castrate; (a una mascota) to neuter, to fix; (a mascotas hembras) to spay

casual ADJ chance, accidental

casualidad F chance, coincidence; **da la — que** it so happens that; **oír por —** to overhear; **por —** by chance

casucha F shack

cata F **— de vinos** wine-tasting

catalán -ana ADJ (del catalán) Catalan; (de Cataluña) Catalonian; MF Catalan; M (lengua) Catalan

catalejo M spyglass

catalizador M catalyst

catalogar[7] VT to catalog, catalogue

catálogo M catalog, catalogue

Cataluña F Catalonia

catar VT to taste

catarata F (cascada) cataract, waterfall; (de los ojos) cataract

catarí ADJ & MF Qatari

catarro M cold

catástrofe F catastrophe

catecismo M catechism

cátedra F (puesto de profesor) chair, professorship; (enseñanza) teaching; (división académica) department; **sentar —** to hold forth

catedral F cathedral

catedrático -ca MF (full) professor

categoría F category; **de —** important; **de mundial** world-class; **de poca —** third-rate

caterpillar M caterpillar

catéter M catheter

cátodo M cathode

catolicismo M Catholicism

católico -ca ADJ Catholic; MF Catholic

catorce NUM fourteen

catre M cot

cátsup M catsup, ketchup

cauce M channel; **— de río** riverbed

cauchero -ra MF rubber gatherer; ADJ **industria cauchera** rubber industry

caucho M rubber; **— sintético** synthetic rubber

caución F security payment

caudal M (conjunto de bienes) wealth; (cantidad de agua) volume of water

caudaloso ADJ mighty

caudillo M leader

causa F cause; (proceso) case; **— noble** worthy cause; **— perdida** lost cause; **a — de** on account of, because of; **con conocimiento de —** wittingly; **hacer — común** to work together

causar VT to cause; **— problemas** to make trouble

cáustico ADJ caustic

cautela F caution

cauteloso ADJ cautious, wary

cauterizar[9] VT to cauterize

cautivar VT (tomar cautivo) to capture; (atraer la simpatía) to captivate

cautiverio M captivity

cautivo -va MF captive

cauto ADJ cautious, wary

cavar VT to dig

caverna F cavern, cave

cavidad F cavity

cavilar VI to muse

cayado M shepherd's crook, staff

cayo M key

caza F (acción de cazar) hunt, hunting; (conjunto de animales) wild game; **— mayor** big game; **— menor** small game; **andar a la — de** to hunt; **dar — a** to hunt down; M (avión) fighter

cazador -ora ADJ hunting; MF hunter; F windbreaker[tm]

cazar[9] VI/VT (buscar presas) to hunt; (matar presas) to shoot, to bag; (atrapar presas) to trap; MF SG **cazatalentos** talent scout; **cazatorpedero** destroyer, torpedo-boat

cazo M (para agua) dipper; (para sopa) ladle

cazoleta F pipe bowl

cazuela F (recipiente) casserole; (cazo) pan

CD M CD; **— ROM** CD-ROM

cebada F barley

cebador M pump primer

cebar VT (un animal) to fatten; (bombas) to prime; (anzuelos) to bait; **—se** to vent one's anger

cebo M (para peces) bait, lure; (para animales)

feed

cebolla F onion

cebollar M onion patch

cebollino M scallion

cebra F (animal) zebra; (paso) crosswalk

cecear VI to lisp

ceceo M lisp

cecina F jerky

cedazo M sieve

ceder VT (propiedad) to cede, to assign; (un sitio) to yield, to give up; VI (disminuir) to diminish; (perder resistencia) to give way

cedro M cedar

cédula F — **de identidad** identification card

céfiro M zephyr

cegar[1,7] VT to blind

ceguera F blindness

ceja F (sobre el ojo) eyebrow; (en una encuadernación) tab; **quemarse las** — to cram for an exam

cejar VI to back down

cejijunto ADJ with thick eyebrows

celada F ambush

celador -ora MF school monitor

celar VT to watch over jealously

celda F cell

celebración F (fiesta) celebration; (acto solemne) performance

celebrar VT (festejar) to celebrate; (una reunión) to hold; (un rito) to perform

célebre ADJ famous, noted

celebridad F celebrity

celeste ADJ (relativo al firmamento) celestial; (del color del cielo) azure, light blue

celestial ADJ celestial, heavenly

célibe ADJ celibate; MF unmarried person

cellisca F sleet; **caer** — to sleet

celo M (diligencia) zeal; (excitación sexual) heat; **estar en** — to be in heat; —**s** jealousy; **tener —s** to be jealous

celofán M cellophane

celosía F window lattice

celoso ADJ (que tiene celos) jealous; (diligente) zealous

célula F cell; — **adiposa** fat cell; — **estaminal embrional** stem cell

celular ADJ cellular; M mobile phone

celulitis F cellulite

celuloide M celluloid

celulosa F cellulose

cementar VT to cement

cementerio M cemetery, graveyard

cemento M cement; — **armado** reinforced concrete

cena F supper, dinner

cenagal M quagmire, swamp

cenagoso ADJ marshy, swampy

cenar VI to eat supper, to eat dinner; **vamos a — pescado** we're having fish for dinner

cencerro M cowbell

cenicero M ashtray

ceniciento ADJ ashen

cenit M zenith

cenizas F PL ashes, cinders

censar VI/VT to take a census (of)

censo M census

censor -ora MF censor; — **de cuentas** auditor

censura F (reprobación) censure; (control) censorship

censurador ADJ censuring

censurar VT (criticar) to censure; (examinar) to censor

centavo M cent

centella F sparkle; **pasar como una** — to go by in a flash

centelleante ADJ sparkling

centellear VI to sparkle, to scintillate

centelleo M sparkle

centenar M group of a hundred; —**es** hundreds

centenario M centennial; ADJ centenarian

centeno M rye

centésimo ADJ & M hundredth

centígrado ADJ centigrade

centímetro M centimeter

céntimo M cent

centinela MF INV sentry, sentinel

centrado ADJ true; M truing

central ADJ central; F plant; — **de teléfonos** telephone exchange; — **eléctrica** power plant; — **lechera** milk processing plant; — **nuclear** nuclear power plant

centralita F switchboard

centrar VT to center; —**se** to focus, to be focused

céntrico ADJ central

centrífugo ADJ centrifugal

centrípeto ADJ centripetal

centro M center; (de ciudad) downtown; — **comercial** shopping center; — **de gravedad** center of gravity; — **de mesa** centerpiece

Centroamérica F Central America

ceñido ADJ tight

ceñir[5,18] VT (rodear) to gird; (abrazar) to encircle; — **la corona** to be crowned; VI (estar apretado) to be tight; —**se a** (limitarse) to limit oneself to; (arrimarse) to get close to

ceño M **fruncir el** — to frown, to scowl

cepa F (de árbol) stump; (de viña) stock; (de bacteria) strain; **de pura** — of good stock

cepillar VT (dientes, pelo) to brush; (madera)

to plane, to shave

cepillo M (para el pelo, los dientes) brush; (para madera) carpenter's plane; **— de dientes** toothbrush

cepo M (para cazar) trap; (para inmovilizar coches) boot

cera F wax; **— de oídos** earwax; **— para muebles** polish

cerámica F (arte) ceramics; (conjunto de artículos) pottery, earthenware

cerámico ADJ ceramic

cerbatana F blowpipe

cerca ADV near, nearby, close; **— de** near, close to; **de —** at close range; F fence

cercado M (terreno cercado) enclosure; (cerca) fence

cercanía F proximity, nearness, closeness

cercano ADJ (lugar) near, nearby; (pariente) close; **— Oriente** Near East

cercar[6] VT (rodear con una cerca) to fence, to enclose; (sitiar) to besiege

cercenar VT (cortar) to chop off; (reducir) to curtail, to encroach upon

cerciorarse VI **— (de)** to make sure (of)

cerco M (sitio) siege; (cerca) *Am* fence

cerda F bristle

cerdo -da M (animal, persona sucia) hog, pig; (carne) pork; F sow

cerdoso ADJ bristly

cereal M cereal; **—es** breakfast cereal; **cultivo —** cereal crop

cerebral ADJ cerebral

cerebro M brain (también genio); **lavarle el — a** to brainwash

ceremonia F ceremony

ceremonial ADJ & M ceremonial

ceremonioso ADJ ceremonious

cereza F cherry

cerezo M cherry tree

cerilla F match

cerner[1] VT to sift; **—se** (un ave) to hover; (un desastre) to loom

cernícalo M kestrel

cero M zero; (en deportes) nothing, goose egg, zip; (en tenis) love; **— absoluto** absolute zero; **partir de —** to start from scratch; **ser un — a la izquierda** to be a nobody

cerrado ADJ (no abierto) closed; (denso, tonto) dense; (poco comunicativo) reserved; (intransigente) closed-minded; (curva) sharp; M enclosure

cerradura F lock; **— de combinación** combination lock

cerrajería F locksmith's shop

cerrajero -ra MF locksmith

cerrar[1] VT (la puerta, un cajón) to close, to

shut; (un trato) to close, to clinch; (un terreno) to enclose; (el gas, un grifo) to turn off; (una fábrica) to shut down, to close; **— filas** to close ranks; **— el paso** to block passage; VI to close; **—se** (una flor, una tienda) to close; (un plazo) to end; **—se el cielo** to become overcast

cerrazón F closed-mindedness

cerro M hill

cerrojo M bolt

certamen M contest; **— de belleza** beauty contest

certero ADJ sure

certeza F certainty

certidumbre F certainty

certificación F certification

certificado ADJ certified; M certificate; **— de nacimiento** birth certificate

certificar[6] VT (la autenticidad de algo) to certify; (una carta) to register

cervatillo M fawn

cervecera F brewery

cervecería F bar

cerveza F beer; **— de barril** draft beer

cérvix M (uterino) cervix

cerviz F (del cuello) cervix

cesar VI to cease; **— de trabajar** to stop working; **— en un cargo** to resign from a position; **— a** to dismiss

cesárea F Caesarean section

cese M cessation; **— el fuego** ceasefire; **— de actividades** shutdown

cesión F (de propiedad) assignment; (de derechos) waiver

césped M lawn, grass; (para deportes) turf

cesta F basket

cestería F basketry

cesto M (cesta) basket; (para ropa) hamper

cetrino ADJ olive-colored

chabacano ADJ (modales) crude; (gustos) tacky; M *Méx* apricot

chacal M jackal

chacha F servant girl

cháchara F small talk

chacota F joke; **tomarse algo a la —** to take lightly

chacra F small farm

Chad M Chad

chadiano -na ADJ & MF Chadian

chal M shawl, wrap

chala F *Am* husk; **quitar la —** to husk

chalán M horse trader

chalé M cottage

chaleco M waistcoat, vest; **— antibalas** bulletproof vest; **— de fuerza** straitjacket; **— salvavidas** life jacket

chalupa F small canoe; *Méx* tortilla with

sauce

chamaco -ca M *Méx* boy; F *Méx* girl

chamarra F sheepskin jacket

chambergo M wide-brimmed hat

chambón ADJ clumsy

champán M champagne

champaña F champagne

champiñón M mushroom

champú M shampoo

chamuscadura F scorch

chamuscar[6] VT to scorch, to singe; **—se** to get scorched, to get singed

chamusquina F scorching, singeing

chance MF chance

chancearse VI **— de** to make fun of

chancho M hog

chanchullo M *fam* monkey business

chancleta F thong, flip-flop; **tirar la —** to kick up one's heels

chanclo M galosh, overshoe; **—s** rubbers

chándal M sweatsuit

chantaje M blackmail

chantajear VT to blackmail

chanza F jest

chao INTERJ bye-bye

chapa F (de metal) sheet metal; (identificación de policía) badge; (tapa de botella) bottle top; (de madera) veneer; **— en la puerta** shingle on the door; **hacerle — y pintura** to fix the bodywork and paint

chapado ADJ **— a la antigua** old-fashioned

chapalear VI to splash

chapar VT to plate

chaparro M scrub oak; ADJ *Méx* short

chaparrón M cloudburst

chaperón -ona MF chaperon(e); **ir de —** to chaperon(e)

chapitel M spire, steeple

chapotear VI to splash

chapoteo M splash, splashing

chapucear VT to botch, to bungle

chapucería F (cosa chapuceada) botched job; (cualidad de chapucero) sloppiness

chapucero ADJ shoddy, slipshod

chapurrear VT to speak a language poorly

chapuz M dive

chapuza F botched job

chapuzar[9] VI to dive

chaqueta F jacket; **— de sport** sport jacket

charada F charades

charca F pond

charco M puddle, pool; **cruzar el —** to cross the ocean

charcutería F (tienda) delicatessen; (industria) sausage-making

charla F chat, talk

charlar VI to chat, to gab

charlatán -ana ADJ talkative; MF (parlanchín) chatterbox, windbag; (curandero) charlatan, quack

charlotear VI to chatter, to jabber

charloteo M chatter, jabber

charol M (barniz) varnish; (cuero barnizado) patent leather

charolar VT to varnish

charqui M beef jerky

charro ADJ flashy, tawdry

chárter M charter flight

chascar VT (los nudillos, un hueso) to crack; (los labios) to smack; (la lengua) to click

chascarrillo M funny anecdote

chasco M (broma) prank; (decepción) dud; **llevarse un —** to be disappointed

chasis M frame, chassis

chasquear VI (decepcionar) to disappoint; (una cerradura, la lengua) to click; (un látigo) to crack; (los labios) to smack; (los dedos) to snap; **—se** to be disappointed

chasquido M (de látigo, madera, las articulaciones) crack; (de los labios) smack; (de la lengua, una cerradura) click; (de los dedos) snap

chata F bedpan

chatarra F scrap iron

chatarrería F junkyard

chato ADJ (nariz) snub-nosed; (zapatos, pecho) flat; **— como una tabla** as flat as a pancake

chaucha F green bean

chaval -la M *Esp* boy; F *Esp* girl

chaveta F cotter pin; **perder la —** *fam* to go bonkers

che INTERJ *RP* say! hey!

checo -ca ADJ & MF Czech

chef MF chef

cheque M check; **— de viajero** traveler's check

chequear VT to check

chequera F checkbook

chic ADJ & M chic

chicha F (bebida alcohólica) *Am* corn liquor; (carne) *Esp fam* meat; **de — y nabo** two-bit; **ni — ni limonada** neither fish nor fowl

chicharra F (insecto) cicada; (timbre eléctrico) buzzer

chichón M bump, lump, knot

chicle M chewing gum; **— de globo** bubblegum

chico -ca ADJ small, little; M boy; F girl; **mis —s** my kids

chicote M *Am* whip

chicotear VT *Am* to whip

chicoteo M *Am* whipping
chiflado ADJ *fam* nuts, cuckoo, loony
chifladura F craziness
chiflar VI (silbar) to whistle; VT (volver loco) to drive crazy; **—se** to go crazy
chiflido M whistle
chifón M chiffon
chile M chili
Chile M Chile
chileno -na ADJ & MF Chilean
chillar VI (persona) to shriek; (puerta, ratón) to squeak; (cerdo) to squeal
chillido M (de persona) shriek; (de puerta, ratón) squeak; (de cerdo) squeal
chillón ADJ (sonido) shrill; (color) loud, gaudy
chimenea F (de casa) chimney; (hogar) fireplace; (de volcán, baño, mina) vent; (de fábrica) smokestack
chimpancé M chimpanzee
china F (porcelana) china; (piedra) pebble
China F China
chinche MF (insecto) bedbug; (chincheta) thumbtack; (persona molesta) pain
chinchilla F chinchilla
chinchorro M rowboat
chino -na ADJ Chinese; M (lengua) Chinese; MF Chinese; **eso es —** that's Greek to me
chip M (de ordenador, en golf) chip; (de patata) potato chip
Chipre M Cyprus
chipriota ADJ & MF Cypriot(e)
chiquilín -ina M little boy; F little girl
chiquito ADJ tiny, wee
chiripa F stroke of good luck; **por / de —** by a fluke
chirivía F parsnip
chirona F jail
chirriante ADJ squeaky
chirriar[16] VI (puerta, freno) to squeak; (ave, freno) to screech
chirrido M (de puerta, freno) squeak; (de ave, freno) screech
chisgarabís M pipsqueak
chisguete M squirt
chisme M (noticia) gossip, piece of gossip; (objeto) *fam* gizmo, thingamajig
chismear VI to gossip
chismoso -sa ADJ gossipy; MF gossip
chispa F (partícula incandescente) spark; (ingenio) wit; **echar —s** to be furious; **pasar echando —s** to whiz by
chispeante ADJ (que echa chispas) sparkling; (ingenioso) witty
chispear VI (echar chispas) to spark; (lloviznar) to sprinkle
chisporrotear VI (leña) to sputter;

(cigarrillo) to fizzle; (carne) to sizzle
chisporroteo M (de leña) sputter; (de carne) sizzle
chiste M (verbal) joke; (visual) cartoon; (ocurrencia) wisecrack; **— verde** dirty joke; **no le veo el —** I don't see the humor in it
chistera F top hat
chistoso ADJ funny, amusing, humorous
chivar VI/VT to snitch (on), to rat (on)
chivatar VI/VT to squeal (on), to snitch (on)
chivato -ta MF (delator) informer, snitch, stool pigeon; (chivito) kid
chivo M kid; **— expiatorio** scapegoat; **estar como un —** to be crazy as a loon
chocante ADJ shocking, jarring
chocar[6] VI (dar con) to bump, to collide; (estar en conflicto) to clash; VT (sorprender) to shock; (causar un accidente) to wreck; **— los cinco** to shake hands
chocarrería F coarseness
chochear VI to be in one's dotage
chochera F senility, dotage
chochez F senility, dotage
chocho ADJ senile; **estar —** to be in one's dotage; **estar — con** to dote on
choclo M ear of corn
chocolate M chocolate; (bebida) cocoa, hot chocolate
chocolatera F chocolate pot
chocolatina F chocolate bar
chófer, chofer MF chauffeur, driver
cholo -la MF (mestizo) person of mixed race; (indio) Europeanized Indian
chopo M poplar
choque M (de objetos móviles) collision, bump, crash; (eléctrico, emocional, cultural) shock
chorizo M sausage
chorlito M plover
chorrear VI/VT (poco) to drip; (mucho) to gush
chorro M spurt, jet; **a —s** in buckets
chotearse VI **— de** to make fun of
choteo M mocking
chovinismo M chauvinism
choza F hut, shack, hovel
chubasco M squall, shower
chuchería F trinket, knick-knack
chueco ADJ *Am* crooked
chuleta F (papel para copiar) cheat sheet; **— de cerdo** pork chop; **— de ternera** veal cutlet
chulo -la M (proxeneta) pimp; (dandi) dandy, dude; (bravucón) tough guy; MF working-class resident of Madrid; ADJ

(fanfarrón) boastful; (bonito) cute

chupada F (de cigarro) puff; (de bebida) sip

chupar VI/VT (succionar) to suck; (fumar) to
puff (on); VT (absorber) to absorb; (vivir a
costa de) to sponge off of; **chúpate esa**
put that in your pipe and smoke it; M SG
chupasangre leech

chupete M pacifier

chupetín M *RP* lollipop, sucker

churrasco M *Am* barbecued steak

churro M fritter

chusma F rabble, riffraff

chutar VI (drogas) to shoot up; (un balón) to
shoot

chute M narcotic fix

chuzo M watchman's pike

CIA F CIA

cianotipo M blueprint

cianuro M cyanide

ciberespacio M cyberspace

cibernética F cybernetics

ciberpunk M cyberpunk

cicatero ADJ stingy

cicatriz F scar

cicatrizar VI to form a scar, to heal up

cíclico ADJ cyclical

ciclista MF bicycle rider, cyclist

ciclo M cycle; **—motor** moped; **— vital** life
cycle

ciclón M cyclone

ciclotrón M cyclotron

cicuta F hemlock

ciego ADJ (que no ve) blind; (por borrachera)
plastered; (por los efectos de drogas) high;
quedarse — to go blind; **a ciegas**
blindly

cielo M (firmamento) sky; (paraíso) heaven;
— abierto open mining; **— raso** ceiling;
¡—s! good heavens! **estar en el séptimo
—** to be in seventh heaven; **me cayó del
—** it's a godsend; **poner el grito en el
—** *fam* to hit the ceiling

ciempiés M centipede

cien, ciento NUM hundred; **por ciento**
percent

ciénaga F swamp, mire, marsh

ciencia F (campo de estudio) science;
(conocimiento) knowledge; (arte) art; **—
ficción** science fiction; **—s políticas**
political science; **a — cierta** with
certainty; **las — ocultas** the occult; **no
tiene —** nothing to it

cieno M mud, mire, ooze

científico -ca ADJ scientific; MF scientist

cierre M (cosa para cerrar) clasp, fastener; (de
cremallera) zipper; (acción de cerrar)
closing, closure; **— patronal** lock-out; **al**

— at press time

cierto ADJ certain; (verdadero) true; (seguro)
sure; **en — sentido** in a sense; **hasta —
punto** to a certain extent; **por —** by the
way; INTERJ you're right!

ciervo -va M deer; (macho) stag; **— volante**
stag beetle; F (hembra) doe, hind

cierzo M north wind

cifra F (0-9) digit; (número) figure; (clave)
cipher, key; **poner en —** to encode

cifrar VT to write in code; **— la esperanza
en** to place one's hopes on; **—se en** to
amount to

cigarra F cicada

cigarrera F cigar case, cigarette case

cigarrillo M cigarette

cigarro M cigarette; (puro) cigar

cigoto M zygote

cigüeña F stork

cigüeñal M crankshaft

cilíndrico ADJ cylindrical

cilindro M cylinder

cima F summit

cimarrón -ona ADJ wild; MF runaway slave

címbalo M cymbal

cimbel M decoy

cimbrar VT to sway, to vibrate

cimentar VT (una casa) to lay the foundation
of; (una victoria) to secure

cimiento M foundation

cinc M zinc

cincel M chisel

cincelar VT to chisel

cincha F cinch, girth

cinchar VT to cinch, to girth

cinco NUM five

cincuenta NUM fifty

cine M cinema, movies

cinematografiar VI/VT to film

cinematográfico ADJ **industria
cinematográfica** motion-picture
industry

cingalés -esa ADJ & MF Sri Lankan

cínico -ca ADJ cynical; MF cynic

cinismo M cynicism

cinta F (para adornar) ribbon; (adhesiva)
tape; (cinematográfica) film; **— aislante**
electrical tape; **— de vídeo** video tape; **—
magnetofónica** recording tape; **—
métrica** tape measure; **— rodante**
treadmill; **— transportadora** conveyor
belt

cinto M belt

cintura F (de persona) waist; (de cosa)
middle

cinturón M belt; **— de seguridad** safety
belt

ciprés M cypress
circo M circus
circonio M zirconium
circuitería F circuitry
circuito M circuit; **— cerrado** closed circuit;
  — impreso circuit board; **— integrado**
  integrated circuit
circulación F circulation; **poner en —** to
  circulate
circular VI to circulate; **hay que — por la
  derecha** you have to drive on the right; F
  circular letter
círculo M circle; **— vicioso** vicious circle
circuncidar VT to circumcise
circundante ADJ surrounding
circundar VT to surround
circunferencia F circumference
circunlocución F circumlocution
circunscribir[51] VT to circumscribe
circunspecto ADJ circumspect
circunstancia F circumstance
circunstancial ADJ circumstantial
cirio M candle
cirro M cirrus
cirrosis F cirrhosis
ciruela F plum; **— pasa** prune
ciruelo M plum tree
cirujano -na MF surgeon
cirujía F surgery; **— de corazón abierto**
  open-heart surgery; **— plástica / estética**
  plastic surgery
cisne M swan
cisterna F cistern
cita F (romántica) date; (con el médico)
  appointment; (textual) quotation, quote;
  — a ciegas blind date; **darse —** to meet
citación F citation, summons
citar VT (a un testigo) to summon; (a un
  autor) to cite, to quote; **—se con** (el
  médico) to make an appointment with;
  (un amigo) to make a date with
cítrico ADJ citric; M citrus
ciudad F city
ciudadanía F citizenship
ciudadano -na MF citizen
Ciudad del Vaticano F Vatican City
ciudadela F citadel
cívico ADJ civic
civil ADJ (no criminal, no religioso) civil; (no
  military) civilian
civilidad F civility
civilización F civilization
civilizador ADJ civilizing
civilizar[9] VT to civilize; **—se** to become
  civilized
cizalla F metal shears
cizaña F **sembrar —** to sow discord

clamar VT to clamor for; **— por** to clamor
  for
clamor M clamor, outcry
clamorear VI/VT to shout
clamoreo M shouting
clamoroso ADJ clamorous
clan M clan
clandestino ADJ clandestine
claqué M tap dance
clara F egg white
claraboya F skylight
clarear VI (ponerse claro) to become clear;
  (amanecer) to grow light; (volverse menos
  espeso) to grow less dense; VT to
  illuminate; **—se** to grow light
claridad F clarity; (luz) brightness, lightness
clarificar[6] VT to clarify, to clear
clarín M bugle
clarinete M clarinet
clarividente ADJ & MF clairvoyant
claro ADJ clear; (franco) straightforward; (que
  tiene mucha luz) light, bright; **azul —**
  light blue; **a las claras** clearly; ADV
  clearly; INTERJ of course! M (espacio) gap;
  (en un bosque) clearing; **— de luna**
  moonlight
clase F (grupo social, sesión docente,
  conjunto de alumnos) class; (aula)
  classroom; (tipo) kind, sort; **— alta** upper
  class; **— obrera** working class; **— turista**
  economy class; **dar —** to teach a class;
  toda — de all sorts of
clasicismo M classicism
clásico ADJ (destacado, consabido) classic; (de
  un período histórico) classical; M classic
clasificación F classification; (deportiva)
  qualification
clasificado M want ad
clasificar[6] VT to classify; (en deportes) to
  qualify; **—se para** to qualify for; **—se
  segundo** to come in second
claustro M cloister; **— de profesores**
  university faculty
claustrofobia F claustrophobia
claustrofóbico ADJ claustrophobic
cláusula F clause
clausura F closing
clavadista MF diver
clavado ADV exactly; M nailing
clavar VT to nail, to drive a nail into;
  (pinchar) to stick, to poke; **—le la
  mirada / los ojos a alguien** to stare at
  someone; **— los frenos** to stomp on the
  brakes; **me clavaron** I got a raw deal
clave F (sistema de signos) code; (tabla de
  correspondencias, base) key; (signo
  musical) clef; (clavicémbalo) harpsichord;

(de mapa) legend; — **de fa** bass clef; — **de seguridad** password; — **de sol** treble clef; ADJ key

clavel M carnation

clavetear VT to put pegs on

clavicémbalo M harpsichord

clavícula F collarbone, clavicle

clavija F (de guitarra) peg; (de enchufe) pin

clavo M (pieza de metal) nail; (capullo) clove; (de zapato) spike; **dar en el —** to hit the nail on the head

claxon M car horn

clearing M clearing

clemencia F clemency, mercy

clemente ADJ forgiving

clerecía F (funciones de clérigo) ministry; (conjunto de clérigos) clergy

clerical ADJ clerical

clérigo M clergyman, minister

clero M clergy

clic M click; **hacer —** to click; **hacer doble — ** to double-click

cliché M (placa fotográfica) photographic plate; (expresión muy usada) cliché

cliente MF (de un profesional) client; (de un negocio) customer; (de un restaurante) patron; (de un hotel) guest

clientela F clientele

clientelismo M patronage

clima M climate

climatización F air conditioning

clímax M climax

clinch M clinch

clínica F clinic

clip M paper clip

cloaca F sewer

clon M clone

clonación F cloning

clonaje M cloning

clonar VT to clone

cloquear VI to cluck

cloqueo M cluck, clucking

cloro M chlorine

clorofila F chlorophyll

cloroformo M chloroform

cloruro M chloride

club M club (también palo de golf); **— nocturno** nightclub

coacción F compulsion, coercion; **bajo —** under duress

coagular VI to coagulate; (sangre) to clot

coágulo M clot

coalición F coalition

coartada F alibi

coartar VT (una libertad) to restrict; (a una persona) to inhibit; (la creatividad) to strangle

cobalto M cobalt

cobarde ADJ cowardly; MF coward

cobardía F cowardice

cobertizo M shed

cobertor M cover

cobertura F (de nieve, aérea) cover; (de noticias, telecomunicativa) coverage

cobija F cover; (manta) blanket

cobijar VT to shelter; **—se** to seek shelter

cobra F cobra

cobrador -ora MF (persona que cobra) collector; M (perro) retriever

cobranza F collection

cobrar VT (impuestos) to collect; (una cuenta) to charge; (un cheque) to cash; (el sueldo) to earn; (víctimas) to claim; (adquirir) to gain; **— ánimo** to take heart; **— caro** to charge a lot; **— de más** to overcharge; **vas a —** you're in for it

cobre M (elemento) copper; (objetos de cobre) copper utensils

cobrizo ADJ copper-colored

cobro M collection

coca F (planta, hoja) coca; (cocaína) *fam* coke

cocaína F cocaine

cocear VI/VT to kick

cocer[2,10c] VI/VT (huevos) to boil; (verduras) to cook; (cerámica) to fire; **— al vapor** to steam; **a medio —** half-cooked; **romper a —** to break into a boil; **¿qué se cuece aquí?** what's up?

coche M (automóvil, vagón) car; (autobús) coach; (vehículo tirado por caballerías) carriage; **— bomba** car bomb; **— cama** sleeper; **—comedor** dining car; **— de bebé** stroller, baby carriage; **— de bomberos** fire engine; **— de choque** bumper car; **— de línea** city bus; **— deportivo** sports car; **— fúnebre** hearse; **ir en —** to go by car, to drive; **pasear en — ** to go on a drive

cochera F carport

cochinada F (acto asqueroso) filthy action; (acto perverso) dirty trick

cochinilla F woodlouse

cochino ADJ filthy; M pig

cocido M stew

cociente M quotient

cocina F (habitación) kitchen; (aparato para cocinar) range, stove; (arte de guisar) cuisine, cookery

cocinar VI/VT to cook; (tramar) to cook up

cocinero -ra MF cook

cócker MF cocker spaniel

coco M (fruto del cocotero) coconut; (cabeza) *fam* dome; (fantasma) bogeyman; **comerse el —** to get all worked up

cocodrilo M crocodile

cóctel M (fiesta) cocktail party; (bebida) cocktail, mixed drink

codazo M jab with the elbow; **dar —s to** elbow

codear VI/VT to elbow, to jab; **—se** to nudge one another; **—se con** to rub elbows with

codeína F codeine

codicia F (deseo de poseer) greed; (deseo sexual) lust

codiciar VT (una cosa) to covet; (sexualmente) to lust after

codicioso ADJ covetous, greedy

codificar[6] VT to codify, to encrypt

código M elbow; **— de barras** bar code; **— genético** genetic code; **— postal** zip code

codo M elbow; **— a —** side by side; **— de tenista** tennis elbow; **empinar el —** to drink too much; **hablar por los —s** to talk one's head off; **hasta los —s** up to one's elbows

codorniz F quail

coeficiente M coefficient; **— de inteligencia** intelligence quotient

coerción F compulsion

coetáneo ADJ contemporary

coexistencia F coexistence; **— pacífica** peaceful coexistence

cofre M coffer

coger[11b] VT (a un criminal) to catch; (con las manos) to grasp; (flores) to gather; to pick; (a un empleado) to hire; (una emisora) to receive; (cosas del suelo) to pick up; (espacio) to take up; (un pez) to land, to catch; (un camino, tren, curso) to take; **— de sorpresa** to catch by surprise; **— el sueño** to fall asleep; **— hacia el castillo** to turn toward the castle; **—le miedo a algo** to get scared of something; **—le el tranquillo a algo** to get into the swing of things; **—se un resfriado** to come down with a cold; **coge y le dice** he ups and says

cognado ADJ & M cognate

cognitivo ADJ cognitive

cogollo M heart

cogote M neck

cohabitar VI to live (with); (sin casarse) to cohabitate

cohecho M bribe

coheredero -ra MF joint heir

coherencia F (consecuencia) consistency; (lógica) coherence

coherente ADJ (consecuente) consistent; (lógico) coherent

cohesión F cohesion

cohesivo ADJ coherent

cohete M rocket

cohetería F rocketry

cohibición F inhibition

cohibido ADJ inhibited, self-conscious

cohibir VT to inhibit

coincidencia F coincidence

coincidir VI to coincide

coito M coitus

cojear VI to limp; **saber de qué pie cojea alguien** to know someone's weaknesses

cojera F limp

cojín M cushion

cojinete M bushing; **— de bolas** ball bearing

cojo ADJ lame, crippled

cok M coke

col F cabbage; **— de Bruselas** Brussels sprouts

cola F (de perro, ave, avión) tail; (de vestido) train; (hilera de gente) line; (pegamento) glue; **— de caballo** ponytail; **hacer —** to stand in line; **no pegar ni con —** not to go together; **traer —** to have consequences

colaboración F collaboration

colaborador -ora MF (de periódico) contributor; (con el gobierno) collaborator

colaborar VI to collaborate; (con un periódico) to contribute

colación F **sacar a —** to bring up

colacionar VT to collate

colador M (para té) strainer; (para verduras) colander

colágeno M collagen

colapso M collapse

colar[2] VT (té) to strain; (metal líquido) to pour; VI to go through, to slip through; **esa excusa no va a —** that excuse won't wash; **—se en una fiesta** to crash a party

colateral ADJ collateral

colcha F bedspread

colchón M mattress; (recurso de emergencia) cushion

colchoneta F mat

colear VI (un perro) to wag the tail; (un tema) to be pending; (un auto) to fishtail

colección F collection

coleccionar VT to collect

coleccionista MF collector

colecta F charity collection

colectivo M (grupo) collective; (autobús) Am bus

colector M (de aguas negras) sewer; (eléctrico) collector; (de coche) manifold

colega MF INV colleague

colegio M (escuela privada) private school; (centro de enseñanza primaria) elementary school; (asociación de profesionales) association, college

colegir[5,11] VI to gather

cólera F rage, wrath; **montar en —** to fly into a rage; M cholera

colérico ADJ irritable

colesterol M cholesterol

coleta F pigtail

coletilla F tag

coleto M **decir para su —** to say to oneself

colgadero M hanger; ADJ hanging

colgado ADJ high and dry

colgadura F drapery; **—s** hangings

colgante ADJ hanging; M pendant

colgar[2,7] VT (suspender, ahorcar) to hang; (un teléfono, un abrigo) to hang up; VI (un espejo) to hang; (un andrajo) to dangle; (un asunto) to be pending; **esa falda te cuelga por atrás** that dress hangs down in the back; **—se (un ordenador)** to crash; **—se de** to get hooked on; **—se del teléfono** to tarry on the phone

colibrí M hummingbird

cólico M colic

coliflor F cauliflower

colilla F cigarette butt

colina F hill, knoll

colindante ADJ neighboring

colindar VI **— con** to border (on), to adjoin

coliseo M coliseum

colisión F collision

collage M collage

collar M (de perlas) necklace; (de perro) collar; **— antipulgas** flea collar

collera F horse collar

collie M collie

colmar VT (un vaso) to fill; (una demanda) to satisfy; **— de alabanzas** to lavish praise upon

colmena F beehive

colmillo M (de persona) eyetooth; (de elefante) tusk; (de víbora) fang

colmo M **— de la locura** height of folly; **¡eso es el —!** that takes the cake; **para —** to top it all

colocación F (ubicación) placement; (puesto) position

colocar[6] VT (poner, encontrar un puesto para) to place; (casar) to marry off; (invertir) to invest; **—se** to get a job

coloide M colloid

Colombia F Colombia

colombiano -na ADJ & MF Colombian

colon M colon

colón M (moneda de El Salvador y Costa Rica) colon

colonia F (territorio, grupo de insectos) colony; (comunidad de inmigrantes) community, settlement; (vivienda) development; (perfume) cologne

colonial ADJ colonial

colonización F colonization

colonizador -ora MF colonist

colonizar[9] VT to colonize, to settle

colono -na MF (habitante de una colonia) colonist, settler; (arrendatario) tenant farmer

coloquial ADJ colloquial

coloquio M colloquium

color M color; (pintura) paint; (maquillaje) rouge; (de naipes) flush; **—es primarios** primary colors; **a todo —** full color; **de — of color**

coloración F coloring

colorado ADJ & M red; **ponerse —** to blush

colorante ADJ & M coloring

coloreado ADJ colored; M coloring

colorear VT to color

colorete M rouge

colorido M (de un caballo) coloring; (de un comentario, paisaje) color; ADJ colorful

colosal ADJ (grande) colossal; (estupendo) wonderful

columbrar VT to glimpse

columna F column; **— de dirección** steering column; **— vertebral** spinal column, backbone

columnista MF columnist

columpiar VI/VT to swing

columpio M swing

colza F (planta) rape; (aceite) rapeseed oil

coma F (signo) comma; M (falta de conciencia) coma

comadre F (chismosa) gossip; (partera) midwife

comadreja F weasel

comadrona F midwife

comandancia F command

comandante M (rango militar) major; (militar que ejerce el mando) commander; **— en jefe** commander in chief

comandar VT to command; **— un avión** to pilot an airplane

comando M (militar) commando; (orden dada al ordenador) command

comarca F district

comatoso ADJ comatose

comba F (de una pared) bulge; (de madera) warp; **saltar a la —** to jump rope

combar VI (una pared) to sag; (madera) to warp

combate M combat; **fuera de —** out of the competition

combatiente MF combatant
combatir VI/VT to combat
combativo ADJ combative
combinación F combination; (billete) transfer ticket
combinar VT to combine; **—se para hacer algo** to agree to do something
combo M combo
combustible ADJ combustible; M fuel
combustión F combustion
comedero M trough
comedia F comedy; (farsa) farce; **— de situación** situation comedy, sitcom; **hacer la — de** to play the part of
comediante MF comedian
comedido ADJ moderate; *Am* obliging
comedirse⁵ VI to show restraint; **— a hacer algo** *RP* to volunteer to do something
comedor M dining room; (de empresa) cantina
comensal MF fellow diner
comentador -ora MF commentator
comentar VI/VT to comment (on), to remark (on)
comentario M (análisis) commentary; (observación) comment, remark
comentarista MF commentator
comenzar¹,⁹ VI/VT to begin, to start; **— a comer** to begin to eat; **— comprando** to begin by buying
comer VI/VT to eat; (al mediodía) to eat lunch; (en ajedrez) to take; (en el juego de las damas) to jump; **dar de —** to feed; **sin —lo ni beberlo** through no fault of one's own; **—se** (ácido) to eat away; (completamente) to eat up; **—se las eses** to dróp s; **—se las palabras** to eat one's words; **—se un semáforo rojo** to run a red light
comercial ADJ commercial
comercialización F marketing, merchandising
comercializar⁹ VT (dar carácter comercial) to commercialize; (llevar al mercado) to market
comerciante MF merchant, trader, dealer
comerciar VI to trade
comercio M commerce, trade; **— exterior** foreign trade; **— minorista** retail trade
comestible ADJ edible; M **—s** groceries
cometa M (cuerpo celeste) comet; F (juguete) kite
cometer VT to commit
cometido M function
comezón F itch; **tener —** to itch
comic M comic book
comicios M PL polls

cómico -ca ADJ comic, comical; MF comedian
comida F (alimento que se toma de una vez) meal; (conjunto de cosas para alimentarse) food; (de mediodía) lunch; **— basura** junk food; **— macrobiótica** health food; **— rápida** fast food
comienzo M beginning; **a —s de** toward the beginning of; **al —** at first; **desde un / el —** from the start
comilla F quotation mark; **entre —s** in quotes
comilón -ona MF big eater; F binge
comino M cumin seed; **me importa un —** *fam* I don't give a hoot; **no vale un —** *fam* it's not worth a hoot
comisaría F **— de policía** police station, precinct
comisario -ria MF (comisionado) commissioner; (jefe de policía) police chief
comisión F (acción de cometer, porcentaje ganado) commission; (conjunto de personas) committee
comisionar VT to commission
comistrajo M bad food
comisura F **— de los labios** corner of the mouth
comité M committee
comitiva F retinue
como ADV (del mismo modo que) as, like; **ella pinta — yo** she paints like I do; (aproximadamente) about; **pesa — diez kilos** it weighs about ten kilos; CONJ (puesto que) since; **— no tenemos dinero** since we have no money; **— no me pagues** if you don't pay me; **era — que muy viejo** he was, like, real old; **— que te voy a permitir** like I would let you; **— quieras** as you please; **— si** as if; **— si me lo fuera a creer** a likely story
cómo ADV INTERR & PRON (de qué manera) how; (¿perdón?) what? **¡— brillan las estrellas!** how the stars are shining! **¿— no?** of course; **¿a — me lo vende?** what does that cost?
cómoda F bureau, chest of drawers, dresser
comodidad F (cualidad de cómodo) comfort; (cosa cómoda) convenience; **—es** amenities
comodín M joker, wild card
cómodo ADJ (mueble) comfortable; (horario) convenient; (persona) lazy
Comoras F PL Comoros
compactar VT to compact
compacto ADJ compact
compadecer¹³ VT to pity; **—se de** to take pity on
compadre M pal, crony

compañero -ra MF companion; (de un zapato) mate; **— de clase** classmate; **— de cuarto** roommate

compañía F company; **en — de** in the company of

comparable ADJ comparable

comparación F comparison

comparar VI/VT to compare; **—se con** to compare with

comparativo ADJ comparative

comparecer[13] VI to appear

compartimiento M compartment

compartir VT (bienes) to share; (el tiempo) to divide

compás M (instrumento de dibujo) compass; (ritmo) beat; (espacio entre barras) measure, bar; (división de música en partes iguales) time signature; **marcar el —** to beat time

compasión F compassion

compasivo ADJ compassionate, sympathetic

compatible ADJ compatible

compatriota MF compatriot

compeler VT to compel

compendiar VT to summarize

compendio M digest, condensation

compenetración F bonding

compensación F compensation

compensar VT to compensate

competencia F (pugna, competición deportiva, conjunto de competidores) competition; (cualidad de competente) competence

competente ADJ competent

competición F athletic competition, meet

competidor -ora ADJ competing; MF competitor

competir[5] VI to compete, to vie

competitivo ADJ competitive

compilador M compiler

compilar VT to compile

compinche M chum, crony

complacencia F satisfaction

complacer[37] VT to please, to gratify; **—se (en)** to take pleasure (in)

complaciente ADJ (que complace) obliging; (que consiente) indulgent

complejidad F complexity

complejo ADJ complex; M complex; **— de inferioridad** inferiority complex

complementar VT to complement, to supplement

complemento M complement; **— alimenticio** dietary supplement; **— directo** direct object; **— indirecto** indirect object; **—s** fringe benefits

completar VT to complete; **—se** to be completed

completo ADJ complete; (baño, pensión, hotel) full; **hoy tenemos el —** today we have a full house; **por —** completely

complexión F build

complicación F complication

complicado ADJ complicated

complicar[6] VT to complicate; **—le a alguien la vida** to give someone trouble

cómplice MF accomplice

complicidad F complicity

complot M plot

componenda F (arreglo provisional) quick fix; (arreglo ilegal) shady deal

componente ADJ & M component

componer[39] VT (un grupo) to compose, to make up; (imprenta) to set; (un coche descompuesto) to fix; (música) to compose; **—se de** to be composed of; **componérselas** to deal with one's problems alone

comportamiento M conduct, behavior

comportarse VI/VT to conduct oneself, to behave

composición F composition

compositor -ora MF composer

compostura F (arreglo) repair; (dignidad) composure

compra F purchase; **ir de —s** to go shopping

comprador -ora MF (persona que compra) buyer, purchaser; (persona que está de compras) shopper

comprar VT to buy, to purchase

comprender VT (entender) to understand, to comprehend; (abarcar) to cover, to include

comprensible ADJ comprehensible, understandable

comprensión F (intelectual) understanding, comprehension; (emocional) sympathy, understanding

comprensivo ADJ understanding

compresa F compress

compresión F compression

comprimido ADJ compressed; M tablet

comprimir VT to compress

comprobación F verification, check

comprobante M proof; **— de compra** proof of purchase

comprobar[2] VT (verificar) to verify, to check; (probar) to prove; (darse cuenta) to realize

comprometer VT (obligar) to commit; (poner en peligro) to jeopardize, to compromise; **—se** (prometer) to promise; (tomar partido) to commit oneself; (para casarse) to get engaged

compromiso M (ideología, obligación, promesa) commitment; (acuerdo)

agreement; (cita) appointment,
engagement; (de matrimonio)
engagement; (solución) compromise; **no
me pongas en —** don't compromise me;
sin — de compra without obligation to
buy
compuerta F sluice gate, floodgate
compuesto ADJ (ojos, tiempo, interés)
compound; **estar — de** to be composed
of; M compound
compulsión F compulsion
compulsivo ADJ compulsive
compungirse[11] VI to feel sorry
computación F computing
computadora F *Am* computer; **— personal**
Am personal computer
computar VT to compute
computarizar[9] VT to computerize
cómputo M computation
comulgar[7] VI (recibir el sacramento) to take
communion; (estar de acuerdo) to agree
común ADJ common; **en —** in common; **por
lo —** generally; **el — de las gentes** the
majority of the people
comuna F commune
comunicable ADJ communicable
comunicación F communication; (ponencia)
presentation; **se nos cortó la —** we got
disconnected
comunicar[6] VI/VT to communicate; **—se
con** (entenderse) to communicate with;
(tener acceso a) to open into; (ponerse en
contacto con) to reach
comunicativo ADJ communicative
comunidad F community
comunión F communion
comunismo M communism
comunista ADJ & MF communist
con PREP with; **— lo que come, tendría
que estar obesa** given what she eats, she
should be obese; **— mucho** by far; **—
que le digas alcanza** just telling him is
enough; **— tal que** provided that; **—
todo** all things considered
conato M minor problem
concavidad F hollow
cóncavo ADJ concave
concebible ADJ conceivable
concebir[5] VT (engendrar) to conceive;
(explicarse) to conceive of
conceder VT (dar) to grant; (admitir) to
concede, to allow
concejal MF councilor
concejo M council
concentración F concentration;
(manifestación) rally, demonstration
concentrar VT to concentrate; **—se** (prestar

atención) to concentrate; (manifestar) to
rally
concepción F conception
concepto M concept; (literario) conceit
concernir[50] VT to concern
concertar[1] VT (arreglar) to arrange;
(concretar) to finalize; (planear) to
concert; **—se** to agree
concesión F (admisión) concession;
(otorgamiento) grant; (permiso comercial)
franchise
concha F shell
conchabarse VI to conspire
conciencia F (vida moral) conscience; (vida
mental) consciousness; **tomar — de** to
come to grips with
concienzudo ADJ conscientious, thorough
concierto M (música) concert; (armonía)
harmony; (acuerdo) agreement
conciliar VT (personas) to conciliate; (ideas)
to reconcile; **— el sueño** to get to sleep
concilio M council
concisión F conciseness
conciso ADJ concise, brief
conciudadano -na MF fellow citizen
concluir[31] VI/VT to conclude
conclusión F conclusion
concluyente ADJ conclusive
concomitante ADJ attendant
concordancia F agreement
concordar[2] VI to agree
concordia F concord
concretar VT (cerrar) to finalize; (especificar)
to be specific about; (realizar) to realize;
—se a to focus on
concreto ADJ concrete; **en—** specifically
concubina F concubine
concurrencia F gathering
concurrido ADJ well-attended
concurrir VI (confluir) to come together;
(asistir) to attend
concursante MF contestant
concurso M (para un premio) contest; (como
parte de una licitación) call for bids; (para
un puesto de trabajo) competitive
examination; **— de belleza** beauty
pageant
concusión F graft
concusionario -ria MF grafter
condado M county
conde M count
condecoración F decoration
condecorar VT to decorate
condena F (castigo) sentence; (crítica)
condemnation; **¡qué —!** what a pain!
condenación F condemnation
condenar VT (criticar) to condemn;

(sentenciar) to sentence; **eso le condenó al fracaso** that doomed him to failure; **—se** to go to hell

condensación F condensation

condensar VT to condense

condesa F countess

condescendencia F (tolerancia) acquiescence; (superioridad) condescension

condescender[1] VI (acomodarse) to acquiesce; (dignarse) to condescend

condición F condition; **— social** social station; **a — de que** on the condition that; **condiciones** (físicas) condition; (de un contrato) terms, provisos

condicional ADJ & M conditional

condicionamiento M conditioning

condicionar VT to condition

condimentar VT to season

condimento M condiment, seasoning

condiscípulo -la MF classmate

condolencias F PL condolences; **dar las —** to offer one's condolences

condolerse[2] VI to offer one's condolences

condominio M condominium

cóndor M condor

conducente ADJ conducive

conducir[24] VT (a un grupo) to lead; (una orquesta, electricidad) to conduct; (un coche) to drive, to steer; **—se** to behave

conducta F (moral) conduct, behavior; (biológica) behavior

conducto M (de agua) conduit; (anatómico) duct; **por — de** through

conductor -ora M (de electricidad, calor) conductor; MF (de coches) driver

conectar VI/VT to connect

conejillo M **— de Indias** Guinea pig

conejo M rabbit

conexión F connection

confabulación F collusion

confección F (fabricación) confection; (calidad) workmanship; **de —** ready-made

confeccionar VT to manufacture

confederación F confederation

confederado -da ADJ & MF confederate

confederar VI to form a confederacy

conferencia F (discurso) lecture; (reunión) conference; **— de prensa** press conference; **dar una —** to give a lecture

conferenciante MF lecturer

conferenciar VI to confer

conferencista MF lecturer, speaker

conferir[3] VT to confer, to bestow; (un título) to confer

confesar[1] VI/VT to confess

confesión F confession

confesionario M confessional

confesor -ora MF confessor

confiabilidad F reliability

confiable ADJ reliable

confiado ADJ (seguro de sí) confident; (crédulo) trusting

confianza F confidence, trust; **en —** in confidence; **tener —** to be confident; **tener — en** to have confidence in; **tomar —s** to be overly familiar with

confianzudo ADJ over-familiar

confiar[16] VT (un secreto) to confide; (una cosa) to entrust; **— en** to rely on; **confío que Dios me proteja** I trust that God will protect me

confidencia F confidence

confidencial ADJ confidential

confidente MF confidant; M (mueble) love seat

configuración F configuration

confinamiento M confinement

confinar VT to confine

confines M PL bounds, confines

confirmación F confirmation

confirmar VT to confirm

confiscación F confiscation, seizure

confiscar[6] VT to confiscate

confitar VT to candy

confite M candy

confitería F confectionery

confitura F confection

conflicto M conflict

confluencia F (de calles) junction; (de ríos) confluence

conformar VT to adapt; **—se con** to settle for

conforme ADJ in agreement, content; **— a** in accordance with; **— amanece** as dawn breaks

conformidad F conformity, agreement; **estar de / en — con** to be in accordance with

conformismo M conformity

confort M comfort

confortable ADJ comfortable

confortar VT to comfort

confraternidad F fraternity, fellowship

confraternizar[9] VI to fraternize

confrontar VT (a un enemigo) to confront; (dos listas) to compare

confundido ADJ confused, mixed-up

confundir VT to confuse, to perplex, to baffle; **—se** (personas) to become confused; (cosas) to mingle

confusión F (mental) confusion; (de cosas) clutter, disarray

confuso ADJ (que no comprende, falto de

orden) confused; (difícil de comprender) confusing

congelación F freezing

congelado ADJ frozen

congelador M freezer

congelar VT to freeze

congeniar VI — **con** to get along with

congénito ADJ congenital

congestión F congestion

conglomeración F conglomeration

conglomerado M conglomeration

Congo M Congo

congoja F anguish, grief

congoleño -ña ADJ & MF Congolese

congregación F congregation

congregar[7] VI to congregate

congresista MF (representante) member of Congress; (asistente a un congreso) conventioneer

congreso M (cuerpo legislativo, edificio) congress; (reunión periódica) convention

congresual ADJ congressional

congruencia F congruence

conífera F conifer

conjetura F conjecture, surmise

conjeturar VT to conjecture, to surmise

conjugación F conjugation

conjugar[7] VT to conjugate

conjunción F conjunction

conjuntivitis F conjunctivitis

conjunto M (grupo de cosas) set; (totalidad) total, aggregate; (de ropa) outfit; — **musical** ensemble; **en** — as a whole, all told; ADJ joint

conjuración F conspiracy

conjurado -da MF conspirator

conjurar VT (conspirar) to conspire, to plot; (alejar un daño) to ward off

conjuro M incantation, spell

conmemorar VT to commemorate

conmemorativo ADJ memorial

conmigo PRON with me

conmiseración F commiseration

conmoción F commotion; — **cerebral** brain concussion

conmovedor ADJ moving, touching

conmover[2] VT to move, to touch

conmovido ADJ moved, touched

conmutador M switch

conmutar VT to commute

connatural ADJ inborn

connotación F connotation

cono M cone

conocedor -ora ADJ who know(s); MF connoisseur, expert

conocer[13] VT to know (también en sentido carnal); (reconocer) to recognize; (tratar

por primera vez) to meet; — **el paño** to know the ropes; **se conoce que** it is clear that

conocido -da ADJ well-known; MF acquaintance

conocimiento M knowledge, acquaintance; — **de embarque** bill of lading; **perder el** — to lose consciousness; **poner en** — to inform; —**s** knowledge

conque CONJ so

conquista F conquest

conquistador -ora MF conqueror; ADJ conquering

conquistar VT (un terreno) to conquer; (el amor de alguien) to win

consabido ADJ habitual

consagración F consecration

consagrar VT (declarar consagrado) to consecrate; (dedicar) to devote

consciente ADJ conscious; — **del problema** aware of the problem

consecución F attainment, achievement

consecuencia F (hecho que resulta de otro) consequence; (cualidad de consecuente) consistency; **a** — **de** as a result of

consecuente ADJ (que se sigue de) consequent, logical; (fiel en sus actos) consistent

consecutivo ADJ consecutive

conseguible ADJ obtainable

conseguir[5, 12] VT to get; (un objetivo) to achieve; (un puesto de trabajo) to land, to get; — **hacer algo** to manage to do something

consejero -ra MF (persona que da consejos) adviser; (miembro del consejo) board member

consejo M (opinión) counsel, advice; (comité) council; — **de guerra** court-martial

consenso M consensus

consentimiento M consent, acquiescence

consentir[3] VT (permitir) to consent to, to acquiesce to; (mimar) to pamper, to indulge; — **en** to permit

conserje MF (limpiador) janitor; (portero) superintendent; (recepcionista) hotel clerk

conserva F canned food; **en** — canned

conservación F conservation, preservation

conservador -ora MF (en política) conservative; (de museo) curator; ADJ (de las tradiciones) conservative; (de comida) preservative

conservadurismo M conservatism

conservante M preservative

conservar VT (guardar) to keep; (seguir teniendo) to retain; (no destruir) to preserve; (no malgastar) to conserve

conservatorio M conservatory
considerable ADJ considerable
consideración F consideration; **de —** considerable; **tomar / tener en —** to take into consideration
considerado ADJ considerate, thoughtful
considerar VT to consider
consigna F watchword
consignación F consignment
consignar VT to consign
consignatario -ria MF consignee
consigo PRON with oneself / himself / herself / themselves
consiguiente ADJ consequent; **por —** consequently
consistencia F consistency
consistente ADJ (que consiste) which consists; (firme) consistent
consistir VI **— en** to consist of
consocio -cia MF fellow member
consola F console
consolación F consolation
consolar² VT to console
consolidar VT to consolidate
consonante ADJ & F consonant
consorcio M consortium
consorte MF consort
conspicuo ADJ conspicuous
conspiración F conspiracy, plot
conspirador -ora MF conspirator, plotter
conspirar VI to conspire, to plot
constancia F (en el amor) constancy; (en el esfuerzo) perseverance; (en el trabajo) steadiness; (prueba) documentary proof
constante ADJ & F constant; **—s vitales** vital signs
constar VI to be stated; **— de** to consist of, to be composed of; **hacer —** to mention; **me consta que** I am aware that; **que conste** let it be known
constatar VT to verify
constelación F constellation
consternación F consternation, dismay
consternar VT to dismay
constipación F constipation
constipado ADJ *Esp* suffering from a cold; *Am* constipated; M *Esp* head cold
constitución F constitution
constitucional ADJ constitutional
constituir³¹ VT to constitute
constitutivo ADJ (constituyente) constituent; (inherente) inherent; **— de un delito** which constitutes a crime
constituyente ADJ constituent
constreñimiento M constraint
constreñir⁵,¹⁸ VT (limitar) to constrain; (apretar) to constrict, to constrain

constricción F constriction
construcción F (acción y actividad de construir, cosa construida) construction, building; (gramatical) construction; **construcciones** building blocks
constructivo ADJ constructive
construir³¹ VI/VT to construct, to build
consuelo M consolation, comfort, solace
consuetudinario ADJ (acción) habitual; (derecho) common
cónsul MF consul
consulado M consulate
consulta F (acción de consultar) consultation; (pregunta) question; (consultorio del médico) doctor's office
consultar VT to consult; **—lo con la almohada** to sleep on it
consultoría F consulting
consultorio M doctor's office
consumado ADJ consummate, accomplished
consumar VT to consummate
consumidor -ora MF consumer; ADJ consuming
consumir VT to consume; **—se** (agua) to boil off; (neumático) to wear out; **—se de** to be consumed by
consumismo M consumerism
consumo M consumption
consunción F consumption
contabilidad F accounting, bookkeeping
contable MF accountant, bookkeeper
contactar VI/VT to contact; **—(se) con** to get in contact with
contacto M contact; **en — con** in touch with
contado M **al —** in cash; ADJ **—s** few
contador -ora ADJ counting; M (de dinero) counter; (de electricidad) meter; **— Geiger** Geiger counter; MF accountant; **— público** certified public accountant
contaduría F accountant's office
contagiar VT to infect
contagio M contagion; (de ordenador) infection
contagioso ADJ contagious, catching, infectious
contaminación F (del agua, de la comida) contamination; (del medio ambiente) pollution
contaminante M contaminate
contaminar VT (agua, alimentos, cultura) to contaminate; (el medio ambiente) to pollute; **—se** (agua) to become contaminated; (medio ambiente) to become polluted
contar² VI/VT (medir una cantidad) to count; (decir historias) to tell; **el hotel cuenta**

con una piscina the hotel has a swimming pool; **cuento con mi hermano** I count on my brother; **esto no cuenta** this doesn't count; **¿me lo vas a contar a mí?** you can say that again; **mi padre cuenta 55 años** my father is 55 years old; **tienes que — con el tiempo** you have to watch the time; M SG **cuentakilómetros** (marcador de kilómetros) odometer; (velocímetro) speedometer

contemplación F contemplation

contemplar VT (mirar, tener en cuenta) to contemplate; (consentir) to spoil; VI to contemplate

contemporáneo ADJ contemporary

contender[1] VI to contend

contenedor M container

contener[44] VT (un líquido) to contain; (risa, lágrimas) to hold back; (entusiasmo) to restrain; (el aliento) to hold

contenido ADJ restrained; M content(s)

contentar VT to satisfy; **—se** to be satisfied

contento ADJ (conforme) content, contented; (feliz) happy; M contentment

contera F (de paraguas) tip; (de bolígrafo) cap

contestación F answer, reply

contestador M answering machine

contestar VT to answer; VI to talk back, to mouth off

contexto M context

contextura F makeup; (de persona) build

contienda F (guerra) conflict; (encuentro deportivo) competition

contigo PRON with you

contiguo ADJ contiguous; **estar — a** to adjoin

continental ADJ continental

continente M continent, mainland; ADJ continent

contingencia F contingency

contingente ADJ & M contingent

continuación F continuation; (de película) sequel; **a —** after that; **a — hubo una guerra** there ensued a war

continuar[17] VI/VT to continue

continuidad F continuity

continuo ADJ (ininterrumpido) continuous; (repetido) continual

contonearse VI (mujer) to swing one's hips; (hombre) to swagger

contoneo M (de mujer) swinging of the hips; (de hombre) swagger

contorno M (forma) outline, contour; (tamaño de árbol, persona) girth

contorsión F contortion

contra PREP against; M **el pro y el —** the pros and cons; **en —** against; F drawback; **llevar a alguien la —** to contradict someone

contraatacar[6] VI/VT to counterattack

contraataque M counterattack

contrabajo M double bass; MF INV double bass player

contrabandear VI/VT to smuggle

contrabandista MF smuggler

contrabando M (introducción de mercancías) smuggling; (mercancías introducidas) contraband; **hacer —** to smuggle

contracción F contraction

contrachapado M plywood

contractual ADJ contractual

contracultura F counterculture

contradecir[26b] VT to contradict

contradicción F contradiction

contradictorio ADJ contradictory

contraejemplo M counterexample

contraer[45] VT to contract; (limitar) to limit; **— matrimonio** to get married

contraespionaje M counterespionage

contrafuerte M (de muro) buttress; (de zapato) counter

contrahecho ADJ deformed

contralor -ora MF comptroller, controller

contralto M (voz) alto; MF (persona) alto

contramandar VT to countermand

contraoferta F counteroffer

contraorden F countermand

contrapartida F compensation

contrapelo LOC ADV **a —** against the grain

contrapesar VT to counterbalance

contrapeso M counterbalance

contraproducente ADJ counterproductive

contrariar[16] VT to annoy; **—se** to get annoyed

contrariedad F (fastidio) annoyance; (dificultad) snag

contrario ADJ (opuesto) opposite; (discrepante) conflicting; **al —** on the contrary; **de lo —** otherwise; **llevar la contraria** to be contrary; **por el —** on the contrary; **soy — al doblaje de películas** I'm against the dubbing of films; **todo lo —** just the opposite

contrarrestar VT to counteract

contrarrevolución F counterrevolution

contraseña F password, watchword

contrastar VI/VT to contrast

contraste M contrast

contrata F contract

contratación F hiring

contratar VT (a un empleado) to hire; (un

servicio) to contract for; **—se** to be hired
contratiempo M mishap
contratista MF contractor, builder
contrato M contract
contravenir[47] VT to contravene
contraventana F shutter
contribución F (cosa contribuida)
contribution; (impuesto) tax
contribuir[31] VT to contribute
contribuyente MF taxpayer
contrincante MF opponent
contrito ADJ contrite
control M (dominio, dirección) control;
(médico) checkup; (vigilancia) check;
(puesto) checkpoint; **— de calidad**
quality control; **— de la natalidad** birth
control; **— remoto** remote control; **bajo**
— under control
controlador -ora MF comptroller
controlar VT (ejercer control) to control;
(llevar a cabo un control) to check on
controversia F controversy
contumacia F obstinacy
contumaz ADJ stubborn
contusión F bruise
convalecer[13] VI to convalesce
convección F convection
convencer[10a] VT (por medio de la lógica) to
convince; (por insistencia) to persuade
convencimiento M (creencia) conviction;
(acción de convencer) convincing
convención F convention
convencional ADJ conventional
conveniencia F (lo cómodo) convenience;
(lo aconsejable) desirability; **a su —** at
your convenience
conveniente ADJ (cómodo) convenient;
(aconsejable) advisable
convenio M agreement; **— colectivo**
collective bargaining
convenir[47] VI (ser apropiado) to be suitable;
(llegar a un acuerdo) to agree
convento M convent
converger[11b] VI to converge
conversación F conversation; **trabar —**
con to engage in a conversation with
conversar VI to converse
conversión F conversion
converso -sa MF convert
convertible ADJ convertible
convertidor M converter
convertir[3] VT to convert; **—se en** to become
convexo ADJ convex
convicción F conviction
convicto -ta ADJ convicted; MF convict
convidar VT to invite; *Am* to offer
convincente ADJ convincing, compelling

convite M (invitación) invitation; (banquete)
banquet
convocación F convocation
convocar[6] VT to convoke, to call together;
(una reunión, un concurso) to convene
convoy M convoy
convoyar VT to convoy
convulsión F convulsion
conyugal ADJ conjugal, marital
cónyuge MF spouse
coñac M cognac, brandy
cooperación F cooperation
cooperar VI to cooperate
cooperativa F cooperative, co-op
cooperativo ADJ cooperative
coordenada F coordinate
coordinación F coordination
coordinado ADJ coordinate
coordinar VT to coordinate
copa F (vaso) goblet, wineglass; (de árbol)
top; (de sombrero) crown; (palo de la
baraja) card in the suit of copas; (trofeo,
parte de un sujetador) cup; **ir de —s** to go
for a drink
copete M (de pelo) tuft; (de plumas) crest;
estar hasta el — to be fed up
copia F copy; (de foto) print; **— de**
seguridad backup copy
copiadora F copy machine
copiar VT (reproducir) to copy; (en un
examen) to cheat
copión -ona MF copycat
copioso ADJ copious, plentiful
copla F (canción) popular song; (estrofa)
stanza
copo M (de nieve) snowflake; (masa de lana)
wad; **—s de maíz** cornflakes
copropietario -ria MF joint owner
coprotagonista MF co-star
copular VI to copulate
copyright M copyright
coque M coke
coqueta F (mujer) coquette; (mueble)
dressing table
coquetear VI to flirt
coquetería F flirtation
coqueto ADJ flirtatious
coraje M (valentía) courage; (enojo) anger
coral M (marino) coral; (musical) chorale
coralino ADJ coral
coraza F armor
corazón M heart; (de manzana) core;
(vocativo) honey; **con el — en la boca**
really tired; **de buen —** kindhearted; **de**
todo — wholeheartedly; **romper el — a**
alguien to break someone's heart
corazonada F hunch

corbata F necktie, tie, cravat

corcel M charger, steed

corchea F eighth note; **— con puntillo** dotted eighth note

corchete M (en costura) hook and eye; (paréntesis recto) square bracket; (llave) brace

corcho M (para botella) cork; (para pescar) float

corcova F hump, hunchback

corcovear VI to buck

cordel M string

cordero M lamb; (piel) lambskin

cordial ADJ cordial

cordillera F mountain range

cordón M cord; (al borde de la calle) *Am* curb; **— de apertura** rip cord; **— de zapatos** shoelace, shoestring; **— policial** police cordon; **— umbilical** umbilical cord

cordoncillo M ridge, rib

cordura F sanity

Corea F Korea; **— del Norte** North Korea; **— del Sur** South Korea

coreano -na ADJ & MF Korean

corear VI/VT to chant

coreografía F choreography

cornada F goring

cornear VT to gore

corneja F crow

corneta F cornet; M bugler

cornisa F cornice, ledge

corno M horn; **— francés** French horn

cornudo ADJ horned; M cuckold

coro M (grupo de cantantes) choir, chorus; (pieza de música) chorus; (parte de la Iglesia) loft; **cantar a —** to sing in unison

corolario M corollary

corona F crown

coronación F coronation

coronar VT to crown

coronel M colonel

coronilla F crown of the head; **estar hasta la —** to be fed up

corpiño M bodice; (sujetador) *Am* bra

corporación F guild

corporal ADJ corporal, bodily

corpulento ADJ stout, corpulent

corpus M corpus

corpúsculo M corpuscle

corral M (de granja) barnyard, farmyard; (para ganado) corral, pen

correa F leather strap; (de ventilador) belt; (de perro) leash

corrección F (acción de corregir) correction; (cualidad de correcto) correctness

correcto ADJ (apropiado) correct, proper; (acertado) right

corrector -ora MF editor; **— de pruebas** proofreader

corredizo ADJ sliding

corredor -ora ADJ running; MF (persona que corre) runner; (deportista automovilístico, ciclista) racer; (intermediario) broker, agent; M (pasillo) hallway, corridor

corregir[5,11] VT to correct; (exámenes) to grade; **—se** to mend one's ways

correlacionar VT to correlate

correlato M correlate

correo M mail; (edificio) post office; **— aéreo** air mail; **— certificado** certified mail; **— electrónico** e-mail; **echar al —** to mail

correoso ADJ tough

correr VI (persona, agua, calle) to run; (coche) to go fast; (una puerta) to slide; (dinero, tiempo) to pass; **— con los gastos** to take on the costs; VT (una cortina) to draw; (una carrera, un riesgo) to run; **—se** (moverse) to scoot over; (colores) to run, to bleed; (tinta) to smear

correría F foray

correspondencia F correspondence

corresponder VI (ser adecuado, estar en consonancia) to correspond; (pertenecer) to belong; VT (amor, favores) to reciprocate; **a mí me corresponde llamarla** it's up to me to call her

correspondiente ADJ corresponding; MF correspondent

corresponsal MF correspondent

corretaje M broker's / agent's commission

corretear VI to run around

corrida F (acción de correr) running; (competición) race; (de banco) run; **— de toros** bullfight; **de —** without stopping

corrido ADJ (que tiene mucha experiencia) worldly; (continuo) uninterrupted; **de —** without stopping; M ballad

corriente ADJ (que corre) running; (común) usual; (franco) frank; **el — mes** the current month; **estar al —** to be up-to-date; F (de agua, electricidad) current; (de dinero) flow; (de pesimismo) wave; (de aire) draft; **— alterna** alternating current; **— continua** direct current; **— del Golfo** Gulf Stream; **dejarse llevar por la —** to conform; **llevarle la — a alguien** to humor someone

corrillo M group of gossips

corro M circle of people

corroborar VT to corroborate

corroer[50] VT to corrode

corromper VT (a una persona) to corrupt; (un alimento) to rot; **—se** (una persona) to become corrupt; (un alimento) to rot

corrompido ADJ corrupt

corrosión F corrosion

corrupción F corruption

corrupto ADJ corrupt

corsé M corset

cortada F shortcut

cortador -ora MF (persona) cutter; F (aparato) cutter; **cortadora de césped** lawn mower

cortadura M cut

cortante ADJ (comentario, instrumento) cutting; (frío, viento) biting; (tono, instrumento) sharp

cortar VT to cut; (un vestido, el uso de algo) to cut out; (a un locutor, una rama, el gas) to cut off; (un árbol) to cut down; (las uñas) to clip; (el césped) to mow; — **el paso** to block; — **por lo sano** to take drastic action; M SG **cortacésped** lawn mower; **cortacircuitos** circuit breaker; **cortafuego** fire line; **cortapapeles** paper cutter; **cortaplumas** penknife; **cortauñas** nail cutter; VI (el frío) to bite; (la piel) to crack; **—se** (una persona) to be intimidated; (la leche) to curdle, to sour; **—se el pelo** to get a haircut

corte M (de un traje, herida) cut; (acción de cortar) cutting; (de televisión) commercial break; (estilo) style; — **de pelo** haircut; — **transversal** cross section; — **y confección** dressmaking; **eso me da —** that embarrasses me; F court; (séquito) retinue; **—s** Spanish parliament; **hacer la —** to court

cortedad F shortness

cortejar VT to court, to woo

cortejo M (séquito) entourage; (acción de cortejar) courtship

cortés ADJ courteous, polite

cortesano -na MF courtier

cortesía F courtesy

córtex M cortex

corteza F (de árbol) bark; (de pan, de la Tierra) crust; (de queso, fruta) rind; — **cerebral** cerebral cortex

cortijo M country house

cortina M (de ventana) curtain; (de lluvia) sheet; — **de humo** smokescreen

cortisona F cortisone

corto ADJ (bajo, no largo) short; (no inteligente) short on brains; (encogido) bashful; **—circuito** short circuit; — **de vista** short-sighted; **a — plazo** in the short run; **quedarse —** to come up short; **vestirse de —** to wear a short dress; M short (film)

cosa F thing; **como quien no quiere la —** without realizing it; **como si tal —** as cool as a cucumber; **como son las —s** what a surprise; **decir una — por otra** to tell a lie; **esperamos — de cinco minutos** we waited about five minutes; **las —s como son** let's be honest; **las —s de la vida** that's life; **no es gran —** it's no big deal; **otra —** something else

cosecha F crop, harvest; **de su —** of his invention; **vino — 1975** wine of 1975 vintage

cosechadora F combine

cosechar VT (cultivos) to harvest; (resultados) to reap

coser VI/VT to sew

cosignatario -ria MF cosigner

cosmético ADJ & M cosmetic

cósmico ADJ cosmic

cosmología F cosmology

cosmonauta MF cosmonaut

cosmopolita ADJ cosmopolitan

cosmos M cosmos

cosmovisión F worldview

coso M doodad

cosquillas F **hacer —** to tickle; **tener —** to be ticklish

cosquillear VT to tickle

cosquilleo M tickle

cosquilloso ADJ ticklish

costa F (del mar) coast, shore; **a toda —** at all costs; **—s** costs

Costa de Marfil F Ivory Coast

costado M side; **al —** alongside; **de —** edgewise; **por los cuatro —s** from all sides

costal M sack

costanero ADJ coastal

costar² VI/VT to cost; — **trabajo** to be difficult; — **un dineral** to cost a fortune; — **un ojo de la cara** to cost an arm and a leg

Costa Rica F Costa Rica

costarricense, costarriqueño -ña ADJ & MF Costa Rican

coste M cost; — **de (la) vida** cost of living

costear VT (pagar) to defray costs; VI to sail along the coast

costero ADJ coastal

costilla F rib; **lo hizo a —s de su padre** he did it at his father's expense

costo M cost; — **de (la) vida** cost of living

costoso ADJ costly

costra F (de pan) crust; (de herida) scab

costroso ADJ (de pan) crusty; (de heridas) scabby

costumbre F (manera habitual) habit; (uso

tradicional) custom; **de —** habitual; **tener la — de** to be accustomed to

costura F (acción de coser) sewing; (línea de puntadas) stitching; (unión de dos piezas) seam; **alta —** high fashion

costurero -ra M (caja) sewing box; (sastre) tailor; F seamstress

costurón M large scar

cota F (nivel del agua) height above sea level; (estándar) benchmark

cotejar VT to check against

cotejo M comparison

cotidiano ADJ everyday

cotización F price quote / quotation

cotizar[9] VT to quote

coto M **— de caza** game preserve; **poner — a** to put an end to

cotorra F (loro) parrot; (persona) chatterbox

cotorrear VI to chatter

covacha F small cave

coyote M coyote

coyuntura F joint; **aprovechar la —** to take advantage of the situation

coz F kick; **dar coces** to kick

crack M (cocaína) crack; (deportista) ace

cráneo M cranium, skull

craso ADJ crass

cráter M crater

crayola® F crayon

creación F creation

creacionismo M creationism

creador -ora MF creator; ADJ creative

crear VI/VT to create

creativo ADJ creative

crecer[13] VI to grow; (masa, río) to rise; (madera, mar) to swell; (la luna) to wax

crecida F rise of a river

crecido ADJ (adulto) grown; (grande) large; (demasiado alto) overgrown

creciente ADJ (que crece) growing; (luna) crescent; M (luna) crescent; (marea) high tide

crecimiento M growth

credencial F credential

crédito M (solvencia, unidad de estudios) credit; (hecho de creer) credence; (fama) reputation; (préstamo) loan; **dar — a** to believe; **—s** film credits; **vender a —** to sell on credit

credo M creed

crédulo ADJ credulous, gullible

creencia F belief

creer[14] VI/VT (tomar como cierto) to believe; (opinar) to think, to feel; **—se** to fall for; **¿quién se cree que es?** who does he think he is? **se cree artista** he fancies himself an artist; **¡ya lo creo!** I should

say so!

creíble ADJ credible, believable

crema F cream (también cosmético); **— de espárragos** cream of asparagus

cremallera F (de coche) rack; (de prenda) zipper; **— y piñón** rack and pinion

cremar VT to cremate

cremoso ADJ creamy

creosota F creosote

crepitación F crackle

crepitar VI to crackle

crepúsculo M twilight

crespo ADJ wiry, kinky

crespón M crepe

cresta F (de ola, montaña) crest; (de ave) tuft; (de gallo) comb

creyente MF believer; ADJ believing

cría F (acción de criar) breeding; (camada) litter; (animal joven) young

criadero M **— de peces** hatchery; **— de pollos** chicken farm

criado -da MF servant; F maid

criador -ora MF breeder

crianza F (de animales) breeding; (de hijos) upbringing; (modales) manners

criar[16] VT (animales) to breed; (hijos) to bring up, to rear, to raise; **estar criando malvas** *fam* to be pushing up daisies; **—se** to grow up

criatura F (ser extraño) creature; (bebé) baby

criba F sieve

cribar VT to sift

crimen M (delito grave) serious crime; (asesinato) murder; **— de guerra** war crime

criminal ADJ & MF criminal

criminalidad F crime

crin F mane

criollo ADJ (nacido en América) born in Spanish America; (tradicionalmente americano) traditionally Spanish American; M (lengua) Creole

críquet M cricket

crisálida F chrysalis

crisantemo M chrysanthemum

crisis F crisis

crisma F crown of the head

crisol M crucible, melting pot

crisparse VI (un músculo) to contract; (los puños) to clench; (los nervios) to be on edge

cristal M (mineral, vidrio de gran calidad) crystal; (vidrio de ventana) *Esp* glass, pane; (lente) lens; **— labrado** cut glass

cristalería F (objetos de cristal) glassware; (establecimiento) glassware store; (fábrica) glassworks

cristalino ADJ (de cristal) crystalline; (transparente) crystal clear; M lens of the eye

cristalizar[9] VI/VT to crystallize

cristiandad F Christendom

cristianismo M Christianity

cristiano -na ADJ & MF Christian; **hablar en —** (claramente) to speak clearly; (español) to speak Spanish

criterio M criterion

crítica F criticism; (de un libro) review

criticar[6] VT to criticize

crítico -ca ADJ critical; MF critic; (de un libro) reviewer

criticón -ona ADJ critical; MF faultfinder

Croacia F Croatia

croar VI to croak

croata ADJ & MF INV Croatian

crocante ADJ crisp, crunchy

croché, crochet M crochet; **hacer —** to crochet

croissant M croissant

crol M crawl

cromado ADJ chroming

cromo M chromium, chrome

cromosoma M chromosome

crónica F (narración de eventos) chronicle; (reportaje) feature; **— policial** police report

crónico ADJ chronic

cronología F chronology

cronológico ADJ chronological

cronometrador -ora MF timer, timekeeper

cronometraje M timing

cronometrar VT to time

cronómetro M chronometer, stopwatch

croquet M croquet

croquis M rough sketch

cross M cross-country race

cruasán M croissant

cruce M (acción de cruzar, lugar donde cruzar) crossing; (de dos calles) crossroads, intersection; (de razas) crossbreeding; (animal procedente de una mezcla) cross; **— peatonal** crosswalk

crucero M (buque) cruiser; (viaje de placer) cruise

cruceta F crosspiece

crucial ADJ crucial

crucificar[6] VT to crucify

crucifijo M crucifix

crucigrama M crossword puzzle

crudo ADJ (comida, seda) raw; (tiempo, invierno, imágenes) harsh; (petróleo, lenguaje) crude; **agua cruda** hard water; **color —** yellowish white

cruel ADJ cruel, mean

crueldad F cruelty, meanness

cruento ADJ grisly, gruesome

crujido M (de puerta, piso) creak; (de un tallo al quebrarse) crack; (de hojas) rustle; (de un fuego) crackle

crujiente ADJ (manzana, tocino) crisp, crispy; (nueces) crunchy

crujir VI (puerta, piso) to creak; (dientes) to grate; (hojas) to rustle; (nueces) to crunch; (fuego) to crackle

cruz F cross; (de moneda) tails; **hacerse cruces de** to dread

cruzada F crusade

cruzado -da MF crusader; ADJ (cheque) crossed; (fuego) cross; (traje) double-breasted

cruzamiento M (de piernas, razas) crossing; (de calles) crossroads; (de razas) cross

cruzar[9] VT to cross; (un cheque) to write across; **—le la cara a alguien** to backhand someone's face; **cruzo los dedos** I'll keep my fingers crossed; **—se con alguien** to bump into someone; **—se de brazos** to fold one's arms; **se me cruzó un ciervo** a deer crossed in front of me

cuaderno M notebook; **— de bitácora** logbook; **— de espiral** spiral notebook

cuadra F (establo) stable; (distancia entre calles) *Am* block

cuadrado ADJ square; **estar —** to be fat; M square; **es (un) —** he's a square; **dos al —** two squared; **elevar al —** to square

cuadrar VT (trabajar en ángulo recto) to square; VI (corresponder) to fit; (ser conveniente) to be convenient; (ser iguales) to balance, to add up; **— con** to be in agreement with

cuadricular VT to divide into squares

cuadrilátero ADJ quadrilateral; M (en boxeo) ring; (polígono) quadrilateral

cuadrilla F (de ladrones) gang; (de obreros) crew; (baile) square dance

cuadro M (cuadrado) square; (pintura) picture; (de bicicleta) frame; (de jardín) bed; (de tela) checker; (de fútbol) team; **— clínico** symptoms; **— sinóptico** table; **a / de —s** checked

cuadrúpedo ADJ & M quadruped

cuajada F curd

cuajar VI (leche) to curdle; (queso, cemento) to set; (gelatina) to jell; (un movimiento literario) to come about; **—se** to curdle; **la cosa no cuajó** that didn't pan out

cuajarón M clot

cual PRON REL which; **el / la —** (cosa) which; (persona) who; **lo —** which; **sea —** sea whichever it may be; ADV like; — **hoja al viento** like a leaf in the wind

cuál PRON INTERR which; **¿cuáles son los tuyos?** which ones are yours?

cualidad F quality

cualquiera ADJ INDEF any; **de cualquier manera / forma** anyhow; **en cualquier lado** anywhere; PRON INDEF (cosa) any; (persona) anyone; — **que sea su nacionalidad** whatever his nationality may be; — **que elijas** whichever one you choose; — **podría hacer eso** anyone could do that

cuando ADV REL when; — **la guerra** during the war; — **menos** at least; — **mucho** at most; **se rompió** — **lo usaba** it broke while she was using it

cuándo ADV INTERR & PRON when

cuantía F (cantidad) quantity; (importancia) importance

cuantificar[6] VT to quantify

cuantioso ADJ considerable

cuanto ADJ REL any; **lee** — **libro ve** she reads any book she sees; PRON REL **unos** —**s** a few; CONJ **hice** — **pude** I did as much as I could; ADV — **antes** as soon as possible; — **más trabajo, menos consigo** the more I work, the less I accomplish; **en** — as soon as possible; **en** — **a** regarding; **en** — **que** as

cuánto ADJ, ADV & PRON INTERR (dinero, agua) how much; (personas, libros) how many; **¿cada** —**?** how often? **¿— piensas quedarte?** how long do you plan to stay?

cuarenta NUM forty; **cantarle las** — **a alguien** to bawl someone out

cuarentena F quarantine; **una** — **de libros** forty-odd books

cuarentón -ona MF person in his or her forties

cuaresma F Lent

cuarta F (marcha) fourth gear; (palmo) span of a hand

cuartear VT (una res) to quarter; (los labios) to chap; —**se** to chap

cuartel M barracks; — **general** headquarters; **no dar** — to give no quarter

cuartelada F military coup

cuartelazo M military coup

cuarteto M quartet

cuartilla F sheet of paper

cuarto ADJ one-fourth, quarter; M (cuarta parte) fourth, quarter; (habitación) room; (cantidad) quarter, one fourth; — **de baño** bathroom; — **de estar** living room; — **de final** quarter finals; — **oscuro**

darkroom; **¡ni que ocho** —**s!** no way! **tres** —**s** three fourths

cuarzo M quartz

cuásar M quasar

cuate M *Méx* pal, buddy

cuatrero -ra MF cattle rustler

cuatrillizo -za MF quadruplet

cuatro NUM four; — **ojos** four-eyes; **más de** — a good number

cuba F (barril) cask, barrel; (tina) tub, vat

Cuba F Cuba

cubano -na ADJ & MF Cuban

cubeta F (recipiente triangular) tray; (balde) pail; — **de hielo** ice tray

cúbico ADJ cubic

cubículo M cubicle

cubierta F (de libro) cover; (cosa para cubrir) covering; (neumático) tire; (de buque) deck

cubierto M place setting; — **de plata** silverware; **a** — sheltered

cubismo M cubism

cubo M (cuerpo geométrico, tercera potencia) cube; (balde) bucket; (de rueda) hub; (juguete) building block; — **de basura** trash can

cubrir[51] VT to cover; (con carteles) to plaster; (una vacante) to fill; (con pintura) to coat; (con crema batida) to smother; (de niebla) to shroud; —**se** (nublarse) to fog up; (ponerse el sombrero) to put on one's hat

cucaracha F cockroach

cuchara F spoon; (de excavadora) bucket; (para helado) scoop; — **sopera** soup spoon; **meter la** — to butt in

cucharada F (lo que cabe en una cuchara) spoonful; (medida) tablespoonful; (de helado) dip

cucharadita F teaspoonful

cucharear VT to spoon

cucharita F teaspoon

cucharón M (para helado) scoop, dipper; (para sopa) ladle

cuchichear VI/VT to whisper

cuchicheo M whisper

cuchilla F (cuchillo grande) large knife, cleaver; (de afeitar, de licuadora) blade; (de patín) runner

cuchillada F (golpe) stab, slash; (herida) stab wound, gash

cuchillería F (conjunto de cuchillos) cutlery; (tienda) cutlery store

cuchillo M knife; **pasar a** — to kill with a knife

cuclillas LOC ADV **en** — squatting; **sentarse en** — to squat

cuclillo M cuckoo

cuco ADJ cute

cucú INTERJ cuckoo

cucurucho M (de papel) paper cone; (para helado) ice-cream cone; (capirote) hood

cuello M (parte del cuerpo) neck; (parte de una prenda) collar; **— de botella** bottleneck; **— uterino** cervix; **— vuelto** turtleneck; **estoy hasta el — en deudas** I'm up to my neck in debts

cuenca F (conjunto de tierras) basin; (cavidad del ojo) eye socket

cuenco M earthen bowl

cuenta F (cálculo) count, calculation; (factura) bill, check; (relación de ingresos y gastos) account; (bolita) bead; (depósito bancario) bank account; **— conjunta** joint account; **— corriente** checking account; **— de ahorros** savings account; **— de crédito** charge account; **— de gastos** expense account; **— regresiva / atrás** countdown; **abrir / cerrar una —** to open / close an account; **a fin de —s** when all is said and done; **ajustar —s** to settle old scores; **caí en (la) — de que** it just dawned on me that; **dar — de** to finish off; **dar —s** to give an accounting; **darse —** to realize; **en resumidas —s** in short; **eso corre por mi** that is my responsibility; **habida — de** bearing in mind; **más de la —** more than necessary; **pasar la —** to call in a favor; **tomar / tener en —** to take into account; **trabajar por — propia** to freelance; M SG **cuentagotas** eyedropper

cuento M story, tale; **— chino** tall tale; **— de hadas** fairy tale; **— de nunca acabar** never-ending tale; **déjese de —s** come to the point; **traer a —** to bring up; **venir a —** to be to the point

cuerda F (soga) cord, rope; (parte de un arco) bowstring; (de guitarra) string; (de reloj) spring; **— floja** tight rope; **—s vocales** vocal cords; **bajo —** under-the-table; **contra las —s** on the ropes; **dar — a** to wind

cuerdo ADJ sane

cuerno M horn (también instrumento de viento); (de caracol) feeler; (de ciervo) antler; **— de la abundancia** horn of plenty; **coger el toro por los —s** to take the bull by the horns; **poner —s a** to be unfaithful to

cuero M (piel de animal) hide; (piel curtida) leather; **— cabelludo** scalp; **en —s** naked

cuerpo M body; (torso) torso; **¡— a tierra!** hit the deck! **— de bomberos** fire department; **— de policía** police force; **—**

de prensa press corps; **— docente** teaching staff; **a — de rey** in great luxury; **dar — a** to flesh out; **de — entero** through and through; **ganó por tres —s de ventaja** he won by three lengths; **ir de —** to have a bowel movement

cuervo M crow, raven

cuesta F slope; **— abajo** downhill; **— arriba** uphill; **a —s** piggyback

cuestión F question; **en — de** in a matter of; **poner en —** to question; **ser — de** to be a matter of

cuestionable ADJ questionable

cuestionador ADJ questioning

cuestionar VT to question

cuestionario M questionnaire

cueva F cave

cuidado M (atención) care; (preocupación) worry; **— con el perro** beware of the dog; **— de la casa** housekeeping; **al — de** in care of; **eso me trae sin —** I don't care about that; **tener —** to be careful; **un enfermo de —** a severely ill patient; INTERJ look out!

cuidador -ora MF caregiver, caretaker

cuidadoso ADJ careful

cuidar VT to take care of, to look after; **— de** to take care of; **— la casa** to keep house; **— niños** to babysit; **—se de** to beware of

culata F (anca) haunch; (de rifle) butt; (de motor) cylinder head

culatazo M (golpe) blow with the butt of a rifle; (rebote al disparar) recoil

culebra F snake

culebrear VI to slither

culebrilla F shingles

culinario ADJ culinary

culminar VI to culminate

culpa F (responsabilidad) fault, blame; (sentimiento) guilt; **echar la — a** to blame; **por — de** because of; **tener la —** to be to blame

culpabilidad F guilt

culpable ADJ guilty; MF culprit

culpar VT to blame

cultivado ADJ (tierra) cultivated; (perlas) cultured

cultivador -ora MF (persona) cultivator; F (aparato) cultivator

cultivar VT (cosechas) to grow, to raise; (la tierra) to farm; (relaciones, inteligencia) to cultivate; (microbios) to culture

cultivo M (de plantas) growing; (de la tierra) farming; (de microbios) culture; (de relaciones) cultivation; **de —** cultured

culto ADJ educated, cultured; M worship;

libertad de — freedom of religion
cultura F culture; **— general** general knowledge
cultural ADJ cultural
culturismo M body-building
cumbre F summit
cumplido ADJ (cortés) polite; (perfecto) perfect; M compliment; **hacer algo de** — to do something out of duty; **hacer un** — to pay a compliment
cumplimiento M (de un contrato) performance; (de una promesa, obligación) fulfillment; (de un plazo) expiration
cumplir VT (una obligación) to fulfill, to discharge; (una promesa) to keep; (una condena) to complete, to serve; **— diez años** to turn ten; **hacer —** to enforce; VI (acceder a las relaciones sexuales) to have sexual relations; (vencer) to expire; **— con** to meet a goal; **me cumple informarle que** it is my duty to inform you that
cúmulo M (grupo) host; (tipo de nube) cumulus
cuna F (que se puede mecer) cradle; (con barandas) crib
cundir VI (extenderse) to spread; (rendir) to go a long way
cuneta F roadside ditch; **en la —** out to pasture
cuña F (pieza para hender) wedge; (recipiente de excrementos) bedpan
cuñado -da M brother-in-law; F sister-in-law
cuño M die; **de — hispano** with a Hispanic stamp
cuota F (cantidad que le corresponde a uno) quota; (cantidad que hay que pagar) dues; (mensualidad) installment
cupé M coupé
cupo M (cantidad) quota; (capacidad) *Am* room
cupón M coupon
cúpula F dome
cura F cure, remedy; M priest
curable ADJ curable
curación F cure
curandero -ra MF healer
curar VT (una enfermedad, carne) to cure; (una herida) to heal; VI to heal; **—se** to heal; **—se en salud** to take precautionary measures
curiosear VI to look around; (en asuntos ajenos) to pry
curiosidad F curiosity
curioso ADJ curious
curita F *Am* adhesive bandage, Band-Aid™
currículum M résumé

curro M *Esp* job
curruca F warbler
curry M curry
cursar VT (un curso) to take; (un telegrama) to send
cursi ADJ (afectado) affected; (de mal gusto) tacky
cursivo ADJ cursive; **escribir en —** to write in cursive
curso M (de río, enfermedad, acontecimientos, moneda) course; (período docente) academic year; (grupo de estudiantes que siguen el mismo curso) class; (libro de texto) textbook; **— legal** legal currency; **el mes en —** the current month
cursor M cursor
curtiduría F tannery
curtiembre F tannery
curtir VT (cuero) to tan; (cutis) to weather; (hacer adquirir experiencia) to harden; **—se** (envejecerse) to get weathered; (acostumbrarse a las dificultades) to become accustomed to hardships
curva F curve
curvatura F curvature
curvo ADJ curved
cúspide F summit
custodia F custody, keeping; **en —** in escrow
custodiar VT to guard
custodio -dia MF guardian
cutícula F cuticle
cutis M facial skin
cuyo ADJ REL whose
cyborg M cyborg

Dd

dádiva F gift
dadivoso ADJ generous
dado ADJ given; M die; **jugar a los —s to** throw dice
dador -ora MF giver; **— de sangre** blood donor
daga F dagger
dalia F dahlia
daltónico ADJ color-blind
dama F lady; (en el juego de la dama) king; **jugar a las —s** to play checkers; **— de honor** bridesmaid
damajuana F demijohn
damasco M (fruta) apricot; (árbol) apricot tree

damisela F damsel

dandi M dandy

danés -esa ADJ Danish; MF Dane; M (lengua) Danish

danza F dance; **— del vientre** belly dance; **en —** in action

danzante MF dancer

danzar[9] VI/VT to dance

dañar VT to harm, to damage; **—se** to suffer harm

dañino ADJ harmful

daño M damage, harm; **— emergente** actual damage; **— físico** bodily harm; **—s y perjuicios** damages; **hacer —** to harm

dañoso ADJ harmful

dar[25] VT (un regalo) to give; (un golpe, naipes) to deal; (sal) to add; (una fiesta) to throw; (la hora) to strike; (un olor) to give off; (la alarma) to raise; (un paseo) to take; **— a** (un edificio) to face; (una calle) to lead to; **— a conocer** to announce; **— a entender** to intimate; **— con** to hit upon, to find; **— de alta** to discharge, to release from the hospital; **— de baja** to discharge; **— de comer** to feed; **— de sí** to perform at capacity; **esta tela da de sí** this fabric gives; **— en la pared** to hit the wall; **—le con** to scrub with; **lo misma da** it makes no difference; **¿qué más da?** what difference does it make? **dale que dale** on and on; **hoy no doy una** today I can't get anything right; **le doy cincuenta años** he must be about fifty; **me da rabia / miedo** that makes me angry / afraid; **no me da el tiempo para ir al cine** I don't have time to go to the movie; **que no le dé el sol** don't let the sun shine on it; **y dale** enough already; **—se** to be found; **—se a** to indulge in; **—se por conforme** to be satisfied; **dárselas de** to boast of being

dardo M dart

dársena F dock

datar VT to date; **— de** to date from

dátil M date

dato M piece of information; **—s** data

de PREP **— la familia** of the family; **— Madrid** from Madrid; **habló — la guerra** he talked about the war; **el hombre — gafas** the man with glasses; **el mejor estudiante — la clase** the best student in the class; **fácil — hacer** easy to do; **más — tres** more than three; **llevar — la mano** to lead by the hand; **— regreso a España** upon returning to Spain; **— venta en farmacias** on sale in pharmacies; **ancianos — respeto** older

people to be respected; **— lo más lindo** really pretty; **tonto — mí** silly me

deambular VI to amble, to saunter

deán M dean

debacle M debacle

debajo ADV under, underneath; PREP **— de** under, below; **por — de** under

debate M debate

debatir VT to debate; **—se** to struggle

debe M debit

deber V AUX **deben apoyarme** they should support me; **debe de ser** it must be; **deberías sentarte** you should sit down; VT to owe; **me debes una** you owe me one; **me debo a mis alumnos** I'm devoted to my students; M duty; **—es** homework

debidamente ADV duly

debido ADJ due; **— a** due to, owing to; **a su — tiempo** in due time

débil ADJ (que tiene poca fuerza) weak; (endeble) frail, feeble; (sonido) faint

debilidad F weakness; (cualidad de endeble) frailty; (de un sonido) faintness

debilitamiento M weakening

debilitar VT to weaken, to debilitate

débito M debit

debutar VI to make a debut

década F decade

decadencia F (moral) decadence, decay; (cultural, económica) decline

decadente ADJ decadent

decaer[23] VI (fuerza) to weaken; (energía) to ebb; (salud) to fail; (ánimo) to flag

decaimiento M (decadencia) decline; (debilidad) weakness

decano -na ADJ senior; MF dean

decapitar VT to behead, to decapitate

decatlón M decathlon

decencia F decency

decenio M decade

decente ADJ decent; **muy —** rather good

decepción F disappointment

decepcionante ADJ disappointing

decepcionar VT to disappoint

decibelio M decibel

decidido ADJ resolute, determined; **una decidida preferencia** a decided preference

decidir VI/VT to decide; **—se** to make up one's mind; **—se a** to resolve to

deciduo ADJ deciduous

décima F tenth

decimal ADJ decimal

décimo ADJ & M tenth

decir[26] VT (palabras, oraciones) to say; (una mentira, un chiste, la verdad) to tell; **—**

tonterías to talk nonsense; **con —te que** suffice it to say that; **este tipo no me dice nada** this guy leaves me cold; **¿que me lo digan a mí?** you're telling me that? vi to say; **diga** hello (al contestar el teléfono); **es** — that is to say; **he dicho** I have spoken; **no es prometedor que digamos** it's hardly promising; **no me digas** you don't say; **querer** — to mean; M saying

decisión F decision; **tomar una** — to make a decision

decisivo ADJ decisive

declaración F (de amor, independencia, guerra) declaration; (de un hecho) statement; (de un testigo) deposition; — **de derechos** bill of rights; — **de impuestos/de la renta** tax return; — **jurada** affidavit

declarar VT (amor, independencia, ingresos) to declare; (un hecho) to state; — **culpable** to find guilty; **os declaro marido y mujer** I pronounce you man and wife; VI (como testigo) to testify; —**se** (un amante) to declare one's love; —**se culpable** to plead guilty; —**se en huelga** to go on strike; —**se en quiebra** to declare bankruptcy

declinar VI/VT to decline

declive M (pendiente) slope, drop; (decadencia) decline

decoración F decoration; — **de interiores** interior decorating

decorado M (de una casa) decoration; (de un escenario) scenery

decorar VT to decorate

decorativo ADJ decorative

decoro M decorum, propriety

decoroso ADJ decorous, proper

decrépito ADJ decrepit

decretar VT to decree

decreto M (disposición ejecutiva) decree; (ley) act

dedal M thimble

dedicación F dedication

dedicar[6] VT (la vida) to dedicate, to devote; (un libro) to dedicate; —**se** to dedicate oneself; (a los estudios) to apply oneself

dedicatoria F dedication

dedo M (de la mano) finger; (del pie) toe; — **anular** ring finger; — **índice** index finger; — **mayor/del corazón** middle finger; — **meñique** little finger; — **pulgar** thumb; **chuparse el** — to be a fool; **chuparse los —s** to lick one's fingers; **cruzar los —s** to keep one's fingers crossed; **elegir a** — to appoint

directly; **hacer** — to hitch a ride; **no mover un** — not to lift a finger

deducción F deduction

deducible ADJ deductible

deducir[24] VT (concluir) to deduce, to conclude; (descontar) to deduct

defecar[6] VI/VT to defecate

defección F defection

defecto M defect, flaw

defectuoso ADJ defective, faulty

defender[1] VT to defend; (una causa) to champion; (los derechos) to stand up for, to stick up for; **se defiende en francés** he can hold his own in French

defendible ADJ defensible

defensa F defense; **aprende** — **personal** he's learning self-defense; **lo dijo en** — **propia** he said it in self-defense

defensivo ADJ defensive; **a la defensiva** on the defensive

defensor -ora MF defender; (de una causa) champion

deferencia F deference

deficiencia F deficiency

deficiente ADJ deficient

déficit M deficit

definición F definition

definido ADJ definite

definir VT to define

definitivo ADJ (superior) definitive; (final) final; **en definitiva** all things considered

deflación F deflation

deflector M baffle

deforestación F deforestation

deformación F deformation

deformar VT to deform; —**se** to become deformed

deforme ADJ deformed

deformidad F deformity

defraudar VT (cometer fraude) to defraud; (decepcionar) to disappoint

defunción F death

degenerado -da ADJ & MF degenerate

degenerar VI to degenerate

degollar[2] VT to slash someone's throat

degradación F degradation

degradar VT (envilecer) to degrade, to debase; (rebajar el rango) to demote; —**se** to degrade

degüello M throat-slashing; **lucha a** — fight to the death

dehesa F pasture

deidad F deity

dejadez F slovenliness

dejado ADJ slovenly

dejar VT (abandonar, no comer, legar) to leave; (a un enamorado) to leave, to dump; (permitir) to let; (soltar) to let go; **— de** to stop; **— caer** to drop; **déjame en paz** leave me alone; **me dejó atónito** it left / rendered me speechless; **no dejes de venir** don't fail to come; **te lo dejo en mil dólares** I'll sell it to you for one thousand dollars; **—se** to let oneself go; **—se crecer la barba** to grow a beard; **déjate de joder** give me a break

deje M slight accent

dejo M (sabor) aftertaste; (acento) slight accent; (toque) hint; **tener un — de** to smack of

delantal M apron

delante ADV in front; **— de** in front of, ahead of

delantera F (de carrera) lead; (de vestido) front; **llevar la —** to be in the lead; **tomar la —** to take the lead

delantero ADJ (pata) front; (línea) forward; M front

delatar VT to inform against, to squeal on; **— la edad** to betray one's age

delator -ora MF accuser, informer

delegación F delegation

delegado -da MF delegate

delegar[7] VT to delegate

deleitar VT to delight; **—se en algo** to revel in something; **—se la vista con** to feast one's eyes on

deleite M delight

deletrear VT to spell; **— mal** to misspell

deleznable ADJ despicable

delfín M dolphin

delgadez F thinness

delgado ADJ thin, slender, slim

deliberación F deliberation

deliberado ADJ deliberate

deliberar VI/VT to deliberate

delicadeza F (tacto) gentleness; (fineza) delicacy; **con —** gently; **tuvo la — de llamar** he was kind enough to call

delicado ADJ (suave, fácil de romper, controvertido) delicate; (enfermizo) frail; (exquisito) dainty; (quisquilloso) squeamish

delicatessen F PL delicacies

delicia F delight

delicioso ADJ delicious, delectable

delimitar VT to delimit

delincuencia F crime

delincuente ADJ & MF delinquent, criminal; **— juvenil** juvenile delinquent

delineador M eyeliner

delinear VT to delineate, to outline

delirante ADJ delirious, raving

delirar VI to be delirious, to rave

delirio M delirium; **— paranoico** paranoid delusion; **—s de grandeza** delusions of grandeur

delito M crime, offense

demacrado ADJ drawn, gaunt, haggard

demagogo -ga MF demagog

demanda F (de mercancías) demand; (de seguros) insurance claim; (pleito) lawsuit; **por —** on demand; **entablar una —** to file a lawsuit

demandado -da MF defendant

demandante MF plaintiff

demandar VT (pedir) to ask for; (poner pleito) to sue, to file a suit against

demarcar[6] VT to demarcate

demás ADJ (restante) remaining; PRON the others, the rest; **lo —** the rest; **y —** and whatnot; ADV **por lo —** moreover; **por —** useless

demasía LOC ADV **en —** excessively

demasiado ADV too; too much; **eso es — para mí** that's too much for me; **él es — alto** he's too tall; ADJ too much; too many; **— dinero** too much money; **demasiadas cosas** too many things

demencia F (locura) insanity; (senilidad) senility

demente ADJ demented, insane, deranged

democracia F democracy

demócrata MF INV democrat

democrático ADJ democratic

demografía F demographics

demográfico ADJ demographic

demoler[2] VT to demolish, to tear down

demonio M demon; **¿qué —s haces?** what the heck are you doing? **un frío de —s** bitter cold

demora F delay

demorar VT to delay; **—se** to linger

demostración F demonstration; **— de fuerza** show of force

demostrar[2] VT (mostrar) to demonstrate, to show; (hacer ver la verdad) to prove, to demonstrate

demostrativo ADJ demonstrative

demudar VT to change, to alter

denigrar VT to denigrate, to disparage

denodado ADJ untiring

denominación F (valor) denomination; (nombre) designation

denominar VT to designate, to term

denostar[2] VT to revile

denotación F denotation

denotar VT to denote

densidad F density

denso ADJ dense; (líquido) heavy

dentado ADJ (rueda) toothed; (montaña)

ragged

dentadura F set of teeth; — **postiza** false teeth

dental ADJ dental

dentellada F (mordedura) bite; (señal de diente) tooth mark; **a —s** biting

dentífrico M dentifrice

dentista MF dentist

dentro ADV inside; PREP — **de la casa** inside the house; — **de la ley** within the law; — **de quince días** (en el plazo de) within two weeks; (al cabo de) in two weeks; **por — within**

denuncia F (acusación) denunciation; (de mina, de seguro) claim

denunciar VT (un hecho negativo) to denounce; (una mina) to claim; (un delito) to report

deparar VT to have in store for

departamento M (división) department; (piso) small apartment

departir VI *lit* to commune

dependencia F (hecho de depender) dependence; (habituación) dependency; (filial) branch office

depender VI to depend; — **de** to depend on

dependiente -ta ADJ dependent; MF clerk

depilar VT to remove hair

depilatorio ADJ & M depilatory

deplorable ADJ deplorable

deplorar VT to deplore

deponer[39] VT (las armas) to lay down; (a un ministro) to depose, to remove; VI to defecate

deportar VT to deport

deporte M sport; **me gusta el** — I like sports/athletics

deportista ADJ athletic; MF athlete

deportivo ADJ athletic; **revista deportiva** sports magazine

deposición F (de un testigo) deposition; (de un ministro) removal; (movimiento de vientre) bowel movement

depositante MF depositor

depositar VT to deposit; —**se** to settle

depositario -ria MF repository

depósito M (en el banco) deposit; (de gasolina) tank; (de agua) reservoir; (de cadáveres) morgue; (de armas) depot, dump; (de mercancías) stock room, storehouse; **hacer un** — to make a deposit; **en** — on consignment

depravado ADJ depraved

depreciar VI to depreciate

depredador -ora MF predator

depresión F depression

deprimente ADJ depressing

deprimido ADJ depressed

deprimir VT to depress

deprisa ADV quickly

depuración F purification; (de un programa) debugging

depurar VT to purify; (un programa) to debug

derby M derby

derecha F (política) right wing; **a la** — to the right; **de —s** right-wing

derechista ADJ right-wing; MF rightist

derecho ADJ (no izquierdo) right; (recto) straight; **ponerse** — to hold oneself erect; ADV straight; **volver — a casa** to go straight home; **todo** — straight ahead; M (preceptos, disciplina) law; (posibilidad legal) right; — **consuetudinario** common law; — **de admisión** fee; — **internacional** international law; —**s** fees; —**s aduaneros** tax on imports; —**s civiles** civil rights; —**s de autor** copyright; —**s de la mujer** women's rights; —**s de los animales** animal rights; **estar en su** — to be entitled; **poner al** — to put on right side out; **registrar los —s** to copyright

derechura F straightness

deriva F drift; **ir a la** — to be adrift

derivación F derivation

derivado M (subproducto) by-product; (palabra) derivative

derivar VT to derive

dermatología F dermatology

dermatólogo -ga MF dermatologist

derogación F repeal

derogar[7] VI to repeal

derramamiento M spill, spilling; — **de sangre** bloodshed

derramar VT (un líquido) to spill; (sangre, lágrimas) to shed; —**se** to spill over, to run over

derrame M spill; — **cerebral** stroke, cerebral hemorrhage

derredor LOC ADV **en** — all around

derrengar[7] VT (dañar la espalda) to sprain one's back; (cansar) to exhaust

derretir[5] VT to melt; —**se por alguien** to be crazy about someone

derribar VT (un edificio) to demolish, to tear down; (a una persona) to knock down; (un gobierno) to topple, to overthrow; (un avión) to shoot down, to down

derrocamiento M overthrow

derrocar[6] VT (un gobierno) to overthrow, to topple; (a un dictador) to depose

derrochador -ora ADJ extravagant; MF (de dinero) spendthrift; (de recursos) squanderer

derrochar VT (dinero) to squander; (salud) to radiate

derroche M (de recursos) waste, extravagance; (de color) profusion

derrota F defeat

derrotar VT to defeat

derrotero M course

derrubio M washout

derruido ADJ dilapidated

derrumbadero M precipice

derrumbamiento M collapse

derrumbar VT to demolish; —**se** (edificio) to collapse; (túnel, caverna) to cave in

derrumbe M (de tierra) landslide; (de un edificio) collapse

desabotonar VT to unbutton, to undo

desabrido ADJ (comida) tasteless; (persona) *Am* dull; *Esp* surly

desabrigado ADJ exposed

desabrochado ADJ undone, unfastened

desabrochar VT to undo; (ganchos) to unhook; (hebillas, cinturones) to unbuckle; (botones) to unbutton; —**se** to come undone

desacato M disrespect; — **al tribunal** contempt of court

desacelerar VI to decelerate

desacierto M mistake

desaconsejable ADJ inadvisable

desaconsejar VT to caution against

desacoplar VT to uncouple, to disconnect

desacostumbrado ADJ unusual

desacostumbrar VT to break of a habit; —**se** to lose a habit

desacreditar VT to discredit

desactivar VT (explosivo, situación) to defuse; (mecanismo) to disable; (virus) to deactivate

desacuerdo M disagreement; **estar en** — to be at odds

desafiar[16] VT (retar) to challenge, to dare; (enfrentar) to defy

desafilado ADJ dull

desafilar VT to dull; —**se** to become dull

desafinado ADJ out of tune, off-key

desafinar VT to be out of tune

desafío M (reto) challenge; (desobediencia) defiance

desafortunado ADJ unfortunate, unlucky

desafuero M (de un diputado) withdrawal of immunity; (ultraje) outrage

desagradable ADJ disagreeable, unpleasant

desagradar VT to displease

desagradecido ADJ ungrateful

desagrado M displeasure

desagraviar VI to make amends, to redress

desagravio M redress

desaguadero M drainpipe

desaguar[8] VI to drain

desagüe M (acción de desaguar) drainage; (de lavabo) drain, drainpipe; (en la azotea) gutter

desaguisado M mess

desahogado ADJ (cómodo) comfortable; (espacioso) spacious

desahogar[7] VT (aliviar) to relieve; (expresar) to pour out one's feelings

desahogo M relief; **vivir con** — to live an easy life

desairar VT to slight, to snub, to rebuff

desaire M slight, snub, rebuff

desajustar VT to loosen; —**se** to come loose

desalentado ADJ despondent

desalentador ADJ disheartening

desalentar[1] VT to discourage, to dishearten; —**se** to get discouraged

desaliento M discouragement, dismay

desaliñado ADJ disheveled, slovenly, unkempt

desaliño M slovenliness

desalmado ADJ heartless

desalojar VT (una piedra) to dislodge; (un tribunal) to clear; (por peligro) to evacuate; (por no pagar) to evict; (dejar vacío) to vacate

desamparado ADJ helpless, forlorn

desamparar VT to forsake

desamparo M abandonment, helplessness

desamueblado ADJ unfurnished

desangrar VT to bleed

desanimado ADJ (persona) discouraged; (jornada) dull

desanimar VT to discourage

desánimo M discouragement

desaparecer[13] VI to disappear, to vanish; (morir) to pass away

desaparición F disappearance; (muerte) demise

desapasionado ADJ dispassionate

desapego M detachment

desapercibido ADJ unnoticed

desaprobación F disapproval

desaprobar[2] VT to disapprove of

desarmado ADJ unarmed

desarmar VT (quitar las armas) to disarm; (desmontar) to take apart

desarme M disarmament

desarraigar[7] VT to uproot

desarreglar VT to disturb, to mess up

desarreglo M (nervioso) disorder; (falta de arreglo) mess

desarrollar VT (aumentar) to develop; (extender algo arrollado) to unroll; (llevar a cabo) to carry out; (aclarar) to elaborate, to flesh out; **—se** to unfold

desarrollo M development; (de una ecuación) expansion; **en —** developing

desarticulado ADJ disjointed

desaseado ADJ slovenly

desaseo M slovenliness

desasir[21] VT to let go of

desasosiego M uneasiness

desastrado ADJ (desaseado) untidy; (funesto) ill-fated

desastre M disaster

desastroso ADJ disastrous

desatado ADJ (ambición) unfettered; (zapatos) untied

desatar VT (un nudo) to untie, to loosen; (una ola de violencia) to unleash; **—se** to come untied; **—se en insultos** to let out a string of insults

desatascador M plunger

desatascar[6] VT (un inodoro) to unclog; (una cosa) to dislodge

desatención F lack of attention

desatender[1] VT (no ocuparse de algo) to neglect; (ignorar) to ignore

desatendido ADJ (descuidado) neglected; (ignorado) ignored

desatento ADJ inattentive

desatinado ADJ imprudent

desatornillar VT to unscrew

desatracar[6] VI/VT to shove off

desavenencia F discord

desayunar VT **desayuné huevos** I had eggs for breakfast; **—se** to have breakfast; **—se (con que)** to find out (that)

desayuno M breakfast

desazón F uneasiness

desbandarse VI to disband

desbaratar VT (un plan) to disrupt; (un hechizo) to break

desbocado ADJ (caballo) runaway; (collar) loose

desbordamiento M overflow

desbordante ADJ overflowing

desbordar VI (derramar) to overflow; VT (abrumar) to overwhelm; **—se** to overflow, to spill over

desbravar VT to break

descabalgar[7] VI to dismount

descabellado ADJ harebrained

descabezar[9] VT to behead; **— un sueño** to take a nap

descafeinado ADJ decaffeinated

descalabrar VT to split someone's head open

descalabro M disaster

descalificar VT to disqualify

descalzar[9] VT to take off someone's shoes;

—se to take off one's shoes

descalzo ADJ barefoot

descaminado ADJ **andar / ir —** to be on the wrong track

descamisado ADJ (sin camisa) shirtless; (pobre) poor

descansar VI/VT to rest; **— en paz** to rest in peace; **—se en** to rely on

descanso M (acción de descansar) rest; (de escalera) staircase landing; (tiempo en que se descansa) break; **en —** at ease

descapotable ADJ & M convertible

descarado ADJ shameless, impudent, brazen; **a la descarada** shamelessly

descarga F (de batería, agua, armas) discharge; (de buques) unloading; (emocional) outpouring; (de electricidad) shock

descargar[7] VT (una batería, agua) to discharge; (un buque, un arma de fuego) to unload; (bombas) to drop; (un programa de computadora) to download; **—se** (una batería) to drain; (ira) to vent

descargo M **en su —** in his defense

descarnado ADJ (realidad) stark; (cara) emaciated

descaro M effrontery, impudence, nerve

descarriar[16] VT to lead astray; **—se** to go astray

descarrilarse VI to derail, to jump the track

descartar VT (un naipe) to discard; (una posibilidad) to dismiss, to discard

descarte M discard; **por —** by elimination

descascararse VI (en jirones) to peel; (en fragmentos) to chip, to flake

descendencia F (linaje) descent; (descendientes) descendants

descendente ADJ descending, downward

descender[1] VI to descend; **— de** to descend from

descendiente MF descendant

descenso M descent

descifrar VT to decipher

descodificar[6] VT to decode

descolgar[2,7] VT (una cortina) to take down; (un teléfono) to pick up; **—se con** to come up with; **—se de** to come down from

descollar[2] VI to excel

descolorido ADJ (persona) pale; (cosa) colorless

descomponer[39] VT (disgustar) to upset; (dar diarrea) to give diarrhea; (dar náuseas) to make nauseous; (productos químicos) to break down; (cadáveres) to decompose; (un reloj) to break; **— en factores** to factor; **—se** (productos químicos) to break

down; (cadáveres) to decompose; (un
reloj) to break; (sentir náuseas) to be
nauseous; (tener diarrea) to have diarrhea;
(disgustarse) to go to pieces

descomposición F (de cadáveres)
decomposition; (de productos químicos)
breaking down; (diarrea) diarrhea

descompuesto ADJ (roto) broken; (caótico)
chaotic; (con diarrea) having diarrhea

descomunal ADJ enormous

desconcertado ADJ disconcerted

desconcertante ADJ disconcerting

desconcertar[1] VT to disconcert, to puzzle, to
baffle; **—se** to become disconcerted

desconchar VT to chip

desconcierto M confusion

desconectado ADJ disconnected

desconectar VT to disconnect

desconexión F (acción de desconectar)
disconnecting; (incomunicación)
disconnect

desconfiado ADJ mistrustful, suspicious

desconfianza F mistrust

desconfiar[16] VT to distrust, to mistrust, to be
wary of

descongelación F thawing

descongestionante M decongestant

desconocer[13] VT (no reconocer) to fail to
recognize; (no saber) not to know

desconocido -da ADJ unknown; **un
actividad desconocida** an unheard-of
activity; MF stranger

desconocimiento M ignorance

desconsideración F thoughtlessness

desconsiderado ADJ thoughtless,
inconsiderate

desconsolado ADJ disconsolate, dejected

desconsolador ADJ disheartening

desconsolar[2] VT to dishearten; **—se** to
become disheartened

desconsuelo M dejection

descontar[2] VT (bajar el precio) to discount;
(excluir) to exclude; (quitar del sueldo) to
dock

descontentadizo ADJ hard to please

descontentar VT to displease

descontento ADJ & M discontent

descorazonado ADJ disheartened

descortés ADJ discourteous, impolite

descortesía F discourtesy, impoliteness

descortezar[9] VT to strip the bark from

descoser VT to rip; **—se** to come unsewn

descosido ADJ unsewn; M unsewn place;
hablar como un — to talk one's head
off

descostrar VT to remove the crust from

descoyuntado ADJ dislocated, out of joint

descoyuntar VT to dislocate; **—se** to become
dislocated

descrédito M discredit

descreído -da ADJ unbelieving; MF unbeliever

descreimiento M unbelief

describir[51] VT to describe

descripción F description

descriptivo ADJ descriptive

descuartizar[9] VT to quarter

descubierto ADJ (destapado) uncovered; (sin
sombrero) hatless; **al —** in the open;
estar al — to be exposed; **poner al —** to
expose, to lay bare; **en —** overdrawn; M
overdraft

descubridor -ora MF discoverer

descubrimiento M discovery

descubrir[51] VT (hallar) to discover; (destapar)
to uncover; **—se** to take off one's hat; **—
el pastel** to spill the beans

descuento M discount

descuidado ADJ (en lo que se hace) careless,
negligent; (en el arreglo de su persona)
slovenly

descuidar VT to neglect; **descuida, yo me
ocupo de eso** don't worry, I'll take care
of that; **—se** to be negligent

descuido M (falta de cuidado) neglect;
(acción descuidada) oversight; **al —** offhand; **por —** by chance

desde PREP (origen) from; (tiempo) since; **—
Madrid** from Madrid; **— el martes** since
Tuesday; **— luego** of course; **— el
principio** from the start; **— el vamos**
from the word go; **— entonces** ever since

desdecirse[26] VI (decir lo contrario) to
contradict oneself; (negar lo dicho) to
retract

desdén M disdain, scorn

desdentado ADJ toothless

desdeñar VT to disdain, to scorn

desdeñoso ADJ disdainful, scornful

desdicha F misfortune; **por —** unfortunately

desdichado ADJ wretched

desdoblamiento M division

desdoblar VT (desplegar) to unfold; (dividir)
to divide

deseabilidad F desirability

deseable ADJ desirable

desear VT to desire

desecación F drying

desecar[6] VT to dry; **—se** to dry up

desechar VT (ropa vieja) to discard; (una
oferta) to refuse; (una posibilidad) to
dismiss

desecho M waste material; **—s** refuse, waste

desembalar VT to unpack

desembarazar[9] VT to rid of; **—se** to get rid

of

desembarcadero M dock

desembarcar[6] VI (de un buque) to disembark, to go ashore; (de un avión) to deplane

desembarco M landing

desembarque M landing

desembocadura F mouth

desembocar[6] VI to flow; — **en** to flow into; **la calle Ocho desemboca en la Rambla** eighth street feeds into la Rambla

desembolsar VT to disburse, to pay out

desembolso M disbursement, outlay.

desembragar[7] VI/VT to disengage (the clutch)

desempacar[6] VT to unpack

desempañar VT to wipe clean

desempeñar VT to redeem; — **un cargo** to perform the duties of a position; — **un papel** to play a part; —**se** to get out of debt

desempeño M (de un cargo o papel) performance; (de una cosa en prenda) redemption

desempleado ADJ unemployed

desempleo M unemployment

desempolvar VT to dust off

desencadenar VT (quitar las cadenas) to unchain; (producir algo) to trigger, to spark

desencajado ADJ (mandíbula) dislocated; (mirada) wild; **estaba — en el funeral** he was deeply disturbed at the funeral

desencajar VT (un cajón) to unstick; (la mandíbula) to dislocate

desencantar VT (desilusionar) to disillusion; (quitar un hechizo) to remove a spell from

desencanto M disillusion

desenchufar VI/VT to unplug

desenfadado ADJ uninhibited

desenfado M lack of inhibition

desenfrenadamente ADV with wild abandon

desenfrenado ADJ (sin moderación) unbridled, wanton, rampant; (muy rápido) reckless

desenganchar VT to unhook

desengañar VT to disabuse; —**se** (de un error) to become disabused; (de una ilusión) to become disillusioned

desengaño M disillusion

desengranar VT to take out of gear

desenmarañar VT to disentangle

desenmascarar VT to unmask, to expose

desenredar VT to disentangle

desenrollar VT to unroll

desenroscar VT to untwist

desentenderse[1] VI to pay no attention

desentendido ADJ **hacerse el** — to pretend not to notice / know

desenterrar[1] VT (una cosa) to unearth, to dig up; (un cadáver) to disinter

desentonado ADJ out of tune

desentonar VI (cantar mal) to sing off key; (estar fuera de lugar) to be out of place

desentrañar VT to unravel

desenvoltura F self-assurance

desenvolver[2,51] VT (desenrollar) to unroll; (quitar la envoltura) to unwrap; —**se** to behave

desenvuelto ADJ self-assured

deseo M desire, wish; (sexual) desire; **pedir un** — to make a wish

deseoso ADJ desirous

desequilibrado -da ADJ unbalanced; MF unbalanced person

desequilibrar VT to unbalance

desequilibrio M imbalance

deserción F desertion

desertar VI/VT to desert; — **de** to defect from

desértico ADJ desert

desertor -ora MF deserter

desesperación F desperation

desesperado ADJ desperate

desesperanza F despair, hopelessness

desesperanzado ADJ hopeless

desesperanzar[9] VT to discourage, to deprive of hope; —**se** to despair

desesperar VI to despair; VT to drive crazy

desestabilizar[9] VT to destabilize

desestimación F rejection

desestimar VT to reject

desfachatez F audacity

desfalcar[6] VT to embezzle

desfalco M embezzlement

desfallecer[13] VI (debilitarse) to grow weak; (desmayarse) to faint

desfallecimiento M (debilidad) weakness; (desmayo) faint

desfavorable ADJ unfavorable

desfibrilar VT to defibrillate

desfigurar VT (el rostro) to disfigure; (una estatua) to deface

desfiladero M narrow passage

desfilar VI to file by; (soldados, modelos) to parade

desfile M parade

desgana F (falta de apetito) lack of appetite; (falta de entusiasmo) lack of enthusiasm

desganado ADJ without enthusiasm

desgarbado ADJ ungainly, gawky

desgarrado ADJ (prenda) torn; (grito) heart-rending

desgarradura F tear
desgarrar VT (rasgar) to tear; (causar dolor)
to break one's heart; —**se** to tear, to pull
desgarro M muscle pull
desgarrón M tear
desgastar VT to wear away; —**se** to get worn
away
desgaste M wear and tear
desglosar VT (una suma) to itemize; (un
documento) to separate out
desgracia F (infortunio) misfortune;
(infelicidad) unhappiness; —**s personales**
casualties; **caer en** — to fall into disgrace /
disfavor
desgraciado -da ADJ (desafortunado)
unfortunate; (infeliz) unhappy; MF
(persona desafortunada) unfortunate
person
desgranar VT (granos) to thrash, to thresh;
(guisantes) to shell
desgravable ADJ tax-deductible
desgreñado ADJ disheveled, unkempt
desgreñar VT to dishevel; —**se** to muss up
one's hair
desguazar[9] VT to scrap
deshabitado ADJ (territorio) uninhabited;
(casa) vacant
deshacer[30] VT (una acción) to undo; (una
cama) to strip; (una cosa) to destroy; (un
sólido en un líquido) to dissolve; (un
nudo) to untie; — **la maleta** to unpack
the suitcase; —**se de** to get rid of; —**se en
elogios** to rave about
desharrapado ADJ ragged
deshelar[1] VT to thaw
desheredar VT to disinherit
deshielo M thaw
deshierbar VT to weed
deshilachar VT to unravel
deshojado ADJ leafless
deshojar VT to strip of leaves; —**se** (un árbol)
to shed leaves; (un libro) to lose pages
deshonestidad F (falta de honradez)
dishonesty; (falta de recato) immodesty
deshonesto ADJ (no honrado) dishonest; (no
modesto) immodest
deshonra F dishonor, disgrace
deshonrar VT to dishonor, to disgrace
deshonroso ADJ dishonorable
deshora LOC ADV **a** — at an inopportune
time; **comer a** — to eat between meals
deshuesar VT (un fruto) to stone; (un
animal) to bone
deshumanizar[9] VT to dehumanize
desidia F indolence
desierto ADJ (lugar) deserted; (premio)
unawarded; M (región árida) desert;

(región poco fértil y no habitada)
wilderness
designación F (acción de designar, nombre)
designation; (nombramiento)
appointment
designar VT to designate; (a un funcionario)
to appoint
designio M design
desigual ADJ (pelea) one-sided; (actuación)
uneven; (números) not equal; (rango)
unequal; (terreno) uneven
desigualdad F inequality; (del terreno)
roughness
desilusión F disillusion, disappointment
desilusionar VT to disillusion, to disappoint;
—**se** to become disillusioned /
disappointed
desinencia F ending
desinfectante ADJ & M disinfectant
desinfectar VT to disinfect
desinflado ADJ (globo, persona) deflated;
(neumático) flat; M flat tire
desinflar VT to deflate
desinformación F disinformation
desinformar VT to misinform
desinhibido ADJ uninhibited
desintegración F disintegration; —
atómica atomic decay
desintegrarse VI to disintegrate; (materia
radiactiva) to decay
desinterés M (falta de interés) lack of
interest; (generosidad) unselfishness
desinteresado ADJ (que no muestra interés)
disinterested; (generoso) unselfish, selfless
desistir VI to desist
deslavado ADJ faded
deslavar VT (quitar color) to fade; (lavar
ligeramente) to wash superficially
desleal ADJ (persona) disloyal, faithless;
(competencia) unfair
desleír[15] VT to mix with a liquid
deslindar VT to mark off
desliz M slipup
deslizamiento M slide, glide
deslizar[9] VT (un patín) to slip, to slide, to
glide; (una tarjeta) to swipe; —**se** (un
patín) to slide, to glide; (un error) to slip
by
deslucido ADJ (actuación) dull; (color) dingy
deslucir[13b] VT (un espectáculo) to tarnish;
(color) to make dingy
deslumbramiento M dazzle
deslumbrante ADJ dazzling
deslumbrar VT to dazzle; —**se** to be dazzled
deslustrar VT to tarnish
deslustre M tarnish
desmadejado ADJ (fatigado) exhausted;

(desgarbado) ungainly

desmadejar VT to exhaust

desmán M abuse

desmantelar VT to dismantle

desmañado ADJ awkward, clumsy

desmayar VI to lose courage; **—se** to faint, to pass out

desmayo M faint, swoon; **peleó sin —** he fought unflaggingly

desmedido ADJ excessive

desmejorar VI (empeorar el aspecto) to look worse; (debilitarse) to get worse

desmembrar VT to dismember

desmentido M denial

desmentir[3] VT to deny

desmenuzar[9] VT (pan) to crumble; (zanahorias) to mince

desmerecer[13] VT **no — de** to compare favorably with

desmesurado ADJ (esfuerzo) inordinate; (orejas) too large

desmigajar VT to crumb, to crumble

desmitificar[6] VT to debunk

desmochar VT to top, to cut the top off of

desmontar VT (limpiar un monte) to clear; (desarmar) to dismantle, to take apart; (derribar de una caballería) to throw; **—se** to dismount

desmoralizar[9] VT to demoralize; **—se** to become demoralized

desmoronar VT to crumble

desmovilizar[9] VT to demobilize

desnatar VT to skim

desnaturalizado ADJ (madre) unnatural; (aceite) denatured

desnudar VT to undress; **—se** to get undressed

desnudez F nakedness

desnudo ADJ nude, naked

desnutrición F malnutrition

desnutrido ADJ underfed, malnourished

desobedecer[13] VT to disobey

desobediencia F disobedience; **— civil** civil disobedience

desobediente ADJ disobedient

desocupación F (paro) unemployment; (abandono de vivienda) vacating

desocupado ADJ (asiento, casa) unoccupied, empty; (tiempo) idle; (que no trabaja) unemployed

desocupar VT to vacate; **—se** to get free

desodorante M deodorant

desoír[35] VT to turn a deaf ear to

desolación F desolation

desolado ADJ desolate, bleak

desolar VT to lay waste to, to desolate; **—se** to be desolated

desollar[2] VT to skin; **— vivo** to skin alive

desorbitado ADJ out of proportion; (ojos) bulging

desorden M disorder, disarray; **— público** public disturbance; **en —** in disarray

desordenado ADJ (persona, situación) messy; (niño, vida) wild; (cuarto) untidy, disorderly; (archivo) disorganized

desordenar VT to mess up

desorganización F disorganization

desorganizado ADJ disorganized

desorientar VT to disorient; (confundir) to confuse; **—se** to lose one's bearings, to become disoriented

desovar VT to spawn

desoxidar VT to deoxidize

despabilado ADJ (despierto) wide-awake; (listo) on the ball

despabilar VT (cortar el pabilo) to trim the wick of; (despertar) to awaken; **—se** to wake up

despachar VT (problemas) to dispatch; (una carta) to mail; (a un cliente) to take care of; (mercancías) to ship; (a una víctima) to bump off; (un pedido) to fill; **— al público** to sell to the public; **—se a su gusto** to speak one's mind

despacho M (oficina) office; (comunicación) dispatch; (envío de cartas) mailing; (envío de mercancías) shipping

despachurrar VT to squash

despacio ADV slow, slowly

desparasitar VT to worm

desparejo ADJ uneven

desparpajo M (desenvoltura) ease; (descaro) impudence

desparramar VT to scatter; **—se** to be scattered

desparramo M (lío) commotion; (de libros) clutter

despatarrarse VT (caerse) to sprawl; (abrirse de piernas) to spread one's legs

despecho M spite; **por —** out of spite

despectivo ADJ derogatory, pejorative

despedazar[9] VT to tear to pieces

despedida F farewell; **— de soltero** bachelor party

despedir[5] VT (acompañar a una persona que se va) to see off; (echar de un empleo) to fire, to dismiss; (emitir un dolor) to emit, to give off; **despídeme de tus padres** say good-bye to your parents for me; **—se (de)** to take leave (of), to say good-bye (to)

despegar[7] VT (dos cosas pegadas) to detach; VI (un avión) to take off; (un cohete) to blast off; **—se** to become detached

despegue M (de avión) takeoff; (de cohete) blastoff, liftoff

despeinado ADJ unkempt

despejado ADJ (el cielo) clear, cloudless; (un camino) clear; (la frente) with one's hair pulled back; (una persona) bright

despejar VT (el campo) to clear; VI (una duda, el cielo) to clear up; **—se** to sober up

despellejar VT to skin

despensa F pantry

despeñadero M cliff

despeñar VT to push off a precipice; **—se** to fall down a precipice

despepitar VT (una granada) to seed; (una manzana) to core; **—se por una cosa** to be crazy about something

desperdiciar VT to waste; **—se** to go to waste

desperdicio M waste; **—s** scraps

desperdigar[7] VT to scatter; **—se** to be scattered

desperezarse[9] VI to stretch

desperezo M stretch

desperfecto M damage; **— mecánico** mechanical breakdown

despertador M alarm clock

despertar[1] VT (a una persona) to awaken, to wake up; (sospecha) to arouse; (interés, deseo) to kindle; **—se** to wake up

despiadado ADJ merciless, heartless, ruthless

despido M dismissal, termination

despierto ADJ (no dormido) awake; (vivaracho) alert

despilfarrador ADJ wasteful

despilfarrar VT to squander

despilfarro M waste

despistado ADJ absent-minded

despistar VT to throw off the track; (a un perseguidor) to lose; **—se** to get confused

desplantador M trowel

desplante M rude remark

desplazar[9] VT to displace; **—se** to move

desplegar[1,7] VT (algo plegado) to unfold; (una bandera) to unfurl; (tropas) to deploy; (interés) to display

despliegue M display

desplomarse VI (edificio, precios) to collapse; (una persona) to slump

desplome M collapse

desplumar VT (un ave) to pluck; (a una víctima) to fleece

despoblado ADJ uninhabited; **— de árboles** treeless; M open country

despojar VT to despoil; **—se** to shed leaves

despojos M PL (de batalla) spoils; (mortales) remains

desportilladura F chip

desportillar VT to chip

desposeer VT to dispossess

déspota MF INV despot

despótico ADJ despotic

despotismo M despotism

despotricar[6] VI to rant

despreciable ADJ (vil) contemptible, despicable, worthless; (insignificante) negligible

despreciar VT (menospreciar) to despise, to look down on; (rechazar) to snub

desprecio M (menosprecio) contempt, disdain; (rechazo) snub

desprender VT (un cierre) to unfasten; (algo prendido) to detach; (gases) to give off; **—se de algo** to part with something; **—se la ropa** to undo one's clothes; **de lo dicho se desprende que** from what has been said it follows that

desprendimiento M (de retina) detachment; (de energía) release; (de tierra) landslide; (generosidad) generosity

despreocupado ADJ carefree

desprestigiar VT to discredit; **—se** to lose one's prestige

desprestigio M loss of prestige

desprevenido ADJ unprepared; **tomar —** to take by surprise

desproporcionado ADJ disproportionate, out of proportion

despropósito M nonsense

desprovisto ADJ **— de** lacking in

después ADV after, afterward; **— de** after; **— de todo** after all

despuntar VI/VT to blunt; **—se** to become blunt

desquiciar VT to unhinge; **—se** to come unhinged

desquitarse VI to get even

desquite M getting even

desregular VT to deregulate

destacado ADJ outstanding

destacamento M military detachment, military detail

destacar[6] VT (tropas) to detach; (una cualidad) to accentuate; VI to stand out; **—se** to stand out

destajo LOC ADV **a —** by the job

destapar VT (una cacerola) to take the top off of; (un plan, a un niño) to uncover; **—se** (en la cama) to uncover; (desnudarse) to bare all

destartalado ADJ dilapidated

destellar VI to flash

destello M flash

destemplado ADJ (persona) feverish; (sonido)

out of tune

desteñido ADJ washed-out

desteñir[5, 18] VI/VT to fade; VI to run; **—se** to fade

desternillarse VI **— de risa** to die laughing

desterrado -da ADJ exiled, banished; MF exile

desterrar[1] VT to exile, to banish

destetar VT to wean

destierro M exile, banishment

destilación F distillation

destilar VT to distill

destilería F distillery

destinar VT (determinar el destino) to destine; (dirigir) to address; (asignar) to commit

destinatario -ria MF addressee, recipient

destino M (hado) destiny, fate, lot; (uso) use; (lugar adonde se viaja) destination

destitución F dismissal

destituir[31] VT to dismiss

destornillador M screwdriver

destoxificación F detoxification

destrabar VT to untie

destreza F dexterity, skill

destripar VT to gut

destronar VT to dethrone

destrozar[9] VT (estropear) to ruin; (causar grandes daños) to destroy; (derrotar) to rout

destrozo M damage

destrucción F destruction

destructible ADJ destructible

destructivo ADJ destructive

destructor -ra ADJ destructive; M (buque) destroyer; MF (persona) destroyer

destruir[31] VT (reducir a pedazos) to destroy, to obliterate; (estropear) to ruin

desunir VT to divide; **—se** to come apart

desusado ADJ (no frecuente) unusual; (no usado) obsolete

desuso M disuse, obsolescence; **caer en —** to fall into disuse

desvaído ADJ faded

desvainar VT to hull, to husk

desvalido ADJ helpless

desvalijar VT (un cuarto) to ransack; (a una persona) to clean out

desvalimiento M helplessness

desván M attic

desvanecer[13] VT (un color) to fade; (un contorno) to blur; **—se** (una persona) to faint; (un color, arrugas) to fade; (un sonido) to trail off

desvanecido ADJ (una persona) fainted; (un color) faded; (un contorno) blurred

desvanecimiento M (de una persona)

fainting; (de colores) fading; (de un contorno) blurring

desvariar[16] VI to rave

desvarío M raving

desvelado ADJ sleepless

desvelar VT to keep awake; **—se** to be sleepless

desvelo M (falta de sueño) sleeplessness; **—s** (esfuerzos) efforts

desvencijado ADJ dilapidated, rickety; **estoy —** I'm all beat up

desventaja F disadvantage; **estar en —** to be at a disadvantage

desventura F misfortune

desventurado ADJ unfortunate

desvergonzado ADJ shameless

desvergüenza F shamelessness

desvestir[5] VT to undress; **—se** to get undressed, to undress

desviación F (de una norma) deviation, divergence; (para coches) detour; (de fondos) diversion; (de la columna vertebral) curvature; **— estándar** standard deviation

desviar[16] VT (la vista) to avert; (fondos, tráfico) to divert; (un golpe) to ward off; (una conversación) to steer; (un tren) to sidetrack; **—se de** (un camino) to stray from; (una norma) to deviate from

desvío M (camino secundario) side road; (desviación) detour

desvirtuar[17] VT to distort; **—se** to become distorted

desvivirse VI **— por hacer algo** to bend over backward to do something; **— por alguien** to go out of one's way for someone

detallado ADJ detailed

detallar VT to detail, to go into detail about

detalle M (pormenor) detail; (venta al por menor) retail; (lista) list; **¡qué —!** how thoughtful! **con / al / en —** in detail

detallista ADJ (cuidadoso) meticulous; (considerado) thoughtful; M (comercio) retail; MF retailer

detectar VT to detect

detective M detective; **— privado** private eye

detención F (arresto) detention, arrest; (de un vehículo) stop; **— domiciliaria** house arrest; **— ilegal** false arrest

detener[44] VT (arrestar) to detain, to arrest; (parar) to stop; **—se** to stop; **—se en** to linger on; **—se a pensar** to stop to think

detenido ADJ thorough

detenimiento LOC ADV **con —** with care

detergente ADJ & M detergent

deteriorar VT to deteriorate
deterioro M deterioration
determinación F determination
determinar VT to determine
detestable ADJ detestable
detestar VT to detest
detonación F detonation; **hacer detonaciones** to backfire
detonar VI/VT to detonate
detrás ADV behind; **— de** (en el espacio) behind; (en el tiempo) after; **por —** behind
detritus M debris
deuda F debt
deudor -ora ADJ & MF debtor; **— hipotecario** mortgagor
devaluación F devaluation
devanar VT to spool; **—se los sesos** to rack one's brain
devaneo M (acción de pasatiempo) idle pursuit; (amorío) fling
devastar VT to devastate
devengar[7] VT to earn
devoción F devotion
devolución F return
devolver[2,51] VT (volver al dueño) to return; VI (vomitar) to throw up
devorar VT to devour
devoto ADJ (pío) devout; (que muestra devoción) devoted
dextrosa F dextrose
día M day; **— a —** day-to-day; **— tras —** day after day; **al —** up-to-date; **al otro —** on the next day; **de —** by day; **de todos los —s** everyday; **el — de mañana** in the future; **hoy —** nowadays; **no veo el —** I can't wait; **ponerse al —** to catch up; **por —** by the day; **todo el —** all day; **todos los —s** every day; **un — sí y otro no** every other day; **vivir al —** to live from hand to mouth
diabetes F SG diabetes
diablo M devil; **pobre —** poor devil; **¿por qué —s dices eso?** *fam* why the heck are you saying that?
diablura F deviltry, mischief
diabólico ADJ diabolic, devilish
diácono M deacon
diacrítico ADJ & M diacritic
diafragma M diaphragm
diagnosticar[6] VT to diagnose
diagonal ADJ & F diagonal
diagrama M diagram; **— de flujo** flow chart
dial M dial
dialéctica F dialectic
dialéctico ADJ dialectic
dialecto M dialect

dialectología F dialectology
diálisis F dialysis
dialogar[7] VI to dialog, to hold talks
diálogo M dialog, conversation; **— de sordos** conversation in which no one listens
diamante M diamond; **— en bruto** diamond in the rough
diámetro M diameter
diana F bull's eye
diapasón M tuning fork
diapositiva F slide
diario ADJ daily; M (periódico) newspaper; (de sucesos personales) journal, diary; (de navegación) log; **a —** every day; **de —** everyday; **llevar un —** to keep a diary
diarrea F diarrhea
diatriba F diatribe
dibujante MF illustrator
dibujar VT to draw; **—se** to appear, to loom
dibujo M (arte de dibujar, cosa dibujada) drawing; (diseño) design; **— al carbón** charcoal drawing; **—s animados** animated cartoon
dicción F diction
diccionario M dictionary
dicha F happiness
dicharachero ADJ witty
dicho ADJ aforementioned; M saying
dichoso ADJ happy; **todo el — día** the whole blessed day
diciembre M December
dicotomía F dichotomy
dictado M (ejercicio) dictation; (orden) dictate; **escribir al —** to take dictation
dictador -ora MF dictator
dictadura F dictatorship
dictamen M (opinión) report; (judicial) ruling
dictaminar VI (dar una opinión) to report; (fallar) to rule
dictar VT to dictate; **— clase** to teach class; **— sentencia** to rule
diecinueve NUM nineteen
dieciocho NUM eighteen
dieciséis NUM sixteen
diecisiete NUM seventeen
diente M (de persona, sierra) tooth; (de víbora) fang; (de rueda dentada) cog; (de tenedor) prong; **— de león** dandelion; **— de leche** baby tooth; **—s postizos** false teeth; **entre —s** under one's breath; **tener buen —** to have a good appetite
diesel M diesel
diestra F right hand
diestro -tra ADJ (habilidoso) skillful, deft; (no zurdo) right-handed; MF right-handed

person; **a diestra y siniestra** on all sides
dieta F diet; **estar a —** to be on a diet
diez NUM ten
diezmar VT to decimate
diezmo M tithe; **pagar el —** to tithe
difamación F (oral) slander; (escrito) libel
difamar VT to defame, to malign; (oralmente) to slander; (por escrito) to libel
difamatorio ADJ slanderous
diferencia F difference; **a — de** unlike; **hacer —s entre** to treat differently; **partir la —** to split the difference
diferencial ADJ & M (distancia, pieza de coche) differential; F (matemática) differential
diferenciar VT to differentiate; **—se de** to differ from
diferente ADJ different
diferir[3] VT (aplazar) to defer; VI (ser diferente) to differ
difícil ADJ difficult, hard
dificultad F difficulty
dificultar VT to make difficult
dificultoso ADJ difficult
difteria F diphtheria
difundir VT (luz) to diffuse; (noticias) to broadcast
difunto -ta ADJ & MF deceased
difusión F (de luz) diffusion; (de noticias) broadcasting
difuso ADJ diffuse
digerible ADJ digestible
digerir[3] VT to digest
digestible ADJ digestible
digestión F digestion
digestivo ADJ digestive
digesto M digest
digital ADJ digital
dígito M digit
dignarse VI to deign
dignatario -ria MF dignitary
dignidad F dignity
digno ADJ (respetable) worthy; (orgulloso) dignified; **— de confianza** trustworthy; **— de elogio** praiseworthy
digresión F digression
dije M charm
dilación LOC ADV **sin —** without delay
dilatación F (de un metal, parte dilatada) expansion; (del ojo) dilation
dilatar VT (pupila, capilares, útero) to dilate; (metal, músculo) to expand; (posponer) to defer; **—se en un asunto** to dwell on a subject
dilema M dilemma
diletante MF dilettante

diligencia F (laboriosidad) diligence, industry; (vehículo) stagecoach
diligente ADJ diligent, industrious
dilucidar VT to elucidate
diluido ADJ dilute
diluir[31] VT (una solución) to dilute; (pintura, sopa) to thin
diluvio M deluge
dimensión F dimension
dimes M PL **— y diretes** gossip; **andar en — y diretes** to quibble
diminutivo ADJ & M diminutive
diminuto ADJ (tamaño) diminutive; (cantidad) minute
dimisión F resignation
dimitir VI to resign
Dinamarca F Denmark
dinámica F dynamics
dinámico ADJ dynamic
dinamismo M vigor
dinamita F dynamite
dinamitar VT to dynamite
dínamo M dynamo
dinastía F dynasty
dineral M fortune
dinero M money; **— contante y sonante** ready cash, hard cash; **— de plástico** plastic, credit card; **— sucio** dirty money
dinosaurio M dinosaur
diodo M diode; **— electroluminiscente** light-emitting diode
Dios M God; **dios** god; **— dirá** we'll see; **los cría y ellos se juntan** birds of a feather flock together; **— mediante** God willing; **¡— mío!** my God! **— te lo pague** may God reward you; **— y su madre** everybody and their dog; **a la buena de —** any old way; **como — manda** as it should be; **¡por —!** oh, my! **que — te oiga** I hope you're right
diosa F goddess
diploma M diploma
diplomacia F diplomacy
diplomático -ca ADJ diplomatic; MF diplomat
diptongo M diphthong
diputación F council
diputado -da MF representative
dique M (presa) dike; (al lado de un río) levee; **— seco** dry dock
dirección F (sentido, rumbo) direction; (domicilio) address; (administración) management; (oficina de administración de una escuela) principal's office; (mecanismo para conducir, acción de conducir) steering; **— asistida** power steering

directiva F (orden) directive; (norma) guideline; (junta de directores) board of directors

directivo -va ADJ leadership; MF officer

directo ADJ (sin desviaciones, intermediarios) direct; (derecho) straight; **en —** live

director -ora MF (de una empresa) director, manager; (de una escuela) principal; (de orquesta) conductor; **— de correos** postmaster

directorio M (índice) directory; (junta directiva) board of directors

dirigente MF leader; **— sindical** union leader

dirigible M dirigible

dirigir[11] VT (una obra teatral) to direct; (una empresa) to manage; (una orquesta) to conduct; (a un turista) to guide; (un saludo, una carta, una pregunta, una crítica) to address; **—se a** (hablar con) to address; (ir a) to go to; (tratar de) to be aimed at.

discar[6] VI/VT *Am* to dial

discernimiento M discernment, insight

discernir[1] VT to discern

disciplina F discipline

disciplinar VT to discipline

discípulo -la MF disciple

disco M (cartílago, objeto plano y circular) disk; (fonográfico) record; **— compacto** compact disk; **— duro** hard disk; **es un — rayado** he's a broken record

díscolo ADJ unruly

disconforme ADJ dissatisfied

discontinuo ADJ discontinuous

discordancia F discord

discordia F discord

discoteca F (lugar donde bailar) discotheque; (colección de discos) record collection

discreción F discretion; **a —** at one's own discretion

discrepancia F discrepancy

discrepar VI to disagree; **— de** to take issue with

discreto ADJ (prudente) discreet; (de unidades indivisibles) discrete; **un partido —** a sorry game

discriminación F discrimination; **— positiva** affirmative action

discriminar VI to discriminate; **— a** to discriminate against

disculpa F (excusa) excuse; (perdón) apology

disculpable ADJ excusable

disculpar VT (excusar) to excuse; (perdonar) to forgive, to pardon; **—se** to apologize

discurrir VI (transcurrir) to pass; (exponer) to discourse

discursear VI to make speeches

discurso M (enunciado) discourse; (alocución pública) speech, address; **— de apertura** keynote address

discusión F (charla) discussion; (riña) argument

discutible ADJ debatable, questionable

discutir VT (hablar sobre) to discuss; (oponerse a) to dispute; VI (reñir) to argue

disecar[6] VT (cortar) to dissect; (preparar para conservar) to stuff

diseminación F dissemination

diseminar VT to disseminate

disensión F dissension, dissent

disenso M dissent

disentería F dysentery

disentir[3] VI to dissent, to disagree

diseñador -ora MF designer

diseñar VT to design

diseño M design; **— de interiores** interior design; **— gráfico** graphic design

disertación F lecture

disertar VI to lecture

disfraz M (para ocultarse) disguise; (de carnaval) costume

disfrazar[9] VT to disguise

disfrutar VI/VT to enjoy; **— de** to enjoy

disfrute M enjoyment

disfunción F dysfunction

disgustado ADJ (molesto) upset; (enojado) angry

disgustar VT to upset; **—se** (molestarse) to get upset; (enfadarse) to get angry

disgusto M (desagrado) unpleasantness; (discusión) quarrel; **a —** (con desgana) against one's will; (con incomodidad) uncomfortably; (en disconformidad) in conflict; **esa niña no da más que —s** that girl keeps us upset all the time

disidente ADJ & MF dissident

disimulado ADJ **hacerse el —** to pretend not to notice

disimular VI (fingir) to dissemble; (ocultar) to conceal

disimulo M (fingimiento) dissimulation; (ocultamiento) concealment

disipación F dissipation

disipar VT (niebla, calor) to dissipate; (dudas) to dispel; (miedo) to allay; (dinero) to squander; **—se** to dissipate; (miedo, dudas) to allay, to lift

dislocar[6] VT to dislocate; **—se** to get dislocated

disminuir[31] VT to diminish, to decrease, to lessen; (despreciar) to belittle

disolución F dissolution

disoluto ADJ dissolute, loose

disolvente M solvent; **— de pintura** paint thinner

disolver[2,51] VT to dissolve; (una reunión) to break up

disonancia F discord

dispar ADJ disparate

disparar VT (un arma de fuego) to shoot, to fire; (una cámara) to click; (la inflación) to trigger; VI (en fútbol) to shoot; **—le a alguien** to shoot at someone; **—se** (aumentar) to take off; (salir) to shoot out

disparatado ADJ absurd

disparatar VI to talk nonsense

disparate M absurdity, nonsense; **decir —s** to talk nonsense; **un — de plata** a ton of money

disparo M (acción de disparar) shooting; (tiro, herida) shot

dispensa F dispensation

dispensación F dispensation

dispensar VT to dispense; **— de** to exempt from

dispensario M dispensary

dispersar VT to disperse

dispersión F dispersal

display M display

displicencia F flippancy

displicente ADJ (comportamiento) flippant; (actitud) cavalier

disponer[39] VT (colocar) to arrange; (preparar) to prepare, to dispose; (mandar) to order; **— de** to have; **—se** to get ready; **—se a** to set about

disponible ADJ available

disposición F (voluntad) disposition; (colocación) arrangement; (de ánimo) mood; **a — de** at the disposal of

dispositivo M device; **— intrauterino** intrauterine device

dispuesto ADJ ready; **bien —** willing; **no estar — a** to be unwilling to

disputa F (controversia) dispute; (riña) argument

disputar VI/VT to dispute; **—se el poder** to vie / challenge / contend for power; **—se la posición** to jockey for position

disquete M floppy disk

disquetera F disk drive

distancia F distance; **a —** at arm's length; **guardar —s** to keep at a distance; **¿a qué — está?** how far away is it?

distanciar VT to distance

distante ADJ distant

distar VI **dista mucho de** it's a far cry from; **dista diez kilómetros de** it's ten kilometers from

distender[1] VT (aflojar) to relax; (dilatar) to expand

distinción F distinction

distinguido ADJ distinguished

distinguir[12] VT to distinguish

distintivo ADJ distinctive, distinguishing; M distinguishing characteristic

distinto ADJ (diferente, no el mismo) different; (que se percibe con claridad) distinct

distorsión F distortion

distorsionar VT to distort

distracción F distraction

distraer[45] VT (la atención) to distract; (fondos, mano de obra) to divert; **—se** to entertain oneself

distraído ADJ distracted, absent-minded; **hacerse el —** to play dumb

distribución F distribution

distribuidor -ora MF (persona) distributor; M (pieza de un motor) distributor

distribuir[31] VT to distribute

distrito M district

Distrito de Columbia M District of Columbia

disturbio M disturbance, trouble

disuadir VT (mediante palabras) to dissuade; (mediante acciones) to deter

diurético ADJ & M diuretic

diurno ADJ (actividad) daytime; (animal) diurnal

divagación F rambling

divagar[7] VI to ramble on, to digress

diván M divan; (de psiquiatra) couch

divergencia F divergence

divergir[11] VI to diverge

diversidad F diversity

diversión F (pasatiempo) amusement, entertainment, fun; (hecho de distraer la atención) diversion

diverso ADJ diverse; **—s** various

divertido ADJ amusing, entertaining

divertir[3] VT to amuse, to entertain; **—se** to have a good time, to have fun

dividendo M dividend

dividir VT to divide; (un territorio conquistado) to partition

divieso M boil

divinidad F divinity

divino ADJ divine; **estuvo —** it was heavenly; **lo pasé —** I had a wonderful time

divisa F (señal) emblem; (moneda) currency; (moneda extranjera) foreign currency

divisar VT to make out, to catch sight of

división F division; (de un territorio conquistado) partition

divisorio ADJ dividing

divorciar VT to divorce; **—se** to get divorced

divorcio M divorce

divulgar[7] VT (un secreto) to divulge; (información) to disseminate

dobladillo M hem; **hacer —s** to hem

doblaje M dubbing

doblar VT (una sábana) to fold; (el capital) to double; (una esquina) to turn; (la voz de un actor) to dub; VI (un coche) to turn; (una campana) to knell; **—se** to bend over

doble ADJ double; **— agente** double agent; **— personalidad** split personality; **— visión** double vision; **de — caño** double-barreled; **de — filo** double-edged; **de — sentido** two-way; MF (persona muy parecida, actor sustituto) double; M (repique) knell; **—s** doubles; **el — double**

doblegar[7] VT to break

doblez M fold; F deceitfulness

doce NUM twelve

docena F dozen; **— del fraile** baker's dozen

docente ADJ teaching

dócil ADJ (persona, animal) docile, pliant; (pelo) manageable

docto ADJ learned

doctor -ora MF doctor

doctorado M doctorate

doctrina F doctrine

documental ADJ & M documentary

documentar VT to document

documento M document

dogma M dogma

dogmático ADJ dogmatic

dogo M pug

dólar M dollar

dolencia F ailment

doler[2] VI to ache, to hurt; **me duele el brazo** my arm aches, my arm is sore; **—se** (compadecerse) to feel sorry for; (arrepentirse) to regret

doliente MF mourner

dolor M (físico) pain, ache; (espiritual) sorrow, pain; **— de barriga** bellyache; **— de cabeza** headache; **— de espalda** backache; **— de muela** toothache; **— de oídos** earache; **— de garganta** sore throat

dolorido ADJ aching, sore

doloroso ADJ painful

doma F (de caballos) breaking; (de leones) taming

domado ADJ (caballo) broken; (león) tamed

domador -ora MF (de perros) trainer; (de leones) lion tamer

domar VT (caballos, personas) to break; (leones) to tame

domesticar[6] VT to domesticate, to tame

doméstico -ca ADJ domestic; MF servant

domiciliarse VI to take up residence; **¿dónde se domicilia usted?** where do you reside?

domicilio M (casa) dwelling; (dirección) address

dominación F domination

dominador ADJ (predominante) dominant; (tiránico) domineering

dominante ADJ (predominante) dominant; (tiránico) domineering, overbearing

dominar VT (tener bajo su autoridad, ser más alto) to dominate; (reprimir los impulsos) to control, to rein in; (tener sometido a su voluntad) to domineer

domingo M Sunday; **— de Ramos** Palm Sunday; **— de Pascua** Easter Sunday

Dominica F Dominica

dominicano -na ADJ & MF Dominican

dominio M (sobre una tierra, derecho de usar una cosa) dominion; (de sí mismo) control; (de una lengua) mastery, command; (hecho de dominar) domination; (ámbito, campo) domain; **— público** public domain

dominiqués -esa ADJ & MF Dominican

dominó M (pieza) domino; (juego) dominoes

domo M dome

don M (gracia) gift; (título, jefe mafioso) don; **un — nadie** a nobody

dona F _Méx_ doughnut

donación F donation

donador -ora MF donor

donaire M grace

donante MF donor

donar MF to donate

doncella F _lit_ maiden

donde ADV REL where; **de — whence, from which; ir — el herrero** to go to the blacksmith's shop; **— no** otherwise; **—quiera** wherever

dónde ADV INTERR where

donoso ADJ graceful

doña F doña

dopar VT to dope

dorado ADJ (cubierto de oro) gilt; (del color de oro) golden; M dolphinfish

dorar VT to gild; **— la píldora** to sweeten the pill

dormido ADJ asleep

dormir[4] VI/VT to sleep; **— a** to put to bed; **— a un paciente** to anesthetize a patient; **— la mona** to sleep it off; **— la siesta** to take a nap; **se me ha dormido el brazo** my arm has fallen asleep; **—se** to fall asleep

dormitar VI to doze, to snooze

dormitorio M bedroom

dorso M back, reverse

dos NUM two; **— puntos** colon; **— veces** twice; **cada — por tres** constantly; **en un — por tres** in a jiffy; **los —** both of them

DOS M DOS

dosel M canopy

dosificar[6] VT to dose

dosis F (de medicamento) dose; (de droga) hit

dotación F (de fondos) endowment; (de personal) complement

dotar VT to endow

dote F dowry; **—s** talents

draga F dredge

dragado M dredging

dragar[7] VT (para limpiar) to dredge; (para buscar objetos) to drag; M SG **dragaminas** minesweeper

dragón M (animal fantástico) dragon; (planta) snapdragon

drama M drama

dramático ADJ dramatic

dramatizar[9] VT to dramatize

dramaturgo -ga MF playwright, dramatist

drapear VI to drape

drástico ADJ drastic

drenaje M drainage

drenar VI/VT to drain

dribbling M dribble, dribbling

driblar VI/VT to dribble

dril M drill

drive M drive

drive-in M drive-in

driver M (de golf) driver

droga F drug; **—s de diseño** designer drugs; **tomar —s** to do drugs; MF **drogadicto -ta** drug addict

drogar[7] VT to drug

drogata MF INV junkie

drogota MF INV junkie

droguería F (tienda) drugstore; (industria) drug industry

droguero -ra MF druggist

ducado M dukedom

ducha F shower

ducharse VI to shower

ducho ADJ skillful

dúctil ADJ (metal) ductile; (persona) flexible, supple

duda F doubt; **en —** in doubt; **fuera de —** beyond doubt; **no cabe —** there's no doubt; **poner en —** to cast doubt on; **sin — without** a doubt, undoubtedly; **sin lugar a —s** without doubt; **tengo una**

— I have a question

dudar VT to doubt; (vacilar) to hesitate; **— de** to have doubts about

dudoso ADJ doubtful; **de dudosa honestidad** of dubious honesty

duela F stave

duelo M (combate) duel; (luto) mourning; (pena) grief; (dolientes) mourners; **estar de —** to be in mourning

duende M (gnomo) goblin, gremlin; (gracia) charm

dueño -ña MF owner; **me sentí — de la situación** I felt like I was in control of the situation; M landlord; F landlady

dueto M duet

dulce ADJ (sabor, personalidad) sweet; (clima) pleasant; (agua) fresh; **—amargo** bittersweet; M (cosa dulce) sweet; (mermelada) preserves, conserve

dulcería F confectionery

dulcificar[6] VT to sweeten

dulzón ADJ unpleasantly sweet

dulzor M sweetness

dulzura F sweetness

duna F dune

dúo M duet; **decir a —** to say in unison

dúplex M duplex

duplicado ADJ & M duplicate; **por —** in duplicate

duplicar[6] VT to duplicate

duplicidad F duplicity

duque M duke

duquesa F duchess

durabilidad F durability

duración F duration; (de una película, vocal) length

duradero ADJ (ropa) durable, serviceable; (pilas) long-lasting

durante PREP during; **— el mandato de los demócratas** under the Democrats; **— muchos años** for/over many years

durar VI/VT to last

duraznero M peach tree

durazno M (fruto) peach; (árbol) peach tree

dureza F (de metal) hardness; (del clima, de la expresión, de una tempestad) severity; (del invierno) harshness; (de un boxeador) toughness; (del cuero) stiffness

durmiente ADJ sleeping; M railroad tie, sleeper

duro ADJ (metal, golpe, droga, agua) hard; (clima, tormenta) severe; (invierno, expresión, sonido) harsh; (soldado) tough; (grifo) stuck; (viento) strong; (autoridad) inflexible; (pan) stale; (cuero) stiff; **— de corazón** hard-hearted; **— de entendederas** slow on the uptake; **a**

duras penas barely; M five peseta coin;
no tengo un — I'm flat broke
DVD M DVD

Ee

e CONJ and
ebanista MF cabinetmaker
ébano M ebony
ebrio ADJ drunk, inebriated
ebullición F boiling
eccema M eczema
echar VT (una pelota, redes) to throw, to cast;
(yemas, hojas) to sprout; (a un empleado)
to fire; (humo, olor) to give off; (un
líquido) to pour; (a un borracho) to throw
out; **— abajo** to knock down; **— a la
basura** to throw away; **— al mar** to put
out to sea; **— al correo** to mail; **— anclas** to
drop anchor; **— a pique** to sink; **—
carnes** to get fat; **— de menos** to miss;
— de ver to notice; **— mano de** to seize
upon; **— la culpa** to blame; **— por la
borda** to jettison; **— raíces** to take root;
— sangre to bleed; **— suertes** to draw
lots; **— una carta** to mail a letter; **—
una siesta** to take a nap; **— un vistazo
a** to glance at, to take a look at; **te echo
una carrera** I'll race you; **—le el
muerto a alguien** to pass the buck to
someone; **—se** to lie down; **—se a correr**
to bolt; **—se a** to start to; **—se a perder**
to spoil; **—se a reír** to burst out laughing;
—se a un lado to dodge; **—se para
atrás** to lean back; **—se atrás** to back
down
ecléctico ADJ eclectic
eclesiástico ADJ & M ecclesiastic
eclipsar VT to eclipse; (superar) to eclipse, to
outshine, to overshadow; **—se** to fade
eclipse M eclipse; **— de sol** solar eclipse; **—
de luna** lunar eclipse
eco M echo; **hacer —** to echo; **hacerse —
de** to repeat
ecología F (medio ambiente) environment;
(ciencia) ecology
ecológico ADJ environmental
ecologista ADJ environmental; MF
environmentalist
economato M commissary
economía F (conjunto de actividades de
producción) economy; (ciencia)
economics; (familiar) finances; **—**

doméstica home economics; **—s** savings;
hacer —s to be thrifty
económico ADJ (relativo a la economía)
economic; (que gasta poco) frugal, thrifty;
(que cuesta poco) economical
economista MF economist
economizar[9] VT to economize, to save
ecosistema M ecosystem
ecuación F equation
ecuador M equator
Ecuador M Ecuador
ecualizar[9] VT to equalize
ecuatoriano -na ADJ & MF Ecuadorian
ecuménico ADJ ecumenical
edad F age; **— avanzada** ripe old age; **—
mental** mental age; **— de Piedra** Stone
Age; **— Media** Middle Ages; **— de
merecer** marriageable age
edición F (tienda, ejemplar) edition; (acción
de editar) publication; **— de sobremesa**
desktop publishing
edicto M edict
edificación F building
edificar[6] VT (construir) to build; (infundir
sentimientos morales) to edify, to uplift
edificio M building
editar VT to edit, to publish
editor -ora ADJ publishing; MF editor
editorial ADJ publishing; F publishing house;
M editorial
editorializar[9] VI to editorialize
edredón M comforter
educación F (en la escuela) education; (de
normas sociales) breeding; **— a distancia**
distance learning; **— cívica** civics; **—
especial** special education; **— física**
physical education
educado ADJ (cortés) well-bred; (instruido)
educated
educador -ora MF educator
educar[6] VT (a una persona en la escuela) to
educate; (a una persona en la casa, la voz)
to train
educativo ADJ educational
edulcorante M sweetener
EEUU (Estados Unidos) M SG USA
efectivo ADJ (eficaz) effective; (real) actual;
hacer — (un cheque) to cash; (una
deuda) to pay off; (una amenaza) to make
good on; M cash; **en —** in cash; **—s** troops
efecto M (resultado) effect, result; (letra
comercial) bill of exchange; (rotación)
English, spin; **en —** in fact; **llevar a —** to
carry out; **surtir —** to work; **—
invernadero** green house effect; **—s
especiales** special effects; **—s personales**
personal effects; **perder —** to wear off;

rebotar con — to glance off; **a estos —s** to this effect; **para los —s** to all intents and purposes; **por — de** as a consequence of

efectuar[17] VT to effect; **—se** to be carried out

eficacia F efficacy; **— de una ley** force of law

eficaz ADJ effective

eficiencia F efficiency

eficiente ADJ efficient

efigie F effigy; **quemar en** — to burn in effigy

efímero ADJ ephemeral, fleeting

efusivo ADJ effusive

egipcio -cia ADJ & MF Egyptian

Egipto M Egypt

égloga F pastoral

ego M ego

egocéntrico ADJ egocentric, self-centered

egoísmo M selfishness

egoísta ADJ selfish; MF selfish person

egotismo M egotism

egresado -da MF graduate

eje M (de la Tierra) axis; (de un vehículo) axle; **— del pistón** piston rod; **eso me parte por el** — that messes me up

ejecución F (de un condenado) execution; (de un plan, una orden) carrying out, execution; (de una tarea) performance; (de una propiedad) foreclosure

ejecutar VT (a un condenado) to execute; (un plan, una orden) to carry out; (una tarea, música) to perform; (una propiedad) to foreclose on

ejecutivo -va ADJ & MF executive

ejemplar ADJ exemplary, model; M (libro) copy; (individuo) specimen

ejemplificar[6] VT to exemplify

ejemplo M (cosa típica) example; (modelo) model; **a — de** on the example of; **dar —** to set an example; **por —** for example

ejercer[10a] VT (una profesión) to practice; (influencia, fuerza) to exert; (poder) to wield

ejercicio M exercise; (de una profesión) practice; **hacer —** to take exercise; **— contable** accounting period; **— físico** physical exercise; **en —** active

ejercitar VT (la vista, los músculos) to exercise; (a soldados) to drill; (a alumnos) to train; **—se** to train

ejército M army; **el —** the military

ejido M common

ejote M *Méx* green bean

el ART DEF M the; **— de la derecha** the one on the right; **— que** the one that; **— que sepa** whoever knows

él PRON PERS M SG (como sujeto) he; **— dijo** he said; (como objeto) him; **para —** for him; **le di el libro a —** I gave the book to him; **estamos hablando de —** we're talking about him; **el libro de —** his book

elaboración F (de miel, comida) making; (de un método) development; (de un informe) drafting

elaborado ADJ elaborate

elaborar VT (un método) to elaborate, to develop; (comida) to make; (un informe) to draft

elasticidad F elasticity

elástico ADJ (sustancia) elastic; (cuerpo) supple; (horario) flexible; M elastic

elección F (votación) election; (selección) choice, selection; **no tuve —** I had no choice

electo ADJ elect

elector -ora ADJ electoral; MF elector

electoral ADJ electoral

electricidad F electricity; **— estática** static electricity

electricista MF electrician

eléctrico ADJ (aparato) electric; (instalación, corriente) electrical

electrificar[6] VT to electrify

electrizado ADJ electrified

electrizante ADJ electrifying

electrizar[9] VT (suministrar electricidad) to electrify; (emocionar) to galvanize, to electrify

electrocardiograma M electrocardiogram

electrocutar VT to electrocute

electrodo M electrode

electrodoméstico M electrical appliance

electroencefalograma M electroencephalogram

electroimán M electromagnet

electrólisis F electrolysis

electromagnético ADJ electromagnetic

electrón M electron

electrónica F electronics

electrónico ADJ electronic

elefante M elephant

elegancia F elegance

elegante ADJ (que tiene gracia) elegant; (en el vestir) stylish, smart

elegible ADJ eligible

elegir[5,11] VT to choose, to select; (votar) to elect

elemental ADJ (sencillo) elementary; (básico) elemental

elemento M element

elenco M cast

elevación F elevation; **tirar por —** to throw

high in the air

elevado ADJ (pensamiento, estilo) elevated; (fiebre, montaña) high; (precios) high

elevador M elevator

elevar VT (en una jerarquía) to elevate; (precios, voz, objeto) to raise; (el espíritu) to uplift; — **la vista** to look up; — **al cuadrado** to square; — **al cubo** to cube; —**se a** to go up to, to rise to; **el rascacielos se eleva sobre la ciudad** the skyscraper towers over the city

elfo M elf

eliminación F elimination

eliminar VT to eliminate

eliminatoria F heat

elíptico ADJ elliptical

elite / élite F elite

elitista ADJ & MF elitist

ella PRON PERS F SG (como sujeto) she; — **dijo** she said; (como objeto) her; **para** — for her; **le di el libro a** — I gave the book to her; **el libro de** — her book

ellas PRON PERS F PL (como sujeto) they; — **dijeron** they said; (como objeto) them; **para** — for them; **les di el libro a** — I gave them the book; **el libro de** — their book

ello PRON it; — **es que** the fact is that

ellos PRON M PL (como sujeto) they; — **dijeron** they said; (como objeto) them; **para** — for them; **les di el libro a** — I gave them the book; **el libro de** — their book

elocuencia F eloquence

elocuente ADJ eloquent; **las estadísticas son** —**s** the statistics speak for themselves

elogiar VT to praise

elogio M praise

elote M *Méx* corn on the cob

elucidación F elucidation

elucidar VT to elucidate

eludir VT to elude, to avoid, to dodge

emanación F emanation, flow

emanar VI/VT to emanate

emancipación F emancipation

emancipar VT to emancipate; —**se** to become free

emascular VT to emasculate

embadurnar VT to daub

embajada F embassy

embajador -ora MF ambassador

embalador -ora MF packer

embalaje M packing

embalar VT to pack; VI to accelerate

embaldosar VT to tile

embalsamar VT (a un muerto) to embalm; (un animal) to stuff

embalse M reservoir

embanderar VT to adorn with flags

embarazada F pregnant

embarazar[9] VT (impedir) to hamper; (fecundar) to make pregnant; —**se** to get pregnant

embarazo M (obstáculo) impediment; (estado de embarazada) pregnancy

embarazoso ADJ embarrassing, awkward

embarcación F boat, embarkation, craft

embarcadero M wharf, pier

embarcar[6] VT (pasajeros) to embark; (mercancías) to load; —**se** to embark, to go aboard; —**se en** to embark upon

embargar[7] VT to seize; **estar embargado de emoción** to be overcome with emotion

embargo M embargo; — **judicial** seizure; **imponer un** — to embargo; **sin** — nevertheless, however

embarque M (de mercancías) loading; (de pasajeros) embarkation

embarrado ADJ smeared with mud

embarrar VT to smear with mud, to muddy

embate M lashing

embaucador M confidence man

embaucar[6] VT to dupe

embeber VT to soak up; —**se** to be enraptured

embelesar VT to enrapture

embeleso M rapture

embellecer[13] VI/VT to beautify

embestida F charge

embestir[5] VI/VT to charge

embetunar VT to polish

emblanquecer[13] VI/VT to whiten

emblema M emblem

embobar VT to amaze; —**se** to be amazed

embolia F embolism

émbolo M piston, plunger

embolsar VT (dinero) to pocket; (una compra) to bag

emborrachar VT (a una persona) to intoxicate; (el carburador) to flood; —**se** to get drunk

emborronar VT (manchar) to blot; (hacer impreciso) to blur

emboscada F ambush

emboscar[6] VT to ambush; —**se** to lie in ambush

embotamiento M (efecto de embotar) dullness, bluntness; (acción de embotar) dulling

embotar VT to dull

embotelladora F bottling plant

embotellamiento M (acción de embotellar) bottling; (de tráfico) traffic jam, bottleneck

embotellar vt (cerveza) to bottle; (tráfico) to bottle up

embozar[9] vt to conceal

embragar[7] vi to engage the clutch

embrague M clutch

embriagado ADJ drunken

embriagar[7] vt to intoxicate; **—se** to become intoxicated

embriaguez F intoxication, drunkenness

embridar vt to bridle

embrión M embryo

embrollar vt to embroil

embrollo M muddle

embromar vt to kid

embrujar vt to bewitch

embrujo M spell

embrutecer[13] vt to stupefy

embudo M funnel

embuste M lie

embustero -ra MF liar, trickster

embutido M sausage

embutir vt to cram, to jam

emergencia F emergency

emerger[11b] vi to emerge; (del agua) to surface

emigración F (de personas) emigration; (de animales) migration

emigrante ADJ & MF emigrant

emigrar vi (personas) to emigrate; (animales) to migrate

eminencia F eminence; **— gris** gray eminence

eminente ADJ eminent

emisario -ria MF emissary; M outlet

emisión F (de acciones, billetes) issue; (de un olor) discharge; (de programas) broadcast; (de vapor) emission

emisor ADJ emitting; M transmitter

emisora F radio/television station

emitir vt (un olor, vapor) to emit; (juicios) to pronounce; (dinero, acciones) to issue; vi/vt (programas) to broadcast; **—se** to be on the air

emoción F emotion; **¡qué —!** what a thrill!

emocional ADJ emotional

emocionante ADJ (conmovedor) touching; (apasionante) exciting

emocionar vt (apasionar) to excite; (conmover) to move, to touch; **—se** (estar apasionado) to be excited; (estar conmovido) to be touched

emotivo ADJ emotional

empacador -ora MF packer

empacar[6] vt (regalos, mercancías) to pack; (algodón) to bale

empachar vi to cause indigestion; **—se** to suffer indigestion; **—se de** to get sick on,

to stuff oneself with

empacho M (indigestión) indigestion; (cohibición) inhibition; **no tener — en** to have no qualms about

empalagar[7] vi/vt to cloy

empalagoso ADJ cloying, saccharine

empalar vt to impale

empalizada F stockade, palisade

empalmar vt to splice; **— con** to join

empalme M (de caminos) junction; (de cuerdas) splice; **— genético** gene splicing

empanada F turnover, pie

empanar vt to bread

empañado ADJ (vidrio) misty, foggy; (metal, reputación) tarnished

empañar vt (vidrio) to fog up, to blur; (metal, reputación) to tarnish

empapado ADJ soggy, sopping wet

empapamiento M soaking

empapar vt (mojar) to soak, to drench; (recoger con algo) to soak up; **—se** (mojarse) to get soaked; (enterarse) to find out all about

empapelado M wallpapering

empapelar vt to paper, to wallpaper; **— las calles** to plaster the streets

empaque M (acción de empacar) packing; (envoltorio) packaging

empaquetadura F gasket

empaquetar vt to pack, to package; **—se** to get dolled up

emparedado M sandwich

emparejar vt (una carga, un partido) to even up; vi/vt (los enamorados) to pair up

emparentado ADJ akin, related

emparentarse vi to become related by marriage

empastar vt to fill

empaste M filling

empatar vi to tie

empate M tie

empatía F empathy

empecinado ADJ stubborn

empedernido ADJ (criminal) hardened; (mujeriego) incorrigible; (solterón) confirmed

empedernirse[50] vi to become hardened

empedrado M (acción) paving with stones; (cosa) cobblestone pavement; ADJ paved with stones

empedrar[1] vt to pave with stones

empeine M (del pie) instep; (del vientre) groin

empellón M shove; **a empellones** with shoves, shoving

empeñar vt to pawn; **— la palabra** to pledge; **—se** (endeudarse) to go into debt; (obstinarse) to insist; (esforzarse) to apply oneself; **—se en** to engage in

empeño M (prenda) pawn; (insistencia) insistence; (deseo) desire; (esfuerzo) exertion; **poner — en** to strive for

empeorar VT to make worse, to aggravate; VI to worsen; **—se** to get worse

empequeñecer[13] VT to make smaller; VI to get smaller

emperador -triz M emperor; F empress

emperifollarse VI to deck oneself out, to doll oneself up

empezar[1,9] VI/VT to begin, to start; **— a** to start to; **— de cero** to start from scratch; **para —** for starters; **no tengo ni para — con él** I can't touch him; **— por** to begin with; **empezamos mal** we got off to a bad start; **un tubo sin —** an unopened tube; **por algo se empieza** you have to start somewhere

empinado ADJ steep

empinar VT to raise; **— el codo** to drink; **—se** (una persona) to stand on tiptoes; (un caballo) to rear; (una torre) to tower

empírico ADJ empirical

empizarrar VT to cover with slate

emplastar VT to plaster

emplasto M plaster

empleado -da MF employee

emplear VT (usar) to employ, to use; (dar trabajo) to employ; **—se en** to be employed in

empleo M (ocupación) employment, work; (puesto de trabajo) job; (utilización) use

emplumado ADJ feathery

emplumar VT (poner plumas a algo) to adorn with feathers; (pegar plumas en el cuerpo) to tar and feather; VI (echar plumas) to grow feathers

empobrecer[13] VI/VT to impoverish

empollar VT (huevos) to hatch, to brood; VI/VT (para un examen) to cram

empollón -ona MF grind, egghead

empolvar VT to cover with dust; **—se** (con cosméticos) to powder oneself; (con polvo) to get dirty

emponzoñar VT to poison

empotrado ADJ built-in

emprendedor ADJ enterprising

emprender VT (una tarea) to undertake; (un viaje) to embark on; **—la con alguien** to attack someone

empresa F (cosa que se emprende) undertaking; (compañía) company, enterprise; **— libre** free enterprise; **— privada** private enterprise; **— pública** public company

empresario -ria MF entrepreneur

empréstito M loan

empujar VT to push; (con violencia) to shove; (apresurar) to hurry

empuje M (ánimo) drive; (fuerza de propulsión) thrust; (fuerza hacia arriba) lift

empujón M shove, push; **dar empujones** to jostle

empuñadura F (espada) hilt; (cuchillo) handle

empuñar VT to grasp

emular VT to emulate

en PREP in; **— Asturias** in Asturias; (sobre una superficie) on, upon; **— la mesa** on the table; **sentarse — el suelo** to sit down on the floor; **me lo vendió — mil pesetas** she sold it to me for a thousand pesetas; **— la parada del autobús** at the bus stop; **— la noche** at night; **ir — tren** to go by train

enaguas F PL petticoat

enajenación M (mental) insanity; (cambio de dueño) transfer

enajenar VT (trasladar) to transfer; (alienar) to alienate; **—se** (a los amigos) to alienate

enaltecer[13] VT to extol

enamorado -da ADJ in love; MF lover

enamoramiento M crush

enamorar VT to make fall in love; **—se (de)** to fall in love (with)

enano -na MF (de los cuentos de hada, persona deforme) dwarf; (de proporciones normales) midget

enarbolar VT (una bandera) to raise on high; (un garrote) to brandish

enardecer[13] VT to inflame; **—se** to become inflamed

enardecimiento M inflaming

encabezamiento M heading

encabezar[9] VT (una carta, una obra, un gobierno) to head; (un desfile) to lead

encabritarse VI (un caballo) to rear (up); (enfurecerse) to get furious

encadenar VT (poner en cadenas) to chain; (unir) to link

encajar VI/VT to fit; **el policía me encajó una multa** the policeman stuck me with a fine; **tu historia no encaja** your story doesn't hold water

encaje M (tejido) lace; (reserva bancaria) reserve; (acción de encajar) fitting together

encajonar VT (meter en una caja) to box; (apretar) to squeeze in

encallar VI to run aground, to strand; (una ballena) to beach; VT to ground

encamarse VI **— con** to go to bed with

encaminar VT to direct; **—se hacia** to head for

encanecer[13] VI to go gray; VT to cause to go gray

encanijado ADJ sickly

encanijarse VI to get sickly

encantado ADJ (a gusto) delighted; (hechizado) enchanted; **— de conocerla** pleased to meet you

encantador -ora ADJ charming, delightful; MF charmer

encantamiento M enchantment

encantar VT to enchant; **eso me encanta** I love that

encanto M (encantamiento) enchantment; (atractivo) charm; **un — de persona** a delightful person; **como por —** as if by magic

encapotado ADJ overcast

encapotarse VI to become overcast

encapricharse VI **— con / de / por** to become infatuated with

encapuchar VT (a una persona) to hood; (un bolígrafo) to put the top on

encaramar VT to raise; **—se** to climb up on; **—se al primer puesto** to rise to first place

encarar VT to face; **me encaró el fusil** he pointed the rifle at me; **—se con** to face

encarcelamiento M imprisonment

encarcelar VT to imprison, to jail, to incarcerate

encarecer[13] VI (subir de precio) to increase in price; VT (rogar) to beg

encarecidamente ADV earnestly

encargado -da MF person in charge; **— de curso** lecturer

encargar[7] VT (dar cargo) to put in charge; (pedir) to order; (mandar) to commission, to order; **— a alguien una tarea** to charge someone with a task; **—se de** to take care of

encargo M (pedido) order; (tarea) assignment, charge, errand; **construido por / de —** custom-built; **hecho por —** made-to-order

encariñarse VI **— de** to become fond of

encarnado ADJ (rojo) red; (uña) ingrown

encarnar VT (un ideal) to embody; (a un personaje) to play; **se me encarnó una uña** one of my nails got ingrown

encarnizado ADJ fierce

encarnizarse[9] VI **— con alguien** to attack someone viciously

encarte M insert

encasillar VT to pigeonhole

encauzamiento M channeling

encauzar[9] VT to channel

encendedor M cigarette lighter

encender[1] VT (un cigarro, fuego) to light; (un fósforo) to strike; (una luz, radio) to switch on, to turn on; (pasión) to arouse; VI **—se** (una persona, sexualmente) to get aroused; (una lámpara) to turn on

encendido ADJ (rojo) bright; (sexualmente) aroused; M ignition

encerado M (pizarrón) blackboard; (acción de encerar) waxing; (capa de cera) wax coating; ADJ waxed

encerar VT to wax, to polish

encerrar[1] VT (palabras entre paréntesis) to enclose; (una oveja) to pen; (a una persona) to lock up; (un contenido) to contain; (un peligro) to involve; **—se** (aislarse) to isolate oneself; (obstinarse) to become fixated

enchapar VT (metal) to plate; (madera) to veneer

enchilada F enchilada

enchufar VT (un aparato eléctrico) to plug in; (a un protegido) to fix up; **— un tubo con otro** to fit one pipe into another

enchufe M (de aparatos eléctricos) socket, plug-in, electrical outlet; (situación ventajosa) connection

encías F PL gums

enciclopedia F encyclopedia

encierro M (confinamiento) confinement; (lugar) enclosure

encima ADV (arriba) on top; (además) in addition; **— de** on top of; **por — de** above; **sacar de —** to get rid of; **orinarse —** to urinate on oneself; **ya tenía el coche —** the car was already on top of me; **no lleves tanto dinero —** don't carry so much money on you; **los exámenes están —** the exams are upon us; **mi madre siempre me está —** my mother is always on me; **lo leí por —** I scanned it

encimera F counter

encina F oak

encinta ADJ pregnant

enclaustrar VT to cloister

enclavarse VI to be located

enclave M enclave

enclenque ADJ (endeble) sickly; (desvencijado) rickety

encoger[11b] VI/VT to shrink; **—se** (una prenda) to shrink; (una persona) to be intimidated; **—se de hombros** to shrug one's shoulders

encogido ADJ (tímido) shy; M (acción de encoger) shrinkage

encogimiento M (acción de encoger) shrinking, **— de hombros** shrug

encolar VT to glue

encolerizar[9] VT to incense; **—se** to become incensed, to lose one's temper

encomendar[1] VT to entrust; **—se** to commend oneself

enconar VT to inflame; VI **—se** (discusión) to become inflamed; (herida) to fester

encono M animosity

encontrado ADJ contrary, opposing

encontrar[2] VT (hallar) to find; (converger) to meet; **— a** to run into; **—se** (estar ubicado) to be located; (hallarse) to feel; **—se con** (verse, según plan) to meet with; (verse, por coincidencia) to run into; (enterarse) to find out; **vas a encontrarte la casa en obras** you'll find the house under construction

encontronazo M collision

encordar[2] VT to string

encorvado ADJ stoop-shouldered

encorvamiento M slouch, stoop

encorvar VT to stoop; **—se** to bend over

encostrarse VI to scab

encrespar VT (el pelo) to curl; (el mar) to make choppy; **—se** (el pelo) to get curly; (el mar) to get choppy

encrucijada F crossroads

encuadernación F (oficio) bookbinding; (lo encuadernado) binding

encuadernar VT to bind

encuadrar VT to frame; **la poesía de esta época se encuadra en tres tendencias** the poetry of this period can be classified into three tendencies

encubierto ADJ covert

encubrimiento ADJ (de un delincuente) concealment; (de un escándalo) cover-up

encubrir[51] VT (un secreto) to conceal; (un escándalo) to cover up, to hush up

encuentro M (casual) encounter; (planeado) meeting; (partido) game; (de atletismo) meet; **salir al — de** (ir a encontrar) to go out to meet; (prevenir) to counter

encuerar VT to strip

encuesta F survey, poll

encuestar VI/VT to survey, to poll

encumbrado ADJ elevated, lofty

encumbramiento M elevation

encumbrar VT to elevate

encurtido M pickle

encurtir VT to pickle

ende LOC ADV **por —** hence

endeble ADJ (persona) feeble; (material, argumento) flimsy; (mesa) rickety

endémico ADJ endemic

endemoniado ADJ (poseído por el diablo) possessed by the devil; (niño) devilish; (pregunta) tough

enderezar[9] VT to straighten; **enderézate** stand up straight; **la niña se enderezó con los años** the girl straightened out after a few years

endeudarse VI to get into debt

endiablado ADJ devilish

endócrino ADJ endocrine

endomingado ADJ dressed in one's Sunday best

endorfina F endorphin

endosante MF endorser

endosar VT to endorse

endoso M endorsement

endulzante M sweetener

endulzar[9] VT to sweeten; **se endulzó el tiempo** the weather became milder

endurecer[13] VT to harden; **—se** (músculos) to get hard; (cola) to set

endurecimiento M hardening

enebro M juniper

eneldo M dill

enema MF enema

enemigo -ga ADJ & MF enemy; **buques —s** enemy ships; **ser — de una cosa** to dislike a thing

enemistad F enmity

enemistar VT to cause enmity between; **—se con** to become an enemy of

energético ADJ (política energética) energy policy

energía F energy; **— nuclear** nuclear energy; **— hidráulica** water power; **— solar** solar energy; **— térmica** thermal energy

enérgico ADJ (persona) energetic; (protesta, medida, tono) forceful

enero M January

enervar VT (debilitar) to enervate; (irritar) to irritate

enfadado ADJ angry

enfadar VT to anger; VI **—se** to get angry

enfado M anger

enfadoso ADJ annoying

enfardar VT to bale

énfasis M emphasis

enfático ADJ emphatic

enfatizar[9] VT to emphasize

enfermar VT to sicken; VI to become sick; **—se** to become ill

enfermedad F (estado de enfermo) sickness, illness; (cardiovascular, de Parkinson) disease; (social) ill; **— contagiosa** contagion; **— coronaria** heart disease; **— mental** mental illness

enfermería F infirmary

enfermero -ra M male nurse; F nurse

enfermizo ADJ (persona) sickly, infirm; (obsesión, aspecto) unhealthy; (imaginación) sick

enfermo -ma ADJ sick, ill; **me tiene — que vengan tarde** I'm sick of them coming late; MF patient; **— del corazón** person with a heart condition

enfisema M emphysema

enflaquecer[13] VI to get thin

enfocar[6] VT (los ojos) to focus; (un faro) to point; (una cámara) to train; (un tema) to approach

enfoque M approach

enfrentamiento M clash

enfrentar VT to confront; (una dificultad) to face, to tackle; **— a** to pit against; **—se con** to clash with

enfrente ADV opposite; **— de** in front of, opposite

enfriamiento M (del aire) cooling; (de una persona) chill; (de la economía, las relaciones) cooling off

enfriar[16] VT to cool, to chill; VI **—se** to cool off

enfundar VT to sheathe

enfurecer[13] VT to infuriate, to enrage; VI **—se** to become enraged, to rage

enfurruñado ADJ sulky

enfurruñarse VI to sulk

engalanar VT (una mesa) to decorate; (a una muchacha) to dress up; **—se** to dress up

enganchar VT (bueyes) to hitch; (una red) to snag; (un teléfono) to hook up; (a los televidentes, a un adicto) to hook; VI **—se** to get hooked

enganche M (del gas, teléfono) connection, hookup; (de drogas) addictiveness; (de vagones) coupling; (de caballos) team; (entrada) *Méx* down payment

enganchón M snag

engañador ADJ deceitful

engañar VT (mentir) to deceive; (ser infiel) to cheat on; **— el hambre** to ward off hunger; **—se** to deceive oneself

engaño M deceit, deception

engañoso ADJ deceitful

engastar VT to set

engaste M setting

engatusar VT to coax, to cajole

engendrar VT (emociones) to engender; (hijos) to procreate

englobar VT to encompass

engomar VT to glue

engordar VT to get fat, to put on weight; VT to make fat, to fatten; **esta semana he engordado dos kilos** I gained two kilos this week

engorroso ADJ irksome

engoznar VT to hinge

engranado ADJ meshed, interlocking; **estar — to** be in gear

engranaje M gears, gearing; **el — del partido** the party apparatus

engranar VT (meter una marcha) to put in gear, to throw into gear; (encajar) to mesh; **— la marcha atrás** to put (the car) in reverse

engrandecer[13] VT (la fama) to aggrandize; (un palacio) to make more grandiose

engrapar VT to staple, to cramp

engrasar VT (untar) to grease; (manchar) to make greasy; (sobornar) to grease someone's palm; **—se** to get greasy

engrase M grease job

engreído ADJ conceited

engreírse[15] VI to get conceited

engrillar VT to shackle

engrosar VT (una manifestación) to swell; (un volumen) to grow; (una persona) to get fat

engrudo M paste

engullir[19] VT to gobble

enhebrar VT (un hilo) to thread; (cuentas) to string; **— idioteces** to string together a bunch of idiocies

enhorabuena F congratulation; INTERJ congratulations

enigma M (misterio) enigma, conundrum; (adivinanza) riddle; (problema) puzzle

enjabonar VT (poner jabón) to soap, to lather; (adular) to flatter

enjaezar[9] VT to harness

enjalbegar[7] VT to whitewash

enjambre M swarm

enjaular VT (un animal) to cage; (a una persona) to jail

enjuagar[7] VT to rinse; (ropa) to rinse out; (platos) to rinse off

enjuague M (limpieza) rinse, rinsing; (trama) scheme; **— bucal** mouthwash

enjugar[7] VT (la frente) to wipe; (lágrimas) to wipe away

enjuiciar VT to prosecute, to try

enjuto ADJ dry; (delgado) thin

enlace M (de trenes) link; (químico) bond; (boda) marriage; (persona) liaison

enladrillado M brick pavement

enladrillar VT to brick, to pave with bricks

enlatar VT to can

enlazar[9] VT (unir) to link; (sujetar con lazo) to rope, to lasso; VI to connect; **—se** to connect

enlodar VT to muddy; **—se** to get muddy

enloquecedor ADJ maddening

enloquecer[13] VT to drive crazy; VI to go crazy; **—se** to go crazy

enlosado M flagstone pavement

enlosar VT to pave with flagstones

enmantecar[6] VT to butter

enmarañar VT (pelo) to entangle; (problema) to complicate

enmarcar[6] VT (un cuadro) to frame; **se enmarca dentro de** it takes place in the context of

enmascarar VT to mask

enmendar[1] VT (una ley) to amend; (un texto) to revise; **— la situación** to mend matters; **no me enmiendes la plana** don't correct me; VI **—se** to mend one's ways

enmienda F (de una ley) amendment; (de un texto) revision

enmohecer[13] VT to mold; **—se** to get moldy, to mold

enmudecer[13] VT to silence; VI to go silent

ennegrecer[13] VI/VT to blacken

ennoblecer[13] VT to ennoble

enojadizo ADJ hotheaded

enojado ADJ angry, mad

enojar VT to anger; **—se** to get angry

enojo M anger

enojoso ADJ bothersome

enorgullecer[13] VT to fill with pride; **—se de** to take pride in

enorme ADJ enormous

enramada F bower

enrarecido ADJ thin, rare

enrarecimiento M rarity, thinness

enredadera F creeper

enredar VT (enmarañar) to entangle; (complicar) to complicate; (involucrar) to mix up; VI to cause trouble; **—se** to get tangled up; **—se con** to become involved with

enredijo M tangle, snarl

enredo M (enredijo) snarl; (lío) mess; (amancebamiento) affair

enredoso ADJ complicated

enrejado M (conjunto de rejas) grating, grate; (entrecruzamiento de varillas) lattice

enrejar VT to install a grate on

enrevesado ADJ involved

enriquecer[13] VT to enrich; **—se** to become rich

enrojecer[13] VI/VT to redden

enrollar VT (manga, alfombra) to roll up; (hilo, cuerda, cinta magnética) to wind up; **—se con** to become involved with

enronquecer[13] VT to make hoarse; VI to become hoarse

enroscar[6] VT (soga) to coil, to roll up; (tuerca) to screw in; (tapa) to screw on; **—se** (vid) to twine; (serpiente) to coil up

ensacar[6] VT to sack

ensalada F salad

ensalzar[9] VT to extol

ensanchar VT to widen; **—se** (una calle) to widen; (una falda) to flare

ensanche M (de una calle) widening; (de una ciudad) expansion

ensangrentado ADJ gory, bloody

ensangrentar VT to smear blood on; **—se** to get covered with blood

ensartar VT (cuentas) to string; (aguja) to thread; (con un pincho) to pierce; (historias) to rattle off

ensayar VT (probar) to try out; (intentar) to try; (analizar un metal) to assay; (practicar una obra teatral) to rehearse

ensayo M (intento) trial, attempt; (de teatro) rehearsal; (obra literaria) essay; (nuclear) testing; (de un metal) assay; **— general** dress rehearsal; **por — y error** by trial and error

ensenada F cove

enseña F ensign

enseñanza F teaching, education; **—s** teachings

enseñar VT (mostrar) to show; (instruir) to teach; **— a** to teach how to

enseres M PL household utensils

ensillar VT to saddle, to saddle up

ensimismarse VI to lose oneself in thought

ensoberbecer[13] VT to make haughty; **—se** to become haughty

ensombrecer[13] VT (oscurecer) to make shadowy; (entristecer) to sadden

ensoñación F dream

ensordecedor ADJ deafening

ensordecer[13] VT to deafen

ensortijar VT to curl

ensuciar VT to dirty, to sully; **—se** (ponerse sucio) to get dirty; (defecar) to soil oneself; **—se en** to defecate on

ensueño M reverie, dream

entablar VT (relaciones) to establish; (un conflicto) to start; (una conversación) to strike up; (una demanda) to file; (una pelea) to pick

entablillar VT to splint

entallar VT to take in

entarimar VT to floor with planks

ente M (ser) entity; (excéntrico) weirdo; (agencia) agency

enteco ADJ sickly

entender[1] VT to understand; (oír) to hear; **— de** to know about; **—se con** (comunicar) to communicate with; (llevarse bien) to get along with; **dar a —** to intimate; **yo me entiendo** I know what I'm doing; **se entiende** of course

entendido -da ADJ (comprendido) understood; (experto) expert; **tengo — que** I understand that; **caridad mal entendida** misguided charity; MF expert

entendimiento M understanding

enterado ADJ informed; **darse por —** to acknowledge; **estar — de** to be privy to

enterar VT to inform; **—se (de)** to find out (about); **recién me entero** I just found out; **para que te enteres** just so you know

entereza F fortitude

enternecedor ADJ touching

enternecer[13] VT to touch; **—se** to be touched

entero ADJ (completo) entire, whole; (número) whole; **se mantuvo — durante el funeral** he held himself together during the funeral; M integer, whole number

enterrar[1] VT to bury

entibiar VT to make lukewarm; **—se** to become lukewarm

entidad F entity; **de —** significant; **— bancaria** banking institution

entierro M burial, funeral

entintar VT to stain with ink

entoldar VT to cover with an awning

entomología F entomology

entonación F intonation

entonar VT to sing; VI to sing in tune; **— con** to go well with; **—se** to get tipsy

entonces ADV then; **desde —** ever since; **hasta —** until then; **el — presidente** the then president; CONJ (así que) so

entornado ADJ half-open

entornar VT (una puerta) to leave ajar; (los ojos) to partially close

entorpecer[13] VT (los sentidos) to dull; (el paso) to hinder; **—se** to become sluggish

entorpecimiento M (de los sentidos) dullness; (del paso) hindrance

entrada F (sitio por donde se entra, de un actor) entrance; (acción de entrar, artículo de diccionario) entry; (conjunto de personas que asisten) gate; (oportunidad para actuar) opening; (billete, derecho, precio de entrar) admission; (llegada) arrival; (primer plato) entrée; (pago inicial) down payment; (tiempo en béisbol) inning; **—s** cash receipts; **— de coches** driveway; **— por partida doble** double entry; **de —** from the start

entramado M lattice

entrante ADJ (alcalde, etc.) incoming; (año) next; M recess

entrañas F PL (intestinos) entrails, *fam* guts; (sentimientos) heart, core; **— de la tierra** bowels of the earth; **de mis —** of my own flesh and blood

entrar VI to enter; (a trabajar) to come in; (en un lugar) to fit; VT (datos) to enter, to input; **le entré dos pastillas** I brought in two pills for him; **me entró miedo** I became afraid; **me entró sueño** I got sleepy; **no sé cómo —le a esa chica** I don't know how to approach that girl; **la física no me entra** I can't learn physics; **no entra entre mis favoritos** it is not included among my favorites; **la semana que entra** next week; **este vestido no me entra** this dress doesn't fit me; **seis entra dos veces en doce** six goes into twelve two times; **dejar —** to let in; **hacer — en razón** to bring to reason; **hazle —** show him in; **— a medicina** to go into medicine; **— en calor** to warm up; **— en coma** to go into a coma; **— en/a un cuarto** to enter a room; **— en una discusión** to take part in a discussion; **— en materia** to get to the meat of a matter; **— en vigencia/vigor** to go into effect

entre PREP (dos) between; (muchos) among; **— vaso y vaso** between glasses; **— dientes** under one's breath

entreabierto ADJ ajar, half-open

entreabrir[51] VT (puerta) to crack open; (los ojos) to half-open

entreacto M intermission

entrecano ADJ graying

entrecejo M space between the eyebrows

entrecortado ADJ (voz) faltering; (respiración) irregular

entrecortarse VI to falter

entrecruzar[9] VT to interlace; **—se** to cross

entredicho LOC ADV **en —** in doubt

entrega F (de un paquete) delivery; (de un manuscrito) submission; (al vicio) surrender; (de una novela) installment; (de revista) issue; **por —s** serial; **— a domicilio** home delivery; **— de premios** presentation of awards; **— inicial** down payment

entregar[7] VT (un paquete) to deliver; (a un rehén, prisionero) to hand over; (a un delincuente) to turn in; (a una hija en matrimonio) to give; (premios) to hand out, to present; (los deberes) to hand in; (el coche) to trade in; **—se (a)** to surrender (to), to dedicate oneself to

entrelazar[9] VT to intertwine

entremés M (obra de teatro) interlude; (comida) hors d'oeuvre

entremeter VT to insert; **—se en** (meterse) to get mixed up in; (inmiscuirse) to meddle in

entremetido -da ADJ meddlesome, nosy; MF meddler

entremezclar VT to intermingle

entrenador -ora MF trainer, coach

entrenamiento M training

entrenar VI/VT to train

entrepierna F (de personas) crotch; (de pantalón) inseam

entrepiso M mezzanine

entresacar[6] VT (seleccionar) to cull; (hacer menos espeso) to thin

entresuelo M (de hotel) mezzanine; (de cine) balcony

entretanto ADV meanwhile

entretejer VT (el pelo, una tela) to weave; (una historia) to weave together

entretener[44] VT (hacer atrasar) to delay; (distraer) to distract; (divertir) to entertain; **—se** (divertirse) to amuse oneself; (detenerse) to delay

entretenido ADJ entertaining

entretenimiento M entertainment, amusement

entrever[48] VT (apenas) to catch a glimpse of; (a lo lejos) to make out

entreverar VT to intersperse; **—se** to meddle

entrevía F gauge

entrevista F interview

entrevistar VT to interview; **—se con** to have an interview with

entristecer[13] VT to sadden; **—se** to become sad

entrometerse VI to meddle, to interfere

entrometido -da ADJ meddlesome, nosy; MF meddler, busybody

entronque M (ferroviario) junction; (parentesco) relationship

entropía F entropy

entumecido ADJ (dedo, diente) numb; (músculo) stiff

entumecimiento M (de los dedos, dientes) numbness; (de los músculos) stiffness

enturbiar VT (el agua) to muddy; (una decisión) to muddle; (el juicio, la alegría) to cloud; **—se** (agua) to get muddy; (alegría) to be marred

entusiasmado ADJ enthusiastic

entusiasmar VT to excite; **—se** to be excited

entusiasmo M enthusiasm, excitement

entusiasta MF enthusiast; ADJ enthusiastic

enumerar VT to enumerate

enunciado M utterance

enunciar VT (palabras) to enunciate; (una teoría) to articulate, to enunciate

envainar VT to sheathe

envalentonar VT to make bold; **—se** to get bold

envanecer[13] VT to make vain; **—se** to become vain

envarado ADJ stiff

envaramiento M stiffness

envasar VT to package; **— al vacío** to vacuum-pack

envase M packaging

envejecer[13] VT to make old; **ese maquillaje te envejece** that makeup makes you look old; VI to grow old, to age

envenenamiento M poisoning

envenenar VT to poison

envergadura F (de un avión) wingspan; (de un ave) wingspread; (de un evento, proyecto) importance

envés M back

enviado -da MF (político) envoy; (periodístico) correspondent

enviar[16] VT to send

enviciar VT to corrupt; **—se con** to get hooked on

envidia F envy

envidiable ADJ enviable

envidiar VT to envy

envidioso ADJ envious, jealous

envilecer[13] VT to debase

envío M (de mercancías) shipment; (de un manuscrito) submission

envite M bet

envoltorio M (cosa envuelta) bundle; (envoltura) wrapper

envoltura F wrapping, wrapper

envolver[2,51] VT (involucrar) to involve; (cubrir) to wrap; (atrapar) to entangle; (rodear) to surround; **—se** to become involved

enyesar VT (enlucir con yeso) to plaster; (escayolar) to put in a cast

enzima MF enzyme

épica F epic

epicentro M epicenter

épico ADJ epic

epidemia F epidemic

epidémico ADJ epidemic

epidermis F epidermis

epifanía F epiphany

epilepsia F epilepsy

epílogo M epilog

episódico ADJ episodic

episodio M episode

epitafio M epitaph

epítome M epitome

época F (momento) time, period; (período histórico) age; (temporada) season; (período geológico) epoch

epopeya F epic poem

equidad F equity

equidistante ADJ equidistant

equilibrar VT to balance

equilibrio M equilibrium, balance; **perder el —** to lose one's balance; **hacer —s** to do a balancing act

equino ADJ & M equine

equinoccio M equinox

equipaje M baggage, luggage

equipamiento M equipment

equipar VT to equip, to outfit

equiparar VT to equate

equipo M (materiales) equipment; (grupo de personas) team; **— de vida** life-support system; **— deportivo** sweatsuit; **— de esquí** ski gear

equitación F horsemanship

equitativo ADJ equitable

equivalente ADJ equivalent

equivaler[46] VI to be equivalent; **lo que equivale a decir** which amounts to saying

equivocación F mistake

equivocado ADJ mistaken, wrong; **estar —** to be wrong/mistaken

equivocar[6] VT to mistake; **—se** to be mistaken, to make a mistake; **—se de sala** to choose the wrong room; **si no me equivoco** unless I'm mistaken

equívoco ADJ (ambiguo) equivocal; (moralmente dudoso) questionable; M misunderstanding

era F (período) era, age; (lugar donde se trilla) threshing floor; (parcela) plot

erario M treasury

erecto ADJ erect; (postura) upright

erguido ADJ erect, upright

erguir[3b] VT to lift, to raise; **—se** to rise

erial M uncultivated land

erigir[11] VT (construir) to erect; (fundar) to found; **—se en** to set oneself up as

Eritrea F Eritrea

eritreo -a ADJ & MF Eritrean

erizado ADJ bristly; **— de** bristling with

erizar[9] VT to set on end; **—se** to bristle

erizo M hedgehog; **— de mar** sea urchin; **ser un —** to be a grouch

ermitaño -ña MF (persona) hermit; M (cangrejo) hermit crab

erógeno ADJ erogenous

erosión F erosion

erótico ADJ erotic

erradicar[6] VT to eradicate, to root out

errado ADJ erroneous, in error

errante ADJ wandering

errar[27] VT to miss; **— el cálculo** to miscalculate; VI (estar equivocado) to be mistaken; (vagar) to roam, to rove, to wander

errata F misprint, typographical error

errático ADJ erratic

erróneo ADJ erroneous

error M error, mistake; **— de imprenta** misprint

eructar VI to belch, to burp

eructo M belch, burp

erudición F learning, scholarship

erudito -ta ADJ (persona) erudite; (obra) scholarly, learned; MF scholar

erupción F eruption; **hacer —** to erupt

esbelto ADJ slender

esbozar[9] VT to outline; **— una sonrisa** to give a hint of a smile

esbozo M sketch, outline; **— de una sonrisa** hint of a smile

escabechar VT to pickle

escabroso ADJ (agreste) rugged; (espinoso) thorny; (sórdido) lurid, sordid

escabullirse[19] VI (ladrones) to slip away, to steal away; (lagartijas) to scurry away/off; **— de** to wriggle out of

escafandra F (en el agua) scuba gear; (en el espacio) spacesuit

escala F (escalera, escalafón) ladder; (serie de grados, notas, relación de importancia) scale; (parada) stopover; **hacer — en** to stop over at; **— salarial** wage scale; **a — nacional** nationwide; **de gran —** large-scale; **sin —s** nonstop

escalada F (de una montaña) climb; (de violencia) escalation

escalador -ora MF climber

escalar VT to scale, to climb

escaldadura F scald

escaldar VT (la piel) to scald; (las verduras) to blanch; **—se** to get scalded

escalera F (en un edificio) stairs, staircase; (de mano) ladder; (de naipes) flush; **— mecánica** escalator; **— de caracol** spiral/winding staircase; **— de color** straight flush; **— de incendios** fire escape; **— real** royal flush

escalfar VT to poach

escalinata F grand staircase

escalofriante ADJ chilling, hair-raising

escalofrío M chill; **—s** the shivers

escalón M (peldaño) step, stair; (terraza) terrace; (de escalera de mano, de escalafón) rung; (formación militar) echelon

escalonar VT (distribuir) to stagger; (aterrazar) to terrace

escalope M scallop

escama F (de animal) scale; (de piel, de corteza) flake

escamar VT to scale

escamoso ADJ (animal) scaly; (piel) flaky

escamotear VT (esconder) to palm; (robar) to snatch; (eludir) to shirk

escampar VI to clear up

escandalizar[9] VT (chocar) to scandalize; (causar escándalo) to cause a scandal; **—se** to be shocked

escándalo M (suceso vergonzoso) scandal; (riña) uproar

escandaloso ADJ (chocante) scandalous, shocking; (ruidoso) raucous

escandir VT *lit* to scan

escanear VT to scan

escáner M scanner

escaño M seat in parliament

escapada F (escape) escape

escapar VI (de un lugar, una situación) to escape; (de una persona, responsabilidad) to run away; **—se** (persona) to escape; (gas) to leak; **se me escapó una sonrisa** I inadvertently smiled; **Matilde se me está escapando de las manos** Matilde is getting out of hand

escaparate M shop window

escapatoria F escape, way out

escape M (de fantasía, escapatoria) escape; (de motor) exhaust; (de gas, agua) leak

escarabajo M beetle

escaramuza F skirmish

escaramuzar[9] VI to skirmish

escarbar VI/VT to dig, to scratch; **— en los archivos** to dig around in the files; **— los dientes** to pick one's teeth

escarcha F frost

escarchar VI to frost

escardar VT to weed

escarlata ADJ & M (color) scarlet; F (enfermedad) scarlet fever

escarlatina F scarlet fever

escarmentar[1] VI to learn one's lesson; VT to teach a lesson

escarmiento M lesson; **que te sirva de —** let that be a lesson to you

escarnecer[13] VT to deride

escarnio M derision

escarpa F steep slope

escarpado ADJ steep, precipitous; M steep slope

escasear VI (estar escaso) to be scarce; (acabarse) to grow scarce

escasez F (falta) shortage; (carestía) scarcity, want

escaso ADJ sparse, scarce; **una docena escasa** a scant dozen; **— de** short on; **— de personal** short-handed

escatimar VT to skimp on; **no — gastos** to spare no expense

escena F (fragmento de una obra de teatro, episodio) scene; (escenario) stage; **montar una —** to make a scene; **en —** on stage; **poner en —** to stage; **entrar en —** to go on stage

escenario M stage

escenificación F staging

escepticismo M skepticism

escéptico -ca ADJ skeptical; MF skeptic

escisión F split

esclarecer[13] VT to elucidate

esclavitud F slavery

esclavizar[9] VT to enslave

esclavo -va MF slave

esclerosis F sclerosis; **— múltiple** multiple sclerosis

esclusa F (de un canal) lock; (de una presa) floodgate, sluice gate

escoba F broom

escobilla F whisk broom

escocer[2,10c] VI to sting

escocés -esa ADJ Scottish; **(cuadros) escoceses** plaid; MF Scot; M (whisky) Scotch; (lengua) Scottish

Escocia F Scotland

escoger[11b] VT to choose

escolar MF pupil; ADJ **año —** school year

escoliosis F scoliosis

escollo M (en el mar) reef; (obstáculo) obstacle

escolta F (policial) escort; MF INV (persona) escort

escoltar VT to escort

escombros M PL rubble, debris

esconder VT to hide; VI **—se** to hide

escondidas LOC ADV **a —** on the sly; **entrar a —** to sneak in; **meter algo a —** to sneak something in; **jugar a las —** to play hide and seek

escondite M hiding place; (de ladrón) hideout; (de cazador) blind; **jugar al —** to play hide and seek

escondrijo M hiding place

escopeta F shotgun

escoplo M chisel

escora F listing

escorar VI to list

escoria F (de metales) slag; (de la sociedad) scum, dregs

escorpión M scorpion

escotado ADJ low-cut

escote M (parte del vestido) neckline; (parte del cuerpo) cleavage; **pagar a —** to go Dutch

escotilla F hatch

escozor M smarting sensation

escribiente MF clerk

escribir[51] VI/VT to write; **¿cómo se escribe?** how do you spell it? **— a máquina** to type

escrito ADJ written; **— a máquina** typewritten; **no —** unwritten; **por —** in writing; M document

escritor -ora MF writer, author

escritorio M (mueble) desk; (oficina) office

escritura F (acción de escribir) writing; (certificado de propiedad) deed; **— de traspaso** conveyance; **— de venta** bill of sale

escrúpulo M scruple, qualm; **sin —s** unscrupulous

escrupuloso ADJ scrupulous

escrutar VT (a una persona) to scrutinize; (el horizonte) to scan; (votos) to count

escrutinio M (examen) scrutiny; (recuento) vote count

escuadra F (de buques, soldados) squadron; (instrumento) square

escuadrilla F (de aviones) flight of aircraft; (de buques) squadron

escuadrón M squadron; **— de la muerte** death squad

escualidez F (delgadez) skinniness; (suciedad) squalor

escuálido ADJ (sucio) squalid; (delgado) thin

escuchar VT to listen to; (oír) to hear; VI to listen; **— a hurtadillas** to eavesdrop

escudar VT to shield

escudo M (arma defensiva) shield; (moneda de Portugal) escudo; **— de armas** coat of arms

escudriñar VT (a una persona) to scrutinize, to peer at; (el horizonte) to scan

escuela F school; **— industrial** trade school; **— normal** school of education; **— pública** public school; **— primaria** elementary school; **— secundaria** secondary school; **tener —** to have good technique

escueto ADJ (explicación) succinct; (verdad) simple

esculpir VI/VT to sculpture, to sculpt

escultor -ora MF sculptor

escultura F sculpture

escupir VI/VT to spit

escupitajo M spit

escurridizo ADJ (acera) slippery; (ladrón) elusive, slippery

escurrir VI/VT (platos, verduras) to drain; (ropa) to wring out; **—se** to slink away

ese ADJ that, those; **esa chica se llama Matilde** that girl is named Matilde; **esas ciudades son antiguas** those cities are old; PRON that one, those; **ese es el mayor** that one is the oldest; **esos son mis hijos** those are my children

esencia F essence

esencial ADJ essential; **lo —** gist, bottom line, name of the game

esfera F (sólido) sphere; (espacio, ámbito) realm, sphere; (de reloj) face, dial

esférico ADJ spherical; M soccer ball

esforzado ADJ valiant

esforzarse[9] VI to try hard, to exert oneself; **— por** to strive to, to make an effort to

esfuerzo M effort

esfumar VT to tone down; **—se** to vanish

esgrima F fencing; **practicar —** to fence

esgrimir VT (armas) to brandish, to wield; (argumentos) to employ

eslabón M chain link; **— perdido** missing link

eslabonar VT to link

eslavo -va ADJ Slavic; MF Slav

eslogan M slogan

eslovaco ADJ & MF Slovakian; M (lengua) Slovakian

Eslovaquia F Slovakia

Eslovenia F Slovenia

esloveno -na ADJ & MF Slovene; M (lengua) Slovene

esmaltar VT to enamel

esmalte M enamel; **— de uñas** nail polish

esmerado ADJ painstaking, careful

esmeralda F emerald

esmerarse VI to take pains

esmerilado ADJ frosted; M frosting

esmerilar VT to frost

esmero M care

esmirriado ADJ scrawny

esmoquin M tuxedo

esnifar VT to snort

esnob M snob

esnórquel M snorkel

eso PRON DEM that; **— es** that's true; **— sí** granted; **a — de las tres** at about three o'clock; **de —, nada** no way! **en — llega y me dice** at that moment he arrives and says to me; **y — que le dije que viniese temprano** even when I told him to come early

esófago M esophagus

esotérico ADJ esoteric

espaciado M pitch, spacing

espacial ADJ spatial; **nave —** space ship
espaciar VT to space; **—se** to space out
espacio M (capacidad) space, room;
(superficie) expanse; (separación entre
líneas) space, spacing; (en un formulario)
blank space; (porción de tiempo) span; **—
aéreo** aerospace; **— exterior** outer space;
— noticioso newscast; **a doble —**
double-spaced; **a un —** single-spaced; **por
— de una semana** for a week
espacioso ADJ spacious, roomy
espada F sword; **—s** (palo de naipes) swords;
— de doble filo double-edged sword;
estar entre la — y la pared to be
between a rock and a hard place
espalda F back; **a —s de alguien** behind
one's back; **caerse de —s** to fall on one's
back; **nadar de —** to do the backstroke;
tener las —s anchas to take a lot of
abuse; **volver las —s** to turn one's back
espaldar M chair back
espantadizo ADJ easily scared
espantoso ADJ frightened
espantado ADJ frightened
espantajo M scarecrow
espantar VT to frighten, to scare; (ahuyentar)
to frighten away, to scare away; **—se** to
get scared; M SG **espantapájaros**
scarecrow
espanto M fright, dread; **estás hecho un —**
you look a sight; **estoy curado de —**
nothing surprises me anymore
espantoso ADJ frightful, dreadful
España F Spain
español -ola ADJ Spanish; MF Spaniard; M
(lengua) Spanish
esparadrapo M surgical tape
esparcimiento M (recreo) relaxation;
(reparto) spreading
esparcir[10b] VT to scatter, to spread; **—se** to
amuse oneself
espárrago M asparagus
espasmo M spasm, jerk
espasmódico ADJ jerky
espástico ADJ spastic
espátula F spatula
especia F spice
especial ADJ & M special; **en —** in particular
especialidad F specialty, specialization
especialista MF specialist
especialización F specialization
especializar[9] VT to specialize; **—se en** to
specialize in
especie F (en ciencias naturales) species;
(clase) kind; **—s en peligro de
extinción** endangered species; **pagar en
—** to pay in kind; **una — de** a kind of
especiero M spice rack

especificar[6] VT to specify
específico ADJ & M specific
espécimen M specimen
espectacular ADJ spectacular
espectáculo M (escándalo) spectacle;
(actuación pública) show; (vista) sight;
dar el — to make a spectacle of oneself
espectador -ora MF (de un espectáculo)
spectator; (de un suceso) onlooker
espectro M (fantasma) specter; (de luz,
medicina) spectrum
especulación F speculation
especulador -ora MF speculator
especular VT to speculate; ADJ mirror;
imagen — mirror image
espejismo M (en el desierto) mirage; (ilusión)
illusion
espejo M mirror; **— de cuerpo entero** full-
length mirror; **— retrovisor** rearview
mirror
espeluznante ADJ hair-raising
espeluznar VT to terrify; **—se** to be terrified
espera F (acción de esperar) wait;
(aplazamiento) extension; **estar en — de**
to be waiting for
esperanza F hope; **— de vida** life
expectancy; **con una — de voto de
12,5%** expected to get 12.5% of the vote
esperanzado ADJ hopeful
esperanzador ADJ hopeful
esperanzar[9] VT to give hope to
esperar VT (tener esperanza) to hope; (llevar
a un hijo, creer que sucederá algo) to
expect; (aguardar) to wait for; VI to wait;
era de — it was to be expected; **espera
sentado** don't hold your breath; **estoy
esperando un milagro** I'm hoping for a
miracle; **todavía espera confirmación**
it still awaits confirmation
esperma MF sperm
esperpento M grotesque person or thing
espesar VT to thicken
espeso ADJ (pelo, sopa, niebla) thick; (cejas)
bushy
espesor M thickness
espesura F (espesor) thickness; (lugar
poblado de matorrales) thicket
espetar VT (decir bruscamente) to blurt out;
(atravesar con un espeto) to run a spit
through
espía MF INV spy
espiar[16] VI to spy; VT to spy on
espichar VI *fam* to croak, to bite the dust
espiga F spike
espigar[7] VT to glean; VI to grow spikes; **—se**
to grow tall
espina F (de planta) thorn; (de pez) fish

bone; — **dorsal** spinal column; **me quedé con la** — I was left wondering

espinaca F spinach

espinal ADJ spinal

espinazo M spine, backbone

espinilla F (de persona) shin; (de animal) shank; (grano) blackhead

espino M thorny shrub

espinoso ADJ thorny

espionaje M espionage

espiración F expiration

espiral ADJ & F spiral

espirar VI/VT to exhale, to breathe out, to expire

espíritu M (ser no físico, fantasma, de una ley) spirit; (alma) soul; — **fuerte** free spirit; — **deportivo** sportsmanship; — **emprendedor** can-do attitude; — **Santo** Holy Spirit

espiritual ADJ & M spiritual

espita F spigot

espléndido ADJ (estupendo) splendid; (generoso) lavish

esplendor M splendor

esplendoroso ADJ magnificent

espliego M lavender

espolear VT to spur

espoleta F bomb fuse

espolón M (de gallo, planta, estímulo) spur; (de buque) ram

espolvorear VT to dust, to sprinkle

esponja F (animal, utensilio) sponge; (borracho) souse

esponjado ADJ spongy

esponjar VT to make spongy; **—se** to become spongy

esponjoso ADJ spongy

esponsales M PL betrothal

espontaneidad F spontaneity

espontáneo ADJ spontaneous

espora F spore

esposar VT to handcuff

esposo -sa M husband; F wife; **esposas** handcuffs

espuela F spur

espulgar[7] VT to delouse

espuma F (de cerveza) froth; (de jabón) suds, lather; (de la boca) foam; (de colchón) foam rubber; (de mar) foam, spray; **echar** — **por la boca** to foam at the mouth; **hacer** — to make suds

espumar VT (quitar la espuma) to skim; (formar espuma) to foam

espumarajo M foam; **echar —s por la boca** to foam at the mouth

espumillón M tinsel

espumoso ADJ foamy

esputo M sputum

esquela F note; — **mortuoria** death notice

esqueleto M (huesos) skeleton; (armazón) framework; **mover el** — (bailar) to dance; (moverse) to move

esquema M outline; **romperle los —s a alguien** (planes) to ruin one's plans; (conceptos) to shatter one's preconceptions

esquí M (tabla) ski; (deporte) skiing; — **acuático** (tabla) water ski; (deporte) water skiing; **hacer** — **acuático** to water-ski

esquiar[16] VI to ski

esquila F (cencerro) cowbell; (acción de esquilar) shearing

esquilador -ora MF sheep shearer

esquilar VT to shear, to clip

esquileo M shearing

esquimal ADJ & MF Eskimo; M (lengua) Eskimo

esquina F corner; **en cada** — everywhere

esquirol M strikebreaker; *pey* scab

esquivar VT (a una vecina) to avoid; (un golpe) to dodge

esquivo ADV (tímido) shy, coy; (huraño) aloof; (reservado) elusive

esquizofrenia F schizophrenia

estabilidad F stability

estabilizar[9] VT to stabilize

estable ADJ (mesa) stable; (precio) firm; (huésped) long-term

establecer[13] VT to establish; (averiguar) to ascertain; — **una cita** to set up an appointment; **—se** to settle

establecimiento M establishment

establishment M establishment

establo M stable

estaca F (con punta) stake; (gruesa) club

estacada F stockade; **dejar en la** — to leave in the lurch

estacar[6] VT (atar) to stake; (delimitar) to stake off

estación F (de tren, autobús, radio) station; (parte del año) season; — **bípeda** bipedal stance; — **de bomberos** fire station; — **de esquí** ski resort; — **de servicio** filling station; — **de trabajo** work station; — **espacial** space station

estacionamiento M (acción) parking; (lugar) parking lot

estacionar VT (tropas) to station; (un vehículo) to park; **—se** (un coche) to park; (precios) to level off

estacionario ADJ stationary

estadía F stay

estadio M (recinto con graderías) stadium; (fase) stage

estadista M statesman; F stateswoman

estadística F (ciencia) statistics; **—s** (datos numéricos) statistics

estado M (manera de estar, unidad política) state; **— civil** marital status; **— de cuenta** bank statement; **— de alarma** state of emergency; **— de ánimo** state of mind; **— de excepción** martial law; **— de guerra** state of war; **— de sitio** state of siege; **— mayor** chiefs of staff; **— policíaco** police state; **de — sólido** solid state; **en — interesante** expecting; **en — vegetativo** brain-dead

Estados Unidos M PL / SG United States

estadounidense ADJ & MF American

estafa F swindle, scam, racket

estafador -ora MF swindler

estafar VT to swindle

estalactita F stalactite

estalagmita F stalagmite

estallar VI (una bomba) to explode; (un globo) to burst; (una guerra) to break out; (una persona) to snap; **— de risa** to burst with laughter; **— en una carcajada** to burst out laughing; **hacer —** to set off

estallido M (de bomba, color) explosion; (ruido) bang, report

estampa F (de revista) illustration; (imagen) image; (apariencia) appearance; **de buena — good-looking; la viva — de la madre** the spitting image of her mother; **la viva — de la desolación** the very picture of desolation

estampado ADJ printed; M (tela) print; (acción) printing

estampar VT (en tela, papel) to print; (con un molde, en metal) to stamp; **—le un beso a alguien** to plant a kiss on someone

estampida F stampede

estampido M bang

estampilla F stamp

estampillar VT to stamp

estancado ADJ stagnant

estancar[6] VT to stem; to dam; to block; **—se** to stagnate

estancia F (estadía) stay; (habitación) hall; (hacienda) RP cattle ranch

estanco ADJ waterproof; M government store

estándar ADJ INV & M standard

estandarización F standardization

estandarizar[9] VT to standardize

estandarte M standard, banner

estanque M pond

estante M (tabla) shelf; (mueble) bookcase

estantería F (mueble) bookcase; (en una biblioteca) stack

estañar VT to tin-plate

estaño M tin

estar[28] VI to be; **— a tres kilómetros de aquí** to be three kilometers from here; **— bien** to be all right; **— del corazón** to have heart trouble; **— de más** to be unnecessary; **— para** to be about to; **— por** (a favor de) to be in favor of; (a punto de) to be about to; **— trabajando duro** to be working hard; **¿a cuántos estamos?** what day of the month is it? **ahí está** that's it; **¿está Alice?** is Alice there? **están muy buenos tus zapatos nuevos** your new shoes are nice; **estáte tranquilo** don't worry; **no —** to be out; **cuarto de —** living room

estático ADJ static

estatua F statue

estatura F (importancia) stature; (altura de una persona) height

estatuto M (ley) statute; (de una sociedad) bylaw

este ADJ DEM this, these; **esta chica se llama Hilary** this girl is named Hilary; **estas ciudades son antiguas** these cities are old; PRON DEM this one, these; **— es el mayor** this one is the oldest; **estos son mis hijos** these are my children; M & ADJ east; **hacia el —** eastward

estela F (de una embarcación) wake; (de humo, polvo) trail; **dejar una —** to leave a trail

estelar ADJ stellar

estenotipista MF court reporter

estentóreo ADJ booming

estepa F steppe

estera F mat

estercolar VT to fertilize with manure

estercolero M dunghill

estéreo ADJ & M stereo; **en —** in stereo

estereotipo M stereotype

estéril ADJ sterile; (mujer) barren

esterilidad F sterility

esterilizar[9] VT to sterilize

esternón M sternum

esteroide M steroid

estertor M death rattle

estética F aesthetics

estético ADJ aesthetic

estetoscopio M stethoscope

estibador M longshoreman

estibar VT to stow

estiércol M manure

estigma M stigma

estigmatizar[9] VT to stigmatize

estilarse VI to be in style

estilo M (literario, estético) style; (de

natación) stroke; — **de vida** lifestyle; —
espalda backstroke; — **indirecto**
reported speech; — **libre** freestyle; —
mariposa butterfly stroke; — **pecho**
breaststroke; — **perrito** dog paddle;
cosas por el — things like that

estima F esteem, regard

estimación F (cálculo) estimate; (estima)
estimation

estimado ADJ esteemed; — **Sr.** Dear Sir

estimar VT (apreciar) to esteem; (determinar
el valor) to estimate; (opinar) to think

estimulación F stimulation

estimulante ADJ stimulating; M stimulant

estimular VT to stimulate; (alentar) to
encourage

estímulo M stimulus

estío M *lit* summer

estipendio M stipend

estipulación F stipulation

estipular VT to stipulate

estirado ADJ stuck-up

estirar VT (alargar) to stretch; — **el cuello** to
crane one's neck; — **la pata** *fam* to kick
the bucket; (crecer) to grow; —**se** to
stretch

estirón M growth spurt; **pegar un** — to
have a growth spurt

estirpe F lineage

estival ADJ **vacaciones —es** summer
vacation

esto ADJ & PRON this; — **es** that is to say; **a
todo** — meanwhile; **en** — at this point

estocada F thrust; **lanzar una** — to thrust

estofa F type; **de baja** — low-class

estofado M stew

estofar VT to stew

estoico -ca ADJ & MF stoic

estolón M runner

estómago M stomach

Estonia F Estonia

estonio -nia ADJ & MF Estonian; M (lengua)
Estonian

estopa F tow

estorbar VT (obstaculizar) to hinder, to
impede; (ser una molestia) to be a
nuisance

estorbo M (obstáculo) hindrance,
impediment; (molestia) nuisance

estornino M starling

estornudar VI to sneeze

estornudo M sneeze

estrado M bench

estrafalario ADJ bizarre, outlandish

estragar[7] VT (físicamente) to devastate;
(moralmente) to corrupt

estrago M havoc; **hacer —s** to wreak havoc

estrangular VT to strangle

estratagema F stratagem

estrategia F strategy

estratégico ADJ strategic

estrato M stratum, layer; — **social** social
class

estratosfera F stratosphere

estrechamiento M constriction

estrechar VT (hacer más estrecho) to narrow;
(abrazar) to embrace; **la estrechó en sus
brazos** he held her in his arms; —**se** to
get narrower; —**se la mano** to shake
hands

estrechez F (cualidad de estrecho)
narrowness; (estrechamiento) narrowing;
(aprietos) dire straits

estrecho ADJ narrow; **la falda le quedaba
estrecha** the skirt was too tight for her;
M strait

estrella F star; — **binaria** binary star; — **de
cine** movie star; — **de mar** starfish; —
fugaz shooting star, falling star; **ver las
—s** to see stars

estrellado ADJ (como una estrella) starlike;
(cubierto de estrellas) starry

estrellar VT (aplastar) to smash; (romper) to
crack; —**se** (avión) to crash; (intento) to
fail; —**se contra** to smash into

estremecer[13] VT to make shudder; **el
terremoto estremeció París** the
earthquake rocked Paris; VI to shudder

estremecimiento M shudder

estrenar VT (un vestido) to wear for the first
time; (una obra de cine, teatro) to debut;
(una bicicleta) to try out for the first time;
(un título) to use for the first time; —**se** to
debut

estreno M (de una película) premiere; (de un
objeto) first use; (de una actividad) debut

estreñido ADJ (constipado) constipated;
(antipático) uptight

estreñimiento M constipation

estreñir[5,18] VT to constipate; —**se** to become
constipated

estrépito M racket, clatter; **causar** — to
clatter

estrepitoso ADJ noisy

estrés M stress

estresar VT to stress (out)

estría F (en la piel) stretch mark; (en una
columna) flute

estriado ADJ (piel) covered with stretch
marks; (columna) fluted; (piedra) streaked

estriar[16] VT to flute; —**se** to get stretch
marks

estribación F spur

estribar VI — **en** (apoyarse en) to lean on;

(radicar en) to lie in

estribillo M refrain

estribo M (de silla, oído) stirrup; (de coche) running board; **perder los —s** to fly off the handle

estribor M starboard

estricnina F strychnine

estricto ADJ strict

estridente ADJ strident

estrofa F verse, stanza

estrógeno M estrogen

estropajo M scrubber; **tengo la boca que es un —** my mouth is as dry as a bone

estropajoso ADJ sinewy

estropear VT to ruin

estructura F structure

estructural ADJ structural

estruendo M din, racket

estruendoso ADJ thunderous

estrujamiento M (para romper) crushing; (para sacar jugo) squeezing

estrujar VT (aplastar) to crush; (apretar) to squeeze

estrujón M squeeze

estuario M estuary

estucar[6] VT to stucco

estuche M (para joyas) jewelry box; (para pastillas) pill box; (para lentes) glasses case

estuco M stucco

estudiantado M student body

estudiante MF student

estudiantil ADJ **vida —** student life

estudiar VI/VT to study

estudio M (acción de estudiar, investigación, habitación de casa) study; (habitación de artista) studio; (apartamento pequeño) studio apartment; **en —** understudy

estudioso -sa ADJ studious; MF scholar

estufa F (para calentar) heater, stove; (para cocinar) *Méx* stove

estupefaciente ADJ & M narcotic

estupefacto ADJ stunned, speechless

estupendo ADJ stupendous, terrific; **me la pasé — en la casa de Hilary** I had a great time at Hilary's house

estupidez F stupidity; **estupideces** nonsense

estúpido ADJ stupid

estupor M stupor

estupro M statutory rape

etapa F stage; **por —s** by stages

etcétera CONJ etcetera, and so forth

éter M ether

eternidad F eternity

eternizarse[9] VI to drag on

eterno ADJ eternal, everlasting

ética F ethics

ético ADJ ethical

etimología F etymology

etíope ADJ & MF Ethiopian

etiqueta F (normas de comportamiento) etiquette; (en una lata, botella) label; (en una prenda) tag; **— adhesiva** sticker; **— de identificación** name tag; **— de precio** price tag; **nos trataron con —** they treated us very formally; **vestirse de —** to dress formally

etiquetar VT (latas, botellas, personas) to label; (prendas) to tag

etnicidad F ethnicity

étnico ADJ ethnic

etnografía F ethnography

etnología F ethnology

eucalipto M eucalyptus

eufemismo M euphemism

euforia F euphoria

eunuco M eunuch

euro M euro

Europa F Europe

europeo -a ADJ & MF European

eutanasia F euthanasia

evacuación F (de un lugar) evacuation; (del vientre) bowel movement; (de agua) drainage

evacuar VT (un lugar, a una persona) to evacuate; (el vientre, los excrementos) to void; (agua) to drain

evadir VT to evade; **—se** to escape

evaluación F evaluation

evaluar[17] VT (analizar) to evaluate, to assess; (tasar) to estimate; (calificar) to test

evangélico ADJ evangelical

evangelio M gospel

evaporación F evaporation

evaporar VT to evaporate; **—se** to vanish

evasión F (fiscal) evasion; (de prisioneros, de la realidad) escape; **— de capitales** capital flight

evasiva F **salirse con —s** to beat around the bush

evasivo ADJ evasive

evasor -ora MF evader

evento M event

evidencia F evidence; **dejar / poner en —** to show up; **quedar / ponerse en —** to become apparent

evidenciar VT to make evident; **—se** to become evident

evidente ADJ evident, obvious

evitar VT (eludir) to avoid; (ahorrar) to spare

evocar[6] VT (una memoria) to evoke; (a los espíritus) to conjure up

evolución F evolution

evolucionar VI to evolve

ex MF *fam* ex

exacerbar VT (intensificar) to exacerbate; (irritar) to aggravate

exactitud F accuracy, precision

exacto ADJ exact, precise, accurate; INTERJ exactly

exageración F exaggeration

exagerado ADJ exaggerated; **Jorge es un —** Jorge always exaggerates

exagerar VI/VT to exaggerate

exaltar VT to exalt; **—se** to get excited

examen M (inspección) examination; (prueba) examination, test, exam; **— de ingreso** entrance examination; **— final** final examination; **— médico** checkup; **dar un —** to take a test; **poner un —** to give a test

examinar VT (inspeccionar) to examine; (someter a un examen) to test

exasperar VT to exasperate, to aggravate

excavación F excavation; (arqueológica) dig

excavador -ora MF (persona) excavator; F (aparato) excavator, earthmover

excavar VT to excavate, to dig

excedente ADJ & M surplus

exceder VT (sobrepasar) to exceed; (superar) to surpass; **— de** to go beyond

excelencia F excellence; **por —** par excellence

excelente ADJ excellent, great

excentricidad F eccentricity

excéntrico ADJ eccentric

excepción F exception; **a — de** with the exception of

excepcional ADJ exceptional

excepto ADV & PREP except

exceptuar[17] VT to except

excesivo ADJ excessive

exceso M excess; **— de equipaje** excess baggage; **beber en —** to drink to excess; **comer en —** to overeat

excitación F (de músculos) excitement; (sexual) arousal

excitante ADJ stimulating

excitar VT (un órgano) to excite; (sexualmente) to arouse; **—se** (sexualmente) to get aroused; (átomos) to be excited

exclamación F exclamation

exclamar VT to exclaim

excluir[31] VT to exclude

exclusión F exclusion

exclusivo ADJ exclusive

excomulgar[7] VT to excommunicate

excremento M excrement

excretar VT to excrete

excursión F excursion, outing

excusa F excuse

excusable ADJ excusable

excusado M *Méx* toilet

excusar VT to excuse

exención F exemption

exento ADJ exempt; **— de impuestos** tax-exempt

exequias F PL funeral rites

exhalar VI/VT (aire) to exhale, to breathe out; (un olor) to give off; **— un suspiro** to sigh

exhaustivo ADJ exhaustive, thorough

exhausto ADJ exhausted

exhibición F (manifestación) exhibition; (despliegue) display

exhibir VT (fotos) to exhibit; (mercancías) to display; (el carnet de identidad) to show; **—se** to be shown

exhortar VT to exhort, to urge

exigencia F demand

exigente ADJ demanding, exacting

exigir[11] VT to demand; **exigen a alguien que sepa inglés** they require someone who knows English

exiguo ADJ meager; **exigua mayoría** scant majority

exiliado -da MF exile

exiliar VT to exile

exilio M exile

eximio ADJ illustrious

eximir VT (de impuestos) to exempt; (de sospecha) to clear; (de una responsabilidad) to excuse

existencia F existence; **complicarle la — a alguien** to cause someone trouble; **la lucha por la —** the fight for survival; **—s** stock on hand; **en —** in stock, on hand

existente ADJ extant, existing

existir VI to exist

éxito M success; (musical) hit; **— de taquilla** blockbuster; **tener —** to be successful; **tiene — con las mujeres** he's popular with women

exitoso ADJ successful

éxodo M exodus

exonerar VT to exonerate

exorbitante ADJ exorbitant

exorcisar VT to exorcise

exorcismo M exorcism

exótico ADJ exotic

expansión F (crecimiento) expansion; (diversión) relaxation

expansivo ADJ (que expande) expansive; (efusivo) effusive

expatriado -da MF expatriate

expatriar VT to expatriate, exile

expectación F anticipation

expectativa F (esperanza) expectation;

(posibilidad) prospect; **estar en — de algo** to be on pins and needles; **— de vida** life expectancy

expectorar VI/VT to expectorate, to cough up

expedición F (viaje) expedition; (de documentos) issuing; (de mercancías) delivery

expedicionario -ria ADJ expeditionary; MF member of an expedition

expedidor -ora ADJ shipping; MF shipper

expediente M (administrativo) file, dossier; (policial, académico) record

expedir[5] VT (enviar) to dispatch; (emitir) to issue

expeler VT to expel

experiencia F experience

experimentado ADJ experienced

experimental ADJ experimental

experimentar VI (hacer experimentos) to experiment; VT (tener experiencia de) to experience

experimento M experiment

experto -ta ADJ & MF expert

expiación F atonement

expiar[16] VT to atone for

expirar VI to expire

explayarse VI to become extended; **— sobre** to enlarge upon

explicable ADJ explainable, explicable

explicación F explanation

explicar[6] VT to explain; **—se** to make oneself clear; **no me explico por qué** I can't figure out why

explicativo ADJ explanatory

explícito ADJ explicit

exploración F exploration

explorador -ora ADJ exploring; MF (expedicionario) explorer; (militar) scout

explorar VI/VT to explore; (con fines diagnósticos) to scan; (con fines militares) to scout

explosión F explosion; **hacer —** to explode

explosivo ADJ & M explosive

explotación F exploitation

explotar VT (sacar provecho) to exploit; (hacer explosión) to explode

exponente M exponent

exponer[39] VT (al sol, al peligro) to expose; (al público) to exhibit, to display; (explicar) to state, to set forth; **—se al peligro** to expose oneself to danger

exportación F (acción) exportation, export; (cosa) export

exportar VI/VT to export

exposición F (feria) exposition; (de arte) exhibition; (explicación) explanation; (al sol, a una influencia, al peligro) exposure

expresar VT to express

expresión F expression; **valga la —** so to speak

expresivo ADJ expressive

expreso ADJ (explícito) express; (rápido) fast; M express train

exprimidor M juicer

exprimir VT (naranjas) to squeeze; (zumo) to squeeze out

expropiar VT to expropriate

expuesto ADJ exposed; **lo —** what has been said

expulsar VT to expel; (de un bar) to throw out; (de un partido) to eject

expulsión F expulsion

exquisito -ta ADJ exquisite; (comida) delicious; MF effete snob

extasiado ADJ rapt

extasiarse[16] VI to be enraptured

éxtasis M ecstasy (también droga)

extender[1] VT (el brazo, radio de acción, gratitud) to extend; (un tapete, una masa, un idioma) to spread; (un cheque) to draw up; **—se** to extend; **—se sobre** to enlarge upon; **la fiesta se extendió hasta las 3** the party lasted until 3 o'clock

extendido ADJ (brazos) outstretched; (costumbre) widespread

extensión F (del antebrazo, semántica, telefónica) extension; (de terreno) expanse; (de un texto) length; (eléctrica) extension cord; **por —** by extension; **tener mucha —** to be widespread

extensivo ADJ extensive; **hacer —** to extend

extenso ADJ (calendario, plan, grupo) extensive; (narración, programa de radio) extended

extenuado ADJ exhausted

exterior ADJ (de fuera) exterior, outer; (mundo) outside; (política) foreign; M (parte de afuera) exterior, outside; (aspecto) outward appearance; **en —es** on location

exteriorizar[9] VT to externalize

exterminación F extermination

exterminar VT to exterminate

exterminio M extermination

externo ADJ external

extinción F extinction

extinguidor M fire extinguisher

extinguir[12] VT (un fuego) to extinguish, to put out; (una especie) to make extinct, to wipe out; **—se** (animal, volcán) to go extinct

extinto ADJ extinct

extintor M fire extinguisher

extirpación F removal

extirpar VT to remove

extorsión F extortion

extorsionar VT to extort money from

extorsionista MF racketeer

extra ADJ extra; **horas —s** overtime; MF INV (de película) extra; M (cosa accesoria) extra; F (pago extraordinario) bonus

extracto M (resumen) abstract; (de café) extract

extraditar VT to extradite

extraer[45] VT (esencia) to extract; (minerales) to mine; (un diente) to pull

extramarital ADJ extramarital

extranjero -ra ADJ foreign; MF foreigner; **en el —** abroad

extrañar VT (sorprender) to surprise; (echar de menos) to miss; **no es de — que** it's no wonder that; **no me extraña** it doesn't surprise me; **—se** to be surprised

extrañeza F surprise

extraño -ña ADJ (persona, costumbre) strange; (partícula) foreign; MF stranger

extraoficial ADJ unofficial

extraordinario ADJ extraordinary

extrapolar VI/VT to extrapolate

extrasensorial ADJ extrasensory

extraterrestre ADJ & M alien, extraterrestrial

extravagancia F (cualidad de extravagante) extravagance; (comportamiento extravagante) outrageous behavior

extravagante ADJ flamboyant, outrageous

extraviar[16] VT (perder) to misplace; (confundir) to lead astray; **—se** to lose one's way, to get lost

extravío M loss

extremado ADJ extreme

extremar VT to maximize

extremidad F extremity

extremo ADJ (máximo, mínimo, extraordinario) extreme; (más lejos) farthest; **con — cuidado** with utmost care; M (punto más alejado) extreme; (de una región) end; **llegar al — de** to go so far as to; **— Oriente** Far East; **extrema izquierda** far left; **extrema unción** last rites

extrovertido -da ADJ extroverted; MF extrovert

exuberante ADJ (vegetación, jóvenes) exuberant; (mujer) voluptuous

exudar VI/VT to exude

exultante ADJ exhilarated, exultant

exultar VI to exult

eyacular VI/VT to ejaculate

eyectar VT to eject

Ff

fábrica F factory, plant; (de acero, de textiles) mill

fabricación F manufacture, manufacturing

fabricante MF manufacturer; (de coches) maker

fabricar[6] VT (producir) to manufacture, to make; (construir) to build; (inventar) to concoct, to fabricate

fabril ADJ manufacturing

fábula F (relato) fable; (mentira) falsehood

fabuloso ADJ (imaginario) imaginary; (magnífico) awesome, fabulous

facción F faction; **facciones** facial features

faceta F facet

facha F **estaba hecho una —** he was a sight

fachada F façade

facial ADJ facial

fácil ADJ easy; (promiscuo) easy, loose; **— de entender** self-explanatory; **— de usar** user-friendly

facilidad F ease; (habilidad) facility, knack

facilitar VT (hacer más fácil) to facilitate; (proporcionar) to furnish

facsímil M fax

factible ADJ feasible

fáctico ADJ factual

factor M factor

factoría F trading post

factura F bill, invoice

facturable ADJ billable

facturación F billing

facturar VT to invoice; (equipaje) to check

facultad F (habilidad) faculty; (autoridad) authority; (división de una universidad) college

facundia F gift of gab

faena F (trabajo corporal) chore; (labor) task; (molestia) nuisance

fagot M bassoon

fairway M fairway

faisán M pheasant

faja F (en la cintura) sash; (prenda interior) girdle; (de tierra) ribbon, strip

fajar VT (ceñir) to gird; (envolver) to wrap up; (golpear) to thrash

fajo M (de dinero) wad; (de papel, paja) sheaf

falacia F fallacy

falaz ADJ fallacious

falda F (prenda de vestir) skirt (también mujer o mujeres); (de una montaña) slope

faldón M (de una camisa) tail, shirttail; (de un saco) coattail

falible ADJ fallible

falla F (en un argumento) flaw; (en un motor) miss; (de una máquina) failure; (geológica) fault; **las Fallas** Valencian holiday

fallar VI (no funcionar) to fail; (un motor) to miss; VI/VT (un juez) to find, to rule

fallecer[13] VI to pass away, to decease

fallecimiento M demise, decease

fallo M (de una computadora) bug, failure; (de la memoria) lapse; (de un juez) ruling, finding

falsear VT to falsify

falsedad F (dicho falso) falsehood; (condición de falso) falseness

falsificación F (de dinero) counterfeit; (de un documento) forgery

falsificar[6] VT to falsify, to fake; (dinero) to counterfeit; VI/VT (una firma) to forge

falso ADJ (incorrecto) false, untrue; (no auténtico) fake, phony; (dinero) counterfeit; (promesa) hollow; (amigo) faithless, two-faced; (excusa) made-up; **falsa alarma** false alarm; **jurar en —** to perjure oneself; **paso en —** a false step; **salida en —** false start

falta F (defecto) fault; (carencia) lack, want; (ausencia) absence, miss; (jugada ilícita) foul; (de ortografía) mistake; **— de aire** shortness of breath; **— de respeto** disrespect; **a — de** for want of, in the absence of; **hacer —** to be necessary; **me hace —** I need; **sin —** without fail

faltar VI (ausentarse) to be absent; (no haber) to be lacking; **— a la palabra** to break a promise; **— a la verdad** to misstate oneself; **—le el respeto a** to disrespect; **— poco para las cinco** to be almost five o'clock; **me falta tiempo** I don't have enough time; **¡no faltaba más!** (con indignación) that's the last straw; (no hay de qué) don't mention it! (no te molestes) I wouldn't hear of it

falto ADJ lacking; **— de esperanza** devoid of hope

fama F (condición de conocido) fame; (reputación) reputation

famélico ADJ ravenous

familia F family; **— nuclear** nuclear family; **en —** in the family; **jefe de —** head of household; **la señora de Juan tuvo —** John's wife had a baby

familiar ADJ (de familia) (of the) family; (amistoso, coloquial, conocido) familiar; (de tamaño grande) family-size; **coche —** family car; **vida —** family life; MF relative; **—es** next of kin

familiaridad F familiarity

familiarizar[9] VT to familiarize, to acquaint; **—se** to acquaint oneself, to become familiar with

famoso ADJ famous

fanático -ca ADJ fanatic; MF fanatic, zealot; (de deportes) freak

fanatismo M fanaticism

fanega F bushel

fanfarria F fanfare

fanfarrón -ona MF braggart, show-off; ADJ blustering

fanfarronear VI to bluster

fanfarronería F bluster, swagger

fango M mire

fangoso ADJ miry

fantasear VI to fantasize

fantasía F (imaginación) imagination; (imagen) fantasy; **de —** fake, artificial

fantasioso ADJ (niño) imaginative; (idea) fanciful

fantasma M ghost, phantom

fantasmagórico ADJ ghostly

fantástico ADJ fantastic

farándula F show business

fardo M (paquete) bundle; (de heno, algodón) bale

farfolla F husk

farfulla F jabber

farfullar VI to jabber

faringe F pharynx

faríngeo ADJ pharyngeal

farmacéutico -ca MF pharmacist, druggist; ADJ pharmaceutical

farmacia F pharmacy, drugstore

farmacología F pharmacology

faro M (torre) lighthouse; (luz) beacon; **— delantero** headlight

farol M (portátil) lantern; (del alumbrado público) street lamp, streetlight; (pie de hierro) lamppost; (jactancia, envite) bluff; **darse —** to show off, to put on airs

farra F spree; **ir de —** to go on a spree

farsa F (engaño) sham, hoax; (obra teatral, imitación ridícula) farce, mockery

farsante MF fraud, fake

fascículo M installment

fascinación F fascination

fascinante ADJ fascinating

fascinar VI/VT to fascinate

fascismo M fascism

fascista ADJ & MF fascist

fase F phase

fastidiado ADJ irked

fastidiar VT to irk

fastidio M annoyance
fastidioso ADJ annoying, wearisome
fatal ADJ (mortal) fatal; (terrible) terrible;
   mujer — femme fatale; ADV very badly
fatalidad F (desgracia) misfortune; (destino)
   destiny
fatídico ADJ ill-fated
fatiga F fatigue, exhaustion; **—s** hardships
fatigado ADJ tired, weary
fatigar[7] VT to tire out
fatigoso ADJ (cansado) tiring; (aburrido)
   tiresome
fauces F PL jaw
favor M favor; **a — de** in favor of; **por —**
   please
favorable ADJ favorable
favorecer[13] VT to favor
favoritismo M favoritism
favorito -ta ADJ favorite; MF favorite; (en una
   elección) front-runner; (de la maestra) pet
fax M fax
faxear VT to fax
faz F face
FBI M FBI
fe F faith; **— de bautismo** baptismal
   certificate; **— de erratas** list of errors; **—
   de nacimiento** birth certificate; **de
   buena —** in good faith; **dar — de** to
   vouch for
fealdad F ugliness
febrero M February
febril ADJ (con fiebre) feverish; (actividad)
   feverish, hectic
fecha F date
fechado ADJ dated
fechar VT to date
fechoría F misdeed
fecundar VT to fertilize; (una hembra) to
   impregnate
fecundo ADJ fertile
federación F federation
federal ADJ federal
felicidad F happiness; **¡—es!** congratulations
felicitación F congratulation;
   ¡felicitaciones! congratulations!
felicitar VT to congratulate
feligrés -esa MF parishioner; **feligreses**
   congregation
felino ADJ feline; M cat
feliz ADJ happy
felpa F plush
felpudo M door mat
femenino ADJ (como una mujer, de género
   gramatical) feminine; (de la mujer) female
feminidad F femininity
feminismo F feminism
fémur M femur

fenómeno M phenomenon
feo ADJ ugly, homely; (dentadura) bad;
   (accidente) nasty
féretro M coffin
feria F (mercado) market; (exposición) fair;
   (espectáculo) carnival; (celebración)
   holiday
feriante MF trader at fairs
fermentación F fermentation
fermentar VT to ferment; (cerveza) to brew
fermento M ferment
ferocidad F ferocity
feroz ADJ ferocious, fierce
férreo ADJ iron; (disciplina) harsh
ferretería F (tienda) hardware store;
   (artículos) hardware
ferrocarril M railroad, railway
ferroviario -ria ADJ railroad; MF railroad
   employee
ferry M ferryboat
fértil ADJ fertile
fertilidad F fertility
fertilizante M fertilizer
fertilizar[9] VT to fertilize
ferviente ADJ fervent
fervor M fervor, zeal
fervoroso ADJ zealous
festejar VT to celebrate
festejo M celebration
festín M feast; **darse un —** to treat oneself
festival M festival
festividad F festivity
festivo ADJ festive, gay; **día —** holiday
festón M scallop
festonear VT to scallop
fetal ADJ fetal
fetiche M fetish
fétido ADJ foul-smelling
feto M fetus
feudal ADJ feudal
feudo M manor
fiabilidad F reliability
fiable ADJ reliable
fiador -ora MF guarantor, voucher;
   (prestamista) backer; (de un preso)
   bondsman
fiambre M (carne) cold cut; (cadáver) *fam*
   stiff
fianza F security, guaranty; (de un preso) bail
fiar[16] VT (garantizar) to vouch for; **—se de** to
   trust
fiasco M fiasco
fibra F fiber; **— de vidrio** fiberglass; **—
   óptica** optical fiber
fibroso ADJ fibrous
ficción F fiction
ficha F (pieza) token; (de dominó) domino;

(de damas) checker; (en poker, ruleta) chip; (tarjeta) index card; MF INV (persona con antecedentes penales) delinquent

fichar VT to open a file on; VI to punch in

fichero M (de computadora) file; (archivador) filing cabinet

ficticio ADJ (no real) fictitious; (novelesco) fictional

fidedigno ADJ trustworthy

fideicomisario -ria MF trustee

fideicomiso M trusteeship

fidelidad F fidelity, faithfulness; (de una traducción) closeness; (a la bandera) allegiance

fideo M noodle

fiduciario -ria ADJ & MF fiduciary

fiebre F fever; — **aftosa** foot-and-mouth disease; — **amarilla** yellow fever; — **de candilejas** stage fright; — **del oro** gold rush; — **tifoidea** typhoid fever; **tener** — to run a fever

fiel ADJ faithful; (exacto) true, accurate; M pointer on a scale; **los —es** the congregation

fieltro M felt; (sombrero de fieltro) felt hat

fiera F beast; **ponerse hecho una** — to go berserk

fiereza F ferocity

fiero ADJ fierce; (muy grande) huge

fierro M piece of iron

fiesta F (festejo) party; (día feriado) holiday; **aguar una** — to ruin a party

fiestero -ra ADJ fond of parties; MF merrymaker, party animal

figura F figure

figurado ADJ figurative

figurar VI (aparecer) to feature; (lucirse) to be seen; (incluirse) to figure, to enter into; **—se** (imaginarse) to imagine; **¡figúrate!** imagine!

figurativo ADJ figurative

figurín M fashion plate

figurón M dummy

fijación F fixing

fijador M hairspray

fijar VT (un cartel) to fix, to fasten; (una fecha) to set; **—se en** (notar) to notice; (prestar atención) to pay attention to, to focus on

fijo ADJ (sujeto, que no cambia) fixed; (inmóvil) fixed, stationary; (firme) firm; (definitivo) definite; (permanente) permanent

fila F (uno detrás del otro) row, file; (hombro a hombro) rank; (de espera) line; — **india** single file; **cerrar —s** to close ranks; **romper —s** to break ranks

filamento M filament

filantropía F philanthropy

filarmónica F philharmonic

filarmónico ADJ philharmonic

filete M (de carne) fillet; (de un plato) rim

filetear VT to fillet

filial ADJ filial; F affiliate

filibusterismo M filibustering

filigrana F filigree

Filipinas F Philippines

filipino -na ADJ & MF Philippine

filmar VT to film, to shoot

filo M (de una navaja) cutting edge; (biológico) phylum; **de doble** — two-edged; **al** — **de las dos** at around two o'clock

filón M seam, vein, pocket

filoso ADJ sharp

filosofía F philosophy

filosófico ADJ philosophical

filósofo -fa MF philosopher

filtración F (acción de filtrar) filtration; (de información) leak

filtrar VT to filter; **—se** to leak through

filtro M filter; — **de aire** air filter; — **de amor** love potion

fin M (conclusión, objetivo) end; — **de año** New Year's Eve; — **del mundo** (lugar apartado) boondocks; — **de semana** weekend; — **de siglo** turn of the century; **al** — at last; **al** — **y al cabo** at any rate; **a** — **de que** so that; **a** — **de mes** toward the end of the month; **en** — in conclusion; **poner** — **a** to put an end to; **por** — at last; **sin** — (ilimitado) myriad; (continuo) endless

finado ADJ late

final ADJ final, last; F (deportiva) final; M (de una historia) ending; (de un terreno) end; (de una carrera) finish; (de una filmación) wrap

finalista MF finalist

finalización F completion

finalizar[9] VT to finish

finalmente ADV at last

financiación F (para una compra) financing; (para un proyecto científico) funding

financiamiento M (para una compra) financing; (para un proyecto científico) funding

financiar VT (una compra) to finance; (un proyecto) to fund, to underwrite

financiero -ra ADJ financial; MF financier

finanza F finance; **—s** finances

finca F property

finés -esa MF Finn; M (lengua) Finnish; ADJ Finnish

fineza F (atención) courtesy; (suavidad) smoothness

fingir[11] VI/VT (sorpresa) to feign; (un ataque al corazón) to fake; **fingió que la quería** he pretended to love her

finiquito M settlement

finito ADJ finite

finlandés -esa MF Finn; M (lengua) Finnish; ADJ Finnish

Finlandia F Finland

fino ADJ (vino, arena, pelo, metal) fine; (sentidos) keen, sharp; (medias) sheer; (hielo, alambre, voz) thin; (modales) smooth, refined

firma F (compañía) firm; (rúbrica) signature

firmamento M sky

firmante MF signer

firmar VI/VT to sign

firme ADJ firm; (control) tight; (colores) fast; (amarras) secure; (mano) steady, sure; (resistencia) stiff; (apoyo, resistencia) strong, staunch, steadfast; **mantenerse —** to stand one's ground; **¡—s!** attention!

firmeza F firmness; (de la mano) steadiness; (de la resistencia) stiffness; (del apoyo) strength

fiscal ADJ fiscal; MF public prosecutor, district attorney

fiscalía F prosecution

fisgar[7] VI to snoop

fisgón -ona ADJ snooping; MF snoop

fisgonear VI to snoop

física F physics

físico -ca ADJ physical; MF (persona) physicist; M (cuerpo) physique

fisiología F physiology

fisiológico ADJ physiological

fisonomía F features

fisura F fissure

fiyano ADJ Fijian

Fiyi M Fiji

flácido, fláccido ADJ (sin firmeza) limp; (gordo) flabby

flaco ADJ thin, skinny; **su lado —** his weakness

flacura F thinness

flagrante ADJ (injusticia) gross; **en — delito** in the act

flamante ADJ brand-new

flamear VI (llamear) to flame; (ondear) to flap

flamenco -ca ADJ Flemish; MF Flemish person; M (lengua) Flemish; (ave) flamingo; (baile) flamenco

flamígero ADJ flaming

flan M caramel custard

flanco M (de un animal, ejército) flank; (de un neumático) sidewall

flanquear VT to flank

flaquear VI (intención) to waver; (salud) to wane

flaqueza F weakness

flash M (noticias, visión) flash; (lámpara) flashbulb, flash

flashback M flashback

flatulencia F flatulence

flauta F flute; **— dulce** recorder

flautín M piccolo

flecha F arrow

flechar VT to wound with an arrow

flechazo M (herida) wound from an arrow; (enamoramiento) love at first sight

fleco M (de una alfombra) fringe; (de pelo) bangs

flema F phlegm

flequillo M bangs

fletamento M charter

fletar VT to charter

flete M (contratación) charter; (envío) transport; (precio de transporte) freight

flexibilidad F flexibility; (libertad) latitude

flexible ADJ flexible; (cuerpo humano) limber, supple; (opinión) pliant, pliable

flojear VT to slacken

flojedad F laxity, looseness; (debilidad) weakness

flojera F (debilidad) weakness; (pereza) laziness

flojo ADJ (no ajustado) loose, slack; (holgazán) lazy; (inferior) crummy; (débil) weak; (sin fundamento) flimsy

floppy M floppy disk

flor F flower, blossom, bloom; (cumplido) compliment; **— de la edad** prime of life; **— de Pascua** poinsettia; **— y nata** the cream of the crop; **a — de** flush with; **en — in bloom**

floración F blooming, blossoming

floral ADJ flowery

floreado ADJ flowery

florear VT (adornar con flores) to decorate with flowers; (adornar) to adorn

florecer[13] VI (echar flores) to flower, to bloom; (prosperar) to flourish, to thrive

floreciente ADJ (que prospera) flourishing, prosperous; (que echa flores) blooming

florecimiento M flourishing

floreo M flourish

florería F florist's shop

florero M flower vase

florete M fencing foil

florido ADJ flowery

florista MF florist

floritura F flourish

flota F fleet

flotador M (cosa que flota) float; (de un avión) pontoon; ADJ floating

flotante ADJ floating, buoyant

flotar VI (estar suspendido, variar en valor) to float; (moverse en la superficie) to drift; (en el aire) to waft

flote M flotation; **a —** afloat; **poner a —** to set afloat

fluctuación F fluctuation; (amplitud de variación) range

fluctuar[17] VI to fluctuate

fluidez F (lo fluido) fluency; (lo aguado) thinness

fluido ADJ (que fluye) fluid, flowing; (no vacilante) fluent; M fluid

fluir[31] VI to flow

flujo M flow; (uterino) discharge; **— de caja** cash flow

flúor M (elemento gaseoso) fluorine; (sal) fluoride

fluorescente ADJ fluorescent

fluoruro M fluoride

flux M flush

fluyente ADJ flowing

fobia F phobia

foca F seal

foco M (punto central) focus; (bombilla) bulb; (lámpara potente) spotlight

fofo ADJ mushy

fogata F bonfire; (en un campamento) campfire

fogonazo M flash

fogonero M fireman

fogoso ADJ fiery, spirited

folclore M folklore

folio M folio

folíolo M leaflet

follaje M foliage

folleto M pamphlet, brochure

follón M (confusión) mess; (alboroto) ruckus

fomentar VT (estudio) to promote; (amistad) to foster; (discordia) to foment; (apoyo) to drum up

fomento M encouragement

fonda F inn

fondear VI to anchor

fondillos M PL seat of pants

fondista MF (posadero) innkeeper; (corredor) long-distance runner

fondo M (parte más profunda de algo) bottom; (de un salón) rear; (del mar) bed; (de un cuadro, foto) background; (de dinero) fund; (de una biblioteca) holdings; **— común** pool; **— físico** endurance; **— musical** background music; **— mutuo** mutual fund; **—s** funds; **a —** in depth; **carrera de —** long-distance race; **de cuatro en —** four abreast; **de —** in depth; **sin —** bottomless; **tocar —** to hit rock bottom

fonética F phonetics

fonógrafo M phonograph

fonología F phonology

fontanería F plumbing

fontanero -ra MF plumber

forajido -da MF outlaw

foráneo ADJ foreign; **influencia foránea** outside influence

forastero -ra MF stranger, outsider

forcejear VI to struggle

forcejeo M struggle

fórceps M forceps

forense ADJ forensic; MF forensic scientist

forja F (fogón) forge; (acción de forjar) forging; (taller) blacksmith's shop

forjado ADJ wrought

forjar VT (metales, un acuerdo) to forge; (un acuerdo) to hammer out; (un documento) to frame

forma F (figura) form, shape; (manera) manner; **ponerse en —** to get in shape; **no hay —** no way; **dar — a** to shape

formación F formation

formal ADJ (que atañe a la forma) formal, serious; (fiable) reliable

formalidad F (convencionalidad) formality; (fiabilidad) reliability

formalismo M formality

formalizar[9] VT to make official; **—se** to settle down

formar VT to form; (reunir tropas) to muster; (entrenar) to train; **—se** (montañas) to form; (estudiantes) to be educated

formatear VT to format

formateo M formatting

formativo ADJ formative

formato M format

formidable ADJ formidable

formón M wood chisel

fórmula F formula

formular VT to formulate; (un plan, una pregunta) to frame; (un documento) to word

formulario M form

fornicar[6] VI to fornicate

fornido ADJ stout, sturdy

foro M forum; (de un escenario) back

forrado ADJ (con un forro) lined; (bien provisto) flush

forraje M forage, fodder

forrajear VI to forage

forrar VT (un saco) to line; **—se** to line one's pockets

forro M lining; (de un libro) jacket
fortalecer[13] VT to fortify, to strengthen
fortaleza F (construcción) fortress, fort; (fuerza) fortitude
fortificación F fortification
fortificar[6] VT to fortify
fortuito ADJ fortuitous, accidental
fortuna F fortune; **por —** fortunately; **probar —** to try one's luck; **hacer —** to become rich
forúnculo M boil
forzar[9] VT to force, to coerce; **— la entrada** to break into
forzoso ADJ (por la fuerza) forcible; (inevitable) necessary; (aterrizaje) forced
fosa F (sepultura) grave; (de la nariz) cavity; (en el fondo del mar) trench
fosfato M phosphate
fósforo M (sustancia) phosphorus; (cerilla) match
fósil ADJ & M fossil
foso M (de un castillo) moat; (de un taller, teatro) pit
foto F snapshot, photo
fotocopia F photocopy
fotocopiadora F photocopier
fotocopiar VI/VT to photocopy
fotoeléctrico ADJ photoelectric
fotogénico ADJ photogenic
fotografía F (foto) photograph; (arte) photography
fotografiar[16] VT to photograph
fotógrafo -fa MF photographer
fotón M photon
fotosíntesis F photosynthesis
foul M foul
frac M tails
fracasar VI to fail; (una película) to bomb; (una embarcación) to break up
fracaso M failure; (una película) flop, bomb
fracción F fraction
fractura F fracture, break
fracturar VT to fracture, to break; **se fracturó la cadera** she broke her hip
fragancia F fragrance
fragante ADJ fragrant; **en —** in the act
fragata F frigate
frágil ADJ (delicado) delicate; (que se quiebra) fragile, brittle; (una paz) tenuous
fragilidad F (condición de quebradizo) brittleness, delicacy; (debilidad) frailty
fragmento M fragment; (de metal, piedra) scrap; (de una conversación) snatch; (de un texto) extract, excerpt
fragoso ADJ rugged
fragua F (fogón) forge; (taller) blacksmith's shop

fraguar[8] VT to forge; (una trama) to hatch; VI (cemento, yeso) to set
fraile M friar
frambuesa F raspberry
frambueso M raspberry bush
francés -esa ADJ French; M (lengua) French; (hombre) Frenchman; F (mujer) Frenchwoman
franchute -uta MF *pey* frog
Francia F France
franco ADJ (sincero) frank, candid; (exento) free; **una franca mayoría** a clear majority; **un tratado —americano** a Franco-American treaty
francotirador -ora MF sniper
franela F flannel
franja F ribbon
franquear VT (una frontera) to cross; (una carta) to frank; **—se** to be frank
franqueo M postage
franqueza F frankness
franquicia F (concesión) franchise; (exención) exemption
frasco M (recipiente de vidrio) flask; (de medicina, perfume) bottle; (de mermelada) jar
frase F phrase
frasear VI/VT to phrase
fraternal ADJ fraternal, brotherly
fraternidad F fraternity
fraternizar[9] VI fraternize
fraterno ADJ fraternal
fraude M fraud
fraudulento ADJ fraudulent
frazada F blanket
frecuencia F frequency; **con —** frequently
frecuentar VT to frequent; (una tienda) to patronize
frecuente ADJ frequent
fregadero M sink
fregado M scrubbing
fregar[7] VT to scour, to scrub
fregona F (persona) scrubwoman, drudge; (utensilio) mop
freír[15] VI/VT to fry
frenar VT (un coche) to brake; (la inmigración) to restrain; (los impulsos) to bridle; VI to brake, to apply the brakes
frenesí M frenzy; (de actividad) flurry
frenético ADJ frantic
freno M (de coche) brake; (de caballo) bit; (contra el contrabando) curb
frente F forehead; **el sudor de la —** the sweat of one's brow; M (parte delantera, zona de combate, zona meteorológica) front; (de un edificio) face; **— a** (ante) in the face of; (al otro lado) facing; **— a —**

face to face; **de** — head-on; **en** — **de** in
front of; **hacer** — to face; **pasar al** — to
come to the fore

fresa F (fruta) strawberry; (herramienta) mill

fresadora F milling machine

fresar VT to mill

frescachona F buxom woman

fresco ADJ (que acaba de producirse,
descansado) fresh; (frío) cool, brisk; (de
poco abrigo) light; (no cocinado) raw;
(pintura) wet; M (frío) coolness; (pintura)
fresco

frescor M (de verduras) freshness; (del aire)
coolness

frescura F (de verduras, del carácter)
freshness; (del tiempo) coolness;
(comentario) impudent remark

fresno M ash tree

friabilidad F looseness

frialdad F coldness, coolness

fricción F friction, rubbing

friccionar VT to rub

friega F rubbing, massage

frigorífico M (electrodoméstico) refrigerator;
(cámara) refrigeration chamber

frijol M bean

frío ADJ cold; (muy frío) frigid; M cold; **tener**
— to be cold

friolento ADJ sensitive to cold

friolera F **la** — **de $50,000** a trifling
$50,000

fritada F dish of fried food

frito ADJ fried; M dish of fried food

fritura F (acción de freír) frying; (comida
frita) dish of fried food

frivolidad F frivolity

frívolo ADJ frivolous

fronda F foliage

frondoso ADJ leafy

frontera F frontier, border

fronterizo ADJ frontier

frontón M (juego) jai alai; (pista) jai alai
court

frotación F rubbing

frotar VI/VT to rub

frote M rub

frotis M smear

fructífero ADJ fruitful

fructificar[6] VI to bear fruit

fructosa F fructose

frugal ADJ frugal

frunce M (volante) ruffle; (defecto) pucker

fruncir[10b] VT to gather; — **el ceño** to frown,
to knit one's brow; — **los labios** to purse
one's lips

fruslería F trifle

frustración F frustration

frustrar VT (los planes) to frustrate, to
thwart, to foil; (las esperanzas) to shatter,
to dash; —**se** to fail, to miscarry

fruta F fruit

frutero -era MF fruit vendor; M fruit dish

fruto M fruit; —**s del mar** seafood

fuego M fire; (para un cigarro) light; —
antiaéreo anti-artillery fire; —**s
artificiales** fireworks; **abrir el** — to
begin to fire; **alto el** — cease-fire; **bajo** —
under fire; **arma de** — firearm; **entre
dos** —**s** between a rock and a hard place;
hacer — to fire; **poner / pegar /
prender** — **a** to set fire to

fuelle M bellows

fuel-oil M fuel oil

fuente F (surtidor) fountain; (manantial,
referencia) spring; (caracteres de imprenta)
font; **de buena** — from the horse's
mouth

fuera ADV outside, out; — **de** outside of; —
de borda outboard; — **de combate** out
of commission; — **de serie** one of a kind;
INTERJ out!

fuero M (jurisdicción) jurisdiction;
(privilegio) privilege, charter

fuerte ADJ strong; (ruido) loud; (cuero)
tough; (personalidad) forceful; (estantería)
sturdy; (comida) hearty; M (castillo) fort;
(talento especial) strong point; ADV (tirar)
strongly; (respirar) heavily; (gritar) loud;
soplar — to bluster; **pisar** — to stomp;
atar — to tie tight

fuerza F (capacidad de mover algo) force; (de
una persona, animal) strength; — **aérea**
air force; — **bruta** brute force; — **de la
naturaleza** force of nature; — **de tarea**
task force; — **de voluntad** willpower; —**s
armadas** armed forces; **a** — **de** by dint
of; **hacer** — to press on; **por la** — by
force; **sacar** — **de flaqueza** to pull
oneself together

fuga F (escape) escape, flight; (de la cárcel)
jailbreak; (de gas) leak; (de capitales) drain

fugarse[7] VI to flee, to escape; — **con** to
abscond with

fugaz ADJ fleeting

fugitivo -va ADJ fugitive; MF fugitive

fulano -na MF so-and-so; —, **zutano y
mengano** Tom, Dick and Harry; F tart,
tramp

fulgor M radiance

fulgurar VI to flash

full M full house

fullero -ra MF (tramposo) cheat; (en naipes)
card sharp

fulminante M cap; ADJ devastating

fulminar VT to strike with lightning; to thunder; **lo fulminó con la mirada** she gave him a withering look

fumadero M crackhouse

fumador -ora MF smoker

fumar VI/VT to smoke; **—se mucho dinero** to blow a lot of money

fumigar[7] VT to fumigate, to fog

función F (uso) function; (de una obra de teatro) performance; (cargo) office

funcionamiento M operation, working

funcionar VI to function, to work; (motor) to run

funcionario -ria MF government employee, official

funda F cover; (de una almohada) pillowcase, slip; (de navaja) sheath

fundación F foundation

fundador -ora MF founder

fundamental ADJ (básico) fundamental; (importante) crucial

fundamentarse VI to be based

fundamento M foundation, basis; **—s** fundamentals

fundar VT (un instituto) to found, to establish; (un argumento) to base

fundición F (fábrica) foundry; (acción de fundirse) fusing

fundido ADJ molten; M (en cinematografía) fade-in/out

fundidor -ora MF foundry worker

fundir VT (combinar) to fuse; (derretir) to melt; (moldear) to mold; **—se** (combinarse) to fuse; (romperse una bombilla) to burn out

fúnebre ADJ funeral

funeral ADJ & M funeral

funerario -ria ADJ funeral; F funeral parlor; MF funeral director

funesto ADJ ill-fated, unlucky

funicular M cable car

funky ADJ funky

furgón M (vagón) boxcar; (camioneta de policía) police van; **— de cola** caboose

furia F fury

furibundo ADJ furious, livid

furioso ADJ furious; (tempestad) fierce

furor M fury; **hacer —** to be all the rage

furtivo ADJ furtive, stealthy

fuselaje M fuselage

fusible M electric fuse

fusil M rifle

fusilar VT to execute with firearms

fusión F (derretimiento) melting; (nuclear) fusion; (empresarial) merger

fusionar VT (metales) to fuse; (compañías) to merge

fusta F crop

fustigar[7] VT to lash, to whip; (criticar) to lash out at

fútbol M soccer; **— americano** football

fútil ADJ futile, trivial

futilidad F triviality

futuro ADJ future; M future; **—s** futures

Gg

gabacho -cha ADJ & MF (francés) *pey* frog; (americano) *pey* American

gabán M overcoat

gabardina F trench coat

gabinete M (ministerial) cabinet; (oficina) office

Gabón M Gabon/Gabun

gabonés -esa ADJ & MF Gabonese

gacela F gazelle

gaceta F gazette

gacetilla F short news item

gachas F PL **— de avena** oatmeal

gacho ADJ (orejas) drooping; (cabeza) bowed; (ojos) lowered

gachupín -ina MF *Méx pey* Spaniard

gafar VT to jinx

gafas F PL glasses

gafe M jinx

gaffe M gaffe, faux pas

gag M gag

gaita F bagpipe

gaje M **—s del oficio** occupational hazards

gajo M (rama) branch; (de naranja) section

gala F (cena) banquet; **—s** finery; **hacer — de** to boast of, to flaunt; **vestirse de —** to dress up

galán M gallant, suitor; (en un drama) leading man

galante ADJ gallant

galantear VT to court

galanteo M courting

galantería F (caballerosidad) gallantry; (cumplido) compliment

galardón M award

galaxia F galaxy

galera F galley (también prueba de imprenta); *RP* top hat

galerada F galley proof

galería F gallery; (pasillo) corridor; (tiendas) mall, gallery; (de coro) loft; (subterráneo) tunnel; **—s** *Esp* department store

Gales M Wales

galés -esa ADJ & MF Welsh

galgo M greyhound

Galicia F Galicia

gallardete M pennant

gallardía F (elegancia) elegance; (valentía) bravery

gallardo ADJ (elegante) elegant; (valiente) brave

gallego -ga ADJ Galician; M (lengua) Galician; MF Galician

gallera F cockpit

galleta F (salada) cracker; (dulce) cookie

gallina F (pollo) chicken; (hembra) hen; MF coward; **— ciega** blind man's bluff; **la — de los huevos de oro** the goose that laid the golden egg

gallinero M (de gallinas) chicken coop; (de teatro) gallery; **alborotarse el —** to raise a ruckus

gallito ADJ cocksure, cocky

gallo M cock, rooster; (de la voz) break; **tener —s en la garganta** to have a frog in one's throat; **en menos que canta un —** before you can say Jack Robinson

galón M (de líquido) gallon; (de tela) stripe

galopar VI/VT to gallop

galope M gallop; **al —** at a gallop

galvanizar[9] VT to galvanize

gama F gamut, range

gamba F large shrimp

gamberro -rra MF punk, hoodlum

Gambia F Gambia

gambiano -na ADJ & MF Gambian

gamo M buck

gamuza F chamois (también piel); (piel de venado) buckskin, deerskin; (de vaca) suede

gana F urge; **con —s** with a vengeance; **de buena —** willingly; **tener —s de** to feel like; **tengo —s** I have to go (to the bathroom); **no me da la —** I absolutely don't want to

ganadero -ra M cattleman; F cattlewoman; ADJ **industria ganadera** cattle industry

ganado M livestock; **— ovino** sheep; **— porcino** swine; **— vacuno** cattle

ganador -ora MF winner; ADJ winning

ganancia F profit, gain, return; **—s** (recaudación de un evento) proceeds; (de un juego) winnings; (de un negocio) earnings

ganapán M (obrero) menial worker; (trabajo) bread-and-butter

ganar VI/VT (una guerra, la lotería) to win; (kilos, en eficacia) to gain; VT (un sueldo) to earn; (tiempo, espacio) to save; (tierra) to reclaim; **dejarse — por algo** to give in to something; **nos ganaron el**

partido they beat us; **—se la vida** to make a living

ganchillo M crochet

gancho M hook (también en boxeo, baloncesto); (rama) snag; (para sujetar) clip; (atractivo) lure; **echar a uno el —** to hook someone; **tener —** to be attractive

gandul -la MF loafer

ganga F bargain, steal

gangoso ADJ twangy

gangrena F gangrene

gangrenarse VI to gangrene

gángster M gangster

ganguear VI to twang

ganso M (animal) goose; (macho) gander; (tonto) *fam* ding-a-ling

ganzúa F picklock

gañido M yelp

gañir[18] VI to yelp

garabatear VI to scribble

garabato M scribble; **hacer —s** to scribble

garaje M garage

garante MF. voucher

garantía F (de producto) guarantee, warranty; (de promesa) security, guaranty; (de un derecho) guarantee

garantizar[9] VT (un producto) to guarantee, to warranty; (prometer) to warrant

garañón M stud, horse

garbanzo M chickpea

garbo M grace

garboso ADJ graceful

garfio M hook

garganta F (interno) throat; (todo) neck; (valle estrecho) gorge

gárgara F gargle; **hacer —s** to gargle

gargarismo M gargle

garita F sentry box

garito M gambling house

garra F (de ave) claw; (de león) paw with claws; **caer en las —s de alguien** to fall into someone's clutches

garrafa F decanter

garrapata F tick

garrapatear VI to scribble

garrapiñar VT to candy

garrocha F pole

garrote M club

garrucha F pulley

gárrulo ADJ garrulous

garza F heron

gas M gas; **—es** (de motor) fumes; (de intestino) gas; **— lacrimógeno** tear gas; **— mostaza** mustard gas; **— natural** natural gas; **— nervioso** nerve gas; **a todo —** at full speed

gasa F gauze; (para heridas) dressing
gaseosa F soda, soft drink
gaseoso ADJ gaseous
gasoducto M pipeline
gasolina F gasoline, gas
gasolinera F gas station
gastado ADJ (neumático) smooth; (ropa) worn-out, shabby
gastador -ora ADJ extravagant, wasteful; MF spendthrift
gastar VT (dinero, tiempo) to spend; (energía) to expend; (neumáticos, ropa) to wear out, to use up; **— una broma** to play a trick; **—se** to wear out
gasto M (dinero) expense, expenditure, outlay; (desgaste) wear
gástrico ADJ gastric
gastritis F gastritis
gastroenteritis F gastroenteritis
gastrointestinal ADJ gastrointestinal
gastronomía F gastronomy
gatas LOC ADV **a —** on all fours
gatear VI to creep, to crawl
gatillo M (en un arma de fuego) trigger; (de dentista) forceps
gatito M kitten
gato M (felino) cat; (aparato para levantar) jack; **— montés** wildcat, mountain lion; **aquí hay — encerrado** I smell a rat; **a gatas** on all fours; **dar — por liebre** to sell someone a pig in a poke
gaucho M gaucho
gaveta F small drawer
gavilán M hawk
gavilla F (de maíz) sheaf; (de maleantes) gang
gaviota F seagull
gayola F big house
gazmoñería F prudery
gazmoño -ña MF prude; ADJ prudish
gaznate M gullet
gazpacho M *Esp* cold vegetable soup
geco M gecko
géiser M geyser
gel M gel
gelatina F gelatin
gélido ADJ frigid
gema F gem, jewel
gemelo -la ADJ & MF twin; **—s** (mellizos) twins; (binoculares) binoculars, opera glasses; (de camisa) studs
gemido M (de dolor) moan, groan; (de queja) whine
gemir[5] VI (gruñir) to moan, to groan; (lloriquear) to whine
gen, gene M gene
genealogía F genealogy

generación F generation
generador M generator
general ADJ & M general; **por lo —** generally
generalidad F generality
generalizar[9] VI/VT to generalize; **—se** to become widespread
generar VT generate
genérico ADJ generic
género M (clase) kind; (gramatical) gender; (tela) material; (literario) genre; (biológico) genus; **— humano** human race; **—s** dry goods
generosidad F generosity
generoso ADJ generous
genética F genetics
genético ADJ genetic
genial ADJ brilliant
genio MF (persona inteligente) genius; M (inteligencia) genius, brilliance; (temperamento) temperament, nature; (mal humor) temper; **de mal —** mean; **de buen —** genial
geniudo ADJ quick-tempered
genocidio M genocide
genoma M genome
gente F (personas) people; **— de campo** country folk; **— de color** persons of color; **— joven** young people; **— menuda** small fry; **buena —** good person
gentil ADJ (cortés) gracious; (no judío) gentile; MF gentile
gentileza F graciousness
gentío M crowd
gentuza F rabble, riffraff
genuino ADJ genuine
geocéntrico ADJ geocentric
geoestacionario ADJ geostationary
geofísica F geophysics
geografía F geography
geográfico ADJ geographical
geología F geology
geológico ADJ geological
geometría F geometry
geométrico ADJ geometric
Georgia F Georgia
georgiano -na ADJ & MF Georgian
geotérmico ADJ geothermal
geranio M geranium
gerencia F management
gerente -ta MF manager
geriátrico ADJ geriatric
germen M germ
germinar VI to germinate, to sprout
gerundio M gerund, present participle
gestación F gestation
gesticular VI to gesture; (exageradamente) to

gesticulate

gestión F (acción) step, maneuver; (empresarial) management; (política) administration; **—es** negotiations; **hacer —es para** to take steps to

gestionar VT (negociar) to negotiate; (administrar) to administer

gesto M (con la cara) face; (con las manos) gesture; **hacer —s a** to make faces at

Ghana F Ghana

ghanés -esa ADJ & MF Ghanaian

giba F hump, hunch

gibón M gibbon

Gibraltar M Gibraltar

gibraltareño -ña ADJ & MF Gibraltarian

giga F jig

gigabyte M gigabyte

gigante ADJ giant, gigantic; MF giant

gigantesco ADJ gigantic

gimnasia F gymnastics

gimnasio M gymnasium, gym

gimotear VI to whimper

gimoteo M whimper

ginebra F gin

ginecología F gynecology

ginecólogo -a MF gynecologist

gingivitis F gingivitis

gira F tour

girar VI/VT (una llave, un volante, un coche, a la derecha) to turn; VI (repetidas veces) to revolve, to spin, to whirl; VT (dinero) to wire

girasol M sunflower

giratorio ADJ rotary, revolving

giro M (movimiento circular) rotation, spin; (cambio de dirección) turn; (expresión) turn of phrase; (monetario) draft, remittance; **— postal** money order

giroscopio M gyroscope

gitano -na ADJ & MF gypsy

glacial ADJ glacial, bitter

glaciar M glacier

gladiador M gladiator

glamoroso ADJ glamorous

glamour M glamour

glándula F gland

glandular ADJ glandular

glaseado M (de una torta) glaze; ADJ (papel) glossy

glasear VT to glaze

glaucoma M glaucoma

glicerina F glycerin

global ADJ (mundial) global; (de conjunto) blanket, overall

globo M (esfera) globe; (de árbol de Navidad) ball; (lleno de gas) balloon; (en tenis) lob; **— ocular** eyeball; **— terráqueo** globe

glóbulo M globule; (de sangre) corpuscle

gloria F glory

glorieta F (pérgola) arbor; (rotonda) traffic circle

glorificar[6] VT to glorify

glorioso M glorious

glosa F gloss

glosar VT to gloss

glosario M glossary

glotón -ona ADJ gluttonous; MF glutton

glotonería F gluttony

glucosa F glucose

gluglutear VI to gobble

gobernador -ora ADJ governing; MF governor

gobernante ADJ governing; MF ruler

gobernar[1] VI/VT to govern, to rule; (un buque) to steer

gobierno M government

goce M enjoyment

gofre M waffle

gol M goal

goleador -ora MF shooter

goleta F schooner

golf M golf

golfo -fa M (mar) gulf; (sinvergüenza) rascal; F tramp

gollería F delicacy

golondrina F swallow

golosina F sweet, goody, tidbit

goloso ADJ sweet-toothed

golpazo M bang, whack

golpe M (físico) blow, knock, whack; (emocional) blow; (estafa) sting; (robo) holdup; (de viento) buffet; (con el codo) to jab; (con los nudillos) rap; **— bajo** low blow; **— de calor** heat stroke; **— de estado** coup; **— de gracia** coup de grâce; **— de sol** sunstroke; **de —** suddenly; **de un —** all at once

golpear VI/VT to strike, to hit; (a la puerta) to knock, to rap; (dar una paliza a una persona) to beat, to batter; (con el codo) to jab

golpecito M tap

golpetear VI to tap; (lluvia) to patter; (motor) to knock; (algo suelto) to rattle

golpeteo M tap; (de lluvia) patter; (de un motor) knock; (de algo suelto) rattle

goma F (de mascar) gum; (caucho) rubber; (neumático) tire; **— de borrar** eraser; **— de mascar** chewing gum; **— elástica** rubber band; **— espuma** foam

gomero M rubber tree

gomoso ADJ slimy

góndola F gondola

gong M gong

gonorrea F gonorrhea, *fam* the clap
gordinflón ADJ *pey* fatso
gordito ADJ chubby
gordo ADJ fat; **se armó la gorda** all hell
 broke loose; **hacer la vista gorda** to
 turn a blind eye
gordura F (cualidad de gordo) fatness; (sebo)
 fat
gorgojo M weevil
gorila M gorilla; (en un bar) bouncer;
 (guardaespaldas) bodyguard
gorjear VI (ave) to warble, to chirp, to
 twitter; (niño) to gurgle
gorjeo M (de ave) warble, twitter, chirp; (de
 niño) gurgle
gorra F cap; **de —** at someone else's expense;
 vivir de — to sponge
gorrino M piglet
gorrión M sparrow
gorro M cap, bonnet
gorrón M sponge, sponger
gorronear VI/VT to mooch, to freeload
gospel M gospel
gota F (de líquido) drop; (de sudor) bead;
 (enfermedad) gout; **— a —** drop by drop;
 ser dos —s de agua to be like two peas
 in a pod; **sudar la — gorda** (sudar) to
 sweat profusely; (trabajar) to work hard
gotear VI (caer gota a gota) to drip;
 (rápidamente) to dribble, to trickle;
 (salirse) to leak; (llover) to sprinkle
goteo M drip (también intravenoso); (rápido)
 dribble, trickle
gotera F leak
gotero M dropper
gótico ADJ Gothic; M (lengua) Gothic
gourmet ADJ & MF gourmet
gozar[9] VT to enjoy; **— de** to enjoy
gozne M hinge
gozo M pleasure, enjoyment
gozoso ADJ enjoyable
grabación F recording
grabado M engraving; (con ácido) etching
grabador -ora MF (persona) engraver; F
 (instrumento) tape recorder; (empresa)
 recording company
grabar VI/VT (marcar) to engrave; (con ácido)
 to etch; (en cinta magnetográfica) to
 record, to tape; **— en la memoria** to
 etch/imprint on one's memory
gracejo M wit
gracia F (garbo, desenvoltura) grace,
 gracefulness; (humor) humor; (monería)
 antic; (favor) favor; (indulto) pardon; **¡—s!**
 thanks! thank you! **—s a Dios** thank God;
 caer en — to please; **dar —s** to say the
 blessing; **dar las —s** to thank; **hacer —**

to amuse; **tener —** to be funny
grácil ADJ supple, graceful
gracioso ADJ (chistoso) amusing, funny;
 (gentil) gracious
grada F step, bleachers
gradación F gradation
graderías F PL bleachers
grado M (de temperatura, de parentesco, de
 un ángulo, de universidad) degree;
 (militar) rank; (de alcohol) proof; **de
 buen —** willingly; **en alto —** to a great
 extent; **en mayor o menor —** to some
 extent; **quemadura de primer —** first-
 degree burn
graduación F (de una escuela) graduation,
 commencement; (rango militar) military
 rank; (de alcohol) proof; (de un lente
 óptico) correction
graduado -da MF graduate
gradual ADJ gradual
graduar[17] VT (ajustar) to adjust; (regular) to
 calibrate; **—se** to graduate, to get a degree
graffiti M graffiti
grafiar[16] VT to graph
gráfica F (arte) graphics; (representación)
 graph, chart
graficar[6] VT to chart
gráfico -ca ADJ graphic; **acento —** written
 accent; M (representación) graph, chart; MF
 (empleado) printer
grafito M graphite
grama F lawn
gramática F grammar
gramatical ADJ grammatical
gramo M gram
grana ADJ INV & F scarlet
granada F (fruta) pomegranate; (proyectil)
 grenade; **— de mano** hand grenade
Granada F Grenada
granadino -na ADJ & MF Grenadian
granado M pomegranate tree; ADJ notable
granate M garnet
Gran Bretaña F Great Britain
grande ADJ large, big; (importante) great; **un
 gran poeta** a great poet; **divertirse en
 —** to have a whale of a time; **a —s
 alturas** at high altitudes; **de gran
 alcance** far-reaching; **de gran escala**
 large-scale; **en gran parte** in large
 measure; **gran almacén** department
 store
grandeza F greatness; **delirios de —**
 delusions of grandeur
grandiosidad F grandeur
grandioso ADJ grandiose, grand
granero M (edificio) granary, grain barn;
 (recipiente) bin, crib

granito M granite

granizada F hailstorm

granizar[9] VI to hail

granizo M hail

granja F farm

granjearse VI to win for oneself

granjero -ra MF farmer

grano M (de una foto, arena, semilla) grain; (cereal) cereal, grain; (barrito) pimple; — **de café** coffee bean; **ir al —** to come to the point

granuja MF ragamuffin

granular VT to granulate; **—se** to become granulated

grapa F (para sujetar madera) clamp; (para sujetar papel) staple

grapadora F stapler

grasa F (aceite) grease; (animal) fat

grasiento ADJ greasy

grasoso ADJ greasy

gratificación F bonus

gratificar[6] VT to gratify

gratis ADV free

gratitud F gratitude, thankfulness

grato ADJ pleasant

gratuito ADJ (gratis) free; (arbitrario) wanton, gratuitous

grava F gravel

gravamen M (impuesto) tax, assessment; (carga sobre una propiedad) lien

gravar VT to tax, to assess

grave ADJ (enfermedad, decisión) grave, serious; (sonido) low, deep; (injuria) grievous; (de carácter) earnest

gravedad F (fuerza de atracción) gravity; (de una situación) seriousness; (de una tormenta) severity; (de un tono) depth; (de una personalidad) earnestness

gravitación F gravitation

gravoso ADJ burdensome

graznar VI (cuervo) to caw, to croak; (pato) to quack; (ganso) to honk

graznido M (de cuervo) caw, croak; (de pato) quack; (de ganso) honk

Grecia F Greece

greda F clay

green M (de golf) green

gregario ADJ gregarious

gremial ADJ **acuerdo —** union agreement

gremio M (conjunto de personas) trade; (asociación histórica) guild; (sindicato) trade union

greña F mop of hair

grey F flock, fold

griego -ga ADJ & MF Greek

grieta F crevice, crack

grifo M faucet, spigot, tap

grillete M fetter, shackle

grillo M (insecto) cricket; **—s** shackles

grima F uneasiness; **dar —** (disgustar) to be upsetting; (dar asco) to be disgusting

gringo -ga ADJ & MF *pey* American

gripe F flu, influenza

gris ADJ & M gray

grisáceo ADJ grayish

gritar VI/VT to shout, to yell; (chillar) to scream

gritería F shouting

grito M shout, cry; (chillido) scream; **el último —** the last word; **estar en un —** to be in agony; **pedir a —s** to clamor for; **poner el — en el cielo** to hit the ceiling

grosella F currant

grosellero M currant

grosería F (cualidad) rudeness; (hecho, dicho) profanity, something rude

grosero ADJ (descortés) rude, ill-mannered, boorish; (vulgar) vulgar, profane; (sin arte) coarse, unrefined

grosor M thickness

grotesco ADJ grotesque

grúa F (máquina) crane; (automóvil para remolcar coches) wrecker, tow truck

gruesa F gross

grueso ADJ (persona) thick-set, heavy; (tabla) thick; (palabra, arena) coarse; M (grosor) thickness; (parte más numerosa) majority

grulla F crane

grumo M lump

grumoso ADJ lumpy

gruñido M (de perro) growl, snarl; (de cerdo) grunt; (humano) grumble

gruñir[18] VI (el cerdo) to grunt; (el perro) to growl, to snarl; (el ser humano) to grumble

gruñón -ona ADJ grumpy; MF grumpy person

grupa F rump; **volver —s** to turn around

grupo M group; — **de apoyo** support group; — **de presión** lobby; — **étnico** ethnicity; — **paritario** peer group; — **sanguíneo** blood type

gruta F grotto, cavern

guacal M crate

guacamole M *Méx* guacamole

guacho M (cría de ave) chick; *Am* (animal huérfano) orphan

guadaña F scythe

guagua F (fruslería) trifle; *Caribbean* bus; MF *Chile* baby; LOC ADV **de —** for nothing, free

guaje -ja MF urchin

guano M guano, bird dung

guantada F slap

guante M glove; — **de boxeo** boxing glove;

arrojar el — to challenge; **echarle el — a alguien** to capture someone; **te queda como un —** it fits you like a glove

guantelete M gauntlet

guantera F glove compartment

guapetón -ona MF *fam* fox

guapo ADJ (de hombre) good-looking, handsome; (de mujer) good-looking, pretty; (valiente) brave; **¡hola —!** hey, good-looking!

guarapo M cane syrup

guarda MF INV (guardián) guard; F (almacenamiento) storage

guardar VT (almacenar) to keep, to store; (observar) to observe; (datos) to save; (proteger) to guard; **— rencor** to hold a grudge; **— un secreto** to keep a secret; **—se de** to guard against; M SG **guardabarros** fender; **guardacostas** Coast Guard cutter; **guardaespaldas** bodyguard; **guardafangos** fender; **guardapelo** locket; **guardarropa** (armario, ropa) wardrobe; (en un local) cloakroom; MF SG **guardabosques** forest ranger, forester; **guardafrenos** brake operator; **guardagujas** switch operator; **guardameta** goalie

guardería F nursery, day-care center

guardia MF (persona) guard; **— civil** civil guard; F (vigilancia) guard; **bajar la —** to let down one's guard; **de —** on duty, on watch; **en —** en garde; **hacer / montar —** to stand guard

guardián -ana MF guardian, keeper

guarecerse[13] VT to take shelter

guarida F den, lair

guarismo M cipher

guarnecer[13] VT (un plato) to garnish; (un vestido) to trim; (una fortaleza) to man, to garrison

guarnición F (de tropas) garrison; (de comida) trimmings; **guarniciones** harness

guarro ADJ filthy; M pig

guasa LOC ADV **de / a —** in jest, as a joke

guasón -ona MF joker

guata F padding

Guatemala F Guatemala

guatemalteco -ca ADJ & MF Guatemalan

guau INTERJ woof

guay ADJ cool, great

guayaba F guava

guayabera F tropical pleated shirt

gubernamental ADJ governmental

gubernativo ADJ governmental

gubia F gouge

guedeja F shock of hair

guepardo M cheetah

guerra F war, warfare; **dar —** to aggravate; **en pie de —** at war; **— fría** cold war

guerrear VI to war

guerrero -rra MF warrior; **operación —** war operation; **espíritu —** warrior spirit

guerrilla F group of guerrillas

guerrillero -ra MF guerrilla

gueto M ghetto

guía MF (persona) guide, leader; F (cosa o animal) guide; **— telefónica** telephone directory

guiar[16] VT to guide, to lead; **—se por** to follow

guijarro M pebble

güinche M hoist

guinda F cherry

guindilla F *Esp* small hot pepper

Guinea F Guinea

guineano -na ADJ & MF Guinean

guingán M gingham

guiñada F wink

guiñapo M rag

guiñar VI/VT to wink

guiño M wink

guión M (ortografía) hyphen; (libreto) script, screenplay

guionista MF screenwriter

guirnalda F garland; (de Navidad) tinsel

guisa F **a — de** by way of

guisado M stew, hash

guisante M pea

guisar VI/VT to cook; (en guisado) to stew

guiso M stew, casserole

guitarra F guitar

gula F gluttony

gusano M worm; **— de seda** silkworm

gustar VT (agradar) to be pleasing to; **ella me gusta** I like her; **le gustan los perros** he likes dogs; **no me gustan las fiestas** I dislike parties; **te guste o no te guste** whether you like it or not; **cuando gustes** whenever you want; **— de** to be fond of; (saborear) to taste

gusto M (sentido, sabor, aprecio estético) taste; (agrado) pleasure; (preferencia personal) like; **a —** at ease; **a mi —** to my liking; **dar —** to be a pleasure; **darle — a alguien** to humor someone; **darse el —** to indulge oneself; **de mal —** in bad taste; **el — es mío** the pleasure is mine; **estar a —** to be comfortable; **mucho —** nice to meet you; **por —** for fun; **tener el — de** to have the pleasure of; **tomar el — a una cosa** to become fond of something

gustoso ADJ (que gusta de) fond of;

(agradable) pleasant; ADV willingly
Guyana F Guyana
guyanés -esa ADJ & MF Guyanese

Hh

haba F bean; (verde) Lima bean
habano M cigar
haber[29] V AUX to have; — **comido cuatro veces en un día** to have eaten four times in a day; **habérselas con** (un problema) to grapple with; (una persona) to have it out with; **ha de llegar mañana** he is to arrive tomorrow; **hay** there is, there are; **hay viento** it is windy; **hubo** there was/were; **había** there was/were; **hay que** it is necessary to; **no hay de qué** don't mention it; **no hay forma** no way; **no hay problema** no problem; **¿qué hay?** what's up?; **todo lo habido y por haber** everything possible; M (hacienda) assets; (columna en una cuenta) credit; **—es** earnings
habichuela F bean; — **verde** string bean
hábil ADJ adept, able; **día** — workday
habilidad F ability, skill
habilidoso ADJ deft, skillful
habilitar VT (equipar) to outfit; (autorizar) to authorize
habitación F (vivienda) dwelling; (cuarto) room
habitante MF inhabitant; (de un barrio) resident
habitar VT to inhabit
hábitat M habitat
hábito M habit (también vestimenta religiosa)
habitual ADJ habitual, usual
habituar[17] VT to accustom; **—se** to get used to
habla F (lenguaje) speech; (modalidad local) dialect; — **infantil** baby talk; **al** — in communication with; **quedarse sin** — to be left speechless
hablador ADJ talkative
habladurías F idle talk, gossip
hablar VI/VT to talk, to speak; — **de** to talk about; — **hasta por los codos** to talk one's head off; — **no cuesta nada** talk is cheap; — **por señas** to use sign language; — **por teléfono** to talk on the phone; — **sin rodeos** to speak one's mind; — **solo/para sí** to talk to oneself; **hablando**

mal y pronto pardon my French; **no —se** not to be on speaking terms; **no me hagas** — don't get me started on it
hablilla F malicious tale
hacedor -ora MF maker
hacendado -da MF landowner
hacendoso ADJ industrious, diligent
hacer[30] VT (crear) to do, to make; (causar) to make; (decir) to go; (resolver) to do; — **frío/calor/viento** to be cold/hot/windy; — **una torta** to make a cake; — **un crucigrama** to do a crossword puzzle; **me hizo llorar** he made me cry; **la vaca hace 'mu'** the cow goes moo; **hace mucho tiempo** a long time ago; **hace poco** a short while ago; **hizo como si estuvieras presente** he acted as if you were here; **a lo hecho, pecho** you've got to face the music; **la hiciste buena** you've really screwed up; **¿qué le vamos a hacer?** that's life; **¿qué se hizo de Juan?** whatever became of Juan? **haz el trabajo** do the work; **—se rico** to become rich; **—se el tonto** to play the fool; **—se el listo** to pull a stunt; **—se pasar por el jefe** to pose as the boss; **—se a un lado** to step aside; **—se amigo de** to befriend; **—se a la oscuridad** to get used to the dark; **—se rogar** to play hard to get
hacha F (grande) ax(e); (pequeña) hatchet
hachís M hashish
hacia PREP (en dirección) toward; (aproximadamente) about; — **abajo** downward; — **adelante** forward; — **adentro** inward; — **afuera** outward; — **arriba** upward; — **atrás** backward; — **el este** eastward; — **la izquierda** to the left; **dar** — to face
hacienda F estate; (de ganado) ranch; (impositiva) Internal Revenue Service
hacina F shock
hacinar VT (liar) to shock; (atestar) to crowd in
hada F fairy
hado M fate
Haití M Haiti
haitiano -na ADJ & MF Haitian
halagar[7] VT to flatter
halago M flattery
halagüeño ADJ (palabras) flattering; (perspectiva) promising
halcón M falcon
hálito M breath
hallar VT to find; **—se** to be; **—se en un aprieto** to be in a pickle; **—se mal de salud** to be in a bad way

hallazgo M (resultado científico) finding; **ese documento fue un — sensacional** that document was a real find

halo M halo

halógeno ADJ & M halogen

halterofilia F weight training, weightlifting

hamaca F hammock

hambre F (deseo de comer) hunger; (hambruna) famine; **tener —** to be hungry; **pasar —** to hunger; **morirse de —** to starve

hambrear VI/VT to starve

hambriento ADJ (que tiene hambre) hungry; (que se muere de hambre) famished, starving

hambruna F famine

hamburguesa F hamburger

hampa F underworld

hámster M hamster

handicapar VT to handicap

hangar M hangar

haragán -ana ADJ indolent; MF loafer

haraganear VI to loaf

haraganería F laziness

harapiento ADJ ragged, tattered

harapo M rag, tatter

hardware M hardware

harén M harem

harina F (fino) flour; (grueso) meal; **— de avena** oatmeal; **— de maíz** cornmeal; **es — de otro costal** that's another kettle of fish

hartar VT to satiate; **—se** (de comida) to have one's fill; (de aburrimiento) to get sick

hartazgo M surfeit, excess

harto ADJ (satisfecho) full; **estar —** to be fed up; **ese asunto me tiene —** I'm sick and tired of the whole business

hasta PREP (temporal) till, until; (espacial) (up) to; **— ahora** to date / so far; **— cierto punto** to a certain extent; **— luego** good-bye, see you later; **— pronto** see you later; **caminó — la esquina** he walked to the corner; **lo llenó — el borde** he filled it up to brim; **estar — la coronilla** to be fed up; ADV even; **— mi madre lo notó** even my mother noticed it; **— que** until

hastiado ADJ jaded

hastial M gable

hastiar[16] VT to cloy, to tire; **—se** to grow weary of

hastío M tedium

hato M (envoltorio) bundle; (rebaño) herd

hay ver haber

haya F beech

hayuco M beechnut

haz M (de leña) bundle; (de luz) beam; (de flechas) sheaf

hazaña F deed, exploit, feat

hazmerreír M laughingstock

he VT IMPERSONAL **he aquí la lista** here's the list

hebilla F buckle

hebra F (de hilo) thread; (vegetal) fiber

hebreo -a ADJ & MF Hebrew

heces F PL (de vino, cafe) dregs; (excremento) feces

hechicería F enchantment

hechicero -ra ADJ bewitching; M sorcerer; F sorceress

hechizar[9] VT to bewitch, to enchant; (al público) to enthrall

hechizo M charm, spell

hecho M fact; **los —s de la noche del 17** the events of the night of the 17th; **de —** in fact

hechura F cut

hectárea F hectare

heder[1] VI to stink, to reek

hediondez F stench

hediondo ADJ stinking, smelly

hedonismo M hedonism

hedor M stink, stench

hegemonía F hegemony

helada F (frente frío) freeze; (escarcha) frost

heladera F refrigerator

heladería F ice-cream parlor

helado ADJ (muy frío) frozen, freezing; (con hielo) icy; M ice cream

helar[1] VI/VT to freeze

helecho M fern

hélice F (espiral) helix; (de avión) propeller; (de barco) screw, propeller

helicóptero M helicopter

helio M helium

hematoma M hematoma

hembra F (de animal) female; (del venado) doe; (de la ballena, foca) cow; (ave) hen

hemisferio M hemisphere

hemofilia F hemophilia

hemoglobina F hemoglobin

hemorragia F hemorrhage

hemorroides F PL hemorrhoids

henchir[5,18] VT to swell

hender[1] VI/VT to cleave, to split

hendido ADJ cleft, split

hendidura F rift, rent

henil M hayloft

heno M hay; **fiebre de —** hay fever

hepatitis F hepatitis

heraldo M herald

herbicida M weedkiller, herbicide

herbívoro ADJ herbivorous; M herbivore

herboso ADJ grassy

heredad F homestead

heredar VI/VT (recibir en herencia) to inherit; (dar en herencia) to bequeath

heredero -ra M heir; F heiress

hereditario ADJ hereditary

hereje MF heretic

herejía F heresy

herencia F (económica) inheritance; (cultural) heritage; (genética) heredity

herida F injury; (abierta) wound; **respirar por la —** to reopen an old wound

herido ADJ injured; (con herida abierta) wounded

herir[3] VI/VT to injure; (con herida abierta) to wound; (sentimientos) to hurt

hermanastro -tra M stepbrother; F stepsister

hermandad F (de hombres) brotherhood; (de mujeres) sisterhood

hermanito -ta M little brother; F little sister

hermano -na M brother (también religioso); **— mayor** big brother; **— menor** little brother; F sister (también religiosa); **— mayor** big sister; **— menor** little sister

herméticamente ADV tight

hermético ADJ hermetic, airtight; (a prueba de agua) watertight; (que no revela secretos) secretive

hermosear VT to beautify

hermoso ADJ beautiful, lovely

hermosura F beauty

hernia F hernia

héroe M hero

heroico ADJ heroic

heroína F (droga) heroin; (personaje) heroine

heroísmo M heroism

herpes M herpes; (en la boca) cold sore

herradura F horseshoe

herraje M ironwork

herramienta F tool

herrar[1] VT (un caballo) to shoe; (una vaca) to brand

herrería F blacksmith's shop

herrero -ra MF blacksmith

herrumbre F rust

hervidero M swarm

hervidor M kettle

hervir[3] VI/VT to boil; **— a fuego lento** to simmer; **— de** to be swarming with; **me hervía la sangre** I was seething

hervor M (acción de hervir) boiling; **levantar el —** to come to a boil

heterodoxo ADJ unorthodox

heterogéneo ADJ heterogeneous

heterosexual ADJ heterosexual; *fam* straight

hexágono M hexagon

hiato M hiatus

hibernar VI to hibernate

híbrido ADJ & M hybrid

hidalgo M hidalgo

hidalguía F (nobleza) nobility; (generosidad) generosity

hidrato M hydrate

hidráulico ADJ hydraulic

hidroavión M hydroplane, seaplane

hidrocarburo M hydrocarbon

hidroeléctrico ADJ hydroelectric

hidrofobia F hydrophobia

hidrógeno M hydrogen

hiedra F ivy

hiel F gall

hielo M ice; **— seco** dry ice; **romper el —** to break the ice

hiena F hyena

hierba F (pasto) grass; (especia) herb; (marihuana) *fam* weed; **— buena** mint; **mala —** weed; **y otras —s** and so on

hierro M iron (también de golf); **— corrugado** corrugated iron; **— forjado** wrought iron; **— fundido** cast iron; **—s** handcuffs

hígado M liver; **malos —s** ill will

higiene F hygiene

higo M fig; **me importa un —** I couldn't care less

higuera F fig tree

hijastro -tra M stepson; F stepdaughter

hijo -ja M son; **— de su madre** *vulg* son of a gun; **John Smith, —** John Smith, Jr.; **sin —s** childless; F daughter

hilachas F loose threads

hilado M spinning

hilandería F (fábrica) spinning mill; (técnica) spinning

hilandero -ra MF spinner

hilar VI/VT to spin; **— fino** to split hairs

hilaridad F mirth

hilera F row, line

hilo M (para coser) thread; (para tejer, hilar) yarn; (alambre) filament; **— de agua** trickle; **— de pensamiento** train of thought; **— de perlas** string of pearls; **— de voz** thin voice; **— dental** floss; **al —** in a row; **mover —s** to pull strings; **seguir el —** to keep track of; **pender de un —** to be hanging by a thread; **perder el —** to lose track

hilván M basting

hilvanar VT to baste, to tack

himno M (religioso) hymn; (patriótico) anthem

hincapié M emphasis; **hacer —** to emphasize

hincar⁶ VT — **los dientes en** to sink one's teeth into; —**se** to kneel

hincha MF INV (aficionado) supporter; F (antipatía) *Esp* grudge

hinchado ADJ (inflamado) swollen; (exagerado) inflated

hinchar VI to swell; (un globo) to blow up; — **por el equipo de Uruguay** to pull for the Uruguayan team; —**se** (cuerpo) to swell; (pulmones) to inflate; (las mejillas) to bulge; (de orgullo) to puff up; (el pan) to rise

hinchazón F swelling

hindi M Hindi

hindú ADJ & MF Hindu

hinojos LOC ADV **de** — on one's knees

hipar VI hiccup

hiperactivo ADJ hyperactive, overactive

hipermétrope ADJ farsighted

hipersensible ADJ hypersensitive; (a la crítica) touchy

hipertensión F high blood pressure

hiperventilar VI to hyperventilate

hipnosis F hypnosis

hipnotizar VI/VT to hypnotize, to mesmerize

hipo M (espasmo) hiccup; (sollozo) sob; **tengo** — I have the hiccups

hipoalérgico ADJ hypoallergenic

hipocondríaco -ca, hipocondriaco -ca ADJ & MF hypochondriac

hipocresía F hypocrisy

hipócrita ADJ INV hypocritical, two-faced; MF INV hypocrite

hipódromo M racetrack

hipogloso M halibut

hipoglucemia F hypoglycemia

hipopótamo M hippopotamus

hipoteca F mortgage

hipotecar⁶ VT to mortgage

hipotecario ADJ **banco** — mortgage bank

hipótesis F hypothesis

hiriente ADJ hurtful; (comentario) nasty, catty

hirviente ADJ boiling

hisopo M swab

hispano -na ADJ Hispanic, Spanish-speaking; MF Spanish-speaking person

Hispanoamérica F Spanish America

hispanoamericano ADJ Spanish-American

histamina F histamine

histerectomía F hysterectomy

histérico ADJ hysterical

historia F (el pasado, estudio del pasado) history; (relato) story; — **clínica** case history; (relato) story; — **clínica** case history; **dejarse de** — s to stop fooling around; **esa es otra** — that's another story; **la** — **se repite** history repeats

itself; **pasar a la** — to be a thing of the past

historiador -ora MF historian

historial M record

histórico ADJ (de importancia histórica) historic; (pertinente a la historia) historical

historietas F PL. funnies

histrionismo M histrionics

hito M landmark, milestone; **de** — **en** — fixedly; **marcar un** — to be a milestone

hobby M hobby

hocicar⁶ VI/VT (un cerdo) to root; (un caballo) to nose

hocico M snout, muzzle

hockey M hockey

hogaño ADV LIT nowadays

hogar M (lumbre) hearth, fireplace; (casa, asilo) home

hogareño ADJ domestic; **persona hogareña** homebody

hoguera F bonfire, campfire

hoja F (de planta) leaf; (de mesa plegadiza) flap; (de papel) sheet; (de un libro) page; (de navaja) blade; — **de afeitar** razor blade; — **de metal** foil; **echar** —**s** to leaf; — **de servicio** record; —**lata** tin plate

hojaldre M puff pastry

hojarasca F fallen leaves

hojear VT to page through, to flip through, to browse

hojuela F flake; —**s de maíz** cornflakes

hola INTERJ hello

Holanda F Holland

holandés -esa ADJ Dutch; M (hombre) Dutchman; (lengua) Dutch; F Dutchwoman

holding M holding company

holgado ADJ (vida) comfortable; (pantalón) loose-fitting, baggy; (cuarto) roomy

holganza F (haraganería) idleness; (diversión) leisure[7]

holgar²,⁷ VI to loaf; **huelga decir** it is needless to say

holgazán -ana ADJ lazy, idle; MF idler, loafer, slouch

holgazanear VI to idle, to loaf

holgazanería F laziness

holgura F (de movimiento) ease; (financiera) comfort; (de la ropa) looseness

holístico ADJ holistic

hollejo M skin

hollín M soot, smut

holocausto M holocaust

hombre M man; — **anuncio** sandwich man; — **de bien** a man of good will; — **de familia** family man; — **de las cavernas** caveman; — **de la calle** man in the

street; — **de negocios** businessman; —
del saco bogeyman; — **de paja** straw
man; — **lobo** werewolf; — **orquesta** one-
man band; — **rana** frogman; **es bien** —
he's a real he-man; INTERJ come on!

hombro M shoulder; **encogerse de** —**s** to
shrug; **cargar al** — to shoulder; **en / a**
—**s** piggyback; **poner el** — to lend a
hand

hombruno ADJ mannish

homenaje M homage, tribute

homeopatía F homeopathy

homeopático ADJ homeopathic

homicida MF INV murderer

homicidio M homicide, murder

homogeneizar VT to homogenize

homogéneo ADJ homogeneous

homólogo -ga MF counterpart

homóplato M shoulder blade

homosexual ADJ homosexual; *fam* gay

honda F sling, slingshot

hondo ADJ deep; M hollow

hondonada F hollow, dell

hondura F depth; **meterse en** —**s** to get in
over one's head

Honduras F Honduras

hondureño -ña ADJ & MF Honduran

honestidad F (castidad) chastity, modesty;
(honradez) honesty

honesto ADJ chaste, modest; (honrado)
honest, straightforward

hongo M (seta) mushroom; (moho) fungus;
aburrirse como un — to be bored stiff

honor M honor; **con** —**es** with honors;
tener el — **de** to have the honor of;
hacer los —**es a** to be appreciative of

honorable ADJ honorable

honorario ADJ honorary; M —**s** fee

honra F honor

honradez F honesty

honrado ADJ honest

honrar VT to honor; (hacer más digno) to do
credit to

honroso ADJ honorable

hora F hour; — **de dormir** bedtime; —
oficial standard time; —**s extras**
overtime; **a esta** — at this time; **¿a qué**
—**?** at what time? **a todas** —**s** at all
hours; **a última** — at the last minute;
decir la — to tell time; **en** — on time; **es**
— **de** it is time to; **es** — **de que me**
vaya it's time for me to go; **kilómetros**
por — kilometers per hour; **no ver la** —
de to be dying to; **por** — by the hour;
¿qué — **es?** what time is it? **ya era** — it
was about time

horadar VT to bore

horario M schedule, timetable; (manecilla del
reloj) hour hand

horca F (cadalso) gallows; (herramienta con
púas) pitchfork; — **de ajos** string of garlic

horcajadas LOC ADV **a** — astraddle, astride

horda F horde

horizontal ADJ horizontal

horizonte M horizon; (de una ciudad)
skyline

horma F (de zapato) shoe last; (de queso)
wheel

hormiga F ant; — **blanca** termite

hormigón M concrete

hormigonera F cement mixer

hormiguear VI (moverse animales) to
swarm; (sentir hormigueo) to tingle

hormigueo M tingle

hormiguero M anthill

hormona F hormone

hornada F batch

horneado M baking

hornear VI/VT to bake

hornilla F burner

horno M (industrial) furnace; (doméstico)
oven; (para cerámica) kiln; — **de**
microondas microwave oven; **alto** —
blast furnace; **el** — **no está para bollos**
it's not a good time; **recién salido del** —
brand-new

horóscopo M horoscope

horquilla F (para el pelo) hairpin; (horca)
pitchfork

horrendo ADJ horrendous, horrid; (feo)
hideous, ghastly

horrible ADJ horrible

horripilante ADJ gruesome, hair-raising

horror M (miedo, repulsión) horror; (cosa
monstruosa) abomination; (espectáculo)
sight; **tenerle** — **a** to be scared of

horrorizar[9] VT to horrify, to shock, to
appall

horroroso ADJ appalling, awful

hortaliza F vegetable; —**s** produce, truck

hortera ADJ INV tacky, uncool, cheesy

horticultura F horticulture

hosco ADJ sullen, surly

hospedaje M lodging

hospedar VT to lodge, to accommodate; —**se**
to lodge, to room

hospicio M (para peregrinos) hospice; (para
huérfanos) orphanage

hospital M hospital

hospitalario ADJ hospitable

hospitalidad F hospitality

hostal M hostel

hostería F hostelry

hostia F (oblea) host, wafer; (golpe) whack

hostigar[7] VT to harass, to harry
hostil ADJ hostile
hostilidad F hostility
hotel M hotel
hotelero·-ra MF hotel keeper
hoy ADV today; — **(en) día** nowadays; **de — en adelante** from now on; **— por —** at present
hoya F river basin
hoyo M hole (también de golf); (muy profundo) pit
hoyuelo M dimple
hoz F sickle
hozar[9] VI to root
HTML M HTML
hucha F piggy bank
hueco ADJ (vacío) hollow; (vanidoso) vain, affected; **palabras huecas** empty words; M (entre los dientes) gap; (cavidad) hollow; (del ascensor) shaft
huelga F strike, work stoppage; — **de hambre** hunger strike; **declararse en —** to strike; **en —** on strike
huelguista MF striker
huella F (señal dejada al pasar) trace, trail; (de pie) footprint, track; (de rueda) track; **— dactilar / digital** fingerprint; **seguir las —s de alguien** to follow in someone's footsteps
huérfano·-na ADJ & MF orphan
huerta F (de verduras) large vegetable garden; (de árboles frutales) large orchard; **la — valenciana** the farming region of Valencia
huerto M (de verduras) vegetable garden; (de árboles frutales) orchard
hueso M (de animal) bone; (de una fruta) stone, pit; **calado hasta los —s** soaked to the bone; **la sin — the** tongue; **no dejarle un — sano** to break someone's bones; **un — duro de roer** a hard pill to swallow
huésped MF (invitado) guest; (anfitrión) host (también de parásitos)
hueste F host
huesudo ADJ bony
hueva F spawn
huevo M egg; **— de Pascua** Easter egg; **— duro** hard-boiled egg; **— estrellado / frito** fried egg; **— pasado por agua** soft-boiled egg; **—s revueltos** scrambled eggs; **ir pisando —s** to walk on eggshells
huída F flight
huir[31] VI to flee, to fly
hule M oilcloth
hulla F soft coal; **— blanca** hydroelectric power

humanidad F (cualidad y condición) humanity; (conjunto de los seres humanos) mankind; **—es** humanities
humanismo M humanism
humanitario ADJ (organización, ayuda) humanitarian; (generoso) humane
humano ADJ (del hombre) human; (generoso) humane; M human
humareda F cloud of smoke
humeante ADJ smoking
humear VI (echar humo) to give off smoke; (echar vapor) to give off steam
humedad F (del aire) humidity; (de un paño) dampness; (en la tierra) moisture; (mancha) moisture stain
humedal M wetland
humedecer[13] VT (sello, ojo) to moisten; (paño) to dampen; **se le humedecieron los ojos** his eyes grew teary
húmedo ADJ damp; (aire) humid; (tierra) moist; (tiempo) wet, soggy
humero M flue, funnel
humidificar[6] VT to humidify
humildad F (actitud de humilde) humility; (condición) lowliness
humilde ADJ (actitud) humble; (condición) low, lowly, mean
humillación F humiliation
humillar VT (dañar el amor propio) to humiliate; (hacer sentirse disminuido) to humble; **—se** to grovel
humo M smoke; (vapor) vapor; **—s** conceitedness; **bajarle los —s a alguien** to cut someone down to size; **echar —** to put out smoke; **estar que echa —** to be fuming; **hacerse —** to vanish into thin air
humor M (actitud risueña) humor; (estado de ánimo) mood
humorada F witty remark
humorismo M (humor) humor; (profesión) comedy
humorístico ADJ humorous
humoso ADJ smoky
hundimiento M (acción de hundirse) sinking; (hoyo) sinkhole
hundir VT (un barco) to sink, to scuttle; (arruinar) to destroy; (enterrar) to bury; **—se** (barco) to sink; (empresa, edificio, precios) to collapse; (tierra) to subside; (sol) to go down
húngaro·-ra MF Hungarian
Hungría F Hungary
huracán M hurricane
huraño ADJ sullen, unsociable
hurgar[7] VI (en una bolsa) to rummage; (en la basura) to scavenge; **—se las narices**

to pick one's nose
hurón M ferret
huronear VI to ferret out
hurra INTERJ hurrah
hurtadillas LOC ADV **a** — stealthily
hurtar VT to steal, to swipe; — **el cuerpo** to dodge; —**se** to hide
hurto M theft, larceny; — **con escalo** break-in
husky M (perro) husky
husmear VT (un pedazo de carne) to sniff at; (a un delincuente) to smell out; (peligro) to smell; (en los asuntos ajenos) to nose around in, to poke around in
husmeo M sniff
huso M spindle; — **horario** time zone
huy INTERJ (sorpresa) wow; (pena) oh

Ii

ibérico ADJ Iberian
iceberg M iceberg
ictericia F jaundice
ida F —**s y venidas** comings and goings
idea F (reflexión) idea, thought; (intuición) inkling
ideal ADJ & M ideal
idealismo M idealism
idealista ADJ idealistic; MF idealist
idear VT to devise, to think out, to plan; (un método) devise; (un plan) to conceive; (una solución) to engineer; (un complot) to hatch
ídem PRON & ADV ditto
idéntico ADJ identical
identidad F identity
identificación F identification
identificar[6] VT to identify
ideología F ideology
idilio M idyll
idioma M language
idiosincrasia F idiosyncrasy
idiota ADJ INV idiotic, lamebrained; MF INV *fam* idiot
idiotez F idiocy
idolatrar VT to idolize
idolatría F idolatry
ídolo M idol
idóneo ADJ (calificado) expert; (ideal) ideal
iglesia F church
iglú M igloo
ignición F ignition
ignifugar[7] VT to fireproof

ignorancia F ignorance
ignorante ADJ ignorant, uneducated
ignorar VT (no saber) to be unaware of; (hacer caso omiso de) to ignore, to disregard; (despreciar) to shrug off, to discount
igual ADJ (idéntico) equal; (semejante) same, alike; (liso) even; **me da** — it's all the same to me; **al** — **que** just like; M equal sign
igualar VT (alisar) to level; (ser igual a) to equal; (hacer iguales) to equalize; (compararse con) to match
igualdad F equality
ijada F loin
ijar M loin
ilegal ADJ illegal, unlawful, lawless
ilegítimo ADJ illegitimate
ileso ADJ unharmed, unhurt
ilícito ADJ illicit
ilimitado ADJ unlimited; (energía) boundless; (horizonte) limitless
iluminación F illumination, lighting; (moral) enlightenment
iluminado ADJ lit
iluminar VT (un cuarto) to illuminate, to brighten; (moralmente) to enlighten
ilusión F (idea o imagen falsa) illusion; (deseo) dream, fond hope; (entusiasmo) thrill; — **óptica** optical illusion; **me da** — I'm looking forward to
iluso ADJ naive
ilusorio ADJ illusory
ilustración F illustration; **la** — the Enlightenment
ilustrador -ora MF illustrator
ilustrar VT illustrate; (intelectualmente) to enlighten
ilustre ADJ illustrious
imagen F (representación, reputación) image; (foto, televisión) picture; (unidad de película fotográfica) frame; — **especular** mirror image; **la** — **del tacto** the soul of tact; — **por resonancia magnética** magnetic resonance imaging
imaginable ADJ conceivable
imaginación F imagination
imaginar VT to imagine, to picture; (idear) to dream up
imaginario ADJ imaginary
imaginativo ADJ imaginative
imán M magnet
imantar VT to magnetize
imbatible ADJ unbeatable
imbécil ADJ idiotic; MF *ofensivo* imbecile, moron
imbuir[31] VT to imbue

imitación F imitation
imitador -ora MF (que imita) imitator; (que imita gestos y voces) imitator; **un — de Elvis** an Elvis wannabe
imitar VT to imitate; (en gestos y voces) to mimic, to impersonate
impaciencia F impatience
impaciente ADJ impatient; *fam* antsy
impactar VI/VT to impact
impacto M impact
impagado ADJ unpaid
impala M impala
impar ADJ odd, uneven
imparcial ADJ impartial, unbiased; (justo) evenhanded; (que no toma partido) nonpartisan
imparcialidad F impartiality
impartir VT to impart
impasible ADJ impassive
impasse M impasse
impávido ADJ undaunted
impeachment M impeachment
impecable ADJ (perfecto) flawless; (limpio) spick and span
impedimento M impediment, hindrance; (incapacidad) handicap
impedir[5] VT to impede, to prevent, to hinder; (acceso) to bar
impeler VT (empujar) to impel; (inducir) to drive
impenetrable ADJ impenetrable
impensable ADJ unthinkable
imperar VI to prevail
imperativo ADJ & M imperative
imperceptible ADJ imperceptible
imperdible M safety pin
imperecedero ADJ undying
imperfecto ADJ & M imperfect
imperial ADJ imperial
imperialismo M imperialism
impericia F lack of skill
imperio M (forma de gobierno) empire; (hecho de imperar) rule
imperioso ADJ (mandón) imperious; (necesario) imperative
impermeabilizar[9] VT to waterproof
impermeable ADJ (al agua) waterproof; (a la crítica) impervious; M raincoat, slicker
impersonal ADJ impersonal
impertinencia F (actitud) impertinence, impudence; (réplica) backtalk
impertinente ADJ impertinent, impudent
ímpetu M impetus
impetuoso ADJ impetuous, brash
impío ADJ godless
implacable ADJ implacable, relentless
implantar VT to implant

implante M implant
implementar VT to implement
implemento M implement
implicar[6] VT (involucrar) to implicate, to involve; (conllevar) to entail
implícito ADJ implicit
implorar VI/VT to implore
imponente ADJ (impresionante) imposing; (espantoso) forbidding
imponer[39] VT to impose, to force upon; (gravar) to assess; **—se** to get one's way
impopular ADJ unpopular
importación F import
importancia F importance
importante ADJ important; (cantidad) substantial; (tema, asunto) weighty; (suceso, ocasión) momentous
importar VI (ser de importancia) to matter; **me importa un comino** I don't give a hoot; **no importa** it makes no difference; VT (introducir bienes) to import
importe M amount
importunar VT to besiege
importuno ADJ inopportune
imposibilidad F impossibility
imposibilitar VT to make impossible
imposible ADJ impossible
imposición F imposition; (de impuestos) assessment
impostor -ora MF impostor, fraud
impotencia F impotence
impotente ADJ powerless; (sexualmente) impotent
impreciso ADJ inaccurate
impredecible ADJ unpredictable
impregnar VT to impregnate
impremeditado ADJ unpremeditated
imprenta F (arte, oficio) printing; (máquina) press, printing press
imprescindible ADJ indispensable
impresión F (efecto en el ánimo) impression; (acción de imprimir) printing; (huella) imprint
impresionante ADJ (logro) impressive, imposing; (edificio) grand, imposing; (panorama) breathtaking
impresionar VT to impress; **—se** to be overwhelmed
impreso M printed matter
impresor -ora MF (persona) printer; F (aparato) printer; **impresora de inyección de tinta** ink-jet printer; **impresora gráfica** plotter; **impresora láser** laser printer
imprevisible ADJ unpredictable
imprevisto ADJ unforeseen; M unforeseen event

imprimir[51] VI/VT to print; (marcar con presión) to imprint
improbable ADJ improbable, unlikely
improductivo ADJ unproductive
impromptu M impromptu
impropio ADJ (inadecuado) unbecoming; (atípico) atypical
improvisación F improvisation, role-playing
improvisado ADJ impromptu
improvisando ADV ad lib
improvisar VI/VT to improvise
improviso LOC ADV **de** — all of a sudden
imprudencia F (actitud) recklessness; (acción) reckless act
imprudente ADJ imprudent, unwise
impublicable ADJ unprintable
impúdico ADJ immodest
impuesto M tax, duty; — **de sucesión** inheritance tax; —**s** taxation; — **sobre ingresos** income tax; — **sobre las ventas** sales tax; — **sobre rentas** income tax
impugnar VT to contest, to dispute
impulsar VT (empujar) to propel, to drive; (estimular) to boost
impulsivo ADJ impulsive
impulso M (estímulo) boost; (deseo espontáneo) impulse, urge
impunidad F impunity
impureza F impurity
impuro ADJ (sustancia) impure; (pensamiento) impure, unclean
inacabado ADJ unfinished
inaccesible ADJ inaccessible
inaceptable ADJ unacceptable, inadequate
inacostumbrado ADJ unwonted
inactividad F inactivity
inactivo ADJ inactive
inadaptado -da ADJ maladjusted; MF misfit
inadecuado ADJ unsuitable
inadvertido ADJ unnoticed, unobserved
inagotable ADJ (recursos) inexhaustible; (optimismo) unfailing
inaguantable ADJ unbearable
inalámbrico ADJ cordless, wireless
inalterable ADJ unalterable, unchangeable
inalterado ADJ unchanged
inamovible ADJ immovable
inanición F starvation
inanimado ADJ inanimate
inapetencia F lack of appetite
inapreciable ADJ (invalorable) invaluable; (muy pequeño) too small to be seen
inapropiado ADJ unsuitable
inasequible ADJ inaccessible
inaudible ADJ Inaudible
inaudito ADJ unheard-of, unprecedented;

(sufrimiento) untold
inauguración F (de un gobierno) inauguration; (de una carretera, etc.) dedication
inaugurar VT (un gobierno) to inaugurate; (una carretera) to dedicate
incalculable ADJ untold
incandescencia F glow
incandescente ADJ incandescent, glowing
incansable ADJ untiring, tireless
incapacidad F inability
incapacitar VT to disable, to incapacitate
incapaz ADJ incapable
incautación F seizure
incauto ADJ unwary
incendiar VT to set fire to; VI/VT to burn; —**se** to catch fire, to burn down
incendiario -ria ADJ incendiary; MF arsonist
incendio M conflagration, fire, blaze; — **doloso** arson; — **forestal** forest fire
incentivo M incentive, inducement
incertidumbre F uncertainty, suspense
incesante ADJ incessant, ceaseless
incesto M incest
incidencia F incidence
incidental ADJ incidental
incidente M incident
incienso M incense
incierto ADJ uncertain
incinerar VT to incinerate
incipiente ADJ incipient
incisión F incision
incisivo ADJ incisive; M incisor
incitar VT to incite, to whip up
incivilizado ADJ uncivilized
inclemencia F **las** —**s del tiempo** foul weather
inclemente ADJ inclement, foul
inclinación F (de personalidad) inclination, bent, disposition; (acto de inclinar) tilting; (estado de inclinado) tilt; (de un techo) slant; (del terreno) slope; (sesgo) bias
inclinar VT (ladear) to tilt; (bajar la cabeza) to hang; —**se** (doblarse en la cintura) to bend over; (tener tendencia a) to tend; (hacer una reverencia) to bow
incluir[31] VT (incorporar) to include; (abarcar) to include, to comprise
inclusive ADV even
inclusivo ADJ inclusive
incluso ADV even
incógnita F unknown (quantity)
incógnito LOC ADV **de** — incognito
incoherente ADJ incoherent
incoloro ADJ colorless
incomestible ADJ inedible
incomformista ADJ & MF nonconformist

incomible ADJ inedible
incomodar VT to inconvenience
incomodidad F uneasiness
incómodo ADJ (silla) uncomfortable; (situación) awkward, inconvenient; (baúl) cumbersome; (silencio) uneasy; (que siente molestia) ill at ease
incomparable ADJ incomparable, peerless
incompatible ADJ incompatible
incompetente ADJ incompetent
incompleto ADJ incomplete
incomprensible ADJ incomprehensible
incomunicación F disconnect
inconcebible ADJ inconceivable
inconcluso ADJ unfinished
incondicional ADJ unconditional, unqualified
inconexo ADJ disconnected
inconformista MF nonconformist
inconfundible ADJ unmistakable
inconsciente ADJ (sin sentido) unconscious, senseless; (ignorante) unaware, oblivious
inconsecuencia F inconsistency
inconsecuente ADJ inconsistent
inconsolable ADJ heartbroken
inconstancia F inconstancy
inconstante ADJ inconstant, changeable
inconstitucional ADJ unconstitutional
incontable ADJ countless
incontenible ADJ uncontrollable
incontinente ADJ incontinent
incontrolable ADJ uncontrollable
incontrovertible ADJ incontrovertible
inconveniencia F inconvenience
inconveniente ADJ improper; M inconvenience, downside
incorporado ADJ built-in
incorporar VT to incorporate, to build into; (incluir) to incorporate; —**se** (erguirse) to sit up
incorrecto ADJ incorrect, wrong
incorregible ADJ incorrigible
incredulidad F disbelief
incrédulo ADJ incredulous
increíble ADJ (que no puede creerse) incredible, unbelievable; (extraordinario) amazing
incrementar VT to augment
incremento M increment, increase
incriminar VT to incriminate
incrustación F inlay
incrustado ADJ (en piedra) embedded; (joyas) inlaid
incrustar VT to embed; (oro) to inlay; —**se en** to become embedded in
incubadora F incubator
incuestionable ADJ unquestionable

inculcar[6] VT to inculcate, to instill
inculto ADJ (sin modales) uncultured, unrefined; (sin instrucción) uneducated
incumbencia F **no es de tu** — it's none of your business
incurable ADJ incurable
incurrir VI — **en** (una deuda) to incur; (un error) to fall into
incursión F raid, foray
incursionar VI to foray
indagación F investigation, probe
indagar[7] VI/VT to investigate, to inquire into
indebido ADJ undue
indecencia F indecency
indecente ADJ indecent
indecible ADJ unspeakable
indecisión F indecision
indeciso ADJ (que no ha decidido) undecided; (que suele vacilar) wishy-washy
indecoroso ADJ improper
indefendible ADJ indefensible
indefenso ADJ defenseless
indefinible ADJ indefinable
indefinido ADJ indefinite
indeleble ADJ indelible
indelicado ADJ indelicate
indemnización F indemnity; (de guerra) reparation; (de un pleito) recovery
indemnizar[9] VT to indemnify
independencia F independence; (de un individuo) self-reliance
independiente ADJ independent
indescriptible ADJ indescribable
indeseable ADJ undesirable, unwelcome
indestructible ADJ indestructible
indeterminado ADJ indeterminate
indexar VT to index
India F India
indicación F indication; (instrucción) instruction; **indicaciones** directions
indicador M pointer
indicar[6] VT to indicate, to point out; (aparato de medida) to read, to register; (mostrar) to show
indicativo ADJ & M indicative
índice M (lista alfabética) index; (tabla de materias) table of contents; (dedo) index finger
indicio M clue, sign
Indico M **Océano** — Indian Ocean
indiferencia F indifference; (frialdad) coolness
indiferente ADJ (apático) indifferent, unconcerned; (frío) cool; (sin entusiasmo) lukewarm; (no conmovido) unmoved; **esa chica me es** — I don't care about that

girl
indígena ADJ INV indigenous; MF INV native
indigente ADJ destitute, indigent
indigestión F indigestion
indignación F indignation
indignado ADJ indignant
indignar VT to make indignant; **—se** to become indignant
indigno ADJ unworthy
índigo M indigo
indio -dia ADJ & MF Indian
indirecta F hint
indirecto ADJ indirect; (ruta) roundabout
indisciplinado ADJ unruly
indiscreción F indiscretion
indiscreto ADJ indiscreet
indiscutible ADJ unquestionable
indispensable ADJ indispensable
indisponer[39] VT to indispose; **—se** to become indisposed
indispuesto ADJ (disgustado) upset; (enfermo) indisposed
indistinto ADJ indistinct, vague
individual ADJ individual; (habitación) single
individualidad F individuality
individualismo M individualism
individualista MF individualist
individuo ADJ & M individual
indivisible ADJ indivisible
índole F type
indolencia F indolence
indolente ADJ indolent
indoloro ADJ painless
indomable ADJ indomitable
indomado ADJ unbroken
Indonesia F Indonesia
indonesio -sia ADJ & MF Indonesian
inducción F induction
inducir[24] VT to induce, to prompt
indudablemente ADV undoubtedly
indulgencia F indulgence
indulgente ADJ indulgent, lenient
indultar VT to pardon
indulto M pardon
indumentaria F apparel
industria F industry, trade
industrial ADJ industrial; MF industrialist
industrioso ADJ industrious
inédito ADJ unpublished
inefable ADJ ineffable
ineficaz ADJ ineffective, ineffectual
ineficiente ADJ inefficient
inelegible ADJ ineligible
inepto ADJ inept
inequívoco ADJ unequivocal
inercia F inertia

inerte ADJ inert
inescrutable ADJ inscrutable
inesperado ADJ unexpected
inestabilidad F instability
inestable ADJ unstable; (andar) unsteady
inestimable ADJ inestimable, invaluable
inevitable ADJ inevitable; (accidente) unavoidable
inexacto ADJ inaccurate
inexcusable ADJ inexcusable
inexorable ADJ inexorable
inexperto ADJ inexperienced, unskilled; (ojo) untrained
inexplicable ADJ inexplicable
inexpresivo ADJ inexpressive, wooden
infalible ADJ infallible, foolproof; (confiable) unfailing
infame ADJ infamous
infamia F infamy
infancia F childhood
infante -ta MF (hijo -ja del rey) infante -ta; M (soldado) infantrymen
infantería F infantry; **— de marina** marine corps
infantil ADJ (como niño) childlike; (aniñado) childish, infantile
infección F infection
infeccioso ADJ infectious
infectar VT to infect; **—se** to become infected
infecto ADJ foul, repugnant
infelicidad F misery
infeliz ADJ unhappy, wretched, miserable; MF poor wretch
inferencia F inference
inferior ADJ (en calidad) inferior; (en posición) lower
inferioridad F inferiority
inferir[3] VT to infer
infernal ADJ infernal; (ruido) unholy
infestar VT to infest
infiel ADJ unfaithful, faithless, untrue
infierno M hell; (lugar donde hace mucho calor) inferno; **en el quinto —** in the middle of nowhere
infinidad F infinity; **una — de** a large number of
infinitivo ADJ & M infinitive
infinito ADJ infinite; M infinity
inflación F inflation
inflado M inflation
inflamable ADJ flammable
inflamación F inflammation
inflamar VT to inflame; **—se** to become inflamed
inflar VT (neumáticos) to inflate, to pump up; (globos) to blow up; (precios) to

balloon

inflexible ADJ (rígido) inflexible; (testarudo) unbending, adamant

infligir[11] VT to inflict

influencia F influence, pull, clout; (sobre las masas) sway

influir[31] VI — **en / sobre** to influence; (las masas) to sway

influjo M influence

influyente ADJ influential

infomercial M infomercial

información F information; (periodística) story

informal ADJ (no formal) informal, casual; (poco fiable) unreliable

informante MF (para un estudio) informant; (de la policía) informer

informar VT to inform, to appraise; (un militar) to debrief; (un periodista) to report; (un abogado) to advise; **—se** to become informed

informática F computer science

informatizar[9] VT to computerize

informe M report; (militar) debriefing; **—s** information; ADJ shapeless

infortunio M misfortune

infracción F (de reglamentos) infraction; (de contrato) breach; (de tránsito) violation

infractor -ora MF lawbreaker

infraestructura F infrastructure

infrarrojo ADJ & M infrared

infrascrito -ta MF undersigned

infringir[11] VT to infringe, to breach, to violate

infructuoso ADJ fruitless, unsuccessful

ínfulas F PL airs; **darse —** to put on airs

infundado ADJ groundless, unfounded

infundir VT to infuse, to imbue

infusionar VT to steep

ingeniar VT to contrive; **ingeniárselas para** to contrive to

ingeniería F engineering; **— genética** genetic engineering; **— química** chemical engineering

ingeniero -ra MF engineer; **— civil** civil engineer; **— electricista** electrical engineer

ingenio M (mental) ingenuity, cleverness; (verbal) wit; (artefacto) artifact; **— de azúcar** (refinería) sugar refinery, sugar mill; (plantación) sugar plantation

ingeniosidad F ingenuity

ingenioso ADJ ingenious, resourceful

ingenuo -nua ADJ (inocente) naive; (crédulo) gullible; MF dupe

ingerir VI/VT to ingest

ingestión F ingestion

ingle F groin

inglés -esa ADJ English; M Englishman; (lengua) English; F Englishwoman

ingobernable ADJ unruly

ingratitud F ingratitude

ingrato -ta ADJ thankless, ungrateful; MF ingrate

ingrávido ADJ weightless

ingrediente M ingredient; **—s** makings

ingresar VT (datos) to input; (dinero en una cuenta) to deposit; VI (a un hospital) to be admitted

ingreso M (permiso para entrar) entrance, entry; (depósito bancario) deposit; (renta) income; **—s** (de una firma) earnings; (del Estado) revenue

inhábil ADJ unskilled

inhabilidad F inability

inhabilitar VT to disqualify

inhalar VI/VT to breathe in, to inhale

inherente ADJ inherent

inhibición F inhibition

inhibir VT to inhibit

inhospitalario ADJ inhospitable

inhóspito ADJ inhospitable

inhumano ADJ inhuman

iniciación M initiation, induction

inicial ADJ initial; (pago) up-front; F initial

inicializar[9] VT to initialize

iniciar VT (comenzar) to initiate; (admitir) to induct

iniciativa F initiative

inimitable ADJ inimitable

ininflamable ADJ fireproof

ininteligible ADJ unintelligible

ininterrumpido ADJ continuous, unbroken

injertar VT to graft

injuria F (insulto) insult, verbal abuse; (daño) damage

injuriar VT to insult, to abuse verbally

injurioso ADJ insulting, injurious, verbally abusive

injusticia F injustice; (acto injusto) wrong; (error judicial) miscarriage of justice

injustificable ADJ unjustifiable

injustificado ADJ uncalled-for, unwarranted

injusto ADJ unjust, unfair

inmaculado ADJ immaculate, spotless

inmaduro ADJ immature

inmanejable ADJ unmanageable

inmaterial ADJ immaterial

inmediación F vicinity

inmediato ADJ immediate, instant; **de —** at once

inmensidad F immensity, vastness

inmenso ADJ immense, vast

inmigración F immigration

inmigrante ADJ & MF immigrant
inmigrar VI to immigrate
inminente ADJ imminent, impending
inmiscuir[31] VI to mix; **—se** to meddle
inmoral ADJ immoral
inmoralidad F immorality
inmortal ADJ & MF immortal
inmortalidad F immortality
inmóvil ADJ motionless, immobile
inmovilizar[9] VT to immobilize; (en una pelea) to pin
inmune ADJ immune
inmunidad F immunity
inmutable ADJ unchangeable, immutable
innato ADJ innate, inborn
innecesario ADJ unnecessary, needless
innegable ADJ undeniable
innoble ADJ ignoble
innocuo ADJ innocuous
innovación F innovation
innumerable ADJ innumerable, countless
inocencia F innocence
inocente ADJ innocent, guiltless; MF dupe
inocuo ADJ harmless
inodoro ADJ odorless; M toilet, commode
inofensivo ADJ inoffensive, harmless
inolvidable ADJ unforgettable
inoperable ADJ inoperable
inoportuno ADJ inopportune, untimely
inorgánico ADJ inorganic
inoxidable ADJ rustproof
inquietar VT to worry
inquieto ADJ (movedizo) restless; (preocupado) uneasy
inquietud F (intranquilidad) restlessness; (preocupación) alarm
inquilino -ina MF (de un apartamento) tenant, renter; (de una pensión) lodger
inquina F spite
inquirir[34] VI/VT to inquire
inquisición F inquisition
inquisitivo ADJ inquisitive
insaciable ADJ insatiable
insalubre ADJ unhealthy
insatisfactorio ADJ unsatisfactory
insatisfecho ADJ dissatisfied, unhappy
inscribir[51] VT (grabar) to inscribe; (matricular) to register, to enroll; **—se** to register, to enroll
inscripción F (grabado) inscription; (matriculación) registration, enrollment
insecticida M insecticide
insectívoro ADJ insectivorous
insecto M insect
inseguro ADJ (personalidad) insecure; (vehículo) unsafe; (el andar) unsteady
insensato -ta ADJ foolish; MF fool

insensibilizar[9] VT to desensitize
insensible ADJ (cruel) insensitive, callous; (imperturbable) unfeeling, thick-skinned; (entumecido) numb
inseparable ADJ inseparable
inserción F insertion
insertar VT to insert
inservible ADJ useless
insidioso ADJ insidious
insigne ADJ famous
insignia F insignia, badge
insignificante ADJ insignificant, unimportant
insincero ADJ insincere
insinuación F insinuation; (sexual) innuendo
insinuante ADJ suggestive
insinuar[17] VT to insinuate, to suggest; **—se** to insinuate oneself
insípido ADJ insipid, flavorless
insistencia F insistence; (perseverancia) persistence
insistente ADJ insistent; (perseverante) persistent
insistir VI/VT to insist; (perseverar) to persist; **— en** to insist on; **— sobre** to harp on
insolación F (por sol) sunstroke; (por calor) heatstroke
insolencia F insolence; (comentario) smart remark
insolente ADJ insolent, sassy
insólito ADJ unusual; (accidente) freak, freakish
insoluble ADJ insoluble
insolvente ADJ insolvent
insomne ADJ wakeful, unable to sleep
insoportable ADJ unbearable, impossible; (dolor) excruciating
insospechado ADJ unsuspected
insostenible ADJ untenable
inspección F inspection; (encuesta) canvass
inspeccionar VT to inspect, to survey
inspector -ora MF inspector
inspiración F (idea) inspiration; (inhalación) inhalation
inspirar VI/VT to inspire; VI to inhale, to breathe in
instalación F installation
instalar VT to install; **—se** to take up residence
instancia LOC ADV **a —s de** at the request of
instantánea F snapshot
instantáneo ADJ instantaneous
instante M instant; **al —** right away
instar VT to enjoin
instigar[7] VT to instigate, to abet
instintivo ADJ instinctive

instinto M instinct; **— suicida** death wish
institución F institution; **— benéfica** charity
instituir[31] VT to institute
instituto M institute; (escuela secundaria) high school
institutriz F governess
instrucción F instruction, schooling
instructivo ADJ instructive
instructor -ora MF instructor
instruir[31] VT to instruct, to school
instrumental ADJ instrumental
instrumentar VT (un plan) to implement; (música) to do the instrumentation for
instrumento M instrument; **— de metal** brass instrument; **— de viento** wind instrument
insubordinado ADJ insubordinate
insuficiencia F insufficiency; (de los órganos) failure
insuficiente ADJ insufficient, inadequate
insufrible ADJ insufferable
insulina F insulin
insulso ADJ bland
insultar VT to insult
insulto M insult, put-down
insuperable ADJ (resultado) insuperable; (obstáculo) insurmountable
insurgente ADJ & MF insurgent
insurrección F insurrection
insurrecto -ta ADJ rebellious; MF rebel
intachable ADJ blameless
intacto ADJ intact, unbroken
intangible ADJ intangible
integral ADJ integral; (harina) whole-grain
integrante ADJ integral
integrar VT to form; (ser miembro de) to be a member of
integridad F integrity
íntegro ADJ whole; (moralmente) upright
intelecto M intellect
intelectual ADJ & MF intellectual
inteligencia F intelligence (también militar); (persona) mind; **— artificial** artificial intelligence
inteligente ADJ intelligent, bright, smart
inteligible ADJ intelligible
intemperie LOC ADV **a la —** exposed to the weather
intención F intention, intent
intencional ADJ intentional
intensidad F intensity
intensificar[6] VT to intensify; **—se** to intensify; (violencia) to escalate
intensivo ADJ intensive
intenso ADJ intense; (debate) fierce; (calor) severe

intentar VI/VT to try; VT to attempt
intento M (tentativa) try, attempt; (propósito) intention
interactivo ADJ interactive
interactuar[17] VI to interact
intercalación F insertion
intercalar VT to insert
intercambiador M interchange
intercambiar VI/VT to exchange
intercambio M exchange
interceder VI to intercede
interceptación F interception
interceptar VT to intercept
intercesión F intercession
intercesor -ora MF advocate
interés M (intelectual, financiero) interest; (preocupación) concern; (participación comercial) stake; **— compuesto** compound interest
interesado ADJ interested; (preocupado) concerned; (egoísta) self-serving
interesante ADJ interesting
interesar VT to interest; **—se por** to become interested in
interestatal ADJ interstate
interestelar ADJ interstellar
interface MF interface
interfaz MF (electrónica / informática) interface
interferencia F interference; (en una transmisión) interference, static
interferir VT to jam; VI to interfere
ínterin M interim; **en el —** meanwhile
interino ADJ acting, interim
interior ADJ (de un edificio) interior; (no costeño) inland; (dentro de una organización) internal; (hacia dentro) inward; M interior
interiorizar[9] VT to internalize
interjección F interjection
interlineal ADJ interlinear
interlock M interlock
interlocutor -ora MF interlocutor
interludio M interlude
intermediario -ria M middleman; MF (mensajero) go-between
intermedio ADJ intermediate; M intermission; **por — de** through
interminable ADJ interminable, unending, endless
intermitente ADJ intermittent; M turn signal
internacional ADJ international
internado -da M (escuela) boarding school; (período de práctica) internship; MF (alumno) boarding student; (en un hospital) inmate
internalizar[9] VT to internalize

internar VT (en una cárcel) to intern; (en un hospital) to admit; (en un manicomio) to commit

internet M Internet

internista MF internist

interno -na ADJ internal; MF (alumno) boarding-school student; (prisionero, médico) intern

interpersonal ADJ interpersonal

interponer[39] VT to interpose; —**se** to intervene

interpretación F interpretation; (artístico) performance, rendition

interpretar VT to interpret; (música) to perform; (intenciones) to construe

intérprete MF interpreter; (músico) artist

interracial ADJ interracial

interrelacionado ADJ interrelated

interrogación F interrogation

interrogador -ora MF questioner; ADJ questioning

interrogar[7] VI/VT (por la policía) to interrogate; (con intensidad) to grill; (a un testigo) to question, to cross-examine

interrogativo ADJ interrogative

interrogatorio M interrogation, questioning

interrumpir VI/VT to interrupt; VT (servicios) to disrupt, to cut off; (producción de un modelo) to discontinue; (en una conversación) to intrude, to cut in

interrupción F interruption; (en una conversación) intrusion; (de producción) stoppage

interruptor M switch

intersección F intersection

intersticio M interstice

intervalo M interval; (en el teatro) intermission, interlude

intervención F intervention; — **de teléfono** wiretap

intervenir[47] VI to intervene; — **un teléfono** to wiretap

interviú F interview

intestino ADJ & M intestine; — **delgado** small intestine; —**s** bowels

intimar VI to become friendly

intimidad F intimacy

intimidar VT (una persona) to intimidate; (una tarea) to daunt

íntimo ADJ intimate, close

intitular VT to entitle; —**se** to be entitled

intolerable ADJ intolerable

intolerancia F intolerance, bigotry

intolerante ADJ intolerant, narrow-minded

intoxicación F intoxication, poisoning; — **con plomo** lead poisoning; — **por alimentos** food poisoning

intoxicar[6] VT to poison, to intoxicate

intransigente ADJ intransigent, uncompromising

intransitivo ADJ intransitive

intravenoso ADJ intravenous

intrepidez F fearlessness

intrépido ADJ (sin miedo) intrepid, fearless; (aventurero) adventurous

intriga F intrigue

intrigante MF schemer; ADJ scheming

intrigar[7] VI/VT to intrigue, to scheme

intrincado ADJ intricate

intrínseco ADJ intrinsic

introducción F introduction

introducir[24] VT (incorporar) to introduce; (colocar) to put in, to insert

introspección F introspection

introvertido -da ADJ introverted; MF introvert

intrusión F intrusion

intrusivo ADJ intrusive

intruso -sa ADJ intruding; MF intruder

intuición F intuition

intuir[31] VT to sense

intuitivo ADJ intuitive

inundación F flood

inundar VI/VT to inundate, to flood; (de regalos) to shower

inusitado ADJ unusual

inútil ADJ useless, pointless; (esfuerzo) futile; (persona) worthless, good-for-nothing

inutilidad F uselessness; (de un esfuerzo) futility

inutilizar[9] VT to render useless, to put out of commission

invadir VI/VT to invade

invalidar VT to render invalid

inválido -da ADJ (discapacitado) invalid; (nulo) void; MF invalid

invalorable ADJ priceless, invaluable

invariable ADJ invariable

invasión F invasion

invasor -ora MF invader; ADJ invading

invencible ADJ invincible

invención F invention (también mentira); (mental) construct

inventar VT to invent; (una historia) to fabricate, to make up

inventariar[16] VT to inventory

inventario M inventory

inventiva F ingenuity

inventivo ADJ inventive

invento M invention

inventor -ora MF inventor

invernadero M greenhouse, hothouse

invernal ADJ wintry

invernar[1] VI to winter

inverosímil ADJ unlikely, farfetched

inversión F (trueque) inversion; (financiero) investment

inversionista MF investor

inverso ADJ inverse, reverse; **a la inversa** the other way around

inversor -ora MF investor

invertir[3] VT to invert, to reverse; VI/VT (dinero) to invest

investidura F inauguration, investment

investigación F (policial) investigation, inquiry; (científico) research

investigador -ora MF investigator; (científico) researcher

investigar[7] VI/VT to investigate, to look into; (científico) to research

investir VI/VT to invest; — **de un cargo** to induct into office

invicto ADJ unbeaten

invierno M winter

invisible ADJ invisible; (oculto) unseen

invitación F invitation

invitado -da MF guest

invitar VI/VT to invite

invocación F invocation

invocar[6] VT to invoke; (espíritus) to conjure

involucrar VT (implicar) to implicate; (consistir de) to involve

involuntario ADJ involuntary; (accidental) inadvertent

inyección F injection, shot; (en coches) fuel injection

inyectado ADJ — **de sangre** bloodshot

inyectar VT to inject

ión M ion

ionizar[9] VT to ionize

ir[32] VI to go; (deber estar situado) to belong; — **a caballo** to ride horseback; — **a pie** to walk; — **a por** to fetch; — **aprendiendo** to learn gradually; — **corriendo** to run; — **de mal en peor** to go from bad to worse; — **en coche** to drive / ride in a car; — **tirando** to scrape along; **no me va ni me viene** it's all the same to me; **¿cómo te va?** how are you? **¡vaya!** well now! **¡vaya a saber uno!** go figure! **¡vamos!** let's go! come on! **¡vaya hombre!** what a man! **¡ve a freír espárragos!** take a hike! **va por dos años que me casé** it's going on two years since I got married; **voy a comer** I'm going to eat; **va y se come un hongo venenoso** she goes and eats a poisonous mushroom; **en lo que va del año** since the beginning of the year; **ya van siete veces que me lo dice** that makes seven times that she's told me; **voy**

a ir de rojo I'm going dressed in red; **para que no vayas a creer** lest you should think; **no vayas a caerte** don't fall; **¡qué va!** no way! **—se** to go away, to leave; **—se a la quiebra** to go broke; **—se a las manos** to come to blows; **—se a pique** to founder; **—se de vacaciones** to take a vacation

ira F ire, wrath

Irak M Iraq

Irán M Iran

iraní ADJ & MF Iranian

iraquí ADJ & MF Iraqi

irascible ADJ irascible, quick-tempered

iridiscente ADJ iridescent

iris M iris

Irlanda F Ireland

irlandés -esa MF Irish; ADJ Irish

ironía F irony

irónico ADJ ironic, wry

irracional ADJ irrational, unreasonable

irradiar VT to radiate, to irradiate

irreal ADJ unreal

irreconocible ADJ unrecognizable

irrecuperable ADJ irretrievable

irreflexivo ADJ thoughtless

irrefutable ADJ irrefutable

irregular ADJ irregular; (borde, filo) ragged; (pulso) unsteady; (superficie) rough, uneven; (comportamiento) erratic, haphazard

irremediable ADJ hopeless

irremplazable ADJ irreplaceable

irreparable ADJ irreparable

irreprochable ADJ irreproachable, flawless

irresistible ADJ irresistible

irrespetuoso ADJ disrespectful

irresponsable ADJ irresponsible

irreverente ADJ irreverent

irrevocable ADJ irrevocable

irrigación F irrigation

irrigar[7] VI/VT to irrigate

irritable ADJ irritable

irritación F irritation

irritante ADJ (molesto) irritating, grating; (agresivo) abrasive

irritar VI/VT to irritate, to aggravate

irrumpir VI to burst into

isla F island, isle; **—s Fiyi** Fiji Islands; **—s Malvinas** Falkland Islands; **—s Marshall** Marshall Islands; **—s Salomón** Solomon Islands; **—s Vírgenes** Virgin Islands

islamismo M Islam

islandés -esa MF Icelander; ADJ Icelandic

Islandia F Iceland

isleño -ña MF islander

isobara F isobar

isométrico ADJ isometric
isótopo M isotope
Israel M Israel
israelí ADJ & MF Israeli
istmo M isthmus
Italia F Italy
italiano -na ADJ & MF Italian
itálico ADJ italic
ítem M item
itinerante ADJ itinerant
itinerario M itinerary
IVA (impuesto al valor añadido / agregado) M sales tax
izar⁹ VT to hoist, to raise
izquierda F left (también política); (mano) left hand; **a la —** to the left
izquierdista ADJ & MF leftist
izquierdo ADJ left

Jj

jab M jab
jabalí M (wild) boar
jabalina F javelin
jabón M soap
jabonera F soap dish
jabonoso ADJ soapy
jaca F nag
jacinto M hyacinth
jactancia F boastfulness
jactancioso ADJ boastful, blustering
jactarse VI to boast, to brag
jacuzzi M Jacuzzi™, hot tub
jade M jade
jadear VI to pant, to gasp
jadeo M panting, gasping
jaez M harness
jaguar M jaguar
jalar VI/VT to pull, to tug
jalea F jelly
jaleo M (lío) mess; (barahúnda) ruckus
jam M jam session
Jamaica F Jamaica
jamaicano -na ADJ & MF Jamaican
jamaiquino -na ADJ & MF Jamaican
jamás ADV never
jamelgo M hack
jamón M ham
Japón M Japan
japonés -esa ADJ & MF Japanese
jaque M check; **— mate** checkmate; **tener a uno en —** *fam* to have someone by the short hairs

jaqueca F migraine
jarabe M syrup
jarana F revelry; **ir de —** to paint the town red
jarcia F rigging
jardín M (de flores) garden; (de césped) yard; **— de niños** kindergarten; **— infantil** nursery
jardinero -ra MF gardener
jarra F (cántaro) jug, pitcher; (taza) mug; **en —s** akimbo
jarro M pitcher, jug
jarrón M vase
jaspe M jasper; (mármol) veined marble
jaula F cage, coop
jauría F pack
jazmín M jasmine
jazz M jazz
jeans M PL jeans
jefatura F headquarters
jefe -fa MF (en un lugar de trabajo) boss; (militar) commander; (departamental) chair, head; (policial) chief; **— del estado mayor** chief of staff
jején M gnat
jengibre M ginger
jerarquía F hierarchy
jerez M sherry
jerga F jargon, slang
jerigonza F gibberish, gobbledygook; (juego lingüístico) pig Latin
jeringa F syringe
jeringar⁷ VT to annoy
jeroglífico ADJ & M hieroglyphic
jersey M sweater
jesuita ADJ INV & M Jesuit
Jesús INTERJ God bless you! gesundheit!
jeta F (hocico) snout; (cara) mug
jet-set M jet set
jilguero M goldfinch
jinete -ta MF rider
jinetear VI to ride horseback
jingle M jingle
jirafa F giraffe
jobar INTERJ holy cow! holy Moses! holy mackerel!
jockey M jockey
jocoso ADJ jocular
jofaina F basin
jolgorio M rumpus
Jordania F Jordan
jordano -na ADJ & MF Jordanian
jornada F (día laboral) workday; (coloquio) colloquium
jornal M daily wage
jornalero -ra MF day laborer
joroba F hump

jorobado -da ADJ & MF hunchback
jorobar VT (molestar) to hassle; (estropear) to gum up
jota F jay; **no saber ni —** to know zilch
joven ADJ young; M (muchacho) youth
jovial ADJ jolly
joya F jewel; (persona apreciada) gem; **—s** jewelry
joyería F jewelry store
joyero -ra MF jeweler
joystick M joystick
juanete M bunion
jubilación F retirement; (pagos) pension
jubilar VT to pension, to retire; **—se** to retire
jubileo M jubilee
júbilo M glee
jubiloso ADJ jubilant, joyous
judía F bean; **— blanca** navy bean; **— pinta** pinto bean; **— verde** green bean
judicial ADJ judicial
judío -ía ADJ Jewish; MF Jew
judo M judo
juego M (actividad recreativa) play; (partido de pelota) game; (conjunto de tazas) set; (conjunto de muebles) suite; **— de damas** checkers; **— de palabras** pun, play on words; **—s Olímpicos** Olympic Games; **estar en —** to be at stake; **hacer —** to match
juerga F binge; **irse de —** to go on a binge
juerguista MF merrymaker
jueves M Thursday
juez -za MF judge; (en deportes) referee; **— de paz** justice of the peace
jugada F play, move
jugador -ora MF player; (apostador) gambler
jugar[33] VI to play; (apostar) to gamble; **— a la baraja / a los naipes** to play cards; **— con fuego** to play with fire; **— limpio** to play fair; **—se** to risk
jugarreta F bad turn
jugo M juice
jugoso ADJ juicy
juguete M plaything, toy
juguetear VI to toy with, to fiddle with
juguetón -ona ADJ playful
juicio M (criterio) judgment; (proceso) trial; **perder el —** to lose one's mind; **a mi —** in my estimation
juicioso ADJ judicious
juke-box M jukebox
julio M July
jumbo ADJ jumbo; M jumbo jet
jumper M jumper
junco M rush, reed; (barco chino) junk
jungla F jungle
junio M June

junta F (reunión) meeting; (concejo) council; (juntura) joint; (pieza de coche) gasket
juntar VT (tubos) to attach; (valentía) to muster; (flores) to gather, to pick; (ganado) to round up, to wrangle; **— polvo** to gather dust; **— valor** to muster courage; **—se** (acumularse) to gather; (asociarse) to band together; (reunirse) to come together
junto ADJ together; LOC ADV **— a** next to; **— con** together with
juntura F (lugar) juncture; (articulación) joint
jurado -da MF juror; M (conjunto de jurados) jury
juramentar VI/VT to swear in; **—se** to be sworn in
juramento M oath
jurar VI/VT to swear, to vow; **— en falso** to perjure oneself; **— la bandera** to pledge allegiance to the flag
jurisdicción F jurisdiction
jurisprudencia F (doctrina) jurisprudence; (derecho) law
justa F joust, tilt
justamente ADV precisely, fairly
justicia F justice
justificación F justification
justificar[6] VT to justify
justo ADJ just; (equitativo) equitable; (pío) righteous, upright; **— después de** right after; **— en ese momento** exactly at that moment
juvenil ADJ (inmaduro) juvenile; (de apariencia joven) youthful
juventud F youth
juzgado M court
juzgar[7] VI/VT to judge, to pass judgment (on); **— mal** to misjudge

Kk

kaki M khaki
kart M go-cart
kayak M kayak
Kazajstán M Kazakhstan
kazako -ka ADJ & MF Kazakh(h)
Kenia F Kenya
keniata ADJ INV & MF INV Kenyan
kermés F bazaar
keroseno M kerosene
ketchup M catsup, ketchup
kilo M kilo

kilobyte M kilobyte
kilociclo M kilocycle
kilogramo M kilogram
kilometraje M mileage
kilómetro M kilometer
kilovatio M kilowatt; F —-hora kilowatt-
    hour
Kirguistán M Kyrgyzstan
Kiribati M Kiribati
kosher ADJ kosher
Kuwait M Kuwait
kuwaití ADJ & MF Kuwaiti

Ll

la ART DEF F the; — **de** the one with, that one
    with; PRON PERS it, her; PRON REL — **que**
    she who, the one that
laberinto M labyrinth, maze
labia F gift of gab
labio M lip; — **leporino** harelip
labor F (trabajo) labor; (tarea) task;
    (manualidad) handiwork
laboral ADJ **legislación** — labor legislation
laboratorio M laboratory
laborioso ADJ (trabajoso) laborious; (amante
    del trabajo) hard-working
labrado ADJ carved
labranza F plowing
labrar VT to till; —**se una carrera** to carve
    out a career
laca F lacquer
lacar[6] VT to lacquer
lacayo M lackey, flunky
laciar VT *RP* to straighten
lacio ADJ straight
lacónico ADJ (persona) laconic; (comentario)
    terse
lacra F (física) scar; (moral) blight
lacre M sealing wax
lacrimógeno ADJ tear-producing
lactar VT to nurse
lácteo ADJ (parecido a la leche) milky; (hecho
    de leche) dairy
ladeado ADJ (torcido) awry, askew;
    (asimétrico) lopsided
ladear VT to tilt; (la cabeza) to cock; (un
    avión) to bank; (ignorar) to snub, to
    ignore; —**se** to tilt, to lean
ladeo M tilt
ladera F hillside
ladillas F PL crabs
ladino ADJ artful

lado M side; — **a** — side by side; **al** —
    nearby; **¡a un** —! gangway! **de** —
    sideways; **hacerse a un** — to move over
ladrar VI to bark; VI/VT (hablar de modo
    áspero) to snap (at)
ladrido M bark, barking
ladrillo M brick
ladrón -ona MF (de casas) burglar; (con
    violencia) robber; (con astucia) thief
lagartija F lizard; (ejercicio) push-up
lagarto M alligator
lago M lake
lágrima F tear, teardrop
lagrimear VI to weep
laguna F lagoon; (de la memoria,
    conocimiento) gap; (legal) loophole
laico -ca MF layperson; ADJ lay
laja F slab
lamentable ADJ (desafortunado) lamentable,
    regrettable; (ruinoso) woeful
lamentación F lamentation
lamentar VT to lament, to regret; —**se** to
    lament, to wail
lamento M lament, lamentation
lamer VT to lick; VI/VT (el mar) to lap
lamida F lick
lámina F (de vidrio, metal) sheet; (de metal)
    plate; (grabado) print
laminar VT to laminate
lámpara F lamp
lamparilla F night-light
lampiño ADJ (sin pelo) hairless; (sin barba)
    beardless
lana F wool; — **de acero** steel wool
lanar ADJ wool-bearing
lance M incident
lancear VT to lance, to spear
lanceta F lancet, lance
lancha F launch, boat; — **a motor**
    motorboat
langosta F (crustáceo) lobster; (insecto)
    locust
langostino M prawn
languidecer[13] VI to languish, to wilt
languidez F languor
lánguido ADJ languid, listless
lanilla F flannel
lanolina F lanolin
lanudo ADJ wooly, shaggy
lanza F lance, spear; **romper una — por
    alguien** to stick one's neck out for
    someone; M SG —**llamas** flame thrower
lanzadera F shuttle
lanzador -ora MF pitcher
lanzamiento M (de un cohete, producto)
    launch; (de suministros) drop; (de una
    roca grande) heave; (de una pelota) pitch

lanzar[9] VT (un cohete, un producto) to launch; (una pelota) to throw; (una bala) to fire; (algo pesado) to heave; (lodo) to sling; VI/VT (vomitar) to puke; **—se** to launch forth/out

lanzazo M thrust with a lance

Laos M Laos

laosiano -na ADJ & MF Laotian

lápida F stone tablet; (de sepultura) gravestone, tombstone

lapidar VT to stone

lapidario ADJ & M lapidary

lápiz M pencil; **— de color** crayon; **— de labios** lipstick

lapso M lapse, span

lapsus M lapse, slip of the tongue

laptop M laptop

laquear VT to lacquer

largar[7] VI (soltar) to cough up; **—se** fam to scram, to buzz off, to shove off

largo ADJ long; (discurso) lengthy; **¡— de aquí!** scram! **—metraje** feature film; **a la larga** in the long run; **a lo —** lengthwise; M length

largueza F generosity

larguirucho ADJ lanky

largura F length

laringe F larynx

laringitis F laryngitis

larva F larva

lascivia F (deseo) lust; (perversión) lewdness

lascivo ADJ (pervertido) lascivious, lewd

láser M laser

lástima F (compasión) pity; **¡qué —!** what a shame!

lastimadura F hurt

lastimar VT to hurt; (insultar) to hurt one's feelings; **—se** to get hurt

lastimoso ADJ pitiful

lastrar VT to ballast

lastre M ballast

lata F tin can, can; (con tapa) canister; (pesadez) bore; **dar la —** to be a nuisance

latente ADJ latent, dormant

lateral ADJ lateral, side

látex M latex

latido M (individual) beat, throb; (colectivo) beating; (del corazón) heartbeat

latifundio M large estate

latigazo M (golpe) lash; (chasquido) crack of a whip

látigo M whip

latín M Latin

latino -na ADJ (relativo a los hispanos) Latino; (relativo a la lengua latina) Latin; M Latino; F Latina

Latinoamérica F Latin America

latinoamericano ADJ Latin American

latir VI to beat, to throb

latitud F latitude (también flexibilidad)

latón M brass

latrocinio M larceny

laudable ADJ laudable

laurel M laurel; **dormirse sobre los —es** to rest on one's laurels

lava F lava

lavable ADJ washable

lavabo M (retrete) lavatory, toilet; (recipiente) sink

lavadero M laundry

lavado M wash, washing; **— de cerebro** brain washing; **— de dinero** money laundering; **— en seco** dry cleaning

lavadora F washing machine

lavanda F lavender

lavandera F washerwoman

lavandería F laundry

lavar VI/VT to wash; (ropa) to launder; **—se** to wash up; **—se las manos** to wash one's hands; M SG **lavaplatos / lavavajillas** dishwasher

lavativa F enema

lavatorio M washroom

laxante M laxative

laxitud F laxity

laxo ADJ lax

lazada F bowknot

lazar[9] VT to lasso

lazarillo M (persona) guide for the blind; (perro) guide dog

lazo M (soga) lasso, rope; (vuelta) loop; (nudo corredizo) noose; (relación) tie, bond

le PRON PERS **— dije** I told you/him/her; **— vi** Esp I saw him; **se — murió el perro** his/her dog died on him/her

leal ADJ loyal, trusty

lealtad F loyalty, allegiance

lección F lesson, assignment; **darle una — a alguien** to teach someone a lesson

lechada F whitewash

leche F (de vaca) milk; **— desnatada** skim milk; **— en polvo** powdered milk; **— entera** whole milk; **— homogeneizada** homogenized milk; **— malteada** malted milk; **¿qué —s quieres?** Esp fam what the hell do you want? **mala —** nasty disposition; **ir a toda —** to barrel along; **ese tío es la —** that guy's a case; **es un mala —** Esp fam he's a nasty creep

lechería F dairy

lechero -ra ADJ dairy; M milkman; F milkmaid

lecho M bed (también de río)

lechón M suckling pig

lechoso ADJ milky
lechuga F lettuce
lechuza F screech owl, barn owl
lector -ora MF reader
lectura F (acción) reading; (material) reading matter
leer[14] VI/VT to read
legación F legation
legado M legacy, bequest
legajo M file
legal ADJ legal, lawful
legalizar[9] VT to legalize
legar[7] VT to will, to bequeath
legendario ADJ legendary
leggings M PL leggings
legible ADJ legible
legión F legion
legislación F legislation
legislador -ora MF legislator, lawmaker
legislar VI/VT to legislate
legislativo ADJ legislative
legislatura F legislature
legítimo ADJ legitimate, lawful, rightful
lego -ga MF layperson; ADJ lay
legua F league
leguleyo -ya MF *pey* shyster
legumbre F legume
leído ADJ well-read
lejanía F distance
lejano ADJ distant, faraway; (parentesco) remote
lejía F (producto de limpieza) bleach; (de sosa) lye
lejos ADV far away, far; **a lo —** in the distance; **— de** far from; **desde —** from afar
lelo ADJ silly
lema M motto; (político) slogan
lencería F lingerie
lengua F (órgano) tongue; (idioma) language; **— materna** mother tongue
lenguado M sole
lenguaje M language (también en informática); **— corporal** body language; **— de máquina** machine language; **— de signos** sign language; **— ensamblador** assembly language
lenguaraz ADJ gossipy
lengüeta F (de un instrumento de viento) reed; (de un zapato) tongue
lengüetazo M lick
lente MF lens; **— filtrador** filter lens; **—s** eyeglasses; **—s de contacto** contact lenses; **—s negros / oscuros** sunglasses, shades
lenteja F lentil
lentitud F slowness

lento ADJ (no rápido) slow; (no inteligente) dull; (letárgico) sluggish
leña F firewood
leñador -ora MF woodcutter, lumberjack
leñera F woodshed
leño M log
leñoso ADJ woody
león M lion; **— marino** sea lion
León M Leon
leona F lioness
leonés ADJ Leonese
leopardo M leopard
lepra F leprosy
lerdo ADJ slow
lesbiano -na ADJ lesbian; F lesbian
lesión F injury, lesion
lesionar VT to injure; **—se** to get injured
Lesotho M Lesotho
letal ADJ lethal
letargo M lethargy
letón -ona ADJ & MF Latvian
Letonia F Latvia
letra F (del alfabeto) letter; (caligrafía) handwriting; (de una canción) lyrics, words; **— bastardilla / cursiva** italics; **— chica** fine print; **— de cambio** bill of exchange; **— de imprenta** block letter; **— manuscrita** longhand; **sin —s** uneducated
letrado ADJ learned, literate
letrero M sign
letrina F latrine
leucemia F leukemia
leudar VI to rise; VT to leaven
leva F (de tropas) levy; (de motor) cam
levadura F leaven, yeast
levantamiento M (revuelta) uprising; (suspensión) suspension; **— de pesas** weight-lifting
levantar VT (la mano) to raise; (una caja) to lift; (un interruptor) to switch; (algo caído) to pick up; (perdices) to flush; (a un dormido) to wake up, to rouse; (un edificio) to put up; **— el campamento** to break camp; **— falso testimonio** to bear false witness; **— la mesa** to clear the table; **— la sesión** to adjourn the meeting; **— vuelo** to take flight; **—se** (de la cama) to get up, to rise, to arise; (de una silla) to stand up, to get up; (un edificio) to go up
levar VT **— anclas** to weigh anchor
leve ADJ (brisa) light; (resfrío) mild; (problema) slight
levedad F (de una brisa) lightness; (de un resfrío) mildness
léxico M lexicon, dictionary; ADJ lexical

lexicografía F lexicography
ley F law, statute; **— de prescripción** statute of-limitations; **— marcial** martial law; **de buena —** of good quality
leyenda F (mitología) legend; (texto que acompaña una figura) caption
liar[16] VT (paquetes) to bundle; (cigarros) to roll; **—se** to get involved
libanés -esa ADJ & MF Lebanese
Líbano M Lebanon
libelo M libel
libélula F dragonfly
liberación F liberation; (de pecados) deliverance; (de presos) release
liberal ADJ & MF liberal
liberalidad F liberality
liberalismo M liberalism
liberar VT (de un deber) to relieve; (a un pueblo) to liberate; (del sufrimiento) to deliver; (a un preso) to free, to release
Liberia F Liberia
liberiano -na ADJ & MF Liberian
libertad F liberty, freedom; **— condicional** parole; **— de expresión** free speech; **poner en —** to set free; **poner en — bajo fianza** to let out on bail; **poner en — condicional** to parole
libertador -ora MF liberator
libertar VT to liberate
libertinaje M licentiousness
libertino -na MF libertine
Libia F Libya
libido F libido
libio -bia ADJ & MF Libyan
libra F pound (también moneda británica)
librar VT to free, to set free; (de una obligación) to release; (un cheque) to write; (una letra de cambio) to draft; (una guerra) to wage; **—se de** to get rid of
libre ADJ free; (asiento) vacant; (camino) clear; (traducción) loose; (de una obligación) exempt; **— albedrío** free will; **— cambio / comercio** free trade; **— de impuestos** duty-free; **— pensador** free thinker
librería F bookstore
librero -ra MF bookseller
libresco ADJ bookish
libreta F small notebook
libreto M libretto
libro M book; **— de bolsa** pocket book; **— de cocina** cookbook; **— de texto** textbook; **— en rústica** paperback; **— mayor** ledger
licencia F (carnet de conducir, libertad poética) license; (permiso) leave
licenciado -da MF college graduate

licenciar VT to discharge; **—se** to graduate from college
licenciatura F bachelor's degree
licencioso ADJ licentious
liceo M high school
licitación F bid
lícito ADJ lawful, permissible
licor M liqueur, cordial
licuadora F blender
líder MF leader
lidiar VI/VT to contend, to grapple
liebre F hare; **levantar la —** to let the cat out of the bag
Liechtenstein M Liechtenstein
liechtensteiniano -na MF Liechtensteiner
lienzo M canvas
lifting M face-lift
liga F (alianza, grupo deportivo) league; (cinta elástica) garter; **— mayor** major league
ligado M slur
ligadura F ligature
ligamento M ligament
ligar[7] VT to bind; (conectar notas) to slur; (perseguir sexualmente) to hit on; (conquistar sexualmente) to score; VI **—se** to bind; **—se las trompas** to have one's tubes tied
ligereza F (de peso) lightness; (de temperamento) levity
ligero ADJ (poco pesado) light; (rápido) swift; (pequeño) slight; **a la ligera** lightly
liguero M garter belt
lija F sandpaper
lijar VI/VT to sandpaper, to sand
lila ADJ & MF INV lilac
lima F (fruta) lime; (árbol) lime tree; **— de uñas** nail file
limar VI/VT to file
limero M lime tree
limitación F (restricción) limitation; (defecto) shortcoming
limitar VT to limit; (gastos) to curb; **—se a** to limit oneself to
límite M limit; (de una región) boundary; (de la paciencia) bounds; **— de velocidad** speed limit
limítrofe ADJ bordering
limo M slime
limón M lemon
limonada F lemonade
limonero M lemon tree
limosna F alms, handout
limpiador M cleanser
limpiar VI/VT to clean; VT (una superficie) to wipe; (la piel) to cleanse; (un camino, una pantalla de computadora, la reputación) to

clear; (animales) to dress; (zapatos) to shine; (un derrame) to mop up, to wipe up; (dejar sin dinero) to clean out; M SG **limpiaparabrisas** windshield wiper; **limpiavidrios** squeegee

límpido ADJ limpid

limpieza F cleanliness, neatness; (operación militar) mop-up; — **étnica** ethnic cleansing

limpio ADJ clean, neat; (piel, conciencia) clear; (juego) fair; (sin dinero) broke; **pasar en** — to make a clean copy

limusina F limousine

linaje M lineage, ancestry

linaza F linseed

lince M (animal) lynx; (persona astuta) sly fox; **con ojos de** — sharp-eyed

linchar VT to lynch

lindante ADJ neighboring

lindar VI to border, to adjoin

linde MF boundary

lindero ADJ adjoining; M boundary

lindo ADJ pretty; **un día** — a nice day; **de lo** — a lot

línea F line; — **de conducta** course of action; — **de crédito** credit line; — **de montaje** assembly line

lineal ADJ linear

linfa F lymph

lingüista MF linguist

lingüística F linguistics

lingüístico ADJ linguistic

linimento M liniment

lino M (tela) linen; (fibra) flax

linóleo M linoleum

linterna F flashlight; (de un faro) lantern

lío M (bulto) bundle; (enredo, molestia) mess, hassle; (amorío) affair, fling; **armar un** — to raise a rumpus; **meterse en un** — to get oneself into a mess

liposucción F liposuction

liquidación F (ajuste de cuentas, de bienes) settlement, liquidation; (rebaja) sale, clearance sale; (pago completo) payment in full

liquidar VT (bienes, mercancías) to liquidate; (una cuenta, herencia) to settle; (a una persona) *fam* to waste, to off

liquidez F liquidity

líquido ADJ & M liquid

lira F lira

lírico ADJ lyric, lyrical

lirio M iris; — **de los valles** lily of the valley

lirismo M lyricism

lisiado ADJ (descapacitado) handicapped; (lesionado) injured

lisiar VT to handicap

liso ADJ (neumático) bald; (camino) even, smooth; (terreno) flat; (pelo) straight; **azul** — solid blue

lisonja F flattery

lisonjear VI/VT to flatter

lisonjero -ra MF flatterer; ADJ flattering

lista F list; (de miembros) roster; (de alumnos) roll; (banda) stripe; (de precios) schedule, list; — **de control** checklist; — **de espera** waiting list; **pasar** — to call the roll

listado ADJ striped; M listing, printout

listo ADJ (preparado) ready, set; (inteligente) clever, smart; **hacerse el** — to pull a stunt

listón M (tabla) board; (en salto de altura) crossbar

lisura F smoothness

litera F (cama en el tren, barco) berth; (cama superpuesta) bunk bed

literal ADJ literal

literario ADJ literary

literato -ta MF writer

literatura F literature

litigio M (pleito) lawsuit; (acción de litigar) litigation

litio M lithium

litoral ADJ seaside; M seaboard, seacoast

litro M liter

Lituania F Lithuania

lituano -na ADJ & MF Lithuanian

liviano ADJ (leve) light; (promiscuo) promiscuous

lívido ADJ livid

living M living room

llaga F sore

llama F (fuego) flame; (animal) llama

llamada F call; (grito) hail; (nota al pie) footnote; — **de cobro revertido / por cobrar** collect call

llamador M knocker

llamamiento M (conversación) call; (exhortación) appeal; **hacer un** — to appeal

llamar VT (un nombre, una huelga, por teléfono) to call; (a la puerta) to knock; (grito) to hail; — **la atención** to call attention; **me llamo Juan** my name is Juan

llamarada F blaze, flare

llamativo ADJ (impactante) striking, bold; (chabacano) gaudy, flashy

llameante ADJ flaming

llamear VI to flare, to flame

llana F trowel

llano ADJ (sencillo) plain; (liso) flat, smooth, level; (de poca profundidad) shallow; M

plain
llanta F (reborde metálico) rim; (neumático) tire
llanto M crying, weeping
llanura F plain, prairie
llave F (para puertas) key; (de armas de fuego) lock; (en lucha libre) lock, hold; (grifo) faucet, tap; (interruptor) light switch; (de gas) cock; **— de tuercas** wrench; **— inglesa** pipe wrench; **— maestra** master key
llavero M key ring
llegada F arrival
llegar[7] VI (arribar) to arrive, to get there/here; (alcanzar) to reach; **— a las manos** to come to blows; **— a ser** to become; **— a un arreglo** to cut a deal; **— tarde** to be late
llenar VT to fill; (un formulario) to fill out; **— el tanque** to tank up, to gas up; **— el vacío** to take up the slack; **—se** to fill up; **—se de** to get filled with; **—se de oro** to make a killing
lleno ADJ full; **— de** full of; **de —** totally; **un — completo** a full house
llevadero ADJ bearable
llevar VT (transportar) to carry, to take; (transportar en coche) to drive; (tener puesto) to wear; (contener) to hold; (inducir) to lead, to drive; **— a cabo** to carry out; **— la cuenta** to keep score; **— la ventaja** to have an advantage; **— los libros** to keep the books; **— un mes aquí** to have been here one month; **le llevo dos años a mi hermano** I'm two years older than my brother; **llevo las de perder** the odds are against me; **—se** to carry away, to take away; **—se bien con** to get along with
llorar VI (con ruido) to cry, to bawl; (con lágrimas) to weep; VT (una pérdida) to lament; (una muerte) to mourn
lloriquear VI to whimper
lloriqueo M whimper
llorón -ona ADJ weeping; MF crybaby, whiner
lloroso ADJ tearful, weeping
llovedizo ADJ **agua llovediza** rainwater
llover[2] VI/VT to rain; **— a cántaros** to rain cats and dogs; **llueva o truene** rain or shine
llovizna F drizzle
lloviznar VI to drizzle, to mist
lluvia F rain; (de preguntas, críticas) barrage; (de protestas, flechas, piedras) volley; (de golpes, de chispas) shower; **— ácida** acid rain
lluvioso ADJ rainy

lo PRON PERS **— bueno** the good thing; **— de la protesta** the matter of the protest; **— que quiero** what I want; **sé — bueno que eres** I know how good you are; **yo — vi** I saw it/him/you
loable ADJ laudable, praiseworthy
loar VT to laud
lobato M wolf cub
lobbista, lobista MF lobbyist
lobby M lobby
lobezno M wolf cub
lobo M wolf
lobotomía F lobotomy
lóbrego ADJ gloomy
lóbulo M lobe
local ADJ local; M premises
localidad F (pueblo) town, locality; (en un teatro) seat
localización F location
localizar[9] VT (encontrar) to locate; (limitar) to localize
loción F lotion
loco -ca ADJ insane, mad, crazy; **— de remate** stark raving mad; MF lunatic, insane person; M madman
locomotora F locomotive, train engine
locuaz ADJ garrulous, loquacious
locura F madness, insanity
locutor -ora MF radio announcer
lodazal M quagmire
lodo M mud
lodoso ADJ muddy
logaritmo M logarithm
logia F lodge
lógica F logic
lógico ADJ logical; (bien fundado) sound
logística F logistics
lograr VT to achieve, to accomplish; **logré convencerle** I managed to/succeeded in convincing him
logro M accomplishment, achievement; (hazaña) feat
loma F knoll
lombriz F (de tierra) earthworm; (de estómago) tapeworm
lomo M (de animal) back ridge; (corte de carne) loin
lona F canvas
longaniza F cured sausage
longevidad F longevity
longevo ADJ long-lived
longitud F (distancia angular) longitude; (largo) length; **— de onda** wavelength
lonja F (mercado) commodity exchange; (loncha) slice of meat
loquería F *fam* booby hatch, funny farm
loquero -ra MF (psiquiatra) *fam* shrink; M

(manicomio) *fam* funny farm
lord M lord
loro M parrot
losa F slab; (baldosa) flagstone
lote M lot
lotería F lottery
loza F (basto) crockery; (fino) china
lozanía F freshness, bloom
lozano ADJ fresh, blooming
LSD MF LSD
lubina F bass
lubricante ADJ & M lubricant
lubricar[6] VI/VT to lubricate
lucero M morning star; — **del alba** morning
  star
lucha F (de clases) struggle; (pelea) fight; —
  libre wrestling
luchador -ora MF fighter; (en lucha libre)
  wrestler
luchar VI/VT (contra un enemigo) to fight;
  (con un problema) to struggle; (en lucha
  libre) to wrestle; — **por** to strive for
lúcido ADJ lucid, clear-headed
luciérnaga F firefly, glowworm
lucio M pike
lucir[13b] VI (mostrarse) to look; VT (llevar) to
  model, to sport; (alardear de) to flaunt;
  —**se** (sobresalir) to excel; (ostentar) to
  show off
lucrativo ADJ lucrative, profitable
lucro M **sin fines de** — not for profit
luctuoso ADJ sad, mournful, dismal
luego ADV afterwards, then, next; — **de** after;
  desde — of course; **hasta** — so long
lugar M place; — **común** platitude; — **de
  nacimiento** birthplace; — **de trabajo**
  workplace; **dar** — **a** to give rise to; **no
  hay** — there's no room; **en** — **de** instead
  of
lúgubre ADJ mournful, gloomy
lujo M luxury; **darse un** — to indulge
  oneself; **con** — **de detalles** in great
  detail
lujoso ADJ luxurious; (hotel) plush
lujuria F lust
lujurioso ADJ lustful
lumbre F fire
luminosidad F brilliance
luminoso ADJ luminous
luna F moon; (espejo) large mirror; — **de
  miel** honeymoon; **estar en la** — to be
  distracted; — **llena** full moon
lunar ADJ lunar; M (en la piel) mole; (en una
  tela) polka dot
lunático -ca ADJ & MF lunatic
lunes M Monday
lupa F magnifying glass

lúpulo M hops
lustrar VT to shine, to polish
lustre M luster, shine
lustroso ADJ (revista) glossy; (pelo) shining,
  sleek
luto M mourning
Luxemburgo M Luxembourg
luxemburgués -esa MF Luxembourger; ADJ
  Luxembourgian
luz F light (también aparato); (del sol)
  sunshine; (abertura) aperture; — **trasera**
  tail light; — **verde** green light; **dar a** —
  to give birth; **sacar a** — to disclose

Mm

macabro ADJ grim
macanudo ADJ cool
Macao M Macao
macarrones M PL macaroni
Macedonia F Macedonia
macedonio -nia ADJ & MF Macedonian
maceta F flowerpot
machacar[6] VT (aplastar) to pound, to crush;
  (insistir) to harp on
machacón ADJ persistent
machetazo M hack with a machete
machete M machete
machismo M (male) chauvinism
macho M (animal masculino) male; (mulo)
  he-mule; (varón) man; (hombre muy
  varonil) he-man; — **cabrío** he-goat; — **y
  hembra** hook and eye; ADJ (masculino)
  male; (fuerte) strong; INTERJ man!
machote ADJ butch
machucar[6] VT to bruise
macilento ADJ pale
macizo ADJ massive; M plateau
Madagascar M Madagascar
madama F madam
madeja F skein
madera F wood; (árboles maderables) timber;
  (madera para construcción) lumber; —
  contrachapada plywood; — **flotante**
  driftwood; — **noble** hardwood; —**s**
  woodwinds; **tocar** — to knock on wood
maderaje M woodwork
madero M trunk
madrastra F stepmother
madre F mother; — **de alquiler** surrogate
  mother; — **patria** mother country;
  —**perla** mother-of-pearl; — **política**
  mother-in-law; —**selva** honeysuckle;

ciento y la — everybody and their dog
madriguera F burrow, hole
madrileño -ña ADJ & MF (person) from Madrid
madrina F godmother
madrugada F early morning hours; **a las dos de la** — at two in the morning
madrugador -ra ADJ & MF early bird
madurar VI to mature, to grow up
madurez F (de personas) maturity; (de frutas) ripeness
maduro ADJ (de personas) mature; (de frutas) ripe
maestría F master's degree
maestro -tra MF (docente) (school)teacher; (artesano) master
mafia F mafia
mafioso -sa MF mafioso
magia F magic
mágico ADJ magic, magical
magistrado -da MF magistrate
magistral ADJ masterful, masterly
magma M magma
magnánimo ADJ magnanimous
magnate MF magnate, tycoon
magnesia F magnesia
magnesio M magnesium
magnético ADJ magnetic
magnetismo M magnetism
magnetizar[9] VT to magnetize
magnificar[6] VT to magnify
magnificencia F magnificence
magnífico ADJ magnificent; (día) glorious
magnitud F magnitude
magno ADJ great
magnolia F magnolia
magnolio M magnolia tree
mago M magician, wizard
magro ADJ lean
magulladura F bruise
magullar VI/VT (machucar) to bruise; (mutilar) to mangle
mahonesa F mayonnaise
maicena® F cornstarch
maíz M corn, maize
maizal M cornfield
majadería F stupidity
majadero ADJ stupid
majar VT to pound
majestad F majesty
majestuoso ADJ majestic, stately
majo ADJ (atractivo) good-looking; (agradable) charming
mal M (maldad) evil; (enfermedad) malady, affliction; (daño) harm; — **de altura** altitude sickness; — **de ojo** evil eye; ADV wrong, badly; — **aconsejado** misguided;

— **adquirido** ill-gotten; — **hablado** foulmouthed; **hablar** — **de alguien** to speak ill of someone; **hacer** — to do wrong
malabarista MF juggler
malandanza F misfortune
malaria F malaria
Malasia F Malaysia
malasio -sia ADJ & MF Malaysian
Malawi M Malawi
malawiano -na ADJ & MF Malawian
malbaratar VT to undersell
malcontento ADJ discontented
malcriado ADJ spoiled
malcriar VT to spoil
maldad F evil, wickedness
maldecir[26b] VI/VT to curse
maldición F curse
maldito ADJ accursed
Maldivas F PL Maldives
maldivo -va ADJ & MF Maldivian
maleable ADJ malleable
maleante MF gangster, hoodlum
malear VT to corrupt
maleducado ADJ ill-mannered, ill-bred
maleficio M evil spell
maléfico ADJ evil
malentendido M misunderstanding
malestar M (de estómago) upset; (físico) discomfort; (espiritual) malaise; (social) unrest
maleta F suitcase, bag; **hacer la** — to pack one's suitcase
maletero M car trunk
maletín M briefcase
malévolo ADJ malevolent; (comentario) snide
maleza F underbrush, scrub
malgache ADJ & MF Madagascan
malgastar VI/VT to waste, to throw away
malgasto M waste
malhechor -ora MF evildoer, criminal
malhumorado ADJ grumpy, ill-humored
Malí M Mali
malí ADJ & MF Malian
malicia F malice
malicioso ADJ malicious, spiteful
maligno ADJ vicious, evil; (tumor) malignant
malinterpretar VI/VT to misunderstand
malla F (de armadura) mail; (de metal) mesh
malo ADJ bad; (calidad, letra) poor; (enfermo) ill; **mal estado** disrepair; **mal humor** bad mood; **mala fama** ill repute; **mala hierba** weed; **mala pasada** bad turn; **mala racha** slump; **mala suerte** bad luck; **mala voluntad** ill will
malograr VT to spoil, to ruin; —**se** to miscarry

malpagar[7] VI/VT to underpay
malparto M miscarriage
malsano ADJ unhealthy, unwholesome
malta F malt
Malta F Malta
maltés -esa ADJ & MF Maltese
maltratar VT to mistreat, to abuse
maltrato M mistreatment, abuse
maltrecho ADJ battered
malvado ADJ wicked, evil
malversación F misuse, misappropriation
malversar VT to misuse, to embezzle
mamá F mama, mamma, mom
mamado ADJ drunk
mamar VI (un bebé) to suckle, to nurse; VI/VT
to suck
mamarracho M sight
mami F mommy
mamífero ADJ mammalian, mammal; M
mammal
mamografía F mammography
mampara F partition
mamut M mammoth
manada F (de ballenas) pod; (de vacas) herd;
(de lobos) pack
manantial M (naciente) spring; (cantidad
inagotable de algo) wellspring
manar VI to stream out
mancha F (marca) stain, spot; (de tinta) blot;
(cosa borrosa) blur; (aceitosa) smear,
smudge; (menoscabo) tinge; (en la piel)
blemish
manchado ADJ spotted
manchar VI/VT (ensuciar) to spot;
(menoscabar) to stain, to blemish
manchón M large spot
mancilla F blemish
mancillar VT to defile, to sully
manco ADJ one-armed
mancuerna F dumbbell
mandado M errand
mandamiento M commandment
mandante MF principal
mandar VI/VT (dar órdenes) to command, to
order; (enviar) to send; **— buscar a** to
send for; **— decir** to send word; **¿quién
manda?** who's in charge? **—se hacer un
traje** to have a suit made
mandarina F tangerine
mandatario -ria MF (mediante contrato)
agent; (de estado) head of state
mandato M (orden) command, order; (cargo
político) term, mandate
mandíbula F jaw; (hueso) jawbone
mandil M apron
mandioca F manioc
mando M (de un estado) rule; (de un

aparato) control; **— a distancia** remote
control
mandolina F mandolin
mandón -ona ADJ bossy, domineering; MF
bossy person, control freak
mandonear VI/VT to domineer, to boss
around
manea F hobble
manear VT to hobble
manecilla F clock hand
manejable ADJ manageable
manejar VT (un vehículo) to drive, to steer;
(un negocio) to run, to manage; (una
máquina) to operate
manejo M (de un negocio) running,
management; (de asuntos) handling; (de
una máquina) operation
manera F manner, way; **a — de** like; **de
alguna —** somehow; **de cualquier —**
anyway; **de ninguna —** on no account;
de — que so that
manga F (de una camisa) sleeve; (de una
nave) beam; (de agua) hose; **— de viento**
windsock; **en —s de camisa** not wearing
a jacket; **ser de — ancha** to be broad-
minded; **sacar algo de la —** to pull
something out of a hat
manganeso M manganese
mangle M mangrove
mango M (agarradera) handle, grip; (fruta,
árbol) mango
mangosta F mongoose
manguera F hose
manguito M muff
maní M peanut
manía F (moda, estado patológico) mania;
(hábito) bad habit; (tic) tic
maníaco -ca ADJ maniacal; MF maniac
maníacodepresivo ADJ manic-depressive
maniatar VT to tie the hands; (manear) to
hobble
maniático ADJ (que tiene manías) crotchety;
(melindroso) fastidious
manicomio M insane asylum
manicura F manicure
manicurar VT to manicure
manido ADJ hackneyed
manifestación F (muestra) manifestation;
(protesta) demonstration
manifestar[1] VT to manifest, to show;
(expresar) to air; (protestar en público) to
demonstrate; (declarar) to state
manifiesto ADJ & M manifest; **poner de —**
to underscore; M (dogma) manifesto
manija F handle
maniobra F (militar) maneuver; (para llamar
la atención) stunt

maniobrar VI/VT to maneuver

manipulación F (de la opinión pública) manipulation; (de alimentos) handling

manipular VT (influir) to manipulate; (tocar con las manos) to handle

maniquí M (muñeco) mannequin; MF (modelo) model

manivela F crank

manjar M delicacy

mano F hand (también de naipes); (de pintura) coat; — **a** — one on one; — **de obra** workforce; —**s a la obra** let's get to work; —**s de mantequilla** butterfingers; **a** — (presente) at hand; (con la mano) by hand; **a** — **armada** at gunpoint; **dar una** — to lend a hand; **dar una** — **de pintura** to put on a coat of paint; **darle una** — **a alguien** to lend someone a hand; **darse la** — (saludo) to shake hands; (señal de afecto) to hold hands; **de primera** — firsthand; **de segunda** — secondhand; **estar a** — **con alguien** to be even with someone; **hecho a** — handmade; **poner las** —**s en el fuego por alguien** to go out on a limb for someone; **quedar a** — to break even; **se le fue la** — he got carried away; **ser** — to lead (in a card game); **tener buena** — **con / para algo** to have a knack for something; **tomarse de la** — to hold hands

manojo M handful; (de llaves) bunch

manómetro M pressure gauge

manopla F mitten

manosear VT (a una persona) to fondle, to grope; (tocar una cosa) to feel, to finger

manoseo M feel, grope

manotazo M swat; **tirarle un** — **a alguien** to take a swipe at someone

manotear VI to swat at

mansalva LOC ADV **a** — at will

mansedumbre F gentleness

mansión F mansion

manso ADJ (humilde) meek; (domesticado) tame; (apacible) gentle

manta F blanket, cover; (liviana) throw

manteca F lard, shortening; *RP* butter; — **cacao** cocoa butter

mantecoso ADJ rich, buttery

mantel M tablecloth

mantener[44] VT (conservar, sostener) to maintain; (dejar prolongadamente) to keep; (alimentar, costear a alguien) to provide for; (apoyar a lo largo del tiempo) to sustain; — **a flote** to buoy up; — **el orden público** to keep the peace; — **en suspenso** to keep in suspense; — **la**

calma to remain calm; —**se** (quedarse) to remain; (ganarse la vida) to support oneself; —**se al corriente** to keep abreast; —**se al tanto** to stay informed; —**se firme** to stand pat, to stick to one's guns

mantenimiento M maintenance, upkeep

mantequera F (platillo) butter dish; (aparato para hacer mantequilla) churn

mantequilla F butter; — **de maní** peanut butter

mantilla F mantilla

manto M mantle (también geológico); (de juez) robe

mantón M shawl

mantra M mantra

manual ADJ & M manual

manubrio M handlebar

manufactura F manufacture

manufacturar VT to manufacture

manufacturero -ra ADJ manufacturing; MF manufacturer

manuscrito ADJ written by hand; M manuscript

manutención F maintenance

manzana F (fruta) apple; (de calles) block; — **de discordia** bone of contention

manzanar M apple orchard

manzano M apple tree

maña F (destreza) skill, knack; (artimaña) cunning

mañana F (división del día) morning; (futuro) tomorrow; ADV tomorrow; — **por la** — tomorrow morning

mañanero -ra MF early bird

mañoso ADJ tricky

mapa M map; — **en relieve** relief map

mapache M raccoon

maple M maple

maqueta F mock-up

maquillaje M makeup

maquillarse VI to put on makeup

máquina F (aparato) machine; (motor) engine; — **de búsqueda** search engine; — **de coser** sewing machine; — **de escribir** typewriter; — **de lavar** washing machine; — **de vapor** steam engine; — **expendedora** vending machine; — **fotográfica** camera

maquinación F scheming, plotting

maquinador -ora MF schemer

maquinal ADJ automatic

maquinar VI/VT to plot, to scheme

maquinaria F machinery, apparatus; (de un gobierno) machine

maquinilla F clipper; — **de afeitar** razor

maquinista M (de locomotora) locomotive

engineer; (obrero) machinist
mar MF sea; **— de fondo** undercurrent;
llover a mares to rain cats and dogs; **en
alta —** on the high seas; **un — de cosas**
a lot of things; **hacerse a la —** to put to
sea
maraca F maraca
maraña F tangle, snarl; (de pelo) mat
marañón M cashew
maratón M marathon
maravilla F wonder, marvel; (flor) marigold;
a las mil —s wonderfully
maravillar VT to amaze; **—se** to be amazed,
to marvel
maravilloso ADJ marvelous, wonderful
marca F (récord) record; (de ganado) brand;
(de producto) brand, brand-name, label;
(de coche) make; **— de fábrica**
trademark; **— registrada** registered
trademark; **de —** name-brand
marcado ADJ (acento) thick; (contraste)
sharp, stark; (descenso) steep; (parecido)
strong
marcador M marker; **— de libros**
bookmark; **— genético** genetic marker
marcar[6] VT to mark; (ganado) to brand; (el
ritmo) to beat; (la hora) to say; (un tanto)
to score; (medida) to read, to show; (un
número telefónico) to dial
marcha F (caminata, pieza musical) march;
(partida) leaving; (progreso) course; (modo
de andar) gait; (cambio en un coche) gear;
(animación) nightlife; **— atrás** reverse;
ponerse en — to get going; **puesta en
—** beginning; **sobre la —** as you go
marchante MF (vendedor) art dealer;
(cliente) customer
marchar VI (soldado) to march; (máquina,
vehículo) to run; **—se** to go away
marchista MF walker
marchitar VT to wither; **—se** to wither, to
shrivel up
marchito ADJ withered, shriveled up
marcial ADJ martial
marco M (de un cuadro, de una puerta, de
referencia) frame; (moneda alemana) mark
marea F tide; **— baja** low tide
mareado ADJ (en una embarcación) seasick;
(en un coche) carsick; (de alegría) giddy;
(con vértigo) dizzy, lightheaded
marear VT to make dizzy; (en un barco) to
make seasick; **—se** to get dizzy; (en un
barco) to get seasick
marejada F tidal wave
maremoto M tidal wave
mareo M (en una embarcación) seasickness;
(en un vehículo) motion sickness;

(vértigo) dizziness
marfil M ivory
marfileño -ña ADJ & MF Ivorian
margarina F margarine
margarita F daisy; **echar —s a los cerdos**
to cast pearls before swine
margen M margin; (de la sociedad) fringe; MF
(de un río) bank; **al —** on the outside
marginado -da ADJ & MF outcast
marginal ADJ marginal
marginar VT to marginalize
mariachi M mariachi
marido M husband
marihuana F marijuana; *fam* pot
marimba F marimba
marina F navy; **— mercante** merchant
marine
marinar VT to marinate
marinero -ra ADJ (buque) seaworthy;
(nación) seafaring; MF sailor
marino -na ADJ marine; MF sailor; (oficial)
naval officer
marioneta F marionette
mariposa F (insecto) butterfly (también
natación); (tuerca) wing nut; **—
nocturna** moth
mariquita F ladybug
mariscal M marshal; **— de campo** field
marshal
mariscos M PL shellfish
marítimo ADJ maritime
marketing M marketing
marmita F pot
mármol M marble
marmóreo ADJ marble
marmota F groundhog
maroma F rope
marrano M hog
marrón ADJ brown
marroquí ADJ & MF Moroccan
Marruecos M Morocco
marshalés -esa ADJ & MF Marshallese
marsopa F porpoise
martes M Tuesday
martillar VI/VT to hammer
martillo M hammer (también hueso del
oído, pieza de revólver); (de juez) gavel; **—
neumático** jackhammer
martinete M (martillo grande) pile driver;
(pieza de piano) piano hammer
martini M martini
mártir MF martyr
martirio M martyrdom
martirizar[9] VT to martyr, to torment
marxismo M Marxism
marzo M March
mas CONJ but

más ADJ more; PREP plus; ADV more; (más tiempo) longer; — **allá de** beyond; — **bien** rather; — **de tres** more than three; — **o menos** more or less; — **que nunca** more than ever; — **que tú** more than you; **a lo** — at best; **a** — **tardar** at the latest; **de** — extra; **el** — **allá** the hereafter; **es de lo** — **simpático** he's really nice; **es** — furthermore; **está de** — it is superfluous; **otro** — yet another; **por** — **que** no matter how much; **y** — **todavía** and then some

masa F mass; (de agua) body; (harina líquida) batter; (harina para amasar) dough; **en** — en masse, in large numbers; **las** —**s** the masses; — **de hojaldre** puff pastry

masacrar VT to massacre, to slaughter

masacre M massacre

masaje M massage

masajear VT to massage

masajista M masseur; F masseuse

mascar[6] VI/VT to chew; (con ruido) to crunch

máscara F mask; — **de gas** gas mask

mascarada F masquerade

mascota F (animal doméstico) pet; (emblema de un equipo) mascot

masculino ADJ (como un hombre) masculine; (del hombre) male

mascullar VI/VT to mumble

masilla F putty

masivo ADJ massive

masón M mason

masonería F masonry

masoquismo M masochism

mastectomía F mastectomy

masticar[6] VT to chew

mástil M (en un barco) mast; (para una bandera) flagpole, flagstaff

mastín M mastiff

masturbar VI to masturbate

mata F bush; — **de pelo** head of hair

matadero M slaughterhouse

matador ADJ horrendous; M bullfighter

matanza F slaughter, killing

matar VT to kill; (animales) to butcher, to slaughter; — **a tiros** to gun down; — **con hambre** to starve; **matasellar** to cancel a stamp; M SG **matamoscas** flyswatter; **matasellos** postmark; **matasanos** quack (doctor)

mate M (en ajedrez) checkmate; (planta, bebida) mate; ADJ (pintura) flat

matemática, matemáticas F mathematics

matemático -ca ADJ mathematical; MF mathematician

materia F matter; (tema de estudio) school subject; (tema) topic; — **extraña** extraneous matter; — **fecal** fecal matter; — **gris** gray matter; — **prima** raw material

material ADJ (necesidades) material; (autor) real; M material

maternal ADJ (instinto) maternal; (amor) motherly

maternidad F (pertinente al nacimiento) maternity; (estado de ser madre) motherhood

materno ADJ maternal

matiné M matinee

matiz M (de un color) tint, shade, hue; (de ironía) tinge; (de sentido) nuance

matizar[9] VT (mezclar colores) to blend, to tinge; (moderar) to qualify

matón M (que intimida a los pequeños) bully; (pendenciero) thug

matorral M (mata) thicket; (región) bush

matraz M flask

matriarca F matriarch

matrícula F (de alumnos) enrollment, matriculation; (de un coche) registration; (placa) license plate; (en la universidad) tuition fees

matriculación F matriculation

matricular VT to matriculate, to enroll

matrimonio M matrimony, marriage; (pareja) married couple

matriz F (en matemáticas) matrix; (útero) womb; (plantilla) stencil; **casa** — main office

matrona ADJ frumpy; F matron

matutino ADJ of the morning

maullar VI to mew

maullido M mew

mauriciano -na ADJ & MF Mauritian

Mauricio M Mauritius

Mauritania F Mauritania

mauritano -na MF Mauritanian

maxilar M jawbone

máxima F maxim

máximo ADJ & M maximum; (autoridad) ultimate; (cuidado) utmost

mayo M May; (palo) maypole

mayonesa F mayonnaise

mayor ADJ (de tamaño) greater, larger; (de edad) older, elder; (rango, clave) major; **al por** — wholesale; **dedo** — middle finger; **el** — **número de votos** the most votes; M (adulto) adult

mayoral M boss

mayordomo M butler

mayoreo M wholesale

mayoría F majority; — **de edad** legal age, majority

mayorista M wholesale dealer

mayúsculo -la ADJ (letra) capital; (problema) major; F capital letter

mazmorra F dungeon

mazo M mallet

mazorca F ear of corn; (sin maíz) corncob

me PRON PERS **él — vio me** he saw me; **él — habló** he talked to me; **se — murió el perro** my dog died on me

mecánico -ca ADJ mechanical; MF mechanic; F mechanics

mecanismo M mechanism; **— de seguridad** safety device

mecanografía F typewriting

mecanografiar[16] VI/VT to type

mecanógrafo -fa MF typist

mecedora F rocking chair, rocker

mecenas MF SG/PL patron, sponsor

mecenazgo M patronage

mecer[10a] VI/VT (cuna) to rock; (columpio) to swing

mecha F (de una vela) wick; (de explosivos) fuse; **—s** (en el pelo) highlights

mechar VT (rellenar con tocino) to lard; (robar) to shoplift

mechero -ra MF shoplifter; M burner; **— Bunsen** Bunsen burner

mechón M lock, strand

medalla F medal

médano M dune

media F (hasta el muslo) stocking; (hasta la cintura) pantyhose; (calcetín) sock; (promedio) mean

mediación F mediation

mediador -ra MF mediator

mediados LOC ADV **a — de mayo** in mid-May

mediana F median

mediano ADJ (intermedio en tamaño) medium; (intermedio en calidad) average; **de tamaño —** middle-sized; **de mediana edad** middle-aged

medianoche F midnight

mediante PREP by means of

mediar VI (intervenir en un asunto) to mediate, to intervene; (transcurrir tiempo) to intervene; **mediaba febrero** it was mid-February

medible ADJ measurable

medicación F medication

medicamento M medicine, drug

medicina F medicine

medición F measurement; (de un terreno) survey

médico -ca MF doctor, physician; **— forense** coroner; **— general** general practitioner; ADJ medical

medida F (dimensión) measure; (acto de medir) measurement; **— para áridos** dry measure; **a — que** as; **en la — en que** to the extent that; **hacer a la —** to make to measure; **hecho a la —** made-to-measure; **tomar —s** to take measures; **tomarle las —s a alguien** to measure someone

medidor M gauge, meter

medieval ADJ medieval

medio ADJ **—día** noon, midday; **— hermano** half brother; **a media asta** at half mast; **clase media** middle class; **el — americano** the average American; **hacer una cosa a medias** to do something halfway; **ir a medias** to go halves; **media hora** half an hour; **mi media naranja** my better half; **temperatura media** mean temperature; ADV half; **a — camino** halfway; **a — derretir** half-melted; **de — tiempo** part-time; M (centro) middle; (ambiente) medium; **— ambiente** environment; **— tiempo** halftime; **—s** means, resources; **en (el) — de** in the middle of; **en — de la calle** in the middle of the street; **meterse de por —** to intervene; **por — de** by means of; **—s de comunicación** the media; **por todos los —s** by all possible means

medioambiental ADJ environmental

mediocre ADJ mediocre; (actuación) lackluster

mediocridad F mediocrity

medir[5] VI/VT to measure; VT (consecuencias) to gauge; (terreno) to survey; **— a pasos** to step off; **—se** to be moderate

meditación F meditation

meditar VI to meditate, to ponder

médium MF medium, psychic

medroso ADJ fearful

médula F marrow, pith; **— espinal** spinal cord; **— ósea** bone marrow

medusa F jellyfish, man-of-war

megabyte M megabyte

megáfono M megaphone

megahercio, megahertz M megahertz

mejilla F cheek

mejor ADJ better; **el — the** best; **en el — de los casos** at best; **te deseo lo —** I wish you the best; ADV better; **a lo —** maybe; **tanto —** so much the better

mejora F improvement

mejoramiento M improvement

mejorar VT to improve, to improve upon; (las posibilidades de uno) to better; VI (ventas) to pick up; **—se** to get better/well

mejoría F improvement
melancolía F melancholy, gloom
melancólico ADJ melancholy, gloomy
melanoma M melanoma
melaza F molasses
melena F mane
melindre M affectation
melindroso ADJ affected, finicky
mella F notch; **hacer —** to make a dent
mellar VT to notch
mellizo -za ADJ & MF twin
melocotón M peach
melocotonero M peach tree
melodía F melody
melodioso ADJ melodious
melodrama M melodrama
melómano -na ADJ music-loving; MF music-lover
melón M melon, cantaloupe
membrana F membrane; (en los patos) web
membrete M letterhead
membrillo M (fruta) quince; (árbol) quince tree
membrudo ADJ stout
memorable ADJ memorable
memorándum M memorandum
memoria F (facultad de recordar, recuerdo) memory; (obra autobiográfica) memoir; (actas) proceedings; **— de acceso directo** random access memory (RAM); **— de sólo lectura** read only memory (ROM); **— intermedia** buffer; **— residente** internal memory; **de —** by heart; **hacer —** to try to remember/recollect
memorial M memorial
memorizar[9] VI/VT to memorize
mención F mention
mencionar VT to mention
mendigar[7] VI to beg
mendigo -ga MF beggar
mendrugo M large crumb
menear VT (las caderas) to wiggle, to wriggle, to shake; (la cola) to wag
meneo M (de las caderas) wiggle; (de la cola) wag
menesteroso ADJ needy, destitute
mengua F diminution, waning
menguante ADJ waning
menguar[8] VI (luna) to wane; (energía) to flag; (provisiones) to dwindle
meningitis F meningitis
menjurje M concoction
menopausia F menopause
menor ADJ (de tamaño) smaller; (de cantidad) lesser, smaller; (de edad) younger; (de importancia, en música) minor; **el —** (de tamaño) the smallest; (de

cantidad) the least, the smallest; (de edad) the youngest; MF **— de edad** minor; **al por —** retail
menos ADV less; **— de** less than; **— mal** just as well; **a — que** unless; **al —** at least; **dar de —** to shortchange; **echar de —** to miss; **lo —** the least; **no es para menos** there is good reason; **por lo —** at least; **signo de menos** minus sign; **venir a —** to decline; **el que trabaja —** the one who works the least; **las cinco — cuarto** quarter to five; **no puede — de hacerlo** he cannot help doing it; **tienes — que yo** you have less than I; **trabaja — que yo** she works less than I; PREP (salvo) except, but; ADJ & PRON less, least; **— agua** less water; **— problemas** fewer problems; M minus
menoscabar VT to impair, to undermine
menoscabo M impairment
menospreciar VI/VT (despreciar) to despise; VT (burlarse de) to belittle, to demean
menosprecio M contempt
mensaje M message
mensajería F carrier
mensajero -ra MF messenger, courier
menstruación F menstruation
mensual ADJ monthly
mensualidad F (recibida) monthly allowance; (pagada) monthly installment
mensuario ADJ monthly
mensurable ADJ measurable
menta F mint, peppermint; **—verde** spearmint
mental ADJ mental
mentalidad F mentality
mente F mind
mentecato -ta ADJ foolish, simple; MF simpleton
mentir[3] VI to lie
mentira F lie, falsehood
mentirilla F fib, white lie
mentiroso -sa ADJ lying; MF liar
mentón M chin
mentor -ora MF mentor
menú M menu (también de computadoras); **— del día** daily special
menudeo LOC ADV **al —** retail
menudo ADJ (pequeño) small; (insignificante) insignificant; **a —** often; **dinero —** small change; **— perro** that's some dog; M (entrañas) entrails
meñique ADJ little (finger); M little finger, *fam* pinkie
meollo M (médula) marrow; (parte sustancial de un asunto) marrow, pith, core; (seso) brain

mequetrefe M runt, pipsqueak

mercachifle M peddler, huckster

mercadear VT to market

mercadeo M merchandising

mercader M merchant

mercadería F merchandise

mercado M market; **— alcista** bull market; **— bajista** bear market; **— de pulgas** flea market; **— de valores** stock market; **— libre** free market; **— negro** black market

mercadotecnia F marketing

mercancía F merchandise, goods

mercante ADJ merchant

mercantil ADJ mercantile

merced LOC ADV **— a** thanks to; **a (la) — de** at the mercy of

mercenario -ria ADJ & MF mercenary

mercería F notions

mercurio M mercury, quicksilver

merecedor ADJ deserving

merecer[13] VT to deserve, to merit

merecido M deserved punishment, due

merendar[1] VI to have a snack

merendero M picnic area

meridiano ADJ & M meridian

meridional ADJ southern; MF southerner

merienda F afternoon snack

mérito M merit

meritorio ADJ meritorious, worthy

merluza F hake

merma F decrease

mermar VI/VT to decrease, to dwindle

mermelada F jam; (de cítricos) marmalade

mero ADJ mere; **la mera idea** the very idea; M grouper

merodear VI to loiter

mes M month

mesa F table; (consejo) board; (formación geológica) mesa; **— de noche** nightstand; **levantar la —** to clear the table; **poner la —** to set the table

mesada F monthly allowance

mesero -ra M waiter; F waitress

meseta F plateau

mesón M inn, lodge

mesonero -ra MF innkeeper

mestizo -za ADJ (persona) *pey* half-breed; (perros) mongrel; MF *pey* half-breed; (mezcla de europeo e india) mestizo; (perro de raza mezclada) mongrel

mesura F moderation

mesurado ADJ moderate; (respuesta) measured

meta F (objetivo) goal; (en una carrera) finish line

metabolismo M metabolism

metafísica F metaphysics

metáfora F metaphor

metafórico ADJ metaphorical

metal M metal; **— precioso** precious metal

metálico ADJ metallic; M cash

metalurgia F metallurgy

metamorfosis F metamorphosis

metano M methane

metástasis F metastasis

meteorito M meteorite

meteoro M meteor

meteorología F meteorology

meteorólogo -ga M weatherman; F weatherwoman

meter VT to put (into), to stick (into); (un lío) to get (into); (invertir) to invest; **— el estómago** to suck in one's stomach; **— la pata** to make a mistake; **— miedo** to scare; **— ruido** to make noise; **— un gol** to score a goal; **—se** to meddle; **—se a bailar** to begin to dance; **—se con** to mess with; **—se en camisa de once varas** to get oneself into a fix

metódico ADJ methodical

método M method

metralleta F portable machine gun

métrico ADJ metric

metro M (medida) meter; (cinta de medir) measuring tape; (tren subterráneo) subway

metrónomo M metronome

metrópoli F metropolis

metropolitano ADJ metropolitan; M subway

mexicano -na ADJ & MF Mexican

México M Mexico

mezcla F mixture, mix; (en albañilería) mortar; (de café, especias) blend

mezclador -ora MF (persona) mixer; F (aparato) mixer

mezclar VT to mix, to blend; (naipes) to shuffle; (números) to scramble; **—se** (combinarse) to mix; (tener trato con) to mingle; (entrometerse) to meddle

mezcolanza F hodgepodge

mezquindad F (crueldad) meanness; (tacañería) stinginess

mezquino ADJ (cruel) mean, mean-spirited, petty; (insignificante) small, petty; (tacaño) tight, stingy

mezquita F mosque

mi ADJ POS my

mí PRON PERS me; **es para —** it's for me; **me vio a —** he saw me; **me la dio a —** he gave it to me

miau M meow

mico M long-tailed monkey

micra F micron

micro M (autobús) bus; (micrófono) microphone

microbio M microbe, germ
microcirujía F microsurgery
microcomputadora F microcomputer
microeconomía F microeconomics
microficha F microfiche
microfilm M microfilm
micrófono M microphone
Micronesia F Micronesia
micronesio -sia ADJ & MF Micronesian
microonda F microwave; M SG **—s**
   microwave oven
microordenador M microcomputer
microorganismo M microorganism
microprocesador M microprocessor
microscópico ADJ microscopic
microscopio M microscope; **— electrónico**
   electron microscope
miedo M fear; **— al escenario** stage fright;
   tener — to be afraid
miedoso ADJ fearful
miel F honey
miembro M member; (extremidad) limb
mientras CONJ (durante) while, as; (siempre
   y cuando) as long as; **— que** while; **—**
   tanto meanwhile; ADV in the meantime
miércoles M Wednesday
mies F grain; **—es** fields of grain
miga F crumb; **hacer buenas —s** to get
   along well
migaja F crumb
migración F migration
migrante ADJ migrant
migraña F migraine
mil NUM thousand; **— millones** billion;
   llegamos a las — y quinientas we got
   there very late
milagro M miracle, wonder
milagroso ADJ miraculous
milano M kite
milenio M millennium
milicia F militia
miligramo M milligram
mililitro M milliliter
milímetro M millimeter
militante ADJ & MF militant
militar ADJ military; MF soldier; VI to militate
milla F mile
millaje M mileage
millar M thousand
millón M million
millonario -ria MF millionaire
millonésimo ADJ & M millionth
mimar VT to pamper, to spoil, to coddle
mimbre M wicker
mímico ADJ mimic; F mimicry
mimo M (trato cariñoso) caressing, cuddling;
   MF (actor) mime

mimoso ADJ cuddly
mina F (yacimiento) mine; (explosivo) (land)
   mine; (de un lápiz) lead; (fuente)
   storehouse
minado M mining
minar VT (sembrar minas) to mine; (socavar)
   to undermine; VI (cavar) to burrow
mineral M mineral; (de oro) ore; ADJ mineral
minería F mining
minero -ra MF miner; ADJ mining
mingitorio M urinal
miniatura F miniature
minicomputadora F minicomputer
minifalda F miniskirt
minifundio M subsistence farm
minimizar[9] VT (gastos) to minimize; (a una
   persona) to belittle; VI (un incidente) to
   play down
mínimo ADJ (cantidad) least; (tamaño)
   smallest; M minimum; **como —** at least;
   en lo más — at all
minino M kitty
miniordenador M minicomputer
ministerio M (religioso) ministry;
   (gubernamental) ministry, department
ministro -tra MF minister, secretary; **— de
   Justicia** Attorney General
minoría F minority
minoridad F minority
minorista MF retailer
minoritario ADJ minority
minucioso ADJ (detalle) minute; (trabajo)
   thorough; (persona) fastidious
minúsculo ADJ small, minuscule; **letra —**
   lowercase letter
minusválido ADJ disabled
minuta F (honorarios) lawyers' fees; (actas)
   minutes
minutero M minute hand
minuto M minute
mío PRON mine; **este libro es —** this book
   is mine; **un amigo —** a friend of mine
miope ADJ shortsighted, nearsighted
miopía F near-sightedness, myopia
mira F (dispositivo de arma) gun sight;
   (intención) intention; **con —s a** with a
   view to
mirada F gaze, look; **— asesina** dirty look;
   — de soslayo side glance; **— fija** stare
mirador M vantage point, overlook
miramiento M consideration
mirar VI/VT to look (at); (un partido,
   televisión) to watch; **— de soslayo** to
   look askance (at); **— fijamente** to stare
   (at); **¡mira (tú)!** you don't say!
miríada F myriad
mirilla F peephole

mirlo M blackbird
mirón M onlooker; (erótico) voyeur
mirto M myrtle
misa F mass
misántropo -pa MF misanthrope
misceláneo ADJ miscellaneous
miserable ADJ (vil, pobre) wretched,
    unhappy; (insignificante) paltry; (tacaño)
    miserly
miseria F (desgracia) misery; (pobreza)
    poverty, squalor; (cantidad despreciable)
    trifle
misericordia F mercy
misericordioso ADJ merciful, gracious
mísero ADJ miserable
misil M missile; **— balístico** ballistic missile;
    — crucero cruise missile
misión F mission
misionero -ra MF missionary
mismo ADJ same; **ese — día** that very day;
    se nombró a sí — he named himself; **lo
    —** the same thing; **me da lo —** it's all the
    same to me; **yo —** I myself
misoginia F misogyny
misterio M mystery
misterioso ADJ mysterious
místico -ca ADJ mystical; MF mystic
mitad F half; **por la —** in half; **en la — de**
    in the middle of; **a — del camino**
    midway
mitigar[7] VT to mitigate
mitin M political meeting
mito M myth
mitología F mythology
mixto ADJ mixed; **escuela mixta** coed
    school
mobiliario M furniture
mocasín M (zapatilla de indio, culebra)
    moccasin; (zapato sin cordones) loafer
mochar VT to chop off
mochila F knapsack, backpack
moción F motion
moco M mucus
moda F fashion; **de —** fashionable, in style;
    ponerse de — to catch on
modales M PL manners
modelar VI/VT to model
modelo ADJ & MF model
módem M modem
moderación F moderation, restraint
moderado -da ADJ moderate; (invierno)
    mild; (precio) reasonable; (respuesta)
    measured; (clima) temperate; MF moderate
moderar VT (restringir) to moderate, to
    restrain; (presidir) to moderate
moderno ADJ modern
modestia F modesty

modesto ADJ modest
módico ADJ moderate, reasonable
modificación F modification
modificar[6] VT to modify
modismo M idiom
modista MF dressmaker
modo M (manera) mode, manner, way;
    (categoría gramatical) mood; (de
    computadora/ordenador) mode; **a — de**
    by way of; **del mismo —** in like manner;
    de ningún — by no means; **de — que**
    so that; **de otro —** otherwise; **de ningún
    —** not at all; **de todos —s** anyway; **en
    cierto —** in a way; **ni —** no dice; **no
    hay —** no way
modorra F drowsiness
modular VT to modulate
mofa F jeer, ridicule
mofarse VT **— de** to make fun of, to scoff at
mofeta F skunk
moflete M fat cheek
mohair M mohair
mohín M grimace
moho M mold, mildew
mohoso ADJ moldy
mojado -da ADJ wet
mojadura F wetting
mojar VT to wet; (impregnar) to dip; **—se** to
    get wet
mojigatería F prudery
mojigato -ta ADJ prudish; MF prude
mojo M dip
mojón M (hito) landmark
molar ADJ molar
Moldavia F Moldova
moldavo -va ADJ & MF Moldovan
molde M (norma) mold, cast; (tortera)
    cakepan; (patrón) pattern; (de imprenta)
    die; **letras de —** block letters
moldeado M molding
moldear VT to mold, to cast
moldura F molding
mole F mass
molécula F molecule
moler[2] VI/VT to mill, to grind; **— a palos** to
    beat thoroughly
molestar VT to bother, to pester; **no te
    molestes** don't bother
molestia F bother, nuisance; **no te tomes la
    —** don't go to the trouble
molesto ADJ bothersome, irksome; (situación)
    uneasy
molibdeno M molybdenum
molienda F grinding
molinero -ra MF miller
molinete M (puerta) turnstile; (juguete)
    pinwheel

molinillo M mill, grinder

molino M mill; **— de viento** windmill

mollete M muffin

molusco M mollusk

momentáneo ADJ momentary

momento M (tiempo) moment; (movimiento) momentum; **al —** immediately; **a cada —** continually; **en todo —** all the time; **no veo el —** I can't wait; **se oscurecía por —s** it was getting darker by the minute

momia F mummy

Mónaco M Monaco

monada F (acción graciosa) antic; (persona atractiva) *fam* peach

monarca MF INV monarch

monarquía F monarchy

monasterio M monastery

mondar VT to pare; **—se los dientes** to pick one's teeth; M SG **mondadientes** toothpick

moneda F (dinero metálico) coin; (divisa) currency; **— corriente** common currency; **— de curso legal** legal tender; **— falsa** counterfeit money

monegasco -ca ADJ & MF Monegasque

monería F antic

monetario ADJ monetary

mongol -la ADJ & MF Mongolian

Mongolia F Mongolia

monigote M puppet

monitor -ora M (aparato) monitor; MF (persona) monitor

monja F nun

monje M monk

mono -na MF (simio) monkey; **— araña** spider monkey; M (mimo) mimic; (prenda de trabajo) overalls, coverall; (síndrome de abstinencia) withdrawal symptoms; **dormir la mona** to sleep it off; ADJ cute

monogamia F monogamy

monokini M topless swimsuit

monólogo M monolog, monologue

mononucleosis F mononucleosis

monopatín M skateboard; (con manillar) scooter; (de nieve) snowboard

monopolio M monopoly

monopolizar[9] VT to monopolize; (un mercado) to corner

monotonía F monotony

monótono ADJ monotonous

monserga F nonsense

monstruo M monster; (persona grotesca) freak

monstruosidad F monstrosity

monstruoso ADJ monstrous

monta F mount; **de poca —** of little value

montaje M (de un aparato) assembly, set up; (de una película) editing

montante M (total) total; (ventana de puerta) transom; (columna) upright

montaña F mountain; **— rusa** roller coaster

montañés -esa ADJ mountain; MF mountain dweller

montañismo M mountaineering

montañoso ADJ mountainous

montar VT (ir a caballo, en bicicleta) to ride; (un aparato) to assemble; (una película) to edit; (subirse al caballo) to mount, to get on; **— en cólera** to fly into a rage; **— una escena** to make a scene; **—se a caballo** to mount a horse

montaraz ADJ coarse

monte M (montaña) mount; (zona agreste) wilderness; **— de piedad** pawnshop

montés ADJ (salvaje) wild; (de la montaña) of the mountains

montículo M mound

montón M pile, heap; (de papel) stack; (de nieve) drift; (de flores) basketful; (de gente) bunch; **a montones** in abundance; **del —** run-of-the-mill

montura F (animal) mount; (silla) saddle; (armazón de gafas) frame, rim

monumental ADJ monumental

monumento M monument

moño M (de pelo) bun; (adorno) bow

mopa F mop

moquearse VI to be snotty

moquillo M distemper

mora F blackberry, mulberry; **en —** in default

morada F dwelling, abode

morado ADJ purple; **ojo —** black eye

morador -ora MF dweller

moral ADJ moral; F (principios éticos) morals; (estado de ánimo) morale; M mulberry tree

moraleja F moral

moralidad F morality

moralista MF moralist

moralizar[9] VI/VT to moralize

morar VI to dwell, to abide

mórbido ADJ morbid

morboso ADJ (mórbido) morbid; (atractivo) sexy

morcilla F black pudding

mordacidad F sharpness

mordaz ADJ (comentario) cutting, sharp; (persona) sharp-tongued

mordaza F (de la boca) gag; (de un torno) vise jaw

mordedor ADJ biting, snappy

mordedura F bite

morder[2] VI/VT to bite; **—se la lengua** to bite one's tongue

mordida F (mordisco) bite; (comisión ilegal) bribe, kickback

mordiscar[6] VI/VT to nibble; to nip

mordisco M nibble, nip

mordisquear VI/VT to nip; to nibble

mordisqueo M nibble

moreno ADJ (piel) dark, dark-skinned, swarthy; (pelo) dark, brunette

moretón M bruise

morfina F morphine

morgue F morgue

moribundo ADJ dying, moribund

morir[4,51] VI to die; (una calle) to end; **—se de envidia** to eat one's heart out; **—se de hambre** to starve; **—se de miedo** to die of fear; **—se de risa** to die laughing; **—se por algo** to crave something; **—se por alguien** to be crazy about someone

morisco ADJ Moorish

moro -ra ADJ Moorish; MF Moor; **—s y cristianos** beans and rice; **no hay —s en la costa** the coast is clear

morocho ADJ dark-haired, brunet, brunette

moroso ADJ delinquent, deadbeat

morrear VI to make out

morriña F homesickness

morro M (monte) knoll; (caradura) gall, nerve; (de un avión) nose; (de animal) snout

morrón M bell pepper

morsa F walrus

mortaja F shroud

mortal ADJ mortal, deadly; MF mortal

mortalidad F mortality

mortandad F death toll

mortecino ADJ fading

mortero M mortar

mortífero ADJ deadly

mortificación F chagrin

mortificar[6] VT to mortify, to chagrin

mortuorio ADJ **casa mortuaria** funeral home

mosaico M mosaic

mosca F fly; (dinero) dough; **— muerta** hypocrite; **no se oía volar una —** you could have heard a pin drop

mosquear VT (crear desconfianza) to cause distrust; (hacer enfadarse) to enrage; **—se** (desconfiar) to distrust; (enfadarse) to become enraged

mosquetero M (de ventana) window screen; (de tienda de campo) mosquito net

mosquito M mosquito

mostacho M mustache, moustache

mostaza F mustard

mostrador M counter

mostrar[2] VT to show; **—se reticente** to

appear reticent

mostrenco ADJ stray

mota F speck, speckle

mote M nickname

moteado ADJ speckled, spotted

motear VT to speck, to speckle

motejar VI **— de** to brand as

motel M motel

motín M (en un barco) mutiny; (de prisioneros) riot

motivación F motivation

motivar VT (impulsar) to motivate; (causar) to cause

motivo M (causa) motive, reason; (figura repetida) motif, theme; **con — de** on the occasion of

moto F bike, motorcycle

motocicleta F motorcycle

motociclista MF biker, motorcyclist

motor ADJ of motion; M motor, engine; **— de reacción** jet engine; **— de búsqueda** search engine; **— de combustión interna** internal combustion engine; **— fuera de borda** outboard engine

motriz ADJ **fuerza —** motive power

movedizo ADJ restless

mover[2] VT to move; **— palancas** to pull strings; **—se** to move, to budge

movible ADJ movable

movido ADJ eventful; (foto) blurred

móvil M (motivo) motive; (teléfono) mobile telephone; (adorno, juguete) mobile; ADJ (que se mueve) mobile; (que puede ser movido) movable; **un blanco —** a moving target

movilizar[9] VI/VT to mobilize

movimiento M movement, motion; (organización, pieza de reloj) movement; (comercial) traffic; **los rojos tienen poco —** the red ones don't sell well; **un cuerpo en —** a moving body

Mozambique M Mozambique

mozambiqueño -ña ADJ & MF Mozambican

mozárabe ADJ Mozarabic

mozo -za ADJ young; **en mis años —s** in my youth; M (joven) young man; **buen —** handsome man; (siervo) servant; **— de cordel** porter; F (joven) young woman; (sierva) servant

mucama F chambermaid

muchacho -cha M boy, youngster; F girl; (de servicio) maid

muchedumbre F crowd, throng

mucho ADJ a lot of; (cosas contables) many; (cosas incontables, en oraciones interrogativas y/o negativas) much; **¿tienes — tiempo?** do you have much

time? **no tenemos — tiempo** we don't
have much time; **tenemos —s
problemas** we have many problems; ADV
much; (demasiado) too much; **hace —
que no lo veo** I haven't seen him for a
long time; **ni con —** not by a long shot;
ni — menos not by any means; **por —
que** no matter how much; PRON a lot,
many; (en preguntas y oraciones
negativas) much
mucoso ADJ mucous
muda F (de ropa, voz) change; (de plumas,
piel de serpiente) molt
mudable ADJ fickle
mudanza F move
mudar VT to change; (el pelo) to shed; **— la
piel** to molt; **— las plumas** to molt;
—se (de casa) to move (house); **—se de
ropa** to change clothes
mudez F dumbness, muteness
mudo -da ADJ mute, dumb; (por emoción)
speechless; (película) silent; MF mute
mueble M piece of furniture; **—s** furniture
mueblería F (tienda) furniture store; (fábrica)
furniture factory
mueca F grimace; **hacer —s** to grimace
muela F (diente) molar tooth; (piedra)
grindstone; **— del juicio** wisdom tooth
muelle M (para embarcaciones) wharf, pier;
(resorte) spring; **— en espiral** coil; **—
real** mainspring
muérdago M mistletoe
muerte F death; **dar —** to kill; **sus clases
son la —** his classes are unbearable; **de
mala —** disreputable
muerto ADJ dead, lifeless; **— de cansancio**
dead tired; **— de hambre** famished;
estoy — de sed I'm parched; **echarle el
— a uno** to pass the buck; **ni — ** not in a
million years
muesca F notch, indentation
muestra F (ejemplo) sample; (señal) sign,
token; **— de orina** urine specimen; **dar
—s de impaciencia** to show impatience
muestrear VT to sample
muestreo M sampling
mugido M moo, lowing
mugir[11] VI to moo, to low
mugre F dirt, grime, crud
mugriento ADJ grimy, dirty
mujer F woman; (esposa) wife
mujeriego ADJ womanizing; M womanizer
mulato -ta ADJ & MF mulatto
muleta F crutch
muletilla F cliché
mullido ADJ fluffy
mullir[19] VT to fluff

mulo -la MF mule (también en el tráfico de
drogas)
multa F fine, penalty; (de tránsito) ticket
multar VT to fine; (en tránsito) to ticket
multicultural ADJ multicultural
múltiple ADJ multiple
multiplicación F multiplication
multiplicar[6] VI/VT to multiply; **—se** to
breed
multiplicidad F multiplicity
múltiplo M multiple
multitarea F multitasking
multitud F multitude, throng
mundano ADJ mundane, worldly
mundial ADJ global, worldwide; **la guerra
—** the world war
mundo M world; **todo el —** everybody;
tener — to be worldly; **el tercer —** the
third world; **el — al revés** the world
upside-down
munición F ammunition, munition
municipal ADJ municipal; **servicios —es**
city services
municipalidad F municipality
municipio M municipality; (ayuntamiento)
city hall
muñeca F (juguete) doll; (articulación del
brazo) wrist; **— de trapo** ragdoll
muñeco M (juguete) boy doll; (de
ventrílocuo) dummy; **— de nieve**
snowman
muñón M stump
mural ADJ & M mural
muralla F wall
murciélago M bat
murmullo M murmur; (de agua) babble
murmuración F gossip
murmurar VI/VT to murmur; VI (agua) to
babble
muro M wall
murria F the blues; **tener —** to have the
blues
musa F muse
musaraña F shrew
muscular ADJ muscular
músculo M muscle
musculoso ADJ muscular
muselina F muslin
museo M museum
musgo M moss
musgoso ADJ mossy
música F music; **— de cámara** chamber
music; **— folclórica** folk music; **—
incidental** incidental music
musical ADJ & M musical
músico -ca ADJ musical; MF musician
musitar VI to mutter

muslo M thigh

mustio ADJ sad, humble; (marchito) limp; (deslucido) faded

musulmán -ana ADJ & MF Moslem, Muslim

mutación F mutation

mutante ADJ & MF mutant

mutilar VT to mutilate, to mangle; (a un ser vivo) to maim, to mutilate; (una estatua) to deface

mutuo ADJ mutual

muy ADV very; **estás — grande para eso** you're too big for that

Myanmar M Myanmar

Nn

nabo M turnip

nácar M mother-of-pearl

nacarado ADJ pearly

nacer[13] VI to be born; (una calle) to begin; **— de** (río) to spring from; **— de nuevo** to have a new lease on life

naciente ADJ (tendencia) incipient; (sol) rising; M (de río) origin

nacimiento M birth; (pesebre) nativity scene; (naciente) origin (of a river)

nación F nation

nacional ADJ national; MF national

nacionalidad F nationality

nacionalismo M nationalism

nacionalizar[9] VT to nationalize

nada PRON nothing; **— del otro mundo** nothing special; **— en absoluto** nothing at all; **como si —** as if nothing were going on; **de —** you are welcome, don't mention it; **no es por —, pero** I hope you don't mind my saying this, but; **no sirve para —** it's useless; **no tener — que ver con** to have nothing to do with; **no tengo — de dinero** I don't have any money; **para —** in the least; **quedar en la —** to fall through; **salir de la —** to come out of nowhere; ADV not at all; **no me gusta —** I don't like it at all; F nothingness

nadador -ora MF swimmer

nadar VI/VT to swim; **— en la abundancia** to be in the lap of luxury

nadería F trifle, nothing

nadie PRON nobody; **— más** no one else; **no vi a — en el parque** I didn't see anyone in the park; **un don —** a nobody

nafta F gasoline

nailón M nylon

naipe M playing card

nalgada F smack on the bottom

nalgas F PL buttocks

Namibia F Namibia

namibio -bia ADJ & MF Namibian

nana F (canción de cuna) lullaby; (lastimadura) boo-boo; (niñera) baby-sitter

nanosegundo M nanosecond

napalm M napalm

napias F PL *fam* snout

naranja F (fruta) orange; ADJ & M (color) orange; **— de ombligo** navel orange; **mi media —** my better half

naranjal M orange grove

naranjo M orange tree

narcisismo M narcissism

narciso M narcissus, daffodil

narcolepsia F narcolepsy

narcótico ADJ & M narcotic

narcotizar[9] VT to drug

narcotráfico M narco-trafficking

nariz F nose; **— chata** pug nose; **sonarse la —** to blow one's nose; F PL **narices** nostrils; **se dio de narices contra la ventana** he bumped his nose on the window; **estoy hasta las narices** I've had it up to here

narración F narration

narrador -ora MF narrator

narrar VT to narrate, to recount

narrativa F narrative

narrativo ADJ narrative

NASA F NASA

nasal ADJ nasal

nata F skin of boiled milk; *Esp* cream

natación F swimming

natal ADJ natal; (suelo) native

natillas F PL custard

nativo -va ADJ & MF native

nato ADJ **es un músico —** he's a born musician

natural ADJ natural; (nacido en un lugar) native; (nacido fuera del matrimonio) illegitimate; M nature; **al —** unprocessed; (sin afectación) unaffected

naturaleza F nature; **— muerta** still life

naturalidad F naturalness

naturalista MF naturalist

naturalización F naturalization

naturalizar[9] VT to naturalize; **—se** to become naturalized

naturalmente ADV (de forma natural) naturally; (desde luego) of course

naufragar[7] VI to shipwreck; (una empresa) to fail

naufragio M shipwreck

náufrago -ga MF shipwrecked person
Nauru M Nauru
nauruano -na ADJ & MF Nauruan
náusea F nausea; **—s** morning sickness; **dar —s** to nauseate; **hasta la —** ad nauseam; **tener —s** to be nauseated, to be sick to one's stomach
nauseabundo ADJ nauseating
nauseoso ADJ queasy
náutica F navigation
náutico ADJ nautical
navaja F jackknife, pocketknife; (de barbero) razor
navajazo M (golpe) stab with a jackknife; (herida) stab wound
naval ADJ naval
nave F (embarcación) vessel; (parte de una catedral) nave; **— espacial** spaceship
navegable ADJ navigable
navegación F navigation; (deportiva) boating
navegador M computer browser
navegante M navigator; ADJ navigating
navegar[7] VI/VT to navigate; (barco o vela) to sail; (en el Internet) to browse, to surf
Navidad F Christmas
navideño ADJ **fiesta navideña** Christmas party
navío M ship
neblina F mist
neblinoso ADJ misty
nebuloso ADJ (poco claro) nebulous; (que tiene niebla) foggy
necesario ADJ necessary
neceser M toiletry bag
necesidad F need; (cosa necesaria) necessity; **hacer sus —es** to relieve oneself; **de primera —** indispensable
necesitado ADJ needy
necesitar VT to need
necio -cia ADJ asinine, foolish; MF *pey* clod
necrología F necrology
néctar M nectar
nectarina F nectarine
nefasto ADJ unholy
nefritis F nephritis
negación F (que sirve para negar) negation; (que no acepta) denial
negar[1,7] VT (decir que no es verdad) to deny; (no dar a alguien algo que ha pedido) to refuse; (no reconocer públicamente) to disavow; **—se** to refuse; **—se a** to refuse to
negativa F (rechazo verbal) denial; (ausencia de cooperación) refusal
negativo ADJ negative; **signo —** minus sign; M (photographic) negative
negligencia F negligence, neglect; (médica) malpractice

negligente ADJ negligent, neglectful
negociación F negotiation
negociante MF business person
negociar VI/VT (tratar condiciones) to negotiate; (realizar un negocio) to trade
negocio M (tienda, actividad comercial) business; (transacción) business deal, business transaction; **hombre de —s** businessman; **mujer de —s** businesswoman; **hacer —** to make a profit
negrear VI to appear black; VT to blacken
negritas F boldface type
negro -ra ADJ black (también aplicado al café sin leche); (futuro) bleak; **pasarlas negras** to undergo hardships; F (nota) quarter note; MF (persona) person of color, black
negrura F blackness
negruzco ADJ blackish
némesis F nemesis
nene -na M baby boy; F baby girl
nenúfar M water lily
neologismo M neologism
neón M neon
neozelandés -esa MF New Zealander
Nepal M Nepal
nepalés -esa ADJ & MF Nepalese
nepalí ADJ & MF Nepalese
nepotismo M nepotism
nervado ADJ veined
nervio M nerve; **perder los —s** to lose one's cool; **tener los —s de punta** to be on edge
nerviosismo M nervousness
nervioso ADJ (relativo a los nervios) nervous; (inquieto) nervous, jumpy; (carne) sinewy
nervudo ADJ sinewy, wiry
neto ADJ (mejoría) distinct; (ganancia) net
neumático M tire; ADJ pneumatic
neural ADJ neural
neurona F nerve cell
neurosis F neurosis
neurótico -ca ADJ & MF neurotic
neutral ADJ neutral
neutralidad F neutrality
neutralizar[9] VT to neutralize
neutro ADJ neutral; (género) neuter
neutrón M neutron
nevada F snowfall
nevado ADJ snowy
nevar[1] VI to snow
nevera F icebox, refrigerator
nevisca F snow flurry
ni CONJ & ADV **— con mucho** not by a long shot; **— hablar** forget it; **— habló conmigo** he didn't even talk to me; **—**

idea (it) beats me; — **modo** no way; — **que esto fuera un hotel** it's not like this is a hotel; — **siquiera** not even; — **soñar** fat chance; — **trabaja — estudia** he neither works nor studies; — **una palabra** not a word; **no tiene amigos — enemigos** he has no friends nor enemies; **no es rico — mucho menos** he's not even close to being rich

Nicaragua F Nicaragua

nicaragüense ADJ & MF Nicaraguan

nicho M niche, recess

nicotina F nicotine

nidada F (huevos) nest of eggs; (crías) hatch, brood

nido M nest

niebla F fog

nieto -ta M grandson; F granddaughter; —s grandchildren

nieve F snow (también cocaína, heroína)

Níger M Niger

Nigeria F Nigeria

nigeriano -na ADJ & MF Nigerian

nigerino -na ADJ & MF Nigerien

nigua F chigger

nihilismo M nihilism

nilón M nylon

nimio ADJ insignificant

ninguno PRON **no tengo —** I have none/I don't have any; **ningún amigo mío** no friend of mine; **no tengo ningún libro** I don't have any books; **— de los dos** neither one; **de ningún modo** in no way

niñera F (ocasional) baby-sitter; (permanente) nanny

niñería F childish act

niñez F childhood; (de niño) boyhood; (de niña) girlhood

niño -ña M child, kid, boy; F child, kid, girl; **— del ojo** pupil (of the eye); ADJ childish

níquel M nickel

niquelado ADJ nickel-plated

níspero M loquat

nitidez F sharpness

nítido ADJ sharp

nitrato M nitrate

nitrógeno M nitrogen

nitroglicerina F nitroglycerine

nivel M level (también herramienta); (grado jerárquico) echelon; **— de mar** sea level; **— de vida** standard of living; **a —** straight; **a — de level** with

nivelar VT to level; (un camino de tierra) to grade

níveo ADJ snowy

no ADV no; — **quiero** I don't want to; — **bien llegaron** no sooner had they

arrived; — **sólo** not only; — **sea que** lest; **a — ser que** unless

noble ADJ noble; M nobleman; F noblewoman

nobleza F nobility

nócaut M knockout

noche F night; (horas de la noche) nighttime; **—buena** Christmas Eve; **—vieja** New Year's Eve; **— y día** day and night; **de —** at night; **de la — a la mañana** overnight; **esta —** tonight; **por la —** at night

noción F notion; **no tener ni —** to have no clue

nocivo ADJ harmful, noxious

nocturno ADJ (que actúa de noche) nocturnal; (que sucede todas las noches) nightly

nodo M node

nodriza F wet nurse

nódulo M node

nogal M walnut tree

nómada MF INV nomad

nombramiento M appointment; (militar) commission

nombrar VT to name, to appoint; (a un oficial militar) to commission

nombre M name; **— de pila** first name; **— de soltera** maiden name; **en — de** on behalf of; **eso no tiene —** that's unheard of; **hacerse un —** to make a name for oneself

nomenclatura F nomenclature

nomeolvides M SG forget-me-not

nómina F payroll

nominación F nomination

nominal ADJ nominal

nominar VT to nominate

non ADJ odd; M odd number

nopal M prickly pear

noquear VT to knock out

norcoreano -na ADJ & MF North Korean

nordeste ADJ & M northeast

nórdico ADJ Nordic

noreste ADJ & M northeast

norma F norm, standard

normal ADJ normal, standard; F (escuela) teacher's college; (línea) perpendicular line

normalizar[9] VT to normalize

noroeste ADJ & M northwest

norte ADJ & M north

norteamericano -na ADJ & MF (de América del Norte) North American; (de EEUU) American

norteño -ña ADJ northern; MF northerner

Noruega F Norway

noruego -ga ADJ & MF Norwegian

nos PRON us; **él — vio** he saw us; **— dio el**

libro he gave us the book, he gave the book to us

nosotros -as PRON we; **para —** for us

nostalgia F nostalgia

nostálgico ADJ nostalgic

nota F (musical) note; (anotación) annotation; (calificación) grade, mark; **— al pie de página** footnote; **de —** of note; **exagerar la —** to overdo something

notable ADJ notable, noteworthy, remarkable

notación F notation

notar VT (percibir) to note, to notice; (señalar) to note

notariar VT to notarize

notario -ria MF notary

noticia F piece of news; **—s** news; **tener —s de alguien** to hear from someone

noticiario M newscast, news bulletin

noticiero M newscast

notificación F notification; (policial) summons

notificar[6] VT to notify

notorio ADJ (conocido públicamente) well-known; (evidente) obvious

novato -ta MF novice; (policía, atleta) rookie

novedad F novelty; **—es** news; **sin —** all's well

novedoso ADJ novel

novela F novel

novelesco ADJ fictional

novelista MF novelist

noveno ADJ ninth

noventa NUM ninety

noviazgo M engagement

novicio -cia MF novice

noviembre M November

novillo -lla M steer; **hacer —s** to play hooky; F heifer

novio -via M (comprometido) fiancé; (no formal) boyfriend; (de boda) bridegroom; F (comprometida) fiancée; (no formal) girlfriend; (de boda) bride

nubarrón M thunderhead

nube F cloud; (de humo) billow; **poner por las —s** to praise to the skies; **está en las —s** his head is in the clouds; **los precios están por las —s** prices have gone through the roof

nublado ADJ (cielo) cloudy, overcast; (los ojos, de emoción) misty; (los ojos, por falta de sueño) bleary

nublar VT to blur; **—se** (cielo) to become overcast; (ojos) to cloud over

nuboso ADJ cloudy

nuca F nape

nuclear ADJ nuclear

núcleo M nucleus; (de imán, reactor) core

nudillo M knuckle

nudismo M nudism

nudista ADJ & MF nudist

nudo M knot (también en la madera, medida de velocidad); (de una obra teatral) turning point; (en el pelo) tangle; (en plantas) node; (en la garganta) lump; **— corredizo** slipknot; **— de rizo** square knot

nudoso ADJ knotty, gnarled

nuera F daughter-in-law

nuestro ADJ POS our; **— hijo** our son; PRON ours; **esto es —** this is ours

nueve NUM nine

nuevo ADJ new; **de —** again; **¿qué hay de — ?** what's new?

nuez F walnut; **— de Adán** Adam's apple; **— moscada** nutmeg

nulidad F nonentity

nulo ADJ null and void, invalid

numeral ADJ & M numeral

numerar VT to number

numérico ADJ numerical

número M (dígito) number; (en un espectáculo) act; (de una revista) issue; (cifra) figure

numeroso ADJ numerous

nunca ADV never, not ever; **no viene —** he never comes, he doesn't ever come; **más que —** more than ever; **casi —** hardly ever; **peor que —** worse than ever

nupcial ADJ nuptial, bridal

nupcias F PL nuptials

nutria F otter

nutrición F nutrition

nutrido ADJ **el congreso tuvo una nutrida concurrencia** the conference was well attended

nutriente M nutrient

nutrir VT to nourish

nutritivo ADJ nutritious, nourishing

Ññ

ñandú M rhea

ñato ADJ *Am* pug-nosed

ñoño ADJ bland

ñu M gnu

Oo

o CONJ or; **— se casa — lo mato** either he gets married or I'll kill him; **— sea** that is

oasis M oasis

obedecer[13] VI/VT to obey; **esto obedece a que** this is due to the fact that

obediencia F obedience

obediente ADJ obedient

obertura F musical overture

obesidad F obesity

obeso ADJ obese

obispo M bishop

obituario M obituary

objeción F objection

objetar VI/VT to object, to take exception (to)

objetivo ADJ objective; M (lente) objective; (meta) aim, objective

objeto M object

oblea F wafer

oblicuo ADJ (inclinado) oblique; (sesgado) biased

obligación F (deber) obligation, duty; (título financiero) bond

obligar[7] VT to force, to compel, to oblige; **—se (a)** to obligate oneself (a)

obligatorio ADJ obligatory, compulsory

oboe M oboe

obra F (artística, literaria, de construcción) work; (lugar de construcción) construction site; **— maestra** masterpiece; **en —s** under construction

obrar VI to act; **obra en nuestro poder** we acknowledge receipt of

obrero -ra MF worker; ADJ working

obscenidad F obscenity; **—es** filth

obsceno ADJ obscene

obsequiar VT to present, to give; **me obsequió perfume** he gave me perfume

obsequio M gift

obsequioso ADJ obsequious

observación F observation; (comentario) remark

observador -ora MF observer; ADJ observant

observancia F observance

observar VI/VT to observe; (hacer un comentario) to remark, to observe

observatorio M observatory

obsesión F obsession

obsesionar VT to obsess; **—se con** to obsess over, to be obsessed with

obsesivo-compulsivo ADJ obsessive-compulsive

obstaculizar VT to impede

obstáculo M obstacle, hindrance, impediment; (en carreras) hurdle

obstante LOC PREP **no — tu oposición** notwithstanding your opposition; LOC ADV **no —, voy a ir** nevertheless, I am going to go

obstar VT to preclude

obstetricia F obstetrics

obstinación F obstinacy

obstinado ADJ obstinate, bullheaded

obstinarse VI to be obstinate

obstrucción F obstruction, blockage

obstruir[31] VT to obstruct, to block; (un aparato) to jam; VI **—se** to get jammed

obtención F acquisition

obtener[44] VT to obtain, to get; (permiso) to secure; (con dificultad) to procure

obturador M (de una cámara fotográfica) shutter; (de un coche) choke

obviar VT to circumvent

obvio ADJ obvious

ocasión F occasion; (oportunidad) opportunity; (ganga) bargain; **de —** reduced

ocasional ADJ occasional

ocasionar VT to occasion, to cause

ocaso M sunset, twilight

occidental ADJ occidental, western; MF westerner

occidente M west

océano M ocean

oceanografía F oceanography

ocelote M ocelot

ochenta NUM eighty

ocho NUM eight

ocio M (diversión) leisure; (inacción) idleness

ociosidad F idleness

ocioso ADJ (inactivo) idle; (no usado) unused

octágono M octagon

octano M octane

octava F octave

octavilla F tract

octavo ADJ & M eighth

octeto M byte

octógono M octagon

octubre M October

ocular M eyepiece; ADJ **infección —** eye infection

oculista MF oculist

ocultar VT to conceal; (información) to withhold

ocultismo M the occult

oculto ADJ unseen, occult

ocupación F occupation

ocupado ADJ busy; (asiento, aseo) occupied

ocupante MF occupant

ocupar VT to occupy; (contratar) to employ;
—**se de** to take care of
ocurrencia F witticism, quip
ocurrente ADJ witty
ocurrir VI to occur
oda F ode
odiar VI/VT to hate
odio M hatred, hate
odioso ADJ (tarea) odious; (persona) hateful
odontología F dentistry
odre M wineskin
**OEA (Organización de Estados
     Americanos)** F OAS
oeste ADJ & M west
ofender VI/VT to offend; —**se** to get
     offended, to take offense
ofensa F offense
ofensiva F (militar) offensive; (deportiva)
     offense
ofensivo ADJ offensive, obnoxious
oferta F offer; (rebaja) special offer; **en —** on
     sale
offset M offset
oficial -la ADJ official; MF (militar) officer;
     (obrero calificado) skilled worker; —
     general high-ranking officer
oficiar VI to officiate; — **de** to serve as
oficina F office; (dependencia
     gubernamental) bureau
oficinista MF office worker
oficio M (actividad laboral) trade, craft;
     (comunicación oficial) official
     communication; **tiene mucho —** he
     knows his stuff; **buenos —s** good offices
oficioso ADJ (entrometedor) officious; (no
     oficial) unofficial
ofrecer[13] VT to offer; (en una subasta) to bid;
     (una cena) to give; — **resistencia** to put
     up resistance; **¿qué se le ofrece a Vd.?**
     how can I help you?
ofrecimiento M (acción de ofrecer) offering;
     (oferta) offer
ofrenda F offering
ofuscar[6] VT to bewilder
ogro M ogre
ohmio M ohm
oído M (facultad) hearing; (órgano) inner ear;
     (musical) ear; — **medio** middle ear; **al —**
     confidentially; **de —** by ear
oír[35] VI/VT (percibir) to hear; (atender) to
     listen; — **decir que** to hear that; —
     hablar de to hear about; — **misa** to
     attend mass; **¡oye!** listen! hey!
ojal M buttonhole
ojalá INTERJ — **estuviera aquí** I wish he
     were here; — **que venga** I hope that he
     comes

ojeada F glimpse
ojear VT to glimpse
ojera F dark circle under the eye
ojeriza F animosity
ojeroso ADJ with dark circles under the eyes
ojiva F (arco) pointed arch; (explosivo)
     warhead
ojo M (órgano, centro de huracán, instinto,
     yema de patata) eye; **¡—!** careful! look out!
     a — de buen cubero as a rule of thumb;
     a —s vistas clearly; **me costó un — de
     la cara** it cost me an arm and a leg; **¿no
     tienes —s en la cara?** are you blind?
     dichosos los —s que te ven you're a
     sight for sore eyes; — **de buey** porthole;
     — **de la cerradura** key hole; — **de
     lince** eagle-eye; — **morado** black eye; —
     por — an eye for an eye
ola F wave; (de un olor) waft; (de protesta)
     storm
oleada F wave, surge
oleaje M swell, surge
óleo M oil painting
oleoducto M pipeline
oleoso ADJ oily
oler[36] VI/VT to smell (también sospechar); —
     a to smell of
olfatear VI/VT to scent, to sniff
olfateo M sniff, sniffing
olfato M (facultad) sense of smell; (instinto)
     nose
olfatorio ADJ olfactory
olimpiada F Olympiad; —**s** Olympic games
olímpico ADJ Olympian
oliva F olive
olivar M olive grove
olivo M olive tree
olla F pot; — **de grillos** snake pit; —
     podrida stew of mixed vegetables and
     meat
olmo M elm
olor M smell, odor
oloroso ADJ odorous
olvidadizo ADJ forgetful
olvidar VI/VT to forget; —**se (de)** to forget;
     se me olvidó algo I forgot something
olvido M oblivion; **caer en el —** to be
     forgotten; **echar al —** to cast into
     oblivion; **tus —s** your forgetfulness
Omán M Oman
omaní ADJ & MF Omani
ombligo M navel
omisión F omission
omiso ADJ **hacer caso — (de)** to ignore
omitir VT to omit, to leave out; (no notar) to
     overlook
ómnibus M bus

omnipotencia F omnipotence
omnipotente ADJ omnipotent
omnisciencia F omniscience
omnisciente ADJ omniscient
omnívoro ADJ omnivorous
once NUM eleven
oncología F oncology
onda F wave; **— corta** short wave; **—
    expansiva** shock wave; **— sonora** sound
    wave; **agarrarle la — a algo** to get in
    the swing of things; **captar la —** to get
    the drift
ondeado ADJ wavy
ondeante ADJ flying
ondear VI to wave
ondulación F ripple, ruffle, roll
ondulado ADJ wavy
ondulante ADJ undulating
ondular VI to undulate; VI/VT to wave
ónix M onyx
onomatopeya F onomatopoeia
**ONU (Organización de las Naciones
    Unidas)** F UN
onza F ounce
opacar[6] VT (oscurecer) to dull; (eclipsar) to
    overshadow
opaco ADJ (no transparente) opaque; (no
    brillante) dull
ópalo M opal
opción F option; **opciones** stock options
opcional ADJ optional
**OPEP (Organización de Países
    Exportadores de Petróleo)** F OPEC
ópera F (composición) opera; (teatro) opera
    house
operable ADJ operable
operación F operation
operador -ora M (en matemáticas) operator;
    MF (de teléfono) operator
operar VI/VT to operate; VT (intervenir
    quirúrgicamente) to operate on; (llevar a
    cabo) to carry out; VI (hacer cuentas) to do
    mathematical operations
operario -ria MF operator, operative
opinar VI/VT to hold an opinion, to think
opinión F opinion, view, feeling; **cambiar
    de —** to change one's mind
opio M opium
oponer[39] VT to oppose; **—se** to conflict; **—se
    a** to oppose, to be against
oporto M port wine
oportunidad F opportunity, chance;
    (pretexto) opening
oportunista ADJ & MF opportunistic
oportuno ADJ (en el momento conveniente)
    opportune, timely; (adecuado) appropriate
oposición F opposition; **oposiciones**
    competitive examinations
opositor -ora MF opponent
opresión F oppression
opresivo ADJ oppressive
opresor -ora MF oppressor
oprimir VT (al pueblo) to oppress; (un
    botón) to press
optar VI to choose; **— por** to choose
optativo ADJ optional
óptico -ca ADJ optical; MF optician; F optics
optimismo M optimism
optimista ADJ optimistic; MF optimist
optometría F optometry
opuesto ADJ opposite, contrary; **se mostró
    — al casamiento** he was against the
    marriage; **dos fuerzas opuestas** two
    opposing forces; **lo —** the opposite;
    dirección opuesta the opposite/reverse
    direction
opulencia F opulence
opulento ADJ opulent; (sociedad) affluent
oración F (frase) sentence; (súplica) prayer
oráculo M oracle
orador -ora MF orator, speaker
oral ADJ oral
orangután M orangutan
orar VI/VT to pray
oratoria F oratory
oratorio M oratory
órbita F (de los cuerpos celestes) orbit; (de
    los ojos) eye socket
orbitador M orbiter
orbital ADJ orbital
orbitar VI/VT to orbit
orca F killer whale
orden M (limpieza, secuencia) order; **— del
    día** order of the day; **perturbar el —
    público** to disturb the peace; **sin — ni
    concierto** haphazard; F (mando)
    command, order; (de religiones) order; (de
    cateo) warrant; **a sus órdenes** at your
    service
ordenado ADJ orderly, neat
ordenador M computer
ordenanza F ordinance; M orderly
ordenar VT (arreglar) to put in order;
    (mandar) to order, to command; (conferir
    órdenes) to ordain; **—se** to become
    ordained
ordeñar VT to milk
ordeño M milking
ordinal ADJ ordinal
ordinariez F vulgarity
ordinario ADJ (corriente) ordinary; (vulgar)
    vulgar
orear VT to air out
orégano M oregano

oreja F (outer) ear; (de un martillo) claw; (en un utensilio) flap; **aguzar la —** to prick up one's ears; **sonreír de — a —** to smile from ear to ear; **estar hasta las —s en algo** to be up to one's neck in something

orejera F ear muff

orfanato M orphanage

orfebre MF (con oro) goldsmith; (con plata) silversmith

orgánico ADJ organic

organismo M organism

organista MF organist

organización F organization

organizador -ora MF organizer

organizar[9] VT to organize; (un ataque) to stage; (una fiesta) to give, to throw

órgano M organ

orgía F orgy

orgullo M pride; **es mi —** she's my pride and joy

orgulloso ADJ proud

orientación F orientation, guidance; (de velas) trim; (de estudios) track; (de un objeto) lie; (del terreno) lay

oriental ADJ oriental, eastern; MF oriental

orientar VT to orient; **—se** to get one's bearings

oriente M orient, east

orificio M orifice

origen M origin; (de un problema, conflicto) source; (antecedentes familiares) birth

original ADJ original; M original; (de una cinta magnética) master

originalidad F originality

originar VT to originate, to give rise to; **—se** to originate, to arise

orilla F (de un lago, mar) shore, bank; (de una cama) edge; (de una prenda) hem

orillar VT (una calle) to border; (una prenda) to hem

orín M rust; M PL **orines** urine

orina F urine

orinal M chamber pot

orinar VI/VT to urinate

oriundo ADJ **ser — de** (persona) to hail from; (cosa) to originate in

orla F (de un uniforme) trimming; (de una alfombra) fringe

orlar VT to fringe

orlón[tm] M Orlon[tm]

ornamental ADJ ornamental

ornamentar VT to ornament, to embellish

ornamento M ornament

ornar VT to adorn

ornitología F ornithology

oro M gold; **— blanco** white gold; **— en lingotes** gold bullion; **— negro** black gold; **— puro** solid gold; **prometer el — y el moro** to promise the moon

orondo ADJ self-satisfied

oropel M tinsel

oropéndola F oriole

orquesta F orchestra

orquestar VT to orchestrate

orquídea F orchid

ortiga F nettle

ortodoncia F orthodontics

ortodoxo ADJ orthodox

ortografía F orthography, spelling

oruga F caterpillar

orujo M rape

orzuelo M sty

osadía F boldness, daring

osado ADJ bold, daring

osamenta F skeleton

osar VI/VT to dare

oscilación F oscillation

oscilar VI to oscillate, to seesaw; **— entre** to range between

oscuridad F (lugar sin luz) dark, darkness; (condición de oscuro) darkness; (falta de claridad conceptual, anonimato) obscurity

oscuro ADJ (sin luz) dark; (nublado) murky; (poco claro, poco conocido) obscure; **lentes —s** dark glasses; **gris —** dark gray; **a oscuras** in the dark

óseo ADJ bony

osezno M bear cub

ósmosis F osmosis

oso -sa M bear; F she-bear; **— blanco / polar** polar bear; **— hormiguero** anteater

ostentación F ostentation, show, display; **hacer de —** to flaunt

ostentar VI/VT to display, to show off, to flaunt

ostentoso ADJ ostentatious, showy

osteoporosis F osteoporosis

ostión M large oyster

ostra F oyster

OTAN (Organización del Tratado del Atlántico Norte) F NATO

otero M hillock

otoñal ADJ autumnal

otoño M autumn, fall

otorgamiento M grant

otorgar[7] VT (permiso) to grant, to concede; (un premio) to award

otro ADJ (uno adicional) another; (uno diferente) other; **otra vez** again; **otra cosa** something else; **— más** another one; **al — día** the next day; **de — modo** otherwise; **en otra parte** somewhere else; **la otra cara de la moneda** the flip side; **por otra parte** on the other hand;

PRON (uno más) another one; (una persona diferente) someone else; (una cosa diferente) something else

ovación F ovation, acclaim

oval ADJ oval

ovalado ADJ oval

óvalo M oval

ovario M ovary

oveja F sheep; (hembra) ewe

ovejero M sheepdog

overoles M PL overalls

ovillar VT to ball; **—se** to curl up into a ball

ovillo M ball of yarn; **hacerse un —** to curl up

OVNI (objeto volador no identificado) M UFO

ovular VI to ovulate

óvulo M egg

oxidado ADJ oxidized, rusty

oxidar VI/VT to oxidize, to rust

óxido M (cuerpo químico) oxide; (herrumbre) rust

oxígeno M oxygen

oyente MF (que oye) listener, hearer; (alumno no oficial) auditor

ozono M ozone

Pp

pabellón M (de feria) pavilion; (parte de un edificio) wing; (bandera) flag; (departamento de hospital) ward; **— de la oreja** outer ear

pabilo M wick

paca F bale

pacana F (fruto) pecan; (árbol) pecan tree

pacer[13] VI to pasture, to graze; VT to crop, to graze

paciencia F patience; **tener —** to be patient

paciente ADJ & MF patient

pacificar[6] VT to pacify

pacífico ADJ peaceful; M **Océano Pacífico** Pacific Ocean

pacifismo M pacifism

pacto M pact, covenant

paddock M (de caballos) paddock; (de coches) pit

padecer[13] VI/VT to suffer; **— de cáncer** to suffer from cancer

padecimiento M suffering

padrastro M (marido de la madre) stepfather; (uñero) hangnail

padre M father; **—s** parents, folks; **— de familia** male head of the household; **—nuestro** the Lord's Prayer; **John Smith, —** John Smith, senior; **ser —** to become a father; **un lío —** a real mess

padrino M (de bautizo) godfather; (de boda) best man; (en un duelo) second

paella F paella

paga F pay; (para un niño) allowance

pagadero ADJ payable, due

pagado ADJ **— de sí mismo** self-satisfied

pagador -ora MF payer

paganismo M paganism

pagano -na ADJ & MF pagan

pagar[7] VT (cuentas, deudas) to pay; (mercancías) to pay for; **—se de** to be proud of; **— el pato** to be left holding the bag; **pagan justos por pecadores** the just pay for the sins of others; **— a plazos** to pay in installments; **— al contado** to pay cash; **— con la misma moneda** to pay in kind; **— en especie** to pay in kind

pagaré M promissory note

página F page

paginar VT to paginate

pago M payment; **— en efectivo** cash payment

paila F large pan

país M country

paisaje M landscape, scenery

paisajismo M landscape architecture

paisano -na M countryman; F countrywoman

paja F straw (también para beber de un vaso); **a humo de —s** thoughtlessly; **por un quítame allá esas —s** for a trifle

pajar M hayloft

pájaro M bird; **— carpintero** woodpecker; **— pinto** cautious person; **un — francés** a French guy

paje M page

pajizo ADJ straw-colored

pajonal M *Am* grassland

pala F (para cavar) shovel; (para recoger basura) dustpan; (de hélice, remo) blade; (de zapato) upper; (para remar, de ping-pong) paddle; **— mecánica** power shovel; **lo tuvimos que recoger con —** he was exhausted

palabra F (unidad léxica) word; (facultad) speech; **— clave** key word; **—s mayores** a big deal; **cuatro —s** a few words; **cumplir con la —** to keep one's word; **dejar con la —** **en la boca** to cut someone off in mid-sentence; **en pocas —s** in a nutshell; **faltar a la —** to break a promise; **la última —** the final say; **ni**

una — not a word; **no dijo** — he didn't breathe a word; **un hombre de** — a man of his word; **tener la** — to have the floor; **tomar la** — to take the floor; **traducción — por** — word for word translation; **tragarse / comerse las propias** —s to eat one's words

palabrerío M verbiage

palabrero ADJ long-winded

palabrota F curse word, four-letter word; —s profanity

palacio M palace

paladar M palate; — **hendido** cleft palate

paladear VT to relish

paladín M champion, crusader

palanca F (mecanismo para levantar algo) lever; (para abrir algo) crowbar; (fuerza) leverage; — **del cambio** gearshift lever; — **de juegos** joystick; — **del regulador** throttle lever; **hacer** — to use leverage

palangana F basin

Paláu M Palau

palco M box

palenque M fence

paleontología F paleontology

paleta F (de pintor) palette; (de albañil) trowel; (de ping-pong, para mezclar, batir) paddle; (hélice) blade; (pirulí) lollipop, sucker

paletilla F shoulder

paleto -ta MF hayseed, hick

paliar VT to alleviate

palidecer[13] VI to turn pale

palidez F pallor, paleness

pálido ADJ pallid, pale

palillo M (de dientes) toothpick; (de tambor) drumstick; (para comida china) chopstick; **tocar todos los** —s to try everything

palique M chit-chat

paliza F beating, whipping; **dar una** — to beat, to whip

palma F (árbol) palm (tree); (hoja) palm leaf; (de mano) palm (of the hand); **batir** —s to clap; **llevarse la** — to take the prize; **conocer como la — de la mano** to know like the back of one's hand

palmada F (en la espalda) slap; (aplauso) clap; (en el trasero) spank; **dar una** — (en la espalda) to slap; (en el trasero) to spank

palmear VT to slap on the back

palmera F palm tree

palmípedo M web-footed bird

palmo M span; — **a** — inch by inch

palmotear VT to slap on the back

palo M (de madera) stick; (de barco) mast; (de naipes) suit; — **de golf** golf club; — **de**

escoba broomstick; **dar** —s to hit with a stick; **de tal — tal astilla** a chip off the old block

paloma F dove, pigeon

palomar M pigeon loft

palomilla F wing nut

palomitas F PL popcorn; **hacer** — to pop corn

palote M rolling pin

palpable ADJ palpable

palpar VT to feel

palpitación F palpitation

palpitante ADJ palpitating; **una cuestión** — a burning question

palpitar VI to palpitate

palta F Am avocado

paludismo M malaria

pampa F Am prairie

pamplinas F PL baloney, hogwash

pan M bread; (pieza) loaf of bread; — **comido** piece of cake, cinch; — **de cada día** everyday occurrence; — **rallado / molido** bread crumbs; **al —, — y al vino, vino** to call a spade a spade; **contigo, — y cebolla** love is all we need; **ganarse el** — to make a living

pana F corduroy

panacea F panacea, magic bullet

panadería F bakery

panadero -ra MF baker

panal M honeycomb

Panamá M Panama

panameño -ña ADJ & MF Panamanian

panamericano ADJ Pan-American

panceta F bacon

páncreas M pancreas

panda M panda bear

pandearse VT to buckle, to sag

pandeo M sag

pandereta F tambourine

pandilla F gang, band

panecillo M roll

panegírico M eulogy

panel M panel

panera F breadbasket

panfleto M pamphlet

pánico ADJ & M panic

panoja F ear of corn

panorama M panorama; (horizonte) outlook

panorámico ADJ panoramic

panqueque M pancake

pantaletas F PL panties

pantalla F (de lámpara) lampshade; (de monitor, para películas) screen; (para actividades ilícitas) cover, front; **la — grande** the silver screen; — **dividida** split screen; — **táctil** touchscreen

pantalón M trousers, pants; — **corto** shorts; **pantalones** trousers, pants; **llevar bien puestos los pantalones** to be master in one's own house
pantano M swamp, marsh
pantanoso ADJ swampy, marshy
panteón M vault
pantera F panther
pantomima F mime, pantomime
pantorrilla F calf
pantufla F slipper
panty M pantyhose
panza F paunch, belly
panzudo ADJ pot-bellied
pañal M diaper; **estar en —es** to be in infancy
paño M (trozo de tela) cloth; (de lana) woolen cloth; (para limpiar) rag; — **higiénico** sanitary napkin; — **mortuorio** pall; — **de manos** towel; — **de cocina** dishcloth; — **de mesa** tablecloth; **ella es mi — de lágrimas** I always cry on her shoulder; **—s menores** underwear
pañuelo M (para la nariz) handkerchief; (de cuello) scarf
papa M pope; F *Am* potato; **no saber ni —** not to know a thing; **—s fritas** French fries
papá M papa, dad
papacito M daddy
papada F double chin
papado M papacy
papagayo M parrot
papaíto M daddy
papar VT to eat; MF SG **papamoscas** (pájaro) flycatcher; (tonto) half-wit; **papanatas** twerp
paparruchas F PL baloney, bull
papaya F papaya
papel M paper; (dramático) role, part; — **aluminio** aluminum foil; — **carbón** carbon paper; — **cuadriculado** graph paper; — **de cartas** stationery; — **de estaño** tin foil; — **de estraza** brown paper; — **de lija** sandpaper; — **de seda** tissue paper; — **encerado** wax paper; — **higiénico** toilet paper; — **moneda** paper money; — **tisú** tissue paper; **desempeñar un —** to play a role; **en el —** on paper; **hacer buen —** to cut a good figure
papelera F (fábrica) paper factory; (cubo) wastepaper basket
papelería F stationery store
papeleta F slip of paper; (para votar) ballot
paperas F PL mumps

papito M daddy
páprika F paprika
papú ADJ & MF Papua New Guinean
paquete M (envuelto) package; (atado) bundle; (conjunto de programas) package
Paquistán M Pakistan
paquistano -na ADJ & MF Pakistani
par ADJ even; M (de cosas idénticas) pair; (de cosas diferentes) couple; (título) peer; (en golf) par; **a la —** at par; **sin —** peerless; **de — en —** wide-open
para PREP in order to, for; **lo hice — ganar dinero** I did it in order to earn money; **demasiado — mí** too much for me; **trabajo — mi padre** I work for my father; **— ser perro es inteligente** for a dog he's smart; **— mi sorpresa** to my surprise; **voy — Madrid** I'm going to Madrid; **— las dos** by two o'clock; **— atrás** backwards; **— empezar** for starters; **— llevar** to go; **¿— qué?** what for? **— que** so that, so as to; **— siempre** forever; **habla — sí** he talks to himself; **— mis adentros** to myself; **— morirse de risa** hilarious; **no es — tanto** it's no big deal; **sin qué ni — qué** without rhyme or reason
parabién M congratulations; **dar el —** to congratulate
parada F (acción de parar) stop; (de perro de caza) point; (de taxis) stand; (militar) parade; (relevo de guardia) changing the guard; (de balón) parry
paradero M whereabouts
paradigma M paradigm
parado ADJ (que no se mueve) stationary; (que no tiene trabajo) unemployed, idle; **salir bien —** to come out on top
paradoja F paradox
paradójico ADJ paradoxical
parafernalia F paraphernalia
parafina F paraffin
parafrasear VI/VT to paraphrase
paráfrasis F paraphrase
paraguas M SG umbrella
Paraguay M Paraguay
paraguayo -ya ADJ & MF Paraguayan
paraíso M paradise
paraje M spot
paralela F parallel line; **—s** parallel bars
paralelo ADJ & M parallel; **hacer —s** to draw parallels
parálisis F paralysis
paralítico -ca ADJ & MF paralytic
paralización F (de tránsito) gridlock; (del cuerpo) paralysis
paralizar⁹ VT to paralyze; (negociaciones) to

stall; **—se** to gridlock
paramédico -ca ADJ & MF paramedic
parámetro M parameter
paramilitar ADJ & MF paramilitary
páramo M cold highland, moor
parangón M comparison; **sin —**
    incomparable
parangonar VT to compare
paraninfo M auditorium
paranoia F paranoia
paranoico -ca ADJ & MF paranoid
paranormal ADJ paranormal
parapsicología F parapsychology
parar VI/VT (detener) to stop; (motor) to stall;
    VT (un pase de pelota) to block; (un golpe)
    to parry; **— de hacer algo** to stop doing
    something; **y para de contar** and that's
    it; **— en seco** to stop short; **ir a —** to end
    up; **habló sin —** he talked non-stop; **—se**
    to stop; *Am* to stand up; **—se a pensar** to
    stop to think; M SG **parabrisas**
    windshield; **paracaídas** parachute;
    paracaidismo skydiving; **parachoques**
    bumper; **pararrayos** lightning rod;
    parasol parasol; MF **paracaidista**
    parachutist
parásito M parasite
parcela F parcel, plot
parcelación F subdivision
parcelar VT to parcel (out)
parche M (para remendar) patch; (de tambor)
    drum head; **— de ojo** eye patch
parcial ADJ partial
pardillo M linnet
pardo ADJ (color) gray-brown; (mulato)
    mulatto
pareado M couplet
parear VT to match
parecer [13] VI to seem; **— que** to seem like, to
    look like; **¿qué te parece?** what do you
    think? **—se a** to resemble, to look like; M
    (opinión) opinion; (aspecto) appearance;
    al — apparently; **a mi —** to my mind /
    way of thinking; **del mismo —** like-
    minded
parecido ADJ alike, similar; **bien —** good-
    looking; M similarity, resemblance
pared F wall; **poner a alguien contra la
    —** to corner; **subirse por las —es** to be
    furious; **de — a —** wall-to-wall; **reloj de
    —** wall clock
paredón M execution wall
pareja F (de personas) couple; (de cosas) pair,
    match; (compañero) partner
parejo ADJ (hermanos) alike; (carrera) even;
    (dientes) straight; **correr al —** to go hand
    in hand

parental ADJ parental
parentela F kin
parentesco M kinship, relation
paréntesis M parenthesis
pargo M red snapper
paria MF INV pariah, outcast
paridad F parity
pariente -ta MF relative, relation; **—
    consanguíneo** blood relative
parir VI/VT to give birth (to)
parlamentar VI to parley
parlamentario -ria ADJ parliamentary; MF
    member of parliament
parlamento M (en una obra de teatro)
    speech; (negociación) parley; (cuerpo
    legislativo) parliament
parlanchín ADJ talkative
parlotear VI to chatter, to rattle on
parloteo M chatter
paro M (pequeña huelga) stoppage; (situación
    de no tener trabajo) unemployment; (ave)
    tit; **— cardiaco** cardiac arrest
parodia F parody
parodiar VT to parody
parpadear VI (un ojo) to blink; (una vela) to
    flicker; (una estrella) to twinkle
parpadeo M (del ojo) blink; (de una vela)
    flicker; (de una estrella) twinkle
párpado M eyelid
parque M park; **— automotor** fleet of cars;
    — de atracciones amusement park; **—
    zoológico** zoo
parra F grapevine
párrafo M paragraph; **echar un — con** to
    have a chat with
parral M grape arbor
parranda F binge, spree; **andar de —** to go
    on a spree
parrandear VI to revel
parrandero -ra MF party animal
parrilla F (sobre el fuego) grill; (en el horno)
    broiler; (de calles) grid; (de coche) grille
parrillada F barbecue dish
párroco M parish priest
parroquia F (distrito) parish; (iglesia) parish
    church
parroquial ADJ parochial
parroquiano -na MF (de iglesia) parishioner;
    (de tienda) regular
parte F (sección) part; (lugar) place; (papel en
    un drama) lines; (persona) party; **—s
    pudendas** private parts; **a otra —**
    somewhere else; **a —s iguales** fifty-fifty;
    de un tiempo a esta — for some time;
    de — de on behalf of; **de — a —**
    completely; **echar a mala —** to take
    amiss; **en —** partly; **en gran —** in large

measure; **en otra —** elsewhere; **en / por todas —s** everywhere; **formar — de** to be part of; **ir por —s** to proceed by steps; **la mayor — de** most of; **la — del león** the lion's share; **no está en ninguna —** it's nowhere to be found; **no va a ninguna —** it's going nowhere; **por otra —** on the other hand; **tomar — en** to take part in; M report; **dar —** to report; **dar — de enfermo** to report sick; **dar — de un crimen** to report a crime

partera F midwife

participación F participation; (en un negocio) interest; **— de nacimiento** birth announcement

participante MF participant; (en una carrera) entrant; (en un concurso) contestant

participar VI to participate; VT to announce; **— de / en** to participate in, to share in

partícipe MF participant

participio M participle

partícula F particle

particular ADJ (específico) particular; (poco usual) peculiar; (privado) private; **en —** in particular; **clases —es** private lessons; M (detalle) particular; (asunto) matter; MF private citizen

partida F (fondos) appropriation; (de caza) party; (cantidad de mercancía) parcel, lot; (de ajedrez) game; (acción de partir) departure; **— de nacimiento** birth record; **jugar una mala —** to play a mean trick; **por — doble** double-entry

partidario -ria MF (de una medida) supporter, advocate; (de partido político) partisan

partido M (grupo político) party; (de golf) round; (de tenis, fútbol) game, match; **es un buen —** he's a good match; **sacar — de** to take advantage of; **tomar —** to take sides; ADJ split, cleft

partir VT (dividir) to divide; (repartir) to share; (quebrar) to break; **eso me parte por el eje** that screws me up; **que te parta un rayo** go jump in the lake; VI (salir) to depart, to leave; **a — de entonces** since then; **a — del lunes** starting Monday; **—se de risa** to die of laughter

partisano -na MF partisan

partitura F musical score

parto M childbirth, delivery; **estar en trabajo de —** to be in labor

parvulario M kindergarten, nursery

párvulo -la MF nursery school child

pasa F raisin

pasable ADJ passable

pasada F (acción de pasar) passing; (con una máquina) pass; **una mala —** a mean trick; **de —** by the way

pasadizo M secret passage

pasado M past; ADJ (anterior) past; (demasiado maduro) overripe; **— mañana** day after tomorrow; **el año —** last year; **el — mes de septiembre** last September

pasador M pin

pasaje M (sitio por donde se pasa, fragmento de texto) passage; (billete) ticket; (pasajeros) passengers

pasajero -ra ADJ fleeting, transitory; MF passenger

pasaporte M passport

pasar VI (no querer jugar, ir de un lado a otro, seguir su proceso, transcurrir) to pass; (ocurrir) to happen; (mantenerse) to get by on; **— a ser** to become; **— de moda** to go out of style; **— por** to pass by; **—le por la cabeza a alguien** to occur to someone; **pasan de los 80 años** they're over 80 years old; **te pasaste la casa** you missed the house; **—se de la raya** to cross the line; **—se de sol** to get too much sun; **—se de listo** to outsmart oneself; **—se** to spoil; **se me pasó ir a buscarte** I totally forgot to pick you up; **me la paso bien** I have a good time; VT (la sal, una prueba, la plancha) to pass; (un sofocón) to endure; (una tarde) to spend; **—las de Caín** to go through hell; **— en limpio** to make a new copy; **— por alto** to overlook; **— los 50 kmh** to exceed 50 kmh; **— revista** to pass in review; **nos pasó un Volvo** a Volvo passed us; **no lo paso** I can't stand him; M **tienen un buen —** they have a comfortable life; **pasamano** (de barco) guard rail, gangway; (de escalera) banister, railing; **pasatiempo** pastime

pasarela F (en un barco) gangplank; (para modelos) runway

Pascua F Easter; (fiesta judía) Passover; **— Florida / de Resurrección** Easter Sunday; **— de Navidad** Christmas

pase M pass

pasear VI (a pie) to take a walk; (en bici, a caballo) to go on a ride; (en coche) to go for a drive, to go on a ride; **—se** to parade, to take a walk; **—se a caballo** to go horseback riding; VT (un perro) to walk a dog

paseo M (a pie) walk, stroll; (a caballo, en bicicleta) ride; (en coche) drive, ride; (lugar donde pasear) mall; **irse a —** to go jump in a lake; **dar un —** (a pie) to take a walk; (a caballo, en bicicleta) to go on a ride; (en coche) to go on a drive

pasillo M (de un teatro) aisle; (de un edificio) hallway, corridor; (para vuelo aéreo) corridor

pasión F passion

pasivo ADJ passive; **voz pasiva** passive voice; M SG (en un negocio) liabilities; (de una cuenta) debit side

pasmado ADJ astounded

pasmar VT to astound, to stun; **—se** to be astounded, to be stunned

pasmo M astonishment

pasmoso ADJ astonishing, stunning

paso M (acción de pasar, lugar donde pasar) pass; (de pie, de danza, distancia, de un proceso) step; (velocidad) pace; (de caballerías) walk; (de tornillo) pitch; (de coche) wheelbase; **— elevado** overpass; **— a nivel** grade crossing; **— de tortuga** snail's pace; **— a paso** step by step; **dar — (dejar pasar)** to let pass; (dejar actuar) to make possible; **dar —s** to take steps; **de —** by the way, in passing; **estar de —** to be passing through; **marcar el —** to set the pace; **al — que** while; **salir del — to** get out of a difficulty; **dicho sea de — incidentally; a cada —** at every turn; **— del tiempo** passage of time; **abrir — para** to make way for; **abrirse —** to plow through, to press through; ADJ dried

pasta F (de almidón) paste; (de harina) dough; (de fideos) pasta; (de libro) hard cover, binding; (dinero) *fam* dough; **de buena —** of good disposition; **— dentífrica / dental** toothpaste

pastar VI/VT to pasture, to graze

pastel M (torta) cake; (tarta) pie; (pintura, cuadro) pastel; **— de cumpleaños** birthday cake; **— de limón** lemon pie; **— de carne** meat pie; **descubrir el —** to spill the beans; ADJ pastel

pastelería F (establecimiento) pastry shop; (conjunto de pasteles) pastry

pastelero -ra M pastry cook

pasterizar, pasteurizar[9] VT to pasteurize

pastilla F (de medicina) tablet, pill; (para la tos) drop; (de jabón) bar

pastizal M grassland

pasto M (terreno) pasture, grassland; (hierba) grass; **ser — de** to be a victim of

pastor -ora MF (de ovejas) shepherd; (sacerdote protestante) pastor, minister; M **— alemán** German shepherd

pastoral ADJ pastoral; F pastoral letter

pastoril ADJ pastoral

pastoso ADJ pasty

pastura F feed

pata F (de animal, mueble) foot, leg; (de pollo) drumstick; (de un enchufe) pin; **— palmada** webfoot; **— de gallo** crow's-foot; **en cuatro —s** on all fours; **a (la) — coja** skipping on one leg; **estirar la —** *fam* to kick the bucket; **mala —** bad luck; **metedura de —** faux pas; **meter la —** to slip up; **—s arriba** upside down; ADJ **patihendido** cloven-hoofed; **patitieso** dumbfounded; **patizambo** (hacia adentro) knock-kneed; (hacia afuera) bow-legged

patada F kick; **libros a —s** tons of books; **en dos —s** in a jiffy; **dar —s** to kick; **echar a —s** to kick out

patalear VI (en el aire) to kick; (en el suelo) to stamp

pataleo M (en el aire) kick; (en el suelo) stamp

pataleta F fit; **dar una —** to throw a fit

patán M boor

patata F *Esp* potato; **—s fritas** French fries; **— caliente** hot potato

patear VT (algo, a alguien) to kick; (el suelo) to stamp; VI to tramp around

patentar VT to patent

patente ADJ & F patent; **se hizo — su ignorancia** he betrayed his ignorance; **— en trámite** patent pending

paternal ADJ (del padre) paternal; (como padre) fatherly

paternidad F paternity, fatherhood; **prueba de —** paternity test

paterno ADJ paternal

patético ADJ moving

patetismo M pathos

patíbulo M gallows scaffold, gallows

patilla F (de gafas) arm; **—s** sideburns

patín M skate; (de trineo) runner; **— de ruedas** roller skate; **— de cuchilla / de hielo** ice skate

patinaje M skating

patinar VI (una persona) to skate; (un coche sobre hielo) to skid; (un embrague) to slip; (en un examen) to blank out

patinazo M (de embrague) slip; (de coche) skid

patio M (de casa) patio, courtyard; (de escuela) playground

pato M duck; (macho) drake; **pagar el —** to take the rap

patochada F blunder

patógeno M pathogen

patología F pathology

patológico ADJ pathological

atoso ADJ clumsy

atraña F tall tale

atria F fatherland, homeland

atriarca M patriarch

atriarcal ADJ patriarchal

atrimonio M patrimony; — **cultural** cultural heritage; — **personal** personal assets

atriota MF patriot

atriótico ADJ patriotic

atriotismo M patriotism

atrocinador -ora MF sponsor

atrocinar VT to sponsor

atrocinio M sponsorship

atrón -ona MF (protector) patron; (jefe) employer; (de navío) skipper; M (dueño de pensión) landlord; (de costura) pattern; (punto de referencia) yardstick, standard; (planta) stock; (de un parásito) host; — **de oro** gold standard; F (dueña de pensión) landlady

atronato M board of trustees

atrono -na MF patron

atrulla F (grupo de policías o soldados) patrol, squad; (coche) squad car

atrullar VI/VT to patrol

atrullero M patrol car, squad car

ausa F (musical) pause, rest; **trabajar con** — to work slowly; **hacer** — to pause

auta F guideline

avimentar VT to pave

avimento M pavement

avo M turkey; — **real** peacock; — **frío** cold turkey; ADJ silly

avón M peacock

avonearse VI to strut, to swagger

avoneo M strut, swagger

avor M dread

avoroso ADJ frightful

ayasada F clownish act or remark; —**s** antics, horseplay

ayasear VI to clown around, to horse around

ayaso M (de circo) clown; (persona poco seria) buffoon; **hacer el** — to clown around

az F peace; **estamos en** — we are even; **en** — **descanse** may she rest in peace; **hacer las paces** to make up; **dejar en** — to leave alone

C M PC

eaje M toll; (lugar donde se paga) tollbooth

eatón -ona MF pedestrian

eca F freckle

ecado M sin; — **mortal** mortal sin

ecador -ora MF sinner; ADJ sinful

ecaminoso ADJ sinful

pecar[6] VI to sin; — **contra** to transgress against; — **de bueno** to be too good; — **de generoso** to be too generous; — **de oscuro** to be exceedingly unclear

pecera F aquarium

pechera F (de camisa) front; (de delantal) bib

pecho M (parte del cuerpo) chest; (mama) breast; **dar el** — to nurse; **nadar** — to do the breaststroke; **tomar a** —**(s)** to take to heart; **sacar** — to puff out one's chest

pechuga F breast

pechugona ADJ buxom

pecio M flotsam and jetsam

pecoso ADJ freckled

pectoral ADJ & M pectoral

peculado M embezzlement

peculiar ADJ peculiar

peculiaridad F peculiarity

pedagogía F pedagogy, education

pedagogo -ga MF pedagogue

pedal M pedal

pedalear VI/VT to pedal

pedante ADJ pedantic; MF pedant

pedazo M piece; — **de idiota** absolute idiot; **él es un** — **de pan** he's a saint; **hacer** —**s** to tear to pieces; **caerse a** —**s** to fall to pieces; — **por** — piece by piece

pedernal M flint

pedestal M pedestal

pedestre ADJ pedestrian

pediatra MF INV pediatrician

pediatría F pediatrics

pedido M order, requisition; **hacer un** — to place an order; — **fijo** standing order; — **urgente** rush order

pedigrí M pedigree

pedigüeño ADJ **no seas** — stop asking me for things

pedir[5] VT (requerir) to ask for, to request; (exigir) to demand; (encargar) to order, to requisition; — **limosna** to beg; — **prestado** to borrow; — **socorro** to cry for help; — **un deseo** to make a wish; — **que** to ask/pray that; — **la mano** to ask in marriage; — **por alguien** to ask to speak to someone

pedrada F **dar una** — to hit with a stone; **matar a** —**s** to stone to death

pedregal M rocky ground

pedregoso ADJ stony

pedrería F precious stones

pedrusco M boulder

pedúnculo M stem

pega F snag

pegadizo ADJ catchy

pegajoso ADJ sticky, tacky

pegamento M glue

pegar[7] VT (con el puño) to hit, to strike; (algo con pegamento) to stick, to glue; (botones) to sew on; (una devisa) to peg; **— con** to match; **— contra** to touch; **— un grito** to yell; **— un susto** to give a scare; **— un salto** to jump; **—le un tiro a alguien** to shoot someone; **—se** (adherir) to stick together, to cling; (contagiarse) to be contagious; **—se a** to latch onto; **no — un ojo** not to sleep a wink

pegote M glob

pegotear VT to gum up

peinado M (estilo) coiffure, hairdo; (acción) combing

peinador -ora MF hairdresser

peinar VT to comb (también registrar); (en una peluquería) to style; **— a contrapelo** to rub the wrong way

peine M comb

pelada F bald spot

pelado ADJ (pobre) poor; (sin cáscara) peeled; (sin pelo) hairless; (sin árboles) treeless; (sin plumas) plucked; (sin dinero) broke

pelador M peeler

pelaje M coat, fur

pelar VT (el pelo) to cut the hair of; (las plumas) to pluck the feathers from; (frutas, verduras) to peel; (a un jugador) to fleece; **duro de —** hard to deal with; **el agua está que pela** the water is really hot; **—se** to peel; M SG **pelagatos** nobody

peldaño M step, stair

pelea F (de palabra) fight, quarrel; (de obra) fight, scrape; (de boxeo) fight; **— a puñetazos** fistfight; **— de perros** dogfight

pelear VI (con palabras) to fight, to quarrel; (con obras) to fight, to scuffle; **—se con alguien** to have a fight with someone

pelechar VI (perder la piel) to shed; (mejorar) to get better

pelele M (persona sin carácter) wimp; (muñeca) straw doll

peletería F (tienda) fur store; (comercio) fur trade

pelícano M pelican

película F film (también membrana); (obra cinematográfica) motion-picture film, movie; **de —** extraordinary; **dar una —** to show a film; **— muda** silent film

peligrar VI to be in danger

peligro M danger, peril; **ese muchacho es un —** that boy is dangerous; **en —** in danger; **poner en —** to imperil / endanger / jeopardize

peligroso ADJ dangerous, perilous

pellejo M (piel de animal) hide, pelt; (odre) wineskin; **salvar el —** to save one's skin; **ser todo —** to be skin and bones; **jugarse el —** to risk one's life

pellizcar[6] VT to pinch

pellizco M pinching

pelma MF jerk

pelo M (de persona) hair; (de animal) fur; (de alfombra) pile; **con —s y señales** with every possible detail; **de medio —** low-class; **eso me viene al —** that suits me perfectly; **montar en —** to ride bareback; **ni un —** not at all; **no tener —s en la lengua** not to mince words; **se le ponen los —s de punta** his hair stands on end; **se salvó por un —** he was saved by the skin of his teeth; **tomar el — a** to make fun of; **traído de los —s** far-fetched; ADJ **pelirrojo** redheaded

pelón ADJ bald

pelota F (objeto) ball; (juego) ball game; **— vasca** jai-alai; **en —s** naked; **pasar la —** to pass the buck

pelotera F brawl

pelotón M (pelota grande) large ball; (de tierra seca) clod; (de ciclistas) pack; (de soldados) platoon; (de fusilamiento) firing squad

peltre M pewter

peluca F wig

peludo ADJ (persona) hairy; (animal) furry; (perro) shaggy

peluquería F (para hombres) barbershop; (para mujeres) salon

peluquero -ra MF (de hombres) barber; (de mujeres) hairdresser

peluquín M toupee

pelusa F (de tela) lint; (de melocotón, cara) fuzz; (de plantas) hair; (de ropa) fluff, lint; (de polvo) dust bunny

pelvis F pelvis

pena F (castigo) penalty; (tristeza) sorrow; **— de muerte** death penalty, capital punishment; **—s** hardships; **a duras —s** with great difficulty; **me da —** it grieves me; **hecho una —** in a mess; **sería una — perder** it would be a shame to lose; **so — de** on pain of; **valer la —** to be worthwhile

penacho M (de plumas) tuft, crest; (de humo) plume

penal ADJ penal; M penitentiary

penalidad F (penuria) hardship; (castigo) penalty

penalizar[9] VT to penalize

penalty M penalty kick

penar VI to suffer; VT to punish

enco M plug, nag
endejo -ja MF (persona licenciosa) *pey* swine; (persona tonta) *fam* dummy
endencia F wrangle, fight
endenciero ADJ quarrelsome
ender VI to hang, to dangle
endiente F slope, incline; M *Esp* earring; ADJ (aretes) dangling; (negocio) pending, unfinished; (pago) outstanding; **vive — de su hija** she lives for her daughter
endón M banner
éndulo M pendulum
ene M penis
enetración F penetration
enetrante ADJ (mirada, sonido) penetrating, piercing; (frío) biting; (comentario) cutting; (inteligencia) keen
enetrar VT (pasar al interior) to penetrate, to pierce; (comprender) to comprehend
enicilina F penicillin
enínsula F peninsula
eninsular ADJ peninsular
enitencia F penance
enitenciaría F penitentiary
enitente ADJ & MF penitent
enoso ADJ (que produce tristeza) painful, grievous; (que lleva consigo penalidades) trying
ensador -ora MF thinker; ADJ reflective
ensamiento M (facultad, acción, efecto) thought; (flor) pansy
ensar[1] VI/VT to think; **— en** to think about/over; **— hacer algo** to intend to do something; **eso da que —** that seems questionable; **no lo pienses dos veces** don't think twice
ensativo ADJ pensive, thoughtful
ensión F (asignación periódica) pension, allowance; (comidas) board; (hostal) boardinghouse; **— completa** room and board; **tener en —** to have as a boarder
ensionado M boarding school
ensionar VT to pension
ensionista MF (que vive en una pensión) boarder; (que cobra una pensión) pensioner
entágono M pentagon
entagrama M musical staff
enthouse M penthouse
enúltimo ADJ next to the last, penultimate
enumbra F semi-darkness, dimness
enuria F (escasez) shortage; (pobreza) poverty
eña F boulder; **— folklórica** folklore club
eñasco M crag
eñascoso ADJ craggy
eñón M crag

peón -ona MF (obrero) unskilled laborer, farm hand; **— caminero** road worker; M (en ajedrez) pawn; (en damas) piece
peonada F gang of laborers
peonaje M gang of laborers
peonza F toy top
peor ADJ worse, worst; **este libro es —** this book is worse; **el — libro** the worst book; ADV worse; **trabaja —** he works worse; **— que** worse than; **— que nunca** worse than ever; **en el — de los casos** if worst comes to worst; **lo —** the worst (thing); **tanto —** so much the worse
pepa F **es un viva la —** it's bedlam
pepino M cucumber
pepita F (simiente) seed; (tumor de gallina) pip; (masa de oro) nugget
pequeñez F (cualidad de pequeño) smallness; (cosa insignificante) trifle
pequeño -ña ADJ (de poco tamaño) small, little; (de corta edad) young; (de poca importancia) trivial
pera F pear; **pedirle —s al olmo** to ask the impossible
peral M pear tree
perca F perch; **— americana** black bass
percal M percale
percance M accident, mishap
percebe M barnacle
percepción F perception
perceptible ADJ perceptible, noticeable
perceptivo ADJ perceptive
percha F (para el armario) clothes hanger; (palo para colgar cosas) peg; (palo para aves) perch; (perchero) coat rack
perchero M coat rack
percibir VT (experimentar) to perceive, to sense; (recibir) to collect
percudir VT to make grimy; **—se** to get grimy
percusión F percussion
percutor M firing pin
perdedor -ora MF loser
perder[1] VT (dejar de tener algo, extraviar) to lose, to mislay; (echar a perder) to spoil, to ruin; (ser derrotado) to lose; (no sacar el provecho debido) to waste; (no llegar a tiempo, no disfrutar) to miss; **— el conocimiento** to lose consciousness; **— el tiempo** to waste time; **— los estribos** to fly off the handle; **— hojas** to shed leaves; **— pie** to lose one's footing; **— terreno** to lose ground; **echarse a —** to spoil; **el vaso pierde agua** the glass leaks water; **llevo las de —** the odds are against me; **—se** (extraviarse) to lose one's way, to get lost; (pervertirse) to go astray,

to go stray; **se han perdido las llaves** the keys have gotten lost; **—se de vista** to disappear; **—(se) una oportunidad** to pass up an opportunity

perdición F perdition, damnation

pérdida F (acción de perder, cosa perdida) loss; **entrar en —** to nosedive; **— de tiempo** waste of time

perdido -da ADJ (extraviado) lost, missing; (aislado) isolated; (promiscuo) promiscuous; **un borracho —** an utter drunkard; **estar — por alguien** to be crazy about someone; M degenerate; F slut

perdigón M (pollo de perdiz) young partridge; (grano de plomo) birdshot, buckshot

perdiz F partridge

perdón M forgiveness; (oficial) pardon; **con — de los presentes** present company excepted; **no tener —** to be unforgivable; INTERJ excuse me

perdonar VT to forgive; (oficial) to pardon

perdurable ADJ lasting

perdurar VI to last

perecedero ADJ perishable

perecer[13] VI to perish

peregrinación F pilgrimage

peregrinar VI to go on a pilgrimage

peregrino -na MF pilgrim; ADJ far-fetched

perejil M parsley

perenne ADJ perennial

pereza F laziness, idleness, sloth

perezoso ADJ lazy, idle; M (animal) sloth

perfección F perfection; **a la —** to perfection

perfeccionamiento M perfecting

perfeccionar VT to perfect

perfecto ADJ perfect, flawless; **es un — tarado** he's an utter idiot

perfil M profile; **de —** from the side

perfilar VT to outline; **—se** (marcarse) to be outlined; (definirse) to become clear

perforación F perforation; (de un pozo) drilling

perforar VT (agujerear) to perforate; (para petróleo) to drill

perfumar VT to perfume, to scent

perfume M perfume, scent

perfumería F perfumery

pergamino M parchment

pérgola F arbor

pericia F expertness

perico M (loro) parakeet; (cocaína) *fam* snow

periferia F periphery, fringe

periférico ADJ & M peripheral

perilla F (adorno, remate) knob; (pelo de barbilla) goatee; **de —** apt

perímetro M perimeter

periódico M newspaper; **— mensual** monthly periodical; ADJ periodic

periodismo M journalism

periodista MF journalist

periodístico ADJ journalistic

período M period (también menstruación); (de materia radiactiva) half-life; **— glaciar** ice age

peripecia F vicissitude

peripuesto ADJ dressed up, dolled up, decked out

periquito M parakeet

periscopio M periscope

perito -ta ADJ expert, practiced; MF technician

peritonitis F peritonitis

perjudicar[6] VT to harm

perjudicial ADJ harmful, detrimental

perjuicio M harm

perjurar VT to swear; VI to commit perjury; **—se** to commit perjury

perjurio M perjury

perla F (de nácar) pearl; (persona) gem; (gota de sudor) bead; (de sabiduría) nugget; (frase desafortunada) blooper; **de —s** perfectly

perlado ADJ pearly

permanecer[13] VI to remain, to stay

permanencia F (carácter de permanente) permanence; (acción de permanecer) stay

permanente ADJ permanent

permeable ADJ permeable

permear VT to permeate

permisible ADJ permissible

permisivo ADJ permissive

permiso M permission; (para faltar al servicio militar) furlough; (para faltar al trabajo) leave; (licencia) license, permit; **con —** excuse me

permitir VT (dar posibilidad moral) to permit, to allow; (dar posibilidad física) to enable; **—se** (una libertad) to take the liberty of; (un lujo) to allow oneself; **¿me permite?** may I cut in?

permuta F exchange

permutación F permutation

permutar VT to exchange

pernetas LOC ADV **en —** barelegged

pernicioso ADJ pernicious

pernicorto ADJ short-legged

perno M bolt, pin

pero CONJ but; ADV **muy — muy lindo** very, very pretty; M objection; **no hay — que valga** no buts about it

perogrullada F platitude

perorar VI to hold forth

perorata F lecture

peróxido M peroxide
perpendicular ADJ perpendicular
perpetrar VT to perpetrate
perpetuar[17] VT to perpetuate
perpetuo ADJ perpetual
perplejidad F perplexity, bewilderment
perplejo ADJ perplexed, bewildered; VT **dejar** — to perplex
perrera F (lugar donde guardar perros) pound; (rabieta) tantrum
perrero -ra MF dogcatcher; ADJ dog-loving
perro M dog; — **caliente** hot dog; — **cobrador** retriever; — **de caza** hunting dog; — **faldero** lapdog; — **callejero** stray dog; — **de lanas** poodle; — **esquimal** husky; — **guía** guide dog; — **guardián** watchdog, guard dog; — **pastor** sheepdog; — **policía** police dog; ADJ miserable; **en la perra vida** never
perruno ADJ canine
persa ADJ & MF Persian; M (lengua) Persian
persecución F (religiosa) persecution; (acción de seguir) pursuit, chase
perseguidor -ora MF (que sigue) pursuer; (que acosa) persecutor
perseguir[5,12] VT (seguir para alcanzar) to pursue, to chase; (seguir para encontrar) to track down; (acosar) to hound; (tratar de destruir) to persecute
perseverancia F perseverance
perseverar VI to persevere
persiana F blind, shade
persistencia F persistence
persistente ADJ persistent
persistir VI to persist
persona F person; — **legal** legal entity; **en** — in person; — **mayor** adult
personaje M (persona importante) personage; (de obra literaria) character; **es todo un** — he's quite a character
personal ADJ personal; M personnel, staff
personalidad F personality
personificar[6] VT to personify, to embody
perspectiva F (punto de vista, distancia, técnica de representación) perspective; (panorama) view, vista; (posibilidad) prospect; **tener en** — to have planned
perspicacia F insight, sharpness
perspicaz ADJ perspicacious, perceptive
persuadir VT to persuade
persuasión F persuasion
persuasivo ADJ persuasive
pertenecer[13] VI to belong
perteneciente ADJ belonging
pertenencias F PL belongings
pértiga F pole
pertinente ADJ pertinent, relevant

pertrechos M PL military supplies
perturbación F disturbance
perturbar VT to perturb, to disturb
Perú M Peru
peruano -na ADJ & MF Peruvian
perversidad F (distorsión) perversity; (maldad) wickedness
perversión F perversion
perverso ADJ (distorsionante) perverse; (malvado) wicked
pervertido -da MF pervert
pervertir[3] VT (hacer vicioso) to pervert; (alterar negativamente) to distort; **—se** to become perverted
pesa F weight; **—s y medidas** weights and measures
pesadez F (cualidad de pesado) heaviness; (tedio) tiresomeness; (persona pesada) tiresome person
pesadilla F nightmare
pesado -da ADJ (que pesa mucho, difícil de digerir) heavy; (aburrido) tiresome; (robusto) heavy-set; (tardo) slow; MF bore, pest
pesadumbre F grief, sorrow
pésame M condolence, expression of sympathy
pesar VT (apenar) to sadden; (medir el peso de) to weigh; (recaer sobre) to weight down; VI (tener peso, importancia) to weigh; M grief, sorrow; LOC ADV **a** — **de** in spite of
pesaroso ADJ (triste) sad; (arrepentido) repentant
pesca F (acción de pescar) fishing; (lo pescado) catch; **ir de** — to go fishing
pescadería F fish market
pescado M fish
pescador -ora MF fisherman
pescar[6] VI/VT (capturar peces) to fish; (sacar del agua, coger, comprender, sorprender, pillar) to catch; (obtener) to land, to nail
pescozón M blow to the back of the head
pescuezo M neck
pesebre M (para pienso) manger, crib; (belén) nativity scene
peseta F peseta
pesimismo M pessimism
pesimista MF pessimist
pésimo ADJ dismal, wretched
peso M (fuerza, importancia) weight; (que oprime moralmente) burden; (cosa pesada) load; **vender al** — to sell by weight; **levantar en** — to lift off the ground
pesquería F fishery
pesquero ADJ fishing; M fishing boat
pesquisa F inquiry

pestaña F (del ojo) eyelash; (en costura) fringe; (de papel) tab; **quemarse las —s** to burn the midnight oil

pestañear VI to blink; **sin —** unflinchingly

pestañeo M blink

peste F (enfermedad) plague; (persona molesta) pest; (hedor) stench; — **bubónica** bubonic plague; — **negra** black death; **hablar —s de alguien** to speak badly of someone

pestilencia F pestilence

pestillo M deadbolt, latch

petaca F (para tabaco) tobacco pouch; (para whisky) flask

pétalo M petal

petardear VI to backfire

petardeo M backfire

petate M bundle; **liar el —** to pack up and go

petición F petition, request

peticionar VT to petition

petirrojo M robin

pétreo ADJ stony

petróleo M petroleum; — **crudo** crude oil

petrolera F oil company

petrolero M oil tanker

petulancia F smugness

petulante ADJ smug

petunia F petunia

peyorativo ADJ pejorative

peyote M peyote

pez M fish; — **dorado** goldfish; — **espada** sword fish; — **gordo** *fam* fat cat, big shot; — **vela** sail fish; — **volador** flying fish; **como — en el agua** perfectly at ease; F pitch

pezón M nipple

pezuña F hoof

piadoso ADJ pious, saintly

piafar VI to stamp

piano M piano; — **de cola** grand piano; — **vertical** upright piano

pianola F player piano

piar[16] VI to peep, to chirp

pica F (lanza) pike; (palo de baraja) spade

picada F (de insecto) bite; (de avión) nosedive; **bajar en —** to dive

picadillo M meat and vegetable hash

picado ADJ (mar) rough, choppy; (carne) chopped; (de viruela) pocked; M (de avión) nosedive

picador M picador; ADJ stinging

picadora F grinder

picadura F (de serpiente) bite; (de insecto) sting, bite

picante ADJ (obsceno) risqué; (especia) spicy, hot; (queso) sharp; M (especia fuerte) strong seasoning; (cualidad) spiciness

picar[6] VI/VT (un pez) to bite; (un ave) to peck; (comer en pequeñas cantidades) to nibble; VT (tomates) to chop up; (carne) to mince; (una vaca) to goad, to poke; (la curiosidad) to pique; (con espuelas) to spur; VI (una comida picante) to sting; (el sol) to burn; (la piel) to itch, to smart; (un avión) to dive; — **alto** to aim high; — **en** to border on; —**se** to spoil; **se pica el mar** the sea is getting rough; **se me picó un diente** I got a cavity; M SG

picapleitos *pey* shyster; **picaporte** latch

picardía F mischief

picaresco ADJ picaresque

pícaro -ra MF rogue, rascal; ADJ roguish, mischievous

picazón F (en la piel) itch; (en la garganta) tickle

picea F spruce

pichi M jumper

pichón M (paloma) pigeon; (cría de ave) chick

picnic M picnic

pico M (de ave) beak, bill; (de montaña) peak; (herramienta) pick; (de tetera) spout; **cuarenta y —** forty-odd; **cerrar el —** to shut one's mouth; **tener el — de oro** to be very eloquent

pícolo M piccolo

picotazo M peck

picotear VI/VT (aves) to peck; (personas) to nibble

pídola F leapfrog

pie M (del cuerpo, de calcetín, de cama, medida) foot; (de foto) caption; (de copa) stem; (de lámpara) stand; (de página) bottom; (para un actor) cue; (de árbol) trunk; (de mueble) leg; — **de atleta** athlete's foot; — **de autor** byline; — **de imprenta** printer's mark; **a —** on foot; **un soldado de —** a foot soldier; — **de banco** silly remark; **a — juntillas** firmly; **al — de la letra** to the letter; **caer de —** to have good luck; **con un — en el estribo** with one foot out of the door; **dar —** (a una crítica) to give rise to; (a un actor) to cue; **de / en —** standing; **en — de guerra** (enojado) on the warpath; (belicoso) on a war footing; **estar de —** to be standing; **estar en — de igualdad con** to be on a par with; **esto no tiene ni —s ni cabeza** I can't make heads or tails of this; **ir a —** to walk; **perder —** to lose one's footing; **ponerse de —** to stand up

piedad F (cualidad de pío) piety;

(misericordia) mercy; **tener —** to show
mercy

piedra F stone; **— angular** cornerstone,
keystone; **— caliza** limestone; **— de
afilar** whetstone; **— de toque**
touchstone; **— pómez** pumice; **—
preciosa** gemstone; **ser — de escándalo**
to be an object of scandal

piel F (humana) skin; (animal) hide, pelt;
(prenda de piel) fur; **— de gallina** goose
bumps; **— de naranja** cellulite

pienso M feed; **ni por —** no way

pierna F leg; **— de ternera** leg of lamb;
dormir a — suelta to sleep like a log

pieza F (de artillería, de tela, de música, de
teatro, mueble) piece; (habitación) room;
de una — astonished; **menuda —** a
piece of work

pífano M fife

pifia F goof, miscue

pifiar VT to goof up, to miscue

pigmento M pigment

pigmeo -a MF pygmy

pijama M pajamas

pila F (recipiente) basin; (bautismal)
baptismal font; (cúmulo) pile, heap, stack;
(generador) battery; **— atómica** atomic
reactor

pilar M pillar

píldora F pill; **—s para dormir** sleeping
pills

pillaje M pillage, plunder

pillar VT (saquear) to pillage, to plunder;
(atrapar, coger) to catch; (en el juego
infantil) to tag

pillo -lla ADJ (travieso) naughty; (taimado)
sly; MF (adulto) scoundrel; (niño) scamp

pilluelo -la MF urchin

pilón M (de fuente) large basin; (de puente)
pylon

pilotar, pilotear VT to pilot, to fly

pilote M pile, stilt

piloto MF pilot; (llama pequeña de gas) pilot
light; **— automático** autopilot; **— de
pruebas** test pilot

pimentar VT to pepper

pimentero M pepper shaker

pimentón M paprika

pimienta F pepper; **— de cayena** red
pepper; **— negra** black pepper

pimiento M pepper, bell pepper; **— verde**
green pepper

pimpollo M (de rosa) rosebud; (de vid) shoot

PIN M PIN

pináculo M pinnacle

pinar M pine grove

pincel M artist's brush

pincelada F stroke; **dar las últimas —s** to
put on the final touches

pinchadura F flat tire

pinchar VT to prick, to puncture; (apuñalar)
to poke; (inyectar) to inject; (intervenir un
teléfono) to wiretap; (provocar) to needle;
VI to have a flat; **ni corta ni pincha** he
doesn't count; M SG **pinchadiscos** disk
jockey, DJ

pinchazo M (acción de pinchar) puncture,
prick; (neumático) flat tire; (puñalada)
stab; (de teléfono) wiretap

pincho M (palo afilado) spike; (de roticería)
spit

pingajo M (harapo) tatter; (persona
harapienta) person dressed in rags

ping-pong M ping-pong

pingüe ADJ abundant

pingüino M penguin

pino M (árbol) pine; (ejercicio) handstand; **en
el quinto —** in the boondocks

pinta F (mancha) dot; (aspecto) looks;
(medida de líquidos) pint

pintar VT (colorear) to paint; (describir) to
depict; **este marcador no pinta** this
marker won't write; **no — nada** to count
for nothing; **las cosas no pintaban
bien** things did not look well; **—se** to put
on makeup

pintarrajear VT to daub, to smear with
paint

pinto ADJ paint, dapple(d)

pintor -ora MF painter; **— de brocha
gorda** house painter

pintoresco ADJ picturesque, colorful

pintorrear VT to smear with paint

pintura F (acción de pintar, obra) painting;
(sustancia) paint; **— al óleo** oil painting;
— en aerosol spray paint; **— fresca** wet
paint

pinza F (de cangrejo) claw; (de vestido) dart;
(instrumento) clothespin; **—s** tweezers

piña F (fruto del pino) pine cone; (ananás)
pineapple; (bomba) hand grenade

piñata F piñata

piñón M (semilla del pino) pine nut; (rueda
del engranaje) pinion; (de bicicleta)
sprocket

pío ADJ pious; INTERJ peep; **ni —** not a word

piojo M louse; **como —s en costura** like
sardines

piojoso ADJ lousy

pionero -ra MF pioneer

pipa F pipe; (semilla) sunflower seed;
pasarlo — to have a great time

pipí M pee; **hacer —** *fam* to pee

pipiolo -la MF novice

pique M (rivalidad) rivalry; (desavenencia) falling-out; **echar a —** to sink; **irse a —** to capsize

piquete M picket

piragua F dugout canoe

pirámide F pyramid

pirata MF INV pirate

piratear VT to pirate

pirómano -na MF pyromaniac

piropo M compliment

pirotecnia F pyrotechnics

pirulí M sucker, lollipop

pisada F (paso) footstep; (huella) footprint; **seguir las —s de** to follow in the footsteps of

pisar VT (oprimir con el pie) to step on, to tread on; (apisonar) to mash; **jamás pisó una plaza de toros** he never set foot in a bullfight; **ir pisando huevos** to walk on eggshells; M SG **pisapapeles** paperweight; VI to step on; **— fuerte** to throw one's weight around

piscifactoría F fishery

piscina F swimming pool

piso M (suelo) floor; (planta) story; (vivienda) apartment; **de — a techo** from the ground up

pisotear VT to tramp on, to trample, to stomp on

pisotón M stamp; **dar un —** to stamp

pista F (rastro) track, scent; (noticia) clue; (de aterrizaje) runway; (de circo) arena, ring; (de patinaje) skating ring; (de tenis) court; (de baile) floor; (de carreras) track, racetrack; **seguir la —** to track; **— para bicicletas** bike lane

pistola F pistol; (para pintura) gun

pistolera F holster

pistolero M gunman

pistón M piston; (explosivo) cap

pitada F drag, puff

pitar VI to toot, to whistle; VI/VT (rechiflar) to boo

pitazo M honk

pitido M whistle, toot

pitillo M cigarette

pito M whistle; **no vale un —** *fam* it is not worth a damn; **entre —s y flautas** when all is said and done; **¿qué —s toca?** what's his role here?

pitón M (serpiente) python; (punta de cuerno) tip of a bull's horn

pituitario ADJ pituitary

pivotar VI to pivot

pivote M pivot; **— central** kingpin

píxel M pixel

pizarra F (roca) slate; (tablero de escuela) blackboard, chalkboard

pizarrón M blackboard, chalkboard

pizca F (de sal) pinch, dash; (de evidencia) shred; (de verdad) grain; (de suciedad) speck; **no entiendo ni —** I don't understand a bit / jot

pizza F pizza

placa F (fotográfica) plate; (de policía) badge; (condecoración, dental) plaque; (de coche) license plate; (de computadora) board, card

placaje M tackle

placar[6] VI/VT to tackle

placebo M placebo

placenta F placenta, afterbirth

placentero ADJ pleasant

placer[37] M pleasure, enjoyment; VT *lit* to please

plácido ADJ placid

plaf INTERJ plop

plaga F plague; (persona, insecto) pest

plagar[7] VT to infest; **—se de** to become infested with

plagio M plagiarism

plan M plan; **— de estudios** curriculum; **se vistió en — de vampiresa** she was dressed to kill

plana F newspaper page; **— mayor** top brass; **enmendar la — a uno** to correct a person's mistakes

plancha F (electrodoméstico) iron; (lámina) metal plate; (parrilla) griddle; **hacer la —** to float; **tirarse una —** to fall flat on one's face

planchado M ironing

planchar VT to iron, to press; **me dejó planchado** it left me speechless

plancton M plankton

planeador M glider

planear VI/VT to plan; VI (volar) to glide, to plane; VT (madera) to plane

planeo M gliding

planeta M planet

planetario M planetarium

planificar[6] VI/VT to plan

planilla F payroll; *Am* **— de cálculo** spreadsheet

plano ADJ flat, even; M (superficie) plane; (de un edificio) plan; (de calles) map; **— inclinado** inclined plane; **caer de —** to fall flat; **de —** flatly; **primer —** foreground

planta F (vegetal) plant; (del pie) sole; **— baja** ground floor

plantación F plantation

plantar VT (una planta, cruz) to plant; (a un novio) to dump; (a un colega) to make

wait; —**se** to stand firm, to refuse to
move; — **a alguien una bofetada** to
give someone a slap; **dejar plantado** to
stand up

plantear VT (presentar) to present; **me
planteó sus planes** she explained her
plans to me; (provocar) to give rise to; **eso
plantea un problema** that gave rise to
a problem; —**se** to occur to; **¿te has
planteado lo que pasa si te quedas
sin trabajo?** have you thought about
what will happen if you become
unemployed?

plantel M (personal) staff; (almáciga) nursery

plantilla F (pieza suelta) insole; (patrón)
pattern, stencil

plantío M grove

plasma M plasma

plasta ADJ INV tiresome; F (cosa informe)
lump; (persona) bore

plástico ADJ & M plastic

plata F (metal, color, objeto de plata) silver;
Am money; **hablar en** — to speak in
plain language

plataforma F platform (también política); —
de lanzamiento launching pad; —
petrolífera oil rig; — **continental**
continental shelf

platanar M banana grove

plátano M (fruta) banana; (bananero) banana
tree; (árbol ornamental) plane tree

platea F main floor of a theatre

plateado ADJ & M (color) silver; M (acción de
platear) silver-plating

platear VT to silver-plate

platero -ra MF silversmith

plática F chat

platicar[6] VI to chat

platija F flounder

platillo M (plato pequeño) saucer;
(instrumento musical) cymbal; —
volador flying saucer

platino M platinum

plato M (recipiente) plate; (comida) dish; —
fuerte main dish/course; — **hondo**
bowl; — **sopero** soup dish

plausible ADJ plausible

playa F beach

playboy M playboy

plaza F (espacio amplio) plaza, public square;
(puesto de trabajo) job; **de cuatro** —**s**
four-seater; — **de toros** bullring; —
mayor main square

plazo M term; **a corto** — short-term; **a
largo** — long-term; **a** — **fijo** fixed-term;
a —**s** on credit; **cumplir un** — to meet a
deadline

plazoleta F court

plazuela F court

pleamar M high tide

plebe F rabble

plebeyo -ya ADJ & MF plebeian

plegable ADJ folding

plegadera F paper folder

plegadizo ADJ folding

plegar[1,7] VT to fold; —**se (a)** to yield (to)

pleitesía F compliance

pleito M dispute; (judicial) litigation, lawsuit;
poner — to sue

plenario ADJ & M plenary

plenitud F — **de la vida** prime of life

pleno ADJ complete; **en** — **día** in broad
daylight; **en** — **invierno** in the dead of
winter; **en** — **rostro** right on the face; **en**
— **verano** in midsummer; **en plena
vista** in plain sight; M full session

pliego M leaflet

pliegue M (en papel) fold; (en tela) pleat

plomada F plumb

plomería F plumbing

plomero -ra MF plumber

plomizo ADJ leaden

plomo M (metal, color) lead; (pesos) lead
weight; (perdigón) shot; **a** — plumb; **caer
a** — to fall vertically; **sin** — unleaded; ADJ
tiresome

pluma F (de ave) feather, quill; (para escribir)
pen; — **fuente** fountain pen

plumaje M plumage

plumero M dust mop, duster

plumífero ADJ feathery

plumón M down

plural ADJ & M plural

pluralidad F plurality

pluscuamperfecto ADJ & N pluperfect

plutonio M plutonium

pluvial ADJ **aguas** —**es** rain water

pluviómetro M rain gauge

PNB (producto nacional bruto) M GNP

población F (conjunto de personas)
population; (acción de poblar) settlement;
(pueblo) town

poblado M hamlet

poblador -ora MF settler

poblar[2] VT (habitar) to populate; (colonizar)
to settle; —**se** to become covered with

pobre ADJ poor; MF **los** —**s** the poor

pobrecito -ta MF poor thing

pobreza F poverty; (escasez) scarcity

pocilga F pigsty, pigpen

pocillo M cup

poción F potion

poco ADJ (no mucho) little; **poca paciencia**
little patience; **al** — **rato** after a little

while; (no muchos) few; **—s pasajeros**
few passengers; **al — tiempo** shortly; **a
los —s meses** after a few months; **como
—** at least; **de pocas luces** stupid; **en
pocas palabras** in a nutshell; ADV
trabaja — he works little; **— caritativo**
not very charitable; **— a —** little by little;
— más o menos about; **hace —** a short
while ago; **por — me caigo** I almost fell;
tener en — to hold in low esteem; M a
little, a bit; **un —** a little bit, a little while;
unos —s a few

poda F trim

podadera F pruning hook

podar VT to prune, to trim

poder[38] VI to be able to; **no puedo llegar
antes de las cinco** I can't get there
before five; **¿puedo sentarme?** may I be
seated? **puede que venga** she may come;
a más no — to the utmost; **no puedo
más** I can't go on; **nadie puede con
ella** nobody can deal with her; **no puede
menos que venir** he can't help but
come; **no puede menos de hacerlo** he
cannot help doing it; M (fuerza) power;
(escrito que da autoridad) proxy, power of
attorney; **— judicial** the judiciary
branch; **por —** by proxy

poderío M power, might

poderoso ADJ powerful, mighty

podio M podium

podredumbre F rot

podrido ADJ rotten

podrir ver pudrir

poema M poem

poesía F poetry; (poema) poem

poeta -tisa MF poet

poética F poetics

poético ADJ poetic

polaco -ca ADJ Polish; M (lengua) Polish; MF
Pole

polaina F legging

polar ADJ polar

polaridad F polarity

polarización F polarization

polca F polka

polea F pulley

polémica F polemic, controversy

polémico ADJ polemic

polen M pollen

poli MF cop; F cops

policía F (en conjunto) police; (mujer)
policewoman; M policeman

policíaco ADJ police

poliéster M polyester

poliestireno M Styrofoam[tm]

poligamia F polygamy

políglota ADJ & MF INV polyglot

polígrafo M polygraph

poliinsaturado ADJ polyunsaturated

polilla F moth

polímero M polymer

polinizar[9] VT to pollinate

polio F polio

pólipo M polyp

política F (actividad relativa al gobierno)
politics; (conjunto de orientaciones)
policy; **— exterior** foreign policy

político -ca ADJ (relativo a la política)
political; (diplomático) politic; MF
politician

poliuretano M polyurethane

póliza F policy; **— de seguros** insurance
policy

polizón -ona MF stowaway

polizonte M *pey* cop

polla F pullet

pollada F brood

pollera F woman who raises and sells
chickens; *Am* skirt

pollo M (cría de ave) young chicken; (carne)
chicken

polo M (extremo) pole; (juego) polo; **—
acuático** water polo; **— de atención**
focus of attention; **— Norte** North Pole

Polonia F Poland

poltrona F easy chair

polvareda F cloud of dust; **levantar una —**
(causar escándalo) to raise a ruckus;
(causar una nube de polvo) to kick up the
dust

polvera F compact

polvo M (suciedad) dust; (partículas) powder;
— de hornear baking powder; **juntar —**
to gather dust; **limpio de — y paja** net

pólvora F gunpowder

polvoriento ADJ dusty

polvorín M (almacén de pólvora) magazine;
(situación explosiva) powder keg

pomada F salve

pomelo M grapefruit

pómez M pumice

pomo M doorknob

pompa F (boato) pomp; (burbuja) soap
bubble; **—s fúnebres** funeral

pomposo ADJ pompous

pómulo M cheekbone

ponche M punch

ponchera F punch bowl

poncho M poncho

ponderación F (acción de ponderar)
pondering; (valor relativo) weighting

ponderar VT (considerar) to ponder, to
consider; (exagerar) to exaggerate; (ajustar

estadísticas) to weight
ponencia F presentation
poner[39] VT to put, to place; (la mesa, un
reloj) to set; (huevos) to lay; (azúcar) to
add; (un examen) to give; (el televisor) to
turn on; (un pleito) to file; — **a alguien
a hacer algo** to have someone do
something; — **en claro** to clarify; — **en
limpio** to recopy, to make a clean copy;
— **nombre a un niño** to name a child;
cada uno pone mil pesetas each
person contributes a thousand pesetas;
pongamos que let us suppose that; —**se**
(volverse) to become; (el sol) to set; (ropa)
to put on; —**se a** to begin to; —**se al
corriente** to become informed; —**se de
acuerdo** to come to an agreement; —**se
de pie** to stand up
póney M pony
poniente M (oeste) west; (viento del oeste)
west wind
pontón M pontoon
ponzoña F poison
ponzoñoso ADJ poisonous
pool M pool
popa F poop, stern
populacho M mob
popular ADJ (conocido y citado) popular;
(del pueblo) folk
popularidad F popularity
populoso ADJ populous
popurrí M potpourri; (musical) medley
por PREP — **barco** by boat; — **casualidad**
by chance; — **Dios** by God; — **etapas** by
stages; — **las buenas o** — **las malas** by
hook or by crook; — **litro** by the liter;
multiplicar — to multiply by; **lo
agarró por la mano** he grabbed him by
the throat; **mi amor** — **ella** my love for
her; — **poco tiempo** for a short time; —
primera vez for the first time; — **vía de
argumento** for the sake of argument; —
ejemplo for instance; — **el momento**
for the time being; **hazlo** — **mí** do it for
my sake; **trabaja** — **mí** work on my
behalf; **no me gustan** — **su olor** I don't
like them because of their smell; **lo supe
— él** I found out through him; **pasé** —
Londres I passed through London; **un
viaje** — **la costa** a trip along the coast;
— **lo que cuentas** from what you're
telling me; — **adelantado** in advance; —
escrito in writing; — **la mañana** in the
morning; — **lo general** in general; —
rachas in spurts; **está** — **Badajoz** it's
near Badajoz; — **fin** at last; — **el mes de
marzo** around the month of March; —

ciento percent; — **consiguiente**
consequently; — **escrito** in writing; —
poco se muere he almost died; **está** —
hacer it is yet to be done; **él está** —
hacerlo he is in favor of doing it;
recibir — **esposa** to take as a wife;
tener — to consider, to think of as; **¿—
qué?** why? for what reason?
porcelana F porcelain, china
porcentaje M percentage
porche M porch, stoop
porcino ADJ **ganado** — swine; M pig
porción F (parte) portion, share; (de
alimento) helping
pordiosear VT to panhandle
pordiosero -ra MF panhandler
porfía F obstinacy
porfiado ADJ willful
porfiar[16] VT to insist
pormenor M detail
pormenorizar[9] VT to detail, to go into
detail about
pornografía F pornography
pornográfico ADJ pornographic
poro M pore
poroso ADJ porous
poroto M *Am* bean
porque CONJ because
porqué M why
porquería F (suciedad) filth; (acción
despreciable) dirty trick; (cosa de mala
calidad) crud; (comida de mala calidad)
junk food; (persona despreciable) *pey*
dirtbag
porra F club, cudgel
porrista MF cheerleader
portada F title page
portador -ora MF (de enfermedad) carrier;
(de cheque) bearer; — **del féretro**
pallbearer
portal M portal, doorway
portar VT to carry; —**se** to behave; —**se mal**
to misbehave; M SG **portaaviones** aircraft
carrier; **portaequipajes** luggage bin;
portaestandarte standard-bearer;
portafolio briefcase; **portalámparas**
socket; **portaligas** garter belt;
portamonedas coin purse; **portaobjeto**
slide
portátil ADJ portable
portavoz MF spokesperson
portazo M slam; **dar un** — to slam the door
porte M (envío) freight; (por correo) postage;
(aspecto) bearing, carriage; (capacidad de
carga) capacity; (tamaño) size; — **de
armas** the carrying of arms; **enviar** —
pagado to send prepaid

portear VT to carry
portentoso ADJ portentous
portería F (de un edificio) entrance area; (en fútbol) goal
portero -ra MF (de un edificio) doorkeeper, superintendent; (en fútbol) goalkeeper; M — **automático** intercom
portón M gate
Portugal M Portugal
portugués -esa ADJ & MF Portuguese; M (lengua) Portuguese
porvenir M future
pos LOC PREP **en — de** after
posada F inn, lodge
posaderas F PL *fam* rear end
posadero -ra MF innkeeper
posar VT (la mano, los ojos) to rest; VI (en el suelo) to sit down; (como modelo) to pose; **—se** (partículas) to settle; (mariposa) to alight; (pájaro) to perch
posdata F postscript
pose F pose
poseedor -ora MF possessor
poseer[14] VT to possess
posesión F possession
posesivo ADJ & M possessive
posibilidad F possibility
posible ADJ possible; **hacer lo —** to do one's best; **es —** it's possible
posición F position; (opinión) stance; (rango) standing; **— fetal** fetal position
positivo ADJ & M positive
poso M dregs; (de café) grounds
posponer[39] VT (aplazar) to postpone, to defer, to put off; (relegar) to put after
posta F (relevo) relay; (perdigón) buckshot
postal ADJ postal; F (tarjeta) postcard
poste M post; (de portería) upright
póster M poster
postergar[7] VT to neglect
posteridad F posterity
posterior ADJ (en el espacio) back, rear; (anatómico) posterior; (temporal) later; **nuestro divorcio fue posterior a nuestra boda** our divorce came after our wedding
postigo M shutter
postizo ADJ false; **familia postiza** adoptive family; M hairpiece
postrado ADJ prostrate, prone
postrar VT to prostrate
postre M dessert; **a la —** at last
postulado M postulate
postulante MF candidate
postular VT to postulate
póstumo ADJ posthumous
postura F posture (también opinión)

potable ADJ drinkable, potable
potasio M potassium
pote M (cilíndrico) jar; (panzudo) jug
potencia F (sexual) potency; (de una fuerza, nación) power; **es un asesino en —** he's a potential murderer; **— naval** sea power; **de alta —** high-powered; **segunda —** the second power
potencial ADJ & M potential
potentado -da MF potentate
potente ADJ potent, powerful
potranco -ca M colt; F filly
potrero M pasture; *Am* cattle ranch, stock farm
potro M (caballo) colt; (en gimnasia) vaulting horse; **— de tormento** rack
pozo M (de agua, petróleo) well; (hoyo profundo) pit; (minero) mine shaft; **sacar del —** to rescue; **— negro** sink; **— sin fondo** bottomless pit; **— séptico** septic tank
práctica F (repetición, costumbre) practice; (destreza) skill; **en la —** in practice; **poner en —** to put into practice
practicante ADJ practicing; MF (que practica) practitioner; (asistente de médico) physician's assistant
practicar[6] VI/VT to practice; (un agujero) to make
práctico ADJ practical; (adiestrado) skillful; M **— de puerto** harbor pilot
pradera F prairie, grassland
prado M meadow, pasture
pragmático ADJ pragmatic
preadolescente ADJ & MF preteen, preadolescent
preámbulo M preamble
precalentamiento M warmup
precario ADJ precarious
precaución F precaution
precaverse VT to take precautions
precavido ADJ cautious
precedencia F precedence
precedente ADJ preceding; M precedent; **sin —** unprecedented; **sentar —** to set a precedent
preceder VI/VT to precede
precepto M precept
preciado ADJ (estimado) prized; (valioso) valuable
preciarse VI **— de** to be proud of
precintar VT to seal
precinto M seal
precio M price; **poner — a** to put a price on; **no tener —** to be priceless; **— de lista** list price; **— de mercado** market price
preciosista ADJ precious

precioso ADJ (de gran valor, metal, piedra) precious; (muy bonito) beautiful, adorable
precipicio M precipice, cliff
precipitación F precipitation (también atolondramiento)
precipitado ADJ precipitate, hasty, rash; M precipitate
precipitar VI to precipitate; VT to hurl; **—se** (apresurarse) to be hasty; (arrojarse) to plunge, to plummet; (depositarse) to precipitate; (adelantarse) to come to a head
precisar VT (determinar) to determine precisely; (necesitar) to need
precisión F precision, accuracy; **precisiones** clarifications
preciso ADJ precise, accurate; **es — que vengas** you must come; **en este — instante** at this very moment
precoz ADJ (niño) precocious; (diagnóstico) early
precursor -ora MF precursor, forerunner
predecesor -ora MF predecessor
predecir[26b] VT to predict, to foretell
predestinar VT to predestine
predicación F preaching
predicado ADJ & M predicate
predicador -ora MF preacher
predicar[6] VI/VT to preach
predicción F prediction
predilección F predilection
predilecto ADJ favorite, pet
predisponer[39] VT to predispose
predominante ADJ predominant, prevailing
predominar VI to predominate
predominio M predominance
preeminente ADJ foremost
preescolar ADJ nursery; MF nursery school child
preestreno M preview
prefacio M preface
preferencia F preference; (en el tráfico) right of way; **de —** predominately
preferente ADJ preferential; (acciones) preferred
preferible ADJ preferable
preferido ADJ preferred, favorite
preferir[3] VT to prefer
prefijar VT to prefix
prefijo M prefix
pregonar VT (noticias) to make public; (mercancías) to hawk
pregunta F question; **hacer una —** to ask a question
preguntar VI/VT to ask, to inquire; **— por** (pedir información) to inquire about; (pedir para hablar) to ask for; **—se** to

wonder
preguntón ADJ inquisitive
prehistórico ADJ prehistoric
prejuicio M prejudice, bias
prejuzgar[7] VT to prejudge
preliminar ADJ & M preliminary
preludiar VT to prelude
preludio M prelude
prematrimonial ADJ premarital
prematuro ADJ premature; (muerte) untimely
premeditado ADJ premeditated
premiar VT to reward; **las obras premiadas** the award-winning works
première M premiere
premio M (galardón) prize, award; (de la moneda) appreciation; **Juan Pérez, — nacional de poesía** Juan Pérez, winner of the national poetry award; **— gordo** jackpot
premisa F premise
premonición F premonition
prenatal ADJ prenatal
prenda F (fianza) pawn, pledge; (de vestir) article of clothing, garment; **dejar en —** to pawn; **en — de** as a token of
prendar VT to charm; **—se de** to fall in love with
prendedor M brooch, pin
prender VT (agarrar) to grab; (sujetar) to clasp; (enganchar) to fasten; (detener) to arrest; (arraigar) to take root; (encender) to turn on, to switch on; **— fuego** to set on fire; **la vacuna no prendió** the vaccination didn't take
prensa F press; **tener mala —** to have bad press
prensar VT to press
prensil ADJ prehensile
prenupcial ADJ prenuptial
preñada ADJ pregnant
preñez F pregnancy
preocupación F worry, concern
preocupado ADJ worried, concerned, anxious
preocupante ADJ worrisome
preocupar VT to worry, to concern; **—se de** to worry about; **—se por** to be concerned about
preocupón -ona MF worrywart
preparación F preparation
preparado ADJ ready; M preparation
preparar VT to prepare; **—se** to get ready, to brace oneself
preparativo ADJ preparatory; M preparation
preparatorio ADJ preparatory
preponderancia F preponderance
preponderante ADJ preponderant

preponderar VI to predominate
preposición F preposition
prepucio M foreskin
prerequisito M prerequisite
prerrogativa F prerogative
presa F (animal de caza) prey, quarry; (dique) dam
presagiar VT to forebode
presagio M omen, sign
présbita ADV & MF INV farsighted
prescindible ADJ dispensable
prescindir VI — **de** to dispense with
prescribir[S1] VT to prescribe
prescripción F prescription
presencia F presence; — **de ánimo** presence of mind
presenciar VT to witness
presentable ADJ presentable
presentación F presentation; (a una persona) introduction
presentador -ora MF (de televisión) host; (de noticiero) anchor
presentar VT to present; (a una persona) to introduce; (la declaración de impuestos, una demanda) to file; (un informe) to submit; (documentos) to produce; (una queja) to lodge; (una renuncia) to tender; —**se** (aparecer) to appear; (hacerse conocer) to introduce oneself
presente ADJ present; M (tiempo) present; (regalo) present, gift; **al** — at the present time; **tener** — to bear in mind; **en el** — **(contrato)** herein; **por la** — **(carta)** hereby
presentimiento M presentiment, foreboding, hunch
presentir[3] VT to have a presentiment of
preservación F (protección) preservation; (ahorro) conservation
preservar VT (proteger) to preserve; (ahorrar) to conserve
presidencia F presidency
presidencial ADJ presidential
presidente -ta MF (de un país) president; (de una reunión, junta) chair
presidiario -ria MF prisoner
presidio M prison
presidir VI to preside; VT to preside over
presilla F loop
presión F pressure; — **atmosférica** atmospheric pressure; — **arterial** blood pressure; — **de aire** air pressure
presionar VT (un botón) to press; (al gobierno) to lobby
preso -sa MF prisoner, inmate
prestación F provision; **prestaciones** benefits

prestador -ora MF lender
prestamista MF lender; (en un montepío) pawnbroker
préstamo M loan
prestar VT to loan, to lend; — **ayuda** to give help; — **atención** to pay attention; — **juramento** to take an oath; — **servicio** to render service
prestatario -ria MF borrower
prestidigitación F sleight of hand
prestigio M prestige
prestigioso ADJ prestigious
presumido ADJ conceited, presumptuous
presumir VT (suponer) to presume; VI (ostentar) to show off; — **de valiente** to boast of one's valor
presunción F presumption
presunto ADJ (autor) presumed; (asesino) alleged; — **heredero** heir apparent
presuntuoso ADJ presumptuous
presuponer[39] VT to presuppose
presupuesto M (de gastos e ingresos) budget; (de costo) estimate
presuroso ADJ hasty
pretencioso ADJ pretentious
pretender VI (sostener) to claim, to purport; — **ser** to claim to be; — **al trono** to pretend to the throne; VT (intentar) to attempt
pretendiente -ta MF (al trono) pretender; (a un puesto) aspirant; M (de una mujer) suitor, admirer
pretensión F pretension
pretérito ADJ past; M past tense; — **perfecto** present perfect
pretexto M pretext, pretense; **so** — **de** under pretense of
pretil M railing
pretina F waistband
prevalecer[13] VI to prevail
prevaleciente ADJ prevalent
prevención F (protección) prevention; (recelo) caution
prevenido ADJ forewarned
prevenir[47] VT (precaver) to prevent; (prever) to foresee; (advertir) to warn; — **contra** to protect oneself against
preventivo ADJ preventive
prever[48] VT to foresee, to anticipate
previo ADJ previous, prior; — **examen de salud** after undergoing a health examination
previsión F foresight, anticipation
prieto ADJ swarthy
prima F (cuota de seguro) premium; (recargo) surcharge; (pago extraordinario) bonus
primario ADJ primary

primate M primate
primavera F spring
primaveral ADJ springlike
primero ADJ & ADV first; **primer ministro** prime minister; **— piso** second floor; **primer plano** foreground; **primera enseñanza** primary education; **primera persona** first person; **—s auxilios** first aid; **a primera vista** at first sight; **de — grado** first degree; **de primera** top-notch; **de primera mano** firsthand; **por primera vez** for the first time; **— del mes** first of the month; F (marcha) first gear; (clase) first-class
primicia F (fruto primero) first fruit; (noticia) scoop
primitivo ADJ primitive
primo -ma MF (hijo de tío) cousin; (persona incauta) sucker, dupe; **— hermano** first cousin; **— segundo** second cousin; ADJ prime
primogénito -ta ADJ & MF firstborn
primogenitura F birthright
primor M (esmero) care; (cosa fina) lovely thing
primordial ADJ primordial
primoroso ADJ exquisite
princesa F princess
principal ADJ principal, main; **la causa — de muerte** the leading cause of death; **el dormitorio —** the master bedroom
príncipe M prince
principesco ADJ princely
principiante MF beginner; ADJ beginning
principiar VT to commence
principio M (fundamento, regla de conducta) principle, tenet; (hecho de empezar, tiempo, lugar) beginning, start; **a —s de** towards the beginning of; **— activo** active ingredient; **al —** at the beginning, at first; **de — a fin** from beginning to end; **desde el —** from the beginning; **en —** in principle
pringar[7] VT (ensuciar) to get greasy; (mojar) to dip
pringoso ADJ greasy
pringue MF grease
prioridad F (autoridad, preferencia) priority, precedence; (en el tráfico) right of way
prisa F haste, hurry; **a toda —** at full speed; **correr —** to be urgent; **darse —** to hurry; **las —s comienzan a la una** the rush starts at one; **tener —** to be in a hurry; **sin —** leisurely
prisión F prison; **— perpetua** life in prison
prisionero -ra MF prisoner; **— de guerra** prisoner of war

prisma M prism
prismáticos M PL binoculars
privacidad F privacy
privación F privation; **pasar privaciones** to suffer want
privado ADJ private; **en —** in private
privar VT to deprive; **—se de** to deprive oneself of
privativo ADJ exclusive
privilegiado ADJ privileged
privilegiar VT to favor, to give a privilege to
privilegio M privilege
pro M advantage; **en — de** in favor of; **en — y en contra** for and against
proa F prow, bow
proaborto ADJ pro-choice
probabilidad F probability; **tienes pocas —es de ganar** you have little chance of winning; **¿qué —es tiene?** what are her odds?
probable ADJ probable, likely
probador M dressing room
probar[2] VT (alimento, bebida) to taste, to try, to sample; (una hipótesis) to prove; (una guitarra) to try out; (un coche) to test-drive; **—se un vestido** to try on a dress; **prueba a venir más temprano** try to come earlier; **no — bocado** not to eat a bite; **— fortuna** to try one's luck
probeta F test tube
problema M problem; **él sólo da —s** he's nothing but trouble
problemático ADJ problematic
procedente ADJ **— de** from
proceder VI to proceed; **— de** to come from; **— a** to proceed to; **— contra** to take action against
procedimiento M procedure; **—s** proceedings
procesado -da MF accused; M processing
procesamiento M prosecution; **— de datos** data processing; **— de textos** word processing
procesar VT to prosecute, to try
procesión F procession; **la — va por dentro** he doesn't let it show
proceso M (conjunto de fases) process; (juicio) trial, legal proceedings
proclama F proclamation
proclamación F proclamation
proclamar VT to proclaim; **—se campeón** to be proclaimed winner
proclive ADJ prone
procrear VI/VT to procreate
procurador -ora MF attorney
procurar VT (intentar) to endeavor; (obtener) to procure, to obtain

prodigar[7] VT to lavish; **—se** to be lavish
prodigio M prodigy
prodigioso ADJ prodigious
pródigo -ga ADJ (derrochador) prodigal; (muy generoso) lavish; MF spendthrift
producción F (acción de producir) production; (cantidad producida) production, yield; **— masiva** mass production
producir[24] VT (efectos, mercancías, películas) to produce; (fruta, resultados) to yield, to bear; **—se** to happen
productivo ADJ productive
producto M product; **— interno bruto** gross national product
productor -ora MF producer; ADJ **un país — de petróleo** an oil-producing country
proeza F exploit
profanación F desecration
profanar VT to profane, to desecrate
profano ADJ profane
profecía F prophecy
proferir[3] VT to utter
profesar VT to profess
profesión F profession
profesional ADJ & MF professional
profesionista MF *Méx* professional
profesor -ora MF (universitario) professor; (de enseñanza secundaria) teacher; (de tenis, perros) instructor
profesorado M faculty
profeta MF INV prophet
profético ADJ prophetic
profetizar[9] VI/VT to prophesy
profilaxis F prevention
prófugo -ga ADJ & MF fugitive
profundidad F (del mar, de comprensión, de un armario) depth; (sabiduría) profundity
profundizar[9] VT to deepen; VI to do into deeply
profundo ADJ (trascendente) profound; (mar, pozo, armario, voz) deep
profuso ADJ profuse
progesterona F progesterone
programa M (de boxeo) card; (de televisión) show, program; (de un curso) syllabus
programación F programming
programador -ora MF programmer
programar VT (una computadora) to program; (un evento) to schedule
progresar VT to progress, to advance
progresista ADJ & MF progressive
progresivo -va ADJ & MF progressive
progreso M progress
prohibición F prohibition, ban
prohibido ADJ forbidden; **prohibida la entrada** no admittance

prohibir VT to prohibit, to ban; **se prohibe fumar** no smoking
prohijar VT to adopt
prójimo -ma MF fellow human
prole F offspring
proletariado M proletariat
proletario -ria ADJ & MF proletarian
proliferación F spread
prolífico ADJ prolific
prolijo ADJ (verboso) wordy; (esmerado) overly careful
prologar[7] VT to preface
prólogo M prologue, foreword, preface
prolongación F prolongation
prolongado ADJ extended
prolongar[7] VT to prolong; **—se** to wear on
promediar VT to average
promedio M average, mean; **de / en —** on average
promesa F promise; **romper una —** to break a promise; **un joven —** a promising young player
prometedor ADJ promising
prometer VT to promise; VI to show promise; **—se** to trust that
prometido -da ADJ engaged; M fiancé; F fiancée
prominente ADJ prominent
promiscuo ADJ promiscuous
promisorio ADJ promissory
promoción F promotion; (conjunto de personas) class
promocionar VT to promote
promontorio M promontory
promotor -ora MF promoter
promover[2] VT (ideas, producto, a un alumno) to promote; (mutua comprensión, una causa) to foster, to further
promulgación F enactment
promulgar[7] VT to promulgate, to enact
pronombre M pronoun
pronominal ADJ pronominal
pronosticar[6] VT to forecast
pronóstico M (del tiempo, de la economía) forecast; (de una enfermedad) prognosis
pronto ADJ (rápido) quick; (listo) ready; ADV soon, promptly; **de —** suddenly; **¡hasta —!** see you soon! **tan — como** as soon as
pronunciación F pronunciation
pronunciado ADJ pronounced
pronunciar VT (un sonido, una sentencia) to pronounce; (un discurso) to make, to deliver; **—se** (acusarse) to be pronounced; (expresarse) to declare one's opinion
propagación F propagation, spread
propaganda F (de ideas) propaganda; (de

mercancías) advertising, publicity; **hacer**
— to advertise
propagar[7] VT to propagate
propalar VT to spread
propano M propane
propasarse VI to go too far
propensión F propensity
propenso ADJ prone
propiciar VT to favor
propicio ADJ propitious, auspicious
propiedad F (cualidad, pertenencia, finca)
property; (derecho de dueño) ownership;
(corrección) precision; **—es** estate
propietario -ria M (de una tienda)
proprietor, owner; (de un apartamento)
landlord; F (de una tienda) owner; (de un
apartamento) landlady
propina F tip, gratuity; **dar (una)** — to tip
propinar VT — **una paliza** to give a
beating
propio ADJ (correcto) proper; **el significado**
— the proper meaning; (típico) like; **no es
— de él quejarse así** it's not like him to
complain like that; (conveniente)
appropriate; **una expresión propia** an
appropriate expression; (que le pertenece)
own; **su — hijo** his own son; **un hijo —**
a son of his own; **por tu — bien** for your
own good; (mismo) same; **al — tiempo**
at the same time
proponente MF proponent
proponer[39] VT to propose; **—se** to set out to
proporción F proportion, ratio;
proporciones dimensions
proporcionar VT (ajustar a proporción) to
proportion; (brindar) to furnish, to
provide
proposición F proposition; (de matrimonio)
proposal; **proposiciones deshonestas**
indecent proposals
propósito M purpose, intent; **a —** (adecuado)
apropos; (voluntariamente) on purpose,
intentionally; (además) by the way,
incidentally; **a — de** apropos of
propuesta F proposal
propugnar VT to urge
propulsar VT to propel
propulsión F propulsion; **— a chorro** jet
propulsion
propulsor -ora ADJ propelling; MF promoter
prorratear VT to prorate
prórroga F (plazo) extension of time; (de un
préstamo) renewal; (de un encuentro
deportivo) overtime
prorrogar[7] VT (un pago) to put off, to defer;
(un tiempo) to extend; (un préstamo) to
renew

prorrumpir VI to burst; **— en llanto** to
burst into tears; **— en carcajadas** to
burst out laughing
prosa F prose
prosaico ADJ prosaic
proscribir[51] VT to banish, to disenfranchise
proscripción F banishment
proseguir[5,12] VI to proceed
prosódico ADJ prosodic
prospectar VT to prospect
prospector -ora MF prospector
prosperar VI to prosper, to flourish, to thrive
prosperidad F prosperity
próspero ADJ prosperous
próstata F prostate (gland)
prostituir[31] VT to prostitute
prostituta F prostitute
protagonista MF protagonist
protagonizar[9] VT to star in
protección F protection
proteccionista ADJ & MF protectionist
protector -ora ADJ protective; MF protector;
— de tensión surge protector; **— solar**
sunblock
protectorado M protectorate
proteger[11b] VT to protect; (a un artista) to
sponsor
protegido -da MF protégé(e)
proteína F protein
prótesis F prosthesis
protesta F protest
protestante MF Protestant
protestar VI/VT to protest
protocolo M protocol
protón M proton
protoplasma M protoplasm
prototipo M prototype
protozoario M protozoan
protuberancia F protuberance, bulge, bump
protuberante ADJ bulging
provecho M (beneficio) benefit; (eructo)
burp; **¡buen —!** bon appétit! **sacar —
(de)** to benefit (from), to profit (from)
provechoso ADJ beneficial, advantageous
proveedor -ora MF provider
proveer[14,51] VT to provide; **— de** to provide
with; **—se de** to provide oneself with
provenir[47] VI to arise; **— de** to stem from
proverbio M proverb
providencia F providence
providencial ADJ providential
provincia F province
provincial ADJ provincial
provinciano -na ADJ & MF provincial
provisión F provision, supply, store
provisional ADJ temporary, provisional
provisorio ADJ temporary

provocación F provocation

provocar[6] VT (ira) to provoke; (sexualmente) to excite; (un incendio) to start; (una respuesta) to elicit

provocativo ADJ provocative

proximidad F proximity, nearness; **en las —es** in the vicinity

próximo ADJ (después) next; (cercano) near, nearby; **el lunes — pasado** last Monday; **de próxima aparición** forthcoming

proyección F projection

proyectar VT (ira) to project; (una película) to screen; (una sombra) to cast; **—se** to overhang, to jut

proyectil M projectile

proyecto M project; (arquitectónico) plan; **— de ley** bill

proyector M (para películas) projector; (en el teatro) spotlight

prudencia F prudence

prudente ADJ prudent

prueba F (de imprenta, argumento irrefutable) proof; (argumento parcial) evidence; (intento, dificultad) trial, test; (examen) examination; (de ropa) fitting; **a — de incendio** fireproof; **— de fuego** trial by fire; **poner — a** to put to the test

psicodélico ADJ & M psychedelic

psicología F psychology

psicológico ADJ psychological

psicólogo -ga MF psychologist

psicópata MF INV psychopath

psicosis F psychosis

psicosomático ADJ psychosomatic

psicoterapia F psychotherapy

psicótico ADJ psychotic

psiquiatra MF INV psychiatrist

psiquiatría F psychiatry

psíquico ADJ psychic

psoriasis F psoriasis

púa F (con punta aguda) spike; (de alambre) barb; (de guitarra) pick; (de erizo) quill; (de horca) prong

puaf, puaj INTERJ yuck, ugh

pubertad F puberty

publicación F publication

publicar[6] VT to publish; (revelar) to divulge

publicidad F publicity, advertising; **hacer —** to advertise

público ADJ public; M (la gente) public; (en un espectáculo) audience; **en —** in public

puchero M (vasija) pot; (gesto) pout; **hacer —s** to pout

puck M puck

pudiente ADJ wealthy

pudor M (sexual) modesty; (reserva) reserve

pudrir[5] VI to rot

pueblerino ADJ provincial

pueblo M (población) town; (nación) people, folk

puente M bridge (también dental, de gafas, de nariz); (fin de semana) long weekend; **— aéreo** (regular) shuttle; (de emergencia) airlift; **— colgante** suspension bridge; **— levadizo** drawbridge

puénting M bungee jumping

pueril ADJ childish

puerta F door; (de aeropuerto, de ciudad) gate; (medio de acceso) entrance; **vender de — en —** to sell door-to-door; **dar a alguien con la — en las narices** to slam the door in someone's face; **llamar a la —** to knock on the door; **— trasera** back door; **a — cerrada** behind closed doors

puerto M port (también en informática); **llegar a buen —** to bring to a satisfactory conclusion

puertorriqueño -ña ADJ & MF Puerto Rican

pues CONJ (puesto que) since, for; ADV (entonces) then; **— bien** well then, now

puesta F **— al día** update; **— del sol** sunset, setting of the sun; **— en marcha** (de un proyecto) setting in motion; (de un coche) starting; **— en libertad** freeing

puestero -ra MF vendor, seller

puesto ADJ **bien —** (casa) well-appointed; (persona) well made-up; **llevar —** to have on; M (posición) place; (de venta) booth, stand; (de trabajo) post, position; **— de socorros** first-aid station; **quedarse con lo —** to be left with only the clothes on one's back; CONJ **— que** since

pugilato M fight

pugilista M boxer, prizefighter

pugna F struggle; **estar en — con** to be in conflict with

pugnaz ADJ feisty

puja F (del viento) push; (en una subasta) bid

pujanza F vigor

pujar VI (para dar a luz) to push; (en una subasta) to bid; **— por** to strive to

pujo M contraction

pulcritud F neatness

pulcro ADJ neat

pulga F flea; **tener malas —s** to be ill-tempered

pulgada F inch

pulgar M thumb

pulido ADJ polished; M polishing

pulimento M (de modales) refinement; (de metales) buffing; (sustancia) scouring powder

pulir VT (metal, oración) to polish; (madera)

to sand
pulla F taunt, dig
pulmón M lung; — **de acero** iron lung
pulmonar ADJ **capacidad** — lung capacity
pulmonía F pneumonia
pulpa F pulp
púlpito M pulpit
pulpo M octopus
pulque M *Méx* pulque
pulquería F *Méx* pulque bar
pulsación F pulse
pulsar VT (una tecla) to hit; (cuerdas de guitarra) to pluck; (la opinión pública) to gauge
púlsar M pulsar
pulsera F bracelet; (de reloj) watchband; **reloj de** — wristwatch
pulso M pulse; (firmeza de mano) steadiness; **echar un** — to arm-wrestle; **tomar el** — to take the pulse; **a** — with great effort
pulular VI to swarm, to teem with
pulverizar[9] VT to pulverize
puma F mountain lion, cougar
puna F cold, arid tableland of the Andes
punitivo ADJ punitive
punk ADJ & M punk
punkero -ra MF punk
punta F (de cuchillo, lengua) point; (de espárrago, lápiz) tip; (de calcetín) toe; — **de lanza** spearhead; **una** — **de** a bunch of; **a** — **de cuchillo** at knifepoint; — **de flecha** arrowhead; **de** — on end; **iba caminando de** —s he was tiptoeing; **sacar** — **a un lápiz** to sharpen a pencil; **en la** — **de la lengua** on the tip of the tongue; **me pone los nervios de** — it makes me nervous; M —**pié** kick; ADJ **puntiagudo** sharp, pointed
puntada F stitch, prick
puntal M (de un edificio) prop; (de la economía) mainstay
puntear VT (una guitarra) to pluck; (un mapa) to make dots on; (una lista) to check off
puntería F aim; **tener buena** — to be a good shot
puntero M pointer
puntilla F point lace; **de** —s on tiptoe
punto M (puntuación) period; (de cinturón) notch; (signo) point, dot; (tanteo, tema, lugar) point; (puntada) stitch; — **álgido** fever pitch; — **de apoyo** foothold; — **de condensación** dewpoint; — **de congelación** freezing point; — **de ebullición** boiling point; — **de partida** point of departure; — **de referencia** point of reference, benchmark; — **de**

vista viewpoint, point of view; — **muerto** (en un negocio) stalemate, deadlock; (en un coche) neutral; — **y coma** semicolon; **al** — at once; **a** — ready; **a** — **de** on the point / verge of; **cogerle el** — to figure out; **dos** —**s** colon; **el** — **medio** the halfway mark; **en** — on the dot; **hacer** — to knit; **hasta cierto** — to a certain extent; **poner los** —**s sobre las íes** to dot the i's and cross the t's
puntuación F punctuation
puntual ADJ punctual, prompt; (específico) specific
puntualidad F punctuality
puntualizar[9] VT to point out
puntuar[17] VT to punctuate
punzada F (de dolor) stab; (de remordimiento, hambre) pang, twinge
punzante ADJ sharp, piercing
punzar[9] VT to prick
punzón M (en papel) hole punch; (en cuero) awl
puñado M handful; **a** —**s** by the handful
puñal M dagger
puñalada F stab; **coser a** —**s** to stab to death
puñetazo M punch, slug; **dar un** — to punch; **dar un** — **en la mesa** to bang on the table
puño M (mano cerrada) fist; (en un mango) cuff; (de espada) handle; **arreglarlo con los** —**s** to duke it out; **de mi** — **y letra** by my own hand
pupa F *Esp* boo-boo
pupila F pupil
pupilo -la MF ward
pupitre M school desk
puré M purée; — **de patatas** mashed potatoes; **hacer** — to smash
pureza F purity
purga F (política) purge; (medicinal) purgative
purgación F atonement
purgante ADJ & M purgative, laxative
purgar[7] VT (el vientre, a un rival) to purge; (frenos) to bleed; (pecados) to atone for
purgatorio M purgatory
purificar[6] VT to purify
purista ADJ & MF purist
puritano ADJ puritanical
puro ADJ pure; **lo hizo de** — **bueno** he did it out of sheer kindness; **a pura fuerza** by sheer force; **la pura verdad** the plain truth; **son puras mentiras** that's a lot of bull; **de purasangre** thoroughbred; M cigar

púrpura ADJ & M purple
pus M pus
putrefacto ADJ putrid
putter M putter

Qq

Qatar M Qatar
quásar M quasar
que PRON REL that; (antecedentes no
humanos) which; (antecedentes humanos)
who, whom; **el / la —** the one that; **lo —
tú dices** what you say; **vino la suegra,
lo — complicó la visita** the mother-in-
law came, which complicated the visit;
CONJ that; **no creo — haya tiempo** I
don't think (that) there's time; **estoy —
me muero** I feel like I'm about to die;
Carlos es más alto — Luis Carlos is
taller than Luis; **más (menos) —** more
(less) than; **déjalo aquí — lo voy a
necesitar después** leave it here because I
will need it later; **por mucho —** no
matter how much; **a — gana** I bet he'll
win; **— yo sepa** as far as I know
qué ADJ INTERR & PRON what, which; **¿—
libro vas a usar?** what / which book are
you going to use? **¿— dices?** what are
you saying? **no sé — dijo** I don't know
what he said; **¡— bonito!** how beautiful!
¡— de gente! what a lot of people! **y eso
—** so what! **no hay de —** don't mention
it; **¿ — sé yo?** what do I know? **¿— tal?**
how are you? **¡— más —!** so what!
quebrada F ravine
quebradizo ADJ breakable, brittle
quebrado ADJ (roto) broken; (rajado)
cracked; (sin dinero) broke; M fraction
quebrantar VT (una casa, la salud) to
weaken; (la ley) to violate
quebranto M weakening
quebrar[1] VT (romper) to break; (rajar) to
crack; VI (irse a bancarrota) to go
bankrupt, to go under, to fail; **—se** to
break (up); **se quebró la muñeca** he
broke his wrist; **—se uno la cabeza** to
rack one's brain
queda F curfew
quedar VI (permanecer) to remain; (no
haberse terminado) to be left; (estar
ubicado) to be located; (sentar bien la
ropa) to suit; **queda leche en el vaso**

there's milk in the glass; **la iglesia
queda en la esquina** the church is
located on the corner; **— bien** to come
out well; **— en** to agree to; **—se** to
remain, to stay; **—se con una cosa** to
take (buy) something
quehacer M chore
queja F complaint; (oficial) grievance
quejarse VI to complain; (ruidosamente) to
gripe, to squawk; (incesantemente) to
whine
quejica ADJ INV whiny; MF INV nag, whiner
quejido M (de sonido grave) moan, groan;
(agudo) squawk
quejoso ADJ whiny
quema F burning
quemado -da MF burn victim
quemador M burner
quemadura F (lugar quemado) burn;
(enfermedad de plantas) blight
quemar VT to burn; (del sol) to sunburn;
—se to burn up / down
quemazón F burning sensation
querella F lawsuit
querellante MF plaintiff
querellarse VI to file suit
querer[40] VI/VT (desear) to want; (amar) to
love; **como quieras** as you please;
cuando quieras whenever you want; **no
quiso hacerlo** he refused to do it;
quiere llover it is about to rain; **sin —**
unwillingly; **— decir** to mean
querido -da ADJ beloved, dear; MF
sweetheart; (como tratamiento) dear,
darling
queroseno M kerosene
quesería F dairy, cheese factory
queso M cheese; **— crema / de untar** cream
cheese; **— suizo** Swiss cheese
quiche M quiche
quicio M hinge; **sacar a uno de —** to drive
someone up the wall
quiebra F bankruptcy (también moral); (de
un mercado) crash; (de un comercio)
failure
quiebre M break
quien PRON REL who, whom; **Juan, —
recién cumplió cuarenta años** Juan,
who just turned forty; **hizo eso**
whoever did that; **a — corresponda** to
whom it may concern; **—quiera**
whoever; **de —** whose; **con —** with
whom
quién PRON INTERR & PRON who; **¿— es?** who
is it? **no sé — entró** I don't know who
came in; **¿a — se lo diste?** who did you
give it to? to whom did you give it?

quieto ADJ still
quietud F stillness
quijada F jaw
quilate M carat
quilla F keel
química F chemistry
químico -ca ADJ chemical; MF chemist
quimioterapia F chemotheraphy
quince NUM fifteen
quincena F (de cosas) group of 15; (de días) two-week period
quincha F thatch
quinchar VT to thatch
quingombó M okra
quinqué M oil lamp
quinta F (casa) villa; (reclutamiento) draft
quinto ADJ, ADV, & M fifth
quiosco M kiosk, newsstand
quiquiriquí INTERJ cock-a-doodle-doo
quirófano M surgery, operating room
quiropráctico -ca ADJ chiropractic; MF chiropractor; F chiropractic
quirúrgico ADJ surgical
quisquilloso ADJ particular, fussy
quiste M cyst
quitar VT (una mancha) to remove; (una prenda de vestir) to take off; (despojar de) to take away; M SG **quitaesmalte** nail polish remover; **quitanieves** snowplow; **quitamanchas** spot remover; VI **—se** to take off; **—se a alguien de encima** to get rid of someone; **quítate de ahí** move over
quite M **salir al — de** to go to the rescue of
quizá, quizás ADV perhaps, maybe

Rr

rabadilla F (coxis) tailbone; (de un ave) rump
rábano M radish; **me importa un —** I couldn't care less
rabia F (hidrofobia) rabies; (enojo) rage; **me tiene —** he hates me; **dar —** to anger
rabiar VI to rage, to fume; **guapa a —** drop-dead beautiful
rabieta F tantrum
rabino -na MF rabbi
rabioso ADJ (hidrofóbico, apasionado) rabid, mad; (enojado) mad, furious
rabo M (cola) tail; (cabo) stem; **mirar con el — del ojo** to look out of the corner of one's eye; **con el — entre las piernas**

with his tail between his legs
rabón ADJ bobtail
racha F (de suerte) streak; (de viento) gust
racial ADJ racial
racimo M (de plátanos, personas) bunch; (de uvas) cluster
raciocinio M reasoning
ración F ration, allowance; (de comida) portion
racional ADJ rational (también número)
racionalizar[9] VT to rationalize
racionamiento M rationing
racionar VT to ration
racismo M racism
racista ADJ & MF racist
radar M radar
radiación F radiation
radiactivo ADJ radioactive
radiador M radiator
radial ADJ radial
radiante ADJ radiant
radiar VT to radiate; (por radio) to broadcast
radical ADJ (extremo) radical; (hojas, células) root; M (en ciencias) radical; (en gramática) root
radicalismo M radicalism
radicar[6] VI to be located; **— en** to lie in; **—se** to take up residence
radio M (hueso, segmento de un círculo) radius; (elemento radiactivo) radium; F (aparato, difusión) radio; (emisora) radio station; **— de acción** sphere of influence
radiodifusión F broadcasting
radiodifusora F radio station
radioescucha MF INV radio listener
radiofónico ADJ radio
radiografía F X-ray
radiografiar[16] VT to x-ray; (examinar con cuidado) to examine carefully
radiología F radiology
radiotelescopio M radio telescope
radiotransmisor M radio transmitter
radón M radon
raer[23] VI/VT to scrape (off); (un artículo de ropa) to wear out
ráfaga F (de viento) gust, blast; (de luz) flash; (de ametralladora) burst
raído ADJ threadbare
raigón M stump
raíz F root; **— cuadrada** square root; **a — de** due to; **arrancar de —** to uproot; **cortar de —** to nip in the bud; **echar raíces** to take root
raja F (de melón) slice; (de falda) slit; (de leña) stick
rajadura F (en piedra, metal) crack; (en tela) rent, rip

rajar VT (una piedra) to crack; (un tronco) to split; **—se** (partir) to split open; (acobardarse) to chicken out, to blink; ADV **a rajatabla** strictly

ralea F ilk

ralear VI to thin out

ralentización F (de la economía) slump; (de un motor) idle

rallador M grater

rallar VT to grate, to shred

ralo ADJ sparse, thin

rama F branch, limb; (delgada) twig; **andarse por las —s** to beat around the bush; **algodón en —** raw cotton

ramaje M foliage

ramal M (de soga) strand; (de vía férrea) branch, spur

ramificarse[6] VI to divide into branches, to branch off

ramillete M bouquet, bunch, spray

ramo M (de flores) bouquet; (de una ciencia) branch; (de una actividad) line; **— de olivo** olive branch

rampa F ramp

ramplón ADJ vulgar

rana F frog

ranchero -ra MF rancher

rancho M (comida para soldados) mess; (comida mala) swill; (finca) ranch; **hacer — aparte** to keep to oneself

rancio ADJ (alimento) rancid; **de — abolengo** of ancient lineage

rango M (militar) rank; (categoría) standing

ranilla F frog (of a hoof)

ranura F (corte) groove; (para insertar monedas, cartas) slot

rapar VT (pelo) to shave off; (cabeza) to shave

rapaz ADJ (animal) predatory; (destructivo) rapacious

rape M **cortar al —** to crop

rapé M snuff

rapear VI to rap

rapidez F (de un coche) speed; (de un movimiento) rapidity, quickness

rápido ADJ (con mucha velocidad) fast; (en poco tiempo) quick; M rapids; ADV (con mucha velocidad) fast; (en poco tiempo) quickly

rapiña F pillage

raptar VT to kidnap, to abduct

rapto M (secuestro) abduction, kidnapping; (arrebato) fit

raqueta F racket

raquítico ADJ feeble, sickly

raramente ADV seldom

rareza F (escasez) rarity; (cosa rara) oddity;
(cualidad de extraño) strangeness

raro ADJ (infrecuente, de gases, tierras) rare; (extraño) strange, funny; **rara vez** seldom; **sentirse —** to feel funny

ras LOC ADV **a — de la tierra** low to the ground

rascar[6] VT to scratch; M SG **rascacielos** skyscraper

rasgado ADJ **ojos —s** slit eyes

rasgadura F tear, rip

rasgar[7] VT to tear, to rip

rasgo M (propiedad) trait, feature; **a grandes —s** in broad strokes

rasgón M tear

rasguñar VT to scratch

rasguño M scratch

raso ADJ (superficie) smooth; (cucharada) level; **al —** in the open air; M satin

raspado M scrape

raspador M scraper

raspadura F scrape

raspar VT to scrape

raspón M scrape

rastra F harrow; **a —s** dragging, pulling

rastrear VT (a un animal) to trail, to track, to trace; (un terreno) to search

rastreo M sweep, search

rastrero ADJ (planta) creeping; (persona) contemptible

rastrillar VT to rake

rastrillo M rake

rastro M (huella) track, trail; (olor) scent; (mercado) flea market; **ni —s** no trace

rastrojo M stubble

rasurado M shave

rasurador -ora MF razor

rasurar VT to shave

rata F rat

ratear VT to pilfer

ratería F petty larceny

ratero -ra MF pickpocket

ratificar[6] VT to ratify

rato M while; **—s perdidos** leisure hours; **a cada —** frequently; **a —s** from time to time; **pasar el —** to kill time; **pasar un buen —** (divertirse) to have a pleasant time; (permanecer) to spend a long time; **un largo —** a great while

ratón M mouse; **— almizclero** muskrat

ratonera F mousetrap

raudal LOC ADV **a —es** in great quantities

raudo ADJ swift

raya F line; (linde) boundary; (lista) stripe; (en el pelo) part; (en un pantalón) crease; (ortografía) dash; (en un zapato) scuff; (pez marino) stingray; **tener a —** to hold in check; **pasarse de la —** to be out of

line
rayado ADJ (papel) lined; (vestido) striped; **hablaba como disco —** he talked like a broken record
rayar VT (papel) to rule, to make lines on; (discos, espejo) to scratch; (zapatos) to scuff; **— el alba** to dawn; **— en** to border on
rayo M (de luz) ray, beam, streak; (de relámpago) flash of lightning; (de rueda) spoke; (de esperanza) ray, flicker; **—s infrarrojos** infrared rays; **—s X** X-rays
rayón M rayon
raza F (de personas) race; (de animal) breed
razón F (facultad) reason; (proporción) ratio; **— social** company name; **a —** de at the rate of; **¡con —!** no wonder! **entrar en —** to listen to reason; **te doy la —** I admit you're right; **perder la —** to lose one's mind; **tener —** to be right
razonable ADJ reasonable
razonamiento M reasoning
razonar VI (pensar) to reason; (arguir) to argue
reabastecer[13] VT to replenish
reabrir[51] VT to reopen
reacción F reaction; **— en cadena** chain reaction; **— nuclear** nuclear reaction
reaccionar VI to react
reaccionario ADJ & MF reactionary
reacio ADJ averse, reluctant
reacondicionar VT to rebuild
reactivo M reagent
reactor M reactor; **— nuclear** nuclear reactor
readaptación F readjustment
readaptar VT to readjust
reagrupar VT to regroup
reajustar VT to readjust
reajuste M readjustment
real ADJ (verdadero) real, actual; (del rey) royal; M fairground
realce M **dar —** to enhance
realeza F royalty
realidad F reality, actuality; **en —** really, actually; **— virtual** virtual reality
realismo M realism
realista ADJ (auténtico) realistic; (partidario del rey) royalist; MF (no idealista) realist; (partidario del rey) royalist
realización F (de un sueño) realization, fulfillment; (de una tarea) realization; (de una película) production
realizar[9] VT (un sueño) to realize, to fulfill; (película) to produce
realzar[9] VT (mejorar) to enhance; (destacar) to accentuate; (intensificar) to heighten

reanimar VT (devolver fuerzas) to revive; (dar ánimos) to rally
reanudación F renewal
reanudar VT (una amistad) to renew; (una reunión) to resume
reaparecer[13] VI to reappear
reasumir VT to resume
reata F lariat, lasso
reavivar VT to revive
rebaja F markdown, price cut; **de —s** cut-rate
rebajar VT (precios) to cut, to lower, to slash; (una bebida) to water down; (una crítica) to tone down; VI/VT (los cambios) to downshift; **—se** to lower oneself; **—se a** to stoop to
rebanada F slice
rebanar VT to slice
rebaño M flock, fold
rebasar VT (un coche) to overtake; (un límite) to exceed
rebatir VT to refute
rebato M alarm
rebelarse VI to rebel, to revolt
rebelde ADJ rebellious; (pelo) unruly; MF rebel
rebeldía F rebelliousness, defiance; (no comparecencia) default
rebelión F rebellion
rebenque M whip
rebobinar VT to rewind
reborde M edge
rebosante ADJ (de líquido) brimming, overflowing; (de salud) flush, glowing
rebosar VI (líquido) to overflow, to brim over; (de alegría) to bubble over; (de salud) to glow
rebotar VI (botar para atrás) to rebound, to bounce; (chocar) to bounce; (cambiar de dirección una bala) to ricochet; (cambiar de dirección una pelota) to carom
rebote M rebound, bounce; (de bala) ricochet
rebozar[9] VT to cover with batter; **—se** to muffle up
rebozo M shawl; **sin —** frankly
rebullir[19] VI to stir
rebuscado ADJ (estilo) overly elaborate; (persona) affected
rebuscar[6] VT (espigar) to glean; VI **— en** (la memoria) to search through; (un cajón) to rummage in
rebuznar VI to bray
rebuzno M bray, braying
recabar VT to raise (money)
recado M (mensaje) message; (quehacer) errand; **— de escribir** writing materials
recaer[23] VI to relapse; **— sobre** to fall to
recaída F relapse
recalar VI to make a stop at

recalcar[6] VT to accentuate

recalcitrante ADJ obstinate

recalentar[1] VT (volver a calentar) to warm over; (calentar en exceso) to overheat

recamar VT to embroider

recámara F (de un arma de fuego) chamber; *Méx* bedroom

recapitular VI/VT to recapitulate, to sum up

recargado ADJ busy, fussy

recargar[7] VT to overload, to burden

recargo M (emocional) burden; (de precio) surcharge, premium

recatado ADJ (cauteloso) cautious; (modesto) modest

recato M (cautela) caution; (modestia) modesty

recaudación F collection, levy; **— de fondos** fund-raising

recaudador -ora MF tax collector

recaudar VT (impuestos) to collect, to levy; (fondos) to raise; **— en bruto** to gross; **lo recaudado** proceeds

recaudo M **estar a buen —** to be in a safe place

rección F government

recelar VT to suspect; **— de** to be suspicious of

recelo M misgivings

receloso ADJ mistrustful

recepción F reception

receptáculo M receptacle, holder

receptor M receiver

recesión F recession

receta F (de cocina) recipe; (de médico) prescription

recetar VT to prescribe

rechazar[9] VT to reject; (un ataque) to repel, to repulse; (una oferta) to decline, to turn down, to refuse; (una acusación) to deny; (a un amante) to spurn, to reject

rechazo M (de un amante) rejection; (de un ataque) repulse; (de una oferta) refusal; (de una acusación) denial

rechifla F whistling, booing

rechiflar VT to whistle, to boo

rechinamiento M (de una puerta) creaking, squeaking; (de los dientes) grinding

rechinante ADJ squeaky

rechinar VI (una puerta) to squeak, to creak; VI/VT (los dientes) to grind; **eso me rechina** that grates on my nerves

rechoncho ADJ plump, chubby, roly-poly

recibidor -ora MF receiver; M reception room

recibimiento M reception

recibir VT to receive, to get; (visitas) to receive, to welcome; (una noticia trágica) to take; **— noticias de** to hear from; **—se** to graduate; **—se de médico** to graduate from medical school

recibo M receipt; **de —** acceptable; **al — de** upon receipt of; **acusar — to** acknowledge receipt; **acuse de —** acknowledgment of receipt

reciclar VI/VT to recycle

recién ADV recently; **— casado** newlywed; **— comprado** brand-new; **— llegado** newly arrived; **— me entero** it's news to me; **— nacido** newborn

reciente ADJ recent

recinto M enclosure

recio ADJ strong, rugged

recipiente M container

recíproco ADJ reciprocal

recitación F recitation

recital M recital

recitar VT to recite, to speak

reclamación F (protesta) protest; (demanda) claim

reclamante MF claimant

reclamar VT (protestar) to protest; (demandar) to claim; VI (aves) to call

reclamo M (reclamación) claim; (voz de animal) call, cry; (dispositivo) bird call; (señuelo) decoy

reclinar VT to lean; **—se** to recline

recluir[31] VT to confine; **—se** to be a recluse

recluso -sa MF inmate

recluta F recruitment; M (voluntario) recruit; (forzoso) conscript

reclutamiento M (voluntario) recruitment; (forzoso) conscription

reclutar VT (voluntariamente) to recruit; (por la fuerza) to draft, to conscript

recobrar VI to recover, to recuperate; VT to recover, to regain

recodo M bend, turn

recoger[11b] VT (el cabello) to gather; (un cuarto) to tidy up; (citas en un texto) to collect; (la mesa) to clear; (polvo) to sweep up; (a un desamparado) to shelter; (los frutos del campo) to glean; **—se** (retirarse) to retire, to withdraw; (acumularse) to gather

recogida F (del cabello) gathering; (de un cuarto) tidying up; (de la mesa) clearing; (de un desamparado) sheltering

recogimiento M (aislamiento) seclusion; (meditación) meditation

recolección F (de frutos, datos) collecting, gathering; (de carga) pickup; (cosecha) harvest

recolectar VT to gather, to forage

recomendable ADJ advisable

recomendación F recommendation
recomendar[1] VT to recommend
recompensa F recompense, reward
recompensar VT to recompense, to reward
reconcentrar VI to concentrate intensely; **—se** to concentrate, to become absorbed in thought
reconciliación F reconciliation
reconciliar VT to reconcile
recóndito ADJ remote
reconfortante ADJ heart-warming, comforting
reconfortar VT to comfort
reconocer[13] VT (identificar) to recognize; (admitir) to admit, to acknowledge; (explorar) to reconnoiter
reconocimiento M (identificación) recognition; (admisión, agradecimiento) acknowledgment; (exploración) scouting; **hacer un —** to reconnoiter
reconsiderar VT to reconsider
reconstrucción F reconstruction
reconstruir[31] VT to reconstruct, to rebuild
recopilar VT to compile
récord M record
recordar[2] VT (acordarse) to remember, to recollect, to recall; (hacer acordar) to remind
recordatorio M reminder
recorrer VT (andar una distancia) to cover; (examinar) to go over, to look over
recorrido M (ruta) run; (distancia) distance
recortado ADJ jagged
recortar VT (pelo, hilos, presupuesto) to trim; (uñas, periódicos) to clip; (una película) to shorten; **—se** to be outlined
recorte M (de pelos, hilos) trimming; (de uñas, periódicos) clipping; (de sueldo) cut; (sobrante) trimming
recostar[2] VT (sobre) to lay; (contra) to lean; **—se** to recline
recoveco M (en un camino) turn; (rincón) cranny
recreación F recreation
recrear VT to entertain; **—se** to amuse oneself
recreo M recreation, relaxation; (tiempo de descanso) recess; (lugar de juego) playground
recriminar VT to recriminate
recrudecer[13] VI to flare up
recrudecimiento M flareup
rectángulo M rectangle
rectificar[6] VT to rectify
rectitud F uprightness, righteousness
recto ADJ (no curvo) straight; (honrado) upright, righteous; (estricto) strict; **todo**

**— straight ahead; M rectum
rector -ora MF university president, chancellor
recua F herd
recuento M account; **— sanguíneo** blood count
recuerdo M (acción de recordar, cosa recordada) memory, recollection; (objeto que hace recordar) souvenir, token; **—s** regards
recular VI (ir hacia atrás) to move backward; (en un coche) to back up; (ante un desafío) to back down
recuperación F recovery
recuperar VT (una cosa perdida) to recover; (tiempo perdido) to make up; **—se** to recuperate
recurrir VT to appeal; **— a** to resort to, to have recourse to
recurso M (acción de recurrir) recourse; (reclamación) appeal; **—s** resources; **—s naturales** natural resources
recusar VT (a una persona) to reject; (a un juez) to challenge
red F (para pescar) net; (tejido de mallas) mesh; (conjunto de mallas) network; (para engañar) snare; (internet) World Wide Web, Internet
redacción F (ensayo) composition; (acción de redactar) drafting; (en un periódico) editorial department
redactar VT to draft; (en la escuela) to compose
redactor -ora MF editor
redada F (de peces) catch, haul; (por la policía) raid
redar VT to net
redecilla F hairnet
redención F redemption
redil M sheepfold, sheep pen; **volver al —** to come back into the fold
redimir VT (a un pecador) to redeem; (a un esclavo) to set free
rédito M (de ahorros) interest; (de acciones) yield
reditar[17] VT to yield
redoblar VT to double; VI/VT (un tambor) to roll
redoble M drumroll
redoma F flask
redonda F whole note; **a la —** all around
redondear VT to make round
redondel M ring
redondez F roundness
redondo ADJ round; **en —** all around; **caer —** to collapse; **salir —** to turn our perfect
reducción F reduction, cutback; **hacer — de**

personal to cut back on personnel
reducir[24] VT to reduce; (un hueso) to set;
(actividades) to curtail, to cut down on;
—se to limit oneself; **—se a** to boil down
to
redundante ADJ redundant
reedificar[6] VT to rebuild
reelección F reelection
reelegir[11] VT reelect
reembolsar VT to reimburse, to refund
reembolso M reimbursement, refund
reemplazable ADJ replaceable
reemplazar[9] VT to replace
reemplazo M replacement, substitute
reencarnación F reincarnation
reescribir[51] VT to rewrite
reexpedir[5] VT to forward
referencia F reference
referéndum M referendum
referente LOC ADV — **a** relative to
referir[3] VT (narrar) to narrate; **—se a** to refer
to
refinación F refinement
refinado ADJ refined, genteel
refinamiento M refinement
refinar VT to refine
refinería F refinery
reflector M (en una bicicleta) reflector; (en
deportes) floodlight; (militar, policial)
searchlight
reflejar VT (luz) to reflect; (imagen) to
mirror; **—se** to be reflected
reflejo M (luz) reflection; (movimiento)
reflex; **—s** frosting; ADJ reflex
reflexión F reflection
reflexionar VI to reflect; **— sobre** to think
over
reflexivo ADJ (gramatical) reflexive;
(pensativo) thoughtful
reflujo M ebb
reforma F (política) reform; (religiosa)
reformation
reformador -ora MF reformer
reformar VT (un gobierno, a un delincuente)
to reform; (ropa) to make alterations in;
—se to mend one's ways
reformatorio M reformatory
reformista MF reformer
reforzar[2,9] VT to reinforce; (las defensas) to
beef up; (un argumento) to bolster, to
buttress
refracción F refraction
refractario ADJ refractory
refrán M proverb, saying
refrenar VT (un caballo) to rein in;
(emociones) to restrain, to check
refrendar VT (una sentencia) to uphold; (un

documento) to countersign, to endorse
refrendario -ria MF endorser
refrendo M endorsement
refrescante ADJ refreshing
refrescar[6] VT to refresh; (el tiempo) to get
cool; **—se** to cool off
refresco M refreshment
refriega F fray, scuffle
refrigeración F refrigeration
refrigerador ADJ refrigerating; M refrigerator
refrigerante ADJ cooling; M coolant
refrigerar VT to cool, to refrigerate
refrigerio M refreshment
refrito ADJ (comida) refried; M (obra) rerun
refuerzo M (acción de reforzar)
reinforcement; (de tela) backing; (de una
vacuna) booster
refugiado -da MF refugee
refugiar VT to shelter; **—se** to take shelter
refugio M refuge, shelter; **— antiaéreo**
bomb shelter; **— fiscal** tax shelter
refulgente ADJ resplendent
refundir VT to recast
refunfuñar VI to grumble, to mutter
refunfuño M grumbling, muttering
refunfuñón -ona ADJ grouchy, grumpy; MF
grouch
refutar VT to refute
regadera F watering can
regadío M (tierra irrigada) irrigated land;
(riego) irrigation
regalar VT (dar como presente) to give as a
gift; (vender barato, donar) to give away;
(agasajar) to regale
regaliz M licorice
regalo M (presente, cosa barata) present, gift;
(para los sentidos) treat, delight
regañar VI (un perro) to snarl; VT (a un
niño) to scold, to reprimand;
(constantemente) to nag; **a**
regañadientes reluctantly
regaño M scolding, reprimand
regañón -ona MF scold
regar[1,7] VT (campos) to irrigate; (flores) to
water
regatear VI to haggle, to bargain
regateo M bargaining
regazo M lap
regente MF regent; ADJ ruling
reggae M reggae
régimen M (gobierno) regime; (dieta) diet; **—
de vida** lifestyle
regimiento M regiment
regio ADJ regal
región F region
regir[5,11] VT to govern; VI to be in force; **—se
por** to be guided by

registrar VT (buscar en) to search; (indicar) to record, to register

registro M (de la voz, lingüístico) register; (de nacimientos) record, register; (del equipaje) search; (de un órgano) stop

regla F (norma) rule; (utensilio para medir) ruler; (menstruación) period; **en —** in order; **por — general** as a general rule

reglamento M regulations

regocijar VT to gladden; **—se** to rejoice

regocijo M joy, rejoicing

regodearse VI (en la desgracia propia) to wallow; (en la desgracia ajena) to gloat

regodeo M (en la desgracia propia) wallowing; (en la desgracia ajena) gloating

regordete ADJ plump

regresar VI to return

regreso M return; **estar de —** to be back

reguero M trail; **correr como un — de pólvora** to spread like wildfire

regulación F (acción de regular) regulation; (de una máquina) adjustment

regulador M regulator, governor, throttle; **— de voltaje** dimmer

regular VT to regulate; (ajustar una máquina) to adjust; ADJ regular; **una paliza —** quite a beating; ADV so-so

regularidad F regularity

regularizar[9] VT to regulate; (formalizar) to formalize; **—se** to become regular

regurgitar VI/VT to regurgitate

rehabilitador ADJ remedial

rehacer[30] VT to remake; **—se** to recover

rehén MF hostage

rehuir[31] VT to shun; (responsabilidades) to shirk

rehusar VT to refuse; **—se a** to refuse to

reimpresión F reprint

reina F queen

reinado M reign

reinante ADJ prevailing

reinar VI to reign

reincidencia F relapse

reincidir VI to relapse

reino M (territorio de un rey) kingdom, realm; (período de reinado) reign; (división biológica) kingdom; (ámbito) realm

reintegrar VT to rebate; **—se a** to return to

reintegro M rebate

reír[15] VI to laugh; **—se de** to laugh at

reiterar VT to reiterate

reivindicar[6] VT to vindicate

reja F grate, grating; (pieza de arado) plowshare; **entre —s** behind bars

rejilla F (para equipaje) luggage rack; (de coche) grille

rejuvenecer[13] VT to rejuvenate; VI to become rejuvenated

relación F relation, connection; (interpersonal) relationship; (relato) account, report; (lista) list; **relaciones** (conocidos) connections; (trato) dealings; **relaciones públicas** public relations; **con — a** in relation to

relacionado ADJ related, germane

relacionar VT to relate, to connect; **—se con** to relate to

relajación F relaxation

relajamiento M relaxation

relajar VT to relax; **—se** to become lax

relajo M (aflojamiento) relaxation; (desorden) mess

relamerse VI to lick one's lips

relámpago M lightning

relampaguear VI to lightning; (los ojos, cosa reluciente) to flash

relampagueo M flash of lightning

relatar VT to relate, to recount

relativo ADJ relative; **— a** relative to

relato M (informe) account; (cuento) story, tale

relé M relay

relegar[7] VT to relegate

relevar VT to relieve

relevo M (soldado) relief; (carrera) relay

relicario M reliquary, locket

relieve M relief; **de —** (mapa) relief; (persona) prominent; **poner de —** to emphasize; **letras en —** raised letters

religión F religion

religioso -sa ADJ religious; M monk; F nun

relinchar VI to neigh

relincho M neigh

reliquia F relic

rellenado M filling

rellenar VT (un vaso) to refill, to replenish; (un tanque de gasolina) to fill, to fill up; (un formulario) to fill out; (un hueco) to fill in; (una almohada) to stuff

relleno ADJ (un pimiento) stuffed; (el cuerpo) full; M (de comida) stuffing, dressing; (de un colchón) padding

reloj M (de pared) clock; (de muñeca, bolsillo) watch; (de horno) timer; **— de pulsera** wristwatch; **— de sol** sundial; **— despertador** alarm clock; **contra —** against the clock; **como un —** regularly, like clockwork

relojería F (tienda) watch shop; (actividad) clock-making

relojero -ra MF watchmaker

reluciente ADJ shining

relucir[13b] VI to shine; **sacar a —** to bring

up
relumbrar VI to glare
relumbre M glare
REM M REM
remachar VT (una victoria, un clavo) to clinch; (un remache) to rivet
remache M (acción de remachar) clinching; (clavo) clinching; (clavija) rivet
remanente M remainder
remar VI/VT to row, to paddle
rematador -ora MF auctioneer
rematar VT (acabar) to finish; (matar) to finish off; (perfeccionar) to give the finishing touches to; (patear un balón) to take a shot; (subastar) to auction
remate M (de una obra) finishing touch; (tiro) shot; (subasta) auction; — **de un chiste** punch line; **loco de** — stark raving mad
remedador -ora MF mimic
remedar VT to mimic, to ape, to mock
remediar VT to remedy
remedio M remedy, cure; **sin** — unavoidable; **no tiene** — it can't be helped; **no tengo más** — I can't help it; **el** — **es peor que la enfermedad** the remedy is worse than the disease
remedo M mockery
remendar[1] VT to mend, to patch; (calcetines) to darn; (zapatos) to repair
remendón -ona MF cobbler
remero -ra MF rower
remesa F (de mercancías) shipment; (de dinero) remittance
remiendo M (de ropa) patch; (de zapatos) repair
remilgado ADJ fussy, prim
remilgo M fussiness, primness
reminiscencia F reminiscence
remisión F remission
remitente MF sender
remitir VT (enviar) to remit; (mandar a otra parte) to refer; —**se** to yield; **a las pruebas me remito** the evidence speaks for itself
remo M (pala) oar, paddle; (deporte) rowing
remodelar VI/VT to remodel
remojar VT to soak
remojo M soaking; **poner en** — to soak
remojón M soaking
remolacha F beet
remolcador M tugboat
remolcar[6] VT to tow
remolino M swirl, whirl; (de viento) whirlwind; (de agua) whirlpool, eddy; (de pelo) cowlick; (juguete) pinwheel; — **de gente** throng, crowd

remolón -ona ADJ dallying; MF dallier
remolonear VI to dally
remolque M (acción de remolcar) tow; (vehículo remolcado) towed vehicle; (vehículo que remolca) tow truck; (de camión) trailer; **llevar a** — to tow
remontar VT (una cometa) to fly; (una pendiente, un río) to go up; —**se** to rise; **el coche se remonta a los años 20** the car dates from the '20s; **para comprenderlo, debemos remontarnos a su juventud** in order to understand him, we must go back to his youth
remorder[2] VT to gnaw at
remordimiento M remorse
remoto ADJ remote, distant; **no tiene la más remota idea** he doesn't have the slightest idea
remover[2] VT (un cargo, un obstáculo) to remove; (un asunto problemático) to stir up
remuneración F compensation
remunerado ADJ gainful
renacer[13] VI to be reborn
renacimiento M revival; (período histórico) Renaissance
renacuajo M tadpole; (hombre esmirriado) shrimp
rencilla F quarrel
rencor M rancor; **guardar** — to bear a grudge
rencoroso ADJ resentful
rendición F surrender
rendido ADJ exhausted
rendija F crack
rendimiento M (lo rendido) yield, output; (productividad) performance
rendir[5] VT (someter) to subdue; (producir) to yield; (fatigar) to fatigue; — **homenaje** to pay homage; — **cuentas a** to answer to; VI (obtener buenos resultados) to perform well; —**se** (darse por vencido) to surrender, to give in; (fatigarse) to become fatigued
renegado -da MF renegade
renegar[1,7] VT (negar) to deny insistently; (repudiar) to renounce; — **de** to gripe about
renglón M line; **a** — **seguido** immediately following
rengo ADJ lame
renguear VI to limp
renguera F limp
reno M reindeer
renombrado ADJ renowned
renombre M renown; **de** — of note

renovación F renewal; **— urbana** urban renewal

renovar[2] VT (un edificio) to renovate; (ataques, temores) to renew

renquear VT to limp

renta F (de una persona) income; (de un gobierno) revenue; (alquiler) rent; **— anual** annuity; **—s internas** internal revenue; **vivir de la —** to live on the interest

rentable ADJ profitable; (idea) viable

renuencia F reluctance

renuente ADJ reluctant, loath; **ser — a** to be loath to

renuevo M sprout

renuncia F (dimisión) resignation; (de un derecho) waiver; (de una herencia) renunciation

renunciar VI **— a** (un cargo) to resign; (la ciudadanía) to renounce; (un derecho) to relinquish, to waive

reñido ADJ contested

reñir[5, 18] VI (discutir) to quarrel, to bicker, to argue; (pelear) to fight, to scuffle; (rezongar) to scold

reo -a MF defendant, accused

reojo M **mirar de —** to look out of the corner of one's eye

reorganizar[9] VT to reorganize, to regroup

repantigarse[7] VI to lounge

reparación F (compensación) reparation, redress; (arreglo) repair

reparador ADJ refreshing; M serviceman

reparar VT (arreglar) to repair; (compensar) to redress; **— en** to notice

reparo M **no tener —s en** to have no qualms about; **sin —s** freely; **hacer —s to** object

repartición F distribution

repartir VT (tierras, un botín) to distribute; (volantes) to hand out; (periódicos) to deliver; (naipes) to deal; (días libres) to space out

reparto M (de tierras) distribution; (entrega de periódicos) delivery; (de naipes) dealing; (ruta de entrega) route; (lista de actores) cast; **— proporcional** apportionment

repasar VT (una lección) to review, to go over again; (en la memoria) to retrace; (leer por encima) to skim

repaso M review

repelente ADJ repellent

repeler VT to repel, to repulse

repente M **de —** suddenly

repentino ADJ sudden

repercusión F repercussion

repercutir VI to have repercussions

repertorio M repertoire

repetición F repetition

repetido ADJ repeated; **repetidas veces** repeatedly

repetir[5] VI/VT to repeat; VI to belch; (tomar una segunda ración) to have seconds; **— como loro** to parrot; **—se** to recur

repicar[6] VI/VT to ring

repique M ringing, ring

repiquetear VI/VT to ring

repiqueteo M ringing

repisa F shelf

replegar[1, 7] VT to fold; **—se** to retreat

repleto ADJ replete

réplica F (contestación) reply, comeback; (copia) replica; (temblor secundario) aftershock

replicar[6] VI/VT to reply, to rejoin; (una célula) to replicate

repliegue M (pliegue marcado) crease; (retirada) retreat

repollo M cabbage

reponer[39] VT (reemplazar) to replace; (restituir) to restore; (replicar) to reply; (una obra de teatro) to revive; (una película) to show again; **—se** to recover one's health

reportaje M feature story

reportar VT (beneficios) to yield; VI (en una jerarquía) to answer to; **—se enfermo** to call in sick

reportero -ra MF reporter

reposado ADJ quiet, calm

reposar VI to repose, to rest; **dejar —** to let steep; M SG **reposacabezas** headrest

reposición F (reemplazo) replacement; (de una obra de teatro) revival

reposo M (descanso) repose, rest; (sosiego) calm

repostería F (establecimiento) pastry shop; (actividad) baking

repostero -ra MF pastry cook

reprender VT to reprimand, to scold, to rebuke

reprensión F rebuke

represa F (dique) dam; (reservorio de agua) reservoir

represalia F reprisal

represar VT to dam

representación F representation; (delegación) delegation; (de un papel) portrayal; (de una obra de teatro) performance

representante MF representative; (comercial) agent

representar VT to represent, to depict; (una

obra de teatro) to perform; (un personaje) to portray; **tiene treinta años, pero no los representa** he's thirty years old, but he doesn't look it; **tu presencia representa mucho para mí** your presence means a lot to me

representativo ADJ representative

represión F (psicológica) repression; (política) suppression, crackdown

reprimenda F reprimand, rebuke

reprimido ADJ repressed, pent-up

reprimir VT (impulsos) to repress; (una tendencia) to check; (enemigos políticos) to suppress, to crack down on; (una rebelión) to quell

reprobación F reproof

reprobar[2] VT to reprove; VI/VT (no aprobar un examen) to flunk, to fail

reprochar VT to reproach, to rebuke

reproche M reproach, rebuke

reproducción F reproduction

reproducir[24] VI/VT to reproduce; —**se** to reproduce, to breed

reproductor -ora ADJ breeding; MF breeding animal; F (aparato) VCR

reptar VI to crawl

reptil M reptile

república F republic

republicano -na ADJ & MF republican

repudiar VT (a la sociedad) to repudiate; (a un hijo) to disown; (una herencia) to renounce

repuesto M (pieza de reemplazo) spare part; **de** — spare

repugnancia F repugnance, disgust, revulsion

repugnante ADJ repugnant, disgusting, loathsome

repugnar VI to be repugnant; VT to disgust, to cloy

repulir VT to polish up

repulsa F rebuff, repulse

repulsar VT to repulse

repulsivo ADJ repulsive, creepy

repuntar VI to rally

reputación F reputation

reputado ADJ reputable

requemar VT to burn

requerimiento M request

requerir[3] VT to require

requesón M cottage cheese

requiebros M PL advances

requisa F requisition

requisar VT to commandeer, to requisition; (registrar) to search

requisito M requirement, requisite

res F animal; — **lanar** sheep; — **vacuna**

cow

resabio M (dejillo) aftertaste; (vicio) bad habit

resaca F (de mar) undertow; (malestar físico) hangover

resaltar VI (sobresalir) to stand out; (poner de relieve) to highlight

resarcir[10b] VT to compensate for

resbaladizo ADJ slippery, slick

resbalar VI (deslizar) to slip; (ser / estar resbaladizo) to be slippery

resbalón M slip; **darse un** — to slip

resbaloso ADJ slippery; *Méx fam* sleazy

rescatar VT (a un secuestrado) to ransom; (a una persona en peligro) to rescue

rescate M (para un secuestrado) ransom; (de una persona en peligro) rescue

rescindir VT to rescind

rescoldo M embers

resecar[6] VT to dry; —**se** to dry out

reseco ADJ dried-up, parched

resentido ADJ resentful

resentimiento M resentment, grudge; **guardar** — to hold a grudge

resentirse[3] VI to hurt, to suffer; — **de** to resent

reseña F book review

reseñar VT to review

reserva F (de provisiones, de oro, de jugadores, del ejército) reserve; (de localidades, de hotel, de indios) reservation; (de animales) preserve; **sin** —**s** without reservations; **tener** —**s** to have reservations

reservación F *Am* reservation

reservado ADJ (distante) aloof; (discreto) reserved

reservar VT to reserve; **me reservo mi opinión** I'll spare you my opinion

resfriado M common cold; **estoy** — I've got a cold

resfriarse VI to catch cold

resfrío M cold, head cold

resguardar VT to shelter; —**se de** to seek shelter from

resguardo M (abrigo) shelter; (comprobante) deposit slip

residencia F residence

residencial ADJ residential; (en las afueras) suburban

residente ADJ & MF resident

residir VI to reside

residuo M residue

resignación F resignation

resignarse VI to resign oneself

resina F resin

resistencia F resistance; (de la calefacción)

element; (aguante) endurance, stamina

resistente ADJ resistant, tough

resistir VT (una tentación) to resist; (un ataque) to withstand; **—se a un arresto** to resist arrest; VI to resist, to hold (up)

resollar[2] VI (por enfermedad) to wheeze; (después de un esfuerzo) to pant; (por alivio) to sigh

resolución F (acción de resolver) resolution; (ánimo) determination, resolve

resolver[2,51] VT (decidir) to decide; (solucionar) to solve; **—se a** to resolve to

resonancia F resonance

resonar[2] VI (sonidos) to resound, to boom; (una polémica) to resonate

resoplar VI (con enfado) to huff and puff; (un caballo) to snort

resoplido M (con enojo) puff; (de caballo) snort

resorte M spring

respaldar VT to back, to stand behind

respaldo M (parte de una silla) back; (apoyo) support, backing

respectivo ADJ respective

respecto LOC ADV **— a / de** with respect to, concerning; **a ese —** on that score; **con — a** with regard to, regarding, vis-à-vis

respetable ADJ respectable

respetar VT to respect

respeto M respect, regard; **con todo —** with all due respect; **faltar el / al —** to slight, to disregard

respetuoso ADJ respectful

respingar[7] VI (dar respingos) to buck; (asustarse) to shy away

respingo M (salto) buck; (susto) start

respiración F respiration, breathing; **— boca a boca** mouth-to-mouth resuscitation

respirar VI/VT to breathe; (sentir alivio) to breathe easy; **dejar —** to give a breather

respiro M (acto de respirar) breathing; (descanso) respite

resplandecer[13] VI (brillar) to glare; (de felicidad) to glow

resplandeciente ADJ resplendent, radiant

resplandor M brilliance, radiance

responder VI (reaccionar) to respond; VT (contestar) to answer; (corresponder) to correspond

respondón ADJ saucy

responsabilidad F (obligación de aceptar consecuencias) responsibility; (obligación de informar) accountability

responsable ADJ (que debe aceptar las consecuencias) responsible; (obligado legalmente) liable for; (que tiene que informar) accountable

respuesta F response, answer

resquebrajadura F crack

resquebrajar VI to crack

resquicio M (rendija) crack; (laguna legal) loophole

resta F subtraction

restablecer[13] VT to reestablish; (una costumbre) to revive; **—se** to recover

restante ADJ remaining

restañar VT to stanch / staunch

restar VT (sustraer) to subtract; (quitar) to take away from; (quedar) to remain; **— importancia a** to make light of

restauración F restoration

restaurante M restaurant

restaurar VT to restore; (muebles) to refurbish

restitución F restitution

restituir[31] VT to pay back, to give back

resto M (lo demás) rest; (sobrante) remainder; **—s** (de un edificio) remains; (de una comida) leftovers; **echar el —** to go all out

restorán M restaurant

restregar[1,7] VT to scrub, to scour

restricción F restriction

restringir[11] VT to restrict, to curtail

resucitación F resuscitation, revival

resucitar VT to resuscitate, to revive

resuello M (por enfermedad) wheeze; (por fatiga) panting

resuelto ADJ (de carácter decidido) resolute, strong-willed; (de actitud decidida) determined

resulta LOC ADV **de —s** as a result

resultado M result; (de un suceso) outcome; (de un partido) score; **—s científicos** findings; **—s electorales** returns; **como — as** a result; **dar buen —** to pan out; **dar por —** to result in

resultante ADJ resulting, consequent

resultar VI to result; (acabar siendo) to turn out, to prove; **— de** to result from; **resulta que** it turns out that

resumen M summary, abstract; **en —** in sum, in brief

resumir VT to summarize, to sum up; **—se a** to be condensed to, to boil down to

resurgimiento M revival

resurgir[11] VI to arise again

resurrección F resurrection

retablo M altarpiece

retaguardia F rear guard

retal M remnant

retama F broom

retar VT to challenge

retardar VI/VT to retard

retardo M lag

retazo M remnant

retén M (aparato) retainer; (de vigilancia) squad

retención F retention

retener[44] VT (una pelota, la atención) to hold; (salarios, fondos) to garnish, to withhold

retina F retina

retintín M (en los oídos) ringing; (de cascabeles) jingle

retirada F (de tropas) retreat, withdrawal; (de un diplomático, producto) recall

retirar VT (apartar) to move away; (dinero) to withdraw; (algo dicho) to take back, withdraw; (un producto) to recall; **—se** (para descansar, de un trabajo) to retire; (un ejército) to retreat, to pull back

retiro M (refugio) retreat; (jubilación) retirement; (de fondos) withdrawal

reto M challenge

retocar[6] VT to retouch, to touch up

retoñar VI to sprout

retoño M sprout, shoot, bud

retoque M retouching

retorcer[2,10c] VT (una toalla mojada) to wring out; (la muñeca) to wrench, to twist; **—se** (de dolor) to writhe; (de inquietud) to squirm

retorcido ADJ (persona) devious; (rama) gnarled

retorcimiento M (de dolor) writhing; (de inquietud) squirming

retórica F rhetoric

retornar VT to return

retorno M return; (de una costumbre, moda) revival

retozar[9] VI to frolic, to romp; (en juegos eróticos) to cavort

retozo M frolic, romp

retractarse VI to take back one's words

retraer[45] VT (las garras) to retract; **—se** to withdraw

retraído ADJ shy

retraimiento M shyness

retrasado ADJ (falto de desarrollo) backward; (deficiente mental) retarded

retrasar VT to delay; (un reloj) to set back; **—se** to fall behind

retraso M delay, lag

retratar VT to portray; (pintar un retrato) to paint a portrait

retrato M (pintura) portrait; (descripción) portrayal

retreta F retreat

retrete M lavatory

retroactivo ADJ retroactive

retroalimentación F feedback

retroceder VI to step back; (de horror) to recoil, to shrink back; (en un coche) to back up; (al mecanografiar) to backspace; (dar marcha atrás) to backtrack; (tropas) to retreat, to fall back; (una inundación) to recede

retroceso M (de un arma de fuego) recoil; (económico) recession; (en un teclado) backspace

retrogradismo M backwardness

retrógrado ADJ backward

retroproyector M overhead projector

retrovirus M retrovirus

retrucar[6] VT to counter

retruécano M play on words

retumbar VI to rumble, to roll

retumbo M rumble

reubicar[6] VT to relocate

reuma M rheumatism

reumatismo M rheumatism

reunión F meeting; (informal) get-together; (de ex-alumnos) reunion

reunir VT (juntar) to gather; (hacer que acudan al mismo lugar) to reunite, to bring together; (coleccionar) to collect; (juntar coraje) to muster; (juntar dinero) to raise; **—se** (formal) to meet; (mucha gente) to gather; (informal) to get together

revancha F (venganza) revenge; (en deportes) return game

revelación F revelation

revelado M film development

revelador ADJ revealing

revelar VT to reveal; (película) to develop; (un escándalo) to expose; (información) to disclose; **—se** to show oneself

revendedor -ora MF (de mercadería) middleman; (de entradas) scalper

revender VT (vender de nuevo) to resell; (billetes) to scalp

reventar[1] VI/VT (estallar) to burst, to bust; (morir) to die; (fastidiar) to annoy

reventón M (acción de reventar) bursting; (de un neumático) blowout

reverberar VI to reverberate

reverdecer[13] VI (ponerse verde de nuevo) to become green again; (renovarse) to gain new strength

reverencia F reverence; (gesto) bow

reverenciar VT to revere

reverendo -da ADJ & MF reverend

reverente ADJ reverent

reverso M reverse

revertir[3] VI to revert; **— en beneficio de** to be of benefit to

revés M (cosa opuesta) reverse; (en tenis)

backhand; (contratiempo) setback, downturn; **al —** (con lo de adelante hacia atrás) backwards; (con lo de arriba hacia abajo) upside down; **dar vuelta al —** to turn inside out

revestimiento M overlay

revestir[5] VT (un camino) to surface; (una pared) to cover; (conllevar) to be marked by

revisar VT (examinar) to review, to go over; (un coche) to service

revisión F review; (de una película vieja) revival

revisor -ora MF (en un tren, autobús) conductor

revista F (inspección) inspection; (de tropas) muster; (publicación) magazine, journal, periodical; (espectáculo) revival; **— de historietas** comic book; **— electrónica** e-zine; **pasar —** to pass in review

revistar VT to inspect

revivir VI/VT to revive

revocación F revocation; (de una ley) repeal

revocar[6] VT (un fallo) to reverse; (una ley) to repeal; (una pared) to plaster

revolcar[6] VT (derribar) to knock over; **—se** (cerdos) to wallow; (niños) to roll around

revolear VT to roll

revolotear VI to flutter, to flit

revoltijo M (de cosas) jumble; (de pelo) muss

revoltoso -sa ADJ unruly, disorderly; MF troublemaker

revolución F (cambio radical) revolution; (giro) revolution, turn; **revoluciones por minuto** revolutions per minute

revolucionario -ria ADJ revolutionary, earthshaking; MF revolutionary

revolver[2,51] VT (remover) to stir up; (registrar) to rummage in; (desordenar) to mess up; (huevos) to scramble; (ensalada) to toss; **eso me revuelve el estómago** that makes my stomach turn; **—se** to toss and turn

revólver M revolver, pistol

revuelo M stir, commotion

revuelta F revolt

revuelto ADJ (el mar) rough; (los ánimos) restless; (el pelo) disheveled; **huevos —s** scrambled eggs

rey M king; **los —es Magos** the Wise Men

reyerta F melee, squabble

rezagarse[7] VI to straggle behind, to lag behind

rezar[9] VI/VT (a Dios) to pray; (un letrero) to say

rezo M prayer

rezongar[7] VI/VT (murmurar) to grumble;

(quejarse) to gripe

rezongón -ona ADJ grumpy; MF grouch

rezumar VT to ooze

riachuelo M brook

riada F flash flood

ribazo M steep bank

ribera F shore, bank; (de río) riverbank

ribereño ADJ on the bank

ribete M (de uniforme) trimming; (de alfombra) binding; (de ropa) piping; (de mosaico) border; **tener —s de** to have hints of

ribetear VT (un uniforme) to trim; (una alfombra) to bind; (un diseño) to border

ricacho ADJ very rich

rico ADJ (persona) rich, wealthy, affluent; (suelo) rich; (piso) exquisite; (manjar) delicious; (niño) cute

ridiculizar[9] VT to ridicule, to deride

ridículo ADJ ridiculous; (medio absurdo) ludicrous; **hacer el —** to act the fool; **poner en —** to ridicule; **ponerse en —** to make a spectacle of oneself

riego M irrigation

riel M rail

rienda F rein; **dar — suelta** to give a free hand

riesgo M risk; **correr un —** to run a risk

rifa F raffle

rifar VT to raffle

rifirrafe M free-for-all

rifle M rifle

rigidez F rigidity

rígido ADJ rigid

rigor M (exactitud) rigor; (del invierno) harshness; **en —** in reality; **de —** indispensable

riguroso ADJ rigorous; (invierno) harsh

rima F rhyme

rimar VI/VT to rhyme

rimbombante ADJ grandiose

rímel M mascara

rin M rim

rincón M corner; (lugar retirado) nook, alcove

rinconera F (mueble) corner cupboard; (mesa) corner table

ring M boxing ring

ringlera F row

rinoceronte M rhinoceros

rinoplastia F *fam* nose job

rinovirus M rhinovirus

riña F (discusión) quarrel; (pelea) scrap, fight, spat

riñón M kidney; (región lumbar) lower back

río M river; **— abajo** downstream

ripio M rubble

riqueza F wealth; **—s** riches

risa F (carcajada) laugh; (acción, sonido de reír) laughter; **reventar / desternillarse de —** to burst with laughter; **morirse de —** to die laughing; **¡qué —!** what a joke!

risco M crag, bluff

risible ADJ laughable

risita F (burlona) snicker; (ahogada) chuckle

risotada F guffaw, gale of laughter

ristra F string

risueño ADJ (sonriente) smiling; (alegre) cheerful

rítmico ADJ rhythmical

ritmo M rhythm; **— cardíaco** heart rate; **— de vida** pace of life

rito M rite

ritual ADJ & M ritual

rival ADJ & MF rival

rivalidad F rivalry

rivalizar[9] VI to rival; **— con** to compete with

rizado ADJ curly; M curling

rizar[9] VT (pelo) to curl, to crimp; (agua) to ripple

rizo M (en el pelo) curl, ringlet; (en el agua) ripple, ruffle; (hecho por un avión) loop

robar VT (algo a una persona) to rob; (dinero) to steal

roble M oak tree

robledal M oak grove

robo M (violento) robbery; (furtivo) theft; **— con allanamiento** burglary

robot M robot

robótica F robotics

robusto ADJ robust; (grueso) stout, stocky; (sólido) sturdy

roca F rock

roce M (acción de rozar) graze; (en una prenda) rub; (conflicto) brush

rociada F (acción de rociar) sprinkling, spraying; (de insultos) volley

rociar[16] VI/VT to spray, to sprinkle; (carne) to baste

rocín M nag

rocío M (del alba) dew; (en aerosol) spray, mist

rock M rock

rocoso ADJ rocky

rodada F track; (profunda) rut

rodadura F rolling

rodaja F flat round slice

rodaje M (de un coche) running; (de una película) shoot

rodar[2] VI (girar) to roll; (caer) to tumble down; (vagar) to roam; (filmar) to shoot

rodear VT (cercar) to surround; (cubrir) to wrap around; (evitar) to go around

rodeo M (desvío) detour; (modo de expresarse) circumlocution; (fiesta) rodeo

rodilla F knee; **de —s** on one's knees; **hincarse de —s** to kneel down

rodillo M (para pintar) roller; (para cocinar) rolling pin; (para caminos) road roller

rododendro M rhododendron

roedor M rodent

roer[50] VI/VT to gnaw

rogar[2,7] VT to pray, to beg, to beseech; **hacerse —** to play hard to get; **se ruega no molestar** please do not disturb

rojez F redness

rojizo ADJ reddish

rojo ADJ & M red; **al — vivo** red-hot

rollizo ADJ plump; M log

rollo M (de papel, de película, de grasa) roll; (de árbol) log; (de cuerda) reel; (de tela) bolt; (discurso aburrido) story; (mentira) lie; (lío) mess, hassle; (relación amorosa) affair; (manuscrito) scroll; (de alambre) coil; **dar el —** to hassle

ROM M ROM

romance ADJ Romance; M (lengua románica) Romance language; (español) Spanish language; (relación amorosa) romance; (composición métrica) ballad; **en buen —** in plain language

románico ADJ (arte) Romanesque; (lengua) Romance

romano -na ADJ & MF Roman

romanticismo M (corriente literaria) romanticism; (sentimentalismo) romance

romántico -ca ADJ & MF romantic

rombo M diamond

romería F pilgrimage

romero -ra M (persona) pilgrim; M rosemary

romo ADJ (sin punta) blunt; (sin filo) dull

romper[51] VI/VT to break; VT (relaciones) to sever; **— a** to start to; **— con** to break up with; **— el alba** to dawn; **— filas** to break ranks; **rompió las aguas / la fuente** her water broke; **de rompe y rasga** coarse; M SG **rompecabezas** jigsaw puzzle; **rompehuelgas** strikebreaker; **rompeolas** breakwater

rompible ADJ breakable

rompientes M PL surf

rompimiento M (con el pasado) break; (de una promesa) breach

rompope M *Méx* eggnog

ron M rum

roncar[6] VI to snore

roncha F (de sarampión) spot; (de mosquito) bite

ronco ADJ hoarse, raspy

ronda F (de policía) patrol, beat; (de niños)

circle; (de bebidas, de negociaciones) round

rondar VT (patrullar) to patrol; (acercarse por interés) to hang around; (cantar serenatas) to serenade; **rondaba los cuarenta** she was around forty years old

ronquera F hoarseness

ronquido M snore

ronronear VI to purr

ronroneo M purr

ronzal M halter

roña F (enfermedad de plantas) scab; (sorna) mange; MF INV (tacaño) skinflint

roñoso ADJ (planta) scabby; (animal) mangy; (persona) stingy

ropa F clothing, clothes; — **blanca** linen; — **vieja** stew made from leftover meat

ropaje M apparel

ropería F checkroom

ropero M (armario) wardrobe; (cuarto) closet

roque M castle

rorro M baby

rosa F (flor) rose; (marca) blemish; — **de los vientos** mariner's compass; ADJ (rosado) rose colored, pink

rosado ADJ (saludable) rosy; (de color de rosa) rose-colored, pink; M rosé wine

rosal M rosebush

rosario M rosary

rosbif M roast beef

rosca F (de tornillo) screw; (pan) ring-shaped roll; **pasarse de** — to go off the deep end

rostro M (cara) face; (morro) nerve

rotación F rotation

rotar VI/VT to rotate

rotativo ADJ (movimiento) rotary; (cultivos) rotating; M Esp newspaper

rotatorio ADJ rotary

roto ADJ broken; (cansado) exhausted; (ropa, voz) ragged

rotor M rotor

rótula F kneecap

rotular VT to label

rótulo M (título) title; (etiqueta) label

rotundo ADJ resounding; **una negativa rotunda** a categorical denial

rotura F break; (de un órgano, tubo) rupture

roturar VT to plow

round M (asalto) round

rozadura F chafing

rozamiento M friction

rozar[9] VT (herir levemente) to graze; (arañar) to scrape; (irritar) to rub, to chafe; (limpiar un terreno) to clear; **—se con alguien** to have dealings with someone; **rozaba en los cuarenta** she was almost forty years old

Ruanda F Rwanda

ruandés -esa ADJ & MF Rwandan

rubí M ruby; (en un reloj) jewel

rubicundo ADJ (permanente) ruddy; (temporal) flush

rubio -a ADJ & MF blond

rubor M blush, flush; (de las mejillas) bloom, glow

ruborizarse[9] VI to blush

rúbrica F (trazo) flourish; (título) title

rucio ADJ gray

rudeza F rudeness, coarseness

rudo ADJ rude, coarse; — **golpe** hard blow

rueca F spinning wheel

rueda F (de coche) wheel; (de personas) circle; (rodaja) slice; — **de prensa** news conference; **ir sobre —s** to be smooth sailing

ruedo M ring; (de vestido) hem

ruego M prayer, plea, entreaty

rufián M ruffian

rugby M rugby

rugido M roar

rugir[11] VI to roar; (estómago) to growl

rugoso ADJ rough

ruibarbo M rhubarb

ruido M noise; **mucho — y pocas nueces** much ado about nothing

ruidoso ADJ noisy, loud

ruin ADJ (persona, cosa) vile; (animal) puny

ruina F (acción de arruinar) destruction; (edificio, estado de pobreza) ruin; (persona) wreck; (perjuicio) downfall; **en —s** in ruins

ruindad F (actitud) vileness; (acto) vile act

ruinoso ADJ ruinous

ruiseñor M nightingale

rulero M RP roller, curler

ruleta F roulette

rulo M roller, curler

Rumania F Romania, Rumania

rumano -na ADJ & MF Romanian, Rumanian

rumba F rumba

rumbear VI to head in a certain direction

rumbo M course, route; — **a** toward

rumiar VI (meditar) to ruminate; (reflexionar) to ruminate, to mull over, to brood over

rumor M rumor

runrún M (rumor) rumor; (sonido sordo) humming

ruptura F (de relaciones) break; (de órganos internos) rupture

rural ADJ rural

Rusia F Russia

ruso -sa ADJ & MF (persona) Russian; M (lengua) Russian

rústico ADJ (rural) rustic, rural; (tosco) coarse; **en rústica** paperback
ruta F route; (carretera) highway
rutina F routine

Ss

sábado M Saturday
sábalo M shad
sábana F bed sheet
sabañón M chilblain
saber[41] VI/VT to know; — **nadar** to know how to swim; **supo la verdad** he found out the truth; — **a** to taste like; — **a ciencia cierta** to know for sure; — **de biología** to know all about biology; **a** — namely; **hacer** — to let know; **las vacaciones me han sabido a poco** my vacation was too short; **para que sepas** for your information; **sabe bien** it tastes good; **sabérselas todas** to know the ropes; **vaya a** — who knows? M knowledge, learning; **a mi leal** — **y entender** as far as I know; **sabelotodo** know-it-all
sabiduría F wisdom
sabiendas LOC ADV **a** — knowingly
sabihondo -da ADJ & MF wise guy; know-it-all
sabio -bia ADJ wise, sage; MF (estudioso) scholar; (sabedor) sage, wise person
sable M saber
sabor M taste, flavor
saborear VT to savor, to relish
sabotaje M sabotage
sabotear VT to sabotage
sabroso ADJ (comida) savory, tasty; (cuento) juicy
sabueso M (perro) bloodhound; (detective) sleuth
sacar[6] VT (cosas de la maleta, a pasear) to take out; (manchas, dinero del banco) to get out; (los zapatos) to take off; (malas notas, carnet de conducir) to get; (una copia) to make; (una foto) to take; (una conclusión) to draw; (la lengua, la cabeza por la ventana) to stick out; (una pelota de tenis) to serve; (una asignatura escolar) *Esp* to pass; — **ampollas** to blister; — **brillo** to polish up; — **provecho (de)** to benefit (from); — **a bailar** to ask to dance; — **a colación** to broach; — **a luz** to divulge; — **de un apuro** to bail out;

me saca de quicio he gets my goat, he gets on my nerves; — **el cuerpo** to dodge; — **el mejor partido de** to make the best of; —**le el jugo a algo** to make the most of; — **en limpio** to deduce; — **el sombrero** *Am* to take off one's hat; **¡sáquese de allí!** *Am* get out of there! — **punta** to sharpen; M SG **sacabocados** punch; **sacacorchos** corkscrew; **sacamuelas** quack dentist; **sacapuntas** pencil sharpener
sacarina F saccharine
sacerdocio M priesthood
sacerdote M priest
saciar VT to satiate; —**se** to be satiated
saco M (bolsa) sack; (prenda) blazer, sport coat; (de boxeo) punching bag; — **de dormir** sleeping bag; — **de noche** overnight bag; **echar en** — **roto** to waste one's effort
sacramento M sacrament
sacrificar[6] VT to sacrifice; (una mascota) to put to sleep
sacrificio M sacrifice
sacrilegio M sacrilege
sacrílego ADJ sacrilegious
sacristán M sexton
sacudida F shake, jolt; (de terremoto) tremor; (de la cabeza) toss; (eléctrica) shock
sacudir VT to shake; (las alfombras) to beat; (el polvo) to dust; **ir sacudiéndose** to rattle along, to jolt along; —**se de alguien** to get rid of someone
sádico ADJ sadistic
sadismo M sadism
saeta F arrow
safari M safari
sagaz ADJ shrewd, astute
sagrado ADJ sacred, holy; **Sagrada Escritura** Holy Scripture
sahumar VT to perfume with incense
sahumerio M burning of incense
sainete M one-act farce; **esa familia es un** — that family is a complete mess
sal F (mineral) salt; (gracia) wit; — **gorda** cooking salt; — **yodada** iodized salt; — **de mesa** table salt; **dar** — to spice up; — **y pimienta** life, spark
sala F (de estar) parlor, living room; (grande) large room; — **de justicia** courtroom; — **de clase** classroom; — **de espera** waiting room; — **de directorio** boardroom; — **de lectura** reading room; — **de operaciones** operating room
salado ADJ salty; (gracioso) witty; M (acción) salting
salamandra F salamander

salar VT to salt; **—se** to become salty

salario M pay, wages; **— base** base pay; **— mínimo** minimum wage

salchicha F sausage

saldar VT to settle

saldo M (resultado final) balance; (venta especial) sale

salegar[7] VT to give salt to; M salt lick

salero M (dispensador) saltcellar, saltshaker; (gracia) charm

saleroso ADJ charming

salida F (partida) departure; (puerta) exit, way out; (de una carrera) start; (militar) sally; (eléctrica, computadora) output; (de una crisis) way out; **este artículo tiene mucha —** this article sells well; **dar la —** to start a race; **— del sol** sunrise; **— de emergencia** emergency exit; **— en falso** false start

saliente ADJ (roca) salient, projecting; (gobierno) outgoing; M salient, projection, overhang

salina F salt mine

salino ADJ saline

salir[42] VI (del interior al exterior, para divertirse) to go out; (de un país) to depart, to leave; (del trabajo) to quit; (manchas de tinta) to come out; (un anillo del dedo) to come off; (el sol) to rise; (una publicación) to appear; (flores) to sprout; **trabajando no se puede — de pobre** you can't work your way out of poverty; **salió a su madre** she takes after her mother; **— a la luz** to surface; **— adelante** to overcome difficulties; **— bien** to turn out well; **— con** to date; **— ganando** to come out ahead; **— mal** to go wrong; **¿a cuánto sale?** how much is it? **no me sale ser amable con él** I can't bring myself to be nice to him; **—se** (gotear) to leak; (rebosar) to overflow; (proyectarse) to stick out

saliva F saliva

salmón M salmon

salmonela F salmonella

salmuera F brine

salobre ADJ salty

salomonense ADJ & MF Solomon Islander

salón M (de estar) living room, parlor; (de conferencias) hall; **— de belleza** beauty parlor; **— de clase** classroom; **— de exposición y ventas** showroom; **— de exhibición** exhibition hall; **— de té** tearoom

salpicadero M dashboard

salpicadura F spatter, splash, splatter

salpicar[6] VI/VT to sprinkle, to spatter, to splash; (adornar) to punctuate; (dispersar) to intersperse

salpicón M meat salad

salpimentar[1] VT to salt and pepper

salsa F sauce; **en su —** in her element; **— tártara** tartar sauce; **— de soya** soy sauce; **— de tomate** ketchup

saltar VI (brincar) to jump, to leap; (cinco metros) to jump; (una cerca) to jump over, to vault; (un renglón) to skip; VT (los fusibles) to trip; (una ley) to ignore; **— a la vista** to be obvious; **— sobre** to pounce on; **se le saltaron los ojos** his eyes bugged out; **se le saltó un botón** one of his buttons popped off; **se me saltaban las lágrimas** it brought tears to my eyes; M SG **saltamontes** grasshopper

salteador -ora MF bandit

saltear VT to stir-fry

salto M jump, leap; **— de agua** waterfall; **a — de mata** from hand to mouth; **— de cama** dressing gown; **dar un —** (saltar) to jump; (el corazón) to skip a beat; **— alto** high jump; **— con esquí** ski jump; **— con pértiga** pole vault; **— de longitud** broad jump; **— del ángel** swan dive; **— mortal** somersault; **— triple** triple jump

saltón ADJ jumping; (ojo) bulging; M grasshopper

salubridad F sanitation

salud F health; **— mental** mental health; **curarse en —** to take precautions; INTERJ cheers!

saludable ADJ healthy, healthful

saludar VT (decir hola) to greet; (recibir bien) to salute, to hail; (en el militar) to salute; (hacer un gesto amistoso con la mano) to wave

saludo M (hola) greeting, salutation; (gesto) wave; (militar) salute; **retirar el — a alguien** to stop speaking to someone; **—s** best wishes, regards

salva F salvo

salvación F salvation

salvado M bran

salvador -ora MF savior; ADJ saving

salvadoreño -ña ADJ & MF Salvador(i)an

salvaguarda F safeguard

salvaguardar VT to safeguard

salvajada F (acción) savage act; (comentario) savage remark

salvaje ADJ (feroz) savage; (no domesticado) wild; MF savage

salvajismo M savagery

salvamento M (de gente) rescue; (de

propiedad) salvage

salvar VT (la vida, el alma) to save; (de un peligro) to rescue; (propiedad) to salvage; (un obstáculo) to clear; (un camino difícil) to negotiate; — **el pellejo** to save one's skin; **el puente salva el río** the bridge spans the river; **—se** to pull through; **—se por poco** to have a narrow escape; **sálvese quien pueda** every man for himself; M SG **salvavidas** (aparato) life preserver, life jacket; MF (persona) lifeguard

salvia F sage

salvo ADJ safe; **a —** safe; **—conducto** safe-conduct; PREP save, except; **— en caso de desastre** barring a disaster

Samoa F Samoa

samoano -na ADJ & MF Samoan

sanar VI/VT to heal; M **sanalotodo** cure-all

sanatorio M (para convalecientes) sanitarium; (hospital) hospital

sanción F sanction

sancionar VT to sanction

sandalia F sandal

sandez F (acción) stupidity, foolishness; (dicho) foolish remark

sandía F watermelon

saneamiento M sanitation

sanear VT to drain

sangrar VI/VT to bleed; VT (un árbol) to tap; (un párrafo) to indent

sangre F blood; **— fría** coolness under pressure; **a — fría** in cold blood; **hacerse mala —** to get upset; **eso lo llevo en la —** that's in my blood; **de — caliente** warm-blooded; **— azul** blue blood; **sudar — to sweat bullets; de pura —** thoroughbred; **chupar la — a alguien** to be a parasite on someone

sangría F (bebida) wine punch; (acción de sangrar) bleeding; (espacio tipográfico) indentation; (pérdida de recursos) drain

sangriento ADJ (manchado de sangre, que provoca la pérdida de sangre) bloody; (sanguinario) bloodthirsty

sanguijuela F leech

sanguinario ADJ bloody, vicious

sanidad F public health

sanitario ADJ sanitary; M **—s** bathroom fittings

sanmarinense ADJ & MF San Marinese

sanmarinés -esa ADJ & MF San Marinese

sano ADJ (persona) healthy; (juicio) sound; (dieta) healthful; (vaso) unbroken; **— y salvo** safe and sound; **en su — juicio** of sound mind

sánscrito M Sanskrit

sanseacabó INTERJ **te quedas y —** you're staying and that's that

santalucense ADJ & MF St. Lucian

santiamén LOC ADV **en un —** in a jiffy, lickety-split

santidad F sanctity, holiness

santificar[6] VT to sanctify

santiguarse[8] VI to cross oneself

santo -ta ADJ saintly, holy; **esperar todo el — día** to wait the whole blessed day; MF saint; **día del —** saint's day; **quedarse para vestir —s** to be a spinster; **¿a — de qué?** for what reason? **¡por todos los —s!** my goodness!

santotomense ADJ & MF São Tomean

santuario M sanctuary

santurrón -ona ADJ & MF goody-goody

saña F fury

sañudo ADJ furious

sapo M toad (también hombre); **echar —s y culebras** to swear, to curse; **sentirse como un — de otro pozo** to feel like a fish out of water

saque M tennis serve, tennis service

saquear VT to sack, to plunder, to pillage

saqueo M sacking, plundering, pillaging

sarampión M measles

sarape M *Méx* serape

sarcasmo M sarcasm

sarcástico ADJ sarcastic

sarcófago M sarcophagus

sarcoma M sarcoma

sardina F sardine

sardo -da ADJ & MF Sardinian

sardónico ADJ sardonic

sargento -ta MF sergeant; F battle-ax(e)

sarmentoso ADJ gnarled

sarmiento M vine

sarna F mange

sarnoso ADJ mangy

sarpullido M rash

sarro M tartar, plaque

sarta F string

sartén F frying pan, skillet

sastre -tra MF tailor

sastrería F tailor shop

satánico ADJ satanic

satélite M satellite; **— artificial** man-made satellite

satén M satin

sátira F satire

satírico ADJ satirical

satirizar[9] VT to satirize

satisfacción F satisfaction

satisfacer[30,51] VT to satisfy; (una deuda) to pay; **—se** to be satisfied

satisfactorio ADJ satisfactory

satisfecho ADJ contented, satisfied

saturar VT to saturate; (un mercado) to glut; (líneas de teléfono) to overload

sauce M willow; **— llorón** weeping willow

saudí, saudita ADJ & MF Saudi Arabian

savia F sap

saxofón M saxophone

sazón F season; **a la —** at that time; **en —** ripe

sazonar VT (condimentar) to season, to flavor; (llegar a su sazón) to ripen

scooter M scooter

scout MF scout

se PRON PERS **— coronó a sí mismo** he crowned himself; **— lavó la cara** he washed his face; **— besaron** they kissed each other; **— habla español** Spanish is spoken; **— lo puede combatir** it can be fought

sebo M tallow, fat

secador M hair dryer

secadora F clothes dryer

secante ADJ drying

secar[6] VT to dry; (las manos) to dry off; **—se** (planta) to dry up; (río) to run dry; (madera) to season

sección F (militar) platoon; (de un almacén) department

seccionar VT to section

seco ADJ dry; (río) dried-up; (planta) withered; (respuesta) curt, brief; **en —** on dry land; **parar en —** to stop short; **quedar —** to fall dead; **estar —** to be broke; **lavar en — to** dry-clean; **a secas** plain

secreción F secretion

secretar VT to secrete

secretaría F secretariat

secretariado M (profesión) secretarial profession; (secretaría) secretariat; (conjunto de secretarias) secretarial pool

secretario -ria MF secretary; **— general** secretary general

secretear VI to whisper

secreto ADJ secret; (de policía sin uniforme) undercover; M (cosa oculta) secret; (condición de oculto) secrecy; **— a voces** open secret; **en —** in secret; **— bancario** client confidentiality

secta F sect

sector M sector

secuaz M henchman

secuela F consequence; **—s** aftermath

secuencia F sequence

secuenciar VT to sequence

secuestrador -ora MF kidnapper

secuestrar VT (a una persona) to kidnap, to abduct; (propiedad) to seize; (un avión) to hijack

secuestro M (de una persona) kidnapping; (de propiedad) seizure; (de un avión) hijacking

secular ADJ secular

secundar VT to second; (imitar) to imitate; (seguir) to follow suit

secundaria F secondary school

secundario ADJ secondary

sed F thirst; **tener —** to be thirsty

seda F silk; **como una —** (suave) soft as silk; (afable) sweet-tempered

sedación F sedation

sedán M sedan

sedante ADJ & M sedative

sedar VT to sedate

sedativo ADJ & M sedative

sede F (gubernamental) seat; (religiosa) see

sedentario ADJ sedentary

sedería F (conjunto de artículos de seda) silk goods; (tienda de sedas) silk shop

sedero -ra MF (que vende) silk dealer; (que fabrica) silk weaver; ADJ **industria sedera** silk industry

sedición F sedition

sediento ADJ thirsty; **estar — de** to thirst for

sedimento M sediment

sedoso ADJ silken, silky

seducción F seduction

seducir[24] VT (corromper) to seduce; (atraer) to entice; (persuadir con argucias) to lure

seductivo ADJ alluring

seductor -ora ADJ alluring; M seducer; F seductress

sefardí ADJ Sephardic; MF Sephardi; M (variedad del español) Sephardi

sefardita ADJ & MF Sephardi

segador -ora MF (persona) mower, reaper; F (máquina) mower, reaper

segar[1,7] VT (hierba) to mow; (mies) to reap

seglar ADJ secular; M layman; F laywoman

segmento M segment

segregar[7] VT (separar) to segregate; (producir una sustancia) to secrete

seguida LOC ADV **en —** at once, immediately

seguido ADJ in a row; **dos horas seguidas** two hours in a row; ADV straight through; **trabajaron —** they worked continuously

seguidor -ora MF follower

seguimiento M (persecución) pursuit; (atención continuada) follow-up

seguir[5,12] VT to follow; (estudios) to pursue; (progreso de un avión) to track; **sigue trabajando** he keeps on working; **sigue allí** he is still there; **de lo anterior se sigue que** from the preceding it follows that; **— los pasos de** to follow in the footsteps of; **—le la corriente a alguien** to play along with someone; **— el tren** to keep up; **— el hilo de** to keep track of; **— la pista de** to trail

según PREP according to; **— se mire** depending on how you see it; **— pasa el tiempo** as time goes by; **— tus instrucciones** per your instructions; CONJ as; **lo haré — me digas** I will do it as you tell me to

segundero M (de reloj) second hand

segundo -da ADV, ADJ & M second; **segunda intención** ulterior motive; **de —** second-rate; **de segunda mano** secondhand; MF second in command

segundón -ona MF (hijo) second-born child; (persona mediocre) also-ran

seguridad F (contra el delito) security; (contra accidentes) safety; **— en sí mismo** self-confidence; **— social** social security

seguro ADJ (a prueba de delincuencia) secure; (que no ofrece, siente duda) sure, certain; (libre de peligro) safe; (firme) stable; **es — que** it is certain that; **su — servidor** yours truly; **— de sí mismo** self-assured; M (contrato contra riesgos) insurance; (dispositivo) safety device, restraint; **— contra daños a terceros** liability insurance; **— contra incendios** fire insurance; **— contra todo riesgo** comprehensive insurance; **— médico** health insurance; **— de vida** life insurance; **en —** in safety; **sobre —** without risk

seis NUM six

selección F selection, choice; **— natural** natural selection; **— nacional** national team

seleccionar VT to select, to choose

selectivo ADJ selective

selecto ADJ select, choice

sellar VT (poner sello) to stamp; (precintar) to seal

sello M (de correo) stamp; (de documento oficial) seal; (instrumento) seal, stamp; (de discos) label; **— de goma** rubber stamp; **— fiscal** revenue stamp

selva F forest; (tropical) jungle; **— virgen** virgin forest

semáforo M traffic light

semana F week; **entre —** during the week

semanal ADJ weekly

semanario M weekly publication

semántica F semantics

semblante M countenance

semblanza F biographical sketch

sembrado M sown ground

sembradora F planting machine

sembrar[1] VT (plantar) to sow, to plant; (esparcir) to scatter; (minas) to lay; (pánico, alegría) to spread

semejante ADJ similar, like; **— afirmación** such a statement; **un tipo —** such a guy; MF fellow human being

semejanza F resemblance, similarity; **a — de** in the manner of

semejar VT to resemble

semental ADJ stud; M stud, stallion

semestre M semester

semicírculo M semicircle

semiconductor M semiconductor

semifinal ADJ & F semifinal

semilla F seed

semillero M seedbed; **— de vicios** hotbed of vice

seminario M (religioso) seminary; (universitario) seminar

semítico ADJ Semitic

senado M senate

senador -ora MF senator

sencillez F simplicity

sencillo ADJ (no complicado, de clase humilde) simple; (fácil) easy, simple; (sin adornos) plain; (no afectado) straightforward

senda F (construida) path, pathway; (natural) track, trail

sendero M (construido) path, pathway; (natural) track, trail

sendos ADJ one for each

Senegal M Senegal

senegalés -esa ADJ & MF Senegalese

senil ADJ senile

senilidad F senility

seno M (pecho) breast; (hueco) sinus; (útero) womb; **— de la familia** bosom of the family

sensación F (física) sensation; (mental) feeling, impression; **tengo la — de que** I have the feeling that; **fue la — de la fiesta** she was the life of the party

sensacional ADJ sensational

sensatez F common sense

sensato ADJ sensible, level-headed

sensibilidad F (modo de pensar) sensibility; (percepción) sensitiveness

sensibilizar[9] VT to sensitize

sensible ADJ sensitive; (notable) perceptible; **tengo el brazo muy — por el accidente** my arm is very tender because of the accident; **Juana es muy — en estas ocasiones** Juana is very emotional on these occasions

sensiblería F sentimentality
sensiblero ADJ sentimental, mushy
sensitivo ADJ sensitive
sensor M sensor
sensorial ADJ sensory
sensual ADJ (carnal) sensual; (de los sentidos) sensuous
sensualidad F sensuality
sentada F sitting; (protesta) sit-in; **de una —** at one sitting
sentado ADJ **dar por —** to take for granted
sentar[1] VT to seat; **— bien** to agree with; **me sentó muy mal lo que dijo** what he said did not sit well with me; **este peinado no te sienta** this hairdo does not become you; **no te sienta ese traje** that suit does not fit you; **— precedente** to set a precedent; **—se** to sit down
sentencia F maxim; (fallo) ruling; (condena) sentence; (indemnización) award
sentenciar VT (condenar) to sentence; (fallar) to rule
sentido ADJ heartfelt; M (facultad) sense; (significado) meaning; (dirección) way; **— común** common sense; **aguzar el —** to prick up one's ears; **de un sólo —** one-way; **de dos —s** two-way; **dejar sin —** to render unconscious; **en cierto —** in a sense; **perder el —** to faint; **quedar —** to have one's feelings hurt; **sin —** meaningless; **tener —** to make sense
sentimental ADJ sentimental
sentimentalismo M sentimentalism
sentimiento M feeling, sentiment
sentir[3] VT to feel; (oír) to hear; (lamentar) to regret; **—se** to feel; **—se capaz de** to feel up to; **—se de los pies** to have pains in the feet
seña F (gesto) sign; (rasgo) trait; (marca) mark; **—s** name and address; **por mas —s** as an additional proof; **—s de vida** life signs; **hablar por —s** to use sign language; **hacer —s** to signal
señal F (de tráfico, violencia, vida, de la cruz) sign; (de violencia) mark; (de radio) signal; (pago anticipado) deposit; **en — de** in token of
señalar VT (marcar, señalar) to mark; (mostrar, mencionar) to point out; (fijar) to fix; **—se** to distinguish oneself
señor M (título) mister; (forma de tratamiento) sir; (dueño) lit master, lord; **el Señor** the Lord; **un gran —** a great man
señora F (dama) lady; (forma de tratamiento) madam, ma'am; (título) Mrs., Ms.; (esposa) wife

señorear VI to dominate
señoría F lordship; **su —** your honor
señorial ADJ lordly
señorío M (dominio) dominion; (dignidad) lordship
señorita F miss
señorito M (joven) master; (dandi) dandy
señuelo M decoy, lure
separación F separation
separado ADJ (apartado) separate; (estado civil) separated; **por —** separately
separar VT to separate; (clasificar) to sort out; (despedir de un cargo) to remove; **—se** to separate, to part company
separata F offprint, reprint
septentrional ADJ northern
septicemia F blood poisoning
septiembre, setiembre M September
séptimo ADJ & M seventh
sepulcro M tomb
sepultar VT to bury, to inter
sepultura F (acción) burial; (lugar) grave, tomb; **dar —** to bury
sepulturero -ra MF gravedigger
sequedad F dryness
sequía F drought
séquito M retinue, entourage
ser[43] VI to be; **— de Valencia** to be from Valencia; **— de madera** to be made of wood; **a no — que** unless; **así es** that's right; **érase una vez** once upon a time; **es decir** that is to say; **es de esperar** it is to be expected; **es más** what's more; **la boda es hoy** the wedding takes place today; **son las nueve** it is nine o'clock; **somos cuatro** there are four of us; V AUX to be; **fue elegido presidente** he was elected president; M (entidad viviente) being; (esencia) essence; (existencia) existence; **un — humano** a human being
serenar VI to quiet; **—se** (el alma) to become serene, to calm down; (el tiempo) to clear up
serenata F serenade; **dar —** to serenade
serenidad F serenity
sereno ADJ (mar, alma) serene; (cielo) clear; **al —** in the night air; M night watchman
serie F series; **en —** serial
seriedad F seriousness, earnestness
serio ADJ serious; (persona) earnest, serious; **en —** seriously
sermón M (prédica) sermon; (reprimenda) lecture
sermonear VI/VT (predicar) to preach; (reprender) to lecture
serpentear VI to wind, to meander
serpiente F snake

serrado ADJ serrated
serranía F mountainous region
serrano -na M mountain man; F mountain
  woman; ADJ **zona —** mountain region
serrín M sawdust
serrucho M handsaw
servicial ADJ helpful
servicio M service; (sirvientes) servants; (para
  un comensal) place setting; (aseo) rest
  room, facilities; **— de entrega** delivery service; **—
  a la habitación** room service; **poner en
  —** to commission, to put into service;
  estar en — to be in commission; **a su —**
  at your service
servidor -ora MF (persona) servant; **un —**
  yours truly; **su seguro —** yours truly; M
  (ordenador) server
servidumbre F servitude
servil ADJ (personalidad) servile; (trabajo)
  menial
servilleta F napkin
servir[5] VI to serve; **— de** to serve as; **— para**
  to be used for; **para —le** at your service;
  no — para nada to be of no use; **¿en
  qué le puedo —?** how can I help you?
  —se de to make use of; **sírvase usted
  hacerlo** please do it
sésamo M sesame; **¡abre —!** open sesame!
sesenta NUM sixty
sesgado ADJ biased
sesgar[7] VT (una tela) to cut on the bias; (una
  opinión) to slant; (las estadísticas) to skew
sesgo M (en la tela) bias; (de los ojos, de
  orientación) slant; **al —** obliquely
sesión F (reunión, periodo) session; (para
  fotografías) sitting; (de una película)
  showing
seso M brain; **de poco —** foolish; **devanarse
  los —s** to rack one's brain
sestear VI to take a nap
sesudo ADJ (persona) brainy; (explicación)
  intelligent; (testarudo) *Méx* stubborn
set M set
seta F mushroom
setenta NUM seventy
seto M hedge
sétter M setter
seudónimo M pseudonym, pen name
severidad F severity, harshness
severo ADJ severe, stern, harsh
sexar VT to sex
sexismo M sexism
sexo M sex; **el — bello** the fair sex
sexto ADV, ADJ & M sixth
sexual ADJ sexual
sexualidad F sexuality

sexy ADJ sexy
Seychelles F PL Seychelles
shock M shock
short, shorts M shorts
si CONJ if; **yo voy — tú vas** I'm going if
  you're going; **no sé — viene o no** I don't
  know whether she's coming or not; **¡— ya
  te lo dije!** but I already told you! **— bien**
  although; **por — acaso** just in case; **—
  Dios quiere** God willing; **— no me
  equivoco** unless I'm mistaken
sí ADV yes; **¿—?** really? **— que fui** I did go;
  creo que — I think so; M consent; **me
  dio el —** she said yes; PRON himself,
  herself, itself, oneself, themselves; **de por
  —** in itself; **estar sobre —** to be on the
  alert; **volver en —** to come to; **pagado
  de —** self-satisfied; **estar fuera de —** to
  be beside oneself; **hablar para —** to talk
  to oneself; **dio todo de —** she gave her
  all; **cada cual para —** every man for
  himself
sicario M hitman
sicomoro M sycamore
**SIDA (síndrome de inmunodeficiencia
  adquirida)** M AIDS
siderurgia F steel industry
sidra F cider
siega F (de la hierba) mowing; (de las mieses)
  reaping
siembra F (acción de sembrar) sowing;
  (época) sowing time
siempre ADV always; **desde —** since forever;
  para / por — forever; **por — jamás**
  forevermore; **— que** (en cualquier
  momento) whenever; (con tal que)
  provided that; **— y cuando** provided
  that; **como —** as usual; **hoy no eres el
  mismo de —** you're not yourself today
sien F temple
sierpe F *lit* serpent
sierra F saw; (cordillera) small mountain
  range; **— de cadena** chain saw
siesta F siesta, afternoon nap; **dormir la —**
  to take an afternoon nap
siete NUM seven
sífilis F syphilis
sifón M (para líquidos) siphon; (tubo) trap
sigilo M stealth
sigla F acronym
siglo M century
signatario -ria MF signer
significación F (sentido) meaning;
  (importancia) significance
significado M meaning, sense
significar[6] VT to mean, to signify
significativo ADJ significant

signo M sign; **— de admiración** exclamation point; **— de igual** equal sign; **— de interrogación** question mark; **— de más** plus sign; **— de menos** minus sign; **— de multiplicación** multiplication sign; **—s vitales** vital signs

siguiente ADJ following; **al día —** the next day

sílaba F syllable

silbar VI to whistle; (rechiflar) to hiss

silbato M whistle

silbido M whistle

silenciador M (de arma) silencer; (de coche) muffler

silenciar VT to silence

silencio M silence, quiet; **guardar —** to keep quiet

silencioso ADJ silent, quiet

silicio M silicon

silla F chair; (de montar) saddle; **— de ruedas** wheelchair; **— eléctrica** electric chair; **— plegadiza** folding chair

sillín M saddle, seat

sillón M armchair

silo M silo

silogismo M syllogism

silueta F silhouette

siluro M catfish

silvestre ADJ wild

silvicultura F forestry

sima F chasm

simbiosis F symbiosis

simbólico ADJ symbolic

simbolismo M symbolism

símbolo M symbol; **— de status** status symbol; **— sexual** sex symbol

simetría F symmetry

simétrico ADJ symmetrical

simiente F seed

símil M simile

similar ADJ similar

simio M ape

simpatía F friendliness; **no le tengo mucha —** I don't like him much

simpático ADJ (amistoso) nice, friendly, congenial; (sistema nervioso) sympathetic

simpatizar[9] VI (con alguien) to like; (con una idea) to be sympathetic toward

simple ADJ (no complicado) simple; (mero) mere; (tonto) simpleminded

simpleza F (sencillez) simplicity; (estupidez) stupidity

simplicidad F simplicity

simplificar[6] VT to simplify

simplista ADJ simplistic; (explicación) glib, simplistic

simplón -ona ADJ simpleminded; MF

simpleton

simposio M symposium

simulacro M **— de batalla** mock battle; **— de incendio** fire drill

simular VT to simulate, to feign

simultáneo ADJ simultaneous

sin PREP without; **— aliento** out of breath; **— amueblar** unfurnished; **— azúcar** sugar-free; **— comentarios** no comment; **— compromiso** without obligation; **— duda** without doubt, undoubtedly; **— embargo** nevertheless; **— escrúpulos** unscrupulous; **— falta** without fail; **— sentido** meaningless

sinagoga F synagogue

sincerarse VI to clear the air

sinceridad F sincerity

sincero ADJ sincere; (opinión) candid; (agradecimiento) heartfelt, wholehearted

sincronización F timing

sincronizar[9] VT to synchronize

sindicar[6] VT to unionize, to syndicate

sindicato M syndicate, trade union, labor union

síndico -ca MF receiver, trustee

síndrome M syndrome; **— de Down** Down's syndrome; **— de abstinencia** withdrawal symptoms

sinfín M **un — de cosas** a lot of things

sinfonía F symphony

Singapur M Singapore

singapurense ADJ & MF Singaporean

singular ADJ (número) singular; (excepcional) unique

siniestro ADJ sinister; M disaster

sinnúmero M myriad

sino CONJ but; **no vino — que llamó** she didn't come, but instead called; **no tengo dos — tres** I don't have two but three; **no es — madera** it's only wood

sinónimo ADJ synonymous; M synonym

sinopsis F synopsis

sinrazón F injustice

sinsabor M trouble

sinsonte M mockingbird

sintaxis F syntax

síntesis F synthesis

sintético ADJ synthetic; (fibras) man-made

sintetizar[9] VT to synthesize

síntoma M symptom

sintonía F tuning

sintonizador M tuner

sintonizar[9] VT (una emisora) to tune in; (un sintonizador) to fine-tune; **los dos sintonizan bien** the two are on the same wavelength

sinuoso ADJ (camino) sinuous, winding;

(comportamiento) devious

sinvergüenza MF creep

siquiera ADV at least; **dame — unos días** give me a few days at least; **ni —** not even

sirena F (ninfa, bocina) siren; (mitad mujer, mitad pez) mermaid

Siria F Syria

sirio -ria ADJ & MF Syrian

sirviente -ta MF servant

sisar VT to pilfer, to swipe

sisear VI to hiss

siseo M hiss, hissing

sísmico ADJ seismic

sistema M system; **— operativo** operating system; **— binario** binary system; **— mundial de posicionamiento** global positioning system; **— experto** expert system; **— inmune** immune system; **— nervioso central** central nervous system; **— solar** solar system

sistemático ADJ systematic

sistematizar[9] ADJ/VT to systematize

sistémico ADJ systemic

sitial M seat of honor

sitiar VT to besiege

sitio M (espacio vacío) room; (ubicación) place, site; (asedio) siege; **no hay —** there's no room; **esto no está en su —** this is out of place; **— web** website; **poner — a** to lay siege to; **poner a alguien en su —** to put someone in his place

sito ADJ situated

situación F situation; (legal, financiero, social) status

situado ADJ situated; **estar —** to be located

situar[17] VT to locate, to place; **—se** to be located

sketch M sketch, skit

slalom M slalom

smog M smog

smoking M dinner jacket

so PREP **— pena de** under penalty of; **— pretexto de** under the pretext of; INTERJ whoa; ADV **— tonto** you stupid idiot!

sobaco M armpit

sobar VT (la masa) to knead; (a una persona) to fondle; (un traje) to wear out

soberanía F sovereignty

soberano -na ADJ & MF sovereign

soberbia F pride, haughtiness

soberbio ADJ proud, haughty

sobornar VT to bribe

soborno M (acción) bribery; (mordida) bribe

sobra F surplus; **—s** leftovers, leavings; **de — sabes** you know full well; **está de —** it is

superfluous; **las piezas de —** spare parts

sobrado ADJ more than enough

sobrante ADJ leftover; M surplus

sobrar VI (dinero, libros) to be left over, to remain; (personas) to be in the way

sobre PREP (encima de) above, over; (en contacto con) on, upon; (acerca de) about; **un préstamo — su coche** a loan on his car; **— todo** above all; **— las 9:30** at about 9:30; **marchar — Madrid** to march toward Madrid; M (para cartas) envelope; (de sopa) packet; **— manila** manila envelope; **irse al —** to hit the sack

sobreactuar[17] VI to ham it up

sobrealimentador M supercharger

sobrecalificado ADJ overqualified

sobrecarga F overload

sobrecargar[7] VT to overload

sobrecogedor ADJ awesome

sobrecoger[11b] VI/VT to awe; **—se** to be in awe; **—se de pánico** to be panic-stricken

sobrecogimiento M awe

sobredosis F overdose

sobreentenderse[1] VI to be understood

sobreentendido ADJ understood; M assumption

sobreexcitado ADJ overexcited, wired

sobreexcitar VT to overexcite

sobregirar VT to overdraw

sobregiro M overdraft

sobrehumano ADJ superhuman

sobrellevar VT to bear, to endure

sobremanera ADV beyond measure

sobremesa F after-dinner conversation

sobrenadar VI to float

sobrenatural ADJ supernatural

sobrenombre M nickname

sobrepasar VT to exceed

sobrepeso M overweight

sobreponerse[39] VT to superimpose; VI **— a** (valer más que) to outweigh; (recuperarse) to get over

sobreproteger[11b] VT to smother

sobrepujar VT to surpass

sobresaliente ADJ outstanding; MF understudy

sobresalir[42] VI (ser notable) to stand out; (estar en un plano más saliente) to project, to jut out; (ser excelente) to excel

sobresaltar VT to startle, frighten; **—se** to be startled, to start

sobresalto M start, scare

sobrestante M foreman

sobresueldo M extra pay

sobretodo M overcoat

sobrevenir[47] VI to happen unexpectedly

sobrevivencia F survival
sobreviviente MF survivor; ADJ surviving
sobrevivir VI/VT to survive
sobriedad F sobriety
sobrino -na M nephew; — **nieto** great-nephew; F niece
sobrio ADJ sober
socarrar VT to singe
socarrón ADJ sarcastic
socarronería F sarcasm
socavar VT (excavar por debajo) to dig under; (debilitar) to undermine, to undercut
socavón M sinkhole; shaft, tunnel
sociable ADJ sociable, gregarious
social ADJ social
socialismo M socialism
socialista ADJ & MF socialist
socializar[9] VT to socialize
sociedad F society; (firma) company, partnership; — **anónima** corporation; — **de consumo** consumer society; **alta** — high society
socio -ia MF (de una firma) partner; (de un club) member
socioeconómico ADJ socioeconomic
sociología F sociology
sociópata MF INV sociopath
socorrer VT to help
socorro INTERJ & M help; **acudir al** — **de** to go to the rescue of; **pedir** — to cry out for help
soda F soda
sodio M sodium
sodomía F sodomy
soez ADJ vulgar
sofá M sofa, couch; —**-cama** sleeper, sofa bed
sofisma M fallacy
sofisticado ADJ sophisticated
sofocante ADJ suffocating, oppressive
sofocar[6] VI/VT to suffocate; (una rebelión) to quash, to quell, to suppress; (un incendio) to put out
sofoco M suffocation
softball M softball
software M software
soga F rope; **estar con la** — **al cuello** to have a rope around one's neck
soja F (planta) soy; (semilla) soybean
sojuzgar[7] VT to subjugate, to subdue
sol M sun; **de** — **a** — from sunrise to sunset; **hace** — it is sunny; **tomar el** — to sunbathe; **ella es un** — she's a gem; **arrimarse al** — **que más calienta** to know which side one's bread is buttered on
solamente ADV only

solana F sunny place
solapa F lapel
solapado ADJ underhanded
solar M (terreno) lot; (casa ancestral) manor; ADJ solar
solaz M *lit* recreation
soldado M soldier; — **raso** private; — **de línea** regular soldier
soldador M soldering iron
soldadura F (acción, con estaño) soldering; (resultado) solder; (acción, sin estaño) welding; (resultado) weld; — **autógena** arc welding
soldar[2] VI/VT (con estaño) to solder; (sin estaño) to weld; —**se** to mend
soleado ADJ sunny
solear VT to put in the sun; —**se** to sun oneself
soledad F solitude, loneliness
solemne ADJ solemn; — **disparate** downright foolishness
solemnidad F solemnity
solenoide M solenoid
soler[2,50] VI **suelo levantarme a las siete** I usually get up at seven; **solía acostarme tarde** I used to go to bed late
solferino ADJ reddish-purple
solicitante MF applicant
solicitar VT (permiso) to request; (un puesto, una beca) to apply for
solícito ADJ solicitous
solicitud F (para beca, puesto) application; (de información, permiso) request; **a** — **de** at the request of
solidaridad F solidarity
solidez F solidity
solidificar[6] VT to solidify
sólido ADJ solid; (mueble) sturdy; (argumento) strong; M solid
solista MF soloist
solitario -ria ADJ solitary; MF (persona) recluse; M (juego de cartas, brillante) solitaire; F tapeworm
sollozar[9] VI to sob
sollozo M sob
solo ADJ (desamparado) lonely, lonesome; (no acompañado) alone; **tengo un** — **coche** I only have one car; **a solas** alone; **habla solo** he talks to himself; **ni una sola palabra** not a single word; M solo
sólo ADV just, only; — **quiero saber** I just / only want to know
solomillo M sirloin
solsticio M solstice
soltar[2] VT (a un prisionero) to let go, to release; (el vientre) to loosen; (una carcajada) to let out; (bombas) to drop;

(un disparate) to say; — **amarras** to cast
off; — **el hervor** to come to a boil; —
tacos to swear; —**se** to loosen up; —**se el
pelo** to kick up one's heels
soltero -ra ADJ single, unmarried; M
bachelor; F unmarried woman
solterón -ona M old bachelor; F *pey* spinster
soltura F ease; **hablar con** — to speak
fluently
soluble ADJ soluble
solución F solution
solucionar VT to solve
solventar VT to settle
solvente ADJ & M solvent
somalí ADJ & MF Somalian
Somalia F Somalia
sombra F (de una figura) shadow; (protección
del sol) shade; (para ojos) eye shadow;
hacer — to overshadow; **dar** — to shade;
no fiarse ni de su propia — to be
scared of one's own shadow; **a la** — in
the shade; **sin** — **de duda** without a
shadow of a doubt
sombreado ADJ (con protección del sol)
shady; (oscuro) shadowy
sombrear VT to shade
sombrerería F millinery
sombrerero -ra MF milliner
sombrero M hat; — **de copa** top hat; —
hongo derby
sombrilla F parasol
sombrío ADJ (oscuro) dark; (triste) somber,
gloomy
somero ADJ shallow
someter VT (proponer algo) to submit; (poner
bajo dominio) to subject; —**se a** to
undergo
sometimiento M (proposición) submission;
(dominio) subjection
somnífero M sleeping pill
somnolencia F drowsiness, sleepiness
somnoliento ADJ drowsy
son LOC ADV **al** — **de** to the sound of;
venimos en — **de paz** we come in peace
sonaja F rattle
sonajero M rattle
sonámbulo -la MF sleepwalker
sonar[2] VI (hacer un sonido) to sound;
(mencionarse) to be mentioned; (ser
familiar) to sound familiar; — **a** to sound
like; VT (bocina) to sound; (tambor) to
beat; (campana, timbre) to ring; —**se la
nariz / los mocos** to blow one's nose;
suena que it is rumored that; M sonar
sonda F (de médico) catheter; (cohete) probe;
tirar una — to sound
sondear VT (medir la oportunidad) to sound,

to fathom; (investigar la opinión) to
sound out
sondeo M survey
soneto M sonnet
sonido M sound
sonoro ADJ sonorous
sonreír[15] VI to smile
sonriente ADJ smiling
sonrisa F smile
sonrojarse VI to blush
sonrojo M blush, flush
sonrosado ADJ rosy
sonsacar[6] VT to extract
soñador -ora MF dreamer
soñar[2] VI/VT to dream; — **con / en** to dream
of; — **despierto** to daydream; — **que** to
dream that; **ni** — *fam* fat chance
soñoliento ADJ sleepy
sopa F (líquido) soup; (pan mojado) sop;
estar hecho una — to be sopping wet;
— **crema** cream soup
sopapo M smack
sopera F soup tureen
sopesar VT to weigh
sopetón LOC ADV **de** — all of a sudden
soplador -ora MF blower
soplar VI/VT to blow; (la sopa) to blow on;
(en un examen) to whisper; (a un amante)
to steal
soplete M blowtorch
soplo M breath, puff; **en un** — in a jiffy; —
cardíaco heart murmur
soplón -ona MF informer, snitch, stool
pigeon
sopor M lethargy
soportar VT (apoyar) to support, to bear;
(aguantar) to stand, to endure
soporte M support; (de una bicicleta)
kickstand
soprano M (voz) soprano; F (cantante)
soprano
sorber VI/VT to sip; —**se los mocos** to sniffle
sorbete M sherbet
sorbo M sip; **de un** — in one gulp
sordera F deafness
sórdido ADJ sordid, tawdry, sleazy
sordina F mute
sordo -da ADJ (que no oye) deaf; (dolor) dull;
(sonido) dull, muffled; **hacerse oídos** —**s**
to turn a deaf ear; MF deaf person;
hacerse el — to pretend not to hear
sordomudo -da ADJ deaf and dumb; MF deaf-
mute
sorna F irony
sorprendente ADJ surprising, startling
sorprender VT to surprise; —**se** to be
surprised

sorpresa F surprise; **— de cumpleaños** party favor; **para mi —** to my surprise; **pillar por —** to catch by surprise

sortear VT (elegir al azar) to draw lots, to raffle; (esquivar) to dodge

sorteo M drawing, raffle

sortija F (anillo) ring; (de pelo) ringlet

sortilegio M spell, charm

SOS M SOS

sosa F soda

sosegado ADJ composed, sedate

sosegar[1,7] VT to calm, to quiet; **—se** to quiet down, to compose oneself

sosiego M quiet, calm

soslayo LOC ADV **de —** oblique, slanting; **mirar de —** to look at out of the corner of one's eye

soso ADJ tasteless, insipid; (persona) dull

sospecha F suspicion

sospechar VT to suspect

sospechoso -sa ADJ suspicious; MF suspect

sostén M (apoyo, sustento) support, prop; (persona que sostiene) supporter, provider; (prenda) brassiere; **— de la familia** breadwinner

sostener[44] VT (una nota musical) to hold, to sustain; (una familia) to support; (un peso) to support, to hold; (una opinión) to claim, to uphold

sostenido ADJ sustained; M sharp

sota F jack, knave

sótano M cellar, basement

soto M thicket

soya F (semilla) soybean; (planta) soy

squash M squash

Sr. M Mr.

Sra. F (casada) Mrs.; (sin indicación de estado civil) Ms.

S.R.C. (Se Ruega Contestar) LOC RSVP

status M status

stop M stop sign

su ADJ POS (de él) his; (de ella) her; (de usted, ustedes) your; (de ellos, ellas) their

suave ADJ (pelo, piel) soft; (tiempo, droga) mild; (brisa, persona, animal) gentle; (coñac) smooth; **hablan —** they speak gently

suavidad F (pelo, piel) softness; (coñac) smoothness; (tiempo, droga) mildness; (brisa, persona, animal) gentleness

suavizante M fabric softener

suavizar[9] VT to soften

suazi ADJ & MF Swazi

Suazilandia F Swaziland

subalterno -na ADJ & MF subordinate

subarrendar VI/VT to sublet

subasta F auction

subastador -ora MF auctioneer

subastar VT to sell at auction, to auction

subconsciente ADJ subconscious

subcontratar VT to subcontract

subdesarrollado ADJ underdeveloped

súbdito -ta MF subject

subdivisión F subdivision

subempleado ADJ underemployed

subestimar VT to underestimate

subida F (de precios, de río) rise; (de montaña) climb; (de drogas) high; (cuesta) slope; **—s y bajadas** ups and downs

subido ADJ (color) bright; **— de tono** risqué

subir VI to rise, to go up; (la marea) to surge; (a un tren) to board; (a un autobús, coche) to get into; VT (algo del sótano) to bring up; (una montaña) to climb; (precios) to raise; **—se** to ride up; **el vino se me sube a la cabeza** the wine goes to my head; M **subibaja** seesaw

súbito ADJ sudden

subjetivo ADJ subjective

subjuntivo ADJ & M subjunctive

sublevación F revolt

sublevar VT to incite to rebellion; (indignar) to infuriate; **—se** to revolt

sublime ADJ sublime

submarino ADJ underwater; M submarine

subordinado -da ADJ & MF subordinate

subordinar VT to subordinate

subproducto M by-product

subproletariado M underclass

subrayar VT (con una línea) to underline; (enfatizar) to emphasize

subrepticio ADJ surreptitious

subrutina F subroutine

subsanar VT (una deficiencia) to remedy; (un error) to correct

subsecretario -ia MF undersecretary; **— de Justicia** Solicitor General

subsidiario ADJ subsidiary

subsiguiente ADJ subsequent

subsistencia F survival

subsistir VI to subsist, to survive

subteniente MF second lieutenant

subterfugio M subterfuge

subterráneo ADJ subterranean, underground; M subway

subtítulo M (de un capítulo, película) subtitle; (pie de foto) caption

suburbano -na ADJ of shantytowns; MF shantytown resident

suburbio M shantytown

subvaluar[17] VT to underestimate

subvención F subsidy

subvencionar VT to subsidize

subversivo ADJ subversive

subyacer[49] VI to underlie
subyugar[7] VT (dominar) to subjugate; (hechizar) to charm
succión F suction
sucedáneo -a MF substitute
suceder VI to happen, to occur; **— al trono** to succeed to the throne; VT to succeed
sucesión F succession; (heredero) descendant
sucesivo ADJ successive; **en lo —** in the future
suceso M (evento) event, occurrence; (incidente) incident
sucesor -ora MF successor
suciedad F (porquería) dirt, filth; (cualidad de sucio) filthiness
sucinto ADJ concise
sucio ADJ dirty, filthy; (trabajo, chiste) dirty; (conciencia) guilty; **blanco —** off-white; **este traje es —** this suit gets dirty easily
sucumbir VI to succumb
sucursal F branch, subsidiary
sudadera F sweatshirt
sudado ADJ sweaty
Sudáfrica F South Africa
sudafricano -na ADJ & MF South African
Sudamérica F South America
sudamericano -na ADJ & MF South American
Sudán M Sudan
sudanés -esa ADJ & MF Sudanese
sudar VT to sweat; **— la gota gorda** to sweat blood
sudeste ADJ southeast, southeastern; M southeast
sudoeste ADJ southwest, southwestern; M southwest
sudor M sweat
sudoroso ADJ sweaty
Suecia F Sweden
sueco -ca ADJ Swedish; M (lengua) Swedish; MF Swede; **hacerse el —** to pretend not to understand
suegro -a M father-in-law; F mother-in-law
suela F (de zapato) sole; (pez) flounder
sueldo M salary
suelo M (tierra) soil, ground; (piso) floor; **arrastrar por el —** to drag; **por los —s** at rock-bottom
suelto ADJ (no atado) loose, unattached; (flojo) loose; (libre) free; M loose change
sueño M (hecho de dormir) sleep; (hecho de soñar) dream; (ganas de dormir) sleepiness; **en —s** dreaming; **conciliar el —** to get to sleep; **tener —** to be sleepy; **ni en —(s)** never; **perder el —** to lose sleep; **— profundo** sound sleep; **estar en el séptimo —** to be deeply asleep

suero M serum; **— de leche** buttermilk; **— fisiológico** saline solution
suerte F (destino) fate; (fortuna) luck; (clase) kind; **de —** in luck; **dejar a su —** to leave to his own devices; **echar —s** to cast lots; **mala —** (desgracia) bad luck; (lo siento) too bad; **tener —** to be lucky; **tentar a la —** to court danger; **tocarle en —** to be one's lot
suertudo -da ADJ lucky; MF lucky devil
suéter M sweater
suficiencia F adequacy; **tiene una —** she's so arrogant
suficiente ADJ (adecuado) sufficient, adequate; (arrogante) smug; M (calificación mínima) lowest passing grade; PRON enough; **ser —** to be enough; **más que —** ample
sufijo M suffix
sufragar[7] VT to defray; **— los gastos** to meet the expenses
sufragio M suffrage
sufrido ADJ (madre) long-suffering; (pantalón) durable
sufrimiento M suffering
sufrir VI/VT to suffer; VT to stand; (una lesión) to sustain; (un cambio) to undergo; (una pena) to grieve; **— de** to suffer from; **— de los pies** to have foot pains
sugerencia F suggestion
sugerir[3] VT to suggest
sugestión F suggestion
suicida MF suicide
suicidarse VI to commit suicide
suicidio M suicide
suite F suite
Suiza F Switzerland
suizo -za ADJ & MF Swiss; M sweet roll
sujeción LOC ADV **con — a** subject to
sujetar VT (fijar) to attach; (unir) to hold; (someter) to subdue, to hold down; **—se** to hold on; M SG **sujetalibros** bookend; **sujetapapeles** paper clip
sujeto ADJ held by; **— a** subject to; M (de oración, de experimento) subject; (individuo) individual
sulfato M sulphate
sulfurarse VI to hit the roof
sulfúrico ADJ sulfuric
sulfuro M sulfide
suma F (resultado aritmético) sum; (operación aritmética) addition; (cantidad) amount, sum; **en —** in sum
sumadora F adding machine
sumar VT to add, to add up; **—se a** to join
sumario M brief; ADJ summary
sumergible ADJ waterproof

sumergir[11] VT to submerge, to dip; —**se** to dive; —**se en** to immerse oneself in

sumidero M (socavón) sinkhole; (desagüe) drain

suministrar VT to furnish, to supply with

suministros M PL supplies

sumir VT to immerse

sumisión F submission

sumiso ADJ submissive

súmmum M ultimate; **el — de la moda** the cat's meow

sumo ADJ utmost, paramount; **a lo —** at the most

suntuoso ADJ sumptuous, luxurious

superar VT (las expectativas) to surpass; (un límite) to exceed; (una dificultad) to overcome, to surmount; (una prueba) to pass; —**se** to improve oneself

superávit M surplus

supercomputadora F supercomputer

superdirecta F overdrive

superdotado ADJ gifted

superego M superego

superestrella F superstar

superficial ADJ (conocimiento, herida, persona) superficial; (persona) shallow

superficialidad F shallowness

superficie F (parte exterior) surface; (de una figura geométrica) area

superfluo ADJ superfluous

superintendente MF superintendent

superior ADJ (mejor) superior; (más alto) higher; (más grande, intenso) greater; MF superior

superioridad F superiority

superlativo ADJ & M superlative

supermercado M supermarket

superordenador M supercomputer

superponer[39] VT to superimpose

superpotencia F superpower

supersónico ADJ supersonic

superstición F superstition

supersticioso ADJ superstitious

supervisar VT to supervise

supervisión F supervision

supervisor -ora MF supervisor

supervivencia F survival; **la — del más apto** the survival of the fittest

superyó M superego

suplantar VT to supplant

suplementar VT to supplement

suplemento M supplement

suplente ADJ & MF substitute

súplica F entreaty, plea

suplicar[6] VT to plead, to beseech

suplicio M ordeal

suplir VT (sustituir) to substitute for; (compensar) to make up for

suponer[39] VT (dar por sentado) to suppose, to presume, to surmise; (implicar) to involve

suposición F supposition, surmise

supositorio M suppository

supremacía F supremacy

supremo ADJ supreme

supresión F (de una idea) suppression; (de una palabra) deletion

suprimir VT (una idea) to suppress; (la esclavitud) to abolish; (una palabra) to delete

supuesto ADJ supposed; — **que** supposing that; **dar por —** to consider certain; **por — de** course; M supposition

supuración F discharge

supurante ADJ festering, running

supurar VI to fester, to discharge

sur ADJ & M south; **hacia el —** southward; **rumbo al —** southward

surcar[6] VT to plow

surco M (en la tierra) furrow; (en un camino) rut; (en un disco) groove; (en el rostro) wrinkle

surcoreano -na ADJ & MF South Korean

sureño -ña ADJ southern; MF southerner

sureste ADJ southeast, southeastern; M southeast

surfear VI/VT to surf (también en el internet)

surfing M surfing; **hacer —** to surf

surgimiento M rise

surgir[11] VI (situación) to arise; (manantial) to rise; (problema) to emerge, to crop up

Surinam M Surinam, Suriname

surinamés -esa ADJ & MF Surinamer

surmenage M burnout

suroeste ADJ southwest, southwestern; M southwest

surrealismo M surrealism

surtido M stock, assortment; ADJ assorted

surtidor M (bomba) pump; (chorro, pieza de carburador) jet

surtir VT to provide; — **efecto** to produce the desired effect; — **un pedido** to fill an order

susceptible ADJ susceptible

suscitar VT to stir up

suscribir[51] VT (una opinión) to subscribe to, to endorse; (un seguro) to underwrite; —**se a** to subscribe to

suscripción F subscription

suscriptor -ora MF subscriber

susodicho ADJ above-mentioned

suspender VT (colgar) to suspend, to hang; (interrumpir) to suspend, to stop; (cancelar) to cancel; (no dejar trabajar) to suspend; VI/VT (no aprobar) to fail, to flunk

suspense M suspense

suspensión F suspension

suspenso ADJ hanging; **quedarse —** to freeze; M (en un examen) failure; (en una película) suspense; **en —** in suspense

suspensorio M jock (strap)

suspicaz ADJ suspicious

suspirar VT to sigh; **— por** to yearn for

suspiro M sigh; **dame un —** give me a breather

sustancia F substance

sustancial ADJ substantial

sustancioso ADJ substantial

sustantivo M noun; ADJ substantive

sustentar VT to sustain

sustento M (alimento) sustenance; (apoyo) support; **ganarse el —** to earn a living

sustitución F substitution

sustituible ADJ replaceable

sustituir[31] VI/VT to substitute for, to replace; **Juan sustituyó a María** John substituted for Mary; **sustituí la leche por agua** I substituted water for milk

sustituto -ta MF substitute

susto M scare, fright

sustracción F subtraction

sustraer[45] VT to take away; **—se a** to avoid

susurrar VI/VT (una persona, el viento) to whisper; (agua) to murmur, to ripple; (hojas) to rustle

susurro M (de una persona, del viento) whisper; (del agua) murmur; (de las hojas) rustle

sutil ADJ subtle

sutileza F subtlety; (exagerada) nicety, quibble

sutilizar[9] VT to quibble over

sutura F suture

suyo ADJ (de él) his; (de ella) her; (de usted, de ustedes) your; (de ellos, de ellas) their; PRON (de él) his; (de ella) hers; (de usted, de ustedes) yours; (de ellos, de ellas) theirs; **salirse con la suya** to get one's own way; **hacer de las suyas** to be up to one's tricks; **los —s** his / her / your / their family

swing M swing

Tt

tabaco M tobacco

tábano M horsefly

tabaquismo M smoking

taberna F tavern, saloon

tabernero -ra MF bartender

tabicar[6] VT to partition

tabique M partition

tabla F (tablero) board, plank; (teatro) stage; (pliegue) pleat; (gráfica) table, chart; **— de surf** surfboard; **— de planchar** ironing board; **—s** (escenario) stage; **—s de la ley** the tables of the law; **—s de multiplicar** multiplication tables; **— periódica** periodic table; **— de contenidos** table of contents; **— de cortar** cutting board; **hacer —s** to tie

tablado M stage

tablero M (para juegos de mesa) board; (de instrumentos) panel, instrument panel; (de coche) dashboard; (pizarra) blackboard; (para noticias) bulletin board; **— de mando** control panel

tableta F (de aspirina) tablet; (de chocolate) bar

tablilla F (de arcilla) tablet; (de cama) slat; (para fracturas) splint

tabloide M tabloid

tablón M plank

tabú M taboo

tabulador M tab

tabular VT to tabulate, to chart

taburete M stool, footstool

TAC (tomografía axial computarizada) F CAT scan

tacañería F stinginess, tightness

tacaño -ña ADJ stingy, miserly; MF miser

tacha F blemish; (al honor) blot

tachar VT (borrar) to cross out, to delete; (atribuir una tacha) to accuse of

tachón M crossing out

tachonar VT to stud

tachuela F tack, thumbtack

tácito ADJ tacit

taciturno ADJ taciturn

taco M (de artillería) wad; (palo de billar) billiard cue; (comida ligera) snack; (palabrota) swear word; (comida mexicana) *Méx* taco; **soltar —s** *Esp* to swear

tacómetro M tachometer

tacón M heel

taconear VI to click the heels

taconeo M clicking

táctica F tactics

táctil ADJ tactile

tacto M (acción de tocar) touch; (sentido) sense of touch; (habilidad diplomática) tact

tahúr -ura MF gambler

tailandés -esa ADJ & MF Thai, Thailander

Tailandia F Thailand

taimado ADJ sly, devious

Taiwán M Taiwan

taiwanés -esa ADJ & MF Taiwanese

tajada F (de pan, carne) slice; (de carne) slab; **sacar —** to take one's cut

tajante ADJ (inequívoco) unequivocal; (cortante) sharp

tajar VT to slice

tajear VI/VT to slash

tajo M (corte) slash, hack; (cañón) gorge; (separación) gap

tal ADJ such; **— cual** just so; **— vez** perhaps; **un — García** a certain García; **a — grado** to such an extent; **de — palo — astilla** a chip off the old block; **en — caso** in such a case; CONJ **— como** like, just as; **con — (de) que** provided that; ADV **¿qué —?** how is it going? PRON **y — y así** and so on; **como si —** as if nothing had happened

taladrar VT to bore, to drill

taladro M drill

talante M temperament

talar VT (un árbol) to chop down; (un bosque) to lumber

talco M talcum

talento M talent

talentoso ADJ talented, gifted

talismán M charm

talla F (altura) height; (moral, intelectual) stature; (de ropa) size; (de madera) carving

tallado M carving

tallar VT to carve; (madera) to whittle, to carve; (naipes) to deal

tallarín M noodle

talle M (cintura) waist, waistline; **tiene buen — she has a good figure; corto de — short-waisted**

taller M (para trabajo manual, para enseñanza artística) workshop; (de artista plástico) studio; (de mecánico) garage, shop

tallo M stalk, stem

talón M (de pie, calcetín) heel; (de cheque) stub; **— de Aquiles** Achilles' heel; **girar sobre los talones** to turn on one's heels; **pisarle los talones a alguien** to be hot on someone's heels

talonario M checkbook

talonear VI to walk briskly

tamal M *Méx* tamale

tamaño M size; **— mediano** medium-sized; **de — natural** life-sized; ADJ such a big, so big a

tambalearse VI (un borracho) to stagger; (un boxeador) to reel; (un viejo) to dodder

tambaleo M stagger

también ADV also, too, as well

tambor M (instrumento musical, pieza de máquina) drum; (músico) drummer; (cilindro) cylinder; **a — batiente** with fanfare

tamborilear VI to drum, to tap

tamborilero -ra MF drummer

tamiz M sieve

tamizar[9] VT to sift

tampoco CONJ either; **no lo hizo —** he did not do it either; **ni yo —** me either

tampón M tampon

tan ADV **es — rica** she is so rich; **— alto como Juan** as tall as Juan; **— pronto como** as soon as; **es — idiota** he's such an idiot; **vecinos — simpáticos** such nice neighbors

tanda F (de personas) group; (de galletas) batch; (de ejercicios) set

tándem M tandem

tanga F thong

tangente ADJ & F tangent; **salirse por la — (irse de tema)** to go off on a tangent; (evadir) to beat about the bush

tangerina F tangerine

tangible ADJ tangible

tango M tango

tanque M tank

tantán M African drum

tantear VT (calcular) to estimate roughly; (averiguar) to sound out, to feel out; (apuntar) to score; (palpar) to grope

tanteo M (cálculo) estimate; (número de tantos) score; **al —** approximately

tanto ADJ, PRON & ADV **lloró — que se le enrojecieron los ojos** he cried so much his eyes got red; **yo tengo — como tú** I have as much as you do; **me quiere —** he loves me so; **no te quiero —** I don't love you that much; **a cada —s pasos** every so many steps; **cuarenta y —s** forty-odd; **a — el kilo** at so much per kilo; **el — por ciento** at such and such a percentage; **estar al —** to be in the know; **no es para —** it's not such a big deal; **da —** it's all the same; **— como** as much as; **— en la ciudad como en el campo** both in the city and in the country; **entre/mientras —** meanwhile; **mantenerse al —** to stay informed; **otros —s** just so many more; **por lo —** therefore; **a las tantas** until late at night; M (en los juegos) points

Tanzania F Tanzania

tanzano -na ADJ & MF Tanzanian

tañer [18] VT *lit* (una guitarra) to play; VI (una campana) to ring, to toll

tañido M (de guitarra) twang; (de campanas) toll

tapa F (de botella) cap; (de libro) cover; (de coche) hood; (de olla, bote) lid, top; *Esp* bar-snack

tapadera F (de recipiente) lid; (de un fraude) cover

tapar VT (una olla) to cover; (una salida) to block; (un caño) to plug up, to stop up; (encubrir) to cover up for; M SG **tapacubos** hubcap; **tapajuntas** flashing; **taparrabos** loincloth

tapete M runner

tapia F garden wall

tapiar VT to board up

tapicería F (para paredes) tapestry; (para muebles) upholstery; (tienda de textiles de decoración) tapestry shop; (arte de hacer tapices) tapestry making; (tienda de tapicero) upholstery shop

tapioca F tapioca

tapir M tapir

tapiz M tapestry, wall hanging

tapizar [9] VT to upholster

tapón M stopper; (de lavabo) plug; (de corcho) cork; **— de oídos** earplug

taponazo M pop of a cork

taquigrafía F shorthand

taquígrafo -fa MF stenographer

taquilla F ticket office, box office

tarambana MF INV dork, knucklehead

tarántula F tarantula

tararear VI/VT to hum

tarareo M hum, humming

tarascada F (mordedura) snap, bite; (réplica) rude answer

tardanza F lateness

tardar VI to take time; **¿cuánto tarda el trámite de divorcio?** how long does it take to get divorced? **—se** to take a long time; **tu padre se tarda** your father is taking a long time; **a más —** at the latest

tarde F afternoon; (hacia el anochecer) evening; **buenas —s** good afternoon; ADV late; **ya es —** it is late; **— o temprano** sooner o later; **más —** later on; **llegar —** to be late

tardío ADJ late

tardo ADJ *lit* slow

tarea F task, chore; (escolar) homework

tarifa F (impuesto) tariff; (lista de precios) list of prices; (de transporte) fare; (precio estipulado) rate

tarima F platform

tarjeta F card (también dispositivo de computadora); **— comercial** business card; **— postal** postcard; **— de cobro automático / de débito** debit card; **— de crédito** credit card; **— de Navidad** Christmas card; **marcar —** to punch in

tarro M jar

tarta F tart, pie

tartajear VI to stutter

tartamudear VI to stutter, to stammer

tartamudeo M stutter, stammer

tartamudez F stuttering

tartamudo -da MF stutterer, stammerer; ADJ stuttering, stammering

tártaro M tartar

tartera F round baking pan

tarugo M (trozo de madera) piece of wood; (tonto) blockhead

tasa F (índice) rate; (impuesto) tax; **— de desempleo** rate of unemployment; **— de interés** interest rate; **— de mortalidad** death rate; **— de natalidad** birth rate; **— prima** prime rate

tasación F valuation, appraisal

tasajo M jerky

tasar VT to appraise, to assess

tatarabuelo -la M great-great-grandfather; F great-great-grandmother

tataranieto -ta M great-great-grandson; F great-great-granddaughter

tatuaje M tattoo

tatuar [17] VT to tattoo

tauromaquia F bullfighting

taxi M taxi, taxicab

taxidermia F taxidermy

taxista MF taxi driver, cab driver

taxonomía F taxonomy

Tayikistán M Tajikistan

tayiko -ka ADJ & MF Tajik

taza F (de té, café) cup; (del inodoro) bowl

tazón M (para beber) mug; (de comida) bowl

té M (bebida) tea; (fiesta) tea party

te PRON you; **yo — amo** I love you; **— digo mañana** I'll tell you tomorrow; **no — mires en el espejo** don't look at yourself in the mirror

teatral ADJ theatrical

teatro M theater; **— de títeres** puppet show; **no hagas —** don't make such a production

techado M (techo) roof; (acción de techar) roofing

techar VT to roof

techo M (exterior) roof; (interior) ceiling

techumbre F roof

tecla F key; **— para mayúsculas** capital letter key; **— de cambio** shift key; **— de control** control key; **— de función**

function key; — **de retroceso** backspace
key; — **de tabulación** tab key; **dar uno
en la** — to hit the nail on the head
teclado M keyboard; — **numérico** keypad
teclear VT (pulsar las teclas) to key in; (hacer
ruido) to click
tecleo M keying in, clicking
técnica F (método) technique; (tecnología)
technology
técnico -ca ADJ technical; MF technician
tecnología F technology
tectónica F tectonics
tedio M boredom
tedioso ADJ tedious
tee M tee
teja F (de cerámica) tile; (de madera u otros
materiales) shingle
tejado M roof
tejar M tile factory; VT to cover with tiles
tejedor -ora MF weaver
tejer VI/VT (cesta, tela) to weave; (suéter) to
knit; M **tejemaneje** (fraude) hanky-
panky; (actividad) goings-on
tejido M (tela) textile, fabric; (de células)
tissue; (acción de tejer tela) weaving;
(acción de tejer un suéter) knitting
tejo M disk
tejón M badger
tela F (paño) cloth, fabric; (lienzo para pintar)
canvas; (de araña) web; (dinero) money;
(película) film; — **adhesiva** adhesive
tape; — **de cebolla** onion skin; **en** —
hardbound; **poner en** — **de juicio** to
call into question
telar M loom
telaraña F cobweb, spider's web
tele F TV
telebobo -ba MF couch potato
telecomunicaciones F PL
telecommunications
teleconferencia F teleconference
teledifusión F telecast
teledirección F remote guidance
teleférico M cable car
telefonazo M buzz, ring
telefonear VI/VT to telephone, to phone
telefónico ADJ **llamada telefónica**
telephone call
telefonista MF telephone operator
teléfono M telephone, phone; (número)
telephone number
telegrafiar[16] VI/VT to telegraph, to wire
telegráfico ADJ telegraphic
telégrafo M telegraph
telegrama M telegram
telemarketing M telemarketing
telemercadeo M telemarketing

telémetro M range finder
telenovela F soap opera
teleobjetivo M zoom lens
telepatía F telepathy
telescopio M telescope
telesquí M ski lift
teletipo M Teletype[tm]
televidente MF television viewer
televisión F television
televisor M television set; — **a / en color**
color television
telón M theater curtain; — **de acero** iron
curtain
tema M (de una obra literaria, musical)
theme; (de conversación) topic, subject;
(de un CD) song
temario M agenda
temático ADJ thematic
temblar[1] VI (la mano, la tierra) to tremble;
(la voz) to shake, to quaver; (de frío) to
shiver; (de miedo) to shudder; (la luz) to
flicker
temblequear VI to dodder
temblón ADJ trembling
temblor M (acción de temblar) trembling;
(de tierra) tremor; (de una llama) flicker;
(de la voz) quaver; (de frío) shiver; (de
miedo) shudder; — **de tierra** earthquake
tembloroso ADJ (mano) shaky; (llama)
flickering; (voz) quavering; (de miedo)
shuddering; (de frío) shivering
temer VI/VT to fear, to be afraid (of); — **por**
to fear for; **mucho me temo que** I fear
that
temerario ADJ rash, reckless
temeridad F temerity, recklessness
temeroso ADJ fearful
temible ADJ dreadful, dread
temor M fear
témpano M (bloque de hielo) block of ice;
(persona fría) cold fish
temperamento M temperament, disposition
temperancia F temperance
temperatura F temperature
tempestad F tempest, storm; **una** — **en un
vaso de agua** a tempest in a teapot
tempestuoso ADJ tempestuous, stormy
templado ADJ (clima) moderate, temperate;
(ánimo) serene; (actitud) moderate
templanza F temperance
templar VT (moderar, dar fuerza) to temper;
(calentar) to warm up; (una guitarra) to
tune
temple M (dureza) temper; (coraje) mettle;
de mal — in a bad mood
templo M temple
temporada F season; — **baja** off-season; —

de caza hunting season

temporal ADJ (del tiempo) temporal; (secular) worldly; (no permanente) temporary; M storm; **capear el —** to weather the storm

tempranero -ra ADJ early rising; MF early riser

temprano ADJ & ADV early

tenacidad F tenacity

tenaz ADJ tenacious

tenazas F PL (de cangrejo) pincers; (de mecánico) pliers; (de dentista) forceps; (para hielo) tongs

tendedero M clothesline

tendencia F tendency; (orientación) orientation; (de la moda) trend; **de — mayoritaria** mainstream; **— a la baja** downturn; **— al alza** upturn

tender[1] VT (un mantel) to spread out; (la ropa) to hang out; (la mano) to extend; (un cable) to lay; (una trampa) to set; VI **— a** to tend to; **—se** to stretch out

tendero -ra MF storekeeper; (de comestibles) grocer

tendido M (de cables) laying; (de ropa mojada) hanging out; (conjunto de cables) cables

tendinitis F tendonitis

tendón M tendon, sinew; **— de Aquiles** Achilles' tendon

tenebroso ADJ (oscuro) dark; (sombrío) gloomy

tenedor -ora M (utensilio) table fork; MF holder, payee; **— de libros** bookkeeper

teneduría F **— de libros** bookkeeping

tener[44] VT to have; **tiene el pelo castaño** she has brown hair, her hair is brown; **— en mucho** to esteem highly; **— por** to consider; **— que** to have to; **— ganas** to feel like; **tengo escrita la carta** I have the letter written; **— éxito** to be successful; **— miedo** to be afraid; **— sueño** to be sleepy; **— frío** to be cold; **— hambre** to be hungry; **tiene cinco años** she is five years old; **—se** to stand straight; **no — más remedio** to have no other choice; **— que ver con** to have to do with

tenería F tannery

tenia F tapeworm

teniente MF lieutenant

tenis M (juego) tennis; (zapatos) sneakers, tennis shoes

tenista MF tennis player

tenor M (voz, estilo) tenor; (tono) tone, tenor; ADJ **saxofón —** tenor saxophone

tensión F tension

tenso ADJ tense; (extendido) taut

tentación F temptation

tentáculo M tentacle

tentador ADJ tempting

tentar[1] VT to tempt; **— a la suerte** to court danger; **— por todos los medios** to try everything

tentativa F attempt, try

tentativo ADJ tentative

tentempié M snack

tenue ADJ (tela) delicate; (luz) tenuous, dim, faint; (sonido) feeble

tenuidad F faintness, softness

teñir[5,18] VT (de color) to dye; (de tristeza) to tinge

teología F theology

teoría F theory

teórico ADJ theoretical

tepe M sod

tequila M tequila

terabyte M terabyte

terapeuta MF INV therapist

terapéutico ADJ therapeutic

terapia F therapy

tercero ADJ third; **tercera persona** third person; **tercera edad** old age; **tercer mundo** third world; M third party

terciar VI/VT to arbitrate

tercio M third

terciopelo M velvet

terco ADJ obstinate, stubborn

tergiversación F distortion, misrepresentation

tergiversar VT (palabras) to distort; (datos) to skew

termal ADJ thermal

terminación F termination, completion; (de una palabra, cuento) ending; (de un piso) finish

terminal ADJ terminal; MF (de aeropuerto, de omnibus) terminal; M (de computadora, eléctrico) terminal

terminante ADJ (negativa) flat; (prohibición) absolute

terminar VI/VT (completar) to finish, to conclude; VI (tener como final) to end; **— por** to end up; **no termino de entender** I still can't understand; **terminó con las ratas** he got rid of the rats; **sin —** unfinished

término M (final) end; (período de tiempo) period; (límite) boundary; (palabra) term; **a —** with a deadline; **estar en buenos —s** to be on good terms; **por — medio** on average; **— medio** medium; **en primer —** first of all; **poner —** to end; **en —s generales** in general terms; **en**

último — as a last resort
terminología F terminology
termita F termite
termo M thermos
termodinámico ADJ thermodynamic
termómetro M thermometer
termonuclear ADJ thermonuclear
termostato M thermostat
ternero -ra MF (animal) calf; F (carne) veal
terneza F tenderness
terno M three-piece suit
ternura F tenderness
terquedad F obstinacy, stubbornness
terraplén M embankment
terrateniente MF landholder
terraza F (terreno) terrace; (de casa) veranda; (delante de un bar) deck; (azotea) flat roof
terremoto M earthquake
terrenal ADJ earthly
terreno M (campo) piece of land, tract of land; (lote) lot; (formación geológica) terrain; (campo científico) field; **todo —** with four-wheel drive; **ganarle — a alguien** to gain on someone; **tantear el —** to put out feelers; **perder —** to lose ground
terrestre ADJ terrestrial, earthly
terrible ADJ terrible, awful
terrier M terrier
territorio M territory
terrón M (de tierra) clod; (de azúcar) lump
terror M terror, dread
terrorismo M terrorism
terrorista MF INV terrorist
terso ADJ (liso) smooth; (pulido) polished
tersura F smoothness
tertulia F social gathering
tesis F thesis; **— doctoral** dissertation
tesón M determination
tesonero ADJ determined
tesorería F treasury
tesorero -ra MF treasurer
tesoro M treasure; (público) treasury
test M test
testaferro M straw man
testamentaría F (gestiones) execution; (bienes) estate
testamento M testament, will
testarudez F stubbornness
testarudo ADJ stubborn, headstrong
testículo M testicle
testificar[6] VI to testify
testigo MF witness; **— de cargo** witness for the prosecution; **— ocular** eyewitness; M proof
testimoniar VI to give testimony
testimonio M testimony, proof, evidence;

levantar falso — to bear false witness; **en — de su amor** as a testament to his love
testosterona F testosterone
teta F teat
tétanos M tetanus
tetera F teapot, teakettle
tetilla F nipple
tetina F nipple
tetraplégico -ca ADJ & MF quadriplegic
tétrico ADJ gloomy
teutónico ADJ Teutonic
textil ADJ & M textile
texto M text; (libro de texto) textbook
textual ADJ verbatim
textura F texture
tez F complexion
ti PRON PERS you; **para —** for you; **te lo doy a —** I give it to you
tibieza F (poco fervor, afecto) lukewarmness; (calor) warmth
tibio ADJ (ni caliente ni frío) tepid, lukewarm; (templado) warm
tiburón M shark
tic M twitch, tic
tictac M **hacer —** to tick
tiempo M (cronológico) time; (climático) weather; (gramatical) tense; (de un partido de cuatro tiempos) quarter; (de un partido de dos tiempos) half; **— completo** full time; **— extra** overtime; **— y medio** time and a half; **— libre** leisure hours, free time; **— pretérito** past tense; **a —** on time; **al mismo —** at the same time; **antes de —** ahead of time; **a su —** in due course; **a un —** at the same time; **con —** in advance; **de medio —** part-time; **en aquel —** back then; **en mis —s** in my day; **hace buen —** the weather is nice; **hace mucho —** a long time ago; **mal —** rough weather; **motor de dos —s** two-stroke motor; **perder el —** to goof off, to waste time; **tener — de sobra** to have time to spare; **todo el —** all the time; **tomar el —** to clock
tienda F (de venta) store; (de campaña) tent
tientas LOC ADV **a —** blindly; **andar a —** to feel one's way
tiento M care; **coger el —** to get the hang of something
tierno ADJ (fácil de cortar) tender; (joven) young; (cariñoso) affectionate
tierra F (planeta) earth; (superficie seca) land; (país) country; (suelo) soil; **— adentro** inland; **—s altas** highlands; **—s bajas** lowlands; **— de nadie** no-man's land; **— firme** mainland; **—s raras** rare earths;

bajo — underground; **caer a** — to fall to the ground; **dar en — con alguien** to overthrow someone; **echar por** — to knock down; **por** — overland; **tomar** — to land

tieso ADJ stiff; **quedarse** — *fam* to kick the bucket

tiesto M flowerpot

tiesura F stiffness

tifoideo -a ADJ & F typhoid

tifón M typhoon

tifus M typhoid fever

tigre M tiger

tijeretada F snip

tijeretazo M snip

tijeretear VT to snip

tildar VT to brand

tilde F (en la ñ) tilde; (en las vocales) accent (mark)

tilín M *fam* ding-a-ling

timador M confidence man

timbrar VT to stamp

timbrazo M ring

timbre M (aparato) buzzer, doorbell; (cualidad de la voz) timbre; (sello) stamp; (insignia heráldica) crest

timidez F timidity, shyness

tímido ADJ timid, shy, bashful

timo M confidence game, scam

timón M helm, rudder

timonear VT to steer

timonel M pilot

timorato ADJ timorous, faint-hearted

tímpano M eardrum

tina F (bañera) tub; (de tintorero) vat

tinaja F large earthen jar

tinglado M (armazón) shed; (plataforma) platform

tinieblas F PL darkness; **en** — in the dark

tino M (buen juicio) good judgment; (puntería) marksmanship

tinta F ink; **medias** —s wishy-washiness

tinte M (sustancia) dye, stain; (matiz) tint

tintero M inkwell; **eso se me quedó en el** — I never got to that

tintín M clink

tintinear VI to tinkle, to clink

tintineo M tinkle, tinkling

tinto ADJ red

tintorería F dry cleaner

tintorero -ra MF dry cleaner

tintura F (medicina) tincture; (tinte) dye, tint

tiñoso ADJ scabby

tío -a M (hermano de madre o padre) uncle; — **abuelo** great uncle; (tipo) guy; F (hermana de madre o padre) aunt; (tipa)

woman, gal

tiovivo M merry-go-round

típico ADJ typical

tiple M treble

tipo -pa M (especie, imprenta) type; (tío) *fam* guy, dude; *Am* rate of interest; *Am* — **de cambio** rate of exchange; — **de interés** interest rate; **un buen** — a good-looking fellow, a regular guy; **tiene buen** — he's good looking; F (tía) woman, gal

tipografía F printing

tipología F typology

tira F (de papel, tocino, tela) strip; (de cuero, zapato) strap; — **cómica** comic strip

tirada F (de una pelota) throw; (de una publicación) issue, print run; (distancia) stretch; **de una** — all at once

tirador -ora MF (persona que dispara) shooter; M (tirachinas) slingshot; (pomo) knob

tiranía F tyranny

tiránico ADJ tyrannical

tirano -na ADJ tyrannical; MF tyrant

tirante ADJ (cable) taut; (relaciones) strained; M (de caballería) trace; (de vestido) strap; (apoyo) brace, strut; —s suspenders

tirantez F tension, strain

tirar VT (pelota) to throw, to toss, to pitch; (derechos, dinero) to throw away; (una bala) to shoot; (una moneda) to flip, to toss; (dados) to cast; (una cuerda) to pull, to tug; — **la cadena** to flush; — **la casa por la ventana** to live it up; — **la chancleta** to kick up one's heels; **no me tira la política** I'm not attracted to politics; **el coche tira a un lado** the car pulls to one side; — **al suelo** to throw down; — **a** to tend toward; — **abajo** to knock over; — **de** to tug at; **ir tirando** to get along; —**se** to lie down; —**se solo** to go it alone; **tirárselas** de to pretend to be; **trabajar con él es un constante tira y afloja** working with him is a roller-coaster; M **tirabuzón** (sacacorchos) corkscrew; (espiral) coil; M SG **tirachinas** slingshot

tiritar VI (de frío) to shiver; (de miedo) to shudder

tiro M (lanzamiento) throw; (disparo) shot; (deporte) shooting; (de cocaína) hit; (de dados) roll; (de caballos) team; (de chimenea) draft; — **al arco** archery; — **al blanco** target practice; — **de penalidad** penalty kick; **errar el** — to miss the mark; **matar a** —**s** to gun down; **ni a** —**s** absolutely not; **pegarle un** — **a alguien** to shoot someone; **me salió el** — **por la**

culata the plan backfired on me
tiroides ADJ & M thyroid
tirón M jerk, tug, pull; (atracción fuerte,
lesión de un músculo) pull; **de un —** all
at once; **un — de orejas** a slap on the
wrist
tironear VI/VT to jerk, to tug at
tirotear VI to shoot; **—se** to exchange shots
tiroteo M shooting, gunfire
tirria F dislike; **tenerle — a una persona**
to have a strong dislike for someone
tisana F herbal tea
tísico ADJ consumptive
tisis F consumption
titánico ADJ titanic
titanio M titanium
títere M (marioneta) puppet; (persona)
puppet, dupe; **—s** puppet show; **no dejar
— sin cabeza** to leave no one standing
titilación F flicker
titilar VI to flicker, to twinkle
titileo M twinkle
titubear VI (vacilar) to hesitate, to waver;
(oscilar) to totter, to dodder
titubeo M hesitation
titular VT to entitle; **—se** to graduate; ADJ
permanent; M (de periódico) headline; MF
(de cargo) incumbent
titularidad F tenure
título M (de una obra, persona, liga) title;
(derecho) claim, legal right; (universitario)
degree, diploma; **—s de crédito** credits;
— de propiedad title deed; **a — de** by
way of
tiza F chalk
tiznado ADJ sooty
tiznar VT to smear with soot
tizne M soot
tizón M (leña) burning log; (parásito) smut
TNT M TNT
toalla F towel; **tirar la —** to throw in the
towel
toallero M towel rack
tobillo M ankle
tobogán M slide
tocado M headdress; ADJ touched
tocador M (mueble) dressing table, vanity
table; (habitación) *lit* boudoir
tocante a PREP concerning
tocar[6] VT (con los dedos) to touch; (un
instrumento musical) to play; (una
campana) to ring; (un timbre) to buzz; (a
la puerta) to knock; (la bocina) to honk,
to blast; (una alarma) to sound;
(mencionar) to touch upon; **— en** to stop
over in; **—le a uno** to be one's turn; **—
fondo** to hit bottom; M SG **tocadiscos**

· record player
tocayo -ya MF namesake
tocino M bacon
tocón M stump
todavía ADV still, as yet, yet; **— está aquí**
she's still here; **¿— no has comido?** have
you not eaten yet? **— no ha llegado** she
still has not arrived, as yet she has not
arrived; **me dio — más** she gave me even
more
todo ADJ all; (cada uno) every, each; **—
hombre** every man; **—s los días** every
day; **a — correr** at top speed; **a toda
costa** at all costs; **a toda marcha** in
high gear; **a toda vela** under full sail; **a
toda velocidad** at full speed; **a —
volumen** at full blast; **de — corazón**
whole-heartedly; **de —s modos** still,
anyway, all the same; **del —** entirely; **en
— caso** in any case, at any rate, in any
event; **es — un personaje** he's quite a
character; **por — lados** everywhere; **— el
día** all day; **— el tiempo** all the time; **—
el mundo** everyone; **todas las noches**
nightly; **toda la noche** all through the
night; **toda clase de** all sorts of; **en / por
todas partes** everywhere, for and wide;
con toda el alma from the bottom of
one's heart; **con toda sinceridad** in all
earnestness; PRON **de una vez por todas**
once and for all; **— se vale** anything
goes; **—s** everybody; **—s juntos** all
together; ADV **— derecho** straight ahead;
— lo contrario quite the opposite; **—
recto** straight ahead; **— sucio** all dirty;
ante — first of all; **así y — in** spite of
that; **con — in** spite of that; **del —**
completely; **sobre —** especially; M whole;
—poderoso almighty
toga F (de catedrático) gown; (de juez) robe
Togo M Togo
togolés -esa ADJ & MF Togolese
toldería F Indian village
toldo M awning, canopy
tolerancia F tolerance
tolerante ADJ tolerant, broad-minded
tolerar VT to tolerate; **no lo puedo —** I
can't stand it
tolete M oarlock
toma F (de una ciudad) taking;
(cinematográfica) take; (de juramento)
administration; (de teléfono) jack; **— de
agua** faucet; **— de corriente** electric
outlet; **— de poder** takeover; **toma y
daca** give and take
tomar VT to take; (un juramento) to
administer; (un vestido) to take in; (a un

criado) to hire; (una bebida) to drink; **— a pecho** to take to heart; **— asiento** to take a seat; **— desprevenido** to take by surprise; **— el sol** to sunbathe; **—lo a mal** to take the wrong way; **— el pelo a** to make fun of, to kid, to pull someone's leg; **— medidas** to take action; **— una decisión** to make a decision; **—le las medidas a alguien** to measure someone for clothes; **—se de la mano** to hold hands; **—se la molestia** to bother to

tomate M tomato

tomillo M thyme

tomo M volume

tomografía F scan; **— axial computarizada** CAT scan

ton LOC ADV **sin — ni son** for no reason

tonada F tune

tonel M (barril) barrel; (persona) *pey* fatso

tonelada F ton

tóner M toner

Tonga F Tonga

tongano -na ADJ & MF Tongan

tongo M setup

tónica F (tono) tone; (agua) tonic (water)

tónico ADJ & M tonic

tono M tone; (tono musical) pitch; (intervalo musical) step; **— de ocupado** busy signal; **— menor** low key; **a —** on key; **bajar el —** to lower the volume; **darse —** to put on airs; **de buen —** in good taste; **fuera de —** out of place; **subido de —** risqué

tontear VI to fool around

tontería F (cualidad de tonto) stupidity; (hecho o dicho) foolishness, nonsense

tonto -ta ADJ (ingenuo) foolish; (de poca inteligencia) stupid, dumb; **a tontas y a locas** haphazardly; MF (persona ingenua) fool; (persona de poca inteligencia) *fam* dummy, blockhead, dimwit; **— de capirote** dunce; **hacer(se) el —** to play the fool

topacio M topaz

topar VT to butt; **—se con** to bump into

tope M (de precios) ceiling, cap; (de tren) bumper; (de puerta) doorstop; **a —** a lot; **hasta el —** to the maximum; **estar hasta el —** to be completely full

topetazo M butt

tópico M (lugar común) cliché; (tema) topic; ADJ topical

topless ADJ topless

topo M mole (también espía)

toque M (con la mano) touch; (de campana) ringing; (de tambor) beat; (de trompeta) blare; (de pintura) dab; **— de queda** curfew; **dar los últimos —s** to put the

finishing touches on; **dar —s** to dab; **un — femenino** a woman's touch

toquetear VI/VT to finger

toqueteo M feel

tórax M thorax

torbellino M whirlwind

torcedura F twist, sprain, strain

torcer[2,10] VT to twist; (una articulación) to sprain, to strain; (tergiversar) to distort; **—le el pescuezo a alguien** to wring someone's neck; VI (un río) to bend

torcido ADJ crooked

tordo M thrush

torear VT (lidiar) to fight a bull; (provocar) to provoke

torero -ra MF bullfighter

tormenta F storm; **— de arena** sandstorm; **— eléctrica** electrical storm

tormento M torment

tormentoso ADJ stormy

tornadizo ADJ changeable

tornado M tornado, twister

tornar VI (regresar) to return; VT (cambiar) to turn; **— a hacer algo** to do something again

tornasolado ADJ iridescent

tornear VT to turn on a lathe

torneo M tournament

tornillo M screw; **— de banco** vise; **faltarle a uno un —** to have a screw loose

torniquete M (eje giratorio) turnstile; (contra hemorragia) tourniquet

torno M (para levantar pesos) hoist, winch; (para cerámicas) lathe, pottery wheel; **en —** around

toro M bull; **coger / agarrar el — por los cuernos** to take the bull by the horns

toronja F grapefruit

torpe ADJ (poco habilidoso) clumsy, awkward; (lento) slow, sluggish

torpedear VT to torpedo

torpedero M (barco) torpedo boat; (avión) torpedo plane

torpedo M torpedo

torpeza F (falta de habilidad) clumsiness; (lentitud) slowness, sluggishness

torpor M torpor

torrar VT to roast

torre F (de castillo) tower; (de buque de guerra) turret; (en ajedrez) castle; **— de control** control tower; **— de marfil** ivory tower; **— de perforación** oil derrick; **— de vigilancia** watch tower

torrencial ADJ torrential

torrente M torrent; **— de lágrimas** flood of tears; **— sanguíneo** bloodstream

torreón M large tower

torreta F turret

tórrido ADJ torrid

torsión F torsion

torso M torso

torta F (postre) cake; (bofetada) slap

tortícolis F kink

tortilla F (de huevo) omelet; (de harina) *Méx* tortilla; **se dio vuelta la** — the tables have turned

tórtola F turtledove

tortuga F tortoise, turtle; — **marina** sea turtle; **a paso de** — at a snail's pace

tortuoso ADJ (camino) tortuous; (carácter) devious

tortura F torture

torturante ADJ torturous

torturar VT to torture

torvo ADJ fierce

tos F cough; — **ferina** whooping cough

tosco ADJ coarse, crude

toser VI to cough

tosquedad F coarseness, crudeness

tostada F toast

tostado ADJ (pan) toasted; (café) roasted; M (acción de tostar pan) toasting; (color, bronceado) tan; (acción de tostar café) roasting

tostador -ora MF toaster

tostar² VT (el pan) to toast; (la piel) to tan; (el café) to roast

total ADJ & M total; **en** — altogether; —, **a mí no me importa** anyway, I don't care

totalidad F **la** — **del dinero** all the money; **en su** — as a whole

totalitario ADJ totalitarian

tour M tour

tóxico ADJ toxic

toxina F toxin

traba F (estorbo) hindrance; (de caballo) hobble

trabajador -ora ADJ (esforzado) hard-working; (proletario) working; MF worker

trabajar VI/VT to work; — **un taxi** to drive a taxi; VI (una tienda) to be open; — **duro** to work hard

trabajo M work; (acción de trabajo) working; (puesto) job; (informe académico) paper; **da mucho** — it's a lot of work; **sin** — unemployed

trabajoso ADJ laborious

trabar VT (una puerta) to jam; (un caballo) to hobble; (a un boxeador) to clinch; (una salsa) to thicken; (negociaciones) to impede; — **amistad con alguien** to strike up a friendship with someone; — **batalla** to join battle; — **conversación** to strike up a conversation; M SG **trabalenguas** tongue twister

tracción F traction

tractocamión M tractor-trailer

tractor M tractor

tradición F tradition

tradicional ADJ traditional

traducción F translation

traducir²⁴ VI/VT to translate

traductor -ora MF translator

traer⁴⁵ VT to bring; (llevar puesto) to have on; (contener) to feature; — **a colación** to bring up; — **a mal a alguien** to mistreat someone; **este niño se las trae** this child is something else; **¿qué te traes entre manos?** what are you up to? —**se secretos** to have secrets

tráfago M bustle

traficante MF dealer

traficar⁶ VI to traffic, to trade

tráfico M traffic

tragar⁷ VI/VT to swallow; (comer) *fam* to feed one's face; (consumir gasolina) to guzzle; (aguantar) to stand; (hacer desaparecer) to engulf; —**se algo** to swallow (accidentally); **no me lo trago** I don't buy that; M **tragaluz** skylight; MF SG **tragamonedas / tragaperras** slot machine

tragedia F tragedy

trágico ADJ tragic

trago M swallow; (bebida alcohólica) shot, slug; **a** —**s** (bebiendo) in sips; (poco a poco) little by little; **echar / tomar un** — to take a drink; **pasar un mal** — to suffer a difficulty

traición F (política) treason; (personal) betrayal; (acto desleal) treachery; **a** — by treachery

traicionar VT to double-cross

traicionero ADJ treacherous

traidor -ora ADJ treacherous; MF (político) traitor; (personal) betrayer

trailer M trailer

traílla F leash

traje M (conjunto) suit; (de fiesta) gown; — **de baño** swimsuit

trajeado ADJ **bien** — well-dressed

trajín M hustle and bustle

trajinar VI to rush around

trama F (argumento) plot; (intriga) scheme; (conjunto de hilos) woof

tramador -ora MF plotter

tramar VT (con hilos) to weave; (intrigar) to plot, to scheme

tramitar VT to take steps to obtain

trámite M procedure, paperwork

tramo M (de carretera) stretch; (de puente) span; (de hielo) patch; (de escalera) flight

tramoyista MF stagehand

trampa F (de caza) trap, snare; (engaño) trick; **hacer —** to cheat, to trick; **tender una —** to set a trap

trampear VI to cheat

trampilla F trap door

trampolín M (de piscina) springboard; (de circo) trampoline

tramposo -sa ADJ deceitful; MF cheat

tranca F crossbar

trance M (momento difícil) pass, difficult moment; (estado de suspensión) trance; **el último —** the last moment of life; **a todo —** at any cost

tranco M stride; **a —s** hurriedly; **en dos —s** in a jiffy

tranquera F wooden fence

tranquilidad F tranquility, calm, quiet

tranquilizante M tranquilizer

tranquilizar[9] VT to quiet, to calm down; **—se** to calm down, to wind down

tranquilo ADJ (no ruidoso) quiet, peaceful; (no excitado) calm, cool; (no preocupado) calm, at ease; (no excitable) sedate; (mar) smooth, tranquil

transacción F transaction; **— comercial** business transaction

transar VI to compromise

transatlántico ADJ transatlantic; M transatlantic liner

transbordar VI to transfer

transbordo M transfer

transcribir[51] VT to transcribe

transcripción F transcript

transcultural ADJ cross-cultural

transcurrir VI to elapse

transcurso M passing, passage; **en el — de un año** in the course of a year

transeúnte MF passer-by, transient

transferencia F transfer

transferible ADJ transferable

transferir[3] VT to transfer

transformación F transformation

transformador M transformer

transformar VT to transform

transfusión F transfusion

transgredir[50] VT to transgress

transgresión F transgression

transgresor -ora MF lawbreaker

transición F transition

transigir[11] VI to compromise

transistor M transistor

transitable ADJ passable

transitar VI/VT to travel

transitivo ADJ transitive

tránsito M (acción de viajar) transit, passage; (tráfico) traffic; **de / en —** in transit

transitorio ADJ transitory

transmisible ADJ communicable

transmisión F transmission; **— automática** automatic transmission

transmisor M transmitter; ADJ transmitting

transmitir VI/VT to transmit; (una enfermedad) to communicate; (por radio o televisión) to broadcast

transparencia F transparency

transparente ADJ transparent

transpiración F perspiration

transpirar VI/VT to transpire, to perspire

transportación F transportation, transport

transportar VT (mercancías, gente) to transport; (mercancías) to ship, to haul

transporte M (acción) transport, transportation; (vehículo de transporte) transport (vessel); **— de locura** fit of madness; **— público** mass transit

transportista MF teamster, trucker

transversal ADJ transverse; F transversal

transverso ADJ transverse

tranvía M (transporte urbano) streetcar, trolley; (tren de cercanías) local train

trapacería F racket

trapacero -ra MF racketeer

trapeador M mop

trapear VT *Am* to mop

trapecio M trapeze

trapezoide ADJ & M trapezoid

trapiche M sugar mill

trapisonda F trick

trapo M rag; **—s** *fam* duds; **a todo —** at full speed; **tratar a alguien como un —** to treat someone like dirt; **—s sucios** dirty laundry

tráquea F trachea, windpipe

traquetear VI (hacer sonido) to rattle, to clatter; (llevar a todos lados) to drag from place to place

traqueteo M rattle, clatter

tras PREP (temporal) after; (espacial) after, behind, in back of; **correr —** to run after; **día — día** day after day; **una vez — otra** time after time

trascendencia F transcendence

trascendental ADJ transcendental; (importante) momentous

trascendente ADJ transcendental

trascender VT to transcend; VI (surgir) to emerge; (extender) to extend

trasegar[1,7] VT (vino) to pour from one container to another; (objetos) to move around; (papeles) to shuffle

trasero ADJ (punto, asiento) rear, back; (pata)

hind; M (de persona) *fam* rear, rear end, bottom
traslación F transfer
trasladar VT (a un empleado) to transfer; (una reunión) to postpone; **—se** to travel
traslado M transfer
traslapo M overlap
trasnochar VI to stay up late
traspapelar VT to mislay, to misplace; **—se** to become mislaid
traspasar VT (pasar por) to transfix; (ir más allá de) to go beyond; (pasar un límite) to transgress, to cross over; (una propiedad) to transfer
traspaso M transfer
traspié M stumble, slip; **dar un —** to stumble
trasplantar VT to transplant
trasplante M transplant
trasponer[39] VT to transpose
trasquilar VT (una oveja) to shear; (a una persona) to fleece
trastabillar VI to stumble
trastazo M bump
traste M (de guitarra) fret, stop; (trasero) buttocks; **dar al — con** to destroy; **irse al —** to go down the drain
trasto M piece of junk; **—s** stuff
trastocar[6] VT to disrupt
trastornar VT (alterar psíquicamente) to disturb; (alterar el funcionamiento) to disrupt; **—se** to go crazy
trastorno M (molestia) trouble; (patología) disorder; **— bipolar** bipolar disorder; **— de personalidad múltiple** multiple personality disorder
trasudar VI/VT to perspire
trata F trade
tratable ADJ (curable) treatable; (amistoso) approachable
tratado M (acuerdo) treaty; (libro) treatise
tratamiento M (acción de tratar) treatment; (fórmula de cortesía) form of address; **— de textos** *Esp* word processing
tratante MF dealer, trader
tratar VT (una enfermedad, a un paciente, un asunto) to treat; VI (intentar) to try; **— como** to treat like; **— con** to have dealings with; **— de** to try to, to attempt; **— sobre** to be about; **lo trató de imbécil** she called him an idiot; **—le a uno de** to address someone as; **— en** to deal in; **—se con** to have to do with; **—se de** to be a question of, to be
trato M (acuerdo) treatment; (acción de tratar) dealings; (convenio) deal; (comercio) trade; (modales) manners; **¡—**

hecho! it's a deal! **tener buen —** to have good manners; **cerrar un —** to strike a bargain
trauma M trauma
traumático ADJ traumatic
traumatismo M trauma
través LOC ADV **a / al — de** through, across; **a — de las declaraciones** throughout the declarations; **de —** across; **mirar de —** to look askance (at)
travesaño M crossbar
travesía F crossing, sea voyage, passage
travesura F mischief, prank; **hacer —s** to play pranks
traviesa F railway tie
travieso ADV mischievous, naughty
trayecto M course, route
trayectoria F (de proyectil) trajectory, path; (profesional) career
traza F (huella) trace; (aspecto) appearance; **tiene —s de no acabar nunca** it looks as if it will never end
trazado M (de ciudad) layout; (de edificio) blueprint; (de un plan) outline
trazador M **— gráfico** plotter
trazar[9] VT to trace, to sketch; (un plan) to outline; (un edificio) to blueprint; **— el curso** to plot a course
trébol M clover
trece NUM thirteen
trecho M (distancia) stretch; **a —s** at intervals; **de — en —** at intervals
tregua F (de guerra) truce; (descanso) lull, respite
treinta NUM thirty
tremendo ADJ (extraordinario) tremendous; (terrible) terrible
trementina F turpentine
tremolar VI (bandera) to flutter; (voz) to trill
trémolo M quaver
trémulo ADJ tremulous, trembling
tren M train; **— de aterrizaje** landing gear; **— de carga / de mercancías** freight train; **— de cercanías** local train; **— de vida** lifestyle; **— expreso** express train; **a todo —** at top speed; **perder el —** to miss the boat; **seguir el —** to keep up
trenza F braid
trenzar[9] VT to braid
trepador ADJ (planta) climbing; (ciclista) climber
trepadora F climbing plant
trepar VI to climb
trepidar VI to tremble
tres NUM three
treta F trick, wile
triaje M triage

triangular ADJ triangular

triángulo M triangle; **— recto** right triangle

tribu F tribe

tribulación F tribulation

tribuna F (de orador) rostrum; (de un público) grandstand

tribunal M (judicial) tribunal, court; (cuerpo de jueces) body of judges

tributar VT to pay tribute with; VI to pay taxes

tributario ADJ & M tributary

tributo M (pago obligatorio) tribute; (impuesto) tax

triceps M triceps

triciclo M tricycle

tridimensional ADJ three-dimensional

trifulca F fight

trigo M wheat

trigueño ADJ (tez) swarthy; (pelo) dark-blond

trillado ADJ trite

trilladora F threshing machine

trillar VT to thresh

trillizo -za ADJ & MF triplet

trilogía F trilogy

trimestral ADJ quarterly

trimestre M quarter

trinar VI to trill; **está que trina** she is furious

trinchante M carving knife

trinchar VT to carve

trinche M pitchfork

trinchera F trench; (gabardina) trench coat

trinchero M carving table

trineo M sleigh, sled

trinitense ADJ & MF Trinidadian

trino M trill

trinquete M ratchet

trío M trio

tripas F PL guts; **hacer de — corazón** to pluck up one's courage

triple ADJ triple

triplicar[6] VT to triple, to treble

trípode M tripod

triptongo M triphthong

tripulación F crew

tripular VT to man

triquiñuela F caper

triquitraque M firecracker

triscar[6] VI to frisk

triste ADJ sad, sorrowful

tristeza F sadness, sorrow

tristón ADJ glum

tritón M newt

trituradora F (para desechos) garbage disposal unit; (para papel) paper shredder

triturar VI/VT (documentos) to shred; (granos) to grind

triunfal ADJ triumphal

triunfante ADJ triumphant

triunfar VT to triumph

triunfo M triumph

trivial ADJ trivial, commonplace, trite

trizas F PL **hacer —** to tear into shreds

trocar[2,6] VT (transformar) to change into; (cambiar una cosa por otra) to exchange

trocear VT to divide into pieces

trocha F trail

trofeo M trophy

troje M granary

trola F whopper

trole M trolley

trolebús M trolley bus

tromba F waterspout; **salir en —** to storm out

trombón M trombone

trompa F (de elefante) trunk; (instrumento musical) horn; **— de Falopio** Fallopian tube

trompada F blow with the fist

trompeta F trumpet

trompetazo M trumpet blast

trompetear VI to trumpet

trompo M spinning top

tronada F thunderstorm

tronar[2] VI to thunder

tronchar VT to chop off

tronco M (de árbol) trunk, log; (del cuerpo) trunk, torso; **dormir como un —** to sleep like a log

tronera F (de buque) gun port; (de mesa de billar) pocket

trono M throne (también wáter)

tropa F (grupo) troop; (oficiales) rank and file; **—s de asalto** storm troops; **—s de choque** shock troops

tropel LOC ADV **en —** in droves

tropezar[1,9] VI to stumble, to trip; **—(se) con alguien** to meet up with someone; **— con algo** to come across something

tropezón M stumble, trip; **salir a tropezones** to stumble out; **darse un —** to stumble

tropical ADJ tropical

trópico M tropic

tropiezo M stumble

troquel M die

trotar VI to trot

trote M trot; **al —** at a trot; **no estoy para estos —** I'm too old for this

troza F log

trozar[9] VT to cut up

trozo M (de roca, madera, torta) piece; (de un texto) section; (de carbón) lump; (de carne) slab

trucha F trout

truco M clever trick

truculento ADJ gruesome

trueno M thunder

trueque M barter

truhán -ana MF scoundrel

truja F cigarette

trust M trust

tu ADJ POS your

tú PRON PERS you

tuba F tuba

tuberculosis F tuberculosis

tubería F (tubo) pipe; (conjunto de tubos) piping

tubo M (cilindro hueco) tube; (de agua, órgano) pipe; (digestivo) tract; **— de ensayo** test tube; **— de escape** tailpipe

tubular ADJ tubular

tuerca F nut

tuerto ADJ one-eyed

tuétano M marrow; **hasta los —s** through and through

tufillo M whiff

tufo M (humo) fumes; (hedor) stench

tugurio M hovel; **—s** slums

tulipán M tulip

tullido -da ADJ crippled; MF *pey* cripple

tullir VT to cripple; **—se** to become crippled

tumba F (panteón) tomb; (sepultura) grave; **soy una —** my lips are sealed

tumbar VT to knock down, to flatten; **—se** to lie down, to stretch out

tumbo M tumble, somersault; **dar —s** (persona) to stagger; (coche) to bump along

tumor M tumor

tumulto M (alboroto) tumult, uproar; (muchedumbre) mob

tumultuoso ADJ tumultuous

tuna F prickly pear; *Esp* minstrel group

tunante -ta MF scamp

tunda F thrashing

túnel M tunnel

tunesino -na ADJ & MF Tunisian

Túnez M Tunisia

tungsteno M tungsten

túnica F tunic; **— de laboratorio** lab gown

tupido ADJ dense, compact

tupir VT (hacer tupido) to compact; (cubrir) to cover; **—se** to stuff oneself

turba F (muchedumbre) mob; (carbón fósil) peat

turbación F confusion

turbamulta F throng

turbante M turban

turbar VT to disturb; **—se** to become disturbed

turbina F turbine

turbio ADJ (pasado, secreto) dark; (agua, materia) murky

turbocompresor M turbocharger

turborreactor M turbojet

turbulento ADJ turbulent

turco -ca ADJ Turkish; MF Turk; M (lengua) Turkish

turcomano -na ADJ & MF Turkmen

turismo M (actividad) tourism; (conjunto de turistas) tourists; **hacer —** to go sightseeing

turista MF tourist

Turkmenistán M Turkmenistan

turnarse VI to take turns

turno M turn; (de trabajo) shift

turquesa F turquoise

Turquía F Turkey

turrón M nougat

tutear VT to address as "tú"

tutela F guardianship

tutelar VT to have charge of

tutor -ora MF (de un menor) guardian; M (de planta) prop

Tuvalu M Tuvalu

tuvaluano -na ADJ & MF Tuvaluan

tuyo PRON your, yours; **el amigo —** your friend; **esto es —** this is yours

tweed M tweed

Uu

u CONJ or

ubicación F location

ubicar[6] VT (situar) to locate; (identificar) to place; **—se** to be located

ubicuo ADJ ubiquitous

ubre F udder

UCP (unidad central de proceso) F CPU

Ucrania F Ukraine

ucraniano -na ADJ & MF Ukrainian

ufanarse VI to glory (in), to be proud (of)

ufano ADJ proud

Uganda F Uganda

ugandés -esa ADJ & MF Ugandan

ujier M bailiff

úlcera F (lesión superficial) sore; (en el estómago) sore; (en la boca) canker, sore

ulterior ADJ ulterior

últimamente ADV of late

ultimar VT to finalize

ultimátum M ultimatum

último ADJ last, final; (destino) ultimate;

(más reciente) latest; **estar en las últimas** to be on one's last legs; **la última palabra** the last word; **en los —s tiempos** lately; **a última hora** at the last moment

ultrajante ADJ outrageous

ultrajar VT to outrage

ultraje M outrage, indignity

ultraligero M ultralight

ultramar LOC ADV **de** — overseas

ultramoderno ADJ ultramodern

ultratumba LOC ADV **de** — from beyond the grave

ultravioleta ADJ INV & M ultraviolet

ulular VI to howl, to hoot

ululato M hoot

umbral M threshold, doorstep

umbrío ADJ shady

un, uno, una ART INDEF a, an; **un hombre** a man; **un actor** an actor; **una mujer** a woman; **una manzana** an apple; NUM one; **de a** — one at a time; **es la una** it is one o'clock; **yo tengo** — I have one; PRON one; **— por** — one by one; **—s** some; **—s cuantos** some; **— tiene que cuidarse** you've got to take care of yourself; **— tras otro** one after the other; **— al lado del otro** side by side; **los —s a los otros / el — al otro** one another / each other

unánime ADJ unanimous

unanimidad F unanimity

uncir[10b] VT to yoke; (a un carro) to hitch

ungüento M ointment, salve

único ADJ only; (extraordinario) unique

unidad F (indivisibilidad) unity; (ejemplar) unit; (fracción militar) unit, outfit; — **central de proceso** central processing unit

unificar[6] VT to unify

uniformar VT (estandarizar) to standardize; (dar uniformes) to furnish with uniforms

uniforme ADJ & M uniform

uniformidad F uniformity

unilateral ADJ unilateral

unión F (acción de unir, cosas unidas) union; (lugar en que se unen dos cosas) junction; (indivisibilidad) unity

unir VT to unite; (dos construcciones) to join; (cinta magnética, genes) to splice; (caños) to couple; VI/VT (con lazos) to bind

unisex ADJ unisex

unísono ADJ unison; **al** — in unison

universal ADJ universal

universidad F (de enseñanza e investigación) university; (de enseñanza) college

universitario ADJ university; (relativo a los deportes) collegiate

universo M universe

untar VT (la piel con crema) to oil; (pan con mantequilla) to spread on; (la cara con pintura) to smear; — **la mano a alguien** to grease someone's palm

untuoso ADJ (graso) oily; (zalamero) slick, unctuous

uña F fingernail; (de gato) claw; **como — y carne** thick as thieves; **con —s y dientes** tooth and nail

uranio M uranium

urbanidad F refinement, polish

urbanización F development

urbanizar[9] VT to build up

urbano ADJ (relativo a la ciudad) urban; (refinado) suave; **autobus** — city bus

urbe F metropolis

urdimbre F warp

urdir VT (una tela) to weave; (una historia) to concoct; (un plan) to devise, to work out

uretra F urethra

urgencia F (prisa) urgency; (crisis médica) emergency; **con** — urgently; **—s** emergency room

urgente ADJ urgent, pressing

urgir[11] VT to urge; VI to be urgent

úrico ADJ uric

urinario ADJ urinary; M urinal

URL M URL

urna F (para cenizas) urn; (electoral) ballot box; **acudir a las** — **s** to go to the polls

urólogo -ga MF urologist

urraca F (ave) magpie; (persona acaparadora) packrat

urticaria F hives

Uruguay M Uruguay

uruguayo -ya ADJ & MF Uruguayan

usado ADJ used; (desgastado) worn

usar VT to use; (ropa) to wear; **—se** to be in use; **sin** — unused

uso M (empleo) use; (costumbre) usage, custom; **al** — **de la época** according to the custom of the time

usted PRON PERS you; **—es** you, you all, y'all

usual ADJ usual

usuario -ria MF user; (en una biblioteca) borrower

usufructo M enjoyment

usufructuar[17] VT to enjoy the use of

usura F usury

usurero -ra MF usurer, loan shark

usurpar VT to encroach upon, to usurp

utensilio M utensil

útero M uterus, womb

útil ADJ useful, helpful; M PL **—es** utensils
utilidad F usefulness, utility
utilitario ADJ utilitarian
utilización F use, utilization
utilizar[9] VT to utilize; (explotar) to use
utopía F utopia
uva F grape
úvula F uvula
uvular ADJ uvular
Uzbekistán M Uzbekistan
uzbeko -ka ADJ & MF Uzbek

Vv

vaca F cow; **— marina** sea cow
vacaciones F PL vacation
vacante ADJ vacant; F vacancy, opening
vaciar[16] VT to empty; (casa) vacant; (una naranja) to hollow out; (una estatua) to cast
vacilación F hesitation
vacilante ADJ vacillating, hesitating; (tembloroso) shaky
vacilar VI to vacillate, to hesitate, to waver; **— (con)** *Esp fam* to make fun (of)
vacío ADJ empty; (casa) vacant; (comentarios) idle; (expresión) blank; M (condición) emptiness; (lugar) void; (espacio sin aire) vacuum; **envasado al —** vacuum-packed; **hacer el —** to give the cold shoulder
vacuna F vaccine
vacunación F vaccination
vacunar VI/VT to vaccinate
vadear VT to ford
vado M ford, crossing
vagabundear VI to wander idly
vagabundo -da ADJ vagabond, vagrant; MF (pordiosero) tramp, bum; (trabajador errante) drifter, transient; (en la playa) beachcomber
vagancia F vagrancy
vagar[7] VI to wander, to roam
vagina F vagina
vago -ga ADJ (idea) vague; (silueta) shadowy; (impresión) faint, vague; (persona) lazy; MF vagrant, tramp
vagón M railway car; **— restaurante** dining car
vaguedad F faintness
vahído M dizzy spell
vaho M steam
vaina F (de una espada) sheath; (de legumbres) pod, shell; (molestia) nuisance
vainilla F vanilla

vaivén M swaying, swinging; **vaivenes** ups and downs
vajilla F tableware, dishes; **— de barro** earthenware; **— de porcelana** chinaware
vale M voucher
valedero ADJ valid
valentía F courage, valor, bravery
valentón -ona ADJ cocky; MF cocky person
valer[46] VT (tener un determinado valor) to be worth; VI (ser válido) to be valid; (estar permitido) to be allowed; (ser de utilidad) to be useful; **— la pena** to be worthwhile; **— más que** to outweigh; **—se de** to avail oneself of; **—se por sí mismo** to be self-sufficient; **¿cuánto vale?** how much is it? **— los derechos** to assert one's rights; **hacerse —** to stand up for oneself; **le valió una paliza** that earned him a beating; **más vale sólo que mal acompañado** better alone than in poor company; **no hay pero que valga** no buts about it; **no vale ni un comino** it's not worth a hoot; **no vale** that's not fair; **¡vale!** OK; **¡válgame Dios!** gracious! **todo —** anything goes
valeroso ADJ valorous, brave
valía F worth
validez F validity
válido ADJ valid; (cheque) good; (argumento) solid
valiente ADJ valiant, brave, courageous
valija F valise, suitcase; (para el correo) pouch
valioso ADJ valuable
valla F fence; (en carreras) hurdle
vallar VT to fence
valle M valley, vale
valor M (precio) value, worth; (valentía) valor, mettle; **— contable** book value; **—es** securities; **—es en cartera** holdings; **— nominal** face value; **armarse de —** to muster up one's courage
valoración F valuation
valorar VT (apreciar el valor) to value; (determinar el valor) to appraise
valorizar[9] VT to make more valuable; **—se** to become more valuable
vals M waltz
valsar VI to waltz
valuación F valuation, appraisal
valuar[17] VT to appraise
valva F valve
válvula F valve; **— reguladora de aceleración** throttle
vampiresa F vamp
vampiro M vampire

vanagloria F boastfulness
vanagloriarse VI to boast
vanaglorioso ADJ boastful
vándalo -la MF vandal
vanguardia F vanguard; **a la —** at the forefront
vanidad F vanity, conceit
vanidoso ADJ vain
vano ADJ vain; **en —** in vain
Vanuatu M Vanuatu
vanuatuense ADJ & MF Vanuatuan
vapor M (de agua) vapor, steam; (buque) steamship; **—es** fumes; **cocer al —** to steam; **echar —** to give off steam
vapulear VT to thrash
vapuleo M thrashing
vaquería F cowshed
vaqueriza F cowshed
vaquero -ra M cowboy; **—s** blue jeans; F cowgirl; ADJ **botas —s** cowboy boots
vaqueta F cowhide
vaquilla F heifer
vara F (rama) stick; (palo) rod
varadero M dry dock
varano M monitor lizard
varar VT to beach, to strand; VI to run aground
varear VT to whip with a stick
variable ADJ variable, changeable; F variable
variación F variation
variado ADJ varied
variante F variant
variar[16] VI/VT to vary
varicela F chicken pox
várices, varices F PL varicose veins
varicoso ADJ varicose
variedad F variety, assortment
varilla F small rod; (para azotar) switch; (de paraguas) rib
vario ADJ varied; **—s** various, several
variopinto ADJ variegated
varita F wand
varón M male (person)
varonil ADJ manly; (hombruno) mannish
vasco -ca ADJ & MF Basque; M (lengua) Basque
vascuence ADJ Basque; M (lengua) Basque
vascular ADJ vascular
vasectomía F vasectomy
vaselina F Vaseline[tm]
vasija F vessel
vaso M (de vidrio) glass; (de papel, plástico) cup; (corto y grueso) tumbler; (sanguíneo) vessel; **— de precipitado** beaker
vástago M (de planta) shoot, sprout; (de persona) offspring; (de motor) rod
vasto ADJ vast

vataje M wattage
vaticinar VT to foretell
vaticinio M prediction
vatio M watt
vecindad F (cercanía) vicinity; (barrio) neighborhood
vecindario M neighborhood
vecino -na MF (de al lado) neighbor; (residente) resident; ADJ neighboring
vedar VT to prohibit
vega F fertile plain
vegan ADJ & MF INV vegan
vegetación F vegetation
vegetal ADJ vegetable; M plant; MF (persona paralizada) vegetable
vegetar VI to vegetate
vegetariano -na ADJ & MF vegetarian
vehemencia F vehemence
vehemente ADJ vehement
vehículo M vehicle
veinte NUM twenty
veintena F (aproximadamente) group of (about) twenty; (exactamente) score
veintiuno NUM twenty-one; M (juego de naipes) blackjack
vejancón -ona M codger; F old woman
vejar VT to humiliate
vejestorio -ria M codger; F old woman
vejete M codger
vejez F old age
vejiga F bladder; (ampolla) blister
vela F (período de vigilancia) vigil, watch; (de cera) candle; (de un navío) sail; **a toda —** under full sail; **en —** without sleep; **hacerse a la —** to set sail
velada F (noche) evening; (fiesta) evening party
velador M nightstand
velar VI (no dormir) to keep vigil, to stay awake; (cubrir con velo) to veil; (exponer a la luz una película fotográfica) to expose; **— por** to look after
velatorio M wake
veleidoso ADJ fickle
velero M sailboat; ADJ swift-sailing
veleta F weathervane; MF INV fickle person
vello M (del cuerpo) body hair; (de frutas) fuzz
vellón M fleece
velloso ADJ fuzzy
velludo ADJ hairy
velo M veil; **— del paladar** soft palate
velocidad F velocity, speed; **a toda —** at full speed
velocímetro M speedometer
velorio M wake
veloz ADJ swift, fast

vena F (vaso sanguíneo, veta) vein; (estado de ánimo) mood; (de locura) streak; **estar en — to be in the mood, to be inspired

venado M deer; (macho) stag; (carne de venado) venison

vencedor -ora ADJ winning; MF winner, victor

vencer[10a] VT (a un enemigo) to conquer, to vanquish; (a un equipo) to defeat, to beat; (obstáculos) to overcome; (en valor, inteligencia) to surpass; VI **—se** (un plazo) to expire; (el asiento de una silla) to cave in

vencido ADJ (derrotado) defeated; (a pagar) due, overdue; **darse por — to give up, to surrender

vencimiento M (de una deuda) maturity; (de un contrato) expiration

venda F bandage; (sobre los ojos) blindfold

vendaje M bandage

vendar VT (una herida) to bandage; (los ojos) to blindfold

vendaval M gale

vendedor -ora MF vendor, seller, salesperson; **— mayorista** wholesaler

vender VI/VT to sell; (traicionar) to betray; **—se a** to go over to; **se vende** for sale

vendetta F vendetta

vendible ADJ marketable

vendimia F vintage

veneciana F venetian blind

veneno M poison; (de víboras) venom

venenoso ADJ poisonous; (de víboras) venomous

venerable ADJ venerable

veneración F veneration, reverence

venerar VT (a una persona) to venerate, to revere; (a Dios) to worship

venéreo ADJ venereal

venezolano -na ADJ & MF Venezuelan

Venezuela F Venezuela

vengador -ora ADJ avenging; MF avenger

venganza F vengeance, revenge

vengar[7] VT to avenge; **—se de** to retaliate for, to avenge, to take revenge

vengativo ADJ vindictive, vengeful

venida F coming

venidero ADJ forthcoming

venir[47] VI to come; **— a colación** to come up (in conversation); **— al caso / a cuento** to be relevant; **— bien** to be convenient; **—le a uno bien** to be suitable to someone; **—se abajo** to collapse; **¿a qué viene eso?** what is the point of that? **el año que viene** next year; **lo mejor esta por — the best is yet to come; **no me vengas con excusas** no

excuses; **venga lo que venga** come what may

venta F sale; **— al por mayor** wholesale; **— al por menor** retail; **en — for sale; **poner a la — to put up for sale

ventaja F advantage; (en una carrera) head start

ventajoso ADJ advantageous

ventana F window; **tirar por la — to throw out the window

ventanilla F (de coche, avión) window; (de la nariz) nostril

ventarrón M gale, high wind

ventear VI to sniff the wind

ventilación F ventilation; (hueco para el aire) vent

ventilado ADJ airy

ventilador M (abertura) ventilator; (aparato) electrical fan

ventilar VT to ventilate, to air out; (una cuestión) to air

ventisca F blizzard

ventisquero M (lugar ventoso) place prone to blizzards; (lugar nevado) snowfield

ventolera F gust of wind; **darle a uno la — de** to take a notion to

ventosear VI to break wind

ventoso ADJ windy, breezy

ventrículo M ventricle

venturoso ADJ **futuro — bright future

ver[48] VI/VT to see; (televisión, espectáculos) to watch; **a — let's see; **eso aún está por —se** that is still to be seen; **no lo puedo — I can't stand him; **no — la hora de** to be dying for something to happen; **no tener nada que — con** not to have anything to do with; **te veo preocupado** you look worried; **a mi modo de — in my opinion; **—se obligado a** to be obliged to; **vérselas con algo** to confront something; **vérselas negras** to have a hard time

vera LOC ADV **a la — beside

veracidad F truthfulness

veranear VI to spend the summer

veraneo M summer vacation

veraniego ADJ summer

verano M summer

veras LOC ADV **de — really

veraz ADJ truthful

verbal ADJ verbal

verbena F carnival

verbo M verb

verborrágico ADJ long-winded

verboso ADJ verbose, wordy

verdad F truth; **¿—?** really? **— de — indeed; **una pistola de — a real pistol; **faltar a

la — to fib
verdadero ADJ true, real
verde ADJ green (también inmaduro, sin
experiencia, ecologista); (chiste) off-color;
— oliva olive-green; **ponerse** — to stuff
oneself; M green; **poner — a alguien** to
run someone down
verdear VI/VT to turn green
verdín M scum
verdor M greenness
verdoso ADJ greenish
verdugo M executioner, hangman
verdugón M welt
verdulero -ra MF vegetable vendor
verduras F PL produce
vereda F *Am* sidewalk; **entrar en** — to toe
the line
veredicto M verdict
verga F yard
vergonzoso ADJ (que da vergüenza)
shameful, disgraceful; (que siente
vergüenza) sheepish, bashful
vergüenza F (humillación) shame;
(incomodidad) embarrassment; (escándalo)
disgrace; **tener** — to be ashamed; **es una**
— it's a shame
vericueto M twists and turns
verídico ADJ truthful, true
verificación F verification, cross-check
verificar[6] VT to verify, to check; **—se** to take
place
verja F grate
vermú M vermouth
vernáculo ADJ & M vernacular
verruga F wart
versado ADJ versed
versar VI **— sobre** to deal (with), to treat
versátil ADJ versatile
versículo M Bible verse
versión F version; (traducción) translation;
(de una canción) rendition; **— original**
original (of a film)
verso M line (of poetry); **— libre** free verse;
— suelto / blanco blank verse
versus PREP versus
vértebra F vertebra
vertebrado ADJ & M vertebrate
vertebral ADJ spinal
vertedero M dump, landfill
verter[1] VT (echar líquido) to pour; (vaciar) to
pour out; (derramar) to spill; **— en** to
empty into; **—se** to spill
vertical ADJ vertical; (erguido) upright;
(empinado) sheer
vertiente F (pendiente) slope; (cuenca)
watershed; ADJ flowing
vertiginoso ADJ dizzy, giddy

vértigo M (falta de equilibrio) vertigo;
(frenesí) hectic pace
vertigoso ADJ dizzy, giddy
vesícula F gall bladder
vestíbulo M (de un edificio) vestibule, lobby;
(de una casa) hallway
vestido M dress; **— de noche** evening gown;
— de novia bridal dress
vestidura F attire
vestigio M vestige, trace, remnant
vestimenta F attire, dress; (estrafalaria) getup
vestir[5] VT to dress, to clothe; **—se** to get
dressed; **—se de gala** to dress up
vestuario M wardrobe; (en el teatro)
costumes; (lugar para vestirse) changing
room
veta F (de minerales) vein, seam; (de madera)
grain; (de humor) strain
vetar VT to veto
veteado ADJ veined
veterano -na ADJ & MF veteran
veterinario -ria MF veterinarian; ADJ
veterinary; F veterinary medicine
veto M veto
vetusto ADJ ancient
vez F time; **a la** — at the same time; **a su** —
in turn; **a veces** sometimes; **cada** — **más**
more and more; **cada** — **que** whenever;
de — **en cuando** from time to time; **de
una** — (por entero) all at once; (por fin)
one and for all; **de una** — **por todas**
once and for all; **en** — **de** instead of; **por
primera** — for the first time; **otra** —
again; **una** — **(que)** once; **una** — **tras
otra** over and over; **una y otra** — over
and over again; **raras veces** seldom;
hacer las veces de to take the place of
vía F (camino) road; (de ferrocarril) track;
(medio de acceso) avenue; **— Láctea**
Milky Way; **— navegable** waterway; **por
— de** by means of; **en —s de** in the
process of; PREP via
viable ADJ viable
viaducto M tunnel
viajante MF traveler; **— de comercio**
traveling salesman / saleswoman
viajar VI to travel, to journey; (por mar) to
voyage; (con drogas) to trip
viaje M trip, journey; (por mar) voyage; (en
coche, caballo) ride; (por efecto de las
drogas) trip; **— de ida y vuelta** round
trip; **buen** — have a nice trip; **de** — out
of town
viajero -ra MF traveler
viandante MF passer-by
viático M (de viaje) per diem; (religioso) last

rites

víbora F viper; **— de cascabel** rattlesnake

vibración F vibration; (de la lengua) trill

vibrador M vibrator

vibrante ADJ vibrating

vibrar VI/VT to vibrate

vicegobernador -ora MF lieutenant governor

vicepresidente -ta MF vice-president

vicerrector -ora MF provost

viceversa ADV vice versa

viciado ADJ (aire) stale; (costumbre) stuffy; (corrupto) foul

viciar VT to foul; (corromper) to corrupt

vicio M (mala costumbre) vice, bad habit; **de —** unjustifiably; **quitarse el — de** to wean oneself of

vicioso ADJ (persona) having bad habits; (gasto) unjustifiable; (gramática) faulty

vicisitud F vicissitude

víctima F victim; (en un accidente) casualty, victim

victimizar[9] VT to victimize

victoria F victory

victorioso ADJ victorious

vid F vine, grapevine

vida F life; **— mía** sweetheart; **— nocturna** night life; **— sentimental** love life; **así es la —** that's life; **de toda la —** lifelong; **de — o muerte** life and death; **en la — voy a hacer eso** I would never do that; **esto es —** this is the life; **ganarse la —** to earn a living; **sin —** lifeless

vidente MF seer; ADJ seeing

vídeo, video M (aparato) VCR; (técnica) video; (cinta) videocassette

videocasete F videocassette

videoconferencia F videoconference

videojuego M video game

vidriado M glaze; ADJ glazed

vidriar VT to glaze

vidriera F show window

vidriero -ra MF glazier, glassmaker

vidrio M (sustancia) glass; (en una ventana) pane; **pagar los —s rotos** to be left holding the bag

vidrioso ADJ glassy

vieira F scallop

viejo -ja ADJ old; (chiste) stale; M old man; (padre) father; **— verde** dirty old man; **los —s** the old folks; F old woman; (madre) mother

viento M wind; **hace —** it is windy; **a los cuatro —s** in all directions

vientre M abdomen; (barriga) belly; (de mujer) womb

viernes M Friday

Vietnam M Vietnam

vietnamita ADJ & MF INV Vietnamese

viga F (de madera) beam, rafter; (de metal) girder

vigencia F **entrar en —** to go into effect; **estar en —** to be in force

vigente ADJ effective, in force

vigía F lookout, reef; MF INV lookout

vigilancia F vigilance; (en una tienda) surveillance

vigilante ADJ vigilant; M watchman; F watchwoman

vigilar VI/VT to keep watch (over); VT to keep an eye on; (policía) to stake out

vigilia F vigil, watch

vigor M vigor; **en —** in force; **entrar en —** to become effective

vigorizar[9] VT to invigorate

vigoroso ADJ vigorous

VIH (virus de inmunodeficiencia humana) M HIV

vil ADJ vile, base, low

vileza F villainy, baseness

vilipendiar VT to revile

villa F village

villancico M Christmas carol

villanía F villainy

villano -na ADJ villainous; MF villain

vilo LOC ADV **en —** (en el aire) suspended; (en ascuas) in suspense

vinagre M vinegar

vincular VT to link; **—se** to link up

vínculo M link, tie

vindicar[6] VT to vindicate

vinilo M vinyl

vino M wine; **— blanco** white wine; **— espumoso** sparkling wine; **— rosado** rosé wine; **— tinto** red wine

viña F vineyard

viñatero -ra MF winegrower

viñedo M vineyard

viola F viola

violación F violation; (sexual) rape

violado ADJ violet; M violet

violar VT (una ley) to violate, to break; (una mujer) to rape, to ravish; (una promesa) to breach; (una cerradura) to pick; (derechos) to infringe upon; (mandamientos) to trespass against

violencia F violence; **— doméstica** domestic violence

violentar VT (a una persona) to manhandle; (una casa) to break into; **—se** to get mortified

violento ADJ violent, rough; (marido) abusive; (entrada) forcible; (ataque) vicious

violeta ADJ INV & M violet

violín M violin; (para música folklórica) fiddle

violinista MF violinist

violonchelo M cello

virada F veer

viraje M swerve

virar VI/VT (vehículo) to swerve, to veer; VI (barco) to tack

virgen ADJ & MF virgin; ADJ (cassette) blank; (selva) undisturbed

virginal ADJ virginal

viril ADJ virile, manly

virilidad F virility, manhood

virreinato M viceroyalty

virrey M viceroy

virtual ADJ virtual

virtud F (moral) virtue; (práctica) asset

virtuoso -sa ADJ (moral) virtuous; ADJ & MF (artístico) virtuoso

viruela F smallpox

virulento ADJ virulent

virus M virus (también de computadoras)

viruta F wood shaving

visa F visa

visado M visa

visar VT to endorse

visceral ADJ visceral

viscoso ADJ viscous

visera F visor

visible ADJ visible

visigodo -da ADJ Visigothic; MF Visigoth

visillo M window shade

visión F vision; (persona fea) sight

visionario -ria ADJ & MF visionary

visita F (acción de visitar) visit; (persona) visitor, caller; (a un edificio) tour; **— de médico** house call

visitación F visitation

visitador -ora MF visitor, caller; (inspector) inspector; (vendedor de medicamentos) pharmaceutical sales representative

visitante MF caller, visitor; ADJ visiting

visitar VT to visit; (un médico) to make a house call

vislumbrar VT to make out

viso M slip

visón M mink

víspera LOC ADV **en —s de** on the eve of

vista F (panorama) view, vista; (visión) eyesight; **a la —** in sight; **a primera —** at first sight; **a simple —** with the naked eye; **bajar la —** to lower one's eyes; **conocer de —** to know by sight; **con —s a** with a view to; **en — de** considering; **hacer la — gorda** to look the other way; **¡hasta la —!** good-bye; **perder de —** to lose sight of; **tener a la —** to have before

one's eyes; **tener — a** to look out on

vistazo M glance, glimpse, look; **dar / echar un — a** to glance over

visto ADJ **bien —** well thought of; **mal —** looked down upon; **— que** whereas; M **— bueno** approval; **dar el — bueno** to approve

vistoso ADJ showy

visual ADJ visual

visualizador M display

visualizar[9] VT to visualize; (en pantalla) to display

vital ADJ vital; **fuerzas —es** life force

vitalicio ADJ life; M lifetime pension

vitalidad F vitality

vitamina F vitamin

viticultor -ora MF winegrower

vítor M cheer

vitorear VI/VT to cheer

vitral M stained-glass window

vitrina F (ventana) shop window; (armario) showcase

vituperación F vituperation

vituperar VT to revile

vituperio M vituperation

viudo -da M widower; F widow; **viuda negra** black widow spider

vivacidad F vivacity

vivaracho ADJ vivacious

vivaz ADJ vivacious, lively

víveres M PL provisions

vivero M nursery

viveza F (vivacidad) liveliness; (inteligencia) cleverness

vívido ADJ vivid

vivienda F (casa) dwelling; (alojamiento) housing

viviente ADJ living

vivir VI/VT to live; **vive una vida normal** he leads a normal life; **¡viva!** hurrah! long live!

vivisección F vivisection

vivo ADJ (no muerto) alive, living; (ágil) lively; (vistoso, intenso) vivid; (listo) clever; **en —** before a live audience; **en — y en directo** live; **de viva voz** by word of mouth

vocablo M word

vocabulario M vocabulary

vocación F vocation, calling; (religioso) call

vocal ADJ vocal; (no consonántico) vowel; F vowel; MF member

vocálico ADJ vocalic

vocear VI/VT to cry out; (anunciar) to page

vocerío M clamor

vocero -ra MF spokesperson

vociferante ADJ vociferous

vociferar VI to clamor
vodevil M vaudeville
vodka M vodka
volado ADJ (drogado) high; (escrito arriba) superscript
volador ADJ flying
volante ADJ flying; M (en un vestido) ruffle, frill; (en un coche) steering wheel; (en un motor) flywheel; (folleto) leaflet, handbill
volar[2] VI/VT to fly; — **por su cuenta** to fly solo; **ir volando** to hurry; VT (un puente) to blow up; VI (hojas) to blow; **—se** (hacer explosión) to blow up; (enojarse) to lose one's temper; (irse volando) to fly away
volátil ADJ volatile
volcán M volcano
volcánico ADJ volcanic
volcar[2,6] VT (voltear) to tip over, to knock over; (derramar) to spill; (vaciar) to empty; VI to roll over; **—se** to tip over, to overturn
volea F volley
volear VI/VT to volley
voleibol M volleyball
volición F volition
volquete M dump truck
voltaje M voltage
voltear VT (una lámpara) to knock over, to turn over; (la cara) to turn away
voltereta F somersault, tumble; **dar una —** to somersault; **dar —s** to tumble
voltio M volt
voluble ADJ (malhumorado) moody; (mercado de valores) volatile
volumen M volume
voluminoso ADJ voluminous, bulky
voluntad F will; **a —** at will; **buena —** good will, willingness; **mala —** ill will; **por su propia —** of his own volition
voluntario -ria ADJ (por la propia voluntad) voluntary; MF volunteer
voluntarioso ADJ (bien dispuesto) willing; (testarudo) willful
voluptuoso ADJ voluptuous
voluta F scroll; **—s de humo** spirals of smoke
volver[2,51] VI (ir al punto de partida) to return, to come back; (ir de nuevo) to return, to go back, to go again; **— a comer** to eat again; **— del revés** to turn inside out; **— en sí** to regain consciousness; **—se** (regresar) to go back; (ponerse) to become; **—se contra** to turn against; **—se atrás** to turn back; **—se hacia** to go toward; **—se loco** to go crazy; VT (la cara) to turn away; **— las espaldas** to turn one's back

vomitar VI/VT to vomit, to throw up
vómito M vomit
voraz ADJ voracious, ravenous
vórtice M vortex
vosotros -as PRON PERS you, you guys; (sur de EEUU) you all, y'all
votación F vote
votante MF voter
votar VI to vote; VT (elegir) to vote for; (aprobar) to vote into law; **— a / por** to vote for
voto M (opinión) vote; (promesa) vow; **— de confianza** vote of confidence
voz F (sonido, aptitud, voto) voice; (cabeza de entrada) headword; **a — en cuello** at the top of one's lungs; **alzar la —** to raise one's, voice; **correr la —** to be rumored; **en — alta** aloud; **a voces** shouting; **dar voces** to shout
vozarrón M loud voice
vudú M voodoo
vuelco M **todo daría un —** everything would change radically; **me dio un — el corazón** my heart skipped a beat; **dar un —** to overturn, to turn over
vuelo M flight; (de una falda) flare; **al — on** the fly; **de alto —** prestigious; **levantar / alzar el —** to fly away
vuelta F (movimiento circular) turn; (regreso, devolución) return; (carrera ciclista) tour; (en una pista) lap; (curva) twist; (de un collar) loop; (en deportes) round; (dinero) change; **— de tuerca** unforeseen event; **a la — de la esquina** around the corner; **a — de correo** by return mail; **dar —** to turn upside down; **dar — al revés** to turn inside out; **dar — a una página / una llave** to turn a page / a key; **dar —s** to spin; **dar —s en la cama** to toss and turn; **dar — a algo** to turn something upside down; **dar la —** to turn around; **dar una —** to take a walk, to take a spin; **darse —** to roll over; **estar de —** (de regreso) to be back; (desencantado) to be jaded; **me da —s la cabeza** my head is spinning; **no tiene — de hoja** there are no two ways about it
vuelto M *Am* change
vuestro ADJ POS **— hermano** your bother; **un amigo —** a friend of yours; PRON **el — yours**
vulgar ADJ (común) ordinary; (tosco) vulgar
vulgo M common people
vulnerable ADJ vulnerable

Ww

wafle M waffle
waflera F waffle iron
wáter M toilet
web F World Wide Web
whisky M whisk(e)y; **— escocés** scotch
windsurf M windsurfing
wok M wok

Xx

xenofobia F xenophobia
xilofón, xilófono M xylophone

Yy

y CONJ and
ya ADV (desde antes) already; (ahora) now;
  (pronto) soon; **¡—! enough! — era hora**
  it was about time; **¡— lo creo!** I should
  say so! **— no** no longer; **— que** since; **—
  sea que** whether; **— te arreglo** I'll fix
  you; **— verás** mark my words; **— voy** I
  am coming
yacer[49] VI to lie
yacimiento M (de minerales) deposit; (de
  petróleo) field
yanqui ADJ & MF *pey* American
yarda F yard
yate M yacht
yegua F mare
yelmo M helmet
yema F (de huevo) egg yolk; (de una planta)
  bud, shoot; **— del dedo** fingertip
Yemen M Yemen
yemení ADJ & MF Yemeni
yen M yen
yermo ADJ (estéril) barren; (desolado) bleak,
  stark
yerno M son-in-law
yesca F tinder
yeso M (mineral) gypsum; (en construcción,
  medicina) plaster (of Paris); (escayola) cast
Yibuti M Djibouti

yibutiano -na ADJ & MF Djiboutian
yo PRON PERS I; M (ego) ego
yodo M iodine
yoduro M iodide
yoga M yoga
yogur M yogurt
yo-yo M yo-yo
yuca F (ornamental) yucca; (comestible)
  manioc
yugo M yoke
Yugoslavia F Yugoslavia
yugoslavo -va ADJ & MF Yugoslavian
yugular ADJ & F jugular
yunque M anvil
yunta F yoke
yuppie MF yuppie
yuxtaponer[39] VT juxtapose

Zz

zafar VT to release; **—se** (soltarse) to slip off;
  (no cumplir) to cop out; **—se de un
  aprieto** to squirm out of a difficulty
zafio ADJ boorish
zafiro M sapphire
zafra F (sugar) harvest
zaga LOC ADV **a la —** behind; F **ir a la —** to
  be behind; **quedar a la —** to fall behind
zaguán M vestibule, hall
zaino ADJ chestnut-colored
zalamería F (tacto) smoothness; (lisonja)
  flattery
zalamero -ra MF flatterer; ADJ (empalagoso)
  smooth, unctuous; (lisonjero) flattering
Zambia F Zambia
zambiano -na ADJ & MF Zambian
zambo ADJ knock-kneed
zambullida F dive, plunge
zambullir[19] VT to plunge, to dip; **—se** to
  dive, to plunge
zanahoria F carrot
zanca F leg of a wading bird
zancada F stride; **dar —s** to stride
zancadilla F intentional tripping; **hacer
  una —** to trip
zanco M stilt
zancudo ADJ long-legged, lanky; M *Am*
  mosquito
zángano M drone (también holgazán)
zangolotear VI/VT to jiggle
zangoloteo M jiggle
zanja F ditch, trench
zanjar VT to settle

zapapico M pickax(e)
zapata F brake shoe
zapatear VI to tap the feet in dancing
zapateo M tapping with the feet in dance
zapatería F shoe store
zapatero -ra MF (que fabrica) shoemaker; (que vende) shoe dealer; (que remienda) cobbler
zapatilla F (pantufla) slipper; (de vestir) pump; —s sneakers
zapato M shoe
zar M czar
zarandear VT to jiggle; —se to flop around
zarandeo M jiggle
zarcillo M (arete) earring; (de planta) tendril
zarigüeya F opossum
zarpa F claw
zarpar VI to sail, to set sail
zarpazo M blow with a claw; dar —s to claw
zarza F bramble, briar
zarzamora F blackberry
zepelín M blimp, zeppelin
zigoto M zygote
zigzag M zigzag
zigzaguear VI to zigzag, to weave one's way
Zimbabue M Zimbabwe
zimbabuo -ua ADJ & MF Zimbabwean
zirconio M zirconium
zócalo M baseboard
zodíaco M zodiac
zombi M zombie
zona F (área) zone; (culebrilla) shingles; — gris gray area; — tampón buffer zone
zonzo ADJ silly, foolish
zoo M zoo
zoología F zoology
zoológico ADJ zoological; M zoo
zoom M zoom lens
zopenco -ca MF dolt, numbskull
zorrillo M skunk
zorro -a MF fox; F (hembra) vixen; ADJ (astuto) foxy, cunning; (promiscuo) loose
zorzal M thrush
zozobra F anxiety, worry
zozobrar VI to founder
zueco M clog
zumbar VI (hacer sonidos los insectos) to buzz, to drone, to hum; (hacer ruidos las máquinas) to whir, to whiz; (tintinear los oídos) to ring; (dar golpe) to sock
zumbido M (sonido de insectos) buzz, drone, hum; (sonido de máquinas) whir, whiz; (sonido en los oídos) ring
zumo M fruit juice
zurcido M (remiendo) darn; (acción de remendar) darning
zurcir[10b] VT to darn

zurdo ADJ left-handed, southpaw
zuro M corncob
zurra F whipping
zurrar VT to whip, to thrash
zutano -na M so-and-so, what's-his-name; F what's-her-name

ista de abreviaturas / List of Abbreviations

dj	adjective	adjetivo
dv	adverb, adverbial	adverbio, adverbial
m	America	América
rt	article	artículo
onj	conjunction	conjunción
ef	definite	definido
em	demonstrative	demostrativo
	feminine	femenino
am	familiar	familiar
def	indefinite	indefinido
aterj	interjection	interjección
aterr	interrogative	interrogativo
av	invariable	invariable
t	literary	literario
oc	locution	locución
n	masculine	masculino
lex	Mexico	México
	noun	sustantivo
um	numeral	numeral
ej	pejorative	peyorativo
l	plural	plural
oss	possessive	posesivo
rep	preposition, prepositional	preposición, preposicional
ron	pronoun	pronombre
el	relative	relativo
P	River Plate	Río de la Plata
g	singular	singular
p	Spain, Spanish	España
aux	auxiliary verb	verbo auxiliar
i	intransitive verb	verbo intransitivo
t	transitive verb	verbo transitivo
ulg	vulgar	vulgar

Pronunciación inglesa

I. VOCALES

Símbolo fonético	Ortografía inglesa	Explicación
[i]	see, pea	como la i en hilo
[ɪ]	bit	el sonido más aproximado es la i en *virtud*, pero la [ɪ] inglesa es más abierta, tirando a e
[e]	late, they	equivale aproximadamente a *ei*
[ɛ]	set	semejante a la e de *perro*, pero más abierta
[ɝ]	work, bird	como la u de *cud* (ver abajo) pero articulada simultáneamente con una r
[æ]	sat	sonido intermedio entre e y a
[ɑ]	hot	como la vocal de *pan*
[ɔ]	saw, laud	sonido intermedio entre a y o
[o]	low, mode	equivale aproximadamente a *ou*
[ʊ]	book, pull	como la u de *turrón*, pero más abierta
[u]	June, moon	como la u de *uno*
[ʌ]	cud	una e muy relajada
[ə]	adept	una e muy relajada y átona
[ɚ]	teacher	una e átona relajada articulada simultáneamente con una r

II. DIPTONGOS

Símbolo fonético	Ortografía inglesa	Explicación
[aɪ]	pie, aisle	como *ai* en *aire*
[aʊ]	now, foul	como *au* en *causa*
[ɔɪ]	boy	como *oy* en *hoy*
[ju]	use	como *iu* en *ciudad*

III. CONSONANTES

Símbolo fonético	Ortografía inglesa	Explicación
[b]	bat	semejante a la b española, pero seguida de aspiración
[d]	day	semejante a la d española, pero articulada en los alvéolos y con más tensión
[f]	fun, photo	como la f española
[g]	go	como la g de *goma*, pero con más tensión

274

[h]	hat	muy suave como la *j* de los dialectos caribeños del español
[j]	year	como la *i* del diptongo de *hielo*
[k]	cat, kill	como la *c* de *carro*, pero seguida de aspiración
[l]	let	como la *l* de *lado*
[ɫ]	ball	como la *l* final catalana
[m]	much	como la *m* española
[n]	no	como la *n* española
[p]	pea	como la *p* española, pero seguida de aspiración
[r]	red	no tiene equivalente en español; se pronuncia con la punta de la lengua enrollada hacia arriba, sin tocar el paladar
[s]	sea	como la *s* hispanoamericana (no la castellana)
[t]	tea	como la *t* española pero articulada en los alvéolos y seguida de aspiración
[v]	very	se articula con los dientes incisivos superiores colocados en el labio inferior
[w]	weed	equivale a la *u* del diptongo de *fui*
[z]	zero, rose	como la *s* de *mismo* cuando se sonoriza, pero aun más sonora
[ɒ]	latter, ladder	como la *r* de *para*
[θ]	thin	como la *z* del español castellano en *zagal*
[ð]	this	como la *d* de *cada*
[ʃ]	sheet, machine, notation	una *s* muy palatal como en francés *chapeau* o italiano *lasciare*
[ʒ]	measure, beige	como la *ll* argentina en *valle*, cuando es sonora
[tʃ]	church	como la *ch* de *charla*
[dʒ]	judge	como la *y* de *inyectar*
[n̩]	eaten, button	representa la *n* silábica, articulada sin la vocal anterior
[ŋ]	ring	como la *n* española en *mango* y *banco*
[l̩]	able	representa la *l* silábica, articulada sin la vocal anterior
[hw]	where	combinación de los sonidos [h] y [w] arriba descritos

Notas sobre gramática inglesa

El sustantivo

Género. En la gramática inglesa el género solo desempeña un papel importante en el sistema pronominal, p. ej. **he runs** 'él corre', **she runs** 'ella corre', **I see him** 'lo veo', **I see her** 'la veo'. En los sustantivos que designan a personas, se emplean varios métodos para distinguir entre los sexos, v. gr. por el agregado de un sufijo, como en **actor** 'actor', **actress** 'actriz', por el agregado de una palabra, como en **baby boy** 'niño', **baby girl** 'niña', **she-bear** 'osa', **male nurse** 'enfermero', o utilizando palabras completamente distintas, como en **uncle** 'tío', **aunt** 'tía'.

Número. Generalmente se forma el plural añadiendo -s al singular: **paper, papers** 'papel, papeles', **books, books** 'libro, libros', **chief, chiefs** 'jefe, jefes'.

Los sustantivos que terminan en **-ss, -x, -sh, -z,** y **-o** añaden **-es** para formar el plural: **kiss, kisses** 'beso, besos', **box, boxes** 'caja, cajas', **dish, dishes** 'plato, platos', **buzz, buzzes** 'zumbido, zumbidos', **hero, heroes** 'héroe, héroes'. Esto vale también por **-ch** cuando se pronuncia [č], como en **arch, arches** 'arco, arcos', pero no cuando se pronuncia [k], como en **monarch, monarchs** 'monarca, monarcas'.

Los sustantivos que terminan en **-fe,** y ciertos sustantivos que terminan en **-f**, cambian estas letras en **v** y añaden **-es** en el plural: **leaf, leaves** 'hoja, hojas', **life, lives** 'vida, vidas', **wife, wives** 'esposa, esposas', **knife, knives** 'cuchillo, cuchillos' (pero **reef, reefs** 'arrecife, arrecifes').

Para formar el plural de los sustantivos terminados en **-y** precedida de consonante se cambia la **-y** en **-ies: fly, flies** 'mosca, moscas', **family, families** 'familia, familias'. En cambio, los sustantivos terminados en **-y** precedida de vocal forman el plural añadiendo **-s** al singular: **day, days** 'día, días'.

Ciertos sustantivos forman el plural de una manera irregular: **man, men** 'hombre, hombres', **woman, women** 'mujer, mujeres', **mouse, mice** 'ratón, ratones', **louse, lice** 'piojo, piojos', **goose, geese** 'ganso, gansos', **tooth, teeth** 'diente, dientes', **foot, feet** 'pie, pies', **ox, oxen** 'buey, bueyes'.

Ciertos sustantivos que terminan en **-is** forman el plural cambiando la **i** de la terminación en **e: axis, axes** 'eje, ejes', **crisis, crises** 'crisis' (sg., pl.).

El adjetivo

El adjetivo inglés es invariable en cuanto a género y número. Normalmente se coloca delante del sustantivo: **an interesting woman** 'una mujer interesante', **a large man** 'un hombre grande', **beautiful birds** 'aves hermosas'.

Los comparativos y superlativos. Aunque no hay una regla general, por lo común los adjetivos monosílabos, los adjetivos acentuados en la última sílaba y algunos bisílabos comunes forman el comparativo de aumento y el superlativo añadiendo **-er** y **-est** (como en **tall**). Los demás adjetivos van precedidos de **more** (para el comparativo) y **most** (para el superlativo) (como en **careful**). Nótese que (1) si la palabra termina en **-e** muda, se añaden **-r** y **-st** en vez de **-er** y **-est** (ver **wise**), (2) los adjetivos terminados en **-y** cambian esta letra en **i** (ver **happy**), (3) los adjetivos terminados en consonante precedida de vocal doblan la consonante (ver **fat**):

Positivo	*Comparativo*	*Superlativo*
tall alto	**taller** más alto	**the tallest** el más alto
careful cuidadoso	**more careful** más cuidadoso	**the most careful** el más cuidadoso
wise sabio	**wiser** más sabio	**the wisest** el más sabio
happy feliz	**happier** más feliz	**the happiest** el más feliz
fat gordo	**fatter** más gordo	**the fattest** el más gordo

Los adjetivos siguientes forman el comparativo y el superlativo de una manera irregular:

good	better	best
bad, ill	worse	worst
much	more	most

El adverbio

Muchos adverbios se forman añadiendo **-ly** al adjetivo: **courteous** 'cortés', **courteously** 'cortésmente', **bold** 'atrevido', **boldly** 'atrevidamente'. Existen las irregularidades ortográficas siguientes en la formación de los adverbios que terminan en **-ly:** (1) los adjetivos terminados en **-ble** cambian la **-e** en **-y: possible, possibly,** (2) los terminados en **-ic** añaden **-ally: poetic, poetically,** (3) los terminados en **-ll** añaden sólo **-y: full, fully,** (4) los terminados en **-ue** pierden la **-e** final: **true, truly,** (5) los terminados en **-y** cambian la **-y** en **i: happy, happily.**

La mayor parte de los adverbios forman el comparativo y el superlativo con los adverbios **more** 'más' y **most** 'el/la más'. Asimismo los adverbios monosílabos añaden **-er** y **-est:**

Positivo	*Comparativo*	*Superlativo*
boldly	**more boldly**	**most boldly**
generously	**more generously**	**most generously**
soon	**sooner**	**soonest**
early	**earlier**	**earliest**
late	**later**	**latest**
fast	**faster**	**fastest**

Los adverbios siguientes forman el comparativo y el superlativo de una manera irregular:

well	**better**	**best**
badly	**worse**	**worst**
little	**less**	**least**
far	**farther, further**	**farthest, furthest**

Sufijos comunes del inglés

-dom   a partir de bases nominales, forma sustantivos con los sentidos de dominio, jurisdicción, estado, condición: **kingdom** 'reino' (**king** 'rey'), **martyrdom** 'martirio' (**martyr** 'mártir'), **freedom** 'libertad' (**free** 'libre')

-ee   a partir de verbos, forma sustantivos indicando a la persona que recibe una acción: **addressee** 'destinatario' (**to address** 'dirigir'), **employee** 'empleado' (**to employ** 'emplear').

-eer   a partir de bases diversas, forma sustantivos que denotan oficio u ocupación: **auctioneer** 'subastador' (**to auction** 'subastar'), **puppeteer** 'titiritero' (**puppet** 'títere')

-en   *a.* forma adjetivos que denotan la sustancia de que está hecha una cosa: **golden** 'dorado' (**gold** 'oro'), **wooden** 'de madera' (**wood** 'madera')

    b. forma verbos a partir de adjetivos: **to whiten** 'blanquear' (**white** 'blanco'), **to darken** 'oscurecer' (**dark** 'oscuro')

-er   *a.* forma sustantivos a partir de verbos para indicar agente: **player** 'jugador' (**to play** 'jugar'), **speaker** 'hablante' (**to speak** 'hablar'), **baker** 'panadero' (**to bake** 'hornear')

    b. forma sustantivos a partir de sustantivos para denominar al residente de un lugar: **New Yorker** 'neoyorkino' (**New York** 'Nueva York'), **islander** 'isleño' (**island** 'isla')

-ess   se usa para formar el género femenino de ciertos sustantivos: **princess** 'princesa' (**prince** 'príncipe'), **countess** 'condesa' (**count** 'conde')

-fold   indica el número de veces que se repite algo: **twofold** 'dos veces' (**two** 'dos'), **hundredfold** 'cien veces' (**hundred** 'cien')

-ful   *a.* forma adjetivos a partir de sustantivos para indicar la presencia de una cualidad: **hopeful** 'esperanzado' (**hope** 'esperanza'), **careful** 'cuidadoso' (**care** 'cuidado'), **willful** 'voluntarioso' (**will** 'voluntad')

    b. forma adjetivos a partir de verbos para indicar tendencia: **forgetful** 'olvidadizo' (**to forget** 'olvidar')

    c. forma sustantivos a partir de sustantivos indicando la capacidad: **handful** 'puñado' (**hand** 'mano'), **spoonful** 'cucharada' (**spoon** 'cuchara')

-hood   forma abstractos a partir de sustantivos concretos: **motherhood** 'maternidad' (**mother** 'madre'), **childhood** 'niñez' (**child** 'niño'), **likelihood** 'probabilidad' (**likely** 'probable')

-ing   *a.* forma adjetivos a partir de verbos: **running water** 'agua corriente' (**to run** 'correr'), **drinking water** 'agua potable' (**to drink** 'beber'), **waiting room** 'sala de espera' (**to wait** 'esperar'), **washing machine** 'máquina lavadora' (**to wash** 'lavar')

    b. se usa para formar sustantivos que denominan la acción de un verbo: **understanding** 'entendimiento' (**to understand** 'entender'), **supplying** 'abastecimiento' (**to supply** 'abastar')

    c. se usa para formar sustantivos que denominan una cosa que desempeña una acción: **clothing** 'ropa' (**to clothe** 'vestir'), **covering** 'cobertura' (**to cover** 'cubrir')

-ish forma adjetivos a partir de sustantivos indicando semejanza o atenuación: **boyish** 'como un niño' (**boy** 'niño'), **womanish** 'como mujer, mujeril' (**woman** 'mujer'), **whitish** 'blancuzco' (**white** 'blanco')

-less se agrega a sustantivos para indicar falta de algo: **childless** 'sin hijos' (**child** 'hijo'), **penniless** 'sin dinero' (**penny** 'centavo'), **endless** 'interminable, sin fin' (**end** 'fin')

-like se añade a sustantivos para indicar semejanza: **lifelike** 'que parece vivo' (**life** 'vida'), **childlike** 'infantil' (**child** 'niño'), **tigerlike** 'como un tigre' (**tiger** 'tigre')

-ly *a.* se añade a adjetivos para formar adverbios: **slowly** 'lentamente' (**slow** 'lento'), **happily** 'felizmente' (**feliz** 'happy')

b. deriva adjetivos a partir de sustantivos indicando manera: **motherly** 'maternal' (**mother** 'madre'), **gentlemanly** 'caballeroso' (**gentleman** 'caballero'), **friendly** 'amistoso' (**friend** 'amigo')

c. deriva adjetivos o adverbios de tiempo a partir de sustantivos: **daily** 'diario', 'diariamente' (**day** 'día'), **weekly** 'semanal', 'semanalmente' (**week** 'semana')

-ness forma sustantivos abstractos a partir de adjetivos: **goodness** 'bondad' (**good** 'bueno'), **darkness** 'oscuridad' (**dark** 'oscuro'), **foolishness** 'tontería' (**fool** 'tonto')

-ship se emplea para derivar sustantivos a partir de sustantivos y verbos para denotar

a. cualidades abstractas: **friendship** 'amistad' (**friend** 'amigo')

b. arte o destreza: **horsemanship** 'equitación' (**horseman** 'jinete')

c. dignidad, oficio, cargo, o título: **professorship** 'cátedra' (**professor** 'catedrático'), **lordship** 'señoría' (**lord** 'señor')

d. la duración de una acción: **courtship** 'cortejo' (**to court** 'cortejar')

-some se añade a verbos para formar adjetivos que expresan tendencia excesiva: **tiresome** 'aburrido' (**to tire** 'aburrir'), **quarrelsome** 'pendenciero' (**to quarrel** 'discutir')

-th es el sufijo que forma números ordinales a partir de los cardinales: **fifth** 'quinto' (**five** 'cinco'), **tenth** 'décimo' (**ten** 'diez')

-ward se añade a sustantivos y adverbios para indicar movimiento hacia un lugar: **homeward** 'hacia casa' (**home** 'casa'), **downward** 'hacia abajo' (**down** 'abajo')

-wise, -ways	se añaden a sustantivos para indicar dirección o posición: **edgewise** 'de lado' (**edge** 'borde'), **lengthwise** 'a lo largo' (**length** 'largo'), **sideways** 'de lado' (**side** 'lado')

-y	a.	es un sufijo diminutivo: **doggy** 'perrito' (**dog** 'perro'), **Johnny** 'Juanito' (**John** 'Juan')
	b.	se añade a sustantivos para formar adjetivos que indican abundancia: **rocky** 'rocoso' (**rock** 'roca'), **rainy** 'lluvioso' (**rain** 'lluvia'), **hairy** 'peludo' (**hair** 'pelo'), **angry** 'enojado' (**anger** 'enojo')
	c.	se añade a sustantivos para formar adjetivos que expresan semejanza: **rosy** 'rosado' (**rose** 'rosa')

Verbos irregulares de la lengua inglesa

Se denominan verbos irregulares los que no forman el pretérito o el participio pasivo con la adición de **-d** o **-ed** al presente. Obsérvese que en ciertos verbos (aquí señalados con asterisco) coexiste la forma regular al lado de la irregular. Las formas poco usadas aparecen entre paréntesis.

Presente	Pretérito	Participio pasivo
*abide	(abode)	abode
am, is, are	was, were	been
arise	arose	arisen
*awake	awoke	awoke, awoken
bear	bore	borne
beat	beat	beat, beaten
become	became	become
befall	befell	befallen
beget	begat	begotten
begin	began	begun
behold	beheld	beheld
bend	bent	bent
beseech	(besought)	(besought)
beset	beset	beset
bet	bet	bet
bid 'offer'	bid	bid
bid 'command'	bade	bidden
bind	bound	bound
bite	bit	bitten, bit
bleed	bled	bled
blow	blew	blown
break	broke	broken
breed	bred	bred
bring	brought	brought
build	built	built
*burn	burnt	burnt

Presente	*Pretérito*	*Participio pasivo*
burst	burst	burst
buy	bought	bought
cast	cast	cast
catch	caught	caught
choose	chose	chosen
cling	clung	clung
*clothe	(clad)	(clad)
come	came	come
cost	cost	cost
creep	crept	crept
*crow	crew	crowed
cut	cut	cut
deal	dealt	dealt
dig	dug	dug
*dive	dove	dived
do	did	done
draw	drew	drawn
*dream	dreamt	dreamt
drink	drank	drunk
drive	drove	driven
*dwell	dwelt	dwelt
eat	ate	eaten
fall	fell	fallen
feed	fed	fed
feel	felt	felt
fight	fought	fought
find	found	found
*fit	fit	fit
flee	fled	fled
fling	flung	flung
fly	flew	flown
forbear	forbore	forborne
forbid	forbade	forbidden
foresee	foresaw	foreseen
foretell	foretold	foretold
forget	forgot	forgotten, forgot
forgive	forgave	forgiven
forsake	forsook	forsaken
freeze	froze	frozen
get	got	got, gotten
*gild	gilt	gilt
*gird	girded	girt
give	gave	given
go	went	gone
grind	ground	ground

Verbos irregulares

Presente	Pretérito	Participio pasivo
grow	grew	grown
hang[1]	hung	hung
have, has	had	had
hear	heard	heard
*hew	hewed	hewn
hide	hid	hidden, hid
hit	hit	hit
hold	held	held
hurt	hurt	hurt
keep	kept	kept
*kneel	knelt	knelt
*knit	knit	knit
know	knew	known
lay	laid	laid
lead	led	led
*lean	(leant)	(leant)
*leap	leapt	leapt
*learn	(learnt)	(learnt)
leave	left	left
lend	lent	lent
let .	let	let
lie[2]	lay	lain
*light	lit	lit
lose	lost	lost
make	made	made
mean	meant	meant
meet	met	met
mistake	mistook	mistaken
*mow	mowed	mown
pay	paid	paid
*plead	pled	pled
put	put	put
quit	quit	quit
read [rid]	read [red]	read [red]
rend	rent	rent
*rid	rid	rid
ride	rode	ridden
ring	rang	rung
rise	rose	risen
run	ran	run
*saw	sawed	sawn
say	said	said
see	saw	seen
seek	sought	sought

1. Es regular cuando significa 'ahorcar'.
2. Es regular cuando significa 'mentir'.

Presente	*Pretérito*	*Participio pasivo*
sell	sold	sold
send	sent	sent
set	set	set
*sew	sewed	sewn
shake	shook	shaken
*shave	shaved	shaven
*shear	sheared	shorn
shed	shed	shed
shine[3]	shone	shone
shoe	shod	shod
shoot	shot	shot
*show	showed	shown
*shred	shred	shred
shrink	shrank (shrunk)	shrunk (shrunken)
shut	shut	shut
sing	sang	sung
sink	sank	sunk
sit	sat	sat
slay	slew	slain
sleep	slept	slept
slide	slid	slid, slidden
sling	slung	slung
slink	slunk	slunk
slit	slit	slit
*smell	(smelt)	(smelt)
smite	smote	smitten
*sneak	snuck	snuck
*sow	sowed	sown
speak	spoke	spoken
*speed	sped	sped
*spell	(spelt)	(spelt)
spend	spent	spent
*spill	spilt	spilt
spin	spun	spun
spit	spat, spit	spat, spit
split	split	split
*spoil	(spoilt)	(spoilt)
spread	spread	spread
spring	sprang, sprung	sprung
stand	stood	stood
*stave	stove	stove
steal	stole	stolen
stick	stuck	stuck
sting	stung	stung
stink	stank	stunk

3. Suele ser regular cuando es transitivo, en el sentido 'pulir, dar brillo'.

Verbos irregulares

Presente	Pretérito	Participio pasivo
*strew	strewed	strewn
stride	strode	stridden
strike	struck	struck, stricken
string	strung	strung
*strive	strove	striven
swear	swore	sworn
*sweat	sweat	sweat
sweep	swept	swept
*swell	swelled	swollen
swim	swam	swum
swing	swung	swung
take	took	taken
teach	taught	taught
tear	tore	torn
tell	told	told
think	thought	thought
throw	threw	thrown
thrust	thrust	thrust
tread	trod	trodden
understand	understood	understood
undertake	undertook	undertaken
undo	undid	undone
uphold	upheld	upheld
upset	upset	upset
*wake	woke	woken
wear	wore	worn
weave	wove	woven
*wed	wed	wed
weep	wept	wept
*wet	wet	wet
win	won	won
wind	wound	wound
withdraw	withdrew	withdrawn
withhold	withheld	withheld
withstand	withstood	withstood
wring	wrung	wrung
write	wrote	written

Aa

a [ə, e] INDEF ART un *m*, una *f*; **what — fool!**
¡qué tonto! **such — fool** tan tonto; **I'm
— teacher / Catholic** soy maestro/
católico

aback [əbǽk] ADV **to be taken —** estar
desconcertado

abandon [əbǽndən] VT abandonar; N **with
wild —** desenfrenadamente

abandonment [əbǽndənmənt] N abandono
m, desamparo *m*

abashed [əbǽʃt] ADJ humillado, avergonzado

abate [əbét] VI/VT disminuir, mitigar(se);
(storm) calmarse, atenuarse

abbey [ǽbi] N abadía *f*

abbot [ǽbət] N abad *m*

abbreviate [əbríviet] VT abreviar

abbreviation [əbriviéʃən] N (act of
abbreviating) abreviación *f*; (short form)
abreviatura *f*

abdicate [ǽbdiket] VI/VT abdicar

abdomen [ǽbdəmən] N abdomen *m*, vientre
m

abdominal [æbdámənəł] ADJ abdominal

abduct [æbdʌ́kt] VT secuestrar, raptar

abduction [æbdʌ́kʃən] N rapto *m*, secuestro
m

aberration [æbəréʃən] N anomalía *f*,
aberración *f*

abet [əbét] VT instigar

abeyance [əbéəns] ADV LOC **in —** pendiente,
en suspenso

abhor [əbhɔ́r] VT aborrecer

abhorrence [əbhɔ́rəns] N aborrecimiento *m*

abhorrent [əbhɔ́rənt] ADJ aborrecible

abide [əbáɪd] VT (tolerate) soportar; VI (dwell)
morar, permanecer; **to — by** acatar,
atenerse a

ability [əbíłɪDi] N (skill) habilidad *f*;
(aptitude) capacidad *f*

abject [ǽbdʒékt] ADJ abyecto; **in — poverty**
en extrema miseria

ablaze [əbléz] ADJ en llamas

able [ébəł] ADJ hábil, capaz; **—-bodied** de
cuerpo sano; **to be — to** (be capable of)
poder; (have an acquired skill) saber

abnegate [ǽbnɪget] VT renunciar

abnormal [æbnɔ́rməł] ADJ anormal

aboard [əbɔ́rd] ADV a bordo; **all —!** (train)
¡viajeros al tren! (ship) ¡pasajeros a bordo!
to go — embarcarse

abode [əbód] N morada *f*; **place of —**

domicilio *m*

abolish [əbálɪʃ] VT abolir, suprimir

abolition [æbəlíʃən] N abolición *f*

abominable [əbámənəbəł] ADJ abominable

abomination [əbamənéʃən] N (action)
abominación *f*; (condition, habit) horror
m

aboriginal [æbəríʤənəł] ADJ aborigen

aborigine [æbəríʤəni] N aborigen *mf*;
Australian — aborigen australiano -na
mf

abort [əbɔ́rt] VT (fetus) abortar; VI/VT
(mission) suspender

abortion [əbɔ́rʃən] N aborto *m*

abortionist [əbɔ́rʃənɪst] N abortador -ra *mf*,
abortero -ra *mf*

abortive [əbɔ́rDɪv] ADJ frustrado

abound [əbáund] VI abundar; **to — with**
abundar en

about [əbáut] PREP (concerning) acérca de,
tocante a; (near, surrounding) alrededor
de, por; **to be — one's business** atender
a su negocio; ADV más o menos, alrededor
de; **at — ten o'clock** a eso de las diez,
sobre las diez; **to be — to do something**
estar por / para hacer algo, estar a punto
de hacer algo

above [əbʌ́v] PREP **you could see the
towers — the buildings** se veían las
torres sobre los edificios; **everyone —
five years of age** todos los de más de
cinco años; **he's — me in the company**
es mi superior en la compañía; **to be —
suspicion** estar libre de toda sospecha; **I
thought you were — such things** no
pensaba que te rebajarías a eso; **the
apartment —** el apartamento de arriba;
books of fifty pages and — libros de
cincuenta páginas y más; **the remark
quoted —** la observación anteriormente
citada; **— all** sobre todo; **—-mentioned**
susodicho, ya mencionado; **from —** de
arriba, del cielo, de Dios

abrasion [əbréʒən] N abrasión *f*

abrasive [əbrésɪv] ADJ (material) abrasivo;
(person, tone) irritante

abreast [əbrést] ADV al lado; **to keep —**
mantenerse al corriente; **four —** de cuatro
en fondo

abridge [əbríʤ] VT abreviar

abroad [əbrɔ́d] ADV en el extranjero; **to go
—** ir al extranjero

abrupt [əbrʌ́pt] ADJ abrupto

ABS (antilock braking system) [ebiés] N
SFA *m*

abscess [ǽbses] N absceso *m*

abscond [æbskánd] VI fugarse

absence [ǽbsəns] N (nonpresence) ausencia *f*; (lack) falta *f*; **in the — of** a falta de

absent [ǽbsənt] ADJ ausente; **—-minded** distraído, despistado; **to be — from school** faltar a la escuela

absentee [ǽbsəntí] N ausente *mf*

absenteeism [æbsəntíizəm] N ausentismo *m*

absolute [ǽbsəlút] ADJ absoluto; (prohibition) terminante

absolutely [æbsəlútli] ADV **— not** en absoluto; INTERJ **—!** ¡sí, señor!

absolve [æbzálv] VT absolver

absorb [əbzɔ́rb] VT (emission) absorber; (shock) amortiguar; (people, information) asimilar

abstain [æbstén] VI abstenerse; **— from** abstenerse de

abstinence [ǽbstənəns] N abstinencia *f*

abstract [ǽbstrækt] ADJ abstracto; N resumen *m*, extracto *m*; **in the —** en abstracto

abstraction [æbstrǽkʃən] N abstracción *f*

absurd [əbsɚd] ADJ absurdo, disparatado

absurdity [əbsɚ́-DIDi] N (quality) absurdo *m*; (action) disparate *m*

abundance [əbándəns] N abundancia *f*

abundant [əbándənt] ADJ abundante

abuse [əbjús] N (of privileges) abuso *m*; (of authority) desmán *m*; (physical) maltrato *m*; (verbal) injuria *f*; [əbjúz] VT (privileges) abusar de; (physically) maltratar; (verbally) injuriar

abusive [əbjúsɪv] ADJ (physically) violento; (verbally) injurioso

abysmal [əbízməl] ADJ abismal; **— ignorance** ignorancia supina *f*; **— results** resultados desastrosos *m pl*

abyss [əbís] N abismo *m*

A/C (air conditioning) [esí] N aire acondicionado *m*

academic [ǽkədémɪk] ADJ (university) académico; (school) escolar; N profesor -ra universitario -ria *mf*

academy [əkǽDəmi] N academia *f*

accede [æksíd] VI acceder; **to —** acceder a

accelerate [æksélaret] VI/VT acelerar

acceleration [æksélaɾéʃən] N aceleración *f*

accelerator [æksélaɾeDɚ] N acelerador *m*

accent [ǽksent] N (pronunciation) acento *m*; (written) tilde *f*, acento escrito *m*; [ǽksént] VT (stress, syllable) acentuar

accentuate [ækséntʃuet] VT (differences, facts) acentuar, recalcar; (beauty) realzar

accept [æksépt] VT aceptar

acceptable [æksɛ́ptəbəl] ADJ aceptable

acceptance [æksɛ́ptəns] N (action) aceptación *f*; (approval) aprobación *f*

access [ǽkses] N acceso *m*

accessible [ækséssəbəł] ADJ accesible

accessory [æksésəri] ADJ accesorio; N accesorio *m*; (to a crime) cómplice *mf*

accident [ǽksɪDənt] N accidente *m*; (mishap) percance *m*; **by —** por casualidad

accidental [æksɪdɛ́ntł] ADJ (injury) accidental; (discovery, meeting) casual, fortuito

acclaim [əklém] VT aclamar; N aclamación *f*, ovación *f*

acclamation [ækləméʃən] N aclamación *f*

acclimate [ǽkləmet] VI/VT (to physical conditions) aclimatar(se); (to an ambiance) acostumbrar(se)

accolade [ǽkəled] N elogio *m*

accommodate [əkámədet] VT (adjust) tener en cuenta; (lodge) hospedar, alojar; (contain) tener capacidad para; VI **to — oneself** adaptarse

accommodation [əkamədéʃən] N (adjustment) acomodación *f*, adaptación *f*; **—s** (lodging) alojamiento *m*; (facilities) comodidades *f pl*

accompaniment [əkámpənɪmənt] N acompañamiento *m*

accompanist [əkámpənɪst] N acompañante *mf*

accompany [əkámpəni] VI/VT acompañar

accomplice [əkámplɪs] N cómplice *mf*

accomplish [əkámplɪʃ] VT (objective) lograr; (mission) completar

accomplished [əkámplɪʃt] ADJ (actor, athlete) consumado; (musician) talentoso

accomplishment [əkámplɪʃmənt] N (achievement) logro *m*; (skill) habilidad *f*; (completion) realización *f*

accord [əkɔ́rd] N acuerdo *m*, convenio *m*; **of one's own —** voluntariamente; VT otorgar, conceder

accordance [əkɔ́rdəns] ADV LOC **in — with** de acuerdo con, de conformidad con

according [əkɔ́rdɪŋ] ADV LOC **— to** según

accordingly [əkɔ́rdɪŋli] ADV (therefore) por consiguiente; (correspondingly) como corresponde

accordion [əkɔ́rDiən] N acordeón *m*

accost [əkɔ́st] VT abordar

account [əkáunt] N (bill) cuenta *f*; (story) relato *m*, relación *f*; **to open (close) an —** abrir (cerrar) una cuenta; **on — of** a causa de, debido a; **on my —** por mí; **on one's own —** por cuenta propia; **on no —** de ninguna manera; **of no —** de ningún valor; **to take into —** tener en cuenta; VI **to — for** dar cuenta de; **how do you — for that?** ¿cómo se explica eso?

accountable [əkáʊntəbəl] ADJ responsable

accountant [əkáʊntn̩t] N *Am* contador -ra *mf*; *Sp* contable *mf*

accounting [əkáʊntɪŋ] N contabilidad *f*; **— firm** empresa de contadores públicos *f*; **— period** ejercicio contable *m*

accredit [əkrɛ́Dɪt] VT acreditar

acculturate [əkʌ́ltʃəret] VI/VT aculturar(se)

accumulate [əkjúmjəlet] VI/VT acumular(se)

accumulation [əkjumjəléʃən] N acumulación *f*

accuracy [ǽkjə-əsi] N precisión *f*, exactitud *f*

accurate [ǽkjə-ɪt] ADJ (measure, instrument) preciso, exacto; (translation) fiel

accursed [əkɜ́-sɪd] ADJ maldito

accusation [ǽkjuzéʃən] N acusación *f*

accuse [əkjúz] VT acusar

accused [əkjúzd] ADJ acusado; N acusado -da *mf*, reo -a *mf*, procesado -da *mf*

accuser [əkjúzə-] N acusador -ra *mf*

accustom [əkʌ́stəm] VT acostumbrar, habituar; **to — oneself** acostumbrarse, habituarse; **to be —ed to** tener la costumbre de, estar acostumbrado a

AC/DC (alternating current / direct current) [ésídísí] ADJ alterna y continua

ace [es] N (cards, athlete, aviator) as *m*; VT sacarse la máxima nota en

acetone [ǽsəton] N acetona *f*

ache [ek] N dolor *m*; **—s and pains** achaques *m pl*; VT doler; **my stomach —s** me duele el estómago

achieve [ətʃív] VT (a goal) conseguir, lograr; (a level) alcanzar

achievement [ətʃívmənt] N (attainment) consecución *f*; (success) logro *m*, realización *f*

achy [éki] ADJ dolorido

acid [ǽsɪd] ADJ ácido; N ácido *m*; (hallucinogen) LSD *m*; **— rain** lluvia ácida *f*; **— test** prueba de fuego *f*

acidic [əsíDɪk] ADJ ácido

acidity [əsíDɪDi] N acidez *f*

acknowledge [æknálɪdʒ] VT (merits) reconocer; (faults) admitir, reconocer; **to — receipt** acusar recibo

acknowledgment [æknálɪdʒmənt] N (of merits) reconocimiento *m*; (of merits, faults) reconocimiento *m*, admisión *f*; (gratefulness) agradecimiento *m*; **— of receipt** acuse de recibo *m*

acme [ǽkmi] N súmmum *m*

acne [ǽkni] N acné *m*

acorn [ékɔrn] N bellota *f*

acoustics [əkústɪks] N acústica *f*

acquaint [əkwént] VT informar, familiarizar; **to — oneself with** informarse de,

familiarizarse con; **to be —ed with** (a person, city, country) conocer; (a piece of news) estar enterado de

acquaintance [əkwéntn̩s] N (with facts) conocimiento *m*; (a person) conocido -a *mf*

acquiesce [ækwiés] VT asentir, condescender; (unwillingly) consentir

acquiescence [ækwiésəns] N asentimiento *m*, consentimiento *m*, condescendencia *f*

acquire [əkwáɪr] VT (knowledge, skill, purchase) adquirir; (fortune, information) obtener; (disease) contraer

acquisition [ækwəzíʃən] N (knowledge, skill, purchase) adquisición *f*; (fortune, information) obtención *f*

acquisitive [əkwízɪDɪv] ADJ codicioso

acquit [əkwít] VT absolver

acquittal [əkwídl] N absolución *f*

acre [ékə-] N acre (0,405 hectáreas) *m*

acrid [ǽkrɪd] ADJ acre

acrimony [ǽkrəmoni] N acritud *f*

acrobat [ǽkrəbæt] N acróbata *mf*

acrobatic [ækrəbǽDɪk] ADJ acrobático; **—s** acrobacia *f*

acronym [ǽkrənɪm] N acrónimo *m*, sigla *f*

acrophobia [ækrəfóbiə] N acrofobia *f*

across [əkrɔ́s] PREP **to lay one stick — the other** poner dos palos cruzados; **there's a bridge — that river** hay un puente sobre ese río; **he came — his old love letters** encontró sus viejas cartas de amor; **the library is — the street** la biblioteca está al otro lado de la calle; ADV **cut the boards —** corta los tablones a lo ancho; **five hundred miles —** de quinientas millas de ancho; **the meaning doesn't come —** el significado no se entiende; **to come / run —** encontrarse con, tropezar con

acrylic [əkrílɪk] ADJ & N acrílico *m*

act [ækt] N (deed, part of play) acto *m*; (part of show) número *m*; (law) ley *f*, decreto *m*; VI (behave) actuar, comportarse; (take measures) obrar; (play a part, chemical process) actuar; (on someone's behalf) representar; (mechanism) funcionar; **to — up** (child) portarse mal; (car) funcionar mal; **to — out** (event) representar; (feelings) exteriorizar

acting [ǽktɪŋ] N actuación *f*; representación *f*; ADJ (interim) interino; (substitute) suplente

action [ǽkʃən] N (practical measure, plot of a play) acción *f*; (deed) acto *m*; (mechanism) funcionamiento *m*; **to take —** tomar medidas

activate [ǽktɪvet] VT activar

active [ǽktɪv] ADJ activo

activism [ǽktɪvɪzəm] N activismo *m*

activist [ǽktɪvɪst] N activista *mf*

activity [æktívɪɖi] N actividad *f*

actor [ǽktə] N actor *m*

actress [ǽktrɪs] N actriz *f*

actual [ǽktʃuəł] ADJ verdadero, real

actually [ǽktʃuəli] ADV en realidad

actuary [ǽktʃueri] N actuario -ria *mf*

acuity [əkjúɪɖi] N agudeza *f*

acumen [ǽkjəmən] N perspicacia *f*, agudeza *f*

acupuncture [ǽkjupʌŋktʃə] N acupuntura *f*

acupuncturist [ækjupʌ́ŋktʃə-ɪst] N acupuntor -ra *mf*

acute [əkjút] ADJ (pain, illness) agudo; (observation) perspicaz, penetrante

A.D. [edí] ADV d.C.

adamant [ǽdəmənt] ADJ inflexible, firme

adapt [ədǽpt] VT adaptar; VI **to — to** adaptar(se) a, acomodar(se) a

adaptation [ædəptéʃən] N adaptación *f*

add [æd] VT añadir, agregar; (sum) sumar; **to — to** aumentar; **to — up** (sum) sumar; (make sense) cuadrar; N **—-on** accesorio *m*

addict [ǽdɪkt] N adicto -ta *mf*

addicted [ədíktɪd] ADJ adicto

addiction [ədíkʃən] N adicción *f*

addition [ədíʃən] N (of numbers) suma *f*; (to a collection, staff) adición *f*, adquisición *f*; (to a building) anexo *m*; **in — (to)** además (de)

additional [ədíʃənəł] ADJ adicional

additive [ǽdɪtɪv] N aditivo *m*

address [ədrɛ́s] N (street) dirección *f*, domicilio *m*; (speech) discurso *m*; **form of —** tratamiento *m*; VT (write the address) dirigir; (speak to) dirigirse a; (deal with) vérselas con

addressee [ædresí] N destinatario -ria *mf*

adept [ədǽpt] ADJ hábil

adequacy [ǽdɪkwəsi] N suficiencia *f*

adequate [ǽdɪkwɪt] ADJ (sufficient) suficiente; (acceptable) aceptable

adhere [ædhír] VI adherirse; **to — to** adherirse a

adherence [ædhírəns] N adhesión *f*

adhesion [ædhíʒən] N (thing or tissue that adheres) adherencia *f*; (act of sticking together) adhesión *f*

adhesive [ædhísɪv] ADJ adhesivo; **— tape** cinta adhesiva *f*

adjacent [ədʒésənt] ADJ adyacente

adjective [ǽdʒɪktɪv] ADJ & N adjetivo *m*

adjoin [ədʒɔ́ɪn] VT lindar con, colindar con; VI estar contiguo a

adjourn [ədʒɝn] VT **to — the meeting** levantar la sesión; **meeting —ed** se levanta la sesión

adjournment [ədʒɝnmənt] N levantamiento de la sesión *m*

adjudge [ədʒʌ́dʒ] VT (declare) declarar; (deem) calificar

adjudicate [ədʒúdɪket] VI arbitrar; VT declarar

adjunct [ǽdʒʌŋkt] ADJ adjunto; N agregado -da *mf*

adjust [ədʒʌ́st] VT (fix) ajustar, graduar; (adapt a machine) regular; VI ajustarse, adaptarse

adjustment [ədʒʌ́stmənt] N ajuste *m*; (on a machine) regulación *f*

ad lib [ædlíb] ADV improvisando

administer [ædmínɪstə] VT (control) administrar, gestionar; (punishment) aplicar; (oath) tomar

administration [ædmɪnɪstréʃən] N administración *f*; (period in power) gestión *f*; (of punishment) aplicación *f*; (of an oath) toma *f*

administrative [ædmínɪstreɖɪv] ADJ administrativo

administrator [ædmínɪstreɖə] N administrador -ra *mf*

admirable [ǽdmə-əbəł] ADJ admirable

admiral [ǽdmə-əł] N almirante *m*

admiration [ædmə-réʃən] N admiración *f*

admire [ædmáɪr] VT admirar

admirer [ædmáɪrə] N admirador -ra *mf*; (suitor) pretendiente *mf*

admissible [ædmísəbəł] ADJ admisible

admission [ædmíʃən] N (acceptance) admisión *f*; (access, ticket price) entrada *f*; (confession) confesión *f*

admit [ædmít] VT (allow entry) admitir; (to a hospital) internar; (acknowledge) reconocer, admitir

admittance [ædmítns] N entrada *f*; **no —** prohibida la entrada

admonish [ædmɑ́nɪʃ] VT amonestar; **to — for** amonestar por

admonition [ædməníʃən] N (warning) amonestación *f*; (reproof) advertencia *f*

adobe [ədóbi] N (mud) adobe *m*; (house) casa de adobe *f*

adolescence [ædlɛ́səns] N adolescencia *f*

adolescent [ædlɛ́sənt] ADJ & N adolescente *mf*

adopt [ədɑ́pt] VT (child, custom) adoptar; (suggestion) aprobar

adoption [ədɑ́pʃən] N (of a child, custom) adopción *f*; (of a suggestion) aprobación *f*

adoptive [ədɑ́ptɪv] ADJ adoptivo

adorable [ədɔ́rəbəł] ADJ adorable, precioso

adoration [ædəréʃən] N adoración *f*

adore [ədɔ́r] VT adorar; **I — playing tennis**

me encanta jugar al tenis

adorn [ədɔ́rn] VT adornar, ornar

adornment [ədɔ́rnmənt] N adorno *m*

adrenal [ədrín] ADJ — **gland** glándula
suprarrenal *f*

adrenalin [ədrénəlɪn] N adrenalina *f*

adrift [ədríft] ADJ & ADV a la deriva

adult [ədʌ́lt] ADJ & N adulto -ta *mf*

adulterate [ədʌ́ltəret] VT adulterar

adulterer [ədʌ́ltərə-] N adúltero -ra *mf*

adultery [ədʌ́ltəri] N adulterio *m*

advance [ædvǽns] VI (move forward)
avanzar; (make progress) avanzar,
progresar; (bring forward) adelantar; VT
(promote) promover; (propose) proponer;
(pay beforehand) adelantar, anticipar; N
(movement) avance *m*; (progress) adelanto
m; (loan) adelanto *m*, anticipo *m*; —**s**
(sexual) requiebros *m pl*; **in** — por
adelantado, con anticipación

advanced [ædvǽnst] ADJ (idea, stage)
avanzado; (country) adelantado

advancement [ædvǽnsmənt] N (movement)
avance *m*; (rank) ascenso *m*; (knowledge)
progreso *m*

advantage [ædvǽntɪdʒ] N ventaja *f*; **it
would be to your** — te convendría; **to
take** — **of** aprovecharse de

advantageous [ædvæntédʒəs] ADJ ventajoso,
provechoso

advent [ǽdvent] N advenimiento *m*

adventure [ædvéntʃə-] N aventura *f*

adventurer [ædvéntʃərə-] N aventurero -ra *mf*

adventuresome [ædvéntʃə-səm] ADJ osado

adventurous [ædvéntʃə-əs] ADJ (seeking
adventure) aventurero, intrépido; (daring)
atrevido, audaz

adverb [ǽdvə-b] N adverbio *m*

adversary [ǽdvə-seri] N adversario -ria *mf*

adverse [ædvə́-s] ADJ adverso

adversity [ædvə́-sɪdi] N adversidad *f*

advertise [ǽdvə-taiz] VT anunciar, hacer
publicidad/propaganda para; VI hacer
propaganda/publicidad; **to** — **for a
cook** poner un anuncio buscando
cocinero

advertisement [ædvə-táizmənt] N anuncio
publicitario *m*, aviso *m*

advertiser [ǽdvə-taizə-] N anunciante *mf*

advertising [ǽdvə-taizɪŋ] N publicidad *f*

advice [ædváís] N consejo *m*; (expert)
asesoramiento *m*

advisable [ædváizəbəl] ADJ aconsejable,
recomendable

advise [ædváiz] VI/VT (counsel) aconsejar,
advertir; VT (inform) avisar, informar;
(expertly) asesorar

adviser, advisor [ædváizə-] N consejero -ra
mf, asesor -ora *mf*

advocacy [ǽdvəkəsi] N defensa *f*

advocate [ǽdvəkɪt] N (promoter) partidario
-ria *mf*; (defender) defensor -ra *mf*,
intercesor -ra *mf*; (lawyer) abogado -da *mf*;
[ǽdvəket] VT abogar por, defender

aerial [ériəl] ADJ aéreo; N antena *f*

aerobic [ɛróbɪk] ADJ (exercise) aeróbico; (air-
breathing) aerobio; —**s** aeróbic *m*

aerodynamic [ɛrodaɪnǽmɪk] ADJ
aerodinámico; —**s** aerodinámica *f*

aeronautics [ɛrənɔ́dɪks] N aeronáutica *f*

aerosol [érəsɑl] N aerosol *m*

aerospace [érospes] N espacio aéreo *m*; ADJ
aeroespacial

aesthetic [esθédɪk] ADJ estético; N —**s** estética
f

affable [ǽfəbəl] ADJ afable

affair [əfér] N (social) acontecimiento social
m; (business) asunto *m*, negocio *m*; (love)
aventura amorosa *f*, affaire *m*

affect [əfékt] VT (have effect on) afectar;
(move) conmover; (feign) fingir

affectation [æfektéʃən] N afectación *f*,
melindre *m*

affected [əféktɪd] ADJ (moved) afectado,
conmovido; (feigned) fingido, artificioso,
melindroso

affection [əfékʃən] N afecto *m*, cariño *m*

affectionate [əfékʃənɪt] ADJ afectuoso,
cariñoso

affidavit [æfidévit] N declaración jurada *f*

affiliate [əfíliet] VT afiliar; VI afiliarse,
asociarse; [əfíliɪt] N filial *f*

affinity [əfínɪdi] N afinidad *f*

affirm [əfə́-m] VT afirmar

affirmation [æfə-méʃən] N afirmación *f*

affirmative [əfə́-mədɪv] ADJ afirmativo; N —
action discriminación positiva *f*; **reply
in the** — dar una respuesta afirmativa

affix [əfíks] VT fijar; **to** — **one's signature**
poner su firma, firmar

afflict [əflíkt] VT aquejar; **to be** —**ed with**
padecer de, sufrir de

affliction [əflíkʃən] N (misery) aflicción *f*;
(ailment) achaque *m*, mal *m*

affluent [ǽfluənt] ADJ (society) opulento;
(person) rico

afford [əfɔ́rd] VT **I cannot** — **a car** no me
alcanza el dinero para un coche; **he
cannot** — **to waste time** no puede
darse el lujo de perder tiempo; **I cannot**
— **the risk** no me puedo permitir ese
riesgo; **we will** — **you every
opportunity** se te darán todas las
oportunidades

affordable [əfɔ́rⅮəbəl] ADJ asequible

affront [əfrʌ́nt] N afrenta f

Afghan, Afghani [ǽfgæn / æfgǽni] ADJ & N afgano -na mf

Afghanistan [æfgǽnɪstæn] N Afganistán m

afire [əfáɪr] ADJ & ADV en llamas

afloat [əflót] ADJ & ADV flotando, a flote

afraid [əfréd] ADJ asustado; **to be — (of)** temer, tener miedo (de)

afresh [əfréʃ] ADV de nuevo, desde el principio

Africa [ǽfrɪkə] N África f

African [ǽfrɪkən] ADJ & N africano -na mf

African-American [ǽfrɪkənəméríkən] ADJ & N afroamericano -na mf

after [ǽftə] PREP (temporal) después de, tras; (spatial) detrás de; **— all** después de todo; ADV después; CONJ después (de) que

afterbirth [ǽftə-bɚ-θ] N placenta f

afterlife [ǽftə-laɪf] N el más allá

aftermath [ǽftə-mæθ] N secuelas f pl

afternoon [ǽftə-nún] N tarde f; INTERJ **good — buenas tardes**

aftershave [ǽftə-ʃev] N loción para después del afeitado f

aftershock [ǽftə-ʃak] N réplica f

aftertaste [ǽftə-test] N (in the mouth) dejo m; (bad memory) resabio m

aftertax [ǽftə-tæks] ADJ **— profit** ganancia neta f

afterthought [ǽftə-θɔt] N **it was just an —** se nos ocurrió después

afterward, afterwards [ǽftə-wə-d(z)] ADV después, luego

again [əgén] ADV otra vez, de nuevo; (on the other hand) por otra parte; **— and —** repetidas veces; **to fall —** volver a caerse

against [əgénst] PREP contra; **— the grain** a contrapelo; **— all odds** a pesar de todo

age [edʒ] N (of a person) edad f; (era) era f, época f; **— of —** mayor de edad; **old —** vejez f; **to come of —** llegar a la mayoría de edad; **under —** menor de edad; VI/VT envejecer

aged [edʒd] ADJ (wine) añejo; **— forty** de cuarenta años; [édʒɪd] anciano

ageless [édʒlɪs] ADJ (everlasting) eterno; (not showing age) siempre joven; (classic) clásico

agency [édʒənsi] N agencia f; **through the — of** por mediación de

agenda [ədʒéndə] N temario m, orden del día m

agent [édʒənt] N agente mf; (commercial) representante mf; (legal) apoderado -da mf

aggrandize [əgrǽndaɪz] VT engrandecer

aggravate [ǽgrəvet] VT (worsen) exacerbar, agravar; (annoy) irritar, exasperar, exacerbar

aggregate [ǽgrɪgɪt] N conjunto m; (rock) agregado m; ADJ total, global

aggression [əgréʃən] N agresión f

aggressive [əgrésɪv] ADJ (violent) agresivo; (dynamic) emprendedor

aggressor [əgrésə-] N agresor -ra mf

aghast [əgǽst] ADJ horrorizado

agile [ǽdʒəl] ADJ ágil

agility [ədʒílɪDi] N agilidad f

agitate [ǽdʒɪtet] VT (shake) agitar; (perturb) turbar; (campaign) alborotar

agitation [ædʒɪtéʃən] N agitación f

agitator [ǽdʒɪteⅮə-] N agitador -ra mf

agnostic [ægnástɪk] ADJ & N agnóstico -ca mf

ago [əgó] ADV **many years —** hace muchos años; **long —** hace mucho tiempo

agog [əgóg] ADJ planchado, boquiabierto

agonize [ǽgənaɪz] VI sufrir angustiosamente; **to — over** atormentarse por

agony [ǽgəni] N (pain) dolor m, tormento m; (anguish) angustia f

agoraphobia [ægə-əfóbiə] N agorafobia f

agrarian [əgrérian] ADJ agrario

agree [əgrí] VI (be in agreement) estar de acuerdo; (in grammar, mathematics) concordar; (color, food) sentarle bien a uno; **they —d to buy the car** quedaron en comprar el coche

agreeable [əgríəbəl] ADJ (nice) agradable; (willing) conforme

agreement [əgrímənt] N (concord, document) acuerdo m, convenio m; (grammatical) concordancia f; **to be in —** estar de acuerdo; **to come to an —** ponerse de acuerdo

agricultural [ægrɪkʌ́ltʃə-əl] ADJ (related to crops) agrícola; (related to crops and cattle) agropecuario

agriculture [ǽgrɪkʌltʃə-] N agricultura f

aground [əgráund] ADV **to run —** encallar, varar

ahead [əhéd] ADV delante; **— of time** adelantado, antes de tiempo; **to go —** ir adelante, adelantarse; **to get —** prosperar; **our team is —** nuestro equipo va primero; **the years —** los años venideros

aid [ed] N (help) asistencia f; (assistant) ayudante mf; VT ayudar; **to — and abet** instigar

AIDS (acquired immune deficiency syndrome) [edz] N SIDA m

ail [el] VI/VT **what —s you?** ¿qué tienes? ¿qué te aflige? **he's —ing** está enfermo

aileron [élərɑn] N alerón m

ailment [élmənt] N achaque m, dolencia f

aim [em] N (with a weapon) puntería f;
(objective) objetivo m; VT (a weapon)
apuntar; (a question, blow) dirigir; **to —
to please** tratar de agradar

aimless [émlɪs] ADJ (purposeless) sin
propósito; (directionless) sin rumbo

air [er] N aire m; **up in the —** en el aire,
incierto; **in the open —** al aire libre; **to
be on the —** estar en el aire, emitirse; **to
put on —s** presumir, darse ínfulas; **to
vanish into thin —** evaporarse; ADJ
aéreo; **—bag** airbag m, bolsa de aire f;
—borne (troops) aerotransportado;
(particles) transportado por el aire;
—brake freno neumático m; **—
conditioned** con aire acondicionado; **—
conditioner** acondicionador de aire m;
— conditioning aire acondicionado m,
climatización f; **—craft** aeronave f;
—craft carrier portaaviones m sg;
—field aeródromo m; **— Force** Fuerza
Aérea f; **—head** cabeza de chorlito mf;
—lift puente aéreo m; **—line** línea aérea
f; **— mail** correo aéreo m; **—plane** avión
m; **— piracy** piratería aérea f; **—port**
aeropuerto m; **— power** fuerza aérea f; **—
pressure** presión de aire f; **— raid** ataque
aéreo m; **— rifle** escopeta de aire
comprimido f; **—ship** dirigible m; **—
strike** bombardeo aéreo m; **—strip** pista
de aterrizaje f; **—tight** hermético;
—-to-— aire-aire; **— traffic control**
control del tráfico aéreo m; VT (an
opinion) manifestar; **to —lift**
aerotransportar; **to — out** orear, ventilar

aisle [aɪl] N pasillo m; (of a church) nave
lateral f

ajar [əʤár] ADJ entornado, entreabierto

akin [əkín] ADJ (related) emparentado;
(similar) semejante

à la mode [alamód] ADV con helado

alarm [əlárm] N (warning) alarma f; (worry)
inquietud f; **— clock** despertador m; **to
sound an —** tocar a rebato; VT (worry)
alarmar; (frighten) asustar

Albania [æłbéniə] N Albania f

Albanian [æłbéniən] ADJ & N albanés -esa mf

albatross [æłbɑtrɑs] N albatros m

albino [æłbáɪno] N albino -na mf

album [æłbəm] N álbum m

alcohol [æłkəhɔł] N alcohol m

alcoholic [æłkəhɔ́łɪk] ADJ & N alcohólico -ca
mf

alcoholism [æłkəhɔ́łɪzəm] N alcoholismo m

alcove [æłkov] N rincón m

ale [eł] N cerveza inglesa f

alert [əlɝ́t] ADJ (vigilant) alerta; (awake)
despierto; **to be —** (on guard) estar alerta;
(lively) ser despierto; N alerta f; VT alertar,
avisar

alfalfa [æłfǽłfə] N alfalfa f

algae [ǽłʤi] N algas f pl

algebra [ǽłʤəbrə] N álgebra f

Algeria [æłʤíriə] N Argelia f

Algerian [æłʤíriən] ADJ & N argelino -na mf

algorithm [ǽłgəríðəm] N algoritmo m

alias [éliəs] N alias m sg

alibi [ǽləbaɪ] N coartada f

alien [éliən] N (visitor from space)
extraterrestre mf; (foreigner) extranjero -ra
mf; ADJ ajeno

alienate [éliənet] VT (people) ofender,
ganarse la antipatía de; (property)
enajenar

alight [əláɪt] VI (rider) apearse; (bird, insect)
posarse

align [əláɪn] VI/VT alinear(se)

alignment [əláɪnmənt] N alineación f

alike [əláɪk] ADJ parecido, igual; **to be —**
parecerse, ser iguales; ADV del mismo
modo

alimony [ǽləmoni] N pensión alimenticia f

alive [əláɪv] ADJ (living) vivo; **— with** lleno
de; **the symphony came — under his
direction** la sinfonía cobró vida bajo su
dirección

alkali [ǽłkəlaɪ] N álcali m

alkaline [ǽłkəlɪn] ADJ alcalino

all [ɔł] ADJ todo; **— the time** todo el tiempo;
N todo m; **he gave his —** dio todo de sí;
PRON todo; **is that —?** ¿eso es todo? ADV
completamente, todo; **— at once**
(uninterrupted) de una vez; (sudden) de
repente; **— told** en conjunto; **he's —
dirty** está todo sucio; **it is — over** se
acabó; **not at —** de ninguna manera;
nothing at — nada en absoluto; **once
(and) for —** de una vez por todas; **she's
— right** está bien; INTERJ **— right** bueno

allay [əlé] VT (fear, doubt) calmar, disipar;
(anger) aplacar

allegation [ælɪgéʃən] N acusación f

allege [əléʤ] VT afirmar

allegiance [əlíʤəns] N lealtad f, fidelidad f;
to pledge — to the flag jurar la bandera

allegory [ǽlɪgɔri] N alegoría f

allergic [əlɝ́ʤɪk] ADJ alérgico

allergist [ǽlɚʤɪst] N alergólogo -ga mf

allergy [ǽlɚʤi] N alergia f

alleviate [əlíviet] VT (suffering) aliviar;
(hunger) paliar

alley [ǽli] N callejón m; **right up her —**
ideal para ella

alliance [əláɪəns] N alianza f

allied [əláɪd, ǽlaɪd] ADJ aliado

alligator [ǽlɪɡeɒə] N caimán *m*; *Am* lagarto *m*

alliterate [əlídəret] VI hacer aliteración

allocate [ǽləket] VT asignar

allot [əlát] VT asignar

allow [əláu] VI/VT (permit) permitir; (admit) admitir; **— an hour to change trains** date una hora para cambiar de trenes; **to — for** tener en cuenta

allowable [əláuəbəɬ] ADJ admisible, permisible

allowance [əláuəns] N (regular payment) asignación *f*, pensión *f*; (monthly payment) mensualidad *f*; (for a child) paga *f*, mesada *f*; (payment for a particular purpose) pago *m*; (food) ración *f*; **to make — for** tener en cuenta

alloy [ǽlɔɪ] N aleación *f*; [əlɔ́ɪ] VT alear

allude [əlúd] VI aludir; **to — to** aludir a

allure [əlúr] VI/VT seducir, atraer; N atractivo *m*

alluring [əlúrɪŋ] ADJ seductivo, atractivo

allusion [əlúʒən] N alusión *f*

ally [ǽlaɪ] N aliado -da *mf*; [əláɪ] VT **to — oneself with** aliarse con

almanac [ɔ́ɬmənæk] N almanaque *m*

almighty [ɔ̀ɬmáɪdi] ADJ todopoderoso

almond [ɔ́mənd] N almendra *f*; **— tree** almendro *m*

almost [ɔ́ɬmost] ADV casi; **I — fell down** por poco me caigo

alms [ɑmz] N limosna *f*

aloe vera [ǽlovírə] N áloe *m*

alone [əlón] ADJ solo; **— among his contemporaries** único entre sus contemporáneos; ADV sólo, solamente; **she — knew that** sólo ella sabía eso; **all — a** solas; **to leave —** no tocar, dejar en paz

along [əlɔ́ŋ] PREP **he was walking — the street** andaba por la calle; **all — the coast** a lo largo de toda la costa; **— with** junto con; **all —** desde el principio; **to carry — with oneself** llevar consigo; **to go — with** acceder a; **to get — with** llevarse bien con

alongside [əlɔ́ŋsaɪd] PREP al lado de; **— the boat** al lado del bote; ADV al lado, al costado; **the dog ran —** el perro corría al costado

aloof [əlúf] ADJ reservado, esquivo; ADV apartado

aloud [əláud] ADV en voz alta

alphabet [ǽɬfəbet] N alfabeto *m*, abecedario *m*

alphanumeric [æɬfənumérɪk] ADJ alfanumérico

alpine [ǽɬpaɪn] ADJ alpino

already [ɔɬrédi] ADV ya

also [ɔ́ɬso] ADV también, además; **—-ran** (horse, candidate) caballo / candidato vencido *m*; (loser) nulidad *f*, segundón -ona *mf*

altar [ɔ́ɬtə] N altar *m*; **—piece** retablo *m*

alter [ɔ́ɬtə] VI/VT (change) alterar; (neuter) capar, castrar

alteration [ɔ̀ɬtəréʃən] N (change) alteración *f*, cambio *m*; **—s** arreglos *m pl*, reformas *f pl*

altercation [ɔ̀ɬtəkéʃən] N altercado *m*

alternate [ɔ́ɬtə-nɪt] ADJ alternativo, alterno; **— route** ruta alternativa *f*; **— spelling** ortografía alterna *f*; **he visits us on — Mondays** nos visita un lunes sí y otro no; N suplente *mf*; [ɔ́ɬtə-net] VI/VT alternar

alternative [ɔɬtə́-nədɪv] ADJ alternativo; N alternativa *f*

alternator [ɔ́ɬtə́-nedə-] N alternador *m*

although [ɔɬðó] CONJ aunque, si bien

altimeter [æɬtímɪdə-] N altímetro *m*

altitude [ǽɬtɪtjud] N altura *f*, altitud *f*; **— sickness** mal de altura *m*

alto [ǽɬto] N contralto *mf*; ADJ alto

altogether [ɔ̀ɬtəɡéðə-] ADV (completely) completamente; (all included) en total

altruism [ǽɬtruizəm] N altruismo *m*

aluminum [əlúmənəm] N aluminio *m*; **— foil** papel de aluminio *m*

always [ɔ́ɬwez] ADV siempre

a.m. [eém] ADV de la mañana

amalgamate [əmǽɬɡəmet] VI/VT (metals) amalgamar(se); (companies) fusionar(se)

amass [əmǽs] VT acumular, amasar

amateur [ǽmətʃə-] ADJ amateur; N aficionado -da *mf*

amaze [əméz] VT maravillar, asombrar

amazement [əmézmənt] N asombro *m*

amazing [əmézɪŋ] ADJ asombroso, increíble

Amazon [ǽməzan] N (region) Amazonia *f*; (river) Amazonas *m sg*

ambassador [æmbǽsədə-] N embajador -ra *mf*

amber [ǽmbə-] N ámbar *m*; ADJ (quality) ambarino; (material) de ámbar; (color) (de) color ámbar

ambiance [ǽmbiəns] N ambiente *m*

ambidextrous [æmbidékstrəs] ADJ ambidiestro

ambient [ǽmbiənt] ADJ ambiental; **— temperature** temperatura ambiente *f*

ambiguity [æmbɪɡjúdi] N ambigüedad *f*

ambiguous [æmbíɡjuəs] ADJ ambiguo

ambition [æmbíʃən] N ambición *f*, aspiración *f*

ambitious [æmbíʃəs] ADJ ambicioso
ambivalent [æmbívələnt] ADJ ambivalente
amble [æmbəł] VI deambular
ambulance [æmbjələns] N ambulancia f
ambush [æmbuʃ] N emboscada f, celada f; **to lie in —** acechar; VT emboscar
ameliorate [əmílíərət] VI/VT mejorar
amen [ámén] INTERJ amén
amenable [əmínəbəł] ADJ bien dispuesto
amend [əménd] VT enmendar; **to make —s (for)** compensar (por)
amendment [əméndmənt] N enmienda f
amenities [əménídiz] N PL comodidades f pl
America [əmérikə] N América f
American [əmérikən] ADJ & N (continental) americano -na mf; (USA) americano -na mf, norteamericano -na mf, estadounidense mf
amethyst [æməθɪst] N amatista f
amiable [émiəbəł] ADJ amable
amicable [æmɪkəbəł] ADJ amistoso
amid [əmíd] PREP en medio de
amino acid [əmínóæsɪd] N aminoácido m
amiss [əmís] ADV **something is —** algo anda mal
ammonia [əmónjə] N amoníaco m
ammunition [æmjəníʃən] N munición f
amnesia [æmníʒə] N amnesia f
amnesty [æmnɪsti] N amnistía f
amniocentesis [æmniosɪntísɪs] N amniocentesis f
amoeba [əmíbə] N ameba f
among [əmʌ́ŋ] PREP entre
amoral [emɔ́rəł] ADJ amoral
amorous [æmərəs] ADJ (sexually aroused) excitado; (loving) amoroso
amorphous [əmɔ́rfəs] ADJ amorfo
amortize [æmə-taɪz] VT amortizar
amount [əmáunt] N cantidad f; (of money) suma f, importe m; VI ascender (a); **that —s to stealing** eso equivale a robar
ampere [æmpír] N amperio m
amphetamine [æmfédəmin] N anfetamina f
amphibian [æmfíbiən] N anfibio m
amphibious [æmfíbiəs] ADJ anfibio
amphitheater [æmfəθiədə-] N anfiteatro m
ampicillin [æmpɪsílɪn] N ampicilina f
ample [æmpəł] ADJ (in quantity) suficiente; (in size) amplio
amplifier [æmpləfaɪə-] N amplificador m
amplify [æmpləfaɪ] VT (an explanation) ampliar; (a sound) amplificar
amplitude [æmplɪtud] N amplitud f
amputate [æmpjətət] VT amputar
amuck, amok [əmák] ADV **to run —** (kill people) perpetrar un ataque homicida; (go crazy) volverse loco

amulet [æmjəlɪt] N amuleto m
amuse [əmjúz] VT (make laugh) divertir; (help pass time) entretener; **to — oneself** divertirse, entretenerse, recrearse
amusement [əmjúzmənt] N diversión f, entretenimiento m
amusing [əmjúzɪŋ] ADJ (entertaining) divertido; (funny) gracioso, chistoso
an [ən, æn] INDEF ART un m, una f
anachronism [ənǽkrənɪzəm] N anacronismo m
anaerobic [ænəróbɪk] ADJ anaerobio
anal [énəł] ADJ anal
analgesic [ænəłdʒízɪk] N & ADJ analgésico m
analog [ænəłɔg] ADJ análogico
analogical [ænəłádʒɪkəł] ADJ analógico
analogous [ənǽləgəs] ADJ análogo
analogy [ənǽlədʒi] N analogía f
analysis [ənǽlɪsɪs] N análisis m
analytic [ænəlídɪk] ADJ analítico
analytical [ænəlídɪkəł] ADJ analítico
analyze [ænəlaɪz] VT analizar
anarchist [ænə-kɪst] N anarquista m
anarchy [ænə-ki] N anarquía f
anathema [ənǽθəmə] N anatema m
anatomical [ænətámɪkəł] ADJ anatómico
anatomy [ənǽdəmi] N anatomía f
ancestor [ænsestə-] N antepasado -da mf, ascendiente m
ancestral [ænséstrəł] ADJ de los antepasados; **— home** casa solariega f
ancestry [ænsestri] N linaje m, ascendencia f, abolengo m
anchor [æŋkə-] N ancla f; **— man** presentador m; **—woman** presentadora f; **to drop —** anclar, echar anclas; VT (a boat) anclar; (an argument) basar; VI echar anclas, fondear
anchovy [æntʃovi] N anchoa f
ancient [énʃənt] ADJ antiguo; pej vetusto
and [ænd] CONJ y; (before i, hi) e; **— so forth** etcétera, y así sucesivamente; **more — more** cada vez más
Andalusia [ændəlúʒə] N Andalucía f
Andalusian [ændəlúʒən] ADJ & N andaluz -za mf
Andes [ændiz] N Andes m pl
Andorra [ændɔ́rə] N Andorra f
Andorran [ændɔ́rən] ADJ & N andorrano -na mf
androgynous [ændrádʒənəs] ADJ andrógino
anecdote [ænɪkdot] N anécdota f
anemia [ənímiə] N anemia f
anemic [ənímɪk] ADJ anémico
anesthesia [ænɪsθíʒə] N anestesia f
anesthesiology [ænɪsθiziálədʒi] N anestesiología f

anesthetic [ænɪsθέDɪk] ADJ anestésico; N (substance) anestesia *f*

aneurysm [ǽnjərɪzəm] N aneurisma *m*

anew [ənjú] ADV otra vez

angel [éndʒəl] N ángel *m*

angelic [ændʒélɪk] ADJ angélico, angelical

anger [ǽŋgə] N enojo *m*, enfado *m*; VT enojar, enfadar

angina [ændʒáɪnə] N — **pectoris** angina de pecho *f*

angioplasty [ǽndʒiəplæstɪ] N angioplastia *f*

angle [ǽŋgəl] N (geometrical) ángulo *m*; (point of view) punto de vista *m*, perspectiva *f*; VI pescar

Anglo-Saxon [ǽŋglosǽksən] ADJ & N anglosajón -na *mf*

Angola [æŋgólə] N Angola *f*

Angolan [æŋgólən] ADJ angolano -na *mf*, angoleño -ña *mf*

angry [ǽŋgri] ADJ enojado, enfadado

angst [áŋkst] N angustia *f*

anguish [ǽŋgwɪʃ] N angustia *f*, ansia *f*, congoja *f*

angular [ǽŋgjələ] ADJ angular; (face) anguloso

animal [ǽnəməl] ADJ & N animal *m*; — **rights** derechos de los animales *m pl*

animate [ǽnəmɪt] ADJ animado; [ǽnəmet] VT (enliven) animar; (encourage) alentar; —**d cartoon** dibujo animado *m*

animation [ænəméʃən] N animación *f*

animosity [ænəmásɪDɪ] N animosidad *f*, ojeriza *f*, encono *m*

anise [ǽnɪs] N anís *m*

ankle [ǽŋkəl] N tobillo *m*

annals [ǽnlz] N anales *m pl*

annex [ǽnɛks] N anexo *m*; [ənéks] VT anexar

annexation [ænɛkséʃən] N anexión *f*

annihilate [ənáɪəlet] VT aniquilar

anniversary [ænəvə́-səri] N aniversario *m*

annotate [ǽnətet] VT anotar

annotation [ænətéʃən] N (action, result) anotación *f*; (result) nota *f*

announce [ənáɪuns] VT anunciar; (an engagement, birth) participar

announcement [ənáɪunsmənt] N anuncio *m*; (of an engagement, birth) participación *f*

announcer [ənáɪunsə] N anunciador -ra *mf*; (on radio) locutor -ra *mf*

annoy [ənɔ́ɪ] VI/VT fastidiar, contrariar

annoyance [ənɔ́ɪəns] N fastidio *m*, contrariedad *f*

annual [ǽnjuəl] ADJ anual; N (book) anuario *m*; (plant) planta anual *f*

annuity [ənjúɪDɪ] N anualidad *f*, renta anual *f*

annul [ənʌ́l] VT anular

annulment [ənʌ́lmənt] N anulación *f*

anomalous [ənáməlas] ADJ anómalo

anomaly [ənáməli] N anomalía *f*

anonymous [ənánəmas] ADJ anónimo

anorak [ǽnəræk] N anorak *m*

anorexia [ænəréksiə] N anorexia *f*

anorexic [ænəréksɪk] ADJ anoréxico

another [ənʌ́ðə] ADJ otro; — **day** otro día; PRON otro; **I want** — quiero otro; **one** — el uno al otro, los unos a los otros

answer [ǽnsə] N (to a question) respuesta *f*, contestación *f*; (to a problem) solución *f*; VI contestar, responder; **to** — **for** ser responsable de/por; VT contestar

answering [ǽnsə-ɪŋ] ADJ — **machine** contestador automático *m*; — **service** servicio telefónico contratado *m*

ant [ænt] N hormiga *f*; —**eater** oso hormiguero *m*; —**hill** hormiguero *m*

antacid [æntǽsɪd] N & ADJ antiácido *m*

antagonism [æntǽgənɪzəm] N antagonismo *m*

antagonist [æntǽgənɪst] N antagonista *mf*

antagonize [æntǽgənaɪz] VT antagonizar

antarctic [æntárktɪk] ADJ antártico

Antarctica [æntárktɪkə] N Antártida *f*

antecedent [æntəsídɪnt] ADJ & N antecedente *m*

antelope [ǽntəlop] N antílope *m*

antenna [ænténə] N antena *f*

anterior [æntíriə] ADJ anterior

anthem [ǽnθəm] N himno *m*

anthology [ænθálədʒi] N antología *f*

anthracite [ǽnθrəsaɪt] N antracita *f*

anthrax [ǽnθræks] N ántrax *m*

anthropologist [ænθrəpáləʤɪst] N antropólogo -ga *mf*

anthropology [ænθrəpáləʤi] N antropología *f*

anthropomorphize [ænθrəpəmɔ́rfaɪz] VI/VT antropomorfizar

antiabortion [æntiəbɔ́rʃən] ADJ antiaborto *inv*

antiaircraft [æntiérkræft] ADJ antiaéreo

antibacterial [æntibæktíriəl] ADJ antibacteriano

antiballistic [æntibəlístɪk] ADJ antibalístico

antibiotic [æntibaɪáDɪk] N & ADJ antibiótico *m*

antibody [ǽntibaDi] N anticuerpo *m*

anticipate [æntísəpet] VI/VT prever, calcular

anticipation [æntɪsəpéʃən] N previsión *f*; **with great** — con gran expectación

anticlimactic [æntikləmǽktɪk] ADJ decepcionante

antics [ǽntɪks] N payasadas *f pl*, monerías *f pl*, monadas *f pl*

antidepressant [æntidɪprésənt] ADJ & N antidepresivo *m*

antidote [ǽntidot] N antídoto *m*

antifreeze [ǽntifriz] N anticongelante *m*

Antigua and Barbuda [æntígəændbɑrbúdə] N Antigua y Barbuda *f*

Antiguan [æntígən] ADJ & N antiguano -ana *mf*

antihistamine [æntihístəmin] N antihistamínico *m*

anti-inflammatory [æntiɪnflǽmətɔri] ADJ & N antiinflamatorio *m*

antilock [ǽntilak] ADJ antibloqueo

antimony [ǽntəmoni] N antimonio *m*

antioxidant [æntiáksɪdənt] N antioxidante *m*

antipathy [æntípəθi] N antipatía *f*

antiperspirant [æntipɝ́spərənt] N antitranspirante *m*

antiquated [ǽntɪkweɪdɪd] ADJ anticuado; (words) desusado

antique [æntík] ADJ antiguo; N antigüedad *f*

antiquity [æntíkwɪdi] N antigüedad *f*

anti-Semitism [æntisémɪtɪzəm] N antisemitismo *m*

antiseptic [æntiséptɪk] ADJ & N antiséptico *m*

antisocial [æntisóʃəɫ] ADJ antisocial

antithesis [æntíθəsɪs] N antítesis *f*

antitrust [æntitrást] ADJ antimonopolio, antitrust

antler [ǽntlɚ] N asta *f*, cuerno·*m*

antonym [ǽntənɪm] N antónimo *m*

antsy [ǽntsi] ADJ (impatient) impaciente; (anxious) ansioso

anvil [ǽnvəɫ] N yunque *m*

anxiety [æŋzáɪɪDi] N ansiedad *f*, angustia *f*

anxious [ǽŋkʃəs] ADJ (worried) ansioso, preocupado; (desirous) ansioso, deseoso

any [éni] ADJ & PRON cualquier(a), cualesquier(a); — **woman** cualquier mujer, una mujer cualesquiera; — **man** cualquier hombre, un hombre cualquiera; — **houses** unas casas cualesquiera; *lit* cualesquiera casas; **in** — **case** en todo caso; **do you have** — **money?** ¿tienes dinero? **I don't have** — no tengo

anybody [énibaDi] PRON alguien, cualquiera; — **could do that** cualquiera podría hacer eso; **is** — **here?** ¿hay alguien aquí? **he does not know** — no conoce a nadie

anyhow [énihau] ADV de todos modos

anymore [énimɔ́r] ADV **he doesn't work** — ya no trabaja, no trabaja más

anyone [éniwʌn] PRON alguien, cualquiera; — **could do that** cualquiera podría hacer eso; **is** — **here?** ¿hay alguien aquí? **he does not know** — no conoce a nadie

anyplace [éniples] ADV en cualquier parte / lugar; **you can buy it** — se puede comprar en cualquier lugar; **he's not going** — no va a ninguna parte

anything [éniθɪŋ] PRON cualquier cosa, algo; — **is fine** cualquier cosa me viene bien; — **you wish** todo lo que quieras; **do you have** — **for a cough?** ¿tienes algo para la tos? **I don't know** — no sé nada

anytime [énitaɪm] ADV en cualquier momento

anyway [éniwe] ADV de todos modos, de cualquier manera

anywhere [énihwɛr] ADV en cualquier parte / lugar; **you can buy it** — se puede comprar en cualquier lugar; **he's not going** — no va a ninguna parte

aorta [eɔ́rDə] N aorta *f*

apart [əpárt] ADV **they are three miles** — están a tres millas de distancia; **they kept him** — **from the group** lo apartaron del grupo; **each factor viewed** — cada factor visto por separado; **to take** — desarmar, desmontar; **to tear** — despedazar, hacer pedazos; **to tell** — distinguir

apartment [əpártmənt] N apartamento *m*; *Sp* piso *m*

apathetic [æpəθéDɪk] ADJ apático

apathy [ǽpəθi] N apatía *f*, abulia *f*

ape [ep] N simio *m*; VT remedar

aperture [ǽpɚtʃɚ] N abertura *f*; (of a pipe) luz *f*

apex [épɛks] N (of tongue) ápice *m*; (of a mountain) cumbre *f*

aphasia [əféʒə] N afasia *f*

apiece [əpís] ADV cada uno

apnea [ǽpniə] N apnea *f*

apocalypse [əpákəlɪps] N apocalipsis *m*

apogee [ǽpədʒi] N apogeo *m*

apologetic [əpalədʒéDɪk] ADJ lleno de disculpas

apologize [əpáladʒaɪz] VI disculparse

apology [əpáladʒi] N disculpa(s) *f (pl)*; (justification) apología *f*

apostle [əpásəɫ] N apóstol *m*

apostrophe [əpástrəfi] N (punctuation) apóstrofo *m*; (invocation) apóstrofe *m*

appall [əpáɫ] VT horrorizar

appalling [əpáɫɪŋ] ADJ horroroso

apparatus [æpərǽDəs] N (single) aparato *m*; (group) maquinaria *f*

apparel [əpǽrəɫ] N indumentaria *f*, ropa *f*; (fine) ropaje *m*

apparent [əpǽrənt] ADJ (visible) visible; (clear) obvio, evidente; (seeming) aparente

apparition [æpəríʃən] N aparición *f*,

fantasma *m*

appeal [əpíł] N (legal) apelación *f*, recurso *m*; (request) ruego *m*, llamamiento *m*; (attraction) atractivo *m*; VT apelar, recurrir (contra); VI **to — to** atraer

appear [əpír] VI (show up) aparecer(se); (seem) parecer, aparentar; (a publication) salir; (before a judge) comparecer

appearance [əpírəns] N (looks) apariencia *f*, traza *f*, estampa *f*; (act of appearing) aparición *f*

appease [əpíz] VT aplacar, apaciguar

appeasement [əpízmənt] N aplacamiento *m*, apaciguamiento *m*

appellate [əpélɪt] N **— court** tribunal de apelaciones *m*

append [əpénd] VT adjuntar

appendage [əpéndɪʤ] N apéndice *m*

appendectomy [æpɪndéktəmi] N apendicectomía *f*

appendicitis [əpendəsáɪdɪs] N apendicitis *f*

appendix [əpéndɪks] N apéndice *m*

appetite [æpɪtaɪt] N apetito *m*

appetizer [æpɪtaɪzɚ] N aperitivo *m*

appetizing [æpɪtaɪzɪŋ] ADJ apetecible, apetitoso

applaud [əplɔ́d] VI/VT aplaudir

applause [əplɔ́z] N aplauso(s) *m* (*pl*)

apple [æpəł] N manzana *f*; **— grove** manzanar *m*; **— of my eye** niña de mis ojos *f*; **—sauce** compota de manzana *f*; **— tree** manzano *m*; **Adam's —** nuez de Adán *f*

appliance [əpláɪəns] N aparato *m*; (electric) (aparato) electrodoméstico *m*

applicable [æplɪkəbəł] ADJ aplicable

applicant [æplɪkənt] N aspirante *mf*, solicitante *mf*

application [æplɪkéʃən] N (act of applying) aplicación *f*; (form) solicitud *f*, formulario *f*

apply [əpláɪ] VT aplicar; **to — for** solicitar, pedir; **are you —ing for the scholarship?** ¿te presentas para la beca? ¿estás solicitando la beca? **to — oneself** aplicarse, dedicarse

appoint [əpɔ́ɪnt] VT (designate) nombrar, designar; (furnish) amueblar, equipar; **a well —ed house** una casa bien amueblada

appointee [əpɔɪntí] N persona nombrada *f*

appointment [əpɔ́ɪntmənt] N (designation) nombramiento *m*, designación *f*; (engagement) cita *f*; **doctor's —** cita / hora con el médico *f*; **—s** mobiliario *m sg*, accesorios *m pl*

apportion [əpɔ́rʃən] VT repartir

proporcionalmente

apportionment [əpɔ́rʃənmənt] N reparto proporcional *m*

appraisal [əprézəł] N tasación *f*, valuación *f*

appraise [əpréz] VT avaluar, valorar, tasar

appreciable [əpríʃəbəł] ADJ apreciable

appreciate [əpríʃiet] VT (value) apreciar, estimar; (recognize) darse cuenta, percibir; (thank) agradecer; **to — in value** apreciarse

appreciation [əpriʃiéʃən] N (esteem) aprecio *m*; (thanks) agradecimiento *m*; (monetary value) apreciación *f*, alza *f*

apprehend [æprɪhénd] VT (arrest) aprehender; (understand) comprender

apprehension [æprɪhénʃən] N (arrest) aprehensión *f*; (worry) aprensión *f*

apprehensive [æprɪhénsɪv] ADJ aprensivo

apprentice [əpréntɪs] N aprendiz -iza *mf*; VT poner de aprendiz

apprenticeship [əpréntɪʃɪp] N aprendizaje *m*

apprise [əpráɪz] VT informar

approach [əprótʃ] N (act of approaching) aproximación *f*; (method) enfoque *m*, aproximación *f*, acercamiento *m*; (means of access) acceso *m*, entrada *f*; VI acercarse, aproximarse; VT (a problem) abordar, enfocar; **to — someone about a problem** plantearle a alguien un problema

approachable [əprótʃəbəł] ADJ tratable

approbation [æprəbéʃən] N aprobación *f*

appropriate [əpróprɪt] ADJ apropiado, adecuado; [əprópriet] VT apropiarse; (funds) asignar

appropriation [əpropriéʃən] N (act of appropriation) apropiación *f*; (assignment of funds) asignación *f*; (assigned funds) partida *f*

approval [əprúvəł] N aprobación *f*

approve [əprúv] VI/VT aprobar

approximate [əpráksəmɪt] ADJ aproximado; [əpráksəmet] VT aproximarse a

apricot [æprɪkɑt] N albaricoque *m*; *Am* damasco *m*; *Mex* chabacano *m*

April [éprəł] N abril *m*

apron [éprən] N (for a cook) delantal *m*; (for a workman) mandil *m*

apropos [æprəpó] ADV a propósito; ADJ oportuno, pertinente; **— of** a propósito de

apt [æpt] ADJ (prone, able) capaz; (suited) pertinente; **is he — to be at home?** ¿estará en casa?

aptitude [æptɪtud] N aptitud *f*, capacidad *f*

aquamarine [akwəmarín] N aguamarina *f*

aquarium [əkwériəm] N (tank) acuario *m*, pecera *f*; (building) acuario *m*

aquatic [əkwádɪk] ADJ acuático

aqueduct [ǽkwɪdʌkt] N acueducto m

Arab [ǽrəb] ADJ & N árabe mf

Arabic [ǽrəbɪk] ADJ árabe, arábigo; N (language) árabe m

Aragonese [ærəgəníz] ADJ & N aragonés -esa mf

arbiter [árbɪdə-] N árbitro -ra mf

arbitrary [árbɪtreri] ADJ arbitrario

arbitrate [árbɪtret] VI/VT (mediate) arbitrar (en), terciar (en); (submit to mediation) someter al arbitraje

arbitration [arbɪtréʃən] N arbitraje m

arbitrator [árbɪtredə-] N árbitro mf

arbor [árbə-] N pérgola f, glorieta f

arboreal [arbóriəł] ADJ arbóreo

arc [ark] N arco m

arcade [arkéd] N (series of arcs) arcada f; (shops) galería f; (of video games) sala de juegos electrónicos f

arcane [arkén] ADJ arcano

arch [artʃ] N arco m; (curved roof) bóveda f; —way arcada f; VI/VT arquear(se)

archaeology [arkiáləʤi] N arqueología f

archaic [arkéik] ADJ arcaico

archaism [árkeɪzəm] N arcaísmo m

archbishop [artʃbíʃəp] N arzobispo m

archenemy [artʃénəmi] N archienemigo -ga mf

archery [ártʃəri] N tiro al arco m

archetype [árkɪtaɪp] N arquetipo m

archipelago [arkəpélago] N archipiélago m

architect [árkɪtekt] N arquitecto -ta mf; (creator) artífice mf

architectural [arkɪtéktʃə-əł] ADJ arquitectónico

architecture [árkɪtektʃə-] N arquitectura f

archive [árkaɪv] N archivo m

arctic [árktɪk] ADJ ártico

ardent [árdnt] ADJ ardiente

ardor [árdə-] N ardor m, fervor m

arduous [árʤuəs] ADJ arduo

area [ériə] N área f; (region) zona f; (of a geometric figure) superficie f, área f

arena [ərínə] N estadio m; (in circus) pista f

Argentina [arʤəntínə] N Argentina f

Argentinian [arʤəntíniən] ADJ & N argentino -na mf

argon [árgan] N argón m

argue [árgju] VT (reason) argüir, argumentar; VI (bicker) discutir, reñir

argument [árgjəmənt] N (reason) argumento m; (altercation) disputa f, discusión f

arid [ǽrɪd] ADJ árido

arise [əráɪz] VI (get up) levantarse; (appear) surgir; (result) provenir, resultar

aristocracy [ærɪstákrəsi] N aristocracia f

aristocrat [ərístəkræt] N aristócrata mf

aristocratic [ərɪstəkrǽdɪk] ADJ aristocrático

arithmetic [əríθmətɪk] N aritmética f; ADJ aritmético

ark [ark] N arca f; **Noah's** — arca de Noé f

arm [arm] N brazo m; **—chair** sillón m, butaca f; **—pit** sobaco m, axila f; **—rest** (in a car) apoyabrazos m sg; (on a sofa) brazo m; **— in** del brazo; **at —'s length** a distancia; **with open —s** con los brazos abiertos; **—s armas** f pl

armada [armádə] N armada f, flota f

armament [árməmənt] N armamento m

Armenia [armíniə] N Armenia f

Armenian [armíniən] ADJ & N armenio -nia mf

armful [ármfuł] N brazada f

armistice [ármɪstɪs] N armisticio m

armoire [armwár] N armario m

armor [ármə-] N (of a knight) armadura f; (on a vehicle) blindaje m; (on insects) coraza f; VT (a car) blindar; (a tank) acorazar

armored [ármə-d] ADJ (van) blindado; (tank) acorazado

armory [árməri] N armería f

army [ármi] N ejército m; (multitude) muchedumbre f

aroma [ərómə] N aroma m

aromatic [ærəmǽdɪk] ADJ aromático

around [əráund] ADV **there were books all —** había libros por todos lados; **there is a supermarket — here** hay un supermercado por aquí; **it was the only farm for miles —** era la única granja en millas a la redonda; **the tree is forty centimeters —** el árbol tiene cuarenta centímetros de circunferencia; **we drove — the block** dimos vuelta a la manzana; **I'll show you —** te enseño el lugar; **the wheels turned —** las ruedas giraban; **turn —** date la vuelta; **she finally came — al final** la convencimos; **he hasn't been —** no ha estado por aquí; **a town with mountains — it** un pueblo rodeado de montañas; **we walked — town** dimos una vuelta por el pueblo; **five o'clock** a eso de las cinco; PREP **a ribbon — her wrist** una cinta alrededor de su muñeca; **tie a string — your finger** atate un hilo al dedo; **stay — the house** quédate cerca de la casa; **he wandered — the park** deambuló por el parque; **the church — the corner** la iglesia a la vuelta de la esquina; **motion — its axis** movimiento en torno a su eje; **—-the-clock** veinticuatro horas al día

aro–ask

298

arouse [əráuz] VI despertar; VT (suspicion) despertar; (sexual response) excitar
arraign [ərén] VT hacer comparecer ante un juez
arrange [əréndʒ] VT arreglar
arrangement [əréndʒmənt] N arreglo *m*; (of objects) disposición *f*; (agreement) acuerdo *m*; **to make —s (for)** hacer arreglos (para)
array [əré] N (arrangement) abanico *m*, selección *f*; (of troops) orden *m*; (attire) gala *f*; VT (troops) formar; (attire) ataviar
arrears [ərírz] ADV LOC **in —** atrasado
arrest [ərést] N arresto *m*, detención *f*; VI/VT arrestar, detener
arrhythmia [əríðmiə] N arritmia *f*
arrival [əráivəl] N llegada *f*; *lit* arribo *m*; **the new —s** los recién llegados
arrive [əráiv] VI llegar; *lit* arribar
arrogance [ǽrəgəns] N arrogancia *f*
arrogant [ǽrəgənt] ADJ arrogante
arrow [ǽro] N flecha *f*; *lit* saeta *f*; **—head** punta de flecha *f*
arsenal [ársənəl] N arsenal *m*
arsenic [ársənik] N arsénico *m*
arson [ársən] N incendio doloso *m*
art [art] N arte *m* (sg) *f* (pl); (works) obras *f pl*; (skill) destreza *f*; **fine —s** bellas artes *f pl*; **master of —s** maestría en humanidades *f*; **— deco** art déco *m*
arteriosclerosis [artirioskləróSıs] N arteriosclerosis *f*
artery [árdəri] N arteria *f*
artful [ártfəl] ADJ (esthetic) artístico; (deceitful) artero, ladino
arthritis [arθráidıs] N artritis *f*
arthroscopic [arθrəskápik] ADJ artroscópico
artichoke [árditʃok] N alcachofa *f*
article [árdikəl] N artículo *m*; **— of clothing** prenda de vestir *f*
articulate [artíkjəlıt] ADJ (clear) claro; (eloquent) elocuente; **he's very —** se expresa muy bien; [artíkjəlet] VI/VT (pronounce, join) articular; (express) enunciar
articulation [artıkjəléʃən] N articulación *f*
artifact [árdəfækt] N artefacto *m*, ingenio *m*
artifice [árdəfıs] N artificio *m*
artificial [ardəfíʃəl] ADJ artificial; (affected) afectado; **— insemination** inseminación artificial *f*; **— intelligence** inteligencia artificial *f*
artillery [artíləri] N artillería *f*
artisan [árdızən] N artesano -na *mf*, artífice *mf*
artist [árdıst] N artista *mf*; (performer) intérprete *mf*

artistic [artístık] ADJ artístico
Aruba [ərúbə] N Aruba *f*
as [æz] CONJ **— for me** en lo que a mí respecta; **— if** como si; **— it were** por decirlo así; **— large** tan grande como; **— long — you wish** todo el tiempo que quieras; **— much** tanto como; **— of a** partir de; **— per** según; **— well** también; **— the illness worsened** a medida que empeoraba la enfermedad; **— yet** hasta ahora, todavía; **the same —** lo mismo que; **it broke — I was using it** se rompió cuando lo usaba; **she knitted — we talked** tejía mientras conversábamos; **he played — never before** jugó como nunca; PREP **— a child, I always felt loved** de niño, siempre me sentí querido; **— a teacher, I must be tough** como maestro, tengo que ser estricto; ADV tan, tanto; **it's not — important** no es tan importante
asbestos [æzbéstəs] N asbesto *m*, amianto *m*
ascend [əsénd] VI ascender
ascent [əsént] N ascenso *m*
ascertain [æsə-tén] VT averiguar, establecer
ascetic [əsédık] ADJ ascético; N asceta *mf*
ascorbic [əskɔ́rbık] ADJ ascórbico
ascribe [əskráıb] VT atribuir, imputar
asexual [əsékʃuəł] ADJ asexual
ash [æʃ] N (residue, remains) ceniza *f*; (species of tree) fresno *m*; **—tray** cenicero *m*; **— Wednesday** miércoles de ceniza *m*
ashamed [əʃémd] ADJ avergonzado; **to be —** tener vergüenza, avergonzarse
ashen [ǽʃən] ADJ ceniciento
ashore [əʃɔ́r] ADV (movement) a tierra; (location) en tierra; **to go —** desembarcar
Asia [éʒə] N Asia *f*
Asian [éʒən] ADJ & N asiático -ca *mf*
aside [əsáıd] ADV **all kidding —** bromas aparte; **his father took him —** su padre lo llamó aparte; **he threw his coat —** tiró su saco a un lado; PREP **— from** aparte de, además; N (theater) aparte *m*
asinine [ǽsənaın] ADJ necio
ask [æsk] VT (inquire) preguntar; (request) pedir; **to — a question** hacer una pregunta; **to — about** preguntar por; **to — for** pedir; **to — for someone** pedir para hablar con alguien; **to — out** invitar a salir; **what's your —ing price?** ¿cuánto pides? **you —ed for it** te lo has buscado
askance [əskǽns] ADV **to look —** (obliquely) mirar de soslayo/través/reojo; (suspiciously) mirar con recelo
askew [əskjú] ADJ ladeado

asleep [əslíp] ADJ dormido; **to fall —** dormirse; **my arm is —** se me ha dormido / entumecido el brazo

asparagus [əspǽrəgəs] N espárrago *m*

aspect [ǽspekt] N aspecto *m*

aspen [ǽspən] N álamo temblón *m*

asphalt [ǽsfɔlt] N asfalto *m*

aspiration [æspəréʃən] N aspiración *f*

aspire [əspáɪr] VI aspirar

aspirin [ǽsprɪn] N aspirina *f*

ass [æs] N (animal) asno *m*, burro *m*, borrico *m*

assail [əséɫ] VT (physically) asaltar, atacar; (verbally) atacar

assailant [əsélənt] N atacante *mf*, agresor -ra *mf*

assassin [əsǽsɪn] N asesino -na *mf*

assassinate [əsǽsənet] VT asesinar

assassination [əsæsənéʃən] N asesinato *m*

assault [əsɔ́ɫt] N asalto *m*, agresión *f*; **— rifle** rifle de asalto *m*; **— and battery** agresión con lesiones *f*; VT asaltar, agredir; (sexually) violar

assay [əsé] VT (situation) examinar, analizar; (metal) ensayar; [ǽse] N ensayo *m*

assemble [əsémbəɫ] VI/VT (call together) reunir(se), congregar(se); VT (put together) armar, montar

assembly [əsémbli] N (meeting) asamblea *f*, reunión *f*; (putting together) montaje *m*, armado *m*; **— language** lenguaje ensamblador *m*; **— line** cadena de producción *f*, línea de montaje *f*

assent [əsént] N asentimiento *m*; VI asentir

assert [əsɚt] VT (declare) aseverar; **to — one's rights** hacer valer los derechos de uno; **to — oneself** obrar con firmeza

assertion [əsɚʃən] N (declaration) aseveración *f*, afirmación *f*, aserto *m*; **an — of ownership** una afirmación de los derechos de propiedad

assess [əsés] VT (evaluate for tax purposes) tasar; (impose tax) gravar, imponer

assessment [əsésmənt] N (estimate) avalúo *m*, tasación *f*; (tax) imposición *f*, gravamen *m*; (testing) evaluación *f*

asset [ǽset] N (useful thing) ventaja *f*; (useful quality) virtud *f*; **—s** activo *m*, bienes *m pl*; (on balance sheet) haber *m*, activo *m*; **personal —s** bienes muebles *m pl*; **real —s** bienes inmuebles *m pl*

assiduous [əsíʤuəs] ADJ (constant) asiduo; (industrious) diligente

assign [əsáɪn] VT (give out) asignar; (appoint, designate) designar; (transfer property) ceder

assignment [əsáɪnmənt] N (act of assigning) asignación *f*; (task) encargo *m*; (mission) misión *f*; (transfer of property) cesión (de bienes) *f*; (homework) tarea *f*; (lesson) lección *f*

assimilate [əsíməlet] VI/VT asimilar(se)

assist [əsíst] VI/VT ayudar, asistir

assistance [əsístəns] N ayuda *f*, asistencia *f*

assistant [əsístənt] N ayudante *mf*, asistente *mf*; ADJ auxiliar

assistantship [əsístəntʃɪp] N ayudantía *f*

associate [əsóʃit] ADJ asociado; N (acquaintance) compañero -ra *mf*; (co-worker) colega *mf*; (employee) empleado -da *mf*; [əsóʃiet] VI/VT asociar(se)

association [əsosiéʃən] N asociación *f*

assonance [ǽsənəns] N asonancia *f*

assorted [əsɔ́rdɪd] ADJ variado, surtido

assortment [əsɔ́rtmənt] N (act of assorting) clasificación *f*; (of wares) surtido *m*; (of tools, etc.) colección *f*

assume [əsúm] VT (responsibility, role) asumir; (right) arrogarse; (suppose) dar por sentado, suponer

assumption [əsʌ́mpʃən] N (premise) suposición *f*; (unstated belief) sobreentendido *m*; (seizure) toma *f*

assurance [əʃúrəns] N (promise) promesa *f*, palabra *f*; (reassurance) palabras de apoyo *f pl*; (certainty) certeza *f*; (confidence) confianza *f*

assure [əʃúr] VT asegurar; (encourage) infundir confianza

assuredly [əʃúrɪdli] ADV seguramente, sin duda

asterisk [ǽstərɪsk] N asterisco *m*

asteroid [ǽstərɔɪd] N asteroide *m*

asthma [ǽzmə] N asma *f*

asthmatic [æzmǽdɪk] ADJ asmático

astigmatism [əstígmətɪzəm] N astigmatismo *m*

astonish [əstánɪʃ] VT asombrar, pasmar

astonishing [əstánɪʃɪŋ] ADJ asombroso, pasmoso

astonishment [əstánɪʃmənt] M asombro *m*, pasmo *m*

astound [əstáʊnd] VT pasmar, asombrar

astraddle [əstrǽdl̩] ADV a horcajadas

astray [əstré] ADV **to go —** perderse, extraviarse; **to lead —** (seduce) llevar por mal camino, seducir; (perplex) confundir

astride [əstráɪd] ADV a horcajadas

astringent [əstrínʤənt] ADJ & N astringente *m*

astrology [əstráləʤi] N astrología *f*

astronaut [ǽstrənɔt] M astronauta *mf*

astronautics [æstrənɔ́dɪks] N astronáutica *f*

astronomer [əstrúnəmɚ] N astrónomo

-ma *mf*

astronomy [əstránəmı] N astronomía *f*

astrophysics [æstrofízıks] N astrofísica *f*

Asturian [æstúriən] ADJ & N asturiano -na *mf*

Asturias [æstúriəs] N Asturias *f sg*

astute [əstút] ADJ astuto, sagaz

asylum [əsáıləm] N asilo *m*

asymmetric [esımétrık] ADJ asimétrico

at [æt] PREP — **the end of the story** al final de la historia; — **five o'clock** a las cinco; — **high altitude** a grandes alturas; — **the table** a / en la mesa; — **five dollars a kilo** a cinco dólares el kilo; — **Easter** en Pascua; — **home** en casa; — **war** en guerra; **wait** — **the door** espera en la puerta; **he is** — **peace with himself** está en paz consigo mismo; **the children are** — **play** los niños están jugando; **look** — **that** mira eso; **amazed** — pasmado por; **he laughed** — **me** se rió de mí; — **last** por fin, al fin

atheism [éθiızəm] N ateísmo *m*

atheist [éθiıst] N ateo -a *mf*

athlete [æθlit] N deportista *mf*; (track and field) atleta *mf*; —'**s foot** pie de atleta *m*

athletic [æθlédık] ADJ deportivo; (concerning track and field; well-built) atlético

athletics [æθlédıks] N deporte *m*; (track and field) atletismo *m*

Atlantic [ætlǽntık] ADJ atlántico; N — **Ocean** Océano Atlántico *m*

atlas [ǽtləs] N atlas *m*

atmosphere [ǽtməsfır] N (air) atmósfera *f*; (mood) ambiente *m*

atmospheric [ætməsfírık] ADJ atmosférico

atom [ǽDəm] N átomo *m*; — **bomb** bomba atómica *f*

atomic [ətámık] ADJ atómico; — **age** era atómica *f*; — **energy** energía atómica *f*; — **number** número atómico *m*; — **weight** peso atómico *m*

atomize [ǽDəmaız] VT atomizar

atone [ətón] VI **to** — **for** expiar, purgar

atonement [ətónmənt] N expiación *f*, purgación *f*

atrium [étriəm] N (of office building, hotel) vestíbulo *m*, patio central *m*; (of church) atrio *m*

atrocious [ətróʃəs] ADJ atroz

atrocity [ətrásıdi] N atrocidad *f*, barbaridad *f*

atrophy [ǽtrəfi] N atrofia *f*; VI/VT atrofiar(se)

attach [ətǽtʃ] VI/VT (pipe, cable) unir(se), juntar; (paper) sujetar; (wages) retener; (significance) atribuir; **to be** —**ed to someone** estar apegado a alguien

attaché [ætəʃé] N agregado -da *mf*

attachment [ətǽtʃmənt] N (act of attaching)

unión *f*; (pipe, cable) conexión *f*; (affection) apego *m*, cariño *m*; (of wages) retención *f*; (significance) atribución *f*; (accessory) accesorio *m*

attack [ətǽk] N ataque *m*, acometida *f*; VI/VT atacar, acometer

attain [ətén] VT alcanzar; VI llegar a

attainment [əténmənt] N (act) alcance *m*; (accomplishment) logro *m*, consecución *f*

attempt [ətémpt] N tentativa *f*, intento *m*; (murder) atentado *m*; VT tratar (de), intentar

attend [əténd] VT (meeting) asistir a, acudir a; VI **to** — **to** (a sick person) atender, cuidar; (a speaker) prestar atención

attendance [əténdəns] N asistencia *f*

attendant [əténdənt] N (at a gas station) encargado -da *mf*; (servant) sirviente -ta *mf*; ADJ concomitante

attention [əténʃən] N atención *f*; (courtesy) atenciones *f pl*; **to pay** — prestar atención; **to pay** — **to** atender a; **to call** — llamar la atención; INTERJ —! ¡firmes!

attentive [əténtıv] ADJ (focused) atento; (courteous) cortés

attenuate [əténjuet] VT atenuar

attest [ətést] VT (bear witness to) atestiguar; (manifest) demostrar; VI certificar, dar fe, atestar

attic [ǽdık] N desván *m*, altillo *m*

attire [ətáır] N atavío *m*, vestidura *f*; VT ataviar

attitude [ǽdıtud] N (mental) actitud *f*; (physical) postura *f*; (insolence) insolencia *f*, descaro *m*

attorney [ətɚ́ni] N abogado -da *mf*; — **General** Ministro -tra de Justicia *mf*

attract [ətrǽkt] VT atraer; **to** — **attention** llamar la atención

attraction [ətrǽkʃən] N (act, power) atracción *f*; (charm) atractivo *m*

attractive [ətrǽktıv] ADJ atractivo; (beautiful) atractivo, agraciado

attractiveness [ətrǽktıvnıs] N atractivo *m*

attribute [ǽtrəbjut] N atributo *m*; [ətríbjut] VT atribuir

attribution [ætrəbjúʃən] N atribución *f*

attrition [ətríʃən] N (wearing out) desgaste *m*; (casualties) bajas *f pl*; **war of** — guerra de agotamiento *f*

auburn [ɔ́bɚn] N & ADJ castaño rojizo *m*

auction [ɔ́kʃən] N subasta *f*, remate *m*; VI/VT subastar, rematar

auctioneer [ɔkʃənír] N subastador -ra *mf*, rematador -ra *mf*

audacious [ɔdéʃəs] ADJ audaz, atrevido

audacity [ɔdǽsıdi] N desfachatez *f*,

atrevimiento *m*

audible [ɔ́dəbəɬ] ADJ audible

audience [ɔ́diəns] N público *m*, auditorio *m*; (TV, radio) audiencia *f*

audio [ɔ́dio] ADJ de audio; **— book** audiolibro *m*; **— frequency** audiofrecuencia *f*; **—visual** audiovisual; **—visuals** audiovisuales *m pl*; N audio *m*

audiology [ɔdiálədʒi] N audiología *f*

audit [ɔ́dɪt] VI/VT (class) asistir de oyente; (accounts) auditar; N auditoría *f*

audition [ɔdíʃən] N audición *f*

auditor [ɔ́dɪdə·] N (of accounts) auditor -ra *mf*, censor -ora *mf*; (of a class) oyente *mf*

auditorium [ɔdɪtɔ́riəm] N auditorio *m*, paraninfo *m*

auditory [ɔ́dɪtɔri] ADJ auditivo

augment [ɔgmɛ́nt] VT incrementar, aumentar

August [ɔ́gəst] N agosto *m*

aunt [ænt] N tía *f*

aura [ɔ́rə] N aura *f*

aurora [ərɔ́rə] N aurora *f*; **— borealis** aurora boreal *f*

auspices [ɔ́spɪsɪz] N auspicios *m pl*

auspicious [ɔspíʃəs] ADJ propicio

austere [ɔstír] ADJ austero

austerity [ɔstɛ́rɪdi] N austeridad *f*

Australia [ɔstréljə] N Australia *f*

Australian [ɔstréljən] ADJ & N australiano -na *mf*

Austria [ɔ́striə] N Austria *f*

Austrian [ɔ́striən] ADJ & N austríaco -ca *mf*

authentic [ɔθɛ́ntɪk] ADJ auténtico

authenticate [ɔθɛ́ntɪket] VT autenticar

author [ɔ́θə·] N (professional) escritor -ra *mf*; (creator) autor -ra *mf*

authoritarian [əθɔrɪtɛ́riən] ADJ autoritario

authoritative [əθɔ́rɪtedɪv] ADJ (official) autorizado; (dictatorial) autoritario

authority [əθɔ́rɪdi] N autoridad *f*; (permission) autorización *f*; **to have on good —** saber de buena fuente; **it's not within your —** no está dentro de tus facultades

authorization [ɔθə·ɪzéʃən] N autorización *f*

authorize [ɔ́θəraɪz] VT autorizar, habilitar

autism [ɔ́tɪzəm] N autismo *m*

autobiography [ɔdobaiágrəfi] N autobiografía *f*

autocrat [ɔ́dəkræt] N autócrata *mf*

autograph [ɔ́dəgræf] N autógrafo *m*

autoimmune [ɔdoɪmjún] ADJ autoinmune

automated [ɔ́dəmeɪdd] ADJ automatizado

automatic [ɔdəmǽdɪk] ADJ automático; (response) maquinal; **— pilot** piloto automático *m*; **— transmission** transmisión automática *f*

automation [ɔdəméʃən] N automatización *f*

automobile [ɔ́dəməbiɬ] N automóvil *m*

automotive [ɔdəmódɪv] ADJ (sport) automovilístico; (industry) automotor -ra, automotriz

autonomy [ɔtánəmi] N autonomía *f*

autopilot [ɔ́dopaɪlət] N piloto automático *m*

autopsy [ɔ́tapsi] N autopsia *f*

autumn [ɔ́dəm] N otoño *m*

autumnal [ɔtámnəɬ] ADJ otoñal

auxiliary [ɔgzíləri] ADJ & N auxiliar *mf*

avail [əvéɬ] VI/VT servir; **to — oneself of** aprovechar; N **of no —** de ninguna utilidad; **to no —** en vano

available [əvélabəɬ] ADJ disponible, asequible

avalanche [ǽvəlæntʃ] N avalancha *f*, alud *m*

avarice [ǽvərɪs] N avaricia *f*

avaricious [ævəríʃəs] ADJ avaro, avariento

avenge [əvɛ́ndʒ] VT vengar

avenger [əvɛ́ndʒə·] N vengador -ra *mf*

avenue [ǽvənu] N avenida *f*; (means of access) vía *f*

aver [əvə́·] VT afirmar

average [ǽvrɪdʒ] N promedio *m*; **on —** de promedio; ADJ medio, mediano; **just —** (person) del montón; (thing) nada del otro mundo; VT promediar; **he —s 20 miles an hour** hace un promedio de 20 millas por hora

averse [əvə́·s] ADJ reacio; **he's not — to a glass of wine** no se opone a una copa de vino

aversion [əvə́·ʒən] N aversión *f*

avert [əvə́·t] VT (eyes) desviar; (danger) evitar

aviation [eviéʃən] N aviación *f*

aviator [éviedə·] N aviador -ra *mf*

avid [ǽvid] ADJ ávido

avocado [ævəkádo] N aguacate *m*; RP palta *f*

avocation [ævəkéʃən] N pasatiempo *m*

avoid [əvɔ́id] VI/VT (stay away from) evitar; (dodge) esquivar

avow [əváu] VT confesar

avowal [əváuəɬ] N confesión *f*

avuncular [əvʌ́ŋkjələ·] ADJ propio de un tío; **— attitude** actitud paternal y amistosa

await [əwét] VT aguardar

awake [əwék] ADJ despierto; VI/VT despertar(se)

awaken [əwékən] VI/VT despertar(se)

award [əwɔ́rd] N premio *m*, galardón *m*; (judicial) adjudicación *f*; VT otorgar

aware [əwér] ADJ consciente, enterado; **I'm — of that** eso me consta

away [əwé] ADV **far —** lejos; **— from his family** lejos de su familia; **she looked —** apartó la vista; **she's —** no está; **he's been painting — all day** se ha pasado todo el día pintando; **right** — ahora mismo, ahorita; **ten miles** — a diez millas de distancia; **to give** — regalar; **to go** — irse; **to take** — quitar; **to blow** — (hacer) volar

awe [ɔ] N sobrecogimiento *m*; **to be in** — sobrecogerse; VT sobrecoger

awesome [ɔ́sǝm] ˈADJ (awe-inspiring) sobrecogedor; (impressive) fabuloso

awestruck [ɔ́strʌk] ADJ pasmado

awful [ɔ́fǝł] ADJ terrible, horroroso; ADV espantoso; **it's — hot here** hace un calor horrible

awhile [ǝhwáɪł] ADV un rato

awkward [ɔ́kwǝd] ADJ (clumsy) torpe, desmañado; (embarrassing) embarazoso; (unwieldy) incómodo

awl [ɔł] N punzón *m*

awning [ɔ́nɪŋ] N toldo *m*

awry [ǝráɪ] ADJ (clothes) mal puesto; (hat) ladeado; **my plans went** — mis planes fracasaron rotundamente

ax, axe [æks] N hacha *f*; VT eliminar

axis [ǽksɪs] N eje *m*

axle [ǽksǝł] N eje *m*

Azerbaijan [æzɚbaɪdʒán] N Azerbaiyán *m*

Azerbaijani, Azerbaijanian [æzɚbaɪdʒúni(ǝn)] ADJ & N azerbaijano -na *mf*, azerbaiyano -na *mf*

azure [ǽʒɚ] ADJ (azul) celeste; N azul celeste *m*

Bb

babble [bǽbǝł] N (baby talk) balbuceo *m*; (chatter) parloteo *m*; (murmur) murmullo *m*; VI (to talk like a baby) balbucear; (to chatter) parlotear; (to murmur) murmurar

baboon [bæbún] N babuino *m*

baby [bébi] N bebé *mf*; **who's the — in your family?** ¿quién es el menor/ benjamín en tu familia? — **blue** celeste *m*; — **boomer** persona nacida entre 1946 y 1965 *f*; — **carriage** cochecito de bebé *m*; — **food** comida para bebés *f*; — **girl** nena *f*; — **sister** hermanita *f*; — **sitter** niñera *f*; — **talk** habla infantil *f*; — **tooth** diente de leche *m*; **to —sit** cuidar niños; **she had a** — dio a luz; VT mimar

baccalaureate [bækǝlɔ́riǝt] N bachillerato *m*

bachelor [bǽtʃǝlɚ] N soltero *m*; —**'s degree** licenciatura *f*; — **of Arts** (degree) licenciatura en filosofía y letras *f*; (person)

licenciado -da en filosofía y letras *mf*

bacillus [bǝsíłǝs] N bacilo *m*

back [bæk] N (human body part) espalda *f*; (animal body part) lomo *m*; (opposite side) dorso *m*; (of chair) respaldo *m*, espaldar *m*; —**ache** dolor de espalda *m*; —**bone** columna vertebral *f*, espinazo *m*; —**pack** mochila *f*; **behind one's** — a espaldas de uno; **he has no —bone** no tiene carácter; **in — of** detrás de, tras; **in the — of the house** atrás de la casa; **to fall on one's** — caer de espaldas; **to turn one's** — volver las espaldas; ADJ — **door** puerta trasera *f*; — **issues** números atrasados *m pl*; **on the — burner** en suspenso; VT respaldar, apoyar; VI dar marcha atrás; **to — down** echarse (para) atrás, recular, cejar; ADV (look) atrás/ para atrás; (fall) de espaldas; — **and forth** de aquí para allá; —**-and-forth movement** movimiento de vaivén *m*; **he ran** — to **the house** volvió corriendo a la casa; **he's — from work** está de vuelta del trabajo

backbite [bǽkbaɪt] VI/VT difamar

backer [bǽkɚ] N (financial) fiador -ra *mf*; (political) partidario -ria *mf*

backfire [bǽkfaɪr] VI (automobile) petardear, hacer detonaciones; (plan) ser contraproducente; N petardeo *m*

backgammon [bǽkgæmǝn] N backgammon *m*

background [bǽkgraʊnd] N (of a picture) fondo *m*; (experience) antecedentes *m pl*; **I have a — in computers** tengo conocimientos de informática; **I know what goes on in the** — sé lo que pasa entre bastidores; **a humble** — orígenes humildes *m pl*

backhand [bǽkhænd] N revés *m*

backing [bǽkɪŋ] N respaldo *m*, apoyo *m*; (fabric) refuerzo *m*

backlash [bǽklæʃ] N reacción violenta *f*

backlog [bǽklɑg] N atraso *m*

backseat [bǽksit] N asiento trasero *m*

backslide [bǽkslaɪd] VI volver a las andadas, reincidir

backspace [bǽkspes] N retroceso *m*; VI retroceder

backstage [bækstédʒ] ADV entre bastidores

backtrack [bǽktræk] VI retroceder, dar marcha atrás

backup [bǽkʌp] N (support) respaldo *m*; (software) copia de seguridad *f*

backward [bǽkwǝd] ADV hacia atrás, para atrás; **to go** — recular; ADJ (underdeveloped) atrasado; (reactionary) retrógrado

backwardness [bǽkwə-dnɪs] N
(underdevelopment) atraso *m*;
(conservatism) retrogradismo *m*; (timidity)
timidez *f*

backyard [bǽkjárd] N patio trasero *m*

bacon [békən] N tocino *m*, *Sp* beicon *m*

bacteria [bæktíriə] N bacteria(s) *f* (*pl*)

bacteriology [bæktiríáləʤi] N bacteriología *f*

bad [bæd] ADJ malo; (man) perverso; (teeth)
feo; (drug) dañoso; (flood) grave; (fruit)
podrido; — **blood** enemistad *f*; **to go
from** — **to worse** ir de mal en peor; **he
has a** — **heart** está enfermo del corazón;
to —**mouth** difamar (a); **to look** —
tener mal aspecto; *fam* quedar mal; ADV
mal; **not** — no está nada mal; **too** — ¡qué
pena!

badge [bæʤ] N insignia *f*, chapa *f*

badger [bǽʤɚ] N tejón *m*; VT acosar

baffle [bǽfəɫ] VT (confuse) confundir;
(frustrate) desconcertar; N deflector *m*

bag [bæg] N bolsa *f*, bolso *m*; (baggage)
maleta *f*; — **lady** vagabunda *f*; —**pipe**
gaita *f*; VT empacar, embolsar; (hunting)
cazar

baggage [bǽgɪʤ] N (suitcases) equipaje *m*;
(impediments) bagaje *m*; — **car** vagón de
equipajes *m*; — **check** contraseña de
equipajes *f*; — **tag** etiqueta *f*; —
inspection revisión de equipaje *f*

baggy [bǽgi] ADJ flojo, holgado

Bahamas [bəháməz] N Bahamas *f pl*

Bahamian [bəhémiən] ADJ & N bahameño
-ña *mf*

Bahrain [barén] N Bahréin *m*

Bahraini [baréni] ADJ & N bahreiní *mf*

bail [beɫ] N fianza *f*; **to let out on** — poner
en libertad bajo fianza; VT pagar la fianza;
to — **someone out** pagarle la fianza a
alguien; **to** — **someone out of a
predicament** sacar a alguien de un
apuro; **to** — **out water** achicar, vaciar; VI
to — **out** (of a plane) tirarse con
paracaídas de un avión; (of a situation)
abandonar

bailiff [béɫɪf] N ujier *m*

bait [bet] N cebo *m*; VT (prepare hook) cebar;
(attract customers) seducir; (harass) acosar

bake [bek] VI/VT hornear; (sun) calcinar,
abrasar; **I'm baking in this heat** me
estoy asando, me muero de calor

baker [békɚ] N panadero -ra *mf*; — **'s dozen**
la docena del fraile *f*

bakery [békəri] N panadería *f*

baking [békɪŋ] N (act of baking) horneado
m; (activity) repostería *f*; — **powder**

polvo de hornear *m*; — **soda** bicarbonato
de sodio *m*

balance [bǽləns] N (instrument) balanza *f*;
(equilibrium) equilibrio *m*; (debit, credit)
saldo *m*, balance *m*; — **of payments**
balanza de pagos *f*; — **of trade** balanza
comercial *f*; — **sheet** balance *m*; **to lose
one's** — perder el equilibrio; VT equilibrar,
hacer equilibrio con; **to** — **the risks
with the benefits** sopesar los riesgos y
los beneficios; VI cuadrar

balcony [bǽɫkəni] N balcón *m*; (in a theater)
palco *m*, entresuelo *m*

bald [bɔɫd] ADJ (person) calvo, pelón;
(mountain) pelón; (tire) liso; — **eagle**
águila americana de cabeza blanca *f*;
—**headed** calvo; — **spot** calva *f*; **he
went** — se quedó calvo

bale [beɫ] N paca *f*, fardo *m*; VT empacar,
enfardar

balk [bɔk] VI oponerse, rehusarse a

ball [bɔɫ] N (tennis, baseball, golf) pelota *f*;
(basketball, football, soccer) balón *m*; (of
string, thread) ovillo *m*; (cannon) bala de
cañón) *f*; (dance) baile *m*; — **and chain**
grillete *m*; — **bearing** cojinete de bolas
m; — **game** juego de pelota *m*; (baseball)
partido de béisbol *m*; VT (string) ovillar

ballad [bǽləd] N balada *f*; (historical)
romance *m*

ballast [bǽləst] N lastre *m*; (railroad) balasto
m; VT lastrar

ballerina [bælərínə] N bailarina de ballet *f*

ballet [bælé] N ballet *m*

ballistic [balístɪk] ADJ balístico; — **missile**
misil balístico *m*; N —**s** balística *f*

balloon [bəlún] N globo *m*; VI (travel in a
balloon) pasear en globo; VI/VT (grow)
inflar(se)

ballot [bǽlət] N (system of voting) votación *f*;
(paper) papeleta *f*; *Mex* boleta *f*; — **box**
urna *f*

balm [bɑm] N bálsamo *m*

balmy [bámi] ADJ templado

baloney [bəlóni] N pamplinas *f pl*,
paparruchas *f pl*

balsa [bóɫsə] N (wood) madera balsa *f*; (raft)
balsa *f*

balsam [bóɫsəm] N (resin) bálsamo *m*; (tree)
especie de abeto *m*

bamboo [bæmbú] N bambú *m*

ban [bæn] N prohibición *f*; (church)
excomunión *f*; VT prohibir

banal [bénəɫ] ADJ banal

banana [bənǽnə] N plátano *m*, banana *f*; —
grove platanar *m*; — **split** banana split
m; — **tree** plátano *m*, banano *m*

band [bænd] N (group) banda f, pandilla f;
(musicians) banda f, conjunto m; (cloth)
banda f; (ribbon) cinta f; (leather) tira f;
to join the —wagon subirse al carro/
tren; **—width** amplitud de banda f; VI/VT
to — together unirse, juntarse

bandage [bǽndɪdʒ] N venda f, vendaje m; VT
vendar

bandit [bǽndɪt] N bandido -da mf, bandolero
-ra mf, salteador -ora mf

bang [bæŋ] N (blow) golpe m, golpazo m;
(sound) estampido m, estallido m; **—s**
fleco m, flequillo m; **I get a — out of
seeing my grandkids** me emociona ver
a mis nietos; VI/VT (hit) golpear; (make
noise) hacer estrépito

Bangladesh [bæŋglədɛ́ʃ] N Bangladesh m

Bangladeshi [bæŋglədɛ́ʃi] ADJ & N
bangladeshí mf

banish [bǽnɪʃ] VT desterrar

banishment [bǽnɪʃmənt] N destierro m,
proscripción f

banister [bǽnɪstɚ] N barandal m,
pasamano(s) m, balaustrada f

banjo [bǽndʒo] N banjo m

bank [bæŋk] N (financial institution) banco
m; (in gambling) banca f; (of a body of
water) orilla f, ribera f, margen m; (slope)
escarpa f; **— statement** estado de cuenta
m; **— vault** cámara f; ADJ bancario, de
banco; VT (money) depositar en un banco;
VI (snow, sand) amontonar; (airplane)
ladear; **to — on** contar con; **to —roll**
financiar

banker [bǽŋkɚ] N (bank owner) banquero
-ra mf; (bank employee) bancario -ria mf

banking [bǽŋkɪŋ] N (activity) actividad
bancaria f; (industry) banca f; ADJ
bancario, de banco

banknote [bǽŋknot] N billete m

bankrupt [bǽŋkrʌpt] ADJ en bancarrota; VT
arruinar, quebrar

bankruptcy [bǽŋkrʌptsi] N bancarrota f,
quiebra f; **to go into —** declararse en
quiebra

banner [bǽnɚ] N estandarte m, pendón m;
ADJ sobresaliente

banquet [bǽŋkwɪt] N banquete m, gala f

baptism [bǽptɪzəm] N (sacrament) bautismo
m; (action) bautizo m

baptize [bǽptaɪz] VT bautizar

bar [bɑr] N (of iron, sand, of a tavern) barra f;
(of chocolate) barra f, tableta f; (vertical
rod) barrote m; (obstacle) barrera f,
obstáculo m; (in music) compás m;
(saloon) bar m; **—bell** barra para pesas f;
—code código de barras m; **— graph**

gráfica de barras f; **—keeper** tabernero -ra
mf, cantinero -ra mf; **—room** bar m;
—room brawl pelea de borrachos f;
—tender tabernero -ra mf, cantinero -ra
mf; **behind —s** tras las rejas; **to be
admitted to the —** recibirse de abogado;
VT (door, exit) atrancar; (access) impedir;
(from a group) excluir; **— none** sin
excepción; **—ring a disaster** salvo en
caso de desastre

barb [bɑrb] N púa f; **—ed wire** alambre de
púas m; Sp alambre de espino m

Barbadian [bɑrbéɪdiən] ADJ & N barbadense
mf

Barbados [bɑrbéɪdos] N Barbados m

barbarian [bɑrbériən] ADJ & N bárbaro -ra mf

barbaric [bɑrbérɪk] ADJ bárbaro

barbarous [bɑrbɚəs] ADJ bárbaro

barbecue [bɑ́rbɪkju] N (meat dish) barbacoa
f, asado m, parrillada f; **— sauce** adobo de
barbacoa m; VI/VT asar con adobo

barber [bɑ́rbɚ] N peluquero m, barbero m;
—shop peluquería f, barbería f

barbiturate [bɑrbítʃɚɪt] N barbitúrico m

bard [bɑrd] N bardo m

bare [bɛr] ADJ (legs, walls) desnudo; (cabinet)
vacío; **—back** a pelo; **—faced** descarado;
—foot descalzo; **the — necessities** lo
imprescindible; **—headed** con la cabeza
descubierta; **—legged** con las piernas
desnudas; **— majority** escasa mayoría f;
to lay — poner al descubierto; **with his
— hands** con las propias manos

barely [bérli] ADV apenas

bargain [bɑ́rgɪn] N (agreement) trato m;
(inexpensive purchase) ganga f, ocasión f;
— basement sección de ofertas f; **into
the —** por añadidura; **to strike a —**
cerrar un trato; VI (haggle) regatear;
(expect) contar con

barge [bɑrdʒ] N barcaza f; VI **to — in**
interrumpir; **to — into** irrumpir en

baritone [bérɪton] N & ADJ barítono m

barium [bériəm] N bario m

bark [bɑrk] N (of a dog) ladrido m; (on a
tree) corteza f; VI/VT ladrar; **to — out an
order** gritar una orden

barley [bɑ́rli] N cebada f

barn [bɑrn] N (for animals) establo m; (for
grain) granero m; **— owl** lechuza f;
—yard corral m

barnacle [bɑ́rnəkəl] N percebe m

barometer [bərɑ́mɪdɚ] N barómetro m

baron [bérən] N barón m

baroque [bərók] ADJ & N barroco m

barracks [bérəks] N cuartel m

barracuda [bærəkúdə] N barracuda f

barrage [bərázʒ] N (of artillery fire) barrera de fuego f; (of questions) lluvia f, aluvión m

barrel [bǽrəɫ] N barril m, tonel m; (gun) cañón m, caño m; **he's a — of laughs** es un payaso; **he is scraping the bottom of the —** está desesperado; **to — along** ir disparado

barren [bǽrən] ADJ (land) árido, yermo; (female) estéril

barrette [bərɛ́t] N broche m

barricade [bǽrɪkéd] N barricada f; VT cerrar con barricadas; VI atrincherarse

barrier [bǽriə˞] N barrera f; **— reef** barrera de coral f

barrio [bárió] N barrio hispano m

barter [bárrɔ˞] VI hacer trueque; VT trocar; N trueque m

basal cell carcinoma [bésəɫsɛɫkɑrsɪnómə] N carcinoma de célula basal m

basalt [bésɔɫt] N basalto m

base [bes] N base f; **— pay** salario base m; **—ball** beisbol m; **—board** zócalo m; ADJ bajo, vil; (metal) de baja ley; VI/VT basar, fundar; **to be —d on** fundamentarse en; **the general is —d in Berlin** el general está estacionado en Berlín

baseless [bésɫɪs] ADJ sin fundamento

basement [bésmənt] N sótano m

baseness [bésnɪs] N bajeza f, vileza f

bash [bæʃ] VT golpear

bashful [bǽʃfəɫ] ADJ tímido, vergonzoso

bashfulness [bǽʃfəɫnɪs] N timidez f

basic [bésɪk] ADJ básico

basin [bésɪn] N (bowl) palangana f, jofaina f; (of a fountain) pilón m; (geographical formation) cuenca f; (pond) estanque m

basis [bésɪs] N fundamento m, base f; **on the — of** en base a, con base en; **on a regular —** regularmente

bask [bæsk] VI (in the sun) asolearse; (in praise) deleitarse

basket [bǽskɪt] N canasta f, cesta f, cesto m; **—ball** baloncesto m, básquetbol m

basketful [bǽskɪtfʌɫ] N (contents of a basket) canasto m; (large amount) montón m

basketry [bǽskɪtri] N cestería f

Basque [bæsk] ADJ & N (person) vasco -ca mf; (language) vascuence m, vasco m

bass [bes] N (voice, bass guitar) bajo m; (double bass) contrabajo m; **— clef** clave de fa f; **— drum** bombo m; **— horn** tuba f; [bæs] (marine fish) lubina f; (freshwater fish) perca f

bassoon [bæsún] N fagot m

bastard [bǽstə˞d] N & ADJ (illegitimate) bastardo -da mf

baste [best] VT (fabric) hilvanar; (meat) rociar

bat [bæt] N (baseball, cricket) bate m; (animal) murciélago m; VT golpear; **not to — an eye** no pestañear; VI (baseball) batear

batch [bætʃ] N (of cookies) hornada f; (of cement) tanda f; (of data) colección f

bath [bæθ] N baño m; **—robe** bata (de baño) f; Sp albornoz m; **—room** (in a house) baño m, cuarto de baño m; (public) Sp aseo m; Am servicio m, baño m; **—tub** bañera f

bathe [beð] VI/VT bañar(se); **bathing beauty** muchacha en traje de baño f; **bathing suit** traje de baño m

bather [béðə˞] N bañista mf

baton [bətán] N batuta f

battalion [bətǽljən] N batallón m

batter [bǽɾə˞] N pasta f, masa f; (baseball) bateador m; VT golpear

battery [bǽɾəri] N (of car, artillery) batería f; (of electronic devices) pila f; (of tests) serie f; (assault) asalto m

battle [bǽdɫ] N batalla f; **—-ax(e)** (weapon) hacha de guerra f; (woman) sargenta f; **— cry** grito de guerra m; **—field** campo de batalla m; **—ship** acorazado m; VI batallar; **to — cancer** luchar contra el cáncer

bawl [bɔɫ] VI berrear; **to — somebody out** echarle bronca a uno; **to — out orders** bramar órdenes

bay [be] N (body of water) bahía f; (howl) aullido m; **— leaf** hoja de laurel f; **— window** ventana saliente f; **to hold at —** tener a raya; ADJ bayo; VI aullar

bayonet [beənɛ́t] N bayoneta f

bazaar [bəzár] N (market place) bazar m; (benefit) kermés f

bazooka [bəzúkə] N bazuca f

be [bi] VI **I am from Uruguay** soy de Uruguay; **there were four of us** éramos cuatro; **he is a doctor** es médico; **it's her** es ella; **sugar is sweet** el azúcar es dulce; **London is in England** Londres está en Inglaterra; **this water is cold** esta agua está fría; **the windows were open** las ventanas estaban abiertas; **there is a problem** hay un problema; **to — cold / warm / hungry / right / in a hurry** tener frío / calor / hambre / razón / prisa; **it is cold / hot / windy** hace frío / calor / viento

beach [bitʃ] N playa f; **—comber** vagabundo -da mf; **—head** cabeza de playa f; VT varar, encallar

beacon [bíkən] N faro m

bead [bid] N cuenta f; (of sweat) gota f, perla f; **to get a — on somebody** apuntarle a

alguien; **to tell one's —s** rezar el rosario;
VT (string) enhebrar/ensartar cuentas;
(decorate) adornar con cuentas

beagle [bígəł] N beagle *m*

beak [bik] N pico *m*

beaker [bíkə] N vaso de precipitados *m*

beam [bim] N (of light) rayo *m*, haz *m*; (in a
building) viga *f*; (of a ship) manga *f*; (of a
scale) brazo *m*; **broad in the —** ancho de
caderas; VI/VT (light, radio) emitir; (smile)
estar radiante

bean [bin] N judía *f*, habichuela *f*; *Sp* alubia *f*;
Am frijol *m*, *Am* poroto *m*; **Lima —** haba
f; **—stalk** tallo de habas/frijol *m*; **Jack
and the —stalk** Juanito y las
habichuelas; **I don't know —s about
that** no sé ni papa/jota de eso

bear [bɛr] N oso *m*; **— hug** abrazo fuerte *m*;
— market mercado bajista *m*; VT (hold
up, tolerate) soportar, aguantar; (suffer)
sobrellevar; (have a child) dar a luz;
(produce young) parir; (produce fruit)
producir; **to — down** (mash) apretar;
(push) pujar; **to — a grudge** guardar
rencor; **to — in mind** tener en cuenta;
to — oneself with dignity portarse con
dignidad; **to — out** confirmar; **to —
testimony** dar testimonio; **to — gifts**
traer regalos; **to — a resemblance**
parecerse; **to — the cost of something**
asumir el costo de algo; **it doesn't —
repeating** no merece repetirse

bearable [bérəbəł] ADJ llevadero

beard [bird] N (on a man) barba *f*; (of wheat)
aristas *f pl*

bearded [bírDɪd] ADJ barbado, barbudo

bearer [bérə] N portador -ra *mf*

bearing [bérɪŋ] N porte *m*; **to lose one's —s**
perder el rumbo, desorientarse; **it has no
— on our situation** no tiene relación
con nuestra situación

bearish [bérɪʃ] ADJ (of bears) osuno; (of stock
market) bajista

beast [bist] N bestia *f*

beat [bit] VT (wings, eggs) batir; (a person)
golpear; (a drum) tocar; (an opponent)
vencer; (tempo) marcar; VI (heart) latir;
(drum) sonar; **to — around the bush**
andarse por las ramas; **to — off** rechazar;
to — up dar una paliza; **—s me!** ¡ni idea!
N (blow) golpe *m*; (drum) toque *m*; (heart)
latido *m*; (tempo) compás *m*; (policeman's
territory) ronda *f*

beaten [bítn] ADJ (mixed) batido; (defeated)
vencido; (tired) fatigado; **— path** camino
trillado *m*

beater [bíDə] N batidor *m*

beating [bíDɪŋ] N (whipping) paliza *f*;
(pulsation) latido *m*

beau [bo] N pretendiente *m*

beautiful [bjúDəfəł] ADJ hermoso; **— people**
jet set *mf*

beautify [bjúDəfaɪ] VT embellecer, hermosear

beauty [bjúDi] N belleza *f*, hermosura *f*;
(woman) beldad *f*; **— contest** concurso/
certamen de belleza *m*; **— pageant**
concurso/certamen de belleza *m*; **—
parlor** salón de belleza *m*

beaver [bívə] N castor *m*

because [bɪkʌ́z] CONJ porque; **— of** por, a
causa de

beckon [békən] VT llamar por señas

become [bɪkʌ́m] VT (through effort) hacerse;
he became rich se hizo rico; (emotional
or physical condition) ponerse; **she
became ill** se puso enferma; (long
process) llegar a ser; **he became a
doctor** llegó a ser médico; (turn into)
convertirse en; **the water became ice** el
agua se convirtió en hielo; (drastic
change) volverse; **he became crazy** se
volvió loco; (suit) sentar bien; **to —
angry** enojarse; **to — frightened**
asustarse; **to — old** envejecer(se); **what
has — of him?** ¿qué ha sido de él?

becoming [bɪkʌ́mɪŋ] ADJ (appropriate)
propio; **that dress is — to you** te sienta
bien ese vestido

bed [bed] N (furniture) cama *f*; *lit* lecho *m*; (of
a river) cauce *m*; (of the sea) fondo *m*; (in
a garden) cuadro *m*; **—bug** chinche *mf*;
—clothes ropa de cama *f*; **—pan** cuña *f*,
chata *f*; **—ridden** postrado en cama;
—rest reposo *m*; **—rock** lecho de roca *m*;
—room alcoba *f*, dormitorio *m*; *Mex*
recámara *f*; **at the —side** al lado de la
cama; **—side table** mesita de noche *f*;
—side manner manera agradable de
tratar a los pacientes *f*; **—sore** llaga *f*;
—spread colcha *f*; **—spring** resorte del
colchón *m*; **—time** hora de dormir *f*;
—wetting enuresis nocturna *f*; **to go to
—** acostarse; **to put to —** acostar

bedding [bédɪŋ] N ropa de cama *f*

bee [bi] N (insect) abeja *f*; (social gathering)
tertulia *f*; **to have a — in one's bonnet**
tener una idea metida en la cabeza;
—hive colmena *f*; **— sting** picadura de
abeja *f*

beech [bitʃ] N haya *f*; **—nut** hayuco *m*

beef [bif] N (meat) carne de vaca/res *f*;
(complaint) queja *f*; **— jerky** cecina *f*;
—steak bistec *m*; VI quejarse; **to — up**

reforzar

beep [bip] N pitazo *m*; VI/VT **the alarm is —ing** la alarma está sonando; **he —ed his horn** tocó el claxón

beeper [bípə-] N buscapersonas *m sg*

beer [bir] N cerveza *f*

beet [bit] N remolacha *f*

beetle [bídl̩] N escarabajo *m*

befall [bɪfɔ́l] VT acontecerle a

befit [bɪfít] VT convenir

before [bɪfɔ́r] ADV (temporal) antes; (spatial) delante; PREP (temporal) antes de; (spatial) delante de; *lit* ante; CONJ antes (de) que, antes de; **— beginning** antes de que comiences, antes de comenzar

beforehand [bɪfɔ́rhænd] ADV de antemano

befriend [bɪfrénd] VT hacerse amigo de

beg [beg] VT **to — for mercy** implorar misericordia; **she —ged me to do it** me rogó que lo hiciera; **to — the question** dar por sentado lo mismo que se arguye; VI mendigar, pedir limosna

beget [bɪgét] VT engendrar; **money —s money** la plata llama a la plata

beggar [bégə-] N mendigo -ga *mf*

begin [bɪgín] VI/VT comenzar, empezar; **the ten dollars won't — to cover the expense** los diez dólares ni siquiera cubren los gastos

beginner [bɪgínə-] N principiante *mf*

beginning [bɪgínɪŋ] N principio *m*; (temporal only) comienzo *m*; **— with** comenzando con / por; **at the —** al / por el principio

begrudge [bɪgrʌ́ʤ] VT aceptar de mala gana

behalf [bɪhǽf] PREP LOC **in / on — of** (in place of) por, en nombre de; (in favor of) a favor de

behave [bɪhév] VI portarse, comportarse; **— yourself!** ¡pórtate bien!

behavior [bɪhévjə-] N comportamiento *m*, conducta *f*

behead [bɪhéd] VT decapitar, descabezar

behind [bɪháɪnd] ADV detrás; (in payments, schedule) atrasado; **he fell — his competitors** quedó a la zaga de sus competidores; **an hour —** una hora de retraso; **from —** desde atrás; **to fall —** atrasarse; **to leave something —** dejar atrás algo; PREP detrás de, tras; **we're all — you** todos te apoyamos; **who's — this evil plot?** ¿quién está detrás de este plan macabro? **— one's back** a espaldas de uno

behold [bɪhɔ́ld] VT contemplar; **— the future king!** ¡he aquí el futuro rey!

behoove [bɪhúv] VI corresponderle a uno

beige [beʒ] ADJ & N beige *m*

being [bíɪŋ] N ser *m*; **for the time —** por ahora

Belarus [belərús] N Bielorrusia *f*

belated [bɪlédɪd] ADJ atrasado

belch [bɛltʃ] VI eructar, repetir; **to — from** salir de; N eructo *m*

belfry [bélfri] N campanario *m*

Belgian [béldʒən] ADJ & N belga *mf*

Belgium [béldʒəm] N Bélgica *f*

belief [bɪlíf] N creencia *f*; (strong opinion) convicción *f*

believable [bɪlívəbəl] ADJ creíble

believe [bɪlív] VI/VT creer

believer [bɪlívə-] N creyente *mf*; (proponent) partidario -ria *mf*

belittle [bɪlídl̩] VT (a person) menospreciar, disminuir; (a situation) minimizar

Belize [bəlíz] N Belice *m*

Belizean [bəlíziən] ADJ & N beliceño -ña *mf*

bell [bɛl] N campana *f*; (small) campanilla *f*; **—boy** botones *m sg*; **—flower** campanilla *f*, campánula *f*; **—hop** botones *m sg*; **— jar** campana de cristal *f*; **— pepper** pimiento *m*, morrón *m*; **— tower** campanario *m*; **with all the —s and whistles** con todos los accesorios

bellicose [bélɪkos] ADJ belicoso

belligerent [bəlíʤə-ənt] ADJ & N beligerante *mf*

bellow [bélo] VI/VT bramar, berrear; N bramido *m*; **—s** fuelle *m*

belly [béli] N barriga *f*, vientre *m*; **—ache** dolor de barriga *m*; **— button** ombligo *m*; **— dance** danza del vientre *f*; **— laugh** carcajada *f*

belong [bɪlɔ́ŋ] VI (ownership) pertenecer; **this car —s to me** este coche me pertenece; (correspondence) corresponder; **this key —s to this door** esta llave corresponde a esta puerta; (placement) ir; **this —s on the shelf** esto va en el estante

belongings [bɪlɔ́ŋɪŋz] N pertenencias *f pl*

beloved [bɪlʌ́vid] ADJ querido; N amado -da *mf*

below [bɪló] ADV abajo; **five — (zero)** cinco bajo cero; PREP bajo, debajo de, abajo de

belt [bɛlt] N (for the waist) cinturón *m*, cinto *m*; (for a machine) correa *f*; (region) zona *f*; **— line** cintura *f*; VT pegar; **to — out a song** cantar una canción a voz en cuello

bemoan [bɪmón] VT lamentarse de, quejarse de

bench [bɛntʃ] N banco *m*; (without a back) banqueta *f*; (in sports) banquillo *m*; (in court) estrado *m*; **—mark** (upper limit) cota *f*; (parameter) punto de referencia *m*;

opinion of the — opinión del tribunal *f*
bend [bɛnd] VI/VT (make curved) doblar(se); (force) someter; **to — over** inclinarse; **to — over backward** desvivirse; **to — the rules** hacer una excepción; N (road) curva *f*, recodo *m*; —**s** enfermedad de los buzos *f*
beneath [bɪníθ] ADV abajo, bajo; (in rank) inferior a; — **contempt** totalmente despreciable; **that's — me** no es digno de mí
benediction [bɛnɪdíkʃən] N bendición *f*
benefactor [bɛnəfæktɚ] N benefactor -ra *mf*; *lit* bienhechor -ra *mf*
beneficent [bənɛ́fɪsənt] ADJ benéfico
beneficial [bɛnəfíʃəl] ADJ beneficioso
beneficiary [bɛnəfíʃieri] N beneficiario -ria *mf*
benefit [bɛ́nəfɪt] N beneficio *m*; — **performance** función de beneficencia *f*; VI/VT beneficiar(se), sacar provecho; **he —ed by the medicine** le hizo bien la medicina
benevolence [bənɛ́vələns] N benevolencia *f*
benevolent [bənɛ́vələnt] ADJ benévolo
benign [bɪnáɪn] ADJ benigno
Benin [bɛnín] N Benín *m*
Beninese [bɛnɪníz] ADJ & N beninés -esa *mf*
bent [bɛnt] N inclinación *f*; **to be — on** estar resuelto a
benzine [bɛ́nzin] N bencina *f*
bequeath [bɪkwíð] VT legar, heredar
bequest [bɪkwɛ́st] N legado *m*
berate [bɪrét] VT reprender
bereaved [bɪrívd] ADJ de luto
beret [bəré] N boina *f*
berry [bɛ́ri] N baya *f*
berserk [bɚrzɝk] ADJ fuera de sí; **he went —** se puso hecho una fiera, se enfureció
berth [bɚθ] N litera *f*; **to give a wide — to** mantener una distancia prudencial de
beseech [bɪsítʃ] VT suplicar, rogar
beset [bɪsɛ́t] VT (attack) acosar; (surround) rodear
beside [bɪsáɪd] PREP al lado de; **sit down — me** siéntate a mi lado; **to be — oneself** estar fuera de sí; **that is — the point** eso no viene al caso; ADV al lado
besides [bɪsáɪdz] ADV además; **they have a table but not much —** tienen una mesa pero poca cosa más; PREP además de, aparte de
besiege [bɪsídʒ] VT (lay siege) sitiar, cercar; (importune) importunar, asediar
best [bɛst] ADJ mejor; —**-case scenario** la mejor situación; — **man** padrino de boda *m*; — **seller** bestseller *m*; **she's the —** ella es la mejor; ADV mejor; **at —** a lo más, en el mejor de los casos; N **the — is still to**

come lo mejor está por venir; **to do one's —** hacer lo mejor posible; **to get the — of a person** ganarle a una persona; **to make the — of** sacar el mejor partido de
bestial [bɛ́stʃəl] ADJ bestial
bestow [bɪstó] VT conferir; **to — gifts upon** dar regalos a
bet [bɛt] N apuesta *f*; VI/VT apostar; **to — on** apostar por
betray [bɪtré] VT (a person) traicionar; (a secret) revelar; (a feeling) traslucir, delatar; **to — one's ignorance** hacer patente su ignorancia
betrayal [bɪtréəl] N traición *f*
betrayer [bɪtréɚ] N traidor -ra *mf*
betrothal [bɪtróðəl] N esponsales *f pl*
better [bɛ́dɚ] ADJ mejor; — **half** media naranja *f*; **the — part of a year** la mayor parte de un año; ADV mejor; **he lives — than a mile away** vive a más de una milla; **so much the —** tanto mejor; —**-off** en mejor posición económica; **to be — off** estar mejor así; **to change for the —** cambiar para bien; **to get —** mejorar(se), aliviarse; VT mejorar; **to — oneself** mejorarse, mejorar de situación; N **the — of the two** el / la mejor de los dos; **don't contradict your —s** no contradigas a tus superiores
better, bettor [bɛ́dɚ] N apostador -ra *mf*
between [bɪtwín] PREP entre; ADV en medio
bevel [bɛ́vəl] N bisel *m*; VT biselar
beverage [bɛ́vrɪdʒ] N bebida *f*
bevy [bɛ́vi] N (of birds, people) bandada *f*; (of deer) manada *f*
beware [bɪwɛ́r] VI cuidarse (de); — **of the dog** cuidado con el perro
bewilder [bɪwíldɚ] VT dejar perplejo, ofuscar, aturdir; **to be —ed** estar perplejo
bewilderment [bɪwíldɚmənt] N perplejidad *f*, aturdimiento *m*
bewitch [bɪwítʃ] VT hechizar, embrujar
beyond [bijánd] ADV más allá; PREP más allá de; — **my reach** fuera de mi alcance; N **the great —** el más allá
Bhutan [bután] N Bután *m*
Bhutanese [butníz] ADJ & N butanés -esa *mf*
bias [báɪəs] N (prejudice) prejuicio *m*; (in fabric) sesgo *m*; ADJ sesgado, oblicuo; VT predisponer
bib [bɪb] N babero *m*; (of an apron) pechera *f*
Bible [báɪbəl] N Biblia *f*
biblical [bíblɪkəl] ADJ bíblico
bibliography [bɪbliágrəfi] N bibliografía *f*
bicarbonate [baɪkárbənɪt] N bicarbonato *m*
bicep, biceps [báɪsɛp(s)] N bíceps *m sg*

bicker [bíkə-] VI reñir

bicycle [báɪsɪkəł] N bicicleta f; VI andar en bicicleta

bid [bɪd] N (in an auction, contest) licitación f, puja f; (in card games) apuesta f; (attempt) tentativa f; VI/VT (offer) ofrecer; (command) mandar; (invite) rogar; (enter a bid in cards) apostar; **to — good-bye** despedirse; **to — up** pujar el precio

bidding [bídɪŋ] N (in auction) puja f; **at someone's —** por orden de alguien; **to do someone's —** cumplir con los deseos de alguien

bide [baɪd] VI/VT **to — one's time** esperar una oportunidad

biennium [baɪéniəm] N bienio m

bifurcate [báɪfə-ket] VI/VT bifurcar(se)

big [bɪg] ADJ grande; **— Bang theory** teoría del Big Bang f; **— brother** hermano mayor m; **— bucks** mucha plata f; **— business** el gran capital; **— deal** asunto importante m; **— deal!** ¡no es para tanto! **— Dipper** Osa Mayor f; **-headed** cabezón, cabezudo; **-hearted** magnánimo; **— house** fam gayola f; **— name** personalidad prominente f; **— picture** panorama general m; **— shot** pez gordo m; **— sister** hermana mayor f; **-ticket** caro; **-wig** pez gordo m; **— with child** embarazada; **jazz was — in the 1920s** el jazz era popular en los años veinte; **she's a — deal** es una persona importante; **a — problem** un gran problema; ADV **-time** un montón; **she wants to go -time** se muere por ir; **to talk —** jactarse; Am lucirse; **to go over —** tener éxito; **to be — on** ser entusiasta de

bigamy [bígəmi] N bigamia f

bigot [bígət] N intolerante mf

bigotry [bígətri] N intolerancia f

bike [baɪk] N bici f

biker [báɪkə-] N motociclista mf

bikini [bɪkíni] N bikini m

bilateral [baɪlǽɾə-əł] ADJ bilateral

bile [baɪł] N (secretion) bilis f; (ill temper) mal genio m; **— duct** conducto biliar m

bilingual [baɪlíŋgwəł] ADJ & N bilingüe mf

bilingualism [baɪlíŋgwəlɪzəm] N bilingüismo m

bill [bɪł] N (statement) factura f; (in a restaurant) cuenta f; (poster) cartel m; (bank note) billete m; (for movies, theater) programa m; (of a bird) pico m; (legislative) proyecto de ley m; **-board** cartelera f; **-fold** cartera f, billetera f; **— of exchange** letra de cambio f; **— of lading** conocimiento de embarque m; **— of rights** declaración de derechos f; **— of sale** escritura de venta f; **-s payable** efectos a pagar m pl; VT cobrar, mandar la factura a

billable [bíləbəł] ADJ facturable

billiards [bíljə-dz] N billar m

billing [bílɪŋ] N (theater) orden de importancia en espectáculos m; (business) facturación f

billion [bíljən] NUM mil millones m pl

billow [bílo] N (of smoke) nube f; (of water) ola f; VI ondular, hacer olas

bin [bɪn] N (for clothes, food) cajón m, recipiente m; (on an airplane) portaequipajes m sg; (for coal) carbonera f; (for grain) granero m

binary [báɪneri] ADJ binario; **— star** estrella binaria f

bind [baɪnd] VI/VT (unite) unir; (connect) ligar; (tie) atar; (put a cover on a book) encuadernar; (press tightly) apretar; (oblige by contract) obligar

binding [báɪndɪŋ] N (of a book) encuadernación f; (on a rug) ribete m; ADJ obligatorio

binge [bɪndʒ] N (alcoholic) juerga f, parranda f; (food) comilona f; VI (on alcohol) emborracharse; (on food) atiborrarse

bingo [bíŋgo] N bingo m

binoculars [bənákjələ-z] N gemelos m pl, prismáticos m pl

binomial [baɪnómiəł] N binomio m; ADJ binomial

biochemistry [baɪokémɪstri] N bioquímica f

biodegradable [baɪodɪgrédəbəł] ADJ biodegradable

bioengineering [baɪoendʒəníríŋ] N bioingeniería f

biofeedback [baɪofídbæk] N biofeedback m, retroalimentación biológica f

biography [baɪágɾəfi] N biografía f

biology [baɪúlədʒi] N biología f

biopsy [báɪɑpsi] N biopsia f

biorhythm [báɪoɾɪðəm] N biorritmo m

biotechnology [baɪotɛknálədʒi] N biotecnología f

bipartisan [baɪpárɾɪzən] ADJ bipartidista

bipolar [baɪpólə-] ADJ bipolar; **— disorder** trastorno bipolar m

birch [bə-tʃ] N abedul m

bird [bə-d] N ave f; (small) pájaro m; **— of prey** ave de rapiña f; **— seed** alpiste m; **odd —** persona peculiar f

birth [bə-θ] N (act of being born) nacimiento m; (act of giving birth) parto m; (lineage) linaje m; (origin) origen m; **— certificate**

certificado de nacimiento *m*, fe / acta de
nacimiento *f*; **— control** (policy) control
de la natalidad *m*; (devices)
anticonceptivos *m pl*; **—day** cumpleaños
m sg; **in his / her —day suit** como Dios
lo / la trajo al mundo; **—mark** antojo *m*;
—place lugar de nacimiento *m*; **—rate**
tasa de natalidad *f*; **—right** derechos de
nacimiento *m pl*; (of oldest child)
primogenitura *f*; **to give —** dar a luz,
parir, alumbrar; **by —** de nacimiento
biscuit [bískɪt] N panecillo *m*
bisect [báɪsekt] VT bisecar
bishop [bíʃəp] N obispo *m*; (in chess) alfil *m*
bison [báɪsən] N bisonte *m*, búfalo *m*
bit [bɪt] N (small piece) pedacito *m*, trocito *m*;
(some) poquito *m*; (of a bridle) bocado *m*,
freno *m*; (of a drill) broca *f*, barrena *f*;
(computer) bit *m*; **I don't care a —** no
me importa en absoluto
bitch [bɪtʃ] N perra *f*
bite [baɪt] VI / VT morder; (be duped) dejarse
engañar; (insect, fish, snake) picar; **to —
off** arrancar de un mordisco; N (act,
wound) mordedura *f*, dentellada *f*;
(morsel, small meal) bocado *m*, bocadito
m; (of an insect) picadura *f*, roncha *f*
bitter [bídɚ] ADJ (taste) amargo; (cold)
glacial; (enemy) acérrimo; **—sweet**
dulceamargo, agridulce; **to fight to the
— end** luchar hasta morir; N **—s** cerveza
amarga *f*
bitterness [bídɚnɪs] N (taste) amargor *m*;
(feelings) amargura *f*; (anger) rencor *m*,
resentimiento *m*
bizarre [bɪzár] ADJ (event) extraño;
(appearance) estrafalario
blab [blæb] VI parlotear; VT descubrir el pastel
black [blæk] ADJ (color, ethnicity) negro;
(night) oscuro; **—and-blue** lleno de
moretones, amoratado; **— bean** frijol
negro *m*; **—berry** zarzamora *f*, mora *f*;
—bird mirlo *m*; **—board** pizarrón *m*,
pizarra *f*; **— death** peste negra *f*; **— eye**
ojo amoratado / morado *m*; **—head**
espinilla *f*; **— hole** agujero negro *m*;
—jack (weapon) cachiporra *f*; (card game)
black-jack *m*, veintiuno *m*; **— magic**
magia negra *f*; **—mail** chantaje *m*; **—
mark** mancha *f*; **— market** mercado
negro *m*; **—out** apagón *m*; **— pepper**
pimienta negra *f*; **— pudding** morcilla *f*;
— sheep oveja negra *f*; **—smith** herrero
m; **—smith's shop** herrería *f*, forja *f*;
—top asfalto *m*; **— widow spider** viuda
negra *f*; N negro -a *mf*; **to put down in
— and white** poner por escrito; VT **to**

—mail chantajear; VI **to — out**
desmayarse
blacken [blǽkən] VT ennegrecer, negrear; VI
(sky) oscurecerse
blackness [blǽknɪs] N negrura *f*
bladder [blǽDɚ] N vejiga *f*
blade [bled] N (of a knife) hoja *f*; (of grass)
brizna *f*; (of a sword) espada *f*; (of an oar)
pala *f*, paleta *f*; (of a propeller) aspa *f*
blame [blem] VT culpar, echar la culpa a,
achacar la culpa a; **to be to —** tener la
culpa; N (responsibility) culpa *f*; (reproof)
reproche *m*
blameless [blémlɪs] ADJ intachable
blanch [blænʧ] VI palidecer; VT (whiten)
blanquear; (scald) escaldar
bland [blænd] ADJ insulso
blank [blæŋk] ADJ (not written on) en
blanco; (not recorded on) virgen;
(unadorned, expressionless) vacío;
(confused) desconcertado; **— cartridge**
cartucho de fogueo *m*; **— check** cheque
en blanco *m*; **— verse** verso libre *m*; N
(place to be filled in on a form) espacio
(en blanco) *m*; (gap) vacío *m*; VI **to — out**
quedarse en blanco
blanket [blǽŋkɪt] N manta *f*, frazada *f*; *Am*
cobija *f*; ADJ global; VT cubrir
blare [blɛr] VI hacer un ruido estruendoso; N
estruendo *m*; (of a trumpet) toque *m*
blaspheme [blæsfím] VI / VT blasfemar (contra)
blasphemy [blǽsfəmi] N blasfemia *f*
blast [blæst] N (of wind) ráfaga *f*; (of
criticism) lluvia *f*; (of a trumpet)
trompetazo *m*; (explosive charge) carga *f*;
(explosion) explosión *f*; **— furnace** alto
horno *m*; **—off** despegue *m*; **we had a —**
lo pasamos bomba; **at full —** a todo
volumen; VI / VT (blow horn) pitar, tocar;
(shatter) volar; (criticize) criticar
duramente; (blow hard) azotar; **to — off**
despegar
blatant [blétṇt] ADJ descarado
blaze [blez] N (flame) llamarada *f*; (fire)
incendio *m*; (glow) resplandor *m*; (mark)
señal *f*; **— of anger** arranque de ira *m*; VI
(burn) arder; (shine) resplandecer; **to — a
trail** marcar una senda
blazer [bléza] N blazer *m*, saco *m*
bleach [bliʧ] VI / VT (intentional)
blanquear(se); (accidental) desteñir(se); N
blanqueador *m*; *Sp* lejía *f* *pl*
bleachers [blíʧɚz] N gradas *f pl*
bleak [blik] ADJ (terrain) yermo, desolado;
(winter) crudo; (wind) helado; (future)
negro
bleary [blíri] ADJ nublado

bleat [blit] N balido *m*; VI balar

bleed [blid] VI (lose blood) sangrar; (run, as in colors) correrse, desteñir(se); **my heart —s for the poor** los pobres me dan lástima; VT (let blood) desangrar; (extort) extorsionar; (clean brakes) purgar

blemish [blέmɪʃ] N mancha *f*, tacha *f*; VT manchar

blend [blɛnd] VI/VT (intermix) mezclar, entremezclar; (have no separation) fundirse; (harmonize voices) armonizar; N mezcla *f*

blender [blέndə·] N licuadora *f*

bless [blɛs] VT bendecir; INTERJ **— you!** ¡salud!

blessed [blέsɪd] ADJ (beatified) beato; (happy) bienaventurado, feliz; **— event** feliz acontecimiento *m*; **the whole — day** todo el santo día; **not a — drop of rain** ni una bendita gota de agua; [blest] **— with** dotado de

blessing [blέsɪŋ] N bendición *f*; **to say the — dar gracias**

blight [blaɪt] N (plant disease) quemadura *f*, añublo *m*; (scourge) lacra *f*; VT (cause to wither) marchitar; (ruin) arruinar

blimp [blɪmp] N zepelín *m*

blind [blaɪnd] ADJ ciego; **— alley** callejón sin salida *m*; **— date** cita a ciegas *f*; **—fold** venda para los ojos *f*; **to —fold** vendar los ojos a; **— man's bluff** juego de la gallina ciega *m*; **— spot** ángulo muerto *m*; **to fly —** volar a ciegas; **to go —** quedarse ciego; N (shade) persiana *f*; (hunter's hiding place) escondite *m*; VT (make blind) cegar; (darken) oscurecer

blinder [blaɪndə·] N anteojera *f*

blindly [blaɪndli] ADV a ciegas

blindness [blaɪndnɪs] N ceguera *f*

blink [blɪŋk] VI/VT (move eyelids) pestañear, parpadear; (go on and off, as of a light) parpadear; (ignore) pasar por alto; (flee a challenge) rajarse; N parpadeo *m*, pestañeo *m*; **on the —** averiado

blip [blɪp] N (on radar) punto *m*; (of a movie) interrupción *f*; (moment) bache *m*

bliss [blɪs] N dicha *f*, felicidad absoluta *f*

blister [blístə·] N ampolla *f*; (small) vejiga *f*; VT sacar ampollas; VI ampollarse

blitz [blɪts] N ataque relámpago *m*

blizzard [blízə·d] N ventisca *f*

bloat [blot] VI hinchar(se), abotagar(se)

blob [blɑb] N pedazo de algo sin forma *m*

block [blɑk] N (piece of stone, cement) bloque *m*; (piece of wood) trozo de madera *m*; (toy) cubo *m*; (sports play) bloqueo *m*; (length from one street to the next) cuadra *f*; (square block) manzana *f*;

(obstacle) obstáculo *m*; (group of tickets) sección *f*; **—buster** éxito de taquilla *m*; **—head** tarugo -ga *mf*, alcornoque *m*; VT (obstruct) bloquear, tapar; (stop a pass) parar; **to — out** (an essay) esbozar, bosquejar; (the sun) ocultar

blockade [blɑkéd] N bloqueo *m*; VT bloquear

blockage [blɑkɪʤ] N obstrucción *f*

blond [blɑnd] ADJ & N rubio -a *mf*

blood [blʌd] N sangre *f*; **—bank** banco de sangre *m*; **—bath** carnicería *f*, baño de sangre *m*; **— count** recuento sanguíneo *m*; **— group** grupo sanguíneo *m*; **—hound** sabueso *m*; **— plasma** plasma sanguíneo *m*; **— poisoning** septicemia *f*; **— pressure** presión arterial *f*; **— relative** pariente consanguíneo *mf*; **—shed** derramamiento de sangre *m*; **— vessel** vaso sanguíneo *m*; **in cold —** a sangre fría; ADJ **—shot** inyectado de sangre; **—thirsty** sanguinario, sangriento

bloody [blʌdi] ADJ (violent) sangriento; (smeared) ensangrentado

bloom [blum] N (flower) flor *f*; (flowering) floración *f*; (youthfulness) lozanía *f*; (flush) rubor *m*; **in —** en flor; VI florecer

blooming [blúmɪŋ] ADJ (flowering) floreciente; (thriving) lozano

blooper [blúpə·] N perla *f*.

blossom [blɑsəm] N (flower) flor *f*; (flowering) floración *f*; VI florecer

blot [blɑt] N (on paper) mancha *f*, borrón *m*; (on honor) tacha *f*; VI/VT manchar(se), emborronar(se); **to — out** (obscure) borrar, tachar; (obliterate) destruir

blotch [blɑtʃ] VT borronear, manchar, cubrir con manchas; N mancha *f*, borrón *m*

blouse [blaʊs] N blusa *f*

blow [blo] VI (wind) soplar; (leaf) volar; (siren) sonar; (horse) resoplar; VT (play a horn) sonar; **to — a fuse** quemar un fusible; **to — away** dejar atónito; **to — down** tirar abajo; **to —-dry** secar con secador; **to — one's nose** sonarse las narices / la nariz; **to — on the soup** soplar la sopa; **to — one's brains out** levantarse la tapa de los sesos; **to — out** reventar(se); **to — over** (knock down) derribar; (dissipate) disiparse; **to — up** (a balloon) inflar, hinchar; (a bridge) volar; N (stroke, shock) golpe *m*; (wind) tempestad *f*; (breath) soplo *m*; **—out** (tire failure) reventón *m*; (party) fiestón *m*; **—pipe** cerbatana *f*; **—torch** soplete *m*; **—up** (fight) pelea *f*, riña *f*; (photo) ampliación *f*; **to come to —s** irse a las manos

blower [blóə·] N (artisan) soplador *m*;

(machine) aventadora *f*

blue [blu] ADJ azul; (sad) triste, melancólico; (from cold) amoratado; **—bell** campanilla *f*; **—bird** pájaro azul *m*; **—blood** sangre azul *f*; **— book** lista de precios de mercado *f*; **--chip** de primera línea; **—-collar** de clase obrera; **—jay** arrendajo *m*; **— jeans** vaqueros *m pl*; **—print** (of a building) cianotipo *m*; (of a project) plan *m*, trazado *m*; **—-ribbon** distinguido; **— whale** ballena azul *f*; N azul *m*; **light —** (azul) celeste *m*; **the —s** (sadness) melancolía *f*, murria *f*; (genre of music) blues *m pl*; VI ponerse azul, azulear; VT azular, teñir de azul; **to —print** trazar

bluff [blʌf] N (cliff) acantilado *m*, risco *m*; (false boast) bluff *m*; (in poker) farol *m*; VT hacer un bluff; **to call a —** poner en evidencia

bluffer [blʌfɚ] N bluff *m*

bluing [blúɪŋ] N añil *m*

bluish [blúɪʃ] ADJ azulado

blunder [blʌ́ndɚ] N disparate *m*, patochada *f*; VI meter la pata; **to — upon / into** tropezar con

blunt [blʌnt] ADJ (not sharp) romo; (frank) directo, franco; VT despuntar

blur [blɚ] VT (to obscure) emborronar, desvanecer; (to make vision blurry) nublar; VI empañarse, nublarse; N (indistinct sight) mancha *f*; **it's a — in my mind** sólo tengo un recuerdo vago de eso

blurry [blɚ́i] ADJ borroso

blurt [blɚt] VT **to — (out)** espetar

blush [blʌʃ] VI sonrojarse, ponerse colorado, ruborizarse; N (act of blushing) sonrojo *m*; (effect of blushing) rubor *m*; **at first —** a primera vista

bluster [blʌ́stɚ] VI (blow hard) soplar fuerte, rugir; (boast) fanfarronear; N (noise) ventarrón *m*; (attitude) fanfarronería *f*

blustering [blʌ́stərɪŋ] ADJ fanfarrón, jactancioso; **— wind** ventarrón *m*

boa constrictor [bóəkənstríktɚ] N boa *f*

boar [bɔr] N jabalí *m*

board [bɔrd] N (wood) tabla *f*, listón *m*; (game) tablero *m*; (meals) pensión *f*; (of directors) directorio *m*, mesa *f*; (for bulletins) cartelera *f*; **—ing school** pensionado *m*, internado *m*; **—inghouse** pensión *f*; **— of trustees** patronato *m*; **—room** sala de directorio *f*; **on —** a bordo; **to go by the —** irse por la borda; VI (lodge) alojarse; **to — up** tapiar, cerrar con tablas; VT (boat, plane, train) abordar; (provide lodging) alojar

boarder [bɔ́rdɚ] N pensionista *mf*

boast [bost] N alarde *m*; VI jactarse, vanagloriarse, blasonar; VT **the town —s two new schools** el pueblo ostenta dos escuelas nuevas

boastful [bóstfəl] ADJ jactancioso, vanaglorioso

boastfulness [bóstfəlnɪs] N jactancia *f*, vanagloria *f*

boat [bot] N (any water vessel) embarcación *f*; (open and small) bote *m*, lancha *f*; (closed, larger) barco *m*; **—house** cobertizo para botes *m*; **—man** barquero *m*, botero *m*

boating [bóɾɪŋ] N navegación *f*; **to go —** navegar

bob [bab] N (of horsetail) cola cortada *f*; (of the head) sacudida *f*; (haircut) melena corta *f*; (of a pendulum) pesa *f*, plomada *f*; **—tail** rabón *m*; VI sacudirse; (a ship) cabecear; VT **to — one's hair** cortarse el pelo en melena

bobbin [bábɪn] N carrete *m*, bobina *f*

bobcat [bábkæt] N lince rojo *m*

bode [bod] VI **that doesn't — well** eso no augura nada bueno

bodice [bádɪs] N corpiño *m*

bodily [bádli] ADJ corporal; **— harm** daño físico *m*

body [bádi] N (of a person, animal, wine, fabric) cuerpo *m*; (torso) tronco *m*; (corpse) cadáver *m*; (of a text, army, etc.) parte principal *f*; (of water) masa *f*; (of a car) carrocería *f*; (of an airplane) fuselaje *m*; **— bag** bolsa para cadáveres *f*; **—-building** culturismo *m*; **— count** número de muertos *m*; **—guard** guardaespaldas *m sg*; **— language** lenguaje corporal *m*; **— temperature** temperatura *f*; **to —search** cachear; **— shop** taller de carrocería *m*

bog [bag] N pantano *m*; VI hundir(se); **to get —ged down** atascarse

bogeyman [búgimæn] N coco *m*; RP cuco *m*

bogus [bógəs] ADJ falso

Bohemian [bohímiən] ADJ & N bohemio -a *mf*

boil [bɔɪl] VI/VT (water) hervir; (eggs) cocer; (ocean) bullir; (angry person) echar chispas; **to — down to** reducirse a; **to — over** derramarse; **—ing point** punto de ebullición *m*; N (inflammation) forúnculo *m*, divieso *m*; (act of boiling) hervor *m*; **to come to a —** soltar / romper el hervor

boiler [bóɪlɚ] N caldera *f*

boisterous [bóɪstəəs] ADJ bullicioso

bold [bold] ADJ (not fearful) atrevido, osado; (unconventional) audaz; (visually striking)

llamativo; —**-faced** descarado; —**face
type** negrita f

boldness [bółdnıs] N (courage) atrevimiento
m, osadía f, arrojo m; (unconventional
attitude) audacia f

Bolivia [bəlívia] N Bolivia f

Bolivian [bəlívian] ADJ & N boliviano -na mf

bolster [bółsta] N cojín cilíndrico m; VT
reforzar; **to — someone's courage**
alentar a alguien

bolt [bołt] N (door lock) pestillo m, cerrojo
m; (crossbar) aldaba f; (pin) perno m,
tornillo grande m; (of cloth) rollo m; **it
came as a — from the blue** cayó como
bomba; VT (fasten) atornillar; (lock door)
cerrar con tranca, atrancar; (devour)
engullir; (break with) romper con; VI
echarse a correr

bomb [bam] N bomba f; —**shell** bomba f; —
shelter refugio antiaéreo m; VT (attack
with bombs) bombardear; VI (fail) fracasar

bombard [bambárd] VT bombardear

bombardier [bamba-dír] N bombardero -ra
mf

bombardment [bambárdmant] N
bombardeo m

bombastic [bambéstık] ADJ grandilocuente,
ampuloso

bomber [báma-] N bombardero m, avión de
bombardeo m

bona fide [bónafaıd] ADJ genuino; — **offer**
oferta seria f

bonbon [bánban] N caramelo m; (chocolate)
bombón m

bond [band] N (tie) lazo m; (fetter) cadenas f
pl; (financial instrument) bono m,
obligación f; (adhesion) adherencia f;
(chemical) enlace m; VI/VT (stick to)
adherirse; (connect) establecer vínculos

bondage [bándıdʒ] N servidumbre f,
esclavitud f

bonding [bándıŋ] N (mother-child) lazos
afectivos m pl; (male) compenetración f

bondsman [bándzman] N fiador -ra mf

bone [bon] N hueso m; (of fish) espina f; —
china porcelana fina f; —**head** estúpido
-da mf; —**yard** cementerio m; — **of
contention** manzana de discordia f; **to
make no —s about it** no andarse con
rodeos; **to** deshuesar; (fish) quitar las
espinas; **to — up on something** estudiar
algo

bonfire [bánfaır] N hoguera f, fogata f

bonnet [bánıt] N gorro m

bonus [bónəs] N (extra salary) gratificación f,
prima f; (at Christmas) aguinaldo m

bony [bóni] ADJ (with large bones) huesudo;

(made of bones) óseo

boo [bu] VI/VT abuchear, rechiflar; INTERJ ¡bu!
N rechifla f, abucheo m

boo-boo [búbu] N lastimadura f; Sp fam pupa
f; Am nana f; **to make a —** meter la pata

booby [búbi] N (fool) bobo -a mf; (bird) bobo
m; — **hatch** fam loquería f; — **prize**
premio al peor competidor m; — **trap**
trampa explosiva f

book [buk] N libro m; —**binding**
encuadernación f; —**case** estante m,
estantería f, biblioteca f; —**end**
sujetalibros m sg; —**keeper** tenedor -ra de
libros mf; Sp contable mf; —**keeping**
teneduría de libros f, contabilidad f;
—**mark** marcador de libros m; —**mobile**
biblioteca móvil f; — **review** reseña f;
—**seller** librero -ra mf; —**shelf** estante m;
—**store** librería f; — **value** valor contable
m; **by the —** según las reglas; **on the —s**
registrado en los libros; **to keep —s** llevar
los libros; VT (reserve) reservar; (hire)
contratar; (record charges against) fichar

bookish [búkıʃ] ADJ (person) estudioso;
(allusion) libresco

booklet [búklıt] N cartilla f

boom [bum] VI (resound) resonar; (prosper)
prosperar; N (noise) explosión f; (increase)
auge m

boon [bun] N (blessing) bendición f; (favor)
favor m

boondocks [búndaks] ADV LOC **(out) in the
—** fam en los quintos infiernos, en el
quinto pino

boondoggle [búndagəł] N despilfarro m

boor [bur] N patán -ana mf

boorish [búrıʃ] ADJ grosero, zafio

boost [bust] VT (to shove) empujar (desde
abajo o detrás); (to promote) estimular,
impulsar; N (shove) empujón (desde abajo)
m; (aid) estímulo m, impulso m; — **in
prices** alza de precios f

booster [bústə] N (person) animador -ra mf;
(rocket) acelerador m; (electronic device)
amplificador m; (vaccination) refuerzo m

boot [but] N (shoe) bota f; (trunk of a car)
cajuela f; (clamp for cars) cepo m;
—**black** limpiabotas m sg; —**legger**
contrabandista de licores m; **to — por**
añadidura; **to give the —** poner de
patitas en la calle; VT dar una patada a; **to
— (out)** echar a patadas

booth [buθ] N (telephone) cabina f; (stand)
puesto m; (ticket) taquilla f

booty [búpi] N botín m

booze [buz] N fam bebercio m, bebida
alcohólica f

borax [bóræks] N bórax *m*

border [bórɖəˑ] N (line between countries) frontera *f*; (edge, brink) borde *m*; (bed of flowers) ariete *m*; (design) ribete *m*; **—line** (on a border) fronterizo; (not up to standards) dudoso; VI/VT (make a design) ribetear; **to — on** colindar con; **it —s on madness** raya en la locura

bordering [bórɖəˑɪŋ] ADJ limítrofe

bore [bɔr] N (hole) agujero *m*; (of a gun, cylinder) calibre *m*; (uninteresting person) aburrido -da *mf*, pesado -da *mf*; (uninteresting thing) lata *f*; VT (make a hole) taladrar, horadar; (fail to interest) aburrir; **to — a hole** hacer un agujero

bored [bɔrd] ADJ aburrido; **I'm —** estoy aburrido

boredom [bórɖəm] N aburrimiento *m*, tedio *m*

boric acid [bórɪk ǽsɪd] N ácido bórico *m*

boring [bórɪŋ] ADJ aburrido; **he's —** es aburrido

born [bɔrn] ADJ nacido; **he's a — dancer** es un bailarín nato; **she's a — liar** es una mentirosa de nacimiento; **to be —** nacer

boron [bóran] N boro *m*

borrow [báro] VT pedir prestado; **I —ed money from Fred** le pedí dinero prestado a Fred; **may I — your car?** ¿me prestas tu coche? **I —ed these books from the library** saqué estos libros de la biblioteca

borrower [bároˑ] N (money) prestatario -ria *mf*; (books) usuario -ria *mf*

Bosnia and Herzegovina [báznɪæn d hɑ·rtsəgəvínə] N Bosnia-Herzegovina *f*

Bosnian [báznɪən] ADJ & N bosnio -nia *mf*

bosom [búzəm] N pecho *m*, seno *m*; **in the — of the family** en el seno de la familia; **— buddy** amigo -ga íntimo -ma *mf*

boss [bɔs] N jefe -fa *mf*; (on a plantation) mayoral *m*, capataz *m*; (political) dirigente *m*; (mafia) capo *m*; VT **to — around** mandonear

bossy [bósi] ADJ mandón

botanical [bətǽnɪkəl] ADJ botánico

botany [bátn̩i] N botánica *f*

botch [bátʃ] VT chapucear, estropear; N chapucería *f*, chapuza *f*

both [boθ] ADJ & PRON ambos, los dos

bother [báɖəˑ] VT molestar, fastidiar; VI molestarse, tomarse la molestia; N molestia *f*

bothersome [báɖəˑsəm] ADJ (activity) molesto, enojoso; (person) enfadoso, molesto

Botswana [batswánə] N Botsuana *f*

bottle [bádl̩] N botella *f*; (for medicine, perfume) frasco *m*; **—neck** atascadero *m*, embotellamiento *m*; **— top** chapa de botella *f*; VT embotellar; **to — up** atascar, embotellar

bottom [báɖəm] N (of a hole) fondo *m*; (of a hall, pile, page, bed) pie *m*; (lower part) base *f*, parte de abajo *f*; (buttocks) trasero *m*; **to be at the — of the class** ser el último de la clase; **to hit —** tocar fondo; **to — out** tocar fondo; **who is at the — of all this?** ¿quién está detrás de todo esto? ADJ de abajo; **— line** (business) balance final *m*; (essential element) lo esencial

bottomless [báɖəmlɪs] ADJ sin fondo; **— supply** recursos ilimitados *m pl*; **— accusation** acusación infundada *f*; **he's a — pit** es un barril sin fondo

boudoir [búdwar] N tocador *m*

bough [baʊ] N rama *f*

bouillon [búljɑn] N caldo *m*

boulder [bóldəˑ] N peña *f*, pedrusco *m*

boulevard [búləvard] N bulevar *m*

bounce [baʊns] N (of a ball) bote *m*, rebote *m*; (vitality) vitalidad *f*; VT echar, botar; **to — a check** rebotar un cheque; VI rebotar; **to — back** recuperarse

bouncer [baʊnsəˑ] N gorila *m*

bound [baʊnd] N (jump) salto *m*; **—s** límite *m*, confín *m*; ADJ (tied up) atado; (confined) confinado; (obliged) obligado; (as a book) encuadernado; **to be — for** ir rumbo a; **to be — up in one's work** estar absorto en su trabajo; **it is — to happen** es seguro que pasará; **I am — to do it** estoy resuelto a hacerlo; VI (jump) saltar; (be contiguous) lindar

boundary [báʊndri] N (of a country, city) límite *m*, término *m*; (of a property) linde *mf*, lindero *m*

boundless [báʊndlɪs] ADJ ilimitado, sin límites

bountiful [báʊntəfəl] ADJ abundante

bounty [báʊnti] N (abundance) abundancia *f*; (reward) recompensa *f*

bouquet [bukéˑ] N (flowers) ramo *m*; (small) ramillete *m*; (of wine) aroma *m*, bouquet *m*

bourgeois [burʒwá] ADJ & N burgués -sa *mf*

bout [baʊt] N encuentro *m*; **a — of flu** una gripe

boutique [butík] N boutique *f*

bow [baʊ] N (gesture) reverencia *f*; (prow) proa *f*; VI (bend at the waist) hacer una reverencia; (yield) someterse; **to — out**

retirarse; vt inclinar; [bo] n (for arrows, violin) arco *m*; (curve) curva *f*; (decoration) moño *m*; —**knot** lazada *f*; —-**legged** patizambo; —-**string** cuerda de arco *f*; vi/vt (bend) arquear(se); (play with a bow) tocar con arco

bowel [báuɔł] n —**s** intestinos *m pl*; —**s of the earth** entrañas de la tierra *f pl*; — **movement** evacuación del vientre *f*

bower [báuɔ·] n enramada *f*

bowl [boł] n (container) bol *m*, tazón *m*; (dish) plato hondo *m*; (depression) cuenco *m*; (of a toilet) taza *f*; (of a pipe) cazoleta *f*; vt **to — over** apabullar, deslumbrar

bowling [bólɪŋ] n boliche *m*, bowling *m*; **let's go —** vamos al boliche; — **alley** boliche *m*, bolera *f*

box [baks] n caja *f*; (for jewelry) estuche *m*; (in the theater) palco de teatro *m*; (for the jury) tribuna *f*; (on a page) cuadro *m*; — **car** vagón de carga *m*; — **office** taquilla *f*; — **seat** asiento de palco *m*; vt (put in a box) meter en una caja; (hit) abofetear; (engage in sport) boxear

boxer [báksɔ·] n boxeador -ra *mf*, pugilista *mf*; (breed of dog) bóxer *m*; — **shorts** calzoncillo *m*

boxing [báksɪŋ] n boxeo *m*, pugilato *m*; — **glove** guante de boxeo *m*; — **ring** ring *m*, cuadrilátero *m*

boy [bɔɪ] n (baby) niño *m*; (young man) muchacho *m*, chico *m*; — **scout** boy scout *m*; —**friend** novio *m*

boycott [bóɪkat] vt boicotear; n boicoteo *m*, boicot *m*

boyhood [bóɪhud] n niñez *f*, juventud *f*

boyish [bóɪʃ] adj de muchacho

brace [bres] n (in construction) tirante *m*; (pair) par *m*; (printed character) corchete *m*; (of a carpenter) berbiquí *m*; —**s** (for teeth) aparato ortodóntico *m*; (for a leg) aparato ortopédico *m*; vt (against a shock) agarrarse; (support) asegurar; (with alcohol) animarse

bracelet [bréslɪt] n brazalete *m*, pulsera *f*

bracket [brékɪt] n (support) soporte *m*, sostén *m*; (typographic sign) paréntesis recto *m*, corchete *m*; (division) banda *f*; vt (fix with brackets) fijar con soportes; (write in brackets) colocar entre paréntesis rectos; (associate) agrupar

brag [bræg] vi jactarse (de), hacer alarde (de)

braggart [brégɔ·t] adj & n fanfarrón -na *mf*

braid [bred] n trenza *f*; vt trenzar

brain [bren] n cerebro *m*; (food) seso *m*; **she blew out his —s** le levantó la tapa de los sesos; **he's short on —s** es corto de

inteligencia; **he is the —s in this operation** él es el cerebro en esta operación; **to rack one's —s** devanarse los sesos, romperse la cabeza; — **drain** fuga de cerebros *f*; — **trust** grupo de expertos *m*; —**storming** brainstorming *m*; vt **to — someone** romperle la crisma a alguien; **to —wash** lavarle el cerebro a; —-**dead** clínicamente muerto, en estado vegetativo

brainy [bréni] adj sesudo

brake [brek] n freno *m*; — **drum** tambor del freno *m*; — **fluid** líquido para frenos *m*; —**man** guardafrenos *m sg*; — **shoe** zapata *f*; **to apply the —s** frenar; vi/vt frenar

bramble [brémbəł] n zarza *f*

bran [bræn] n salvado *m*; (for birds) afrecho *m*

branch [bræntʃ] n (of a plant, of a family) rama *f*; (of a train) ramal *m*; (of antlers) brazo *m*; (of a science) ramo *m*; (of a business) sucursal *f*; (of the armed forces) arma *f*; (in a computer program) bifurcación *f*; (of a river) tributario *m*; vi/vt ramificar(se)

brand [brænd] n (make, mark) marca *f*; (of humor, etc.) tipo *m*; (mark of disgrace) estigma *m*; — **name** marca *f*; —-**new** flamante, recién comprado; vt (burn) herrar, marcar; (stigmatize) estigmatizar; **to — as** tildar de, tachar de

brandish [brændɪʃ] vt blandir, esgrimir

brandy [brǽndi] n (fine) brandy *m*; (cheap) aguardiente *m*

brash [bræʃ] adj (impudent) descarado; (impetuous) impetuoso

brass [bræs] n (metal) latón *m*; (attitude) descaro *m*; (high-ranking officers) la plana mayor; — **instrument** instrumento de metal *m*; **to get down to — tacks** ir al grano; adj de latón

brassiere [brəzír] n sostén *m*

brat [bræt] n mocoso -sa *mf*

bravado [brəvádo] n alarde *m*

brave [brev] adj valiente, gallardo; n guerrero indio *m*; vt desafiar

bravery [brévəri] n valentía *f*, gallardía *f*

brawl [brɔł] n reyerta *f*, riña *f*, pelotera *f*; vi reñir

bray [bre] n rebuzno *m*; vi rebuznar

brazen [brézən] adj (impudent) descarado; (made of brass) de latón

brazier [brézɔ·] n brasero *m*

Brazil [brəzíł] n Brasil *m*

Brazilian [brəzíljən] adj & n brasileño -ña *mf*, brasilero -ra *mf*

breach [britʃ] n (opening) brecha *f*;

(infraction) infracción *f*; (severance)
ruptura *f*; **— of contract** incumplimiento
de contrato *m*; **— of faith** abuso de
confianza *m*; VT abrir una brecha; (violate
a law) violar, infringir

bread [brɛd] N pan *m*; **— basket** panera *f*; **—
box** panera *f*; **—winner** sostén de la
familia *m*; ADJ **—-and-butter** básico; VT
empanar

breadth [brɛdθ] N anchura *f*, ancho *m*; (size)
extensión *f*; (perspective) amplitud *f*

break [brek] VI (fracture) romperse; (pause)
parar; VT (a record) batir; (a code)
descifrar; (a law) violar; (news) dar,
divulgar; (a bone) fracturar; (a horse)
domar, desbravar; (a habit) quitar(se) (una
costumbre); (one's spirit) quebrar,
doblegar; (cause to go bankrupt) arruinar;
to — a promise romper una promesa,
faltar a la palabra; **to — a ten-dollar
bill** conseguir cambio para un billete de
diez dólares; **to — away** escaparse; **to —
down** (a person) descomponerse; (a car)
averiarse; (resistance) vencer; (continuity)
interrumpir; **to — even** quedar a mano;
to — into violentar; **to — loose**
liberarse; **to — out** (war) estallar; (one's
face) brotarse; (from prison) escaparse; **to
— up** (into pieces) quebrarse; (a
relationship) romper con; **—in** hurto con
escalo *m*; **—down** (analysis) análisis *m*;
(automotive) avería *f*; **—through**
adelanto *m*; (military) penetración *f*;
—water rompeolas *m sg*; N (weather)
cambio *m*; (from work) descanso *m*; (with
tradition) quiebre *m*, rompimiento *m*; (of
a bone) fractura *f*; (from prison) fuga *f*;
(opportunity) oportunidad *f*; **lucky —**
golpe de suerte *m*

breakable [brékəbəl] ADJ quebradizo,
rompible

breaker [brékə] N rompiente *f*

breakfast [brékfəst] N desayuno *m*; VI
desayunar

breast [brest] N seno *m*, pecho *m*; *fam* teta *f*;
(bird) pechuga *f*; **— cancer** cáncer de
mama *m*; **—stroke** (estilo) pecho *m*; VI/VT
to —-feed amamantar, dar de mamar

breath [brɛθ] N aliento *m*; *lit* hálito *m*;
(current of air) soplo *m*; **—taking**
impresionante; **in the same —** al mismo
tiempo; **out of —** sin aliento; **to catch
one's —** recobrar el aliento; **to hold
one's —** aguantar la respiración; **to take
a —** inhalar; **to take a deep —** respirar
hondo; **under one's —** entre dientes, por
lo bajo

breathe [brið] VI/VT respirar; **to — in**
inspirar, aspirar; **to — into** infundir; **to
— out** exhalar, espirar; **he did not — a
word** no dijo palabra

breathing [bríðɪŋ] N respiración *f*

breathless [brɛ́θlɪs] ADJ sin aliento

breed [brid] VT (mate) criar; (bring up)
educar; (give rise to) engendrar; VI
reproducirse, multiplicarse; N (species) raza
f; (type) clase *f*

breeder [brídə] N (person who breeds)
criador -ra *mf*; (animal used for breeding)
(animal) reproductor *f*

breeding [brídɪŋ] N (of animals) cría *f*;
(people) educación *f*, modales *m pl*

breeze [briz] N brisa *f*

breezy [brízi] ADJ (windy) ventoso; (jaunty)
ameno

brevity [brɛ́vɪdi] N brevedad *f*

brew [bru] VT (coffee) hacer; (mischief)
fomentar, tramar; (beer) fabricar; VI
(storm) armarse una tormenta; **let the
tea —** deja reposar el té; N (mixture)
mezcla *f*; (beer) cerveza *f*

brewery [brúəri] N cervecera *f*, fábrica de
cerveza *f*

briar [bráɪə] N zarza *f*

bribe [braɪb] N soborno *m*, cohecho *m*; *Mex*
mordida *f*; VT sobornar

bribery [bráɪbəri] N soborno *m*

brick [brɪk] N ladrillo *m*; **—bat** (piece of
brick) pedazo de ladrillo *m*; (insult) insulto
m; **—layer** albañil *m*; **—laying**
albañilería *f*; VT (adorn with bricks)
revestir de ladrillo; (pave with bricks)
enladrillar

bridal [bráɪdl] ADJ nupcial; **— dress** vestido
de novia *m*

bride [braɪd] N novia *f*; **—groom** novio *m*;
—smaid dama de honor *f*

bridge [brɪdʒ] N puente *m*; (of the nose)
caballete *m*; (card game) bridge *m*; VT
tender un puente sobre; **to — a gap**
llenar un vacío, salvar un obstáculo

bridle [bráɪdl] N (harness) brida *f*; (restraint)
freno *m*; VT (put on a bridle) embridar;
(restrain) frenar; VI (be insulted) ofenderse

brief [brif] ADJ (short) breve, escueto;
(concise) conciso, escueto; (curt) seco; N
sumario *m*, resumen *m*; (report)
expediente *m*; **—case** portafolio(s) *m sg*,
maletín *m*; **—s** calzoncillos *m pl*; **in —** en
suma; VT informar

briefing [brífɪŋ] N reunión para dar
instrucciones *f*

brigade [brɪgéd] N brigada *f*

bright [braɪt] ADJ (shining) brillante; (full

with light) iluminado; (smart) inteligente; (future) venturoso, prometedor; (smile) radiante; (color) subido

brighten [bráɪtn̩] VT (a room) iluminar; VI **to — up** (become cheerful) animar(se); (sky) despejarse

brightness [bráɪtnɪs] N (light) claridad *f*; (cheerfulness) viveza *f*; (intelligence) inteligencia *f*

brilliance [bríljəns] N (of hair, of a historical period) brillantez *f*; (intelligence) genio *m*

brilliant [bríljənt] ADJ (shining) brillante; (intelligent) genial; (splendid) espléndido; N brillante *m*, diamante *m*

brim [brɪm] N borde *m*; (hat) ala *f*; **to fill to the —** llenar hasta el borde; **to be filled to the —** estar de bote en bote; **to be —ming with** estar rebosante de; VI **to — over** rebosar

brine [braɪn] N salmuera *f*

bring [brɪŋ] VT traer; (cause) ocasionar, causar; **to — about** producir, ocasionar; **to — down** (kill) bajar; (depress) deprimir; **to — forth** (give birth) dar a luz; (produce) producir; **to — to a stop** parar; **to — together** reunir, juntar; **— oneself to do something** poder hacer algo; **to — a good price** redituar una buena ganancia; **to — up** (raise children) criar, educar; (mention) mencionar

brink [brɪŋk] N borde *m*; **on the — of** al borde de

brisk [brɪsk] ADJ (walk) rápido; (weather) fresco; (trading) activo

bristle [brɪsəl] N cerda *f*; VI erizar(se); **to — with** estar erizado de

bristly [brísli] ADJ (with bristles) erizado, cerdoso; (irascible) irascible

Britain [brítn̩] N Gran Bretaña *f*

British [brídɪʃ] ADJ británico

brittle [brídl̩] ADJ quebradizo, frágil

brittleness [brídl̩nɪs] N fragilidad *f*

broach [brotʃ] VT sacar a colación

broad [brɔd] ADJ (wide) ancho; (vast) vasto; (ample) amplio; **—cast** emisión *f*; **—cast station** emisora *f*; **—casting** (radio) radiodifusión *f*; (TV) transmisión por televisión *f*; **to —cast** (communicate electronically) transmitir, emitir, radiar; **— hint** insinuación clara *f*; **— jump** salto de longitud *m*; **—minded** tolerante; **—side** andanada *f*; **in — daylight** en pleno día; N *pej* tipa *f*

brocade [brokéd] N brocado *m*

broccoli [brákəli] N brócoli *m*, brécol *m*

brochure [broʃúr] N folleto *m*

broil [brɔɪl] VI/VT asar(se) (a la parrilla)

broiler [brɔ́ɪlɚ] N (oven) parrilla *f*; (chicken) pollo (para asar) *m*

broke [brok] ADJ **to be —** estar limpio, estar pelado; **to go —** irse a la quiebra

broken [brókən] ADJ (fragmented) roto, quebrado; (tamed) domado; (not functioning) descompuesto; (not continuous) interrumpido; **—down** averiado, descompuesto; **—English** inglés chapurrado / chapurreado *m*; **—hearted** deshecho, con el corazón destrozado

broker [brókɚ] N (intermediary) agente *mf*; (stock salesman) corredor -ra de bolsa *mf*

brokerage [brókɚɪdʒ] N agencia de corredores de bolsa *f*

bromide [brómaɪd] N bromuro *m*

bromine [brómin] N bromo *m*

bronchial [bráŋkiəl] ADJ bronquial; **— tube** bronquio *m*

bronchitis [braŋkáɪdɪs] N bronquitis *f*

bronco [bráŋko] N caballo no domado *m*

bronze [branz] N bronce *m*; VT broncear

brooch [brutʃ] N broche *m*, prendedor *m*

brood [brud] N pollada *f*, nidada *f*; VI/VT empollar; **to — over** rumiar

brook [bruk] N riachuelo *m*, cañada *f*; VT tolerar

broom [brum] N (tool) escoba *f*; (plant) retama *f*; **—stick** palo de escoba *m*

broth [brɔθ] N caldo *m*

brothel [bráθəl] N burdel *m*

brother [bráðɚ] N hermano *m*; **—-in-law** cuñado *m*; **Oh —!** ¡caray!

brotherhood [bráðɚhud] N hermandad *f*

brotherly [bráðɚli] ADJ fraternal

brow [brau] N (ridge of eye) arco súperciliar *m*; (eyebrow) ceja *f*; (forehead) frente *f*

brown [braun] ADJ (skin) moreno; (eyes, shoes, clothes) café, marrón; (hair) castaño; (dun) pardo; (tanned) bronceado; VI/VT dorar(se); N (color) café *m*, castaño *m*, moreno *m*, pardo *m*; **— bear** oso pardo *m*; **— rice** arroz integral *m*; **— sugar** azúcar moreno -na *mf*

brownie [bráuni] N bizcocho de chocolate *m*

browse [brauz] VT (leaf through) hojear; VI (graze) pacer, pastar; (surf the web) *Sp* navegar (la web); *Am* navegar (en la red)

browser [bráuzɚ] N navegador *m*

bruise [bruz] N (skin) moretón *m*, cardenal *m*, contusión *f*; (fruit) magulladura *f*, cardenal *m*; VI/VT magullar(se), machucar(se)

brunch [brʌntʃ] N brunch *m*, desayuno tardío *m*

Brunei [brunáɪ] N Brunéi *m*

Bruneian [brunáıən] ADJ & N bruneano -na mf

brunet, brunette [brunét] ADJ & N moreno -na mf, morocho -cha mf; *Cuba* trigueño -ña mf

brunt [brʌnt] N impacto m

brush [brʌʃ] N (tooth, clothes) cepillo m; (paint, shaving) brocha f; (artist's) pincel m; (vegetation) maleza f; (contact) roce m; **—-off** despedida brusca f; **—wood** (dead) broza f; (live) maleza f; VT (clean with a brush) cepillar; (touch lightly) rozar; **to — aside** echar a un lado; **to — up on** repasar; **to — off** (clean) quitar con cepillo; (reject) despedir bruscamente a alguien

brusque [brʌsk] ADJ brusco

Brussels sprouts [brásəłsprauts] N coles de Bruselas f pl, repollitos de Bruselas m pl

brutal [brúdl] ADJ brutal

brutality [brutǽlɪɾi] N brutalidad f

brute [brut] N (animal) bestia f; (person) bruto -ta mf; ADJ bruto

bubble [bʌ́bəł] N (in soap) pompa f; (in boiling water) borbollón m; (illusion) encanto m; **— bath** baño de burbujas m; **—gum** chicle de globo m; VI (make bubbles) borbotar, borbollar; (boil) bullir, hervir; **to — over with joy** rebosar de alegría

bubonic plague [bubánıkplég] N plaga bubónica f

buck [bʌk] N (goat) macho cabrío m; (deer) gamo m; (male of other animals) macho m; (leap of horse) respingo m; **— private** soldado raso m; **—shot** posta f, perdigón m; **—skin** gamuza f; **—toothed** de dientes salidos; **—wheat** trigo sarraceno m; **to pass the —** echarle el muerto a uno; VI (horse) respingar, corcovear; **to — a trend** oponerse; **to — up** cobrar ánimo

bucket [bʌ́kɪt] N cubo m, balde m; (of a loader) cuchara f; **— seat** asiento delantero individual m

buckle [bʌ́kəł] N (clasp) hebilla f; (kink in a board) torcedura f; VT (to clasp) abrocharse; (to bend) torcerse, pandearse; **to — down** esforzarse; **to — up** abrocharse

bud [bʌd] N botón m, retoño m; VI (make buds) echar retoños

buddy [bʌ́di] N camarada mf

budge [bʌʤ] VI moverse

budget [bʌ́ʤɪt] N presupuesto m; VT (money) presupuestar; (time, personal resources) administrar

buff [bʌf] N (leather) gamuza f; (tan color)

color beige m; (wheel for polishing) pulidor m; (devotee) aficionado m; **in the —** en cueros; ADJ (beige) de color beige; (muscular) musculoso; VT pulir

buffalo [bʌ́fələo] N bisonte m, búfalo m; **— wings** alitas f pl

buffer [bʌ́fə] N (in a computer) memoria intermedia f; (shock absorber) amortiguador m; (polishing device) pulidor -ra mf; **— zone** zona tampón f

buffet [bʌ́fɪt] N (blow) golpe m, puñetazo m; (shock) azote m; VT (hit) golpear; (hit repeatedly) azotar; [bəfé] N (cabinet) aparador m; (meal) buffet m

buffoon [bəfún] N payaso -a mf, bufón -ona mf

bug [bʌg] N bicho m; (disease-causing) microbio m, virus m; (for eavesdropping) micrófono oculto m; (in a computer program) fallo m, bicho m; VT (bother) molestar; (install microphones) colocar micrófonos ocultos; **his eyes —ged out** se le saltaron los ojos

buggy [bʌ́gi] N (cart) calesa f; (baby carriage) cochecillo m

bugle [bjúgəł] N clarín m; VI tocar el clarín

build [bɪld] VT (construct) construir, edificar; (manufacture) fabricar; **to — into** incorporar; **to — up** (make stronger) fortalecer; (accumulate) acumular; (enhance) desarrollar; (urbanize) urbanizar; **—-up** (of military forces) concentración f; (of substance) acumulación f; (of anticipation) aumento m; N (of human body) complexión f

builder [bɪ́łdə] N contratista mf

building [bɪ́łdɪŋ] N (thing built) edificio m, construcción f, edificación f; (act of building) construcción f, edificación f; (unit in a housing complex) bloque m; **— block** (solid mass) bloque (de construcción) m; (toy) cubo m; (essential element) elemento fundamental m

built [bɪłt] ADJ **—-in** (furniture appliance) empotrado; (feature) incorporado; **—-up** urbanizado

bulb [bʌłb] N (plant) bulbo m; (light) bombilla f; *Am* foco m

bulbous [bʌ́łbəs] ADJ bulboso

Bulgaria [bʌłgéria] N Bulgaria f

Bulgarian [bʌłgérian] ADJ & N búlgaro -ra mf

bulge [bʌłʤ] N bulto m, protuberancia f; VI abultar, hincharse

bulgy [bʌ́łʤi] ADJ abultado

bulk [bʌłk] N (mass) cantidad f, volumen m; (greater part) mayor parte f; **in — a** granel; VI **to — up** echar músculos

bulky [búłki] ADJ voluminoso

bull [buł] N toro m; **—dog** buldog m;
—dozer bulldozer m; **—fight** corrida de
toros f; **—fighter** torero m; **—fighting**
tauromaquia f; **—frog** rana grande f; **—
market** mercado alcista m; **—'s eye** diana
f; **to hit the —'s-eye** dar en el blanco;
ADJ **—headed** terco, obstinado

bullet [búlıt] N bala f; ADJ **—proof** antibalas
inv

bulletin [búlıtıŋ] N boletín m; **— board**
tablero m, cartelera f

bullion [búljən] N oro en lingotes m

bully [búli] N matón -ona mf, bravucón -ona
mf; VT intimidar

bulwark [búłwə·k] N baluarte m

bum [bʌm] N (lazy person) holgazán -ana mf;
(hobo) vagabundo -da mf; (sports fan)
fanático -ca mf; ADJ falso; VI holgazanear;
VT gorronear

bumblebee [bámbəłbi] N abejorro m, abejón
m

bump [bʌmp] VT chocar; **to — along** ir
dando tumbos; **to — off** despachar; **to —
into** toparse con; N (blow) choque m,
trastazo m; (lump) protuberancia f; (lump
on a person) chichón m

bumper [bámpə·] N parachoques m sg, tope
m; **— car** coche de choque m, autito
chocador m; **— crop** cosecha abundante f;
—-to-— traffic caravana de autos f; **—
sticker** autoadhesivo m

bumpy [bámpi] ADJ bacheado, lleno de
baches

bun [bʌn] N (bread) bollo m; (in hair) moño
m

bunch [bʌntʃ] N (group of things) manojo m;
(group of people) montón m, grupo m; (of
grapes, bananas) racimo m; (of flowers)
ramillete m; VI/VT juntar(se), agrupar(se)

bundle [bándł] N paquete m, fardo m,
envoltorio m; (of clothes) lío m, atado m;
(of belongings) hato m, petate m; (of
firewood) haz m; VT (tie together) liar,
atar; **to — up** abrigarse; **to — off**
despachar

bungalow [báŋgəlo] N bungaló m

bungee jumping [bándʒiʤʌmpıŋ] N bungee
m, puénting m

bungle [báŋgəł] VT estropear; VI chapucear

bunion [bánjən] N juanete m

bunk [bʌŋk] N (place to sleep) litera f;
(nonsense) tonterías f pl; **— bed** litera f; VI
dormir en una litera

bunker [báŋkə·] N búnker m

bunny [báni] N conejito m

buoy [búi] N boya f; VI boyar; **to — up**

mantener a flote, animar

buoyant [bóıənt] ADJ (floating) boyante,
flotante; (mood) optimista

bur [bɜ·] N abrojo m

burden [bɜ́·dṇ] N (load) carga f;
(responsibility) peso m; **— of proof** carga
de la prueba f; VT (heavily) recargar;
(oppressively) agobiar

burdensome [bɜ́·dṇsəm] ADJ agobiante,
gravoso

bureau [bjúro] N (government department)
oficina f, agencia f; (chest of drawers)
cómoda f

bureaucracy [bjurákrəsi] N burocracia f

bureaucrat [bjúrəkræt] N burócrata mf

burglar [bɜ́·glə·] N ladrón -ona mf; **— alarm**
alarma antirrobo f; **— proof** a prueba de
robos

burglary [bɜ́·gləri] N robo con allanamiento
m

burial [bériəł] N entierro m; **— place** lugar
de sepultura m

Burkina Faso [bə·kínəfáso] N Burkina Faso
m

burlap [bɜ́·læp] N arpillera f

burlesque [bə·lésk] ADJ burlesco; N
espectáculo de variedades m

burly [bɜ́·li] ADJ corpulento

Burma [bɜ́·mə] N Birmania f

Burmese [bə·míz] ADJ & N birmano -na mf

burn [bɜ·n] N quemadura f; **—out** surmenage
m; VI/VT quemar(se), abrasar(se); (a house)
incendiar(se); (food) quemar(se),
requemar(se); **he got —ed in the
transaction** lo estafaron en el negocio;
the bulb is still —ing la bombilla sigue
prendida; **the house is —ing** la casa se
está quemando; **the iodine —ed his
skin** el yodo le quemó la piel; **to — a
hole** hacer un agujero con algo; VI (by
heat, passion) arder, abrasar; **my skin —s**
me arde la piel; **he's —ing with desire**
arde en deseos; **to — down** incendiarse;
to — off (fog) disiparse; **to — out** (a
fuse) fundirse; (to be exhausted) agotarse;
to — up quemarse completamente

burner [bɜ́·nə·] N (person or thing that burns
something) quemador -ra mf; (on stove)
hornilla f; **Bunsen —** mechero Bunsen m

burning [bɜ́·nıŋ] ADJ (desire) ardiente,
abrasador; (question) urgente

burnish [bɜ́·nıʃ] VT bruñir

burp [bɜ·p] N eructo m; VI eructar, repetir

burrow [bɜ́·o] N madriguera f; VI (dig) hacer
madrigueras; (live) vivir en una
madriguera

burst [bɜ·st] VI reventar(se); **to — into**

irrumpir en; **to — into tears** romper en llanto; **to — out** salir disparado; **to — with laughter** estallar / reventar de risa; N **— of activity** explosión de actividad f; **— of laughter** carcajada f; **— of machine-gun fire** ráfaga de ametralladora f; **— of speed** aceleración f

Burundi [burúndi] N Burundi m

Burundian [burúndiən] ADJ & N burundés -esa mf

bury [béri] VT enterrar; (in sand) hundir; (corpse only) sepultar; **to be buried in thought** estar absorto / meditabundo

bus [bʌs] N autobús m, ómnibus m; Mex camión m; RP colectivo m; Chile micro m; Cuba guagua f; (in a computer) bus m; VT transportar en autobús

bush [buʃ] N (plant) arbusto m, mata f; (region) matorral m; **to beat around the — andarse por las ramas

bushed [buʃt] ADJ fatigado

bushel [búʃəl] N fanega f

bushing [búʃɪŋ] N buje m, cojinete m

bushy [búʃi] ADJ (whiskers) espeso; (plants) poblado de arbustos

business [bíznɪs] N (trade, store) negocio m; (occupation) ocupación f; (commercial activity) comercio m; **— card** tarjeta comercial f; **— day** día hábil m; **— hours** horas hábiles f pl, horario de atención al público m; **it is booming** el negocio florece; **—man** hombre de negocios m, negociante m; **— suit** traje m; **— transaction** negocio m, transacción comercial f; **—woman** mujer de negocios f, negociante f; **I'm tired of the whole — este asunto me tiene harto; **I mean — hablo en serio; **to do — with** comerciar con; **he has no — doing it** no tiene derecho a hacerlo; **it's none of your — no es asunto tuyo; **mind your own — no te metas en lo que no te importa

businesslike [bíznɪslaɪk] ADJ (efficient) eficiente; (cold) impersonal

bust [bʌst] N (statue, body part) busto m; VI/ VT (burst, hit, break) reventar; (force into bankruptcy) hacer quebrar; (lower in rank) degradar

bustle [bʌ́səl] N (noise) bullicio m; (movement) ajetreo m, tráfago m; VI (move busily) ajetrear(se); (be crowded) bullir

busy [bízi] ADJ ocupado, atareado; (overdecorated) recargado; **—body** entrometido -da mf; **— signal** señal de ocupado f; VI **to — oneself** ocuparse

but [bʌt] CONJ (on the contrary) pero; (excepting) sino; PREP menos; **any day — today** cualquier día menos hoy; **he's nothing — trouble** sólo da problemas; ADV **— for you** si no fuera por ti

butane [bjúten] N butano m

butch [butʃ] ADJ machote

butcher [bútʃə] N carnicero -ra mf; **—'s shop** carnicería f; VT (cattle) matar; (people) masacrar; (performance) estropear

butchery [bútʃəri] N carnicería f

butler [bʌ́tlə] N mayordomo m

butt [bʌt] N (rifle part) culata f; (of a cigarette) colilla f; (blow with head) topetazo m, cabezada f, cabezazo m; **the — of ridicule** el blanco de las burlas; VT embestir, topar; **to — in** entrometerse; **to — into a conversation** meter baza; Am meter la cuchara

butter [bʌ́tə] N mantequilla f; VT (bread) untar con mantequilla; (a cakepan) enmantecar; **—cup** botón de oro m; **— dish** mantequera f; **—fingers** manos de mantequilla mf sg; **—milk** suero de leche m; **—scotch** dulce de azúcar y mantequilla m

butterfly [bʌ́təflaɪ] N mariposa f; **— stroke** estilo mariposa m

buttery [bʌ́təri] ADJ mantecoso

buttocks [bʌ́dəks] N nalgas f pl, asentaderas f pl, cachas f pl

button [bʌ́tn] N botón m; **—hole** ojal m; VI/ VT abotonar(se); VT **to —hole** hacer ojales; **to —hole someone** detener a alguien

buttress [bʌ́trɪs] N apoyo m, sostén m; (of a building) contrafuerte m; VT apoyar, reforzar

buxom [bʌ́ksəm] ADJ (full-bosomed) pechugona; (fat and cheerful) frescachona

buy [baɪ] VT comprar; **to — into** dejarse convencer; **I don't — that** no me lo trago; **to — on credit** comprar a crédito; **to — off** sobornar; **to — in installments** comprar a plazos; **to — out** comprar la parte de; **to — up** acaparar; N (purchase) compra f; (bargain) ganga f

buyer [báɪə] N comprador -ra mf

buzz [bʌz] N zumbido m; (feeling of intoxication) borrachera f; (phone call) telefonazo m; **to give someone a — pegarle / echarle un telefonazo a alguien; **— saw** sierra circular f; VI zumbar; (group) murmurar; VT hacer zumbar; **to — the bell** tocar el timbre; **to — off** largarse

buzzard [bʌ́zəd] N buitre m

buzzer [bʌ́zə] N timbre m, chicharra f

by [baɪ] PREP por; **we drove — the church**

pasamos por la iglesia; **a 4 — 3 room** un cuarto de 4 por 3; **multiply 2 — 2** multiplica 2 por 2; — **the liter** por litro; **we live — the church** vivimos al lado de la iglesia; **she had a son — him** tuvo un hijo con él; — **and** — a la larga; — **dint of** a fuerza de; — **far** con mucho; — **night** de noche; — **the way** a propósito; — **chance** por casualidad; **piece — piece** pedazo a / por pedazo; — **this time tomorrow** mañana a esta hora; — **two o'clock** para las dos; ADV **the factory is close** — la fábrica está cerca; **the bus drove** — pasó el autobús

bye-bye [báibái] INTERJ ¡adiós! ¡chaucito!

bygones [báigɔnz] N **let — be** — lo pasado pisado

bylaw [báilɔ] N estatuto *m*

by-line [báilaɪn] N pie de autor *m*

bypass [báipæs] VT evitar; N desvío *m*; — **operation** bypass *m*

by-product [báiprɑdəkt] N subproducto *m*; (chemical) derivado *m*

bystander [báistændɚ] N persona presente *f*

byte [baɪt] N byte *m*, octeto *m*

Cc

cab [kæb] N (taxi) taxi *m*; (of a truck) cabina *f*; — **driver** taxista *mf*

cabaret [kæbəréi] N cabaret *m*

cabbage [kæbɪʤ] N col *f*, repollo *m*, berza *f*

cabin [kæbɪn] N (hut) cabaña *f*; (in an airplane) cabina *f*; (in a ship) camarote *m*

cabinet [kæbɪnɪt] N (for dishes) armario *m*; (for medicines) botiquín *m*; (for display) vitrina *f*; (department heads) gabinete *m*; —**maker** ebanista *mf*

cable [kébəl] N cable *m*; (on ships) amarra *f*; (telegram) telegrama *m*; — **car** funicular *m*, teleférico *m*; — **television** televisión por cable *f*, cablevisión *f*; VI/VT telegrafiar

caboose [kəbús] N furgón de cola *m*

cache [kæʃ] N (of weapons) alijo *m*; (in a computer) caché *m*

cachet [kæʃé] N caché *m*

cackle [kækəl] VI cacarear; (talk) parlotear; N cacareo *m*; (talk) parloteo *m*

cacophony [kəkáfəni] N cacofonía *f*

cactus [kæktəs] N cacto *m*, cactus *m*

cad [kæd] N *pej* canalla *mf*

cadaver [kədévɚ] N cadáver *m*

caddie [kædi] N caddy *m*, caddie *m*

cadence [kédns] N cadencia *f*

cadet [kədét] N cadete *mf*

cadmium [kædmiəm] N cadmio *m*

Caesarian section [sɪzériənsékʃən] N cesárea *f*

café [kæfé] N (coffee only) café *m*; (coffee and food) cafetería *f*

cafeteria [kæfɪtíriə] N cafetería *f*; (in school, factory) cantina *f*

caffeine [kæfín] N cafeína *f*

cage [keʤ] N jaula *f*; VT enjaular

cahoots [kəhúts] ADV LOC **in** — arreglados

cajole [kəʤól] VI/VT engatusar, persuadir con halagos

cake [kek] N pastel *m*, torta *f*; (sponge) bizcocho *m*; (soap) pastilla *f*; **a piece of** — pan comido; **to take the** — ser el colmo; VI/VT apelmazar(se)

calamine [kæləmaɪn] N calamina *f*

calamity [kəlæmɪdi] N calamidad *f*

calcium [kælsiəm] N calcio *m*

calculate [kælkjəlet] VI/VT calcular; **his actions were —d to fool us** con sus acciones trataba de engañarnos

calculating [kælkjəledɪŋ] ADJ calculador

calculation [kælkjəléʃən] N cálculo *m*

calculator [kælkjəlétɚ] N calculadora *f*

calculus [kælkjələs] N cálculo *m*

calendar [kælɪndɚ] N calendario *m*, almanaque *m*; — **year** año civil *m*

calf [kæf] N (animal) ternero -ra *mf*, becerro -rra *mf*; (of leg) pantorrilla *f*, canilla *f*; — **skin** piel de becerro *f*

caliber [kæləbɚ] N calibre *m*

calibrate [kæləbret] VT calibrar, graduar

calico [kæliko] N calicó *m*

caliper [kæləpɚ] N (on brakes) calibrador *m*; (for measuring) calibre *m*

call [kɔl] N (bird call, device for calling birds) reclamo *m*; (telephone call) llamada *f*; (summons) llamamiento *m*; (to the ministry) vocación *f*; **there's no — for panic** no hay motivo de alarma; **it's your —** tú decides; **within —** al alcance de la voz; VT (summon, by telephone, a name, a strike) llamar; (cry out) gritar; (a meeting) convocar; **she —ed me a liar** me llamó mentiroso; — **me back** llámame tú; **to — a meeting to order** abrir la sesión; VI/VT (birds) reclamar; **to — roll** pasar lista; VI (call out) gritar; **to — at a port** hacer escala en un puerto; **to — for** pedir; **to — off** cancelar; **to — on** (visit) visitar; (depend on) acudir a; **to — together** convocar; **to — up** llamar por teléfono

caller [kɔ́lɚ] N visita *f*, visitante *mf*; (by

telephone) persona que llama f; — **ID** identificador de llamadas m
calligraphy [kəlígrəfi] N caligrafía f
calling [kɔ́liŋ] N vocación f
callous [kǽləs] ADJ (having calluses) calloso; (insensitive) insensible
callus [kǽləs] N callo m
calm [kam] ADJ tranquilo, reposado, calmo; N calma f, tranquilidad f, sosiego m; VT calmar, tranquilizar, sosegar; **to — down** calmar(se)
calmness [kámnɪs] N calma f, tranquilidad f
calorie [kǽləri] N caloría f
calumny [kǽləmni] N calumnia f
cam [kæm] N leva f
Cambodia [kæmbóɾiə] N Camboya f
Cambodian [kæmbóɾiən] ADJ & N camboyano -na mf
camel [kǽməł] N camello m
cameo [kǽmio] N camafeo m; — **appearance** actuación especial f
camera [kǽmrə] N cámara fotográfica f; **—man** cámara m, camarógrafo m; **—woman** cámara f, camarógrafa f
Cameroon [kæmərún] N Camerún m
Cameroonian [kæmərúniən] ADJ & N camerunés -esa mf
camouflage [kǽməflɑʒ] N camuflaje m; VT camuflar
camp [kæmp] N (campsite) campamento m; (faction) bando m; **—fire** fogata f, hoguera f; **—ground** campamento m, cámping m; **—site** campamento m; **the Republican —** el campo republicano; VI/VT acampar
campaign [kæmpén] N campaña f; VI hacer campaña
camper [kǽmpɚ] N acampante mf, campista mf
camphor [kǽmfɚ] N alcanfor m
camping [kǽmpɪŋ] N cámping m, acampada f; **let's go —** vamos de camping / acampada
campus [kǽmpəs] N campus m
can [kæn] N lata f, bote m; — **of worms** caja de Pandora f; — **opener** abrelatas m sg; VT enlatar; V AUX — **you come tomorrow?** ¿puedes venir mañana? — **you see me?** ¿me ves? **I — ride a bicycle** sé andar en bicicleta; **a —do attitude** un espíritu emprendedor
Canada [kǽnəɾə] N Canadá m
Canadian [kənéɾiən] ADJ & N canadiense mf
canal [kənǽł] N canal m
canary [kənéri] N canario m
Canary Islands [kənériáɪlənz] N Islas Canarias f pl

cancel [kǽnsəł] VT cancelar; (a stamp) matasellar; (an order) anular; (writing) tachar
cancellation [kænsəléʃən] N cancelación f; (of an order) anulación f
cancer [kǽnsɚ] N cáncer m; — **patient** canceroso -sa mf; ADJ — **causing** cancerígeno
candelabrum, candelabra [kændəlábrəm -brə] N candelabro m
candid [kǽndɪd] ADJ franco, sincero
candidacy [kǽndɪɒəsi] N candidatura f
candidate [kǽndɪdɪt] N (for office) candidato -ta mf; (for a job) aspirante mf, postulante mf
candle [kǽndł] N vela f, candela f; (on the altar) cirio m; **—stick** candelero m
candor [kǽndɚ] N franqueza f
candy [kǽndi] N dulce m, caramelo m, confite m; (with chocolate) bombón m; — **store** bombonería f; VT confitar, acaramelar; (nuts) garapiñar; VI (syrup) cristalizarse
cane [ken] N (sugar) caña f; (walking) bastón m; — **chair** silla de mimbre f; **to beat with a —** bastonear, apalear
canine [kénaɪn] ADJ canino, perruno; N (canid) can m; (tooth) canino m
canister [kǽnɪstɚ] N lata f
canker [kǽŋkɚ] N úlcera f
cannery [kǽnəri] N fábrica de conservas f
cannibal [kǽnəbəł] N caníbal m
cannon [kǽnən] N cañón m; — **fodder** carne de cañón f
canny [kǽni] ADJ sagaz, astuto
canoe [kənú] N canoa f
canon [kǽnən] N (rule, melody) canon m; (priest) canónigo m
canopy [kǽnəpi] N (of a bed) dosel m; (of a building) toldo m
cantaloupe [kǽntlop] N melón m
canteen [kæntín] N (snack bar) cantina f; (container) cantimplora f
canvas [kǽnvəs] N (fabric) lona f; (for painting) lienzo m
canvass [kǽnvəs] VI/VT (poll) encuestar; (solicit votes) solicitar votos en; (solicit sales) buscar pedidos comerciales en; N solicitud f
canyon [kǽnjən] N cañón m
cap [kæp] N (head covering without visor) gorro m; (head covering with visor) gorra f; (of a bottle) tapa f; (of a pen) capucha f, contera f; (limit) tope m; (for capgun) fulminante m, pistón m; VT (to cover, put a cap on) tapar; (to complete) rematar; (to limit) limitar

capability [kepəbíliɒi] N capacidad *f*
capable [képəbəɫ] ADJ capaz
capacious [kəpéʃəs] ADJ amplio
capacity [kəpǽsiɒi] N capacidad *f*
cape [kep] N (clothing) capa *f*; (promontory) cabo *m*
caper [képə-] N (skipping) cabriola *f*; (prank) treta *f*, triquiñuela *f*; (crime) delito *m*; (food) alcaparra *f*; VI retozar
Cape Verde [kepvɝ́-d] N Cabo Verde *m*
Cape Verdean [kepvɝ́-dìən] ADJ & N caboverdiano -na *mf*
capillary [kǽpəleri] N & ADJ (vaso) capilar *m*
capital [kǽpidɫ] N (city) capital *f*; (wealth) capital *m*; (of a column) capitel *m*; (letter) mayúscula *f*; **to make — of** sacar partido de, aprovecharse de; ADJ (city) capital; (financial) de capital; **— gains** ganancias en bienes de capital *f pl*; **— investment** inversión de capital *f*; **— punishment** pena de muerte *f*
capitalism [kǽpidɫizəm] N capitalismo *m*
capitalist [kǽpidɫist] N capitalista *mf*
capitalistic [kæpidɫístik] ADJ capitalista
capitalization [kæpidɫizéʃən] N capitalización *f*
capitalize [kǽpidɫaiz] VT (finance) capitalizar; (write) escribir con mayúscula; **to — on** sacar provecho de
capitol [kǽpidɫ] N capitolio *m*
capitulate [kəpítʃəlet] VI capitular
cappuccino [kæpətʃíno] N capuchino *m*
caprice [kəprís] N capricho *m*
capricious [kəpríʃəs] ADJ caprichoso
capsize [kǽpsaiz] VI/VT volcar(se)
capsule [kǽpsəɫ] N cápsula *f*
captain [kǽptin] N capitán *m*; VT capitanear
caption [kǽpʃən] N (with illustration) pie *m*; (subtitle) subtítulo *m*
captivate [kǽptəvet] VT cautivar
captive [kǽptiv] ADJ & N cautivo -va *mf*; **— animals** animales en cautiverio *m pl*
captivity [kæptíviɒi] N cautiverio *m*
captor [kǽptə-] N captor -ra *mf*
capture [kǽptʃə-] VT (apprehend, record data) capturar; (attract) cautivar; (conquer) tomar; N captura *f*
car [kar] N (automobile) coche *m*, automóvil *m*; *Am* carro *m*, auto *m*; (railroad) vagón *m*, coche *m*; (elevator) cabina *f*; *Am* elevador *m*; **— bomb** coche bomba *m*; **—fare** pasaje *m*; **—jacking** secuestro de vehículo *m*; **—load** carga de un coche *f*; **—port** cochera *f*; **—sick** mareado; **he got —sick** se mareó en el coche; **— wash** túnel de lavado *m*
caramel [kǽrəməɫ] N caramelo *m*

carat [kǽrət] N quilate *m*
caravan [kǽrəvæn] N caravana *f*
carbohydrate [karbəháidret] N carbohidrato *m*, hidrato de carbono *m*
carbon [kárbən] N carbono *m*; **— copy** copia en papel carbón *f*; **— dioxide** dióxido de carbono *m*; **— monoxide** monóxido de carbono *m*; **— paper** papel carbón *m*
carburetor [kárbəreɒə-] N carburador *m*
carcass [kárkəs] N (of an animal) cuerpo muerto *m*; (human) cadáver *m*; (of a ship) casco *m*
carcinogen [karsínədʒən] N cancerígeno *m*, carcinógeno *m*
carcinoma [karsənómə] N carcinoma *m*
card [kard] N (piece of stiff paper) tarjeta *f*; (playing) naipe *m*, carta *f*; (for boxing events) programa *m*; (for textiles) carda *f*; (witty person) gracioso -sa *mf*; (in a computer) tarjeta *f*, placa *f*; **—board** (thick) cartón *m*; (thin) cartulina *f*; **— sharp** fullero -ra *mf*; **pack of —s** baraja *f*; **to play —s** jugar a la baraja, jugar a los naipes; **he's holding all the —s** tiene todas las ventajas; VT (comb) cardar; (ask for identification) pedir identificación
cardiac [kárdiæk] ADJ cardiaco, cardíaco
cardinal [kárdṇɫ] ADJ (number, main) cardinal; (colored red) rojo, bermellón; N (bishop, bird) cardenal *m*
cardiology [kardiáɫədʒi] N cardiología *f*
cardiovascular [kardiovǽskjəɫə-] ADJ cardiovascular
care [ker] N (worry) preocupación *f*; (attention) cuidado *m*, atención *f*, tiento *m*; (extreme attention) esmero *m*, primor *m*; **—free** despreocupado; **—giver** cuidador -ra *mf*; **to take — of** cuidar de, atender; (of a house) casero -ra *mf*; VI (be concerned, object) importarle a uno; **to — about** interesarle a uno, importarle a uno; **to — for** (look after) cuidar de; (love) tenerle cariño a; **to — to** tener ganas de; **I couldn't — less** me importa un rábano; **what does he —?** ¿a él qué le importa? **would you — for a drink?** ¿te puedo ofrecer algo?
careen [karín] VI ladearse a toda velocidad
career [karír] N carrera *f*, trayectoria *f*
careful [kérfəɫ] ADJ (cautious) cuidadoso, cauteloso; (painstaking) esmerado; **to be — tener cuidado
carefulness [kérfəɫnis] N cuidado *m*
careless [kérlis] ADJ descuidado
caress [kərés] N caricia *f*; VT acariciar
cargo [kárgo] N cargamento *m*
Caribbean [kærəbíən] N Caribe *m*; ADJ

caribeño

caricature [kǽrɪkətʃəʳ] N caricatura f; VT caricaturizar

caries [kériz] N caries f

carnage [kárnɪʤ] N carnicería f

carnal [kárnl] ADJ carnal

carnation [karnéʃən] N (flower) clavel m; (color) rosado m

carnival [kárnəvəl] N carnaval m; (traveling) feria f

carnivorous [karnívəəs] ADJ carnívoro, carnicero

carol [kǽrəl] N villancico m; VI cantar villancicos

carom [kǽrəm] N carambola f; VI rebotar

carotid artery [kərádɪdárɾəri] N (arteria) carótida f

carouse [kəráuz] VI andar de parranda

carp [karp] N carpa f; VI (complain) quejarse

carpenter [kárpəntəʳ] N carpintero -ra mf

carpentry [kárpəntri] N carpintería f

carpet [kárpɪt] N alfombra f; **—bagger** político -ca oportunista mf; VT alfombrar

carriage [kǽrɪʤ] N (wheeled vehicle) carruaje m, coche m; (posture) porte m

carrier [kǽriəʳ] N (one who carries) portador -ra mf; (postal worker) cartero -ra mf; (transport company) mensajería f

carrion [kǽriən] N carroña f

carrot [kǽrət] N zanahoria f

carry [kǽri] VT llevar; **do you — Italian wine?** ¿venden vino italiano? **the bill carried** se aprobó el proyecto de ley; **you — yourself well** te comportas bien; **he can't — a tune** no puede seguir una tonada; **this suitcase carries a lot** esta maleta es espaciosa; **to — away** llevarse; **he got carried away** se le fue la mano; **to — on** continuar; **to — out** (complete) llevar a cabo, ejecutar; (take out) sacar; **—on** de mano

cart [kart] N carro m; VT acarrear

cartilage [kárdlɪʤ] N cartílago m

carton [kártn] N caja de cartón f

cartoon [kartún] N (drawing) caricatura f; (strip) tira cómica f; (film) dibujo animado m

cartoonist [kartúnɪst] N caricaturista mf

cartridge [kártrɪʤ] N cartucho m; **— belt** cartuchera f, canana f

carve [karv] VI/VT (piece of wood) tallar; (a career) labrarse; (turkey) trinchar

carving [kárvɪŋ] N (action) tallado m; (figure) talla f; **— knife** trinchante m

cascade [kæskéd] N cascada f

case [kes] N caso m; (box) caja f; (of a pillow) funda f; **in — (that)** en caso de que; **in**

— it rains por si llueve; **in any —** en todo caso; **just in —** por si acaso; **get off my —!** ¡déjame en paz!

cash [kæʃ] N efectivo m; **— advance** anticipo en efectivo m; **— and carry** al contado y sin entrega a domicilio; **— flow** corriente en efectivo f; **— on delivery** entrega contra reembolso f; **— payment** pago en efectivo m; **— register** caja registradora f; **to pay —** pagar al contado; VT cobrar

cashew [kǽʃu] N marañón m, castaña de cajú f, Sp anacardo m

cashier [kæʃír] N cajero -ra mf; **—'s check** cheque de caja m

casino [kəsíno] N casino m

cask [kæsk] N tonel grande m

casket [kǽskɪt] N ataúd m

casserole [kǽsəroɫ] N (container) cazuela f; (food) guiso m

cassette [kəsét] N cassette mf, casete mf

cast [kæst] VT (throw) tirar, echar; (adapt) adaptar; (form an object) moldear, vaciar; (give out dramatic roles) repartir papeles; **to — a ballot** votar; **to — about** buscar; **to — a glance** echar un vistazo; **to — aside** desechar; **to — doubt** poner en duda; **to — light on** aclarar; **to — lots** echar suertes; **to — off** (a ship) soltar amarras; (something rejected) deshacerse de; **to — out** exiliar; **to be — down** estar abatido; N (form) molde m; (in theater) reparto m, elenco m; **— iron** hierro fundido m

castanet [kǽstənet] N castañuela f

caste [kæst] N casta f

castigate [kǽstɪget] VT (criticize) criticar, reprender; (punish) castigar

Castile [kæstíɫ] N Castilla f

Castilian [kæstíljən] N & ADJ castellano -na mf

casting [kǽstɪŋ] N (throwing) tiro m; (piece of metal) pieza fundida f; (selection of actors) cásting m

castle [kǽsəl] N castillo m; (chess piece) torre f, roque m

castor oil [kǽstəɔɪɫ] N aceite de ricino m

castrate [kǽstret] VT castrar; (animals) capar

casual [kǽʒuəɫ] ADJ (informal) informal; (offhand) al pasar

casualty [kǽʒuəɫti] N (of war) baja f; (in an accident) víctima f

cat [kæt] N (domestic) gato -ta mf; (others) felino m; **—'s meow** súmmum m; **—fish** siluro m

Catalan [kǽdlæn] ADJ & N catalán -ana mf; (language) catalán m

catalog, catalogue [kǽdlɔg] N catálogo m;

vt catalogar

Catalonia [kædǀónɪə] N Cataluña f

Catalonian [kædǀónɪən] ADJ catalán

catalyst [kædǀɪst] N catalizador m

cataract [kǽdərækt] N catarata f

catastrophe [kətǽstrəfɪ] N catástrofe f

catch [kæʧ] vt (a criminal, ball) atrapar; *Sp, Cuba* coger; (a fish) pescar, capturar; (someone in an act) pillar; (a bus) agarrar; (what someone said) comprender, agarrar; **to — a glimpse of** vislumbrar; **to — cold** resfriarse; **to — fire** prenderse fuego; **to — on** (understand) caer en cuenta; (become popular) ponerse de moda; **to — oneself** contenerse; **to — one's eye** llamarle a uno la atención; **to — sight of** avistar; **to — unawares** sorprender; **to — up** (with a person) alcanzar; (on work) ponerse al día; vi (get entangled) enredarse; (snap into place) agarrar; N (act of catching prey, quantity caught) captura f, redada f, pesca f; (prey) presa f; (device) pestillo m; (act of catching a ball) atrapada f; **—phrase** eslogan m; **he is a good —** es un buen partido; **to play —** jugar a la pelota; **what's the —?** ¿cuál es la treta?

catching [kǽʧɪŋ] ADJ contagioso

catchy [kǽʧɪ] ADJ pegadizo

catechism [kǽdɪkɪzəm] N catecismo m

category [kǽdɪgɔri] N categoría f

cater [kédə] vi/vt abastecer de alimentos (banquetes, fiestas, etc.); **to — to** atender a

caterpillar [kǽdəpɪlə] N (insect) oruga f; (tractor) tractor oruga m, caterpillar m

cathedral [kəθídrəl] N catedral f

catheter [kǽθɪdə] N catéter m, sonda f

cathode [kǽθod] N cátodo m; **— rays** rayos catódicos m pl

Catholic [kǽθlɪk] N & ADJ católico -ca mf

Catholicism [kəθólɪsɪzəm] N catolicismo m

CAT scan [kǽtskæn] N TAC f, tomografía axial computadorizada f

catsup [kǽʧəp] N cátsup m, ketchup m

cattle [kǽdl] N ganado (vacuno) m; **—man** ganadero m; **— rustler** cuatrero m; **— rustling** abigeato m

catty [kǽdɪ] ADJ hiriente

cauliflower [kólɪflauə] N coliflor f

cause [kɔz] N causa f; **— for celebration** motivo de celebración m; **the democratic —** la causa democrática; **without —** sin motivo; vt causar, ocasionar; (involving volition) motivar; **to — to flee** hacer huir; **the heat —d her to faint** el calor la hizo desmayar

caustic [kóstɪk] ADJ cáustico

cauterize [kódəraɪz] vt cauterizar

caution [kóʃən] N (prudence) cautela f, recato m; (warning) advertencia f; **—!** ¡cuidado! ¡atención! vt advertir; **to — against** desaconsejar

cautious [kóʃəs] ADJ cauto, cauteloso, precavido

cavalier [kævəlír] N caballero m, galán m; ADJ (disdainful) desdeñoso; (overly casual) displicente

cavalry [kǽvəlri] N caballería f

cave [kev] N cueva f, caverna f; **—man** hombre de las cavernas m; vi **to — in** ceder, derrumbarse, desplomarse

cavern [kǽvən] N caverna f, gruta f

cavity [kǽvɪdi] N cavidad f; (in a tooth) caries f; (nasal) fosa f

cavort [kəvórt] vi cabriolar, retozar

caw [kɔ] N graznido m; vi graznar

CD (compact disc) [sidí] N CD m, disco compacto m; **— player** reproductor de discos compactos m; **—-ROM** CD-ROM m

cease [sis] vi cesar; vt interrumpir; **—-fire** alto el fuego m; *Am* cese el fuego m

ceaseless [síslɪs] ADJ incesante

cedar [sídə] N cedro m

cede [sid] vt ceder

ceiling [sílɪŋ] N techo m, cielo raso m; (cap) tope m; (sky) altura máxima f

celebrate [séləbret] vi/vt celebrar, festejar

celebrated [sélabredɪd] ADJ célebre

celebration [seləbréʃən] N (action) celebración f, festejo m; (festivities) fiesta f

celebrity [səlébrɪdi] N celebridad f

celery [séləri] N apio m

celestial [səléstʃəl] ADJ celeste; (heavenly) celestial; **— body** astro m

celibate [sélabɪt] ADJ célibe

cell [sɛl] N (room) celda f; (structural) célula f

cellar [sélə] N sótano m; (for wine) bodega f

cello [ʧélo] N violonchelo m

cellophane [séləfen] N celofán m

cellular [séljələ] ADJ celular; **— phone** celular m; *Sp* móvil m

cellulite [séljəlaɪt] N celulitis f

celluloid [séljələɪd] N celuloide m

cellulose [séljəlos] N celulosa f

cement [sɪmént] N cemento m; (glue) adhesivo m; **— mixer** hormigonera f; vi/vt cementar

cemetery [sémɪteri] N cementerio m

censor [sénsə] N censor -ora mf; vt censurar

censorship [sénsəʃɪp] N censura f

censure [sénʃə] N censura f; vt censurar

census [sénsəs] N censo m; **to take a —** censar

cent [sɛnt] N centavo m, céntimo m

centennial [sɛnténiəł] ADJ & N centenario *m*

center [sɛntə·] N centro *m*; **— of gravity** centro de gravedad *m*; VI/VT centrar(se)

centigrade [sɛntɪgred] ADJ centígrado

centimeter [sɛntəmidə·] N centímetro *m*

centipede [sɛntəpɪd] N ciempiés *m*

central [sɛntrəł] ADJ central; (downtown) céntrico; N central de teléfonos *f*; **— heating** calefacción central *f*; **— nervous system** sistema nervioso central *m*; **— processing unit** unidad central de proceso *f*

Central [sɛntrəł] ADJ **— African Republic** República Centroafricana *f*; **— America** Centroamérica *f*

centralize [sɛntrəlaɪz] VI/VT centralizar(se)

centrifugal [sɛntrífəgəł] ADJ centrífugo

centripetal [sɛntrípɪtəł] ADJ centrípeto

century [sɛntʃəri] N siglo *m*

ceramic [sərǽmɪk] ADJ cerámico; N **—s** cerámica *f*

cereal [síriəł] N (breakfast food) cereal *m*; (the grain itself) grano *m*; ADJ cereal

cerebral [səríbrəł] ADJ cerebral; **— cortex** corteza cerebral *f*

ceremonial [serəmóniəł] ADJ & M ceremonial

ceremonious [serəmóniəs] ADJ ceremonioso

ceremony [sérəmoni] N ceremonia *f*

certain [sɜ́·tn̩] ADJ seguro; **— rules are inviolable** ciertas reglas son inviolables; **death are taxes** — lo único seguro son los impuestos y la muerte; **he's — to come** seguro que viene; **it is — that it rained** es cierto que llovió

certainly [sɜ́·tn̩li] ADV (without doubt) sin duda; **she — gets her way** no cabe duda de que se sale con la suya; INTERJ ¡cómo no!

certainty [sɜ́·tn̩ti] N certeza *f*, certidumbre *f*

certificate [sə·tífɪkɪt] N certificado *m*; **— of baptism** fe de bautismo *f*; **— of deposit** certificado de depósito *m*

certification [sɜ·ɾəfɪkéʃən] N certificación *f*

certify [sɜ́·ɾəfaɪ] VT certificar; **certified check** cheque certificado *m*; **certified mail** correo certificado *m*; **certified public accountant** contador -ora público -ca *f*

cervix [sɜ́·vɪks] N (neck) cerviz *f*; (uterine) cérvix *m*, cuello uterino *m*

cessation [seséʃən] N cese *m*

cesspool [sɛspuł] N pozo séptico *m*, fosa séptica *f*

Chad [tʃæd] N Chad *m*

Chadian [tʃǽdiən] ADJ & N chadiano -na *mf*

chafe [tʃef] VI/VT rozar(se); N rozadura *f*

chaff [tʃæf] N ahechaduras *f pl*

chagrin [ʃəgrín] N mortificación *f*; VT mortificar

chain [tʃen] N cadena *f*; **— reaction** reacción en cadena *f*; **— saw** sierra *f*; **— smoker** persona que fuma como una chimenea *f*; **— store** tienda de cadena *f*; VI/VT encadenar(se)

chair [tʃer] N silla *f*; (academic) cátedra *f*; (of a meeting) presidente -ta *mf*; (of a department) jefe -fa *mf*; **—man** presidente *m*, director *m*, jefe *m*; **—manship** dirección *f*; **—person** presidente -ta *mf*, jefe -fa *mf*; **—woman** presidenta *f*, jefa *f*

chalk [tʃɔk] N (substance) caliza *f*; (piece) tiza *f*; **—board** pizarrón *m*, pizarra *f*; VT marcar con tiza; **to — up** (attribute) atribuir; (score) marcar

chalky [tʃɔ́ki] ADJ de/con/como tiza

challenge [tʃǽlɪndʒ] N desafío *m*, reto *m*; (of a jury) recusación *f*; VT (defy) desafiar, retar; (take exception) cuestionar, disputar; (recuse) recusar; **to be vertically —d** ser muy bajito

chamber [tʃémbə·] N (legislative) cámara *f*; (in a palace) aposento *m*; (of a cannon) recámara *f*; **—maid** camarera *f*, mucama *f*; **— music** música de cámara *f*; **— of commerce** cámara de comercio *f*; **— pot** orinal *m*; **—s** (of a judge) despacho *m*

chameleon [kəmíljən] N camaleón *m*

chamois [ʃǽmi] N gamuza *f*

champagne [ʃæmpén] N champán *m*, champaña *mf*

champion [tʃǽmpiən] N campeón -ona *mf*; (of a cause) defensor -ra *mf*, paladín *m*; VT defender

championship [tʃǽmpiənʃɪp] N campeonato *m*

chance [tʃæns] N (opportunity) oportunidad *f*; (probability) probabilidad *f*; (unpredictable element) casualidad *f*, azar *m*; **by —** por casualidad; **game of —** juego de azar *m*; **to take a —** correr riesgo, arriesgarse; ADJ casual; VI arriesgarse; **we —d to meet him at the bar** nos encontramos con él en el bar por casualidad

chancellor [tʃǽnsələ·] N (chief minister) canciller *m*; (of a university) rector -ora de universidad *mf*

chandelier [ʃændəlír] N araña de luces *f*

change [tʃendʒ] VT cambiar; **to — clothes** cambiarse de ropa; **to — into** transformar; **to — trains** cambiar de tren; N cambio *m*; (money returned) vuelta *f*; *Am* vuelto *m*; (fresh clothes) muda de ropa *f*; **— of heart** cambio de opinión m

changeable [tʃéndʒəbəl] ADJ (variable) cambiante, variable; (fickle) inconstante, tornadizo; **— silk** seda tornasolada f

channel [tʃǽnəl] N canal m; (bed of stream) cauce m; VT canalizar, encauzar

chant [tʃænt] N (plain song) canto llano m; (hymn) cántico m; (repeated slogan) cantinela f; VI/VT (sing) cantar; (repeat a slogan) corear

chaos [kéas] N caos m

chaotic [keáʊɪk] ADJ caótico

chap [tʃæp] VI/VT cuartear(se), agrietar(se); N tipo m

chapel [tʃǽpəl] N capilla f

chaperon, chaperone [ʃǽpəron] N chaperón -ona f; VI ir de chaperón -ona

chaplain [tʃǽplɪn] N capellán m

chapter [tʃǽptə] N capítulo m

char [tʃɑr] VI/VT (reduce to ashes) carbonizar(se); (scorch) chamuscar(se)

character [kǽrɪktə] N carácter m; (of a novel) personaje m; **— actor** actor de carácter m; **Chinese —s** caracteres chinos m pl; **he's quite a —** es todo un personaje; **that's out of — for him** eso no es característico de él

characteristic [kænɪktərístɪk] ADJ característico; N característica f; (genetic) carácter m

characterize [kǽrɪktəraɪz] VT (describe) caracterizar; (attribute) calificar

charade [ʃəréd] N farsa f; **—s** charada f

charcoal [tʃɑ́rkol] N carbón de leña m; **— drawing** dibujo al carbón m

charge [tʃɑrdʒ] VT (ask price) cobrar; (load) cargar; (buy on credit) cargar a cuenta; (attack) embestir; **to — off a loss** restar una pérdida; **to — with a task** encargarle a alguien una tarea; **to — with murder** acusar de homicidio; N (mission) misión f, encargo m; (accusation) cargo m, acusación f; (charge in account) cargo m, débito m; (explosives, electricity) carga f; (attack) embestida f; **— account** cuenta de crédito f; **— card** tarjeta de crédito f; **there will be a — for delivery** se cobra entrega a domicilio; **to be in — of** estar a cargo de; **under my —** a mi cargo

charger [tʃɑ́rdʒə] N (for a battery) cargador m; (horse) corcel m

chariot [tʃǽriət] N carro de guerra m

charisma [kərízmə] N carisma m

charitable [tʃǽrɪɾəbəl] ADJ caritativo

charity [tʃǽrɪɾi] N (virtue, aid to the poor) caridad f; (institution) institución benéfica f, institución de beneficencia f; **to give to**

— dar dinero a las instituciones benéficas; **to live on** — vivir de la caridad

charlatan [ʃɑ́rlətən] N charlatán -ana mf

charm [tʃɑrm] N (attractiveness) encanto m, salero m; (trinket) dije m; (spell) sortilegio m, hechizo m; (amulet) talismán m, amuleto m; VT (delight) encantar; (influence) hechizar, subyugar

charming [tʃɑ́rmɪŋ] ADJ encantador, salero; Sp majo

chart [tʃɑrt] N (table) tabla f; (graph) gráfica f; (marine map) carta f; (of musical hits) lista de éxitos f; VT (in a table) tabular; (in a graph) graficar; (a region) cartografiar; **to — a course** trazar una ruta

charter [tʃɑ́rɾə] N (of a city) fuero m; (of an organization) estatuto m; (document granting rights) constitución f, carta f; (hire) flete m; **— flight** (vuelo) chárter m; **— member** socio fundador mf; VT (a corporation) aprobar los estatutos; (a flight) fletar

chase [tʃes] VT (hunt) cazar; (follow rapidly) perseguir; **to — after** correr tras; **to — away** ahuyentar; N caza f, persecución f

chasm [kǽzəm] N sima f

chassis [tʃǽsi] N chasis m, bastidor m

chaste [tʃest] ADJ casto, honesto

chastise [tʃǽstaɪz] VT (punish) castigar; (criticize) criticar

chastisement [tʃǽstáɪzmənt] N (punishment) castigo m; (criticism) crítica f

chastity [tʃǽstɪɾi] N castidad f, honestidad f

chat [tʃæt] N charla f; Mex plática f; **— room** chat m; VI charlar; Mex platicar

chattel [tʃǽdl] N (movable property) bien mueble m; (slave) esclavo -va mf

chatter [tʃǽdə] VI (jabber) cotorrear, parlotear; VT (click rapidly) castañetear; N (of speech) cotorreo m, parloteo m; (of teeth) castañeteo m; **—box** charlatán -ana mf, cotorra f

chauffeur [ʃofɚ] N chófer m

chauvinism [ʃóvənɪzəm] N (nationalist) chovinismo m; (sexist) machismo m

cheap [tʃip] ADJ (costs little) barato; (stingy) avaro; **life is — there** la vida no vale nada allí; **talk is —** hablar no cuesta nada; **to feel —** sentirse despreciable; **— shot** golpe bajo m; **—skate** tacaño -ña mf

cheapen [tʃípən] VI/VT (lower in price) abaratar(se); VT (lower in esteem) desvalorizar

cheapness [tʃípnɪs] N (low price) baratura f; (stinginess) avaricia f

cheat [tʃit] N tramposo -sa mf, fullero -ra mf; VT engañar; **to — at cards** hacer trampa en / a las cartas, trampear; **to — on a test** copiar; **to — on one's spouse** engañar a la pareja de uno

check [tʃɛk] VT (stop) refrenar; (restrain) reprimir; (hand over luggage) facturar; (hand over coat) dejar; (verify) verificar; *Am* chequear; (in chess) dar jaque; **to — against** cotejar con; **to — into a hotel** registrarse; **to — into something** averiguar algo; **to — off** puntear; **to — out a book** sacar (prestado) un libro; **to — up on** controlar; **—up** examen / control médico *m*; **—out counter** caja *f*; **—point** control *m*; **—room** guardarropa *m*; **that —s out** lo hemos comprobado; N (bank) cheque *m*; (means of restraint) control *m*; (ticket) ficha *f*; (mark) marca *f*; (in a restaurant) cuenta *f*; (in fabric) cuadro *m*; (checked fabric) tela a cuadros *f*; (examination) comprobación *f*; (in chess) jaque *m*; **—book** chequera *f*, talonario *m*; **—ing account** cuenta corriente *f*; **—list** lista de control *f*; **—mate** jaque mate *m*; **— stub** talón *m*

checker [tʃɛkɚ] N (on a fabric) cuadro *m*; (on a checkerboard) casilla *f*; (game piece) ficha *f*; (cashier) cajero -ra *mf*; (person who checks) verificador -ra *mf*; **— board** tablero *m*; **—s** juego de damas *m*; VT cuadricular; **—ed cloth** tela a cuadros *f*; **—ed past** pasado oscuro *m*

cheek [tʃik] N (on face) mejilla *f*; *Am* cachete *m*; (impudence) descaro *m*; (of buttocks) nalga *f*; **— bone** pómulo *m*

cheer [tʃɪr] N (shout) viva *m*, vítor *m*; (applause) aplausos *m pl*; (encouragement) ánimo *m*; (joy) alegría *f*; **—leader** animador -ra *mf*; *Am* porrista *mf*; INTERJ **—s!** ¡salud! VI/VT vitorear; **to — on** dar ánimo; **to — up** animar(se)

cheerful [tʃɪrfəl] ADJ (person) risueño, alegre; (room, etc.) alegre

cheerfulness [tʃɪrfəlnɪs] N alegría *f*

cheerless [tʃɪrlɪs] ADJ triste, sombrío

cheese [tʃiz] N queso *m*; **—burger** hamburguesa con queso *f*; **—cake** tarta de queso *f*

cheesy [tʃizi] ADJ (of cheese) de queso; (cheap) barato; (uncool) *Sp* hortera

cheetah [tʃitə] N guepardo *m*

chef [ʃɛf] N chef *mf*

chemical [kɛmɪkəl] ADJ químico; **— engineering** ingeniería química *f*; **— warfare** guerra química *f*; N producto químico *m*

chemist [kɛmɪst] N químico -ca *f*

chemistry [kɛmɪstri] N química *f*

chemotheraphy [kimoθɛrəpi] N quimioterapia *f*

cherish [tʃɛrɪʃ] VT apreciar; **I — the memory of him** tengo muy buenos recuerdos de él

cherry [tʃɛri] N cereza *f*; **— tree** cerezo *m*

chess [tʃɛs] N ajedrez *m*; **—board** tablero de ajedrez *m*

chest [tʃɛst] N (box) arca *f*; (body part) pecho *m*; **— of drawers** cómoda *f*

chestnut [tʃɛsnʌt] N castaña *f*; **— tree** castaño *m*; ADJ castaño; (horse) zaino

chew [tʃu] VT (food) masticar; (non-food) mascar; **—ing gum** goma de mascar *f*; *Am* chicle *m*; **to — a hole** hacer un agujero a mordiscones; **to — out** reprender; **to — over** meditar sobre; **to — up** romper a mordiscones; N mascada *f*, bocado *m*

chewy [tʃui] ADJ correoso

chic [ʃik] ADJ & N chic *m*

chick [tʃik] N (young chicken) pollito *m*; (young bird) pichón *m*; (young woman) *fam* chavala *f*; **—pea** garbanzo *m*

chicken [tʃikɪn] N (flesh) pollo *m*; (bird) gallina *f*; **— coop** gallinero *m*; **—-hearted** cobarde; **— pox** varicela *f*

chicory [tʃikəri] N achicoria *f*

chide [tʃaɪd] VT regañar

chief [tʃif] N jefe *m*; (of a tribe) cacique *m*; ADJ principal; **— justice** presidente de la Suprema Corte de los Estados Unidos *m*; **— of staff** (military) jefe del estado mayor *m*; (of a division) secretario -ria general *mf*

chieftain [tʃiftən] N cacique *m*

chiffon [ʃifán] N chifón *m*

chigger [tʃigɚ] N nigua *f*

chilblain [tʃɪlblen] N sabañón *m*

child [tʃaɪld] N (young person) niño -ña *mf*; (offspring) hijo -ja *mf*; **—bearing** en edad de procrear; **—birth** parto *m*, alumbramiento *m*; **—like** infantil, aniñado; **—proof** a prueba de niños; **—'s play** cosa de niños *f*; **to be with —** estar embarazada

childhood [tʃaɪldhud] N niñez *f*, infancia *f*

childish [tʃaɪldɪʃ] ADJ infantil, pueril

childless [tʃaɪldlɪs] ADJ sin hijos

Chile [tʃili] N Chile *m*

Chilean [tʃiliən] ADJ & N chileno -na *mf*

chili, chile [tʃili] N (pepper) chile *m*, ají *m*; (meat dish) chile con carne *m*

chill [tʃɪl] N (coldness) frío *m*; (fear, cold with shivering) escalofrío *m*; **it had a —ing effect on the group** le cayó al grupo como un baldazo de agua fría; VI/VT

enfriar(se); **to — out** tranquilizarse
chilly [tʃíli] ADJ frío
chime [tʃaɪm] N (sound) repique *m*;
(instrument) carillón *m*, carrillón *m*; VI
repicar; VT tañer; **to — in** intervenir (en
una conversación)
chimney [tʃímni] N chimenea *f*
chimpanzee [tʃɪmpænzí] N chimpancé *m*
chin [tʃɪn] N barbilla *f*, mentón *m*
china [tʃáɪnə] N (material) porcelana *f*, china
f; (dishes) vajilla de porcelana *f*, china *f*;
—ware vajilla de porcelana *f*
China [tʃáɪnə] N China *f*
Chinese [tʃaɪníz] ADJ chino; N (inhabitant of
China) chino -na *mf*; (language) chino *m*
chink [tʃɪŋk] N grieta *f*
chip [tʃɪp] N (of wood) astilla *f*; (in glass)
desportilladura *f*; (in gambling) ficha *f*; (in
computers) chip *m*; **he's a — off the old
block** de tal palo, tal astilla; **he has a —
on his shoulder** guarda resentimientos;
VI/VT (wood) astillar(se); (glass, plaster)
desportillarse, desconchar(se); (paint)
descascarar(se); **to — in** contribuir; **to —
a tooth** romperse un diente
chipmunk [tʃípmʌŋk] N ardilla listada *f*
chiropractic [kaɪrəpræktɪk] ADJ
quiropráctico; N quiropráctica *f*
chiropractor [káɪrəpræktɚ] N quiropráctico
-ca *mf*
chirp [tʃɚp] N gorjeo *m*; VI/VT piar, gorjear
chisel [tʃízəl] N escoplo *m*; (for stone) cincel
m; (for wood) formón *m*; VT cincelar;
(swindle) estafar
chiseler [tʃízlɚ] N estafador -ra *mf*
chit-chat [tʃíttʃæt] N palique *m*; VI charlar
chivalrous [ʃívəlrəs] ADJ (of knights)
caballeresco; (courteous to women)
caballeroso
chivalry [ʃívəlri] N caballerosidad *f*
chloride [klɔ́raɪd] N cloruro *m*
chlorine [klɔ́rin] N cloro *m*
chloroform [klɔ́rəfɔrm] N cloroformo *m*
chlorophyl, chlorophyll [klɔ́rəfɪl] N
clorofila *f*
chocolate [tʃáklɪt] N chocolate *m*; (piece)
chócolatina *f*; **— pot** chocolatera *f*
choice [tʃɔɪs] N (act of selecting, thing
selected) selección *f*; (alternative) opción *f*;
to have no other — no tener más
remedio; ADJ selecto
choir [kwaɪr] N coro *m*
choke [tʃok] VI/VT (suffocate) ahogar(se);
(strangle) estrangular(se); (on food)
atragantarse, atorarse; (obstruct) tapar(se);
VI (in sports) bloquearse; **I'm all —d up**
estoy muy conmovido; **to — back /**

down contener; N (act of choking on
something) atragantamiento *m*; (act of
choking someone) estrangulación *f*;
(device in cars) obturador *m*; (in sports)
bloqueo *m*
cholera [kálə·ə] N cólera *m*
cholesterol [kaléstɚɔl] N colesterol *m*
choose [tʃuz] VI/VT elegir, seleccionar,
escoger; **to — to** optar por
choosy [tʃúzi] ADJ quisquilloso
chop [tʃap] VI/VT cortar; **to — down** talar;
to — off mochar, tronchar; **to — up**
picar; N (act of chopping) golpe *m*; (cut of
meat) chuleta *f*; **—s** morro *m*; **—stick**
palillo *m*
choppy [tʃápi] ADJ picado, agitado
choral [kɔ́rəl] ADJ coral
chord [kɔrd] N (mathematical) cuerda *f*;
(musical) acorde *m*; **it struck a — in me**
me conmovió
chore [tʃɔr] N tarea *f*, faena *f*, quehacer *m*;
it's such a — es un trabajo asqueroso
choreography [kɔriógrəfi] N coreografía *f*
chorus [kɔ́rəs] N coro *m*
chosen [tʃózən] ADJ **my — profession** la
profesión de mi preferencia; **the — one** el
elegido, la elegida
christen [krísən] VT bautizar
Christendom [krísəndəm] N cristianismo *m*
christening [krísənɪŋ] N bautizo *m*,
bautismo *m*
Christian [krístʃən] ADJ & N cristiano -na *mf*;
— name nombre de pila *m*
Christianity [krɪstʃiǽnɪdi] N cristianismo *m*
Christmas [krísməs] N Navidad *f*, Pascua de
Navidad *f*; ADJ navideño; **— card** tarjeta
de Navidad *f*; **— Eve** Nochebuena *f*; **—
gift** regalo de Navidad *m*; **— tree** árbol
de Navidad *m*
chrome [krom] N cromo *m*; ADJ cromado
chromium [krómiəm] N cromo *m*
chromosome [króməsom] N cromosoma *m*
chronic [kránɪk] ADJ crónico
chronicle [kránɪkəl] N crónica *f*; VT registrar
chronological [krɑnládʒɪkəl] ADJ
cronológico
chronology [krənáləʤi] N cronología *f*
chronometer [krənámɪdɚ] N cronómetro *m*
chrysalis [krísəlɪs] N crisálida *f*
chrysanthemum [krɪsǽnθəməm] N
crisantemo *m*
chubby [tʃʌbi] ADJ rechoncho, gordito
chuck [tʃʌk] N (cut of meat) paletilla *f*; VT (to
throw) lanzar; (to discard) tirar, botar
chuckle [tʃʌkəl] N risita *f*; VI reírse levemente
chum [tʃʌm] N compinche *mf*
chunk [tʃʌŋk] N trozo *m*, pedazo *m*; **a — of**

cash un montón de plata
church [tʃɚtʃ] N iglesia *f*; **—man** clérigo *m*
churn [tʃɚn] N mantequera *f*; VI/VT (make butter) batir; (agitate) agitar, revolver
CIA (Central Intelligence Agency) [siaié] N CIA *f*
cicada [sɪkédə] N chicharra *f*
cider [sáɪdə] N (alcoholic) sidra *f*; (non-alcoholic) *Am* jugo de manzana *m*; *Sp* zumo de manzana *m*
cigar [sɪgár] N puro *m*, habano *m*; **— store** tabaquería *f*; **close, but no —** bien, pero te quedaste corto
cigarette [sɪgarét] N cigarrillo *m*; *Sp* pitillo *m*; *Am* cigarro *m*; **— case** cigarrera *f*; *Sp* pitillera *f*; **— holder** boquilla *f*; **— lighter** encendedor *m*
cinch [sɪntʃ] N (for a saddle) cincha *f*; (something easy) pan comido *m*; (favorite) favorito -ta *mf*; VT cinchar
cinder [síndə] N ceniza *f*, rescoldo *m*
cinema [sínəmə] N cine *m*
cinnamon [sínəmən] N canela *f*; **— tree** canelo *f*
cipher [sáɪfə] N cifra *f*, guarismo *m*; VI/VT cifrar(se)
circle [sɚkəl] N círculo *m*; (literary) ámbito *m*, círculo *m*; VT (draw a circle) encerrar en un círculo; VI (go around) dar una vuelta
circuit [sɚkɪt] N circuito *m*; **— board** circuito impreso *m*; **— breaker** cortacircuitos *m*
circuitry [sɚkɪtri] N circuitería *f*
circular [sɚkjələ] ADJ circular; **— saw** sierra circular *f*; N circular *f*
circulate [sɚkjəlet] VI circular; VT (to pass around) poner en circulación
circulation [sɚkjəléʃən] N circulación *f*
circulatory system [sɚkjələtɔrɪsɪstəm] N aparato circulatorio *m*
circumcise [sɚkəmsaɪz] VT circuncidar
circumcise [sɚkəmsaɪz] VT circuncidar
circumference [səkámfəəns] N circunferencia *f*
circumlocution [sɚkəmlokjúʃən] N circunlocución *f*, rodeo *m*
circumscribe [sɚkəmskráɪb] VT circunscribir
circumspect [sɚkəmspɛkt] ADJ circunspecto
circumstance [sɚkəmstæns] N circunstancia *f*; **—s** condiciones financieras *f pl*
circumstantial [sɚkəmstǽnʃəl] ADJ circunstancial; **— evidence** pruebas circunstanciales *f pl*
circumvent [sɚkəmvént] VT evitar, obviar
circus [sɚkəs] N circo *m*
cirrhosis [sɪrósɪs] N cirrosis *f*
cirrus [síɾəs] N cirro *m*
cistern [sístən] N cisterna *f*, aljibe *m*

citadel [sídədəl] N ciudadela *f*
citation [saɪtéʃən] N (summons) citación *f*; (quote, quotation) cita *f*; (commendation for bravery) mención *f*
cite [saɪt] VT (quote, summon) citar; (comment on) mencionar
citizen [sídɪzən] N (of a nation) ciudadano -na *mf*; (of a city or region) habitante *mf*
citizenship [sídɪzənʃɪp] N ciudadanía *f*
citrus [sítɾəs] ADJ & N cítrico *m*
city [sídi] N ciudad *f*; ADJ municipal, urbano; **— council** concejo *m*; **— hall** ayuntamiento *m*; **— planning** urbanismo *m*
civic [sívɪk] ADJ cívico; N **—s** educación cívica *f*
civil [sívəl] ADJ (civilian) civil; (polite) cortés; **— disobedience** desobediencia civil *f*; **— engineer** ingeniero -ra civil *mf*; **— rights** derechos civiles *m pl*; **— service** administración pública *f*; **— war** guerra civil *f*
civilian [sɪvíljən] ADJ & N civil *mf*
civility [sɪvílɪdi] N civilidad *f*, cortesía *f*
civilization [sɪvəlɪzéʃən] N civilización *f*
civilize [sívəlaɪz] VT civilizar
clad [klæd] ADJ vestido
claim [klem] VT (demand) reclamar, reivindicar; (assert) sostener, pretender; (notify of the existence of) denunciar; **to — to be** pretender ser; N (demand) reclamación *f*, reclamo *m*; (assertion) afirmación *f*; (right) derecho *m*, título *m*; (on insurance) demanda *f*, denuncia *f*
claimant [klémənt] N demandante *mf*, reclamante *mf*; (to the throne) pretendiente *mf*
clairvoyant [klɛrvɔ́ɪənt] ADJ & N clarividente *mf*
clam [klæm] N almeja *f*; VI **to — up** callarse
clamber [klǽmbə] VI/VT (climb with effort) trepar con dificultad; (climb on all fours) subir gateando
clammy [klǽmi] ADJ frío y húmedo
clamor [klǽmə] N clamor *m*, vocerío *m*; VI clamar, vociferar
clamorous [klǽməəs] ADJ clamoroso
clamp [klæmp] N (support) grapa *f*; (vice) tornillo *m*; (wrap-around) abrazadera *f*; VT sujetar; **to — down on** reprimir
clan [klæn] N clan *m*
clandestine [klændéstɪn] ADJ clandestino
clang [klæŋ] VI sonar; N sonido metálico *m*
clap [klæp] N (tap) palmada *f*; (blow) golpe seco *m*; **— of thunder** trueno *m*; VT (on the back) palmear; (in approval) aplaudir; (a book) cerrar de golpe; **to — in jail**

meter en la cárcel
clapper [klǽpɚ] N badajo *m*
clarification [klærəfɪkéʃən] N aclaración *f*
clarify [klǽrəfaɪ] VT aclarar, clarificar
clarinet [klærənét] N clarinete *m*
clarity [klǽrɪDi] N claridad *f*
clash [klæʃ] N (noise) estruendo metálico *m*; (collision) choque *m*; (conflict) conflicto *m*, enfrentamiento *m*; VI/VT (collide) chocar; (oppose, fight) enfrentarse a; (not go with) no combinar, no pegar
clasp [klæsp] N (fastener) broche *m*, cierre *m*; (grip) apretón *m*; VT (fasten) abrochar; (grip) apretar; (embrace) abrazar, prender
class [klæs] N clase *f*; (graduation class) promoción *f*, graduación *f*; **in a — by itself** único; **—mate** compañero -ra de clase *mf*, condiscípulo -la *mf*; **—room** salón de clase *m*, aula *f*; **— struggle** lucha de clases *f*; VI/VT clasificar(se)
classic [klǽsɪk] ADJ & N clásico -ca *mf*
classical [klǽsɪkəl] ADJ clásico
classicism [klǽsəsɪzəm] N clasicismo *m*
classification [klæsəfɪkéʃən] N clasificación *f*
classify [klǽsəfaɪ] VT clasificar; N **classified ad** anuncio clasificado *m*
clatter [klǽDɚ] N (noise) estrépito *m*; (movement) traqueteo *m*; VI (make noise) causar estrépito; (move) traquetear
clause [klɔz] N cláusula *f*
claustrophobia [klɔstrəfóbiə] N claustrofobia *f*
claustrophobic [klɔstrəfóbɪk] ADJ claustrofóbico
clavicle [klǽvɪkəl] N clavícula *f*
claw [klɔ] N (of a bear) garra *f*, zarpa *f*; (of a cat) uña *f*; (of a crab) pinza *f*; (of a hammer) orejas *f pl*; VI/VT arañar; **they —ed their way through** se abrieron paso con las uñas
clay [kle] N arcilla *f*; (for ceramics) greda *f*
clean [klin] ADJ limpio; (free from impurities, not ornate) puro; (honorable) decente; **—cut** (person) acicalado; (concept) bien definido; **— joke** broma inocente *f*; **—shaven** afeitado; **—up** limpieza *f*; **he has a — record** no tiene antecedentes; **you'd better come —** deberías confesar; VI/VT limpiar; **he —ed me out** me limpió, me desvalijó; **to — out** something vaciar algo; **to — up** (a room) limpiar, asear; (a document) pasar en limpio; (get rich) forrarse
cleaner [klínɚ] N limpiador -ra *mf*; **—s** tintorería *f*
cleanliness [klénlinɪs] N limpieza *f*; (personal) aseo *m*

cleanse [klɛnz] VT limpiar
cleanser [klɛnzɚ] N limpiador *m*
clear [klir] ADJ claro; (skin, conscience) limpio; (sky) despejado; (path) libre; **—cut** (clearly defined) bien definido; (obvious) claro; **—headed** lúcido; **— profit** ganancia neta *f*; **to be in the —** estar libre de culpa; **to keep — of someone** evitar a alguien; **to pass — through** pasar de lado a lado; VT (the mind, confusion, voice) aclarar(se); (a road, one's reputation, computer screen) limpiar; (of criminal charges) absolver; (of suspicion) eximir; (liquid) clarificar; (a legislative bill, plan) aprobar, obtener autorización para; (land for farming) desmontar; (a hurdle) salvar; (a net gain) sacar; **to — the air** sincerarse; **to — the table** levantar la mesa; **to — up** (a mystery) aclarar(se); (the sky) despejar(se)
clearance [klírəns] N (space) espacio libre *m*; (vertical) margen de altura *m*; (permission) autorización *f*; **— sale** liquidación *f*
clearing [klírɪŋ] N (terrain) claro *m*; (of checks) clearing *m*; **— house** banco de compensación *m*
cleavage [klívɪʤ] N (cut) hendidura *f*; (in dress) escote *m*
cleave [kliv] VT hender(se); **to — to** adherirse a
cleaver [klívɚ] N cuchilla *f*
clef [klɛf] N clave *f*
cleft [klɛft] N hendidura *f*; ADJ hendido, partido; **— palate** paladar hendido *m*
clemency [klémənsi] N clemencia *f*
clench [klɛntʃ] VT agarrar, asir; (teeth, fist) apretar
clergy [klɝ́ʤi] N clero *m*, clerecía *f*; **—man** clérigo *m*, pastor *m*; **—woman** pastora *f*
clerical [klérɪkəl] ADJ (of the clergy) clerical, eclesiástico; (of office personnel) de oficina; **— error** error de copia *m*; **— work** trabajo de escritorio *m*
clerk [klɝk] N (sales) dependiente -ta *mf*; (office) empleado -da de oficina *mf*; (court) escribiente *mf*, actuario -ria *mf*; VI trabajar como actuario -ria
clever [klévɚ] ADJ (ingenious) ingenioso; (smart) listo, vivo; (dexterous) habilidoso
cleverness [klévɚnɪs] N (intelligence) inteligencia *f*, viveza *f*; (ingenuity) ingenio *m*; (dexterity) habilidad *f*
cliché [kliʃé] N cliché *m*, muletilla *f*; *Sp* tópico *m*
click [klɪk] N clic *m*, chasquido *m*; (sound of heels) taconeo *m*; VI chascar; (on a computer) hacer clic; (heels) taconear; VT

chascar, chasquear

client [kláɪənt] N (of professional or store) cliente -ta *mf*; (of social service) beneficiario -ria *mf*

clientele [klaɪəntéł] N clientela *f*

cliff [klɪf] N precipicio *m*, despeñadero *m*; (by the sea) acantilado *m*

climate [kláɪmɪt] N clima *m*

climax [kláɪmæks] N clímax *m*; VI culminar, alcanzar el clímax

climb [klaɪm] N (ascent) subida *f*; (in alpinism) escalada *f*; VI/VT (ascend) subir; (ascend with effort) trepar(se) (a), encaramar(se) (a); VT (a mountain, wall) escalar; **to — down** bajar

climber [kláɪmə] N (in alpinism) escalador -ora *mf*; (plant) trepadora *f*

clinch [klɪntʃ] VT (resolve) rematar; (hammer down) remachar; (hug, in boxing) trabar; (secure) sujetar; (finalize) cerrar; N (nail) remache *m*; (embrace) abrazo *m*; (in boxing) clinch *m*

cling [klɪŋ] VI (to stick to) pegarse; (to hold onto) aferrarse

clinic [klínɪk] N clínica *f*; (workshop) taller *m*

clink [klɪŋk] N tintín *m*; VI tintinear

clip [klɪp] VT (cut) cortar; (trim) recortar; (shear) esquilar; (shorten) acortar; (hit) tocar; (fasten) abrochar; (attach paper) sujetar con un clip; N (fastener) gancho *m*; (for paper) clip *m*; (of cartridge) cargador *m*; (brooch) broche *m*

clipper [klípə] N (shearer) esquilador -ra *mf*; **—s** (scissors) tijeras *f pl*; (hair trimmer) maquinilla *f*

clipping [klípɪŋ] N recorte *m*

clique [klɪk] N (political) camarilla *f*; (in school) pandilla *f*

cloak [klok] N capa *f*; (military) capote *m*; **—room** guardarropa *m*; VT (put a cloak on) vestirse con una capa; (hide) encubrir

clock [klɑk] N reloj *m*; **—-making** relojería *f*; **— radio** radio reloj *f*; **—work** maquinaria de reloj *f*; **like —work** con precisión, sin falta; VT **you swim and I'll — you** tú nadas y yo te tomo el tiempo; **the police —ed him at 90 mph** la policía lo pescó haciendo noventa millas por hora

clockwise [klókwaɪz] ADV en el sentido de las manecillas de reloj

clod [klɑd] N (piece of dirt) terrón *m*, pelotón *m*; (dolt) tonto -ta *mf*, necio -cia *mf*

clog [klɑg] VI/VT obstruir(se), tapar(se); N (shoe) zueco *m*; **— dance** baile zapateado *m*

cloister [klɔ́ɪstə] N claustro *m*; (monastery)

monasterio *m*; VT enclaustrar

clone [klon] N clon *m*; VT clonar

cloning [klónɪŋ] N clonaje *m*, clonación *f*

close [kloz] VI/VT cerrar(se); VT (a hole) tapar; **to — an account** cerrar una cuenta; **to — a meeting** levantar una sesión; **to — in upon** (oppress) oprimir; (approach) cercar a uno; **to — out** liquidar; N fin *m*; (act of closing) cierre *m*; **—out** saldo *m*; [klos] ADJ (near) cercano; (dense) tupido; (intimate) íntimo; **— attention** mucha atención *f*; **—-fought** reñido; **—-knit** muy unido; **— questioning** interrogatorio minucioso *m*; **— translation** traducción fiel *f*; **—up** primer plano *m*; **at — range** de cerca; **that was a — call** nos salvamos por poco; ADV cerca

closed [klozd] ADJ cerrado; **— circuit** circuito cerrado *m*; **—-minded** cerrado; **—-mindedness** cerrazón *f*

closeness [klósnɪs] N cercanía *f*; (friendship) intimidad *f*; (correctness) fidelidad *f*

closet [klázɪt] N ropero *m*, armario *m*; VI enclaustrarse; ADJ a escondidas

closure [klóʒə] N (conclusion) cierre *m*; (sense of completeness) clausura *f*

clot [klɑt] VI/VT coagular(se); N coágulo *m*, cuajarón *m*

cloth [klɔθ] N tela *f*, tejido *m*; (wool) paño *m*; ADJ de tela; **— bound** encuadernado en tela; **man of the —** clérigo *m*

clothe [kloð] VT vestir; **—s** ropa *f*; **—sline** tendedero *m*; **—spin** pinza *f*

clothier [klóðjə] N comerciante en ropa o paño *mf*

clothing [klóðɪŋ] N ropa *f*

cloud [klaʊd] N nube *f*; **—burst** chaparrón *m*, aguacero *m*; VT nublar, anublar; (make indistinct, place under suspicion) enturbiar; **to — up** nublarse, anublarse; **to be on — nine** estar en el séptimo cielo; **under a —** bajo sospecha

cloudless [kláʊdlɪs] ADJ despejado

cloudy [kláʊdi] ADJ nublado; *Sp* nuboso; (gloomy) sombrío

clout [klaʊt] N influencia *f*

clove [klov] N clavo *m*; **— of garlic** diente de ajo *m*

cloven [klóvən] ADJ hendido; **—-hoofed** patihendido

clover [klóvə] N trébol *m*; **—leaf** trébol *m*; **to be in —** vivir en el lujo

clown [klaʊn] N payaso *m*; VI payasear, bufonear

cloy [klɔɪ] VI/VT (to satiate) hastiar; (to be too sweet for) repugnar

club [klʌb] N (society, nightclub) club *m*;
(stick) porra *f*, garrote *m*; (suit of cards)
basto *m*; **—house** casa de club *f*; VT
aporrear

cluck [klʌk] VI cloquear; N cloqueo *m*

clue [klu] N pista *f*, indicio *m*; **to have no —**
no tener ni noción

clueless [klúlɪs] ADJ (absent-minded)
despistado; (uninformed) en ayunas

clump [klʌmp] N (of bushes) matorral *m*; (of
trees) arboleda *f*; VI/VT apiñar(se)

clumsiness [klámzɪnɪs] N torpeza *f*

clumsy [klámzi] ADJ torpe, desmañado,
chambón; *Sp* patoso

clunker [klʌ́ŋkə] N cacharro *m*

cluster [klástə] N grupo *m*; (of grapes)
racimo *m*; VI/VT agrupar(se), arracimar(se)

clutch [klʌtʃ] N (in a car) embrague *m*; **—
pedal** pedal del embrague *m*; **to step on
the —** pisar el embrague; **—es** garras *f pl*;
VT (seize) asir; (hold) apretar

clutter [klʌ́də] VT **books —ed her desk**
tenía libros desparramados por todo el
escritorio; N desparramo *m*, desorden *m*,
confusión *f*

coach [kotʃ] N (carriage) coche *m*, carruaje *m*,
carroza *f*; (bus) autobús *m*; (trainer)
entrenador -ra *mf*; (in air travel) clase
turista *f*; (tutor) profesor -ra particular *mf*;
—man cochero *m*; VI/VT entrenar

coagulate [koǽgjəlet] VI/VT coagular(se)

coal [kol] N carbón *m*; **— bin** carbonera *f*; **—
tar** alquitrán *m*

coalition [koəlíʃən] N coalición *f*

coarse [kɔrs] ADJ (fabric) burdo, basto; (sand)
grueso; (manners, language) grosero,
tosco, rudo

coarseness [kɔ́rsnɪs] N (fabric) bastedad *f*;
(language, manners) tosquedad *f*, rudeza *f*;
(of a joke) chocarrería *f*

coast [kost] N costa *f*; **— Guard** Guardia
Costera *f*; **—line** costa *f*; **—-to-—** de costa
a costa; VI (on a sled) deslizar(se); (in a car,
on a bike) tirarse por una bajada; **he —ed
through medical school** la Facultad de
Medicina le resultó muy fácil

coastal [kóstəł] ADJ costero

coat [kot] N abrigo *m*; (of paint) capa *f*, mano
f; (on animals) pelaje *m*; **— of arms**
escudo de armas *m*, blasón *m*; **— rack**
percha *f*, perchero *m*; **—tail** faldón *m*; VT
cubrir; (with paint) dar una mano a; (with
grease) engrasar; (with soap) enjabonar;
(with sugar) bañar

coax [koks] VT persuadir con halagos,
engatusar

cob [kɑb] N mazorca *f*, panoja *f*; **—web**
telaraña *f*

cobalt [kóbɔłt] N cobalto *m*

cobbler [káblə] N (person who repairs shoes)
zapatero -ra *mf*, remendón -ona *mf*;
(dessert) budín de bizcocho y fruta *m*

cobblestone [kábəłston] N adoquín *m*

cobra [kóbrə] N cobra *f*

cocaine [kokén] N cocaína *f*

cock [kɑk] N (rooster) gallo *m*; (male bird)
macho de ave de corral *m*; (faucet) llave *f*;
(gun part) martillo *m*; **—fight** riña de
gallos *f*; **—pit** (for cockfights) gallera *f*; (in
an airplane) cabina *f*; **—scomb** cresta de
gallo *f*; **—sure** gallito; VT (a gun)
amartillar; (one's head) ladear

cock-a-doodle-doo [kákədudldú] INTERJ
quiquiriquí

cockatoo [kákatu] N cacatúa *f*

cocker spaniel [kákə-spǽnjəł] N cócker *m*

cockroach [kákrotʃ] N cucaracha *f*

cocktail [káktel] N cóctel *m*; **— party**
cóctel *m*

cocky [káki] ADJ gallito, valentón

cocoa [kóko] N (powder) cacao *m*; (drink)
chocolate *m*

coconut [kókənʌt] N coco *m*

cocoon [kəkún] N capullo *m*

cod [kɑd] N *Sp* abadejo *m*; *Am* bacalao *m*;
—-liver oil aceite de hígado de bacalao *m*

coddle [kádł] VT mimar

code [kod] N código *m*; **— switching**
alternancia de códigos *f*

codeine [kódin] N codeína *f*

codger [kádʒə] N vejete *m*, vejancón *m*

codify [kádəfaɪ] VT codificar

coed [kóed] ADJ mixto; N alumna universitaria
f

coefficient [koəfíʃənt] N coeficiente *m*

coerce [koɚ́s] VT forzar, obligar

coercion [koɚ́ʒən] N coacción *f*

coexistence [koɪgzístəns] N coexistencia *f*

coffee [kɔ́fi] N café *m*; **— bean** grano de café
m; **— break** descanso para tomar el café
m; **— bush** cafeto *m*; **— maker** máquina
de café *f*, cafetera *f*; **—pot** cafetera *f*; **—
shop** (for coffee) café *m*; (for coffee and
light meals) cafetería *f*; **— table** mesa baja
f

coffer [kɔ́fə] N cofre *m*

coffin [kɔ́fɪn] N ataúd *m*, féretro *m*

cog [kɑg] N diente *m*; **—wheel** rueda dentada
f

cogent [kódʒənt] ADJ convincente

cognac [kánjæk] N coñac *m*

cognate [kágnet] ADJ & N cognado *m*

cognitive [kágnɪDIV] ADJ cognitivo

cohabitate [kohǽbɪtet] VI cohabitar

coherent [kohírənt] ADJ coherente; (sticking together) cohesivo

cohesion [kohíʒən] N cohesión *f*

coiffure [kwafjúr] N peinado *m*

coil [kɔɪl] VI/VT arrollar(se), enrollar(se); (snake) enroscar(se); N (roll) rollo *m*; (spiral) tirabuzón *m*; (electric) bobina *f*; — **spring** muelle en espiral *m*

coin [kɔɪn] N moneda *f*; —-**operated** de monedas; VT acuñar (also words)

coinage [kɔ́ɪnɪdʒ] N acuñación *f* (also of words)

coincide [kɔɪnsáɪd] VI coincidir

coincidence [koínsɪdəns] N coincidencia *f*, casualidad *f*

coitus [kóɪɾəs] N coito *m*

coke [kok] N (coal) cok *m*, coque *m*; (cocaine) *fam* coca *f*

cola [kólə] N gaseosa *f*

colander [káləndə-] N colador *m*

cold [kold] ADJ frío; — **cream** cold cream *m*; — **cuts** fiambres *m pl*; — **fish** *fam* témpano *m*; — **snap** ola de frío *f*; — **sore** herpes *m sg*; — **war** guerra fría *f*; **to be** — tener frío; **to be out** — quedar seco; **it is** — **today** hace frío hoy; **he gave me the** — **shoulder** me hizo el vacío; **he quit** — **turkey** dejó de un día para otro; **he got** — **feet** se acobardó; N frío *m*; (illness) resfrío *m*, resfriado *m*, catarro *m*; **to catch a** — resfriarse

coldness [kóldnɪs] N frialdad *f*

colic [kálɪk] N cólico *m*

coliseum [kɑlɪsíəm] N coliseo *m*

collaborate [kəlǽbəret] VI colaborar

collaboration [kəlæbəréʃən] N colaboración *f*

collaborator [kəlǽbəreɾə-] N colaborador -ora *mf*

collage [kəláʒ] N collage *m*

collagen [kálədʒən] N colágeno *m*

collapse [kəlǽps] VI (fold into sections) plegarse; (cave in) hundirse, derrumbarse; (fail) fracasar; (faint) desmayarse; (empty of air, decline in value) colapsar(se); N (falling in) derrumbe *m*, derrumbamiento *m*, desplome *m*; (breakdown) colapso *m*

collar [kálə-] N (for restraining dogs, marking on an animal, necklace) collar *m*; (of a shirt) cuello *m*; —**bone** clavícula *f*; VT acollarar; (grab by the neck) agarrar por el cuello; **I was** —**ed by the boss** el jefe me agarró de charla

collate [kólet] VT (put in order) colacionar; (compare) cotejar

collateral [kəlǽɾə-əl] ADJ (on the side) colateral; (auxiliary) subsidiario; N garantía subsidiaria *f*

colleague [kálig] N colega *mf*

collect [kəlékt] VT (gather) recoger; (make a collection) coleccionar; (receive taxes) recaudar; VI/VT (receive payment) cobrar, percibir; (assemble) reunir(se); (accumulate) acumular(se); **to** — **oneself** calmarse; — **on delivery** pago contra reembolso *m*; — **call** llamada de cobro revertido *f*, llamada por/a cobrar *f*

collection [kəlékʃən] N (set of collectibles, clothes) colección *f*; (for charity) colecta *f*; (of taxes) recaudación *f*, cobranza *f*, cobro *m*; (of data, fruit) recolección *f*

collective [kəléktɪv] N & ADJ colectivo *m*; — **bargaining** convenio colectivo *m*

collector [kəléktə-] N (of taxes) recaudador -ra *mf*; (of collectibles) coleccionista *mf*; (of other things) colector -ora *mf*

college [kálɪdʒ] N (institution) universidad *f*; (division) facultad *f*; (association) colegio *m*; **let's give it the old** — **try** vamos a hacer un esfuerzo supremo

collegial [kəlídʒəl] ADJ cooperador

collegiate [kəlídʒɪt] ADJ universitario

collide [kəláɪd] VI/VT chocar

collie [káli] N collie *m*

collision [kəlíʒən] N colisión *f*, choque *m*

colloid [kálɔɪd] N coloide *m*

colloquial [kəlókwiəl] ADJ coloquial; — **expression** frase familiar *f*

colloquium [kəlókwiəm] N coloquio *m*, jornada *f*

collusion [kəlúʒən] N confabulación *f*

cologne [kəlón] N colonia *f*

Colombia [kəlámbiə] N Colombia *f*

Colombian [kəlámbiən] ADJ & N colombiano -na *mf*

colon [kólən] N (punctuation) dos puntos *m pl*; (bowels) colon *m*; [kəlón] (currency of El Salvador and Costa Rica) colón *m*

colonel [kɝ́nəl] N coronel *m*

colonial [kəlóniəl] ADJ colonial

colonist [kálənɪst] N (settler) colono *m*; (colonizer) colonizador -ra *mf*

colonization [kɑlənɪzéʃən] N colonización *f*

colonize [kálənaɪz] VT colonizar

colony [káləni] N colonia *f*

color [kálə-] N color *m*; (colorfulness) colorido *m*; **the** —**s** la bandera; **he showed his true** —**s** se mostró tal cual era; **persons of** — gente de color *f*; **a** — **TV** un televisor en/a color; ADJ —-**blind** daltónico; —-**fast** de colores firmes; VT (give color) colorear; (make colorful) dar colorido; (taint) teñir; (blush) ruborizarse

colored [kálə-d] ADJ coloreado; (biased) sesgado

colorful [kÁlə-fəł] ADJ (full of color) colorido; (eccentric) pintoresco

coloring [kÁlə-ɪŋ] N (tone) colorido *m*; (action) coloración *f*; (substance) colorante *m*

colorless [kÁlə-lıs] ADJ (without color) incoloro; (bleached) descolorido

colossal [kəlÁsəł] ADJ colosal

colt [kołt] N potro *m*

column [kÁləm] N columna *f*

columnist [kÁləmnıst] N columnista *mf*

coma [kómə] N coma *m*

comatose [kámətos] ADJ comatoso

comb [kom] N (for hair) peine *m*; (of a rooster) cresta *f*; (for wool) carda *f*; (for horses) almohaza *f*; (of honey) panal *m*; VT (hair) peinar; (wool) cardar; (search an area) peinar, batir; **to — one's hair** peinarse

combat [kámbæt] VI/VT combatir; N combate *m*

combatant [kəmbǽtn̩t] ADJ & N combatiente *mf*

combative [kəmbǽDIV] ADJ combativo

combination [kambənéfən] N combinación *f*; **— lock** cerradura de combinación *f*

combine [kəmbáın] VI/VT combinar(se); [kámbaın] N cosechadora *f*

combo [kámbo] N combo *m*

combustible [kəmbÁstəbəł] ADJ & N combustible *m*

combustion [kəmbÁstʃən] N combustión *f*

come [kʌm] VI venir; **an idea came to me** se me ocurrió una idea; **Christmas is coming** llega la Navidad; **milk —s from cows** la leche se saca de las vacas; **no harm will — to you** no te va a pasar nada; **the dress —s to her knees** el vestido le llega a las rodillas; **to — about** suceder; **to — across** (find) encontrar; (make an impression) parecer; **to — along** (accompany) acompañar; (appear) surgir; **how's your paper coming along?** ¿cómo va tu trabajo? **to — again** volver, volver a venir; **to — at** venirse encima; **to — back** volver; **to make a —back** resurgir; (in sports) recuperarse; **to — down with a cold** cogerse un resfriado; **to — downstairs** bajar; **to — from** ser de; **to — in** entrar; **to — off** salir(se); **to — out** salir; **to — over** venir para acá; **to — to** volver en sí; **to — together** (meet) juntarse, unirse; (reach agreement) ponerse de acuerdo; **to — up** subir; **your name came up** tu nombre vino a colación; N **—back** (reply) réplica *f*; (in sports) recuperación *f*

comedian [kəmídiən] N cómico -ca *mf*, comediante *mf*

comedy [kámədi] N (genre) comedia *f*; (profession) humorismo *m*

comet [kámıt] N cometa *m*

comfort [kámfə-t] VT reconfortar; N (feeling of ease) comodidad *f*, confort *m*, holgura *f*; (solace) consuelo *m*

comfortable [kámfə-Dəbəł] ADJ cómodo, confortable; **— income** buen pasar *m*; **— life** vida holgada / desahogada *f*

comforter [kámfə-Də-] N edredón *m*

comic [kámık] ADJ cómico, chistoso, gracioso; **— book** revista de historietas *f*, comic *m*; **—s** tiras cómicas *f pl*, historietas *f pl*; **— strip** tira cómica *f*

comical [kámıkəł] ADJ cómico, gracioso

coming [kámıŋ] N venida *f*; **— of Christ** advenimiento de Cristo *m*; **—s and goings** idas y venidas *f pl*; ADJ que viene, próximo

comma [kámə] N coma *f*

command [kəmænd] VT (order) mandar; (have authority over) comandar; **to — respect** inspirar respeto, imponerse; N (order) mandato *m*, orden *f*; (post) comandancia *f*; (dominance) dominio *m*; (on a computer) comando *m*; **he has a good — of English** domina bien el inglés; **to be in — of** estar al mando de; **to be under the — of** estar al mando de; **at your —** a sus órdenes

commandeer [kamandír] VT apoderarse de; (for the military) requisar

commander [kəmændə-] N (leader) jefe -fa *mf*; (army officer) comandante *mf*; (navy officer) capitán de fragata *m*; **— in chief** comandante en jefe

commandment [kəmændmənt] N mandamiento *m*

commemorate [kəmémə-ret] VT conmemorar

commence [kəméns] VI/VT comenzar, principiar

commencement [kəménsmənt] N (beginning) comienzo *m*; (graduation) graduación *f*, colación *f*

commend [kəménd] VT (praise) alabar; (entrust) encomendar

commendation [kamandéfən] N (praise) alabanza *f*; (mention) mención de honor *f*

commensurate [kəménsə-ıt] ADJ proporcional, acorde

comment [kámɛnt] N comentario *m*; **no —** sin comentarios; VI/VT comentar

commentary [kámənteri] N comentario *m*

commentator [kámənteDə-] N (person who describes) comentador -ra *mf*; (on radio, etc.) comentarista *mf*

commerce [kámɚs] N comercio *m*

commercial [kəmɔ́-ʃəl] ADJ comercial; N (on radio or television) anuncio *m*

commercialize [kəmɔ́-ʃəlaɪz] VT comercializar

commiserate [kəmízəret] VI/VT compadecerse de

commiseration [kəmɪzəréʃən] N conmiseración *f*

commissary [kámɪseri] N economato *m*

commission [kəmíʃən] N (act, committee, payment) comisión *f*; (of a broker) corretaje *m*; (charge) encargo *m*; (mission) misión *f*; (title) nombramiento *m*; **to be in** — estar en servicio; **to be out of** — estar fuera de servicio; **to put out of** — (object) inutilizar; (person) retirar de servicio; VT (authorize) comisionar; (order) encargar; (appoint) nombrar; (get ready) poner en servicio; **—ed officer** oficial *m*

commissioner [kəmíʃənɚ] N comisario -ria *mf*

commit [kəmít] VT (perpetrate) cometer; (entrust) encargar; (direct) destinar; **to — to an asylum** internar; **to — to memory** aprender de memoria; **to — to paper** poner por escrito; **to — to prison** encarcelar

commitment [kəmítmənt] N compromiso *m*

committee [kəmíɖi] N comité *m*, comisión *f*

commode [kəmód] N wáter *m*, inodoro *m*

commodity [kəmáɖiɖi] N (product) mercancía *f*, artículo *m*, producto *m*; (raw material) materia prima *f*

common [kámən] ADJ (shared, frequent) común; (general) general; (vulgar) ordinario; (unremarkable) simple; **— cold** resfriado *m*; **— denominator** denominador común *m*; **— law** derecho consuetudinario *m*; **—place** trivial; **— sense** sentido común *m*, sensatez *f*; **— soldier** soldado raso *m*; **— stock** acciones ordinarias *f pl*; **—wealth** (state) estado *m*; (republic) república *f*; N **—s** (land) ejido *m*

commotion [kəmóʃən] N conmoción *f*, revuelo *m*

commune [kəmjún] VI (communicate) comunicarse, departir; (take communion) comulgar; [kámjun] N comuna *f*

communicable [kəmjúnɪkəbəl] ADJ comunicable; (disease) transmisible

communicate [kəmjúnɪket] VI/VT comunicar(se); (disease) transmitir(se)

communication [kəmjunɪkéʃən] N comunicación *f*

communicative [kəmjúnɪkəɖɪv] ADJ comunicativo

communion [kəmjúnjən] N comunión *f*

communism [kámjənɪzəm] N comunismo *m*

communist [kámjənɪst] N & ADJ comunista *mf*

community [kəmjúnɪɖi] N comunidad *f*

commute [kəmjút] VT (reduce a sentence) conmutar; VI viajar diariamente al trabajo

commuter [kəmjúɖɚ] N persona que viaja diariamente al trabajo *f*

Comoros [kámɚoz] N Comoras *f pl*

compact [kampǽkt] ADJ compacto; (dense) tupido, apretado; (concise) conciso; **— disk** disco compacto *m*; VT compactar; (make denser) tupir; [kámpækt] N (agreement) pacto *m*; (case for powder) polvera *f*

compactness [kampǽktnɪs] N densidad *f*; (conciseness) concisión *f*

companion [kəmpǽnjən] N (comrade, partner) compañero -ra *mf*; (caregiver) acompañante *mf*

companionship [kəmpǽnjənʃip] N compañía *f*

company [kámpəni] N compañía *f*; **to keep — with** codearse con, frecuentar

comparable [kámpəɹəbəl] ADJ comparable

comparative [kəmpǽɹəɖɪv] ADJ comparativo

compare [kəmpér] VI/VT comparar(se); **beyond —** incomparable, sin parangón

comparison [kəmpǽɹɪsən] N comparación *f*; **in — with** comparado con

compartment [kəmpártmənt] N compartimiento *m*

compass [kámpəs] N (for drawing) compás *m*; (for directions) brújula *f*

compassion [kəmpǽʃən] N compasión *f*

compassionate [kəmpǽʃənɪt] ADJ compasivo

compatible [kəmpǽɖəbəl] ADJ compatible (also computer term)

compatriot [kəmpétriət] N compatriota *mf*

compel [kəmpɛ́l] VT (force) obligar; (demand) exigir

compelling [kəmpɛ́lɪŋ] ADJ (argument) convincente; (story) emocionante

compensate [kámpənset] VT (make up for) compensar, resarcir; (pay) remunerar

compensation [kampənséʃən] N (making up for) compensación *f*; (remuneration) remuneración *f*

compete [kəmpít] VI/VT competir

competence [kámpɪɖəns] N competencia *f*

competent [kámpɪɖənt] ADJ competente

competition [kampɪtíʃən] N competencia *f*; (sports match) competición *f*, contienda *f*

competitive [kəmpéɖɪɖɪv] ADJ competitivo; **— examination** *Sp* oposición *f*; *Am*

concurso *m*; — **sports** deportes de
competición *m pl*
competitor [kəmpédɪdə] N competidor -ra
mf
compile [kəmpáɪł] VT recopilar, compilar
compiler [kəmpáɪlə] N compilador *m*
complacency [kəmplésənsi] N confianza
infundada *f*
complacent [kəmplésənt] ADJ confiado
complain [kəmplén] VI quejarse
complaint [kəmplént] N queja *f*; (civil
charge) demanda *f*; (ailment) dolencia *f*
complement [kámpləmənt] N complemento
m; (of staff) dotación *f*; [kámpləmɛnt] VT
complementar
complete [kəmplít] ADJ completo, pleno; **a
— stranger** un perfecto desconocido; VT
completar
completion [kəmplíʃən] N finalización *f*,
terminación *f*; **she brought the project
to —** completó el proyecto
complex [kəmpléks] ADJ complejo; [kámplɛks]
N complejo *m*
complexion [kəmplékʃən] N (skin) cutis *m*;
(color) tez *f*; (perspective) cariz *m*
complexity [kəmpléksɪdi] N complejidad *f*
compliance [kəmpláɪəns] N (obedience)
conformidad *f*, acatamiento *m*; (meek
agreement) pleitesía *f*; **in — with** en
conformidad con
complicate [kámplɪket] VT complicar
complicated [kámplɪkeɪd] ADJ complicado
complication [kamplɪkéʃən] N complicación
f
complicity [kəmplísɪdi] N complicidad *f*
compliment [kámpləmənt] N cumplido *m*;
(on looks) piropo *m*; (from a suitor)
galantería *f*; **to pay someone a —**
hacerle un cumplido a alguien; **to send
one's —s** enviar saludos; [kámpləmɛnt]
VI/VT elogiar
comply [kəmpláɪ] VI obedecer; **to — with**
cumplir con, acatar
component [kəmpónənt] ADJ & N
componente *m*
compose [kəmpóz] VI/VT componer; **to —
oneself** sosegarse
composed [kəmpózd] ADJ sosegado; **to be —
of** estar compuesto de, componerse de,
constar de
composer [kəmpózə] N compositor -ra *mf*
composite [kəmpázɪt] ADJ compuesto; N
amalgama *f*
composition [kampəzíʃən] N (make-up,
musical piece) composición *f*; (aggregate
material) compuesto *m*; (school essay)
composición *f*, redacción *f*

composure [kəmpóʒə] N compostura *f*
compound [kámpaund] ADJ & N compuesto
m; — **fracture** fractura expuesta *f*; —
interest interés compuesto *m*;
[kɑmpáund] VT (combine) combinar;
(worsen) empeorar
comprehend [kamprɪhénd] VT comprender
comprehensible [kamprɪhénsəbəł] ADJ
comprensible
comprehension [kamprɪhénʃən] N
comprensión *f*
comprehensive [kamprɪhénsɪv] ADJ
exhaustivo; — **insurance** seguro contra
todo riesgo *m*
compress [kəmprés] VT comprimir; [kámpres]
N compresa *f*
compression [kəmpréʃən] N compresión *f*
comprise [kəmpráɪz] VT comprender, incluir;
to be —d of comprender, incluir
compromise [kámprəmaɪz] N (arrangement)
arreglo por concesiones mutuas *m*,
compromiso *m*; (intermediate thing) cruce
m, término medio *m*; VI/VT (make
agreement) transigir; *Am* transar;
(jeopardize) comprometer
comptroller [kɑntrólə] N controlador -ra *mf*;
Am contralor -ora *mf*
compulsion [kəmpʌ́łʃən] N (impulse)
compulsión *f*, coacción *f*; (coercion)
coerción *f*
compulsive [kəmpʌ́łsɪv] ADJ compulsivo
compulsory [kəmpʌ́łsəri] ADJ obligatorio
computation [kampjutéʃən] N cómputo *m*,
cálculo *m*
compute [kəmpjút] VI/VT computar, calcular
computer [kəmpjúdə] N *Am* computadora *f*;
Sp ordenador *m*; — **graphics** gráficos por
computadora / ordenador *m pl*; — **science**
informática *f*; — **virus** virus de
computadora / ordenador *m*
computerize [kəmpjúdəraɪz] VI/VT
informatizar, computarizar
comrade [kámræd] N camarada *mf*
concave [kánkev] ADJ cóncavo
conceal [kənsíł] VT encubrir, ocultar,
disimular
concealment [kənsíłmənt] N encubrimiento
m, disimulo *m*
concede [kənsíd] VI/VT (recognize) conceder;
(yield) otorgar
conceit [kənsít] N (vanity) vanidad *f*; (literary
device) concepto *m*
conceited [kənsídɪd] ADJ engreído, presumido
conceivable [kənsívəbəł] ADJ imaginable,
concebible
conceive [kənsív] VI/VT concebir; (a plan)
concebir, idear

concentrate [kánsəntret] VI/VT
concentrar(se)

concentration [kansəntréʃən] N
concentración f; **— camp** campo de
concentración m

concept [kánsept] N concepto m

conception [kənsépʃən] N concepción f

concern [kənsɜ́-n] N (interest) interés m;
(affair) asunto m; (worry) preocupación f;
(company) compañía f; **to be of no —** no
tener consecuencia; VT (be of interest)
concernir, atañer; (worry) preocupar; **to —
oneself with** ocuparse de; **to whom it
may —** a quien corresponda

concerned [kənsɜ́-nd] ADJ (involved)
involucrado; (anxious) preocupado; **as far
as I am —** en lo que a mí respecta; **to be
— about** preocuparse por

concerning [kənsɜ́-nɪŋ] PREP tocante a,
respecto a

concert [kánsɚt] N concierto m; [kənsɜ́-t] VT
concertar

concession [kənséʃən] N concesión f

conciliate [kənsíliet] VI/VT (make
compatible) conciliar; (appease) aplacar

concise [kənsáis] ADJ conciso, sucinto

conciseness [kənsáisnɪs] N concisión f

conclude [kənklúd] VI/VT concluir, terminar;
(deduce) deducir

conclusion [kənklúʒən] N conclusión f

conclusive [kənklúsɪv] ADJ concluyente

concoct [kənkákt] VT (contrive) fabricar,
urdir; (prepare by cooking) preparar

concoction [kənkákʃən] N menjurje m

concord [kánkɔrd] N (peace) concordia f;
(agreement) convenio m, acuerdo m

concrete [kankrít] ADJ concreto; (made of
concrete) de hormigón; [kánkrit] N
hormigón m

concubine [káŋkjəbain] N concubina f

concur [kənkɜ́-] VI estar de acuerdo

concussion [kənkáʃən] N (brain injury)
conmoción cerebral f; (shock) concusión f

condemn [kəndém] VT condenar; (acquire
public ownership) expropiar; (declare
unsafe) declarar ruinoso

condemnation [kandemnéʃən] N
condenación f, condena f

condensation [kandenséʃən] N
condensación f; (of a book) compendio m

condense [kandéns] VI/VT condensar(se)

condescend [kandəsénd] VI condescender a

condescension [kandəsénʃən] N
condescendencia f

condiment [kándəmənt] N condimento m,
aliño m

condition [kəndíʃən] N condición f; **he's**
got a heart — sufre del corazón, tiene
una afección cardíaca; **he's in good
physical —** está en buen estado físico;
the patient is in critical — el paciente
está en estado crítico; **on — that** a
condición de que; VT (restrict on a
condition, establish a conditioned
response) condicionar; (accustom oneself)
acostumbrarse

conditional [kəndíʃənəł] ADJ & N
condicional m

conditioning [kəndíʃənɪŋ] N
condicionamiento m

condolences [kəndólənsɪz] N pésame m,
condolencias f; **to express one's —** dar
las condolencias

condominium [kandəmíniəm] N
, condominio m

condone [kəndón] VT tolerar

conducive [kəndúsɪv] ADJ conducente

conduct [kándʌkt] N conducta f,
comportamiento m; [kəndʌ́kt] VI/VT
(behave) conducirse, comportarse; (carry
out) llevar a cabo; (direct, lead) dirigir;
(serve as channel for) conducir

conductor [kəndʌ́ktɚ] N (substance that
conducts) conductor m; (of an orchestra)
director -ra mf; (of a train) revisor -ra mf

conduit [kánduit] N conducto m

cone [kon] N cono m; (container) cucurucho
m

confection [kənfékʃən] N (of clothes)
confección f; (of candy) confitura f

confectionery [kənfékʃəneri] N confitería f;
(shop) dulcería f; (candies) dulces m pl

confederacy [kənfédɚəsi] N confederación f

confederate [kənfédɚət] ADJ & N
confederado -da mf; [kənfédɚret] VI/VT
confederar(se)

confederation [kənfɛdɚréʃən] N
confederación f

confer [kənfɜ́-] VT (grant) conferir; (consult)
consultar; (negotiate) conferenciar

conference [kánfɚəns] N (consultation)
consulta f; (professional meeting) congreso
m; (legislative) asamblea general f; (sports
league) liga f; **— call** llamada en
conferencia f

confess [kənfés] VI/VT confesar(se)

confession [kənféʃən] N confesión f

confessional [kənféʃənəł] N confesionario m

confessor [kənfésɚ] N confesor m

confidant [kánfidant] N confidente mf

confide [kənfáid] VI/VT (entrust) confiar; VI
(tell secrets to) hacer confidencias a

confidence [kánfɪɾəns] N confianza f;
(certainty) seguridad f; (secret

communication) confidencia *f*; **— game**
timo *m*; **— man** timador *m*, embaucador
m; **in —** en confianza
confident [kánfɪdənt] ADJ seguro; **he's a —
person** tiene mucha confianza
confidential [kɑnfɪdénʃəł] ADJ confidencial;
(secretary, etc.) de confianza
configuration [kənfɪgjəréʃən] N
configuración *f* (also computer term)
confine [kənfáin] VT confinar, recluir; **to —
oneself to** limitarse a; [kánfain] N confín
m
confinement [kənfáinmənt] N
confinamiento *m*
confirm [kənfɚm] VT confirmar
confirmation [kɑnfɚméʃən] N confirmación
f
confiscate [kánfɪsket] VT confiscar
confiscation [kɑnfɪskéʃən] N confiscación *f*
conflagration [kɑnfləgréʃən] N incendio *m*
conflict [kánflɪkt] N conflicto *m*, contienda *f*;
— of interest conflicto de intereses *m*;
[kənflíkt] VI oponerse
confluence [kánfluəns] N confluencia *f*
conform [kənfɔ́rm] VI/VT conformar(se)
conformity [kənfɔ́rmɪDi] N (agreement)
conformidad *f*; (passive acquiescence)
conformismo *m*
confound [kənfáund] VT (bewilder)
desconcertar; (mix) confundir; **— it!** *fam*
¡caramba!
confront [kənfránt] VT (set face to face,
fight) confrontar; (face up to) enfrentarse
a
confuse [kənfjúz] VT confundir
confused [kənfjúzd] ADJ (person)
confundido; (situation) confuso; **to
become —** confundirse
confusing [kənfjúzɪŋ] ADJ confuso
confusion [kənfjúʒən] N confusión *f*
congeal [kəndʒíł] VI/VT cuajar(se)
congenial [kəndʒínjəł] ADJ agradable,
simpático; **to be — with** congeniar con
congenital [kəndʒénɪd] ADJ congénito
congestion [kəndʒéstʃən] N congestión *f*
conglomeration [kənglɑməréʃən] N (unit)
conglomeración *f*; (mass) conglomerado *m*
Congo [káŋgo] N Congo *m*
Congolese [kaŋgəlíz] ADJ & N congoleño -ña
mf
congratulate [kəngrǽtʃəlet] VI/VT felicitar(se)
congratulation [kəngrætʃəléʃən] N
felicitación *f*, parabién *m*; **—s!**
¡enhorabuena! ¡albricias!
congregate [káŋgrɪget] VI/VT congregar(se)
congregation [kaŋgrɪgéʃən] N (worshippers)
fieles *m pl*, feligreses *m pl*; (act of

congregating, committee of cardinals)
congregación *f*
congress [káŋgrɪs] N (professional) congreso
m; (political) asamblea legislativa *f*; (US)
congreso *m*
congressional [kəngréʃənəł] ADJ congresual
congressman [káŋgrɪsmən] N representante
m; (US) congresista *m*
congresswoman [káŋgrɪswumən] N
representante *f*; (US) congresista *f*
congruence [kəngrúəns] N congruencia *f*
conifer [kánəfɚ] N conífera *f*
conjecture [kəndʒéktʃɚ] N conjetura *f*; VI
conjeturar
conjugal [kándʒəgəł] ADJ conyugal
conjugate [kándʒəget] VI/VT conjugar(se)
conjugation [kandʒəgéʃən] N conjugación *f*
conjunction [kəndʒʎŋkʃən] N conjunción *f*
conjunctivitis [kəndʒʎŋktəváɪDɪs] N
conjuntivitis *f*
conjure [kándʒɚ] VT invocar; **to — up**
evocar; VI hacer hechizos
connect [kənékt] VI/VT (join) conectar(se),
enlazar(se); (buildings, callers)
comunicar(se); (concepts) relacionar(se);
(pipes) acoplar(se); **—ing rod** biela *f*
connection [kənékʃən] N (act of connecting,
electrical device) conexión *f*; (of
telephone) comunicación *f*, enganche *m*;
(of concepts) relación *f*; (of pipes) acople
m; (affinity) afinidad *f*; (supplier) contacto
m; **—s** contactos *m pl*, enchufe *m*
connive [kənáɪv] VI conspirar
connoisseur [kɑnəsɚ́] N conocedor -ra *f*
connotation [kɑnətéʃən] N connotación *f*
conquer [káŋkɚ] VI/VT (win) conquistar;
(overcome) vencer
conqueror [káŋkərɚ] N conquistador -ra *mf*;
(one who overcomes) vencedor -ra *mf*
conquest [káŋkwest] N conquista *f*
conscience [kánʃəns] N conciencia *f*
conscientious [kɑnʃiéntʃəs] ADJ concienzudo
conscious [kánʃəs] ADJ consciente
consciousness [kánʃəsnɪs] N conciencia *f*; **to
lose —** perder el conocimiento
conscript [kənskrípt] VT reclutar; [kánskrɪpt]
N recluta *mf*
conscription [kənskrípʃən] N reclutamiento
m
consecrate [kánsɪkret] VT consagrar
consecration [kɑnsɪkréʃən] N consagración *f*
consecutive [kənsékjəDɪv] ADJ consecutivo
consensus [kənsénsəs] N consenso *m*
consent [kənsént] N consentimiento *m*; VI
consentir
consequence [kánsɪkwens] N consecuencia *f*;
(negative) secuela *f*

consequent [kánsɪkwənt] ADJ consiguiente, resultante; N (in mathematics) consecuente m; (in logic) consiguiente m

consequently [kánsɪkwəntli] ADV por consiguiente, en consecuencia

conservation [kɑnsə-véʃən] N conservación f, preservación f

conservatism [kənsɚ-vətɪzəm] N conservadurismo m

conservative [kənsɚ-vədɪv] ADJ & N conservador -ra mf

conservatory [kənsɚ-vətɔri] N conservatorio m

conserve [kənsɚ-v] VT conservar, preservar; [kánsɚv] N dulce m

consider [kənsíɖə] VT considerar

considerable [kənsíɖə-əbəl] ADJ considerable

considerate [kənsíɖə-ɪt] ADJ considerado

consideration [kənsɪɖə-réʃən] N consideración f; (tolerance) miramiento m; (payment) remuneración f

considering [kənsíɖə-ɪŋ] PREP en vista de, teniendo en cuenta; **she cooks well, —** para ser ella, cocina bien

consign [kənsáɪn] VT consignar

consignee [kɑnsaɪní] N consignatario -ria mf

consignment [kənsáɪnmənt] N consignación f; **on —** a consignación

consist [kənsíst] VI consistir (en)

consistency [kənsístənsi] N (adherence to principles) coherencia f, consecuencia f; (density) consistencia f

consistent [kənsístənt] ADJ (adherent to principles) consecuente, coherente; (cohering) consistente

consolation [kɑnsəléʃən] N consuelo m, consolación f

console [kənsóɫ] VT consolar; [kánsoɫ] N consola f

consolidate [kənsálɪdet] VI/VT consolidar(se)

consonant [kánsənənt] N consonante f; ADJ consonante, conforme

consort [kánsɔrt] N consorte mf; [kənsɔrt] VI **to — with** asociarse con

consortium [kənsɔrʃiəm] N consorcio m

conspicuous [kənspíkjuəs] ADJ evidente

conspiracy [kənspírəsi] N conspiración f, conjura f

conspirator [kənspírəɖə-] N conspirador -ora mf, conjurado -da mf

conspire [kənspáɪr] VI conspirar, conjurar

constable [kánstəbəl] N oficial de policía mf; (keeper of fortress) condestable m

constancy [kánstənsi] N constancia f

constant [kánstənt] ADJ & N constante f

constellation [kɑnstəléʃən] N constelación f

consternation [kɑnstə-néʃən] N consternación f

constipate [kánstəpet] VT estreñir

constipated [kánstəpedɪd] ADJ estreñido

constipation [kɑnstəpéʃən] N estreñimiento m

constituent [kənstítʃuənt] ADJ componente, constitutivo; N (component) componente m; (voter) votante mf; (part of a sentence) constituyente m

constitute [kánstɪtut] VT constituir

constitution [kɑnstɪtúʃən] N constitución f

constitutional [kɑnstɪtúʃənəl] ADJ constitucional; N caminata f

constrain [kənstrén] VT constreñir

constraint [kənstrént] N constreñimiento m

constrict [kənstríkt] VT constreñir

constriction [kənstríkʃən] N (action) constricción f; (place) estrechamiento m

construct [kənstrʌ́kt] VT construir; [kánstrʌkt] N invención f

construction [kənstrʌ́kʃən] N construcción f

constructive [kənstrʌ́ktɪv] ADJ constructivo

construe [kənstrú] VT interpretar

consul [kánsəl] N cónsul mf

consulate [kánsəlɪt] N consulado m

consult [kənsʌ́lt] VI/VT consultar; VI (serve as a consultant) asesorar

consultant [kənsʌ́ltənt] N asesor -ra mf

consultation [kɑnsəltéʃən] N consulta f

consulting [kənsʌ́ltɪŋ] N asesoramiento m, consultoría f

consume [kənsúm] VI/VT consumir

consumer [kənsúmə-] N consumidor -ra mf

consumerism [kənsúmərɪzəm] N consumismo m

consuming [kənsúmɪŋ] ADJ **a — need** una necesidad imperiosa; **a — drive** un deseo abrasador

consummate [kánsəmet] VT consumar; [kánsəmɪt] ADJ consumado

consumption [kənsʌ́mpʃən] N (using up) consumo m; (wasting of the body) consunción f; (tuberculosis) tisis f

consumptive [kənsʌ́mptɪv] ADJ tísico

contact [kúntækt] N contacto m; **— lens** lente de contacto mf; VI/VT (touch) tocar; (communicate with) contactar

contagion [kəntédʒən] N (spread) contagio m; (disease spread) enfermedad contagiosa f

contagious [kəntédʒəs] ADJ contagioso

contain [kəntén] VI/VT contener

container [kənténə-] N recipiente m; (on a ship) contenedor m; **—ship** buque portacontenedores m

contaminate [kəntǽmənet] VT contaminar

contamination [kəntæmənéʃən] N

contaminación f

contemplate [kántəmplet] VT (observe)
contemplar; (consider) considerar

contemplation [kɑntəmpléʃən] N
(observation) contemplación f;
(consideration) consideración f

contemporary [kəntémpəreri] ADJ
contemporáneo

contempt [kəntémpt] N desprecio m,
menosprecio m; — **of court** desacato al
tribunal m

contemptible [kəntémptəbəł] ADJ
despreciable, rastrero

contemptuous [kəntémptʃuəs] ADJ
desdeñoso

contend [kənténd] VI (struggle) contender,
lidiar; (argue) disputar; VT afirmar

content, contents [kántent(s)] N contenido
m

content [kəntént] ADJ (happy) contento;
(resigned) conforme; N **to one's heart's**
— a discreción

contented [kənténtɪd] ADJ contento,
satisfecho

contention [kənténʃən] N (opinion) opinión
f; **in** — (disputed) en discusión; (with
possibilities) con posibilidades

contentment [kənténtmənt] N contento m

contest [kántest] N (competition) concurso
m, certamen m; (struggle) contienda f;
[kəntést] VT (compete) contender; (dispute)
disputar; (challenge) impugnar

contestant [kəntéstənt] N concursante mf,
participante mf

context [kántekst] N contexto m

contiguous [kəntígjuəs] ADJ contiguo

continent [kántənənt] N continente m; ADJ
(sexually) continente; (of bodily
functions) capaz de controlar los esfínteres

continental [kántṇéntł] ADJ continental

contingency [kəntíndʒənsi] N contingencia f

contingent [kəntíndʒənt] ADJ & N
contingente m

continual [kəntínjuəł] ADJ continuo

continuance [kəntínjuəns] N continuación f;
(delay) aplazamiento m

continuation [kəntɪnjuéʃən] N continuación
f

continue [kəntínju] VI/VT continuar

continuity [kántṇúɪDi] N continuidad f

continuous [kəntínjuəs] ADJ (uninterrupted
in time) continuo; (uninterrupted in
space) ininterrumpido

contortion [kəntɔ́rʃən] N contorsión f

contour [kántur] N contorno m

contraband [kántrəbænd] N contrabando m

contraception [kɑntrəsépʃən] N

anticoncepción f

contraceptive [kɑntrəséptɪv] ADJ & N
anticonceptivo m

contract [kántrækt] N contrato m; — **killer**
asesino -na a sueldo mf; [kəntrǽkt] VI/VT
contraer(se); (assign by contract) contratar

contraction [kəntrǽkʃən] N contracción f;
(in childbirth) contracción f, pujo m

contractor [kántræktə] N contratista mf

contractual [kəntrǽktʃuəł] ADJ contractual

contradict [kɑntrədíkt] VI/VT contradecir

contradiction [kɑntrədíkʃən] N
contradicción f

contradictory [kɑntrədíktəri] ADJ
contradictorio

contraption [kəntrǽpʃən] N chisme m, coso
m

contrary [kántreri] ADJ contrario, opuesto;
(obstinate) testarudo; N lo contrario; **on
the** — al contrario

contrast [kántræst] N contraste m; [kəntrǽst]
VI/VT contrastar

contravene [kɑntrəvín] VT contravenir

contribute [kəntríbjut] VI contribuir; (to a
newspaper) colaborar; VT contribuir con,
aportar

contribution [kɑntrəbjúʃən] N (donation,
article) contribución f; (scientific) aporte
m, aportación f

contributor [kəntríbjəDə] N colaborador -ra
mf

contrite [kəntráit] ADJ contrito

contrivance [kəntráivəns] N artefacto m

contrive [kəntráiv] VI/VT ingeniar; **he —d to
get their money** se las ingenió para
sacarles el dinero

contrived [kəntráivd] ADJ artificioso

control [kəntrół] VI/VT controlar; N control
m; (of a machine) mando m; **who's in**
—? ¿quién manda? **under** — bajo
control; — **freak** mandón -ona mf; —
key tecla de control/mando f; — **tower**
torre de control f

controller [kəntrólə] N (comptroller)
controlador -ora mf; Am contralor -ora mf;
(device) regulador m

controversy [kántrəvɚsi] N controversia f,
polémica f

conundrum [kənándrəm] N (riddle)
adivinanza f, acertijo m; (mystery) enigma
m

convalesce [kɑnvəlés] VI convalecer

convection [kənvékʃən] N convección f

convene [kənvín] VT convocar; VI reunirse

convenience [kənvínjəns] N (practicality)
conveniencia f; (appliance) comodidad f;
— **store** autoservicio m; **at your** —

cuando le venga bien

convenient [kənvínjənt] ADJ conveniente, oportuno; (at hand) accesible

convent [kánvent] N convento *m*

convention [kənvénʃən] N (political assembly) convención *f*; (professional assembly) congreso *m*; (pact) convenio *m*; (international agreement, acceptable usage) convención *f*

conventional [kənvénʃənəl] ADJ (not original) convencional; (traditional) clásico

conventioneer [kənvenʃənír] N congresista *mf*

converge [kənvɚ́dʒ] VI converger

conversant [kənvɚ́sənt] ADJ — **with** versado en

conversation [kanvɚséʃən] N conversación *f*; — **piece** tema de conversación *m*

converse [kənvɚ́s] VI conversar

conversion [kənvɚ́ʒən] N conversión *f*

convert [kánvɚt] VI/VT convertir(se); [kánvɚt] N converso -sa *mf*

converter [kənvɚ́Dɚ] N convertidor *m*

convertible [kənvɚ́Dəbəl] ADJ convertible; (car) descapotable; N descapotable *m*

convex [kánveks] ADJ convexo

convey [kənvé] VT (carry) llevar; (transfer a title) transferir; (transmit) transmitir; (communicate) comunicar; **to** — **thanks** expresar agradecimiento

conveyance [kənvéəns] N (vehicle) vehículo *m*; (transfer of property) transferencia *f*; (document) escritura de traspaso *f*

conveyer, conveyor [kənvéɚ] N transmisor -ra *mf*; — **belt** cinta transportadora *f*

convict [kánvɪkt] N convicto -ta *mf*; [kənvíkt] VI/VT declarar culpable

conviction [kənvíkʃən] N (belief) convicción *f*, convencimiento *m*; (act of convicting) declaración de culpabilidad *f*; (on one's record) condena *f*

convince [kənvíns] VT convencer

convincing [kənvínsɪŋ] ADJ convincente

convocation [kɑnvəkéʃən] N (act) convocación *f*; (group of people) asamblea *f*

convoke [kənvók] VT convocar

convoluted [kanvəlúɪd] ADJ retorcido

convoy [kánvɔɪ] N convoy *m*; VT convoyar

convulse [kənvʌ́ls] VI/VT convulsionar(se)

convulsion [kənvʌ́lʃən] N convulsión *f*

coo [ku] VI arrullar; N arrullo *m*

cook [kuk] N cocinero -ra *mf*; VT cocinar, guisar; —**book** libro de cocina *m*; **to** — **up a plan** urdir un plan

cookery [kúkəri] N cocina *f*

cookie [kúki] N galletita dulce *f*

cool [kuł] ADJ (not hot) fresco; (indifferent) frío, indiferente; (calm) tranquilo; (good) excelente; *Caribbean* chévere; *RP* macanudo; *Sp* guay; **that's not** — eso no se hace; N (cold) fresco *m*; (composure) tranquilidad *f*; VT (make cooler) enfriar; (air condition) refrigerar; **to** — **off** (get cold) enfriarse; (get cooler) refrescar(se); (calm down) calmarse; —**ing-off period** tregua *f*

coolant [kúlənt] N refrigerante *m*

cooler [kúlɚ] N (room) cámara frigorífica *f*; (container) nevera portátil *f*

coolness [kúlnɪs] N (cold weather) fresco *m*, frescor *m*; (indifference) frialdad *f*, indiferencia *f*

coon [kun] N (raccoon) mapache *m*; **a** —**'s age** una eternidad

co-op [kóap] N cooperativa *f*

coop [kup] N jaula *f*; (for chickens) gallinero *m*; VT enjaular; **to** — **up** encerrar

cooperate [koápɚet] VI cooperar

cooperation [koɑpɚéʃən] N cooperación *f*

cooperative [koɑpɚəDIV] ADJ cooperativo; N cooperativa *f*

coordinate [koɔ́rdnɪt] ADJ coordinado; N coordenada *f*; —**s** conjunto *m*; [koɔ́rdn̩et] VI/VT coordinar

coordination [koɔrdnéʃən] N coordinación *f*

cop [kap] N *fam* poli *mf*, polizonte *m*; VI **to** — **out** zafarse

cope [kop] VI **to** — **with** arreglárselas con; **I cannot** — **with this** no puedo con esto

copious [kópiəs] ADJ copioso

copper [kápɚ] N cobre *m*; (cop) *fam* poli *mf*; ADJ de cobre

copulate [kápjəlet] VI copular

copy [kápi] N (reproduction) copia *f*; (specimen, example) ejemplar *m*; (news story) texto *m*; —**cat** copión -ona *mf*; — **machine** copiadora *f*; —**right** copyright *m*, derechos de autor *m pl*; **this material is** —**righted** reservados todos los derechos; VT copiar; **to** —**right** registrar los derechos

coquette [kokét] N coqueta *f*

coral [kɔ́rəł] N coral *m*; ADJ (related to coral) coralino; (made of coral) de coral; — **reef** arrecife de coral *m*

cord [kɔrd] N (thread) cuerda *f*; (for shoes) cordón *m*; (firewood measure) medida de leña *f*; —**s** pantalones de pana *m pl*

cordial [kɔ́rdʒəł] ADJ cordial; N licor *m*

cordless [kɔ́rdlɪs] ADJ inalámbrico

corduroy [kɔ́rdərɔɪ] N pana *f*; —**s** pantalones de pana *m pl*

core [kor] N (of fruit) corazón *m*; (of a problem) meollo *m*; (of a magnet, reactor) núcleo *m*; VT despepitar

cork [kɔrk] N (woody material) corcho *m*; (stopper, buoy) tapón *m*; **—screw** sacacorchos *m sg*, tirabuzón *m*; **— tree** alcornoque *m*; VT tapar con un corcho

corn [kɔrn] N (plant) maíz *m*; (painful growth) callo *m*; **—bread** pan de maíz *m*; **—cob** mazorca *f*; *Sp* zuro *m*; **— on the cob** choclo *m*; *Mex* elote *m*; **—ed beef** corned beef *m*; **—field** maizal *m*; *Mex* milpa *f*; **—flakes** copos de maíz *m pl*; **—meal** harina de maíz *f*; **—starch** maicena® *f*

corner [kɔ́rnə] N (angle) ángulo *m*; (of a room, of a country) rincón *m*; (of two streets) esquina *f*; (monopoly) monopolio *m*; **—stone** piedra angular *f*; **— table** mesa rinconera *f*; VT (trap) arrinconar, acorralar; (monopolize) monopolizar; VI doblar; *Sp* girar

cornered [kɔ́rnəd] ADJ (animal) acorralado; (person) arrinconado

cornet [kɔrnét] N corneta *f*

cornice [kɔ́rnɪs] N cornisa *f*

corny [kɔ́rni] ADJ sensiblero; (joke) viejo

corollary [kɔ́rəlɛri] N corolario *m*

coronation [kɔrənéʃən] N coronación *f*

coroner [kɔ́rənə] N médico -ca forense *mf*

corporal [kɔ́rpəəl] ADJ corporal; N (rank) cabo *m*

corporation [kɔrpəréʃən] N sociedad anónima *f*

corps [kor] N cuerpo *m*

corpse [kɔrps] N cadáver *m*

corpulent [kɔ́rpjələnt] ADJ corpulento

corpus [kɔ́rpəs] N corpus *m*

corpuscle [kɔ́rpʌsəl] N corpúsculo *m*; (of blood) glóbulo *m*

corral [kəráɛl] N corral *m*; VT acorralar

correct [kərékt] VT corregir; ADJ correcto; **that is —** es cierto

correction [kərékʃən] N corrección *f*; (for glasses) graduación *f*

correctness [kəréktnɪs] N corrección *f*

corrector [kəréktə] N corrector -ra *mf*

correlate [kɔ́rəlet] VI/VT correlacionar; [kɔ́rəlɪt] N correlato *m*

correspond [kɔrəspánd] VI (be in agreement) corresponder, responder; (exchange letters) cartearse, escribirse

correspondence [kɔrəspándəns] N correspondencia *f*

correspondent [kɔrəspándənt] ADJ correspondiente; N (writer of letters) correspondiente *mf*; (news gatherer) corresponsal *mf*, enviado -da *mf*

corresponding [kɔrəspándɪŋ] ADJ correspondiente; (secretary, etc.) encargado de la correspondencia

corridor [kɔ́rɪdɔr] N corredor *m*, pasillo *m*

corroborate [kərɑ́bəret] VT corroborar

corrode [kəród] VI/VT corroer(se)

corrosion [kərózən] N corrosión *f*

corrupt [kərʌ́pt] ADJ (dishonest) corrupto; (rotten) corrompido; **to become —** corromperse; VT corromper, viciar

corruption [kərʌ́pʃən] N corrupción *f*

corset [kɔ́rsɪt] N corsé *m*

cortex [kɔ́rtɛks] N córtex *m*, corteza cerebral *f*

cortisone [kɔ́rDɪzon] N cortisona *f*

cosigner [kósaɪnə] N cosignatario -ria *mf*

cosmetic [kazmɛ́Dɪk] ADJ & N cosmético *m*

cosmic [kázmɪk] ADJ cósmico

cosmology [kazmáɪədʒi] N cosmología *f*

cosmonaut [kázmənɔt] N cosmonauta *mf*

cosmopolitan [kazməpálɪtn] ADJ cosmopolita

cosmos [kázmos] N cosmos *m*

cost [kɔst] N costo *m*; *Sp* coste *m*; **—s** (court costs) costas *f pl*; **at all —s** a toda costa; **— effective** económico; **— of living** costo / coste de vida *m*; **to sell at —** vender al costo / al coste; VT costar; **how much does this —?** ¿cuánto vale / cuesta esto?

co-star [kóstar] N coprotagonista *mf*

Costa Rica [kóstəríkə] N Costa Rica *f*

Costa Rican [kóstəríkən] ADJ & N costarricense *mf*

costly [kɔ́stli] ADJ costoso, caro

costume [kástum] N (style of clothing) vestimenta *f*; (in the theater) vestuario *m*; (disguise) disfraz *m*; **— jewelry** bisutería *f*

cot [kat] N catre *m*

cottage [kɑ́Dɪdʒ] N (small house) casita *f*; (vacation house) cabaña *f*, chalé *m*; **— cheese** requesón *m*

cotter pin [kɑ́Dəpɪn] N chaveta *f*

cotton [kɑtn] N algodón *m*; **— candy** algodón de azúcar *m*; **— gin** desmontadora de algodón *f*; **—seed** semilla de algodón *f*; **—wood** álamo (de Virginia) *m*; **— wool** algodón en rama *m*

couch [kautʃ] N sofá *m*; (psychiatrist's) diván *m*; **— potato** telebobo -ba *mf*; VT expresar

cougar [kúgə] N puma *f*

cough [kɔf] VI toser; **to — up** (spit) expectorar; (hand over) soltar, largar; N tos *f*; **— drop** pastilla para la tos *f*; **— syrup** jarabe para la tos *m*

could [kud] V AUX **I — do it if I wanted** podría hacerlo si quisiera; **— you arrive**

early? ¿podrías llegar temprano? — **I leave early?** ¿puedo salir temprano? **you — be right** quizá tengas razón

council [káunsəł] N (religious) concilio m; (advisory) consejo m, junta f; (provincial) diputación f; (municipal) concejo m; **—man** concejal m; **—woman** concejal f, concejala f

councilor [káunsələ] N concejal mf

counsel [káunsəł] N (advice) consejo m; (lawyer) abogado -da mf; vi/vt (give advice) aconsejar

counselor [káunsələ] N consejero -ra mf; (lawyer) abogado -da mf

count [kaunt] vi/vt contar; **to — in** incluir; **to — on** contar con; **to — oneself lucky** considerarse dichoso; **to — out** excluir; **—down** cuenta regresiva f; N (reckoning) cuenta f; (charge) cargo m; (noble) conde m

countenance [káuntŋəns] N (expression) semblante m; (face) cara f; vt (tolerate) tolerar; (approve) aprobar

counter [káuntə] N (in a kitchen) Sp encimera f; Am mostrador m; (in a store) mostrador m; (in a bar) barra f; (in board games) tablero m; (counting device) contador m; (in a shoe) contrafuerte m; **over the —** sin receta; ADJ contrario, opuesto; ADV **— to** contra; **to run — to** ser contrario a; vt (an argument) retrucar; (a blow) devolver; vi/vt replicar

counteract [kauntəǽkt] vt contrarrestar

counterattack [káuntəətæk] N contraataque m; vi/vt contraatacar

counterbalance [kauntəbǽləns] vi/vt contrapesar; [káuntəbæləns] N contrapeso m

counterculture [káuntəkʌltʃə] N contracultura f

counterespionage [kauntəéspiənaʒ] N contraespionaje m

counterexample [káuntəɪgzæmpəł] N contraejemplo m

counterfeit [káuntəfɪt] N falsificación f; ADJ falso; **— money** moneda falsa f; vt falsificar

countermand [kauntəmǽnd] vt contramandar; [káuntəmænd] N contraorden f

counteroffer [káuntəɔfə] N contraoferta f

counterpart [káuntəpart] N homólogo -ga mf

counterproductive [kauntəprədáktɪv] ADJ contraproducente

counterrevolution [kauntərɛvəlúʃən] N contrarrevolución f

countersign [káuntəsaɪn] N contraseña f; vt refrendar

countess [káuntɪs] N condesa f

countless [káuntlɪs] ADJ incontables, innumerables

country [kántri] N (nation) país m; (territory) territorio m; (homeland) patria f; (rural area) campo m; ADJ (of the countryside) rural; (uncouth) rústico; **— club** club campestre m; **—man** compatriota m; **— music** música country f; **—side** campo m; (scenery) paisaje m; **—woman** compatriota f

county [káunti] N condado m; **— fair** feria (de ganado) f; **— seat** capital de condado f

coup [ku] N (success) golpe maestro m; (putsch) golpe de estado m; **— d'état** golpe de estado m

coupe [kup] N cupé m

couple [kápəł] N (of times, of forces, of people) par m; (romantic) pareja f; vi/vt (pair up) formar parejas; vt (connect) acoplar; vi (copulate) copular

couplet [káplɪt] N pareado m

coupling [káplɪŋ] N (action) acoplamiento m, enganche m; (device) acople m, enganche m

coupon [kjúpan] N cupón m

courage [kɜ́ɪʤ] N valentía f, valor m, coraje m

courageous [kəréʤəs] ADJ valiente

courier [kúriə] N mensajero -ra mf

course [kɔrs] N (of a river, of study, of a disease) curso m; (of a road, route) trayecto m; (of a ship, plane) derrotero m; (progression of time) marcha f; (dish) plato m; **— of action** línea de conducta f, proceder m; **in the — of a year** en el transcurso de un año; **in due — a** la larga; INTERJ **of —** claro, por supuesto, naturalmente; vi correr, fluir

court [kɔrt] N (courtyard) patio m; (atrium) patio interior m; (in sports) cancha, pista f; (in a city) plazuela f, plazoleta f; (tribunal) juzgado m, tribunal m; (session) audiencia f; (royal residence, retinue) corte f; **—-martial** consejo de guerra m; **— of law** tribunal de justicia m; **— reporter** estenotipista mf; **—yard** patio m; **to settle out of —** llegar a un arreglo extrajudicial; **to pay — to** cortejar; vt cortejar, galantear; **to — danger** tentar a la suerte; **to —-martial** someter a consejo de guerra; vi estar de novios

courteous [kɜ́ɪdiəs] ADJ cortés

courtesy [kɜ́ɪDɪsi] N (attitude) cortesía f; (act)

fineza f, atención f

courtier [kórdɪə·] N (member of the court) cortesano -na mf; (sycophant) adulador -ra mf

courtship [kórtʃɪp] N cortejo m

cousin [kázən] N primo -ma mf; **first —** primo -ma hermano -na mf

counterclockwise [kaʊntə·klákwaɪz] ADV en el sentido opuesto al de las manecillas del reloj

cove [kov] N ensenada f

covenant [kávənənt] N pacto m; (religious) alianza f

cover [kávə·] VI/VT cubrir; (with lid, screen) tapar; (replace) sustituir; (include, deal with) comprender; (traverse) recorrer; (sing) hacer una versión; **to — up** (wrap up) tapar bien; (hide) ocultar; **—all** mono m; **—-up** encubrimiento m; N (lid) tapa f; (book) cubierta f, tapa f; (blanket) manta f; (for appliances, furniture) funda f; (front for activity) tapadera f, pantalla f; (shelter) resguardo m, abrigo m; **— charge** entrada f; **—girl** modelo de portada f; **to send under separate —** enviar por separado; **to take —** resguardarse; **under —** de incógnito; **under — of dark** bajo el manto de la noche

coverage [kávə·ɪʤ] N cobertura f; (of a cell phone) alcance m

covering [kávə·ɪŋ] N cubierta f

covert [kovз́·t] ADJ encubierto

covet [kávɪt] VT (desire wrongfully) codiciar; (want) ansiar

covetous [kávɪdəs] ADJ codicioso

cow [kaʊ] N (bovine female) vaca f; (female of other animals) hembra f; **—bell** cencerro m, esquila f; **—boy** vaquero m; **—hide** cuero de vaca m, vaqueta f; **—lick** remolino m; **—shed** vaquería f, vaqueriza f; **to have a —** tener una pataleta; VT intimidar

coward [káʊ·d] N cobarde mf

cowardice [káʊ·dɪs] N cobardía f

cowardly [káʊ·dli] ADJ cobarde

cower [káʊ·] VI achicarse

cowl [kaʊɫ] N capucha f

coy [kɔɪ] ADJ (coquettish) remilgado; (evasive) esquivo

coyote [kaɪódi, káɪot] N coyote m

cozy [kózi] ADJ (warm) acogedor; (beneficial) conveniente; **to — up to** adular

CPU (central processing unit) [sipijú] N UCP f

crab [kræb] N cangrejo m; (mechanism) carro corredizo m; (grouch) cascarrabias mf; **— apple** manzana silvestre f; **—s** ladillas f pl;

VI (fish) pescar cangrejos; (complain) quejarse

crack [kræk] VI (single fissure) rajarse; (multiple fissures) resquebrajarse, agrietarse; (psychological breakdown) sufrir un ataque de nervios; (of voice) quebrarse; VT (knuckles) hacer un chasquido con, chascar, chasquear; (nuts) cascar; (jokes) contar; (a prisoner) quebrar; (a case) resolver; (a code) descifrar; (a door) entreabrir; **to — down on** reprimir; **that —s me up** esto me hace desternillar de risa; N (fissure) rajadura f, grieta f, resquebrajadura f; (sound) chasquido m; (joke) pulla f, chanza f; **— cocaine** crack m; **—down** represión f; **—house** fumadero m; **—pot** excéntrico -ca mf; **at the — of dawn** al romper el alba; **I'd like a — at the championship** me gustaría poder participar en el campeonato

cracked [krækt] ADJ rajado, quebrado; (crazy) chiflado; **it's not all it's — up to be** no es para tanto

cracker [krǽkə·] N galleta f

crackle [krǽkəɫ] N (of paper) crujido m; (of fire) crepitación f; VI crujir, crepitar

cradle [kréd̬ɫ] N cuna f

craft [kræft] N (skill) destreza f; (cunning) astucia f; (occupation) arte m, oficio m; (boat) embarcación f; **—sman** artesano m; **—swoman** artesana f; VT fabricar

crafty [krǽfti] ADJ astuto, taimado

crag [kræg] N risco m, peñasco m, peñón m

craggy [krǽgi] ADJ peñascoso

cram [kræm] VT (pack in) embutir; VI (study intensely) memorizar; Sp empollar; **the bar was —med with people** el bar estaba atestado

cramp [kræmp] N (spasm) calambre m; (staple) grapa f; VI/VT (to suffer a spasm) acalambrar(se); VT (to staple) engrapar; **you're —ing my style** me estorbas

cranberry [krǽnberi] N arándano agrio m

crane [kren] N (bird) grulla f; (machine) grúa f; VT **to — one's neck** estirar el cuello

cranium [kréniəm] N cráneo m

crank [kræŋk] N (mechanism) manivela f; (grouch) cascarrabias mf sg; (overzealous advocate) fanático -ca mf; **—case** cárter superior del aceite m; **—shaft** cigüeñal m; VI/VT arrancar con manivela

cranky [krǽŋki] ADJ (irritable) irritable; (eccentric) excéntrico

cranny [krǽni] N (crevice) rendija f; (corner) recoveco m

crash [kræʃ] VI (collide) estrellarse; (market) quebrar; (overnight with someone) quedarse a dormir; (hang up, as with a computer) colgarse; (sleep) dormir; VT **to — a car** chocar un coche; **to — a party** colarse en una fiesta; N (noise) estallido *m*; (collision) choque *m*; (financial) quiebra *f*; **— landing** aterrizaje forzoso *m*

crass [kræs] ADJ craso

crate [kret] N cajón *m*, guacal *m*; VT poner en cajones

crater [krédə] N cráter *m*

cravat [krəvǽt] N corbata *f*

crave [krev] VT anhelar; **I — chocolate** me muero por un chocolate

craving [krévɪŋ] N antojo *m*

crawl [krɔl] VI (on hands and knees) gatear; (on the belly) arrastrarse, reptar; (proceed slowly) avanzar a paso de tortuga; **to be —ing with** hormiguear de; N (swimming stroke) crol *m*; **traffic is going at a —** el tráfico va a paso de tortuga

crayon [kréan] N lápiz de color *m*, crayola™ *f*

craze [krez] N (vogue) moda *f*; VI/VT enloquecer(se)

craziness [krézinɪs] N locura *f*, chifladura *f*

crazy [krézi] ADJ & N loco -ca *mf*; **I'm — about you** estoy loco por ti; **that's —!** ¡qué locura! **to go —** volverse loco, enloquecerse

creak [krik] N (of wooden floor) crujido *m*; (of a hinge) rechinamiento *m*; VI (a wooden floor) crujir; (a hinge) rechinar

cream [krim] N (milk product) crema *f*; *Sp* nata *f*; (medicament) crema *f*; **— cheese** queso de untar *m*; **— of tomato soup** sopa crema de tomate *f*; **the — of the crop** la flor y nata; VT (decream) desnatar; (butter, sugar) batir; (vegetables) preparar con salsa blanca; (defeat) aplastar

creamy [krími] ADJ cremoso

crease [kris] N (in trousers) raya *f*, repliegue *m*; (wrinkle) arruga *f*; VT (trousers) planchar la raya; (wrinkle) arrugar

create [kriét] VI/VT crear

creation [kriéʃən] N creación *f*

creationism [kriéʃənɪzəm] N creacionismo *m*

creative [kriéDɪv] ADJ creativo

creator [kriéDə] N creador -ra *mf*

creature [krítʃə] N (being) ser *m*; (animal) animal *m*; **a — of your imagination** un producto de tu imaginación

credence [krídn̩s] N crédito *m*

credentials [krɪdéntʃəɫz] N credenciales *f pl*

credible [krédəbəɫ] ADJ creíble

credit [krédɪt] N crédito *m*; (commendation) reconocimiento *m*; **— card** tarjeta de crédito *f*; **— line** línea de crédito *f*; **—s** créditos *m pl*; **— underwriters**

aseguradores de crédito *m pl*; **— union** banco cooperativo *m*; **—worthy** solvente; **on —** a crédito; **to give — to** (believe) dar crédito; (ascribe) acreditar; VT (believe) creer; (enter as credit) acreditar; (attribute) atribuir

creditor [krédɪDə] N acreedor -ra *mf*

credulous [krédʒələs] ADJ crédulo

creed [krid] N credo *m*

creek [krik] N arroyo *m*

creep [krip] VI (crawl on belly) arrastrarse; (crawl on all fours) gatear; (grow upward) trepar; (go slowly) andar a paso de tortuga; **to — up on** acercarse furtivamente a; N (obnoxious person) *pej* repulsivo -va *mf*, sinvergüenza *mf*; **that gives me the —s** eso me da asco; *Sp* eso me da grima

creeper [krípə] N enredadera *f*, planta trepadora *f*

creepy [krípi] ADJ repulsivo

cremate [krímet] VT cremar

Creole [kríoɫ] ADJ & N criollo -lla *mf*

creosote [kríəsot] N creosota *f*

crepe [krep] N (fabric) crespón *m*; (band of fabric) crespón negro *m*

crescent [krésənt] N media luna *f*; ADJ creciente

crest [krest] N (of a wave, rooster) cresta *f*; (of feathers) penacho *m*, copete *m*; (of mountain) cima *f*, cumbre *f*; (of heraldic arms) timbre *m*; **—fallen** alicaído, cabizbajo; VI **the river —ed at two meters above flood-level** el río creció hasta dos metros por encima de lo normal

crevice [krévɪs] N grieta *f*

crew [kru] N (for ships, etc.) tripulación *f*; (of workers) cuadrilla *f*

crib [krɪb] N (bed) cuna *f*; (manger) pesebre *m*; (bin for grain) granero *m*; (cheat notes) hoja para copiar *f*; VI copiar

cricket [kríkɪt] N (insect) grillo *m*; (game) criquet *m*

crime [kraɪm] N (illegal act) delito *m*; (act of violence against people) crimen *m*; (criminal activity) delincuencia *f*, criminalidad *f*

criminal [krímənəɫ] ADJ & N delincuente *mf*, malhechor -ora *mf*; (violent crimes) criminal *mf*

crimp [krɪmp] VT rizar; N rizo *m*

crimson [krímzən] ADJ & N carmesí *m*, carmín *m*

cringe [krɪndʒ] VI **he makes me —** me da asco

cripple [krípəɫ] N *offensive* tullido -da *mf*; (in the legs) *offensive* cojo -ja *mf*; (in the arms) *offensive* manco -ca *mf*; VT tullir

crisis [kráɪsɪs] N crisis *f*

crisp [krɪsp] ADJ (apple, bacon, etc.) crocante, crujiente; (weather) fresco y despejado; (hair) crespo; VI/VT volver crujiente

crispy [kríspi] ADJ crocante, crujiente

criterion [kraɪtíriən] N criterio *m*

critic [krídɪk] N crítico -ca *mf*

critical [krídɪkəl] ADJ crítico

criticism [krídɪsɪzəm] N crítica *f*

criticize [krídɪsaɪz] VT criticar

croak [krok] VI (make the sound of a frog) croar; (make the sound of a crow) graznar; (die) *fam* espichar; N (sound made by frogs) cante de ranas *m*; (sound made by crows) graznido *m*

Croatia [kroéʃə] N Croacia *f*

Croatian [kroéʃən] ADJ & N croata *mf*

crochet [kroʃé] N ganchillo *m*, croché *m*, crochet *m*; — **hook** aguja de croché *f*; VI hacer ganchillo, hacer croché

crock [krak] N (pot) vasija *f*; (lies) pamplinas *f pl*

crockery [krákəri] N loza *f*

crocodile [krákədaɪl] N cocodrilo *m*

croissant [krəsánt] N cruasán *m*, croissant *m*

crony [króni] N compinche *mf*, compadre *m*, comadre *f*

crook [krʊk] N (criminal) delincuente *mf*; (curve) curva *f*; (hook) gancho *m*; (staff) cayado *m*

crooked [krúkɪd] ADJ (bent) torcido; *Am* chueco; (dishonest) deshonesto

crop [krap] N (harvest) cosecha *f*; (group of contemporaries) promoción *f*; (of a bird) buche *m*; (horse whip) fusta *f*; — **rotation** rotación de cultivos *f*; VT (graze) pastar, pacer; (trim) recortar; **to — up** surgir

croquet [kroké] N cróquet *m*

cross [krɔs] N (symbol) cruz *f*; (street intersection) cruce *m*; (act of mixing) cruzamiento *m*; (in boxing) cruzado *m*; —**bar** (soccer) travesaño *m*; (gymnastics) barra *f*; (high jump) listón *m*; (of a door) tranca *f*; —**check** verificación *f*; —**piece** cruceta *f*; **to bear one's** — cargar la cruz; VI/VT (intersect, form a cross, breed, meet) cruzar(se); (make sign of the cross) santiguarse; VT (betray) traicionar; (pass) cruzar, franquear; **to — out** tachar; **to — over** (change allegiance) cambiar de bando; (go to the other side) traspasar; **you've —ed the line** se te fue la mano; **to —check** verificar; ADJ (transverse) transversal; (angry) enojado; —**-country** a campo traviesa; —**-cultural**

transcultural; **to — examine** interrogar; —**-eyed** bizco; **to be —-eyed** bizquear; —**-fertilization** fecundación cruzada *f*; —**-reference** referencia cruzada *f*; **to —-reference** hacer una referencia cruzada; —**road** encrucijada *f*; — **section** corte transversal *m*; —**walk** cruce peatonal *m*, cebra *f*; —**word puzzle** crucigrama *m*

crossing [krɔ́sɪŋ] N (street or railroad intersection, pedestrian path) cruce *m*; (hybridization, act of mixing) cruzamiento *m*; (of ocean) travesía *f*; (of a border) paso *m*; (of a river) vado *m*

crotch [kratʃ] N entrepierna *f*

crotchety [krátʃɪdi] ADJ cascarrabias

crouch [kraʊtʃ] VI (stoop) agacharse; (prepare to spring) agazaparse

croup [krup] N tos *f*, croup *m*

crow [kro] N (bird) cuervo *m*; (sound of rooster) canto del gallo *m*; —**bar** alzaprima *f*; —**'s-foot** pata de gallo *f*; **to eat** — comerse sus propias palabras; VI cantar; (gloat, brag) jactarse

crowd [kraʊd] N (group of people) muchedumbre *f*, gentío *m*, aglomeración *f*; (at a performance) público *m*; (clique) pandilla *f*; VI (push forward) agolparse; VI/VT (gather in large numbers) apiñar(se), amontonar(se), aglomerar(se); (gather in a confined space) hacinar(se)

crowded [kráʊdɪd] ADJ **it is — in here** hay demasiada gente aquí; **the restaurant is —** el restaurante está lleno

crown [kraʊn] N corona *f*; (of head) coronilla *f*, crisma *f*; (of a hat) copa *f*; — **jewels** joyas de la corona *f pl*; VT coronar; (hit on head) dar un coscorrón

crucial [krúʃəl] ADJ (element) fundamental; (moment) crucial

crucible [krúsəbəl] N crisol *m*

crucifix [krúsəfɪks] N crucifijo *m*

crucify [krúsəfaɪ] VT crucificar

crud [krʌd] N (filth) mugre *f*; (worthless thing, sickness, despicable person) *fam* porquería *f*

crude [krud] ADJ (vulgar, unpolished) basto, tosco; — **oil** petróleo crudo *m*; — **sugar** azúcar sin refinar *mf*

cruel [krúəl] ADJ cruel

cruelty [krúəlti] N crueldad *f*

cruise [kruz] VI (take a cruise) tomar un crucero; (patrol) patrullar; — **missile** misil crucero *m*; **cruising speed** velocidad de crucero *f*; N crucero *m*; — **control** control de crucero *m*

cruiser [krúzə-] N crucero *m*

crumb [krʌm] N (small) miga f, migaja f; (large) mendrugo m; VT (break into crumbs) desmigajar; (remove crumbs) sacar las migas

crumble [krámbəl] VI/VT (bread) desmigajar(se); (clods of dirt) desmenuzar(se); (house) desmoronar(se)

crummy [krámi] ADJ (place) fam de mala muerte; (object) fam de porquería; (show) flojo

crumple [krámpəl] VI/VT (crush) arrugar(se); VI (collapse) aplastarse

crunch [krʌntʃ] VI/VT (eat noisily) mascar; N (sound) crujido m; (shortage) crisis f; **—es** abdominales m pl

crunchy [krántʃi] ADJ crocante, crujiente

crusade [kruséd] N cruzada f; VI (engage in a campaign) hacer una campaña

crusader [kruséda-] N cruzado -da mf; **a — for human rights** un paladín de los derechos humanos

crush [krʌʃ] VI/VT aplastar, machacar; (stone) demoler; N (act of crushing) aplastamiento m; (crowd) tumulto m; (infatuation) enamoramiento m

crust [krʌst] N (of bread, earth) corteza f; (of bread) costra f; (of pie) tapa f

crusty [krásti] ADJ (with a crust) costroso; (grouchy) irascible

crutch [krʌtʃ] N muleta f

cry [krai] N (shout) grito m; (weeping) llanto m; (call of an animal) reclamo m; **a far — from** muy distante de, muy lejos de; VI (shout) gritar; (weep) llorar; **—baby** llorón -ona mf; **to — over spilt milk** hacer como la lechera; **to — for attention** reclamar atención; **to — for help** pedir socorro; **to — out** vocear

crystal [kríst] N cristal m; **— ball** bola de cristal f; **— clear** cristalino

crystalline [krístlɪn] ADJ cristalino

crystallize [krístaɪz] VI/VT cristalizar(se)

cub [kʌb] N (lion) cachorro m; (bear) osezno m; (whale) ballenato m; (wolf) lobato m, lobezno m; **— reporter** reportero -ra novato -ta mf

Cuba [kjúbə] N Cuba f

Cuban [kjúbən] ADJ & N cubano -na mf

cubbyhole [kábihoł] N casilla f

cube [kjúb] N cubo m; **— root** raíz cúbica f; VT (cut) cortar en cubos; (raise to the third power) elevar al cubo

cubic [kjúbɪk] ADJ cúbico

cubicle [kjúbɪkəł] N cubículo m

cubism [kjúbɪzəm] N cubismo m

cuckold [kákəłd] N cornudo m, cabrón m; VT poner los cuernos a

cuckoo [kúku] N cuco m, cuclillo m; **— clock** reloj de cucú m; ADJ & N chiflado -da mf; INTERJ cucú

cucumber [kjúkʌmbə-] N pepino m

cud [kʌd] N **to chew the —** rumiar

cuddle [kád] VI/VT hacer(se) mimos; N mimo m

cuddly [kádli] ADJ mimoso

cudgel [kádʒəł] N porra f; VT aporrear

cue [kju] N (in theater) pie m; (stimulus) estímulo m; **— ball** bola blanca f; **— stick** taco de billar m; VT dar pie, dar la señal

cuff [kʌf] N (of sleeve, glove) puño m; (of pants) bajo m; (handcuffs) esposas f pl; (blow) bofetada f; VT (pants) hacer los bajos; (with handcuffs) esposar; (hit) abofetear

cuisine [kwɪzín] N cocina f

cul-de-sac [kʌłdəsæk] N callejón sin salida m

culinary [kjúləneri] ADJ culinario

cull [kʌł] VT (choose) seleccionar, entresacar; (collect) recoger

culminate [kálmənet] VI/VT culminar

culprit [kálprɪt] N culpable mf

cult [kʌłt] N (sect) secta religiosa f; (worship) culto m

cultivate [káłtəvet] VT cultivar

cultivated [káłtəvedɪd] ADJ (land) cultivado; (plant) de cultivo; (educated) culto

cultivation [káłtəvéʃən] N (tillage) cultivo m; (education) cultura f

cultivator [káłtəvedə-] N (person) cultivador -ra mf; (implement) cultivadora f

cultural [káłtʃə-əł] ADJ cultural

culture [káłtʃə-] N cultura f; (microorganisms) cultivo m; **— shock** choque cultural m; VT (microorganisms) cultivar

cultured [káłtʃə-d] ADJ (person) culto; (pearl) cultivado, de cultivo

cumbersome [kámbə-səm] ADJ (bulky) voluminoso; (unwieldy) incómodo

cumulative [kjúmjələdɪv] ADJ acumulativo

cumulus [kjúmjələs] N cúmulo m

cunning [kánɪŋ] ADJ (sly) astuto, zorro; N astucia f, maña f

cup [kʌp] N (with handle) taza f, pocillo m; (without handle) vaso m; (measure) taza f; (trophy, brassiere part) copa f; **—board** armario m, aparador m

cur [kɝ] N (dog) perro m; (villain) pej villano -na mf

curable [kjúrəbəł] ADJ curable

curator [kjúredə-] N conservador -ra mf

curb [kɝb] N (of a street) Sp bordillo m; Mex borde m; RP cordón m; (of a well) brocal

m; (restraint) freno *m*, restricción *f*; VT
(emotions) refrenar; (spending) limitar

curd [kɚd] N cuajada *f*; VI/VT cuajar(se),
coagular(se)

curdle [kɚdl] VI/VT cuajar(se), coagular(se);
my blood —d se me heló la sangre

cure [kjur] N (healing, preserving meat) cura
f, curación *f*; (method) tratamiento *m*; VI/
VT curar(se); **—all** sanalotodo *m*

curfew [kɚfju] N toque de queda *m*, queda *f*

curio [kjúrio] N curiosidad *f*

curiosity [kjuriásɪdi] N curiosidad *f*

curious [kjúrias] ADJ curioso

curl [kɚl] VI/VT (form ringlets) rizar(se),
ensortijar(se); (coil) enroscar(se); (smoke)
alzarse en espirales; **to — up** ovillar(se); N
(of hair) rizo *m*, bucle *m*; (of smoke)
espiral *f*

curler [kɚlə] N *Sp* rulo *m*; *Mex* tubo *m*; *RP*
rulero *m*

curly [kɚli] ADJ rizado

currant [kɚənt] N (fruit) grosella *f*; (tree)
grosellero *m*

currency [kɚənsi] N (money) moneda *f*,
divisa *f*; (acceptance) aceptación *f*

current [kɚənt] ADJ (commonly used)
corriente; (prevalent) actual; **the — issue
of a magazine** el último número de una
revista; **the — month** el corriente mes; N
corriente *f*

curriculum [kəríkjələm] N plan de estudios
m

curry [kɚri] N curry *m*

curse [kɚs] N (ill wish) maldición *f*; (swear
word) palabrota *f*; VI/VT (wish ill) maldecir;
(swear) decir palabrotas

cursive [kɚsɪv] ADJ cursivo; N cursiva *f*

cursor [kɚsɚ] N cursor *m*

curt [kɚt] ADJ (abrupt) seco, brusco; (brief)
breve

curtail [kətél] VT restringir, cercenar

curtain [kɚtn̩] N cortina *f*; (theater) telón *m*;
VT ponerle cortinas a

curvature [kɚvətʃʊr] N curvatura *f*; (of the
spine) desviación *f*

curve [kɚv] N curva *f*; **he threw me a —**
me agarró desprevenido; VI/VT
encorvar(se); (road) torcer(se), desviar(se);
VI **the ball —s** la pelota tiene efecto

curved [kɚvd] ADJ curvo

cushion [kúʃən] N (pad) almohadilla *f*;
(emergency resources, pad of air) colchón
m; (pillow) almohadón *m*; (decorative
pillow) cojín *m*; VT (put pads) poner
almohadones; (soften a blow) amortiguar

cuss [kʌs] VI decir palabrotas; N **—word** *fam*
palabrota *f*; **strange old —** *fam* bicho

raro *m*

custard [kástɚd] N flan *m*, natillas *f pl*

custodian [kʌstódiən] N (caretaker) cuidador
-ra *mf*; (guardian) custodio -dia *mf*

custody [kástədi] N custodia *f*; **to take into
—** detener

custom [kástəm] N costumbre *f*, uso *m*;
—-built construido por encargo;
—-made hecho a medida; **—s**
(government department) aduana *f*;
(taxes) derechos de aduana *m pl*;
—(s)house aduana *f*

customary [kástəmeri] ADJ acostumbrado

customer [kástəmə] N cliente -ta *mf*

customize [kástəmaɪz] VT adaptar por
encargo

cut [kʌt] VI/VT cortar; (shorten) acortar; (trees)
talar; (prices) rebajar; **—! ¡**corte(n)! **to — a
deal** llegar a un arreglo; **to — across**
(take a shortcut) cortar por; (transcend)
trascender; **to — back** reducir; **to —
class** faltar a clase; **to — down on**
reducir; **to — in** (interrupt) interrumpir;
(in traffic) atravesarse; **may I — in?** ¿me
permite? **to — off** (interrupt) interrumpir;
(intercept) interceptar; **to — out** omitir;
to be — out for estar hecho para; **to —
up** (divide) trozar; (misbehave) portarse
mal; **—-and-dried** predeterminado;
—back reducción *f*; **— glass** cristal
labrado *m*; **—off date** fecha límite *f*;
—-rate de rebajas; **—throat** despiadado;
N corte *m*; (in salary) recorte *m*; (of prices)
rebaja *f*; (of a suit) hechura *f*, corte *m*;
(insult) desaire *f*

cute [kjut] ADJ mono, rico; **to act —** ser
afectado, ser melindroso

cuticle [kjúdɪkəl] N cutícula *f*

cutlery [kátləri] N (knives, knife store)
cuchillería *f*; (eating utensils) cubiertos *m
pl*

cutlet [kátlɪt] N filete *m*

cutter [kádɚ] N (person) cortador -ra *mf*;
(device) cortadora *f*; (sleigh) trineo *m*;
Coast Guard — guardacostas *m sg*

cutting [kádɪŋ] ADJ (sharp) cortante; (cold)
penetrante; (sarcastic) mordaz, sarcástico;
— board tabla de cortar *f*; **— edge** filo *m*

cyanide [sáɪənaɪd] N cianuro *m*

cybernetics [saɪbə·nédɪks] N cibernética *f*

cyberpunk [sáɪbə·pʌnk] N ciberpunk *m*

cyberspace [sáɪbə·spes] N ciberespacio *m*

cyborg [sáɪbɔrg] N cyborg *m*

cycle [sáɪkəl] N ciclo *m*

cyclical [síklɪkəl] ADJ cíclico

cyclone [sáɪklon] N ciclón *m*

cyclotron [sáɪklətrɑn] N ciclotrón *m*

cylinder [sílɪndɚ] N cilindro *m*; (of a gun) tambor *m*; **— head** culata *f*
cylindrical [sɪlíndrɪkəl] ADJ cilíndrico
cymbal [símbəl] N címbalo *m*, platillo *m*
cynic [sínɪk] N cínico -ca *mf*
cynical [sínɪkəl] ADJ cínico
cynicism [sínɪsɪzəm] N cinismo *m*
cypress [sáɪprɪs] N ciprés *m*
Cypriot, Cypriote [síprɪət] ADJ & N chipriota *mf*
Cyprus [sáɪprəs] N Chipre *m*
cyst [sɪst] N quiste *m*
czar [zɑr] N zar *m*
Czech [tʃɛk] ADJ & N checo -ca *mf*
Czech Republic [tʃɛkrɪpʌ́blɪk] N República Checa *f*

Dd

dab [dæb] VT (pat) dar toques; (apply) aplicar con golpecitos; N toque *m*
dabble [dǽbəl] VI (splash) chapotear; (be interested superficially) ser aficionado a
dachshund [dɑ́ksənd] N perro salchicha *m*
dad [dæd] N papá *m*
daddy [dǽɾi] N papaíto *m*, papito *m*, papacito *m*
daffodil [dǽfədɪl] N narciso *m*
dagger [dǽgɚ] N daga *f*, puñal *m*; **to look —s at** traspasar con la mirada
dahlia [dǽljə] N dalia *f*
daily [déli] ADJ diario; **— wage** jornal *m*, salario *m*; N diario *m*
dainty [dénti] ADJ (delicate) delicado, exquisito; (finicky) remilgado
dairy [déri] N (milk) lechería *f*; (cheese) quesería *f*; ADJ (industry) lechero; (product) lácteo
daisy [dézi] N margarita *f*; **to be pushing up daisies** *fam* estar criando malvas
dale [del] N valle *m*
dally [dǽli] VI (risk danger) jugar con fuego; (waste time) remolonear
dam [dæm] N presa *f*, represa *f*; VT represar
damage [dǽmɪdʒ] N daño *m*, destrozo *m*; **—s** daños y perjuicios *m pl*; **to pay —s** indemnizar *m*; VI/VT dañar(se)
damaging [dǽmɪdʒɪŋ] ADJ perjudicial
dame [dem] N (noblewoman) dama *f*; (woman) *pej* tipa *f*
damn [dæm] VT condenar; **it's not worth a — no vale un comino**
damnation [dæmnéʃən] N condenación *f*,

perdición *f*
damp [dæmp] ADJ húmedo; N humedad *f*; VT (wet) humedecer; (deaden) amortiguar; (extinguish) apagar
dampen [dǽmpən] VT (wet) humedecer; (depress) deprimir; (deaden) amortiguar
dampness [dǽmpnɪs] N humedad *f*
damsel [dǽmzəl] N damisela *f*
dance [dæns] N (act of dancing, party, activity) baile *m*; (artistic activity, animal courtship movements) danza *f*; **— music** música bailable *f*; VI/VT (at a party) bailar; (in ballet, of animals) danzar; **she —d her way to stardom** llegó al estrellato bailando
dancer [dǽnsɚ] N bailarín -ina *mf*, danzante *mf*
dancercise [dǽnsɚsaɪz] N baile aeróbico *m*
dandelion [dǽndlaɪən] N diente de león *m*
dandruff [dǽndrəf] N caspa *f*
dandy [dǽndi] N (affected man) dandi *m*, señorito *m*; ADJ estupendo
Dane [den] N danés -esa *mf*
danger [déndʒɚ] N peligro *m*
dangerous [déndʒɚəs] ADJ peligroso
dangle [dǽŋgəl] VI/VT (hang) colgar; (sway) bambolear(se); (tempt) tentar con; **her legs were dangling off the bench** sus piernas pendían del banco
Danish [dénɪʃ] ADJ danés; N bollo dulce *m*
dapple, dappled [dǽpəl(d)] ADJ pinto, moteado
dare [der] VI/VT (be brave) atreverse (a), osar; (challenge) desafiar; **how — you?** ¿cómo te atreves? N desafío *m*; **—devil** temerario -ria *mf*
daring [dérɪŋ] N atrevimiento *m*, osadía *f*; ADJ atrevido, osado, arriesgado
dark [dɑrk] ADJ (in color) oscuro; (of hair) moreno, morocho, trigueño; (gloomy) sombrío, tenebroso; (evil, ignorant) oscuro; (hidden) turbio; **— Ages** (Alta) Edad Media *f*; **—room** cuarto oscuro *m*; **—-skinned** moreno; N oscuridad *f*; **after — después de que oscurece**
darken [dɑ́rkən] VI/VT oscurecer(se)
darkness [dɑ́rknɪs] N (complete) oscuridad *f*, tinieblas *f pl*; (partial) penumbra *f*
darling [dɑ́rlɪŋ] ADJ & N amado -da *mf*, querido -da *mf*; **my — vida mía, amor mío**
darn [dɑrn] VT zurcir, remendar; **—ing needle** aguja de zurcir *f*; N zurcido *m*; **it is not worth a — no vale un comino**; INTERJ ¡caramba! ¡caracoles!
dart [dɑrt] N (missile) dardo *m*; (tuck) pinza *f*; (swift movement) movimiento rápido

m; **—board** diana *f*; **to play —s** jugar a los dardos; VI disparar; **to — out** salir disparado

dash [dæʃ] VI/VT (of waves, porcelain) estrellar(se); VT (plans) frustrar; VI (hopes) desplomarse; **to — by** pasar corriendo; **to — off / out** salir disparado; **to — off a letter** escribir de prisa una carta; N (line) raya *f*; (run) corrida *f*; (race) carrera *f*; (small amount) pizca *f*; (splash) salpicadura *f*; **the one-hundred-meter — la carrera de los cien metros llanos / planos; —board** tablero *m*, salpicadero *m*

data [déɾə,dǽɾə] N datos *m pl*; **—base** base de datos *f*; **—bank** banco de datos *m*; **— processing** procesamiento de datos *m*

date [det] N (time) fecha *f*; (appointment) cita *f*; (person) acompañante *mf*; (fruit) dátil *m*; **out of —** anticuado; **to —** hasta ahora; **up to —** al día; VI (be dated) estar fechado; (go out socially) salir; VT (write the date) fechar; (show to be old-fashioned) delatar la edad; (go out socially) salir con; **to — from** datar de, remontarse a

dated [déɾɪd] ADJ (having a date) fechado; (old-fashioned) anticuado

daub [dɔb] VT (smear) embarrar, embadurnar; (apply unskillfully) pintarrajear

daughter [dɔ́ɾə] N hija *f*; **—-in-law** nuera *f*

daunt [dɔnt] VT (intimidate) intimidar; (dishearten) desanimar

dauntless [dɔ́ntlɪs] ADJ intrépido

davenport [dǽvənpɔrt] N sofá grande *m*

dawn [dɔn] N alba *f*, amanecer *m*, aurora *f*; **the — of civilization** los albores de la civilización; VI amanecer, aclarar; **it just —ed on me that** caí en (la) cuenta de que

day [de] N día *m*; **— after tomorrow** pasado mañana *m*; **— before yesterday** anteayer *m*; **—break** amanecer *m*; **at —break** al amanecer; **—care** guardería *f*; **—dream** fantasía *f*; **to —dream** soñar despierto; **— laborer** jornalero -ra *mf*; **—light** luz del día *f*; **—time** día *m*; **—time activity** actividad diurna *f*; **—-to—** día a día; **by — de día; by the — por día; eight-hour — jornada de ocho horas *f*; in my — en mis tiempos; in the old —s antaño; make my — dame el gusto; New Year's — Año Nuevo *m*; ADJ diurno

daze [dez] VT aturdir; N **to be in a —** estar aturdido

dazzle [dǽzəł] VI/VT deslumbrar

deacon [díkən] N diácono *m*

deactivate [diǽktəvet] VI/VT desactivar

dead [ded] ADJ muerto; **— air** aire viciado *m*; **—beat** moroso -sa *mf*; **—bolt** pestillo *m*; **he's a — duck** está muerto; **— end** callejón sin salida *m*; **—-end job** puesto sin perspectivas *m*; **— letter** letra muerta *f*; **—line** fecha límite *f*; **—lock** punto muerto *m*; **to —lock** trancarse; **—pan** de palo; **— ringer** fiel retrato *m*; **— sure** completamente seguro; **— tired** muerto de cansancio; **—wood** (person) persona inútil *f*; (thing) cosa inútil *f*; N **the —** los muertos; **in the — of the night** en el silencio de la noche; **in the — of winter** en pleno invierno

deaden [dédn̩] VT amortiguar

deadly [dédli] ADJ (enemy) mortal; (poison) letal; (weapon) mortífero; ADV mortalmente; **— dull** sumamente aburrido

deaf [def] ADJ sordo; **—-mute** sordomudo -da *mf*

deafen [défən] VT (make deaf) ensordecer; (deaden) amortiguar

deafening [défənɪŋ] ADJ ensordecedor, atronador

deafness [défnɪs] N sordera *f*

deal [dil] VT (cards) dar, repartir; (drugs) vender; (a blow) dar, asestar; **to — in** comerciar en; **biology —s with the study of life** la biología se ocupa del estudio de la vida; **I have to — with all kinds of people** tengo que vérmelas con todo tipo de gente; N (business transaction) trato *m*, negocio *m*; (shady transaction) componenda *f*; (act of dealing) reparto *m*; **a great — of** una gran cantidad de; **it's a —** ¡trato hecho! **I got a raw —** me clavaron

dealer [dílə] N (in cars, antiques) comerciante *mf*; (in drugs, arms) traficante *mf*; (of cards) el / la que reparte *mf*

dealings [dílɪŋz] N trato *m*, relaciones *f pl*; (business) negocios *m pl*

dean [din] N (of university, professional group) decano -na *mf*; (in church) deán *m*

dear [dir] ADJ (beloved) querido; (expensive) caro; (cherished) apreciado; **— Sir / Madam** Estimado señor / Estimada señora; **my —est wish** mi deseo más ferviente; N **he's such a —!** ¡es un amor! **my —** querido mío *m* / querida mía *f*; ADV caro; **that cost me —** eso me costó caro; **— me!** ¡Dios mío! **oh —!** ¡Dios mío!

dearth [dɜθ] N escasez *f*

death [deθ] N muerte *f*; **—bed** lecho de muerte *m*; **— certificate** partida de defunción f; — **penalty** pena de muerte f; — **rate** tasa de mortalidad f; — **row** pabellón de los condenados a muerte m; — **squad** escuadrón de la muerte m; — **toll** mortandad f; —**trap** trampa mortal f; — **wish** instinto suicida m; **to put to** — ejecutar; **we have discussed this to** — hemos discutido esto hasta el hartazgo; **I'm sick to** — **of this job** estoy harto de este trabajo

debacle [dɪbɑ́kəɫ] N debacle f

debase [dɪbés] VT degradar, envilecer

debatable [dɪbénəbət] ADJ discutible

debate [dɪbét] N debate m; VI/VT (discuss) debatir, discutir; (weigh a decision) considerar

debilitate [dɪbílɪtet] VT debilitar

debit [dɛ́bɪt] N débito m, adeudo m; (column in an account) debe m; (total sum owed) pasivo m; — **card** tarjeta de cobro automático f; VT adeudar, cargar a la cuenta

debriefing [dibrífɪŋ] N informe m

debris [dɑbrí] N (ruins) escombros m pl; (detritus) detritus m (pl)

debt [dɛt] N deuda f; **bad** — cuenta incobrable f; **to get into** — endeudarse

debtor [dɛ́bə-] N deudor -ra mf

debug [dibʌ́g] VT depurar

debugging [dibʌ́gɪŋ] N depuración f

debunk [dibʌ́ŋk] VT (ideas, beliefs) desacreditar; (myths) desmitificar

debut [debjú] N (of a play or film) estreno m; (in society) presentación en sociedad f; **to make a** — (an actor) debutar; (in society) presentarse en sociedad; VI/VT (a film) estrenar(se); (a product) lanzar(se) al mercado

decade [dɛ́ked] N década f, decenio m

decadence [dɛ́kədəns] N decadencia f

decadent [dɛ́kədənt] ADJ decadente

decaffeinated [dɪkǽfɪneDɪd] ADJ descafeinado

decal [díkæɫ] N calcomanía f, autoadhesivo m

decanter [dɪkǽntə] N garrafa f

decapitate [dɪkǽpɪtet] VT decapitar

decathlon [dɪkǽθlan] N decatlón m

decay [dɪké] VI/VT (biological matter) descomponer(se); (teeth) cariar(se); VI (health) deteriorarse; (radioactive matter) desintegrarse; N (of morals) decadencia f; (of biological matter) descomposición f; (nuclear) decaimiento f; (tooth) -caries f

decease [dɪsís] N muerte f, fallecimiento m; VI morir, fallecer

deceased [dɪsíst] ADJ & N difunto -ta mf

deceit [dɪsít] N engaño m, trampa f

deceitful [dɪsítfəɫ] ADJ tramposo, engañoso

deceive [dɪsív] VI/VT engañar

decelerate [disɛ́lərɛt] VI desacelerar

December [dɪsɛ́mbə-] N diciembre m

decency [dísənsi] N decencia f

decent [dísənt] ADJ decente

deception [dɪsɛ́pʃən] N engaño m

decibel [dɛ́səbɛɫ] N decibelio m

decide [dɪsáɪd] VT (make a decision) decidir; (award victory) fallar; **what —d you to come?** ¿qué te motivó a venir?

decided [dɪsáɪdɪd] ADJ (resolute) decidido; (clear) claro

deciduous [dɪsídʒuəs] ADJ deciduo, caduco; — **tooth** diente de la primera dentición m

decimal [dɛ́səməɫ] ADJ decimal

decimate [dɛ́səmet] VT diezmar

decipher [dɪsáɪfə-] VT descifrar

decision [dɪsíʒən] N decisión f; (in court) fallo m

decisive [dɪsáɪsɪv] ADJ decisivo

deck [dɛk] N (of a boat) cubierta f; (of a house) terraza f; (of playing cards) baraja f; VT (knock down) tumbar; (decorate) decorar; **to** — **oneself out** emperifollarse; **hit the** —! ¡cuerpo a tierra!

declaration [dɛkləréʃən] N declaración f

declare [dɪklɛ́r] VI/VT declarar, afirmar

decline [dɪklárn] N (deterioration) decadencia f; (slope) declive m; (reduction in prices) baja f; VI/VT declinar; (an offer) rechazar; **to** — **to do something** negarse a hacer algo

decode [dikód] VT descodificar

decompose [dikəmpóz] VI/VT descomponer(se)

decongestant [dikəndʒɛ́stənt] N descongestionante m

decorate [dɛ́kəret] VT decorar; (award medals) condecorar

decoration [dɛkəréʃən] N (embellishment) adorno m; (interior decorating) decoración f; (medal of honor) condecoración f

decorative [dɛ́kəəDɪv] ADJ decorativo

decorous [dɛ́kəəs] ADJ decoroso

decorum [dɪkórəm] N decoro m

decoy [díkɔɪ] N (artifact) señuelo m, reclamo m; (live animal or person) cimbel m; VT atraer con señuelo / cimbel

decrease [díkris] N disminución f, merma f; [díkrís] VI/VT disminuir, mermar

decree [dɪkrí] N decreto m; VI/VT decretar

decrepit [dɪkrɛ́pɪt] ADJ decrépito

decry [dɪkráɪ] VT condenar

dedicate [dɛ́dɪket] VI/VT dedicar(se); VT (mark opening of a highway, etc.) inaugurar

dedication [dɛDɪkéʃən] N (act of dedicating)

dedicación *f*; (in a book) dedicatoria *f*; (of a highway, etc.) inauguración *f*

deduce [dɪdús] VT deducir

deduct [dɪdÁkt] VT deducir

deductible [dɪdÁktəbəl] ADJ deducible, desgravable; N deducible *m*

deduction [dɪdÁkʃən] N deducción *f*

deed [did] N (action) acción *f*; (exploit) hazaña *f*; (certificate of ownership) escritura *f*

deem [dim] VT considerar

deep [dip] ADJ (extending down) hondo, profundo; (dark) oscuro; (of a voice) grave; **— freeze** congelador *m*; **— in debt** cargado de deudas; **— in thought** absorto; **—-sea** de altura; **he's got — pockets** es un ricachón; **he went off the — end with his hobby** se le fue la mano con el pasatiempo; **ten meters —** de diez metros de profundidad; **to —-six** hacer desaparecer; N **the —** el piélago, el abismo; ADV **to dive —** bucear en las profundidades

deepen [dípən] VI/VT ahondar, profundizar

deer [dir] N ciervo *m*, venado *m*; **—-skin** gamuza *f*

deface [dɪfés] VT (disfigure) desfigurar; (smear with paint) pintarrajear; (mutilate) mutilar

defame [dɪfém] VT difamar

default [dɪfɔ́lt] N (negligence) negligencia *f*; (failure to appear in court) rebeldía *f*; (computer setting) opción por defecto *f*; **in —** en mora; **by —** en ausencia de alternativa; (in sports) por abandono de los contrincantes; VI (on a loan) no pagar; (in a sports match) no comparecer

defeat [dɪfít] VT vencer, derrotar; N derrota *f*

defecate [défɪket] VI defecar

defect [dífekt] N defecto *m*; [dɪfékt] VI desertar

defection [dɪfékʃən] N defección *f*

defective [dɪféktɪv] ADJ defectuoso

defend [dɪfénd] VI/VT defender

defendant [dɪféndənt] N (criminal) acusado -da *mf*, reo -a *mf*; (civil) demandado -da *mf*

defender [dɪféndɚ] N defensor -ora *mf*

defense [dɪféns] N defensa *f*

defenseless [dɪfénslɪs] ADJ indefenso

defensible [dɪfénsəbəl] ADJ defendible

defensive [dɪfénsɪv] ADJ defensivo; **on the —** a la defensiva

defer [dɪfɚ́] VT (a meeting) diferir, posponer; (a payment) prorrogar; (an appointment) dilatar; (from military service) eximir; **to — to another's opinion** remitirse a la opinión de otro

deference [défɚəns] N deferencia *f*

defiance [dɪfáɪəns] N (challenge) desafío *m*; (resistance to authority) rebeldía *f*; **in — of** en abierta oposición a

defibrillate [difíbrəlet] VT desfibrilar

deficiency [dɪfíʃənsi] N deficiencia *f*

deficient [dɪfíʃənt] ADJ deficiente

deficit [défɪsɪt] N déficit *m*; **— spending** gastos deficitarios *m pl*

defile [dɪfáɪl] VT (violate) mancillar; (desecrate) profanar; (to make dirty) ensuciar

define [dɪfáɪn] VI/VT definir

defining [dɪfáɪnɪŋ] ADJ decisivo

definite [défənɪt] ADJ (clearly defined) definido; (certain) seguro; **she was — in her demands** ella fue terminante es sus exigencias; **— article** artículo definido *m*

definitely [défənɪtli] ADV sin duda

definition [defəníʃən] N definición *f*

definitive [dɪfínɪtɪv] ADJ (final) definitivo; (authoritative) de mayor autoridad

deflate [dɪflét] VI/VT desinflar(se)

deflation [dɪfléʃən] N deflación *f*

deflect [dɪflékt] VI/VT desviar(se)

deforestation [difɔrɪstéʃən] N deforestación *f*

deform [dɪfɔ́rm] VI/VT deformar(se)

deformed [dɪfɔ́rmd] ADJ deforme

deformity [dɪfɔ́rmɪɾi] N (body part) deformidad *f*; (act or result of deforming) deformación *f*

defraud [dɪfrɔ́d] VT defraudar

defray [dɪfré] VT sufragar, costear

defrost [difrɔ́st] VI/VT descongelar(se)

deft [dɛft] ADJ diestro, habilidoso

defunct [dɪfÁŋkt] ADJ caduco; **the Whig party is now —** el partido de los whigs se disolvió

defuse [difjúz] VT (bomb) desactivar; (situation) distender

defy [dɪfáɪ] VT (challenge) desafiar; (resist) resistir

degenerate [dɪʤénɚɪt] ADJ & N degenerado -da *mf*; [dɪʤénɚet] VI degenerar(se)

degradation [dɛgrədéʃən] N degradación *f*

degrade [dɪgréd] VI/VT degradar(se)

degree [dɪgrí] N (stage) grado *m*; (academic) título *m*; **by —s** gradualmente; **to a —** hasta cierto punto; **to get a —** graduarse

dehumanize [dihjúmənaɪz] VI/VT deshumanizar

dehydrate [diháɪdret] VI/VT deshidratar(se)

deign [den] VI dignarse

deity [díɪti] N deidad *f*

déjà vu [deʒɑvú] N deja vu *m*

dejected [dɪʤéktɪd] ADJ abatido, desconsolado

dejection [dɪdʒékʃən] N abatimiento *m*, desconsuelo *m*

delay [dɪlé] N demora *f*, retraso *m*; VT demorar, retrasar; VI demorar, retrasarse

delectable [dɪléktəbəł] ADJ delicioso; N delicia *f*

delegate [délɪgɪt] N delegado -da *mf*; [délɪget] VT delegar

delegation [delɪgéʃən] N delegación *f*, representación *f*

delete [dɪlít] VT (omit) suprimir; (cross out) tachar

deletion [dɪlíʃən] N supresión *f*

deliberate [dɪlíbə·ɪt] ADJ (intentional) deliberado; (careful) cuidadoso; [dɪlíbə·et] VI/VT deliberar

deliberation [dɪlíbə·éʃən] N deliberación *f*

delicacy [délɪkəsi] N (fineness, precision, sensitivity) delicadeza *f*; (food) manjar *m*, delicatessen *f pl*, gollería *f*; (breakability) fragilidad *f*

delicate [délɪkɪt] ADJ delicado, tenue; (breakable) frágil; (acute) fino

delicatessen [delɪkətésən] N (store) tienda de fiambres *f*, charcutería *f*; RP rotisería *f*; (foods) delicatessen *f pl*

delicious [dɪlíʃəs] ADJ delicioso, rico

delight [dɪláɪt] N (pleasure) deleite *m*, regalo *m*; (source of pleasure) delicia *f*; VI/VT deleitar(se)

delighted [dɪláɪDɪd] ADJ encantado; **to be — to** alegrarse de; **I'm — to meet you** me alegro de conocerla; **I'd be — to dance with you** me encantaría bailar contigo

delightful [dɪláɪtfəł] ADJ encantador

delimit [dɪlímɪt] VT delimitar

delineate [dɪlíniet] VT delinear

delinquent [dɪlíŋkwənt] ADJ & N (debtor) moroso -sa *mf*; (wrong-doer) delincuente *mf*; (juvenile) delincuente juvenil *mf*

delirious [dɪlírɪəs] ADJ delirante; (happy) contentísimo; **to be —** delirar

delirium [dɪlírɪəm] N delirio *m*

deliver [dɪlívə·] VT (hand over) entregar; (hand out) repartir; (liberate) liberar; (pronounce a speech) pronunciar; (administer a blow) dar; (have a baby) dar a luz; (assist a birth) atender en un parto; **— the goods** cumplir

deliverance [dɪlívə·əns] N liberación *f*

delivery [dɪlívə·i] N (handing out) entrega *f*, expedición *f*; (things to be delivered) pedido *m*; (birth) parto *m*; (speaking) ejecución *f*, expresión oral *f*; **— service** servicio de entrega *m*; **— truck** camión de reparto *m*

dell [deł] N hondonada *f*

delude [dɪlúd] VT engañar

deluge [déljudʒ] N diluvio *m*; VT abrumar

delusion [dɪlúʒən] N (act of deluding, state of being deluded) engaño *m*; **—s of grandeur** delirios de grandeza *m pl*

deluxe [dɪláks] ADJ de lujo

demagog, demagogue [déməgɑg] N demagogo -ga *mf*

demand [dɪmǽnd] VT (ask for) exigir; (require) requerir, exigir; N demanda *f*, exigencia *f*; **on —** por demanda

demanding [dɪmǽndɪŋ] ADJ exigente

demarcate [dɪmárket] VT demarcar

demean [dɪmín] VT menospreciar

demeanor [dɪmínə·] N conducta *f*, comportamiento *m*

demented [dɪméntɪd] ADJ demente

demijohn [démɪdʒɑn] N damajuana *f*

demise [dɪmáɪz] N fallecimiento *m*, desaparición *f*

demobilize [dɪmóbəlaɪz] VT desmovilizar

democracy [dɪmákrəsi] N democracia *f*

democrat [déməkræt] N demócrata *mf*

democratic [deməkrǽDɪk] ADJ democrático

demographics [deməgrǽfɪks] N demografía *f*

demolish [dɪmálɪʃ] VT demoler, derrumbar

demon [dímən] N demonio *m*

demonstrate [démənstret] VT (prove) demostrar; (show a product) hacer una demostración; VI manifestar

demonstration [demənstréʃən] N (proof, exhibition) demostración *f*; (protest) manifestación *f*, concentración *f*

demonstrative [dɪmánstrəDɪv] ADJ demostrativo

demoralize [dɪmórəlaɪz] VT desmoralizar

demote [dɪmót] VT degradar, bajar de categoría

den [den] N (of an animal) guarida *f*; (room in a house) cuarto de estar *m*; (cave) cueva *f*; **— of iniquity** antro de perdición *m*

denial [dɪnáɪəł] N (refusal to recognize) negación *f*; (act of denying) negativa *f*, rechazo *m*; (assertion that an allegation is false) desmentido *m*; **he is in —** no lo quiere aceptar

denigrate [dénɪgret] VT denigrar

denim [dénɪm] N tela de vaquero *f*

Denmark [dénmark] N Dinamarca *f*

denomination [dɪnɑmənéʃən] N (name, monetary value) denominación *f*; (sect) secta religiosa *f*

denotation [dinotéʃən] N denotación *f*

denote [dɪnót] VT denotar

denounce [dɪnáʊns] VT denunciar

dense [dens] ADJ (compacted) denso, tupido, cerrado; (stupid) *fam* burro, duro de entendederas

density [dénsɪDɪ] N densidad f

dent [dent] N abolladura f; **to make a — in a task** hacer mella en una tarea; VI/VT abollar(se)

dental [déntl] ADJ dental; **— floss** hilo dental m; **— hygienist** higienista dental mf

dentifrice [déntəfrɪs] N dentífrico m, pasta dental f

dentist [déntɪst] N dentista mf

dentistry [déntɪstri] N odontología f

dentures [déntʃəz] N dientes postizos m pl

denunciation [dɪnʌnsiéfən] N denuncia f, acusación f

deny [dɪnáɪ] VT (state that something is false) negar, desmentir; (refuse to approve) rechazar; **to — oneself** abstenerse

deodorant [dióDə-ənt] N desodorante m

deoxidize [diáksɪdaɪz] VT desoxidar

depart [dɪpárt] VI (leave) salir, partir; (deviate) desviarse, apartarse; (die) dejar de existir

departed [dɪpárDɪd] ADJ & N difunto -ta mf

department [dɪpártmənt] N (of company, school, country) departamento m; (of government) ministerio m; (of a store) sección f; (of knowledge, expertise) especialidad f; **— store** gran almacén m

departure [dɪpártʃə-] N (scheduled) salida f; (not scheduled) partida f; (deviation) desviación f

depend [dɪpénd] VI depender; **to — on** (be conditioned by) depender de; (rely on) contar con

dependable [dɪpéndəbəl] ADJ confiable, fiable

dependence [dɪpéndəns] N dependencia f

dependency [dɪpéndənsi] N dependencia f

dependent [dɪpéndənt] ADJ dependiente; **success is — on perseverance** el éxito depende de la perseverancia; N familiar a cargo mf

depict [dɪpíkt] VT (verbally) describir; (visually) representar

depilate [dépəlet] VT depilar(se)

depilatory [dɪpílətɔri] ADJ & N depilatorio m

deplane [dɪplén] VI desembarcar

deplete [dɪplít] VT agotar

depletion [dɪplíʃən] N agotamiento m

deplorable [dɪplórəbəl] ADJ deplorable

deplore [dɪplór] VT deplorar

deploy [dɪplóɪ] VT desplegar

deport [dɪpórt] VT deportar; VI comportarse

deportment [dɪpórtmənt] N comportamiento m, conducta f

depose [dɪpóz] VT (overthrow) deponer, derrocar; (testify) declarar; (take

testimony) tomar declaración

deposit [dɪpázɪt] VT (add to an account) depositar; Sp ingresar; (place) colocar; N (amount added to an account) depósito m; Sp ingreso m; (of a mineral) yacimiento m; (earnest money) señal f, anticipo m

deposition [depəzíʃən] N (removal from office) deposición f; (testimony) declaración f

depositor [dɪpázɪDə-] N depositante mf

depot [dípo] N (of trains) estación f; (of buses) terminal mf; (for storage) almacén m, depósito m; (for military training) cuartel m

depraved [dɪprévd] ADJ depravado

deprecate [déprɪket] VT despreciar

depreciate [dɪpríʃiet] VT (currency) depreciar(se); (goods) desvalorizar(se), amortizar(se)

depress [dɪprés] VT deprimir

depressed [dɪprést] ADJ deprimido

depressing [dɪprésɪŋ] ADJ deprimente

depression [dɪpréʃən] N depresión f

deprive [dɪpráɪv] VT privar

depth [depθ] N (of hole, feeling) profundidad f, hondura f; (of the voice) gravedad f; **in the —s** en las profundidades; **in — a** fondo; **what is the — of that bookshelf?** ¿cuánto miden estos estantes de fondo? **he has sunk to such —s** ha caído muy bajo; **in the — of the night** bien entrada la noche; **in the — of winter** en lo más crudo del invierno

deputation [depjətéʃən] N delegación f

deputy [dépjəDi] N (elected official) diputado -da mf; (substitute) suplente mf

derail [dɪrél] VI/VT descarrilar(se)

deranged [dɪréndʒd] ADJ trastornado, demente

derby [dɜ́-bi] N (hat) sombrero hongo m; (race) derby m

deregulate [dɪrégjəlet] VT desregular

derelict [dérəlɪkt] ADJ (deserted) abandonado; (negligent) negligente; N (ship) buque abandonado m; (person) vagabundo -da mf

deride [dɪráɪd] VT escarnecer, ridiculizar

derision [dɪríʒən] N escarnio m

derivation [derəvéʃən] N derivación f

derivative [dɪrívəDɪv] ADJ & N derivado m

derive [dɪráɪv] VI/VT derivar(se); **to — pleasure from** disfrutar de

dermatology [dɜ-mətáləʤi] N dermatología f

derogatory [dɪrágətɔri] ADJ despectivo

derrick [dérɪk] N torre de perforación f

descend [dɪsénd] VI/VT descender; **to — upon** caer sobre

descendant [dɪséndənt] ADJ & N descendiente *mf*

descent [dɪsént] N (act of descending, decline) descenso *m*; (slope) bajada *f*; (lineage) descendencia *f*

describe [dɪskráɪb] VT describir

description [dɪskrípʃən] N descripción *f*; **of all —s** de todas clases

descriptive [dɪskríptɪv] ADJ descriptivo

desecrate [désɪkret] VT profanar

desecration [desɪkréʃən] N profanación *f*

desegregate [diségrɪget] VI/VT eliminar la segregación racial

desensitize [disénsɪtaɪz] VT insensibilizar

desert [dézə·t] ADJ (barren, empty) desierto; (of the desert) desértico; N desierto *m*; [dɪzə́·t] VI/VT (a person, place) abandonar; (military service) desertar

deserter [dɪzə́·də·] N desertor -ra *mf*

desertion [dɪzə́·ʃən] N (of a person or place) abandono *m*; (from the military) deserción *f*

deserve [dɪzə́·v] VT merecer

deserving [dɪzə́·vɪŋ] ADJ merecedor

design [dɪzáɪn] VI/VT (prepare a sketch of) diseñar, trazar; (plan) planear, idear; N (model, pattern) diseño *m*; (sketch) esbozo *m*; **he has —s on her** le ha echado el ojo

designate [dézɪgnet] VT designar, denominar

designation [dezɪgnéʃən] N denominación *f*, designación *f*

designer [dɪzáɪnə·] N diseñador -ra *mf*; **— drugs** drogas de diseño *f pl*

desirability [dɪzaɪrəbílɪɾi] N deseabilidad *f*, conveniencia *f*

desirable [dɪzáɪrəbəl] ADJ deseable

desire [dɪzáɪr] VT desear; **I — your cooperation** requiero tu cooperación; N deseo *m*

desirous [dɪzáɪrəs] ADJ deseoso

desist [dɪsíst] VI desistir

desk [dɛsk] N escritorio *m*; (school) pupitre *m*; **—top publishing** edición de sobremesa *f*

desolate [désəlɪt] ADJ (barren) desolado; [désəlet] VT desolar, asolar

desolation [desəléʃən] N desolación *f*, asolamiento *m*

despair [dɪspér] N desesperanza *f*; VI desesperarse, perder la esperanza

despairing [dɪspérɪŋ] ADJ de desesperación

desperate [déspə·ɪt] ADJ desesperado; **— illness** enfermedad gravísima

desperation [despə·réʃən] N desesperación *f*

despicable [dɪspíkəbəl] ADJ despreciable, deleznable

despise [dɪspáɪz] VT despreciar, menospreciar

despite [dɪspáɪt] N despecho *m*; PREP a pesar de

despoil [dɪspɔ́ɪl] VT despojar

despondency [dɪspándənsi] N abatimiento *m*, desaliento *m*

despondent [dɪspándənt] ADJ abatido, desalentado

despot [déspət] N déspota *mf*

despotic [dɪspáɾɪk] ADJ despótico

despotism [déspətɪzəm] N despotismo *m*

dessert [dɪzə́·t] N postre *m*

destabilize [distébəlaɪz] VT desestabilizar

destination [destənéʃən] N destino *m*

destine [déstɪn] VT destinar; **she's —d for greatness** promete grandes cosas

destiny [déstəni] N destino *m*

destitute [déstɪtut] ADJ menesteroso, indigente; **— of** falto de, desprovisto de

destroy [dɪstrɔ́ɪ] VT (demolish) destruir, deshacer; (kill) sacrificar; (ruin a reputation) arruinar

destroyer [dɪstrɔ́ɪə·] N (person who destroys) destructor -ra *mf*; (ship) destructor *m*

destructible [dɪstráktəbəl] ADJ destructible

destruction [dɪstrákʃən] N (act of demolishing) destrucción *f*; (act of killing) matanza *f*; (act of ruining a reputation) ruina *f*

destructive [dɪstráktɪv] ADJ destructivo, destructor

detach [dɪtǽtʃ] VT separar, desprender; (troops) destacar

detachment [dɪtǽtʃmənt] N (physical) separación *f*; (emotional) desapego *m*; (of troops) destacamento *m*; (of the retina) desprendimiento *m*

detail [dítet] N detalle *m*, pormenor *m*; (military) destacamento *m*; **to go into —** detallar, pormenorizar; [dɪtét] VT detallar, pormenorizar; (assign duties) destacar

detain [dɪtén] VT detener

detect [dɪtékt] VT detectar

detective [dɪtéktɪv] N detective *mf*

detector [dɪtéktə·] N detector *m*

detention [dɪténʃən] N detención *f*

deter [dɪtə́·] VT (dissuade) disuadir; (prevent) prevenir

detergent [dɪtə́·dʒənt] N detergente *m*

deteriorate [dɪtíriəret] VI deteriorar(se)

deterioration [dɪtiriəréʃən] N deterioro *m*

determination [dɪtɜ·mənéʃən] N determinación *f*; (resolution) resolución *f*; (persistence) tesón *m*, perseverancia *f*

determine [dɪtə́·mɪn] VT determinar; **to — to do something** decidirse a hacer algo

determined [dɪtə́·mɪnd] ADJ decidido, resuelto; (persistent) tesonero

detest [dɪtést] VT detestar, abominar de

detestable [dɪtéstəbəł] ADJ detestable
dethrone [diθrón] VT destronar
detonate [détnet] VI/VT detonar
detonation [detnéʃən] N detonación f
detour [dítur] N desvío m; VI/VT desviar(se)
detoxification [ditɑksəfikéʃən] N
    destoxificación f
detract [dɪtrǽkt] VT distraer; VI **to — from**
    disminuir
detrimental [detrəméntl] ADJ perjudicial
devaluation [divæljuéʃən] N devaluación f
devastate [dévəstet] VT devastar, asolar
develop [dɪvéləp] VI/VT (mature, elaborate)
    desarrollar(se); (build houses on) construir,
    edificar; (treat film) revelar; **she —ed an**
    allergy le vino una alergia; **—ing**
    countries países en desarrollo m pl
development [dɪvéləpmənt] N (evolution)
    desarrollo m; (buildings) urbanización f,
    colonia f; (of a photograph) revelado m
deviate [díviet] VI/VT desviar(se)
deviation [diviéʃən] N desviación f
device [dɪváɪs] N (gadget) artefacto m;
    (literary convention) recurso m; (emblem)
    divisa f; **they left me to my own —s**
    me dejaron que me las arreglara sola
devil [dévəł] N diablo m; **lucky —!**
    ¡suertudo! **what the — are you saying?**
    ¿qué diablos dices? **—'s advocate**
    abogado del diablo m
devilish [dévəlɪʃ] ADJ (evil) diabólico; (large,
    extreme) endiablado, endemoniado
deviltry [dévəltri] N (mischief) diablura f;
    (witchcraft) brujería f
devious [dívias] ADJ (roundabout) sinuoso,
    tortuoso; (crafty) taimado, retorcido
devise [dɪváɪz] VT idear, urdir
devoid [dɪvɔ́id] ADJ **— of** falto de, desprovisto
    de
devote [dɪvót] VT dedicar; (consecrate)
    consagrar
devoted [dɪvódid] ADJ (friend) leal; (parent)
    dedicado; (worshipper) devoto
devotion [dɪvóʃən] N devoción f
devour [dɪváur] VT devorar
devout [dɪváut] ADJ devoto
dew [dju] N rocío m; **—drop** gota de rocío f;
    —point punto de condensación m
dexterity [dɛkstériɾi] N destreza f
dextrose [dékstros] N dextrosa f
diabetes [daɪəbíɾiz] N diabetes f
diabolic [daɪəbɑ́lɪk] ADJ diabólico
diacritic [daɪəkrídɪk] ADJ & N diacrítico m
diagnose [daɪəgnós] VT diagnosticar
diagonal [daɪǽgənəł] ADJ & N diagonal f
diagram [dáɪəgræm] N diagrama m
dial [dáɪəł] N (of a watch, clock) esfera f; (of

radio) dial m; VI/VT (telephone number) Sp
    marcar; Am discar; **— tone** Sp señal de
    marcar f; Am tono de discar m
dialect [dáɪələkt] N dialecto m
dialectic [daɪəléktɪk] ADJ dialéctico; N
    dialéctica f
dialectology [daɪələktálədʒi] N dialectología f
dialog, dialogue [dáɪəlɑg] N diálogo m; VI
    dialogar
dialysis [daɪǽlɪsɪs] N diálisis f
diameter [daɪǽmiɾə] N diámetro m
diamond [dáɪəmənd] N (stone) diamante m;
    (shape) rombo m
diaper [dáɪpə] N pañal m; VT poner pañales
diaphragm [dáɪəfræm] N diafragma m
diarrhea [daɪəríə] N diarrea f
diary [dáɪəri] N diario m
diatribe [dáɪətraɪb] N diatriba f
dice [daɪs] N PL dados m pl; VT cortar en
    cubos; VI jugar a los dados; **no —!**
    (impossibility) no hay forma; Mex ¡ni
    modo! (refusal) de ninguna manera
dichotomy [daɪkɑ́ɾəmi] N dicotomía f
dicker [díkə] VI regatear
dictate [díktet] VI/VT dictar; N dictado m,
    precepto m
dictation [dɪktéʃən] N dictado m; **to take —**
    escribir al dictado
dictator [díkteɾə] N dictador -ra mf
dictatorship [dɪktéɾəʃɪp] N dictadura f
diction [díkʃən] N dicción f
dictionary [díkʃəneri] N diccionario m
didactic [daɪdǽktɪk] ADJ didáctico
die [daɪ] VI morir(se); **—hard** intransigente
    mf; **to — down / away** disminuir; **to —**
    off irse muriendo; **to — out** morirse,
    extinguirse; **my car —d** se me murió el
    coche; N (game piece) dado m; (press)
    molde m; (stamp) cuño m, troquel m
diesel [dízəł] N diesel m; **— engine** motor
    diesel m
diet [dáɪɪt] N (food) dieta f; (controlled intake
    of food) dieta f, régimen m; **to be / go on**
    a — estar a dieta / régimen; **to put on a**
    — poner a dieta; VI estar a dieta
differ [dífə] VI diferir; **to — with** disentir,
    no estar de acuerdo con; **to — from** ser
    diferente de
difference [dífəəns] N diferencia f; **it**
    makes no — no importa, da igual
different [dífəənt] ADJ diferente, distinto
differential [dɪfərénʃəł] ADJ & N (difference,
    car part) diferencial m; **— equation**
    diferencial f
differentiate [dɪfərénʃiet] VI/VT
    diferenciar(se), distinguir(se)
difficult [dífɪkəłt] ADJ difícil

difficulty [dífɪkʌlti] N dificultad f
diffident [dífidənt] ADJ tímido
diffuse [dɪfjúz] VI/VT difundir; [dɪfjús] ADJ
difuso
diffusion [dɪfjúʒən] N difusión f
dig [dɪg] VI/VT cavar; (by machine) excavar;
(superficially) escarbar; **to — in the files**
escarbar en los archivos; **to — under**
socavar; **to — up** desenterrar; **he dug his**
heels into the ground clavó los talones
en el suelo; **I — your new shoes** están
muy buenos tus zapatos nuevos; N
(archaeological site) excavación f;
(sarcastic remark) pulla f; **a — in the ribs**
un codazo
digest [dɪʤést] VI/VT digerir; [dáɪʤest] N
(summary) compendio m; (legal) digesto
m
digestible [dɪʤéstəbəl] ADJ digerible,
digestible
digestion [dɪʤéstʃən] N digestión f
digestive [dɪʤéstɪv] ADJ digestivo
digit [díʤɪt] N dígito m
digital [díʤɪd]] ADJ digital
dignified [dígnəfaɪd] ADJ digno
dignitary [dígnɪteri] N dignatario -ria mf
dignity [dígnɪDi] N dignidad f
digress [dɪgrés] VI divagar
digression [dɪgréʃən] N digresión f
dike [daɪk] N dique m
dilapidated [dɪlǽpɪdeɪɾɪd] ADJ (machine)
destartalado; (furniture) desvencijado;
(house) derruido, venido abajo
dilate [dáɪlet] VI/VT dilatar(se)
dilation [daɪléʃən] N dilatación f
dilemma [dɪlémə] N dilema m
dilettante [dílɪtɑnt] N diletante mf
diligence [dílɪʤəns] N diligencia f
diligent [dílɪʤənt] ADJ diligente, hacendoso
dill [dɪl] N eneldo m; **— pickle** pepinillo en
vinagre con eneldo m
dilute [dɪlút] VI/VT diluir(se); ADJ diluido
dim [dɪm] ADJ (light) tenue; (outline) difuso;
(room) oscuro, en penumbras; (person)
fam de pocas luces; **—wit** fam tonto,
bobo; VI/VT (make less bright) atenuar; VT
(switch to low beam) bajar
dime [daɪm] N moneda de diez centavos f;
English teachers are a — a dozen
sobran los profesores de inglés
dimension [dɪménʃən] N dimensión f
diminish [dɪmínɪʃ] VI/VT disminuir,
menguar; **the law of —ing returns** la
ley de los rendimientos decrecientes
diminution [dɪmənúʃən] N disminución f,
mengua f
diminutive [dɪmínjətɪv] ADJ (small)

diminuto; N diminutivo m
dimmer [dímə-] N regulador de voltaje m
dimness [dímnɪs] N oscuridad f, penumbra f
dimple [dímpəl] N hoyuelo m; VT formar
hoyuelos
din [dɪn] N estruendo m, estrépito m
dine [daɪn] VI cenar; **to — out** cenar afuera
diner [dáɪnə-] N (restaurant) cafetería f; (on a
train) coche-comedor m; (person)
comensal mf
ding-a-ling [díŋəlɪŋ] N (silly person) ganso
-sa mf; (eccentric person) excéntrico -ca
mf; (sound) tilín m
dingy [díndʒi] ADJ deslucido
dining [dáɪnɪŋ] ADJ **— car** coche-comedor m;
— room comedor m
dinner [dínə-] N (main meal) comida f; (at
midday) almuerzo m; (in the evening)
cena f; **— jacket** smoking m; **—time**
hora de la comida f
dinosaur [dáɪnəsɔr] N dinosaurio m
dint [dɪnt] ADV LOC **by — of** a fuerza de
dip [dɪp] VT (make wet) mojar; (scoop) sacar;
(immerse) sumergir; (in insecticide) bañar;
(in sauce, coffee) pringar, mojar; VI (sun)
hundirse; (stocks) bajar; (road) hacer una
bajada; (airplane) descender súbitamente;
N (act of wetting) mojada f; (of ice-cream)
bola f, cucharada f; (sauce) mojo m;
(decrease) bajada f; (in a road) declive m;
(in the land) hondonada f; (swim) baño
m; (air travel) descenso rápido m;
(irritating person) pej pesado -da mf
diphtheria [dɪpθíriə] N difteria f
diphthong [dɪpθɔŋ] N diptongo m
diploma [dɪplómə] N diploma m
diplomacy [dɪpləmɑsi] N diplomacia f
diplomat [dípləmæt] N diplomático -ca mf
diplomatic [dɪpləmǽɾɪk] ADJ diplomático
dipper [dípə-] N cucharón m, cazo m
dire [daɪr] ADJ terrible, espantoso; **— need**
necesidad acuciante f; **— predictions**
predicciones funestas f pl; **— situation**
situación extrema f
direct [dɪrékt] ADJ directo; **— current**
corriente continua f; **— object**
complemento directo m; **— quotation**
cita textual f; ADV directo, directamente;
VI/VT dirigir; **he —ed me to leave** me
mandó irme
direction [dɪrékʃən] N dirección f; **—s**
indicaciones f pl; **I'm thinking in that**
— me inclino por eso
directive [dɪréktɪv] ADJ directivo; N directiva f
director [dɪréktə-] N director -ra mf
directory [dɪréktəri] N directorio m (also
computer term)

dirigible [dərídʒəbəl] ADJ & N dirigible *m*
dirt [dɚt] N (filth) suciedad *f*; (foul
substance) mugre *f*; (earth) tierra *f*; **—bag**
offensive porquería *f*; **— cheap** baratísimo;
—poor pobrísimo; **I've got some — on
him** le conozco los trapos sucios
dirty [dɚ·Di] ADJ sucio, mugriento; **— joke**
chiste verde *m*; **— look** mirada asesina *f*;
— money dinero sucio *m*; **— shame**
pena horrible *f*; **— trick** trampa *f*; **—
word** palabrota *f*; *Sp* taco *m*; **— work**
trabajo sucio *m*; VI/VT ensuciar; ADV **to
talk —** decir cosas obscenas
disability [dɪsəbílɪɾi] N incapacidad *f*
disable [dɪsébəl] VT (person) incapacitar;
(device) desactivar
disabled [dɪsébəld] ADJ minusválido
disabuse [dɪsəbjúz] VT desengañar
disadvantage [dɪsədvǽntɪdʒ] N desventaja *f*;
to be at a — estar en desventaja
disadvantaged [dɪsədvǽntɪdʒd] ADJ
carenciado
disagree [dɪsəgrí] VI (differ) diferir; (differ in
opinion) disentir, no estar de acuerdo;
pizza —s with me no me cae bien la
pizza
disagreeable [dɪsəgríəbəl] ADJ desagradable
disagreement [dɪsəgrímənt] N (lack of
agreement, argument) desacuerdo *m*;
(discrepancy) discrepancia *f*
disallow [dɪsəláu] VT desaprobar; (in sports)
anular
disappear [dɪsəpír] VI desaparecer
disappearance [dɪsəpírəns] N desaparición *f*
disappoint [dɪsəpɔ́ɪnt] VI/VT decepcionar,
desilusionar; **to be —ed** estar
desilusionado
disappointing [dɪsəpɔ́ɪntɪŋ] ADJ
decepcionante
disappointment [dɪsəpɔ́ɪntmənt] N
decepción *f*, desilusión *f*
disapproval [dɪsəprúvəl] N desaprobación *f*
disapprove [dɪsəprúv] VI/VT desaprobar
disarm [dɪsárm] VI/VT desarmar(se)
disarmament [dɪsárməmənt] N desarme *m*
disarray [dɪsəré] VT desordenar; N confusión
f, desorden *m*; **in —** en desorden
disaster [dɪzǽstɚ] N desastre *m*
disastrous [dɪzǽstrəs] ADJ desastroso
disavow [dɪsəváu] VT negar
disband [dɪsbǽnd] VT disolver; VI
desbandarse
disbelief [dɪsbəlíf] N incredulidad *f*
disbelieve [dɪsbəlív] VI/VT descreer de
disburse [dɪsbɚ́s] VT desembolsar
disbursement [dɪsbɚ́smənt] N desembolso *m*
discard [dɪskárd] VT (a card) descartar;

(garbage) desechar; [dískɑrd] N (card)
descarte *m*; (garbage) desecho *m*
discern [dɪsɚ́n] VT (distinguish mentally)
discernir; (perceive) percibir
discernment [dɪsɚ́nmənt] N discernimiento
m
discharge [dɪstʃárdʒ] VI/VT (battery, load,
firearm) descargar(se); (obligation)
cumplir; (prisoner) poner en libertad,
soltar; (odor) despedir; (soldier) dar de
baja; (patient) dar de alta; (a debt) pagar;
(pus) supurar; [dístʃardʒ] N (of a battery,
load, firearm) descarga *f*; (of an obligation)
cumplimiento *m*; (from a job) despido *m*;
(of a soldier) baja *f*; (of a patient) alta *f*;
(of a debt) pago *m*; (of an odor) emisión *f*;
(of a prisoner) puesta en libertad *f*; (of oil)
pérdida *f*; (of pus) supuración *f*; (uterine,
vaginal) flujo *m*
disciple [dɪsáɪpəl] N discípulo -la *mf*
discipline [dísəplɪn] N disciplina *f*; VT
disciplinar
disclaimer [dɪsklémɚ] N descargo de
responsabilidad *m*
disclose [dɪsklóz] VT revelar
disco [dísko] N discoteca *f*
discolor [dɪskálɚ] VI/VT descolorar(se)
discomfort [dɪskámfɚt] N malestar *m*
disconcert [dɪskənsɚ́t] VT desconcertar
disconnect [dɪskənékt] VI/VT desconectar; N
desconexión *f*
disconnected [dɪskənéktɪd] ADJ (broken)
desconectado; (incoherent) inconexo
disconsolate [dɪskánsəlɪt] ADJ desconsolado
discontent [dɪskəntént] N descontento *m*
discontinue [dɪskəntínju] VT suspender,
interrumpir; VI abandonar
discontinuous [dɪskəntínjuəs] ADJ
discontinuo
discord [dískɔrd] N (lack of concord)
discordia *f*, desavenencia *f*; (dissonance)
disonancia *f*, discordancia *f*
discotheque [dískotɛk] N discoteca *f*
discount [dískaunt] VT (deduct from a
charge, take into account in advance)
descontar; (sell at a reduced price) rebajar;
(disregard) ignorar; N descuento *m*
discourage [dɪskɚ́ɪdʒ] VT desanimar,
desalentar; **to — from** disuadir de
discouragement [dɪskɚ́ɪdʒmənt] N desánimo
m, desaliento *m*
discourse [dískɔrs] N (conversation, talk)
discurso *m*; (treatise) disertación *f*; [dɪskórs]
VI (talk) discurrir; (treat a subject) disertar
discourteous [dɪskɚ́·Diəs] ADJ descortés
discourtesy [dɪskɚ́·Dɪsi] N descortesía *f*
discover [dɪskávɚ] VT descubrir

discoverer [dɪskʌ́vərə] N descubridor -ra *mf*

discovery [dɪskʌ́vəri] N descubrimiento *m*

discredit [dɪskɾɛ́dɪt] VT (injure the reputation of) desacreditar; (give no credence to) no creer; N descrédito *m*

discreet [dɪskɾít] ADJ discreto

discrepancy [dɪskɾɛ́pənsi] N discrepancia *f*

discrete [dɪskɾít] ADJ discreto

discretion [dɪskɾɛ́ʃən] N discreción *f*; **at your own —** a discreción; **at the judge's —** al arbitrio del juez

discriminate [dɪskɾímənət] VI/VT distinguir; **to — against** discriminar a

discuss [dɪskʌ́s] VT discutir

discussion [dɪskʌ́ʃən] N discusión *f*

disdain [dɪsdén] N desdén *m*, desprecio *m*; VT (treat with contempt) desdeñar; (think unworthy of a response) no dignarse a

disdainful [dɪsdénfəl] ADJ desdeñoso

disease [dɪzíz] N enfermedad *f*

diseased [dɪzízd] ADJ enfermo

disembark [dɪsɪmbárk] VI/VT desembarcar

disenfranchise [dɪsɪnfɾǽntʃaɪz] VT (politician) proscribir; (minorities) privar de derechos, desheredar

disengage [dɪsɪngédʒ] VI/VT (a clutch) soltar(se); (from a situation) distanciar(se)

disentangle [dɪsɪntǽŋgəl] VT desenredar, desenmarañar

disfavor [dɪsfévə] N **to fall into —** (a person) caer en desgracia; (a fashion) caer en desuso; VT mirar con malos ojos

disfigure [dɪsfígjə] VT desfigurar

disgrace [dɪsgɾés] N (dishonor) deshonra *f*; (shame) vergüenza *f*; **to fall into —** caer en desgracia; VT deshonrar

disgraceful [dɪsgɾésfəl] ADJ vergonzoso

disgruntled [dɪsgɾántld] ADJ descontento, resentido

disguise [dɪsgáɪz] VT disfrazar(se); N disfraz *m*

disgust [dɪsgʌ́st] VT (repel) asquear, repugnar; (displease) disgustar; N asco *m*, repugnancia *f*

disgusted [dɪsgʌ́stɪd] ADJ asqueado, repugnado

disgusting [dɪsgʌ́stɪŋ] ADJ asqueroso, repugnante

dish [dɪʃ] N (plate, food, quantity) plato *m*; (serving container) fuente *f*; (attractive person) *fam* bombón *m*; **—es** vajilla *f*; **—cloth / towel** paño de cocina *m*, repasador *m*; **—washer** lavaplatos *m sg*, lavavajillas *m sg*; **—water** agua de fregar *f*; VI/VT (serve food) servir; **to — out** repartir

dishearten [dɪshártn] VT desanimar, descorazonar, desalentar

disheartening [dɪshártnɪŋ] ADJ desalentador

dishevel [dɪʃévəl] VT desgreñar

disheveled [dɪʃévəld] ADJ (hair) desgreñado, revuelto; (clothes) desaliñado

dishonest [dɪsánɪst] ADJ deshonesto

dishonesty [dɪsánɪsti] N deshonestidad *f*

dishonor [dɪsánə] N deshonra *f*; VT deshonrar; (a check) no pagar

dishonorable [dɪsánəəbəl] ADJ deshonroso

disillusion [dɪsɪlúʒən] N desilusión *f*, desencanto *m*; VT desilusionar, desencantar

disinfect [dɪsɪnfékt] VT desinfectar

disinfectant [dɪsɪnféktənt] N desinfectante *m*

disinformation [dɪsɪnfəméʃən] N desinformación *f*

disinherit [dɪsɪnhérɪt] VT desheredar

disintegrate [dɪsíntɪgret] VI/VT desintegrar(se)

disintegration [dɪsɪntɪgréʃən] N desintegración *f*

disinterested [dɪsíntɾɪstɪd] ADJ desinteresado

disjointed [dɪsdʒɔ́ɪntɪd] ADJ desarticulado

disk, disc [dɪsk] N disco *m*; (in certain games) tejo *m*; (in a computer) disco *m*, disquete *m*; **— brake** freno de disco *m*; **— drive** disquetera *f*; **— jockey** pinchadiscos *mf sg*

diskette [dɪskét] N disquete *m*

dislike [dɪsláɪk] N aversión *f*, tirria *f*; VT **I — parties** no me gustan las fiestas

dislocate [dɪslóket] VT dislocar, descoyuntar

dislodge [dɪsládʒ] VT (force out) desatascar; (displace) desprender

disloyal [dɪslɔ́ɪəl] ADJ desleal

dismal [dízməl] ADJ pésimo; **a — failure** un fracaso rotundo

dismantle [dɪsmǽntl] VT (a factory) desmantelar; (a car, watch, etc.) desmontar

dismay [dɪsmé] VT (disappoint) consternar; (daunt) desalentar; (alarm) alarmar; N (disappointment) consternación *f*; (loss of courage) desaliento *m*; (alarm) alarma *f*

dismember [dɪsmémbə] VT desmembrar

dismiss [dɪsmís] VT (fire a private employee) despedir; (fire a public employee) destituir, cesar; (reject a possibility) desechar, descartar; (discharge from military service) dar de baja; (reject a claim) desestimar; **class —ed!** ¡pueden retirarse!

dismissal [dɪsmísəl] N (firing) destitución *f*, despido *m*; (of a possibility) rechazo *m*; (from military service) baja *f*; (of a claim) desestimación *f*

dismount [dɪsmáunt] VI (get off a horse) desmontarse, apearse; (take apart) desarmar; N bajada *f*

disobedience [dɪsəbíɾɪəns] N desobediencia f
disobedient [dɪsəbíɾɪənt] ADJ desobediente
disobey [dɪsəbé] VI/VT desobedecer
disorder [dɪsɔ́rɾɚ] N (confusion) desorden m; (public disturbance) desorden público m; (illness) trastorno m, desarreglo m
disorderly [dɪsɔ́rɾɚli] ADJ (untidy) desordenado; (unruly) revoltoso; — **conduct** alteración del orden público f
disorganization [dɪsɔrgənɪzéʃən] N desorganización f
disorganized [dɪsɔ́rgənaɪzd] ADJ desorganizado
disown [dɪsón] VT repudiar
disparage [dɪspǽrɪʤ] VT denigrar
disparate [díspɚɪt] ADJ dispar
dispassionate [dɪspǽʃənɪt] ADJ desapasionado
dispatch [dɪspǽtʃ] VT despachar; N (sending off) envío m; (putting to death) ejecución f; (news story, official communication) despacho m
dispel [dɪspél] VT disipar
dispensable [dɪspénsəbəl] ADJ prescindible
dispensary [dɪspénsəri] N dispensario m
dispensation [dɪspenséʃən] N (relaxation of law) dispensa f; (act of handing out) dispensación f
dispense [dɪspéns] VT (goods) dispensar; (justice) administrar; **to — from an obligation** eximir de una obligación; **to — with** prescindir de
dispersal [dɪspɚ́səl] N dispersión f
disperse [dɪspɚ́s] VI/VT dispersar(se)
displace [dɪsplés] VT (evict) desalojar; (take up space, remove from office) desplazar; **—d person** expatriado -da mf
display [dɪsplé] VT (exhibit) exhibir, exponer; (unfold, flaunt) desplegar, ostentar; (show on a computer screen) visualizar; N (of wares, etc.) exhibición f, despliegue m; (advertisement) cartel m; (flaunting) ostentación f; (computer) visualizador m, display m
displease [dɪsplíz] VT contrariar, desagradar, descontentar; VI molestar
displeasure [dɪspléʒɚ] N disgusto m, desagrado m
disposal [dɪspózəl] N (arrangement) disposición f; (disposing of) eliminación f
dispose [dɪspóz] VT (give inclination) predisponer; (set in order, make ready) disponer; **to — of** descartar, eliminar
disposition [dɪspəzíʃən] N (attitude) temperamento m; (inclination) inclinación f, tendencia f; (arrangement, disposal) disposición f

dispossess [dɪspəzés] VT desposeer
disproportionate [dɪsprəpɔ́rʃənɪt] ADJ desproporcionado
disprove [dɪsprúv] VT refutar
dispute [dɪspjút] N disputa f; VI disputar; VT discutir, impugnar
disqualify [dɪskwɑ́ləfaɪ] VT (deprive of rights) inhabilitar; (exclude from a sport event) descalificar
disregard [dɪsrɪgárd] VT hacer caso omiso de, ignorar; N (neglect) descuido m; (disrespect) falta de respeto f
disrepair [dɪsrɪpér] N mal estado m; **to fall into —** caer en ruina
disreputable [dɪsrɛ́pjəɾəbəl] ADJ (of bad reputation) de mala reputación; (shabby) de mala muerte
disrespect [dɪsrɪspékt] N desacato m, falta de respeto f; VT faltar el respeto
disrespectful [dɪsrɪspéktfəl] ADJ irrespetuoso
disrobe [dɪsrób] VI/VT desvestir(se)
disrupt [dɪsrápt] VT (cause disorder) trastornar, trastocar; (interrupt) interrumpir
dissatisfied [dɪssǽɾɪsfaɪd] ADJ insatisfecho, disconforme
dissatisfy [dɪssǽɾɪsfaɪ] VT no satisfacer
dissect [daɪsékt] VT (cut apart) disecar; (analyze argument) analizar minuciosamente
dissemble [dɪsémbəl] VI/VT (hide) disimular; (feign) fingir
disseminate [dɪsémənet] VT (spread out) diseminar; (publicize) divulgar
dissemination [dɪsemənéʃən] N diseminación f
dissension [dɪsénʃən] N disensión f, disenso m
dissent [dɪsént] VI disentir; N disenso m
dissertation [dɪsɚtéʃən] N (formal discourse) disertación f; (doctoral treatise) tesis de doctorado f
dissident [dísɪdənt] N disidente mf
dissimilar [dɪssímələ] ADJ diferente
dissimulation [dɪsɪmjəléʃən] N disimulo m
dissipate [dísəpet] VI/VT disipar(se)
dissipation [dɪsəpéʃən] N disipación f
dissolute [dísəlut] ADJ disoluto
dissolution [dɪsəlúʃən] N disolución f
dissolve [dɪzɑ́lv] VI/VT disolver(se)
dissuade [dɪswéd] VT disuadir
distance [dístəns] N distancia f, recorrido m; **— learning** educación a distancia f; **in the —** a lo lejos, en la lejanía; VT distanciarse de, distanciar
distant [dístənt] ADJ (far away, aloof) distante; (remote) lejano, remoto; **to be**

— from distar de
distaste [dɪstést] N aversión *f*
distasteful [dɪstéstfəl] ADJ desagradable
distemper [dɪstémpə·] N moquillo *m*
distend [dɪsténd] VI/VT distender(se)
distill [dɪstíł] VI/VT destilar(se)
distillation [dɪstəléʃən] N destilación *f*
distillery [dɪstíləri] N destilería *f*
distinct [dɪstíŋkt] ADJ (different) distinto;
(clear) bien delineado, neto
distinction [dɪstíŋkʃən] N distinción *f*; **he
passed with** — aprobó con sobresaliente
distinctive [dɪstíŋktɪv] ADJ distintivo
distinguish [dɪstíŋgwɪʃ] VI/VT distinguir
distinguished [dɪstíŋgwɪʃt] ADJ distinguido
distinguishing [dɪstíŋgwɪʃɪŋ] ADJ distintivo
distort [dɪstɔ́rt] VT (an object) deformar;
(reports, sound) distorsionar
distortion [dɪstɔ́rʃən] N (object) deformación
f; (image, sound) distorsión *f*; (of a
statement) tergiversación *f*
distract [dɪstrǽkt] VT distraer, entretener
distraction [dɪstrǽkʃən] N distracción *f*; **to
drive to** — volver loco
distraught [dɪstrɔ́t] ADJ angustiado
distress [dɪstrés] N (anxiety) angustia *f*; (pain)
dolor *m*, congoja *f*; **to be in** — (a person)
estar en apuros; (a ship, plane) estar en
peligro; VT (cause anxiety) angustiar,
atribular; (cause pain) acongojar, afligir
distribute [dɪstríbjut] VT distribuir, repartir
distribution [dɪstrəbjúʃən] N distribución *f*,
reparto *m*
distributor [dɪstríbjədə·] N distribuidor *m*
district [dɪstrɪkt] N distrito *m*, comarca *f*; **—
attorney** fiscal de distrito *mf*
District of Columbia [dístrɪktəvkəlámbiə] N
Distrito de Columbia *m*
distrust [dɪstrást] N desconfianza *f*; VT
desconfiar de
distrustful [dɪstrástfəl] ADJ desconfiado
disturb [dɪstɚ́b] VI/VT (interrupt, interfere,
perplex) perturbar; (trouble) turbar; (alter
mentally) trastornar; (mess up) desarreglar;
do not — se ruega no molestar
disturbance [dɪstɚ́bəns] N disturbio *m*;
(weather) perturbación *f*
disuse [dɪsjús] N desuso *m*; **to fall into** —
caer en desuso
ditch [dɪtʃ] N (trench) zanja *f*; (roadside)
cuneta *f*; (for irrigation) acequia *f*; VT
(make ditches) abrir zanjas; (get rid of)
deshacerse de; (crash-land an airplane on
water) hacer un amarizaje; **to —
someone** dejar a alguien
dither [díðə·] VI (hesitate) titubear; N **it
threw her into a** — se puso muy

nerviosa
ditsy [dítsi] ADJ atolondrado, cabeza de
chorlito
ditto [dído] PRON & ADV ídem *m*
diuretic [daɪəɾɛ́dɪk] ADJ & N diurético *m*
diurnal [daɪɚ́nəł] ADJ diurno
divan [dɪvǽn] N diván *m*, canapé *m*
dive [daɪv] VI (into water) zambullirse,
chapuzar; (into an activity) lanzarse;
(with scuba equipment) bucear; (airplane)
bajar en picada; (submarine) sumergirse; N
(of a person) zambullida *f*, chapuz *m*; (of
an airplane) picada *f*; (cheap bar) antro *m*
diver [dáɪvə·] N saltador -ra *mf*; (high-dive)
clavadista *mf*; (scuba) buzo *mf*
diverge [dɪvɚ́ʤ] VI (branch off, differ in
opinion) divergir; VI/VT (deviate) desviar
divergence [dɪvɚ́ʤəns] N (separation,
difference in opinion) divergencia *f*;
(deviation) desviación *f*
diverse [dɪvɚ́s] ADJ (of various kinds) diverso;
(different) diferente
diversify [dɪvɚ́səfaɪ] VI/VT diversificar(se)
diversion [dɪvɚ́ʒən] N (entertainment)
entretenimiento *m*; (distraction)
distracción *f*; (military) diversión *f*;
(turning aside) desvío *m*, desviación *f*
diversity [dɪvɚ́sɪdi] N diversidad *f*
divert [dɪvɚ́t] VI/VT (turn aside) desviar,
distraer; (distract) entretener
divest [dɪvést] VT (strip) despojar; (get rid of)
deshacerse de
divide [dɪváɪd] VI/VT dividir(se); (classify)
clasificar(se); N línea divisoria *f*
dividend [dívidɛnd] N dividendo *m*
divine [dɪváɪn] ADJ divino; VI/VT adivinar
divinity [dɪvínɪdi] N divinidad *f*; (theology)
teología *f*
division [dɪvíʒən] N división *f*
divorce [dɪvɔ́rs] N divorcio *m*; VI/VT
divorciar(se)
divulge [dɪvʌ́łʤ] VT divulgar, publicar
dizziness [dízinɪs] N mareo *m*
dizzy [dízi] ADJ (person) mareado; (height)
vertigoso; (speed) vertiginoso; **— spell**
vahido *m*
DJ (disc jockey) [dídʒe] N pinchadiscos *mf sg*
Djibouti [dʒɪbúti] N Yibuti *m*
Djiboutian [dʒɪbúdiən] ADJ & N yibutiano -na
mf
DNA (deoxyribonucleic acid) [dienέ] N
ADN *m*
do [du] VI/VT hacer; **to — away with**
eliminar; **to — one's hair** arreglarse el
pelo; **to — the dishes** lavar los platos; **to
— drugs** tomar drogas; **to — in** matar;
to — time cumplir una condena; **we**

were —ing 100 kph ibamos a cien kph; to — well prosperar; to — without prescindir de; to have nothing to — with no tener nada que ver con; that will — basta; that won't — eso no sirve; I'm —ing well estoy bien; this will have to — habrá que conformarse con esto; —-it-yourself hágalo usted mismo; v AUX I feel as you — pienso igual que tú; how — you —? ¿cómo estás? — you hear me? ¿me oyes? yes, I — sí; — come again vuelve por favor; N (hairstyle) peinado m; (party) fiesta f

DOA (dead on arrival) [dioé] ADJ muerto -ta antes de ingresar al hospital mf

docile [dásəł] ADJ dócil

dock [dak] N (pier) muelle m; (for landing) desembarcadero m, atracadero m; (water between piers) dique m, dársena f; dry — dique seco m; VI/VT (a boat) atracar; (a space ship) acoplar(se); (wages) descontar

doctor [dáktə] N (physician) médico -ca mf; (Ph.D., scholar) doctor -ra mf; (expert) especialista mf; VT (treat) atender; (cure) curar; (restore) restaurar; (counterfeit) alterar; I —ed up this recipe le hice unos retoques a esta receta

doctorate [dáktəɹt] N doctorado m

doctrine [dáktrɪn] N doctrina f

document [dákjəmənt] N documento m; [dákjəment] VT documentar

documentary [dakjəméntəɹi] N documental m

dodder [dádə] VI (stumble along) tambalearse, titubear; (shake) temblequear

dodge [dadʒ] VT esquivar, sortear; VI (be evasive) dar rodeos; (move sideways) apartarse, echarse a un lado; N evasiva f

doe [do] N cierva f; (female of various animals) hembra f

dog [dɔg] N perro -ra mf; —catcher perrero -ra mf; — collar collar de perro m; —-eared sobado, muy gastado; —fight (dogs) pelea f de perros; (aircraft) combate aéreo m; (people) reyerta f; —gone maldito -ta mf; —house casilla de perro f; Sp caseta f; to be in the —house haber caído en desgracia, estar en capilla; — paddle nado estilo perrito m; to —-paddle nadar estilo perrito; —sled trineo para perros m; — tag placa de identificación f; —wood cornejo m; to go to the —s venirse abajo; VT (follow) seguir la pista de; (harass) hostigar

doggy [dɔ́gi] N perrito -ta mf; — bag bolsa para las sobras f

dogma [dɔ́gmə] N dogma m

dogmatic [dɔgmǽdɪk] ADJ dogmático

doily [dɔ́ili] N mantelito m

doings [dúŋz] N acciones f pl

dole [doł] N (alms) limosna f; to be on the — estar cobrando el seguro de desempleo / paro; to — out repartir

doleful [dółfəł] ADJ apesadumbrado, triste

doll [dɑł] N (toy) muñeco -ca mf; (attractive female) muñeca f; —house casa de muñecas f; VI to get —ed up emperifollarse, empaquetarse

dollar [dálə] N dólar m; — diplomacy diplomacia del dólar f; — sign signo del dólar m

dolly [dáli] N (doll) muñeca f; (cart) carretilla f

dolphin [dɔ́łfɪn] N (mammal) delfín m; (fish) dorado m

dolt [dołt] N zopenco -ca mf

domain [domén] N dominio m

dome [dom] N (roof) cúpula f, domo m; (head) coco m, pelada f; the — of the sky la bóveda celeste

domestic [dəméstɪk] ADJ (appliance, pet, chore) doméstico; (devoted to homemaking) hogareño; (home-loving) casero; (of a country) interno, nacional; — violence violencia doméstica f; N doméstico -ca mf

domesticate [dəméstɪket] VI/VT (animals) domesticar; (plants) aclimatar

domicile [dáməsaɪł] N domicilio m

dominant [dámənənt] ADJ dominante

dominate [dámənet] VI/VT dominar; VI señorear

domination [damənéʃən] N (act of dominating) dominación f; (rule) dominio m

domineer [damənír] VI/VT dominar, mandonear

domineering [damənírŋ] ADJ tiránico, mandón

Dominica [dəmíníkə] N Dominica f

Dominican [dəmíníkən] ADJ & N (of Dominica) dominiqués -esa mf; (of the Dominican Republic) dominicano -na mf

Dominican Republic [dəmíníkənɹipáblɪk] N República Dominicana f

dominion [dəmínjən] N dominio m, señorío m

domino [dáməno] N (game, costume) dominó m; (piece) ficha f

don [dɑn] N (title, form of address, mafia boss) don m; (lecturer) profesor -ra universitario -ria mf; VT ponerse, vestirse

donate [dónet] VI/VT donar

donation [donéʃən] N donación f

done [dʌn] ADJ terminado, acabado; **when you are** — cuando termines; **to be all — in** estar muerto de cansancio; **the meat is well** — está bien asada la carne; **that sort of thing just isn't** — eso no se hace

donkey [dáŋki] N burro *m*, asno *m*, borrico *m*

donor [dónə] N donante *mf*, donador -ora *mf*

doodad [dúdæd] N (trinket) chuchería *f*; (device) chisme *m*, coso *m*

doohickey [dúhıki] N chisme *m*, coso *m*

doom [dum] N perdición *f*; **—sday** día del juicio final *m*; VT condenar; **to be —ed to failure** estar condenado al fracaso

door [dɔr] N puerta *f*; **—-to-** — de puerta a puerta; **—bell** timbre *m*; **—keeper** portero -ra *mf*; **—knob** pomo *m*; **—man** portero *m*; **—mat** felpudo *m*; **—step** umbral *m*; **—way** puerta *f*, portal *m*; **I showed him the** — lo eché

dope [dop] N (narcotic) droga *f*; (stimulant) estimulante *m*; (information) chismes *m pl*; **he is a** — *fam* es un zopenco; VT dopar; **to — oneself up** medicarse en exceso

dork [dɔrk] N *fam* idiota *mf*, tarambana *mf*

dorky [dɔ́rki] ADJ **that's a — dress** *fam* parece una idiota con ese vestido

dormant [dɔ́rmənt] ADJ latente

dormitory [dɔ́rmıtɔri] N residencia estudiantil *f*

DOS (Disk Operating System) [dɑs] N DOS *m*

dose [dos] N dosis *f*; VT dosificar

dossier [dásie] N expediente *m*

dot [dɑt] N punto *m*; (on a tie) pinta *f*; **—-com** punto com; **—-matrix printer** impresora de matriz de puntos *f*; **—ted eighth note** corchea con puntillo *f*; **on the** — en punto; VT marcar con puntos

dotage [dóDɪdʒ] N chochera *f*, chochera *f*; **to be in one's** — chochear, estar chocho

dote [dot] VI **to — on** estar chocho con

double [dʌ́bəɬ] ADJ doble; **— agent** agente *mf*; **—-barreled** de doble caño; **— bass** contrabajo *m*; **— bed** cama doble *f*; **— bind** dilema *m*; **— boiler** baño de María *m*; **—-breasted** cruzado; **— chin** papada *f*; **—-click** hacer doble clic; **— cross** traición *f*; **to —-cross** traicionar; **to —-date** salir dos parejas juntas; **— dealing** duplicidad *f*; **— entry** entrada por partida doble *f*; **— sided** de dos caras; **— shift** turno doble *m*; **— standard** trato discriminatorio *m*; **— vision** doble visión *f*; **to do a — take** quedar atónito;

N doble *m*; **—s** juego de dobles *m*; ADV **to sleep** — dormir de a dos; **to —-check** verificar; **to —-talk** salirse con evasivas; VI/VT duplicar(se); (an effort) redoblar(se); (fold, be twice as old, challenge a bid) doblar(se); **to — up** (bend over) doblarse; (crowd) amontonarse; **this sofa —s as a bed** este sofá sirve también de cama

doubt [daʊt] VI/VT dudar; (not trust) desconfiar; N duda *f*; **beyond a** — indudablemente; **in** — en duda; **no —!** ¡sin duda!

doubtful [dáʊtfəɬ] ADJ dudoso

doubtless [dáʊtlıs] ADV (certainly) sin duda; (probably) probablemente

dough [do] N pasta *f*, masa *f*; (money) pasta *f*, mosca *f*; **—nut** rosquilla *f*; *Mex* dona *f*; *Sp* donut *m*

douse [daʊs] VI/VT empapar; (a flame) apagar (con agua)

dove [dʌv] N paloma *f*

dowdy [dáʊDi] ADJ (article of clothing) pasado de moda; (person) sin gracia

dowel [dáʊəɬ] N clavija *f*

down [daʊn] ADV abajo; **two blocks** — dos calles más abajo; **turn — the volume** bajar el volumen; **to water — a drink** rebajar una bebida con agua; **to get — to work** aplicarse al trabajo; **to fall** — caerse; **to go / come** — bajar; **to come — with a cold** caer con gripe; *Sp* cogerse un resfriado; **to lie** — tumbarse, echarse; **to write** — anotar; **to put — someone** denigrar a alguien; **slow —!** ¡anda más despacio! **the wind died** — amainó el viento; PREP **— the street** calle abajo; ADJ (depressed) abatido; **one — and two to go** hicimos uno y nos quedan dos por hacer; **prices are** — han bajado los precios; **they're — on me** están mal conmigo; N (turn for the worse) revés *m*; (feathers) plumón *m*; VT (knock down, shoot down) derribar; (drink quickly) despachar de un solo trago; (defeat) vencer

down-and-dirty [dáʊnındɜ́-Di] ADJ sucio

down-and-out [dáʊnınáʊt] ADJ tirado

downcast [dáʊnkæst] ADJ abatido, cabizbajo

downfall [dáʊnfɔɬ] N ruina *f*

downgrade [dáʊngred] N declive *m*, pendiente *f*; VT quitarle importancia a

downhill [dáʊnhıl] ADV cuesta abajo; **his health is going** — su salud se deteriora; [dáʊnhıɬ] ADJ **a — slope** una pendiente; N bajada contra-reloj *f*

download [dáʊnlod] VT descargar

down payment [dáʊnpémənt] N entrega

initial *f*, entrada *f*
downplay [dáʊnple] VT quitar la importancia a
downpour [dáʊnpɔr] N aguacero *m*
downright [dáʊnraɪt] ADJ absoluto; — **foolishness** reverenda tontería *f*; **he was — angry** echaba chispas
downshift [dáʊnʃɪft] VI rebajar (el cambio)
downside [dáʊnsaɪd] N inconveniente *m*
downsize [dáʊnsaɪz] VI (cut back) hacer reducción de personal; VT (make smaller) reducir el tamaño de; **he got —d** perdió el trabajo cuando hicieron reducción de personal
downstairs [dáʊnstérz] ADV abajo; (in the apartment one floor lower) en el piso de abajo; [dáʊnsterz] ADJ de abajo; N planta baja *f*
downstream [dáʊnstrím] ADV río abajo
downtime [dáʊntaɪm] N (of a machine) tiempo de inactividad *m*; (of a person) horas de ocio *f pl*
down-to-earth [dáʊntəɾˈθ] ADJ sensato, práctico
downtown [dáʊntáʊn] ADV (toward) al centro; (in) en el centro; ADJ del centro, céntrico; N centro *m*
downturn [dáʊntɚn] N tendencia a la baja *f*
down under [dáʊnándɚ] ADV en / a Australia
downward [dáʊnwɚd] ADJ descendente; — **mobility** descenso social *m*; **—s** hacia abajo
downwind [dáʊnwínd] ADV en la dirección del viento
downy [dáʊni] ADJ sedoso, suave
dowry [dáʊri] N dote *f*
doze [doz] VI dormitar; N siesta *f*
dozen [dázən] N docena *f*
drab [dræb] ADJ triste; N pardo *m*
draft [dræft] N (of air) corriente *f*; (drink) trago *m*; (bank) giro *m*; (outline) esbozo *m*; (military) conscripción *f*, quinta *f*; (of a ship) calado *m*; — **beer** cerveza de barril *f*; — **horse** caballo de tiro *m*; **—sman** dibujante *m*; VT (to sketch) esbozar; (to compose) redactar; (to select for military service) reclutar
drag [dræg] VI/VT (haul slowly) arrastrar(se); (search a body of water) dragar; **don't — me into this** no me metas en esto; **to — on and on** eternizarse; **to — out** estirar; N (dredge) draga *f*; (boring person) pesado -da *mf*; (hassle) lata *f*; (counterforce) resistencia *f*; (on a cigarette) pitada *f*; — **race** carrera de dragsters *f*; — **strip** pista de dragsters *f*

dragon [drǽgən] N dragón *m*; **—fly** libélula *f*
drain [dren] N (channel) desagüe *m*, sumidero *m*; (depletion of resources) sangría *f*, fuga *f*; — **pipe** desaguadero *m*, desagüe *m*; **to go down the —** irse por la borda; VI/VT (empty a sink) desagotar(se), desaguar(se); (exhaust) agotar(se); VT (wetlands) drenar, sanear; VI (a battery) descargarse
drainage [drénɪdʒ] N (act of draining) desagüe *m*, drenaje *m*; (system) drenaje *m*; **—pipe** tubo de desagüe *m*
drake [drek] N pato (macho) *m*
drama [drámə] N drama *m*
dramatic [drəmǽdɪk] ADJ dramático
dramatist [drúmətɪst] N dramaturgo -ga *mf*
dramatize [drúmataɪz] VI/VT dramatizar
drape [drep] VI (hang in folds) colgar, drapear; VT (cover) cubrir; N cortina *f*
drapery [drépəri] N cortinado *m*, colgadura *f*
drastic [drǽstɪk] ADJ drástico
draw [drɔ] VT (a picture) dibujar; (lines, shapes) trazar; (a cart) tirar de; (a curtain) correr; (cards, blood, water, conclusion, strength) sacar; (a crowd) atraer; (withdraw money) retirar, sacar; (receive money) cobrar; (comparison, distinction) hacer; (sword) desenvainar; VI (of a boat) tener calado; (of a fireplace) tirar; (in sports, have the same score) empatar; **to — aside** apartar(se); **to — away** separar(se); **to — a breath** aspirar, tomar aliento; **to — a blank** quedarse en blanco; **to — in** involucrar; **to — lots / straws** echar a la suerte, sortear; **to — near** acercarse; **to — off** irse, retirarse; **to — on** (be based on) basarse en; (have recourse to) recurrir a; **to — out** (remove) sacar; (prolong) alargar, prolongar; **to — up** (approach) acercar(se); (write) redactar; (shrink) encoger; N (tie) empate *m*; (lot) número sorteado *m*; (attraction) atracción *f*; **—back** inconveniente *m*; **—bridge** puente levadizo *m*
drawer [drɔɚ] N cajón *m*; (small) gaveta *f*; **—s** calzones *m pl*
drawing [drɔ́ɪŋ] N (picture) dibujo *m*; (raffle) sorteo *m*; — **room** sala (de recibo) *f*
drawn [drɔn] ADJ demacrado; **—-out** interminable
dread [drɛd] N pavor *m*, terror *m*, espanto *m*; VT **I — going to the dentist** me aterra ir al dentista
dreadful [drɛ́dfəl] ADJ horrendo, espantoso, temible
dream [drim] N sueño *m* (also aspiration); (reverie) ensueño *m*, ensoñación *f*; (fancy)

ilusión *f;* **—land** tierra del ensueño *f;* vi/
vt soñar; **to — of** soñar con; **I wouldn't
— of stealing** no se me ocurriría robar;
to — that soñar que; **to — up** imaginar;
adj **a — holiday** unas vacaciones
perfectas; **— team** dream team *m,* equipo
de estrellas *m;* **— world** mundo de
ensueño *m*

dreamer [drímə] n (impractical person)
soñador -ora *mf;* (visionary) visionario -ria
mf

dreary [dríri] adj sombrío, deprimente

dredge [dredʒ] n draga *f;* vt dragar

dregs [dregz] n heces *f pl,* poso *m;* **— of
society** escoria de la sociedad *f*

drench [drentʃ] vt empapar, calar; **—ed in
blood** bañado en sangre

dress [dres] n (article of clothing for women)
vestido *m;* (attire) ropa *f;* (formal) traje de
etiqueta *m,* ropa de etiqueta *f;* (costume)
vestimenta *f;* **—maker** modista *mf;* **—
rehearsal** ensayo general *m;* **— shirt**
camisa para traje *f;* vi/vt vestir(se); vt
(store window) arreglar; (slaughtered
animals) limpiar; (salad) aderezar; (hides)
adobar; (a wound) vendar; **to — down**
(scold) regañar; (wear casual clothes)
ponerse ropa informal; **to — up** (wear
fine clothes) vestirse de gala; (make more
appealing) embellecer

dresser [drésə] n cómoda *f;* **she is a good
—** se viste con elegancia

dressing [drésɪŋ] n (act, result) vestir(se) *m;*
(for salad) aderezo *m;* (for fowl) relleno *m;*
(for wounds) gasa *f,* vendaje *m;* **—down**
regaño *m;* **— gown** bata *f;* **— room** (in a
theater) camerino *m;* (in a store) probador
m; **— table** tocador *m*

dribble [dríbəl] vt (trickle) gotear; (sliver)
babear; vt (a ball) driblar; (liquid) rociar; n
(trickle) goteo *m;* (small quantity) chorrito
m; (of a ball) dribbling *m*

dried [draɪd] adj seco; **— fig** higo paso / seco
m; **—-up** (without water) seco; (wizened)
arrugado

drift [drɪft] n (direction) deriva *f;* (current)
corriente *f;* (meaning) sentido *m,* tenor *m;*
(pile) montón *m,* acumulación *f;* **do you
get my —?** ¿me captas la onda? vi (float)
flotar; (be adrift) ir a la deriva; (wander)
errar; **he —ed off** se durmió; vi/vt
(deviate) desviar(se); (accumulate)
amontonar(se), acumular(se); **—wood**
madera flotante *f*

drifter [dríftə] n (wanderer) vagabundo -da
mf; (of a worker) itinerante *mf*

drill [drɪl] n (tool) taladro *m;* (training)

ejercicios *m pl;* (procedure) procedimiento
m; (rehearsal) simulacro *m;* (cloth) dril *m;*
vi/vt (make a hole) taladrar, perforar,
barrenar; (train) entrenar(se), adiestrar(se);
vi (train) hacer ejercicios; (practice)
practicar; vt hacer practicar

drink [drɪŋk] vi/vt (person) beber; (animal)
abrevar; (absorb, take in) absorber; **to —
up** apurar el trago; **to — to someone's
health** brindar por alguien; n bebida *f*
(also alcoholic); (a measure of beverage)
trago *m*

drinkable [dríŋkəbəl] adj potable

drip [drɪp] n goteo *m;* (a bore) plasta *mf;* vi
gotear; vt dejar caer gotas

drive [draɪv] vi/vt (a car) conducir, manejar;
vi (go in a vehicle) ir en coche; vt (move
forth) impulsar, impeler; (an animal)
arrear; (convey) llevar (en coche); (force
labor) forzar a trabajar; (a nail) clavar; (a
ball) tirar, golpear; **to — a hard bargain**
regatear mucho; **to — away** ahuyentar;
to — someone mad volver loco a
alguien; **what are you driving at?** ¿qué
quieres decir con eso? **—-by shooting**
tiroteo desde un coche *m;* **—-in** drive-in
m, establecimiento en que el cliente es
atendido en el coche *m;* **—-in movie
theater** autocine *m;* **—way** camino de
entrada *m,* entrada de coches *f;* n (ride)
paseo (en coche) *m;* (of an animal) arreo
m; (urge) impulso *m;* (military offensive)
ofensiva *f;* (road) carretera *f;* (driveway)
camino *f;* (campaign) campaña *f;*
(energy) empuje *m;* (propulsion system)
propulsión *f;* (of a ball) tiro *m;* (in tennis
and golf) drive *m;* **front wheel —**
tracción delantera *f*

drivel [drívəl] n (saliva) baba *f;* (idiocy)
tontería *f;* vi babearse

driveling [drívəlɪŋ] adj baboso; **he's a —
idiot** es un oligofrénico

driver [dráivə] n (chauffeur) chófer *mf,*
conductor -ra *mf;* (of animals) arriero -ra
mf; (golf club) driver *m*

drizzle [drízəl] vi lloviznar; n llovizna *f*

drone [dron] n (male bee; idler) zángano *m;*
(remote-controlled vehicle) nave
teledirigida *f;* (drudge) esclavo *m;* (sound)
zumbido *m;* vi/vt (make a sound) zumbar;
(talk) hablar monótonamente

drool [drul] n baba *f;* vi babear

droop [drup] vi doblarse; (sag) colgarse; (flag)
languidecer; (wither) marchitarse; **his
shoulders —** tiene los hombros caídos;
—ing ears orejas gachas *f pl*

drop [drɑp] n (liquid quantity) gota *f;*

(descent) caída *f*; (incline) declive *m*; (in
value) baja *f*; (lozenge) pastilla *f*; (of mail,
etc.) buzón *m*, punto de recolección *m*; (of
supplies) lanzamiento *m*; vi caer; (let fall)
dejar caer, descargar; **to — a line** mandar
unas líneas; **to — from sight**
desaparecer; **to — in** caer de sorpresa; **to
— out** (sports) retirarse; (school)
abandonar; **—out** (student) estudiante
que abandona *mf*; (marginalized person)
marginado -da *mf*; **to — the curtain**
bajar el telón; **why don't you — by?**
¿por qué no pasas por aquí? **—-dead
beautiful** hermosísima
dropper [dɾɑ́pɚ] N gotero *m*
drought [dɾaʊt] N sequía *f*
drove [dɾov] N tropel *m*
drown [dɾaʊn] vi/vt ahogar(se)
drowse [dɾaʊz] vi (be half-asleep) dormitar;
(feel drowsy) estar amodorrado
drowsiness [dɾáʊzɪnɪs] N modorra *f*,
somnolencia *f*
drowsy [dɾáʊzi] ADJ amodorrado,
somnoliento; **to become —** amodorrarse
drudge [dɾʌʤ] N esclavo del trabajo *m*,
fregona *f*; vi trabajar como un esclavo
drug [dɾʌg] N (chemical substance, narcotic)
droga *f*; (medicine) medicamento *m*; **to
be a — on the market** ser invendible;
— addict drogadicto -a *mf*; **—store**
(drugs) farmacia *f*; (non-drug items)
droguería *f*, perfumería *f*; vt (stupefy with
drugs) drogar; (mix with a drug) adulterar
con droga
druggist [dɾʌ́gɪst] N farmacéutico -ca *mf*,
droguero -ra *mf*
drum [dɾʌm] N (musical instrument) tambor
m; (eardrum) tímpano *m*; (receptacle for
storing liquids) barril *m*; **—head** parche
m; **—stick** (music) palillo de tambor *m*;
(fowl) pata *f*; vi (play a drum) tocar el
tambor; (beat rhythmically) tamborilear;
to — out expulsar; **to — up** fomentar;
**I'm trying to — this idea into his
head** le estoy repitiendo esta idea con
insistencia
drummer [dɾʌ́mɚ] N (classical) tambor *m*;
(folk) tamborilero -ra *mf*; (rock & roll)
baterista *mf*; (sales person) viajante de
comercio *mf*
drunk [dɾʌŋk] ADJ & N borracho -cha *mf*; *fam*
mamado -da *mf*; **to get —** emborracharse
drunkard [dɾʌ́ŋkɚd] N borracho -cha *mf*,
borrachín -ina *mf*
drunken [dɾʌ́ŋkən] ADJ borracho,
embriagado
drunkenness [dɾʌ́ŋkənnɪs] N borrachera *f*,

embriaguez *f*
dry [dɾaɪ] ADJ seco; (sober) sobrio; (topic,
book) árido, aburrido; **— land** tierra firme
f; **— cleaner** (business) tintorería *f*;
(owner of business) tintorero -ra *mf*; **—
cleaning** limpieza en seco *f*; **— county**
condado seco *m*; **— wit** humor agudo *m*;
— goods géneros *m pl*; **— measure**
medida para áridos *f*; **— run** prueba *f*; **—
ice** hielo seco *m*; **— dock** dique seco *m*,
varadero *m*; vi/vt (wet clothes) secar(se);
(leather) resecar(se); **to — up** secarse,
resecarse; **to — out** desintoxicar(se)
dryer [dɾáɪɚ] N (hair) secador *m*; (clothes)
secadora *f*
dryness [dɾáɪnɪs] N (skin, etc.) sequedad *f*;
(land, lecture) aridez *f*
dual [dúəł] ADJ (function) doble; (ownership)
compartido
dub [dʌb] vt doblar
dubious [dúbiəs] ADJ dudoso
duchess [dʌ́tʃɪs] N duquesa *f*
duck [dʌk] N (species) pato *m*; (downward
dodge) agachada *f*; vi/vt (plunge under
water) hundir(se); (bend down)
agachar(se); vt (avoid) esquivar
duckling [dʌ́klɪŋ] N patito *m*
duct [dʌkt] N conducto *m*; **— tape** cinta
aislante *f*
ductile [dʌ́ktl̩] ADJ dúctil
dud [dʌd] N (disappointing thing) chasco *m*;
(unexploded bomb) bomba que no estalla
f; **—s** (clothes) ropa *f*, *fam* trapos *m pl*;
(belongings) pertenencias *f pl*
dude [dud] N (dandy) chulo *m*; (fellow) tipo
m
due [du] ADJ (payable) pagadero;
(immediately owed) vencido; (fitting,
rightful) debido; (adequate) suficiente; **in
— time / course** a su debido tiempo; **the
train is — at two o'clock** se supone
que el tren llega a las dos; ADV **— east**
hacia el este; N (punishment) merecido *m*;
give Mary her —; she's honest tienes
que reconocer que María es honrada; **—s**
cuota *f*
duel [dúəł] N duelo *m*; vi/vt batirse en / a
duelo (con alguien)
duet [duέt] N (played) dúo *m*; (sung) dueto *m*
dugout [dʌ́gaʊt] N (canoe) piragua *f*;
(underground refuge) trinchera *f*
DUI (driving under the influence) [dijuáɪ]
N conducir en estado de ebriedad *m*
duke [duk] N duque *m*; **to put up one's —s**
levantar los puños; vt **to — it out**
arreglarlo con los puños
dukedom [dúkdəm] N ducado *m*

dull [dʌɫ] ADJ (lackluster) opaco; (listless, muted) apagado; (boring) aburrido, soso, desanimado; (blunt) romo, desafilado; (sluggish, stupid) lento; (pain) sordo; VI/VT (a knife) desafilar(se); (color) opacar(se); (sound, impact) amortiguar(se); (pain) aliviar(se); (senses) embotar(se), entorpecer(se)

duly [dúli] ADV debidamente

dumb [dʌm] ADJ (mute) mudo; (dull) tonto; **—bell** (handweight) mancuerna *f*; (stupid person) bobo -ba *mf*; **—founded** patitieso, atónito; VT **to — down** simplificar demasiado

dumbness [dʌ́mnɪs] N (muteness) mudez *f*; (foolishness) estupidez *f*

dummy [dʌ́mi] N (figure) muñeco *m*; (fool) tonto -ta *mf*; *offensive* pendejo -ja *mf*; (front) hombre de paja *m*; ADJ (fake) falso; **a — president** un títere

dump [dʌmp] VT (unload) descargar; (empty) botar; (dismiss) echar, despedir; (discard) tirar la basura, descargar desechos; (flood a market) hacer dumping; (abandon) plantar; **to — on** (criticize) criticar; (unload problems) descargarse; N (place for waste) vertedero *m*, basural *m*, basurero *m*; (of weapons) depósito *m*; (act of discarding) vertido *m*; **—truck** camión volteador *m*, volquete *m*; **to be in the —s** estar deprimido, estar depre

dunce [dʌns] N burro -rra *mf*, tonto -ta de capirote *mf*

dune [dun] N duna *f*, médano *m*

dung [dʌŋ] N boñiga *f*, bosta *f*; **—hill** estercolero *m*

dungeon [dʌ́ndʒən] N mazmorra *f*

dupe [dup] N (gullible person) ingenuo -nua *mf*, inocente *mf*; *Sp* primo -ma *mf*; (manipulated person) títere *m*; VT embaucar

duplex [dúpləks] N & ADJ dúplex *m*

duplicate [dúplɪkɪt] ADJ & N duplicado *m*; **in —** por duplicado; [dúplɪket] VT duplicar(se)

duplicity [duplísɪɾi] N duplicidad *f*

durability [durəbílɪɾi] N durabilidad *f*

durable [dúrəbəɫ] ADJ (long-lasting) duradero; (serviceable) sufrido

duration [duréʃən] N duración *f*

duress [durés] N coacción *f*

during [dúrɪŋ] PREP durante

dusk [dʌsk] N atardecer *m*, anochecer *m*; **at —** al atardecer

dusky [dʌ́ski] ADJ (dark) oscuro; (gloomy) sombrío

dust [dʌst] N polvo *m*; **—pan** pala *f*; **to bite the —** (die) *fam* espichar; (lose) morder el polvo de la derrota; **cloud of —** polvareda *f*; VI/VT (remove dust) quitar / sacudir el polvo (a); VT (sprinkle with powder) espolvorear; VI (become dusty) empolvarse; **to — off** desempolvar

duster [dʌ́stə] N plumero *m*

dusty [dʌ́sti] ADJ polvoriento

Dutch [dʌtʃ] ADJ & N holandés -esa *mf*; **to go —** pagar a escote

Dutchman [dʌ́tʃmən] N holandés *m*

duty [dúɾi] N deber *m*, obligación *f*; (tax on imports) derechos aduaneros *m pl*; (any tax) impuesto *m*; **to be on —** estar de guardia; **to be off —** no estar de guardia; **—-free** libre de impuestos

DVD (digital versatile disc) [dívidí] N DVD *m*

dwarf [dwɔrf] ADJ & N enano -na *mf*; VT hacer parecer pequeño

dwell [dwɛɫ] VI morar, habitar; **to — on a subject** dilatarse en un asunto

dweller [dwɛ́lə] N habitante *mf*, morador -ra *mf*

dwelling [dwɛ́lɪŋ] N vivienda *f*, domicilio *m*

DWI (driving while intoxicated) [dɪdʌbəljuáɪ] N conducir en estado de ebriedad *m*

dwindle [dwíndɫ] VI/VT menguar, mermar

dye [daɪ] N tinte *m*, tintura *f*; VT teñir

dying [dáɪɪŋ] ADJ moribundo

dynamic [daɪnǽmɪk] ADJ dinámico; N **—s** dinámica *f*

dynamite [dáɪnəmaɪt] N dinamita *f*; VT dinamitar; ADJ fabuloso

dynamo [dáɪnəmo] N dínamo *m*

dynasty [dáɪnəsti] N dinastía *f*

dysentery [dísənteri] N disentería *f*

dysfunction [dɪsfʌ́ŋkʃən] N disfunción *f*

Ee

each [itʃ] ADJ cada; **— person** cada persona; PRON cada uno; **— receives a prize** cada uno recibe un premio; **they looked at — other** se miraron el uno al otro

eager [ígə] ADJ (enthusiastic) ansioso; (avid) ávido

eagerness [ígənɪs] N (enthusiasm) ansia *f*, afán *m*; (strong desire) avidez *f*

eagle [ígəɫ] N águila *f*; **—-eye** ojo de lince *m*

eaglet [íɡlɪt] N aguilucho *m*

ear [ir] N (outer organ) oreja *f*; (inner organ, sense of hearing, musical aptitude) oído

m; (of corn) mazorca *f*; *Am* elote *m*;
—**ache** dolor de oídos *m*; —**drops** gotas
para los oídos *f pl*; —**drum** tímpano *m*;
—**lobe** lóbulo de la oreja *m*; — **muff**
orejera *f*; — **of wheat** espiga *f*; —**phone**
audífono *m*; —**ring** pendiente *m*, zarcillo
m; **by** — de oído; **within** —**shot** al
alcance del oído; **he has the** — **of the**
governor el gobernador le presta mucha
atención

earful [írfʊ‡] N **I got an** — (scolding) me
echó un rapapolvo; (gossip) me dio la lata

early [ʒ́·li] ADJ temprano; — **detection**
diagnóstico precoz *m*; — **man** hombre
primitivo *m*; — **reply** respuesta rápida *f*;
— **riser / bird** madrugador -ra *mf*,
mañanero -ra *mf*; **the** — **bird gets the**
worm al que madruga, Dios lo ayuda

earn [ʒ·n] VI/VT (money, admiration, etc.)
ganar; (salary) cobrar, ganar; (interest)
devengar; N **to** — **a living** ganarse la vida

earnest [ʒ́·nɪst] ADJ (sincere) serio, formal;
(grave) grave; **in** — en serio; — **money**
señal *f*; *Mex* enganche *m*

earnestness [ʒ́·nɪstnɪs] N (sincerity) seriedad
f, formalidad *f*; (gravity) gravedad *f*; **in all**
— con toda sinceridad

earnings [ʒ́·nɪŋz] N (of a person) ingresos *m*
pl, haberes *m pl*; (of a business) ganancias
f pl

earth [ʒ·θ] N tierra *f*; —**mover** excavadora *f*;
—**quake** terremoto *m*, temblor de tierra
m; —**shaking** revolucionario; —**worm**
lombriz *f*; **the** — la Tierra

earthen [ʒ́·θən] ADJ (wall) de tierra; (pot) de
barro; —**ware** vajilla de barro *f*, cerámica
f

earthly [ʒ́·θli] ADJ terrenal; — **possessions**
bienes terrenales *m pl*; **to be of no** — **use**
no servir para nada

earthy [ʒ́·θi] ADJ natural; (person)
campechano; (sense of humor, joke) basto;
— **smell** olor a tierra *m*

ease [iz] N (facility) facilidad *f*;
(unaffectedness) soltura *f*, desparpajo *m*;
(comfort) comodidad *f*; (lack of worry)
tranquilidad *f*; (fullness of a garment)
holgura *f*; **at** — (military) en descanso;
(comfortable) tranquilo, a gusto; **a life of**
— una vida desahogada; **ill at** —
incómodo; VT (make easier) facilitar; VI/VT
(relieve pain) aliviar(se); (release from
tension) aflojar(se); (relieve anxiety)
tranquilizar(se); **to** — **up** aflojar

easel [ízə‡] N caballete *m*

east [ist] N este *m*, oriente *m*; ADJ del este,
oriental; ADV — **of here** al este (de aquí);

to go — ir al / hacia el este; **back** — en el
este

Easter [ístɚ] N Pascua *f*; — **egg** huevo de
Pascua *m*; — **Sunday** Domingo de Pascua
m

eastern [ístɚn] ADJ oriental, del este

eastward [ístwɚd] ADV & ADJ hacia el este

easy [ízi] ADJ (simple) fácil, sencillo;
(compliant) fácil; (comfortable) cómodo;
(informal) desenvuelto; (unworried)
tranquilo; — **chair** poltrona *f*; —**going**
calmoso; — **terms** facilidades de pago *f*
pl; **at an** — **pace** a paso moderado;
within — **reach** al alcance de la mano;
go — **on me** sea bueno; **he's on** —
street vive en la abundancia

eat [it] VI/VT comer(se); VT (costs) absorber; **to**
— **away** corroer, comer; **to** — **breakfast**
desayunar(se); **to** — **dinner** (midday)
comer; (evening) cenar; **to** — **lunch**
comer, almorzar; **to** — **one's heart out**
morirse de envidia; **to** — **one's words**
tragarse las palabras; **to** — **supper** cenar;
to — **up** comerse todo; **what's** —**ing**
you? ¿qué bicho te picó?

eating [ídɪŋ] N (act) comer *m*; (food) comida
f; — **utensils** cubiertos *m pl*; — **apples**
manzanas para comer *f pl*

eaves [ivz] N PL alero *m*

eavesdrop [ívzdrɑp] VI escuchar sin ser visto

ebb [eb] N (flowing back) reflujo *m*; (decay)
decadencia *f*; — **tide** reflujo *m*; **to be at**
a low — estar en un punto bajo; VI (tide)
bajar; (energy) decaer

ebony [ébəni] N ébano *m*

eccentric [ekséntrɪk] ADJ & N excéntrico -ca
mf

ecclesiastic [ɪkliziǽstɪk] ADJ & N eclesiástico
m

echelon [éʃəlɑn] N (military formation)
escalón *m*; (rank) nivel *m*, estrato *m*

echo [éko] N eco *m*; VI hacer eco; **the gym**
—**ed with laughter** el gimnasio resonó
de risas; VT repetir

eclectic [ɪkléktɪk] ADJ ecléctico

eclipse [ɪklíps] N eclipse *m*; VT eclipsar

ecology [ɪkɑ́lədʒi] N ecología *f*

e-commerce [íkámɚs] N comercio
electrónico *m*

economic [ekənɑ́mɪk] ADJ económico; —**s**
economía *f*

economical [ekənɑ́mɪkə‡] ADJ económico

economist [ɪkɑ́nəmɪst] N economista *mf*

economize [ɪkɑ́nəmaɪz] VI economizar

economy [ɪkɑ́nəmi] N economía *f* (also
thrift); ADJ — **car** coche económico *m*; —
class clase turista *f*

ecosystem [íkosɪstəm] N ecosistema *m*

ecstasy [ékstəsi] N éxtasis *m* (also drug)

Ecuador [ékwədɔɔr] N Ecuador *m*

Ecuadorian [ɛkwədɔ́riən] ADJ & N ecuatoriano -na *mf*

ecumenical [ɛkjəménɪkəl] ADJ ecuménico

eczema [égzəmə] N eccema *m*

eddy [édi] N remolino *m*; VI arremolinarse

edge [ɛʤ] N borde *m*, canto *m*; (of a knife) filo *m*; (of a cube) arista *f*; **to be on —** estar nervioso; **her voice has an — to it** tiene la voz penetrante; **a competitive —** una ventaja sobre la competencia; VT (make an edge) hacerle el borde; (sharpen) afilar; (move sideways) meterse de costado; **to — out** ganar por un pelito; **to — up** aproximarse; ADV **—wise** de costado

edgy [éʤi] ADJ nervioso

edible [édəbəl] ADJ & N comestible *m*

edict [ídɪkt] N edicto *m*, bando *m*

edifice [édəfɪs] N edificio *m*

edify [édəfaɪ] VT edificar

edit [édɪt] VT (revise, correct) corregir; (serve as editor) editar; (film) montar; **to — out** eliminar; N corrección *f*

edition [ɪdíʃən] N edición *f*

editor [édɪtɚ] N (director of a publication) redactor -ra *mf*; (compiler, radio or film worker) editor -ra *mf*; (proofreader) corrector -ra *mf*

editorial [ɛdɪtɔ́riəl] ADJ editorial; N editorial *f*

editorialize [ɛdɪtɔ́riəlaɪz] VI editorializar

educate [éʤəkét] VT educar

education [ɛʤəkéʃən] N educación *f*, enseñanza *f*; (academic subject) pedagogía *f*; **school of —** escuela normal *f*

educational [ɛʤəkéʃənəl] ADJ educativo

educator [éʤəkéɾɚ] N educador -ra *mf*

eel [il] N anguila *f*

eerie [íri] ADJ misterioso

effect [ɪfɛ́kt] N efecto *m*; **—s** efectos *m pl*; **to go into —** entrar en vigencia, ponerse en operación; **I wrote a letter to that —** le escribí una carta en ese sentido; VT efectuar

effective [ɪfɛ́ktɪv] ADJ efectivo, eficaz; (a law) vigente; **— date** fecha de vigencia *f*

effectively [ɪfɛ́ktɪvli] ADV (well) eficazmente; (in fact) de hecho, en efecto

effectual [ɪfɛ́ktʃuəl] ADJ eficaz

effeminate [ɪfémənət] ADJ afeminado

efficacy [éfɪkəsi] N eficacia *f*

efficiency [ɪfíʃənsi] N eficiencia *f*; **— apartment** estudio *m*

efficient [ɪfíʃənt] ADJ eficiente; (motor) económico

effigy [éfəʤi] N efigie *f*; **to burn in —** quemar en efigie

effort [éfɚt] N (exertion) esfuerzo *m*; (work of art) obra *f*; (campaign) campaña *f*

effrontery [ɪfrántəri] N descaro *m*

effusive [ɪfjúsɪv] ADJ efusivo

egg [ɛg] N huevo *m*; (female gamete) óvulo *m*; (fellow) tipo *m*; **—beater** batidor de huevos *m*; **—head** empollón -na *mf*; **—nog** rompopo *m*, rompope *m*, ponche de huevo *m*; **—plant** berenjena *f*; **—shell** cáscara de huevo *f*; **to have — on one's face** estar avergonzado, quedar mal; **to lay an —** (of a hen) poner un huevo; (fail) fracasar; **to walk on —shells** ir pisando huevos; VT **to — on** incitar

ego [ígo] N (self) yo *m*, ego *m*; (vanity) ego *m*; (self-esteem) amor propio *m*; **winning the prize was an — trip for him** ganar el premio le aceitó el ego

egocentric [igoséntrɪk] ADJ egocéntrico

egotism [ígətɪzəm] N egotismo *m*

Egypt [íʤɪpt] N Egipto *m*

Egyptian [ɪʤípʃən] ADJ & N egipcio -cia *mf*

eight [et] NUM ocho

eighteen [ettín] NUM dieciocho

eighth [etθ] ADJ, N & ADV octavo *m*; **— note** corchea *f*

eighty [éti] NUM ochenta

either [íðɚ] ADJ & PRON **— will do** cualquiera de los dos está bien; **choose — suit** elige uno de los dos trajes; **choose —** elige uno (u otro) de los dos; **there were flowers on — side of the road** había flores a ambos lados de la carretera; ADV **if you don't, I won't —** si tú no lo haces, yo tampoco; **I'll — go by bus or by car** voy (o) en autobús o en auto

ejaculate [ɪʤǽkjəlet] VI/VT eyacular; (exclaim) exclamar

eject [ɪʤékt] VT (throw out) echar, expulsar; VI/VT (from a plane) eyectar(se)

ejection [ɪʤékʃən] N expulsión *f*

elaborate [ɪlǽbɚɪt] ADJ (ornate) elaborado; (detailed) detallado; [ɪlǽbaret] VI/VT (create) elaborar; (develop) desarrollar

elapse [ɪlǽps] VI transcurrir, pasar

elastic [ɪlǽstɪk] ADJ elástico; N elástico *m*; (rubber band) goma elástica *f*

elasticity [ɪlæstísɪdi] N elasticidad *f*

elated [ɪlépɪd] ADJ encantado

elbow [élbo] N codo *m*; **to be within — reach** estar a la mano; VI/VT codear, dar codazos; **to — one's way through** abrirse paso a codazos

elder [éldɚ] ADJ (older) mayor; N (older person) mayor *mf*; (old person) anciano -na *mf*; (in a church) miembro del consejo

de una iglesia *m*; **our —s** nuestros
mayores *m pl*
elderly [éˑldəˑli] ADJ anciano
elect [ɪlékt] ADJ (elected) electo; (chosen by
God) elegido -da *mf*; VI/VT elegir
election [ɪlékʃən] N elección *f*
elector [ɪléktə] N elector -ra *mf*
electoral [ɪléktəˑəl] ADJ electoral
electric [ɪléktrɪk] ADJ eléctrico; (exciting)
electrizante; (excited) electrizado; **— chair**
silla eléctrica *f*; **— eel** anguila eléctrica *f*;
— eye célula fotoeléctrica *f*; **— meter**
contador eléctrico *m*; **— storm** tormenta
eléctrica *f*
electrical [ɪléktrɪkəl] ADJ eléctrico; **—
engineer** ingeniero electricista *mf*; **—
engineering** ingeniería eléctrica *f*; **—
tape** cinta aislante *f*
electrician [ɪlɛktríʃən] N electricista *mf*
electricity [ɪlɛktrísɪdɪ] N electricidad *f*
electrify [ɪléktrəfaɪ] VT (apply electricity)
electrificar; (thrill) electrizar
electrocardiogram [ɪlɛktrokárdɪəgræm] N
electrocardiograma *m*
electrocute [ɪléktrəkjut] VT electrocutar
electrode [ɪléktrod] N electrodo *m*
electroencephalogram [ɪlɛktroɛnséfələgræm]
N electroencefalograma *m*
electrolysis [ɪlɛktrálɪsɪs] N electrólisis *f*
electromagnet [ɪlɛktromǽgnɪt] N
electroimán *m*
electromagnetic [ɪlɛktromægnéDɪk] ADJ
electromagnético
electron [ɪléktrɑn] N electrón *m*; **—
microscope** microscopio electrónico *m*
electronic [ɪlɛktránɪk] ADJ electrónico; **—
banking** banca electrónica *f*; **— mail**
correo electrónico *m*; **—s** electrónica *f*; **—
signature** firma electrónica *f*
elegance [élɪgəns] N elegancia *f*, gallardía *f*
elegant [élɪgənt] ADJ elegante, gallardo; (gift)
de lujo
element [éləmənt] N elemento *m*;
(component part) componente *m*, pieza *f*;
(for heating) resistencia *f*; **the —s** los
elementos
elemental [ɛləmént̬l] ADJ elemental; **—
forces** fuerzas de la naturaleza *f pl*
elementary [ɛləméntri] ADJ elemental; **—
school** escuela primaria *f*
elephant [éləfənt] N elefante -ta *mf*
elevate [éləvet] VT elevar
elevation [ɛləvéʃən] N elevación *f*; (altitude)
altura *f*
elevator [éləvedə] N ascensor *m*; *Am*
elevador *m*; (for grain) elevador *m*
eleven [ɪlévən] NUM once

elf [ɛlf] N elfo *m*; (child) pillo -lla *mf*
elicit [ɪlísɪt] VT provocar; **to — admiration**
despertar admiración; **to — applause**
suscitar el aplauso
eligible [élɪdʒəbəl] ADJ elegible; **an —
bachelor** un buen partido; **you are —
for a scholarship** tienes derecho a
solicitar una beca
eliminate [ɪlímənet] VT eliminar
elimination [ɪlɪmənéʃən] N eliminación *f*
elite [ɪlít] N elite *f*, élite *f*
elitist [ɪlíDɪst] ADJ & N elitista *mf*
elk [ɛlk] N alce *m*
elliptical [ɪlíptɪkəl] ADJ elíptico
elm [ɛlm] N olmo *m*
elongate [ɪlóŋget] VI/VT alargar(se)
elope [ɪlóp] VI fugarse para casarse a
escondidas
eloquence [éləkwəns] N elocuencia *f*
eloquent [éləkwənt] ADJ elocuente
El Salvador [ɛlsǽlvədɔr] N El Salvador *m*
else [ɛls] ADJ & ADV **who — was there?**
¿quién más estaba? **someone —'s son** el
hijo de otro; **somebody —** (algún) otro;
or — si no; **leave town or —** vete del
pueblo o sufre las consecuencias / o verás
lo que es bueno; **nobody —** nadie más;
nothing — nada más; **how —?** ¿de qué
otra forma? ADV **—where** (location) en
otra parte / en otro lado; (movement) a
otra parte / a otro sitio
elucidate [ɪlúsɪdet] VI/VT dilucidar, esclarecer
elucidation [ɪlusɪdéʃən] N elucidación *f*
elude [ɪlúd] VT eludir
elusive [ɪlúsɪv] ADJ (slippery) escurridizo;
(evasive) esquivo; (difficult to understand)
difícil de entender
emaciated [ɪméʃɪeDɪd] ADJ escuálido,
descarnado
e-mail, E-mail [ímel] N correo electrónico *m*
emanate [émənet] VI/VT emanar
emanation [ɛmənéʃən] N emanación *f*
emancipate [ɪmǽnsəpet] VT emancipar
emancipation [ɪmænsəpéʃən] N
emancipación *f*
emasculate [ɪmǽskjəlet] VT castrar; (remove
testicles) castrar, emascular
embalm [ɪmbám] VT embalsamar
embankment [ɪmbǽŋkmənt] N terraplén *m*
embargo [ɪmbárgo] N embargo *m*; VT
imponer un embargo
embark [ɪmbárk] VI/VT embarcar(se)
embarrass [ɪmbǽrəs] VT (shame) hacerle
pasar vergüenza a; (discomfit, financial
difficulties) poner en aprietos; VI
avergonzarse
embarrassing [ɪmbǽrəsɪŋ] ADJ (shameful)

vergonzoso; (impeding) embarazoso

embarrassment [ɪmbǽrəsmənt] N (shame)
vergüenza f, bochorno m; (act of
embarrassing) vergüenza f; (financial
difficulty) aprieto m; **he's an — to the
company** siempre deja mal a la
compañía; **we have an — of riches**
nadamos en la abundancia

embassy [ǽmbəsi] N embajada f

embattled [ɪmbǽd|d] ADJ hostigado,
agobiado

embed [ɪmbéd] VT incrustar

embedded [ɪmbédɪd] ADJ incrustado

embellish [ɪmbélɪʃ] VT adornar, ornamentar

ember [émbə] N ascua f, brasa f

embezzle [ɪmbézəl] VT desfalcar, malversar

embezzlement [ɪmbézəlmənt] N desfalco m,
peculado m

embitter [ɪmbídə] VT amargar

emblem [émbləm] N emblema m, divisa f

embody [ɪmbádi] VT (personify) personificar;
(to provide with a body) encarnar

embolism [émbəlɪzəm] N embolia f

embrace [ɪmbrés] VT (hug, adopt)
abrazar(se); (include) abarcar; N abrazo m

embroider [ɪmbrɔ́ɪdə] VI/VT bordar, recamar

embroidery [ɪmbrɔ́ɪdəri] N bordado m

embroil [ɪmbrɔ́ɪl] VT (involve in a conflict)
meterse en un lío; (throw into confusion)
embrollar

embryo [émbrio] N embrión m

emerald [émərəld] N esmeralda f

emerge [ɪmɝ́ʤ] VI (come into view) emerger;
(arise, as a question, problem) surgir

emergency [ɪmɝ́ʤənsi] N emergencia f; **—
brake** freno de emergencia m; **— exit**
salida de emergencia f; **— room** urgencias
f pl

emigrant [émɪgrənt] ADJ & N emigrante mf

emigrate [émɪgret] VI emigrar

emigration [emɪgréʃən] N emigración f

eminence [émənəns] N eminencia f

eminent [émənənt] ADJ eminente

emissary [émɪseri] N emisario -ria mf

emission [ɪmíʃən] N emisión f

emit [ɪmít] VT (light, sound, etc.) emitir;
(smells) despedir; (sparks) echar

emotion [ɪmóʃən] N emoción f

emotional [ɪmóʃənəl] ADJ (of the emotions)
emocional; (arousing or expressing
emotions) emotivo; (easily moved)
sensible

empathy [émpəθi] N empatía f

emperor [émpərə] N emperador m; **—
penguin** pingüino emperador m

emphasis [émfəsɪs] N énfasis m, hincapié m

emphasize [émfəsaɪz] VT enfatizar, hacer

hincapié en, subrayar

emphatic [ɪmfǽdɪk] ADJ enfático

emphysema [emfɪsímə] N enfisema m

empire [émpaɪr] N imperio m

empirical [empírɪkəl] ADJ empírico

employ [ɪmplɔ́ɪ] VT emplear; (hire) emplear,
ocupar; N empleo m; **to be in someone's
—** trabajar a las órdenes de alguien

employee [ɪmplɔ́ɪí] N empleado -da mf

employer [ɪmplɔ́ɪə] N patrón -na mf

employment [ɪmplɔ́ɪmənt] N empleo m;
(occupation) ocupación f; **—
opportunities** oportunidades laborales f
pl; **place of —** lugar de trabajo m

empower [ɪmpáuə] VT (authorize) autorizar;
(give strength) dar poder

empress [émprɪs] N emperatriz f

emptiness [émptɪnɪs] N vacío m

empty [émpti] ADJ vacío; (devoid of activity)
desocupado; VI/VT vaciar(se), volcar(se);
(debouch) desembocar; **—-handed** con
las manos vacías; **to run on —** (of a car,
person) quedarse sin combustible

emulate [émjəlet] VT emular (also computer
term)

enable [nébəl] VT permitir

enact [ɪnǽkt] VT (a law) promulgar; (a role)
desempeñar

enamel [ɪnǽməl] N esmalte m; VT esmaltar

enamor [ɪnǽmə] VT enamorar; **to be —ed
of** estar enamorado de

encamp [ɪnkǽmp] VI acampar

enchant [ɪntʃǽnt] VT (bewitch) hechizar;
(delight) encantar

enchanting [ɪntʃǽntɪŋ] ADJ encantador

enchantment [ɪntʃǽntmənt] N
encantamiento m, encanto m, hechicería f

encircle [ɪnsɝ́kəl] VT cercar, ceñir

enclave [ánklev] N enclave m

enclose [ɪnklóz] VT (confine someone or
something) encerrar; (fence in) cercar; (put
in the same envelope) adjuntar, anexar

enclosure [ɪnklóʒə] N (wall or fence) cerca f;
(enclosed area) cercado m, recinto m;
(enclosed document) documento adjunto
m; (act of enclosing) encierro m

encompass [ɪnkámpəs] VT (include) abarcar,
englobar; (surround) circundar

encore [ánkɔr] N bis m; INTERJ ¡otra!

encounter [ɪnkáuntə] VI/VT encontrar(se);
they —ed the enemy army se
enfrentaron con el ejército enemigo; N
(meeting) encuentro m (also sports);
(battle) enfrentamiento m

encourage [ɪnkɝ́ɪʤ] VT (inspire with
confidence) alentar, animar; (promote)
fomentar, estimular

encouragement [ɪnkɔ́rɪdʒmənt] N aliento *m*; (inspiration) ánimo *m*; (promotion) estímulo *m*, fomento *m*

encroach [ɪnkróʧ] VT **to — upon** (liberties) cercenar; (territory) usurpar; (time) quitar

encrypt [ɪnkrípt] VT codificar

encumber [ɪnkʌ́mbər] VT (block) impedir; (burden) agobiar

encyclopedia [ɪnsaɪkləpíDiə] N enciclopedia *f*

end [end] N (temporal) fin *m*, término *m*; (limit, boundary) final *m*, extremo *m*; (tip) cabo *m*; (aim) fin *m*; **— to —** uno tras otro; **— table** mesa pequeña *f*; **at the — of the movie** al final de la película; **the north — of town** el barrio norte; **no — of things** un sinfín de cosas; **at the — of the day** al fin y al cabo; **on —** de punta; **for days on —** día tras día; **to put an — to** poner fin a; VI/VT terminar; (a street) morir; **he —ed his life** puso fin a su vida; **a prayer —s the class** la clase termina con una oración; **a war to — all wars** una guerra que supera a todas las anteriores

endanger [ɪndéndʒər] VT poner en peligro; **—ed species** especie en peligro de extinción *f*

endear [ɪndír] VI **to — oneself** congraciarse; **his humor —ed him to her** se ganó la simpatía de ella gracias a su humor

endeavor [ɪndévər] VT (try) tratar de, intentar, procurar; VI (strive) esforzarse por; N esfuerzo *m*

endemic [ɪndémɪk] ADJ endémico

ending [éndɪŋ] N final *m*; (derivational, inflectional) terminación *f*; (inflectional) desinencia *f*

endless [éndlɪs] ADJ interminable; (continuous) sin fin; (infinite) eterno

endocrine [éndəkrɪn] ADJ endócrino

endorphin [ɪndɔ́rfɪn] N endorfina *f*

endorse [ɪndɔ́rs] VT (sign a check) endosar; (support) respaldar; (authorize a document) refrendar, visar

endorsement [ɪndɔ́rsmənt] N (signature) endoso *m*; (backing) respaldo *m*; (authorization) refrendo *m*

endorser [ɪndɔ́rsər] N (check signer) endosante *mf*; (supporter) partidario -ria *mf*; (authorizer) refrendario -ria *mf*

endow [ɪndáu] VT (grant funds) hacer un legado; (furnish powers) dotar

endowment [ɪndáumənt] N (funds granted) legado *m*, dotación *f*; (power) dote *f*; **— annuity** anualidad dotal *f*; **— fund** fondo de un legado *m*

endurance [ɪndúrəns] N (stamina) resistencia *f*, fondo *m*; (power of bearing pain) aguante *m*

endure [ɪndúr] VT (undergo) sobrellevar, soportar, pasar; VI (live on) durar; (bear up) aguantar

enema [énəmə] N enema *m*, lavativa *f*

enemy [énəmi] N enemigo -ga *mf*

energetic [enəʤɛ́Dɪk] ADJ enérgico

energy [énəʤi] N energía *f*; **— policy** política energética *f*

enervate [énə-vet] VT enervar, debilitar

enforce [ɪnfɔ́rs] VT hacer cumplir

enforcement [ɪnfɔ́rsmənt] N **law —** autoridades *f pl*; **the sheriff is responsible for the — of the law** el alguacil es responsable de hacer cumplir la ley

engage [ɪnɡéʤ] VT (hire) contratar; (attract) captar, atraer; (interlock) engranar; **to — the brake** poner el freno; **to — someone in conversation** trabar conversación con alguien; **to — in battle** trabar batalla; **to be —d in something** estar ocupado en algo; **to be —d to be married** estar comprometido (para casarse), estar prometido

engagement [ɪnɡéʤmənt] N (commitment) compromiso *m*; (betrothal) compromiso *m*, noviazgo *m*; (employment) empleo *m*; (battle) batalla *f*; (gear interlocking) engranaje *m*

engender [ɪndʒéndər] VT engendrar

engine [éndʒɪn] N (machine) máquina *f*; (in a vehicle) motor *m*; (locomotive) locomotora *f*; **— block** bloque del motor *m*

engineer [endʒənír] N ingeniero -ra *mf*; (of locomotive) maquinista *mf*; VT (create) idear; (plot) maquinar

engineering [endʒənírɪŋ] N ingeniería *f*

English [íŋɡlɪʃ] ADJ inglés; N (spin) efecto *m*; **the —** los ingleses; **—man, —woman** inglés -esa *mf*

engrave [ɪngrév] VI/VT grabar

engraver [ɪngrévər] N grabador -ora *mf*

engraving [ɪngrévɪŋ] N grabado *m*

engross [ɪngrós] VT absorber

engrossed [ɪngróst] ADJ absorto

engulf [ɪngʌ́lf] VT (swallow) tragar; (overwhelm) abrumar

enhance [ɪnhǽns] VT (intensify) realzar; (improve) mejorar

enigma [ɪnígmə] N enigma *m*

enjoin [ɪndʒɔ́ɪn] VT instar; **to — from** prohibir

enjoy [ɪndʒɔ́ɪ] VI/VT (take pleasure) disfrutar (de), gozar (de); (benefit from) gozar (de);

—! ¡Que lo disfrutes! **to — oneself**
divertirse; **to — the use of** usufructuar
enjoyable [ɪnʤɔ́iəbəl] ADJ (pleasant)
agradable, gozoso; (fun) ameno
enjoyment [ɪnʤɔ́imənt] N (act of enjoying)
goce *m*, disfrute *m*; (right of use) usufructo
m; (pleasure) placer *m*, gozo *m*
enlarge [ɪnlɑ́rʤ] VI/VT agrandar(se); VT (blow
up a photo) ampliar; VI **to — upon**
explayarse sobre, extenderse sobre
enlargement [ɪnlɑ́rʤmənt] N (photo,
building) ampliación *f*; (act of enlarging)
agrandamiento *m*; (temporary swelling)
dilatación *f*
enlighten [ɪnláɪtn̩] VT (morally) iluminar;
(intellectually) explicar, ilustrar
enlightenment [ɪnláɪtn̩mənt] N (moral)
iluminación *f*; (intellectual) explicación *f*;
The — La Ilustración
enlist [ɪnlíst] VI/VT (for the army) alistar(se);
(for a campaign) conseguir el apoyo
enlistment [ɪnlístmənt] N alistamiento *m*
enliven [ɪnláɪvən] VT animar, avivar
enmity [énmɪdi] N enemistad *f*
ennoble [ɪnnóbəl] VT ennoblecer
enormous [ɪnɔ́rməs] ADJ enorme,
descomunal
enough [ɪnʌ́f] ADJ suficiente; ADV **he's tall —**
tiene altura suficiente; **no** lo suficiente; **we
have — to live comfortably** tenemos
lo suficiente como para vivir
cómodamente; **that is —** con eso basta;
more than — bastante; INTERJ ¡basta!
enrage [ɪnréʤ] VT enfurecer
enrapture [ɪnrǽptʃə] VT embelesar
enrich [ɪnrítʃ] VT enriquecer
enroll [ɪnróI] VI/VT matricular(se),
inscribir(se); (in army) alistar(se)
enrollment [ɪnróImənt] N matrícula *f*,
inscripción *f*; **what is your —?** ¿Cuántos
alumnos tienes matriculados?
ensemble [ɑnsámbəl] N conjunto *m*
ensign [énsɪn] N (naval rank) alférez de
fragata *mf*; (flag) enseña *f*; (badge) insignia
f
enslave [ɪnslév] VT esclavizar
ensnare [ɪnsnér] VT atrapar, coger en una
trampa
ensue [ɪnsú] VI (follow) ocurrir después,
suceder; (result from) resultar; **the
ensuing events** los sucesos subsiguientes
ensure [ɪnʃúr] VT asegurar
entail [ɪntél] VT implicar, traer aparejado; (an
inheritance) vincular
entangle [ɪntǽŋgəl] VT enredar
enter [éntə] VT entrar en/a; (join) ingresar
en/a; (write) escribir; (put data in a

computer) dar entrada a; (put data in
account books) asentar; VI/VT (register for
a competition) inscribir(se); **to — into**
(make an agreement) concertar; (form part
of) figurar; VI salir/entrar a escena
enterprise [éntəprɑɪz] N empresa *f*
enterprising [éntəprɑɪzɪŋ] ADJ emprendedor
entertain [entətén] VI/VT (amuse) divertir,
recrear; (host) invitar; **we — a lot**
tenemos invitados muy a menudo;
(consider) contemplar; (harbor) abrigar
entertainer [entəténə] N artista *mf*
entertaining [entəténɪŋ] ADJ (fun) divertido;
(serving as pastime) entretenido;
(pleasant) ameno
entertainment [entəténmənt] N (source of
fun) diversión *f*; (pastime) entretenimiento
m; (of guests) agasajo *m*
enthrall [ɪnθrɔ́l] VT (captivate) cautivar,
hechizar; (make a slave of) esclavizar
enthusiasm [ɪnθúziæzəm] N entusiasmo *m*
enthusiast [ɪnθúziɪst] N entusiasta *mf*
enthusiastic [ɪnθuziǽstɪk] ADJ entusiasta *inv*;
I'm very — about the trip estoy muy
entusiasmado con el viaje
entice [ɪntáɪs] VT (attract) atraer; (lure)
tentar; (seduce) seducir
entire [ɪntáɪr] ADJ (unbroken) entero;
(complete) completo; **the — crew** toda la
tripulación, la tripulación entera
entirety [ɪntáɪrɪdi] N totalidad *f*
entitle [ɪntáɪdl̩] VT (give a title) titular,
intitular; (give a right) dar derecho
entitlement [ɪntáɪdlmənt] N derecho *m*
entity [éntɪdi] N (institution) entidad *f*;
(being) ente *m*, ser *m*
entomology [entəmáləʤi] N entomología *f*
entourage [ántʊrɑʤ] N séquito *m*, cortejo *m*
entrails [éntreɪz] N entrañas *f pl*
entrance [éntrəns] N (act, point of entering)
entrada *f*; (permission to enter) ingreso *m*;
— examination examen de ingreso *m*;
[ɪntrǽns] VT embelesar
entrant [éntrənt] N participante *mf*; **—s in
the law profession** abogados recién
recibidos *m pl*
entrap [ɪntrǽp] VT (ensnare) coger con una
trampa; (deceive) embaucar
entreaty [ɪntrídi] N súplica *f*, ruego *m*
entrench [ɪntréntʃ] VT (establish) afianzar(se);
(dig trenches) atrincherar; **a deeply —ed
habit** un hábito muy arraigado
entrepreneur [ɑntrəprənúr] N empresario
-ria *mf*
entropy [éntrəpi] N entropía *f*
entrust [ɪntrʌ́st] VT confiar, encomendar
entry [éntri] N (act, point of entry) entrada *f*;

(permission to enter) ingreso *m*; (record) anotación *f*; (contestant) participante *mf*; (dictionary definition) entrada *f*, artículo *m*; (computer) entrada *f*; (in bookkeeping) asiento *m*; **double** — contabilidad por partida doble *f*

enumerate [ɪnúməret] VT enumerar

enunciate [ɪnánsiet] VI/VT articular; (state a theory) enunciar; (proclaim) proclamar

envelop [ɪnvéləp] VT envolver

envelope [énvəlop] N sobre *m*

enviable [énviəbəł] ADJ envidiable

envious [énviəs] ADJ envidioso

environment [ɪnváɪə-nmənt] N ambiente *m*, medio ambiente *m*; (biological) medio ambiente *m*, ecología *f*; ADJ ambiental; (biological) medioambiental, ecológico

environmental [ɪnvaɪə-nmént]] ADJ ambiental; (biological) medioambiental, ecológico

environmentalist [ɪnvaɪə-nmént]ɪst] N ecologista *mf*

envisage [ɪnvízɪʤ] VT anticipar, prever

envision [ɪnvíʒən] VT imaginar

envoy [ánvɔɪ] N enviado -da *mf*

envy [énvi] N envidia *f*; VI/VT envidiar

enzyme [énzaɪm] N enzima *f*

ephemeral [ɪfémə-əł] ADJ efímero

epic [épɪk] N (poem) epopeya *f*; (genre) épica *f*; ADJ épico

epicenter [épɪsɛntə-] N epicentro *m*

epidemic [epɪdémɪk] ADJ epidémico; N epidemia *f*

epidermis [epɪdɚ-mɪs] N epidermis *f*

epilepsy [épələpsi] N epilepsia *f*

epilog, epilogue [épələg] N epílogo *m*

epiphany [ɪpífəni] N epifanía *f*

episode [épɪsod] N episodio *m*

episodic [episádɪk] ADJ (sporadic) episódico; (serial) en episodios

epitaph [épɪtæf] N epitafio *m*

epitome [ɪpítəmi] N epítome *m*

epoch [épək] N época *f*; —-**making** trascendental

equal [íkwəł] ADJ igual; — **rights** igualdad de derechos *f*; **an** — **contest** una competición pareja; **to be** — **to a task** capaz de cumplir una tarea; N igual *m*; — **sign** signo de igual *m*; VT igualar

equality [ɪkwálɪti] N igualdad *f*

equalize [íkwəlaɪz] VT igualar; (electronically) ecualizar

equate [ɪkwét] VT equiparar

equation [ɪkwéʒən] N ecuación *f*

equator [ɪkwétə-] N ecuador *m*

Equatorial Guinea [ekwətɔ́riəłgíni] N Guinea Ecuatorial *f*

equidistant [ikwɪdístənt] ADJ equidistante

equilibrium [ikwəlíbriəm] N equilibrio *m*

equine [íkwaɪn] ADJ & N equino *m*

equinox [íkwənaks] N equinoccio *m*

equip [ɪkwíp] VT equipar

equipment [ɪkwípmənt] N (supplies) equipo *m*; (act of equipping) equipamiento *m*

equitable [ékwɪtəbəł] ADJ equitativo, justo

equity [ékwɪti] N equidad *f*, valor libre de hipoteca de una propiedad *m*; **equities** acciones *f pl*

equivalent [ɪkwívələnt] ADJ & N equivalente *m*

equivocal [ɪkwívəkəł] ADJ equívoco

era [íɾə] N era *f*

eradicate [ɪrǽdɪket] VT (extirpate) erradicar; (pull up by roots) arrancar

erase [ɪrés] VI/VT borrar(se)

eraser [ɪrésə-] N (pencil) goma de borrar *f*; (blackboard) borrador *m*

erasure [ɪréʃə-] N (act of erasing) borrado *m*; (smudge) borrón *m*

erect [ɪrékt] ADJ erecto; (posture) erguido; VT erigir

Eritrea [erɪtríə] N Eritrea *f*

Eritrean [erɪtríən] ADJ & N eritreo -a *mf*

ermine [ɚ-mɪn] N armiño *m*

erode [ɪród] VI/VT erosionar(se)

erogenous [ɪrádʒənəs] ADJ erógeno

erosion [ɪróʒən] N erosión *f*

erotic [ɪrádɪk] ADJ erótico

err [er] VI errar

errand [érənd] N mandado *m*, recado *m*; — **boy** mandadero *m*

errant [érənt] ADJ errante

erratic [ɪrǽdɪk] ADJ (unpredictable) irregular, errático; (eccentric) excéntrico; (wandering) errante

erroneous [ɪróniəs] ADJ erróneo, errado

error [érə-] N error *m*; **to be in** — estar errado

erudite [érjədaɪt] ADJ erudito

erupt [ɪrápt] VI (volcano) hacer erupción; (anger) estallar; (pimples) salir

eruption [ɪrápʃən] N erupción *f*

escalate [éskəlet] VI (prices) aumentar; (violence) intensificarse, aumentar

escalator [éskəletə-] N escalera mecánica *f*

escapade [éskəped] N (adventure) aventura *f*; (prank) travesura *f*

escape [ɪskép] N (of gas) escape *m* (also computer term); (from reality) escape *m*, evasión *f*; (of prisoners) fuga *f*, evasión *f*; (means of escaping) escapatoria *f*; VI escapar(se), evadirse; VT (elude) eludir; **his name** —**s me** no me acuerdo de su nombre

escort [éskɔrt] N (people who accompany) escolta *mf*; (male companion) acompañante *m*; (paid female companion) señorita de compañía *f*; [ɪskɔ́rt] VT (protect) escoltar; (accompany) acompañar

escrow [éskro] ADV LOC **in —** en custodia

escudo [ɪskúdo] N escudo *m*

Eskimo [éskəmo] N esquimal *mf*

esophagus [ɪsáfəgəs] N esófago *m*

esoteric [esətérɪk] ADJ esotérico

especial [ɪspéʃəł] ADJ especial

espionage [éspiənɑʒ] N espionaje *m*

espouse [ɪspáʊz] VT defender, abrazar

essay [ése] N ensayo *m*; [esé] VT ensayar

essence [ésəns] N esencia *f*; **time is of the —** el tiempo apremia

essential [ɪsénʃəł] ADJ esencial

establish [ɪstǽblɪʃ] VT establecer; (a university) fundar

establishment [ɪstǽblɪʃmənt] N establecimiento *m*; (authority) establishment *m*

estate [ɪstét] N (piece of land) hacienda *f*; (possessions) bienes *m pl*; (property) propiedades *f pl*; (of a dead person) testamentaría *f*; **— tax** impuesto de sucesión *m*

esteem [ɪstím] VT (regard highly) estimar; (consider) considerar; N estima *f*

estimate [éstəmet] VT estimar, evaluar; VI hacer una estimación; [éstəmɪt] N (calculation) estimación *f*; (approximate charge) presupuesto *m*

estimation [estəméʃən] N (opinion) juicio *m*; (esteem) estima *f*; (estimate) estimación *f*; **in my —** a mi juicio

Estonia [estóniə] N Estonia *f*

Estonian [estóniən] ADJ & N estonio -nia *mf*

estrange [ɪstréndʒ] VT (alienate) enajenar; **to become —d** separarse

estrogen [éstrədʒən] N estrógeno *m*

estuary [éstʃueri] N estuario *m*

etcetera [etsétra] ADV etcétera

etch [etʃ] VI/VT (engrave) grabar; (outline) perfilar(se)

etching [étʃɪŋ] N grabado *m*

eternal [ɪtɜ́-nəł] ADJ eterno

eternity [ɪtɜ́-nɪði] N eternidad *f*

ether [íθɚ] N éter *m*

ethical [éθɪkəł] ADJ ético

ethics [éθɪks] N ética *f*

Ethiopia [iθiópiə] N Etiopía *f*

Ethiopian [iθiópiən] ADJ & N etíope *mf*

ethnic [éθnɪk] ADJ étnico; (dances, clothes) tradicional; **— Chinese** de ascendencia china; **— cleansing** limpieza étnica *f*

ethnicity [eθnísɪdi] N etnicidad *f*; (group) grupo étnico *m*

ethnography [eθnágrəfi] N etnografía *f*

ethnology [eθnáladʒi] N etnología *f*

ethyl alcohol [éθəlǽłkəhɑł] N alcohol etílico *m*

etiquette [édɪkɪt] N etiqueta *f*

etymology [edəmáladʒi] N etimología *f*

eucalyptus [jukalíptəs] N eucalipto *m*

eulogy [júlədʒi] N (praise) elogio *m*; (at a funeral) panegírico *m*

eunuch [júnək] N eunuco *m*

euphemism [júfəmɪzəm] N eufemismo *m*

euphoria [jufɔ́riə] N euforia *f*

euro [júro] N euro *m*

Europe [júrəp] N Europa *f*

European [jurəpíən] ADJ & N europeo -a *mf*

euthanasia [juθənéʒə] N eutanasia *f*

evacuate [ɪvǽkjuet] VI/VT (remove due to danger, defecate) evacuar; (empty a building) desalojar

evade [ɪvéd] VT (taxes, responsibilities) evadir, burlar; (questions) eludir

evaluate [ɪvǽljuet] VT (assess) evaluar; (appraise) avaluar, tasar

evangelical [ivændʒélɪkəł] ADJ evangélico

evaporate [ɪvǽpəret] VI/VT evaporar(se); VI (vanish) esfumarse

evaporation [ɪvæpəréʃən] N evaporación *f*

evasion [ɪvéʒən] N (escape) evasión *f*; (subterfuge) evasiva *f*

evasive [ɪvésɪv] ADJ evasivo

eve [iv] N (day before) víspera *f*; (evening) atardecer *m*; **on the — of** en vísperas de

even [ívən] ADJ (flat) plano, llano; (smooth) liso; (parallel) paralelo; (without fluctuation) parejo; (equal) igual; (divisible by two) par; (placid) tranquilo; **—-handed** imparcial; **—-tempered** apacible; **an — dozen** una docena exacta; **to be — with someone** estar a mano con alguien; **to get — with someone** desquitarse de alguien; ADV (still, yet) aun; (for extreme case) hasta, inclusive, incluso; **— if / though** aun cuando; **— my mother went** hasta mi madre fue; **— so** aun así; **it's — more expensive** es aun más caro; **not —** ni siquiera; VI/VT (make a surface even) nivelar(se); (make accounts even) emparejar

evening [ívnɪŋ] N tarde *f*, velada *f*; (dusk) atardecer *m*; **— gown** vestido de fiesta *m*, vestido de noche *m*; **— party** velada *f*; **— star** lucero de la tarde *m*; **good —!** ¡buenas noches!

event [ɪvént] N (happening) hecho *m*, evento *m*; (of importance) acontecimiento *m*, suceso *m*; **in any —** en todo caso; **in the**

— of en caso de

eventful [ɪvéntfəl] ADJ agitado, movido

eventual [ɪvéntʃuəl] ADJ (later) posterior; (final) final

eventuality [ɪvéntʃuǽlɪɾi] N eventualidad f

eventually [ɪvéntʃuəli] ADV a la larga

ever [évɚ] ADV alguna vez; **—green** (planta de hoja) perenne f; **—lasting** eterno; **—more** para siempre; **— since** desde entonces; **have you — studied French?** ¿alguna vez has estudiado francés? **how did you — do this?** ¿cómo pudiste hacer esto? **for — and —** por/para siempre jamás; **hardly —** casi nunca; **if —** si alguna vez; **more than —** más que nunca; **the best friend I — had** el mejor amigo que he tenido jamás; **for—ever** para/por siempre jamás

every [évri] ADJ (each) cada; **— child is different** cada niño es diferente; (all) todo(s); **we go — Friday** vamos todos los viernes; **—body** todos -das mf pl, todo el mundo m; **— day** todos los días; **—day** (of clothes) de diario, de todos los días; (of occurrences) cotidiano; **— once in a while** de vez en cuando; **—one** todos -das mf pl, todo el mundo m; **— other day** cada dos días, un día sí y otro no; **—thing** todo; **you are —thing to me** eres todo para mí; **—where** (location) por/en todas partes; (direction) a todas partes

evict [ɪvíkt] VT desalojar

evidence [évɪdəns] N evidencia f; (data in court) prueba f; **to be in —** ser evidente; VI/VT evidenciar(se), demostrar(se)

evident [évɪdənt] ADJ evidente

evil [ívəl] ADJ (wicked) malo, malvado; (harmful) maligno; **—doer** malhechor -ora mf; **— eye** mal de ojo m; N (force of nature) mal m; (wickedness) maldad f; **the lesser of two —s** el mal menor

evoke [ɪvók] VT (call up) evocar; (elicit) provocar

evolution [evəlúʃən] N evolución f

evolve [ɪválv] VI/VT desarrollar(se); VI evolucionar

ewe [ju] N oveja f

ex [ɛks] N ex mf

exacerbate [ɪgzǽsɚbet] VI/VT exacerbar

exact [ɪgzǽkt] ADJ exacto; VT exigir

exacting [ɪgzǽktɪŋ] ADJ exigente

exaggerate [ɪgzǽdʒɚret] VT exagerar

exalt [ɪgzɔ́lt] VT exaltar

exam [ɪgzǽm] N examen m

examination [ɪgzæmənéʃən] N examen m (also medical)

examine [ɪgzǽmɪn] VT (inspect) examinar; (analyze) analizar

example [ɪgzǽmpəl] N ejemplo m

exasperate [ɪgzǽspəret] VT exasperar

excavate [ɛ́kskəvet] VT excavar

excavator [ɛ́kskəvəɾɚ] N (person) excavador -ora mf; (machine) excavadora f

exceed [ɪksíd] VT (go beyond) exceder, rebasar; (be superior) superar, sobrepasar

exceedingly [ɪksídɪŋli] ADV sumamente, extremadamente

excel [ɪksɛ́l] VI sobresalir, lucirse, descollar

excellence [ɛ́ksələns] N excelencia f

excellent [ɛ́ksələnt] ADJ excelente

except [ɪksɛ́pt] PREP excepto, menos; **all the students — Pam** todos los estudiantes menos Pam; CONJ excepto, salvo; **the cars are identical — that one is older** los coches son idénticos salvo que uno es más viejo; **we would go to the beach, — for the inclement weather** iríamos a la playa si no fuera por el mal tiempo; VT exceptuar

excepting [ɪksɛ́ptɪŋ] PREP exceptuando

exception [ɪksɛ́pʃən] N excepción f; **with the — of** con/a excepción de; **to take — (object)** objetar; (resent) ofenderse

exceptional [ɪksɛ́pʃənəl] ADJ (unusual) excepcional; (gifted) superdotado; (handicapped) con necesidades especiales

excerpt [ɛ́ksɚpt] N fragmento m; VT seleccionar fragmentos

excess [ɛ́ksɛs] N exceso m, hartazgo m; **— baggage** exceso de equipaje m; **— profits tax** impuesto sobre ganancias excesivas m; **— weight** exceso de peso m; **in — of twenty pounds** más de veinte libras; **to drink to —** beber en exceso

excessive [ɪksɛ́sɪv] ADJ excesivo, desmedido

exchange [ɪkstʃéndʒ] VT (replace with something similar) cambiar; (give mutually) intercambiar; (trade political prisoners, books, CDs) canjear; (barter) permutar; **to — greetings** saludarse; N (replacement) cambio m; (interchange) intercambio m; (barter) permuta f; (of prisoners, books, etc.) canje m; (for stock trading) bolsa f; (for commodity trading) lonja f; (telephone) central de teléfonos f; **— student** estudiante de intercambio mf; **rate of —** tipo de cambio m

excise [ɛ́ksaɪz] N impuesto sobre bienes de consumo m

excite [ɪksáɪt] VT excitar, alborotar; (enthuse) entusiasmar

excited [ɪksáɪɾɪd] ADJ (agitated, aroused) excitado; (enthusiastic) entusiasmado; **to**

get — (enthused) entusiasmarse; (aroused) excitarse

excitement [ıksáıtmənt] N (arousal) excitación f; (enthusiasm) entusiasmo m

exciting [ıksáıdıŋ] ADJ (stimulating) excitante; (thrilling) emocionante

exclaim [ıksklém] VI exclamar

exclamation [ɛkskləméʃən] N exclamación f; **— point** signo de admiración m

exclude [ıksklúd] VT excluir

exclusion [ıksklúʒən] N exclusión f

exclusive [ıksklúsıv] ADJ exclusivo; **— of** sin incluir

excommunicate [ɛkskəmjúnıket] VT excomulgar

excrement [ɛkskrəmənt] N excremento m

excrete [ıkskrít] VI/VT excretar

excruciating [ıkskrúʃiɛdıŋ] ADJ insoportable, atroz

excursion [ıkská-ʒən] N excursión f

excusable [ıkskjúzəbəł] ADJ excusable, disculpable

excuse [ıkskjúz] VT (release from a duty, seek exemption) excusar, eximir; (forgive) disculpar, perdonar; **— me!** (forgive me) disculpe; (let me pass) con permiso; [ıkskjús] N excusa f, disculpa f; **it's a poor — for a car** no merece llamarse un coche

execute [ɛksıkjut] VT ejecutar (also computer term); (by firing squad) fusilar

execution [ɛksıkjúʃən] N ejecución f; **— wall** paredón m

executioner [ɛksıkjúʃənə-] N verdugo mf

executive [ıgzékjədıv] ADJ ejecutivo; N (person) ejecutivo -va mf; (branch of government) poder ejecutivo m

executor [ıgzékjədə-] N albacea mf

exemplary [ıgzémpləri] ADJ ejemplar

exemplify [ıgzémpləfaı] VT ejemplificar

exempt [ıgzémpt] VT eximir, dispensar; ADJ exento, libre

exemption [ıgzémpfən] N exención f, franquicia f

exercise [ɛksə-saız] N ejercicio m; **—s** ceremonia f; VT ejercer; VI hacer ejercicio; **to be —d about something** estar disgustado por algo

exert [ıgzá-t] VT ejercer; **to — oneself** esforzarse, empeñarse

exertion [ıgzá-ʃən] N (use of powers, faculties) ejercicio m; (vigorous action) esfuerzo m, empeño m

exhale [ɛkshéł] VT exhalar; VI espirar

exhaust [ıgzɔ́st] VT agotar, desmadejar; (a topic) tratar exhaustivamente; N (from a car) escape m

exhausted [ıgzɔ́stıd] ADJ rendido, agotado

exhaustion [ıgzɔ́stʃən] N (act or process of exhausting) agotamiento m; (weakness, tiredness) fatiga f

exhaustive [ıgzɔ́stıv] ADJ exhaustivo

exhibit [ıgzíbıt] VI/VT (manifest) exhibir; (put on view) exponer; N exposición f

exhibition [ɛksəbíʃən] N (manifestation, show of skills) exhibición f; (public display of objects) exposición f

exhilarated [ıgzíləreɪd] ADJ exultante

exhort [ıgzɔ́rt] VT exhortar

exile [ɛgzaıł] N exilio m, destierro m; (person exiled) exiliado -da mf, desterrado -da mf; VT exiliar

exist [ıgzíst] VI existir

existence [ıgzístəns] N existencia f

exit [ɛgzıt] N salida f; VI/VT salir (de); (theater) hacer mutis; **he —ed the building** salió del edificio

exodus [ɛksədəs] N éxodo m

exonerate [ıgzánəret] VT exonerar

exorbitant [ıgzɔ́rbıdənt] ADJ exorbitante

exorcise [ɛksɔrsaız] VT exorcisar

exorcism [ɛksɔrsızəm] N exorcismo m

exotic [ıgzɑ́dık] ADJ exótico

expand [ıkspǽnd] VI/VT expandir(se), ampliar(se); (an equation, an idea) desarrollar(se); (through heat) dilatar(se)

expanse [ıkspǽns] N extensión f

expansion [ıkspǽnʃən] N expansión f; (of an equation, of an idea) desarrollo m; (through heat) dilatación f

expansive [ıkspǽnsıv] ADJ expansivo

expatriate [ɛkspétriet] VI/VT expatriar(se); [ɛkspétrıt] N expatriado -da mf

expect [ıkspékt] VT esperar; **we — guests** esperamos visita(s); **I — you to be on time** cuento con que vengas puntualmente; **I'm —ed to work fifty hours a week** tengo que trabajar cincuenta horas por semana; **I — you're tired** estarás cansado; **she's —ing** está embarazada/encinta

expectation [ɛkspɛktéʃən] N (anticipation) expectación f; (expected thing) expectativa f; **he has great —s** tiene grandes expectativas

expectorate [ıkspéktərət] VI/VT expectorar

expedient [ıkspíɾiənt] ADJ conveniente, expeditivo

expedite [ɛkspıdaıt] VT (speed up) acelerar; (deal with promptly) despachar

expedition [ɛkspıdíʃən] N expedición f

expeditionary [ɛkspıdíʃəneri] ADJ expedicionario

expel [ıkspéł] VT (discharge) expeler; (throw out) expulsar

expend [ɪkspénd] VT gastar, agotar

expenditure [ɪkspéndɪtʃə] N gasto *m*

expense [ɪkspéns] N gasto *m*; **— account** cuenta de gastos *f*; **they had fun at my —** se divirtieron a mi costa

expensive [ɪkspénsɪv] ADJ caro

experience [ɪkspíriəns] N experiencia *f*; VT experimentar; **—d** experimentado

experiment [ɪkspérəmənt] N experimento *m*; VI experimentar

experimental [ɪkspɛrəméntl] ADJ experimental

expert [ékspɜt] N experto -ta *mf*; ADJ experto, idóneo, perito; **— system** sistema experto *m*

expertise [ɛkspətíz] N pericia *f*

expiration [ɛkspəréʃən] N (of a contract) vencimiento *m*, caducidad *f*; (breathing out) espiración *f*

expire [ɪkspáɪr] VI (die, terminate) expirar; (breathe out) espirar; (lapse) vencer, caducar

explain [ɪksplén] VT explicar; **he tried to — away his absence** trató de justificar su ausencia

explainable [ɪksplénəbəl] ADJ explicable

explanation [ɛksplənéʃən] N explicación *f*

explanatory [ɪksplǽnətɔri] ADJ explicativo

expletive [éksplɪdɪv] N palabrota *f*

explicable [ɪksplíkəbəl] ADJ explicable

explicit [ɪksplísɪt] ADJ explícito

explode [ɪksplód] VI/VT estallar, hacer explosión, explotar; VT (a theory) hacer añicos; VI (population) dispararse

exploit [éksplɔɪt] N hazaña *f*, proeza *f*; [ɪksplɔ́ɪt] VT explotar

exploitation [ɛksplɔɪtéʃən] N explotación *f*

exploration [ɛkspləréʃən] N exploración *f*

explore [ɪksplór] VI/VT explorar; (a topic) bucear

explorer [ɪksplórə] N explorador -ra *mf*

explosion [ɪksplóʒən] N explosión *f*, estallido *m*

explosive [ɪksplósɪv] ADJ & N explosivo *m*

exponent [ɪkspónənt] N exponente *m*

export [ɪkspórt] VI/VT exportar; [ékspɔrt] N exportación *f*

exportation [ɛkspɔrtéʃən] N exportación *f*

expose [ɪkspóz] VT (to lay open to danger, exhibit, subject to light) exponer; (to make known) revelar; (to unmask) desenmascarar

exposition [ɛkspəzíʃən] N exposición *f*

exposure [ɪkspóʒə] N (to danger, to light, act of exposing) exposición *f*; (disclosure) revelación *f*; **to die of —** morir de frío

expound [ɪkspáʊnd] VI/VT exponer, explicar

express [ɪksprés] VT expresar; (send by mail) enviar por correo expreso; (squeeze out) exprimir; ADJ (clearly indicated) expreso; **— train** tren expreso *m*; ADV por expreso; N expreso *m*

expression [ɪkspréʃən] N expresión *f*

expressive [ɪksprésɪv] ADJ expresivo

expropriate [ɛkspróʊpriet] VT expropiar

expulsion [ɪkspʌ́lʃən] N expulsión *f*

exquisite [ekskwízɪt] ADJ exquisito, primoroso; (pain) penetrante

extant [ékstənt] ADJ existente

extemporaneous [ɪkstɛmpəréniəs] ADJ improvisado

extend [ɪksténd] VI/VT extender(se); (a street) ampliar(se); **he —ed his hand to her** le tendió la mano

extended [ɪksténdɪd] ADJ (extensive) extenso; (prolonged) prolongado; (folded out) extendido

extension [ɪksténʃən] N extensión *f*; (of a deadline) prórroga *f*; (phone line) extensión *f*; (addition) anexo *m*, ampliación *f*; **— cord** extensión *f*

extensive [ɪksténsɪv] ADJ extenso; (agriculture) extensivo

extent [ɪkstént] N extensión *f*; **to a great —** en alto grado; **to such an — that** a tal grado que; **to the — that you are able** en la medida en que seas capaz; **up to a certain —** hasta cierto punto

extenuate [ɪksténjuet] VT atenuar

exterior [ɪkstíriə] ADJ exterior; N exterior *m*

exterminate [ɪkstɜ́mənet] VT exterminar

extermination [ɪkstɜmənéʃən] N exterminio *m*, exterminación *f*

external [ɪkstɜ́nəl] ADJ externo; (concerned with foreign countries) exterior; N exterior *m*

extinct [ɪkstíŋkt] ADJ extinto

extinguish [ɪkstíŋgwɪʃ] VT apagar, extinguir

extol [ɪkstól] VT ensalzar, enaltecer

extort [ɪkstórt] VT extorsionar

extortion [ɪkstórʃən] N extorsión *f*

extra [ékstrə] ADJ de más, adicional; **make some — cakes** haz unos pasteles de más / adicionales / extras; ADV extra; N extra *m* (including newspaper, actor); **—marital** extramarital; **—ordinary** extraordinario; **—sensory** extrasensorial

extract [ékstrækt] N (something extracted) extracto *m*; (passage from a book) fragmento *m*; [ɪkstrǽkt] VT extraer; (a secret) sonsacar

extradite [ékstrədaɪt] VT extraditar

extraneous [ɪkstréniəs] ADJ superfluo

extrapolate [ɪkstrǽpəlet] VI/VT extrapolar

extravagance [ɪkstrǽvəgəns] N (unnecessary

expense) despilfarro *m*, derroche *m*;
(excess) exceso *m*; (oddity) extravagancia *f*
extravagant [ɪkstrǽvəgənt] ADJ (shopper)
gastador, derrochador; (price) exorbitante;
(praise, demand) excesivo
extreme [ɪkstrím] ADJ extremo; N extremo *m*;
to go to —s exagerar, llegar a extremos;
to the — sumamente, extremadamente
extremity [ɪkstrémɪDi] N extremidad *f*
extricate [ékstrɪket] VT sacar; VI **to —
oneself from** conseguir salir de
extrovert [ékstrəvɝt] N extrovertido -da *mf*
extroverted [ékstrəvɝDɪd] ADJ extrovertido
exuberant [ɪgzúbəənt] ADJ exuberante
exude [ɪgzúd] VI/VT (liquid) exudar;
(cheerfulness, confidence) emanar
exult [ɪgzʌ́lt] VI exultar
eye [aɪ] N ojo *m* (also of hurricane, needle,
tools); (look) mirada *f*; **—ball** globo ocular
m; **—brow** ceja *f*; **—dropper** cuentagotas
m sg; **—glass** (of a telescope, microscope)
ocular *m*; **—glasses** anteojos *m pl*, lentes
m pl; **—lash** pestaña *f*; **—lid** párpado *m*;
—liner delineador *m*; **—opener**
revelación *f*; **—piece** ocular *m*; **—sight**
vista *f*; **—sore** monstruosidad *f*; **—
shadow** sombra para ojos *f*; **— socket**
órbita *f*; **—tooth** colmillo *m*; **—witness**
testigo ocular *mf*; **my —s are bad** tengo
mala vista; **in the twinkling of an —**
en un abrir y cerrar de ojos; **her dress
caught his —** su vestido le llamó la
atención; **to keep an — on** cuidar,
vigilar; **to see — to —** estar de acuerdo;
in the —s of the law ante la ley; **to
give someone the —** hacerle ojito a
alguien; **to have —s for someone** estar
prendado de alguien; **to keep one's —
open** tener cuidado; VT mirar
eyeful [áɪfʊɫ] N **we got an —** vimos más
que suficiente
e-zine [ízin] N revista electrónica *f*

Ff

fable [fébəɫ] N fábula *f*
fabric [fǽbrɪk] N tela *f*, tejido *m*; (wool) paño
m; (of society) estructura *f*; **— softener**
suavizante *m*
fabricate [fǽbrɪket] VT (goods) fabricar; (a
story) inventar
fabulous [fǽbjələs] ADJ fabuloso
façade [fəsád] N fachada *f*

face [fes] N (front part of head, coin, cube,
facial expression) cara *f*; (of a building)
frente *m*; (of a watch) esfera *f*; (of the
Earth) faz *f*; **—cloth** toalla para la cara *f*;
—lift lifting *m*; **—-to-—** cara a cara; **—
value** valor nominal *m*; **in the — of**
ante, frente a; **on the — of**
aparentemente; **she put on a brave —**
se comportó con entereza; **to make —s**
hacer muecas; **to lose —** quedar mal; **to
save —** quedar bien; **to show one's —**
aparecerse; VT (stand opposite to) encarar;
(meet defiantly) enfrentar, enfrentarse
con, afrontar; (look forward) mirar a /
hacia; (to have the front toward) dar a /
hacia; (to put on facing) ribetear; **about
—!** ¡media vuelta! **left —!** ¡a la izquierda!
to — down intimidar; **to — the music**
dar la cara; **to — with marble** revestir
de mármol
faceless [féslɪs] ADJ (anonymous) anónimo;
(without a face) sin cara
facet [fǽsɪt] N faceta *f*
facetious [fəsíʃəs] ADJ gracioso
facial [féʃəɫ] ADJ facial; N limpieza de cutis *f*
facilitate [fəsílɪtet] VT facilitar
facility [fəsílɪDi] N (skill) facilidad *f*;
facilities (of a building) instalación *f*;
(restroom) aseo *m*, servicio *m*
fact [fækt] N hecho *m*; **hard —s** datos
concretos *m pl*; **is that a —!** ¡no me
digas! **as a matter of —** de hecho; **in —**
de hecho; **it's a — of life** así son las
cosas
faction [fǽkʃən] N facción *f*
factor [fǽktɝ] N factor *m*; VT descomponer
en factores; VI **to — in** tener en cuenta
factory [fǽktəri] N fábrica *f*
factual [fǽktʃuəɫ] ADJ (of facts) fáctico;
(based on facts) objetivo
faculty [fǽkəɫti] N (ability) facultad *f*; (in a
college) profesorado *m*, cuerpo docente *m*,
claustro *m*
fad [fæd] N moda pasajera *f*
fade [fed] VI/VT (cloth) decolorar(se),
desteñir(se); (color) deslavar(se); VI
(strength) disminuir; (lights) apagarse;
(feelings, colors) desvanecerse
faggot [fǽgət] N (bundle) haz *m*
fail [feɫ] VI (faculties, organs, machinery,
structure) fallar; (experiment, plan)
fracasar, frustrarse; (health) decaer;
(business) quebrar, hacer bancarrota; VI/VT
(exam, student) suspender, reprobar; **he
—ed to remember their anniversary**
no se acordó de su aniversario; **don't —
to come** no dejes de venir; **without —**

sin falta

failure [féljə‧] N (of a plan, a person) fracaso *m*; (of organs) insuficiencia *f*; (of faculties) deterioro *m*; (of machinery) falla *f*; *Sp* fallo *m*; (of business) quiebra *f*, bancarrota *f*; (in an exam) suspenso *m*; **her — to respond puzzled me** su falta de respuesta me confundió

faint [fent] ADJ (sound) débil; (light) tenue; (image) vago; **to feel —** sentirse mareado; **—‑hearted** timorato, cobarde; N desmayo *m*, desfallecimiento *m*; VI desmayarse, desfallecer

faintness [féntnɪs] N (of sound) debilidad *f*; (of light) tenuidad *f*; (of an image) vaguedad *f*

fair [fer] ADJ (just) justo; (by the rules) limpio; (large) considerable; (of weather) bueno; (of sky) despejado; (of wind) propicio; (of complexion) blanco; **— play** juego limpio *m*; **— chance of success** buena probabilidad de éxito *f*; **the — sex** el sexo bello; **that's not —!** ¡no vale! ¡no es justo! ADV **to play —** jugar limpio; N feria *f*; **—‑ground** real de la feria *m*; **—way** calle *f*, fairway *m*

fairly [férli] ADV (justly) justamente; (moderately) medianamente; **— difficult** bastante difícil

fairness [férnɪs] N (justice) justicia *f*; (whiteness) blancura *f*

fairy [féri] N hada *f*; **— godmother** hada madrina *f*; **—land** país de las hadas *m*; **— tale** cuento de hadas *m*

faith [feθ] N fe *f*; (fidelity) fidelidad *f*; **— healing** cura por la fe *f*; **in good —** de buena fe; **to have — in someone** tener confianza en alguien; **to keep —** cumplir con la palabra

faithful [féθfəɫ] ADJ fiel

faithfulness [féθfəɫnɪs] N fidelidad *f*

faithless [féθlɪs] ADJ (disloyal) desleal, falso; (lacking in faith, fidelity) infiel

fake [fek] N (object) objeto falso *m*; (person who fakes) farsante *mf*; ADJ falso; **— pearls** perlas de fantasía *f pl*; VT (render false, counterfeit) falsificar; VI/VT (feign) fingir

falcon [fǽɫkən] N halcón *m*

Falkland Islands [fɔ́kləndáɪləndz] N Islas Malvinas *f pl*

fall [fɔɫ] VI (drop) caer(se); (light upon) detenerse; (slope downward) bajar; (be assigned to) tocar a, recaer sobre; **—ing out** desavenencia *f*, pique *m*; **—ing star** estrella fugaz *f*; **to — asleep** dormirse; **to — back** retroceder; **to — back on**

recurrir a; **to — behind** atrasarse, retrasarse; **to — down** (drop) caerse; (fail) fallar; **to — in love** enamorarse; **to — off** disminuir; **he —s for blondes** se enamora de las rubias; **to — out with** reñir con; **to — through** quedar en la nada; **you — for it** te dejas engañar; N (drop) caída *f*; (of a terrain) declive *m*; (season) otoño *m*; **— guy** cabeza de turco *mf*; **—s** catarata *f*, salto de agua *m*

fallacious [fəléʃəs] ADJ falaz

fallacy [fǽləsi] N (false notion) falacia *f*; (false argument) sofisma *m*

fallible [fǽləbəɫ] ADJ falible

fallout [fɔ́laut] N (particle-settling) precipitación radiactiva *f*; (consequences) repercusiones *f pl*

fallow [fǽlo] ADJ baldío, en barbecho; N barbecho *m*; VT dejar en barbecho

false [fɔɫs] ADJ falso; **to bear — witness** jurar en falso; **— alarm** falsa alarma *f*; **— arrest** detención ilegal *f*; **— pretense** estafa *f*; **— start** salida en falso *f*; **— step** paso en falso *m*; **— teeth** postizo *m*

falsehood [fɔ́lshud] N falsedad *f*, mentira *f*

falseness [fɔ́lsnɪs] N falsedad *f*

falsify [fɔ́lsəfaɪ] VT falsificar, falsear

falter [fɔ́ɫtə‧] VI (hesitate) vacilar, entrecortarse; (stutter) titubear

fame [fem] N fama *f*

famed [femd] ADJ afamado

familiar [fəmíljə‧] ADJ (generally known) familiar, conocido; (informal) familiar; (too friendly) confianzudo; (closely personal) íntimo; **to be — with a subject** conocer bien un tema

familiarity [fəmiljériDi] N familiaridad *f*

family [fǽmli] N familia *f*; **— doctor** médico general *m*; **— man** hombre de familia *m*; **— name** apellido *m*; **— planning** planificación familiar *f*; **— room** cuarto de estar *m*; **— tree** árbol genealógico *m*; **— values** valores tradicionales *m pl*

famine [fǽmɪn] N (lack of food) hambruna *f*, hambre *f*; (scarcity) escasez *f*

famished [fǽmɪʃt] ADJ hambriento, muerto de hambre; **to be —** morirse de hambre

famous [féməs] ADJ famoso

fan [fæn] N (handheld) abanico *m*; (electrical) ventilador *m*; (for cleaning grain) aventadora *f*; (of sports) aficionado -da *mf*; (of a person) admirador -ra *mf*; VT (blow air) abanicar; (enliven) avivar; **to — out** abrirse en abanico; **— belt** correa del ventilador *f*; **— mail** correo de admiradores *m*

fanatic [fənǽDɪk] ADJ & N fanático -ca *mf*

fanaticism [fənǽdɪsɪzəm] N fanatismo *m*

fanciful [fǽnsɪfəɫ] ADJ (whimsical) caprichoso; (imaginary) imaginario; (led by fancy) fantasioso

fancy [fǽnsi] N fantasía *f*; (whim) capricho *m*; **to strike one's** — gustarle a alguien; **to take a** — **to** aficionarse a; **he took a** — **to his teacher** se enamoró de su maestra; ADJ (luxurious) de lujo; (elaborate) elaborado; (strange) estrafalario; —**free** despreocupado; —**work** bordado fino *m*; VT imaginar(se); **he fancies himself an artist** se cree artista; **just — the idea!** ¡figúrate!

fanfare [fǽnfer] N fanfarria *f*; **with great** — con bombo y platillo

fang [fæŋ] N colmillo *m*

fantasize [fǽntəsaɪz] VI fantasear

fantastic [fæntǽstɪk] ADJ fantástico

fantasy [fǽntəsi] N fantasía *f*

far [far] ADV lejos; — **and away** sin duda; — **and wide** por todas partes; — **away / off** lejos, lejano; —**fetched** (implausible) inverosímil, peregrino; (forced) traído por los cabellos; —**flung** remoto; —**off** distante; —**out** radical, poco convencional; —**reaching** de gran alcance; —**sighted** (with defective vision) présbita, hipermétrope; (seeing the future) con visión de futuro; — **be it from me to complain** no es mi intención quejarme; — **more money** mucho más dinero; — **off we could see land** a lo lejos divisábamos tierra; **as** — **as I know** que yo sepa; **as** — **as I'm concerned** en lo que a mí respecta; **by** — con mucho; **how** — **do I need to walk?** ¿cuanto tengo que caminar? **how** — **is the church?** ¿a cuánto queda la iglesia? **so** — hasta ahora; **we talked** — **into the night** hablamos hasta entrada la noche; **we traveled as** — **as Chicago** viajamos hasta Chicago; ADJ lejano; **the** — **corner** la esquina de más allá; **it is a** — **cry from what you said** dista mucho de lo que dijiste

farce [fars] N farsa *f*

fare [fer] N (ticket) billete *m*; (price of transport) tarifa *f*; (food) comida *f*; VI **I** —**d well in the course** me fue bien en el curso; —**well** despedida *f*; **to bid** —**well to** despedirse de; —**well!** ¡adiós!

farm [farm] N (large) hacienda *f*; (small) granja *f*; —**hand** peón *m*; —**house** alquería *f*, caserío *m*; — **produce** productos agrícolas *m pl*; —**yard** (enclosed) corral *m*; (open) patio *m*; VI/VT

cultivar; **to** — **out** (lease) dar en arriendo; (distribute) repartir; (subcontract) subcontratar; (exhaust) agotar

farmer [fármə] N agricultor -ra *mf*; (small) granjero -ra *mf*; (large) hacendado -da *mf*

farming [fármɪŋ] N agricultura *f*; ADJ agrícola *mf*

farther [fárðə] ADV más lejos; **it's an even** — **distance** es una distancia mayor todavía; **the concept was extended** — el concepto se extendió más; — **on** más adelante; ADJ más lejano

farthest [fárðɪst] ADJ el más lejano; ADV lo más lejos

fascinate [fǽsənet] VI/VT fascinar, alucinar

fascination [fæsənéʃən] N fascinación *f*

fascism [fǽʃɪzəm] N fascismo *m*

fascist [fǽʃɪst] N fascista *mf*

fashion [fǽʃən] N (style) moda *f*; (way) manera *f*, modo *m*; — **plate** figurín *m*; **after a** — más o menos; **to be in** — estar de moda; VT hacer; (metal) forjar; (character) formar; (putty, etc.) moldear

fashionable [fǽʃənəbəɫ] ADJ de moda

fast [fæst] ADJ (quick) rápido, veloz; (ahead, of a watch) adelantado; (firm, permanent) firme; (closed) atrancado; (loyal) fiel; (dissolute) disipado; — **food** comida rápida *f*; **to** —**forward** avanzar; **life in the** — **lane** vida loca *f*; — **money** dinero mal habido *m*; ADV (quickly) rápido; (firmly) firmemente; — **asleep** profundamente dormido; N ayuno *m*; VI ayunar

fasten [fǽsən] VT (with buckles, buttons, hooks) abrochar(se), prender; (with ribbon, thread) atar; (door) atrancar

fastener [fǽsənə] N cierre *m*

fastidious [fæstídiəs] ADJ (hard to please) maniático; (painstaking) minucioso

fat [fæt] ADJ gordo; — **cat** pez gordo *m*; — **cell** célula adiposa *f*; — **chance** ¡ni soñar! —**head** idiota *mf*; — **job** trabajo lucrativo *m*; — **profits** pingües ganancias *f pl*; **to get** — engordar; N (oily substance) grasa *f*; (animal tissue) gordura *f*, sebo *m*; **the** — **of the land** la abundancia de la tierra

fatal [fédɫ] ADJ fatal

fatality [fətǽlɪɾi] N víctima fatal *f*

fate [fet] N (lot) destino *m*, fatalidad *f*, hado *m*; (outcome) suerte *f*; VT destinar

father [fáðə] N padre *m*; — **figure** figura paterna *f*; —**in-law** suegro *m*; —**land** patria *f*

fatherhood [fáðə·hud] N paternidad *f*

fatherly [fáðə·li] ADV paternal

fathom [fǽðəm] N braza *f*; VT (measure)

sondear; (understand) comprender

fatigue [fatíg] N fatiga *f*; —**s** ropa de faena *f*; VI/VT fatigar(se), rendir(se)

fatness [fǽtnɪs] N gordura *f*

fatso [fǽtso] N *pej* gordinflón *m*, tonel *m*

fatten [fǽtn] VT engordar, cebar

fatty [fǽɾi] ADJ adiposo; N (insult for fat people) *pej* gordito -ta *mf*

faucet [fɔ́sɪt] N grifo *m*, llave *f*

fault [fɔlt] N (defect, misdeed) falta *f*; (responsibility) culpa *f*; (geological) falla *f*; —**finder** criticón -ona *mf*; **to a —** demasiado cuidadoso; **to be at —** ser culpable; **to find — with** criticar a

faultless [fɔ́ltlɪs] ADJ perfecto

faulty [fɔ́lti] ADJ defectuoso; (grammar) vicioso

faux pas [fopá] N gaffe *f*, metedura de pata *f*

favor [févɚ] N (kind act, goodwill) favor *m*, gracia *f*; (popularity) popularidad *f*; (party gift) sorpresa *f*; VT (give help, show preference) favorecer; (foster) propiciar; (approve of) estar a favor de; **they are —ed to win** son los favoritos; **she —s her mother** se parece a su madre

favorite [févɚɪt] ADJ & N preferido -da *mf*, favorito -ta *mf*, predilecto -ta *mf*

favoritism [févɚɪtɪzəm] N favoritismo *m*

fawn [fɔn] N cervatillo *m*; VI **to — (over)** adular

fax [fæks] N fax *m*, facsímil *m*; VT faxear

FBI (Federal Bureau of Investigation) [ɛfbiái] N FBI *m*

fear [fir] N miedo *m*, temor *m*; **— of God** temor de Dios *m*; VI/VT (be afraid of) temer, tenerle miedo a; (suspect) temerse; **to — for** temer por

fearful [fírfəl] ADJ (causing fear) terrible, espantoso; (showing fear) temeroso, miedoso, medroso

fearless [fírlɪs] ADJ intrépido

fearlessness [fírlɪsnɪs] N intrepidez *f*

feasible [fízəbəl] ADJ factible

feast [fist] N (party, religious celebration) fiesta *f*; (abundant meal) festín *m*, banquete *m*; VI **to — on** darse un festín de; **to — one's eyes on** deleitarse la vista con

feat [fit] N (heroic act) hazaña *f*; (trick) logro *m*

feather [féðɚ] N pluma *f*, **a — in one's cap** un triunfo personal; —**weight** peso pluma *m*; **birds of a — flock together** Dios los cría y ellos se juntan; VI/VT (grow feathers, cover with feathers) emplumar; (change blade angle) poner horizontal

feature [fítʃɚ] N (characteristic) aspecto *m*,

característica *f*; (newspaper article) reportaje *m*; (facial) facción *f*, fisonomía *f*, rasgo *m*; **— article** artículo principal *m*; **— film** largometraje *m*; VT (give prominence to) destacar; (depict) mostrar; **this film —s John Smith** esta película cuenta con la actuación de John Smith; **— that!** ¡imagínate! VI figurar

February [fébjueri] N febrero *m*

feces [físiz] N PL heces *f pl*

federal [fédɚəl] ADJ federal

federation [fedɚéʃən] N federación *f*

fee [fi] N (professional) honorarios *m pl*; (artist) cachet *m*; (admission) derecho de admisión *m*; —**s** (university) matrícula *f*

feeble [fíbəl] ADJ (person) débil, endeble; (sound, light) tenue; —**minded** (retarded) *pej* retrasado; (stupid) tonto

feed [fid] VI/VT (supply with food, materials) alimentar(se); (prompt lines) apuntar; (broadcast) transmitir; **he —s sugar cubes to his horse** le da terrones de azúcar a su caballo; **I fed him a lie** le dije una mentira; **to be fed up** estar harto, estar hasta la coronilla; VI **to — into** desembocar en; —**back** retroalimentación *f*; (response) respuesta *f*, reacción *f*; —**ing frenzy** (of the press) escándalo periodístico *m*; (of sharks, etc.) carnicería *f*; N (fodder) pienso *m*, cebo *m*; (transmission) transmisión *f*

feel [fil] VI/VT (perceive, experience) sentir(se); (examine with the hands) palpar, manosear; (suffer) sufrir; (have an opinion) creer; VI (grope, check out) tantear; (seem) parecer; **to — one's way** tantear el camino, andar a tientas; **I — for you** te compadezco; **it —s soft** está suave al tacto; **I — like a coffee** tengo ganas de tomar un café; **to — up to something** sentirse capaz de algo; N (feeling) sensación *f*; (sense) tacto *m*; (ability) don *m*; (groping) manoseo *m*, toqueteo *m*

feeler [fílɚ] N (of insects) antena *f*; (of snails) cuerno *m*; (person who feels) persona emotiva *f*; **to put out —s** tantear el terreno

feeling [fílɪŋ] N (sense of touch) tacto *m*; (instance of physical perception) sensación *f*; (emotion) sentimiento *m*; (opinion) opinión *f*; (compassion) compasión *f*; **a — of sadness** un sentimiento de tristeza; **with —** con sentimiento; **to hurt someone's —s** herirle los sentimientos a alguien; ADJ sensible

feign [fen] VI/VT fingir, simular, aparentar

feisty [fáɪsti] ADJ (aggressive) pugnaz, belicoso; (energetic) vivaz

feline [fílaɪn] ADJ felino

fell [fɛl] VT (an animal) derribar; (a tree) talar; N (pelt) piel de animal f; **in one — swoop** de un golpe

fellow [félo] N (member) miembro m; (scholar) becario -ria mf; (man or boy) tipo m; **— citizen** conciudadano -na mf; **— man** prójimo m; **— student** compañero -ra de clase mf

fellowship [féloʃɪp] N (friendly relations) amistad f; (community of interest) confraternidad f; (scholarship) beca f

felony [félani] N delito grave m

felt [fɛlt] N fieltro m; ADJ de fieltro

female [fímɛl] N (animal) hembra f; (person) mujer f; ADJ (animal, fastener) hembra; (person) femenino

feminine [fémənɪn] ADJ femenino

femininity [femənínɪti] N feminidad f

feminism [fémənɪzəm] N feminismo m

femur [fíməɹ] N fémur m

fence [fɛns] N (barrier) cerca f, cerco m, valla f; (person who deals in stolen goods) vendedor -ra de artículos robados mf; (store for stolen goods) tienda de artículos robados f; **to be sitting on the —** estar indeciso; VT (enclose) cercar, vallar; **to — in** cercar; **to — off** dividir con una cerca; VI (sport) practicar esgrima

fencing [fénsɪŋ] N (barrier) cerca f; (sport) esgrima f

fender [féndəɹ] N guardabarro(s) m, guardafango m; **— bender** choquecito m

ferment [fɜ́ɹment] N fermento m; [fəɹmént] VI/VT fermentar(se)

fermentation [fɜɹmentéʃən] N fermentación f

fern [fɜɹn] N helecho m

ferocious [fəɹóʃəs] ADJ feroz, fiero

ferocity [fəɹásɪdi] N ferocidad f, fiereza f

ferret [fɛ́ɹɪt] N hurón m; VI **to — out** huronear

Ferris wheel [fɛ́ɹɪshwil] N rueda gigante f

ferry [fɛ́ɹi] N ferry m; **— boat** ferry m; VT transportar de una orilla a otra; VI viajar en ferry

fertile [fɜ́ɹdl] ADJ fértil, fecundo

fertility [fəɹtílɪdi] N fertilidad f

fertilize [fɜ́ɹdlaɪz] VT fertilizar; (female, egg) fecundar; (land) abonar

fertilizer [fɜ́ɹdlaɪzəɹ] N fertilizante m, abono m

fervent [fɜ́ɹvənt] ADJ ferviente

fervor [fɜ́ɹvəɹ] N fervor m

fester [féstəɹ] VI (form pus) supurar; (rankle) enconarse

festival [féstəvəl] N festival m

festive [féstɪv] ADJ festivo

festivity [festívɪdi] N festividad f

fetal [fídl] ADJ fetal; **— position** posición fetal f

fetch [fɛtʃ] VT Sp ir a por; Am ir a buscar; **the ring —ed a fancy price** nos dieron una buena suma por el anillo; VI/VT (dog) buscar

fetish [fédɪʃ] N fetiche m

fetter [fédəɹ] N grillete m; VT engrillar

fetus [fídəs] N feto m

feud [fjud] N enemistad hereditaria f; VI pelear

feudal [fjúdl] ADJ feudal

fever [fívəɹ] N fiebre f, calentura f; **— pitch** punto álgido m

feverish [fívəɹɪʃ] ADJ (related to fever) febril; (having a fever) afiebrado, destemplado

few [fju] ADJ & PRON pocos; **a —** unos pocos, algunos; **the —** una minoría

fiancé [fiɑnsé] N novio m, prometido m; **—e** novia f, prometida f

fiasco [fiǽsko] N fiasco m

fib [fɪb] N mentirilla f; VI decir mentirillas

fiber [fáɪbəɹ] N (textile) fibra f; (animal, vegetable) hebra f; **—optic** de fibra óptica; **—glass** fibra de vidrio f

fibrous [fáɪbɹəs] ADJ fibroso

fickle [fíkəl] ADJ veleidoso, mudable

fiction [fíkʃən] N ficción f

fictional [fíkʃənəl] ADJ novelesco

fictitious [fɪktíʃəs] ADJ ficticio

fiddle [fídl] N violín m; VI (play the violin) tocar el violín; **to — around** perder el tiempo; **to — with** juguetear con; **stop fiddling with the computer** deja de juguetear con la computadora

fidelity [fɪdélɪdi] N fidelidad f; **high —** alta fidelidad f

fidget [fídʒɪt] VI estar inquieto; **stop —ing!** ¡deja de moverte!

fiduciary [fɪdúʃieɾi] ADJ & N fiduciario -ria mf

field [fild] N (land) campo m (also in computers, heraldry, optics); (in sports) campo m; Am cancha f; (of oil) yacimiento m; (group of competitors) participantes mf pl; (of knowledge) campo m, terreno m; **— artillery** artillería de campaña f; **— day** (day for outdoor activity) día de campo m; (for military maneuvers) día de maniobras m; (unrestrained enjoyment) festín m; **— glasses** binoculares m pl; **— mouse** ratón de campo m; **— trip** (in school) paseo escolar m; (in science) viaje de estudio m;

—**work** trabajo de campo *m*; VT (catch) atrapar; (answer) contestar

fiend [find] N (devil) demonio *m*, diablo *m*; (fanatic) fanático -ca *mf*

fierce [firs] ADJ (animals) feroz, fiero; (illness) espantoso; (storms, etc.) furioso, espantoso; (competition, debate) intenso, encarnizado; (a look) torvo

fierceness [fírsnɪs] N ferocidad *f*, bravura *f*

fiery [fáɪəri] ADJ (passionate) fogoso; (hot, causing burning sensation) ardiente

fife [faɪf] N pífano *m*

fifteen [fɪftín] NUM quince

fifth [fɪfθ] ADJ & N quinto *m*; (measure of liquor) tres cuartos de un litro *m pl*

fifty [fɪfti] NUM cincuenta; **to go —- on something** ir a medias; **a —-- chance** un cincuenta por ciento de probabilidades

fig [fɪg] N higo *m*; — **leaf** hoja de higuera *f*; — **tree** higuera *f*; **it's not worth a** — no vale ni un pepino / pito

fight [faɪt] N (combat) lucha *f*, pelea *f*; **the — against AIDS** la lucha contra el SIDA; (argument) pelea *f*, riña *f*; VI/VT (combat) luchar (con), pelear (con); VI (argue) pelear, reñir; **to — a duel** batirse a duelo; **to — back** (to hold back) contener; (resist) resistir; **to — it out** arreglarlo a los golpes; **to — off** rechazar; **to — one's way through** abrirse camino a la fuerza

fighter [fáɪtɚ] N (boxer) boxeador -ra *mf*; (someone who fights) luchador -ra *mf*; (dog, cock) animal de pelea / riña *m*; — **airplane** avión caza *m*

fighting [fáɪdɪŋ] N (fight) lucha *f*; ADJ combativo; —**'chance** posibilidad remota *f*; — **words** palabras incendiarias *f pl*

figurative [fígjɚədɪv] ADJ (art) figurativo; (language) figurado

figure [fígjɚ] N (number, amount) cifra *f*; (form, bodily shape, representation, dance move, syllogism) figura *f*; (character) personaje *m*; —**head** figurón de proa *m*; — **of speech** figura retórica *f*; —**s** (written symbols) números *m pl*; — **skating** patinaje artístico *m*; **to be good at** —**s** ser bueno con los números; **to cut a poor** — dar una mala impresión; VI (appear) figurar; VI/VT (think) imaginar(se), figurar(se); **to — in** tener en cuenta; **to — on** contar con; **to — out** (solve) resolver; (calculate) calcular; **it —s!** no me extraña, era de esperar; VT calcular

Fijian [fídʒiən] N fijiano -na *mf*

Fiji Islands [fídʒiáɪləndz] N Islas Fiji *f pl*

filament [fíləmənt] N filamento *m*

file [faɪl] N (documents) archivo *m*; (for

computers) archivo *m*, fichero *m*; (official report) expediente *m*, legajo *m*; (line) fila *f*; (tool) lima *f*; —**name** nombre de archivo *m*; — **server** servidor *m*; **filing cabinet** fichero *m*, archivador *m*; VT (papers) archivar; (news story) entregar; (tax return, claim, etc.) presentar; **to — a suit** entablar una demanda, querellarse; VI (for a job) presentarse; (walk in a line) desfilar; VI/VT (smooth) limar

filial [fíliəl] ADJ filial

filibuster [fíləbʌstɚ] VI/VT practicar obstrucción parlamentaria; N filibusterismo *m*, obstrucción *f*

filigree [fíləgri] N filigrana *f*

fill [fɪl] VI/VT (glass, container) llenar(se); (a hole, a pastry, land) rellenar; **the smell —ed the room** la habitación se llenó del olor; **the airline —ed the position** la compañía aérea llenó el cargo; **the new employee —ed the vacancy** el nuevo empleado ocupó el cargo vacante; VT (a tooth) empastar; (prescription, order) despachar; (a need) satisfacer; VI (sails) hinchar; **to — out** llenar; **to — in** (inform) informar; (fill out) llenar; (replace) sustituir; **to — up** llenarse hasta el tope

fillet [fɪlé] N filete *m*; VT filetear; [fílɪt] N cinta *f*; (on a book) filete *m*

filling [fílɪŋ] N (act) rellenado *m*; (filler) relleno *m*; (of a tooth) empaste *m*; — **station** estación de servicio *f*, gasolinera *f*

filly [fíli] N potranca *f*

film [fɪlm] N película *f* (also thin coating); (material) película *f*, cinta *f*; — **industry** industria cinematográfica *f*; VI/VT filmar, cinematografiar

filter [fíltɚ] N filtro *m*; VI/VT filtrar(se)

filth [fɪlθ] N (dirt, despicable person) mugre *f*, suciedad *f*; (moral impurity) porquería *f*; (vulgar material) obscenidades *f pl*

filthiness [fílθɪnɪs] N suciedad *f*

filthy [fílθi] ADJ (dirty) cochino, mugriento; (obscene, vile) puerco, cochino; *Sp* guarro; — **rich** riquísimo

filtration [fɪltréʃən] N filtración *f*

fin [fɪn] N aleta *f*

final [fáɪnəl] ADJ (result, conclusion) final; (last) último; (conclusive) definitivo; N (in sports) final *f*; (exam) examen final *m*

finalist [fáɪnəlɪst] N finalista *mf*

finalize [fáɪnəlaɪz] VT completar, ultimar

finance [fáɪnæns] N finanza *f*; —**s** finanzas *f pl*; (to fund) financiar; (to purchase on credit) comprar financiado

financial [fɪnǽnʃəl] ADJ financiero

financier [fɪnænsír] N financiero -ra *mf*

financing [fáɪmænsɪŋ] N financiamiento *m*; *Am* financiación *f*

find [faɪnd] VT hallar, encontrar; (discover) descubrir; (determine innocence or guilt) declarar; VI (determine officially) fallar; **to — fault with** criticar a, censurar a; **to — out** (discover) descubrir; (verify) averiguar; N hallazgo *m*

finding [fáɪndɪŋ] N fallo *m*; **—s** resultados *m pl*

fine [faɪn] ADJ (wine, sand, hair, precious metal) fino; (thread) delgado; (cloth) delicado; (artist, athlete) consumado; (manners) refinado; (good-looking) atractivo, guapo; (weather) bueno; (distinction) sutil; **— arts** bellas artes *f pl*; **— print** letra pequeña *f*, letra chica *f*; **to —tune** (a receiver) sintonizar; (an engine) ajustar; (a plan) afinar; **I'm —** estoy bien; **to feel —** sentirse muy bien de salud; **to have a — time** pasarlo bien; N multa *f*; VT multar

finery [fáɪnəri] N galas *f pl*

finesse [fɪnés] N (subtlety) sutileza *f*; (tact) diplomacia *f*; VI usar artimañas; VT conseguir por artimañas

finger [fíŋɡɚ] N dedo *m*; **—food** canapé *m*, aperitivo *m*; **—nail** uña *f*; **—print** huella dactilar / digital *f*; **—tip** punta del dedo *f*; **at one's —tips** al alcance de la mano; **little —** dedo meñique *m*; **middle —** dedo del corazón *m*; VI/VT toquetear, manosear; VT (guitar) tañer; (squeal on) delatar; **to give someone the —** hacerle un gesto obsceno a alguien; **I'll keep my —s crossed** cruzo los dedos; **to wrap someone around one's —** meterse a alguien en el bolsillo; **I can't put my — on it** no se me ocurre una solución

finicky [fínɪki] ADJ melindroso, dengoso

finish [fínɪʃ] VI/VT (end) terminar(se), finalizar(se); VT (polish) pulir; (varnish) barnizar; (kill) liquidar; **— line** meta *f*; **to — off** acabar con, rematar; **to — up** terminar; N (ending) final *m*; (decisive end) fin *m*; (polish, treatment) acabado *m*; (varnish) barniz *m*; (coat of paint) última mano *f*; **with a rough —** sin pulir

finished [fínɪʃt] ADJ (doomed) acabado; (polished) pulido

finite [fáɪnaɪt] ADJ finito

Finland [fínlənd] N Finlandia *f*

Finn [fɪn] N finlandés -esa *mf*, finés -esa *mf*

Finnish [fínɪʃ] ADJ finlandés, finés

fir [fɚ] N abeto *m*

fire [faɪr] N (flame) fuego *m*; (conflagration) incendio *m*; (passion) ardor *m*; (for cigarettes, hearths) lumbre *f*; **— alarm** alarma contra incendios *f*; **— cracker** triquitraque *m*; **— drill** simulacro de incendio *m*; **— department** cuerpo de bomberos *m*; **— engine** coche de bomberos *m*, autobomba *f*; **— escape** escalera de incendios *f*; **— extinguisher** extinguidor (de incendios) *m*, extintor *m*; **—fly** luciérnaga *f*; **— hydrant** boca de incendio *f*; **— insurance** seguro contra incendios *m*; **—man** (who extinguishes) bombero *m*; (stoker) fogonero *m*; **—place** hogar *m*, chimenea *f*; **—proof** ininflamable, a prueba de incendio; **to —proof** hacer incombustible, ignifugar; **—side** hogar *m*; **— station** estación de bomberos *f*; **— trap** edificio sin medios de escape en caso de incendio *m*; **—wood** leña *f*; **—works** fuegos artificiales *m pl*; **when he finds out, there will be —works** cuando se entere, se va a armar la gorda; **to be on —** estar quemándose; **to catch —** incendiarse, prenderse fuego; **to set —to** prender fuego a, incendiar; **under —** bajo fuego; **to play with —** jugar con fuego; **firing pin** percutor *m*; **firing squad** pelotón de fusilamiento *m*; VT (pottery) cocer; (an employee) despedir; (a projectile) lanzar; VI/VT (a gun) disparar; VI **to — up** entusiasmar; **to — off** (gun) disparar; (letter) despachar

firm [fɚm] ADJ (solid, unwavering) firme; (fixed) fijo; (not fluctuating, as prices) estable; VI/VT **to — up** (finalize) concretar; (harden) endurecer; N firma *f*

firmness [fɚmnɪs] N firmeza *f*

first [fɚst] ADJ primero; **— aid** primeros auxilios *m pl*; **— base** primera base *f*; **to get to — base** comenzar con éxito; **—born** primogénito -ta *mf*; **— chapter** capítulo primero *m*, primer capítulo *m*; **— class** primera clase *f*; **—class** de primera clase; **— cousin** primo hermano; **—degree** (burn) de primer grado; (murder) en primer grado; **— floor** (ground floor) planta baja *f*; **for the — time** por primera vez; **—hand** de primera mano; **— lady** primera dama *f*; **— name** nombre de pila *m*; **— person** primera persona *f*; **—rate** de primera clase; ADV (before anything else) primero; **I'd die —** antes la muerte; **at —** al principio; **— off** al principio; N (first in series) primero -ra *mf*; (low gear) primera *f*

fiscal [fískəl] ADJ fiscal; **— period** año fiscal *m*

fish [fɪʃ] N (in water) pez *m*; (out of water) pescado *m*; **—hook** anzuelo *m*; **— market** pescadería *f*; **— story** patraña *f*; **like a — out of water** como sapo de otro pozo; **neither — nor fowl** ni chicha ni limonada; **I have other — to fry** tengo otras cosas mejores que hacer; VI/VT pescar; **to — out** sacar, rebuscar; **to — for compliments** buscar cumplidos; **to —tail** colear

fisherman [fɪʃɚmən] N pescador *m*

fishery [fɪʃəri] N (for breeding) piscifactoría *f*; (for fishing) pesquería *f*; (industry) industria pesquera *f*

fishing [fɪʃɪŋ] N pesca *f*; **— pole / rod** caña de pescar *f*; **— tackle** aparejos de pescar *m pl*; **to go —** ir de pesca

fishy [fɪʃi] ADJ (of smell, taste) a pescado; (suspicious) sospechoso

fissure [fɪʃɚ] N fisura *f*

fist [fɪst] N puño *m*; **—fight** pelea a puñetazos *f*

fit [fɪt] ADJ (suited) apto; (healthy) en buen estado físico; **are you — for driving?** ¿estás en condiciones de manejar? **he was — to be tied** estaba que trinca; **he didn't see — to greet her** no se le antojó saludarla; N (process of fitting) prueba *f*; (mechanical union) encaje *m*; (attack of a disease) ataque *m*; (sudden outburst) rapto *m*; (of anger, coughing) acceso *m*; **to throw a —** tener una pataleta; **by —s and starts** a trompicones; **that suit is a good —** ese traje le queda bien; VT (be suitable for) adecuarse a; (be in agreement with) cuadrar con, ajustarse a; (measure for clothes) tomarle las medidas a; (make suitable) capacitar, preparar; **to — in with** acomodarse a; **I tried to — you in** traté de incluirte; VI (conform to contours of a person) quedarle bien a alguien; (conform to the contours of a mechanism) encajar

fitness [fɪtnɪs] N (suitability) aptitud *f*; (health) buen estado físico *m*

fitting [fɪdɪŋ] ADJ apropiado; N ajuste *m*; (trying on) prueba *f*

five [faɪv] NUM cinco

fix [fɪks] VT (repair, arrange) arreglar, aviar; **he —ed his eyes on me** me miró fijamente; (place permanently, determine) fijar; (prepare food) preparar; **to — up** arreglar, aviar; **to get an animal —ed** castrar a un animal; **I was —ing to call** estaba a punto de llamar; **I'll — you!** ¡ya te arreglo! N (predicament) apuro *m*, aprieto

m; (temporary repair) arreglo provisorio *m*; (narcotic injection) chute *m*; **to get a — on** localizar

fixed [fɪkst] ADJ (stationary) fijo; (arranged in advance) arreglado

fixture [fɪkstʃɚ] N (thing) artefacto *m*; **she's a permanent — in this office** está siempre en la oficina

fizzle [fɪzəl] VI (fail) fracasar; **to — (out)** (make a noise) apagarse chisporroteando

flabby [flǽbi] ADJ flácido

flag [flæg] N bandera *f*; **—pole** mástil *m*; **—staff** mástil *m*; **—stone** losa *f*, baldosa *f*; VT (adorn with flags) embanderar; (mark) marcar con banderas; **to — (down)** hacer parar; VI (diminish) menguar

flagrant [flégrənt] ADV flagrante

flair [fler] N (aptitude) aptitud *f*, facilidad *f*; (style) estilo *m*

flak [flæk] N (anti-artillery fire) fuego antiaéreo *m*; (criticism) crítica *f*

flake [flek] N (snow) copo *m*; (small thin piece) escama *f*; (eccentric person) chiflado -da *mf*; VI descascararse

flamboyant [flæmbɔ́iənt] ADJ (clothes) llamativo; (behavior) extravagante

flame [flem] N llama *f*; **— thrower** lanzallamas *m sg*; **old —** viejo amor *m*; VI llamear, flamear, encenderse

flaming [flémɪŋ] ADJ (emitting flames) llameante; (like a flame) flamígero; (ardent) ardiente; **— red** rojo encendido

flammable [flǽməbəl] ADJ inflamable

flank [flæŋk] N (of a bastion or army) flanco *m*; (of an animal) ijar *m*; VT flanquear

flannel [flǽnəl] N franela *f*, lanilla *f*

flap [flæp] VI (wings) aletear; (flag) flamear; VT (wings) batir; (arms) sacudir; N (of a jacket, pocket) cartera *f*; (of a saddle, table) hoja *f*; (of an airplane) alerón *m*; (action of flapping) aleteo *m*

flare [fler] VI (burn unsteadily) llamear; (skirt) ensancharse; **to — up** (fire) avivarse; (activity) recrudecer; **the illness —d up** recrudeció la enfermedad; VT (a skirt) levantar; (a flame) avivar; (a pipe) abocinar; (signal by flare) señalar con bengala; N (flaring light, burst of flame) llamarada *f*; (signal light) bengala *f*; (sudden emotional outburst) arranque *m*; (outward curvature) vuelo *m*; **—up** recrudecimiento *m*

flash [flæʃ] N (of light) destello *m*, ráfaga *f*; (of explosion) fogonazo *m*; (news, camera, vision) flash *m*; **— of hope** rayo de esperanza *m*; **— of lightning**

relampagueo *m*, rayo *m*; **in a** — en un instante; VI/VT (shine) destellar (sobre); (expose) exhibir(se); VI (gleam) relucir, fulgurar, relampaguear; (appear) aparecer; VT (display) ostentar; **—back** flashback *m*, escena retrospectiva *f*; **—bulb** flash *m*; — **flood** riada *f*; **—light** linterna *f*; **to — by** pasar como un relámpago

flashing [flǽʃɪŋ] ADJ destellante

flashy [flǽʃi] ADJ (colorful) llamativo; (ostentatious) ostentoso; (tasteless) *Am* charro

flask [flæsk] N (glass container) frasco *m*; (in a laboratory) matraz *m*, redoma *f*; (for alcoholic beverages) petaca *f*

flat [flæt] ADJ (of surfaces) plano; (of land) llano; (smooth) liso; (horizontal) horizontal, acostado; (flattened) arrasado, aplastado; (of shoes, nose) chato; (deflated) desinflado, pinchado; (dull of color) apagado; (without effervescence) sin gas; (lifeless) soso; (without gloss) mate; (absolute) terminante; (of a photo) sin contraste; (of a painting) sin volumen; (too low in pitch) demasiado grave; (of a musical note) bemol; **—footed** con pie plano; **— rate** tarifa fija *f*; **trading was** — hubo poco movimiento económico; **to be — broke** estar completamente pelado; **to fall** — (of a body) caer de plano / redondo; (of a joke) caer mal; (of a plan) fracasar; N (shoe) zapato sin tacón *m*; (flat tire) desinflado *m*, pinchadura *f*, pinchazo *m*; (wooden box) caja para plantas *f*; (musical note) bemol *m*; **—iron** plancha *f*; ADV **—out** (directly) absolutamente; (at full speed) a toda velocidad; **in two minutes** — en dos minutos exactos

flatten [flǽtn̩] VI/VT (make flat) achatar(se), aplanar(se); VT (knock down) tumbar, voltear; (raze) arrasar

flatter [flǽɾɚ] VI/VT lisonjear, adular, halagar; **this picture —s you** esta foto te favorece; **I was —ed by his attentions** me halagaron sus atenciones

flatterer [flǽɾ əɾɚ] N lisonjero -ra *mf*, adulador -ora *mf*

flattering [flǽɾ ə ɪŋ] ADJ (comment) lisonjero, halagüeño; (person) adulón

flattery [flǽɾ ə ɾi] N lisonja *f*, adulación *f*, halago *m*

flatulence [flǽt ʃ ə l ə ns] N flatulencia *f*

flaunt [flɔnt] VI/VT ostentar, lucir(se)

flavor [flévɚ] N (taste, quality) sabor *m*; (flavoring) condimento *m*; VT sazonar

flavorless [fléva lɪs] ADJ insípido

flaw [flɔ] N (in character, in construction) defecto *m*; (in an argument) falla *f*

flawless [flɔ́ lɪs] ADJ (logic) impecable; (behavior) intachable, irreprochable; (appearance) perfecto

flax [flæks] N lino *m*

flea [fli] N pulga *f*; **— collar** collar antipulgas *m*; **— market** *Sp* rastro *m*; *Am* mercado de (las) pulgas *m*

flee [fli] VI huir; VT huir de

fleece [flis] N vellón *m*; VT (shear) trasquilar, esquilar; (defraud) estafar; (in card games) pelar, desplumar

fleet [flit] N (of boats, buses) flota *f*; (of cars) parque *m*; ADJ veloz

fleeting [flíɾɪŋ] ADJ fugaz, efímero, pasajero

Flemish [flémɪʃ] ADJ & N flamenco -ca *mf*

flesh [flɛʃ] N carne *f*; (of a fruit) pulpa *f*; **— and blood** carne y hueso; **of my own — and blood** de mi propria sangre; **in the —** en persona; VI/VT **to — out** (a character) dar cuerpo a; (an argument) desarrollar

fleshy [fléʃi] ADJ (succulent) carnoso; (fat) metido en carnes

flexibility [flɛksəbílɪɾi] N flexibilidad *f*

flexible [flɛksəbəl] ADJ flexible

flicker [flíkɚ] VI (stars) titilar; (candle) parpadear; (of wings, etc.) temblar; N (of light) parpadeo *m*, titilación *f*; (of hope) rayo *m*

flier [fláɪɚ] N (one who flies) volador -ra *mf*; (aviator) aviador -ra *mf*; (leaflet) volante *m*

flight [flaɪt] N (act of flying, trip) vuelo *m*; (trajectory) trayectoria *f*; (flock of birds) bandada *f*; (group of military aircraft) escuadrilla *f*; (escape) fuga *f*, huida *f*; **— attendant** azafato -ta *mf*; **— plan** plan de vuelo *m*; **— school** escuela de aviación *f*; **a — of fancy** una fantasía; **— of stairs** tramo de escalera *m*; **to put to —** poner en fuga; **to take —** darse a la fuga

flimsy [flímzi] ADJ (structure, argument) endeble; (excuse) flojo, pobre

flinch [flɪntʃ] VI pestañear

fling [flɪŋ] VT arrojar, lanzar; **she flung herself at the attacker** se le tiró arriba al atacante; **he flung himself into his work** se dedicó de lleno a su trabajo; **he flung open the door** abrió la puerta de golpe; N (act of flinging) lanzamiento *m*; (sexual affair) aventura *f*; **he had a — at selling cars** intentó vender coches

flint [flɪnt] N pedernal *m*

flip [flɪp] VT (a coin) tirar; (a switch) (up) levantar, (down) bajar; (a pancake) dar vuelta; VI (head over heels) dar una voltereta; (get excited, go crazy) volverse

loco; **to — through** hojear; **—-flop**
(reversal of opinion) giro de 180 grados *m*;
(backward somersault) voltereta para atrás
f; (slipper) chancleta *f*; **— side** la otra cara
de la moneda

flippant [flípənt] ADJ (frivolous) frívolo,
displicente; (impudent) impertinente

flipper [flípə-] N aleta *f*

flirt [flɜ-t] VI coquetear; N coqueto -ta *mf*

flirtation [flɜ-téʃən] N coquetería *f*, coqueteo
m

flit [flɪt] VI revolotear; **a smile —s across
her face** una sonrisa le cruza la cara

float [flot] VI (rest on water, air, etc., fluctuate
freely) flotar; (in soup) sobrenadar; (drift)
errar, ir a la deriva; **she —ed down the
stairs** se deslizó por la escalera; VT (set
afloat) poner a flote; (start a company,
scheme) lanzar; (emit shares) emitir; (let
fluctuate) dejar flotar; (try out an idea)
proponer; N (thing that floats) flotador *m*;
(on a line) corcho *m*, boya *f*; (in a parade)
carro alegórico *m*, carroza *f*; (with soda)
gaseosa con helado *f*

flock [flɑk] N (birds, children) bandada *f*;
(sheep) rebaño *m*; (worshipers) grey *f*;
(people) muchedumbre *f*; VI acudir en
masa, afluir; **to — around someone**
rodear a alguien; **to — together** andar
juntos

flog [flɑg] VT azotar

flood [flʌd] N inundación *f*; **— of tears**
torrente de lágrimas *m*; **the —** El Diluvio
Universal; (of tides) creciente *f*; **—gate** (of
a dam) compuerta *f*; (of a canal lock)
esclusa *f*; **—light** reflector *m*; VI/VT
inundar(se), anegar(se); (car) ahogar(se),
emborrachar(se)

floor [flɔr] N (surface of a room, vehicle)
suelo *m*, piso *m*; (story) piso *m*; (of sea)
fondo *m*; (dance) pista *f*; (minimum level)
mínimo *m*; **to have the —** tener la
palabra; VT (topple over) tumbar, derribar;
(stun, surprise) asombrar; **— it!** ¡acelera!
Sp ¡mete caña!

flop [flɑp] VI (flail) zarandearse; (fish) dar
coletazos; (drop) dejarse caer; (fail)
fracasar; **to — down** dejarse caer,
desplomarse; **to — over** voltear(se)
flojamente; N (failure) fracaso *m*; (sound)
ruido sordo *m*

floppy [flɑpi] ADJ caído; **— disk** disquete *m*,
floppy *m*

florist [flɔrɪst] N florista *mf*; **—'s** (shop)
florería *f*

floss [flɔs] N (silk) seda floja *f*; (for
embroidery) hilo de seda *m*; (dental) hilo

dental *m*; VI/VT pasar hilo dental (por)

flounder [fláʊndə-] VI (in mud, etc.) andar/
moverse con dificultades; (for an answer)
quedarse sin saber qué decir, perder pie; N
platija *f*

flour [flaʊr] N harina *f*

flourish [flɜ́-ɪʃ] VI (prosper) florecer,
prosperar; VT (brandish) blandir; N
(ornament, florid language, brandishing)
floreo *m*; (of music) floritura *f*; (of a
signature) rúbrica *f*; **in full —** en plena
eclosión

flow [flo] VI (run) fluir, correr; (issue forth)
surgir, brotar; (come and go) circular; (fall
loosely) caer; (abound) abundar; (rise)
crecer; **to — into** desembocar en, afluir a;
N (liquid) flujo *m*; (electricity) corriente *f*;
(of traffic, blood, air) circulación *f*;
—chart diagrama de flujo *m*; **— of
words** torrente de palabras *m*

flower [fláʊə-] N flor *f*; (paragon) flor y nata *f*;
in — en flor; **— bed** *Mex, Sp* arriate *m*; *RP*
cantero *m*; **—pot** maceta *f*, tiesto *m*; **—
vase** florero *m*; VI florecer

flowery [fláʊəri] ADJ (of a garden, language)
florido; (of a pattern) floreado; (of a
fragrance) floral

flowing [flóɪŋ] ADJ (liquid) fluyente;
(clothing) suelto

flu [flu] N gripe *f*

fluctuate [flʌ́ktʃuet] VI fluctuar

fluctuation [flʌ̀ktʃuéʃən] N fluctuación *f*

fluency [flúənsi] N fluidez *f*

fluent [flúənt] ADJ fluido; **he is — in
French** habla francés con fluidez/soltura

fluff [flʌf] VT (mullir; (blunder) pifiar; N pelusa
f; (blunder) pifia *f*; **this book is pure —**
este libro es insustancial

fluffy [flʌ́fi] ADJ (airy) mullido; (covered with
fluff) peludo

fluid [flúɪd] ADJ & N fluido *m*; **— ounce** onza
líquida (29,42 mililitros) *f*

fluke [fluk] N (of whale) aleta *f*; (chance)
chiripa *f*; **by a —** por chiripa

flunk [flʌŋk] VI/VT reprobar, suspender; VI **to
— out** abandonar

flunky [flʌ́ŋki] N (lackey, servant) lacayo *m*;
(yes-man) adulón *m*

fluorescent [flʊrésənt] ADJ fluorescente; **—
light** tubo fluorescente *m*

fluoride [flɔ́raɪd] N (chemical) fluoruro *m*;
(dental aid) flúor *m*

fluorine [flɔ́rin] N flúor *m*

flurry [flɜ́-i] N (of snow) nevisca *f*; (of
activity) frenesí *m*

flush [flʌʃ] N (rosy glow, heat) rubor *m*; (of
anger) arranque *m*; (of youth, color)

resplandor *m*; (of embarrassment) sonrojo *m*; (in poker) color *m*; **did you hear the — of the toilet?** ¿oíste el sonido de la cisterna? ADJ (well supplied, rich) forrado; (ruddy, reddish) rubicundo; (full) rebosante; **— with** a(l) ras de; **— against** pegado a; VI/VT (make or turn red) sonrojar(se), ruborizar(se); (activate toilet) tirar la cadena; (rinse) baldear; VT **to — out** levantar

fluster [flÁstə-] VI/VT agitar(se), poner(se) nervioso

flute [flut] N (musical instrument) flauta *f*; (of a column) estría *f*; VT estriar

flutter [flÁdə-] VI (wings) aletear; (butterfly) revolotear; (flag) tremolar; (heart) palpitar; VT (agitate) agitar; N (of wings) aleteo *m*; (of excitement) agitación *f*; (of a fly) tremolar *m*; (of the heart) palpitación *f*

flux [flÁks] N flujo *m*; **a state of —** un estado de cambio continuo

fly [flaɪ] VI (through air) volar; (from danger) huir; (flag) ondear; (kite) remontar; VT (aircraft) pilotar; (air cargo) transportar en avión; **to — at** abalanzarse sobre; **to — away** volando; **to — into a rage** montar en cólera; **to — off the handle** perder los estribos; **to — open (shut)** abrirse (cerrarse) de un golpe; **to — out of a room** salir disparado de un cuarto; **that idea won't —** esa idea no va a ser aceptada; **he flew the coop** se escapó; N (insect) mosca *f*; (over a zipper) bragueta *f*; **—catcher** papamoscas *m sg*; **—leaf** solapa *f*; **—swatter** matamoscas *m sg*; **—wheel** volante *m*; **on the —** al vuelo

flying [flÁɪŋ] ADJ (passing through the air) volador; (fluttering) ondeante; **with — colors** con distinción; **— saucer** platillo volador *m*; **I hate —** no me gusta viajar en avión

foam [fom] N (suds, padding) espuma *f*; **— rubber** goma espuma *f*; VI hacer espuma; **to — at the mouth** echar espuma por la boca

focus [fókəs] N foco *m*; VI/VT (bring into or be in focus) enfocar(se); (concentrate) centrarse; **to — on** fijarse en

fodder [fÁdə-] N forraje *m*

foe [fo] N enemigo -ga *mf*

fog [fɑg] N niebla *f*; **to be in a —** estar confundido; **—horn** sirena de niebla *f*; VI/VT (confuse) ofuscar; (spray with insecticide) fumigar; (film) velar(se); **to — up** (window) empañar(se); (one's sight) nublar(se); **the airport was —ged in** el aeropuerto estaba cerrado por niebla

foggy [fÁgi] ADJ (weather) brumoso, nebuloso; (window) empañado; (confused) confuso; (blurred, as a photograph) velado

foil [fɔɪl] N (any metal) hoja de metal *f*; (aluminum) papel de aluminio *m*; (on mirrors) azogue *m*; (rapier) florete *m*; (thing contrasted) contraste *m*; VT frustrar

fold [fold] VI/VT (sheets) doblar(se); (paper, folding chairs) plegar(se); (wings, flag) replegar(se); (in cards) abandonar; (close a business) cerrar(se); (performance) bajar de cartel; **to — in** (in cooking) incorporar; **to — one's arms** cruzarse de brazos; N (pleat, hollow) pliegue *m*; (crease) doblez *m*; (enclosure) redil *m*, aprisco *m*; (sheep) rebaño *m*; (congregation) grey *f*; **to rejoin the —** volver al redil; **three—** tres veces

folder [fóldə-] N (file) carpeta *f*; (instrument for folding) plegadera *f*

folding [fóldɪŋ] ADJ plegadizo, plegable; **— chair** silla plegadiza *f*; **— screen** biombo *m*

foliage [fólɪɪʤ] N follaje *m*, fronda *f*, ramaje *m*

folic acid [fólɪkǽsɪd] N ácido fólico *m*

folio [fólio] N (page) folio *m*; (book) libro en folio *m*

folk [fok] N (people) gente *f*; (nation) pueblo *m*; ADJ popular; **— dance** baile folclórico *m*; **—lore** folclore *m*; (traditional stories) leyendas tradicionales *f pl*; **— medicine** medicina tradicional *f*; **— music** música folclórica *f*; **old —s** los viejos; **—s** (relatives) parientes *m pl*; (parents) padres *m pl*, viejos *m pl*; **— song** canción tradicional *f*

follow [fálo] VI/VT seguir; VI (be a consequence) seguirse; (come next) ir a continuación; **to — suit** seguir el ejemplo, secundar; **to — through** llevar a cabo; **—through** continuación del movimiento; **to — up (on)** (pursue) obtener más detalles sobre; (develop) desarrollar; **—up** seguimiento *m*

follower [fáloə-] N seguidor -ra *mf*

following [fáloɪŋ] N seguidores -ras *mf pl*; **the —** lo siguiente; ADJ siguiente

foment [fomént] VT fomentar

fond [fand] ADJ **I'm — of strolls** soy amigo de los paseos, soy gustoso de los paseos; **I'm — of Chinese food** me gusta la comida china; **I'm — of John** le tengo cariño a Juan; **— hopes** ilusión *f*; **to become — of** encariñarse de

fondle [fándl] VI/VT (touch affectionately) acariciar; (grope) manosear, sobar

fondness [fándnɪs] N (affection) cariño *m*,

afecto *m*; (liking or weakness) afición *f*

font [fɑnt] N (of water) pila *f*; (of characters) fuente *f*

food [fud] N comida *f*, alimento *m*; — **chain** cadena alimenticia *f*; — **poisoning** intoxicación por alimentos *f*; —**stuff** producto alimenticio *m*; — **for thought** algo para reflexionar

fool [ful] N (foolish person) tonto -ta *mf*, bobo -ba *mf*, necio -cia *mf*; (jester) bufón *m*; **to make a — of someone** hacer quedar como un tonto; **to play the —** hacer el tonto; **I'm a card-playing —** soy loco por los naipes; VI bromear; **to — around** tontear; VT engañar; ADJ —**proof** (plan) infalible; (device) a prueba de tontos

foolish [fúlɪʃ] ADJ tonto, necio

foolishness [fúlɪʃnɪs] N tontería *f*, bobería *f*, sandez *f*

foot [fut] N pie *m*; (of an animal) pata *f*; **on — a pie; to put one's — in it** meter la pata; —**and-mouth disease** fiebre aftosa *f*; —**ball** (American) fútbol americano *m*; (soccer) fútbol *m*; (ball) balón (de fútbol) *m*, pelota (de fútbol) *f*; —**hill** pie de la montaña *m*; —**hold** punto de apoyo *m*; **he has a —hold in the computer business** ha logrado establecerse en el negocio de la informática; —**lights** candilejas *f pl*; —**man** lacayo *m*; —**note** nota al pie de página *f*, llamada *f*; —**path** senda *f*; —**print** huella *f*, pisada *f*; —**race** carrera a pie *f*; — **soldier** soldado de infantería *m*; —**step** pisada *f*, paso *m*; (footprint) huella *f*, pisada *f*; **to follow in the —steps of** seguir los pasos de; —**stool** taburete *m*; —**wear** calzado *m*; —**work** (in sports) juego de piernas *m*; **it'll take some pretty fancy —work to get out of this** va a ser difícil zafar de esto; VI **to —** it andar a pie; VT **to — the bill** pagar la cuenta

footing [fútɪŋ] N (basis) base *f*; (foothold) punto de apoyo *m*; **to be on a friendly — with** tener relaciones amistosas con; **to lose one's —** perder pie

for [fɔr] PREP para; **this gift is — John** este regalo es para John; **we're headed — the beach** vamos para la playa; **this is a device — sorting letters** este es un aparato para clasificar cartas; **they gave me enough food — three people** me dieron comida (como) para tres personas; **she's studying — the bar** está estudiando para el examen de abogacía; **the party is planned — Saturday** la

fiesta está organizada para el sábado; **he has a good eye — talent** tiene buen ojo para descubrir talento; **he works — IBM** trabaja para IBM; **smoking is bad — your health** fumar es perjudicial para la salud; **he's mature — his age** es maduro para su edad; por; **I've come — the money** he venido por el dinero; **she asked — you** pidió por ti; **I walk to work — the exercise** voy al trabajo andando por el ejercicio; **we went to Spain — a month** fuimos a España por un mes; **she did it — the first time** lo hizo por primera vez; **my wife signed — me** mi esposa firmó por mí; **mothers feel love — their children** las madres sienten amor por sus hijos; **they fired him — arriving late** lo echaron por llegar tarde; **run — your life!** ¡corre por tu vida! **she took me — a fool** me tomó por tonto; **thanks — the help** gracias por la ayuda; **I paid ten dollars — the book** pagué diez dólares por el libro; **I'm — gun control** estoy por el control de armas; — **all her intelligence** a pesar de su inteligencia; **that's not — you to decide** a ti no te toca decidir esto; **as — him** en cuanto a él; **it's time — me to go** es hora de que me vaya; **to know — a fact** saber a ciencia cierta; CONJ porque, pues; **I wish to eat, — I'm hungry** quiero comer, pues tengo hambre

forage [fɔ́rɪdʒ] N (feed) forraje *m*; (searching) recolección *f*; VI (gather food) forrajear; VT (feed) dar forraje a; (collect) recolectar

foray [fɔ́re] N incursión *f*, correría *f*; VI (explore) incursionar; (maraud) saquear

forbear [fɔrbér] VT abstenerse de; VI contenerse; [fɔ́rber] N antepasado -da *mf*

forbid [fəbíd] VT prohibir

forbidden [fəbídn] ADJ prohibido

forbidding [fəbídɪŋ] ADJ (strict) severo; (daunting) imponente

force [fɔrs] N fuerza *f*; **in —** (effective) en vigor, vigente; (in large numbers) en masa; **armed —s** fuerzas armadas *f pl*; VT (oblige, compel) obligar; (rape, break open) forzar; **she —d a laugh** soltó una risa forzada; **to — upon** imponer; **to — one's way** abrirse paso a la fuerza; **to — out** echar a la fuerza

forced [fɔrst] ADJ forzado; (of a landing) forzoso

forceful [fɔ́rsfəl] ADJ (of personality) fuerte; (of arguments) convincente; (of behavior) enérgico

forceps [fɔ́rsəps] N (in obstetrics) fórceps *m*;

(in dentistry) tenazas *f pl*, gatillo *m*

forcible [fɔ́rsəbəɫ] ADJ (done by force)
forzoso; (effective) convincente; (by force)
violento; **— entry** allanamiento de
morada *m*

ford [fɔrd] N vado *m*; VT vadear

fore [fɔr] ADJ delantero; (of a ship) de proa; N
frente *m*; **to come to the —** ponerse en
evidencia; INTERJ ¡cuidado!

forearm [fɔ́rɑrm] N antebrazo *m*

forebode [fɔrbód] VT (foretell) presagiar;
(have a presentiment) presentir

foreboding [fɔrbódɪŋ] N (omen) presagio *m*;
(presentiment) presentimiento *m*

forecast [fɔ́rkæst] N pronóstico *m*; VI/VT
pronosticar

foreclose [fɔrklóz] VI ejecutar una hipoteca

foreclosure [fɔrklóʒɚ] N ejecución *f*

forefather [fɔ́rfɑðɚ] N antepasado *m*

forefront [fɔ́rfrʌnt] ADV LOC **at the —** a la
cabeza, a la vanguardia

forego [fɔrgó] VT abstenerse de

foregone [fɔ́rgɔn] ADJ **it's a — conclusion**
eso es de cajón

foreground [fɔ́rgraʊnd] N primer plano *m*

forehead [fɔ́rɪd] N frente *f*

foreign [fɔ́rɪn] ADJ extranjero; (not local)
foráneo; (alien) ajeno; **— affairs**
relaciones exteriores *f pl*; **— aid** ayuda
exterior *f*; **—-born** nacido en el
extranjero; **— currency** divisa *f*; **— debt**
deuda exterior *f*; **— exchange** cambio de
divisas *m*; **— matter** materia extraña *f*; **—
policy** política exterior *f*; **— trade**
comercio exterior *m*

foreigner [fɔ́rənɚ] N extranjero -ra *mf*

foreman [fɔ́rmən] N (in a factory) capataz *m*,
sobrestante *m*; (of a jury) presidente *m*

foremost [fɔ́rmost] ADJ principal,
preeminente

forensic [fərɛ́nzɪk] ADJ forense

forerunner [fɔ́rrʌnɚ] N (precursor) precursor
-ora *mf*; (omen) presagio *m*; (harbinger)
mensajero -ra *mf*

foresee [fɔrsí] VT prever, prevenir

foresight [fɔ́rsaɪt] N previsión *f*

foreskin [fɔ́rskɪn] N prepucio *m*

forest [fɔ́rɪst] N (temperate) bosque *m*;
(tropical) selva *f*; **— fire** incendio forestal
m; **— ranger** guardabosques *m sg*

forestall [fɔrstɔ́ɫ] VT bloquear

forester [fɔ́rɪstɚ] N (forest ranger)
guardabosques *m sg*; (forest animal)
animal silvícola *m*

forestry [fɔ́rɪstri] N silvicultura *f*

foretell [fɔrtɛ́ɫ] VT predecir, vaticinar

forever [fɔrɛ́vɚ] ADV para siempre; **I'm —**

having to pick up after him siempre
tengo que estar juntando sus cosas; **we
can't go on like this —** no podemos
seguir así por toda la vida

foreword [fɔ́rwɚd] N prólogo *m*

forfeit [fɔ́rfɪt] VT perder; N (fine) multa *f*;
(loss) pérdida *f*

forge [fɔrdʒ] N fragua *f*, forja *f*; VT (plans)
fraguar; (metal, agreement) forjar; VI/VT
(signature, legal document) falsificar; **to —
ahead** abrirse paso

forgery [fɔ́rdʒəri] N falsificación *f*

forget [fɚgɛ́t] VI/VT olvidar, olvidarse de; **I
forgot my keys** se me olvidaron las
llaves; **to — oneself** meter la pata; N
—-me-not nomeolvides *mf*

forgetful [fɚgɛ́tfəɫ] ADJ olvidadizo; **— of**
negligente de

forgetfulness [fɚgɛ́tfəɫnɪs] N falta de
memoria *f*

forgive [fɚgív] VI/VT perdonar (also a debt),
disculpar

forgiveness [fɚgívnɪs] N perdón *m*

forgiving [fɚgívɪŋ] ADJ clemente

fork [fɔrk] N (for eating) tenedor *m*; (for hay)
horca *f*, trinche *m*; (for tuning) diapasón
m; (in a road) bifurcación *f*; **—lift**
montacargas de horquilla *m sg*; VI
bifurcarse; **to — over** soltar

forlorn [fɔrlɔ́rn] ADJ desamparado,
abandonado

form [fɔrm] N forma *f*; (physical condition)
condiciones físicas *f pl*; (document to be
filled in) formulario *m*; VI/VT formar(se)

formal [fɔ́rməɫ] ADJ formal; **— attire** ropa
de etiqueta *f*; **— dance** baile de etiqueta
m

formality [fɔrmǽlɪɾi] N (conventionality)
formalidad *f*; (rigidity) formalismo *m*;
(legal step) trámite *m*

format [fɔ́rmæt] N formato *m*; VT formatear

formation [fɔrméʃən] N formación *f*

formative [fɔ́rmədɪv] ADJ formativo

formatting [fɔ́rmædɪŋ] N formateo *m*

former [fɔ́rmɚ] ADJ **the — capital** la
antigua capital; **my — husband** mi ex-
marido; **the — president** el expresidente; **in — times** antiguamente;
PRON aquel (aquella, etc.), ese (esa, etc.)

formidable [fɔ́rmɪɾəbəɫ] ADJ formidable

formula [fɔ́rmjələ] N fórmula *f*; (for babies)
preparado para biberón *m*

formulate [fɔ́rmjəlet] VT formular

fornicate [fɔ́rnɪket] VI fornicar

forsake [fɔrsék] VT abandonar, desamparar

fort [fɔrt] N fuerte *m*, fortaleza *f*; **to hold
(down) the —** quedarse cuidando

forth [fɔrθ] ADV (time) en adelante; (space) hacia adelante; **to go —** irse; **and so —** etcétera, y así sucesivamente

forthcoming [fɔrθkʌmɪŋ] ADJ (approaching) venidero, próximo; (available) disponible; **help wasn't —** no había ayuda disponible; (frank, friendly) abierto; (soon to be published) de próxima aparición

forthright [fɔrθraɪt] ADJ directo

forthwith [fɔrθwɪθ] ADV en seguida, al punto

fortification [fɔrɾəfɪkéʃən] N fortificación f

fortify [fɔrɾəfaɪ] VT (building, body) fortificar; (food) enriquecer; (hair, mind) fortalecer; (argument) reforzar

fortitude [fɔrɾɪtud] N fortaleza f, entereza f

fortress [fɔrtrɪs] N fortaleza f

fortuitous [fɔrtúɪɾəs] ADJ (coincidental) fortuito; (lucky) afortunado

fortunate [fɔrtʃənɪt] ADJ afortunado

fortune [fɔrtʃən] N fortuna f; **— teller** adivino -na mf; **it cost me a —** me costó un dineral; **to tell someone's —** decirle la buenaventura a alguien

forty [fɔrɾi] NUM cuarenta

forum [fɔrəm] N foro m

forward [fɔrwə-d] ADJ (toward the front) hacia adelante; (leading, in the front) delantero; (pushy) descarado; ADV adelante, en adelante; **to bring —** presentar; VT reexpedir; N delantero -ra mf

fossil [fásəl] N fósil m; (old fogey) carcamal m, carca mf; **— fuel** combustible fósil m

foster [fɔstə-] VT (promote) fomentar, promover; (bring up) criar; ADJ adoptivo

foul [faʊl] ADJ (dirty, illicit) sucio; (disgusting) asqueroso; (of a smell) fétido; (of weather) inclemente; (of winds) adverso; (morally offensive) vil; (of air) viciado; **—mouthed** mal hablado; **the police suspect — play** la policía sospecha que fue un crimen; N falta f, foul m; **—up** desastre m; VT (make dirty) ensuciar; (pollute) viciar; (tarnish) manchar; VI cometer una falta; **to — up** estropear

found [faʊnd] VT (establish) fundar; (build) cimentar

foundation [faʊndéʃən] N (establishment, institution) fundación f; (of a building) cimiento m; (of an argument) fundamento m; (cosmetic) base f

founder [fáʊndə-] N (establisher) fundador -ra mf; (smith) fundidor -ra mf; VI (sink) zozobrar, irse a pique; (fail) fracasar

foundry [fáʊndri] N fundición f

fountain [fáʊntṇ] N fuente f; **— pen** pluma

fuente f

four [fɔr] NUM cuatro; **—-eyes** fam cuatro ojos m sg; **—-letter word** palabrota f; **—-score** ochenta; **—-some** grupo de cuatro m

fourteen [fɔrtín] NUM catorce

fourth [fɔrθ] ADJ cuarto; N cuarta parte f; **the Fourth of July** el cuatro de julio

fowl [faʊl] N (domestic) ave de corral m; (wild) ave m

fox [faks] N zorro -rra mf; (crafty person) persona astuta f; (attractive person) guapetón -na mf; **—hole** madriguera f; (military) trinchera f

foxy [fáksi] ADJ (crafty) zorro; (attractive) sexy

foyer [fɔɪə-] N vestíbulo m

fraction [frǽkʃən] N fracción f, quebrado m

fracture [frǽktʃə-] N fractura f; VI/VT fracturar(se)

fragile [frǽdʒəl] ADJ frágil

fragment [frǽgmənt] N fragmento m; [frǽgmént] VI/VT fragmentar(se)

fragrance [frégrəns] N fragancia f

fragrant [frégrənt] ADJ fragante

frail [freɫ] ADJ frágil, débil

frailty [frétɪ] N fragilidad f, debilidad f

frame [frem] N (of a building, airplane, furniture) armazón m; (of eyeglasses) montura f, armadura f; (of a car) chasis m; (of a person's body) estatura f; (of a picture, door) marco m; (for embroidery) bastidor m; (on a strip of film) imagen f; **— of mind** disposición f; **—work** (of a house, structure) armazón m; (of reference) marco m, esquema m; VT (a document) forjar; (a question, plan) formular; (a picture) enmarcar; (a person) tenderle una trampa

franc [fræŋk] N franco m

France [fræns] N Francia f

franchise [frǽntʃaɪz] N (license) concesión f, franquicia f; (voting privilege) derecho al voto m; VT conceder en franquicia, dar la concesión

frank [fræŋk] ADJ franco, abierto; VT franquear; N salchicha alemana f

frankfurter [frǽŋkfɚɾə-] N salchicha alemana f

frankness [frǽŋknɪs] N franqueza f

frantic [frǽntɪk] ADJ (wild) frenético; (desperate) desesperado

fraternal [frətɚnəɫ] ADJ fraternal, fraterno

fraternity [frətɚnɪɾi] N (relationship) fraternidad f, confraternidad f; (student association) asociación estudiantil f

fraternize [frǽɾə-naɪz] VI confraternizar, fraternizar

fraud [frɔd] N (deceit) fraude *m*; (impostor) farsante *mf*, impostor -ra *mf*

fraudulent [frɔ́dʒələnt] ADJ (of a business, etc.) fraudulento; (of a person) engañoso

fray [fre] N (fight) reyerta *f*, riña *f*; (harsh debate) refriega *f*; VI/VT (rub, wear out) desgastar(se); (strain) crispar(se)

freak [frik] N (anomaly) anomalía *f*; (monster) monstruo *m*, anormal *mf*; (enthusiast) fanático -ca *mf*; (pervert) pervertido -da *mf*, ADJ (unusual) insólito; VT chiflar, flipar; **to — out** chiflar(se), flipar(se)

freakish [fríkɪʃ] ADJ insólito

freckle [frékəl] N peca *f*; VI/VT cubrir(se) de pecas

freckled [frékəld] ADJ pecoso

free [fri] ADJ (having liberty, unrestricted, loose, uncombined chemically, independent) libre; (unobstructed, unoccupied) libre, despejado; (without charge) gratis, gratuito; (generous) generoso; (unstinted) sin límites, descontrolado; (frank) franco, abierto; **— and easy** despreocupado; **— enterprise** empresa libre *f*; **— fall** caída libre *f*; **—for-all** rifirrafe *m*; **—lance** freelance *m*; **— lunch / ride** algo gratis *m*; **— market** mercado libre *m*; **— radical** radical libre *m*; **— speech** libertad de expresión *f*; **— spirit** espíritu fuerte *m*; **—style** estilo libre *m*; **— thinker** libre pensador -ra *mf*; **— trade** libre cambio *m*; **— verse** verso libre *m*; **—way** autopista *f*, autovía *f*; **— will** libre albedrío *m*; **to give someone a — hand** dar rienda suelta a alguien; **to set —** poner en libertad; **for —** gratis; **sugar-—** sin azúcar; ADV libremente; **— lance** por cuenta propia; VT (liberate) liberar; (deliver, rid) librar; (untie a knot) desenredar; (drain) desatascar; **to —load** gorronear; **to — up** (time) dejar libre

freedom [frídəm] N libertad *f*; **— of speech** libertad de expresión *f*; **we all want — from fear** todos queremos vivir libres de miedo; **I want — from having to go to work every day** no quiero tener que ir a trabajar todos los días

freeze [friz] VI/VT (of food, water) congelar(se); (of accounts) bloquear(se), congelar(se); **he froze to death** murió congelado; **my computer froze up** se me colgó la computadora / el ordenador; VI (of temperature) helar; N (action or state of being frozen) congelación *f*; (cold snap) helada *f*

freezer [fríza] N congelador *m*

freezing [frízɪŋ] ADJ helado; **— cold** frío glacial *m*; **— point** punto de congelación *m*

freight [fret] N (load) carga *f*; (charge) flete *m*, porte *m*; **— train** tren de carga *m*, tren de mercancías *m*; **by —** por carga

French [frentʃ] ADJ francés; **— dressing** salsa francesa *f*; **— fries** Am papas fritas *f pl*; Sp patatas fritas *f pl*; **— horn** corno francés *m*; **—man** francés *m*; **—woman** francesa *f*; **the —** los franceses

frenzy [frénzi] N frenesí *m*; **he worked himself into a —** se puso histérico

frequency [fríkwənsi] N frecuencia *f*

frequent [fríkwənt] ADJ frecuente; VT frecuentar

fresh [freʃ] ADJ (pure, cool, not stale, not frozen, not tired) fresco; (new) nuevo; (bold) impertinente, atrevido; (healthy) lozano; **— out of school** recién salido de la escuela; **— paint** pintura fresca *f*; **— water** agua dulce *f*; **we're — out of ideas** se nos acabaron las ideas

freshen [fréʃən] VI/VT refrescar(se); **to — up** arreglarse, lavarse

freshman [fréʃmən] N (student) estudiante de primer año *mf*; (novice) novato -ta *mf*

freshness [fréʃnɪs] N (of food, of temperature) frescor *m*, frescura *f*; (of skin, flowers, youth) lozanía *f*; (of an idea) originalidad *f*; (impudence) descaro *m*

fret [fret] VI/VT (worry) preocupar(se); (irritate) irritar(se); N traste *m*

fretful [frétfəl] ADJ preocupado

friar [fráɪə] N fraile *m*

friction [fríkʃən] N fricción *f*, rozamiento *m*

Friday [fráɪde] N viernes *m*

fried [fraɪd] ADJ frito

friend [frend] N amigo -ga *mf*

friendliness [fréndlinɪs] N afabilidad *f*, simpatía *f*

friendly [fréndli] ADJ amistoso, simpático, amigable; **— advice** consejo de amigo *m*; **user-—** fácil de usar

friendship [fréndʃɪp] N amistad *f*

frigate [frígɪt] N fragata *f*

fright [fraɪt] N (fear) espanto *m*, susto *m*; (grotesque thing or person) espantajo *m*, esperpento *m*; **to take —** asustarse

frighten [fráɪtn] VI/VT espantar(se), asustar(se); **to — away** ahuyentar, espantar; **to get —ed** espantarse

frightened [fráɪtnd] ADJ asustado, espantado

frightful [fráɪtfəl] ADJ espantoso, pavoroso; **we had a — time** lo pasamos horrible; **he's a — flatterer** es un adulón espantoso

frigid [frídʒɪd] ADJ (of weather) gélido; (of personal relations) frío

frill [frɪl] N (trimming) volante *m*; (something superfluous) adorno *m*; **with no —s** sin lujos, sencillo

fringe [frɪndʒ] N (of a rug, etc.) fleco *m*, orla *f*; (of a city) periferia *f*; (of a political party) extremo *m*; (of society) margen *m*; **— benefits** prestaciones *f pl*, complementos *m pl*; VT orlar, poner un fleco

frisk [frɪsk] VI/VT (frolic) retozar, triscar; (search) cachear

frisky [fríski] ADJ retozón

fritter [frídə] VI/VT desmenuzar(se); VT **to — away** malgastar; VI irse gastando de poco a poco; N buñuelo *m*, churro *m*

frivolity [frɪváliɪi] N frivolidad *f*

frivolous [frívələs] ADJ frívolo

fro [fro] ADV **to and —** de aquí para allá

frock [frɑk] N (dress) vestido *m*; (habit) hábito *m*

frog [frɑg] N (animal) rana *f*; (fastener) alamar *m*; (of a hoof) ranilla *f*; (French person) *pej* franchute -ta *mf*; **to have a — in one's throat** tener gallos en la garganta; **—man** hombre rana *m*

frolic [frálɪk] N retozo *m*; VI retozar

from [frʌm] PREP desde; **— here to there** desde aquí hasta allá; **— two to four** de las dos a las cuatro; **— what I can tell** por lo que yo veo; **four hours — now** de aquí a cuatro horas, dentro de cuatro horas; **different — the other one** diferente del otro; **to come — Minnesota** ser de Minnesota; **death — starvation** muerte por inanición *f*

front [frʌnt] N frente *m*; (cover for illegal activity) pantalla *f*; **in — of** en frente de, delante de; **—-runner** favorito -ta *mf*; **—-wheel drive** tracción delantera *f*; ADJ delantero; VI/VT (face) dar a; (cover up) servir de pantalla

frontier [frʌntír] N frontera *f*; ADJ fronterizo; **— spirit** espíritu pionero *m*; **— town** pueblo fronterizo *m*

frost [frɔst] N helada *f*, escarcha *f*; VI/VT helar, escarchar; VT (a cake) bañar; (glass) esmerilar; (hair) hacer rayitos / reflejos; **—bite** necrosis por congelación *f*

frosting [frɔstɪŋ] N (of a cake) baño *m*; (for glass) esmerilado *m*; (of hair) rayos *m pl*, reflejos *m pl*

frosty [frɔsti] ADJ (cold, unfriendly) helado; (covered with frost) escarchado

froth [frɔθ] N espuma *f*; VI echar espuma; VT batir

frown [fraʊn] VI fruncir el ceño; **to — on** desaprobar; N ceño *m*

frozen [frózən] ADJ congelado

fructose [frúktos] N fructosa *f*

frugal [frúgəl] ADJ (economical) económico, ahorrativo; (meager) frugal

fruit [frut] N (food) fruta *f*; (plant part, product of labor) fruto *m*; **—cake** (food) torta de frutas secas *f*; (crazy person) *fam* chiflado -da *mf*

fruitful [frútfəl] ADJ fructífero

fruitless [frútlɪs] ADJ infructuoso

frumpy [frʌmpi] ADJ matrona

frustrate [frʌstret] VT frustrar; **to get —d** frustrar(se)

frustration [frʌstréʃən] N frustración *f*

fry [fraɪ] VI/VT (cook, also execute by electrocution) freír(se); **—ing pan** sartén *f*; N (fried potato) papa / patata frita *f*; (gathering with fried food) fiesta con comida frita *f*; (young fish) alevín *m*; **small —** gente menuda *f*

fudge [fʌdʒ] N turrón blando de chocolate *m*; VI (cheat) hacer trampa; (avoid an issue) dar rodeos

fuel [fjúəl] N (combustible) combustible *m*; (topic) tema *m*; **— injection** inyección *f*; **— oil** fuel-oil *m*; VT (a vehicle) llenar el tanque, cargar de combustible; (fire, debate) avivar

fugitive [fjúdʒɪɾɪv] ADJ (fleeing) fugitivo; (transitory) fugaz; N fugitivo -va *mf*, prófugo -ga *mf*

fulfill [fʊlfíl] VT (promise, order) cumplir; (need) satisfacer; **she doesn't feel —ed** no se siente realizada

fulfillment [fʊlfílmənt] N (of a promise, order) cumplimiento *m*; (of a need) satisfacción *f*; (of a person) realización *f*

full [fʊl] ADJ (completely filled) lleno; (complete) completo; (a dress) amplio; (a person's figure) relleno; (sated) harto; **—-blooded** de raza; **—-blown** (of disease) declarado; (complete) auténtico; **—-bodied** con cuerpo; **—-fledged** verdadero; **—-grown** adulto; **— house** full *m*; **—-length** (movie) de largometraje; (mirror) de cuerpo entero; **— moon** luna llena *f*; **—-scale** (model, etc.) de tamaño natural; (war) total; (investigation) exhaustivo; **—-service** de servicio completo; **—-size** (bed) de matrimonio; (model, etc.) de tamaño natural; **— time** tiempo completo *m*, de tiempo completo; **to pay in —** pagar el total de la deuda; ADV **you know — well**

sabes perfectamente; **it hit him — in
the chest** le pegó en pleno pecho
fully [fúli] ADV (entirely) completamente; (at
least) al menos
fumble [fámbəł] VI (search for) buscar a
tientas; (move clumsily) andar a tientas;
(blunder) meter la pata; **he —d his way
into the living room** entró a tientas a
la sala
fume [fjum] VI (be angry) rabiar; (emit
vapors, smoke) emitir humo; N **—s** gases
m pl, vapores *m pl*, tufo *m*
fumigate [fjúmɪget] VT fumigar
fun [fʌn] N diversión *f*; **for —** por gusto; **to
make — of** burlarse de; **to have —**
divertirse; ADJ divertido
function [fáŋkʃən] N (systems, computers,
etc.) función *f*; VI (work) funcionar; (serve)
oficiar
fund [fʌnd] N (of money) fondo *m*; (of
knowledge) acervo *m*; **—raising**
recaudación de fondos *f*; VT financiar
fundamental [fʌndəméntł] ADJ
fundamental; N fundamento *m*
fundamentalism [fʌndəméntłɪzəm] N
fundamentalismo *m*
funding [fándɪŋ] N financiamiento *m*,
financiación *f*
funeral [fjúnəəł] N funeral *m*, entierro *m*,
exequias *f pl*; **— director** director -ora de
pompas fúnebres *mf*; **— home** casa de
pompas fúnebres *f*, funeraria *f*; **— service**
funeral *m*; **it's your —** te estás cavando
tu propia tumba; (march, procession)
fúnebre; (pyre) funerario; (expenses) de
entierro
fungus [fáŋgəs] N hongo *m*
funky [fáŋki] ADJ (of music) funky; (strange)
estrafalario, raro; (smelly) hediondo
funnel [fánəł] N (for liquids) embudo *m*; (in
a chimney) humero *m*; VT canalizar,
encauzar
funny [fáni] ADJ (amusing) cómico, chistoso,
gracioso; (strange) raro; **— farm** *fam*
loquero *m*, loquería *f*; **that's not —** eso
no tiene gracia; **don't get — with me**
no te pases de listo; N **funnies** historietas
f pl, tiras cómicas *f pl*; ADV raro
fur [fɝ] N (hair) pelo *m*; (coat) pelaje *m*;
(hide) piel *f*; **— store** peletería *f*; VT forrar
de piel
furious [fjúriəs] ADJ (angry) furioso, sañudo,
rabioso; (fight, storm) feroz; (activity)
febril
furlough [fɝ́lo] N licencia *f*, permiso *m*; VT
dar licencia
furnace [fɝ́nɪs] N (for heating) caldera *f*; (in

industry) horno *m*
furnish [fɝ́nɪʃ] VT (put in furniture)
amueblar; (equip) equipar; (provide)
proporcionar, suministrar, facilitar
furniture [fɝ́nɪtʃə] N muebles *m pl*,
mobiliario *m*; **— store** mueblería *f*
furrow [fɝ́o] N surco *m*; VT (soil) arar; (face)
fruncir
furry [fɝ́i] ADJ peludo
further [fɝ́ðə] ADV **we want to go —**
queremos ir más lejos; **I refuse to
discuss this —** me niego a seguir
discutiendo esto; (furthermore) (lo que) es
más; ADJ (more distant) más lejano;
(additional) adicional; VT (promote)
promover; ADV **—more** además
furthest [fɝ́ðɪst] ADJ (el) más lejano, (el) más
remoto; ADV más lejos
furtive [fɝ́DIV] ADJ furtivo; (shifty)
sospechoso
fury [fjúri] N furia *f*, furor *m*, saña *f*
fuse [fjuz] N (in an explosive) mecha *f*; (in a
circuit) fusible *m*; **he has a short —** tiene
pocas pulgas; **he blew a —** estalló; VT (to
join) fusionar; VI/VT (to merge)
fusionar(se); (to blend metals) fundir(se)
fuselage [fjúsəlɑʒ] N fuselaje *m*
fusion [fjúʒən] N fusión *f*
fuss [fʌs] N (bustle) alboroto *m*, bulla *f*;
(uproar) escándalo *m*, alharaca *f*;
(argument) discusión *f*; VI (worry about
trifles) preocuparse por naderías;
(complain) quejarse
fussiness [fásɪnɪs] N remilgo *m*, ñoñería *f*
fussy [fási] ADJ (particular) quisquilloso,
remilgado; (overdecorated) recargado;
(whiny) quejica, cargoso
futile [fjúdł] ADJ inútil
futility [fjutílɪDi] N inutilidad *f*
future [fjútʃə] N futuro *m*, porvenir *m*; **—s**
futuros *m pl*; ADJ futuro
fuzz [fʌz] N (fluff) pelusa *f*; (fine hair) vello
fino *m*; (on the lip) bozo *m*
fuzzy [fázi] ADJ (fluffy) cubierto de pelusa;
(hairy) velloso; (blurred) borroso;
(muddled) confuso

Gg

gab [gæb] VI parlotear, charlar; N parloteo *m*,
charla *f*; **gift of —** labia *f*, facundia *f*
gable [gébəł] N hastial *m*; **— roof** tejado de
dos aguas *m*; **— window** buhardilla *f*

Gabon, Gabun [gəbón] N Gabón *m*
Gabonese [gæbəníz] ADJ & N gabonés -esa *mf*
gad [gæd] VI **to — about** callejear
gadget [gǽdʒɪt] N adminículo *m*
gaffe [gæf] N gaffe *f*, metedura de pata *f*
gag [gæg] VT (stop up mouth, silence) amordazar; (cause to choke) dar arcadas; VI tener arcadas; N (thing stuffed into mouth) mordaza *f*; (joke) gag *m*, burla *f*; **— order** orden de supresión de la libertad de expresión *f*
gaiety [géɪDi] N alegría *f*, **gaieties** festejos *m pl*
gain [gen] VT ganar; VI **to — on** irse acercando a; VI/VT (watch) adelantar; N (profit, act of gaining) ganancia *f*; (in weight) aumento *m*
gainful [génfəł] ADJ remunerado
gait [get] N marcha *f*, paso *m*
galaxy [gǽləksi] N galaxia *f*
gale [geł] N ventarrón *m*, vendaval *m*; **—-force winds** vientos huracanados *m pl*; **— of laughter** risotada *f*
Galicia [gəlíʃə] N Galicia *f*
Galician [gəlíʃən] ADJ & N gallego -ga *mf*
gall [gɔł] N (bile, bitterness) hiel *f*; (impudence) morro *m*; (of a plant) agalla *f*; **— bladder** vesícula (biliar) *f*; **—nut** agalla *f*; **—stone** cálculo biliar *m*; VT (irritate) irritar
gallant [gǽlənt] ADJ (brave) valiente; (attentive to women) galante; [gəlónt] N galán *m*
gallantry [gǽləntri] N (courage) valentía *f*, bizarría *f*; (chivalrous attention) galantería *f*
gallery [gǽləri] N (art, shopping) galería *f*; (theater) paraíso *m*, gallinero *m*; (golf) público *m*
galley [gǽli] N (kitchen) cocina *f*; (boat) galera *f*; **— proof** galerada *f*
gallium [gǽliəm] N galio *m*
gallon [gǽlən] N galón (3.7853 liters) *m*
gallop [gǽləp] VI galopar; N galope *m*
gallows [gǽloz] N horca *f*, cadalso *m*
galore [gəlór] ADV en abundancia
galoshes [gəlóʃíz] N chanclos *m pl*
galvanize [gǽłvənaɪz] VT (metals) galvanizar; (a crowd) electrizar
Gambia [gǽmbiə] N Gambia *f*
Gambian [gǽmbiən] ADJ & N gambiano -na *mf*
gamble [gǽmbəł] VI jugar; VT jugarse; **I'll — my whole fortune on this venture** voy a jugarme todo en este negocio; **to — away** perder en el juego; N (risk) riesgo *m*; (bet) apuesta *f*

gambler [gǽmblə] N apostador -ora *mf*, tahúr *m*
game [gem] N juego *m*; (match of chess, etc.) partida *f*; (sports match) partido *m*; (wild animals and their meat) caza *f*; **— show** programa concurso *m*; **to be fair —** ser blanco legítimo; ADJ **I'm — for some tennis** me apunto para jugar al tenis; **he has a — knee from years of rugby** tiene la rodilla lisiada después de años de jugar al rugby
gamut [gǽmət] N gama *f*
gander [gǽndə] N ganso (macho) *m*; **to take a — at** echarle un vistazo a
gang [gæŋ] N (of youths, thieves, etc.) pandilla *f*, gavilla *f*, banda *f*; (group of friends) grupo *m*; **—plank** pasarela *f*; **—way** (passage way) pasillo *m*; (on a ship) pasamano *m*; **—way!** ¡abran cancha! VI **to — up on** conspirar contra, conspirar en masa
gangrene [gǽŋgrin] N gangrena *f*; VI/VT gangrenar(se)
gangster [gǽŋstə] N gángster *m*, maleante *m*
gap [gæp] N (breach) brecha *f*, hueco *m*; (of memory) laguna *f*; (of time) intervalo *m*; **she has a — between her teeth** tiene los dientes separados; VT espaciar (correctamente)
gape [gep] VI mirar boquiabierto
garage [gərúʒ] N (for parking) garaje *m*; (for repairing) taller mecánico *m*; **— sale** venta de garaje *f*; VT estacionar en un garaje
garb [gɑrb] N vestimenta *f*, atavío *m*; VT vestir, ataviar
garbage [gárbɪdʒ] N basura *f*; **— can** bote de basura *m*; **— disposal unit** trituradora *f*; **—man** basurero *m*; **— truck** camión de la basura *m*; **what a lot of —!** ¡qué montón de mentiras!
garden [gárdn̩] N jardín *m*; **— of Eden** jardín del Edén *m*; VI cultivar una jardín
gardener [gárdnə] N jardinero -ra *mf*
gargle [gárgəł] VI hacer gárgaras; VT hacer gárgaras con; N (liquid) gargarismo *m*; (sound) gárgara *f*
garland [gárlənd] N guirnalda *f*
garlic [gárlɪk] N ajo *m*
garment [gármənt] N prenda *f*
garner [gárnə] VT cosechar
garnet [gárnɪt] N granate *m*
garnish [gárnɪʃ] VT (decorate) decorar; (decorate food) aderezar, guarnecer; (withhold wages) retener; N (decoration) adorno *m*, decoración *f*
garret [gǽrɪt] N desván *m*, buhardilla *f*

garrison [gǽrisən] N guarnición f; VT guarnecer

garrulous [gǽrələs] ADJ locuaz, gárrulo

garter [gárdɚ] N liga f; **— belt** liguero m, portaligas m sg; **— snake** culebra de jaretas f; VT sujetar con ligas

gas [gæs] N (vapor) gas m; (fuel) gasolina f; (flatulence) gases m pl; **— chamber** cámara de gas f; **— mask** máscara de gas f; **— pedal** acelerador m; **— station** gasolinera f; **we had a —** lo pasamos bomba; VT asfixiar con gas, matar en la cámara de gas; **to step on the —** acelerar; **to — up** llenar el tanque

gaseous [gǽʃəs] ADJ gaseoso

gash [gæʃ] N tajo m; VT hacer un tajo en

gasket [gǽskit] N junta (de culata) f

gasoline [gǽsəlin] N gasolina f, nafta f

gasp [gæsp] N (cry) grito sofocado m; (pant) jadeo m, boqueada f; VI (cry out) dar un grito sofocado; (in surprise) quedar boquiabierto; (for breath) jadear, boquear

gastric [gǽstrik] ADJ gástrico; **— ulcer** úlcera gástrica f

gastritis [gæstráiðis] N gastritis f

gastroenteritis [gæstroentəráiðis] N gastroenteritis f

gastrointestinal [gæstrointéstinəɫ] ADJ gastrointestinal

gastronomy [gæstránəmi] N gastronomía f

gate [get] N (to a garden) portón m; (to a city) puerta f; (at an airport) puerta de embarque f; **—way** (entrance, access) puerta (de entrada) f; (in computers) portal m

gather [gǽðɚ] VT (bring together) reunir, allegar; (pick) recolectar; (pick up, sort out) juntar; (deduce) deducir, colegir; (sew) fruncir; VI (come together) reunirse; (collect) juntarse; (contract into folds) fruncirse; **to — dust** juntar polvo/tierra; **to — speed** acelerar; N frunce m

gathering [gǽðɚɪŋ] N (meeting) asamblea f; (social) tertulia f; (assemblage of people) concurrencia f, reunión f; (act of gathering fruit, etc.) recolección f

gaudy [gɔ́di] ADJ (of bright color) chillón; (ostentatious) llamativo

gauge [gedʒ] VT (measure) medir; (estimate) estimar; (calibrate) calibrar; N (measurement standard) medida f; (caliber) calibre m; (measuring device) medidor m; (track width) entrevía f

gaunt [gɔnt] ADJ demacrado

gauntlet [gɔ́ntlit] N (glove) guante m; (mailed glove) guantelete m; **to throw down the —** retar, desafiar; **to run the**

— sufrir acosos

gauze [gɔz] N gasa f

gavel [gǽvəɫ] N martillo m

gawk [gɔk] VT mirar boquiabierto

gawky [gɔ́ki] ADJ torpe, desgarbado

gay [ge] ADJ (happy) alegre, festivo; (homosexual) homosexual; N fam homosexual m

gaze [gez] VI mirar fijamente, contemplar; N mirada fija f

gazelle [gəzéɫ] N gacela f

gazette [gəzét] N gaceta f

gear [gir] N (equipment) equipo m; (cog) rueda dentada f; (assembly of cogs) engranaje m; (speed) marcha f, cambio m; (personal property) pertenencias f pl; **—box** caja de cambios f; **—shift lever** palanca de cambios f; **to be in —** estar engranado; **to change —s** cambiar de marcha, poner el cambio; **to put into —** engranar; **to put out of —** desengranar; **to — up** prepararse

gearing [gírɪŋ] N engranaje m

gecko [gɛ́ko] N geco m

Geiger counter [gáigɚkáʊntɚ] N contador Geiger m

gel [dʒɛɫ] VI/VT cuajar(se)

gelatin [dʒɛ́lətn̩] N gelatina f

gem [dʒɛm] N (precious stone) gema f; (valuable person) joya f; **—stone** piedra preciosa f

gender [dʒɛ́ndɚ] N género m; **— gap** diferencias entre los sexos f pl; **—-specific** propio de un solo sexo

gene [dʒin] N gen m; **— marker** marcador genético m; **— pool** conjunto de genes de una población m; **— splicing** empalme genético m; **— therapy** terapia genética f

genealogy [dʒiniáladʒi] N genealogía f

general [dʒɛ́nɚəɫ] ADJ & N general m f; **in —** por lo general; **— practitioner** médico -ca general m f

generality [dʒɛnɚǽliði] N generalidad f

generalize [dʒɛ́nɚəlaiz] VI/VT generalizar

generate [dʒɛ́nɚet] VT generar

generation [dʒɛnɚéʃən] N generación f; **— gap** brecha generacional f, abismo generacional m

generator [dʒɛ́nɚeðɚ] N generador m

generic [dʒənɛ́rik] ADJ genérico

generosity [dʒɛnɚásiði] N generosidad f, larguesa f

generous [dʒɛ́nɚəs] ADJ generoso

genetic [dʒənéðik] ADJ genético; **— code** código genético m; **— engineering** ingeniería genética f; **— fingerprinting** identificación genética f; **— marker**

marcador genético *m*; **—s** genética *f*
genial [dʒínjəł] ADJ afable, de buen genio
genius [dʒínjəs] N genio *m*
genocide [dʒénəsaɪd] N genocidio *m*
genome [dʒínom] N genoma *m*
genre [ʒánrə] N género *m*
genteel [dʒentíł] ADJ refinado
gentile [dʒéntaɪł] ADJ & N gentil *mf*
gentle [dʒéntl] ADJ (kindly) amable; (mild, slow, gradual) suave; (tame) manso
gentleman [dʒéntłmən] N caballero *m*
gentlemanly [dʒéntłmənli] ADJ caballeroso
gentleness [dʒéntłnɪs] N (kindness) amabilidad *f*; (mildness) suavidad *f*; (tameness) mansedumbre *f*
genuine [dʒénjuɪn] ADJ genuino
genus [dʒínəs] N género *m*
geocentric [dʒioséntrɪk] ADJ geocéntrico
geographical [dʒiəgrǽfɪkəł] ADJ geográfico
geography [dʒiágrəfi] N geografía *f*
geological [dʒiəládʒɪkəł] ADJ geológico
geology [dʒiáłədʒi] N geología *f*
geometric [dʒiəmétrɪk] ADJ geométrico
geometry [dʒiámɪtri] N geometría *f*
geophysics [dʒiofízɪks] N geofísica *f*
Georgia [dʒórdʒə] N Georgia *f*
Georgian [dʒórdʒən] ADJ & N georgiano -na *mf*
geostationary [dʒiostéʃəneri] ADJ geoestacionario
geothermal [dʒioθɚ́məł] ADJ geotérmico
geranium [dʒɚéniəm] N geranio *m*
geriatric [dʒeriǽtrɪk] ADJ geriátrico
germ [dʒɚm] N (microorganism) microbio *m*, germen *m*; (bud, embryo, rudiment) germen *m*; **— warfare** guerra biológica *f*
German [dʒɚ́mən] ADJ & N alemán -na *mf*; **— measles** rubeola, rubéola *f*; **— shepherd** pastor alemán *m*
germane [dʒɚmén] ADJ pertinente, relacionado
Germany [dʒɚ́məni] N Alemania *f*
germinate [dʒɚ́mənet] VI germinar; VT hacer germinar
gerund [dʒérənd] N gerundio *m*
gestate [dʒéstet] VI/VT gestar(se)
gestation [dʒestéʃən] N gestación *f*
gesticulate [dʒestíkjəlet] VI gesticular
gesture [dʒéstʃɚ] N gesto *m*, ademán *m*; (token) muestra *f*; VI gesticular
gesundheit [gəzúnthaɪt] INTERJ ¡salud! *Sp* ¡Jesús!
get [get] VT (receive, earn) recibir; (obtain) obtener; (reach by phone, etc.) comunicarse con; (hear, understand) entender; (seize) agarrar; *Sp* coger; (prevail) conseguir, lograr; (affect) afectar; (strike)

pegar, dar; (catch disease) pescar; *Sp* coger; **to — across** comunicar; **to — ahead** prosperar; **to — along (with)** llevarse bien (con); **to — angry** enojarse; **to — around** (skirt) esquivar, evitar; (go out) salir mucho; **to — away** escapar(se); **to — away with** quedar impune; **—away** (escape) escape *m*; (vacation) escapada *f*; **to — back** (return) volver; (recover) recuperar; **to — back at** vengarse de; **to be —ting on in years** ponerse viejo; **to — by** (go past) pasar; (survive) ir tirando; **to — down** (lower oneself) bajar; (depress) deprimir; (swallow) tragar; **to — down to business / brass tacks** ir al grano; **from the —-go** desde el principio; **to — going** ponerse en marcha; **to — in** (enter) entrar; (arrive) llegar; (a vehicle) subir a; **to — it** captar, entender; **to — married** casarse; **to — nowhere** no llegar a ningún lado; **to — off** (dismount, get down) bajar; (not receive punishment) salir impune; (leave work) salir; **to — off on** enloquecerse por; **to — off someone's back** dejar de fastidiar; **to — old** envejecer; **to — on** montarse a; **to — out** (take out) sacar; (exit) salir; **to — over** (recuperate) recuperarse, sobreponerse a; (forgive) olvidar; **to — ready** preparar(se); **to — rich** enriquecerse; **to — rid of** deshacerse de; **to — sick** enfermarse; **to — somewhere** tener resultado; **to — through** (survive an ordeal) sobrevivir; (reach by phone, be understood) comunicarse; (complete) lograr terminar; **to — to someone** afectar a alguien; **to — together** reunirse; **—-together** reunión *f*; **to — up** (arise) levantarse; (prepare) montar; **—up** disfraz *m*, atuendo *m*; **I got him to do it** conseguí / logré que lo hiciera; **I have got to do it** tengo que hacerlo; **we got our house painted** pintamos la casa; **he got a year in jail** le dieron un año de cárcel; **we — to stay up late in summer** en el verano nos dejan quedarnos despiertos hasta tarde; **that —s my goat** eso me fastidia
geyser [gáɪzɚ] N géiser *m*
Ghana [gánə] N Ghana *f*
Ghanaian [gánəjən] ADJ & N ghanés -esa *mf*
ghastly [gǽstli] ADJ (horrible) horrendo, espantoso; (cadaverous) cadavérico
ghetto [gédo] N gueto *m*
ghost [gost] N fantasma *m*; **not a — of a chance** ni la menor posibilidad; **— town** pueblo fantasma *m*; **—writer** colaborador

-ora anónimo -ma *mf*
ghostly [góstli] ADJ fantasmagórico
ghoul [guɬ] N fantasma *m*
giant [dʒáiənt] N & ADJ gigante -ta *mf*
gibberish [dʒíbə‧ɪʃ] N jerigonza *f*
gibbon [gíbən] N gibón *m*
Gibraltar [dʒɪbrɔ́ɬtɚ] N Gibraltar *m*
Gibraltarian [dʒɪbrɔɬtériən] ADJ & N
gibraltareño -ña *mf*
giddy [gídi] ADJ (dizzy) mareado; (of heights)
vertigoso; (of speed) vertiginoso
gift [gɪft] N (thing given, act of giving) regalo
m, presente *m*; (special ability) don *m*; —
certificate vale por un regalo *m*;
—-**wrap** envolver para regalo; VT regalar
gifted [gíftɪd] ADJ (artist) talentoso; (child)
superdotado
gigabyte [gígəbaɪt] N gigabyte *m*
gigantic [dʒaɪgǽntɪk] ADJ gigantesco, gigante
giggle [gígəɬ] VI reír tontamente; N risita
tonta *f*
gild [gɪld] VT dorar
gill [gɪɬ] N agalla *f*
gilt [gɪɬt] ADJ & N dorado *m*
gimmick [gímɪk] N treta *f*, estratagema *f*
gin [dʒɪn] N (liquor) ginebra *f*; — **rummy** gin
rummy *m*
ginger [dʒíndʒɚ] N jengibre *m*; — **ale** ginger
ale *m*; —**bread** pan de jengibre *m*
gingham [gíŋəm] N guingán *m*
gingivitis [dʒɪndʒəváɪdɪs] N gingivitis *f*
giraffe [dʒɚǽf] N jirafa *f*
gird [gɚd] VT ceñir; **to — oneself** prepararse
girder [gɚ́dɚ] N viga *f*
girdle [gɚ́dɬ] N faja *f*; VT rodear
girl [gɚɬ] N (female child) niña *f*; (young
female) muchacha *f*, joven *f*, chica *f*;
(servant) muchacha *f*, chacha *f*; —**friend**
novia *f*
girlhood [gɚ́lhʊd] N niñez *f*
girlish [gɚ́lɪʃ] ADJ de niña
girth [gɚθ] N (of things) circunferencia *f*; (of
persons) contorno *m*; (of horses) cincha *f*;
VT cinchar
gist [dʒɪst] N esencia *f*, lo esencial
give [gɪv] VT dar; (present as a gift) regalar;
(organize a party) organizar; (assign a .
name) poner; (donate) donar; **I don't —
a hoot** me importa un comino; VI dar;
(yield) ceder; (break) romperse; **to —
away** (a gift) regalar, donar; (the bride)
entregar; (the truth) revelar; **to — back**
devolver; **to — in** (acknowledge defeat)
rendirse; (hand in) entregar; **to — off**
emitir, despedir, desprender; **to — out**
(announce) anunciar; (distribute) repartir;
(become exhausted) rendirse; (run out)

acabarse; **to — over** entregar; **to — up**
(surrender) darse por vencido; (stop) dejar
(de); **we'll work on this two years, —
or take a month** vamos a trabajar en
esto dos años, un mes más, un mes
menos; N elasticidad *f*; — **and take** toma
y daca *m*
given [gívən] ADJ (stated, fixed) dado;
(bestowed) regalado; — **name** nombre de
pila *m*; — **that she's not here** dado que
ella no está; — **to** propenso a; N premisa *f*
giver [gívɚ] N dador -ora *mf*, donador -ora *mf*
gizmo [gízmo] N coso *m*, chisme *m*
glacial [gléʃəɬ] ADJ glacial
glacier [gléʃɚ] N glaciar *m*
glad [glæd] ADJ contento; **I'm — to see you**
me alegro de verte; **I'd be — to help**
sería un placer ayudarte
gladden [glǽdn̩] VT alegrar, regocijar,
alborozar
gladiator [glǽdietɚ] N gladiador *m*
glamorous [glǽmɚəs] ADJ glamoroso,
encantador
glamour [glǽmɚ] N (charm) glamour *f*,
encanto *m*; (excitement) atractivo *m*
glance [glæns] VI echar un vistazo; **to — off**
rebotar con efecto; N (look) vistazo *m*;
(bounce) rebote oblicuo *m*
gland [glænd] N glándula *f*
glandular [glǽndʒəlɚ] ADJ glandular
glare [gler] N (bright light) relumbre *m*;
(stare) mirada furiosa *f*; VI (shine)
relumbrar; (stare fiercely) lanzar una
mirada hostil
glaring [glérɪŋ] ADJ (blinding) deslumbrante;
(obvious) evidente; (hostile) hostil
glass [glæs] N (substance) vidrio *m*; (window
pane) vidrio *m*, cristal *m*; (tumbler) vaso
(de vidrio) *m*; (mirror) espejo *m*;
(glassware) cristalería *f*; (magnifier) lupa *f*;
—**blowing** soplado de vidrio *m*; —
cutter cortavidrio *m*; —**es** anteojos *m pl*,
lentes *m pl*, gafas *f pl*; — **eye** ojo de vidrio
m; —**maker** vidriero -ra *mf*; —**ware**
cristalería *f*
glassy [glǽsi] ADJ vidrioso
glaucoma [glɔkómə] N glaucoma *m*
glaze [glez] VT (a window) poner vidrios a;
(ceramic) vidriar; (food) glasear; (varnish)
barnizar; VI vidriarse; N (pottery) vidriado
m, barniz *m*; (food) glaseado *m*
glazier [gléʒɚ] N vidriero -ra *mf*
gleam [glim] N reflejo *m*, brillo *m*; **a — of
hope** un rayo de esperanza; VI brillar,
relucir
glean [glin] VT (grain) espigar; (information)
extraer, deducir

glee [gli] N regocijo *m*, júbilo *m*; **— club** coro *m*

glib [glɪb] ADJ (fluent) de mucha labia; (superficial) simplista, superficial

glide [glaɪd] VI (slide) deslizarse; (fly) planear; N (sliding movement) deslizamiento *m*; (flight) planeo *m*

glider [gláɪdɚ] N planeador *m*

glimmer [glímɚ] N luz trémula *f*; **a — of hope** un destello de esperanza; **the — of an idea** el atisbo de una idea; VI guiñar, emitir una luz trémula

glimpse [glɪmps] N (look) ojeada *f*, vistazo *m*; (hint) atisbo *m*; VT ojear

glint [glɪnt] N destello *m*; VI destellar

glisten [glísən] VI brillar, relucir

glitch [glɪtʃ] N problema técnico *m*

glitter [glídɚ] VI destellar; N (light) destello *m*; (showiness) brillo *m*; (sparkling powder) brillantina *f*

gloat [glot] VI regodearse; N regodeo *m*

glob [glɑb] N pegote *m*

global [glóbəl] ADJ global, mundial; **— positioning system** sistema mundial de posicionamiento *m*; **— warming** calentamiento global *m*

globe [glob] N globo *m*; (map of the Earth) globo terráqueo *m*

globule [glábjul] N glóbulo *m*

gloom [glum] N (darkness) oscuridad *f*; (melancholy) melancolía *f*, tristeza *f*

gloomy [glúmi] ADJ (dark, depressing) sombrío, lúgubre, tenebroso; (melancholic) melancólico, deprimido

glorify [glɔ́rəfaɪ] VT glorificar

glorious [glɔ́riəs] ADJ (wonderful) magnífico, excelente; (related to glory) glorioso

glory [glɔ́ri] N gloria *f*; VI **to — in** regocijarse con

gloss [glɔs] N (shine) brillo *m* (also cosmetics); (marginal note) glosa *f*; (in a dictionary) acepción *f*; VT (polish) lustrar, dar brillo a; (explain) glosar; **to — over** disfrazar, encubrir

glossary [glɔ́səri] N glosario *m*

glossy [glɔ́si] ADJ lustroso; (paper) glaseado

glove [glʌv] N guante *m*; **— compartment** guantera *f*

glow [glo] N incandescencia *f*; (of cheeks) rubor *m*; (of emotion) calor *m*; VI resplandecer; (of metal) estar al rojo vivo; (of cheeks) ruborizarse; **to — with health** estar rebosante de salud; **—worm** luciérnaga *f*

glowing [glóɪŋ] ADJ (with light) incandescente; (colors) vivo; (with health) rebosante; (report, etc.) favorable

glucose [glúkos] N glucosa *f*

glue [glu] N cola *f*, pegamento *m*; VT (put glue on) engomar; (stick together) pegar; (stick wood together) encolar

glum [glʌm] ADJ tristón

glut [glʌt] VI/VT (with food) hartar(se); VT (with products) saturar; N exceso *m*

glutton [glʌ́tn̩] N glotón -ona *mf*

gluttonous [glʌ́tnəs] ADJ glotón

gluttony [glʌ́tn̩i] N glotonería *f*, gula *f*

glycerin [glísəɪn] N glicerina *f*

gnarled [nɑrld] ADJ (knotty) nudoso, sarmentoso; (twisted) retorcido

gnash [næʃ] VI/VT rechinar

gnat [næt] N jején *m*

gnaw [nɔ] VI/VT (bite, corrode) roer; (torment) remorder; **to — a hole** hacer un agujero a mordiscos

GNP (gross national product) [dʒiɛnpí] N PNB *m*

gnu [nu] N ñu *m*

go [go] VI (move) ir; (function) andar, marchar; **to — against** oponerse a; **to — ahead** seguir adelante; **—-ahead** visto bueno *m*; **to — all out** dar todo de sí; **to — along** estar de acuerdo; **to — around** (circumvent) dar la vuelta a; (circulate) circular; (be sufficient) alcanzar; **to — around with** andar con; **to — away** irse; **to — back** volver; **to — back on one's word** faltar a la palabra; **—-between** intermediario -ria *mf*; **to — beyond** traspasar; **to — by** (pass) pasar; (be guided by) guiarse por; **to — by another name** usar otro nombre; **to — crazy** enloquecerse; **—-cart** kart *m*; **to — down** (descend) bajar; (fall) caer, estrellarse; (lose) perder; (be accepted) gustar; **to — for** (attack) atacar; **pizza to — pizza para llevar; **to — in with** participar; **to — it alone** tirarse solo; **to — off** (explode) estallar; (happen) suceder; (leave) irse; **to — on** (happen) pasar; (continue) seguir; **to — out** (extinguish) apagarse; (socialize) salir; **to — over** (review) repasar, revisar; (be accepted) gustar; (read) leer; (cross) cruzar; **to — through** (suffer) sufrir; (examine) examinar; (be approved) ser aprobado; (spend) gastar; **to — through with** llevar a cabo; **to — to sleep** dormirse; **to — under** (go bankrupt) quebrar; (sink) hundirse; **to — up** (building) levantarse; (prices) subir; **to let — soltar(se); **the car went for a good price** el coche se vendió a un buen precio; **he's smart, as dogs — para ser perro, es inteligente;

that old couch **has got to —** hay que deshacernos de ese sofá viejo; **cows — "moo"** las vacas hacen "mu"; **she went straight for the pizza** se fue derechito a la pizza; **she's —ing to buy a house** va a comprar una casa; **anything —s** todo vale; **what I say —s** lo que yo digo, vale; **don't — to any trouble** no te molestes; **— figure!** ¡vaya a saber uno! **I've got to — (to the bathroom)** tengo que ir al baño; N (energy) energía f; (attempt) intento m; **in one —** de una vez; **on the —** a las corridas; **at the first — de** primera; **they made a — of it** tuvieron éxito; **it's a —** ¡trato hecho! **from the word —** desde el vamos

goad [god] N aguijada f; VT aguijonear

goal [goɫ] N (objective) meta f; (score) gol m; **—keeper** portero -ra f

goalie [góli] N guardameta mf

goat [got] N cabra f; **—herd** cabrero -ra mf; **he gets my —** me saca de quicio

goatee [gotí] N perilla f

gobble [gábəɫ] VI/VT (devour) engullir; VI (turkey) gluglutear; **to — up** engullir

gobbledygook [gábəɫdiguk] N jerigonza f

gobbler [gáblə-] N pavo m

goblet [gáblɪt] N copa f

goblin [gáblɪn] N duende m

god, God [gad] N dios m, Dios m; **God bless you!** ¡que Dios te bendiga! (after a sneeze) ¡salud! ¡Jesús! **—child** ahijado -da mf; **—father** padrino m; **—forsaken** de mala muerte; **—given** divino; **—mother** madrina f; **—send** bendición f; **God willing** si Dios quiere; **by God** por Dios; **my God!** ¡Dios mío!

goddess [gádɪs] N diosa f

godless [gádlɪs] ADJ impío

godly [gádlij] ADJ piadoso

goggles [gágəɫz] N gafas protectoras f pl, antiparras f pl

going [góɪŋ] ADJ que marcha bien; **—s-on** tejemaneje m

gold [goɫd] N oro m; **a heart of —** un corazón de oro; **— digger** mujer cazafortunas f; **—finch** jilguero m; **—fish** pez dorado m; **— medal** medalla de oro f; **—smith** orfebre m

golden [góɫdən] ADJ (made of gold) de oro, áureo; (of gold color) dorado; **— eagle** águila dorada f; **— retriever** golden retriever m; **— rule** regla de oro f

golf [gaɫf] N golf m; **— ball** pelota de golf f; **— club** (stick) palo de golf m; (place) club de golf m; **— course** campo de golf m

gondola [gándələ] N (boat, basket under a balloon) góndola f; (cable car) cabina f

gone [gɔn] ADJ **my computer is —** desapareció mi computadora; **the candy is all —** se acabaron los dulces

gong [gaŋ] N batintín m, gong m

gonorrhea [ganəríə] N gonorrea f

good [gud] ADJ bueno; (valid) válido; **—for-nothing** inútil, zanguango; **—looking** guapo, apuesto; **—natured** apacible, bonachón; **for —** para siempre; **a — hour** una hora larga; **a — many** muchos; **to have a — time** divertirse; **to make —** cumplir; **to smell —** oler bien; N (moral act, benefit) bien m; **— for two burritos** vale por dos burritos; **—s** mercancías f pl; **—s and services** bienes y servicios m pl; **for your own —** por tu propio bien; **to deliver the —s** cumplir lo prometido; INTERJ ¡bien! **— afternoon** buenas tardes; **—bye** adiós; **— day** buenos días; **— evening** buenas noches; **— morning** buenos días; **— night** buenas noches

goodly [gúdli] ADJ (considerable) considerable; (of fine appearance) de buen aspecto

goodness [gúdnɪs] N bondad f; (of food) calidad f; INTERJ ¡Dios mío!

goody [gudi] N golosina f; **——** santurrón -ona mf; INTERJ ¡qué bien!

goof [guf] VI pifiar; **to — off** perder el tiempo; **to — up** pifiarla; N pifia f

goofy [gúfi] ADJ (person) bobalicón; (idea) tonto

goose [gus] N ganso -sa mf (also fool); VT sorprender a alguien tocándole entre las nalgas; **—berry** (berry) grosella espinosa f; (bush) grosellero m; **—bumps** carne de gallina f; **— egg** cero m

GOP (Grand Old Party) [dʒiopí] N Partido Republicano m

gopher [gófə-] N ardilla de tierra f

gore [gɔr] N sangre derramada f; VT cornear

gorge [gɔrdʒ] N (body part) garganta f; (ravine) garganta f, tajo m; VI **to — one's self (on)** atracarse (de), darse un atracón (de)

gorgeous [gɔ́rdʒəs] ADJ (woman, outfit) precioso; (weather) espléndido

gorilla [gərílə] N gorila mf; (thug) matón m

gory [gɔ́ri] ADJ (of a battle) sangriento; (of a surface) ensangrentado

gospel [gáspəɫ] N evangelio m; (music) gospel m; **— truth** pura verdad f

gossip [gásəp] N (rumor) chismorreo m, murmuración f, habladurías f pl; (person) chismoso -sa mf; (woman) comadre f; **a**

piece of — us chisme; vi chismear, murmurar

gossipy [gásəpi] ADJ chismoso, lenguaraz

Gothic [gúθik] ADJ gótico (also literature); N (language) gótico *m*; (style) estilo gótico *m*

gouge [gaudʒ] N gubia *f*; vt (scoop) sacar con gubia; (overcharge) cobrar de más; **to — someone's eyes out** arrancarle los ojos a alguien

gourd [gɔrd] N calabaza *f*

gourmet [gɔrmé] N & ADJ gourmet *mf*; **— cheese** queso fino *m*

gout [gaut] N gota *f*

govern [gávən] vi/vt gobernar, regir; vt (in grammar) regir

governess [gávənis] N institutriz *f*

government [gávənmənt] N gobierno *m*; (in grammar) rección *f*

governmental [gavə-nméntl] ADJ gubernamental, gubernativo

governor [gávənə-] N (leader) gobernador -ora *mf*; (of an engine) regulador *m*

gown [gaun] N (woman's dress) vestido *m*; (for sleeping) camisón *m*; (in hospital) bata *f*; (for graduation) toga *f*

grab [græb] vt agarrar, prender; **how does that idea — you?** ¿qué te parece esa idea? vi **to — at** tratar de agarrar; N agarrón *m*; **up for —s** a la rebatiña

grace [gres] N gracia *f*; (of movement) garbo *m*; (of expression) donaire *m*; **to say —** decir la oración; **to be in the good —s of someone** gozar del favor de alguien, disfrutar de la gracia de alguien; vt (adorn) adornar; (honor) honrar, agraciar

graceful [grésfəl] ADJ (of movement) grácil, garboso; (of behavior) donoso

gracefulness [grésfəlnis] N gracia *f*, donaire *m*

gracious [gréʃəs] ADJ (kind) gentil, cortés; (elegant) elegante; (merciful) misericordioso; **—!** ¡válgame Dios!

graciousness [gréʃəsnis] N gentileza *f*

gradation [gredéʃən] N gradación *f*

grade [gred] N (degree) grado *m*; (category) calidad *f*; (year in school) año *m*, curso *m*; (marks) nota *f*, calificación *f*; (slope) declive *m*; **to make the —** alcanzar el nivel deseado; **— point average** promedio de notas *m*; vt (classify) clasificar; (assign grades) calificar, corregir; (level) nivelar

gradual [grǽdʒuəl] ADJ gradual

graduate [grǽdʒuit] N (advanced student) estudiante de posgrado *mf*; (degree-holder) graduado -da *mf*, egresado -da *mf*; ADJ de posgrado; **— school** programa de posgrado *m*; [grǽdʒuet] vi graduarse, titularse; vt (confer a degree) dar un diploma a; (mark a scale) graduar

graduation [grædʒuéʃən] N graduación *f*

graffiti [grəfíDi] N graffiti *m*

graft [græft] N (of plant, tissue) injerto *m*; (corruption) concusión *f*, corrupción *f*; vi/vt injertar(se)

grain [gren] N (cereal, seed) grano *m*, mies *f*; (photographic texture) grano *m*; (of gold) pepita *f*; (of wood, meat, stone) veta *f*; (texture) textura *f*; (small amount) pizca *f*; **against the —** a/al redopelo, a contrapelo

gram [græm] N gramo *m*

grammar [grǽmə-] N gramática *f*

grammatical [grəmǽDikəl] ADJ gramatical

granary [grénəri] N granero *m*, troje *m*

grand [grænd] ADJ (splendid) grandioso, espléndido; (lofty) elevado; (impressive) impresionante; **—child** nieto -ta *mf*; **—children** nietos *m pl*; **—daughter** nieta *f*; **—father** abuelo *m*; **— jury** jurado de acusación *m*; **—mother** abuela *f*; **—ma** abuelita *f*; **—pa** abuelito *m*; **—parent** abuelo *m*; **—parents** abuelos *m pl*; **— piano** piano de cola *m*; **—son** nieto *m*; **—stand** tribuna *f*; **a — old man** un gran señor; **the — total** el total

grandeur [grǽndʒə-] N grandiosidad *f*

grandiose [grǽndios] ADJ (complex) complejo; (of speech) grandilocuente, rimbombante; (imposing) grandioso

granite [grǽnit] N granito *m*

grant [grænt] vt (give) conceder, otorgar, dispensar; (accept) admitir; (transfer) ceder; **to take for —ed** (an assumption) dar por sentado; (a person) no valorar; N (something granted) concesión *f*; (act of granting) concesión *f*, otorgamiento *m*; (subsidy) subvención *f*

granulate [grǽnjəlet] vi/vt granular(se)

grape [grep] N uva *f*; **—fruit** pomelo *m*, toronja *f*; **—vine** vid *f*; (ornamental) parra *f*; **I heard it through the —vine** me lo contó un pajarito

graph [græf] N (curve) gráfica *f*; vt grafiar; **— paper** papel cuadriculado *m*

graphic [grǽfik] ADJ gráfico; **— design** diseño gráfico *m*; N gráfico *m*; **—s** gráfica *f*

graphite [grǽfait] N grafito *m*

grapple [grǽpəl] vi/vt (hold) aferrar; (struggle) luchar, lidiar

grasp [græsp] vt (seize) agarrar, asir, aferrar; (understand) comprender; vi **to — at/for** tratar de agarrar; N (hold) agarre *m*, asidero *m*; (comprehension) comprensión *f;* **within one's —** al alcance; **to have a good — of a subject** dominar una materia

grass [græs] N (plant) hierba *f;* (lawn) césped *m;* (pasture) pasto *m;* **—hopper** saltamontes *m sg,* saltón *m;* **—land** pradera *f,* pastizal *m;* **— roots** las bases *f pl*

grassy [græsi] ADJ herboso

grate [gret] N (of a fireplace) parrilla *f;* (partition, guard) reja *f,* verja *f;* VT (install a grate) enrejar; (mince) rallar; (rub teeth together) crujir, rechinar; VI **to — on** rechinar

grateful [grétfəl] ADJ agradecido

grater [grédə] N rallador *m*

gratification [grædəfikéʃən] N gratificación *f*

gratify [grædəfaɪ] VT complacer, gratificar

grating [grédɪŋ] N reja *f,* enrejado *m,* rejilla *f;* ADJ (discordant) rechinante; (irritating) irritante

gratitude [grædɪtud] N gratitud *f*

gratuitous [grətúɪdəs] ADJ gratuito

gratuity [grətúɪdi] N propina *f*

grave [grev] ADJ grave; N fosa *f,* sepultura *f;* **—digger** sepulturero *m;* **—stone** lápida *f;* **—yard** cementerio *m;* **—yard shift** turno de la noche *m;* **to have one foot in the —** *fam* estar por reventar

gravel [grævəl] N grava *f;* VT cubrir con grava

gravitation [grævitéʃən] N gravitación *f*

gravity [grævɪdi] N gravedad *f* (also seriousness)

gravy [grévi] N jugo de carne *m;* **the rest is —** el resto es fácil

gray [gre] ADJ gris; (hair) canoso; (horses) rucio; **— area** zona gris *f;* **—haired** cano, canoso; **— matter** materia gris *f;* N gris *m;* VI/VT agrisar; (hair) encanecer

grayish [gréɪʃ] ADJ grisáceo

graze [grez] VI/VT (feed) pacer, pastar, apacentar; (brush) rozar; N roce *m*

grease [gris] N grasa *f;* VT engrasar; **to — someone's palm** untarle la mano a alguien, engrasar a alguien

greasy [grísi, grízi] ADJ grasiento, grasoso

great [gret] ADJ (large, numerous) grande; **a — tree blocked the path** un árbol grande bloqueaba el camino; (good, excellent, considerable) gran; **she's a — friend** es una gran amiga; (long) largo; **a — while** un largo rato; (skillful) excelente; **she's — at tennis** juega muy bien al tenis; **a — deal of** mucho; ADV muy bien, excelente; **she did —** le fue muy bien; N **the —s** los/las grandes *mf;* **—grandchild** bisnieto -ta *mf;*

—grandfather bisabuelo *m;* **—grandmother** bisabuela *f;* **———grandchild** tataranieto -ta *mf;* INTERJ ¡qué bien!

greatness [grétnɪs] N grandeza *f*

Greece [gris] N Grecia *f*

greed [grid] N codicia *f*

greedy [grídi] ADJ (covetous) codicioso; (voracious) voraz; (eager) ávido

Greek [grik] ADJ & N griego -ga *mf;* **that's — to me** eso es chino

green [grin] ADJ verde; (verdant, unripe, inexperienced, nauseated, environmentally conscious) verde; N (color) verde *m;* (lawn) césped *m;* (pasture) prado *m;* (in golf) green *m;* (commons) ejido *m;* **—back** dólar *m;* **— bean** *Sp* judía verde *f; Mex* ejote *m; RP* chaucha *f;* **— card** tarjeta verde *f;* **—horn** novato -ta *mf;* **—house** invernadero *m;* **—house effect** efecto invernadero *m;* **— light** luz verde *f;* **— pepper** pimiento verde *m;* **—s** verduras de hoja verde *f pl*

greenish [gríniʃ] ADJ verdoso

greenness [grínnɪs] N verdor *m*

greet [grit] VT (say hello) saludar; (welcome) dar la bienvenida; (receive) recibir

greeting [grídɪŋ] N saludo *m;* **— card** tarjeta de felicitación *f;* **—s!** ¡saludos!

gregarious [grɪgériəs] ADJ (animal) gregario; (person) sociable

gremlin [grémlɪn] N duende *m*

Grenada [grənédə] N Granada *f*

grenade [grənéd] N granada *f*

Grenadian [grənédiən] ADJ & N granadino -na *mf*

greyhound [gréhaʊnd] N galgo *m*

griddle [grídl] N plancha *f*

gridlock [grídlɑk] N paralización *f;* VI paralizarse

grief [grif] N congoja *f,* pesar *m,* pesadumbre *f;* **to come to —** sufrir una desgracia; **to give someone —** meterse con alguien, jorobar a alguien; **good —!** ¡caramba!

grievance [grívəns] N (complaint) queja *f;* (cause for complaint) motivo de queja *m*

grieve [griv] VI estar de duelo; **to — for/over** llorar (la muerte de alguien); **he's grieving over the loss of his dog** lamenta la muerte de su perro; VT **that —s me** eso me apena

grieved [grivd] ADJ apenado

grievous [grívəs] ADJ (painful) doloroso, penoso; (atrocious) grave, atroz; (sorrowful) dolido

grill [grɪl] N (metal grid, restaurant fixture) parrilla *f;* (dish) parrillada *f;* VI/VT asar a la parrilla; (interrogate) interrogar

grille [grɪl] N parrilla *f*

grim [grɪm] ADJ (news, situation) desalentador; (war) cruento; (joke) macabro

grimace [grímɪs] N mueca *f*, mohín *m*; VI hacer muecas

grime [graɪm] N mugre *f*, suciedad *f*

grimy [gráɪmi] ADJ mugriento, sucio; **to make —** percudir; **to get —** percudirse

grin [grɪn] VI sonreír; N sonrisa *f*; **wipe that — off your face** deja de reírte

grind [graɪnd] VI/VT (mill finely) moler; (mill coarsely) triturar; (make shiny) pulir; (rub harshly) rechinar; (study hard) estudiar mucho; *Sp* empollar; **to — to a halt** pararse con un chirrido; N (drudgery) trabajo pesado *m*; (overzealous student) empollón -ona *mf*; **the daily —** la lucha diaria; **—stone** muela *f*; **to keep one's nose to the —stone** matarse trabajando / estudiando

grinder [gráɪndɚ] N (for coffee, pepper) molinillo *m*; (for meat) picadora *f*; (for sharpening tools) afilador *m*

grip [grɪp] N (hold) agarre *m*; (control) control *m*; (handle) mango *m*; **he had a firm — on the tool** tenía bien agarrada la herramienta; **get a — on yourself** contrólate, cálmate; VT (seize) agarrar, asir; (take hold, interest) atrapar

gripe [graɪp] VI quejarse, rezongar, renegar; N queja *f*

grisly [grízli] ADJ cruento, espantoso

gristle [grísəl] N cartílago *m*

grit [grɪt] N (sand) arena *f*; (pluck) firmeza *f*, *fam* cojones *m pl*; **—s** sémola de maíz *f*; VT apretar

gritty [grídi] ADJ (sandy) arenoso; (plucky) resuelto, *fam* cojonudo

grizzly [grízli] ADJ (grayish) grisáceo; **— bear** oso pardo *m*

groan [gron] N quejido *m*, gemido *m*; VI quejarse, gemir; (creak) crujir

grocer [grósɚ] N tendero -ra *mf*; *Mex* abarrotero -ra *mf*; *Caribbean* bodeguero -ra *mf*; *RP* almacenero -ra *mf*

grocery [grósəri] N tienda de comestibles *f*; *Mex* tienda de abarrotes *f*; *Caribbean* bodega *f*; *RP* almacén *m*; **groceries** comestibles *m pl*

groin [grɔɪn] N ingle *f*

groom [grum] N (in a wedding) novio *m*; (in a stable) mozo de cuadra *m*, caballerizo *m*; VT (a horse) almohazar; (prepare for a position) preparar; **to — oneself** arreglarse; **well-—ed** bien arreglado

groove [gruv] N (narrow cut) estría *f*, ranura *f*; (on a record, road) surco *m*; (routine) rutina *f*; VT estriar, acanalar

grope [grop] VI (feel one's way) andar a tientas; (search) buscar a tientas; VT manosear; N manoseo *m*, toqueteo *m*

gross [gros] ADJ (before deductions) bruto; (flagrant) flagrante; (indecent) grosero; (overall) general; (disgusting) asqueroso; **— domestic product** producto interno bruto *m*; N gruesa *f*; VT recaudar en bruto; **to — out** dar asco, asquear

grotesque [grotésk] ADJ grotesco

grotto [gráɾo] N gruta *f*

grouch [graʊtʃ] N cascarrabias *mf sg*, refunfuñón -ona *mf*, rezongón -ona *mf*; VI refunfuñar

grouchy [gráʊtʃi] ADJ cascarrabias, refunfuñón

ground [graʊnd] N (land) tierra *f* (also electrical); (soil) suelo *m*; (basis) fundamento *m*, **—s** (reason) motivo *m*; (dregs) borra *f*, poso *m*; (tract of land) terreno *m*; **— floor** planta baja *f*; **—hog** marmota *f*; **to gain / lose —** ganar / perder terreno; **to stand one's —** ponerse firme; **from the — up** de piso a techo; VT (a wire) conectar a tierra; (a ship) hacer encallar; (punish) poner en penitencia; **the 747 was —ed** se prohibió volar en el 747

groundless [gráʊndlɪs] ADJ infundado

group [grup] N grupo *m*; **— therapy** terapia de grupo *f*; VI/VT agrupar(se)

grouper [grúpɚ] N mero *m*

groupie [grúpi] N admirador -ra *mf*

grove [grov] N arboleda *f*, plantío *m*; **orange —** naranjal *m*

grovel [grávəl] VI arrastrarse, humillarse

grow [gro] VI (naturally increase in size) crecer; (increase) aumentar, acrecentarse; (expand) desarrollarse; VT (crops) cultivar; (beard) dejarse crecer; **to — old** envejecer; **to — up** madurar; **Thai food —s on you** la comida tailandesa acaba gustándote

growl [graʊl] VI gruñir; (of thunder) retumbar; (of stomach) rugir; N gruñido *m*

grown [gron] ADJ adulto; **— man** hombre hecho y derecho *m*; **— up** adulto *m*; **—-up** para adultos

growth [groθ] N (increase in size) crecimiento *m*; (increase in number) aumento *m*, acrecentamiento *m*; (tumor) bulto *m*; (expansion) desarrollo *m*; **a — industry** una industria en expansión

grudge [grʌdʒ] N resentimiento *m*

grueling [grúəlɪŋ] ADJ arduo

gruesome [grúsəm] ADJ cruento, truculento

gruff [grʌf] ADJ (manner) bronco; (voice) ronco

grumble [grʌ́mbəł] VI/VT refunfuñar, rezongar; N refunfuño m, gruñido m

grumpy [grʌ́mpi] ADJ refunfuñón, gruñón, rezongón

grunt [grʌnt] VI/VT gruñir; N gruñido m

guarantee [gærəntí] N (promise, pledge) garantía f; (guaranty) fianza f; VT (promise, pledge) garantizar; (warrant) dar fianza, avalar

guarantor [gǽrəntɔr] N fiador -ora mf

guaranty [gǽrənti] N (guarantee) garantía f; (thing taken as security) fianza f; (guarantor) fiador -ora mf

guard [gɑrd] VT custodiar; (watch over) vigilar; (protect) proteger; VI protegerse; **to — against** guardarse de; N (person that guards) guardia mf, guarda mf; (of a machine) dispositivo protector m; **to be on —** estar alerta / estar en guardia; **— dog** perro guardián m; **—rail** baranda f, pasamano m

guardian [gɑ́rdiən] N guardián -ana mf; (legal) tutor -ora mf; **— angel** ángel de la guarda m

guardianship [gɑ́rdiənʃɪp] N tutela f

Guatemala [gwɑɾəmálə] N Guatemala f

Guatemalan [gwɑɾəmálən] ADJ & N guatemalteco -ca mf

guava [gwávə] N guayaba f

guess [ges] VT (hazard, conjecture) adivinar; (suppose) suponer; N (conjecture) conjetura f; (supposition) suposición f; **I'll give you three —es** te doy tres oportunidades para adivinar

guest [gest] N (to a party, function) invitado -da mf; (to a restaurant) cliente mf; (overnight) huésped mf

guffaw [gəfɔ́] N carcajada f, risotada f

guidance [gáɪdn̩s] N (act of guiding) dirección f; (counsel) orientación f; (in a missile) teledirección f

guide [gaɪd] VT guiar; (force to move) dirigir; (counsel) orientar; N (person) guía mf; (publication, mechanism) guía f; **—book** guía f; **— dog** perro guía m; **—d missile** misil guiado m; **—lines** directivas f pl, pautas f pl

guild [gɪłd] N gremio m, corporación f

guile [gaɪł] N astucia f

guilt [gɪłt] N culpa f; **— trip** manipulación por acusaciones falsas f

guiltless [gɪ́łtlɪs] ADJ inocente

guilty [gɪ́łti] ADJ culpable; **we find the defendant not —** hallamos al acusado inocente

Guinea [gíni] N Guinea f; **— pig** conejillo de Indias m; **—-Bissau** Guinea-Bissau f

Guinean [gínɪən] ADJ & N guineano -na mf

guise [gaɪz] ADV LOC **under the — of** so / bajo pretexto de; **in the — of** a manera de

guitar [gɪtár] N guitarra f

gulf [gʌłf] N (body of water) golfo m; (abyss, gap) abismo m; **— Stream** corriente del Golfo f

gull [gʌł] N (bird) gaviota f; (dupe) crédulo -la mf; Sp primo -ma mf

gullet [gʌ́łɪt] N gaznate m

gullible [gʌ́łəbəł] ADJ crédulo, ingenuo

gully [gʌ́łi] N barranco m, barranca f; (gutter) alcantarilla f

gulp [gʌłp] VT tragar saliva; N trago m

gum [gʌm] N goma f; (for chewing) chicle m; **—s** encías f pl; VT **to — up** (ruin) jorobar; (stick) pegotear

gumption [gʌ́mpʃən] N (initiative) iniciativa f, arranque m; (courage) agallas f pl

gun [gʌn] N (firearm) arma de fuego f; (revolver) revólver m; (rifle) rifle m; (shotgun) escopeta f; (cannon) cañón m; (for painting, nailing) pistola f; VT (an engine) acelerar; **to — down** matar a tiros; **to — for** andar a la caza de; **to stick to one's —s** mantenerse firme; **don't jump the —** no te precipites; **to be under the —** estar bajo mucha presión; **—boat** cañonero m; **—fire** tiroteo m; **—man** pistolero m; **at —point** a mano armada; **—powder** pólvora f; **—shot** disparo m

gung-ho [gʌ́ŋhó] ADJ fanático, entusiasta

gunner [gʌ́nɚ] N (shooting artillery) artillero -ra mf; (shooting a machine gun) ametrallador -ora mf

gurgle [gɚ́gəł] VI (water) borbotar; (baby) gorjear; N (of water) borboteo m; (of a baby) gorjeo m

gush [gʌʃ] VI (liquids) chorrear, brotar; (talk effusively) hablar con efusividad

gust [gʌst] N ráfaga f; **— of wind** racha / ráfaga de viento f, ventolera f; VI soplar en ráfagas

gusto [gʌ́sto] N (pleasure) placer m; (enthusiasm) entusiasmo m

gut [gʌt] N tripa f; (belly) barriga f; **— feeling** corazonada f; **—s** (intestines) entrañas f pl; (courage) fam cojones m pl; VT (eviscerate) destripar; (destroy the insides of) destrozar el interior de; (strip) desarmar

gutter [gÁDɚ] N (in the street) alcantarilla f; (on the roof) canaleta f, desagüe m; (squalor) miseria f

guy [gaɪ] N (man) tipo m; Sp tío m; **you —s** Sp vosotros/vosotras, ustedes; **— wire** cable m

Guyana [gaɪánə] N Guyana f

Guyanese [gaɪəníz] ADJ & N guyanés -esa mf

gym [ʤɪm] N gimnasio m

gymnasium [ʤɪmnéziəm] N gimnasio m

gymnastics [ʤɪmnǽstɪks] N gimnasia f

gynecology [gaɪnəkálaʤi] N ginecología f

gyp [ʤɪp] VT estafar, timar; N estafa f, timo m

gypsum [ʤípsəm] N yeso m

gypsy [ʤípsi] N & ADJ gitano -na mf

gyrate [ʤáɪret] VI girar

gyroscope [ʤáɪrəskop] N giroscopio m

Hh

habit [hǽbɪt] N (custom) hábito m, costumbre f; (clerical dress) hábito m; (vice) vicio m; **—-forming** que genera dependencia

habitat [hǽbɪtæt] N hábitat m

habitual [həbítʃuəl] ADJ habitual

hack [hæk] N (cut) tajo m, machetazo m; (cough) tos seca f; (horse for hire) caballo de alquiler m; (nag) jamelgo m; (writer) escritor -a mercenario -ria mf; VI/VT tajar, cortar a machetazos; VI toser con tos seca; **—saw** sierra para metales f

hag [hæg] N (witch) bruja f; (ugly old woman) vieja fea f

haggard [hǽgɚd] ADJ demacrado

haggle [hǽgəl] VI regatear

hail [hel] N (precipitation) granizo m; (greeting) saludo m; (shout) llamada f; **— Mary** Ave María f; **—storm** granizada f; VI (precipitate) granizar; VT (greet) saludar; (call out) llamar; (acclaim) aclamar; **to — from** ser oriundo de

hair [her] N pelo m; (of the head only) cabello m; (of the body only) vello m; (on plants) pelusa f; **—brush** cepillo para el cabello m; **—cut** corte de pelo m; **to get a —cut** cortarse el pelo; **—do** peinado m; **—dresser** peluquero -ra mf, peinador -ora mf; **— follicle** folículo capilar m; **—piece** postizo m; **—pin** horquilla f; **—-raising** horripilante, espeluznante; **—spray** fijador m

hairless [hérlɪs] ADJ (deprived of hair) pelado;

(growing no hair) lampiño

hairy [héri] ADJ (including head) peludo; (body only) velludo

Haiti [hédi] N Haití m

Haitian [héʃən] ADJ & N haitiano -na mf

hake [hek] N merluza f

half [hæf] N mitad f; **— an apple** media manzana f; ADJ medio; **—-baked** (not fully cooked) a medio cocer; (not fully developed) mal concebido; **—-breed** mestizo -za mf; **— brother** medio hermano m; **—-cocked** mal preparado; **he went off half-cocked** actuó precipitadamente; **—-cooked** a medio cocer; **—-dozen** media docena f; **—-hearted** desganado; **—-hour** media hora f; **—-moon** media luna f; **— note** blanca f; **—-open** entreabierto, entornado; **— past one** la una y media; **—time** medio tiempo m; **—way** a medio camino; **—way measures** medidas parciales f pl; **—way point** punto medio m; **—-wit** pej imbécil mf, papamoscas mf; **at —-mast** a media asta; **to do something —way** hacer algo a medias; **to go halves** ir a medias

halibut [hǽləbət] N hipogloso m

hall [hɔl] N (corridor) corredor m, pasillo m; (large room) salón m; (building) edificio m; **—mark** distintivo m; **—way** (corridor) corredor m, pasillo m; (entrance) zaguán m, vestíbulo m

Halloween [hæləwín] N víspera del día de Todos los Santos f, noche de brujas f

hallucinate [həlúsənet] VI alucinar

halo [hélo] N halo m, aureola f

halogen [hǽləʤən] ADJ halógeno

halt [hɔlt] N **to come to a —** detenerse; VI/VT parar, detener(se); **—!** ¡alto!

halter [hɔ́ltɚ] N cabestro m

halting [hɔ́ltɪŋ] ADJ vacilante

halve [hæv] VT partir por la mitad

ham [hæm] N (meat) jamón m; (attention getter) payaso m; **—string** (human) ligamento de la corva m; (horse) tendón del jarrete m; **to — it up** sobreactuar, exagerar

hamburger [hǽmbɚgɚ] N (meat) carne picada de vaca f; (sandwich or patty) hamburguesa f

hamlet [hǽmlɪt] N aldea f, poblado m, caserío m

hammer [hǽmɚ] N martillo m; VI/VT martillar, amartillar; **to — out** (an agreement) forjar; (differences) negociar

hammock [hǽmək] N hamaca f

hamper [hǽmpɚ] N canasto m, cesto m; VT

impedir, embarazar
hamster [hǽmstɚ] N hámster *m*
hand [hænd] N mano *f*; (of a clock) aguja *f*, manecilla *f*; (farm helper) peón *m*; **—bag** (purse) bolsa *f*, cartera *f*; (valise) maletín *m*; **—ball** (American) pelota *f*, frontón *m*; (European) balonmano *m*; **—bill** volante *m*; **—cuffs** esposas *f pl*; **— grenade** granada de mano *f*, bomba de piña *f*; **—gun** revólver *m*; **—held** de mano; **— in —** (cogidos) de la mano; **—kerchief** pañuelo *m*; **—made** hecho a mano; **—out** (notes) repartido *m*, notas *f pl*; (alms) limosna *f*; **—saw** serrucho *m*; **—shake** apretón de manos *m*; **—s-on** práctico; **—stand** pino *m*, paro de manos *m*; **—work** trabajo manual *m*; **—writing** letra *f*; **at —** (within reach) al alcance; (about to happen) cerca; **on —** disponible, a mano; **on the other —** en cambio, por otra parte; **to have one's —s full** estar ocupadísimo; VT entregar, dar; **to —cuff** esposar; **to — down** (a thing) pasar; (a judgment) pronunciar; **to — in** entregar; **to — over** entregar
handful [hǽndfʊl] N manojo *m*, puñado *m*
handicap [hǽndikæp] N (physical disability) impedimento *m*, (mental disability) retardo *m*; (disadvantage) desventaja *f*; **physically —ped** minusválido físico; **— race** carrera de hándicap *f*; VT (hinder) perjudicar, handicapar; (injure) lisiar
handiwork [hǽndiwɚk] N labor *f*
handle [hǽndl] N (straight) mango *m*; (curved) asa *f*; (of a drawer) manija *f*; (of a knife) empuñadura *f*, puño *m*; **—bar** manubrio *m*; VT (manage) manejar; (touch) manipular, tocar; (deal in) comerciar en; **the car —s easily** el coche tiene buena maniobrabilidad
handling [hǽndlɪŋ] N (dealing) manejo *m*; (touching) manipulación *f*; (charge) porte *m*; (of a car) maniobrabilidad *f*
handsome [hǽnsəm] ADJ guapo, bien parecido; **a — sum** una suma considerable
handy [hǽndi] ADJ (near) a (la) mano; (practical) práctico; (skillful) hábil, diestro; **—man** hombre habilidoso *m*
hang [hæŋ] VI/VT colgar, suspender; **— glider** ala delta *f*; **—man** verdugo *m*; **—nail** padrastro *m*; **—out** sitio frecuentado *m*; **—over** resaca *f*; **—-up** complejo *m*; VT (door) colocar; (one's head) inclinar; VI pender; **— in there!** ¡ánimo! **to — around** quedarse por ahí, rondar; **to — on** (hold tight) agarrarse

bien; (persevere) aguantar; (wait) esperar; **to — out** (be outside) estar fuera; (hang around with) andar (con); **to — over** sobresalir; **to — paper on a wall** empapelar una pared; **to — up** colgar; **sentenced to —** condenado a la horca; N caída *f*; **to get the — of something** agarrarle la onda a algo
hangar [hǽŋɚ] N hangar *m*
hanger [hǽŋɚ] N colgadero *m*; (for clothes) percha *f*
hanging [hǽŋɪŋ] N muerte en la horca *f*; **—s** colgaduras *f pl*, tapiz *m*; ADJ colgante
hanky-panky [hǽŋkipǽŋki] N (deceit) tejemaneje *m*; (illicit sexual activity) aventuras *f pl*
haphazard [hæphǽzɚd] ADV a la buena de Dios; ADJ irregular
happen [hǽpən] VI suceder, pasar, acontecer; **I — to know** da la casualidad de que sé; **to — to pass by** acertar a pasar; **to — upon** encontrarse con, toparse con
happening [hǽpənɪŋ] N acontecimiento *m*, suceso *m*
happiness [hǽpinis] N felicidad *f*, dicha *f*
happy [hǽpi] ADJ (satisfied) feliz, dichoso; (pleased) contento; (lucky) afortunado; **— ending** final feliz *m*; **to be — to** hacer algo de buena gana
harangue [hərǽŋ] N arenga *f*; VT arengar
harass [hərǽs] VT acosar, hostigar
harbor [hárbɚ] N (for ships) puerto *m*; (refuge) refugio *m*; VT (refugees, suspicions) albergar; (hopes) abrigar
hard [hɑrd] ADJ (firm) duro; (difficult) difícil; (arduous) arduo; **to play —ball** ser despiadado; **— cash** dinero contante y sonante *m*; **— coal** antracita *f*; **— copy** copia *f*; **— core** núcleo resistente *m*; **—-core** (pornography) duro; (politics) radical; **— disk** disco duro *m*; **— hat** casco *m*; **—headed** testarudo; **—hearted** duro de corazón; **— liquor** bebida alcohólica fuerte *f*; **— luck** mala suerte *f*; **— of hearing** medio sordo; **—-on** erección *f*; **he had a —-on** la tenía dura; **—-pressed** en aprietos; **—ware** (metal articles) ferretería *f*; (computer) hardware *m*; **—ware store** ferretería *f*; **—wood** madera noble *f*; **— water** agua dura *f*; **— winter** invierno crudo *m*; **—-wired** programado; **—-working** trabajador; ADV (fall, push) con fuerza; (work) duro, con ahínco
harden [hárdn] VI/VT (make or become hard) endurecer(se); (make or become experienced) curtir(se)

hardening [hárdṇɪŋ] N endurecimiento *m*

hardly [hárdli] ADV (scarcely) apenas; (at all) en absoluto; **— anyone** casi nadie; **— surprising** nada sorprendente

hardness [hárdnɪs] N dureza *f*

hardship [hárdʃɪp] N penuria *f*, penalidad *f*

hardy [hárdi] ADJ robusto

hare [her] N liebre *f*; **—brained** descabellado; **—lip** labio leporino *m*

harem [hérəm] N harén *m*

harm [harm] N daño *m*, mal *m*, perjuicio *m*; VT (object) dañar; (person) hacer daño; (chances) perjudicar

harmful [hármfəl] ADJ perjudicial, dañino, nocivo

harmless [hármlɪs] ADJ inocuo, inofensivo

harmonic [harmánɪk] ADJ & N armónico *m*

harmonious [harmóniəs] ADJ armonioso

harmonize [hármənaɪz] VI/VT armonizar

harmony [hármənɪ] N armonía *f*

harness [hárnɪs] N arnés *m*, jaez *m*, guarnición *f*; VT (put on a harness) enjaezar; (utilize) aprovechar

harp [harp] N arpa *f*; VI (play the harp) tocar el arpa; (insist) machacar; **to — on** insistir sobre

harpoon [harpún] N arpón *m*; VT arponear

harpsichord [hárpsɪkɔrd] N clavicémbalo *m*

harrowing [hǽroɪŋ] ADJ angustioso; **— adventure** aventura espeluznante *f*

harry [hǽri] VT acosar, hostigar

harsh [harʃ] ADJ (words) duro; (surface) áspero; (discipline) severo, férreo; (winter) crudo, riguroso

harshness [hárʃnɪs] N (of words) dureza *f*; (of a surface) aspereza *f*; (of character) severidad *f*; (of a winter) rigor *m*

harvest [hárvɪst] N cosecha *f*; (of sugar) zafra *f*; VT cosechar

hash [hæʃ] N guisado *m*, picadillo *m*

hashish [hǽʃɪʃ] N hachís *m*

hassle [hǽsəl] N rollo *m*, lío *m*; VT jorobar

haste [hest] N prisa *f*; **in —** de prisa; **to make —** darse prisa, apresurarse; *Am* apurarse

hasten [hésən] VI apresurarse; *Am* apurarse; VT acelerar, adelantar

hasty [hésti] ADJ apresurado, precipitado, presuroso; *Am* apurado; **to be —** precipitarse, apresurarse

hat [hæt] N sombrero *m*

hatch [hætʃ] VI/VT (chicks) empollar; (plot, scheme) fraguar, maquinar; N (chicks) nidada *f*; (opening) escotilla *f*; **— way** escotilla *f*

hatchet [hǽtʃɪt] N hacha *f*; **— job** crítica feroz *f*; **— man** sicario *m*; **to bury the —**

hacer las paces

hate [het] N odio *m*; VI/VT odiar; **I — to admit it** me molesta admitirlo; **I — eating leftovers** detesto comer restos

hateful [hétfəl] ADJ odioso, aborrecible

hatred [hétrɪd] N odio *m*

haughtiness [hɔ́dɪnɪs] N altivez *f*, altanería *f*, soberbia *f*

haughty [hɔ́di] ADJ altivo, altanero, soberbio

haul [hɔl] VT (transport) transportar; (drag) arrastrar; VI (pull) jalar (de), tirar (de); N (quantity transported) carga *f*; (tug) tirón *m*; (catch of fish) redada *f*; (stolen goods) botín *m*; **long —** distancia larga *f*

haunch [hɔntʃ] N anca *f*

haunt [hɔnt] VI/VT (frequent) frecuentar; (enchant) rondar; **that idea —s me** me obsesiona esa idea; **—ed house** casa embrujada *f*; N (of animals, criminals) guarida *f*; (of people socializing) sitio frecuentado *m*

have [hæv] V AUX haber; VT tener; **to — to** tener que; **to — a baby** dar a luz; **to — a look at** echar una mirada a; **to — a suit made** mandarse hacer un traje; **— him come later** dile que venga más tarde; **what did she — on?** ¿qué tenía puesto? **we've been had** nos estafaron

haven [hévən] N abrigo *m*, refugio *m*

havoc [hǽvək] N estrago *m*; **to wreak —** hacer estragos

hawk [hɔk] N gavilán *m*; VT pregonar

hay [he] N heno *m*; **— fever** alergia al polen *f*; **— loft** henil *m*; **—seed** paleto -ta *mf*; **—stack** almiar *m*; **to look for a needle in a —** buscar una aguja en un pajar

hazard [hǽzə-d] N (chance) azar *m*; (danger) peligro *m*; VT arriesgar, aventurar

hazardous [hǽzə-Dəs] ADJ peligroso

haze [hez] N neblina *f*, calina *f*; VT atormentar (como parte de un rito de iniciación)

hazel [hézəl] N avellano *m*; **—nut** avellana *f*; ADJ de avellano

hazy [hézi] ADJ (weather) brumoso; (idea) confuso, vago

he [hi] PRON él; **—-goat** macho cabrío *m*; **— who** el que, quien

head [hed] N (of body) cabeza *f*; (of bed) cabecera *f*; (chief) jefe -fa *mf*; **—ache** dolor de cabeza *m*; **— cold** resfrío *m*; **—dress** tocado *m*, adorno para la cabeza *m*; **—gear** (hat) sombrero *m*; (helmet) casco *m*; (for a horse) cabezada *f*; **—land** cabo *m*, promontorio *m*; **—light** faro delantero *m*; **—line** titular *m*; **—long** (head first) de cabeza; (hastily) precipitadamente; **— of hair** cabellera *f*; **—-on** de frente; **—phone** audífono *m*, auricular *m*; **—quarters** (military) cuartel general *m*; (police) jefatura *f*; (corporation) oficina central *f*; **—rest** reposacabezas *m sg*; **—set** auriculares *m pl*; **—s or tails** cara o cruz; **I can't make —s or tails of it** esto no tiene ni pies ni cabeza; **— start** ventaja *f*; **— stone** lápida *f*; **—strong** testarudo; **—way** avance *m*; **—word** voz *f*; **to make —way** avanzar, progresar; **to be out of one's —** desvariar; **to come to a —** (a crisis) precipitarse; (an abscess) supurar; **to keep one's —** mantener la calma; VT (lead) encabezar; (steer) dirigir; VI dirigirse; **to — off** atajar; **it went to his —** se le fue a la cabeza

heading [hédɪŋ] N encabezamiento *m*

heal [hiɫ] VT curar; VI (get well) sanar, curarse; (form a scar) cicatrizarse

health [hɛɫθ] N salud *f*; **— care** asistencia médica *f*; **— food** comida macrobiótica *f*; **— insurance** seguro de salud *m*

healthful [héɫθfəɫ] ADJ saludable, sano

healthy [héɫθi] ADJ sano, saludable

heap [hip] N montón *m*, pila *f*; VT amontonar; VI apilar; **to — up** amontonar

hear [hir] VI/VT (perceive) oír; VT (listen) escuchar; **to — about / of someone / something** oír hablar de alguien / algo; **to — from someone** tener noticias de alguien; **I won't — of your leaving** no quiero saber de que te vayas

hearer [hírə] N oyente *mf*

hearing [hírɪŋ] N (sense) oído *m*; (trial) audiencia *f*; **within —** al alcance del oído; **— aid** audífono *m*; **—-impaired** sordo

hearsay [hírse] N testimonio de oídas *m*; **by — de oídas**

hearse [hɚs] N coche fúnebre *m*, carroza *f*

heart [hart] N (organ) corazón *m*; (spirit) ánimo *m*; **—ache** angustia *f*; **— attack** ataque cardíaco *m*; **—beat** latido *m*; **I would do it in a —beat** lo haría sin pestañear; **—broken** inconsolable; **—burn** acidez de estómago *f*; **— disease** enfermedad coronaria *f*; **—felt** sincero, sentido; **— murmur** soplo cardíaco *m*; **my —felt sympathy** mi más sentido pésame; **—-warming** reconfortante; **at — en realidad**, en el fondo; **from the bottom of one's —** de corazón, con toda el alma; **to learn by —** aprender de memoria; **to take —** cobrar ánimo; **to take to —** tomar a pecho

hearten [hártn̩] VT animar

hearth [harθ] N hogar *m*

heartless [hártlɪs] ADJ despiadado, desalmado

hearty [hárdi] ADJ (cordial) cordial; (strong) fuerte; **— appetite** apetito saludable *m*; **a — laugh** una risa desbordante; **— meal** una comida abundante

heat [hit] N (warmth) calor *m*; (passion) ardor *m*; (estrus) celo *m*; (source of heat) calefacción *f*; (preliminary race) eliminatoria *f*; **—stroke** insolación *f*; VI/VT calentar(se); **to — up** acalorarse

heater [hídə] N calentador *m*

heating [hídɪŋ] N calefacción *f*

heave [hiv] VT (raise) levantar; (throw) arrojar, lanzar; (sigh) exhalar; (pull) jalar; VI (pant) jadear; (vomit) hacer arcadas; N (throw) lanzamiento *m*; (pull) tirón *m*

heaven [hévən] N cielo *m*

heavenly [hévənli] ADJ celestial; **— bodies** cuerpos celestes *m pl*; **it was —** estuvo divino

heaviness [hévɪnɪs] N pesadez *f*

heavy [hévi] ADJ (weighty) pesado; (thick) grueso, pesado; (dense) denso; (oppressive) opresivo; **— artillery** artillería pesada *f*; **— breathing** jadeos *m pl*; **—-duty** para uso industrial; **—-handed** severo, autoritario; **with a — heart** abatido; **— rain** lluvia fuerte *f*; **— schedule** agenda cargada *f*; **—weight** peso pesado *m*; N villano -na *mf*

Hebrew [híbru] N & ADJ hebreo -a *mf*; (language) hebreo *m*

heck [hɛk] INTERJ ¡caramba! **what the — are you doing?** ¿qué demonios haces? **that was a — of a good game** fue un partidazo

hectare [héktɛr] N hectárea *f*

hectic [héktɪk] ADJ febril, agitado

hedge [hɛdʒ] N (row of bushes) seto *m*; (precaution) precaución *f*; VI/VT (a bet) cubrir(se); VT (a question) evadir

hedgehog [hédʒhag] N erizo *m*

hedonism [hídnɪzəm] N hedonismo *m*

heebie-jeebies [híbidʒíbiz] N **it gives me the —** me pone los pelos de punta

heed [hid] VT atender; N atención *f*, cuidado *m*; **to pay — to** prestar atención a

heel [hiɫ] VT (of foot or sock) talón *m*; (of shoe) tacón *m*; **kick up one's —s** tirar la chancleta, soltarse el pelo; VT poner tacón a; VI/VT seguir de cerca

hegemony [hɪdʒémənɪ] N hegemonía *f*

heifer [héfə] N novilla *f*, vaquilla *f*

height [haɪt] N (of a building, mountain) altura *f*; (of a person) estatura *f*; (utmost

point) colmo *m*
heighten [háitn̩] VI/VT (increase) aumentar(se); (intensify) realzar
heinous [hénəs] ADJ aborrecible
heir [ɛr] N heredero -ra *mf*; — **apparent** presunto heredero *m*, presunta heredera *f*
heiress [érɪs] N heredera *f*
helicopter [hélɪkaptə-] N helicóptero *m*
helium [híliəm] N helio *m*
helix [hílɪks] N hélice *f*
hell [hɛl] N infierno *m*
hello [heló] INTERJ ¡hola! (on the telephone) hola; *Sp* diga; *Mex* bueno; *RP* olá
helm [hɛlm] N timón *m*
helmet [hɛ́lmɪt] N (for bikes, etc.) casco *m*; (armor) yelmo *m*
help [hɛlp] N (aid) ayuda *f*; (rescue) auxilio *m*; (remedy) remedio *m*; (employee) empleado -da *mf*; INTERJ ¡auxilio! ¡socorro! VI/VT (aid) ayudar, asistir; (rescue) auxiliar, socorrer; — **yourself** sírvete; **he cannot — it** no puede evitarlo; **he cannot — but come** no puede menos que venir; **may I — you?** ¿en qué le puedo servir?
helper [hɛ́lpə-] N ayudante *mf*, asistente *mf*
helpful [hɛ́lpfəl] ADJ (useful) útil; (willing to help) servicial
helping [hɛ́lpɪŋ] N porción *f*
helpless [hɛ́lplɪs] ADJ desamparado, desvalido
helplessness [hɛ́lplɪsnɪs] N desamparo *m*, desvalimiento *m*
hem [hɛm] N dobladillo *m*, orillo *m*; (of a skirt) ruedo *m*; VT hacer dobladillos en, orillar; **to — in** arrinconar; **to — and haw** vacilar
hematoma [himətómə] N hematoma *m*
hemisphere [hémɪsfɪr] N hemisferio *m*
hemlock [hémlɑk] N cicuta *f*
hemoglobin [hímǝglobɪn] N hemoglobina *f*
hemophilia [himəfíliə] N hemofilia *f*
hemorrhage [héməridʒ] N hemorragia *f*
hemorrhoids [hémɔrɔɪdz] N hemorroides *f pl*
hemp [hɛmp] N cáñamo *m*
hen [hɛn] N (chicken) gallina *f*; (female bird) ave hembra *f*; —**pecked** dominado por su mujer
hence [hɛns] ADV de ahí; **a week —** de aquí a una semana
henceforth [hénsfɔrθ] ADV de aquí en adelante, de hoy en adelante
hepatitis [hɛpətáɪdɪs] N hepatitis *f*
her [hə-] PRON I see — la veo; I talk to — le hablo (a ella); I went with — fui con ella; POSS ADJ **this is — dog** este es su perro, este es el perro de ella
herald [hérəld] N heraldo *m*; VT anunciar, proclamar

herb [ɚb] N hierba *f*
herbal [ɚbəl] ADJ de hierbas; — **tea** tisana *f*
herbicide [hɚ́bɪsaɪd] N herbicida *m*
herbivore [hɚ́bəvɔr] N herbívoro *m*
herbivorous [hɚbívərəs] ADJ herbívoro
herd [hɚd] N (of animals) manada *f*; (of goats) hato *m*; (of sheep) rebaño *m*; (of horses, donkeys) recua *f*; **the common —** el populacho, la chusma; —**sman** pastor *m*; VT arrear; VI ir en manada
here [hir] ADV aquí, acá; — **it is** aquí está; **that is neither — nor there** eso no viene al caso; —**after** en adelante; **the —after** el más allá; —**by** (in writing) por la presente; **I —by pronounce you husband and wife** los declaro marido y mujer; —**in** en el presente; —**'s to you!** ¡a tu salud! —**tofore** hasta ahora; —**with** (hereby) por la presente; (attached) adjunto; **the — and now** el presente
hereditary [həréDIteri] ADJ hereditario
heredity [həréDITi] N herencia *f*
heresy [hérɪsi] N herejía *f*
heretic [hérɪtik] N hereje *mf*
heritage [hérɪtɪdʒ] N herencia *f*, patrimonio *m*
hermetic [hɚ-méDIK] ADJ hermético
hermit [hɚ́-mɪt] N ermitaño -ña *mf*; — **crab** ermitaño *m*
hernia [hɚ́-niə] N hernia *f*; —**ted** herniado; —**ted disk** hernia de disco *f*
hero [híro] N (brave man) héroe *m*; (main character) protagonista *mf*
heroic [hɪróɪk] ADJ heroico
heroin [héroɪn] N heroína *f*
heroine [héroɪn] N heroína *f*
heroism [héroɪzəm] N heroísmo *m*
heron [hérən] N garza *f*
herpes [hɚ́-piz] N herpes *m*
herring [hérɪŋ] N arenque *m*
hers [hɚz] PRON **this book is —** este libro es suyo/ de ella; **these things are —** estas cosas son suyas; — **is bigger** el suyo/ la suya es más grande; **a friend of —** un amigo suyo/ de ella
herself [hɚsélf] PRON ella misma; **she — wrote the letter** ella misma escribió la carta; **she's not — today** hoy no es la misma de siempre; **she was sitting by —** estaba sentada sola; **she — did it** lo hizo sola, lo hizo ella misma; **she talks to —** ella habla para sí, habla sola; **she looked at — in the mirror** se miró en el espejo; **she bought — a house** se compró una casa
hesitant [hézɪtənt] ADJ vacilante
hesitate [hézɪtet] VI (pause) vacilar; (stutter)

titubear; (doubt) dudar
hesitating [hézɪtepɪŋ] ADJ vacilante
hesitation [hezɪtéʃən] N (pause) vacilación f;
(stammer) titubeo m; (doubt) duda f
heterogeneous [hɛDəəʤíniəs] ADJ
heterogéneo
heterosexual [hɛDərosékʃuəł] ADJ
heterosexual
hexagon [héksəgɑn] N hexágono m
hey [he] INTERJ ¡oiga!
heyday [héde] N auge m
hiatus [haɪéDəs] N hiato m
hibernate [háɪbə-net] VI hibernar
hiccup, hiccough [híkʌp] N hipo m; VI
hipar, tener hipo
hick [hɪk] N & ADJ paleto -ta mf
hickory [híkəri] N nogal americano m
hide [haɪd] VI/VT ocultar(se), esconder(se); —
and seek Sp escondite m; Am escondidas
f pl; —**out** escondite m; N cuero m, piel f,
pellejo m
hideous [hídiəs] ADJ horrendo, espantoso
hierarchy [háɪərɑrki] N jerarquía f
hieroglyphic [haɪrəglífɪk] ADJ & N jeroglífico
m
high [haɪ] ADJ alto; (intoxicated) ebrio; (on
drugs) volado; — **and dry** (ship) en seco;
(person) colgado; — **blood pressure**
hipertensión f; —**brow** culto; —**class** de
clase; —**er-up** superior; — **explosive**
explosivo de alta potencia m; — **fever**
fiebre elevada f; — **fidelity** alta fidelidad
f; —**grade** de calidad superior;
—**handed** arbitrario; — **jump** salto alto
m; —**lands** tierras altas f pl; —**light** lo
más destacado m; —**lights** claritos m pl,
mechas f pl; **to** —**light** resaltar;
—**minded** idealista; —**pitched** agudo;
—**powered** de alta potencia; —**priced**
caro; —**rise** de muchos pisos; — **school**
escuela secundaria f; Sp instituto m; —
seas alta mar f; —**sounding** altisonante;
—**speed** de alta velocidad; — **spirits**
buen ánimo m; —**strung** nervioso;
—**tech** alta tecnología f; —
temperature temperatura máxima f; —
tide pleamar f; —**way** carretera f, ruta f;
— **wind** ventarrón m; **in** — **gear** a toda
marcha; **two feet** — dos pies de altura; **it
is** — **time** that ya era hora de que; **to
look** — **and low** buscar por todas partes;
N flash m, subida f
highly [háɪli] ADV — **amusing** sumamente
divertido; — **paid** muy bien pagado; **he
spoke** — **of her** habló muy bien de ella
highness [háɪnɪs] N alteza f
hijack [háɪʤæk] VT secuestrar (un vehículo)

hike [haɪk] N caminata f; VI salir a caminar;
take a —! ¡ve a freír espárragos!
hilarious [hɪlériəs] ADJ graciosísimo, para
morirse de risa
hill [hɪł] N (elevated area) colina f, cerro m;
(pile) montón m; —**billy** paleto -ta mf;
—**side** ladera f; —**top** cumbre f, cima f
hillock [hílək] N otero m
hilly [híli] ADJ accidentado
hilt [hɪłt] N empuñadura f; **to the** — al
máximo
him [hɪm] PRON **I see** — lo veo; Sp le veo; **I
talk to** — le hablo; **I went with** — fui
con él
himself [hɪmsélf] PRON él mismo; **he**
wrote the letter el mismo escribió la
carta; **he's not** — **today** hoy no es el
mismo de siempre; **he was sitting by** —
estaba sentado solo; **he talks to** — el
habla para sí / solo; **he looked at** — **in
the mirror** se miró en el espejo; **he
bought** — **a house** se compró una casa
hind [haɪnd] ADJ trasero; —**most** último; **in**
—**sight** a posteriori; N cierva f
hinder [híndə-] VT impedir, entorpecer,
estorbar
Hindi [híndi] N hindi m
hindrance [híndrəns] N obstáculo m,
impedimento m, traba f
Hindu [híndu] ADJ & N hindú mf
hinge [hɪnʤ] N gozne m, quicio m; VT
engoznar, poner goznes; VI **to** — **on**
depender de
hint [hɪnt] N (clue) indirecta f, pista f; (trace)
dejo m; **to take the** — darse por
enterado; VT insinuar
hip [hɪp] N cadera f
hippopotamus [hɪpəpáDəməs] N
hipopótamo m
hire [haɪr] VT (engage for work) contratar; VI/
VT (rent) alquilar(se); **to** — **out** dar en
alquiler, alquilar; N (engagement)
contratación f; (employee) nuevo -va
empleado -da mf; (rent) alquiler m
his [hɪz] POSS ADJ **this is** — **dog** este es su
perro / el perro de él; PRON **these things
are** — estas cosas son suyas; — **is right
here** el suyo / la suya está aquí; **a friend
of** — un amigo suyo / una amiga suya
Hispanic [hɪspǽnɪk] ADJ hispánico, hispano;
N hispano -na mf
hiss [hɪs] VI sisear; (to boo) silbar; N siseo m
histamine [hístəmɪn] N histamina f
historian [hɪstɔ́riən] N historiador -ra mf
historic [hɪstɔ́rɪk] ADJ histórico
historical [hɪstɔ́rɪkəł] ADJ histórico
history [hístəri] N historia f

histrionics [hɪstriánɪks] N histrionismo *m*
hit [hɪt] VT (a target) dar en; (a car) chocar con; (a key) pulsar, tocar; **they — it off well** se llevaron bien desde el principio; **to — the mark** acertar, dar en el blanco; **to — upon** dar con; **to — on** ligar (con); N (blow) golpe *m*; (success) éxito *m*; (dose) dosis *f*; **that was a — with me** me encantó; **—-and-run** que se da a la fuga después de atropellar a alguien; **—man** sicario *m*; **—-or-miss** al azar
hitch [hɪtʃ] VT atar, amarrar; (pants) levantar; (yoke) uncir, enganchar; **to get —ed** casarse; **to —hike** Sp hacer autostop; Am hacer dedo; N (knot) nudo *m*; (difficulty) dificultad *f*; (period) período *m*
hither [híðə] ADV acá; **— and thither** acá y allá; **—to** hasta ahora
HIV (human immunodeficiency virus) [etʃaɪvi] N VIH *m*
hive [haɪv] N (shelter for bees) colmena *f*; (colony of bees) enjambre *m*; **—s** urticaria *f*
hoard [hɔrd] N reserva *f*; VI/VT acaparar
hoarse [hɔrs] ADJ ronco; (of alcoholics) aguardentoso
hoarseness [hɔrsnɪs] N ronquera *f*
hoax [hoks] N engaño *m*
hobble [hábəl] VI (limp) cojear; VT (tie to impede walking) manear; (hinder) trabar; N cojera *f*; (rope) traba *f*, manea *f*
hobby [hábi] N hobby *m*
hobo [hóbo] N vagabundo *m*
hockey [háki] N hockey *m*
hodgepodge [hádʒpadʒ] N mezcolanza *f*, batiburrillo *m*
hoe [ho] N azada *f*, azadón *m*; VI/VT limpiar con azadón
hog [hag] N puerco *m*, cerdo *m*, marrano *m*; Am chancho *m*; **—wash** pamplinas *f pl*; **to live high on the —** vivir en la abundancia; VT acaparar, adueñarse de
hoist [hɔɪst] VT izar; N torno *m*, guinche *m*
hokey [hóki] ADJ sensiblero
hold [hold] VT (bear) llevar, sujetar; (contain) contener; (detain) detener; (decide legally, sustain a note) sostener; (opine) opinar; VI (remain fast) aguantar, resistir; (occupy a position) ocupar; (be valid) ser válido; **to — back** detener; **to — down** sujetar; **to — forth** perorar; **to — hands** tomarse de la mano; **to — in place** sujetar; **to — a meeting** celebrar una reunión; **to — off** mantener(se) a distancia; **to — on** (not let go) agarrar(se), sujetar(se); (stop) esperar; (persist) persistir; **— the pickles on that burger!** una hamburguesa sin pepinillos,

por favor; **to — someone responsible** hacerle a uno responsable; **to — someone to his word** obligar a uno a cumplir con su palabra; **to — oneself erect** ponerse derecho; **to — one's own** defenderse; **to — one's tongue** callarse, morderse la lengua; **to — out** tender; **to — still** quedarse/estarse quieto; **to — tight** agarrarse; **to — to one's promise** cumplir con la palabra; **to — up** (raise) alzar; (detain) detener; (rob) atracar, asaltar; (persevere) aguantar; **how much does it — ?** ¿Qué capacidad tiene? N (grip) agarro *m*; (thing to grasp) asidero *m*; (dominion) dominio *m*; (wrestling move) llave *f*; (in music) calderón *f*; (of a ship) bodega *f*; **—up** golpe *m*, atraco *m*; **to get — of** agarrar; **to take — of** Sp coger, agarrar; **to have a good — on something** agarrarse bien de algo
holder [hóldə] N (person) tenedor -ra *mf*, poseedor -ra *mf*; (device) receptáculo *m*
holding [hóldɪŋ] N propiedad *f*; **— company** holding *m*; **—s** (financial) valores en cartera *m pl*; (of a library) fondos *m pl*
hole [hol] N agujero *m*; (in a wall) boquete *m*; (of an animal) madriguera *f*; (in ground only, golf included) hoyo *m*; **to be in a —** hallarse/estar en un apuro/aprieto
holiday [hálɪde] N día de fiesta *m*; **—s** vacaciones *f pl*
holiness [hólinɪs] N santidad *f*
holistic [holístɪk] ADJ holístico
Holland [háland] N Holanda *f*
hollow [hálo] ADJ (empty) hueco; (concave) cóncavo; (sunken) hundido; (insincere) falso; N (cavity) hueco *m*, concavidad *f*; (valley) hondonada *f*, hondo *m*; VT **to — out** ahuecar, vaciar
holly [háli] N acebo *m*
holocaust [háləkɔst] N holocausto *m*
holster [hólstə] N pistolera *f*, funda de pistola *f*
holy [hóli] ADJ santo, sagrado; **— Bible** Santa Biblia *f*; **— cow/Moses/mackerel!** ¡jobar! **— Ghost** Espíritu Santo *m*; **— Spirit** Espíritu Santo *m*; **— war** guerra santa *f*; **— water** agua bendita *f*
homage [hámɪdʒ] N homenaje *m*; **to pay —** rendir homenaje, honrar
home [hom] N casa *f*, hogar *m*; (for old people, orphans) asilo *m*, hogar *m*; **at —** en casa; ADJ doméstico; **— economics** economía doméstica *f*; **— game** partido en casa *m*; **—land** patria *f*; **—less** sin

techo; —**made** casero; — **office** oficina
central f; —**owner** propietario -ria de un
bien inmueble mf; — **page** página de
inicio f; — **rule** autonomía f; — **run**
jonrón m; **to be** —**sick** echar de menos/
extrañar (a la familia); —**sickness**
morriña f, añoranza f; — **stretch** último
trecho m; —**work** tarea domiciliaria f,
deber m; ADV (direction) a casa; (location)
en casa; **to strike** — dar en el blanco

homely [hómli] ADJ (ugly) feo; (familiar)
familiar, doméstico

homeopathic [homiopǽθɪk] ADJ
homeopático

homeopathy [homiápəθi] N homeopatía f

homestead [hómstɛd] N heredad f, casa de la
familia f

homeward [hómwəd] ADV a casa; — **bound**
camino a casa

homicide [hámɪsaɪd] N homicidio m

homogeneous [homədʒíniəs] ADJ homogéneo

homogenize [həmádʒənaɪz] VT
homogeneizar

homonym [hámənɪm] N homónimo m

homosexual [homosékʃuəł] ADJ & N
homosexual mf

Honduran [handúrən] ADJ & N hondureño
-ña mf

Honduras [handúrəs] N Honduras f

hone [hon] VT afilar; **to** — **one's skills**
desarrollar las destrezas; N piedra de afilar
f

honest [ánɪst] ADJ honrado, honesto; **I'll be**
— **with you** voy a ser franco contigo; —!
¡de veras!

honesty [ánɪsti] N (integrity) honradez f,
honestidad f; (sincerity) franqueza f

honey [háni] N (sweet substance) miel f;
(endearment) querido -da mf; —**bee** abeja
f; —**comb** panal m; —**suckle** madreselva
f

honeymoon [hánimun] N luna de miel f; VI
pasar la luna de miel

honk [haŋk] N (car) bocinazo m, pitazo m;
(goose) graznido m; VI/VT tocar la bocina;
VI graznar

honor [ánə] N (respect, privilege) honor m;
(good reputation) honra f; (title) señoría f;
with —**s** con honores; VT (revere) honrar;
(accept invitation, check) aceptar

honorable [ánərəbəł] ADJ honorable

honorary [ánəreri] ADJ honorario

hood [hud] N (of a coat) capucha f, caperuza
f; (of a car) capó m; Am tapa f; VT
encapuchar

hoodlum [húdləm] N maleante mf, gamberro
-rra mf

hoof [huf] N casco m, pezuña f; VI **to** — **it** ir
andando

hook [hʊk] N (for lifting) gancho m, garfio m;
(for fishing) anzuelo m; — **and eye**
alamar m, macho y hembra m; **by** — **or**
by crook por las buenas o por las malas;
—**up** conexión f, enganche m; VT (snag)
enganchar; (a dress) abrochar; **to** — **up**
conectar, enganchar

hooked [hʊkt] ADJ (shaped like a hook)
ganchudo; (addicted) enganchado

hooky [húki] N **to play** — hacer novillos

hoop [hup] N aro m

hoot [hut] VI/VT (of owl) ulular; (in derision)
abuchear; N (of an owl) ululato m; (cry of
derision) abucheo m; **I don't give a** —
no me importa un comino; **it's a** — es
para morirse de risa

hop [hap] VI saltar, brincar; **to** — **on** subirse
a montar; N (short jump) saltito m, brinco
m; (dance) bailongo m; —**s** lúpulo m

hope [hop] N esperanza f; VI/VT esperar; **to** —
for esperar; **to** — **against** — esperar lo
imposible

hopeful [hópfəł] ADJ (having hopes)
esperanzado; (giving hopes) esperanzador,
alentador

hopefully [hópfəli] ADV — **she'll come**
ojalá (que) venga

hopeless [hóplɪs] ADJ (without hope)
desesperanzado; (with no solution)
irremediable; (unattainable) inalcanzable;
— **cause** causa perdida f; **it is** — no tiene
remedio; **the new secretary is** — **with**
numbers el nuevo secretario es un
desastre con los números

hopelessness [hóplɪsnɪs] N desesperanza f

horde [hɔrd] N (of people) horda f; (of
animals) plaga f

horizon [həráɪzən] N horizonte m

horizontal [hɔrɪzántł] ADJ horizontal

hormone [hórmon] N hormona f

horn [hɔrn] N (of an animal, substance)
cuerno m, asta f; (of an automobile)
bocina f, claxon m; (musical) corno m,
trompa f; — **of plenty** cuerno de la
abundancia m; **to toot one's own** —
darse autobombo; VI **to** — **in**
entremeterse

hornet [hórnɪt] N avispón m̃; —**'s nest**
avispero m

horoscope [hórəskop] N horóscopo m

horrendous [hɔréndəs] ADJ horrendo

horrible [hórəbəł] ADJ horrible

horrid [hórɪd] ADJ horrendo

horrify [hórəfaɪ] VT horrorizar

horror [hórə] N horror m

hors d'oeuvre [ɔrdɚ́v] N entremés *m*

horse [hɔrs] N caballo *m*; **—back** lomo de caballo *m*; **to ride —back** montar a caballo, cabalgar; **—fly** tábano *m*; **—laugh** carcajada *f*; **—man** jinete *m*; **—manship** equitación *f*; **—play** payasadas *f pl*; **—power** caballo de fuerza *m*; **— race** carrera de caballos *f*; **—radish** rábano picante *m*; **— sense** sentido común *m*; **—shoe** herradura *f*; **hold your —s!** ¡para el carro! VI **to — around** payasear

horticulture [hɔ́rdɪkʌltʃɚ] N horticultura *f*

hose [hoz] N (for legs) medias *f pl*; (for irrigation) manguera *f*, manga *f*

hosiery [hóʒəri] N (stockings) medias *f pl*; (shop for stockings) calcetería *f*

hospice [háspɪs] N (inn) hospicio *m*; (hospital) hospital para enfermos terminales *m*

hospitable [hɑspídəbəl] ADJ hospitalario, acogedor

hospital [háspɪd] N hospital *m*

hospitality [hɑspɪtǽlɪdi] N hospitalidad *f*

host [host] N anfitrión *m*; (at home, also for a parasite) huésped *m*; (on television) presentador -ra *mf*; (army) hueste *f*; (multitude) multitud *f*, cúmulo *m*; (wafer) hostia *f*

hostage [hástɪʤ] N rehén *m*

hostel [hástəl] N hostal *m*

hostelry [hástəlri] N hostería *f*

hostess [hóstɪs] N (at home) anfitriona *f*; (on airplanes) azafata *f*

hostile [hástəl] ADJ hostil

hostility [hɑstílɪdi] N hostilidad *f*

hot [hɑt] ADJ (at high temperature) caliente; (sweltry) caluroso; (spicy) picante; (sexy) bueno; (stolen) robado; (recent) de último momento; (popular) popular; **— and heavy** apasionadamente; **—bed** semillero *m*; **— dog** perro caliente *m*; **—headed** impetuoso, exaltado; **—house** invernadero *m*; **— potato** patata caliente *f*; **— seat** situación embarazosa *f*; **—shot** estrella *f*; **— tub** jacuzzi *m*; **(to) —wire** hacerle un puente a; **it is — today** hace calor hoy; **— under the collar** enojado

hotel [hotél] N hotel *m*; **—keeper** hotelero -ra *mf*

hound [haund] N perro de caza *m*, sabueso *m*; VT acosar, perseguir

hour [aur] N hora *f*; **— hand** horario *m*; **his finest —** su mejor momento *m*

hourly [áurli] ADV (by the hour) por horas; (on the hour) cada hora; **— wages** salario por hora *m*

house [haus] N (residence) casa *f*; (legislature) cámara legislativa *f*; **— arrest** detención domiciliaria *f*; **—boat** casa flotante *f*; **—cleaning** limpieza de la casa *f*; **—hold** casa *f*, familia *f*; **—keeper** (in a house) ama de llaves *f*; (in a home) encargado -da de limpieza *mf*; **—keeping** mantenimiento del hogar *m*; **—-to-** puerta a puerta; **—top** techo *m*, tejado *m*; **—wife** ama de casa *f*; **—work** trabajo de casa *m*, quehaceres domésticos *m pl*; **on the —** la casa paga; **to keep —** cuidar la casa; [hauz] VI/VT alojar

housing [háuzɪŋ] N (place to live) vivienda *f*; (protective covering) caja *f*

hovel [hávəl] N (hut) choza *f*, cabaña *f*, tugurio *m*; (open shed) cobertizo *m*

hover [hávɚ] VI (bird) cernerse; (hang in air) estar suspendido; (linger) rondar; **—craft** aerodeslizador *m*

how [hau] ADV cómo; **— about your mom?** ¿y tu mamá? **— beautiful!** ¡qué hermoso! **— come?** ¿por qué? **— early (late, soon)?** ¿cuándo? ¿a qué hora? **— far is it?** ¿a qué distancia está? ¿cuánto dista de aquí? **— long?** ¿cuánto tiempo? **— many?** ¿cuántos? **— much is it?** ¿cuánto vale? **— old are you?** ¿cuántos años tienes? **no matter — much it rains** por mucho que llueva; **he knows — difficult it is** él sabe lo difícil que es

however [hauévɚ] CONJ sin embargo, no obstante; ADV como quieras; **— difficult it may be** por muy difícil que sea; **— much it rains** por mucho que llueva

howl [haul] VI aullar; (wind) ulular; (with laughter) reír a carcajadas; N aullido *m*, alarido *m*

HTML (HyperText Markup Language) [etʃtiemét] N HTML *m*

hub [hʌb] N (center of wheel) cubo *m*; (center of activity) núcleo *m*; **—cap** tapacubos *m sg*

hubbub [hábʌb] N alboroto *m*, barullo *m*

huckster [hákstɚ] N (peddler) vendedor ambulante *m*; (promoter) mercachifle *m*

huddle [hádl] VI/VT (a group) apiñar(se); (curl up) acurrucar(se); (consult) conferenciar; N tropel *m*; (group meeting for consultation) reunión *f*; **to be in a —** estar agrupados; **to get in a —** agruparse

hue [hju] N matiz *m*

huff [hʌf] N **to get into a —** enojarse; **to — and puff** resoplar

hug [hʌg] VI/VT abrazar(se); **to — the coast** costear; N abrazo *m*

huge [hjuʤ] ADJ enorme, fiero

hull [hʌl] N (of a ship, airplane) casco *m*; (of beans, peas) vaina *f*; (of fruits, nuts) cáscara *f*; VT (beans, peas) desvainar; (nuts) cascar

hum [hʌm] VI/VT (person) tararear; (insect, machine) zumbar; (place of activity) hervir; **to — to sleep** arrullar; N (of voice) tarareo *m*; (of insect, machine) zumbido *m*

human [hjúmən] ADJ & N humano *m*; — **being** ser humano *m*

humane [hjumén] ADJ humano, humanitario

humanism [hjúmənɪzəm] N humanismo *m*

humanitarian [hjumænɪtériən] ADJ humanitario

humanity [hjumænɪɾi] N humanidad *f*; **humanities** humanidades *f pl*

humble [hʌ́mbəl] ADJ humilde; VT humillar

humid [hjúmɪd] ADJ húmedo

humidify [hjumídəfaɪ] VT humidificar

humidity [hjumídɪɾi] N humedad *f*

humiliate [hjumíliet] VT humillar, vejar

humiliation [hjumiliéʃən] N humillación *f*

humility [hjumílɪɾi] N humildad *f*

hummingbird [hámɪŋbɚd] N colibrí *m*

humor [hjúmɚ] N humor *m*, humorismo *m*; **out of —** de mal humor, malhumorado; VT complacer a

humorous [hjúmɚəs] ADJ gracioso, chistoso

hump [hʌmp] N joroba *f*, giba *f*, corcova *f*; **we're over the —** ya pasamos lo peor

humpback [hámpbæk] N jorobado -da *mf*; — **whale** ballena jorobada *f*, yubarta *f*

hunch [hʌntʃ] N presentimiento *m*, corazonada *f*; —**back** (person) jorobado -da *mf*; (hump) corcova *f*; VI encorvar

hundred [hándrɪd] NUM cien(to); **a — people** cien personas; **a — and fifty people** ciento cincuenta personas; N cien / ciento *m*; —**s** centenares *m pl*, cientos *m pl*

hundredth [hándrɪdθ] ADJ centésimo

Hungarian [hʌŋgériən] ADJ & N húngaro -ra *mf*

Hungary [háŋgəri] N Hungría *f*

hunger [háŋgɚ] N hambre *f*; VI pasar hambre; **to — for** ansiar, anhelar

hungry [háŋgri] ADJ hambriento; **to be —** tener hambre

hunk [hʌŋk] N pedazo *m*, cacho *m*; **he's a real —** es un cacho de hombre

hunt [hʌnt] VI/VT (seek prey) cazar; **to — down** dar caza a; **to — for** buscar; N (activity of hunting) caza *f*; (instance of hunting) cacería *f*; (search) búsqueda *f*

hunter [hántɚ] N (who captures game) cazador -ra *mf*; (seeker) buscador -ra *mf*; (dog) perro de caza *m*

hunting [hántɪŋ] N caza *f*; — **knife** cuchillo

de caza *m*

huntsman [hántsmən] N cazador *m*

hurdle [hɚ́dl] N (impediment) obstáculo *m*; (in races) valla *f*; VT saltar

hurl [hɚl] VI/VT arrojar, lanzar, precipitar

hurrah [hɚɑ́] INTERJ ¡hurra!

hurricane [hɚ́ɪkən] N huracán *m*

hurried [hɚ́id] ADJ apresurado; *Am* apurado

hurry [hɚ́i] VI darse prisa, apresurarse; *Am* apurarse; VT apresurar; *Am* apurar; **to — in (out)** entrar (salir) de prisa; **to — up** apresurar(se), dar(se) prisa; *Am* apurar(se); N prisa *f*; *Am* apuro *m*; **to be in a —** tener prisa; *Am* estar apurado

hurt [hɚt] VI/VT (to injure) lastimar(se), hacer(se) daño; (damage) dañar(se); (harm) perjudicar(se); VI (suffer pain) doler; **to get —** lastimarse; **to — someone's feelings** lastimar a uno; **my tooth —s** me duele la muela / el diente; N (damage) daño *m*; (wound) herida *f*, lastimadura *f*

hurtful [hɚ́tfəl] ADJ hiriente

husband [házbənd] N marido *m*, esposo *m*; VT administrar

hush [hʌʃ] VI/VT aquietar(se), callar(se); —! ¡chitón! ¡silencio! **to — up a scandal** encubrir un escándalo; N silencio *m*

husk [hʌsk] N (shell) cáscara *f*; (pod) vaina *f*; (of corn) chala *f*; *Sp* farfolla *f*; VT (corn) quitar la chala / farfolla a; (beans, peas) desvainar

husky [háski] ADJ (voice) ronco; (strong) recio; N husky *m*, perro esquimal *m*

hustle [hásəl] VI (work energetically) afanarse; (swindle) estafar; VT (hurry along) empujar; N (bustle) ajetreo *m*; (scheme) timo *m*; — **and bustle** ajetreo *m*, trajín *m*

hut [hʌt] N choza *f*, cabaña *f*

hyacinth [háɪəsɪnθ] N jacinto *m*

hybrid [háɪbrɪd] ADJ híbrido

hydrate [háɪdret] N hidrato *m*; VI/VT hidratar(se)

hydraulic [haɪdrɔ́lɪk] ADJ hidráulico

hydrocarbon [háɪdrəkɑrbən] N hidrocarburo *m*

hydroelectric [haɪdroɪléktrɪk] ADJ hidroeléctrico

hydrogen [háɪdrədʒən] N hidrógeno *m*; — **bomb** bomba de hidrógeno *f*; — **peroxide** peróxido de hidrógeno *m*, agua oxigenada *f*

hydrophobia [haɪdrəfóbiə] N hidrofobia *f*

hydroplane [háɪdrəplen] N hidroavión *m*

hyena [haɪínə] N hiena *f*

hygiene [háɪdʒin] N higiene *f*

hymn [hɪm] N himno *m*

hype [háɪp] N exageración *f*; VT promocionar (exageradamente)

hyper [háɪpɚ] ADJ hiperactivo

hyperactive [haɪpɚǽktɪv] ADJ hiperactivo

hypersensitive [haɪpɚsénsɪdɪv] ADJ hipersensible

hyperventilate [haɪpɚvéntˌlet] VI hiperventilar

hyphen [háɪfən] N guión *m*

hypnosis [hɪpnósɪs] N hipnosis *f*

hypnotize [hípnətaɪz] VT hipnotizar

hypoallergenic [haɪpoælɚdʒénɪk] ADJ hipoalérgico

hypochondriac [haɪpokándrɪæk] N hipocondríaco *mf*, hipocondriaco *mf*

hypocrisy [hɪpákrɪsi] N hipocresía *f*

hypocrite [hípəkrɪt] N hipócrita *mf*

hypocritical [hɪpəkrídɪkəɫ] ADJ hipócrita

hypoglycemia [haɪpoglaɪsímɪə] N hipoglucemia *f*

hypothesis [haɪpáθɪsɪs] N hipótesis *f*

hysterectomy [hɪstəréktəmi] N histerectomía *f*

hysterical [hɪstérɪkəɫ] ADJ (out of control) histérico; (funny) desternillante

Ii

I [aɪ] PRON yo

I-beam [áɪbim] N viga doble *f*

Iberian [aɪbírɪən] ADJ ibérico

ice [aɪs] N hielo *m*; — **age** periodo glaciar *m*; —**berg** iceberg *m*; —**box** Sp nevera *f*; Am refrigerador *m*; — **cream** helado *m*; **cream cone** cucurucho de helado *m*; —**-cream parlor** heladería *f*; — **hockey** hockey sobre hielo *m*; — **skates** patines de cuchilla *m pl*; —**d tea** té helado *m*; — **water** agua helada *f*; **to break the** — romper el hielo; **on** — en suspenso; VI/VT (freeze) helar(se); (cover with ice) cubrir(se) de hielo; VT (cover with icing) bañar; (insure a deal) cerrar; **to** —**-skate** patinar sobre hielo

Iceland [áɪslənd] N Islandia *f*

Icelander [áɪsləndɚ] N islandés -esa *mf*

Icelandic [aɪslǽndɪk] ADJ islandés

icicle [áɪsɪkəɫ] N carámbano *m*

icing [áɪsɪŋ] N (frosting) baño *m*; (formation of ice) formación de hielo *f*

icon [áɪkɑn] N icono *m*, ícono *m* (also computer term)

icy [áɪsi] ADJ helado

idea [aɪdíə] N idea *f*

ideal [aɪdíəɫ] N ideal *m*; ADJ ideal, idóneo

idealism [aɪdíəlɪzəm] N idealismo *m*

idealist [aɪdíəlɪst] N idealista *mf*

idealistic [aɪdíəlístɪk] ADJ idealista

identical [aɪdéntɪkəɫ] ADJ idéntico

identification [aɪdɛntəfɪkéʃən] N identificación *f*; — **card** carnet de identidad *m*, cédula de identidad *f*

identify [aɪdéntəfaɪ] VI/VT identificar(se)

identity [aɪdéntɪdi] N identidad *f*

ideology [aɪdiálədʒi] N ideología *f*

idiocy [ídɪəsi] N idiotez *f*

idiom [ídɪəm] N modismo *m*

idiosyncrasy [ɪdɪosíŋkrəsi] N idiosincrasia *f*

idiot [ídɪət] N idiota *mf*

idiotic [ɪdiádɪk] ADJ idiota

idle [áɪdɫ] ADJ (not active) ocioso; (lazy) perezoso, holgazán; (of a machine, worker) parado; (of an engine) en ralentí; (meaningless) vacío; VI (person) holgazanear; (motor) girar en vacío; VT (cause to be idle) dejar parado / desocupado

idleness [áɪdɫnɪs] N (inactivity) ociosidad *f*, ocio *m*, holganza *f*; (sloth) pereza *f*

idler [áɪdlɚ] N holgazán -ana *mf*, zanguango -ga *mf*

idol [áɪdɫ] N ídolo *m*

idolatry [aɪdálətri] N idolatría *f*

idolize [áɪdˌaɪz] VT idolatrar

idyll [áɪdɫ] N idilio *m*

if [ɪf] CONJ si; — **I were you** en tu lugar / yo que tú; — **only I had known** de haber sabido / ojalá hubiera sabido; **he's tall,** — **a bit stooped** es alto, aunque un poco encorvado; **no** —**s, ands, or buts** no hay pero que valga

igloo [íglu] N iglú *m*

ignite [ɪgnáɪt] VI/VT encender(se), prender fuego (a)

ignition [ɪgníʃən] N ignición *f*, encendido *m*; — **switch** llave de contacto *f*

ignoble [ɪgnóbəɫ] ADJ innoble

ignorance [ígnərəns] N ignorancia *f*

ignorant [ígnərənt] ADJ ignorante

ignore [ɪgnór] VT ignorar

ilk [ɪɫk] N ralea *f*, calaña *f*

ill [ɪɫ] ADJ enfermo, malo; — **fortune** mala suerte *f*; — **nature** mal genio *m*, mala índole *f*; — **repute** mala fama *f*; — **will** mala voluntad *f*; N (unfavorable statement) mal *m*; (sickness) enfermedad *f*; (calamity) calamidad *f*; ADV — **at ease** incómodo; —**-bred** maleducado; —**-fated** fatídico, funesto, desastrado; —**-gotten** mal adquirido; —**-humored**

malhumorado; —-**mannered**
maleducado, grosero; —-**natured** de mal
genio; **we can — afford to stop now**
de ninguna manera podemos detenernos
ahora; **you would be —-advised to
invest** sería desaconsejable que invirtieras
illegal [ɪlíɡəł] ADJ ilegal
illegitimate [ɪlɪʤínəmɪt] ADJ ilegítimo
illicit [ɪlísɪt] ADJ ilícito
illiteracy [ɪlínərəsi] N analfabetismo *m*
illiterate [ɪlínərət] ADJ & N analfabeto -ta *mf*
illness [íłnɪs] N enfermedad *f*
illuminate [ɪlúmənet] VI/VT iluminar(se)
illumination [ɪlumənéʃən] N iluminación *f*
illusion [ɪlúʒən] N ilusión *f*
illusory [ɪlúzəri] ADJ ilusorio
illustrate [íləstret] VI/VT ilustrar
illustration [ɪləstréʃən] N ilustración *f*,
estampa *f*
illustrator [íləstredə-] N ilustrador -ra *mf*,
dibujante *mf*
illustrious [ɪlástriəs] ADJ ilustre, eximio
image [ímɪʤ] N imagen *f*
imagery [ímɪʤri] N conjunto de imágenes *m*
imaginary [ɪmǽʤəneri] ADJ imaginario,
fabuloso
imagination [ɪmæʤənéʃən] N imaginación *f*,
fantasía *f*
imaginative [ɪmǽʤənədɪv] ADJ imaginativo,
fantasioso
imagine [ɪmǽʤɪn] VI/VT imaginar(se); —
that! ¡figúrate!
imbalance [ɪmbǽləns] N desequilibrio *m*
imbecile [ímbəsəł] N imbécil *mf*
imbibe [ɪmbáɪb] VI/VT beber
imbue [ɪmbjú] VT imbuir, infundir
imitate [ímɪtet] VT imitar
imitation [ɪmɪtéʃən] N imitación *f*; ADJ —
leather imitación de cuero *f*
imitator [ímɪtedə-] N imitador -ra *mf*
immaculate [ɪmǽkjəlɪt] ADJ inmaculado
immaterial [ɪmətíriəł] ADJ inmaterial; **it is
— to me** me es indiferente
immature [ɪmətʃúr] ADJ inmaduro
immediate [ɪmídiɪt] ADJ inmediato
immense [ɪméns] ADJ inmenso
immensity [ɪménsɪti] N inmensidad *f*
immerse [ɪmɔ́-s] VT (submerge) sumergir;
(absorb) sumir
immigrant [ímɪɡrənt] ADJ & N inmigrante
mf
immigrate [ímɪɡret] VI inmigrar
immigration [ɪmɪɡréʃən] N inmigración *f*
imminent [ímənənt] ADJ inminente
immobile [ɪmóbəł] ADJ inmóvil
immobilize [ɪmóbəlaɪz] VT inmovilizar
immodest [ɪmádɪst] ADJ impúdico,

deshonesto
immodesty [ɪmádɪsti] N deshonestidad *f*
immoral [ɪmɔ́rəł] ADJ inmoral
immorality [ɪmɔrǽlɪɾi] N inmoralidad *f*
immortal [ɪmɔ́rdł] ADJ & N inmortal *mf*
immortality [ɪmɔrtǽlɪɾi] N inmortalidad *f*
immovable [ɪmúvəbəł] ADJ inamovible
immune [ɪmjún] ADJ inmune; — **system**
sistema inmune *m*
immunity [ɪmjúnɪɾi] N inmunidad *f*
immutable [ɪmjúɾəbəł] ADJ inmutable
impact [ímpækt] N impacto *m*; VI/VT
impactar
impair [ɪmpér] VT dañar, deteriorar,
menoscabar
impairment [ɪmpérmənt] N daño *m*,
deterioro *m*, menoscabo *m*
impala [ɪmpálə] N impala *m*
impale [ɪmpéł] VT empalar
impart [ɪmpárt] VT (bestow knowledge)
impartir; (reveal) revelar
impartial [ɪmpárʃəł] ADJ imparcial
impartiality [ɪmparʃiǽlɪɾi] N imparcialidad *f*
impasse [ímpæs] N impasse *m*
impassioned [ɪmpǽʃənd] ADJ apasionado
impassive [ɪmpǽsɪv] ADJ impasible
impatience [ɪmpéʃəns] N impaciencia *f*
impatient [ɪmpéʃənt] ADJ impaciente
impeach [ɪmpítʃ] VT acusar formalmente; **to
— a person's honor** poner en tela de
juicio el honor de uno
impeachment [ɪmpítʃmənt] N impeachment
m
impede [ɪmpíd] VT obstaculizar, estorbar,
trabar
impediment [ɪmpédəmənt] N impedimento
m, obstáculo *m*; (of speech) defecto *m*
impel [ɪmpéł] VT impeler
impending [ɪmpéndɪŋ] ADJ inminente
impenetrable [ɪmpénɪtrəbəł] ADJ
impenetrable
imperative [ɪmpérədɪv] ADJ (like a
command) imperativo; (necessary)
imperioso; N (command, grammatical
mood) imperativo *m*; (obligation)
obligación *f*
imperceptible [ɪmpə-séptəbəł] ADJ
imperceptible
imperfect [ɪmpɔ́-fɪkt] ADJ & N imperfecto *m*
imperial [ɪmpíriəł] ADJ imperial
imperialism [ɪmpíriəlɪzəm] N imperialismo
m
imperil [ɪmpérəł] VT poner en peligro
imperious [ɪmpíriəs] ADJ imperioso
impersonal [ɪmpɔ́-sənəł] ADJ impersonal
impersonate [ɪmpɔ́-sənet] VT (assume traits
of) hacerse pasar por; (mimic) imitar

impertinence [ɪmpə́-tṇəns] N impertinencia f

impertinent [ɪmpə́-tṇənt] ADJ impertinente

impervious [ɪmpə́-viəs] ADJ impermeable; (to reason) refractario

impetuous [ɪmpétʃuəs] ADJ impetuoso

impetus [ímpəɒəs] N ímpetu m, empuje m

impious [ímpiəs] ADJ impío

implacable [ɪmplǽkəbəł] ADJ implacable

implant [ɪmplǽnt] VT implantar; [ímplænt] N implante m

implement [ímpləmənt] N implemento m, utensilio m; [ímpləmənt] VT implementar, instrumentar

implicate [ímplɪket] VT implicar, involucrar

implicit [ɪmplísɪt] ADJ implícito

implore [ɪmplɔ́r] VI/VT implorar

imply [ɪmpláɪ] VT dar a entender

impolite [ɪmpəláɪt] ADJ descortés

import [ɪmpɔ́rt] VT (bring in) importar; [ímpɔrt] N (act of importing, thing imported) importación f; (significance) significado m

importance [ɪmpɔ́rtṇs] N importancia f

important [ɪmpɔ́rtṇt] ADJ importante

impose [ɪmpóz] VT imponer; **to — (upon)** abusar (de)

imposing [ɪmpózɪŋ] ADJ imponente, impresionante

imposition [ɪmpəzíʃən] N (act of imposing, burden) imposición f; (abuse) abuso m

impossibility [ɪmpɑsəbílɪɒi] N imposibilidad f

impossible [ɪmpɑ́səbəł] ADJ (not possible) imposible; (unbearable) insoportable; **to make —** imposibilitar

impostor [ɪmpɑ́stə-] N impostor -ra mf

impotence [ímpətəns] N impotencia f

impotent [ímpətənt] ADJ impotente

impoverish [ɪmpɑ́və-ɪʃ] VT empobrecer

impregnate [ɪmprégnet] VT (cause to be permeated) impregnar; (make pregnant) fecundar

impress [ɪmprés] VT (make a mark by pressing) estampar; VI/VT (affect deeply) impresionar

impression [ɪmpréʃən] N impresión f; (feeling) impresión f, sensación f

impressive [ɪmprésɪv] ADJ impresionante

imprint [ímprɪnt] N (indentation) impresión f, marca f; (printer's mark) pie de imprenta m; [ɪmprínt] VT (impress on) imprimir; (fix firmly in mind) grabar

imprison [ɪmprízən] VT (in jail) encarcelar; (anywhere) apresar

imprisonment [ɪmprízənmənt] N encarcelamiento m

improbable [ɪmprɑ́bəbəł] ADJ improbable

impromptu [ɪmprɑ́mptu] ADJ improvisado; **he gave the speech —** improvisó el discurso; N impromptu m

improper [ɪmprɑ́pə-] ADJ indecoroso, inconveniente

improve [ɪmprúv] VI/VT mejorar(se); **to — upon** mejorar

improvement [ɪmprúvmənt] N (act & effect of improving) mejora f; (in health) mejoría f

improvisation [ɪmprɑvɪzéʃən] N improvisación f

improvise [ímprəvaɪz] VI/VT improvisar

imprudent [ɪmprúdṇt] ADJ imprudente, desatinado

impudence [ímpjədəns] N impertinencia f, descaro m, desparpajo m

impudent [ímpjədənt] ADJ impertinente, descarado

impulse [ímpʌłs] N impulso m; **to act on —** obrar impulsivamente

impulsive [ɪmpʌ́łsɪv] ADJ impulsivo

impunity [ɪmpjúnɪɒi] N impunidad f

impure [ɪmpjúr] ADJ impuro

impurity [ɪmpjúrɪɒi] N impureza f

in [ɪn] PREP en; **— London** en Londres; **— haste** de prisa; **— the morning** por/en la mañana; **— writing** por escrito; **she was walking — the street** andaba por la calle; **to arrive — London** llegar a Londres; **the books — the box** los libros de la caja; **at two — the morning** a las dos de la mañana; **dressed — white** vestido de blanco; **the tallest — his class** el más alto de su clase; **to come — a week** venir dentro de una semana; ADV adentro, dentro; **is she — or out?** ¿está adentro o afuera? **to be all —** estar rendido; **to be — with someone** estar bien con alguien; **to come —** entrar; **to have it — for someone** tenerle ojeriza a una persona; **to put —** meter; **the doctor is —** el doctor está; **hats are —** los sombreros están de moda; **—patient** paciente internado -da mf; **—seam** entrepierna f; **—step** empeine m; ADJ **the — place to eat** el restaurante de moda; **an — joke** una broma para un grupo selecto

inability [ɪnəbílɪɒi] N inhabilidad f, incapacidad f

inaccessible [ɪnæksésəbəł] ADJ inaccesible, inasequible

inaccurate [ɪnǽkjə-ɪt] ADJ (not precise) inexacto, impreciso; (wrong) incorrecto

inactive [ɪnǽktɪv] ADJ inactivo

inactivity [ɪnæktívɪDɪ] N inactividad *f*
inadequate [ɪnǽDɪkwɪt] ADJ (insufficient)
insuficiente; (unacceptable) inaceptable
inadvertent [ɪnədvɝ́-tŋt] ADJ (unintentional)
involuntario; (careless) descuidado,
negligente
inadvisable [ɪnədváɪzəbəl] ADJ
desaconsejable
inane [ɪnén] ADJ necio
inanimate [ɪnǽnəmɪt] ADJ inanimado
inasmuch as [ɪnəzmǽtʃæz] CONJ puesto que
inattentive [ɪnətɛ́ntɪv] ADJ desatento
inaudible [ɪnɔ́Dəbəl] ADJ inaudible
inaugurate [ɪnɔ́gjəret] VT (initiate)
inaugurar; (induct into office) investir de
un cargo
inauguration [ɪnɔgjəréʃən] N (initiation)
inauguración *f*; (induction) investidura *f*
inboard [ɪ́nbɔrd] ADJ dentro del casco
inborn [ɪnbɔ́rn] ADJ innato
incandescence [ɪnkændésəns] N
incandescencia *f*
incandescent [ɪnkændésənt] ADJ
incandescente
incantation [ɪnkæntéʃən] N conjuro *m*
incapable [ɪnképəbəl] ADJ incapaz
incapacitate [ɪnkəpǽsɪtet] VT incapacitar
incarcerate [ɪnkɑ́rsəret] VT encarcelar
incendiary [ɪnséndieri] ADJ & N incendiario
-ria *mf*; **— bomb** bomba incendiaria *f*
incense [ínsɛns] N incienso *m*; [ɪnséns] VT
encolerizar
incentive [ɪnséntɪv] N incentivo *m*, acicate *m*
inception [ɪnsépʃən] N comienzo *m*
incessant [ɪnsésənt] ADJ incesante
incest [ínsɛst] N incesto *m*
inch [ɪntʃ] N pulgada (2.54 centímetros) *f*; **to
be within an — of** estar a un punto de;
VI avanzar poco a poco
incidence [ínsɪdəns] N incidencia *f*
incident [ínsɪdənt] N incidente *m*, lance *m*;
(crime, accident) suceso *m*
incidental [ɪnsɪdéntl] ADJ (happening in
accordance with) accesorio; N **— music**
música incidental *f*; **—s** gastos imprevistos
m pl
incidentally [ɪnsɪdéntli] ADV a propósito
incinerate [ɪnsínəret] VT incinerar
incipient [ɪnsípiənt] ADJ incipiente, naciente
incision [ɪnsíʒən] N incisión *f*
incisive [ɪnsáɪsɪv] ADJ incisivo
incite [ɪnsáɪt] VT incitar
inclement [ɪnklémənt] ADJ inclemente
inclination [ɪnklənéʃən] N (slope)
inclinación *f*; (tendency) afición *f*,
inclinación *f*
incline [ɪnkláɪn] VI/VT inclinar(se); [ínklaɪn] N

declive *m*, pendiente *f*
include [ɪnklúd] VT incluir
inclusive [ɪnklúsɪv] ADJ inclusivo; **from
Monday to Friday —** de lunes a viernes
inclusive
incoherent [ɪnkohírənt] ADJ incoherente
income [ínkʌm] N *Sp* renta *f*; *Am* ingreso *m*;
— tax *Sp* impuesto sobre la renta *m*; *Am*
impuesto sobre ingresos *m*
incoming [ínkʌmɪŋ] ADJ entrante
incomparable [ɪnkɑ́mpə-əbəl] ADJ
incomparable, sin parangón
incompatible [ɪnkəmpǽɛDəbəl] ADJ
incompatible
incompetent [ɪnkɑ́mpɪtənt] ADJ
incompetente
incomplete [ɪnkəmplít] ADJ incompleto
incomprehensible [ɪnkɑmprɪhénsəbəl] ADJ
incomprensible
inconceivable [ɪnkənsívəbəl] ADJ
inconcebible
inconclusive [ɪnkənklúsɪv] ADJ no
concluyente
inconsiderate [ɪnkənsíDə-ɪt] ADJ
desconsiderado
inconsistency [ɪnkənsístənsi] N (condition)
inconsecuencia *f*; (instance) incoherencia *f*
inconsistent [ɪnkənsístənt] ADJ
inconsecuente
inconspicuous [ɪnkənspíkjuəs] ADJ poco
llamativo; **to be —** pasar inadvertido
inconstancy [ɪnkɑ́nstənsi] N inconstancia *f*
inconstant [ɪnkɑ́nstənt] ADJ inconstante
incontinent [ɪnkɑ́ntənənt] ADJ incontinente
incontrovertible [ɪnkɑntrəvɝ́-Dəbəl] ADJ
incontrovertible
inconvenience [ɪnkənvínjəns] N (state of
being inconvenient) inconveniencia *f*;
(thing that is inconvenient) molestia *f*,
inconveniente *m*; VT incomodar, molestar
inconvenient [ɪnkənvínjənt] ADJ
(bothersome) incómodo; (untimely)
inoportuno
incorporate [ɪnkɔ́rpəret] VI/VT (include)
incorporar(se); (form a corporation)
constituir(se) en sociedad
incorrect [ɪnkərékt] ADJ incorrecto
incorrigible [ɪnkɔ́rɪdʒəbəl] ADJ incorregible
increase [ɪnkrís] VI/VT aumentar(se),
incrementar(se); [ínkris] N aumento *m*,
incremento *m*
increasingly [ɪnkrísɪŋli] ADV cada vez más
incredible [ɪnkrédəbəl] ADJ increíble
incredulous [ɪnkrédʒələs] ADJ incrédulo
increment [ínkrəmənt] N incremento *m*
incriminate [ɪnkrímənet] VT incriminar
incubator [íŋkjəbeDə-] N incubadora *f*

inculcate [ɪnkáɫket] VT inculcar
incumbent [ɪnkámbənt] ADJ **a duty —
upon me** un deber que me incumbe; N
titular *m*
incur [ɪnkɚ́] VT incurrir en
incurable [ɪnkjúrəbəɫ] ADJ incurable
indebted [ɪndéDɪd] ADJ endeudado; **I'm —
to you for your kindness** estoy en
deuda contigo por tu amabilidad
indebtedness [ɪndéDɪdnɪs] N endeudamiento
m, adeudo *m*
indecency [ɪndísənsi] N indecencia *f*
indecent [ɪndísənt] ADJ indecente; **—
exposure** delito de exhibicionismo *m*
indecision [ɪndɪsíʒən] N indecisión *f*
indeed [ɪndíd] ADV de verdad; INTERJ
(ironically) ¡no me digas! (sincerely)
¡tienes razón!
indefensible [ɪndɪfénsəbəɫ] ADJ indefendible
indefinite [ɪndéfənɪt] ADJ indefinido
indelible [ɪndéləbəɫ] ADJ indeleble
indelicate [ɪndélɪkɪt] ADJ (tactless) indelicado;
(offensive) indecoroso
indemnify [ɪndémnəfaɪ] VT indemnizar
indemnity [ɪndémnɪDi] N indemnización *f*
indent [ɪndént] VI/VT sangrar
indentation [ɪndɛntéʃən] N (notch) muesca
f; (blank space) sangría *f*
independence [ɪndɪpéndəns] N
independencia *f*
independent [ɪndɪpéndənt] ADJ
independiente
indestructible [ɪndɪstráktəbəɫ] ADJ
indestructible
indeterminate [ɪndɪtɚ́mənɪt] ADJ
indeterminado
index [índɛks] N índice *m*; **— card** ficha *f*; **—
finger** índice *m*; VT (incorporate into an
index) poner en el índice; (make the
index) poner un índice; (adjust wages)
indexar
India [índiə] N India *f*
Indian [índiən] ADJ & N indio -a *mf*; **—
Ocean** Océano Índico *m*
indicate [índɪket] VT indicar
indication [ɪndɪkéʃən] N indicación *f*
indicative [ɪndíkəDɪv] ADJ & N indicativo *m*
indict [ɪndáɪt] VT acusar
indictment [ɪndáɪtmənt] N acusación *f*
indifference [ɪndífrəns] N indiferencia *f*
indifferent [ɪndífrənt] ADJ indiferente
indigenous [ɪndíʤənəs] ADJ (person)
indígena; (plant, animal) autóctono
indigent [índɪʤənt] ADJ & N indigente *mf*
indigestion [ɪndɪʤéstʃən] N indigestión *f*
indignant [ɪndígnənt] ADJ indignado
indignation [ɪndɪgnéʃən] N indignación *f*

indignity [ɪndígnɪDi] N ultraje *m*, afrenta *f*
indigo [índɪgo] N índigo *m*, añil *m*; **— blue**
azul añil *m*
indirect [ɪndɪrékt] ADJ indirecto; **— object**
complemento / objeto indirecto *m*
indiscreet [ɪndɪskrít] ADJ indiscreto
indiscretion [ɪndɪskréʃən] N indiscreción *f*
indispensable [ɪndɪspénsəbəɫ] ADJ
indispensable, imprescindible
indispose [ɪndɪspóz] VT indisponer
indisposed [ɪndɪspózd] ADJ indispuesto; **to
become —** indisponerse
indistinct [ɪndɪstíŋkt] ADJ indistinto
individual [ɪndəvíʤuəɫ] ADJ individual; N
individuo *m*, persona *f*; *pej* sujeto *m*,
individuo *m*
individualism [ɪndəvíʤuəlɪzəm] N
individualismo *m*
individualist [ɪndəvíʤuəlɪst] N
individualista *mf*
individuality [ɪndəvɪʤuǽlɪDi] N
individualidad *f*
indivisible [ɪndəvízəbəɫ] ADJ indivisible
indoctrinate [ɪndáktrɪnet] VT adoctrinar
indolence [índələns] N indolencia *f*, desidia *f*
indolent [índələnt] ADJ indolente, haragán
indomitable [ɪndámɪDəbəɫ] ADJ indomable
Indonesia [ɪndəníʒə] N Indonesia *f*
Indonesian [ɪndəníʒən] ADJ & N indonesio
-sia *mf*
indoor [índɔr] ADJ interior; [índɔrz] ADV **—s**
dentro; **to go —s** entrar, ir para adentro
induce [ɪndús] VT inducir
inducement [ɪndúsmənt] N aliciente *m*,
incentivo *m*
induct [ɪndákt] VT (initiate) admitir, iniciar;
(draft) reclutar ·
induction [ɪndákʃən] N (philosophical,
electrical) inducción *f*; (into an
organization) admisión *f*, iniciación *f*
indulge [ɪndáɫʤ] VT mimar, consentir; VI **to
— in** darse a, entregarse a; **to — oneself
(in)** darse el gusto (de)
indulgence [ɪndáɫʤəns] N (act or state of
indulging, religious) indulgencia *f*; (thing
indulged in) exceso *m*, lujo *m*
indulgent [ɪndáɫʤənt] ADJ indulgente;
(toward a child) complaciente
industrial [ɪndástriəɫ] ADJ industrial
industrialist [ɪndástriəlɪst] N industrial *mf*
industrious [ɪndástriəs] ADJ (student)
aplicado, diligente; (worker) industrioso
industry [índəstri] N (manufacturing)
industria *f*; (hard work) diligencia *f*
inebriated [iníbrieDɪd] ADJ ebrio
inedible [ɪnédəbəɫ] ADJ incomestible,
incomible

ineffable [ɪnéfəbəɫ] ADJ inefable
ineffective [ɪnɪféktɪv] ADJ (measure) ineficaz; (person) deficiente
ineffectual [ɪnɪféktʃuəɫ] ADJ ineficaz
inefficient [ɪnɪfíʃənt] ADJ ineficiente
ineligible [ɪnélɪdʒəbəɫ] ADJ inelegible
inept [ɪnépt] ADJ inepto
inequality [ɪnɪkwálɪɾi] N desigualdad *f*
inert [ɪnɝ́t] ADJ inerte
inertia [ɪnɝ́ʃə] N inercia *f*
inescapable [ɪnɪsképəbəɫ] ADJ inevitable
inestimable [ɪnéstəməbəɫ] ADJ inestimable
inevitable [ɪnévɪɾəbəɫ] ADJ inevitable
inexcusable [ɪnɪkskjúzəbəɫ] ADJ inexcusable
inexhaustible [ɪnɪgzɔ́stəbəɫ] ADJ inagotable
inexorable [ɪnéksəəbəɫ] ADJ inexorable
inexpensive [ɪnɪkspénsɪv] ADJ económico, barato
inexperienced [ɪnɪkspíriənst] ADJ inexperto
inexplicable [ɪnɪksplíkəbəɫ] ADJ inexplicable
infallible [ɪnfǽləbəɫ] ADJ infalible
infamous [ínfəməs] ADJ infame, de mala fama
infamy [ínfəmi] N infamia *f*
infancy [ínfənsi] N primera infancia *f*
infant [ínfənt] N bebé *m*
infantile [ínfəntaɪɫ] ADJ infantil
infantry [ínfəntri] N infantería *f*; **—man** infante *m*
infatuated [ɪnfǽtʃuedɪd] ADJ enamorado
infect [ɪnfékt] VT (cause disease) infectar; (spread a mood) contagiar
infection [ɪnfékʃən] N infección *f*
infectious [ɪnfékʃəs] ADJ (disease) infeccioso, contagioso; (mood) contagioso
infer [ɪnfɝ́] VT inferir, deducir
inference [ínfəəns] N inferencia *f*, deducción *f*
inferior [ɪnfíriə] ADJ inferior
inferiority [ɪnfiriɔ́rɪɾi] N inferioridad *f*; **— complex** complejo de inferioridad *m*
infernal [ɪnfɝ́nəɫ] ADJ infernal
inferno [ɪnfɝ́no] N (fire) incendio *m*; (hot place) infierno *m*
infest [ɪnfést] VT infestar, plagar
infiltrate [ɪnfíɫtret] VI/VT infiltrar(se); **to — an organization** infiltrarse en una organización
infinite [ínfənɪt] ADJ & N infinito *m*
infinitive [ɪnfínɪɾɪv] ADJ & N infinitivo *m*
infinity [ɪnfínɪɾi] N (large number) infinidad *f*; (space) infinito *m*
infirm [ɪnfɝ́m] ADJ enfermizo, achacoso
infirmary [ɪnfɝ́məri] N enfermería *f*
infirmity [ɪnfɝ́mɪɾi] N enfermedad *f*, achaque *m*
inflame [ɪnflém] VT (with infection)

inflamar(se); (with passion) enardecer(se); (with fire) encender(se)
inflammation [ɪnfləméʃən] N inflamación *f*
inflate [ɪnflét] VI/VT (fill with air) inflar(se), hincharse; (exaggerate) exagerar
inflation [ɪnfléʃən] N (rise in prices) inflación *f*; (introduction of air) inflado *m*
inflexible [ɪnfléksəbəɫ] ADJ inflexible
inflict [ɪnflíkt] VT (impose on) infligir; **to — a blow** asestar un golpe
influence [ínfluəns] N influencia *f*, influjo *m*; VT influir en / sobre; **— peddling** tráfico de influencias *m*
influential [ɪnfluénʃəɫ] ADJ influyente
influenza [ɪnfluénzə] N gripe *f*
influx [ínflʌks] N (of fluid, goods) entrada *f*; (of people) afluencia *f*
infomercial [ínfomɝ̀ʃəɫ] N infomercial *m*
inform [ɪnfɔ́rm] VI/VT (give knowledge) informar(se); VT (inspire) inspirar; **to — against / on** delatar a, denunciar a
informal [ɪnfɔ́rməɫ] ADJ informal
informant [ɪnfɔ́rmənt] N informante *mf*
information [ɪnfəméʃən] N (service) información *f*; (details) informes *m pl*
informer [ɪnfɔ́rmə] N informante *mf*, delator -ora *mf*, *pej* soplón -ona *mf*
infraction [ɪnfrǽkʃən] N infracción *f*
infrared [ɪnfrəréd] ADJ & N infrarrojo *m*
infrastructure [ínfrəstrʌktʃə] N infraestructura *f*
infringe [ɪnfrínɖʒ] VT infringir; VI **to — upon** violar
infuriate [ɪnfjúriet] VT enfurecer, sublevar
infuse [ɪnfjúz] VT infundir
ingenious [ɪnɖʒínjəs] ADJ ingenioso
ingenuity [ɪnɖʒənúɪɾi] N ingenio *m*, inventiva *f*
ingest [ɪnɖʒést] VI/VT ingerir
ingrate [íngret] N ingrato -ta *mf*
ingratitude [ɪngrǽɾɪtud] N ingratitud *f*
ingredient [ɪngrídiənt] N ingrediente *m*
ingrown [íngron] ADJ encarnado
inhabit [ɪnhǽbɪt] VT habitar
inhabitant [ɪnhǽbɪtənt] N habitante *mf*
inhale [ɪnhéɫ] VI/VT inhalar, aspirar
inherent [ɪnhérənt] ADJ inherente
inherit [ɪnhérɪt] VI/VT heredar
inheritance [ɪnhérɪɾəns] N herencia *f*
inhibit [ɪnhíbɪt] VT inhibir, cohibir
inhibition [ɪnɪbíʃən] N inhibición *f*, cohibición *f*
inhospitable [ɪnhɑspíɾəbəɫ] ADJ (person) inhospitalario; (place) inhóspito
inhuman [ɪnhjúmən] ADJ inhumano
inimitable [ɪnímɪɾəbəɫ] ADJ inimitable
initial [ɪníʃəɫ] ADJ & N inicial *f*; VT firmar las

iniciales
initialize [ɪníʃəlaɪz] VT inicializar
initiate [ɪníʃiet] VT iniciar
initiative [ɪníʃədɪv] N iniciativa *f*
inject [ɪndʒékt] VI/VT inyectar(se), pinchar(se)
injection [ɪndʒékʃən] N inyección *f*
injunction [ɪndʒʌ́ŋkʃən] N mandato judicial *m*, orden judicial *f*
injure [índʒə] VI/VT herir(se); (sports) lesionar(se)
injurious [ɪndʒúriəs] ADJ (harmful) perjudicial; (defamatory) injurioso
injury [índʒəri] N herida *f*, lesión *f*
injustice [ɪndʒʌ́stɪs] N injusticia *f*
ink [ɪŋk] N tinta *f*; VT (mark with ink) entintar; (sign) firmar; **—jet printer** impresora de inyección de tinta *f*; **—pad** almohadilla *f*; **—well** tintero *m*
inkling [íŋklɪŋ] N idea *f*
inlaid [ínled] ADJ incrustado; **— work** incrustación *f*
inland [ínlənd] ADJ interior; ADV tierra adentro
inlay [ɪnlé] VT incrustar; [ínle] N incrustación *f*
inmate [ínmet] N (in a prison) preso -sa *mf*, recluso -sa *mf*; (in an asylum) internado -da *mf*; (in a hospital) paciente *mf*
inn [ɪn] N posada *f*, fonda *f*; **—keeper** posadero -ra *mf*, fondista *mf*
innate [ɪnét] ADJ innato
inner [ínə] ADJ (inside) interior; (intimate) íntimo; **— city** zona céntrica empobrecida *f*; **— ear** oído interno *m*; **—most** más recóndito; **— tube** cámara *f*
inning [íniŋ] N entrada *f*
innocence [ínəsəns] N (absence of guilt) inocencia *f*; (naivety) candidez *f*, candor *m*
innocent [ínəsənt] ADJ & N inocente *mf*
innocuous [ɪnákjuəs] ADJ innocuo
innovation [ɪnəvéʃən] N innovación *f*
innuendo [ɪnjuéndo] N insinuación *f*
innumerable [ɪnúmərəbəl] ADJ innumerables
inoculate [ɪnákjəlet] VI/VT inocular(se)
inoffensive [ɪnəfénsɪv] ADJ inofensivo
inoperable [ɪnápə-əbəl] ADJ inoperable
inopportune [ɪnapə-tún] ADJ inoportuno
inordinate [ɪnɔ́rdn̩ɪt] ADJ desmesurado
inorganic [ɪnɔrgǽnɪk] ADJ inorgánico; **— chemistry** química inorgánica *f*
input [ínput] N (electric, computer) entrada *f*; (opinion) opinión *f*; VT ingresar/entrar datos
inquire [ɪnkwáɪr] VI/VT inquirir, preguntar; **to — about / after** preguntar por; **to — into** indagar, investigar

inquiry [íŋkwəri] N (scientific) investigación *f*; (police) pesquisa *f*; **we made — about hotels** hicimos averiguaciones acerca de hoteles
inquisition [ɪnkwɪzíʃən] N inquisición *f*
inquisitive [ɪnkwízɪdɪv] ADJ (curious) inquisitivo, curioso; (asking many questions) preguntón
insane [ɪnsén] ADJ demente, loco; **— asylum** manicomio *m*
insanity [ɪnsǽnɪdi] N locura *f*, demencia *f*
insatiable [ɪnséʃəbəl] ADJ insaciable
inscribe [ɪnskráɪb] VT (mark) inscribir; (engrave) grabar; (dedicate) dedicar
inscription [ɪnskrípʃən] N (marks, engraving) inscripción *f*; (dedication) dedicatoria *f*
inscrutable [ɪnskrúɾəbəl] ADJ inescrutable
insect [ínsekt] N insecto *m*
insecticide [ɪnséktɪsaɪd] N insecticida *m*
insectivorous [ɪnsektívə-əs] ADJ insectívoro
insecure [ɪnsɪkjúr] ADJ inseguro
insensible [ɪnsénsəbəl] ADJ insensible
insensitive [ɪnsénsɪdɪv] ADJ insensible
inseparable [ɪnsépə-əbəl] ADJ inseparable
insert [ɪnsɝ́t] VT insertar, introducir; (into a text) intercalar; [ínsɝt] N encarte *m*
insertion [ɪnsɝ́ʃən] N inserción *f*; (into a text) intercalación *f*
inside [ɪnsáɪd] PREP dentro de; ADV dentro, adentro; [ínsaɪd] N interior *m*; **to turn — out** volver del revés; **—s** entrañas *f pl*; **he passed me on the —** me pasó por la derecha; ADJ (interior) interior; **— job** delito cometido por un empleado *m*; **— track** pista interior *f*
insider [ɪnsáɪdə] N privilegiado -da *mf*; **— trading** abuso de información privilegiada *m*
insidious [ɪnsídiəs] ADJ insidioso
insight [ínsaɪt] N (intuition) perspicacia *f*; (discernment) discernimiento *m*
insignia [ɪnsígniə] N insignia *f*
insignificant [ɪnsɪgnífɪkənt] ADJ insignificante, menudo, nimio
insincere [ɪnsɪnsír] ADJ insincero
insinuate [ɪnsínjuet] VT insinuar
insinuation [ɪnsɪnjuéʃən] N insinuación *f*
insipid [ɪnsípɪd] ADJ insípido, soso
insist [ɪnsíst] VI/VT insistir; **to — on** insistir en
insistence [ɪnsístəns] N insistencia *f*
insistent [ɪnsístənt] ADJ insistente
insole [ínsoɫ] N plantilla *f*
insolence [ínsələns] N insolencia *f*
insolent [ínsələnt] ADJ insolente, atrevido
insoluble [ɪnsáljəbəl] ADJ insoluble
insolvent [ɪnsálvənt] ADJ insolvente

inspect [ɪnspékt] VT inspeccionar; **to — the troops** pasar revista a la tropa, revistar la tropa
inspection [ɪnspékʃən] N inspección f; (of troops) revista f
inspector [ɪnspéktə] N inspector -ra mf
inspiration [ɪnspəréʃən] N inspiración f
inspire [ɪnspáɪr] VI/VT inspirar
instability [ɪnstəbílɪDi] N inestabilidad f
install [ɪnstɔ́l] VT instalar (also computer term)
installation [ɪnstəléʃən] N instalación f (also computer term)
installment [ɪnstɔ́lmənt] N (payment of debt) cuota f; (of a book) entrega f, fascículo m; **to pay in —s** pagar a plazos
instance [ínstəns] N ejemplo m; **for —** por ejemplo; **court of first —** tribunal de primera instancia m
instant [ínstənt] N instante m; **this —** ahora mismo; ADJ inmediato; **— coffee** café instantáneo m
instantaneous [ɪnstənténiəs] ADJ instantáneo
instead [ɪnstéd] ADV **she didn't want a sandwich, so she ordered a hamburger —** no quería un bocadillo, así que pidió una hamburguesa en su lugar; **— of** en lugar de, en vez de
instigate [ínstɪget] VT instigar
instill [ɪnstíl] VT inculcar
instinct [ínstɪŋkt] N instinto m
instinctive [ɪnstíŋktɪv] ADJ instintivo
institute [ínstɪtut] N instituto m; VT instituir
institution [ɪnstɪtúʃən] N institución f
instruct [ɪnstrákt] VT (teach) instruir; (command, advise) dar instrucciones; (command) mandar
instruction [ɪnstrákʃən] N instrucción f (also computer term); **—s** (orders) órdenes f pl; (information) instrucciones f pl, indicaciones f pl
instructive [ɪnstráktɪv] ADJ instructivo
instructor [ɪnstráktə] N (of skills) instructor -ra mf; (of knowledge) profesor -ra mf
instrument [ínstrəmənt] N instrumento m; **— panel** salpicadero m, tablero m
instrumental [ɪnstrəmént]] ADJ instrumental; **to be — in** ser fundamental para
insubordinate [ɪnsəbɔ́rdnɪt] ADJ insubordinado
insufferable [ɪnsáfə·əbəl] ADJ insufrible
insufficiency [ɪnsəfíʃənsi] N insuficiencia f
insufficient [ɪnsəfíʃənt] ADJ insuficiente
insulate [ínsəlet] VT aislar
insulation [ɪnsəléʃən] N aislamiento m

insulator [ínsəleDə·] N (material) aislante m; (device) aislador m
insulin [ínsəlɪn] N insulina f
insult [ínsʌlt] N insulto m, injuria f; [ɪnsʌ́lt] VT insultar, injuriar
insulting [ɪnsʌ́ltɪŋ] ADJ insultante, injurioso
insuperable [ɪnsúpə·əbəl] ADJ insuperable
insurance [ɪnʃúrəns] N seguro m; **— agent** agente de seguros mf; **— company** compañía de seguros f; **— policy** póliza de seguro f
insure [ɪnʃúr] VI/VT asegurar(se)
insurmountable [ɪnsə·máuntəbəl] ADJ insuperable
insurrection [ɪnsərékʃən] N insurrección f
intact [ɪntǽkt] ADJ intacto
intangible [ɪntǽndʒəbəl] ADJ intangible
integer [íntɪdʒə·] N (número) entero m
integral [íntɪgrəl] ADJ (complete) integral; (forming part of) integrante; N integral f; **— calculus** cálculo integral m
integrate [íntɪgret] VT integrar; VI integrarse a
integrity [ɪntégrɪDi] N integridad f
intellect [ínt]ekt] N intelecto m
intellectual [ɪnt]éktʃuəl] ADJ & N intelectual mf
intelligence [ɪntélɪdʒəns] N inteligencia f (also secret information); **— quotient** coeficiente intelectual / de inteligencia m
intelligent [ɪntélɪdʒənt] ADJ inteligente
intelligible [ɪntélɪdʒəbəl] ADJ inteligible
intend [ɪnténd] VT pensar; **to — to do something** pensar hacer algo; **a book —ed for children** un libro destinado / dirigido a los niños
intense [ɪnténs] ADJ intenso
intensify [ɪnténsɪfaɪ] VI/VT intensificar(se)
intensity [ɪnténsɪDi] N intensidad f
intensive [ɪnténsɪv] ADJ intensivo
intent [ɪntént] N intención f, propósito m; **to / for all —s and purposes** en la práctica; ADJ atento; **— on** resuelto a
intention [ɪnténʃən] N intención f
intentional [ɪnténʃənəl] ADJ intencional
intentionally [ɪnténʃənəli] ADV a propósito
inter [ɪntɜ́·] VT sepultar
interact [ɪntə·ǽkt] VI interactuar
interactive [ɪntə·ǽktɪv] ADJ interactivo
intercede [ɪntə·síd] VI interceder
intercept [ɪntə·sépt] VT interceptar
interception [ɪntə·sépʃən] N interceptación f
intercession [ɪntə·séʃən] N intercesión f
interchange [íntə·tʃendʒ] N cambio m; (on road) enlace m; Sp intercambiador m; [ɪntə·tʃéndʒ] VI/VT cambiar, intercambiar
intercourse [íntə·kɔrs] N comunicación f,

trato *m*

interest [íntrɪst] N interés *m*; (financial) interés *m*, rédito *m*; (share in a business) participación *f*; **mining —s** los negocios mineros; **— rate** tasa de interés *f*; VT interesar; **may I — you in a cookie?** ¿te puedo ofrecer una galleta?

interested [íntrɪstɪd] ADJ interesado; **to be / become — in** interesarse en / por

interesting [íntrɪstɪŋ] ADJ interesante

interface [íntɚfes] N interface *mf*, interfaz *f*

interfere [ɪntɚfír] VI interferir; (meddle) entrometerse; **to — with** interferir en

interference [ɪntɚfírəns] N interferencia *f*

interim [íntɚɪm] N ínterin *m*; ADJ (person) interino; (decision) provisional

interior [ɪntíriɚ] ADJ & N interior *m*; **— decoration** decoración de interiores *f*; **— design** diseño de interiores *m*

interjection [ɪntɚdʒékʃən] N interjección *f*, exclamación *f*

interlace [ɪntɚlés] VI/VT entrelazar(se)

interlinear [ɪntɚlíniɚ] ADJ interlineal

interlock [ɪntɚlák] VI/VT (gears) engranar(se); (branches, etc.) entrelazar(se); N interlock *m*

interlocking [ɪntɚlákɪŋ] ADJ (gears) engranado; (branches) entrelazado

interlude [íntɚlud] N (interval) intervalo *m*; (musical) interludio *m*; (theatrical) entremés *m*

intermediate [ɪntɚmídiɪt] ADJ intermedio

interment [ɪntɚmənt] N entierro *m*

interminable [ɪntɚmənəbəl] ADJ interminable

intermingle [ɪntɚmíŋɡəl] VI/VT entremezclar(se)

intermission [ɪntɚmíʃən] N entreacto *m*, intervalo *m*

intermittent [ɪntɚmítn̩t] ADJ intermitente

intern [íntɚn] VT internar, confinar; N (prisoner, doctor) interno -na *mf*

internal [ɪntɚnəl] ADJ interno, interior; **—-combustion engine** motor de combustión interna *m*; **— revenue** rentas internas *f pl*; **— Revenue Service** Hacienda *f*

internalize [ɪntɚnəlaɪz] VT interiorizar, internalizar

international [ɪntɚnǽʃənəl] ADJ internacional; **— law** derecho internacional *m*

Internet [íntɚnet] N internet *m*

internist [íntɚnɪst] N internista *mf*

internship [íntɚnʃɪp] N (medical) internado *m*; (student) práctica *f*

interpersonal [ɪntɚpɚ́sənəl] ADJ interpersonal

interpose [ɪntɚpóz] VI/VT interponer(se)

interpret [ɪntɚ́prɪt] VI/VT interpretar

interpretation [ɪntɚprɪtéʃən] N interpretación *f*

interpreter [ɪntɚ́prɪdɚ] N intérprete *mf*

interracial [ɪntɚréʃəl] ADJ interracial

interrelated [ɪntɚrɪlédɪd] ADJ interrelacionado

interrogate [ɪntɛ́rəget] VI/VT interrogar

interrogation [ɪntɛrəɡéʃən] N interrogación *f*, interrogatorio *m*

interrogative [ɪntɚrágədɪv] ADJ interrogativo; N palabra / oración interrogativa *f*

interrupt [ɪntɚrápt] VI/VT interrumpir

interruption [ɪntɚrápʃən] N interrupción *f*

intersect [ɪntɚsékt] VI/VT (math) intersecar(se); (road) cruzar(se)

intersection [ɪntɚsékʃən] N (math) intersección *f*; (street) cruce *m*, intersección *f*

intersperse [ɪntɚspɚ́s] VT (scatter) esparcir; (intermingle) entremezclar, entreverar; (spice up) salpicar

interstate [íntɚstet] ADJ interestatal; N **— highway** autopista interestatal *f*

interstellar [ɪntɚstélɚ] ADJ interestelar

interstice [ɪntɚ́stɪs] N intersticio *m*

intertwine [ɪntɚtwáɪn] VI/VT entrelazar(se)

interval [íntɚvəl] N intervalo *m*

intervene [ɪntɚvín] VI intervenir; (mediate) interponerse, mediar

intervention [ɪntɚvénʃən] N intervención *f*; (mediation) mediación *f*

interview [íntɚvju] N entrevista *f*; (for entertainment) Sp interviú *f*; VT entrevistar; VI entrevistarse

intestine [ɪntéstɪn] ADJ & N intestino *m*; **small —** intestino delgado *m*; **large —** intestino grueso *m*

intimacy [íntəməsi] N intimidad *f*

intimate [íntəmɪt] ADJ íntimo; (knowledge) profundo; [íntəmet] VT insinuar, dar a entender

intimation [ɪntəméʃən] N insinuación *f*

intimidate [ɪntímɪdet] VT intimidar, acobardar

into [íntu] PREP **she came — the room** entró en la habitación; **he put it — the box** lo metió en la caja; **he translated it — German** lo tradujo al alemán; **he ran — a tree** chocó contra un árbol; **it fell — oblivion** cayó en el olvido; **he went — medicine** entró a medicina; **I'm really — pop music** me ha dado por la música pop

intolerable [ɪntálə‐əbəł] ADJ intolerable
intolerance [ɪntálə‐əns] N intolerancia *f*
intolerant [ɪntálə‐ənt] ADJ intolerante
intonation [ɪntənéʃən] N entonación *f*
intoxicate [ɪntáksɪket] VI/VT embriagar (also exhilarate); (poison) intoxicar
intoxication [ɪntaksɪkéʃən] N (drunkenness) embriaguez *f*; (poisoning) intoxicación *f*
intransigent [ɪntrǽnzɪdʒənt] ADJ intransígente
intransitive [ɪntrǽnzɪdɪv] ADJ intransitivo
intrauterine device [ɪntrəjúdəɹɪndváɪs] N dispositivo intrauterino *m*
intravenous [ɪntrəvínəs] ADJ intravenoso
intrepid [ɪntrépɪd] ADJ intrépido
intricate [íntrɪkɪt] ADJ intrincado
intrigue [ɪntríg] VI/VT intrigar; [íntrig] N intriga *f*
intrinsic [ɪntrínzɪk] ADJ intrínseco
introduce [ɪntrədús] VT (put in, bring) introducir; (to a person) presentar
introduction [ɪntrədákʃən] N (putting in, preface) introducción *f*; (to a person) presentación *f*
introspection [ɪntrəspékʃən] N introspección *f*
introvert [íntrəvɚt] N introvertido -da *mf*
introverted [íntrəvɚDɪD] ADJ introvertido
intrude [ɪntrúd] VI/VT interrumpir; (penetrate, of rock) penetrar
intruder [ɪntrúdɚ] N intruso -sa *mf*
intrusion [ɪntrúʒən] N (interruption) interrupción *f*; (penetration) intrusión *f*
intrusive [ɪntrúsɪv] ADJ (rock) intrusivo; (people) entrometido
intuition [ɪntuíʃən] N intuición *f*
intuitive [ɪntúɪDɪv] ADJ intuitivo
inundate [ínəndet] VT inundar
invade [ɪnvéd] VI/VT invadir
invader [ɪnvédɚ] N invasor -ra *mf*
invalid [ínvəlɪd] ADJ & N (infirm) inválido -da *mf*; [ɪnvǽlɪd] ADJ (not valid) nulo
invaluable [ɪnvǽljuəbł] ADJ invalorable, inestimable
invariable [ɪnvériəbł] ADJ invariable
invariably [ɪnvériəbli] ADV siempre
invasion [ɪnvéʒən] N invasión *f*
invent [ɪnvént] VT inventar
invention [ɪnvénʃən] N (act of inventing, thing invented) invención *f*, invento *m*; (falsehood) invención *f*
inventive [ɪnvéntɪv] ADJ inventivo
inventor [ɪnvéntɚ] N inventor -ra *mf*
inventory [ínvəntɔri] N inventario *m*; VT inventariar
inverse [ɪnvɚ́s] ADJ & N inverso *m*
inversion [ɪnvɚ́ʒən] N inversión *f*

invert [ɪnvɚ́t] VT invertir
invest [ɪnvést] VI/VT (money) invertir; (a rank upon someone) investir
investigate [ɪnvéstɪget] VI/VT investigar, indagar
investigation [ɪnvestɪgéʃən] N investigación *f*
investigator [ɪnvéstɪgedɚ] N investigador -ra *mf*
investment [ɪnvéstmənt] N (of money) inversión *f*; (of rank) investidura *f*; — **broker** corredor -ra de bolsa *mf*
investor [ɪnvéstɚ] N inversionista *mf*, inversor -ra *mf*
invigorate [ɪnvígəret] VT vigorizar
invincible [ɪnvínsəbł] ADJ invencible
invisible [ɪnvízəbəł] ADJ invisible
invitation [ɪnvɪtéʃən] N invitación *f*
invite [ɪnváɪt] VI/VT invitar; **to — trouble** buscarse problemas; [ínvaɪt] N *fam* invitación *f*
inviting [ɪnváɪDɪŋ] ADJ atractivo, seductor
in vitro fertilization [ɪnvítrofɚdlɪzéʃən] N fertilización in vitro *f*
invocation [ɪnvəkéʃən] N invocación *f*
invoice [ínvɔɪs] N factura *f*; VT facturar
invoke [ɪnvók] VT invocar
involuntary [ɪnválənteri] ADJ involuntario
involve [ɪnvátv] VT (take, last) suponer; **how much time will this —?** ¿cuánto tiempo supone esto? (consist of, entail) consistir en, involucrar; **what does your work —?** ¿en qué consiste tu trabajo? (be in question) ser cuestión de; **national security is —d!** ¡es una cuestión de seguridad nacional! (implicate) implicar; **they tried to —** her trataron de implicarla; (wrapped up in) estar metido; **he's very —d in the family business** está muy metido en el negocio familiar; (have a liaison) enredarse; **she got —d with a married man** se enredó con un hombre casado
involved [ɪnvátvd] ADJ complicado, enrevesado
inward [ínwɚd] ADV hacia dentro; ADJ interior
iodide [áɪədaɪd] N yoduro *m*
iodine [áɪədaɪn] N yodo *m*
ion [áɪɑn] N ión *m*
ionize [áɪənaɪz] VT ionizar
IQ (intelligence quotient) [aɪkjú] N coeficiente de inteligencia *m*
Iran [ɪrán] N Irán *m*
Iranian [ɪréniən] ADJ & N iraní *mf*
Iraq [ɪrǽk] N Irak *m*
Iraqi [ɪrǽki] ADJ & N iraquí *mf*
irascible [ɪrǽsəbəł] ADJ irascible

irate [aɪrét] ADJ airado
ire [aɪr] N ira f
Ireland [áɪrlənd] N Irlanda f
iridescent [ɪrɪdésənt] ADJ iridiscente,
  tornasolado
iridium [ɪrídɪəm] N iridio m
iris [áɪrɪs] N (of eye) iris m; (plant, flower)
  lirio m; (rainbow) arco iris m
Irish [áɪrɪʃ] ADJ irlandés; N (language) irlandés
  m; **the** — los irlandeses
irk [ɜ˞k] VT fastidiar; **—ed** fastidiado
irksome [ɜ˞ksəm] ADJ engorroso, molesto
iron [áɪə˞n] N (element, golf club) hierro m;
  (appliance) plancha f; **in —s** en grilletes;
  ADJ férreo, de hierro; **—work** herrajes m
  pl; **—works** fundición f; VI/VT planchar;
  to — out a difficulty allanar una
  dificultad
ironic [aɪránɪk] ADJ irónico
ironing [áɪə˞nɪŋ] N planchado m
irony [áɪrəni] N ironía f; (mockery) ironía f,
  sorna f
irradiate [ɪrédiet] VT irradiar
irrational [ɪrǽʃənəl] ADJ irracional
irrefutable [ɪrɪfjúɾəbəl] ADJ irrefutable
irregular [ɪrégjələ˞] ADJ irregular
irrelevant [ɪréləvənt] ADJ no pertinente;
  your age is — tu edad no viene al caso
irreparable [ɪrépə˞əbəl] ADJ irreparable
irreplaceable [ɪrɪplésəbəl] ADJ irreemplazable
irreproachable [ɪrɪprótʃəbəl] ADJ
  irreprochable
irresistible [ɪrɪzístəbəl] ADJ irresistible
irresponsible [ɪrɪspánsəbəl] ADJ
  irresponsable
irretrievable [ɪrɪtrívəbəl] ADJ irrecuperable
irreverent [ɪrévə˞ənt] ADJ irreverente
irrevocable [ɪrévəkəbəl] ADJ irrevocable
irrigate [ɪrɪget] VI/VT (a garden) irrigar, regar;
  (the eyes) irrigar
irrigation [ɪrɪgéʃən] N riego m, irrigación f;
  — ditch acequia f
irritable [ɪrɪɾəbəl] ADJ irritable, colérico
irritate [ɪrɪtet] VT irritar
irritating [ɪrɪteɾɪŋ] ADJ irritante
irritation [ɪrɪtéʃən] N irritación f
IRS (Internal Revenue Service) [aɪɑɾés] N
  Hacienda f
Islam [ɪzlɑm] N islamismo m, islam m
Islamic [ɪzlámɪk] ADJ islámico
island [áɪlənd] N isla f
Islander [áɪləndə˞] N isleño -ña mf
isle [aɪl] N isla f
isobar [áɪsəbɑr] N isobara f
isolate [áɪsəlet] VT aislar
isolation [aɪsəléʃən] N aislamiento m
isolationism [aɪsəléʃənɪzəm] N

aislacionismo m
isometric [aɪsəmétrɪk] ADJ isométrico
isotope [áɪsətop] N isótopo m
Israel [ízrɪəl] N Israel m
Israeli [ɪzréli] ADJ & N israelí mf
issue [íʃu] N (of printed matter) tirada f; (of
  stock, bonds) emisión f; (copy of a
  magazine) número m, entrega f; (of a
  fluid) flujo m; (problem) problema m,
  tema m; (progeny) descendencia f; **he's
  got —s** es muy complejado; **to take —
  with** discrepar de; VT (written material)
  publicar; (a decree) promulgar; (a permit,
  document) expedir; (shares) emitir; (to
  flow) brotar; (to come out of) salir de; (to
  descend from) descender de
isthmus [ísməs] N istmo m
it [ɪt] PRON **— all started yesterday** todo
  empezó ayer; **— is necessary** es
  necesario; **— is raining** llueve, está
  lloviendo; **— is said that** se dice que; **—
  is two o'clock** son las dos; **— was
  broken** estaba roto; **who is —?** ¿quién
  es? **if — weren't five o'clock** si no
  fueran las cinco; **I saw —** lo/la vi; **he
  talked about —** habló de eso; **what
  time is —?** ¿qué hora es? **how is —
  going?** ¿qué tal? **I don't get —** no
  entiendo; **you're —!** ¡tú te/la quedas!/
  ¡tú la traes!
Italian [ɪtǽljən] ADJ & N italiano -na mf
italic [ɪtǽlɪk] ADJ itálico; N **—s** letra
  bastardilla / cursiva f
italicize [ɪtǽlɪsaɪz] VT poner en bastardilla /
  cursiva
Italy [ɪdli] N Italia f
itch [ɪtʃ] VI/VT picar; **to be —ing to** tener
  ganas de; N comezón f, picazón f;
  (longing) ansia f
itchy [ɪtʃi] ADJ que pica; **it feels — to me**
  me pica
item [áɪɾəm] N (piece of news) artículo m;
  (topic of gossip) tema de conversación m;
  (unit) ítem m; (couple) pareja f
itemize [áɪɾəmaɪz] VT (list) enumerar; (break
  down) desglosar
itinerant [aɪtínə˞ənt] ADJ itinerante,
  ambulante
itinerary [aɪtínə˞eri] N (schedule) itinerario
  m; (guidebook) guía de viajeros f
its [ɪts] POSS ADJ su/sus, de él, de ella, de ello
itself [ɪtsélf] PRON **this story wrote —** esta
  historia se escribió sola; **the bike was
  standing by —** la bici estaba parada sola;
  the dog bit — el perro se mordió (a sí
  mismo); **the fox found — a hole** la
  zorra se encontró una guarida

Ivorian [aɪvɔ́riən] ADJ & N marfileño -ña *mf*
ivory [áɪvri] N marfil *m*; — **tower** torre de marfil *f*
Ivory Coast [áɪvrikóst] N Costa de Marfil *f*
ivy [áɪvi] N hiedra *f*

Jj

jab [dʒæb] VI/VT (hit) golpear; (hit with elbow) codear; N (blow) golpe *m*; (blow with elbow) codazo *m*; (in boxing) jab *m*, puñetazo directo *m*
jabber [dʒǽbə-] VI (unintelligibly) farfullar; (incessantly) charlotear; N (unintelligible) farfulla *f*; (incessant) charloteo *m*
jack [dʒæk] N (tool) gato *m*; (card) sota *f*; (plug-in) hembra *f*, toma *f*; (flag) bandera de proa *f*; —**ass** asno *m*, burro *m* (also person); —**hammer** martillo neumático *m*; —**knife** navaja *f*; — **of all trades** hombre orquesta *m*; —**pot** premio gordo *m*; —**rabbit** liebre americana *f*; **you don't know** — no sabes ni un comino; VT **to** — **up** (a car) alzar con gato; (prices) subir
jackal [dʒǽkəl] N chacal *m*
jacket [dʒǽkɪt] N (clothing) chaqueta *f*; (of a book) forro *m*; (of a potato) piel *f*
jade [dʒed] N jade *m*
jaded [dʒédɪd] ADJ (disenchanted) de vuelta; (sated) hastiado
jagged [dʒǽgɪd] ADJ recortado, desigual
jaguar [dʒǽgwar] N jaguar *m*
jail [dʒel] N cárcel *f*; —**break** fuga *f*; VT encarcelar
jailer [dʒéla-] N carcelero -ra *mf*
jalopy [dʒəlápi] N cacharro *m*
jam [dʒæm] VT (stuff) embutir; (block) atestar; (immobilize) trabar; (make unworkable) obstruir, atascar, atorar; (stop radio signals) interferir; VI (become stuck or unworkable) atascarse; (crowd in) apiñarse; **to** — **on the brakes** frenar de golpe; **to** — **one's fingers** pillarse los dedos; N (jelly) mermelada *f*, dulce *m*; (difficult situation) aprieto *m*; (traffic) embotellamiento *m*; — **session** jam *m*
Jamaica [dʒəméka] N Jamaica *f*
Jamaican [dʒəmékən] ADJ & N jamaicano -na *mf*, jamaiquino -na *mf*
janitor [dʒǽnɪtə-] N conserje *m*
January [dʒǽnjueri] N enero *m*
Japan [dʒəpǽn] N Japón *m*

Japanese [dʒæpəníz] ADJ & N japonés -esa *mf*
jar [dʒar] VI/VT (shake) sacudir(se); (clash) chocar; **to** — **one's nerves** ponerle a uno los nervios de punta; N (container) tarro *m*, frasco *m*, pote *m*; (large earthen container) tinaja *f*; (collision) choque *m*; (shake) sacudida *f*
jargon [dʒárgən] N jerga *f*
jasmine [dʒǽzmɪn] N jazmín *m*
jasper [dʒǽspə-] N jaspe *m*
jaundice [dʒɔ́ndɪs] N ictericia *f*
jaunt [dʒɔnt] N excursión *f*; VI pasear
javelin [dʒǽvlɪn] N jabalina *f*
jaw [dʒɔ] N (of animal) quijada *f*; (of human) mandíbula *f*; (of carnivores) fauces *f pl*; —**bone** mandíbula *f*, maxilar *m*
jay [dʒe] N arrendajo *m*
jazz [dʒæz] N jazz *m*; -VI **to** — **up** animar
jealous [dʒélas] ADJ (possessive) celoso; (envious) envidioso; (protective) protector
jealousy [dʒélasi] N celos *m pl*
jeans [dʒinz] N jeans *m pl*, vaqueros *m pl*
jeer [dʒir] VI/VT (mock) mofarse (de), burlarse (de); (boo) abuchear, befar; N (act of mockery) mofa *f*, burla *f*; (boos) abucheo *m*, befa *f*
jelly [dʒéli] N jalea *f*; —**fish** medusa *f*
jeopardize [dʒépə-daɪz] VT comprometer, poner en peligro
jeopardy [dʒépə-di] ADV LOC **in** — en peligro
jerk [dʒɚk] N (quick pull) tirón *m*; (muscular contraction) espasmo *m*; (idiot) *pej* pelmazo *m*; VI/VT tironear; **to** — **around** manipular; —**water** de mala muerte
jerky [dʒɚki] ADJ espasmódico; N tasajo *m*
jersey [dʒɚzi] N jersey *m*
jest [dʒest] N broma *f*, chanza *f*; **in** — en broma; VI bromear
jester [dʒéstə-] N bufón *m*
Jesuit [dʒézuɪt] N jesuita *m*
jet [dʒet] N (stream) chorro *m*; (spout) surtidor *m*; (stone) azabache *m*; — **(air)plane** avión a reacción *m*; — **engine** motor a reacción *m*; — **lag** jet lag *m*; —**liner** avión a reacción de pasajero *m*; — **propulsion** propulsión a chorro *f*; — **set** jet-set *m*; — **stream** (of air) corriente en chorro *f*; (of a jet) chorro *m*; ADJ -**black** negro como el azabache; VI (stream out) salir a chorros; (travel) volar en avión a reacción; VT (spew out) lanzar a chorros; (transport) transportar en avión a reacción
jettison [dʒétɪsən] VT echar por la borda
Jew [dʒu] N judío -día *mf*
jewel [dʒúəl] N (ornament, prized person) joya *f*, alhaja *f*; (stone) gema *f*; (watch jewel) rubí *m*; — **box** joyero *m*

jeweler [ʤúələ] N joyero -ra *mf*; —**'s shop** joyería *f*

jewelry [ʤúətri] N joyas *f pl*, alhajas *f pl*; —**box** alhajero *m*; — **store** joyería *f*

Jewish [ʤúíʃ] ADJ judío

jiffy [ʤífi] ADV LOC **in a** — en un santiamén

jig [ʤɪg] N giga *f*; —**saw** sierra de vaivén *f*; —**saw puzzle** rompecabezas *m sg*; VI (dance) bailotear; **to — up and down** zangolotearse

jiggle [ʤígəɫ] VI/VT zangolotear(se), zarandear(se); N zangoloteo *m*, zarandeo *m*

jilt [ʤɪɫt] VT dejar plantado

jingle [ʤíŋgəɫ] VI tintinear; VT agitar; N retintín *m*; (short song) jingle *m*

jinx [ʤɪŋks] N gafe *m*; VT gafar

job [ʤab] N (task) tarea *f*; (position) trabajo *m*, empleo *m*; (theft) golpe *m*; **to be out of a** — estar sin trabajo; *Sp* estar en (el) paro; **by the** — a destajo; **to do a good** — hacer buen trabajo; VI trabajar a destajo

jobber [ʤábə] N (day-worker) trabajador -ra a destajo *mf*; (wholesaler) vendedor -ra mayorista *mf*

jobless [ʤáblɪs] ADJ sin trabajo; *Sp* en paro

jock [ʤak] N deportista *mf*; — **(strap)** suspensorio *m*

jockey [ʤáki] N jockey *m*; VI **to — for position** disputarse la posición

jocular [ʤákjələ] ADJ jocoso

jog [ʤag] VI (run) correr; VT (refresh) refrescar; N trote *m*; **to go for a** — salir a correr

join [ʤɔɪn] VI/VT juntar(se); (pipes) acoplar(se), unir(se); (bones) articular(se); (a club) asociarse (a); (the navy, etc.) alistarse (en)

joint [ʤɔɪnt] N (point of contact) juntura *f*, junta *f*; (connection between bones) articulación *f*, coyuntura *f*; (nodule on a plant) nudo *m*; (public place) antro *m*; **out of** — descoyuntado; ADJ (shared) común; —**account** cuenta conjunta *f*; —**action** acción colectiva *f*; —**owner** copropietario -ria *mf*; —**session** sesión plena *f*; —**venture** joint venture *m*

joke [ʤok] N broma *f*, chiste *m*; VI bromear

joker [ʤókə] N (person who jokes) bromista *mf*, guasón -ona *mf*; (card) comodín *m*

jokingly [ʤókɪŋli] ADV en broma

jolly [ʤáli] ADJ jovial

jolt [ʤoɫt] N sacudida *f*; VT sacudir; **to — along** avanzar a los tumbos

Jordan [ʤórdn̩] N Jordania *f*

Jordanian [ʤordénіən] ADJ & N jordano -na *mf*

jostle [ʤásəɫ] VI/VT codear(se), dar empujones (a); N empujón *m*

jot [ʤat] VT **to — down** apuntar; N pizca *f*

journal [ʤə́nəɫ] N (diary) diario *m*; (periodical) revista *f*; (logbook) cuaderno de bitácora *m*

journalism [ʤə́nəlɪzəm] N periodismo *m*

journalist [ʤə́nəlɪst] N periodista *mf*

journalistic [ʤənəlístɪk] ADJ periodístico

journey [ʤə́ni] N viaje *m*; VI viajar

joust [ʤaust] N justa *f*

joy [ʤɔɪ] N (delight) alegría *f*, regocijo *m*, alborozo *m*; (source of delight) deleite *m*; —**ride** paseo en coche robado *m*; —**stick** joystick *m*, palanca de juegos *f*

joyful [ʤɔ́ɪfəɫ] ADJ alborozado

joyous [ʤɔ́ɪəs] ADJ jubiloso, alegre

jubilant [ʤúbələnt] ADJ jubiloso

jubilee [ʤubəlí] N jubileo *m*

judge [ʤʌʤ] N juez -za *mf*; **to be a good** — **of character** saber juzgar a la gente; VI/VT juzgar; (estimate) calcular

judgment [ʤʌ́ʤmənt] N juicio *m*; (in court) fallo *m*; — **day** día del juicio final *m*

judicial [ʤudíʃəɫ] ADJ judicial

judicious [ʤudíʃəs] ADJ juicioso, sensato

judo [ʤúɪo] N judo *m*

jug [ʤʌg] N (pitcher) jarro *m*, jarra *f*; (storage jar) pote *m*

juggle [ʤʌ́gəɫ] VI/VT hacer juegos malabares (con), hacer malabarismo (con); **to — the accounts** manipular las cuentas

juggler [ʤʌ́glə] N malabarista *mf*

jugular [ʤʌ́gjələ] N yugular *f*

juice [ʤus] N jugo *m*; (fruit only) *Sp* zumo *m*

juicer [ʤúsə] N exprimidor *m*

juicy [ʤúsi] ADJ jugoso; **a — story** un cuento sabroso

jukebox [ʤúkbaks] N juke-box *m*

July [ʤulái] N julio *m*

jumble [ʤʌ́mbəɫ] VI/VT revolver(se) *m*; N revoltijo *m*

jumbo [ʤámbo] ADJ jumbo, gigantesco; —**jet** jumbo *m*

jump [ʤʌmp] VI (spring) saltar; (increase, as temperature, prices) dar un salto; VT (capture in checkers) comer; (ride a horse over barrier) hacer saltar; (mug) asaltar; (cross a river, mountains, etc.) salvar; **to — at** abalanzarse sobre; **to — over** saltar; **to — the track** descarrilarse; **to — to conclusions** hacer deducciones precipitadas; N salto *m*; (in prices) subida repentina *f*; —**rope** cuerda de saltar *f*; **to —-start** hacer un puente; —**suit** mono *m*

jumper [ʤʌ́mpə] N (person who jumps) saltador -ra *mf*; (dress) jumper *m*; *Sp* pichi *m*; — **cable** puente *m*

jumpy [ʤʌ́mpi] ADJ nervioso, asustadizo

junction [ʤʌ́ŋkʃən] N (act or state of joining) unión f; (joining of two rivers) confluencia f; (of two railways) empalme m; (of roads) entronque m

juncture [ʤʌ́ŋktʃə] N (point where joined) juntura f; **at this** — en esta coyuntura

June [ʤun] N junio m

jungle [ʤʌ́ŋgəl] N selva f, jungla f; **the law of the** — la ley de la selva

junior [ʤúnjə] ADJ (younger) menor; (more recent) más nuevo, de menos antigüedad; — **college** institución para los dos primeros años de la licenciatura f; **John Smith,** — John Smith, hijo; N estudiante del tercer año mf

juniper [ʤúnəpə] N enebro m

junk [ʤʌŋk] N (useless articles) trastos viejos m pl; (metal) chatarra f; (Chinese boat) junco m; — **dealer** chatarrero -ra mf; — **food** comida basura f, porquerías f pl; — **mail** publicidad por correo f; — **yard** chatarrería f; VT desechar, echar a la basura

junkie [ʤʌ́ŋki] N fam drogata mf, drogota mf

jurisdiction [ʤʊrɪsdíkʃən] N jurisdicción f

jurisprudence [ʤʊrɪsprúdn̩s] N jurisprudencia f

juror [ʤúrə] N miembro de un jurado m, jurado -da mf

jury [ʤúri] N jurado m; — **box** banco de jurado m; **to** —-**rig** chapucear

just [ʤʌst] ADJ justo; ADV (exactly) exactamente; (only) sólo; **he** — **left** acaba de salir; **she is** — **a little girl** no es más que una niña; **you'll** — **have to wait** tendrás que esperar; — **barely** apenas; **the meeting is** — **starting** la reunión está empezando

justice [ʤʌ́stɪs] N (fairness) justicia f; (judge) juez -za mf; **to bring to** — enjuiciar; **the painting doesn't do him** — el retrato no le favorece

justification [ʤʌstəfɪkéʃən] N justificación f

justify [ʤʌ́stəfaɪ] VT justificar

jut [ʤʌt] VI sobresalir, proyectarse

juvenile [ʤúvənaɪl] ADJ juvenil; — **delinquent** delincuente juvenil mf

juxtapose [ʤʌ́kstəpoz] VT yuxtaponer

Kk

kangaroo [kæŋgərú] N canguro m

karat, carat [kǽrət] N quilate m

kayak [káɪæk] N kayak m

Kazak, Kazakh [kəzǽk] ADJ & N kazako -ka mf

Kazakhstan [kəzákstɑn] N Kazajstán m

keel [kił] N quilla f; VI/VT volcar(se); **to** — **over** (ship) volcar(se); (person) caer de cabeza, desplomarse

keen [kin] ADJ (sharp) afilado; (ear) fino; (mind) agudo, penetrante

keenness [kínnɪs] N agudeza f

keep [kip] VI (continue) seguir; (not spoil) aguantar; VT (retain) guardar; (maintain) mantener; (employ) tener; (look after) cuidar; **to** — **a diary** llevar un diario; **to** — **a secret** guardar un secreto; **to** — **at it** persistir; **to** — **away** mantener(se) alejado; **to** — **back** (stay away) tener a raya; (restrain) contener; **to** — **bad company** andar en mala compañía; **to** — **from** (prevent) impedir; (protect) proteger; **to** — **(on) talking** seguir hablando; **to** — **the door open** mantener la puerta abierta; **to** — **off the grass** no pisar el césped; **to** — **up** (perform as well) seguir el tren; (stay informed) mantenerse al tanto; **to** — **one's hands off** no tocar; **to** — **someone posted** mantener al corriente a alguien; **to** — **quiet** estarse callado; **to** — **to the right** mantenerse a la derecha; **to** — **track of** (do accounts) llevar la cuenta de; (consider) no perder de vista; **to** — **watch** vigilar; **he** — **a maid** tiene una criada; **she kept me on the phone** me (re)tuvo en el teléfono; N **for** —**s** (forever) para siempre; (for real) en serio

keeper [kípə] N (of people) guardián m; (of things) custodio m

keeping [kípɪŋ] N custodia f; **in** — **with** en armonía con

keepsake [kípsek] N recuerdo m

keg [keg] N barril m

kennel [kénəł] N residencia de perros f

Kenya [kénjə] N Kenia f

Kenyan [kénjən] ADJ & N keniata mf

kernel [kə́nəł] N (seed) semilla f, grano m; (essence) meollo m

kerosene [kérəsin] N queroseno m

kestrel [késtrəł] N cernícalo m

ketchup [kétʃəp] N salsa de tomate f, cátsup m

kettle [kédł] N caldera f, hervidor m; (for tea) tetera f; — **drum** tímpano / timbal m; **that's another** — **of fish** es harina de otro costal

key [ki] N (for locks) llave f; (secret, book of answers) clave f; (for winding) clavija f;

(for keyboard) tecla *f*; (island) cayo *m*; (music) clave *f*; **—board** teclado *m*; **—hole** ojo de la cerradura *m*; **—note** tónica *f*; **—note address** discurso de apertura *m*; **—pad** teclado numérico *m*; **— ring** llavero *m*; **— signature** armadura *f*; **—stone** piedra angular *f*; **—stroke** pulsación (de la tecla) *f*; **— word** palabra clave *f*; **to sing on —** cantar a tono; ADJ clave; VT (scratch) rayar; **to be —ed up** estar sobreexcitado

khaki [kǽki] N kaki *m*, caqui *m*

kick [kɪk] VI/VT (person) patear; (horse) dar coces (a), cocear; VI (gun) dar un culatazo, retroceder; **to — around** (discuss) discutir; (to mistreat) dar por la cabeza; **to — at** dar patadas; **to — out** echar a patadas; **to — the bucket** estirar la pata; **to — up a lot of dust** levantar una polvareda; **to — a habit** dejar un vicio; N patada *f*, puntapié *m*; (of a horse) coz *f*; *Am* patada *f*; (of a gun) culatazo *m*; (in the air) pataleo *m*; **this whisky has a —** este whisky es fuerte; **I get a — out of swimming** me encanta nadar; **—back** comisión ilegal *f*; *Mex* mordida *f*; **—stand** soporte *m*; **to —start** arrancar

kid [kɪd] N (young goat) cabrito *m*, chivo *m*; (leather) cabritilla *f*; (child) niño -ña *mf*, chico -ca *mf*; **— stuff** juego de niños *m*; VI bromear, embromar, tomar el pelo

kidnap [kídnæp] VT secuestrar, raptar

kidnapper [kídnæpə-] N secuestrador -ra *mf*

kidnapping [kídnæpɪŋ] N secuestro *m*, rapto *m*

kidney [kídni] N riñón *m*; **— bean** judía *f*; **— stone** cálculo renal *m*

kill [kɪɫ] VI/VT matar; (drink completely) terminar; (turn off) apagar; **that comedian —s me** ese cómico me mata de risa; N (animal killed) caza *f*; (slaughter) matanza *f*; **—joy** aguafiestas *mf sg*

killer [kílə-] N asesino -na *mf*; **a — game** un partidazo; **— bee** abeja asesina *f*; **— whale** orca *f*

killing [kílɪŋ] N (slaughter) matanza *f*; (murder) asesinato *m*; (game killed) caza *f*; **to make a —** llenarse de oro

kilo [kílo] N kilo *m*

kilobyte [kílabaɪt] N kilobyte *m*

kilometer [kɪlámɪɾə-] N kilómetro *m*

kilowatt [kílawɑt] N kilovatio *m*; **—-hour** kilovatio-hora *f*

kin [kɪn] N parentela *f*, parientes *m pl*; **—sman** pariente *m*; **—swoman** parienta *f*; **to notify the next of —** avisar a los deudos

kind [kaɪnd] ADJ (benevolent) bondadoso, bueno; (words) amable; **to be — to animals** ser cariñoso con los animales; **—hearted** de buen corazón; **— of tired** algo cansado; N clase *f*, tipo *m*, género *m*; **to pay in —** (without money) pagar en especie; (retaliate) pagar con la misma moneda

kindergarten [kíndə-gɑrtn̩] N jardín de niños *m*; *Sp* parvulario *m*

kindle [kíndl̩] VT (fire) prender; (interest) despertar, provocar; VI encenderse

kindling [kíndlɪŋ] N leña ligera *f*, astillas *f pl*

kindly [káɪndli] ADJ bondadoso, bueno; ADV (with kindness) amablemente; (please) por favor; **we thank you —** le agradecemos mucho; **not to take — to criticism** no aceptar de buen grado las críticas

kindness [káɪndnɪs] N (state) bondad *f*, amabilidad *f*; (act) favor *m*

kindred [kíndrɪd] ADJ emparentado; **— spirits** espíritus afines *m pl*, almas gemelas *f pl*

king [kɪŋ] N rey *m* (also chess, cards); (in checkers) dama *f*; **—fisher** martín pescador *m*; **—pin** (in a mechanism) pivote central *m*; (in bowling) bolo central *m*; (person) figura central *f*; **—-sized** extra grande

kingdom [kíndəm] N reino *m*

kingly [kíŋli] ADJ real

kink [kɪŋk] N (bend) doblez *m*; (pain) tortícolis *f*

kinky [kɪŋki] ADJ crespo

kinship [kínʃɪp] N parentesco *m*; (likeness) afinidad *f*

kiosk [kíɑsk] N quiosco *m*

Kiribati [kɪrəbáɾi] N Kiribati *m*

kiss [kɪs] VI/VT besar(se); N beso *m*

kit [kɪt] N (of tools) caja *f*; (of first aid) botiquín *m*; (of sewing notions) costurero *m*

kitchen [kítʃɪn] N cocina *f*; **—ware** utensilios de cocina *m pl*

kite [kaɪt] N (toy) cometa *f*; (bird) milano *m*

kitten [kítn̩] N gatito *m*

kitty [kíɾi] N (young cat) gatito *m*, minino *m*; (petty cash) caja chica *f*, fondo *m*

knack [næk] N buena maña *f*, maña *f*; **once you get the —** una vez que le agarras la vuelta/onda

knapsack [nǽpsæk] N mochila *f*

knave [nev] N pícaro *m*; (in cards) sota *f*

knead [nid] VT amasar, sobar

knee [ni] N rodilla *f*; **—cap** rótula *f*; **—-deep** hasta las rodillas; **—-jerk liberal** liberal fanático *m*; **—-jerk reaction** reacción

visceral *f*; vt dar un rodillazo
kneel [nil] vi arrodillarse
knell [nɛl] n doble *m*; vi doblar
knickknack [níknæk] n chuchería *f*, baratija *f*
knife [naif] n cuchillo *m*; (big) cuchilla *f*; (folding) navaja *f*; (for carving) trinchante *m*; vt acuchillar; **at —point** a punta de cuchillo
knight [nait] n caballero *m*; (in chess) caballo *m*; **— errant** caballero andante *m*; vt armar caballero
knighthood [náithʊd] n (all knights) caballería *f*; (title) orden de la caballería *f*
knit [nit] vi/vt tejer; **to — one's brow** fruncir el entrecejo/el ceño
knitting [nídiŋ] n tejido *m*; **— needle** aguja de punto *f*
knob [nab] n (on a door) pomo *m*, perilla *f*, tirador *m*; (protuberance) protuberancia *f*
knock [nak] vi (pound) golpear; (of motors) golpetear; (call at the door) llamar; vt (criticize) criticar; **to — a hole in the wall** hacer un agujero en la pared a golpes; **to — down** derribar, echar abajo, tumbar; **to — off** (stop working) terminar; (reduce) rebajar; (make fall) tirar; (kill) liquidar; **— it off!** ¡basta! **to — into** golpearse contra; **to — out** noquear; **to — over** voltear, revolcar; n (pounding) golpe *m*, toque *m*; (criticism) crítica *f*; (in a motor) golpeteo *m*; **—-kneed** patizambo, zambo; **—out** (boxing) nócaut *m*; (attractive person) bomba *f*
knocker [nákə] n (handle on door) llamador *m*, aldaba *f*
knoll [nol] n morro *m*, loma *f*
knot [nat] n nudo *m* (also in wood, unit of speed); (of people) grupo *m*; (swelling) chichón *m*; vi/vt anudar(se)
knotty [nádi] adj (full of knots) nudoso; (difficult) dificultoso, enredado
know [no] vi/vt (to have knowledge of; to know how to) saber; vt (to be acquainted with, have sexual intercourse with) conocer; (to recognize) reconocer; (distinguish) distinguir; **to — how to swim** saber nadar; **to — of** estar enterado de; n **to be in the —** estar al tanto; **—-how** conocimiento *m*; **—-it-all** sabelotodo *mf*
knowing [nóiŋ] adj (complicitous) cómplice; (astute) astuto
knowingly [nóiŋli] adv a sabiendas
knowledge [nálidʒ] n (awareness) conocimiento *m*; (information known) saber *m*, conocimientos *m pl*; **not to my**

— no que yo sepa
knuckle [nákəl] n nudillo *m*; **—head** tarambana *mf*; vi **to — down** arremangarse, aplicarse con empeño; **to — under** someterse
Korean [koríən] adj & n coreano -na *mf*
kosher [kóʃə] adj kosher
Kuwait [kuwét] n Kuwait *m*
Kuwaiti [kuwédi] adj & n kuwaití *mf*
Kyrgyzstan [kəgistán] n Kirguistán *m*

Ll

label [lébəl] n etiqueta *f*, rótulo *m*; (brand) marca *f*; (of recording companies) sello *m*; vt etiquetar, rotular
labor [lébə] n trabajo *m*, labor *f*; (body of workers) mano de obra *f*; (working class) clase obrera *f*; (uterine contractions) trabajo de parto *m*; **—-intensive** que requiere mucha mano de obra; **— union** sindicato *m*; **to be in —** estar de parto; adj laboral; vi (work) trabajar; (dedicate oneself) afanarse; **to — under a disadvantage** sufrir una desventaja
laboratory [lǽbrətɔri] n laboratorio *m*
laborer [lébərə] n jornalero -ra *mf*; (unskilled) peón -ona *mf*
laborious [ləbóriəs] adj (industrious) laborioso; (difficult) trabajoso
labyrinth [lǽbərinθ] n laberinto *m*
lace [les] n (cloth) encaje *m*; (cord) cordón *m*; vt (to adorn with lace) bordar con encaje; (to insert laces into) poner cordones a; (to spike) echar alcohol; vi atarse
lack [læk] n falta *f*, carencia *f*; vi/vt carecer de, faltarle a uno; **he —s courage** le falta valentía; **—luster** mediocre
lackey [lǽki] n lacayo *m*
lacking [lǽkiŋ] adj (deficient) deficiente; **good maids are — in this town** faltan buenas criadas en este pueblo; **— in** falto de, carente de
laconic [ləkánik] adj lacónico
lacquer [lǽkə] n laca *f*; vt lacar, laquear
lactic acid [lǽktikǽsid] n ácido láctico *m*
ladder [lǽdə] n escalera *f*
laden [lédn] adj cargado
ladle [lédl] n cucharón *m*, cazo *m*; vt servir con cucharón
lady [lédi] n señora *f*, dama *f*; **—bug** mariquita *f*; **—like** muy fina; **—love** amada *f*; **ladies' room** *Sp* aseo/servicio

de damas *m*

lag [læg] VI (fall behind) quedarse atrás, rezagarse; (flag) disminuir; N retardo *m*, retraso *m*

lagoon [ləgún] N laguna *f*

lair [lɛr] N guarida *f*

lake [lek] N lago *m*

lamb [læm] N cordero *m*; (yearling) borrego *m*

lame [lem] ADJ cojo; *Am* rengo; **—brained** idiota; **— duck** funcionario -ria cesante *mf*; **— excuse** pretexto tonto *m*; VT dejar cojo

lament [ləmént] N lamento *m*; VI lamentar(se); VT llorar

lamentable [ləméntəbəɬ] ADJ lamentable

lamentation [læməntéʃən] N lamentación *f*, lamento *m*

laminate [læmənet] VT laminar

lamp [læmp] N lámpara *f*; (on a street) farol *m*; **—post** farol *m*; **—shade** pantalla *f*

lance [læns] N lanza *f*; (lancet) lanceta *f*; VT lancear; (a wound) abrir con una lanceta

lancet [lǽnsɪt] N lanceta *f*

land [lænd] N tierra *f*; (lot) terreno *m*; (country) país *m*, tierra *f*; **—fill** vertedero *m*; **— grant** con terrenos concedidos por el estado; **—lady** casera *f*, propietaria *f*; **—lord** casero *m*, propietario *m*; **—mark** hito *m* (also historical), mojón *m*; **— mine** mina *f*; **—owner** hacendado -da *mf*; **—scape** paisaje *m*; **—scape architecture** paisajismo *m*; **—slide** derrumbe *m*, desprendimiento *m*; (election) victoria aplastante *f*; VI/VT (a ship) atracar; (an airplane) aterrizar; VT (a fish) *Sp* coger; *Am* pescar; (a job) conseguir; **you'll — in jail** terminarás en la cárcel

landing [lǽndɪŋ] N (of a ship) desembarco *m*; (of cargo) desembarque *m*; (of an airplane) aterrizaje *m*; (place) desembarcadero *m*; (on stairs) descanso *m*; **— field** campo de aterrizaje *m*; **— gear** tren de aterrizaje *m*; **— strip** pista de aterrizaje *f*

lane [len] N (country road) sendero *m*; (road division) carril *m*; (for ships) ruta *f*

language [lǽŋgwɪdʒ] N lengua *f*, idioma *m*; (faculty, computer) lenguaje *m*

languid [lǽŋgwɪd] ADJ lánguido

languish [lǽŋgwɪʃ] VI languidecer

languor [lǽŋgɚ] N languidez *f*

lanky [lǽŋki] ADJ larguirucho, zancudo

lanolin [lǽnəlɪn] N lanolina *f*

lantern [lǽntɚn] N farol *m*; (of a lighthouse) faro *m*, linterna *f*

Laos [léɑs] N Laos *m*

Laotian [leóʃən] ADJ & N laosiano -na *mf*

lap [læp] N (part of body) regazo *m*; (part of a race) vuelta *f*; **—dog** perro faldero *m*; **—top** laptop *m*; **to live in the — óf luxury** vivir en la abundancia; VI/VT lamer

lapel [ləpéɬ] N solapa *f*

lapidary [lǽpɪdɛri] ADJ & N lapidario -ria *mf*

lapse [læps] N (period of time) lapso *m*; (linguistic error) lapsus *m*; (defect in memory) fallo *m*; (fall) caída *f*; (termination) caducidad *f*; VI (fall) caer; (decline) decaer; (end) caducar, vencer

larceny [lɑ́rsəni] N latrocinio *m*, hurto *m*

lard [lɑrd] N manteca *f*; VT enmantecar; (with bacon) mechar

large [lɑrdʒ] ADJ grande; **—scale** de gran escala; **a — company** una gran compañía/una compañía grande; **at —** (not in jail) suelto, libre; (in general) en general; N tamaño grande *m*

lariat [lǽriət] N reata *f*

lark [lɑrk] N (bird) alondra *f*; (bit of fun) diversión *f*; **to go on a —** ir de jarana

larva [lɑ́rvə] N larva *f*

laryngitis [lærəndʒáɪdɪs] N laringitis *f*

larynx [lǽrɪŋks] N laringe *f*

lascivious [ləsíviəs] ADJ lascivo

laser [lézɚ] N laser *m*; **— printer** impresora laser *f*

lash [læʃ] N (blow with a whip, tail, etc.) azote *m*, latigazo *m*; (blow of waves) embate *m*; (part of eye) pestaña *f*; VT azotar; (tie) amarrar; **to — out at** fustigar

lasso [lǽso] N lazo *m*, reata *f*; VT lazar; *Am* enlazar

last [læst] ADJ (in a series) último; (definitive) final; **—ditch** desesperado; **— minute** de último momento; **— name** apellido *m*; **— night** anoche; **— rites** extrema unción *f*, viático *m*; **— straw** colmo *m*; **— word** última palabra *f*; **— year** el año pasado; **next to the —** penúltimo; ADV último; **to arrive —** llegar al último; **when — seen** cuando se lo vio por última vez; **at —** finalmente; N el último; (of a shoe) horma *f*; VI durar; (live on) perdurar

lasting [lǽstɪŋ] ADJ duradero, perdurable

lastly [lǽstli] ADV por último

latch [lætʃ] N pestillo *m*, picaporte *m*, cierre *m*; VI cerrar con el pestillo; **to — on** agarrarse de; **to — onto** pegarse a

late [let] ADJ (tardy) tardío; (hour) avanzada; (recent) reciente, último; (recently deceased) finado; **—comer** rezagado -da *mf*; — **afternoon** atardecer *m*; ADV tarde; — **in the night** a una hora avanzada de la noche; — **into the night** hasta cualquier hora de la noche; — **in the week** a finales de la semana; **it is** — ya es tarde; **of** — últimamente; **to be** — llegar tarde; **to work** — trabajar hasta tarde; **the train was ten minutes** — el tren llegó con diez minutos de retraso

lately [létli] ADV últimamente

lateness [létnıs] N tardanza *f*

latent [létn̩t] ADJ latente

later [léɾɚ] ADJ posterior; **see you** — hasta luego; — **on** más tarde

lateral [léɾəɹəł] ADJ lateral

latest [léɾıst] ADJ último; **the** — **fashion** la última moda; **the** — **news** las últimas novedades; **at the** — a más tardar; N la última

latex [léteks] N látex *m*

lathe [leð] N torno *m*

lather [léðɚ] N (foam) espuma *f*; (sweat) sudor *m*; **he got into a** — se puso histérico; VT enjabonar; VI hacer espuma

Latin [létn̩] ADJ latino; N latín *m*; — **America** América Latina *f*, Latinoamérica *f*; — **American** latinoamericano -na *mf*

latitude [léɾıtud] N latitud *f*; (freedom) flexibilidad *f*

latrine [lətrín] N letrina *f*

latter [léɾɚ] ADJ último; **in the** — **days of the Roman Republic** en los últimos días de la República Romana; **toward the** — **part of the week** a finales de la semana; **the** — este *m*, esta *f*

lattice [léɾıs] N enrejado *m*, entramado *m*; (of a window) celosía *f*

Latvia [léɾviə] N Letonia *f*

Latvian [léɾviən] ADJ & N letón -ona *mf*

laud [lɔd] VT loar

laudable [lɔ́dəbəł] ADJ laudable, loable

laugh [læf] VI reír(se); **to** — **at** reírse de; **to** — **loudly** reírse a carcajadas; **to** — **up / in one's sleeve** reírse para sus adentros; **she** — **ed in his face** se rió en su cara; N risa *f*; **we did it for** — **s** lo hicimos por diversión

laughable [léfəbəł] ADJ risible

laughingstock [léfıŋstɑk] N hazmerreír *m*

laughter [léftɚ] N risa *f*

launch [lɔntʃ] VT (put into water) botar; (a rocket, new product) lanzar; **to** — **forth / out** lanzarse; N lancha *f*; (act of launching a boat) botadura *f*; (act of launching a rocket) lanzamiento *m*

launder [lɔ́ndɚ] VI/VT (wash) lavar; (money) blanquear, lavar; (wash and iron) lavar y planchar

laundry [lɔ́ndri] N (business establishment) lavandería *f*, lavadero *m*; (room in house) cuarto de lavado *m*, lavadero *m*; (clothes to be washed) ropa sucia *f*; (washed clothes) ropa limpia *f*

laurel [lɔ́rəł] N laurel *m* (also honor); **to rest on one's** — **s** dormirse sobre los laureles

lava [lávə] N lava *f*

lavatory [lévətɔri] N (basin) lavabo *m*; (bathroom) baño *m*, retrete *m*

lavender [lévəndɚ] N espliego *m*, lavanda *f*; ADJ lavanda

lavish [lévıʃ] ADJ INV (generous) pródigo, espléndido; (abundant) abundante, copioso; VT prodigar; **to** — **praise upon** colmar de alabanzas a

law [lɔ] N ley *f*; (discipline) derecho *m*, jurisprudencia *f*; (police) policía *f*; — **and order** orden público *m*; —**breaker** infractor -ora *mf*, transgresor -ora *mf*; —**maker** legislador -ra *mf*; — **student** estudiante de derecho *mf*; —**suit** pleito *m*, litigio *m*; **to practice** — ejercer la abogacía; **to take the** — **into one's hands** hacer justicia por mano propia; ADJ —-**abiding** respetuoso de las leyes

lawful [lɔ́fəł] ADJ (in accordance with the law) legal; (allowed by law) lícito; (recognized by law) legítimo

lawless [lɔ́lıs] ADJ (anarchic) anárquico; (illegal) ilegal

lawn [lɔn] N césped *m*, grama *f*; — **mower** cortadora de césped *f*

lawyer [lɔ́jɚ] N abogado -da *mf*

lax [læks] ADJ laxo

laxative [léksədıv] ADJ & N laxante *m*, purgante *m*

laxity [léksıdi] N flojedad *f*, laxitud *f*

lay [le] VT colocar; (eggs) poner; (a cable) tender; **to** — **aside** (abandon) dejar de lado; (save) guardar; **to** — **a wager** apostar; **to** — **bare** poner al descubierto; **to** — **bricks** poner ladrillos; **to** — **down arms** rendir las armas; **to** — **down the law** imponerse; **to** — **hold of** asir, agarrar; **to** — **into** atacar; **to** — **off a workman** despedir temporalmente a un obrero; **to** — **one's head on a pillow** recostar la cabeza sobre una almohada; **to** — **open** exponer; **to** — **out a plan** trazar un plan; **to** — **up** almacenar; **to be laid up** estar en cama; **to** — **waste** asolar; N situación *f*, orientación *f*; —**man** (non-expert) lego *m*; (clergy) laico *m*; —**out** trazado *m*; ADJ lego, laico

layer [léɚ] N capa *f*; (geological) estrato *m*;

(hen) gallina ponedora *f*; **— cake** tarta de capas *f*

laziness [lézɪnɪs] N pereza *f*, holgazanería *f*, flojera *f*

lazy [lézi] ADJ perezoso, holgazán, flojo

lead [lɛd] N (metal) plomo *m*; (graphite) mina *f*; **— poisoning** intoxicación con plomo *f*; [lid] VT (guide) guiar; (guide a horse) llevar de la rienda; (induce, take) llevar, inducir; (be in charge, be first) encabezar; (direct) dirigir; (be superior to) estar a la cabeza de; **to — a life of ease** llevar una vida fácil; **to — astray** llevar por mal camino; **to — the way** mostrar el camino; VI (afford passage to, result in) llevar a; (be first) estar a la cabeza; N (first position) delantera *f*, primer lugar *m*; (clue) indicio *m*; (most important role) papel principal *m*; **— story** noticia principal *f*

leaden [lɛ́dn] ADJ (of lead) de plomo; (color) plomizo; (oppressive, slow) pesado

leader [líɖɚ] N (in politics) líder *mf*, caudillo *m*; (in a race) líder *mf*; (in music) director -ora *mf*; (as a guide) guía *mf*

leadership [líɖɚʃɪp] N dirección *f*, liderazgo *m*

leading [líɖɪŋ] ADJ (most important) principal; (arriving first) delantero; **— man** primer actor *m*

leadoff [líɖɔf] ADJ comienzo

leaf [lif] N hoja *f*; VI echar hojas; **to — through a book** hojear un libro

leafless [líflɪs] ADJ sin hojas, deshojado

leaflet [líflɪt] N (small leaf) folíolo *m*; (printed matter) volante *m*; (folded printed matter) pliego *m*

leafy [lífi] ADJ (with foliage) frondoso; (in the form of leaves) de hoja

league [lig] N (alliance) liga *f*; (unit of distance) legua *f*; VI/VT aliar(se)

leak [lik] N (in a roof) gotera *f*; (in a boat, bucket, etc.) agujero *m*; (of information) filtración *f*; (of gas, steam, electricity) escape *m*, fuga *f*; VI (roof) gotear(se); (boat) hacer agua; (gas) salirse, escaparse; (information) filtrarse; VT pasar información

leaky [líki] ADJ (roof) que tiene goteras; (boat) que hace agua; (gas, electricity) que pierde

lean [lin] VI/VT (incline) inclinar(se); (support) apoyar(se), reclinar(se), recostar(se); **to — on** presionar; ADJ magro; **— year** mal año *m*

leap [lip] VI/VT saltar; **to — at** aprovechar; **to — to mind** ocurrírsele a uno; N salto *m*;

—frog pídola *f*; **— year** año bisiesto *m*

learn [lɚn] VI/VT aprender; (find out) enterarse de

learned [lɚ́nɪd] ADJ erudito, letrado

learner [lɚ́nɚ] N estudiante *mf*; (driver) aprendiz -za *mf*

learning [lɚ́nɪŋ] N (result) erudición *f*, saber *m*; (process) aprendizaje *m*; **— disability** problema de aprendizaje *m*

lease [lis] N (action) arrendamiento *m*; (contract) contrato de arrendamiento *m*; (period) período de arrendamiento *m*; **to have a new — on life** nacer de nuevo; VI/VT arrendar

leash [liʃ] N traílla *f*, correa *f*

least [list] ADJ **he doesn't have the — chance** no tiene la más mínima posibilidad; **the — amount of money** la menor cantidad de dinero; **— common denominator** denominador mínimo común *m*; ADV menos; **the — important** lo menos importante; **at — al** menos, por lo menos; **I received the — of anyone** yo fui el que recibió menos de todos

leather [léɖɚ] N cuero *m*; ADJ de cuero; **— strap** correa *f*

leave [liv] VT (a person, thing) dejar; (a place) salir de, irse de; VI salir, partir; **to — off** (stop) parar de; (omit) omitir; **to — out** omitir; **I have two books left** me quedan dos libros; N permiso *m*; **to be on — estar de licencia; to take — of** despedirse de

leaven [lévən] N levadura *f*; VT leudar

leavings [lívɪŋz] N (leftovers) sobras *f pl*; (refuse) desperdicios *m pl*; (act of leaving) partida *f*

Lebanese [lɛbəníz] ADJ & N libanés -esa *mf*

Lebanon [lébənɑn] N Líbano *m*

lecherous [létʃɚəs] ADJ lujurioso

lecture [léktʃɚ] N (presentation) conferencia *f*, disertación *f*; (sermon) sermón *m*; (long-winded speech) perorata *f*; VI (present) dar una conferencia, disertar; VT (scold) sermonear

lecturer [léktʃɚɚ] N conferenciante *mf*; (academic rank) profesor -ra *mf*

LED (light-emitting diode) [ɛlidí] N LED *m*

ledge [lɛdʒ] N cornisa *f*

ledger [lédʒɚ] N libro mayor *m*

leech [litʃ] N sanguijuela *f*

leer [lir] VT (sideways) mirar de soslayo; (lecherously) mirar con lujuria; N (sideways) mirada de soslayo *f*; (lecherous) mirada lujuriosa *f*

leeway [líwe] N margen de maniobra *m*; (of a

ship) deriva *f*

left [left] ADJ izquierdo; **—-handed** zurdo, con la mano izquierda; **—-handed compliment** alabanza irónica *f*; **—-handed tool** herramienta para zurdos *f*; **—-wing** de izquierdas; N izquierda *f*; **at / on / to / toward the** — a / hacia la izquierda; **make a** — dobla / gira a la izquierda

leftist [léftɪst] N & ADJ izquierdista *mf*

leg [leg] N (human) pierna *f*; (animal, furniture) pata *f*; (wading bird) zanca *f*; (furniture) pie *m*; (of a trip) etapa *f*; **to be on one's last** —s estar en las últimas; **to pull someone's** — tomarle el pelo a alguien; **to stretch one's** —s estirar las piernas

legacy [légəsi] N legado *m*

legal [lígəɫ] ADJ (in accordance with the law) legal; (permitted by law) lícito; (recognized by law) legítimo; **— age** mayoría de edad *f*; **— fees** honorarios del abogado *m pl*; **— holiday** día feriado *m*; **— procedure** procedimiento jurídico *m*; **— tender** moneda de curso legal *f*

legalize [lígəlaɪz] VT legalizar

legation [lɪgéʃən] N legación *f*

legend [lédʒənd] N leyenda *f* (also inscription); (of a map) clave *f*

legendary [lédʒənderi] ADJ legendario

leggings [légɪŋz] N (ankle to knee) polainas *f pl*; (trousers) leggings *m pl*

legible [lédʒəbəɫ] ADJ legible

legion [lídʒən] N legión *f*

legislate [lédʒɪslet] VI/VT legislar

legislation [ledʒɪsléʃən] N legislación *f*

legislative [lédʒɪsledɪv] ADJ legislativo

legislator [lédʒɪsledə-] N legislador -ra *mf*

legislature [lédʒɪsletʃə-] N legislatura *f*

legitimate [lɪdʒítəmɪt] ADJ legítimo

legitimize [lədʒítəmaɪz] VT legitimar

legume [légjum] N legumbre *f*

leisure [líʒə-] N ocio *m*, holgura *f*; **— hours** horas de ocio *f pl*, tiempo libre *m*; **to be at** — estar desocupado; **do it at your** — hazlo cuando te convenga

leisurely [líʒə-li] ADJ lento, deliberado; ADV sin prisa

lemon [lémən] N limón *m*; ADJ de limón; **— tree** limonero *m*

lemonade [lemənéd] N limonada *f*

lend [lend] VI/VT prestar; **to — a hand** dar una mano

lender [léndə-] N (person who lends) prestador -ora *mf*; (professional) prestamista *mf*

length [leŋkθ] N largo *m*, largura *f*, longitud

f; (of movie) duración *f*; (of a book) extensión *f*; **at** — (in detail) pormenorizadamente; (finally) finalmente; **by two** —s por dos cuerpos; **two meters in** — dos metros de largo; **to go to any** —s hacer lo imposible

lengthen [léŋkθən] VI/VT alargar(se)

lengthwise [léŋkθwaɪz] ADV & ADJ a lo largo

lengthy [léŋkθi] ADJ largo, prolongado

lenient [líniənt] ADJ indulgente

lens [lenz] N lente *m*; (of the eye) cristalino *m*

Lent [lent] N Cuaresma *f*

lentil [léntɫ] N lenteja *f*

Leon [león] N León *m*

Leonese [lianíz] ADJ leonés

leopard [lépə-d] N leopardo *m*

leprosy [léprəsi] N lepra *f*

lesbian [lézbian] ADJ lesbiano; N lesbiana *f*

lesion [líʒən] N lesión *f*

Lesotho [ləsóto] N Lesoto *m*

less [les] ADJ, ADV & PREP menos; **I have — than you do** tengo menos que tú; **— and** — cada vez menos

lessen [lésən] VI/VT disminuir, aminorar

lesser [lésə-] ADJ menor

lesson [lésən] N lección *f*

lest [lest] CONJ no sea que; **— you should think I'm teasing** para que no vayas a creer que estoy bromeando

let [let] VT (permit) dejar, permitir; (rent) alquilar; **— him come** que venga; **—'s do it** hagámoslo; **to — be** dejar en paz; **to — down** (lower) bajar; (disappoint) decepcionar; **to — go** soltar; **to — in** dejar entrar; **to — know** hacer saber; **to — off** dejar ir; **to — through** dejar pasar; **to — up** (permit to stand) dejar incorporarse; (cease) disminuir; N **—down** desilusión *f*; **—up** tregua *f*

lethal [líθəɫ] ADJ letal

lethargy [léθə-dʒi] N letargo *m*, sopor *m*; **to fall into a** — aletargarse

letter [létə-] N (of alphabet) letra *f*; (missive) carta *f*; **— box** buzón *m*; **— carrier** cartero -ra *mf*; **—head** membrete *m*; **—head paper** papel membretado *m*; **—s** letras *f pl*; **the — of the law** la letra de la ley; **to the** — al pie de la letra; VT escribir

lettuce [lédɪs] N lechuga *f*

leukemia [lukímiə] N leucemia *f*

levee [lévi] N dique *m*

level [lévəɫ] ADJ llano, plano; N nivel *m* (also tool); VT (make level) nivelar, igualar; (to demolish) arrasar, allanar; (to knock down a person) tumbar; (to aim criticism) dirigir; (to aim a gun) apuntar; **—-headed** sensato; **— with** a nivel de; **a —**

teaspoon una cucharada al ras; **to be on the** — ser serio; **to** — **off** quedar paralelo al suelo; **to** — **with** hablar en serio con / a

lever [lévə-] N palanca *f*

leverage [lévə-ɪdʒ] N (influence) palanca *f*; (physical) apalancamiento *m*

levity [lévɪdí] N ligereza *f*

levy [lévɪ] N (of taxes) recaudación *f*; (of troops) leva *f*; VT (taxes) recaudar; (troops) reclutar, hacer una leva de

lewd [lud] ADJ lascivo

lewdness [lúdnɪs] N lascivia *f*

lexical [léksɪkəl] ADJ léxico

lexicography [leksɪkágɹəfi] N lexicografía *f*

lexicon [léksɪkən] N léxico *m*

liability [laɪəbílɪdɪ] N (disadvantage) desventaja *f*; (debits) pasivo *m*; (debts) deudas *f pl*; (responsibility) responsabilidad legal *f*; — **insurance** seguro contra daños a terceros *m*; **liabilities** obligaciones *f pl*

liable [láɪəbəl] ADJ responsable; — **to** propenso a; **she's** — **to get angry** es probable que se enoje

liaison [liézən] N enlace *m*; (illicit love affair) aventura *f*

liar [láɪɚ] N mentiroso -sa *mf*, embustero -ra *mf*

libel [láɪbəl] N libelo *m*, difamación *f*; VT difamar

liberal [líbə-əl] ADJ & N liberal *mf*

liberalism [líbə-əlɪzəm] N liberalismo *m*

liberality [lɪbəɹǽlɪdɪ] N (generosity) liberalidad *f*; (tolerance) tolerancia *f*

liberalize [líbə-əlaɪz] VI/VT liberalizar(se)

liberate [líbəɹet] VT (give freedom to) libertar, liberar; (release from obligation) librar; (give off) desprender

liberation [lɪbəɹéʃən] N liberación *f*

liberator [líbəɹedə-] N libertador -ra *mf*

Liberia [laɪbíɹiə] N Liberia *f*

Liberian [laɪbíɹiən] ADJ & N liberiano -na *mf*

libertine [líbə-tin] ADJ & N libertino -na *mf*, calavera *m*

liberty [líbə-DI] N libertad *f*; **at** — autorizado

libido [lɪbído] N libido *f*

librarian [laɪbɹéɹiən] N bibliotecario -ria *mf*

library [láɪbɹeri] N biblioteca *f*

libretto [lɪbɹédo] N libreto *m*

Libya [líbjə] N Libia *f*

Libyan [líbjən] ADJ & N libio -bia *mf*

license [láɪsəns] N permiso *m*; (driver's permit, poetic freedom) licencia *f*; — **plate** placa *f*, matrícula *f*; VT (issue license to) otorgar una licencia; (give permission) autorizar

licentious [laɪsénʃəs] ADJ licencioso

lick [lɪk] VT (touch with tongue) lamer (also waves); (thrash) dar una paliza; (defeat) derrotar; N lamida *f*, lengüetazo *m*; (blow) golpe *m*; **not to do a** — **of work** no mover un dedo

lickety-split [lɪkɪdɪsplít] ADV en un santiamén

licking [líkɪŋ] N paliza *f*

licorice [líkə-ɪʃ] N regaliz *m*

lid [lɪd] N tapadera *f*, tapa *f*; (of eye) párpado *m*; (on prices) tope *m*

lie [laɪ] N (falsehood) mentira *f*, embuste *m*; (orientation of an object) orientación *f*; — **detector** detector de mentiras *m*; **to give the** — **to** desmentir; VI mentir; **to** — **one's way out of a situation** salirse de una situación a mentiras; (be buried) yacer; (to be on a flat surface) estar; (to be situated) estar situado; (be horizontal) tumbarse, acostarse; **he's lying in bed** está acostado en la cama; **to** — **back** recostarse; **to** — **down** acostarse, tumbarse; **to** — **in wait** acechar

Liechtenstein [líktənstaɪn] N Liechtenstein *m*

Liechtensteiner [líktənstaɪnɚ] N liechtensteiniano -na *mf*

lien [lin] N gravamen *m*, carga *f*

lieutenant [luténənt] N teniente *mf*; — **colonel** teniente coronel *mf*; — **governor** vicegobernador -ora *mf*

life [laɪf] N vida *f*; —**-and-death** de vida o muerte; —**boat** bote de salvamento *m*; — **cycle** ciclo vital *m*; — **expectancy** expectativa de vida *f*; —**guard** salvavidas *mf sg*; — **imprisonment** prisión perpetua *f*; — **insurance** seguro de vida *m*; — **jacket** salvavidas *m sg*; —**like** natural, que parece vivo; —**long** de toda la vida; — **of the party** alma de la fiesta *f*; — **preserver** salvavidas *m sg*; — **raft** balsa salvavidas *f*; —**-support system** (in space) equipo de vida *m*; (in a hospital) máquina corazón-pulmón *f*; —**style** estilo de vida *m*; —**time** vida *f*; ADJ (relative to life) vital; (for duration of life) vitalicio; —**-sized** de tamaño natural

lifeless [láɪflɪs] ADJ (without living things) sin vida; (dead) muerto, sin vida; (fainted) desfallecido; (without liveliness) sin animación

lifer [láɪfɚ] N (prisoner) condenado -da a cadena perpetua *mf*; (soldier) militar de carrera *m*

lift [lɪft] VT levantar; (steal) robar; (plagiarize) copiar; VI (disperse) disiparse; (go up) elevarse; N (upward force) empuje *m*; (feeling) mejoría de ánimo *f*; (device for lifting) montacargas *m sg*; **to give someone a —** llevar en coche; *Mex* dar un aventón; **—off** despegue *m*

ligament [lígəmənt] N ligamento *m*

ligature [lígətʃə] N ligadura *f*

light [laɪt] N luz *f*; (device) luz *f*, lámpara *f*; (for traffic) semáforo *m*; (perspective) perspectiva *f*; (for cigarettes) fuego *m*; **—house** faro *m*; ADJ (well-lighted) claro; (of little weight) ligero, leve; (of clothes) fresco; *Am* liviano; **— blue** azul claro *m*; **—emitting diode** diodo electroiluminiscente *m*; **—headed** mareado; **—hearted** alegre; **— rain** lluvia fina *f*; **—skinned** de tez blanca; **— touch** mano delicada *f*; **—weight** de peso ligero; **—year** año luz *m*; **to make — of** restar importancia a; VI/VT (turn on, ignite) encender(se), prender(se); (provide light, brighten) iluminar(se); (land on) posarse en; **to — up** prender, encender, alumbrar; **to — upon** caer sobre

lighten [láɪtn̩] VI/VT (make/become lighter) aligerar(se), aliviar(se); (brighten) iluminar(se); **— up!** ¡No tomes las cosas a la tremenda!

lighter [láɪdə] N encendedor *m*

lighting [láɪdɪŋ] N iluminación *f*; (in the street) alumbrado *m*

lightness [láɪtnɪs] N (little weight) ligereza *f*, levedad *f*; (brightness) claridad *f*

lightning [láɪtnɪŋ] N relámpago *m*; **— bug** luciérnaga *f*; **— rod** pararrayos *m sg*; **it happened at — speed** pasó como rayo; VI relampaguear

likable [láɪkəbəl] ADJ agradable, simpático

like [laɪk] ADV & PREP como; ADJ semejante, parecido; **in — manner** del mismo modo; **to feel — going** tener ganas de ir; **to look — someone** parecerse a alguien; **it looks — rain** parece que va a llover; **—minded** del mismo parecer; N **—s** gustos *m pl*, preferencias *f pl*; VT gustarle a uno; **he —s dogs** le gustan los perros; **do whatever you —** haz lo que quieras; CONJ **he talked — he was crazy** hablaba como si estuviera loco; **she came — you predicted she would** vino, tal como tú pronosticaste; **I'm —, "you're crazy"** yo pensé/dije, "estás loco"; INTERJ **he was, like, way too old** era como que demasiado viejo

likely [láɪkli] ADJ (probable) probable; (believable) creíble; (promising) prometedor; **John is — to win** es probable que gane Juan; ADV probablemente

liken [láɪkən] VT comparar, asimilar

likeness [láɪknɪs] N (similarity) parecido *m*; (portrait) retrato *m*

likewise [láɪkwaɪz] ADV (the same thing) lo mismo; **we did —** hicimos lo mismo; (similarly) asimismo; (also) también

liking [láɪkɪŋ] N preferencia *f*, gusto *m*

lilac [láɪlək] N lila *f*; ADJ lila *inv*

lily [líli] N lirio *m*, azucena *f*; ADJ **—white** (very white) blanquísimo; (pure) puro; (for whites only) exclusivamente para blancos

limb [lɪm] N (branch) rama *f*; (appendage) miembro *m*

limber [límbə] ADJ flexible; VT hacer flexible; VI **to — up** estirarse

lime [laɪm] N (mineral) cal *f*; (fruit, color) lima *f*; **—light** candilejas *f pl*; **in the —light** en el candelero; **—stone** piedra caliza *f*; **— tree** limero *m*, lima *f*

limit [límɪt] N límite *m*; **to the —** al máximo; VT limitar

limitation [lɪmɪtéʃən] N limitación *f*

limitless [límɪtlɪs] ADJ ilimitado

limousine [líməzin] N limusina *f*

limp [lɪmp] N cojera *f*, renguera *f*; VI cojear, renguear, renquear; ADJ (body) flácido; (plants) mustio

limpid [límpɪd] ADJ límpido

line [laɪn] N (bus route, telephone connection) línea *f*; (of words) renglón *m*, línea *f*; (row) raya *f*, hilera *f*; (cord) cuerda *f*; (persons waiting) cola *f*, fila *f*; (business) ramo *m*; (wrinkle) arruga *f*; (boundary) límite *m*; **— of credit** línea de crédito *f*; **—s** (in a play) parte *f*; **—up** hilera de personas *f*; (sports) alineación *f*; **drop me a —** escríbeme unas líneas; **off—** fuera de línea; **on—** en línea; **out of —** irrespetuoso; **to get in —** hacer cola; VI/VT (border) alinear, bordear; (put in a lining) forrar; **to — up** alinear(se)

lineage [líniɪdʒ] N linaje *m*, estirpe *f*

linear [líniə] ADJ lineal

lined [laɪnd] ADJ (with lines) rayado; (with a lining) forrado

linen [línɪn] N (fabric) lino *m*; (bedclothes, etc.) ropa blanca *f*

liner [láɪnə] N (ocean) transatlántico *m*; (air) avión comercial *m*; (eye) delineador *m*

linger [língə] VI (stay) quedarse, demorarse; (persist) persistir; (saunter) rezagarse; (contemplate) detenerse; (delay death) aguantar

lingerie [lɑnʒəré] N lencería *f*

linguist [língwɪst] N lingüista *mf*

linguistics [lɪŋgwístɪks] N lingüística *f*
liniment [línəmənt] N linimento *m*
lining [láɪnɪŋ] N forro *m*; **every cloud has a silver —** no hay mal que por bien no venga
link [lɪŋk] N (of a chain) eslabón *m*; (bond, tie) vínculo *m*; (computer, rail, radio connection) enlace *m*; VI/VT enlazar(se), conectar(se), vincular(se)
linnet [línɪt] N pardillo *m*
linoleum [lɪnólɪəm] N linóleo *m*
linseed [línsid] N linaza *f*; **— oil** aceite de linaza *m*
lint [lɪnt] N pelusa *f*
lion [láɪən] N león *m*; **—'s share** la parte del león
lioness [láɪənɪs] N leona *f*
lip [lɪp] N labio *m*; (of a pitcher) borde *m*; **—stick** lápiz de labios *m*; **to —read** leer los labios; **don't give me no —!** no me contestes
liposuction [láɪposʌkʃən] N liposucción *f*
liqueur [lɪkɚ] N licor *m*
liquid [líkwɪd] ADJ líquido; **— assets** activo líquido *m*; **— measure** medida para líquidos *f*; N líquido *m*
liquidate [líkwɪdet] VI/VT liquidar
liquidation [lɪkwɪdéʃən] N liquidación *f*
liquidity [lɪkwídɪɾi] N liquidez *f*
liquor [líkɚ] N bebida espirituosa *f*
lira [líɾə] N lira *f*
lisp [lɪsp] N ceceo *m*; VI cecear
list [lɪst] N lista *f*; (of a ship) escora *f*; **— price** precio de lista *m*; **— server** servidor de lista *m*; VT (make a list) hacer una lista de; VI (lean) escorar; **this chair —s for two hundred dollars** esta silla está a doscientos dólares
listen [lísən] VI/VT (hear) escuchar, oír; (heed) escuchar, prestar atención; **to — in** (on radio) sintonizar; (eavesdrop) escuchar a hurtadillas
listener [lísənɚ] N oyente *mf*; **radio —** radioescucha *mf*, oyente *mf*
listing [lístɪŋ] N listado *m*
listless [lístlɪs] ADJ lánguido
lit [lɪt] ADJ (provided with light) iluminado; (tipsy) alegre, alumbrado
literacy [líɾəəsi] N (action of making literate) alfabetización *f*; (rate) alfabetismo *m*
literal {líɾəəl} ADJ literal
literary [líɾəɾeri] ADJ literario
literate [líɾəɪt] ADJ (who can read and write) alfabeto; (erudite) erudito, letrado; **he's barely —** apenas sabe leer y escribir
literature [líɾəətʃɚ] N literatura *f*;

(handbills) impresos *m pl*, folletos *m pl*; **the scientific —** la literatura científica
lithium [líθɪəm] N litio *m*
Lithuania [lɪθuénɪə] N Lituania *f*
Lithuanian [lɪθuénɪən] ADJ & N lituano -na *mf*
litigation [lɪtɪgéʃən] N litigio *m*, pleito *m*
litter [líɾɚ] N (young animals) camada *f*, cría *f*; (stretcher) camilla *f*; (straw) cama de paja para animales *f*; (trash) basura *f*; (for cats) arena higiénica *f*; VI/VT (dirty) ensuciar; (strew) esparcir; VI (give birth) parir
little [líɾl] ADJ (small) pequeño, chico; (not much) poco; **— brother** hermano menor *m*, hermanito *m*; **— finger** (dedo) meñique *m*; **— pig** puerquito *m*; **a — coffee** un poco de café; **a — while** un ratito, un poco; ADV & N poco; **— by —** poco a poco
live [lɪv] VI/VT vivir; **to — up to** cumplir; **to — it up** tirar la casa por la ventana; **all the —long day** todo el santo día; [laɪv] ADJ vivo; (ammunition) cargado; **— coal** ascua encendida *f*; **— oak** roble de Virginia *m*; **—stock** ganado *m*; **— wire** (electric) cable cargado *m*; (person) persona vivaz *f*; **before a — audience** en vivo; **—-in** con cama; ADV en vivo y en directo
livelihood [láɪvlihʊd] N sustento *m*
liveliness [láɪvlinɪs] N viveza *f*, animación *f*
lively [láɪvli] ADJ (party) animado; (person) vivaz, avispado; ADV con animación
liver [lívɚ] N hígado *m*
livid [lívɪd] ADJ (bluish) lívido; (angry) furibundo
living [lívɪŋ] N (life) vida *f*; **to earn / make a —** ganarse la vida; ADJ vivo, viviente; **— room** sala *f*, living *m*; **— wage** sueldo suficiente para vivir *m*; **the —** los vivos
lizard [lízɚd] N lagartija *f*
llama [lάmə] N llama *f*
load [lod] N carga *f*; (weight) peso *m*; (of a ship) cargamento *m*; **—s of** montones de; VI/VT cargar; **to — down** colmar; **to — oneself down** agobiarse
loaf [lof] N hogaza de pan *f*, pan *m*; VI holgar, holgazanear, haraganear
loafer [lófɚ] N (idler) holgazán -ana *mf*, haragán -na *mf*, gandul -la *mf*; (shoe) mocasín *m*
loan [lon] N préstamo *m*; (to a government) empréstito *m*; **— shark** usurero -ra *mf*; **—word** préstamo *m*; VI/VT prestar
loath [loθ] ADJ renuente; **to be — to** ser renuente a

loathe [loð] VT aborrecer
loathsome [lóðsəm] ADJ repugnante, abominable
lob [lab] VT tirar por lo alto; N (tennis) globo m
lobby [lábi] N (vestibule) vestíbulo m; (special interest) grupo de presión m, lobby m; VI/VT (influence) presionar
lobbyist [lábiɪst] N lobbista mf, lobista mf
lobe [lob] N lóbulo m
lobotomy [ləbádəmi] N lobotomía f
lobster [lábstɚ] N langosta f
local [lókəɫ] ADJ local; — **train** tren de cercanías m
localize [lókəlaɪz] VT localizar
locate [lóket] VI/VT (establish in a place) situar, ubicar; (find) localizar; VI (settle) radicarse, establecerse
location [lokéʃən] N (position) ubicación f; (finding) localización f; **on** — en exteriores
lock [lak] N (door) cerradura f; (canal) esclusa f; (firearms, wrestling) llave f; (of hair) mechón m; **to have a** — **on the award** tener asegurado el premio; —-**out** cierre patronal m; —**smith** cerrajero -ra mf; VI/VT cerrar con llave; (make immovable) trabar(se); **to** — **in** encerrar; **to** — **out** dejar afuera; **to** — **up** (door) cerrar con llave; (animal) encerrar; (prisoner) encarcelar; (valuables) poner bajo llave
locker [lákɚ] N (for athletic equipment) casillero m; (for frozen food) cámara frigorífica f; — **room** vestuario m
locket [lákɪt] N relicario m, guardapelo m
locomotive [lokəmóDɪv] N locomotora f
locust [lókəst] N langosta f; — **tree** algarrobo m
lodge [ladʒ] N (of fraternal organization) logia f; (cabin) cabaña f; (hotel) posada f, mesón m; VI/VT alojar(se), hospedar(se); **to** — **a complaint** presentar una queja
lodger [ládʒɚ] N inquilino -na mf
lodging [ládʒɪŋ] N alojamiento m, hospedaje m
loft [lɔft] N (attic) desván m; (for choir) coro m; (for hay) pajar m; VT tirar por lo alto
lofty [lɔ́fti] ADJ elevado, encumbrado
log [lɔg] N (log) leño m, madero m, rollizo m; (ship record) cuaderno de bitácora m; (record of activity) diario m; — **cabin** cabaña de troncos f; VI/VT (cut trees) cortar; VT (write down) anotar; **to** — **in** entrar (al sistema); **to** — **off / out** salir (del sistema)
logarithm [lɔ́gəɪðəm] N logaritmo m
logic [ládʒɪk] N lógica f
logical [ládʒɪkəɫ] ADJ lógico

logistics [lədʒístɪks] N logística f
loin [lɔɪn] N ijada f; (in animals) ijar m; (cut of meat) lomo m; —**s** entrañas f pl
loiter [lɔ́ɪDɚ] VI (idly) holgazanear; (with intent) merodear; **to** — **behind** rezagarse
loll [laɫ] VI arrellanarse
lollipop [láIipap] N Sp pirulí m; Mex paleta f; RP chupetín m
lone [lon] ADJ (solitary) solitario; (only) único
loneliness [lónlinɪs] N soledad f
lonely [lónli] ADJ solo
lonesome [lónsəm] ADJ solo
long [lɔŋ] ADJ largo; **a** — **way home** lejos de casa; **to work** — **hours** trabajar muchas horas; — **distance** de larga distancia; — **division** división de más de una cifra f; —**hand** letra manuscrita f; — **johns** calzoncillos largos m pl; — **jump** salto largo m; —-**lasting** duradero, perdurable; —-**lived** (batteries) duradero; (people) longevo; —-**range** de largo alcance; —**shoreman** estibador m; —-**term** a largo plazo; —**underwear** calzoncillo largo m; —-**winded** verborrágico, palabrero; **it's a** — **shot** es muy improbable; — **ago** hace mucho tiempo; — **before** mucho antes; — **live . . . !** ¡viva . . . ! —**suffering** sufrido; **all winter** — todo el invierno; **how** — **did he stay?** ¿cuánto tiempo se quedó ? **not for** — no por mucho tiempo; **so** — ! ¡hasta luego! **to be** — **in coming** tardar en venir; **three meters** — tres metros de largo; **will you be** —? ¿tardarás mucho? **the whole day** — todo el santo día; VI **to** — **for** anhelar
longer [lɔ́ŋgɚ] ADJ más largo; ADV más; **no** — ya no; **how much** —? ¿hasta cuándo?
longevity [landʒévɪDi] N longevidad f
longing [lɔ́ŋɪŋ] N anhelo m; ADJ anhelante
longitude [lándʒɪtud] N longitud f
look [luk] VI (see) mirar; (seem) parecer; **it** —**s good on you** te queda bien, te luce; **to** — **after** atender, cuidar; **to** — **alike** parecerse; **to** — **down on someone** despreciar a alguien; **to** — **for** (search for) buscar; (anticipate) esperar; **I** — **forward to it** lo espero con ansia, me da mucha ilusión; **to** — **into** investigar; **she** —**s her age** aparenta la edad que tiene; **to** — **out on** dar a, tener vista a; **to** — **out of** asomarse a; — **out!** ¡cuidado! **to** — **over** dar un vistazo a; **to** — **up** (upwards) levantar la vista; (in a directory) buscar; **to** — **up to** admirar; N (gaze) mirada f; (examination) vistazo m; —-**alike** doble

mf; **—out** (person) vigía *mf;* (place) mirador *m,* vigía *f;* **to be on the —out** estar alerta; **—s** aspecto *m,* pinta *f;* **good —s** belleza *f*

looking glass [lúkɪŋglæs] N espejo *m*

loom [lum] N telar *m;* VI (appear indistinctly) dibujarse; (threaten) cernerse

loony [lúni] ADJ chiflado

loop [lup] N (for fastening) presilla *f;* (in a rope) lazo *m;* (of a flight) rizo *m;* (electric) circuito cerrado *m;* (computer programming, ice-skating) bucle *m;* **—hole** resquicio *m,* agujero *m;* VI (make a loop) hacer un lazo; (curve around) serpentear; (loop the loop) rizar el rizo; VT enlazar

loose [lus] ADJ (free) suelto; (not tight) flojo; (approximate) libre; (unfettered) desatado; (immoral) disoluto; (promiscuous) fácil; **—cannon** mono con una metralleta *m;* **—change** suelto *m,* cambio *m;* **— end** cabo suelto *m;* **—-fitting** holgado; **—-jointed** de articulaciones flexibles; **—-leaf** (de) hojas sueltas; **to let —** soltar; VT desatar, soltar

loosen [lúsən] VI/VT (untie) soltar(se), desatar; (make / become less tight / dense / strict) aflojar(se)

looseness [lúsnɪs] N (of skin) flojedad *f;* (of morals) relajamiento *m;* (of clothing) holgura *f;* (of soil) friabilidad *f;* (of translation) lo libre

loot [lut] N botín *m;* VI/VT saquear

lop [lɑp] VT (cut) cortar; (eliminate) eliminar; VI caer(se); ADJ **—sided** (leaning to one side) ladeado; (unbalanced) desequilibrado; (listing) escorado

lope [lop] VI correr a pasos largos

loquacious [lokwéʃəs] ADJ locuaz

loquat [lókwɑt] N níspero *m*

lord [lɔrd] N señor *m;* (God) Señor *m;* (British title) lord *m;* **—'s Prayer** Padrenuestro *m;* **my —!** ¡Dios mío! VI **to — it over someone** tratarle a alguien con arrogancia

lordly [lɔ́rdli] ADJ (kingly) señorial; (haughty) altivo

lordship [lɔ́rdʃɪp] N (title) señoría *f;* (power) señorío *m*

lore [lɔr] N saber *m*

lose [luz] VI/VT perder; (a pursuer) dejar atrás; **to — sight of** perder de vista; **to — oneself in thought** ensimismarse

loser [lúzɚ] N perdedor -ra *mf*

loss [lɔs] N (destruction) pérdida *f;* (misplacement) pérdida *f,* extravío *m;* (sports) derrota *f;* **to be at a —** no saber

qué hacer; **to sell at a —** vender con pérdida; **—es** bajas *f pl*

lost [lɔst] ADJ perdido; **— in thought** absorto; **to get —** perderse, extraviarse

lot [lɑt] N (parcel) lote *m;* (luck) suerte *f,* destino *m;* (piece of land) solar *m,* terreno *m;* **the —** todo; **a — of / —s of** mucho(s); **a — of money** mucho dinero; **by —** al azar; **to draw —s** echar suertes; **to fall to one's —** caerle en suerte a uno; ADV **a — better** mucho mejor

lotion [lóʃən] N loción *f*

lottery [lɑ́ɾəri] N lotería *f*

loud [laud] ADJ (noisy) ruidoso; (strong) fuerte; (ostentatious) chillón; ADV fuerte, alto; **—speaker** altavoz *m,* altoparlante *m;* **—mouth** bocazas *mf sg*

lounge [laundʒ] VI repantigarse, arrellanarse; **to — away** pasar holgazaneando; N (waiting-room) sala de espera *f;* (room in bar) salón *m;* (divan) diván *m;* **— chair** diván *m*

louse [laus] N piojo *m*

lousy [láuzi] ADJ (infested with lice) piojoso; (contemptible) despreciable; (poorly done) pésimo

lout [laut] N bruto *m*

lovable [lávəbəl] ADJ adorable

love [lav] N (affection) amor *m;* (fondness) afición *f;* (in tennis) nada *f;* **— affair** aventura *f,* amorío *m;* **— at first sight** amor a primera vista *m,* flechazo *m;* **— life** vida sentimental *f;* **— seat** confidente *m;* **books were her great —** los libros fueron su gran pasión; **to be in —** estar enamorado; **to fall in — with** enamorarse de; **to make — to** hacerle el amor a; VI/VT amar, querer; **I — to eat apples** me encanta comer manzanas

loveliness [lávlinɪs] N (beauty) hermosura *f;* (charm) encanto *m*

lovely [lávli] ADJ (beautiful) hermoso; (charming) encantador; (pleasant) ameno

lover [lávɚ] N (sexually involved) amante *mf;* (in love) enamorado -da *mf,* amante *mf;* (interested in) aficionado -da *mf*

loving [lávɪŋ] ADJ cariñoso, afectuoso

low [lo] ADJ (not high) bajo; (base) vil; (humble) humilde; (downcast) abatido; (deep in pitch) grave; **— beam** luces cortas *f pl;* **—brow** poco culto; **—-cal** de bajas calorías; **—down** verdad *f;* **—-end** barato; **— gear** primera marcha *f;* **—-grade** (inferior) inferior; (low) bajo; **—-key** tranquilo; **—land** tierra baja *f;* **—-level** de bajo nivel; **—life** canalla *f;* **—-tech** sencillo; **— tide** bajamar *f,* marea baja *f*; **dress with a — neck** vestido escotado *m*; **to be — on something** estar escaso de algo; **to be in — spirits** estar abatido/desanimado; ADV bajo; **to buy** — comprar barato; N (sound of a cow) mugido *m*; VI mugir

lower [lóə-] VI/VT bajar; (prices) rebajar; (flag, sail) arriar; ADJ más bajo, inferior; **—case** minúscula *f*; **— house** cámara de diputados *f*

lowliness [lólinıs] N humildad *f*

lowly [lóli] ADJ humilde

loyal [lɔ́ıəł] ADJ leal

loyalty [lɔ́ıəłti] N lealtad *f*

LSD (lysergic acid diethylamide) [ɛlɛsdí] N LSD *m*

lubricant [lúbrıkənt] ADJ & N lubricante *m*

lubricate [lúbrıket] VI/VT lubricar

lucid [lúsıd] ADJ lúcido

luck [lʌk] N suerte *f*; **in** — de suerte; **to be out of** — estar de mala suerte; **to — into** conseguir por un golpe de suerte; **to — out** tener suerte

lucky [lʌ́ki] ADJ afortunado; **— charm** amuleto de la suerte *m*; **to be** — tener suerte

lucrative [lúkrəɑıv] ADJ lucrativo

ludicrous [lúdıkrəs] ADJ ridículo

lug [lʌg] VT acarrear

luggage [lágıʤ] N equipaje *m*; **— rack** rejilla *f*

lukewarm [lúkwɔ́rm] ADJ (not warm or cold) tibio; (indifferent) indiferente

lull [lʌ́ł] VT (put to sleep) arrullar; VI/VT (soothe) calmar(se); N (calm) calma *f*, tregua *f*; (sound) arrullo *m*

lullaby [lʌ́ləbaı] N canción de cuna *f*, nana *f*

lumber [lʌ́mbə-] N madera *f*; **—jack** leñador *m*; **—man** maderero *m*; **— mill** aserradero *m*; **—yard** almacén de maderas *m*; VI/VT (cut trees) talar; (move heavily) moverse pesadamente; (make a low noise) tronar

luminous [lúmənəs] ADJ luminoso

lump [lʌmp] N (in breast) bulto *m*; (in sauce) grumo *m*; (in throat) nudo *m*; (of coal) trozo *m*; (of rice) plasta *f*; (on head) chichón *m*; (of sugar) terrón *m*; **to take one's —s** recibir palos; **— sum** pago global *m*; VT juntar; VI agrumarse

lumpy [lʌ́mpi] ADJ grumoso

lunar [lúnə-] ADJ lunar; **— eclipse** eclipse lunar *m*

lunatic [lúnətık] ADJ & N lunático -ca *mf*, loco -ca *mf*; **— fringe** extremistas *mf pl*

lunch [lʌntʃ] N comida *f*, almuerzo *m*; **—time** hora de almorzar/comer *f*; **out to —** (crazy) en la luna; VI comer, almorzar

lung [lʌŋ] N pulmón *m*

lunge [lʌnʤ] N arremetida *f*; VI arremeter, abalanzarse; **to — at** arremeter contra, abalanzarse sobre

lurch [lɜ-tʃ] N tambaleo *m*; **to give a —** tambalearse; **to leave someone in the —** dejar a alguien en la estacada; VI tambalearse, dar barquinazos

lure [lur] N (thing that attracts) atractivo *m*, gancho *m*; (in hunting) señuelo *m*; (in fishing) cebo *m*; VT atraer, seducir

lurid [lúrıd] ADJ (gruesome) sangriento; (shocking) escabroso

lurk [lɜ-k] VI (lie in wait) estar en acecho, acechar; (move furtively) moverse furtivamente

luscious [lʌ́ʃəs] ADJ (delicious) exquisito, delicioso; (sexy) voluptuoso

lust [lʌst] N (sexual desire) lujuria *f*, lascivia *f*; (craving) deseo *m*, ansia *f*; VI desear; **to — after** codiciar

luster [lʌ́stə-] N lustre *m*, brillo *m*

lustful [lʌ́stfəł] ADJ lujurioso

lusty [lʌ́sti] ADJ (robust) robusto; (full of lust) lujurioso

Luxembourg [lʌ́ksəmbɚg] N Luxemburgo *m*

Luxembourger [lʌ́ksəmbɚgɚ] N luxemburgués -esa *mf*

Luxembourgian [lʌ́ksəmbɚ́giən] ADJ luxemburgués

luxurious [lʌgʒúriəs] ADJ (characterized by luxury) lujoso; (luxuriant) exuberante

luxury [lʌ́gʒəri] N lujo *m*; **— tax** impuesto suntuario *m*; ADJ de lujo

lye [laı] N lejía *f*

lying [láıŋ] ADJ mentiroso

lymph [lımf] N linfa *f*; **— node** nodo linfático *m*

lynch [lıntʃ] VT linchar

lynx [lıŋks] N lince *m*

lyric [lírık] N poema lírico *m*; **—s** letra *f*; ADJ lírico

lyrical [lírıkəł] ADJ lírico

lyricism [lírısızəm] N lirismo *m*

Mm

ma'am [mæm] N señora *f*

Macao [məkáu] N Macao *m*

macaroni [mækəróni] N macarrones *m pl*

Macedonia [mæsıdóniə] N Macedonia *f*

Macedonian [mæsıdóniən] ADJ & N macedonio -nia *mf*

machine [məʃín] N máquina f; (of government) maquinaria f, aparato m; — **gun** (not portable) ametralladora f; (portable) metralleta f; — **language** lenguaje de máquina m; —**made** hecho a máquina; VT trabajar a máquina

machinery [məʃínəri] N maquinaria f

machinist [məʃínɪst] N maquinista mf, operario -ria mf

mackerel [mǽkəəɫ] N caballa f

mad [mæd] ADJ (crazy) loco; (angry) rabioso, enojado; (hydrophobic) rabioso; **to be — about someone** estar loco por alguien; **to drive —** enloquecer, volver loco; **to get —** enojarse; **to go —** volverse loco, enloquecerse; **like —** como loco; —**man** loco m

Madagascan [mædəgǽskən] ADJ & N malgache mf

Madagascar [mædəgǽskɑr] N Madagascar m

madam [mǽdəm] N señora f; (woman who runs a brothel) madama f

maddening [mǽdṇɪŋ] ADJ enloquecedor

made [med] ADJ —**to-measure** hecho a la medida; —**to-order** hecho por encargo; —**up** (invented) inventado, falso; (wearing make-up) maquillado; **to be — of** ser de; **to have something —** mandar hacer algo; **I'm a — man** estoy hecho; **to have it —** estar hecho

madness [mǽdnɪs] N (insanity) locura f; (anger) rabia f

Mafia [máfɪə] N mafia f

mafioso [mafióso] N mafioso m

magazine [mǽgəzin] N (publication) revista f; (room for ammunition) polvorín m; (part of gun) cargador m

magic [mǽdʒɪk] N magia f; ADJ mágico; — **bullet** panacea f; — **wand** varita mágica f

magical [mǽdʒɪkəɫ] ADJ mágico

magician [mədʒíʃən] N mago -ga mf

magistrate [mǽdʒɪstret] N magistrado -da mf

magma [mǽgmə] N magma m

magnanimous [mægnǽnəməs] ADJ magnánimo

magnate [mǽgnet] N magnate m

magnesia [mægníʒə] N magnesia f

magnesium [mægníziəm] N magnesio m

magnet [mǽgnɪt] N imán m

magnetic [mægnéDɪk] ADJ magnético; — **pole** polo magnético m; — **resonance imaging** imagen por resonancia magnética f; — **tape** cinta magnetofónica f

magnetism [mǽgnɪtɪzəm] N magnetismo m

magnetize [mǽgnɪtaɪz] VT magnetizar, imantar

magnificence [mægnífɪsəns] N magnificencia f

magnificent [mægnífɪsənt] ADJ magnífico

magnify [mǽgnɪfaɪ] VT (to make larger) aumentar; (to make louder) amplificar; (to exaggerate) exagerar, magnificar

magnitude [mǽgnɪtud] N magnitud f

magnolia [mægnóljə] N (flower) magnolia f; (tree) magnolio m

magpie [mǽgpaɪ] N urraca f (also hoarder)

mahogany [məhágəni] N caoba f

maid [med] N criada f, sirvienta f; (in hotel) camarera f; — **of honor** dama de honor f

maiden [médṇ] N lit doncella f, virgen f; — **voyage** primer viaje m; — **name** nombre de soltera m

mail [meɫ] N correo m; (electronic) mensaje m; (of metal) malla f; —**bag** cartera f; —**box** buzón m; —**man** cartero m; — **order** pedido por correo m; VT echar al correo

maim [mem] VT mutilar

main [men] ADJ principal; — **office** oficina central f; N (pipe) cañería principal f; (sea) alta mar f; —**frame** Sp ordenador central m, Am computadora central f; —**land** continente m; —**spring** muelle real m; —**stream** tendencia mayoritaria f; —**stay** pilar m, puntal m; —**street** calle principal f

maintain [mentén] VT mantener (also support); (assert) afirmar

maintenance [méntṇəns] N (repairs) mantenimiento m; (monetary support) manutención f

maize [mez] N maíz m

majestic [mədʒéstɪk] ADJ majestuoso

majesty [mǽdʒɪsti] N majestad f; **Your —** Su Majestad

major [médʒɚ] ADJ (greater) mayor, más grande; (large) grande; — **key** mayor m; N (military rank) comandante m; (field of study) especialidad f; — **league** liga mayor f; VI especializarse

majority [mədʒɔ́rɪDi] N mayoría f; **the —** el grueso; (age) mayoría de edad f

make [mek] VT (do) hacer; (create) fabricar; (cause) causar; (earn) ganar; (a speech) pronunciar; **to — a clean breast of** sacarse del pecho; **to — a decision** tomar una decisión; **to — a living** ganarse la vida; **to — a train** llegar a tiempo para tomar un tren; **to — a turn** girar, doblar; **to — away with** fugarse con; **two plus two —s four** dos y dos son cuatro; **to — believe** hacer de cuenta que; **to — out**

(see) vislumbrar, divisar; (read) descifrar; (kiss) *Sp* morrear; *Am* besuquearse; **to — too much of** exagerar; **what do you — of that?** ¿cómo interpretas eso? **to — up** (a story) inventar un cuento; (after a quarrel) hacer las paces; (for a loss) recuperar; (one's face) maquillarse; (one's mind) decidirse; **to — up for** suplir; **you'll — a good teacher** vas a ser un buen profesor; N marca *f;* **—-up** (composition) composición *f;* (character) carácter *m;* (cosmetics) maquillaje *m;* ADJ **—shift** provisional

maker [mékə] N (creator) creador *mf,* hacedor -ora *mf;* (manufacturer) fabricante *m*

makings [mékɪŋz] N (potential) potencial *m;* (ingredients) ingredientes *m pl*

maladjusted [mælədʒʌ́stɪd] ADJ inadaptado

malady [mǽlədi] N mal *m*

malaise [məléz] N malestar *m*

malaria [məlɛ́riə] N malaria *f,* paludismo *m*

Malawi [məláwi] N Malawi *m*

Malawian [məláwiən] ADJ & N malawiano -na *mf*

Malaysia [məléʒə] N Malasia *f*

Malaysian [məléʒən] ADJ & N malasio -sia *mf*

malcontent [mǽłkəntɛnt] ADJ & N descontento -ta *mf*

Maldives [mółdaɪvz] N Maldivas *f pl*

Maldivian [mołdívíən] ADJ & N maldivo -va *mf*

male [mel] ADJ (animal, plant) macho; (person) varón; (trait) masculino; N (animal, plant) macho *m;* (person) varón *m*

malevolent [məlɛ́vələnt] ADJ malévolo

malfunction [mælfʌ́ŋkʃən] N funcionamiento defectuoso *m;* VI funcionar mal

Mali [máli] N Malí *m*

Malian [máliən] ADJ & N malí *mf*

malice [mǽlɪs] N malicia *f;* **with — aforethought** con premeditación y alevosía

malicious [məlíʃəs] ADJ malicioso

malign [məláɪn] VT calumniar, difamar

malignant [məlíɡnənt] ADJ maligno

mall [mɔł] N (closed street) paseo *m;* (enclosed shopping area) galería *f,* centro comercial *m*

mallet [mǽlɪt] N mazo *m*

malnourished [mælnɹ́-rɪʃt] ADJ desnutrido

malnutrition [mælnutríʃən] N desnutrición *f*

malpractice [mælprǽktɪs] N negligencia *f,* mala práctica *f*

malt [mɔłt] N malta *f;* **—ed milk** leche malteada *f*

Malta [mółtə] N Malta *f*

Maltese [mɔłtíz] ADJ & N maltés -esa *mf*

mama, mamma [mámə] N mamá *f;* **—'s boy** nene de mamá *m*

mammal [mǽməł] N mamífero *m*

mammography [mæmágɹəfi] N mamografía *f*

mammoth [mǽməθ] ADJ enorme; N mamut *m*

man [mæn] N hombre *m;* (servant) criado *m;* (in games) pieza *f,* ficha *f;* **— and wife** marido y mujer; **—hunt** persecución *f;* **—kind** humanidad *f;* **—-of-war** (ship) buque de guerra *m;* (jellyfish) medusa *f;* **—power** (for work) mano de obra *f;* (for war) soldados *m pl;* **every — for himself** cada cual para sí; **to a —** unánimamente; ADJ **—-eating** que come carne humana; **—-made** (fiber) sintético; (lake) artificial; INTERJ ¡hombre! VT (a fort) guarnecer; (a ship) tripular; **to —handle** violentar

manage [mǽnɪdʒ] VT (succeed in) conseguir, lograr; (direct) dirigir, administrar; (maneuver) manejar; VI **to — without help** arreglárselas sin ayuda; **—d care** asociación mutualista de salud *f*

manageable [mǽnɪdʒəbəł] ADJ manejable; (hair) dócil

management [mǽnɪdʒmənt] N (act of managing) manejo *m,* dirección *f;* (persons controlling a business) gerencia *f,* gestión *f*

manager [mǽnɪdʒə-] N (of a store) gerente -ta *mf;* (of a company) director -ra *mf*

mandate [mǽndet] N mandato *m;* VT decretar

mandatory [mǽndətɔri] ADJ obligatorio

mandolin [mǽndəlɪn] N mandolina *f*

mane [men] N (of a lion) melena *f;* (of a horse) crin *f*

maneuver [mənúvə-] N maniobra *f;* VI/VT maniobrar

manganese [mǽŋɡəniz] N manganeso *m*

mange [mendʒ] N sarna *f,* roña *f*

manger [méndʒə-] N pesebre *m*

mangle [mǽŋɡəł] VT (mutilate) magullar, mutilar; (ruin) estropear

mango [mǽŋɡo] N mango *m*

mangrove [mǽŋɡrov] N mangle *m*

mangy [méndʒi] ADJ sarnoso

manhood [mǽnhʊd] N virilidad *f;* (men collectively) hombres *m pl;* (adult age) edad adulta *f*

mania [méniə] N manía *f*

maniac [méniæk] N maníaco -ca *mf,* maniaco

-ca *mf*
maniacal [mənáiəkəł] ADJ maníaco
manic-depressive [mǽnɪkdɪprésɪv] ADJ
maníaco-depresivo
manicure [mǽnɪkjur] N manicura *f*; VT
manicurar
manifest [mǽnəfest] ADJ manifiesto; N (list of
cargo) manifiesto *m*, hoja de ruta *f*; VT
(show) manifestar, poner de manifiesto;
(express) declarar
manifestation [mænəfestéʃən] N
manifestación *f*
manifesto [mænɪfésto] N manifiesto *m*
manifold [mǽnəfołd] ADJ diverso; N colector
m
manila [mənílə] N abacá *m*; — **envelope**
sobre manila *m*
manioc [mǽniak] N mandioca *f*, yuca *f*
manipulate [mənípjəlet] VT manipular
manipulation [mənɪpjəléʃən] N
manipulación *f*
manlike [mǽnlaik] ADJ (manly) varonil;
(mannish) hombruna; (resembling a
human) de hombre
manly [mǽnli] ADJ varonil, viril
manner [mǽnə] N (way) manera *f*, modo *m*,
forma *f*; (type) tipo *m*; (air) aire *m*,
ademán *m*; (outward bearing) porte *m*; —**s**
modales *m pl*, crianza *f*; **in the — of** a la
manera de
mannerism [mǽnərɪzəm] N peculiaridad *f*
mannish [mǽnɪʃ] ADJ hombruno, varonil
manor [mǽnə] N feudo *m*, solar *m*; —
house casa solariega *f*
mansion [mǽnʃən] N mansión *f*
mantel [mǽntl] N repisa de chimenea *f*
mantle [mǽntl] N manto *m*
mantra [mǽntrə] N mantra *f*
manual [mǽnjuəł] ADJ & N manual *m*
manufacture [mænjəfǽktʃə] VT fabricar,
manufacturar; (clothes, shoes)
confeccionar; N fabricación *f*, manufactura
f; (of clothes, shoes) confección *f*
manufacturer [mænjəfǽktʃərə] N
fabricante *m*
manufacturing [mænjəfǽktʃə-ɪŋ] N
fabricación *f*, manufactura *f*; ADJ fabril,
manufacturero
manure [mənúr] N estiércol *m*; VT estercolar,
abonar
manuscript [mǽnjəskrɪpt] ADJ & N
manuscrito *m*
many [méni] ADJ muchos; — **apples** muchas
manzanas; — **came** vinieron muchos; —
a time muchas veces; **a great** —
muchísimos; **as** — **as** tantos como; **as** —
as five hasta cinco; **how** — ¿cuántos?

three books too — tres libros de más;
too — demasiados
map [mæp] N (geographical) mapa *m*; (of
streets) plano *m*; VT trazar un mapa de; **to**
— **out** planear
maple [mépəł] N *Sp* arce *m*; *Am* maple *m*; —
syrup miel de arce / maple *m*
mar [mɑr] VT estropear
marathon [mǽrəθan] N maratón *mf*
marble [mɑ́rbəł] N mármol *m*; (toy) canica *f*,
bola *f*; **to play** —**s** jugar a las canicas; ADJ
de mármol, marmóreo
march [mɑrtʃ] N marcha *f*; VI marchar;
(leave) marcharse; **to** — **in** entrar; **to** —
out marcharse; VT hacer marchar
March [mɑrtʃ] N marzo *m*
mare [mer] N yegua *f*
margarine [mɑ́rdʒə-ɪn] N margarina *f*
margin [mɑ́rdʒɪn] N margen *m*
marginal [mɑ́rdʒənəł] ADJ marginal
marginalize [mɑ́rdʒənəlaɪz] VT marginar
marigold [mǽrɪgołd] N caléndula *f*,
maravilla *f*
marijuana, marihuana [mærəwánə] N
marihuana *f*
marinate [mǽrənet] VT marinar
marine [mərín] ADJ (of the sea) marino;
(maritime) marítimo; — **corps** infantería
de marina *f*; N soldado de infantería de
marina *m*
marionette [mæriənét] N marioneta *f*
marital [mǽrɪdl] ADJ conyugal
maritime [mǽrɪtaɪm] ADJ marítimo
mark [mɑrk] N marca *f*, seña *f*; (token) señal
f; (indication) seña *f*; (grade) nota *f*,
calificación *f*; (former German currency)
marco *m*; —**sman** tirador *m*; **he's a good**
—**sman** tiene muy buena puntería / muy
buen tino; **the halfway** — el punto
medio, la mitad; **to hit the** — dar en el
blanco; **on your** —, set, go! ¡en sus
marcas, listos y ya! ¡en sus marcas, listos,
fuera! **to make one's** — distinguirse; **to
miss the** — errar el tiro; **easy** — blanco
fácil *m*; VT marcar; (indicate) señalar;
(observe) observar, notar; (grade) calificar;
—**ed for greatness** destinado a la
grandeza; — **my words!** ¡ya verás! **to** —
down prices rebajar los precios; **to** —
off acotar, deslindar; **to** — **up prices**
subir los precios
markdown [mɑ́rkdaun] N rebaja *f*
marker [mɑ́rkə] N marcador *m*
market [mɑ́rkɪt] N mercado *m*; —**place**
mercado *m*; — **price** precio de mercado
m; — **share** sector del mercado *m*; **I'm in
the** — **for** estoy buscando; VT

comercializar, mercadear
marketable [márkɪdəbəł] ADJ vendible
marketing [márkɪdɪŋ] N (field of study)
mercadotecnia f, marketing m; (selling)
comercialización f
marmalade [mármələd] N mermelada de
naranja f
maroon [mərún] ADJ & N bordó / bordeaux
m; VT abandonar
marriage [mǽrɪʤ] N matrimonio m;
(combination) combinación f; — **license**
licencia de matrimonio f
marriageable [mǽrɪʤəbəł] ADJ casadero
married [mǽrid] ADJ (united in marriage)
casado; (relation to marriage) conyugal; —
couple matrimonio m; **to get** — casarse
marrow [mǽro] N (in the bones) médula f;
(food) tuétano m; (essential part) meollo
m
marry [mǽri] VT (to marry off) casar; (to get
married) casarse con; VI casarse
marsh [marʃ] N pantano m, ciénaga f
marshal [márʃəł] N (military) mariscal m;
(police chief) alguacil m; (of a parade)
maestro de ceremonia m; VT (facts, forces)
reunir; (troops) formar
Marshallese [marʃəlíz] ADJ & N marshalés
-esa mf
Marshall Islands [márʃəláiləndz] N Islas
Marshall f pl
marshmallow [márʃmɛlo] N caramelo de
azúcar y gelatina m
marshy [márʃi] ADJ pantanoso, cenagoso
martial [márʃəł] ADJ marcial; — **arts** artes
marciales f pl; — **law** ley marcial f
martin [mártn] N avión m
martini [martíni] N martini m
martyr [márɖɚ] N mártir m; VT martirizar
martyrdom [márɖɚdəm] N martirio m
marvel [márvəł] N maravilla f; VI
maravillarse
marvelous [márvələs] ADV maravilloso
Marxism [márksɪzəm] N marxismo m
mascara [mæskǽrə] N rímel m
mascot [mǽskɑt] N mascota f
masculine [mǽskjəlɪn] ADJ masculino
mash [mæʃ] VT aplastar, pisar; N (pulpy mass)
puré m; (food for livestock) afrecho m;
(malt) malta remojada f; —**ed potatoes**
puré de papas / patatas m
mask [mæsk] N máscara f, careta f; VT
enmascarar; —**ed ball** baile de máscaras
m
masochism [mǽsəkɪzəm] N masoquismo m
mason [mésən] N (builder) albañil m;
(freemason) masón m
masonry [mésənri] N (bricklaying) albañilería

f; (fraternal order) masonería f
masquerade [mæskəréd] N mascarada f; VI
to — **as** hacerse pasar por
mass [mæs] N masa f; (in church) misa f; —
communication comunicación de masas
f; —-**marketing** comercialización masiva
f; — **media** medios de comunicación (de
masas) m pl; — **production** fabricación
en masa f; — **unemployment**
desempleo / paro masivo m; — **transit**
transporte público m; **the** —**es** las masas
pl; VI/VT juntar(se) en masa; (troops)
concentrar(se)
massacre [mǽsəkɚ] N masacre m; VT
masacrar
massage [məsáʒ] N masaje m; — **parlor**
salón de masajes m; VT (give a massage)
masajear; (change data) manipular
masseur [məsɚ́] N masajista m
masseuse [məsús] N masajista f
massive [mǽsɪv] ADJ (severe) masivo; (solid)
macizo; (large) enorme
mast [mæst] N mástil m, árbol m
mastectomy [mæstéktəmi] N mastectomía f
master [mǽstɚ] N (person in control) amo -a
mf, señor -ora mf; (owner of slave or
animal) amo -a mf; (best representative,
skilled laborer) maestro m; (young boy)
señorito m; (tape or disk) original m; —**'s
degree** maestría f; ADJ (dominant)
dominante; — **bedroom** dormitorio
principal m; — **key** llave maestra f;
—**piece** obra maestra f; VT dominar
masterful [mǽstɚfəł] ADJ magistral
masterly [mǽstɚli] ADJ magistral
mastery [mǽstɚi] N dominio m
mastiff [mǽstɪf] N mastín m, alano m
masturbate [mǽstɚbet] VI/VT masturbar
mat [mæt] N (floor covering) estera f; (for
wiping feet) felpudo m; (in gymnastics)
colchoneta f; (of hair) maraña f; VI
enmarañarse
match [mæʧ] N (pair) pareja f; (chess game)
partida f; (tennis game) partido m; (boxing
encounter) combate m; (device for fire)
fósforo m, cerilla f; —**box** cajita de
fósforos f; —**maker** casamentero -ra mf;
he has no — no tiene igual; **he is a
good** — es un buen partido; **the hat
and coat are a good** — el abrigo y el
sombrero hacen juego; VI/VT hacer juego
(con); VI (to correspond) estar de acuerdo;
the colors don't — los colores no
combinan; VT (equal) igualar; (come to
correspond) poner de acuerdo; (form pairs)
parear
matchless [mǽʧlɪs] ADJ sin par

mate [met] N (one of a pair) pareja *f*; (friend) compañero -ra *mf*; (on a ship) oficial *m*; (in chess) mate *m*; VI/VT aparear(se)

material [mətíríəł] ADJ material; (pertinent) pertinente; N (substance) material *m*; (fabric) tejido *m*, género *m*

materialize [mətíríəlaɪz] VI/VT materializar(se)

maternal [mətə́·nəł] ADJ (motherly) maternal; (on mother's side of family) materno

maternity [mətə́·nɪɾi] N maternidad *f*

math [mæθ] N matemática(s) *f (pl)*

mathematical [mæθəmǽɒɪkəł] ADJ matemático

mathematician [mæθəmətíʃən] N matemático -ca *mf*

mathematics [mæθəmǽɒɪks] N matemática(s) *f (pl)*

matinée [mætŋé] N matiné *f*

matriarch [métrɪɑrk] N matriarca *f*

matriculate [mətríkjəlet] VI/VT matricular(se)

matriculation [mətrɪkjəléʃən] N matriculación *f*, matrícula *f*

matrimony [mǽtrəmoni] N matrimonio *m*

matrix [métrɪks] N matriz *f*

matron [métrən] N matrona *f*; (in a hospital) jefa de enfermeras *f*

matter [mǽɒə·] N (substance, pus) materia *f*; (affair) asunto *m*; (printed) impreso *m*; (reading) material de lectura *m*; **— for complaint** motivo de queja *m*; **a — of two minutes** cosa de dos minutos *f*; **as a — of fact** de hecho; **it is of no —** no tiene importancia; **no — what you say** no importa lo que digas; **to do something as a — of course** hacer algo por rutina; **what is the — ?** ¿qué pasa? VI importar; **it doesn't —** no importa

mattress [mǽtrɪs] N colchón *m*

mature [mətʃúr] ADJ maduro; **a — note** un pagaré vencido / pagadero; **for — audiences** para adultos; VI/VT madurar(se); (a savings bond) vencer(se)

maturity [mətúrɪɾi] N madurez *f*; (of a debt) vencimiento *m*

maul [mɔł] VT atacar, herir gravemente

Mauritania [mɔrɪténiə] N Mauritania *f*

Mauritanian [mɔrɪténiən] ADJ & N mauritano -na *mf*

Mauritian [mɔríʃən] ADJ & N mauriciano -na *mf*

Mauritius [mɔríʃəs] N Mauricio *m*

maverick [mǽvə·ɪk] N cimarrón *m* (also person); (person) inconformista *mf*

maxim [mǽksɪm] N máxima *f*, sentencia *f*

maximum [mǽksəməm] ADJ & N máximo *m*

may [me] V AUX **— I sit down?** ¿puedo sentarme? **— you have a merry Christmas** que pases una feliz Navidad; **it — be that** puede ser que; **it — rain** puede (ser) que llueva, tal vez llueva; **she — have been late** puede (ser) que haya llegado tarde; **be that as it —** sea como fuere

May [me] N mayo *m*; **— Day** primero de mayo *m*; **—pole** mayo *m*

maybe [mébi] ADV quizá(s), tal vez

mayonnaise [méənez] N mayonesa *f*, mahonesa *f*

mayor [méə·] N alcalde *m*

maze [mez] N laberinto *m*

me [mi] PRON **she sees —** me ve; **he talks to —** me habla; **he comes with —** viene conmigo; **he did it for —** lo hizo para mí

meadow [méɒo] N pradera *f*, prado *m*; **—lark** alondra *f*

meager [mígə·] ADJ escaso, exiguo

meal [miɫ] N comida *f*; (flour) harina *f*; **—time** hora de comer *f*

mean [min] ADJ (unkind) cruel; (petty) vil; (humble) humilde; (stingy) mezquino; (difficult) de mal genio; (middle) medio; **—-spirited** mezquino; **I make a — lasagna** me sale muy rica la lasagna; N (average) media *f*, promedio *m*; **—s** medios *m pl*; **the ends justify the —s** el fin justifica los medios; **a man of —s** un hombre adinerado; **by —s of** por medio de; **by all —s** (of course) por supuesto; (using all resources) por todos los medios; **by no —s** de ningún modo; VT (intend) querer, tener intenciones; (signify) querer decir, significar; **he —s well** tiene buenas intenciones; **winning —s everything to them** lo que más les importa es ganar; **they are meant for each other** son el uno para el otro

meander [miǽndə·] VI (be winding) serpentear; (to wander) vagar

meaning [mínɪŋ] N (sense) significado *m*, sentido *m*; (purpose) sentido *m*; ADJ **well-—** bien intencionado

meaningless [mínɪŋlɪs] ADJ sin sentido

meanness [mínnɪs] N (cruelty) crueldad *f*; (pettiness) mezquindad *f*

meantime [míntaɪm] ADV LOC **in the —** mientras tanto

meanwhile [mínhwaɪł] ADV mientras tanto

measles [mízəłz] N sarampión *m*

measurable [méʒə·əbəł] ADJ medible, mensurable

measure [méʒə·] N (dimension) medida *f*;

(criterion) criterio *m*; (in musical bar) compás *m*; (bill) proyecto de ley *m*; **—s** medidas *f pl*; **beyond —** sobremanera; **dry —** medida de áridos *f*; **in large —** en gran parte; VI/VT medir; **to — up** compararse con; **measuring tape** cinta de medir *f*, metro *m*

measured [mɛʒəd] ADJ (rhythmical) acompasado; (moderate) moderado, mesurado

measurement [mɛʒəmənt] N (act of measuring) medición *f*; (dimension) medida *f*, dimensión *f*

meat [mit] N carne *f*; (essential point) meollo *m*; **—ball** albóndiga *f*; **— loaf** pan / pastel de carne *m*

meaty [mídi] ADJ (with meat) con mucha carne; (substantial) sustancioso

mechanic [mɪkǽnɪk] ADJ & N mecánico *m*; N **—s** mecánica *f*

mechanical [mɪkǽnɪkəl] ADJ mecánico

mechanism [mékənɪzəm] N mecanismo *m*

medal [médl] N medalla *f*; VI ganar una medalla

meddle [médl] VI entrometerse, inmiscuirse

meddler [médlə] N entrometido -da *mf*

meddlesome [médlsəm] ADJ entrometido

media [mídiə] N media *m pl*, medios de comunicación (de masas) *m pl*

median [mídiən] ADJ mediano; N (middle value, line) mediana *f*

mediate [mídiet] VI/VT mediar

mediation [midiéʃən] N mediación *f*

mediator [mídiedə] N mediador -ra *mf*

medical [médɪkəl] ADJ médico; **— school** facultad de medicina *f*

medication [mɛdɪkéʃən] N medicación *f*

medicine [médɪsɪn] N medicina *f*, medicamento *m*; **— ball** balón medicinal *m*; **— cabinet** botiquín *m*; **— man** curandero *m*

medieval [mídívəl] ADJ medieval

mediocre [midióka] ADJ mediocre

mediocrity [midiákrɪdi] N mediocridad *f*

meditate [médɪtet] VI meditar

meditation [mɛdɪtéʃən] N meditación *f*, recogimiento *m*

medium [mídiəm] N medio *m*; (person who contacts spirits) médium *mf*; ADJ mediano; ADV término medio; **— of exchange** medio de cambio *m*

medley [médli] N (music) popurrí *m*; (mixture) mezcla *f*

meek [mik] ADJ manso

meet [mit] VT (encounter) encontrarse con; (make acquaintance) conocer; (face in conflict) enfrentar; (satisfy) satisfacer;

(pay) pagar; **to — a deadline** cumplir el plazo; **to — the expenses** sufragar los gastos; **to — halfway** partir la diferencia; **to — a train** esperar un tren; **I will — you at the station** nos encontramos / vemos en la estación; **have you met my brother?** ¿conoces a mi hermano? **we were met with disapproval** se nos recibió con desaprobación; VI (encounter) encontrarse; (make acquaintance) conocerse; (have a meeting) reunirse; (cross) cruzarse; **to — in battle** trabar batalla; **to — with** (intentional) reunirse con; (unintentional) tropezar con; N encuentro deportivo *m*, competición *f*

meeting [mídɪŋ] N reunión *f*, junta *f*; (political) mitin *m*; (crossing of roads) cruce *m*

megabyte [mégəbaɪt] N megabyte *m*

megahertz [mégəhɜtz] N megahertz *m*, megahercio *m*

megaphone [mégəfon] N megáfono *m*, bocina *f*

melancholy [mélənkali] N melancolía *f*; ADJ melancólico

melanoma [mɛlənómə] N melanoma *m*

meld [mɛld] VT fusionar

melee [méle] N reyerta *f*, tumulto *m*

mellow [mélo] ADJ (soft) dulce, suave; (gentle) tranquilo; VI/VT suavizar(se)

melodious [məlódiəs] ADJ melodioso

melodrama [mélodramə] N melodrama *m*

melody [mélədi] N melodía *f*

melon [mélən] N melón *m*

melt [mɛlt] VI/VT (liquefy) derretir(se); (dissolve) disolver(se); **—down** (fusion) catástrofe por fusión nuclear incontrolada *f*; (any developing disaster) catástrofe *f*

melting pot [méltɪŋpat] M crisol *m*

member [mémbə] N miembro *m* (also body part)

membership [mémbəʃɪp] N (number) número de miembros / socios *m*; (state) calidad de miembro / socio *f*

membrane [mémbren] N membrana *f*

memento [məméntó] N recuerdo *m*

memoir [mémwar] N memoria *f*; **—s** memorias *f pl*, autobiografía *f*

memorable [mémərəbəl] ADJ memorable

memorandum [mɛmərǽndəm] N memorándum *m*

memorial [məmóriəl] N (monument) monumento conmemorativo *m*; (petition) memorial *m*; ADJ conmemorativo

memorize [méməraɪz] VI/VT memorizar

memory [méməri] N (faculty) memoria *f*; (recollection) recuerdo *m*

menace [ménis] N amenaza f; VI/VT amenazar

mend [mɛnd] VT remendar; **to — matters** enmendar la situación; **to — one's ways** enmendarse, reformarse; VI (sick person) mejorarse; (bones) soldarse; N remiendo m; **to be on the —** ir mejorando

menial [míniəl] ADJ bajo; (job) servil; N criado -da mf

meningitis [mɛnɪndʒaɪdɪs] N meningitis f

menopause [ménəpɔz] N menopausia f

menstruation [mɛnstruéʃən] N menstruación f

mental [mɛ́nt̬l] ADJ mental; (insane) fam chiflado; **— health** salud mental f; **— illness** enfermedad mental f; **— retardation** retraso mental m

mentality [mɛntǽlɪḏi] N mentalidad f

mention [ménʃən] VT mencionar; **don't — it** no hay de qué; N mención f

mentor [mɛ́ntɔr] N mentor -ra mf

menu [ménju] N (list of dishes) carta f, menú m; (computer) menú m

meow [mjau] INTERJ miau

mercantile [mɝ́kəntil] ADJ mercantil

mercenary [mɝ́səneri] ADJ mercenario

merchandise [mɝ́tʃəndaɪs] N mercancía f, mercadería f

merchandising [mɝ́tʃəndaɪzɪŋ] N mercadeo m, comercialización f

merchant [mɝ́tʃənt] N (trader) comerciante m, mercader m; ADJ mercante; **— marine** marina mercante f

merciful [mɝ́sɪfəl] ADJ misericordioso

merciless [mɝ́sɪlɪs] ADJ despiadado

mercury [mɝ́kjəri] N mercurio m; (on a mirror) azogue m

mercy [mɝ́si] N (compassion) misericordia f, clemencia f, piedad f; **to be at the — of** estar a merced de; **— killing** eutanasia f

mere [mir] ADJ mero, simple; **a — trifle** una nonada

merge [mɝdʒ] VI/VT (join) unir(se); (colors) fundir(se); (companies) fusionar(se)

merger [mɝ́dʒɚ] N fusión f

meridian [mərídiən] ADJ & N meridiano m

merit [mɛ́rɪt] N mérito m; VT merecer

meritorious [mɛrɪtɔ́riəs] ADJ meritorio

mermaid [mɝ́med] N sirena f

merriment [mɛ́rɪmənt] N alegría f, algazara f

merry [mɛ́ri] ADJ alegre; **—go-round** tiovivo m; **—maker** fiestero mf, juerguista mf; **—making** fiesta f, juerga f; **to make — divertirse; INTERJ — Christmas** Feliz Navidad f, Felices Pascuas

mesa [mésə] N mesa f

mesh [mɛʃ] N (of metal) malla f; (of fiber) red f; (of gears) engranaje m; VI engranar

mesmerize [mézməraɪz] VI/VT hipnotizar

mess [mɛs] N (state of confusion) desorden m, desarreglo m; (disorderly person) desordenado -da mf, mugriento -ta mf; (confused person) desastre m; (difficult situation) lío m, jaleo m; (food for soldiers) rancho m; (cafeteria) cantina f; **— hall** cantina f; **— of fish** plato de pescado m; **to make a — of** (a room) ensuciar, desordenar; (a project) estropear; VI/VT **to — around** (waste time) perder el tiempo; (get involved with) meterse con; (philander) correr detrás de las mujeres; **to — up** (a room) alborotar, desordenar; (clothes, hair) desarreglar; (a project) estropear; **to — with** meterse con

message [mésɪdʒ] N mensaje m, recado m; **I get the —** ya caí en cuenta

messenger [mésəndʒɚ] N mensajero -ra mf

messy [mési] ADJ desordenado; (embarrassing) embarazoso

metabolism [mətǽbəlɪzəm] N metabolismo m

metal [méd̬l] N metal m; ADJ de metal, metálico

metallic [mətǽlɪk] ADJ metálico

metallurgy [médlɚdʒi] N metalurgia f

metamorphosis [mɛdəmɔ́rfəsɪs] N metamorfosis f

metaphor [médəfɔr] N metáfora f

metaphysics [mɛdəfízɪks] N metafísica f

metastasis [mətǽstəsɪs] N metástasis f

meteor [mídiɔr] N meteoro m; **— shower** lluvia de meteoritos f

meteorite [mídiəraɪt] N meteorito m

meteorology [midiərálədʒi] N meteorología f

meter [mídɚ] N (unit of length) metro m; (measuring device) contador m, medidor m

methane [méθen] N metano m

method [méθəd] N método m

methodical [məθádɪkəl] ADJ metódico

methodology [mɛθədálədʒi] N metodología f

meticulous [mətíkjələs] ADJ detallista

metric [métrɪk] ADJ métrico

metronome [métrənom] N metrónomo m

metropolis [mətrápəlɪs] N metrópoli f, urbe f

metropolitan [mɛtrəpálɪḏən] ADJ metropolitano

mettle [méd̬l] N temple m, valor m

mew [mju] N maullido m; VI maullar

Mexican [méksɪkən] ADJ & N mexicano -na mf

Mexico [méksɪko] N México m

mezzanine [mézənin] N entrepiso m, entresuelo m

mickey mouse [míkimáus] ADJ poco serio,

informal

microbe [máɪkrob] N microbio *m*

microcomputer [maɪkrokəmpjúdə] N *Am* microcomputadora *f*; *Sp* microordenador *m*

microeconomics [maɪkroekənámɪks] N microeconomía *f*

microfiche [máɪkrofiʃ] N microficha *f*

microfilm [máɪkrofɪłm] N microfilm *m*

micromanage [maɪkromǽnɪʤ] VI/VT administrar con excesivo control

micron [máɪkrɑn] N micrón *m*, micra *f*

Micronesia [maɪkroníʒə] N Micronesia *f*

Micronesian [maɪkroníʒən] ADJ & N micronesio -sia *mf*

microorganism [maɪkroórɡənɪzəm] N microorganismo *m*

microphone [máɪkrofɑn] N micrófono *m*

microprocessor [maɪkroprásesə] N microprocesador *m*

microscope [máɪkrəskɑp] N microscopio *m*

microscopic [maɪkrəskápɪk] ADJ microscópico

microsurgery [maɪkrosə́ʤəri] N microcirujía *f*

microwave [máɪkrowev] N microonda *f*; — **oven** (horno) microondas *m sg*

mid [mɪd] ADJ medio; **—air** en el aire; **—day** (del) mediodía *m*; **—life** madurez *f*; **—night** (de) medianoche *f*; **—shipman** guardiamarina *m*; **in —stream** (of a river) en medio del río; (of a task) en plena actividad; **—summer** pleno verano *m*; **—term examination** examen a mitad del curso *m*; **—way** a medio camino, a mitad del camino; **—wife** partera *f*, comadre *f*

middle [mídl̩] ADJ (average) medio, mediano; (intermediate) intermedio; (central) central; **—aged** de mediana edad; **— Ages** Edad Media *f*; **— ear** oído medio *m*; **— finger** dedo mayor *m*, dedo del corazón *m*; **—man** intermediario *m*, revendedor *m*; **— management** mandos medios *m pl*; **— name** segundo nombre *m*; **—-sized** (de) tamaño mediano *m*; medio *m*; (waist) cintura *f*; **in the — of** en el medio de; **I'm in the — of something** estoy ocupado haciendo algo; **—-of-the-road** moderado; **toward the — of the month** a mediados del mes

midget [mídʒɪt] N enano -na *mf*

midst [mɪdst] N medio *m*, centro *m*; **in the — of** en medio de, entre; **in our —** entre nosotros

mien [min] N porte *m*

might [maɪt] V AUX **it — be that** podría ser que; **he said it — rain tomorrow** dijo que tal vez lloviera mañana; **she — have been late** puede ser que haya llegado tarde; N poder *m*, poderío *m*

mighty [máɪdɪ] ADJ (strong) poderoso, potente; (large) imponente; ADV muy

migraine [máɪgren] N migraña *f*, jaqueca *f*

migrant [máɪgrənt] ADJ migratorio, migrante; N trabajador -ra itinerante *mf*, bracero -ra *mf*

migrate [máɪgret] VI emigrar

migration [maɪgréʃən] N migración *f*

mild [maɪld] ADJ (gentle) suave; (moderate) moderado; (not serious) leve

mildew [mɪ́łdu] N moho *m*

mildness [máɪłdnɪs] N (gentleness) suavidad *f*; (lack of gravity) levedad *f*

mile [maɪl] N milla *f*; **—stone** hito *m*

mileage [máɪlɪʤ] N (distance, odometer reading) millaje *m*, kilometraje *m*; **this car gets good —** este coche es económico; **what kind of — are you getting?** ¿cuántos kilómetros por litro hace tu coche?

milieu [mɪljú] N ambiente *m*

militant [mɪ́lɪtənt] ADJ & N (fanatic) militante *mf*; (combatant) combatiente *mf*

military [mɪ́lɪteri] ADJ militar; N **the —** (armed forces) el ejército; (military personnel) los militares

militia [məlíʃə] N milicia *f*

milk [mɪłk] N leche *f*; **— chocolate** chocolate con leche *m*; **—maid** lechera *f*; **—man** lechero *m*; **— shake** batido *m*; VT ordeñar; (exploit) exprimir; **he's —ing it for all it's worth** le está sacando todo el jugo

milky [mɪ́łki] ADJ (consistency) lechoso; (product) lácteo; **— Way** Vía Láctea *f*

mill [mɪł] N (building) molino *m*; (factory) fábrica *f*; (for sugar) trapiche *m*, ingenio *m*; (rotating tool) fresa *f*; (small grinder) molinillo *m*; **—stone** muela de molino *f*; **a —stone around your neck** una piedra al cuello; VT (grind grain) moler; (cut wood) aserrar; (cut grooves on coins) acordonar; (machine) fresar; **to — around** dar vueltas

millennium [məlíniəm] N milenio *m*

miller [mílə] N (person who mills) molinero *m*; (machine for milling) fresadora *f*; (moth) mariposa nocturna *f*

milligram [mílɪgræm] N miligramo *m*

milliliter [míləlidə] N mililitro *m*

millimeter [mílɪmidə] N milímetro *m*

milliner [mílənə] N sombrerero -ra *mf*

millinery [míləneri] N (shop) sombrerería *f*;

(hats) sombreros de señora *m pl*

million [míljən] N millón *m*; **a — dollars** un millón de dólares

millionaire [miljənér] N millonario -ria *mf*

millionth [míljənθ] ADJ & N millonésimo *m*

mime [maɪm] N (actor) mimo *m*; (technique, performance) pantomima *f*; VI hacer la mímica

mimic [mímɪk] VT imitar, remedar; N mono -na *mf*, remedador -ra *mf*

mince [mɪns] VT picar, desmenuzar; **—meat** picadillo *m*; **not to — words** no tener pelos en la lengua; **I'm going to make —meat of you** te voy a hacer picadillo

mind [maɪnd] N (thinking process) mente *f*; (person of intellect) inteligencia *f*; (opinion) parecer *m*, opinión *f*; **—altering** alucinógeno; **— games** manipulación psicológica *f*; **— over matter** el espíritu sobre la materia; **—set** actitud *f*; **to be out of one's —** estar loco; **to change one's —** cambiar de parecer/opinión; **to give someone a piece of one's —** cantarle a alguien las cuarenta; **I have a — to** me dan ganas de; **to make up one's —** decidirse; **to my —** a mi modo de ver; **to speak one's — freely** hablar con toda franqueza; **what do you have in —?** ¿qué tienes en mente? **to call to —** recordar; **to keep one's — on one's work** concentrarse en el trabajo; VT (take care of) cuidar; (pay attention to) atender a; (obey) obedecer; **I don't —** no tengo inconveniente en ello; **— what you say** cuidado con lo que dices; **to — one's own business** no meterse en lo ajeno

mindful [máɪndfəl] ADJ atento (a)

mine [maɪn] PRON **this book is —** este libro es mío; **these things are —** estas cosas son mías; **— is bigger** el mío/la mía es más grande; **a friend of —** un amigo mío/una amiga mía; N mina *f* (also explosive device); **—field** campo minado *m*; **— sweeper** dragaminas *m sg*, barreminas *m sg*; VT (plant explosives) minar; (dig out minerals) extraer; (exploit an area for minerals) explotar; VI (lay mines) sembrar minas; (dig a mine) cavar una mina; **to — for** extraer

miner [máɪnɚ] N minero -ra *mf*

mineral [mínɚəl] ADJ & N mineral *m*; **— water** agua mineral *f*

mingle [míŋɡəl] VI mezclarse; (sounds) confundirse; VT mezclar

miniature [mínɪətʃɚ] N miniatura *f*; ADJ en miniatura

minicomputer [mɪnikəmpjúdɚ] N *Am* minicomputadora *f*; *Sp* miniordenador *m*

minimal [mínəməl] ADJ mínimo

minimize [mínəmaɪz] VT minimizar

minimum [mínəməm] ADJ & N mínimo *m*; **— wage** salario mínimo *m*

mining [máɪnɪŋ] N (of minerals) minería *f*; (with explosives) minado *m*; ADJ minero; **— engineer** ingeniero -ra de minas *mf*

miniskirt [mínɪskɚt] N minifalda *f*

minister [mínɪstɚ] N (official) ministro -tra *mf*; (pastor) pastor -ora *mf*, clérigo *m*; VI **to — to** atender a

ministry [mínɪstri] N (government agency) ministerio *m*; (functions of pastor) clerecía *f*

minivan [mínɪvæn] N camioneta *f*

mink [mɪŋk] N visón *m*

minnow [míno] N pececillo *m*

minor [máɪnɚ] ADJ (smaller) menor, más pequeño; (of secondary importance) menor; **— key** tono menor *m*; **— league** liga menor *f*; N (young person) menor de edad *mf*; (musical interval) tono menor *m*; (subfield) asignatura secundaria *f*; VI tener como segunda especialización

minority [mənɔ́rɪdi] N (smaller part or group) minoría *f*; (state of being underage) minoridad *f*; (member of a minority) miembro de una minoría *m*; ADJ minoritario

mint [mɪnt] N (flavor) menta *f*, hierbabuena *f*; (candy) pastilla de menta *f*; (money) casa de la moneda *f*; VT acuñar

minus [máɪnəs] PREP **seven — four** siete menos cuatro; **we came — my brother** vinimos sin mi hermano; N signo de menos *m*; ADJ negativo

minuscule [mínəskjul] ADJ minúsculo

minute [mínɪt] N minuto *m*; **— hand** minutero *m*; **—s** actas *f pl*; [mənjút] ADJ (small) diminuto; (detailed) detallado, minucioso

miracle [mírəkəl] N milagro *m*

miraculous [mɪrǽkjələs] ADJ milagroso

mirage [mɪráʒ] N espejismo *m*

mire [maɪr] N (mud) cieno *m*, fango *m*; (muddy place) ciénaga *f*; VI/VT (bog down) atascar(se) en el fango; (be or get covered with mud) enlodar(se)

mirror [mírɚ] N espejo *m*; (large) luna *f*; **— image** imagen especular *f*; VT reflejar

mirth [mɚθ] N risa *f*, hilaridad *f*

mirthful [mɚ́θfəl] ADJ risueño

miry [máɪri] ADJ cenagoso, fangoso

misappropriation [mɪsəpropriéʃən] N malversación *f*

misbehave [mɪsbɪhév] vɪ portarse mal

miscarriage [mískærɪʤ] N aborto espontáneo *m*, malparto *m*; **— of justice** injusticia *f*

miscarry [mɪskǽri] vɪ (abort) abortar espontáneamente; (fail) malograrse, frustrarse

miscellaneous [mɪsəlénɪəs] ADJ diverso; (of texts) misceláneo; **— expenses** gastos varios *mf*

mischief [místʃɪf] N travesura *f*, diablura *f*, picardía *f*; (serious prank) barrabasada *f*, bellaquería *f*; **this will come to —** va a suceder una desgracia

mischievous [místʃəvəs] ADJ travieso, pícaro

misconception [mɪskənsépʃən] N concepto erróneo *m*

misconduct [mɪskándʌkt] N (bad behavior) mala conducta *f*; (malfeasance) mala administración *f*; [mɪskəndʌ́kt] vᴛ administrar mal; **to — oneself** portarse mal

miscue [mɪskjú] N pifia *f*; vɪ/vᴛ pifiar

misdeed [mɪsdíd] N fechoría *f*

misdemeanor [mɪsdɪmínɚ] N delito menor *m*

miser [máɪzɚ] N avaro -ra *mf*, tacaño -ña *mf*

miserable [mízɚəbəl] ADJ infeliz, desdichado, mísero; **a — day** un día asqueroso; **a — failure** un fracaso rotundo

miserly [máɪzɚli] ADJ avariento, tacaño

misery [mízɚri] N (wretchedness) desgracia *f*; (poverty) miseria *f*; (unhappiness) infelicidad *f*

misfit [mísfɪt] N inadaptado -da *mf*

misfortune [mɪsfɔ́rtʃən] N desgracia *f*, desdicha *f*, desventura *f*

misgivings [mɪsgívɪŋz] N aprensión *f*, recelo *m*

misguided [mɪsgáɪdɪd] ADJ mal aconsejado, poco feliz

mishap [míshæp] N contratiempo *m*, percance *m*

misinform [mɪsɪnfɔ́rm] vᴛ desinformar, dar información errónea

misjudge [mɪsʤʌ́ʤ] vᴛ juzgar mal

mislay [mɪslé] vᴛ (lose keys, etc.) extraviar, perder; (lose a document) traspapelar; (lay wrong) colocar mal

mislead [mɪslíd] vᴛ (lead in wrong direction) guiar por mal camino; (lead into error) engañar, confundir

mismanage [mɪsmǽnɪʤ] vᴛ administrar mal

misogyny [mɪsáʤəni] N misoginia *f*

misplace [mɪsplés] vᴛ (lose keys, etc.) extraviar; (lose a document) traspapelar;

(place wrong) colocar mal; **she —d her trust** confió en la persona equivocada

misprint [mísprɪnt] N errata *f*, error de imprenta *m*

misrepresent [mɪsrɛprɪzɛ́nt] vᴛ distorsionar, tergiversar

misrepresentation [mɪsrɛprɪzɛntéʃən] N distorsión *f*, tergiversación *f*

miss [mɪs] vɪ (fail to hit) errar; (misfire) fallar; vᴛ (fail to hit) errar, no acertar; (fail to be on time for) perder; (fail to attend) faltar a; (feel absence of) echar de menos; *Am* extrañar; **he just —ed being killed** por poco se mata; N (of a target) tiro errado *m*; (in a motor) falla *f*; (from class) falta *f*; (young woman) señorita *f*; **— Smith** la señorita Smith

missile [mísəl] N (projectile) proyectil *m*; (guided weapon) misil *m*

missing [mísɪŋ] ADJ (not present) ausente; (lost) perdido; **— link** eslabón perdido *m*; **one book is —** falta un libro

mission [míʃən] N misión *f*

missionary [míʃəneri] ADJ & N misionero -ra *mf*

misspell [mɪsspél] vᴛ (written) escribir mal; (oral) deletrear mal

misstep [místep] N paso en falso *m*

mist [mɪst] N (of water droplets) neblina *f*, bruma *f*; (of perfume) rocío *m*; vɪ lloviznar; vᴛ rociar

mistake [mɪsték] N error *m*, equivocación *f*; (orthographical) falta *f*; **to make a —** equivocarse; vɪ/vᴛ equivocar(se); **I mistook my sister for my mother** confundí a mi hermana con mi madre

mistaken [mɪstékən] ADJ equivocado; **to be —** estar equivocado, equivocarse; **unless I'm —** si no me equivoco

mister [místɚ] N señor *m*

mistletoe [mísəlto] N muérdago *m*

mistreat [mɪstrít] vᴛ maltratar

mistreatment [mɪstrítmənt] N maltrato *m*

mistress [místrɪs] N (of a household) señora *f*; (employing servants, animal owner) ama *f*; (lover) amante *f*

mistrial [místraɪl] N proceso viciado de nulidad *m*

mistrust [mɪstrást] N desconfianza *f*; vᴛ desconfiar de

mistrustful [mɪstrástfəl] ADJ desconfiado, receloso

misty [místi] ADJ (foggy) neblinoso, brumoso; (in tears) nublado; (blurry) empañado

misunderstand [mɪsʌndɚstǽnd] vᴛ comprender mal, malinterpretar

misunderstanding [mɪsʌndɚstǽndɪŋ] N

(confusion) malentendido *m*; (failure to understand) equivocación *f*, mala inteligencia *f*; (argument) desavenencia *f*

misuse [mɪsjús] N (of drugs) abuso *m*; (of a word) mal uso *m*; (of funds) malversación *f*; ⫽mɪsjúz⫽ VT (drugs) abusar de; (a friend) maltratar; (a word) emplear mal; (funds) malversar

mite [maɪt] N ácaro *m*; **a — greedy** un poquito codicioso

mitigate [mídɪget] VT mitigar

mitten [mítn̩] N manopla *f*

mix [mɪks] VI/VT mezclar(se); **to — up** confundir; N mezcla *f*; (for baking) preparado *m*; **—-up** (confusion) confusión *f*; (fight) pelea *f*; **—ed bag** grupo heterogéneo *m*; **—ed drink** cóctel *m*; **—ed-up** confundido

mixed [mɪkst] ADJ mixto

mixer [míksɚ] N (appliance) batidora *f*; (party) fiesta *f*; (soda) refresco *m*; (sound technician) mezclador -ra *mf*; (sound device) mezcladora *f*

mixture [míkstʃɚ] N mezcla *f*

moan [mon] N quejido *m*, gemido *m*; VI gemir, quejarse; VI/VT lamentar

moat [mot] N foso *m*

mob [mɑb] N (disorderly crowd) tumulto *m*, turba *f*; (crowd) muchedumbre *f*, populacho *m*; (Mafia) mafia *f*; VT (attack) asaltar; (crowd) atestar

mobile [móbɚl] ADJ móvil; (personnel) que tiene movilidad; **— home** casa prefabricada *f*; **— phone** (teléfono) móvil *m*, (teléfono) celular *m*

mobilize [móbəlaɪz] VI/VT movilizar(se)

moccasin [mákəsɪn] N mocasín *m* (also snake)

mock [mɑk] VI (ridicule) burlar(se); VT (imitate) remedar; **to — at** burlarse de; ADJ de práctica; **— battle** simulacro de batalla *m*; **—-up** maqueta *f*, modelo *m*

mockery [mákəri] N (ridicule) burla *f*; (imitation) remedo *m*; (travesty) farsa *f*

mockingbird [mákɪŋbɚd] N sinsonte *m*

mode [mod] N modo *m*

model [mádl̩] N (guide) modelo *m*; (person) modelo *mf*, maniquí *mf*; ADJ modelo, ejemplar; **— school** escuela modelo *f*; VI/VT modelar; (display clothes) lucir

modem [módəm] N módem *m*

moderate [mádɚɪt] ADJ (not excessive) moderado, mesurado; (person) comedido; (weather) templado; (price) módico; N moderado -da *mf*; [mádɚet] VI/VT moderar(se) (also preside at meetings)

moderation [mɑdɚéʃən] N moderación *f*,

mesura *f*

modern [mádɚn] ADJ moderno

modernize [mádɚnaɪz] VI/VT modernizar(se)

modest [mádɪst] ADJ (humble) modesto; (chaste) recatado, honesto

modesty [mádɪsti] N (humility) modestia *f*; (chastity) recato *m*, pudor *m*

modification [mɑdɪfɪkéʃən] N modificación *f*

modify [mádɪfaɪ] VT modificar

modulate [mádʒəlet] VI/VT modular(se)

mohair [móher] N mohair *m*

moist [mɔɪst] ADJ húmedo

moisten [mɔ́ɪsən] VI/VT humedecer(se)

moisture [mɔ́ɪstʃɚ] N humedad *f*

moisturizer [mɔ́ɪstʃəráɪzɚ] N (crema) hidrante / humectante *f*

molar [mólɚ] ADJ molar; N muela *f*, molar *m*

molasses [məlǽsɪz] N melaza *f*

mold [moɫd] N (form) molde *m*; (fungi) moho *m*; (mettle) temple *m*; VT (shape) moldear; (adapt) amoldar; (fuse) fundir; VI/VT (become moldy) enmohecer(se)

molder [móɫdɚ] VI/VT descomponerse; (paper) enmohecerse

molding [móɫdɪŋ] N (adornment) moldura *f*; (action of molding) moldeado *m*

Moldova [mɔɫdóvə] N Moldavia *f*

Moldovan [mɔɫdóvən] ADJ & N moldavo -va *mf*

moldy [móɫdi] ADJ mohoso

mole [moɫ] N (blemish) lunar *m*; (animal, spy) topo *m*; (breakwater) rompeolas *m sg*

molecule [málɪkjuɫ] N molécula *f*

molest [məlést] VT abusar sexualmente de

mollify [máləfaɪ] VT apaciguar, aplacar

mollusk [máləsk] N molusco *m*

molt [moɫt] VI (birds) mudar la pluma; (snakes) mudar la piel; N muda *f*

molten [móɫtn̩] ADJ fundido

molybdenum [məlíbdənəm] N molibdeno *m*

mom [mɑm] N mamá *f*; **— and pop store** tienda familiar *f*

moment [mómənt] N momento *m*; **being a parent has its —s** ser padre / madre tiene sus momentos de recompensa

momentary [mómənteri] ADJ momentáneo

momentous [moméntəs] ADJ importante, trascendental

momentum [moméntəm] N (in physics) momento *m*; (in politics, sports) empuje *m*

mommy [mámi] N mami *f*

Monaco [mánəko] N Mónaco *m*

monarch [mánɑrk] N monarca *mf*

monarchy [mánɑrki] N monarquía *f*

monastery [mánəsteri] N monasterio *m*

Monday [mánde] N lunes *m*

Monegasque [manɪgásk] ADJ & N monegasco -ca *mf*

monetary [mánɪteri] ADJ monetario

money [máni] N dinero *m*; — **belt** faltriquera en forma de cinturón *f*; — **changer** cambista *mf*; — **machine** cajero automático *m*; —-**making** lucrativo, rentable; — **market** mercado de valores *m*; — **order** giro postal *m*; **to get one's** —'**s worth** sacar jugo al dinero

Mongolia [maŋgólia] N Mongolia *f*

Mongolian [maŋgólian] ADJ & N mongol -la *mf*

mongoose [máŋgus] N mangosta *f*

mongrel [máŋgrəl] ADJ & N mestizo *m*

monitor [mánɪtə] N monitor *m*; (in a school) celador -ora *mf*; — **lizard** varano *m*

monk [mʌŋk] N monje *m*, religioso *m*

monkey [máŋki] N mono *m*, mico *m* (also child); — **bars** jaula de los monos *f*; — **business** (mischief) picardía *f*; (trickery) chanchullo *m*; — **wrench** llave inglesa *f*; **to have a** — **on one's back** estar adicto; VI **to** — **around** bobear, payasear; **to** — **with** bobear con

monogamy [mənágəmi] N monogamia *f*

monolog, monologue [mánələg] N monólogo *m*

mononucleosis [manonukliósɪs] N mononucleosis *f*

monopolize [mənápəlaɪz] VT monopolizar

monopoly [mənápəli] N monopolio *m*

monotonous [mənátṇəs] ADJ monótono

monotony [mənátṇi] N monotonía *f*

monster [mánstə-] N monstruo *m*; ADJ enorme, monstruo *inv*

monstrosity [manstrásɪdi] N monstruosidad *f*

monstrous [mánstrəs] ADJ monstruoso

month [mʌnθ] N mes *m*

monthly [mánθli] ADJ mensual; — **installment** mensualidad *f*; N publicación mensual *f*, mensuario *m*; ADV mensualmente

monument [mánjəmənt] N monumento *m*

monumental [manjəméntḷ] ADJ monumental

moo [mu] N mugido *m*; VI mugir

mooch [mutʃ] VI/VT gorronear

mood [mud] N (emotional state) humor *m*, vena *f*, ánimo *m*; (grammatical category) modo *m*; **to be in a good** — estar de buen humor; **to be in the** — **to** tener ganas de

moody [múdi] ADJ (sullen) malhumorado; (changing) voluble

moon [mun] N luna *f*; — **beam** rayo de luna *m*; — **light** claro de la luna *m*, luz de la luna *f*; — **shine** bebida alcohólica destilada sin licencia *f*; **once in a blue** — de Pascuas a Ramos; VT *fam* mostrar el culo

moor [mʊr] VI/VT amarrar; N páramo *m*

Moor [mʊr] N moro -ra *mf*

Moorish [múrɪʃ] ADJ morisco, moro

moose [mus] N alce *m*

moot [mut] ADJ **it became a** — **point** dejó de tener importancia

mop [map] N *Sp* fregona *f*, *Sp* mopa *f*; *Mex* trapeador *m*; (for dust) plumero *m*; (of hair) greña *f*; —-**up** (of an enemy) limpieza *f*; (of a task) remate *m*; VI/VT pasar la mopa (sobre); *Am* trapear; **to** — **one's brow** enjugarse la frente; **to** — **up** (a spill) limpiar; (an enemy) acabar con; (a task) rematar

mope [mop] VI andar abatido

moped [móped] N ciclomotor *m*, scooter *m*

moral [mɔ́rəl] ADJ moral; N moraleja *f*; —**s** moral *f*

morale [mərǽl] N moral *f*

moralist [mɔ́rəlɪst] N moralista *mf*

morality [mɔrǽlɪdi] N moralidad *f*

moralize [mɔ́rəlaɪz] VI/VT moralizar

morbid [mɔ́rbɪd] ADJ mórbido, morboso

more [mɔr] ADJ & ADV más; — **and** — cada vez más; — **or less** más o menos; **there is no** — no hay más; —**over** además

morgue [mɔrg] N depósito de cadáveres *m*, morgue *f*

moribund [mɔ́rəband] ADJ moribundo

morning [mɔ́rnɪŋ] N mañana *f*; **good** —! ¡buenos días! **tomorrow** — mañana por la mañana; ADJ de la mañana, matutino; — **glory** dondiego de día *m*; — **sickness** náuseas *f pl*; — **star** lucero del alba *m*

Moroccan [mərákən] ADJ & N marroquí *mf*

Morocco [məráko] N Marruecos *m*

moron [mɔ́ran] N imbécil *m*

morphine [mɔ́rfin] N morfina *f*

morsel [mɔ́rsəl] N bocado *m*

mortal [mɔ́rdḷ] ADJ & N mortal *mf*; — **sin** pecado mortal *m*

mortality [mɔrtǽlɪdi] N (rate) mortalidad *f*; (toll) mortandad *f*

mortar [mɔ́rdə-] N (for pounding) mortero *m* (also ballistics); (for bricks) argamasa *f*, mezcla *f*; —**board** birrete *m*

mortgage [mɔ́rgɪdʒ] N hipoteca *f*; VT hipotecar; ADJ hipotecario

mortgagor [mɔ́rgɪdʒə-] N deudor -ra hipotecario -ria *mf*

mortify [mɔ́rdəfaɪ] VI/VT mortificar(se)

mosaic [mozéɪk] N mosaico *m*

Moslem [mázləm] ADJ & N musulmán -ana *mf*

mosque [mɔsk] N mezquita *f*

mosquito [məskíDo] N mosquito *m*; — **net** mosquitero *m*

moss [mɔs] N musgo *m*

mossy [mɔ́si] ADJ musgoso

most [most] ADJ — **children are good** la mayoría de los niños son buenos; — **people** la mayoría de la gente; **the — money** más dinero *m*; **the — votes** el mayor número de votos; **for the — part** generalmente; PRON **the — that I can do** lo más que puedo hacer; **we ate the —** comimos más que nadie; — **of the guests are here** ha llegado la mayoría de los invitados; ADV **the — ambitious** el más ambicioso; **a — pleasant day** un día de lo más agradable

mostly [móstli] ADV generalmente

motel [motél] N motel *m*

moth [mɔθ] N (pest) polilla *f*; (nocturnal insect) mariposa nocturna *f*; —**ball** bolita de naftalina *f*; —**-eaten** apolillado

mother [máðə] N madre *f*; —**board** plaqueta madre *f*; — **country** madre patria *f*; —**-in-law** suegra *f*; —**-of-pearl** madreperla *f*; —**tongue** lengua materna *f*; VT mimar a, cuidar de/a

motherhood [máðəhud] N maternidad *f*

motherly [máðəli] ADJ maternal

motif [motíf] N motivo *m*

motion [móʃən] N (movement) movimiento *m*; (signal) ademán *m*; (proposal) moción *f*; — **picture** película de cine *f*; —**picture industry** industria cinematográfica *f*; — **sickness** mareo *m*; VI/VT hacer un ademán

motionless [móʃənlɪs] ADJ inmóvil

motivate [móDəvet] VT motivar

motivation [moDəvéʃən] N motivación *f*

motive [móDɪv] N motivo *m*; ADJ motriz

motley [mátli] ADJ abigarrado

motor [móDə] N motor *m*; —**bike** motocicleta pequeña *f*; —**boat** lancha a motor *f*; —**cycle** motocicleta *f*; —**cyclist** motociclista *mf*; — **home** casa rodante *f*, caravana *f*; — **scooter** scooter *m*; — **vehicle** vehículo motorizado *m*; VI pasear en coche

motorist [móDəɪst] N automovilista *mf*

motto [máDo] N lema *f*

mound [maʊnd] N montículo *m*; **burial —** túmulo *m*; — **of laundry** pila de ropa *f*

mount [maʊnt] VI/VT montar; VI (increase) subir; VT (assemble) armar; N (mountain)

monte *m*; (getting on a horse) monta *f*; (animal for riding) montura *f*

mountain [maʊntn̩] N montaña *f*; ADJ (animal, person) montañés; (thing) de montaña; — **bike** bicicleta de montaña *f*; — **climber** alpinista *mf*; — **climbing** alpinismo *m*, montañismo *m*; — **goat** cabra montés *f*; — **lion** puma *f*, gato montés *m*; — **range** (large) cordillera *f*; (small) sierra *f*; —**side** ladera (de una montaña) *f*; —**top** cumbre (de una montaña) *f*

mountaineer [maʊntnír] N alpinista *mf*

mountainous [máʊntnəs] ADJ montañoso

mourn [mɔrn] VI estar de duelo/luto; VT llorar; **to — for** llorar a

mourner [mórnə] N doliente *mf*

mournful [mórnfəl] ADJ lúgubre, triste

mourning [mórnɪŋ] N luto *m*, duelo *m*; **to be in —** estar de luto/duelo; ADJ de luto

mouse [maʊs] N ratón *m* (also computer); — **pad** bandeja del ratón *f*; —**trap** ratonera *f*

mouth [maʊθ] N boca *f*; (of a cave) abertura *f*; (of a river) desembocadura *f*; —**piece** (part of a trumpet) boquilla *f*; (spokesman) portavoz *mf*; —**-to-mouth resuscitation** respiración boca a boca *f*; —**wash** enjuague bucal *m*; —**-watering** delicioso; [maʊð] VT articular silenciosamente una palabra; VI **to — off** contestar

mouthful [máʊθʊl] N (of food) bocado *m*; (of liquid) bocanada *f*, buche *m*

movable [múvəbt] ADJ movible, móvil

move [muv] VI (change position) mover(se) (also board games); (change residence) mudar(se) de casa; (sell) venderse; **to — away** (distance oneself) apartarse; (change residence) irse; **to — forward** avanzar; **to — on** seguir adelante; **to — out** mudarse de casa; **to — up** anticipar; VT (propose) proponer; (affect emotionally) conmover; N (act of moving) movimiento *m*; (change of residence) mudanza *f*; (action toward a goal) paso *m*; (play, in games) jugada *f*; **get a — on there!** ¡date prisa! **he made the first —** dio el primer paso

movement [múvmənt] N (motion, part of a watch) movimiento *m*; **to have a bowel — mover el vientre**

mover [múvə] N compañía de mudanzas *f*; —**s and shakers** la plana mayor

movie [múvi] N película *f*; —**s** cine *m*

moving [múvɪŋ] ADJ (target) móvil; (car) en movimiento; (company) de mudanzas; (story) conmovedor; — **picture** película *f*;

— **van** camión de mudanzas *m*; N **I hate** — no me gusta mudarme de casa

mow [mo] VT cortar; (harvest) segar

mower [móə·] N (for lawns) cortadora de céspedes *f*, cortacésped *m*; (farm implement) segadora *f*; (farm worker) segador -ra *mf*

Mozambican [mozæmbíkən] ADJ & N mozambiqueño -ña *mf*

Mozambique [mozæmbík] N Mozambique *m*

Mozarabic [mozǽrəbɪk] ADJ mozárabe

Mr. [místə·] N Sr. *m*

Mrs. [mísɪz] N Sra. *f*

Ms. [mɪz] N Sra. *f*

much [mʌtʃ] ADJ & ADV mucho; — **the same** casi lo mismo; — **like the others** muy parecido a los demás; **as** — **as** tanto como; **how** — ? ¿cuánto? **too** — demasiado; **very** — muchísimo; **to make** — **of** dar mucha importancia a; — **as I'd like, I won't do it** aunque me gustaría, no lo voy a hacer; **that's not** — **of a book** ese libro no es gran cosa; **she cried so** — **that her eyes turned red** lloró tanto que se le enrojecieron los ojos; **they need water,** — **as they need sun** necesitan agua, del mismo modo que necesitan sol

muck [mʌk] N (manure) estiércol *m*; (mire) cieno *m*, lodo *m*; (filth) porquería *f*

mucous [mjúkəs] ADJ mucoso

mucus [mjúkəs] N mucosidad *f*

mud [mʌd] N lodo *m*, barro *m*; —**slinging** difamación *f*

muddle [mʌdl] VT (confuse) confundir; (make turbid) enturbiar; VI **to** — **along** ir tirando; **to** — **through** salir del paso; N (confusion) confusión *f*; (confused situation) embrollo *m*

muddy [mʌdi] ADJ (path) lodoso, barroso; (shoes) embarrado; (vague) confuso; VT (cover with mud) enlodar, embarrar; (make unclear) enturbiar

muff [mʌf] N manguito *m*; VT estropear

muffin [mʌfɪn] N mollete *m*

muffle [mʌfəl] VT amortiguar

muffler [mʌflə·] N (scarf) bufanda *f*; (exhaust device) silenciador *m*

mug [mʌɡ] N (ceramic) tazón *m*; (glass) jarra *f*; (face) jeta *f*; VT atracar

mugger [mʌɡə·] N asaltante *mf*; atracador -ora *mf*

muggy [mʌɡi] ADJ bochornoso

mulatto [muláɾo] ADJ & N mulato -ta *mf*

mulberry [mʌlberi] N mora *f*; — **tree** moral *m*

mule [mjul] N mulo -la *mf* (also in drug trafficking)

mull [mʌl] VI/VT rumiar

multicultural [mʌltikʌltʃə·əl] ADJ multicultural

multiple [mʌltəpəl] N múltiplo *m*; ADJ múltiple; —**-choice** de opción múltiple; — **personality disorder** trastorno de personalidad múltiple *m*; — **sclerosis** esclerosis múltiple *f*

multiplication [mʌltəplikéʃən] N multiplicación *f*; — **sign** signo de multiplicación *m*; — **table** tabla de multiplicar *f*

multiplicity [mʌltəplísɪdi] N multiplicidad *f*

multiply [mʌltəplaɪ] VI/VT multiplicar(se)

multitasking [mʌltitǽskɪŋ] N multitarea *f*

multitude [mʌltɪtud] N multitud *f*

multi-user [mʌltijúzə·] N multiusuario -ria *mf*

mum [mʌm] ADJ callado; **to keep** — callarse la boca

mumble [mʌmbəl] VI/VT mascullar; N refunfuño *m*

mumbo jumbo [mámboʤámbo] N jerigonza *f*

mummy [mʌmi] N momia *f*

mumps [mʌmps] N paperas *f pl*

munch [mʌntʃ] VT mascar

mundane [mʌndén] ADJ mundano

municipal [mjunísəpəl] ADJ municipal; — **council** concejo *m*

municipality [mjunɪsəpǽlɪdi] N municipio *m*, municipalidad *m*

munition [mjuníʃən] N munición *f*

mural [mjúrəl] ADJ & N mural *m*

murder [mə́·də·] N asesinato *m*, homicidio *m*; **to get away with** — salirse con la suya; **that exam was** — ese examen fue matador; VI/VT asesinar

murderer [mə́·də·ə·] N asesino *mf*, homicida *mf*

murderous [mə́·də·əs] ADJ asesino, homicida

murky [mə́·ki] ADJ (of water, matter) turbio; (of sky) oscuro

murmur [mə́·mə·] N (noise) murmullo *m*, susurro *m*; (complaint) queja *f*; VI/VT (make noise) murmurar, susurrar; (complain) quejarse

muscle [mʌsəl] N músculo *m*

muscular [mʌskjələ·] ADJ (relative to muscles) muscular; (endowed with muscles) musculoso

muse [mjuz] VI meditar; VT cavilar; N musa *f*

museum [mjuzíəm] N museo *m*

mushroom [mʌ́ʃrum] N seta *f*, hongo *m*, champiñón *m*

mushy [mʌ́ʃi] ADJ (soft) fofo; (sentimental)

sensiblero
music [mjúzɪk] N música *f*; **— stand** atril *m*; **— video** *Am* video musical *m*; *Sp* vídeo musical *m*
musical [mjúzɪkəɫ] ADJ (pertaining to music) musical; (fond of music) aficionado a la música, melómano; **— comedy** comedia musical *f*
musician [mjuzíʃən] N músico -ca *mf*
muskrat [mʌ́skræt] N ratón almizclero *m*
Muslim [mʌ́zləm] ADJ & N musulmán -ana *mf*
muslin [mʌ́zlɪn] N muselina *f*
muss [mʌs] VT revolver, alborotar; N revoltijo *m*
mussel [mʌ́səɫ] N mejillón *m*
must [mʌst] V AUX **you — arrive before nine** debes llegar antes de las nueve; **you really — eat at that restaurant** tienes que comer en ese restaurante; **you — be his son** debes (de)/has de ser su hijo; **they — have seen me** deben (de) haberme visto
mustache, moustache [mʌ́stæʃ] N bigote *m*; (large) mostacho *m*
mustard [mʌ́stɚd] N mostaza *f*; **— gas** gas mostaza *m*
muster [mʌ́stɚ] VT (troops) formar; (courage) juntar, reunir; VI (assemble for inspection) formar; (come together) reunirse; **to — out** dar de baja; **to — up one's courage** juntar valor; N revista *f*; **to pass —** ser aceptable
musty [mʌ́sti] ADJ (stale smelling) con olor a encierro/humedad; (antiquated) anticuado
mutant [mjútn̩t] ADJ & N mutante *mf*
mutation [mjutéʃən] N mutación *f*
mute [mjut] ADJ mudo; N (mute person) mudo -da *mf*; (for musical instruments) sordina *f*
mutilate [mjúdl̩et] VT mutilar
mutiny [mjútn̩i] N motín *m*; VI amotinarse
mutter [mʌ́ɾɚ] VI/VT refunfuñar, musitar; N refunfuño *m*
mutton [mʌ́tn̩] N carne de cordero *f*
mutual [mjútʃuəɫ] ADJ mutuo; **— fund** fondo mutuo/mutual *m*
muzzle [mʌ́zəɫ] N (snout) hocico *m*; (mouthguard) bozal *m*; (gun opening) boca *f*; VT (a dog) abozalar, poner bozal a; (critics) amordazar, silenciar
my [maɪ] POSS ADJ mi; **these are — friends** estos son mis amigos; **oh —!** ¡Dios mío! **— foot!** ¡ni lo pienses!
Myanmar [mjɑnmár] N Myanmar *m*
myopia [maɪópiə] N miopía *f*
myriad [míriəd] N miríada *f*, sinfín *m*; **— problems** un sinfín de problemas
myrtle [mɝ́dl̩] N mirto *m*, arrayán *m*
myself [maɪsɛ́ɫf] PRON **I — wrote the letters** yo mismo escribí las cartas; **I'm not — today** hoy no soy la misma de siempre; **I was sitting by —** estaba sentado solo; **I talk to —** hablo solo; **I looked at — in the mirror** me miré en el espejo; **I bought — a house** me compré una casa
mysterious [mɪstíriəs] ADJ misterioso
mystery [místəri] N misterio *m*
mystic [místɪk] ADJ & N místico -ca *mf*
mystical [místɪkəɫ] ADJ místico
myth [mɪθ] N mito *m*
mythology [mɪθálədʒi] N mitología *f*

Nn

nab [næb] VT pescar; *Sp* coger
nag [næg] N (horse) jaca *f*, rocín *m*, penco *m*; (complainer) quejica *mf*; VI/VT regañar, criticar
nail [neɫ] N (for nailing) clavo *m*; (of finger, toe) uña *f*; **—-biter** situación angustiante *f*; **— file** lima *f*; **— polish** esmalte para uñas *m*; **to hit the — on the head** dar en el clavo; VT (fasten) clavar; (nab) pescar; *Sp* coger
naïve [nɑív] ADJ ingenuo, cándido, bonachón
naked [nékɪd] ADJ desnudo
nakedness [nékɪdnɪs] N desnudez *f*
name [nem] N nombre *m*; **—-brand** marca *f*; **—plate** placa *f*; **—sake** tocayo *m*; **—tag** etiqueta de identificación *f*; **— of the game** lo esencial *m*; **to call someone —s** motejar a alguien; **to make a — for oneself** hacerse un nombre; **what is your —?** ¿cómo te llamas? VT nombrar; **— your price** haz una oferta
namely [némli] ADV a saber, en concreto
Namibia [nəmíbiə] N Namibia *f*
Namibian [nəmíbiən] ADJ & N namibio -bia *mf*
nanny [nǽni] N niñera *f*
nanosecond [nǽnosɛkənd] N nanosegundo *m*
nap [næp] N (sleep) siesta *f*; (fibers) pelo *m*; **to take a —** echar/dormir una siesta; VI echar/dormir una siesta
napalm [népɑɫm] N napalm *m*
nape [nep] N nuca *f*

napkin [nǽpkɪn] N servilleta *f*

narcissism [nɑ́rsɪsɪzəm] N narcisismo *m*

narcissus [nɑrsɪ́səs] N narciso *m*

narcolepsy [nɑ́rkəlɛpsi] N narcolepsia *f*

narcotic [nɑrkɑ́dɪk] ADJ & N narcótico *m*, estupefaciente *m*

narco-trafficking [nɑrkotrǽfɪkɪŋ] N narcotráfico *m*

narrate [nǽret] VI/VT narrar

narration [nærɛ́ʃən] N narración *f*

narrative [nǽrədɪv] ADJ narrativo; N narrativa *f*

narrator [nǽrɛdəɹ] N narrador -ora *mf*

narrow [nǽro] ADJ (of little width) estrecho, angosto; (exhaustive) exhaustivo; (limited in scope) limitado; (intolerant) intolerante; **to have a — escape** salvarse por poco; **— gauge** de vía angosta / estrecha; **—-minded** intolerante; N **—s** desfiladero *m*, estrecho *m*, angostura *f*; VI/VT angostar(se), estrechar(se); **to — down** reducir

narrowness [nǽronɪs] N (quality of being narrow) estrechez *f*, angostura *f*; (intolerance) estrechez *f*

nasal [nézəɫ] ADJ nasal

nastiness [nǽstɪnɪs] N (filth) suciedad *f*; (stinkiness) asquerosidad *f*; (rudeness, obscenity) grosería *f*

nasturtium [nəstɚ́ʃəm] N capuchina *f*

nasty [nǽsti] ADJ (mess) sucio; (smell) asqueroso; (comment) hiriente; (accident) feo; (word) grosero; (disposition) malo

natal [nédɫ] ADJ natal

nation [néʃən] N nación *f*; **—wide** a escala nacional

national [nǽʃənəɫ] ADJ nacional; **— park** parque nacional *m*; N ciudadano -na *mf*, nacional *mf*

nationalism [nǽʃənəlɪzəm] N nacionalismo *m*

nationality [næʃənǽlɪdi] N nacionalidad *f*; **adjective of —** gentilicio *m*

nationalize [nǽʃənəlaɪz] VT nacionalizar

native [nédɪv] ADJ nativo; **— language** lengua nativa *f*; **— plants** flora nativa *f*; **my — Italy** mi Italia natal *f*; (innate) innato; N (person born in a place) natural *m*; (member of a tribal group) indígena *mf*, nativo -va *mf*

nativity [natívɪdi] N nacimiento *m*; **— scene** pesebre *m*; **the —** la Natividad

NATO (North Atlantic Treaty Organization) [nédo] N OTAN *f*

natural [nǽtʃəɹəɫ] ADJ natural; (inborn) innato; **— childbirth** parto natural *m*; **— gas** gas natural *m*; **— resources** recursos

naturales *m pl*; **— selection** selección natural *f*; N (musical sign) becuadro *m*; **he is a — for that job** tiene aptitud natural para ese puesto

naturalist [nǽtʃəɹəlɪst] N naturalista *mf*

naturalization [nætʃəɹəlɪzéʃən] N naturalización *f*

naturalize [nǽtʃəɹəlaɪz] VI/VT naturalizar(se)

naturally [nǽtʃəɹəli] ADV (of course) naturalmente; **I have — curly hair** tengo rizos naturales

naturalness [nǽtʃəɹəɫnɪs] N naturalidad *f*

nature [nétʃəɹ] N naturaleza *f*; (disposition) genio *m*, natural *m*

naught [nɔt] N (zero) cero *m*; (nothing) nada *f*

naughty [nɔ́di] ADJ (child) travieso, pícaro, pillo; **— word** picardía *f*

Nauru [naúru] N Nauru *m*

Nauruan [nɑúrʊən] ADJ & N nauruano -na *mf*

nausea [nɔ́ziə] N náusea *f*, mareo *m*

nauseate [nɔ́ziet] VT dar náuseas; **to be —d** tener náuseas

nauseating [nɔ́zieɾɪŋ] ADJ nauseabundo

nauseous [nɔ́ʃəs] ADJ (feeling nausea) mareado; (causing nausea) nauseabundo

nautical [nɔ́dɪkəɫ] ADJ náutico

naval [névəɫ] ADJ naval; **— officer** oficial de marina *m*

nave [nev] N nave *f*

navel [névəɫ] N ombligo *m*; **— orange** naranja de ombligo *f*

navigable [nǽvɪgəbəɫ] ADJ navegable

navigate [nǽvɪget] VI/VT navegar

navigation [nævɪgéʃən] N navegación *f*; (science) náutica *f*

navigator [nǽvɪgeɾəɹ] N navegante *mf*

navy [névi] N marina (de guerra) *f*, armada *f*; **— bean** judía blanca *f*; **— blue** azul marino *m*

nay [ne] N (refusal) no *m*; (negative vote) voto negativo *m*

near [nɪr] ADV cerca; **— at hand** cerca, a la mano; **to come / go / draw —** acercarse; **—sighted** miope; PREP cerca de; **— the end of the month** hacia fines del mes; **to be — death** estar a punto de morir; ADJ cercano, próximo; **— East** Cercano Oriente *m*, Oriente Próximo *m*; **I had a — miss** por poco me sucede un accidente; VI/VT acercarse (a)

nearby [nírbáɪ] ADV cerca; ADJ cercano, próximo

nearly [nírli] ADV casi, cerca de; **I — did it** casi lo hago

nearness [nírnɪs] N cercanía *f*, proximidad *f*

neat [nit] ADJ (clean) limpio, pulcro; (ordered) ordenado; (great) bueno

neatness [nítnɪs] N (cleanness) limpieza f, pulcritud f; (order) orden m

nebulous [nébjələs] ADJ nebuloso

necessary [nésɪseri] ADJ (needed) necesario; (involuntary) forzoso

necessitate [nəsésɪtet] VT requerir

necessity [nəsésɪdi] N necesidad f

neck [nɛk] N (of a human) cuello m; (of an animal) pescuezo m; (of clothes) escote m; (throat) garganta f; **— and —** parejos; **—lace** collar m; **—line** escote m; **— of land** istmo m; **—tie** corbata f

necrology [nəkrúlədʒi] N necrología f

nectar [néktə-] N néctar m

nectarine [nɛktərín] N nectarina f

need [nid] N (lack) necesidad f; (poverty) carencia f; **in —** en aprietos; **if — be** en caso de necesidad; VT necesitar, precisar; **you — to come at four** tienes que venir a las cuatro

needle [nídl] N aguja f; **—point** bordado m; **—work** (embroidery) bordado m; (sewing) costura f; VT pinchar

needless [nídlɪs] ADJ innecesario; **— to say** huelga decir

needy [nídi] ADJ necesitado, menesteroso

ne'er-do-well [nérduwɛl] N inútil mf

negate [nɪgét] VT negar

negation [nɪgéʃən] N negación f

negative [négəDɪv] ADJ negativo; **the search proved —** la búsqueda no dio resultado; N negativa f; (photographic) negativo m; **this plan has one —** este plan tiene una contra; INTERJ ¡negativo!

neglect [nɪglékt] VT postergar; (children) descuidar; (chores) desatender; **you're —ing your friends** tienes abandonados a tus amigos; **to — to** olvidarse de; N negligencia f, descuido m

neglectful [nɪgléktfəl] ADJ negligente, descuidado

negligence [néglɪdʒəns] N negligencia f

negligent [néglɪdʒənt] ADJ negligente, descuidado

negligible [néglɪdʒəbl] ADJ despreciable

negotiate [nɪgóʃiet] VI/VT (a contract) negociar, gestionar; (an obstacle) salvar

negotiation [nɪgoʃiéʃən] N negociación f, gestión f

Negro [nígro] ADJ & N negro -gra mf

neigh [ne] N relincho m; VI relinchar

neighbor [nébə-] N (person who lives near) vecino -na mf; (fellow human) prójimo -ma mf; ADJ vecino; VI **to — with** lindar con

neighborhood [nébə-hud] N vecindario m, barrio m; **in the — of a hundred dollars** alrededor de cien dólares

neighboring [nébərɪŋ] ADJ vecino, colindante

neither [níðə-] PRON ninguno de los dos, ni (el) uno ni (el) otro; **— of the two** ninguno de los dos; ADJ ninguno de los dos; **— one of us** ninguno de nosotros dos; CONJ ni; **— hot nor cold** ni caliente ni frío; **— will I** yo tampoco

nemesis [némɪsɪs] N némesis f

neologism [niálədʒɪzəm] N neologismo m

neon [nían] N neón m

Nepal [nəpɔ́l] N Nepal m

Nepalese [nɛpəlíz] ADJ & N nepalés -esa mf, nepalí mf

nephew [néfju] N sobrino m

nephritis [nəfráɪdɪs] N nefritis f

nepotism [népətɪzəm] N nepotismo m

nerd [nɜ-rd] N (technological adept) persona aficionada a las computadoras/los ordenadores f; (socially inept person) persona socialmente inepta f

nerve [nɜ-v] N (anatomy) nervio m; (courage) presencia de ánimo f; (impertinence) descaro m, morro m; **— cell** neurona f; **— gas** gas nervioso m; **—-(w)racking** angustiante; **he gets on my —s** me saca de quicio

nervous [nɜ́-vəs] ADJ nervioso; **— breakdown** ataque de nervios m

nervousness [nɜ́-vəsnɪs] N nerviosismo m

nest [nɛst] N nido m; (brood) nidada f; **— egg** ahorros m pl; **— of thieves** guarida de ladrones f; VI/VT anidar; (fit together) encajarse

nestle [nésəl] VI acurrucarse; VT apoyar, recostar

net [nɛt] N red f (also network); (in hair) redecilla f; VT (catch a fish) pescar con red; (cover with a net) cubrir con una red; (catch a criminal) atrapar; (hit the tennis net) dar en la red; (make money after expenses) producir/ganar neto; ADJ neto; **— price** precio neto m; **— profit** ganancia neta f; **— assets** activo neto m; **— income** ingreso neto m; **—work** red f; **—working** (social) relaciones profesionales f pl; (computer) diseño de redes y comunicaciones m

Netherlander [néðə-ləndə-] N holandés -esa mf

Netherlands [néðə-ləndz] N Países Bajos m pl

nettle [nédl] N ortiga f

neural [núrəl] ADJ neural

neuron [núran] N neurona f

neurosis [nʊrósɪs] N neurosis f
neurotic [nʊrɑ́ɗɪk] ADJ & N neurótico -ca mf
neuter [núɗɚ] ADJ neutro; VT castrar
neutral [nútrəł] ADJ neutral; (of colors) neutro; N punto muerto m
neutrality [nutrǽlɪɗi] N neutralidad f
neutralize [nútrəlaɪz] VI/VT neutralizar(se)
neutron [nútrɑn] N neutrón m; **— bomb** bomba de neutrones f
never [névɚ] ADV nunca, jamás; **— mind** no te preocupes; **this will — do** esto no va a funcionar; **—-ending** interminable
nevertheless [nevɚðəlɛ́s] ADV & CONJ sin embargo, no obstante
new [nu] ADJ (not old) nuevo; (fresh) otro; **a — sheet of paper** otra hoja de papel; **— Age (music)** new age f; **—-born baby** recién nacido -da mf; **—-comer** recién llegado -da mf; **—-fangled** moderno, recién inventado; **—-found** nuevo; **— year** año nuevo m; **— Year's Eve** fin de año m; Sp nochevieja f
newly [núli] ADV recientemente; **— arrived** recién llegado; **—-wed** recién casado
newness [núnɪs] N novedad f
news [nuz] N noticias f pl; (latest gossip) novedades f pl; (newspaper) periódico m; **it is — to me** recién me entero; **piece of — noticia** f; **— broadcast / bulletin** noticiero m, noticiario m; **—-cast** noticiero m, noticiario m; **— clipping** recorte de diario m; **—-letter** boletín informativo m; **—-paper** periódico m, diario m; **—-print** papel de periódico m; **—-room** sala de redacción f; **—-stand** quiosco m; **—-worthy** de interés periodístico
newt [nut] N tritón m
New Zealand [nuzílənd] N Nueva Zelanda f
New Zealander [nuzíləndɚ] N neozelandés -esa mf
next [nɛkst] ADJ (future) próximo, entrante; (following) siguiente; (contiguous) contiguo, de al lado; **who's —?** ¿quién sigue? ADV después, luego; **— best** segundo en calidad; **when — we meet** cuando nos volvamos a ver; PREP **— door** de al lado; **— of kin** familiares m pl; **— to** junto a, al lado de
nibble [níbəł] VI/VT (bite) mordiscar, mordisquear; (eat) picotear; (of fish) picar; N (bite) mordisco m; (act of nibbling) mordisqueo m
Nicaragua [nɪkərágwə] N Nicaragua f
Nicaraguan [nɪkərágwən] ADJ & N nicaragüense mf
nice [naɪs] ADJ (kind) amable, simpático; (agreeable) Am lindo, Sp majo; **it's — and**

hot está bien calentito
nicety [náɪsɪɗi] N (subtlety) sutileza f; (detail) exactitud f, precisión f
niche [nɪtʃ] N nicho m (also environmental); **I've found my —** he encontrado mi lugar
nick [nɪk] N (chip) muesca f; (cut) corte m; **in the — of time** justo a tiempo; VT (chip) hacer muescas; (cut) cortar
nickel [níkəł] N (metal) níquel m; (coin) moneda de cinco centavos f; **—-plated** niquelado
nickname [níknem] N apodo m, mote m, sobrenombre m; VT apodar
nicotine [níkɑtin] N nicotina f
niece [nis] N sobrina f
Niger [náɪdʒɚ] N Níger m
Nigeria [naɪdʒíriə] N Nigeria f
Nigerian [naɪdʒíriən] ADJ & N nigeriano -na mf
Nigerien [naɪdʒírien] ADJ & N nigerino -na mf
niggardly [nígɚdli] ADJ mezquino
night [naɪt] N noche f; ADJ nocturno, de noche; **—-club** club nocturno m; **—-fall** anochecer m, atardecer m; **—-gown** camisón m; **—-life** vida nocturna f; Sp marcha f; **—-light** lamparilla f; **—-mare** pesadilla f; **— owl** trasnochador -ora mf; **— shift** turno de la noche m; **—-stand** veladora f, mesilla de noche f; **—-time** noche f; **— watchman** sereno m
nightingale [náɪtŋgeł] N ruiseñor m
nightly [náɪtli] ADV todas las noches; ADJ nocturno
nihilism [náɪəlɪzəm] N nihilismo m
nil [nɪł] N; **your chances are —** tus probabilidades son nulas
nimble [nímbəł] ADJ ágil
nincompoop [nínkəmpup] N fam tarambana mf, bobalicón -ona mf
nine [naɪn] NUM nueve
nineteen [naɪntín] NUM diecinueve
ninety [náɪnti] NUM noventa
ninth [náɪnθ] ADJ & N noveno m
nip [nɪp] VT (pinch) pellizcar; (bite) mordiscar, mordisquear; (cause frostbite) helar; **to — in the bud** cortar de raíz; **to — off** despuntar; VI (drink in sips) dar sorbitos; N (pinch) pellizco m; (bite) mordisco m; (sip) traguito m, sorbito m; (cold) frío m; **it's going to be — and tuck** va a ser muy reñido
nipple [nípəł] N (on female breast) pezón m; (on male breast) tetilla f; (on bottle) tetina f
nitpick [nítpɪk] VI criticar detalles insignificantes

nitrate [náɪtret] N nitrato *m*
nitric acid [náɪtrɪkǽsɪd] N ácido nítrico *m*
nitrogen [náɪtrədʒən] N nitrógeno *m*
nitroglycerin [naɪtroglísə·ɪn] N
   nitroglicerina *f*
nitty-gritty [nídigrídi] N **to get down to
   the** — ir al grano
no [no] ADV no; **— longer** ya no; **he was a
   —-show** no se presentó; **a —-win
   situation** una situación insoluble; **there
   is — more** no hay más; ADJ ningun(o); **—
   man's land** tierra de nadie *f*; **— matter
   how much** por mucho que; **— one**
   ninguno, nadie; **— smoking** se prohibe
   fumar; **—where** (location) en ninguna
   parte / ningún lado; (direction) a ninguna
   parte / ningún lado; **I have — friends** no
   tengo amigos; **it's a —-brainer** la
   respuesta es obvia; **— friend of mine
   will go hungry** ningún amigo mío
   pasará hambre; **of — use** inútil; N
   (refusal) no *m*; (negative vote) voto
   negativo *m*
nobility [nobílɪɖi] N nobleza *f*, hidalguía *f*
noble [nóbəl] ADJ & N noble *mf*
nobody [nóbaɖi] PRON nadie, ninguno; N un
   don nadie, pelagatos *mf sg*
nocturnal [naktɝ·nəl] ADJ nocturno
nod [nad] VI/VT (signal affirmation) asentir
   con la cabeza; VI (doze) cabecear, dar
   cabezadas; **to — off** dormirse; N (as
   signal) inclinación de cabeza *f*, saludo con
   la cabeza *m*; (from sleepiness) cabezada *f*
node [nod] N (of cells) nódulo *m*; (in plants)
   nudo *m*; (in physics) nodo *m*
noise [nɔɪz] N ruido *m*; VI **it is being —d
   about that** corre el rumor que
noiseless [nɔ́ɪzlɪs] ADJ silencioso
noisy [nɔ́ɪzi] ADJ ruidoso
nomad [nómæd] N nómada *mf*
nomenclature [nómɪnklɛtʃɚ·] N
   nomenclatura *f*
nominal [námənəl] ADJ nominal
nominate [námənet] VT nominar
nomination [namənéʃən] N nominación *f*
nominee [naməní] N candidato -ta *mf*
nonchalant [nanʃəlánt] ADJ despreocupado
nonconformist [nankənfɔ́rmɪst] ADJ & N
   incomformista *mf*
none [nʌn] PRON ninguno; **I want — of
   that** no me quiero meter en eso; **that is
   — of your business** no es asunto tuyo;
   ADV **— too soon** al último momento;
   —theless sin embargo
nonentity [nanéntɪɖi] N nulidad *f*
nonfiction [nanfíkʃən] N no ficción *f*
nonpartisan [nanpárɖɪzən] ADJ imparcial

nonproductive [nanprədáktɪv] ADJ
   improductivo
nonprofit [nanpráfɪt] ADJ sin fines de lucro
nonresident [nanrézɪdənt] ADJ & N no
   residente *mf*
nonsense [nánsens] N tonterías *f pl*,
   monsergas *f pl*, estupideces *f pl*; **to talk —**
   decir barbaridades / disparates
nonstop [nánstáp] ADJ sin escala, directo;
   ADV sin parar
noodle [núdl] N fideo *m*, tallarín *m*
nook [nʊk] N rincón *m*
noon [nun] N mediodía *m*; **—time** mediodía
   m
noose [nus] N soga *f*, lazo *m*; **with a —
   around his neck** con la soga al cuello;
   VT (catch with a rope) enlazar; (make a
   loop in) hacer un lazo corredizo en
nope [nop] ADV no
nor [nɔr] CONJ ni; **we have neither eggs —
   flour** no tenemos ni huevos ni harina
Nordic [nɔ́rdɪk] ADJ nórdico
norm [nɔrm] N norma *f*
normal [nɔ́rməl] ADJ normal; N (line) normal
   f; **to return to —** volver a la normalidad;
   (perpendicular line) perpendicular *f*
normalize [nɔ́rməlaɪz] VI/VT normalizar(se)
north [nɔrθ] N norte *m*; ADJ (in the north)
   norte, norteño; **the — entrance** la
   entrada norte; (from the north) del norte;
   — America América del Norte *f*; **—
   American** norteamericano -na *mf*; **—east**
   noreste, hacia el noreste; **—eastern** del
   noreste; **— Korea** Corea del Norte *f*; **—
   Korean** norcoreano -na; **— Pole** Polo
   Norte *m*; **—west** noroeste *m*, hacia el
   noroeste; **— wind** cierzo *m*, viento norte
   m; ADV al norte, hacia el norte
northern [nɔ́rðɚ·n] ADJ del norte; (from the
   north) norteño; (in the north)
   septentrional; **— lights** aurora boreal *f*
northerner [nɔ́rðɚ·nɚ] N norteño -ña *mf*
northward [nɔ́rθwɚd] ADJ hacia el norte
Norway [nɔ́rwe] N Noruega *f*
Norwegian [nɔrwíʤən] ADJ & N noruego -ga
   mf
nose [noz] N nariz *f*; (of an airplane) morro
   m; (of an animal) hocico *m*; (perspicacity)
   olfato *m*; **—bleed** hemorragia nasal *f*;
   —dive picado *m*; **— job** rinoplastia *f*;
   keep your — clean no te metas en líos;
   on the — exactamente; VI/VT (move
   forward) entrar de punta; (muzzle)
   hocicar; **to — around** husmear; **to pick
   one's —** hurgarse las narices
nostalgia [nastǽlʤə] N nostalgia *f*
nostalgic [nastǽlʤɪk] ADJ nostálgico

nostrils [nástrəlz] N narices *f pl*, ventanillas de la nariz *f pl*

nosy, nosey [nózi] ADJ entrometido

not [nɑt] ADV no; **I'm — your friend** no soy tu amigo; **— at all** (no way) de ningún modo; (you're welcome) de nada; **— at all sure** nada seguro; **— even a word** ni una palabra

notable [nóɾəbəł] ADJ notable, granado

notarize [nóɾəraɪz] VT notariar

notary [nóɾəri] N notario -ria *mf*; **— public** notario -ria público -ca *mf*

notation [notéʃən] N (system of signs) notación *f*; (act of writing) anotación *f*; (short note) anotación *f*, apunte *m*

notch [nɑtʃ] N (nick) muesca *f*, mella *f*; (degree) grado *m*; **a — above the rest** mejor que los demás; VT hacer una muesca; **he —ed another win** se anotó otra victoria

note [not] N nota *f*; (touch) toque *m*; **—book** cuaderno *m*; (small) libreta *f*; **—s** apuntes *m pl*; **—worthy** notable; **of —** de renombre/de nota; **to take — of** notar; VT (notice) notar; (write down) anotar, apuntar

noted [nóɾɪd] ADJ célebre

nothing [nʌ́θɪŋ] PRON nada; (score) cero, nada; N (insignificant person) don nadie *m*; (insignificant thing) nadería *f*; **— to it** no tiene ciencia; ADV **it was — like that** no fue así para nada; **we did it for — **(free) lo hicimos gratis; (fruitlessly) lo hicimos en balde

notice [nóɾɪs] N (information) aviso *m*; (warning) advertencia *f*; (attention) atención *f*; **a week's — **una semana de plazo; **to give — **renunciar; **to take — **hacer caso; VT (perceive) notar, advertir; (pay attention to) fijarse (en), reparar (en)

noticeable [nóɾɪsəbəł] ADJ perceptible, apreciable

notification [noɾəfɪkéʃən] N notificación *f*

notify [nóɾəfaɪ] VT notificar

notion [nóʃən] N noción *f*, idea *f*; (whim) capricho *m*; **—s** mercería *f*

notorious [notɔ́riəs] ADJ de mala fama; **he's a — liar** tiene fama de mentiroso

nougat [núgət] N turrón *m*

noun [naʊn] N sustantivo *m*

nourish [nɝ́ɪʃ] VT (a person) nutrir, alimentar; (a hope) abrigar

nourishing [nɝ́ɪʃɪŋ] ADJ nutritivo

nourishment [nɝ́ɪʃmənt] N (food) alimento *m*; (act of nourishing) alimentación *f*

novel [návəł] N novela *f*; ADJ novedoso

novelist [návəlɪst] N novelista *mf*

novelty [návəłti] N novedad *f*; **the — soon wore off** se pasó la novedad; **novelties** chucherías *f pl*

November [novémbɚ] N noviembre *m*

novice [návɪs] N novato -ta *mf*, pipiolo -la *mf*; (religious) novicio -cia *mf*

now [naʊ] ADV ahora; **— and then** de vez en cuando; **— that** ahora que; **he left just —** salió hace poco, recién salió; **—, —, calm down!** bueno, bueno, ¡cálmate!

nowadays [náʊədez] ADV hoy (en) día

noxious [nákʃəs] ADJ nocivo

nuance [núɑns] N matiz *m*

nuclear [núkliɚ] ADJ nuclear; **— energy** energía nuclear *f*; **— family** familia nuclear *f*; **— fission** fisión nuclear *f*; **— fusion** fusión nuclear *f*; **— physics** física nuclear *f*; **— weapon** arma nuclear *f*

nucleus [núkliəs] N núcleo *m*

nude [nud] ADJ & N desnudo *m*

nudge [nʌdʒ] VI/VT codear; N golpe suave con el codo *m*

nugget [nágɪt] N (gold) pepita *f*; (chicken) pedacito *m*; (wisdom) perla *f*

nuisance [núsəns] N molestia *f*; Sp pesadez *f*; (legal) perjuicio *m*; **you're such a —!** ¡qué pesado eres tú!; **— tax** impuesto de consumo *m*

nuke [nuk] N arma nuclear *f*; VT (bomb) bombardear con armas nucleares; (cook) calentar en microondas

null [nʌł] ADJ nulo; **— and void** nulo

nullify [nʌ́ləfaɪ] VT anular

numb [nʌm] ADJ entumecido; **to get —** entumecerse; VT entumecer

number [nʌ́mbɚ] N número *m*; **— one** uno mismo *m*; **—-crunching** procesamiento de datos numéricos complejos *m*; VT numerar; VI (total) ascender a; **I — him among my friends** lo cuento entre mis amigos

numberless [nʌ́mbɚlɪs] ADJ sin número

numbskull, numskull [nʌ́mskʌł] N zopenco -ca *mf*

numeral [númɚəł] N número *m*; ADJ numeral

numerical [numérɪkəł] ADJ numérico

numerous [númɚəs] ADJ numeroso

nun [nʌn] N monja *f*, religiosa *f*

nuptial [nʌ́pʃəł] ADJ nupcial; N **—s** nupcias *f pl*

nurse [nɝs] N (for the sick) enfermero -a *mf*; (for children) niñera *f*; VT (give milk) amamantar, lactar; (tend to a sick person) cuidar; **to — a grudge** guardar rencor; **to — a cup of coffee** tomar una taza de café a sorbitos; **to — a cold** cuidarse durante un resfrío; vi (drink milk) mamar

nursery [nə́·sri] N (children's room) cuarto
para niños *m*; (day-care center) guardería
f; (place for growing plants) almáciga *f*,
vivero *m*, plantel *m*; — **rhyme** canción
infantil *f*, ronda *f*; — **school** pre-escolar
m; *Sp* parvulario *m*; *Am* jardín infantil *m*

nursing [nə́·sɪŋ] N (profession) enfermería *f*;
(care) cuidado *m*; — **home** (for old
people) hogar de ancianos *m*; (for sick
people) casa de salud *f*

nurture [nə́·tʃɚ] vt (rear) criar; (feed) nutrir,
alimentar; (encourage) fomentar; N
(rearing) crianza *f*; (feeding) alimentación
f

nut [nʌt] N (fruit) fruto seco *m*; (device)
tuerca *f*; (person) excéntrico -ca *mf*;
—**cracker** cascanueces *m sg*; —**meg** nuez
moscada *f*; **he's** —**s** está loco; —**s and
bolts** los fundamentos; —**shell** cáscara de
fruto seco *f*; **in a** —**shell** en pocas
palabras

nutrient [nútriənt] N nutriente *m*

nutrition [nutríʃən] N nutrición *f*,
alimentación *f*

nutritious [nutríʃəs] ADJ nutritivo,
alimenticio

nylon [náɪlɑn] N nilón *m*, nailon *m*

Oo

oak [ok] N roble *m*, encina *f*; — **grove**
robledal *m*

oar [ɔr] N remo *m*; vi/vt remar, bogar; —**lock**
tolete *m*

OAS (Organization of American States)
[oeʃ] N OEA *f*

oasis [oésɪs] N oasis *m*

oat [ot] N avena *f*; —**meal** (flour) harina de
avena *f*; (breakfast food) gachas de avena *f
pl*; —**s** avena *f*

oath [oθ] N (pledge) juramento *m*; (curse)
maldición *f*; (swear word) palabrota *f*, taco
m; **to take an** — prestar juramento

obedience [obídiəns] N obediencia *f*

obedient [obídiənt] ADJ obediente

obese [obís] ADJ obeso

obesity [obísɪdi] N obesidad *f*

obey [obé] vi/vt obedecer

obituary [obítʃuɛri] N nota necrológica *f*,
obituario *m*

object [ábdʒɪkt] N objeto *m*; (of a verb)
complemento *m*; [əbdʒɛ́kt] vi/vt objetar

objection [əbdʒékʃən] N objeción *f*

objective [əbdʒéktɪv] ADJ objetivo; N objetivo
m

obligate [ábliget] vt obligar

obligation [abligéʃən] N obligación *f*; **under
no** — **to buy** sin compromiso de compra

obligatory [əblígətɔri] ADJ obligatorio

oblige [əbláɪdʒ] vt (make obliged) obligar; vi/
vt (do a favor for) complacer; vi (obey an
order) obedecer; **much** —**d!** ¡muchas
gracias! ¡muy agradecido!

obliging [əbláɪdʒɪŋ] ADJ complaciente; *Am*
comedido

oblique [oblík] ADJ oblicuo

obliterate [əblídəret] vt (blot out) tachar;
(destroy) arrasar, destruir

oblivion [əblíviən] N olvido *m*

oblivious [əblíviəs] ADJ inconsciente; — **to
the danger** ajeno al peligro

obnoxious [əbnákʃəs] ADJ (remark, behavior)
ofensivo; (person) molesto

oboe [óbo] N oboe *m*

obscene [əbsín] ADJ obsceno; **his salary is**
— lo que gana es escandaloso

obscenity [əbsénɪdi] N obscenidad *f*

obscure [əbskjúr] ADJ oscuro; vt oscurecer

obscurity [əbskjúrɪdi] N oscuridad *f*

obsequious [əbsíkwiəs] ADJ obsequioso

observance [əbzɚ́vəns] N observancia *f*

observant [əbzɚ́vənt] ADJ observador

observation [abzɚvéʃən] N observación *f*

observatory [əbzɚ́vətɔri] N observatorio *m*

observe [əbzɚ́v] vt observar; (holidays,
rituals) guardar

observer [əbzɚ́vɚ] N observador -ra *mf*

obsess [əbsés] vi/vt obsesionar(se); **he's**
—**ing over it** está obsesionado

obsession [əbséʃən] N obsesión *f*

obsessive-compulsive [əbsésɪvkəmpʌ́lsɪv]
ADJ obsesivo-compulsivo

obsolescence [absəlésəns] N desuso *m*

obsolete [absəlít] ADJ anticuado, desusado

obstacle [ábstəkəl] N obstáculo *m*

obstetrics [abstétrɪks] N obstetricia *f*

obstinacy [ábstənəsi] N obstinación *f*,
terquedad *f*, porfía *f*

obstinate [ábstənɪt] ADJ obstinado, terco,
recalcitrante; **to be** — obstinarse

obstruct [əbstrʌ́kt] vi/vt obstruir; (traffic)
atascar, obstruir

obstruction [əbstrʌ́kʃən] N obstrucción *f*

obtain [əbtén] vt obtener, procurar; vi
prevalecer

obtainable [əbténəbəl] ADJ conseguible

obviate [ábviet] vt hacer innecesario

obvious [ábviəs] ADJ obvio, evidente

occasion [əkéʒən] N (moment) ocasión *f*;

(chance) oportunidad *f*, ocasión *f*; (cause)
motivo *m*; (event) acontecimiento *m*,
ocasión *f*; VT ocasionar
occasional [əkéʒənəł] ADJ ocasional
occasionally [əkéʒənəli] ADV de vez en
cuando, ocasionalmente
occidental [aksidéntł] ADJ & N occidental *mf*
occult [əkʌ́łt] ADJ oculto; N ocultismo *m*,
ciencias ocultas *f pl*; VT ocultar
occupant [ákjəpənt] N ocupante *mf*
occupation [akjəpéʃən] N ocupación *f*
occupy [ákjəpaɪ] VI/VT ocupar
occur [əkə́˞] VI ocurrir, suceder; **it —red to
me** se me ocurrió
occurrence [əkə́˞əns] N suceso *m*,
acontecimiento *m*
ocean [óʃən] N océano *m*
oceanography [oʃənágrəfi] N oceanografía *f*
ocelot [ásəlat] N ocelote *m*
o'clock [əklák] ADV **it is one —** es la una; **it
is two —** son las dos
octagon [áktəgən] N octágono *m*, octógono
m
octane [ákten] N octano *m*
octave [áktɪv] N octava *f*
October [aktóbə˞] N octubre *m*
octopus [áktəpəs] N pulpo *m*
OD (overdose) [odí] N sobredosis *f*; VI tomar
una sobredosis
odd [ɑd] ADJ (unusual) extraño; (not even)
impar, non; **—ball** excéntrico -ca *mf*; **—
change** suelto *m*, cambio *m*; **— job**
trabajo ocasional *m*; **— shoe** zapato sin
compañero *m*; **thirty-—** treinta y tantos
oddity [ɑ́dɪti] N rareza *f*; (person) excéntrico
-ca *mf*
odds [ɑdz] N (probabilities) probabilidades *f
pl*; **— and ends** cachivaches *m pl*; **—-on
favorite** favorito *m*; **the — are against
me** llevo las de perder; **to be at —** estar
en desacuerdo
ode [od] N oda *f*
odious [ódiəs] ADJ odioso
odor [ódə˞] N olor *m*; (bad) hedor *m*
odorless [ódə˞lɪs] ADJ inodoro
odorous [ódə˞əs] ADJ oloroso
of [ɑv] PREP de; **— course** por supuesto,
desde luego; **a quarter — five** las cinco
menos cuarto; **doctor — medicine**
doctor -ra en medicina *mf*; **the smell —
paint** el olor a pintura; **a friend —
mine** un amigo mío
off [ɔf] ADV **— and on** de vez en cuando; **—
the record** extraoficialmente; **ten cents
—** rebaja de diez centavos *f*; **ten miles —**
a diez millas de distancia; **to take a day
—** tomarse un día libre; ADJ **— chance**

posibilidad remota *f*; **—-color** verde; **—
season** temporada baja *f*; **— year** de
producción decreciente; **our deal is —** se
canceló nuestro plan; **prices are —** los
precios han caído; **you're — by a mile**
estás equivocadísimo; **he's a little —** está
tocadito; **with his hat —** sin el
sombrero; **the electricity is —** está
apagada la electricidad; **to be — to war**
haberse ido a la guerra; **to be well —**
tener mucho dinero; PREP **— course** fuera
de curso; **he drove — the road** se salió
de la carretera; **I bought it — a gypsy** se
lo compré a un gitano; **he's — playing
golf** se fue a jugar al golf; VT liquidar
off-duty [ɔfdúti] ADJ **to be —** no estar de
turno
offend [əfénd] VI/VT (insult) ofender,
afrentar; (affect disagreeably) desagradar
offender [əféndə˞] N delincuente *mf*
offense [əféns] N (sin, insult) ofensa *f*;
(misdemeanor) delito *m*; **no — was
meant** no te lo tomes a mal; [áfens] (in
sports) ofensiva *f*
offensive [əfénsɪv] ADJ ofensivo; N ofensiva *f*
offer [ɔ́fə˞] VT ofrecer; **to — to** ofrecerse a;
N oferta *f*
offering [ɔ́fə˞ɪŋ] N (thing given in worship)
ofrenda *f*; (thing presented for sale) oferta
f; (action of offering) ofrecimiento *m*
offhand [ɔ́fhǽnd] ADV **he remarked —**
mencionó al descuido; ADJ **an — remark**
un comentario descuidado
office [ɔ́fɪs] N (function) cargo *m*, función *f*;
(place) oficina *f*, despacho *m*;
(headquarters) oficinas *f pl*; **— boy**
mandadero de oficina *m*; **— building**
edificio para oficinas *m*; **through the —s
of** por la intervención de
officer [ɔ́fɪsə˞] N (military) oficial *m*; (police)
agente de policía *mf*; (of an organization)
directivo -va *mf*
official [əfíʃəł] ADJ oficial; N funcionario -ria
mf
officiate [əfíʃiet] VI oficiar; (in sports) arbitrar
officious [əfíʃəs] ADJ oficioso
off-key [ɔfkí] ADJ desafinado
off-limits [ɔflímɪts] ADJ vedado
off-season [ɔfsízən] ADJ de temporada baja
offset [ɔfsét] N offset *m*; VT compensar
offshore [ɔfʃɔ́r] ADJ & ADV cerca de la costa;
— drilling explotación petrolífera en el
fondo del mar *f*
offspring [ɔ́fsprɪŋ] N prole *m*
offstage [ɔfstédʒ] ADV & ADJ entre bastidores,
fuera de escena
often [ɔ́fən] ADV a menudo; **how — ?** ¿con

qué frecuencia? ¿cada cuánto?

ogre [óɡə] N ogro *m*

ohm [om] N ohmio *m*

oil [ɔɪl] N (for cars, cooking) aceite *m*; (crude) petróleo *m*; **—can** alcuza *f*, aceitera *f*; **—cloth** hule *m*, tela de hule *f*; **— field** yacimiento petrolífero *m*; **— lamp** quinqué *m*; **— painting** pintura al óleo *f*, óleo *m*; **— pan** cárter *m*; **— rig** plataforma petrolífera *f*; **— slick** mancha de petróleo *f*; **— well** pozo de petróleo *m*; VT (apply oil) aceitar; (bribe) untar

oily [ɔɪli] ADJ aceitoso, oleoso; (unctuous) untuoso

oink [ɔɪŋk] VI gruñir; N gruñido *m*

ointment [ɔɪntmənt] N ungüento *m*

OK [oké] ADJ bueno; ADV bien; **he's an — guy** es un buen tipo; **it's —** (fine) está bien; (adequate) es regular; **to give one's — dar el visto bueno; VT dar el visto bueno, aprobar

okra [ókrə] N quingombó *m*

old [old] ADJ viejo; (objects only) antiguo; (wine) añejo; **— age** vejez *f*, ancianidad *f*; **—fashioned** (unfashionable) pasado de moda; (antiquated) anticuado; (morally prudish) chapado a la antigua; **— fogey** carcamal *m*, carca *m*; **— hat** pasado de moda; **— maid** solterona *f*; **—time** antiguo, viejo; **—timer** (long-time member) miembro de la vieja guardia *m*; (oldster) viejo *m*; **— wives' tale** superstición *f*; **— world** viejo mundo *m*; **days of —** antaño; **how — are you?** ¿cuántos años tienes? **— man** (husband) marido *m*; (father) *fam* viejo *m*; **I'm not — enough to drive** soy muy joven para conducir; **to be an — hand at** ser ducho en

olden [óldən] ADJ **in — days** antaño

oldie [óldi] N viejo éxito *m*

oleander [óliændə] N adelfa *f*

olfactory [ɔlfǽktəri] ADJ olfatorio

olive [álɪv] N (tree) olivo *m*; (fruit) aceituna *f*, oliva *f*; **— branch** ramo de olivo *m*; **— grove** olivar *m*; **— oil** aceite de oliva *m*; **— wood** madera de olivo *m*; ADJ verde oliva

Olympiad [olímpiæd] N olimpiada *f*

Olympic [olímpɪk] ADJ olímpico; **— Games** Olimpiadas *f pl*, Juegos Olímpicos *m pl*

Oman [omán] N Omán *m*

Omani [ománi] ADJ & N omaní *mf*

omelet [ámlɪt] N tortilla francesa *f*

omen [ómən] N agüero *m*, presagio *m*

ominous [ámənəs] ADJ (threatening) amenazador; (like an omen) agorero

omission [omíʃən] N omisión *f*

omit [omít] VT omitir

omnipotence [amnípətəns] N omnipotencia *f*

omnipotent [amnípətənt] ADJ omnipotente

omniscience [amníʃəns] N omnisciencia *f*

omniscient [amníʃənt] ADJ omnisciente

omnivorous [amnívə-əs] ADJ omnívoro

on [an] PREP en, sobre, encima de; **— the table** en/sobre/encima de la mesa; **— all sides** por todos lados; **— arriving** al llegar; **— call** de guardia; **— credit** al fiado; **— drugs** drogado; **— horseback** a caballo; **—line** en línea; **— Monday** el lunes; **— purpose** a propósito; **—screen** en la pantalla; **— the house** la casa paga; **— time** a tiempo; **a book — stamps** un libro sobre sellos; **do you have any cigarettes — you?** ¿tienes cigarros? **— drunk — beer** borracho de cerveza; **to talk — the phone** hablar por teléfono; ADV **— and —** dale que dale; ADJ **his hat is —** lleva puesto el sombrero; **the light is —** está encendida la luz; **there's a war —** estamos en guerra; **you're —** (broadcasting) estás en el aire

once [wʌns] ADV (in the past, a single time) una vez; (if ever) si alguna vez; **— and for all** una vez por todas; **— in a while** de vez en cuando; **—over** vistazo *m*; **— upon a time** érase una vez; **at —** de inmediato; **just this —** sólo por esta vez; **— cousin — removed** primo segundo *m*; CONJ una vez que, cuando; N una vez

oncology [ankáləʤi] N oncología *f*

one [wʌn] ADJ uno; **— book** un libro; **— thousand** mil; **—armed** manco; **—armed bandit** tragaperras *mf sg*; **—eyed** tuerto; **— John Smith** un tal John Smith; **—man band** hombre orquesta *m*; **— on —** mano a mano; **—sided fight** pelea desigual *f*; **—upmanship** competitividad *f*; **—way street** calle de sentido único *f*; **his — chance** su única oportunidad; **the — and only** el único; **this is — smart dog** es un perro muy listo; N & PRON uno *m*; **— at a time** de a uno; **— by —** uno por uno; **love — another** amaos los unos a los otros; **the — who** el/la que; **the green —** el verde; **this —** este/esta

oneself [wʌnsélf] PRON **to be —** ser uno mismo; **to sit by —** estar sentado solo; **to talk to —** hablar para sí; **to look at — in the mirror** mirarse en el espejo; **to buy — a house** comprarse una casa

ongoing [ángoɪŋ] ADJ continuo

onion [ánjən] N cebolla *f*; **— patch** cebollar *m*

onlooker [ánlukə-] N espectador -ra *mf*, mirón -ona *mf*

only [ónli] ADJ único; ADV sólo, solamente; **I — just caught the train** por poco pierdo el tren; CONJ sólo que, pero

onomatopoeia [anəmɑɑəpíə] N onomatopeya *f*

onset [ánset] N comienzo *m*

onto [ántu] PREP en, sobre, encima de; **he placed it — the top of the refrigerator** lo colocó encima de la nevera; **I'm — your plot** conozco tu plan

onward [ánwə-d] ADV hacia adelante

onyx [ániks] N ónix *m*

oops [ups] INTERJ ¡huy!

ooze [uz] VI/VT rezumar(se); N cieno *m*

opal [ópəl] N ópalo *m*

opaque [opék] ADJ opaco

OPEC (Organization of Petroleum Exporting Countries) [ópɛk] N OPEP *f*

open [ópən] VI/VT abrir(se); **to — into** comunicarse con; **to — one's way** abrirse paso; **to — onto** dar a; **to — up** abrirse; **and shut** claro, evidente; **— door policy** política de acceso libre *f*; **—-ended** claro; **—-heart surgery** cirujía de corazón abierto *f*; **—-minded** de amplias miras; **—-mouthed** boquiabierto; **— question** cuestión discutible *f*; **— season** temporada de caza *f*; **— to criticism** expuesto a la crítica; N (outdoors) aire libre *m*; (tournament) abierto *m*

opener [ópənə-] N abridor *m*; (in sports) primer partido *m*; **for —s** para empezar

opening [ópənɪŋ] N (open space) abertura *f*; (act of making or becoming open, ceremony) apertura *f*; (beginning) comienzo *m*; (clearing) claro *m*; (vacancy) vacante *m*; (pretext) oportunidad *f*; **— night** estreno *m*

opera [ápərə] N ópera *f*; **— glasses** gemelos *m pl*; **— house** ópera *f*

operable [ápə-əbəl] ADJ operable

operate [ápəret] VI (function) funcionar; (intervene surgically) operar; **to — on a person** operar a una persona; VT (run a machine) manejar; (administrate) dirigir; (make function) accionar

operating room [ápəreɪ̯ɪŋrum] N sala de operaciones *f*, quirófano *m*

operation [apəréʃən] N (surgical intervention, mission, math function) operación *f*; (function) funcionamiento *m*;

(use of a machine) manejo *m*; **to be in —** (law) estar vigente; (machine) estar funcionando

operative [ápə-ədɪv] ADJ (law) vigente; (contract provision) pertinente; (word) clave; N (machine worker) operario -ria *mf*; (spy) agente *mf*

operator [ápəredə-] N (telephone, math) operador -ra *mf*; (machine) operario -ria *mf*; (stock) especulador -ra *mf*; **he's a smooth —** es un astuto

opinion [əpínjən] N opinión *f*

opium [ópiəm] N opio *m*

opossum [əpásəm] N zarigüeya *f*

opponent [əpónənt] N opositor -ora *mf*, contrincante *mf*, adversario -ria *mf*

opportune [apə-tún] ADJ oportuno

opportunistic [apə-tunístɪk] ADJ oportunista, aprovechado

opportunity [apə-túnɪdi] N oportunidad *f*, ocasión *f*

oppose [əpóz] VI/VT oponer(se)

opposing [əpóʒən] ADJ opuesto, contrario; **— thumb** pulgar oponible *m*

opposite [ápəzɪt] ADJ (contrary) opuesto, contrario; **— frente a**; PREP frente a, en frente de; N contrario *m*, opuesto *m*; ADV en frente

opposition [apəzíʃən] N oposición *f*; **they met with little —** encontraron poca resistencia

oppress [əprés] VT oprimir

oppression [əpréʃən] N opresión *f*

oppressive [əprésɪv] ADJ (harsh) opresivo; (heat) bochornoso, sofocante

oppressor [əprésə-] N opresor -ra *mf*

optic [áptɪk] ADJ óptico; N **—s** óptica *f*

optical [áptɪkəl] ADJ óptico; **— fiber** fibra óptica *f*; **— illusion** ilusión óptica *f*

optician [aptíʃən] N óptico -ca *mf*

optimism [áptəmɪzəm] N optimismo *m*

optimist [áptəmɪst] N optimista *mf*

optimistic [aptəmístɪk] ADJ optimista

option [ápʃən] N opción *f* (also financial); (feature) extra *m*; **to leave one's —s open** no descartar posibilidades

optional [ápʃənəl] ADJ opcional, optativo

optometry [aptámɪtri] N optometría *f*

opulence [ápjələns] N opulencia *f*

opulent [ápjələnt] ADJ opulento

or [ɔr] CONJ o; **seven — eight** siete u ocho

oracle [ɔ́rəkəl] N oráculo *m*

oral [ɔ́rəl] ADJ oral; (hygiene) bucal

orange [ɔ́rɪndʒ] N naranja *f*; **— blossom** azahar *m*; **— grove** naranjal *m*; **— tree** naranjo *m*; ADJ anaranjado

orangutan [ərǽŋətæn] N orangután *m*

orator [ɔ́rəɒ̀ɚ] N orador -ra *mf*
oratory [ɔ́rətɔri] N (skill in speaking) oratoria *f*; (place for prayer) oratorio *m*
orbit [ɔ́rbɪt] N órbita *f*; VI/VT orbitar
orbital [ɔ́rbɪdəł] ADJ orbital
orbiter [ɔ́rbɪdɚ] N orbitador *m*
orchard [ɔ́rtʃɚd] N huerto *m*; (large) huerta *f*
orchestra [ɔ́rkɪstrə] N orquesta *f*
orchestrate [ɔ́rkɪstret] VT orquestar
orchid [ɔ́rkɪd] N orquídea *f*
ordain [ɔrdén] VT (as minister) ordenar; (with an edict) decretar
ordeal [ɔrdíł] N suplicio *m*, tortura *f*; — **by fire** ordalía de fuego *f*
order [ɔ́rdɚ] N (command) orden *f*, mandato *m*; (request, commission) pedido *m*; (obedience to law, sequence, regime) orden *m*; **holy —s** órdenes sagradas *f pl*; **an apology is in —** corresponde una disculpa; **in — to** para; **in working —** en buen estado; **in — that** para que, a fin de que; **to the — of** a la orden de; **out of —** no funciona; **to put in —** ordenar; VI/VT (command, arrange) ordenar, mandar; (ask for) pedir
orderly [ɔ́rdɚli] ADJ ordenado; N (military) ordenanza *m*; (hospital) camillero *m*
ordinal [ɔ́rdnəł] ADJ ordinal
ordinance [ɔ́rdnəns] N ordenanza *f*
ordinary [ɔ́rdneri] ADJ común, corriente, ordinario; **do it the — way** hazlo de la forma habitual
ore [ɔr] N mineral *m*
oregano [ərégəno] N orégano *m*
organ [ɔ́rgən] N órgano *m* (also musical instrument)
organic [ɔrgǽnɪk] ADJ orgánico; **— chemistry** química orgánica *f*
organism [ɔ́rgənɪzm] N organismo *m*
organist [ɔ́rgənɪst] N organista *mf*
organization [ɔrgənɪzéʃən] N organización *f*
organize [ɔ́rgənaɪz] VI/VT organizar(se)
organizer [ɔ́rgənaɪzɚ] N organizador -ra *mf*
orgy [ɔ́rdʒi] N orgía *f*
orient [ɔ́riant] N oriente *m*; [ɔ́rient] VT orientar
oriental [ɔriéntł] ADJ & N oriental *mf*
orientate [ɔ́rientet] VT orientar
orientation [ɔrientéʃən] N (guidance) orientación *f*; (tendency, leaning) tendencia *f*
orifice [ɔ́rəfɪs] N orificio *m*
origin [ɔ́rədʒɪn] N origen *m*; (of a river) naciente *f*, nacimiento *m*
original [ərídʒənəł] ADJ & N original *m*
originality [ərɪdʒənǽlɪɾi] N originalidad *f*
originate [ərídʒənet] VI/VT originar(se)

oriole [ɔ́rioł] N oropéndola *f*
Orlon™ [ɔ́rlɑn] N orlón *m*
ornament [ɔ́rnəmənt] N adorno *m*, ornamento *m*; [ɔ́rnəmɛnt] VT adornar, ornamentar
ornamental [ɔrnəméntł] ADJ ornamental
ornate [ɔrnét] ADJ adornado en exceso; **— style** estilo rebuscado *m*
ornithology [ɔrnəθálədʒi] N ornitología *f*
orphan [ɔ́rfən] ADJ & N huérfano -na *mf*; VT dejar huérfano a
orphanage [ɔ́rfənɪdʒ] N orfanato *m*, hospicio *m*
orthodontics [ɔrθədántɪks] N ortodoncia *f*
orthodox [ɔ́rθədaks] ADJ ortodoxo
orthography [ɔrθágrəfi] N ortografía *f*
oscillate [ásəlet] VI oscilar; VT hacer oscilar
oscillation [asəléʃən] N oscilación *f*
osmosis [azmósɪs] N ósmosis *f*
osprey [áspre] N águila pescadora *f*
ostensible [asténsəbəł] ADJ aparente
ostentation [astentéʃən] N ostentación *f*
ostentatious [astentéʃəs] ADJ ostentoso
osteoporosis [astiopərósɪs] N osteoporosis *f*
ostracize [ástrəsaɪz] VT aislar
ostrich [ástrɪtʃ] N avestruz *m*
other [Áðɚ] ADJ, PRON & N otro -tra *mf*; **— than Bob** salvo Bob; **every — day** cada dos días, un día sí y otro no; **—wise** de otro modo; **—worldly** fantástico
otter [ádɚ] N nutria *f*
ouch [autʃ] INTERJ ¡ay!
ought [ɔt] V AUX **you — to sit down** deberías sentarte; **we — to get up early** deberíamos levantarnos más temprano
ounce [auns] N onza *f*
our [aur] POSS ADJ nuestro
ours [aurz] ADJ nuestro; **this book is —** este libro es nuestro; **these things are —** estas cosas son nuestras; PRON el nuestro; **— is bigger** el nuestro/la nuestra es más grande; **a friend of —** un amigo nuestro
ourselves [aursélvz] PRON **we made the cake —** nosotros mismos hicimos la torta; **we were sitting by —** estábamos sentados solos; **we look at — in the mirror** nos miramos en el espejo; **we bought — a house** nos compramos una casa
oust [aust] VT echar, expulsar
out [aut] ADV (outside) fuera; ADJ (turned off, extinguished) apagado; INTERJ ¡fuera! N escape *m*; VT (expel) expulsar; (expose) descubrir; VI **the truth will —** se descubrirá la verdad; PREP **she ran — the door** salió corriendo por la puerta; **they locked me —** me dejaron fuera; **— and**

— **criminal** criminal empedernido *f*; — **and** — **refusal** una negativa rotunda; — **of commission / order** fuera de servicio; —**-of-date** pasado de moda, anticuado; — **of fashion** pasado de moda; — **of fear** por miedo; — **of joint** dislocado; — **of money** sin dinero; — **of print / stock** agotado; — **of touch with** desconectado de; — **of tune** desentonado; — **of work** desempleado; **made** — of hecho de; **miniskirts are on the way** — las minifaldas se están dejando de usar; **I had it** — **with him** me peleé con él; **you were** — no estabas; **before the week is** — antes de que termine la semana; **the book is just** — acaba de publicarse el libro; **the secret is** — se ha divulgado el secreto; **we had some, but now we're** — teníamos, pero se nos acabó; **I'm** — $10 perdí $10

outage [áutidʒ] N apagón *m*

outbreak [áutbrek] N (of pimples) erupción *f*; (of war) comienzo *m*; (of disease) brote *m*

outburst [áutbə-st] N (emotional) arrebato *m*; (of tears) ataque *m*; (of violence) motín *m*, explosión *f*

outcast [áutkæst] ADJ & N marginado -da *mf*

outcome [áutkʌm] N resultado *m*

outcry [áutkraɪ] N clamor *m*, protesta *f*

outdated [autdéDɪd] ADJ anticuado

outdoor [áutdɔr] ADJ al aire libre; [autdɔ́rz] ADV —**s** al aire libre, afuera

outer [áuDə-] ADJ exterior; — **ear** oído externo *m*; — **space** espacio exterior *m*

outfit [áutfɪt] N (gear) equipo *m*; (clothes) conjunto *m*; (soldiers) unidad *f*; VI/VT equipar, habilitar

outfox [autfáks] VT ser más listo que

outgoing [áutgoɪŋ] ADJ (leaving) saliente; [autgóɪŋ] (extrovert) extrovertido

outgrow [autgró] VT **she will** — **her clothes** le quedará la ropa pequeña; **she will** — **her epilepsy** la epilepsia se le irá con la edad

outing [áuDɪŋ] N excursión *f*, paseo *m*

outlandish [autlǽndɪʃ] ADJ estrafalario

outlast [autlǽst] VT (last longer than) durar más que; (live longer than) sobrevivir a

outlaw [áutlɔ] N bandido -da *mf*, forajido -da *mf*; VT prohibir

outlay [áutle] N gasto *m*, desembolso *m*; [autlé] VT gastar, desembolsar

outlet [áutlɛt] N (exit) salida *f*; (stream) desagüe *m*, emisario *m*; (store) tienda *f*; (electric connection) toma de corriente *f*; **she needs an** — **for her talent** necesita canalizar su talento

outline [áutlaɪn] N (abstract) bosquejo *m*, esbozo *m*, trazado *m*; (boundary) contorno *m*; VT (summarize) bosquejar, esbozar; (draw) delinear; (plan) trazar

outlook [áutluk] N perspectiva *f*, panorama *m*

outlying [áutlaɪɪŋ] ADJ (marginal) periférico; (distant) remoto

output [áutput] N (production) rendimiento *m*; (computer information) salida *f*

outrage [áutredʒ] N (offense) ultraje *m*, agravio *m*, atropello *m*; (indignation) indignación *f*; VT (offend) ultrajar, agraviar; (enrage) indignar

outrageous [autrédʒəs] ADJ (offensive) ultrajante; (exorbitant) exorbitante; (extravagant) extravagante

outreach [áutritʃ] N extensión *f*; [autrítʃ] VT exceder

outright [autráɪt] ADV completamente; **he bought it** — lo compró al contado; **he rejected it** — lo rechazó categóricamente; [áutraɪt] ADJ — **denial** negativa rotunda *f*; — **lie** mentira descarada *f*

outset [áutsɛt] N comienzo *m*, principio *m*

outshine [autʃáɪn] VT eclipsar

outside [autsáɪd] ADV fuera, afuera; PREP fuera de; [áutsaɪd] ADJ (external) exterior; (foreign) foráneo; N exterior *m*; — **chance** posibilidad remota *f*; **in a week, at the** — en una semana, a lo sumo; **to close on the** — cerrar por fuera

outsider [autsáɪDə-] N forastero -ra *mf*

outskirts [áutskə-ts] N alrededores *m pl*, afueras *f pl*

outspoken [autspókən] ADJ franco

outstanding [autstǽndɪŋ] ADJ (excellent) sobresaliente, destacado; (pending) pendiente

outstretched [autstrétʃt] ADJ extendido

outward [áutwə-d] ADJ exterior, externo; — **appearances** apariencias *f pl*; ADV hacia fuera; — **bound** que sale

outweigh [autwé] VT (weigh more) pesar más que; (be more important) sobreponerse a, valer más que

outwit [autwít] VT ser más listo que

oval [óvəɫ] ADJ oval, ovalado; N óvalo *m*

ovary [óvəri] N ovario *m*

ovation [ovéʃən] N ovación *f*

oven [ávən] N horno *m*

over [óvə-] PREP — **here** acá; — **in Japan** allá en Japón; — **many years** durante muchos años; — **the sea** al otro lado del mar; — **the hill** viejo; — **there** allá; **an**

umbrella — his head un paraguas sobre la cabeza; **I heard it — the radio** lo oí por la radio; **he jumped — the fence** saltó por encima de la cerca; **he is — her in the hierarchy** él está por encima de ella en la jerarquía; **not — one year** no más de un año; **he hit him — the head with a rock** le golpeó en la cabeza con una piedra; **all — the city** por toda la ciudad; ADV — **again** de nuevo, otra vez; — **against** en contraste con; — **and —** una y otra vez; —**generous** demasiado generoso; **do it —** hazlo de nuevo, hazlo otra vez; **the world —** por todo el mundo; **it is — with** se acabó; INTERJ — **and out** cambio y fuera

overactive [ovəǽktɪv] ADJ hiperactivo, demasiado activo

overall [ovəɔ́ɫ] ADJ global, total; —**s** mono *m*, overol *m*

overbearing [ovəbérɪŋ] ADJ mandón -ona, dominante

overboard [óvəbɔrd] ADV (into the water) al agua; **she went — on her project** se le fue la mano con su proyecto

overcast [óvəkæst] ADJ nublado, encapotado; **to become —** nublarse, encapotarse

overcharge [ovətʃárʤ] VI/VT cobrar demasiado

overcoat [óvəkot] N sobretodo *m*, gabán *m*

overcome [ovəkám] VI/VT (to get the better of) superar; (to overwhelm) embargar; **to be — by weariness** estar agobiado

overdose [óvədos] N sobredosis *f*; VI tomar una sobredosis

overdraft [óvədræft] N sobregiro *m*, descubierto *m*

overdraw [ovədrɔ́] VI/VT sobregirar(se)

overdrawn [ovədrɔ́n] ADJ en descubierto, sobregirado

overdrive [óvədraɪv] N superdirecta *f*

overdue [ovədú] ADJ (borrowed item) atrasado; (bill) vencido

overeat [ovəít] VI comer en exceso

overexcite [ovərɪksáɪt] VT sobreexcitar

overflow [ovəfló] VI desbordarse, rebosar; [óvəflo] N desborde *m*

overgrown [ovəgrón] ADJ cubierto, crecido; — **boy** muchacho demasiado crecido para su edad *m*

overhang [ovəhǽŋ] VI (jut) proyectarse; (hang over) estar suspendido; [óvəhæŋ] N saliente *m*

overhaul [ovəhɔ́ɫ] VT revisar; [óvəhɔɫ] N revisión *f*

overhead [óvəhed] N gastos generales *mf*; ADJ elevado; — **projector** retroproyector

m; [ovəhéd] ADV en lo alto

overhear [ovəhír] VT oír por casualidad

overkill [óvəkɪɫ] N exageración *f*

overland [óvəlænd] ADV & ADJ por tierra

overlap [ovəlǽp] VI/VT solapar(se), superponer(se); [óvəlæp] N traslapo *m*

overlay [ovəlé] VT cubrir; (with gold, etc.) incrustar; [óvəle] N cubierta *f*; (with metal, wood) revestimiento *m*, chapa *f*

overload [ovəlód] VT sobrecargar, recargar, saturar; [óvəlod] N sobrecarga *f*

overlook [ovəlúk] VT (fail to mention) pasar por alto, omitir; (pardon) perdonar; (look from above) mirar desde arriba; (afford a view of) dar a, tener vista a; [óvəluk] N mirador *m*

overly [óvəli] ADV excesivamente

overnight [óvənaɪt] ADJ — **delivery** entrega al otro día *f*; — **guest** invitado -da a dormir *mf*; [ovənáɪt] ADV **he succeeded — tuvo éxito de la noche a la mañana

overpass [óvəpæs] N paso elevado *m*

overpower [ovəpáʊə] VT vencer

overqualified [ovəkwáləfaɪd] ADJ sobrecalificado

overreach [ovərítʃ] VI **to — oneself** abarcar demasiado

overreact [ovəriǽkt] VI reaccionar exageradamente

override [ovəráɪd] VT anular

overrule [ovərúɫ] VT anular

overrun [ovərán] VT (overflow) desbordarse; (exceed) exceder; (invade) infestar; [óvərʌn] N exceso *m*

overseas [ovəsíz] ADV (beyond the sea) en ultramar; (abroad) en el extranjero

oversee [ovəsí] VI dirigir, supervisar

overseer [óvəsir] N capataz -za *mf*, supervisor -ra *mf*

overshadow [ovəʃǽdo] VT eclipsar, opacar

overshoe [óvəʃu] N chanclo *m*

oversight [óvəsaɪt] N (mistake) descuido *m*; (act of overseeing) supervisión *f*

overstep [ovəstép] VT excederse en

overt [ovə́t] ADJ evidente

overtake [ovəték] VT (pass someone) pasar, rebasar; (befall) abatirse sobre

overtax [ovətǽks] VT (tax too much) gravar excesivamente; (demand too much) exigir demasiado

overthrow [ovəθró] VT derrocar, derribar; [óvəθro] N derrocamiento *m*

overtime [óvətaɪm] N (at work) horas extras *f pl*; (in a game) prórroga *f*; **to work —** hacer horas extras

overture [óvətʃə] N (musical composition) obertura *f*; (initial move) propuesta *f*

overturn [ovəˈtɜ́n] VI/VT volcar(se); VT (a decision) anular; (a government) derrocar

overview [óvəvju] N vista global f, panorama m

overweight [ovəwét] ADJ **he's** — pesa demasiado; [óvəwet] N sobrepeso m

overwhelm [ovəhwɛ́lm] VT abrumar, agobiar

overwhelming [ovəhwɛ́lmɪŋ] ADJ (responsibility, task) abrumador, agobiante; (victory) arrollador

overwork [ovəwɜ́k] VI trabajar demasiado; VT hacer trabajar demasiado; [óvəwɜk] N exceso de trabajo m

ovulate [ávjəlet] VI ovular

owe [o] VI/VT deber; (a sum) adeudar, deber

owing [óɪŋ] ADJ debido; **— to** debido a

owl [aʊl] N lechuza f, búho m

own [on] ADJ & PRON propio; **a house of his —** una casa suya; **to be on one's —** ser independiente; **to come into one's —** conseguir lo que uno se merece; **to hold one's —** mantenerse firme; VT poseer; **to — up (to)** confesar

owner [ónə] N dueño -ña mf, propietario -ria mf

ownership [ónəʃɪp] N propiedad f

ox [aks] N buey m

oxidize [áksɪdaɪz] VI/VT oxidar(se)

oxygen [áksɪdʒən] N oxígeno m; **— tent** cámara de oxígeno f

oyster [ɔ́ɪstə] N ostra f; (large) ostión m

ozone [ózon] N ozono m; **— layer** capa de ozono f

Pp

pace [pes] N paso m; VT (traverse) ir y venir por; (set the pace) marcar al paso; (measure) medir a pasos; **—maker** marcapasos m sg

pacific [pəsífɪk] ADJ pacífico; **— Ocean** Océano Pacífico m

pacifier [pǽsəfaɪə] N chupete m

pacifism [pǽsəfɪzəm] N pacifismo m

pacify [pǽsəfaɪ] VT (a country) pacificar; (a person) apaciguar

pack [pæk] N (of wolves) manada f; (of dogs) jauría f; (of cigarettes) cajilla f, cajetilla f; (of cloth) compresa f; (of cards) baraja f; (of cyclists) pelotón m; **— animal** acémila f, bestia de carga f; **a — of lies** una sarta de mentiras; VT empacar, empaquetar; (carry a gun) portar; (crowd) atestar; (load) cargar; **to — off** despachar; **to — one's bags** hacer las maletas; **— rat** rata urraca f; (person who saves everything) urraca f

package [pǽkɪdʒ] N paquete m (also organized vacation); VT (gift) empaquetar; (food) envasar; (in advertising) presentar

packer [pǽkə] N empacador -ra mf, embalador -ra mf

packet [pǽkɪt] N paquete m; (of soup) sobre m

packing [pǽkɪŋ] N embalaje m (also cushioning material)

pact [pækt] N pacto m

pad [pæd] N (cushion) almohadilla f (also for ink); (block of paper) bloc m; (for aircraft) pista f; (for spacecraft) plataforma de lanzamiento f; VT (stuff with padding) acolchar; (add to dishonestly) rellenar

padding [pǽdɪŋ] N relleno m; (cotton) guata f; (of a speech) ripio m

paddle [pǽdl] N (for rowing) pala f, remo m; (for mixing, beating, ping-pong) paleta f; **— wheel** rueda de paleta f; VI remar; VT hacer avanzar remando; (hit) dar una paletada

paddock [pǽdək] N (field) prado m; (enclosure at racetrack) paddock m

padlock [pǽdlak] N candado m; VT cerrar con candado

pagan [pégən] ADJ & N pagano -na mf

paganism [pégənɪzəm] N paganismo m

page [pedʒ] N (sheet) hoja f, página f; (boy servant) paje m; (hotel employee) botones m sg; VT (number pages) paginar; (call) llamar por altavoz; Mex vocear; **to — through** hojear

pageant [pǽdʒənt] N (parade) desfile m; (show) espectáculo m

pail [pel] N balde m, cubeta f

pain [pen] N dolor m; (suffering) sufrimiento m; **—killer** analgésico m; **—staking** esmerado; **on — of** so pena de; **to take —s** esmerarse; **he's a —** es un chinche; VT (physical) doler; (mental) apenar

painful [pénfəl] ADJ (hurting) doloroso; (distressing) penoso; (difficult) arduo

painless [pénlɪs] ADJ sin dolor, indoloro

paint [pent] N (substance) pintura f; (spotted horse) pinto m; **—brush** (for art) pincel m; (for a house) brocha f; VI/VT pintar; **to — the town red** irse de juerga

painter [péntə] N pintor -ra mf

painting [péntɪŋ] N pintura f

pair [pɛr] N par m; (married couple) pareja f; (span) yunta f; **a — of scissors** unas tijeras, una tijera; VI/VT aparear(se), emparejar(se); **to — off** aparearse

pajamas [pədʒáməz] N pijama/piyama *mf*

Pakistan [pǽkɪstæn] N Paquistán *m*

Pakistani [pækɪstǽni] ADJ & N paquistano -na *mf*

pal [pæl] N compañero -ra *mf*, compadre *m*, comadre *f*

palace [pǽlɪs] N palacio *m*

palate [pǽlɪt] N paladar *m*

palatial [pəléʃəl] ADJ suntuoso

Palau [pəláu] N Paláu *m*

pale [peł] ADJ pálido, macilento; **beyond the — grosero; VI palidecer

paleness [péłnɪs] N palidez *f*

paleontology [peliəntáləʤi] N paleontología *f*

palette [pǽlɪt] N paleta *f*

palisade [pælɪséd] N empalizada *f*; **—s** acantilados *m pl*

pall [pɔł] VT (cover with a cloth) cubrir con un paño mortuorio; (satiate) hartar; VI cansar; N paño mortuorio *m*; **—bearer** portador del féretro *m*; **to cast a — on** empañar

pallid [pǽlɪd] ADJ pálido

pallor [pǽlɚ] N palidez *f*

palm [pɑm] N (part of hand) palma *f*; (tree) palmera *f*, palma *f*; **— Sunday** Domingo de Ramos *m*; VT (hide in palm) escamotear; **to — something off on someone** encajar algo a alguien

palpable [pǽłpəbəł] ADJ (perceptible) palpable; (tangible) tangible

palpitate [pǽłpɪtet] VI palpitar

palpitation [pæłpɪtéʃən] N palpitación *f*

paltry [pɔ́łtri] ADJ miserable, despreciable

pamper [pǽmpɚ] VT mimar, consentir

pamphlet [pǽmflɪt] N (informative) folleto *m*; (political) panfleto *m*

pan [pæn] N (for boiling) cazuela *f*, cacerola *f*; (for frying) sartén *f*; (for baking) molde *m*; **—handle** mango de sartén *m*; **—handler** pordiosero -ra *mf*; VT criticar duramente; VI **to — for gold** extraer oro; **to — out** dar buen resultado; **to —handle** mendigar, pordiosear

panacea [pænəsíə] N panacea *f*

Panama [pǽnəmɑ] N Panamá *f*

Panamanian [pænəméniən] ADJ & N panameño -ña *mf*

Pan-American [pænəmérɪkən] ADJ panamericano

pancake [pǽnkek] N panqueque *m*; **flat as a — chato como una tabla

pancreas [pǽnkriəs] N páncreas *m*

panda [pǽndə] N panda *f*

pander [pǽndɚ] VI consentir

pane [pen] N vidrio *m*, cristal *m*

panel [pǽnəł] N (wall, group of persons) panel *m*; (of instruments) tablero *m*; VT revestir con paneles

pang [pæŋ] N (sharp pain, hunger) punzada *f*; (anguish) remordimientos *m pl*

panic [pǽnɪk] ADJ & N pánico *m*; **—stricken** sobrecogido de pánico

panorama [pænərǽmə] N panorama *m*

panoramic [pænərǽmɪk] ADJ panorámico

pansy [pǽnzi] N (flower) pensamiento *m*

pant [pænt] VI jadear; **to — out** decir jadeando

panther [pǽnθɚ] N pantera *f*

panties [pǽntiz] N *Sp* bragas *f pl*; *Mex* pantaletas *f pl*; *RP* bombacha *f*

pantomime [pǽntəmaɪm] N pantomima *f*

pantry [pǽntri] N despensa *f*, alacena *f*

pants [pænts] N pantalones *m pl*, pantalón *m*

pantyhose [pǽntihoz] N panty *m*

papa [pápə] N papá *m*

papacy [pépəsi] N papado *m*

papaya [pəpáɪə] N papaya *f*; *Cuba* fruta bomba *f*

paper [pépɚ] N (material) papel *m*; (newspaper) periódico *m*; (assignment) trabajo *m*; (oral learned contribution) comunicación *f*; (written learned contribution) artículo *m*; **—back** libro en rústica *m*; **— clip** clip *m*, sujetapapeles *m sg*; **— cutter** guillotina *f*; **— money** papel moneda *m*; **—s** papeles *m pl*; **— shredder** trituradora *f*; **—weight** pisapapeles *m sg*; **—work** trámites *m pl*; **on —** por escrito; VI/VT empapelar

paprika [pæpríkə] N pimentón *m*, páprika *f*

Papua New Guinea [pǽpjuənugíni] N Papúa Nueva Guinea *f*

Papua New Guinean [pǽpjuənugíniən] ADJ & N papú *mf*

par [pɑr] N (financial) paridad *f*; (in golf) par *m*; **at —** a la par; **below —** bajo par; **to be on a — with** estar en pie de igualdad con; **to feel above —** sentirse mejor que lo normal; VT hacer el par

parachute [pérəʃut] N paracaídas *m sg*

parachutist [pérəʃutɪst] N paracaidista *mf*

parade [pəréd] N (procession) desfile *m*; (military review) parada *f*; **— ground** campo de maniobras *m*; **to make a — of** ostentar, hacer ostentación de; VI desfilar; VT hacer ostentación de

paradigm [pérədaɪm] N paradigma *m*

paradise [pérədaɪs] N paraíso *m*

paradox [pérədɑks] N paradoja *f*

paradoxical [pærədɑ́ksɪkəł] ADJ paradójico

paraffin [pérəfɪn] N parafina *f*

paragraph [pǽrəgræf] N párrafo *m*; VT dividir en párrafos

Paraguay [pǽrəgwaɪ] N Paraguay *m*

Paraguayan [pærəgwáɪən] ADJ & N paraguayo -ya *mf*

parakeet [pǽrəkit] N perico *m*, periquito *m*

parallel [pǽrəlɛł] ADJ & N paralelo *m*; (geometry) paralela *f*; VT (run equidistant from) correr paralelo a; (compare) comparar

paralysis [pərǽləsɪs] N (of the body) parálisis *f*; (of a transportation system) paralización *f*

paralyze [pǽrəlaɪz] VT paralizar

paramedic [pærəmɛ́dɪk] ADJ & N paramédico -ca *mf*

parameter [pərǽmɪdɚ] N parámetro *m*

paramilitary [pærəmílɪteri] ADJ & N paramilitar *mf*

paramount [pǽrəmaunt] ADJ supremo, sumo

paranoia [pærənɔ́ɪə] N paranoia *f*

paranoid [pǽrənɔɪd] ADJ & N paranoico -ca *mf*; — **delusion** delirio paranoico *m*

paranormal [pærənɔ́rməł] ADJ paranormal

paraphernalia [pærəfənéljə] N parafernalia *f*

paraphrase [pǽrəfrez] N paráfrasis *f*; VI/VT parafrasear

parapsychology [pærəsaɪkáləʤi] N parapsicología *f*

parasite [pǽrəsaɪt] N parásito *m*

parasol [pǽrəsɔł] N parasol *m*, sombrilla *f*

paratroops [pǽrətrups] N tropas paracaidistas *f pl*

parcel [pɑ́rsəł] N (package) paquete *m*; (lot) partida *f*; (land) parcela *f*; — **post** paquete postal *m*; VT (land) parcelar; **to — out** repartir

parch [pɑrtʃ] VT secar; **I'm —ed** estoy muerto de sed

parchment [pɑ́rtʃmənt] N pergamino *m*

pardon [pɑ́rdn̩] N perdón *m*, gracia *f*; (legal) indulto *m*; **I beg your —** perdone; VT perdonar, disculpar; (legally) indultar

pare [per] VT mondar, pelar; **to — down expenditures** reducir gastos

parent [pérənt] N padre *m*, madre *f*; **—s** padres *m pl*

parental [pərɛ́ntl̩] ADJ parental

parenthesis [pərɛ́nθəsɪs] N paréntesis *m*

pariah [pəráɪə] N paria *mf*

parish [pǽrɪʃ] N parroquia *f*; — **priest** (cura) párroco *m*

parishioner [pəríʃənɚ] N feligrés -esa *mf*, parroquiano -na *mf*

parity [pǽrɪdi] N paridad *f*

park [pɑrk] N parque *m*; (for baseball) estadio de béisbol *m*; VI/VT estacionar, aparcar

parking [pɑ́rkɪŋ] N estacionamiento *m*, aparcamiento *m*; — **lot** estacionamiento *m*, aparcamiento *m*; — **place** lugar de estacionamiento/aparcamiento *m*

parlance [pɑ́rləns] N habla *f*

parley [pɑ́rli] N (peace negotiation) parlamento *m*; (discussion) discusión *f*; VI parlamentar

parliament [pɑ́rləmənt] N parlamento *m*

parliamentary [pɑrləmɛ́ntri] ADJ parlamentario

parlor [pɑ́rlɚ] N sala *f*, salón *m*; — **game** juego de salón *m*; **beauty —** salón de belleza *m*

parochial [pərókiəł] ADJ (of a parish) parroquial; (provincial) pueblerino

parody [pǽrədi] N parodia *f*; VT parodiar

parole [pərół] N libertad condicional *f*; VT poner en libertad condicional

parrot [pǽrət] N loro *m*, papagayo *m*; VT repetir como loro

parry [pǽri] VT (a blow) parar; (a remark) eludir; N parada *f*

parsley [pɑ́rsli] N perejil *m*

parsnip [pɑ́rsnɪp] N chirivía *f*

parson [pɑ́rsən] N pastor *m*

part [pɑrt] N (component) parte *f*; (role) papel *m*; (in hair) raya *f*; — **and parcel** parte esencial *f*; —**-time** a tiempo parcial; **in foreign —s** en el extranjero; **spare —s** piezas de repuesto *f pl*, repuestos *m pl*; VI/VT (cut into parts) partir(se); (divide into parts) dividir(se); (separate, leave) separar(se); (apportion) repartir(se); **to — company** separarse; **to — one's hair** hacerse la raya; **to — with** desprenderse de

partake [pɑrték] VI **to — in** participar; **to — of** (share) compartir; (eat) comer

partial [pɑ́rʃəł] ADJ parcial

participant [pɑrtísəpənt] ADJ & N participante *mf*, partícipe *mf*

participate [pɑrtísəpet] VI participar

participation [pɑrtɪsəpéʃən] N participación *f*

participle [pɑ́rdɪsɪpəł] N participio *m*

particle [pɑ́rdɪkəł] N partícula *f*; — **board** aglomerado *m*

particular [pətíkjələ‑] ADJ particular; (fussy) quisquilloso; N **—s** particulares *m pl*; **in —** en particular

parting [pɑ́rdɪŋ] N (farewell) despedida *f*; (separation) separación *f*; — **of the ways** encrucijada *f*

partisan [pɑ́rdɪzan] N (supporter) partidario -ria *mf*; (guerrilla) partisano -na *mf*; ADJ (of supporters) partidario; (of guerrillas) de partisanos

partition [pɑrtíʃən] N (distribution) reparto *m*; (division) división *f*; (wall) tabique *m*, mampara *f*; VT (distribute) repartir; (divide) dividir; (divide with a wall) tabicar

partly [pártli] ADV en parte

partner [pártnɚ] N (in business) socio -cia *mf*; (in an activity) compañero -ra *mf*; (in dancing, sports, marriage) pareja *f*

partnership [pártnɚʃɪp] N (business) sociedad *f*; (relationship) asociación *f*

partridge [pártrɪdʒ] N perdiz *f*

party [párdi] N (get-together) fiesta *f*; (political group) partido *m*; (group of people) partida *f*; (litigant) parte *f*; **— of four** mesa para cuatro *f*; **— animal** fiestero -ra *mf*, parrandero -ra *mf*

pass [pæs] VI/VT pasar; (a law) aprobar; (an exam, test) aprobar, superar; **to — away** fallecer; **to — for** pasar por; **to — in review** pasar revista; **to — judgment** juzgar; **to — on** (die) fallecer; (approve) aceptar; (refuse) no querer; **to — oneself off as** hacerse pasar por; **to — out** desmayarse; **to — over** no tener en cuenta; **to — up an opportunity** perderse una oportunidad; **he —ed a kidney stone** expulsó un cálculo renal; **— me the salt** pásame la sal, alcánzame la sal; N (road through mountains) paso *m*; (motion, permission) pase *m*; (for transportation) abono *m*; (over a surface) pasada *f*; (on an exam) aprobación *f*; (difficult event) trance *m*; **—key** llave maestra *f*; **—port** pasaporte *m*; **—word** contraseña *f*, clave de seguridad *f*; **he made a — at her** trató de ligar con ella

passable [pǽsəbəl] ADJ (penetrable) transitable; (mediocre) pasable

passage [pǽsɪdʒ] N (fare, musical or textual phrase, alley) pasaje *m*; (passing of time) paso *m*, transcurso *m*; (hallway in a house) pasillo *m*; (secret pathway) pasadizo *m*; (crossing) travesía *f*; (approval of a bill) aprobación *f*; **—way** (corridor) corredor *m*, pasillo *m*; (alley) pasaje *m*

passenger [pǽsəndʒɚ] N pasajero -ra *mf*

passerby [pǽsɚbaɪ] N transeúnte *mf*, viandante *mf*

passing [pǽsɪŋ] ADJ **each — day** cada día que pasa; **a — grade** una nota de aprobado; **a — fancy** un capricho pasajero; **a — mention** una mención al pasar

passion [pǽʃən] N pasión *f*

passionate [pǽʃənɪt] ADJ apasionado

passive [pǽsɪv] ADJ pasivo; N pasiva *f*

past [pæst] ADJ pasado; **— participle** participio pasado *m*; **— perfect** pluscuamperfecto *m*; **— precedents** precedentes anteriores *m pl*; **— tense** tiempo pretérito *m*; **the — president** el expresidente; PREP **— hope** más allá de toda esperanza; **— noon** después de mediodía; **the house — the store** la casa pasando la tienda; **we went — the tower** pasamos al lado de la torre; **half — two** las dos y media; **a woman — forty** una mujer de más de cuarenta años; ADV **for some time —** desde hace algún tiempo; **they drove —** pasaron en coche; N (time) pasado *m*; (tense) pretérito *m*

pasta [pástə] N pasta *f*

paste [pest] N (soft material, purée) pasta *f*; (glue) engrudo *m*; **—board** cartón *m*; VT pegar

pastel [pæstɛl] ADJ & N pastel *m*

pasteurize [pǽstʃəraɪz] VT pasterizar / pasteurizar

pastime [pǽstaɪm] N pasatiempo *m*

pastor [pástɚ] N pastor -ra *mf*

pastoral [pǽstɚəl] ADJ (literary) pastoril; (ecclesiastical) pastoral; N pastoral *f*; (literary work) égloga *f*

pastry [péstri] N (in general) pastelería *f*; (specific) pastel *m*; **— cook** pastelero -ra *mf*, repostero -ra *mf*; **— shop** pastelería *f*, repostería *f*

pasture [pǽstʃɚ] N (grassland) prado *m*; (grass) pasto *m*; (for horses) potrero *m*; VI/VT pastar, pacer, apacentar

pasty [pésti] ADJ pastoso

pat [pæt] ADJ banal; **(down) —** al dedillo; **to stand —** mantenerse firme; VI/VT dar palmaditas (a); N palmadita *f*; **— of butter** porción de mantequilla *f*

patch [pætʃ] N (piece of cloth to repair clothes) remiendo *m*, parche *m* (also for eye); (spot or area, as of ice) tramo (con hielo) *m*; (plot) parcela *f*; VT (repair) remendar; **to — up a quarrel** hacer las paces

patent [pǽtnt] ADJ (evident) patente; (protected by patent) patentado; **— leather** charol *m*; N patente *f*; **— pending** patente en trámite; VT patentar

paternal [pətɚ́nəl] ADJ (fatherly) paternal; (of the father's lineage) paterno

paternity [pətɚ́nɪdi] N paternidad *f*

path [pæθ] N senda *f*, sendero *m*; (of a projectile, storm) trayectoria *f*; **—way** senda *f*, sendero *m*

pathetic [pəθέDɪk] ADJ (moving) patético; (contemptible) lamentable

pathogen [pǽθədʒən] N patógeno *m*

pathology [pæθáləʤi] N patología *f*

pathos [péθɑs] N patetismo *m*

patience [péʃəns] N paciencia *f*

patient [péʃənt] ADJ & N paciente *mf*

patriarch [pétriɑrk] N patriarca *m*

patriarchal [petriárkəl] ADJ patriarcal

patrimony [pǽtrəmoni] N patrimonio *m*

patriot [pétriət] N patriota *mf*

patriotic [petriáDɪk] ADJ patriótico

patriotism [pétriətɪzəm] N patriotismo *m*

patrol [pətróɫ] VI/VT patrullar, rondar; N patrulla *f*, ronda *f*; **— car, — man** patrullero *m*

patron [pétrən] N (customer) cliente -ta *mf*; (benefactor) benefactor -ra *mf*, mecenas *mf*; (saint) patrono *m*

patronage [pétrənɪʤ] N (support of an artist) mecenazgo *m*; (clientele) clientela *f*; (political) clientelismo *m*; **we appreciate your —** agradecemos su preferencia

patronize [pétrənaɪz] VT (be condescending) tratar con condescendencia; (do business with) frecuentar

patter [pǽDɚ] VI (strike lightly) golpetear; (chatter) parlotear; N (small blows) golpeteo *m*; (chatter) parloteo *m*

pattern [pǽDɚn] N (for sewing) molde *m*; (for drawing) plantilla *f*; (of behavior) patrón *m*; VI/VT **to — something after** modelar algo a imitación de, basarse en el modelo de; **to — oneself after** seguir el ejemplo de

paucity [pɔ́sɪDi] N escasez *f*

paunch [pɔntʃ] N panza *f*, barriga *f*

pause [pɔz] N pausa *f*; VI (while talking) hacer pausa; (while moving) detenerse

pave [pev] VT (with asphalt) pavimentar; (with bricks) enladrillar; (with flagstones) enlosar; **to — the way for** preparar el camino para

pavement [pévmənt] N calzada *f*; (of asphalt) pavimento *m*; (of bricks) enladrillado *m*; (of flagstones) enlosado *m*

pavilion [pəvíljən] N pabellón *m*

paw [pɔ] N pata *f*; (with claws) garra *f*; VT (touch with paw) tocar con la pata; (touch with claws) dar zarpazos; (grope) manosear

pawn [pɔn] N (object left in deposit) prenda *f*; (chess piece) peón *m*; (puppet) títere *m*; **—broker** prestamista *mf*; **—shop** casa de empeños *f*, monte de piedad *m*; **in —** en prenda; VT empeñar, dejar en prenda

pay [pe] VT (remit) pagar; VI (be profitable)

ser provechoso, convenir; (be worthwhile) valer la pena; **to — attention** prestar atención, fijarse en; **to — back** (return) restituir; (retaliate) vengarse; **to — a compliment** hacer un cumplido; **to — homage** rendir homenaje; **to — one's respects** saludar; **to — off a debt** cancelar una deuda; **to — a visit** hacer una visita; **to — through the nose** pagar demasiado; **I will — for your meal** te pago la comida; N (payment) pago *m*; (wages) paga *f*, salario *m*; **—back** venganza *f*; **—check** cheque del sueldo *m*; **—day** día de pago *m*; **—load** carga útil *f*; **—off** (pay) pago *m*; (reward) recompensa *f*; (bribe) soborno *m*; **— phone** teléfono público *m*; **—roll** nómina *f*, planilla *f*; **to hit — dirt** encontrar una mina de oro

payable [péəbəɫ] ADJ pagadero

payee [peí] N tenedor -ra *mf*, beneficiario -ria *mf*

payment [pémənt] N pago *m*; **— in full** liquidación *f*

PC [pisí] N (personal computer) PC *m*; (political correctness) lo políticamente correcto; ADJ (politically correct) políticamente correcto

pea [pi] N guisante *m*; *Am* arveja *f*; **—nut** *Sp* cacahuete *m*; *Mex* cacahuate *m*; *Am* maní *m*; **—nut butter** *Sp* crema de cacahuete *f*; *Mex* crema de cacahuate *f*; *Am* manteca / mantequilla de maní *f*

peace [pis] N paz *f*; **— officer** oficial de policía *m*; **at —** en paz; **to keep the —** mantener el orden público; **to hold one's —** callar

peaceful [písfəɫ] ADJ pacífico, tranquilo

peach [pitʃ] N durazno *m*; *Sp* melocotón *m*; (nice thing or person) delicia *f*, monada *f*; **— tree** durazno *m*, duraznero *m*; *Sp* melocotonero *m*

peacock [píkɑk] N pavo real *m*, pavón *m*

peak [pik] N pico *m*, cumbre *f*; (of production, of one's abilities) punto máximo *m*; **— load** carga máxima *f*; **— season** temporada alta *f*; **— time** hora punta *f*

peal [piɫ] N (of bells) repique *m*; (of laughter) carcajada *f*; VI/VT repicar

pear [per] N pera *f*; **— tree** peral *m*

pearl [pɝɫ] N perla *f*; **— necklace** collar de perlas *m*

pearly [pɝ́li] ADJ (color) nacarado, perlado; (with pearls) perlado; **the — Gates** las puertas del cielo

peasant [pézənt] ADJ & N campesino -na *mf*

peat [pit] N turba *f*

pebble [pébəł] N guijarro *m*, piedrecilla *f*; (smooth) canto *m*

pecan [pɪkán] N pacana *f*

peccary [pékəri] N pecarí / pécari *m*

peck [pek] VI/VT (strike with beak) picar; (eat bit by bit) picotear; (kiss) dar un besito; **to — a hole** agujerear a picotazos; N (quick stroke) picotazo *m*; (kiss) besito *m*; (measure) medida de áridos (9 litros) *f*; **you're in a — of trouble** estás metido en un lío

pecking order [pékɪŋɔrdə] N jerarquía *f*

pectoral [péktə-əł] ADJ & N pectoral *m*

peculiar [pɪkjúljə] ADJ peculiar, particular

peculiarity [pɪkjuljénɪdi] N peculiaridad *f*

pedagogue [pédəgag] N pedagogo -ga *mf*

pedagogy [pédəgadʒi] N pedagogía *f*

pedal [pédḷ] N pedal *m*; VI/VT pedalear

pedant [pédṇt] N pedante *mf*

pedantic [pədǽntɪk] ADJ pedante

peddle [pédł] VI/VT ir vendiendo de puerta en puerta; **to — gossip** repartir chismes

peddler [pédlə] N buhonero -ra *mf*, mercachifle *m*

pedestal [pédɪstəł] N pedestal *m*

pedestrian [pədéstriən] N peatón -ona *mf*; ADJ pedestre

pediatrician [pidiətríʃən] N pediatra *mf*

pediatrics [pidiǽtrɪks] N pediatría *f*

pedigree [pédəgri] N (of persons) linaje *m*; (of animals) pedigrí *m*

pee [pi] VI *fam* hacer pipí; N *fam* pipí *m*

peek [pik] VI atisbar; N atisbo *m*

peel [pił] VI/VT (fruit, tree) pelar(se), descortezar(se); (paint) descascarar(se); **to keep one's eyes —ed** mantener los ojos abiertos; N cáscara *f*

peeler [pílə] N pelador *m*

peep [pip] VI/VT (begin to appear) asomar(se); VI (make sound of chicks) piar; **to — at** atisbar; N (look) atisbo *m*; (sound of chicks) pío *m*; **—hole** mirilla *f*

peer [pir] N par *m* (also nobleman); **— group** grupo paritario *m*; VI (look attentively) escudriñar; (peep out) asomar

peerless [pírlɪs] ADJ incomparable, sin par

peeve [piv] VT irritar; **to get —d** ponerse de mal humor; N cosa que irrita *f*

peevish [pívɪʃ] ADJ malhumorado

peg [peg] N percha *f*; (on violin) clavija *f*; **to take a person down a —** bajarle los humos a alguien; VT clavar, clavetear; (price) estabilizar

pejorative [pɪdʒɔ́rədɪv] ADJ peyorativo, despectivo

pelican [pélɪkən] N pelícano *m*

pellet [pélɪt] N (ball) bola *f*, bolita *f*; (shot) perdigón *m*

pell-mell [pélmél] ADJ confuso, tumultuoso; ADV a troche y moche

pelt [pełt] N piel *f*, pellejo *m*; VI/VT acribillar; **to — with stones** apedrear

pelvis [pélvɪs] N pelvis *f*

pen [pen] N (fountain) pluma *f*; (ballpoint) bolígrafo *m*; (for pigs) pocilga *f*; (for sheep) redil *m*; (for cows) corral *m*; **— holder** mango de pluma *m*, portaplumas *m sg*; **— name** seudónimo *m*; VT (write) escribir; (shut in) acorralar, encerrar

penal [pínəł] ADJ penal

penalize [pénəlaɪz] VT penar; (in sports) penalizar

penalty [pénəłti] N (punishment) pena *f*, castigo *m*; (forfeiture) multa *f*; (in sports) penalidad *f*; **— kick** tiro de penalidad *f*, penalty *m*

penance [pénəns] N penitencia *f*

pencil [pénsəł] N (writing instrument) lápiz *m*; (beam of light) haz *m*; **— sharpener** sacapuntas *m sg*

pendant [péndənt] N colgante *m*; ADJ pendiente

pending [péndɪŋ] ADJ pendiente; PREP **— his arrival** hasta que llegue, mientras no llegue

pendulum [péndʒələm] N péndulo *m*

penetrate [pénɪtret] VI/VT penetrar

penetrating [pénɪtredɪŋ] ADJ penetrante

penetration [pénɪtréʃən] N penetración *f*

penguin [péŋgwɪn] N pingüino *m*

penicillin [penɪsílɪn] N penicilina *f*

peninsula [pənínsələ] N península *f*

penis [pínɪs] N pene *m*

penitent [pénɪtənt] ADJ & N penitente *mf*

penitentiary [penɪténʃəri] N penitenciaría *f*, penal *m*

penmanship [pénmənʃɪp] N escritura *f*, caligrafía *f*

pennant [pénənt] N banderín *m*, gallardete *m*

penniless [pénɪlɪs] ADJ pobre, sin dinero

penny [péni] N centavo *m*; **—-pincher** avaro -ra *mf*; **to cost a pretty —** costar un dineral

pension [pénʃən] N (paid to a worker) jubilación *f*; (paid to a worker's survivors) pensión *f*; **— fund** caja de jubilaciones *f*; VT jubilar, pensionar

pensioner [pénʃənə] N pensionista *mf*

pensive [pénsɪv] ADJ pensativo

pent [pent] ADJ encerrado; **—-up** reprimido

pentagon [péntəgɑn] N pentágono *m*

penthouse [pénthaus] N penthouse *m*

penultimate [pɪnʌ́łtəmɪt] ADJ penúltimo

people [pípəł] N gente *f*; (national group)

pueblo *m*; VT poblar
pep [pɛp] N energía *f*; VI **to — up** animar
pepper [pépə] N (black) pimienta *f*; (green) pimiento *m*; (plant, shaker) pimentero *m*; **—mint** menta *f*; VT pimentar; **to — with bullets** acribillar a balazos
peptic [péptɪk] ADJ **— ulcer** úlcera péptica *f*
per [pɝ] PREP (for each) por; (according to) según; **— capita** per capita; **—cent** por ciento; **— diem** viático *m*
percale [pəkél] N percal *m*
perceive [pəsív] VT percibir
percentage [pəséntɪʤ] N porcentaje *m*
percentile [pəséntaɪl] N percentil *m*
perceptible [pəséptəbəl] ADJ perceptible
perception [pəsépʃən] N percepción *f*
perceptive [pəséptɪv] ADJ (pertaining to perception) perceptivo; (having keen perception) perspicaz
perch [pɝtʃ] N (rod for birds) percha *f*; (type of fish) perca *f*; VT posarse; VI/VT (set) encaramar(se)
percolate [pɝkəlet] VI/VT filtrar(se)
percussion [pəkʌʃən] N percusión *f*
perdition [pədíʃən] N perdición *f*
perennial [pəréniəl] ADJ perenne; N **— plant** planta perenne *f*
perfect [pɝfɪkt] ADJ perfecto; **a — stranger** un completo desconocido; [pəfékt] VT perfeccionar
perfection [pəfékʃən] N perfección *f*
perforate [pɝfəret] VI/VT perforar(se); VT calar
perforation [pɝfəréʃən] N perforación *f*
perform [pəfɔ́rm] VT (a task) ejecutar, realizar; (a rite, ceremony) celebrar; (a contract) cumplir; (a play) representar; VI (give a performance) actuar; (play music) interpretar; (function) funcionar; (do well) rendir
performance [pəfɔ́rməns] N (of a task) ejecución *f*; (of a ceremony) celebración *f*; (of a contract) cumplimiento *m*; (of a motor) desempeño *m*, rendimiento *m*; (of a play) representación *f*; (of an actor) actuación *f*; (of music) interpretación *f*
perfume [pɝfjum] N perfume *m*; [pəfjúm] VT perfumar
perfumery [pəfjúməri] N (store) perfumería *f*; (collection) perfumes *m pl*
perhaps [pəhǽps] ADV tal vez, quizá(s), acaso
peril [pérəl] N peligro *m*; VT poner en peligro
perilous [pérələs] ADJ peligroso
perimeter [pərímɪtə] N perímetro *m*
period [píriəd] N período *m*; (historical) época *f*; (punctuation) punto *m*; (menstruation) período *m*, regla *f*; **you**

can't go, —! no puedes ir, y sanseacabó; **within a — of ten days** en el término de diez días
periodic [pɪriɑ́dɪk] ADJ periódico; **— table** tabla periódica *f*
periodical [pɪriɑ́dɪkəl] ADJ periódico; N revista *f*
peripheral [pərífəəl] ADJ & N periférico *m*; **— vision** visión periférica *f*
periphery [pərífəri] N periferia *f*
periscope [pérɪskop] N periscopio *m*
perish [pérɪʃ] VI perecer
perishable [pérɪʃəbəl] ADJ perecedero
peritonitis [pɛrɪtnáɪdɪs] N peritonitis *f*
perjure [pɝʤə] VI **to — oneself** perjurarse, jurar en falso
perjury [pɝʤəri] N perjurio *m*
permanence [pɝmənəns] N permanencia *f*
permanent [pɝmənənt] ADJ permanente; (of a position) titular
permeable [pɝmiəbəl] ADJ permeable
permeate [pɝmiet] VI/VT permear
permissible [pəmísəbəl] ADJ permisible, lícito
permission [pəmíʃən] N permiso *m*
permissive [pəmísɪv] ADJ permisivo
permit [pəmít] VI/VT permitir; [pɝmɪt] N permiso *m*
permutation [pɝmjutéʃən] N permutación *f*
pernicious [pəníʃəs] ADJ pernicioso
peroxide [pəráksaɪd] N peróxido *m*
perpendicular [pɝpɪndíkjələ] ADJ & N perpendicular *f*
perpetrate [pɝpɪtret] VT perpetrar
perpetual [pəpétʃuəl] ADJ perpetuo
perpetuate [pəpétʃuet] VT perpetuar
perplex [pəpléks] VT confundir, dejar perplejo; **—ed** perplejo
perplexity [pəpléksɪdi] N perplejidad *f*
persecute [pɝsɪkjut] VT perseguir
persecution [pɝsɪkjúʃən] N persecución *f*
persecutor [pɝsɪkjudə] N perseguidor -ra *mf*
perseverance [pɝsəvírəns] N perseverancia *f*
persevere [pɝsəvír] VI perseverar, persistir
Persian [pɝʒən] ADJ & N persa *mf*
persist [pəsíst] VI (continue, endure) persistir; (to be insistent) insistir
persistence [pəsístəns] N (endurance) persistencia *f*; (insistence) insistencia *f*
persistent [pəsístənt] ADJ (lasting) persistente; (insisting) insistente, machacón
person [pɝsən] N persona *f*
personable [pɝsənəbəl] ADJ agradable
personage [pɝsənɪʤ] N personaje *m*
personal [pɝsənəl] ADJ personal; **— computer** *Sp* ordenador personal *m*; *Am*

computadora personal f; — **effects** efectos personales m pl; — **identification number** número de identificación personal m; — **pronoun** pronombre personal m; — **property** bienes muebles m pl; **to make a — appearance** presentarse en persona

personality [pɜ-sənǽliɾi] N personalidad f

personify [pɜ-sánəfaɪ] VT personificar

personnel [pɜ-sənɛ́l] N personal m

perspective [pɜ-spɛ́ktɪv] N perspectiva f

perspicacious [pɜ-spɪkéʃəs] ADJ perspicaz

perspiration [pɜ-spəréʃən] N transpiración f

perspire [pɜ-spáɪr] VI transpirar

persuade [pɜ-swéd] VT persuadir, convencer

persuasion [pɜ-swéʒən] N persuasión f; (belief) convicción f

persuasive [pɜ-swésɪv] ADJ persuasivo, convincente

pert [pɜ-t] ADJ (insolent) insolente; (lively) vivaz

pertain [pɜ-tén] VI atañer, corresponder

pertinent [pɜ-tɲənt] ADJ pertinente

perturb [pɜ-tɜ́-b] VT perturbar

Peru [pərú] N Perú m

perusal [pərúzəɫ] N lectura f

peruse [pərúz] VT (read carefully) leer con cuidado; (read carelessly) hojear

Peruvian [pərúviən] ADJ & N peruano -na mf

pervade [pɜ-véd] VT difundirse por

perverse [pɜ-vɜ́-s] ADJ perverso

perversion [pɜ-vɜ́-ʒən] N perversión f

perversity [pɜ-vɜ́-sɪɾi] N perversidad f

pervert [pɜ-vɜ́-t] VT pervertir; (misconstrue) desvirtuar; [pɜ́-vɜ-t] N pervertido -da mf

peso [péso] N peso m

pessimism [pésəmɪzəm] N pesimismo m

pessimist [pésəmɪst] N pesimista mf

pest [pest] N (insect, disease) peste f, plaga f; (person) pesado -da mf

pester [péstɜ-] VT molestar

pesticide [péstɪsaɪd] N pesticida m

pestilence [péstələns] N pestilencia f

pet [pet] N (animal) mascota f; (favorite) favorito -ta mf, preferido -da mf; ADJ predilecto; — **name** apodo cariñoso m; VT (caress) acariciar; (pat) dar palmaditas a

petal [péɾl̩] N pétalo m

petition [pətíʃən] N petición f, solicitud f; VI/VT peticionar, solicitar

petrify [pétrɪfaɪ] VI/VT petrificar(se)

petroleum [pətróliəm] N petróleo m; — **products** productos petrolíferos m pl; — **jelly** vaselina f

petticoat [péɾɪkot] N enaguas f pl

petty [péɾi] ADJ (trivial) trivial; (mean) mezquino; — **cash** caja chica f; —

larceny ratería f; — **officer** suboficial de marina m

petunia [pɪtúnjə] N petunia f

pew [pju] N banco de iglesia m

pewter [pjúɾɜ-] N peltre m

peyote [peóɾi] N peyote m

phantom [fǽntəm] N fantasma m

pharmaceutical [farməsúɾɪkəɫ] ADJ farmacéutico; N producto farmacéutico m

pharmacist [fárməsɪst] N farmacéutico -ca mf

pharmacology [farməkáləʤi] N farmacología f

pharmacy [fárməsi] N farmacia f

pharynx [fǽrɪŋks] N faringe f

phase [fez] N fase f; VI **to — out** retirar por etapas; **to — in** incorporar paulatinamente

pheasant [fézənt] N faisán m

phenomenon [fɪnámənən] N fenómeno m

philanthropy [fɪlǽnθrəpi] N filantropía f

philharmonic [fɪlharmánɪk] ADJ filarmónico; N filarmónica f

Philippine [fíləpin] ADJ & N filipino -na mf

Philippines [fíləpinz] N Filipinas f pl

philosopher [fɪlásəfɜ-] N filósofo -fa mf

philosophical [fɪləsáfɪkəɫ] ADJ filosófico

philosophy [fɪlásəfi] N filosofía f

phlegm [flem] N flema f

phobia [fóbiə] N fobia f

phone [fon] N teléfono m; VI/VT telefonear; — **card** tarjeta telefónica f

phonetics [fənéɾɪks] N fonética f

phonograph [fónəgræf] N fonógrafo m

phonology [fənáləʤi] N fonología f

phony [fóni] ADJ falso

phosphate [fásfet] N fosfato m

phosphorus [fásfɜ-əs] N fósforo m

photo [fóɾo] N foto f; — **finish** final muy reñido m

photocopier [fóɾokapiɜ-] N fotocopiadora f

photocopy [fóɾokapi] N fotocopia f; VI/VT fotocopiar

photoelectric [foɾoɪléktrɪk] ADJ fotoeléctrico

photogenic [foɾəʤénɪk] ADJ fotogénico

photograph [fóɾəgræf] N fotografía f; VT fotografiar

photographer [fətágrəfɜ-] N fotógrafo -fa mf

photography [fətágrəfi] N fotografía f

photon [fóɾan] N fotón m

photosynthesis [foɾosínθəsɪs] N fotosíntesis f

phrase [frez] N frase f; VI/VT expresar; (musical) frasear

phylum [fáɪləm] N filo m

physical [fízɪkəɫ] ADJ físico; — **education** educación física f; — **geography**

geografía física f; — **science** ciencia física f

physician [fɪzíʃən] N médico -ca mf; **—'s assistant** ayudante médico -ca sanitario -ria mf

physicist [fízɪsɪst] N físico -ca mf

physics [fízɪks] N física f

physiological [fɪzɪəládʒɪkəl] ADJ fisiológico

physiology [fɪziáhdʒi] N fisiología f

physique [fɪzík] N físico m

piano [piǽno] N piano m; — **bench** banqueta de piano f; — **hammer** martinete m; — **stool** taburete de piano m

picaresque [pɪkərésk] ADJ picaresco

piccolo [píkəlo] N flautín m, pícolo m

pick [pɪk] VT (choose) escoger, elegir; (gather flowers) juntar; (play a guitar) puntear; (clean teeth) mondarse; (eat with the bill) picotear; (provoke a fight) armar, entablar; VI picar; **to —** at picotear; **to — apart** criticar; **to — a lock** violar una cerradura con ganzúa; **to — on** meterse con; **to — out** (choose) escoger; (distinguish) distinguir; **to — pockets** ratear; **to — up** (gather) recoger; (lift) levantar; (learn) aprender; (order) ordenar; (improve) mejorar; (contact in hope of sex) ligar con; **to — up speed** acelerar la marcha; **—-proof** a prueba de ladrones; N (tool) pico m; (of a guitar) púa f; (act of selecting) selección f; (thing or person selected) elección f; (the best) lo selecto, lo mejor; **—ax(e)** zapapico m; **—lock** ganzúa f; **—pocket** ratero -ra mf, carterista mf; **—up** (taking on freight) recolección f; (improvement in business) recuperación f; (acceleration) aceleración f; **—up truck** camioneta f

picket [píkɪt] N piquete m (also union worker); — **fence** cerca de piquetes f; VT (fence) vallar; (block with workers) bloquear

pickle [píkəl] N pepinillo en vinagre m, curtido m; **to be in a —** hallarse en un aprieto; VT encurtir, escabechar; **—d fish** pescado al/en escabeche m, pescado adobado m

picnic [píknɪk] N picnic m; — **area** merendero m; VI hacer un picnic

picture [píktʃə] N (image) imagen f; (drawing) dibujo m; (photo) fotografía f; (situation) panorama m; (movie) película f; — **frame** marco m; — **gallery** galería de pinturas f; — **tube** tubo de imagen m; **she is the — of unhappiness** es la imagen de la infelicidad; VT (describe) describir; (imagine) imaginar

picturesque [pɪktʃərésk] ADJ pintoresco

pie [paɪ] N pastel m, tarta f; — **chart** gráfica circular f; — **in the sky** castillos en el aire m pl; **it's as easy as —** es pan comido

piece [pis] N (of music, in a board game, of furniture) pieza f; (of wood, rock, pie) pedazo m, trozo m; **—meal** por partes; — **of advice** consejo m; — **of cake** pan comido m; — **of land** parcela f, terreno m; — **of one's mind** regaño m; — **of news** noticia f; **—work** trabajo a destajo m; **to go to —s** descomponerse; VI remendar; **to — together** (assemble) armar; (make sense of) atar cabos

pier [pir] N muelle m, embarcadero m; (breakwater) rompeolas m sg

pierce [pirs] VI/VT (make a hole in) agujerear; (penetrate) penetrar; (cause a sharp pain) punzar; (make a sharp sound) quebrar

piercing [pírsɪŋ] ADJ (glance, sound) penetrante; (pain) punzante

piety [páɪɪdi] N piedad f

pig [pɪg] N puerco m, cerdo m, cochino m; Sp guarro m; **—-headed** testarudo, cabezón; **—-iron** hierro en lingotes m; — **Latin** jerigonza f; **—pen** pocilga f; **—tail** coleta f

pigeon [pídʒən] N paloma f; (young) pichón m; **—hole** casilla f; **to —hole** encasillar; — **loft** palomar m

piggy [pígi] N cerdito m; **—-bank** alcancía f; Sp hucha f; **—-back** a hombros, a cuestas

pigment [pígmənt] N pigmento m

pike [paɪk] N (weapon) pica f; (fish) lucio m

pile [paɪl] N (ordered stack) pila f; (chaotic group) montón m, amontonamiento m; (surface of a carpet) pelo m; (post) pilote m; — **driver** martinete m; **—s** almorranas f pl; **—up** accidente múltiple m; VI/VT apilar(se), amontonar(se)

pilfer [pílfə] VI/VT ratear, sisar

pilgrim [pílgrəm] N peregrino -na mf, romero -ra f

pilgrimage [pílgrəmɪdʒ] N peregrinación f, romería f

pill [pɪl] N píldora f (also birth control), pastilla f; (naughty child) pesado -da mf

pillage [pílɪdʒ] N pillaje m, saqueo m, rapiña f; VI/VT pillar, saquear

pillar [pílə] N pilar m, columna f

pillow [pílo] N almohada f; **—case** funda f

pilot [páɪlət] N piloto mf (also test, light); (of a boat) timonel m, piloto mf; VT pilotar, comandar

pimple [pímpəl] N grano m, barro m

pin [pɪn] N alfiler m; (ornament) prendedor

m; (rod) pasador *m,* perno *m;* (bowling) bolo *m;* (electric) pata *f,* clavija *f;* **—cushion** alfiletero *m;* **—wheel** molinete *m,* remolino *m;* VT (affix with pins) prender; (in wrestling) inmovilizar; **to be on —s and needles** estar en ascuas; **to — someone down** (hold down) inmovilizar; (force to act) hacer que concrete detalles; **to — one's hopes on** poner sus esperanzas en; **to —point** localizar con precisión; **to — up** sujetar con alfileres

PIN (personal identification number) [pɪn] N PIN *m*

pincers [pínsɚz] N (of lobsters) pinzas *f pl;* (tool) tenazas *f pl*

pinch [pɪntʃ] VT (squeeze with fingers) pellizcar; (squeeze tightly, hamper) apretar; (steal) birlar; (arrest) prender; VI (be too tight) apretar; (economize) economizar; N (act of pinching) pellizco *m;* (small amount) pizca *f;* (trying circumstances) aprieto *m,* apuro *m*

pine [paɪn] N pino *m;* **—apple** piña *f,* ananá(s) *m;* **— cone** piña *f;* **— grove** pinar *m;* **— nut** piñón *m;* VI **to — away** languidecer; **to — for** anhelar, suspirar por

ping-pong [píŋpɑŋ] N ping-pong *m,* tenis de mesa *m*

pinion [pínjən] N piñón *m*

pink [pɪŋk] N rosado *m,* rosa *m;* **in the —** rebosante de salud; ADJ rosado, rosa *inv*

pinnacle [pínəkəl] N pináculo *m*

pint [paɪnt] N pinta *f;* **—-sized** diminuto

pinto bean [píntobin] N judía pinta *f*

pioneer [paɪənír] N pionero -ra *mf;* VI ser el primero en hacer algo; VT promover

pious [páɪəs] ADJ (religious) pío, piadoso; (hypocritical) beato

pipe [paɪp] N (for smoking) pipa *f;* (for water) tubo *m,* caño *m;* (of an organ) tubo *m;* (for playing music) caramillo *m,* flauta *f;* **— dream** ilusiones *f pl;* **—line** (for oil) oleoducto *m;* (for gas) gasoducto *m;* (for water) tubería *f;* **in the —line** en trámite; **— wrench** llave inglesa *f;* VT (convey water) conducir por cañerías; (make music) tocar la flauta; VI chillar; **to — down** callarse

piping [páɪpɪŋ] N (many pipes) cañería *f,* tubería *f;* (border on clothes) ribete *m;* (sound of pipes) sonido de la gaita / flauta *m;* **— hot** hirviendo

pipsqueak [pípskwik] N chisgarabís *m,* mequetrefe *m*

pirate [páɪrət] N pirata *mf;* VT piratear

pistol [pístəl] N pistola *f,* revólver *m;* **to —-whip** dar culatazos

piston [pístən] N pistón *m,* émbolo *m;* **— ring** segmento de compresión *m;* **— rod** eje del pistón *m*

pit [pɪt] N (hole) hoyo *m,* pozo *m;* (in a garage, theater) foso *m;* (trap) trampa *f;* (seed) hueso *m;* (part of a racetrack) box *m,* paddock *m;* (part of the stomach) boca *f;* **—fall** (trap) trampa *f;* (difficulty) dificultad *f;* **this is the —s** esto es lo peor; VI/VT (make holes) picarse; VT (set against) oponer, enfrentar

pitch [pɪtʃ] VT (throw) tirar, lanzar; (try to sell) pregonar; **to — a tent** armar una tienda de campaña; VI (plane, ship) cabecear; **to — in** colaborar; N (throw) tiro *m,* lanzamiento *m;* (in music) tono *m;* (in printing) espaciado *m;* (slope) grado de inclinación *m;* (tar) brea *f,* pez *f;* **— dark** oscuro como boca del lobo; **—fork** horca *f,* horquilla *f*

pitcher [pítʃɚ] N (vessel) cántaro *m,* jarro *m,* jarra *f;* (in baseball) lanzador *m*

pith [pɪθ] N (in plants, feathers) médula *f;* (essence) meollo *m*

pithy [píθi] ADJ sustancial

pitiful [pítɪfəl] ADJ (deserving pity) lastimoso; (deserving contempt) despreciable

pitiless [pítɪlɪs] ADJ despiadado

pituitary [pɪtúɪtɛri] ADJ pituitario; **— gland** glándula pituitaria *f*

pity [pídi] N compasión *f,* lástima *f;* **what a —!** ¡qué lástima! VT compadecerse (de)

pivot [pívət] N pivote *m;* VI pivotar

pixel [píksəl] N píxel *m*

pizza [pítsə] N pizza *f*

placard [plǽkɑrd] N cartel *m*

placate [pléket] VT apaciguar

place [ples] N (site) lugar *m,* sitio *m;* (position) puesto *m;* (passage in text) pasaje *m;* **— mat** mantel individual *m;* **— of business** oficina *f;* **— setting** cubierto para una persona *m;* **— of worship** templo *m;* **in — of** en lugar de; **it is not my — to do it** no me corresponde a mí hacerlo; VT colocar; (identify) situar, ubicar; VI clasificarse; **to — an order** hacer un pedido; **to — an ad** poner un anuncio

placebo [pləsíbo] N placebo *m*

placement [plésmənt] N colocación *f*

placenta [pləséntə] N placenta *f*

placid [plǽsɪd] ADJ plácido

plagiarism [pléʤərɪzəm] N plagio *m*

plague [pleg] N plaga *f,* peste *f;* VT

atormentar, apestar
plaid [plæd] N tela escocesa f
plain [plen] ADJ (without embellishment) sencillo, llano; (clear) claro; (downright, unadulterated) puro; (ordinary) común; (unattractive) poco atractivo; — **fool** tonto de capirote; **in — sight** en plena vista; —**clothesman** policía en traje de civil m; —**Jane** sencillo; ADV completamente; N llano m, llanura f
plaintiff [pléntɪf] N demandante mf, querellante mf
plan [plæn] N plan m; (drawing, sketch, map, outline) plano m; VI/VT planear, planificar; (diagram) hacer el plano de
plane [plen] N (airplane) avión m; (surface) plano m; (tool) cepillo m; ADJ plano; — **geometry** geometría plana f; — **tree** plátano m; VI (glide, hover) planear; VT (smooth) cepillar, planear
planet [plǽnɪt] N planeta m
planetarium [plænɪtériəm] N planetario m
plank [plæŋk] N (board) tabla f, tablón m; (tenet) principio m, base f; VT entarimar
plankton [plǽŋktən] N plancton m
plant [plænt] N (vegetation) planta f; (industrial installation) fábrica f, planta f; (mole, spy) topo m; VT (plants) plantar; (ideas) sembrar; (a spy, evidence) colocar
plantation [plæntéʃən] N plantación f
plaque [plæk] N placa f; (on teeth) sarro m, placa f
plasma [plǽzmə] N plasma m
plaster [plǽstə-] N (substance) yeso m; (preparation applied to body) emplasto m; — **of Paris** yeso m; VT: (cover with plaster) revocar; (apply a preparation) emplastar; (cover with posters) cubrir, empapelar; (defeat) aplastar; **to — down one's hair** achatarse el pelo; **he got —ed** se emborrachó
plastic [plǽstɪk] ADJ plástico; — **surgery** cirugía plástica/estética f
plate [plet] N (for food) plato m; (for collections) bandeja f; (metal) plancha f, lámina f; (license) placa f; — **glass** vidrio cilindrado m; — **tectonics** tectónica de placas f; VT apply metal covering) chapar, enchapar; (apply armor) blindar
plateau [plætó] N meseta f, macizo m
platform [plǽtfɔrm] N plataforma f (also political); (railway) andén m; (mobile) tarima f, tinglado m
platinum [plǽtnəm] N platino m
platitude [plǽɾɪtud] N lugar común m, perogrullada f
platter [plǽɾə-] N fuente f

plausible [plɔ́zəbəl] ADJ plausible
play [ple] VT (game) jugar; (an opponent) jugar contra; (an instrument) tocar; (a drama) representar; (a role) desempeñar; (bet on) apostar; VI (divert oneself, gamble) jugar; (kid) bromear; (make music) tocar; **to — a joke** gastar una broma; **to — along** seguir la corriente; **to — cards** jugar a los naipes; **to — down** minimizar; **to — havoc** hacer estragos; **to — tennis** jugar al tenis; **to — the fool** hacerse el tonto; **to be all —ed out** estar agotado; N (recreational activity, looseness) juego m; (instance of playing) jugada f; (theater work) obra de teatro f; — **on words** juego de palabras m; —**boy** playboy m; —**ground** recreo m, patio m; —**ing card** naipe m; —**mate** compañero -ra de juego mf; —**thing** juguete m
player [pléə-] N (one who plays, gambler) jugador -ra mf; (musician) músico -ca mf; (actor) actor m, actriz f; (participant) participante mf; — **piano** pianola f
playful [pléfəl] ADJ juguetón
playwright [plérat] N dramaturgo -ga mf
plea [pli] N (entreaty) súplica f, ruego m; (allegation) alegato m; **to enter a — of guilty** declararse culpable
plead [plid] VI/VT (entreat) suplicar, rogar; (defend) abogar, defender; **to — guilty** declararse culpable
pleasant [plézənt] ADJ agradable, grato, placentero
pleasantry [plézəntri] N cortesía f
please [pliz] ADV por favor; VI/VT agradar, complacer; **as you —** como quieras; **to be —d to** tener el gusto de, tener gusto en; **to be —d with** estar satisfecho con
pleasing [plízɪŋ] ADJ agradable
pleasure [pléʒə-] N placer m, gusto m, agrado m; — **trip** viaje de placer m
pleat [plit] N pliegue m, tabla f; (wide) tabla f; VT plisar; (wide) tablear
pledge [plɛʤ] N (promise) promesa f; (security deposit) prenda f; (in a fraternity) miembro provisorio m; **as a — of** en prenda de; VI/VT (promise) prometer; VT (give as a deposit) empeñar; **to — one's word** dar la palabra; **to — to secrecy** exigir promesa de discreción
plenary [plénəri] ADJ & N plenario m
plentiful [pléntɪfəl] ADJ abundante, copioso
plenty [plénti] N abundancia f; — **of time** suficiente tiempo m; **that's —** con eso basta
pliable [plájəbəl] ADJ (flexible) flexible; (docile) dócil

pliant [pláɪənt] ADJ (flexible) flexible; (docile) dócil

pliers [pláɪəz] N alicates *m pl*, tenazas *f pl*

plight [plaɪt] N aprieto *m*

plod [plɑd] VI (walk) caminar trabajosamente; (work) trabajar laboriosamente

plop [plɑp] VI hacer plaf; VT dejar caer; N plaf *m*

plot [plɑt] N (storyline) trama *f*, argumento *m*; (conspiracy) complot *m*, conspiración *f*; (land) parcela *f*, era *f*; (floor plan) plano *m*; VI/VT (plan secretly) tramar, conspirar, maquinar; VT (make a graph) hacer un gráfico; **to — a course** trazar un curso

plotter [plɑ́də] N (one who plots) conspirador -ora *mf*; (device) trazador de gráficos *m*

plover [plóvə] N chorlito *m*

plow [plaʊ] N arado *m*; **—share** reja de arado *f*; VI/VT arar; (fresh soil) roturar; **to — through** abrirse paso

plowing [pláʊɪŋ] N labranza *f*

pluck [plʌk] VT (a feather, flower) arrancar; (bird) desplumar; (guitar) puntear, pulsar; **to — at** tirar de; **to — out / off** desprender; **to — up courage** animarse, cobrar ánimo; N (act of plucking) tirón *m*; (courage) valor *m*

plug [plʌg] N (stopper) tapón *m*; (horse) *pej* penco *m*; (electric) enchufe *m*; (advertisement) mención favorable *f*; (tobacco) rollo *m*; **—-in** enchufe *m*; VT tapar; (advertise) hacer una mención favorable de; VI **to — along** afanarse; **to — in** enchufar; **to — up** tapar

plum [plʌm] N (fruit) ciruela *f*; **— tree** ciruelo *m*; **that job is a real —** ese trabajo es estupendo

plumage [plúmɪdʒ] N plumaje *m*

plumb [plʌm] N (lead weight) plomada *f*; **to be out of —** no estar a plomo; ADJ (perpendicular) a plomo; **— bob** plomada *f*; ADV (in a vertical direction) a plomo; (completely) completamente; VT (measure depth) sondear; (test for verticality) aplomar; (examine) examinar

plumber [plʌ́mə] N plomero -ra *mf*; *Sp* fontanero -ra *mf*

plumbing [plʌ́mɪŋ] N (work and trade) plomería *f*; *Sp* fontanería *f*; (system of pipes) cañerías *f pl*

plume [plum] N penacho *m*; VT adornar con plumas

plummet [plʌ́mɪt] VI precipitarse; N plomada *f*

plump [plʌmp] ADJ rechoncho, regordete, rollizo; ADV a plomo; VI/VT **to — down**

dejar(se) caer

plunder [plʌ́ndə] N (act of plundering) pillaje *m*, saqueo *m*; (loot) botín *m*; VI/VT pillar, saquear

plunge [plʌndʒ] VI/VT (into water) zambullir(se), sumergir(se); (into something solid) hundir(se); VI (fall) precipitarse; (slope downward) bajar repentinamente; **to — headlong** echarse de cabeza; N zambullida *f*; (rush) salto *m*

plunger [plʌ́ndʒə] N (for a toilet) desatascador *m*; (of a pump) émbolo *m*

pluperfect [plupɜ́-fɪkt] N pluscuamperfecto *m*

plural [plúrəl] ADJ & N plural *m*

plurality [plurǽlɪɾi] N pluralidad *f*

plus [plʌs] PREP más; N signo más *m*; (advantage) ventaja *f*; **two — three** dos más tres *m*; **on the — side** en el lado positivo; **— sign** signo de más *m*

plush [plʌʃ] N felpa *f*; ADJ (fabric) afelpado; (hotel) lujoso

plutonium [plutóniəm] N plutonio *m*

ply [plaɪ] VT (use) manejar; (assail with questions) acosar; (navigate a body of water) surcar; VI (travel regularly) recorrer con regularidad; (work steadily) aplicarse; **to — a trade** ejercer un oficio; N (layer of cloth, rubber) capa *f*; (layer of plywood) chapa *f*; **—wood** madera compensada *f*, contrachapado *m*

pneumatic [numǽɾɪk] ADJ neumático

pneumonia [numónjə] N pulmonía *f*

poach [potʃ] VT (eggs) escalfar; VI/VT (game) cazar furtivamente

pocket [pákɪt] N bolsillo *m*; (vein of ore) filón *m*; (on a pool table) tronera *f*; (of air) bache *m*; (of poverty) bolsa *f*; **—book** cartera *f*, *Sp* bolso *m*; **— book** libro de bolsillo *m*; **—knife** navaja *f*; **— of resistance** foco de resistencia *m*; VT meterse en el bolsillo; (appropriate) embolsar; (knock in a billiard ball) meter en la tronera

pod [pɑd] N (seed vessel) vaina *f*; (herd of cetaceans) manada *f*

podium [pódiəm] N podio *m*

poem [póəm] N poema *m*, poesía *f*

poet [póɪt] N poeta *mf*

poetic [poέɾɪk] ADJ poético; **—s** poética *f*; **— justice** justicia divina *f*

poetry [póɪtri] N poesía *f*

poignant [póɪnjant] ADJ conmovedor

poinsettia [pɔɪnsέɾə] N flor de Pascua *f*

point [pɔɪnt] N (place) punto *m*; (sharp end) punta *f*; **— of view** punto de vista *m*; **—-blank** a quemarropa; **it is not to the — no** viene al caso; **I don't see the —**

no le veo el sentido; **on the — of** a
punto de; vt (direct finger at) apuntar
con, señalar con; (indicate) señalar; **to —
out** señalar, indicar; **to — up** enfatizar

pointed [póɪntɪd] ADJ (having a point)
puntiagudo; (piercing) agudo; (aimed) a
propósito; — **arch** arco ojival *m*

pointer [póɪntɚ] N (stick) puntero *m*; (on a
scale) indicador *m*; (dog) perro de muestra
m; (advice) consejo *m*

pointless [póɪntlɪs] ADJ inútil

poise [pɔɪz] N (balance, steadiness) equilibrio
m; (dignified bearing) aplomo *m*; vi/vt
equilibrar(se); vt (ready) preparar; vi
(hover) cernerse

poison [póɪzən] N veneno *m*, ponzoña *f*; —
ivy hiedra venenosa *f*; vt envenenar,
emponzoñar

poisoning [póɪzənɪŋ] N intoxicación *f*

poisonous [póɪzənəs] ADJ venenoso,
ponzoñoso

poke [pok] vt (jab) clavar, pinchar; (stir a
fire) atizar; (thrust out, as one's head)
asomar; **to — out an eye** sacar un ojo; vi
to — along andar perezosamente; **to —
around** husmear; **to — fun at** burlarse
de; **to — into** meterse en; **to — out**
(project) sobresalir; N pinchazo *m*

Poland [pólənd] N Polonia *f*

polar [pólɚ] ADJ polar; — **bear** oso polar *m*

polarity [pəlérɪɾi] N polaridad *f*

polarization [polɚɪzéʃən] N polarización *f*

polarize [póləraɪz] vi/vt polarizar(se)

pole [pol] N (long piece of wood, metal)
poste *m*; (for a flag) asta *f*; (for vaulting)
pértiga *f*, garrocha *f*; (earth's axis) polo *m*;
(for skiing) bastón *m*; — **vault** salto con
pértiga *m*

Pole [pol] N polaco -ca *mf*

polemic [pəlémɪk] ADJ polémico *m*;
polémica *f*

police [pəlís] N policía *f*; — **car** patrullero *m*;
— **dog** perro policía *m*; — **force** cuerpo
de policía *m*; —**man** policía *m*; — **officer**
oficial de policía *mf*; — **state** estado
policíaco *m*; — **station** comisaría de
policía *f*; —**woman** policía *f*; vt patrullar

policy [pálɪsi] N (procedure) política *f*; (for
insurance) póliza *f*

polio [pólio] N polio *f*

Polish [pólɪʃ] ADJ & N polaco -ca *mf*

polish [pálɪʃ] N (sheen) lustre *m*,
refinamiento *m*; (refinement) urbanidad *f*,
cultura *f*; (substance for furniture) cera *f*;
(substance for shoes) betún *m*; vt (a
speech) pulir; (a metal) sacar brillo; (a car)
encerar; (shoes) lustrar, embetunar; vi

lustrarse; **to — off** despachar; **to — up**
(metal) sacar brillo; (speech) pulir

polite [pəláɪt] ADJ cortés

politeness [pəláɪtnɪs] N cortesía *f*

politic [pálɪtɪk] ADJ diplomático, político

political [pəlíɾɪkəɫ] ADJ político; —
prisoner preso -sa político -ca *mf*; —
science ciencias políticas *f pl*

politically correct [pəlíɾɪklikɔrékt] ADJ
políticamente correcto

politician [palɪtíʃən] N político -ca *mf*

politics [pálɪtɪks] N política *f*

polka [pókkə] N polca *f*; — **dot** lunar *m*

poll [pol] N (survey) encuesta *f*; —**s**
(elections) comicios *m pl*; (voting place)
urna *f*; vt (survey) encuestar; (receive
votes) obtener; (record vote of) registrar

pollen [pálən] N polen *m*

pollinate [pálənet] vt polinizar

pollute [pəlút] vi/vt contaminar

pollution [pəlúʃən] N contaminación *f*

polo [pólo] N polo *m*

polyester [palíéstɚ] N poliéster *m*

polygamy [pəlígəmi] N poligamia *f*

polyglot [páliglɑt] ADJ & N políglota *mf*

polygraph [páligræf] N polígrafo *m*

polymer [páləmɚ] N polímero *m*

polyp [pálɪp] N pólipo *m*

polyunsaturated [paliʌnsǽtʃəreɪɾɪd] ADJ
poliinsaturado

polyurethane [palijúrəθen] N poliuretano *m*

pomegranate [pámɪgrænɪt] N granada *f*; —
tree granado *m*

pomp [pɑmp] N pompa *f*, boato *m*, aparato *m*

pompous [pámpəs] ADJ pomposo, aparatoso

pond [pɑnd] N (natural) charca *f*; (artificial)
estanque *m*; (for irrigation) balsa *f*

ponder [pándɚ] vi meditar; vt considerar

ponderous [pándɚəs] ADJ enorme

pontoon [pɑntún] N (on a bridge) pontón *m*;
(on an airplane) flotador *m*

pony [póni] N póney *m*; —**tail** colita *f*, cola
de caballo *f*; vi **to — up** soltar

poodle [púdl] N caniche *m*

pool [pul] N (puddle of water, blood, etc.)
charco *m*; (swimming place) piscina *f*, *Mex*
alberca *f*; (association of competitors) pool
m; (game) pool *m*, billar *m*; (bets) pozo *m*;
— **table** billar *m*; — **hall** billar *m*; vi
acumularse; vt combinar fondos

poop [pup] N (part of ship) popa *f*;
(excrement) *fam* caca *f*; vi *fam* hacer caca

poor [pur] ADJ (lacking money) pobre;
(deficient) malo; **I'm a — cook** no sé
cocinar; —**house** asilo para los pobres *m*;
— **little thing** pobrecito -ta *mf*; **the —**
los pobres

pop [pɑp] VI reventar, estallar; (eyes, cork) saltar; **to — in** entrar de paso; VT (make explode) hacer reventar; (take out cork) hacer saltar; (put) meter; (take, as pills) tomar (píldoras); **to — a question** espetar una pregunta; **to — corn** hacer palomitas; N estallido m, detonación f; **—corn** palomitas f pl; **— music** música popular f; **— quiz** prueba sorpresa f; **— of a cork** taponazo m

Pope [pop] N Papa m

poplar [páplə-] N álamo m, chopo m; **— grove** alameda f

poppy [pápi] N amapola f

popular [pápjələ-] ADJ popular; **he's very — with the ladies** tiene mucho éxito con las mujeres

popularity [pɑpjəlǽrɪDi] N popularidad f

populate [pápjəlet] VT poblar

population [pɑpjəléʃən] N población f

populous [pápjələs] ADJ populoso

porcelain [pɔ́rsəlɪn] N porcelana f

porch [pɔrtʃ] N porche m

porcupine [pɔ́rkjəpaɪn] N puercoespín m

pore [pɔr] N poro m; VI **to — over a book** estudiar detenidamente un libro

pork [pɔrk] N carne de cerdo f; **— chop** chuleta de cerdo f

pornography [pɔrnágrəfi] N pornografía f

porous [pɔ́rəs] ADJ poroso

porpoise [pɔ́rpəs] N marsopa f

port [pɔrt] N (harbor, computer) puerto m; (wine) oporto m; (left side of ship) babor m; **—hole** ojo de buey m

portable [pɔ́rDəbəl] ADJ portátil

portal [pɔ́rdl] N portal m (also of Internet)

portent [pɔ́rtɛnt] N (omen) presagio m, agüero m; (marvel, prodigy) portento m

portentous [pɔrtɛ́ntəs] ADJ (ominous) de mal agüero; (prodigious) portentoso

porter [pɔ́rDə-] N mozo -za mf

portfolio [pɔrtfólio] N cartera f; (flat case for papers) carpeta f

portion [pɔ́rʃən] N porción f; VI **to — out** repartir

portly [pɔ́rtli] ADJ grueso

portrait [pɔ́rtrɪt] N retrato m

portray [pɔrtré] VT (draw, describe) retratar; (in a drama) representar

portrayal [pɔrtréəl] N (portrait) retrato m; (act of portraying) representación f

Portugal [pɔ́rtʃəgəl] N Portugal m

Portuguese [pɔ́rtʃəgiz] ADJ & N portugués -esa mf

pose [poz] N (posture) pose f, postura f; (affected attitude) afectación f; VI (sit as a model) posar; (act affectedly) afectar una actitud; VT (to make sit as model) hacer posar; (to present) plantear; **to — as** hacerse pasar por

position [pəzíʃən] N (place) posición f; (job) puesto m, colocación f

positive [pázɪDɪv] ADJ positivo; **— proof** prueba certera f; **I am —** estoy seguro

possess [pəzɛ́s] VT poseer

possession [pəzɛ́ʃən] N posesión f

possessive [pəzɛ́sɪv] ADJ & N posesivo m

possessor [pəzɛ́sə-] N poseedor -ra f

possibility [pɑsəbílɪDi] N posibilidad f

possible [pásəbəl] ADJ posible

post [post] N (pole) poste m; (position) puesto m; (mail) correo m; **—card** tarjeta postal f; **— haste** a la brevedad; **—man** cartero m; **—mark** matasellos m; **—master** director de correos m; **— office** oficina de correos f, casa de correos f; **—-office box** apartado postal m; **— paid** porte pagado; VT (affix) fijar; (announce) anunciar; (list) poner en lista; (place) apostar, situar; (mail) echar al correo; **keep me —ed** mantenme al tanto

postage [póstɪdʒ] N franqueo m; **— meter** franqueadora f; **— stamp** sello m; Am estampilla f; Mex timbre m

postal [póstəl] ADJ postal; **to go —** perpetrar un ataque homicida, volverse loco

poster [póstə-] N cartel m, póster m, afiche m; **— child** modelo m

posterior [pɑstíriə] ADJ posterior; N trasero m

posterity [pɑstɛ́rɪDi] N posteridad f

postgraduate [postgrǽdʒuɪt] ADJ de posgrado

posthumous [pástʃəməs] ADJ póstumo

postpone [postpón] VT posponer, aplazar

postponement [postpónmənt] N aplazamiento m

postscript [póstskrɪpt] N posdata f

postulate [pástʃəlet] VT postular; [pástʃələt] N postulado m

posture [pástʃə-] N (carriage, attitude) postura f; (affectation) afectación f; VI darse aires

posy [pózi] N ramillete m

pot [pat] N (vessel) olla f, marmita f; (marijuana) marihuana f; **—-bellied** panzudo, barrigón; **—hole** bache m

potable [pódəbəl] ADJ potable

potassium [pətǽsiəm] N potasio m

potato [pətéDo] N Sp patata f; Am papa f; **— chip** patata / papa frita a la inglesa f, chip m

potency [pótn̩si] N potencia f

potent [pótn̩t] ADJ potente

potentate [pótn̩tet] N potentado -da mf

potential [pətɛ́nʃəl] ADJ & N potencial m

potion [póʃən] N poción f

potter [pάɒə] N alfarero -ra *mf*

pottery [pάɒəri] N (craft, shop) alfarería *f*; (objects) cerámica *f*, objetos de alfarería *m pl*

pouch [pautʃ] N bolsa *f*; (for mail) valija *f*; (for tobacco) petaca *f*

poultry [póʊtri] N aves de corral *f pl*

pounce [pauns] VI saltar; **to — upon/on** abalanzarse sobre; **to — on an opportunity** no dejar pasar una oportunidad; N salto *m*

pound [paund] N (unit of weight, British currency) libra *f*; (blow) golpazo *m*; (place for stray dogs) perrera *f*; VT (a door) golpear; (seeds) machacar; (a military target) bombardear; VI (beat) latir con fuerza

pour [pɔr] VT verter; VI (leave en masse) salir en tropel; (rain) llover a cántaros; **to — out one's feelings** desahogarse

pout [paut] VI hacer pucheros; N puchero *m*

poverty [pάvəɒi] N pobreza *f*, penuria *f*; **—-stricken** indigente

powder [pάudə] N polvo *m*; (for the face) polvos *m pl*; (for guns) pólvora *f*; **— compact** polvera *f*; **— puff** borla *f*; **to take a —** poner pies en polvorosa; VI/VT (use powder) empolvar(se); (pulverize) pulverizar(se)

power [pάuə] N (control) poder *m*, poderío *m*; (might, in physics, in math) potencia *f*; (physical strength) fuerza *f*; (energy) energía *f*; **— of attorney** poder *m*; **— plant** central eléctrica *f*; **— steering** dirección asistida *f*; **legislative —s** atribuciones legislativas *f pl*

powerful [pάuəfəl] ADJ poderoso, potente

powerless [pάuəlis] ADJ impotente

practical [prǽktikəl] ADJ práctico; **— joke** broma pesada *f*; **— nurse** enfermero -ra sin título *mf*

practice [prǽktis] N práctica *f*; (habit) costumbre *f*; (doctor's office) consultorio *m*; (lawyer's office) bufete *m*; VI/VT practicar; VT (a profession) ejercer

practiced [prǽktist] ADJ experto, perito

practitioner [prǽktiʃənə] N practicante *mf*; **general —** médico -ca general *mf*

pragmatic [prǽgmǽɒɪk] ADJ pragmático

prairie [préri] N pradera *f*, llanura *f*

praise [prez] N alabanza *f*, elogio *m*; VT alabar, elogiar; **—worthy** loable, encomiable

prance [præns] VI cabriolar, hacer cabriolas; N cabriola *f*

prank [præŋk] N travesura *f*, chasco *m*; **to play —s** hacer travesuras

prawn [prɔn] N langostino *m*; *Sp* gamba pequeña *f*

pray [pre] VI/VT (religious) rezar, orar; (beg) rogar, suplicar

prayer [prɛr] N (devout petition to God) oración *f*, rezo *m*; (entreaty) ruego *m*, súplica *f*

praying mantis [préɪŋmǽntɪs] N mantis religiosa *f*

preach [pritʃ] VI/VT predicar; (moralize) sermonear

preacher [prítʃə] N predicador -ra *mf*

preamble [prίæmbəl] N preámbulo *m*

precarious [prɪkériəs] ADJ precario

precaution [prɪkɔ́ʃən] N precaución *f*

precede [prɪsíd] VI/VT preceder

precedence [prέsɪdəns] N precedencia *f*, prioridad *f*

preceding [prɪsíɒɪŋ] ADJ precedente, anterior

precept [prίsɛpt] N precepto *m*

precinct [prίsɪŋkt] N distrito *m*; (police station) comisaría *f*; **—s** límites *m pl*

precious [prέʃəs] ADJ precioso; (overly refined) preciosista; **— little** muy poco; **— metal** metal precioso *m*; **— stone** piedra preciosa *f*

precipice [prέsəpɪs] N precipicio *m*, derrumbadero *m*

precipitate [prɪsípɪtet] VI/VT precipitar(se); [prɪsípɪtət] ADJ & N precipitado *m*

precipitation [prɪsɪpɪtéʃən] N precipitación *f*

precipitous [prɪsípɪɒəs] ADJ (steep) escarpado; (hasty) precipitado

precise [prɪsáɪs] ADJ preciso, exacto

precision [prɪsíʒən] N precisión *f*, exactitud *f*; (of expression) propiedad *f*

preclude [prɪklúd] VT excluir; **that doesn't — our considering your application** esto no obsta para que tengamos en cuenta su solicitud

precocious [prɪkóʃəs] ADJ precoz

precursor [prɪkə́sə] N precursor *m*

predator [prέɒəɒə] N depredador *m*

predatory [prέɒətɔri] ADJ (animal) depredador; (persona) rapaz

predecessor [prέɒɪsesə] N predecesor -ra *mf*, antecesor -ra *mf*

predestine [pridéstɪn] VT predestinar

predicament [prɪdíkəmənt] N aprieto *m*

predicate [prέdɪkɪt] ADJ & N predicado *m*; [prέdɪket] VT basar

predict [prɪdíkt] VT predecir

prediction [prɪdíkʃən] N predicción *f*, vaticinio *m*

predilection [predlékʃən] N predilección *f*

predispose [pridɪspóz] VI/VT predisponer

predominance [prɪdámənəns] N

predominio *m*

predominant [prɪdámənənt] ADJ
predominante

predominate [prɪdámənet] VI/VT
predominar, preponderar

preface [préfɪs] N prefacio *m*, prólogo *m*; VT
hacer una introducción; (a book) prologar

prefer [prɪfɚ] VT preferir; **to — a claim**
presentar una demanda

preferable [préfɚəbəl] ADJ preferible

preference [préfɚəns] N preferencia *f*

preferential [prefɚénʃəl] ADJ preferente

preferred [prɪfɚd] ADJ preferido; **— stocks**
acciones preferentes *f pl*

prefix [prífɪks] N prefijo *m*; VT poner un
prefijo

pregnancy [prégnənsi] N embarazo *m*; (of an
animal) preñez *f*

pregnant [prégnənt] ADJ (person)
embarazada, encinta; (animal) preñada;
(full of meaning, rain) preñado, cargado

prehensile [prɪhénsəl] ADJ prensil

prehistoric [prihɪstórɪk] ADJ prehistórico

prejudge [pridʒʌ́dʒ] VT prejuzgar

prejudice [prédʒədɪs] N (bias) prejuicio *m*;
(harm) perjuicio *m*; VT (cause bias against)
predisponer en contra; (harm) perjudicar

preliminary [prɪlímɪneri] ADJ & N
preliminar *m*

prelude [prélud] N preludio *m*; VI/VT
preludiar

premarital [primǽrɪdəl] ADJ prematrimonial

premature [primətʃʊ́r] ADJ prematuro

premeditated [priméDɪteɪd] ADJ
premeditado

premier [prɪmír] N primer ministro/primera
ministra *mf*; ADJ principal

premiere [prɪmír] N estreno *m*, première *f*

premise [prémɪs] N premisa *f*; **—s** local *m*

premium [prímiəm] N (bonus) premio *m*;
(insurance) prima *f*; (surcharge) recargo *m*;
at a — muy escaso; ADJ superior

premonition [premənɪʃən] N premonición *f*

prenatal [prinédl] ADJ prenatal

prenuptial [prinʌ́pʃəl] ADJ prenupcial

preoccupy [priákjəpaɪ] VT absorber

prepaid [pripéd] ADJ pagado de antemano;
to send — enviar porte pagado

preparation [prepəréʃən] N (act of
preparing) preparación *f*; (substance)
preparado *m*; (for a trip) preparativos *m pl*

preparatory [prépəətɔri] ADJ preparatorio,
preparativo

prepare [prɪpér] VI/VT preparar(se)

preponderance [prɪpándəəns] N
preponderancia *f*

preponderant [prɪpándəənt] ADJ
preponderante

preposition [prepəzíʃən] N preposición *f*

preposterous [prɪpástəəs] ADJ absurdo

prerequisite [prirékwəzɪt] N prerequisito *m*

prerogative [prɪrágəDɪv] N prerrogativa *f*

prescribe [prɪskráɪb] VT (order) prescribir;
(medicine) recetar

prescription [prɪskrípʃən] N (order)
prescripción *f*; (of medicine) receta *f*

presence [prézəns] N presencia *f*; **— of mind**
aplomo *m*, presencia de ánimo *f*

present [prézənt] N (time) presente *m*; (gift)
regalo *m*, presente *m*; **at —** ahora; **for
the —** por ahora; ADJ (at a place) presente;
(at this time) actual; **— company
excepted** con perdón de los presentes;
—-day actual; **— participle** gerundio *m*;
— perfect pretérito perfecto *m*; [prɪzént]
VT presentar, entregar

presentable [prɪzéntəbəl] ADJ presentable

presentation [prezəntéʃən] N presentación *f*,
entrega *f*; (talk) ponencia *f*

presentiment [prɪzéntəmənt] N
presentimiento *m*

presently [prézəntli] ADV (soon) pronto;
(now) actualmente

preservation [prezə-véʃən] N preservación *f*,
conservación *f*

preservative [prɪzɚ́-vəDɪv] N conservante *m*

preserve [prɪzɚ́-v] VI/VT (protect) preservar;
(keep food fresh) conservar; N (for game)
coto *m*; (for animals) reserva *f*; **—s**
mermelada *f*, dulce *m*

preside [prɪzáɪd] VI presidir; **to — over a
meeting** presidir una reunión

presidency [prézɪdənsi] N presidencia *f*

president [prézɪdənt] N presidente -ta *mf*

presidential [prezɪdénʃəl] ADJ presidencial

press [pres] VI/VT (bear down, squeeze)
apretar, oprimir; (iron) planchar; (force)
presionar; (extract juice) prensar; (put
under pressure) apremiar; **to — on**
avanzar; **to — one's point** insistir en un
argumento; **to — through** abrirse paso; N
(newspapers) prensa *f*; (printing machine)
imprenta *f*; (crowding) empuje *m*; **—
conference** conferencia de prensa *f*; **—
corps** cuerpo de prensa *m*; **— release**
comunicado de prensa *m*

pressing [présɪŋ] ADJ apremiante, urgente

pressure [préʃɚ] N presión *f*; **— cooker** olla
a presión *f*; **— gauge** manómetro *m*; **—
group** grupo de presión *m*; VT apremiar,
presionar

prestige [prestíʒ] N prestigio *m*

prestigious [prestídʒəs] ADJ prestigioso

presume [prɪzúm] VI (be presumptuous)

presumir; VT (suppose) suponer; (dare)
atreverse a
presumption [prɪzʌ́mpʃən] N presunción f
presumptuous [prɪzʌ́mptʃuəs] ADJ
presuntuoso, presumido
presuppose [prisəpóz] VT presuponer
preteen [pritín] ADJ & N preadolescente mf
pretend [prɪténd] VI/VT (make believe) hacer
de cuenta que; (feign) fingir; VT (claim)
pretender; **to — to the throne** pretender
el trono
pretense [prítens] N (faked action or belief)
engaño m; (false show) apariencia f;
under — of so pretexto de
pretension [prɪténʃən] N pretensión f;
(pretext) pretexto m
pretentious [prɪténʃəs] ADJ (full of
pretension) pretencioso; (showy) ostentoso
pretext [prítekst] N pretexto m
pretrial [pritráɪł] ADJ anterior al juicio
pretty [prídi] ADJ bonito; (human only) Sp
guapo; ADV bastante; VI/VT **to — up**
embellecer
prevail [prɪvéł] VI (win) prevalecer; (be
widespread, dominant) preponderar,
imperar; **to — on (upon)** persuadir
prevailing [prɪvélɪŋ] ADJ (dominant)
predominante; (existing) reinante
prevalent [prévələnt] ADJ prevaleciente,
preponderante
prevent [prɪvént] VT (keep from occurring)
prevenir; VI/VT (impede) impedir
prevention [prɪvénʃən] N prevención f; (of a
disease) prevención f, profilaxis f
preventive [prɪvéntɪv] ADJ preventivo
preview [prívju] N preestreno m
previous [prívɪəs] ADJ previo, anterior
prey [pre] N (animal) presa f; VI **to — on**
alimentarse de cazar; **it —s upon my
mind** me tiene preocupado
price [praɪs] N precio m; **at any — a** toda
costa; **— control** control de precios m; **—
fixing** fijación de precios f; **— index**
índice de precios m; **— tag** etiqueta de
precio f; VT (set price) poner precio a; (ask
price) averiguar el precio de
priceless [práɪsləs] ADJ (without price)
invalorable; (amusing) divertidísimo
prick [prɪk] N (puncture) pinchazo m; (sharp
point) púa f; VI/VT pinchar, punzar; **to —
up one's ears** parar las orejas
prickly [príkli] ADJ espinoso; **— heat**
sarpullido causado por el calor m; **— pear**
tuna f, nopal m
pride [praɪd] N orgullo m; (excessive) soberbia
f; VI **to — oneself on** enorgullecerse de
priest [prist] N sacerdote m; (Catholic only)

cura m; **—hood** sacerdocio m
prim [prɪm] ADJ remilgado
primary [práɪmeri] ADJ primario; (main)
fundamental, principal; **— colors** colores
primarios m pl; **— election** elección
primaria f; **— school** escuela primaria f
primate [práɪmet] N primate m
prime [praɪm] ADJ (principal) fundamental;
(of a number) primo; (select) de primera;
— minister primer ministro m, primera
ministra f; N (stage) flor f; (number)
número primo m; **to be in one's — estar**
en la flor de la edad, estar en la plenitud
de la vida; **— rate** tasa prima f; VT
preparar; (a pump) cebar
primer [prímɚ] N (first book) manual
elemental m; (pump part) cebador m
primitive [prímɪdɪv] ADJ & N primitivo -va
mf
prince [prɪns] N príncipe m
princely [prínsli] ADJ noble, principesco; **a —
sum** una suma muy grande
princess [prínses] N princesa f
principal [prínsəpəł] ADJ principal; N
(money invested) capital m; (giver of
power of attorney) poderdante mf,
mandante mf; (head of a school) director
-ora mf
principle [prínsəpəł] N principio m
print [prɪnt] VI/VT imprimir; (write in block
letters) escribir en letra de molde; **to —
out** imprimir; N (type) letra de imprenta f;
(of art) lámina f; (of photographs) copia f;
(of fingers) huella digital f; (on cloth)
estampado m; **—out** listado m; **in —**
publicado, en venta; **out of —** agotado
printer [prínrɚ] N (person) impresor -ra mf,
gráfico -ca mf; (machine) impresora f
printing [príntɪŋ] N (art, trade) imprenta f;
(process) impresión f, tipografía f; (block
letters) letra de molde f, letra de imprenta
f; **— press** imprenta f; **this book is in
its second —** este libro está en su
segunda edición
prior [práɪɚ] ADJ previo; **— to** anterior a
priority [praɪɔ́rɪdi] N prioridad f
prism [prízəm] N prisma m
prison [prízən] N prisión f, cárcel f, presidio
m
prisoner [prízənɚ] N (captive) prisionero -ra
mf; (in jail) preso -sa mf, presidiario -ria
mf; **— of war** prisionero -ra de guerra mf
pristine [prɪstín] ADJ (immaculate) puro;
(perfect) perfecto
privacy [práɪvəsi] N privacidad f
private [práɪvɪt] ADJ (not public) privado;
(individual) particular; **— enterprise**

empresa privada *f;* — **eye** detective privado -da *mf;* — **parts** partes pudendas *f pl;* — **school** escuela privada *f;* — **sector** sector privado *m;* **a — citizen** un particular; **in —** en privado; N soldado raso *m*

privation [praɪvéʃən] N privación *f*

privilege [prívəlɪʤ] N privilegio *m*

privileged [prívlɪʤd] ADJ privilegiado

privy [prívi] ADJ **to be — to** estar enterado de; N retrete *m*

prize [praɪz] N (reward) premio *m;* (booty) botín *m;* — **fight** pelea de boxeo profesional *f;* — **fighter** boxeador -ora *mf,* pugilista *mf;* VT apreciar

pro [pro] N profesional *mf*

probability [prɑbəbílɪDi] N probabilidad *f*

probable [prábəbəl] ADJ probable

probation [probéʃən] N libertad condicional *f*

probe [prob] VI/VT (explore with a probe) sondear; (examine) examinar; N sonda *f* (also space); (investigation) indagación *f*

problem [prábləm] N problema *m*

procedure [prəsíʤə] N procedimiento *m;* (legal) trámite *m*

proceed [prəsíd] VI (originate) proceder; (continue) proseguir, continuar; **to — against** demandar a; **to — to** proceder a; N —**s** ganancia *f,* lo recaudado

proceedings [prəsídɪŋz] N (events) acontecimientos *m pl;* (record of a conference) actas *f pl,* memoria *f;* (legal action) procedimiento *m*

process [práses] N proceso *m;* **in the — of** en vías de

procession [prəséʃən] N procesión *f*

pro-choice [protʃóɪs] ADJ proaborto

proclaim [prəklém] VT proclamar

proclamation [prɑkləméʃən] N proclamación *f,* proclama *f*

procrastinate [prəkrǽstənət] VI/VT dejar para último momento

procreate [prókriet] VI/VT procrear, engendrar

procure [prəkjúr] VT procurar, obtener; VI ser proxeneta

prod [prɑd] VT aguijonear; **they —ded me into going / to go** insistieron en que fuera

prodigal [prádɪgəl] ADJ & N pródigo -ga *mf*

prodigious [prədíʤəs] ADJ prodigioso

prodigy [prádəʤi] N prodigio *m*

produce [pródus] N (vegetables) verduras *f pl,* hortalizas *f pl;* [prədús] VI/VT producir; VT (present) presentar

producer [prədúsə] N productor -ora *mf*

product [prádəkt] N producto *m*

production [prədákʃən] N producción *f;* (TV, radio) producción *f,* realización *f;* (exaggerated situation) teatro *m*

productive [prədáktɪv] ADJ productivo

profane [profén] ADJ profano; (vulgar) grosero; VT profanar

profanity [prəfǽnɪDi] N groserías *f pl,* palabrotas *f pl*

profess [prəfés] VI/VT (publicly accept, take vows) profesar; VT (express) expresar

profession [prəféʃən] N profesión *f*

professional [prəféʃənəl] ADJ & N profesional *mf*

professor [prəfésə] N profesor -ra universitario -ria *mf;* (full) catedrático -ca *mf*

proffer [práfə] VT ofrecer; N oferta *f*

proficiency [prəfíʃənsi] N competencia *f*

proficient [prəfíʃənt] ADJ competente

profile [prófaɪl] N (contour) perfil *m;* **a high-— case** un caso muy sonado

profit [práfɪt] N (gain) ganancia *f;* — **and loss** ganancias y pérdidas *f pl;* — **sharing** participación en las ganancias de una empresa *f;* **at a —** con ganancia; **to turn a —** dar ganancia; **not for —** sin fines de lucro; VI salir ganando; **to — from** (benefit) aprovechar, sacar provecho de; (use to get an advantage) aprovecharse de; VT servir

profitable [práfɪDəbəl] ADJ (beneficial) provechoso; (lucrative) lucrativo, rentable

profound [prəfáund] ADJ profundo

profundity [prəfándɪDi] N profundidad *f*

profuse [prəfjús] ADJ profuso, pródigo

progesterone [proʤéstəron] N progesterona *f*

prognosis [prɑgnósɪs] N pronóstico *m*

program [prógræm] N programa *m;* VI/VT programar

programmer [prógræmə] N programador -ora *mf*

programming [prógræmɪŋ] N programación *f*

progress [prágres] N progreso *m;* [prəgrés] VI progresar

progressive [prəgrésɪv] ADJ (advancing) progresivo; ADJ & N (liberal) progresista *mf,* progresivo -va *mf*

prohibit [prohíbɪt] VT prohibir, vedar

prohibition [proəbíʃən] N prohibición *f*

project [práʤekt] N proyecto *m;* [prəʤékt] VI/VT proyectar(se); VI (jut out) sobresalir

projectile [prəʤéktaɪl] N proyectil *m;* ADJ arrojadizo

projection [prəʤékʃən] N proyección *f,* (jut) saliente *f*

projector [prədʒéktə·] N proyector *m*
proletariat [prolɪtériət] N proletariado *m*
pro-life [prolái̯f] ADJ antiaborto
prolific [prəlífɪk] ADJ prolífico
prologue [prólɔg] N prólogo *m*
prolong [prəlɔ́ŋ] VT prolongar
prolongation [prolɔŋgéʃən] N prolongación *f*
promenade [prɑmənéd] N paseo *m*; (prom) baile *m*; VI/VT pasear(se)
prominent [prámənənt] ADJ prominente
promiscuous [prəmískjuəs] ADJ promiscuo, liviano
promise [prámɪs] N promesa *f*; **he showed — prometía** mucho; VI/VT prometer
promising [prámɪsɪŋ] ADJ prometedor, halagüeño
promissory [prámɪsɔri] ADJ promisorio; **— note** pagaré *m*
promontory [práməntɔri] N promontorio *m*
promote [prəmót] VT (foster) promover, fomentar; (advance in rank) ascender; (in school) pasar de año, promover; (advertise) promocionar
promoter [prəmódə·] N (fomenter) propulsor -ora *mf*; (organizer) promotor -ora *mf*
promotion [prəmóʃən] N (act of promoting) promoción *f*; (advance in rank) ascenso *m*
prompt [prɑmpt] ADJ (quick) rápido; (punctual) puntual; VT (cause) inducir; (in theater) apuntar; **to give someone a — apuntarle** a alguien
promptly [prámptli] ADV (soon) pronto; (punctually) puntualmente
promulgate [prámə̟lget] VT promulgar
prone [pron] ADJ (disposed) propenso, proclive; (face down) boca abajo; (prostrate) postrado
prong [prɔŋ] N púa *f*, diente *m*
pronoun [prónau̯n] N pronombre *m*
pronounce [prənáu̯ns] VT (enunciate) pronunciar; (declare) declarar
pronounced [prənáu̯nst] ADJ pronunciado
pronunciation [prənʌnsiéʃən] N pronunciación *f*
proof [pruf] N (evidence, test, trial printing) prueba *f*; (of alcohol) graduación *f*, grado *m*; **— of purchase** comprobante de compra *m*; **—reader** corrector -ra de pruebas *mf*; **fifty —** veinticinco por ciento de graduación alcohólica; ADJ **fire— a** prueba de incendios; **water—** impermeable; **bullet— a** prueba de balas
prop [prɑp] N (pole) puntal *m*; (in theater) accesorio *m*; (propeller) hélice *f*; (support) sostén *m*, apoyo *m*; (of a plant) tutor *m*; VT **to — against** apoyar en, sostener en;

to — up apuntalar, sostener
propaganda [prɑpəgǽndə] N propaganda *f*
propagate [prápəget] VI/VT propagar(se)
propagation [prɑpəgéʃen] N propagación *f*
propane [própen] N propano *m*
propel [prəpél] VT propulsar, impulsar
propeller [prəpélə·] N hélice *f*
propensity [prəpénsɪDi] N propensión *f*
proper [prápə·] ADJ (appropriate) apropiado; (decorous) decoroso; (genuine) como Dios manda; (correct) correcto; (in math, grammar) propio; **to be — to** ser propio de
property [prápə·Di] N (characteristic) propiedad *f*; (real estate) propiedad *f*, finca *f*; (assets) bienes *m pl*
prophecy [práfɪsi] N profecía *f*
prophesy [práfɪsai̯] VI/VT profetizar
prophet [práfɪt] N profeta -tisa *mf*
prophetic [prəfédɪk] ADJ profético
propitious [prəpíʃəs] ADJ propicio
proponent [prəpónənt] N (person who proposes) proponente *mf*; (adherent) defensor -ra *mf*
proportion [prəpórʃən] N proporción *f*; **out of —** desproporcionado; VT proporcionar; **well —ed** bien proporcionado
proposal [prəpózə̟l] N (suggestion) propuesta *f*; (of marriage, dishonest) proposición *f*
propose [prəpóz] VI/VT (suggest) proponer; VI (ask in marriage) declararse, hacer una proposición de matrimonio; **to — to do something** proponerse hacer algo
proposition [prɑpəzíʃən] N proposición *f*; VT hacer proposiciones deshonestas
proprietor [prəpráiɪDə·] N propietario -ria *mf*
propriety [prəpráiɪDi] N decoro *m*
propulsion [prəpʌ́lʃən] N propulsión *f*
prorate [prorét] VT prorratear
prosaic [prozéi̯k] ADJ prosaico
prose [proz] N prosa *f*
prosecute [prásɪkjut] VI/VT (take to court) procesar, enjuiciar; VT (pursue) llevar adelante
prosecution [prɑsɪkjúʃən] N (act of prosecuting) procesamiento *m*; (officials who prosecute) ministerio público *m*, fiscalía *f*
prosecutor [prásɪkjuDə·] N fiscal *mf*
proselytize [prásəlɪtai̯z] VT convertir; VI ganar prosélitos
prospect [práspekt] N (outlook, possibility) perspectiva *f*, expectativa *f*; (candidate) candidato -ta *mf*; (possible client) posible cliente -ta *mf*; VT prospectar; VI **to — for** buscar
prospective [prəspéktɪv] ADJ posible,

potencial
prospector [práspɛktə-] N prospector -ora *mf*
prosper [práspə-] VI prosperar
prosperity [prɑspɛ́rɪDi] N prosperidad *f*, bonanza *f*
prosperous [práspərəs] ADJ próspero
prostate [prástet] N próstata *f*; **— gland** próstata *f*
prosthesis [prɑsθísɪs] N prótesis *f*
prostitute [prástɪtut] N prostituto -ta *mf*; VT prostituir
prostrate [prástret] VT postrar; ADJ (lying flat, overcome) postrado; (lying face down) boca abajo
protagonist [protǽgənɪst] N protagonista *mf*
protect [prətɛ́kt] VI/VT proteger, amparar
protection [prətɛ́kʃen] N protección *f*
protectionist [prətɛ́kʃənɪst] ADJ & N proteccionista *mf*
protective [prətɛ́ktɪv] ADJ protector
protector [prətɛ́ktə-] N protector -ra *mf*
protectorate [prətɛ́ktərət] N protectorado *m*
protégé, protégée [próDəʒe] N protegido -da *mf*
protein [prótin] N proteína *f*
protest [prótɛst] N protesta *f*, reclamación *f*; [prətɛ́st] VI/VT protestar, reclamar
Protestant [práDɪstənt] ADJ & N protestante *mf*
protestation [protɛstéʃən] N declaración *f*
protocol [próDəkɔ̀l] N protocolo *m*
proton [prótan] N protón *m*
protoplasm [próDəplæzəm] N protoplasma *m*
prototype [próDətaɪp] N prototipo *m*
protozoan [proDəzóən] N protozoario *m*
protract [protrǽkt] VT prolongar
protrude [protrúd] VI sobresalir, proyectarse
protuberance [prətúbərəns] N protuberancia *f*
proud [praʊd] ADJ orgulloso; (haughty) soberbio; **to be — of** enorgullecerse de, ufanarse de
prove [pruv] VT (demonstrate) probar, demostrar; (verify) resultar; VI resultar; **events have —d me right** los hechos me han dado la razón
proverb [právə-b] N proverbio *m*, refrán *m*
provide [prəváɪd] VT (furnish) proveer, proporcionar; (supply) abastecer, aportar; (stipulate) estipular, prevenir; VI **to — for** (support) mantener; (stipulate) estipular; **to — with** proveer de, proporcionar
provided [prəváɪDɪd] CONJ **— (that)** con tal (de) que, siempre que
providence [právɪDəns] N providencia *f*
provider [prəváɪDə-] N (supplier) proveedor -ra *mf*; (breadwinner) sostén *m*

province [právɪns] N (area) provincia *f*; (competence) competencia *f*
provincial [prəvínʃəl] ADJ (of a province) provincial; (rustic) provinciano, pueblerino; N provinciano -na *mf*
provision [prəvíʒən] N (act of providing, thing provided) provisión *f*, prestación *f*; (precaution) medida *f*, precaución *f*; (clause) estipulación *f*, prevención *f*; **—s** provisiones *f pl*, víveres *m pl*, bastimentos *m pl*
provisional [prəvíʒənəl] ADJ provisional
proviso [prəváɪzo] N condición *f*, estipulación *f*
provocation [prɑvəkéʃən] N provocación *f*
provoke [prəvók] VT provocar
provost [próvost] N vicerrector -ora *mf*
prow [praʊ] N proa *f*
prowess [práʊɪs] N valentía *f*
prowl [praʊł] VI/VT rondar en acecho
proximity [prɑksímɪDi] N proximidad *f*
proxy [práksi] N (person) apoderado -da *mf*; (power of attorney) poder *m*; **by —** por poder
prude [prud] N mojigato -ta *mf*, gazmoño -ña *mf*
prudence [prúdn̩s] N prudencia *f*
prudent [prúdn̩t] ADJ prudente
prudery [prúDəri] N mojigatería *f*, gazmoñería *f*
prudish [prúDɪʃ] ADJ mojigato, gazmoño
prune [prun] N ciruela pasa *f*; VI/VT podar
pry [praɪ] VT curiosear; **to — into** entrometerse; **to — open** abrir por la fuerza; **to — a secret out** extraer / arrancar un secreto
pseudonym [súdn̩ɪm] N seudónimo *m*
psoriasis [səráɪəsɪs] N psoriasis *f*
psychedelic [saɪkɪdɛ́lɪk] ADJ psicodélico
psychiatrist [saɪkáɪətrɪst] N psiquiatra *mf*
psychiatry [saɪkáɪətri] N psiquiatría *f*
psychic [sáɪkɪk] ADJ psíquico; N médium *mf*, psíquico -ca *mf*
psychological [saɪkəláʤɪkəl] ADJ psicológico
psychologist [saɪkáləʤɪst] N psicólogo -ga *mf*
psychology [saɪkáləʤi] N psicología *f*
psychopath [sáɪkəpæθ] N psicópata *mf*
psychosis [saɪkósɪs] N psicosis *f*
psychosomatic [saɪkosəmǽDɪk] ADJ psicosomático
psychotherapy [saɪkoθérəpi] N psicoterapia *f*
psychotic [saɪkáDɪk] ADJ psicótico
puberty [pjúbə-Di] N pubertad *f*
public [páblɪk] ADJ público; **— domain** dominio público *m*; **— relations** relaciones públicas *f pl*; **— school** escuela pública *f*; **— service** servicio público *m*; N

público *m*

publication [pʌblɪkéʃən] N publicación *f*

publicity [pʌblísɪDɪ] N publicidad *f*, propaganda *f*

publish [pʌblɪʃ] VI/VT publicar, editar; **—ing house** editorial *f*

publisher [pʌblɪʃ&] N editor -ra *mf*

puck [pʌk] N puck *m*

pucker [pʌk&-] VI/VT fruncir(se); N frunce *m*

pudding [pʊdɪŋ] N budín *m*

puddle [pʌdl] N charco *m*

Puerto Rican [pɔrDəríkən] ADJ & N puertorriqueño -ña *mf*

Puerto Rico [pɔrDəríko] N Puerto Rico *m*

puff [pʌf] N (air) resoplido *m*, soplo *m*; (smoke) bocanada *f*; (on a cigarette) pitada *f*, chupada *f*; (of a sleeve) bullón *m*; **— pastry** masa de hojaldre *f*; VI (blow) resoplar; (breathe hard) jadear; (smoke a cigarette) echar bocanadas; **to — up** hincharse; **to — up with pride** henchirse de orgullo

pug [pʌg] N dogo *m*; **— nose** nariz chata *f*

puke [pjuk] VI/VT vomitar, lanzar; N vómito *m*

pull [pʊl] VI/VT (tug) tirar, jalar; (extract) arrancar, extraer; (stretch) estirar; (injure) desgarrarse; **to — apart** destrozar; **to — down** (demolish) demoler; (earn) sacar; **to — for** hinchar; **to — off** conseguir; **to — oneself together** calmarse; **to — over** parar; **to — up** parar; **to — through** salvarse; **to — strings** mover palancas; **to — out** (leave a place) salir; (back out) retirarse; **the train —ed into the station** el tren entró a la estación; N (act of pulling) tirón *m*; (force) fuerza *f*; (influence) influencia *f*; (injury) desgarro *m*

pullet [pʊlɪt] N polla *f*

pulley [pʊli] N polea *f*, carrucha *f*

pulp [pʌlp] N (of paper, wood, fruit) pulpa *f*; (residue of grape, sugarcane, olive, etc.) bagazo *m*

pulpit [pʊlpɪt] N púlpito *m*

pulsar [pʌlsar] N púlsar *m*

pulsate [pʌlset] VI latir

pulse [pʌls] N pulso *m*; (single pulsation, act of pulsing) pulsación *f*

pulverize [pʌlvəraɪz] VT pulverizar(se)

pumice [pʌmɪs] N piedra pómez *f*

pump [pʌmp] N bomba *f*; (shoe) zapatilla *f*, zapato escotado *m*; (for gasoline) surtidor *m*; VI/VT bombear; (inflate) inflar; **to — someone for information** sonsacar (información) a alguien

pumpkin [pʌmpkɪn] N calabaza *f*

pun [pʌn] N juego de palabras *m*, retruécano *m*; VI hacer juegos de palabras

punch [pʌntʃ] N (blow) puñetazo *m*; (drink) ponche *m*; (drill) sacabocados *m sg*; (force) fuerza *f*, empuje *m*; **— bowl** ponchera *f*; **— line** remate de un chiste *m*; VI/VT (hit) dar un puñetazo; VT (drive cattle) arriar; (make a hole) agujerear; **to — in / out** marcar tarjeta

punctual [pʌŋktʃuəl] ADJ puntual

punctuality [pʌŋktʃuǽlɪDɪ] N puntualidad *f*

punctuate [pʌŋktʃuet] VI/VT puntuar; (interrupt) interrumpir; (accentuate) salpicar

punctuation [pʌŋktʃuéʃən] N puntuación *f*

puncture [pʌŋktʃ&-] VI/VT pinchar(se); **—d tire** neumático pinchado *m*; N (action of perforating) perforación *f*; (hole) pinchazo *m*

pundit [pʌndɪt] N experto -ta *mf*

pungent [pʌndʒənt] ADJ (acrid) acre; (sarcastic) mordaz

punish [pʌnɪʃ] VT castigar, penar

punishment [pʌnɪʃmənt] N castigo *m*

punitive [pjúnɪDɪv] ADJ punitivo; **— damages** daños punitivos *m pl*

punk [pʌŋk] N (inexperienced boy) mocoso *m*; (hoodlum) gamberro *m*; (rock) punk *m*; (punker) punkero -ra *mf*

punt [pʌnt] N (kick) patada de despeje *f*; (boat) balsa *f*; VI/VT despejar; VI andar en balsa

puny [pjúni] ADJ endeble, ruin

pupil [pjúpəl] N escolar *mf*; **— of the eye** pupila *f*, niña *f*

puppet [pʌpɪt] N títere *m*, monigote *m*; **— show** teatro de títeres *m*

puppy [pʌpi] N cachorro *m*

purchase [p&-tʃəs] VI/VT comprar, adquirir; N compra *f*; (hold) asidero *m*

purchaser [p&-tʃəs&-] N comprador *mf*

pure [pjur] ADJ puro; ADJ & N **—bred** purasangre *m*

puree [pjuré] N puré *m*

purgative [p&-gəDɪv] ADJ & N purgante *m*

purgatory [p&-gətɔri] N purgatorio *m*

purge [p&-dʒ] VI/VT purgar(se); N purga *f*

purify [pjúrəfaɪ] VI/VT purificar(se), depurar(se)

purist [pjúrɪst] N purista *mf*

puritanical [pjurɪtǽnɪkəl] ADJ puritano

purity [pjúrɪDɪ] N pureza *f*

purple [p&-pəl] N morado *m*, púrpura *f*; ADJ púrpura *inv*, morado

purport [p&-pɔrt] N (meaning) significado *m*; (purpose) propósito *m*; [pə-pórt] VT pretender

purpose [pʌ́·pəs] N propósito *m*, objetivo *m*; **on —** adrede, a propósito

purr [pɜ·] N ronroneo *m* (also motors); VI ronronear

purse [pɜ·s] N bolso *m*, cartera *f*; VT **to — one's lips** fruncir los labios

pursuant [pə·súant] ADV LOC **— to** conforme a, de acuerdo con

pursue [pə·sú] VT (follow) perseguir; (strive) dedicarse a; (continue) continuar con; (practice a profession) ejercer

pursuer [pə·súə·] N perseguidor -ora *mf*

pursuit [pə·sút] N (chase) persecución *f*, seguimiento *m*; (striving for) búsqueda *f*; (pastime) pasatiempo *m*; (practice) ejercicio *m*; **in — of** (chasing) detrás de; (striving for) en busca de

pus [pʌs] N pus *m*

push [puʃ] VI/VT (shove) empujar; VT (pressure) presionar, promover; (sell drugs) camellear; VI (in childbirth) pujar; **to — aside / away** apartar; **to — forward** abrirse paso, avanzar; **to — open** abrir con un empujón; **to — through** hacer pasar; **to — a button** apretar un botón; N empujón *m*; (military) ofensiva *f*; **—-button** de botones; **—-up** lagartija *f*

pusher [púʃə·] N camello *mf*

pushy [púʃi] ADJ insistente

pussy [púsi] N (cat) minino *m*, gatito *m*; **— willow** sauce *m*

put [put] VT poner, colocar; **to — a question** plantear una pregunta; **to — across** expresar; **to — away** guardar; **to — down** (write down) apuntar; (suppress) sofocar; (attribute) atribuir; (humiliate) humillar; (make a deposit) hacer un depósito; **to — into** meter; **to — into words** expresar, decir; **to — in writing** poner por escrito; **to — off** (postpone) aplazar, posponer; (perturb) desagradar; **to — on** ponerse; **to — on airs** darse tono; **to — on weight** engordar; **to — out** (extinguish) apagar, extinguir; (annoy) molestar; **to — the blame** echar la culpa; **to — to sea** echar al mar; **to — up** (construct) levantar; (lodge) alojar; **to — up for sale** poner a la venta; **to — up with** aguantar; **—-down** insulto *m*; **I felt —-upon** sentí que se habían aprovechado de mí

putrid [pjútrid] ADJ putrefacto

putter [pʌ́də·] VI entretenerse; N putter *m*

putty [pʌ́di] N masilla *f*; VT rellenar con masilla

puzzle [pʌ́zəl] N (jigsaw) rompecabezas *m sg*; (riddle) acertijo *m*; (problem) enigma *m*;

(crossword) crucigrama *m*; VT dejar perplejo, desconcertar; VI **to — out** desentrañar; **to — over** meditar sobre; **to be —d** estar perplejo

pygmy [pígmi] N pigmeo -a *mf*

pylon [páilɑn] N pilón *m*

pyramid [pírəmid] N pirámide *f*

pyromaniac [pairoméniæk] N pirómano -na *mf*

pyrotechnics [pairətékniks] N pirotecnia *f*

python [páiθɑn] N pitón *mf*

Qq

Qatar [kətár] N Qatar *m*

Qatari [kətári] ADJ & N catarí *mf*

quack [kwæk] N (sound of duck) graznido *m* (charlatan) matasanos *mf*, charlatán -ana *mf*; ADJ charlatán; VI graznar

quadrilateral [kwɑdrəláEDəəł] ADJ & N cuadrilátero *m*

quadriplegic [kwɑdrəplídʒik] ADJ & N tetraplégico -ca *mf*

quadruped [kwɑ́drəped] ADJ & N cuadrúped *m*

quadruplet [kwɑdrúpłit] N cuatrillizo -za *m*/

quagmire [kwǽgmair] N (bog) cenagal *m*, atascadero *m*; (crisis) atolladero *m*, atascadero *m*

quail [kweł] N codorniz *f*

quaint [kwent] ADJ pintoresco

quake [kwek] N (instance of quaking) temblor *m*; (earthquake) terremoto *m*; VI temblar

qualification [kwɑləfikéʃən] N (for a race) clasificación *f*; (requirement) requisito *m*; **without —** sin reservas

qualify [kwɑ́ləfai] VT (characterize) calificar; (moderate) moderar; (provide with credentials) capacitar; VI (for a race) clasificarse; (for a position) estar capacitado

quality [kwɑ́lidi] N (characteristic) cualidad *f*; (excellence) calidad *f*

qualm [kwɔm] N escrúpulo *m*

quantify [kwɑ́ntəfai] VT cuantificar

quantity [kwɑ́ntidi] N cantidad *f*

quantum mechanics [kwɑ́ntəmməkǽniks] N mecánica cuántica *f*

quarantine [kwɔ́rəntin] N cuarentena *f*; VT poner en cuarentena

quarrel [kwɔ́rəł] N riña *f*, rencilla *f*; VI reñir, pelear

quarrelsome [kwɔ́rəɫsəm] ADJ pendenciero

quarry [kwɔ́ri] N (stone) cantera *f*; (game) presa *f*; VT explotar

quart [kwɔrt] N cuarto de galón (0.9463 litros) *m*

quarter [kwɔ́rDɚ] N (one-fourth) cuarto *m*, cuarta parte *f*; (coin) moneda de 25 centavos *f*; (of a sporting match) tiempo *m*; (of a calendar or school year) trimestre *m*; (district) barrio *m*; **— note** negra *f*; **—s** alojamiento *m*; **from all —s** de todas partes; **to give no — to the enemy** no dar cuartel al enemigo; ADJ cuarto; VT (divide) cuartear, dividir en cuartos; (execute) descuartizar; (lodge troops) acuartelar, acantonar

quarterly [kwɔ́rDɚli] ADV trimestralmente; ADJ trimestral; N publicación trimestral *f*

quartet [kwɔrtét] N cuarteto *m*

quartz [kwɔrts] N cuarzo *m*

quasar [kwéːzɑr] N cuásar *m*, quásar *m*

quash [kwɑʃ] VT (a rebellion) sofocar; (a decision) anular

quaver [kwéːvɚ] VI temblar; N temblor *m*; (in music) trémolo *m*

queasy [kwízi] ADJ nauseoso

queen [kwin] N reina *f*

queer [kwir] ADJ (strange) raro; (eccentric) excéntrico; **to feel —** sentirse raro; VT comprometer

quell [kweɫ] VT (suppress) reprimir, sofocar; (calm) calmar

quench [kwentʃ] VT (flames, thirst) apagar; (passions) aplacar, apagar

query [kwíri] N (question) pregunta *f*; (question mark) signo de interrogación *m*; (doubt) duda *f*; VT (ask) preguntar; (question) expresar dudas; (mark with a question mark) marcar con signo de interrogación

quest [kwest] N búsqueda *f*

question [kwéstʃən] N (thing asked) pregunta *f*; (issue) cuestión *f*; **— mark** signo de interrogación *m*; **beyond —** fuera de duda; **that is out of the —** ¡ni pensarlo! VT (ask) preguntar; (interrogate) interrogar; (call into doubt) dudar, cuestionar

questionable [kwéstʃənəbəɫ] ADJ (doubtful) cuestionable, discutible; (morally dubious) equívoco

questioner [kwéstʃənɚ] N interrogador -ra *mf*

questioning [kwéstʃənɪŋ] N interrogatorio *m*; ADJ (asking) interrogador; (doubting) cuestionador

questionnaire [kwestʃənér] N cuestionario *m*

quibble [kwíbəɫ] VI (split hairs) sutilizar; (evade) evadir; (argue) andar en dimes y diretes; N (hairsplitting) sutileza *f*; (evasion) evasiva *f*

quiche [kiʃ] N quiche *f*

quick [kwɪk] ADJ rápido, pronto; **—-tempered** irascible, geniudo; **—-witted** agudo; ADV rápido; N (flesh under nails) carne viva *f*; (the living) los vivos; **to cut to the —** herir en lo vivo; **—sand** arena movediza *f*; **—silver** mercurio *m*, azogue *m*

quicken [kwíkən] VI/VT (speed up) acelerar(se), aligerar(se); (liven) avivar(se)

quickly [kwíkli] ADV rápido, deprisa

quickness [kwíknɪs] N (speed) rapidez *f*; (of wit) agudeza *f*

quiet [kwáɪt] ADJ (not noisy) silencioso; (not talking) callado; (restrained) tranquilo; (peaceful, still) reposado; **be —!** ¡silencio! ¡cállate! N (freedom from noise) silencio *m*; (tranquility) tranquilidad *f*, sosiego *m*; VT (make quiet) acallar; (make tranquil) sosegar, tranquilizar, serenar; VI **to — down** calmarse

quill [kwɪɫ] N (feather) pluma *f*; (hollow base of feather) cañón *m*; (spine on a porcupine) púa *f*

quilt [kwɪɫt] N edredón *m*; VI/VT acolchar

quip [kwɪp] N ocurrencia *f*; VI decir ocurrencias

quirk [kwɝk] N excentricidad *f*

quit [kwɪt] VT (a competition) abandonar; (a place) irse de, salir de; (a job) dejar; **to call it —s** abandonar; **to — smoking** dejar de fumar; VI (withdraw) abandonar; (stop) parar; (resign) renunciar

quite [kwaɪt] ADV (very) bastante; (entirely) del todo, enteramente; **— a person** una persona admirable *f*; **— a lot** bastante; **it's — the fashion** está muy de moda

quiver [kwívɚ] VI temblar; N (shake) temblor *m*; (sheath for arrows) carcaj *m*, aljaba *f*

quiz [kwɪz] N (test) prueba *f*; (show) concurso *m*; VI (give a quiz) examinar, poner una prueba; (interrogate) interrogar

quota [kwóDə] N cuota *f*

quotation [kwotéʃən] N cita *f*; (of a price) cotización *f*; **— marks** comillas *f pl*

quote [kwot] VI/VT citar; (prices) cotizar; **to — from** citar a; N cita *f*; (of a price) cotización *f*; **in —s** entre comillas

quotient [kwóʃənt] N cociente *m*

Rr

rabbi [rǽbaɪ] N rabino -na *mf*

rabbit [rǽbɪt] N conejo *m*

rabble [rǽbəl] N chusma *f*, plebe *f*, gentuza *f*

rabid [rǽbɪd] ADJ rabioso

rabies [rébiz] N rabia *f*

raccoon [rækún] N mapache *m*

race [res] N (lineage) raza *f*; (competition) carrera *f*; **—horse** caballo de carreras *m*; **—track** (for runners) pista *f*; (for horses) hipódromo *m*; VI (participate in competition) correr, competir en una carrera; (hurry) ir corriendo; (of heart) latir rápido; (of a motor) acelerar; VT (a horse) hacer correr; (an engine) acelerar; **I'll — you** te echo una carrera

racer [résə-] N corredor -ra *mf*; (horse) caballo de carreras *m*

racial [réʃəl] ADJ racial

racism [résɪzəm] N racismo *m*

rack [ræk] N (for clothes) perchero *m*; (on a vehicle) baca *f*; (for spices) especiero *m*; (for towels) toallero *m*; (torture) potro de tormento *m*; **— and pinion** cremallera *f* y piñón *m*; VT **to be —ed with pain** estar transido de dolor; **to — one's brain** devanarse los sesos; **to — up** acumular

racket [rǽkɪt] N (sports) raqueta *f*; (noise of an impact) estrépito *m*, estruendo *m*; (noise of voices and movement) barahúnda *f*, batahola *f*; (swindle) estafa *f*; (extortion) extorsión *f*

racketeer [rækitír] N trapacero -ra *mf*; (swindler) estafador -ra *mf*; (extortionist) extorsionista *mf*; VI (swindle) estafar; (extort) extorsionar

radar [rédɑr] N radar *m*

radial [rédiəl] ADJ radial

radiance [rédiəns] N resplandor *m*, fulgor *m*

radiant [rédiənt] ADJ radiante, resplandeciente

radiate [rédiet] VI/VT irradiar, radiar; (health) derrochar

radiation [rediéʃən] N radiación *f*

radiator [rédietə-] N radiador *m*

radical [rǽdɪkəl] ADJ & N radical *mf*

radicalism [rǽdɪkəlɪzəm] N radicalismo *m*

radio [rédio] ADJ **—active** radiactivo, radioactivo; N (device, system of communication) radio *f*; **— announcer** locutor -ra *mf*; **— listener** radioescucha *mf*; **— station** radiodifusora *f*; **—**

telescope radiotelescopio *m*; **— transmitter** radiotransmisor *m*; **by —** por radio; VT (broadcast) transmitir por radio; VI/VT (call) llamar por radio

radiology [rediálədʒi] N radiología *f*

radish [rǽdɪʃ] N rábano *m*

radium [rédiəm] N radio *m*

radius [rédiəs] N radio *m*

radon [rédɑn] N radón *m*

raffle [rǽfəl] N rifa *f*, sorteo *m*; VI rifar, sortear

raft [ræft] N balsa *f*

rafter [rǽftə-] N viga *f*, cabrio *m*

rag [ræg] N (piece of cloth) trapo *m*, guiñapo *m*; (clothes) harapo *m*, andrajo *m*; **— doll** muñeca de trapo *f*

rage [redʒ] N ira *f*, rabia *f*, cólera *f*; **to be all the —** estar de moda; VI enfurecerse; **to — with anger** bramar de ira

ragged [rǽgɪd] ADJ (ill-clothed) andrajoso, harapiento, desharrapado; (voice) ronco, roto; (on an edge) irregular, desigual; **to be on the — edge** estar al borde

raid [red] N (military) incursión *f*; (by police) allanamiento *m*, redada *f*; (by air) bombardeo aéreo *m*; VI/VT hacer una incursión; VT (attack) atacar; (rob) asaltar; (by the police) allanar

rail [rel] N (of a railroad track) riel *m*, carril *m*; (railing) baranda *f*, barandilla *f*; **— fence** barrera *f*; **—road** ferrocarril *m*; **—road company** empresa ferroviaria *f*; **—road crossing** cruce de ferrocarril *m*; **—road employee** ferroviario -a *mf*; **to —road** (goods) transportar por ferrocarril; (laws) hacer aprobar apresuradamente; (a person) condenar injustamente; **—way** ferrocarril *m*; **by —** por ferrocarril

railing [rélɪŋ] N (barrier) baranda *f*; (on a bridge) pretil *m*; (on a stairway) pasamán *m*

rain [ren] N lluvia *f*; **—bow** arco iris *m*; **—coat** impermeable *m*; **—drop** gota de lluvia *f*; **—fall** precipitación *f*; **— forest** selva tropical *f*; **— gauge** pluviómetro *f*; **—storm** temporal de lluvia *f*; **— water** agua llovediza *f*; VI/VT llover; **— or shine** llueva o truene; **to — cats and dogs** llover a cántaros

rainy [réni] ADJ lluvioso

raise [rez] VI/VT (voice, hand, a house, spirit) levantar(se); VT (prices) subir; (an alarm) dar; (a flag) izar; (crops) cultivar; (animal children) criar; (money) recabar, recaudar; **to — a question** plantear una pregunta; **to — a racket** armar un alboroto; N aumento *m*

raisin [rézin] N pasa (de uva) *f*

rake [rek] N rastrillo *m*; VI/VT rastrillar; **to —
in money** amasar dinero

rally [ráli] VI/VT (reorganize troops)
reunir(se), juntar(se); (inspire) reanimar; VI
(demonstrate) concentrarse; (recuperate)
recuperarse; (reinvigorate) recobrar ánimo;
(rise in value) repuntar; **to — around
someone** apoyar a alguien; N
(demonstration) concentración *f*;
(recovery) recuperación *f*; (rise in prices)
subida *f*

RAM (random-access memory) [ræm] N
RAM *m*

ram [ræm] N (male sheep) carnero *m*; (tool
for battering) ariete *m*; (part of a ship)
espolón *m*; VT chocar contra; **to — a
boat** embestir un buque con el espolón

ramble [ræmbəl] VI vagar; **to — on** divagar;
N paseo *m*

ramp [ræmp] N rampa *f*

rampage [ræmpedʒ] N **to go on a —** andar
destrozando todo; VI andar destrozando
todo

rampant [ræmpənt] ADJ desenfrenado

ranch [ræntʃ] N hacienda *f*; *Mex* rancho *m*

rancid [rænsɪd] ADJ rancio

rancor [ræŋkɚ] N rencor *m*

random [rændəm] ADJ aleatorio, azaroso; **at
—** al azar; **— access memory** memoria
de acceso directo *f*

range [rendʒ] N (gamut) gama *f*; (of a gun)
alcance *m*; (amplitude of variation)
fluctuación *f*; (of mountains) cadena *f*; (for
shooting) campo de tiro *m*; (of an aircraft)
autonomía *f*; (grazing place) campo
abierto *m*; (stove) cocina *f*; *Mex* estufa *f*; **—
finder** telémetro *m*; **— of vision** alcance
visual *m*; VT (align) alinear; (of a gun)
tener alcance; VI (vary) oscilar; (be found
in an area) extenderse; **his children —
in age between 2 and 10** sus hijos van
en edad entre 2 y 10

ranger [réndʒɚ] N (in a park) guardabosques
mf; (soldier) guardia de asalto *m*

rank [ræŋk] N (in a hierarchy) rango *m*,
grado *m*; (line) fila *f*; **— and file** (of an
army) tropa *f sg*; **the —s** (soldiers) la
tropa; (union members) bases *f pl*; **a
sculptor of the first —** un escultor de
primer orden; VT (arrange) poner en orden
de importancia; VI (rate) figurar; **to —
high** tener alto rango; **to — second** estar
clasificado en el segundo lugar; ADJ
(smelly) hediondo; (growing vigorously)
exuberante

ransack [rænsæk] VT saquear, desvalijar

ransom [rænsəm] N rescate *m*; VT rescatar

rant [rænt] VI/VT despotricar

rap [ræp] VI/VT (strike) golpear; (chat) charlar;
VI rapear, cantar rap; N (blow) golpe *m*;
(accusation) cargo *m*; **to take the —** ser
el cabeza de turco; **— music** música rap *f*

rapacious [rəpéʃəs] ADJ rapaz

rape [rep] N (violation) violación *f*;
(statutory) estupro *m*; (plant) colza *f*;
(grape pulp) orujo *m*; VT violar

rapid [ræpɪd] ADJ rápido; N **—s** rápidos *m pl*

rapidity [rəpídɪti] N rapidez *f*

rapport [rapór] N relación *f*

rapt [ræpt] ADJ extasiado

rapture [ræptʃɚ] N éxtasis *m*, embeleso *m*; **to
go into a —** arrobarse

rare [rer] ADJ (infrequent) raro, poco
frecuente, extraño; (of gas, earth) raro;
(thin, of air) enrarecido; (excellent)
excepcional; (not well-done) crudo; **—
earths** tierras raras *f pl*

rarity [rérɪti] N rareza *f*; (of air)
enrarecimiento *m*

rascal [ræskəl] N bribón *m*, bellaco *m*, pícaro
m; *Sp* golfo *m*; **you little —!** ¡bandido!
¡sinvergüenza!

rash [ræʃ] ADJ (thoughtless) precipitado,
temerario; N sarpullido *m*

raspberry [ræzberi] N frambuesa *f*; **— bush**
frambueso *m*

raspy [ræspi] ADJ ronco, áspero

rat [ræt] N rata *f*; **I smell a —** aquí hay gato
encerrado; VI (one's hair) cardar; **to — on**
chivar, delatar

ratchet [rætʃɪt] N trinquete *m*

rate [ret] N (amount of interest) tasa *f*;
(charge) tarifa *f*; (unit charge for
insurance) prima *f*; (pace) paso *m*, ritmo
m; **— of exchange** tipo de cambio *m*; **at
any —** en todo caso; **at this —** a este
ritmo; **at the — of** a razón de; VT
(estimate) valorar, estimar; (esteem)
considerar; **he —s as the best** se le
considera como el mejor; **he —s high** se
le tiene en alta estima

rather [ræðɚ] ADV (somewhat) bastante;
(more precisely) más bien; **— than** en vez
de; **I would — die than** antes la muerte
que; **I would — not go** prefiero no ir

ratify [rætəfaɪ] VT ratificar

rating [rédɪŋ] N (act of adjudging)
calificación *f*; (for credit) clasificación *f*;
(TV quotient) rating televisivo *m*, índice
de audiencia *m*

ratio [réʃio] N razón *f*, proporción *f*

ration [ræʃən] N ración *f*; VT racionar

rational [ræʃənəl] ADJ racional

rationale [ræʃənǽɫ] N motivo *m*

rationalize [rǽʃənəlaɪz] VI/VT racionalizar

rationing [rǽʃənɪŋ] N racionamiento *m*

rattle [rǽdl] VI (bang) golpetear; (move noisily) traquetear; **to — on** parlotear; VT hacer sonar, sacudir; **to — off** recitar; N (banging) golpeteo *m*; (movement) traqueteo *m*; (toy) sonaja *f*, sonajero *m*; (of a rattlesnake) cascabel *m*; (of death) estertor *m*; **—snake** víbora de cascabel *f*

raucous [rɔ́kəs] ADJ (loud) estridente; (rowdy) escandaloso

ravage [rǽvɪʤ] VI/VT asolar, arruinar; N estrago *m*

rave [rev] VI (rant) desvariar, delirar; VI/VT (roar) bramar; **to — about** deshacerse en elogios; N crítica muy favorable *f*

raven [révən] N cuervo *m*; ADJ azabache

ravenous [rǽvənəs] ADJ voraz, famélico; **to be —** tener un hambre canina

ravine [rəvín] N quebrada *f*, barranco *m*, cañada *f*

raving [révɪŋ] ADJ delirante; (extraordinary) extraordinario; **— mad** loco de remate; N desvarío *m*

ravish [rǽvɪʃ] VT (kidnap) raptar, secuestrar; (rape) violar

raw [rɔ] ADJ (uncooked, unprocessed, damp and cold) crudo; (of vegetables) fresco, crudo; (unadorned) descarnado; **— flesh** carne viva *f*; **— material** materia prima *f*; **— sugar** azúcar bruto *m*; N **—hide** cuero crudo *m*

ray [re] N (beam) rayo *m*; (stingray) raya *f*

rayon [réan] N rayón *m*

raze [rez] VT arrasar, asolar

razor [réza·] N (device with blade) maquinilla de afeitar *f*, rasuradora *f*; (barber's tool) navaja *f*; (electric) rasuradora electrica *f*; **— blade** hoja de afeitar *f*; **safety —** navaja de seguridad *f*

reach [ritʃ] VI/VT (extend) alcanzar; VT (arrive at) llegar a; (contact) ponerse en contacto con; **to — for** tratar de agarrar; *Sp* tratar de coger; **to — into** meter la mano en; **to — out one's hand** alargar la mano; N alcance *m*; **beyond his —** fuera de su alcance; **within his —** a su alcance; **far —es** zona remota *f*

react [riǽkt] VI reaccionar

reaction [riǽkʃən] N reacción *f*

reactionary [riǽkʃəneri] ADJ & N reaccionario -ria *mf*

reactor [riǽktə·] N reactor *m*

read [rid] VI/VT leer; VT (interpret) interpretar; (give as a reading) decir; (indicate) indicar, marcar; **it —s easily** es fácil de leer; N

lectura *f*

reader [rídə·] N (person who reads) lector -ra *mf*; (schoolbook) libro de lectura *m*, cartilla *f*; (anthology) antología *f*

readily [rédli] ADV fácilmente

readiness [rédɪnɪs] N estado de preparación *m*; (willingness) buena disposición *f*; **to be in —** estar preparado, estar listo

reading [rídɪŋ] N lectura *f*; (interpretation) interpretación *f*; **— room** sala de lectura *f*

readjust [riəʤást] VI/VT (improve fit) reajustar; (acclimate) readaptar

readjustment [riəʤástmənt] N (fitting) reajuste *m*; (acclimation) readaptación *f*

ready [rédi] ADJ (prepared) listo, preparado, pronto; (willing) dispuesto; (available) disponible; (quick) rápido; **—-made** de confección

reagent [riéʤənt] ADJ & N reactivo *m*

real [riɫ] ADJ real, verdadero; **— estate** bienes raíces *m pl*, bienes inmuebles *m pl*

realism [ríəlɪzəm] N realismo *m*

realist [ríəlɪst] N realista *mf*

realistic [ríəlístɪk] ADJ realista

reality [riǽlɪdi] N realidad *f*; **— check** ajuste de perspectiva *m*

realization [riəlɪzéʃən] N (making real) realización *f*; (understanding) comprensión *f*

realize [ríəlaɪz] VT (achieve) realizar; (comprehend) darse cuenta de, comprobar

realm [rɛɫm] N (kingdom) reino *m*; (domain) terreno *m*, esfera *f*

realtor[rm] [ríəɫtə·] N agente inmobiliario -ria *mf*

reap [rip] VI/VT (cut with sickle) segar; (harvest) cosechar; **to — a benefit** obtener, sacar

reaper [rípə·] N (person) segador -ora *mf*; (machine) segadora *f*; (death) la Parca, la Muerte

reappear [riəpír] VI reaparecer

rear [rir] ADJ trasero, posterior; **—guard** retaguardia *f*; N (space at the back) parte de atrás *f*, fondo *m*; (backside) trasero *m*, posaderas *f pl*; **— end** trasero *m*; **—view mirror** espejo retrovisor *m*; VT (raise) criar; VI (rise on back legs) encabritarse, empinarse

reason [rízən] N (faculty) razón *f*; (cause) motivo *m*, razón *f*; **by —** of por causa de; **it stands to —** es lógico; VT razonar; **to — out** resolver por medio de la razón; **to — with** hacer entrar en razón

reasonable [rízənəbəɫ] ADJ razonable; (in price) módico, moderado

reasoning [rízənɪŋ] N razonamiento *m*,

raciocinio *m*; ADJ racional

reassure [riəʃúr] VT tranquilizar

rebate [ríbet] N reembolso *m*, reintegro *m*; VT reembolsar, reintegrar

rebel [rébəl] ADJ & N rebelde *mf*, insurrecto -ta *mf*; [ríbél] VI rebelarse

rebellion [ríbéljən] N rebelión *f*

rebellious [ríbéljəs] ADJ rebelde, insurrecto

rebelliousness [ríbéljəsnıs] N rebeldía *f*

rebound [ríbáund] VI (bounce) rebotar; (recover) recuperarse; [ríbaund] N rebote *m*; **on the** — de rebote

rebuff [ríbáf] N desaire *m*, repulsa *f*; VT desairar, rechazar

rebuild [ríbíld] VI/VT reconstruir, reedificar; (auto engine) reacondicionar

rebuke [ríbjúk] VT reprender, reprochar; N reproche *m*, reprimenda *f*

recall [ríkɔ́l] VT (remember) recordar; (call back) retirar; (remove from office) destituir; [ríkɔ́l] N (memory) memoria *f*; (of a diplomat, product) retirada *f*; (from office) destitución *f*

recapitulate [rikəpítʃəlet] VI/VT recapitular

recast [ríkǽst] VT refundir

recede [rısíd] VI retroceder; (of hairline) tener entradas

receipt [rısít] N recibo *m*; **upon** — **of** al recibo de; —**s** entradas *f pl*, ingresos *m pl*

receive [rısív] VI/VT recibir; (suggestions) acoger, recibir; (a broadcast) captar, recibir

receiver [rısívə] N recibidor -ora *mf*; (of a telephone) auricular *m*; (of a television or radio, in sports) receptor *m*; (of a business) síndico *m*

recent [rísənt] ADJ reciente

receptacle [rıséptəkəl] N receptáculo *m*

reception [rıséfʃən] N (hotel, social event, TV) recepción *f*; (act of receiving) recibimiento *m*, acogida *f*; — **room** recibidor *m*

recess [ríses] N (niche) nicho *m*, entrante *m*; (pause) descanso *m*; (playtime) recreo *m*; **in the** —**es of** en lo más recóndito de; VI/VT (a meeting) interrumpir; VT (a wall) hacer un nicho en

recession [rıséʃən] N (act of receding) retroceso *m*; (economic) recesión *f*

recipe [résəpi] N receta *f*

recipient [rısípiənt] N destinatario -ria *mf*

reciprocal [rısíprəkəl] ADJ recíproco

reciprocate [rısíprəket] VI/VT corresponder (a)

recital [rısáıdl] N recital *m*

recitation [resıtéfʃən] N recitación *f*

recite [rısáıt] VI/VT recitar

reckless [réklıs] ADJ (driver) temerario, imprudente; (speed) desenfrenado

recklessness [réklısnıs] N temeridad *f*, imprudencia *f*

reckon [rékən] VI/VT calcular; (consider) considerar; (think) suponer

reckoning [rékənıŋ] N (computation) cálculo *m*; (settlement of accounts) ajuste de cuentas *m*; **the day of** — el día del juicio final

reclaim [ríklém] VT (win back, recover) recuperar; (make land usable) ganar, sanear

recline [rıkláın] VI/VT reclinar(se), recostar(se)

recluse [réklus] ADJ & N solitario -ria *mf*, ermitaño -ña *mf*

recognition [rekəgnífʃən] N reconocimiento *m*

recognize [rékəgnaız] VT reconocer

recoil [ríkɔ́ıl] VI (firearm) dar un culatazo; (move back) retroceder; [ríkɔıl] N (of a gun) culatazo *m*; (move back) retroceso *m*

recollect [rekəlékt] VI/VT recordar

recollection [rekəlékʃən] N recuerdo *m*

recommend [rekəménd] VI/VT recomendar

recommendation [rekəmendéfʃən] N recomendación *f*

recompense [rékəmpens] VI/VT recompensar; N recompensa *f*

reconcile [rékənsaıt] VT (persons) reconciliar; (statements) conciliar; **to** — **oneself to** resignarse a, conformarse con

reconciliation [rekənsıliéfʃən] N reconciliación *f*

reconnoiter [rikənɔ́ıdə] VT reconocer; VI hacer un reconocimiento

reconsider [rikənsídə] VI/VT reconsiderar

reconstruct [rikənstrákt] VT reconstruir

reconstruction [rikənstrákʃən] N reconstrucción *f*

record [rékəd] N (account) registro *m*, asiento *m*; (account of a meeting) acta *f*; (of criminal acts) antecedentes *m pl*; (of past activities) historial *m*, hoja de servicios *f*; (phonographic) disco *m*; (best performance) récord *m*, marca *f*; — **player** tocadiscos *m sg*; **off the** — extraoficialmente; [ríkórd] VI/VT (write down) registrar, apuntar; (cut a recording) grabar

recorder [ríkɔ́rdə] N (archivist) archivero -ra *mf*; (sound device) grabadora *f*; (musical instrument) flauta dulce *f*

recording [ríkɔ́rdıŋ] N grabación *f*; — **company** grabadora *f*

recount [ríkáunt] VT (tell) narrar, relatar; [ríkáunt] (count again) recontar

recourse [ríkɔrs] N recurso *m*; **to have** — **to**

recurrir a

recover [rɪkávɚ] vɪ/vт recobrar(se), recuperar(se); vɪ (lost health) restablecerse; vт (lost time, property) recuperar; (damages) obtener indemnización

recovery [rɪkávəri] N recuperación f, recobro m; (from a lawsuit) indemnización f

recreation [rɛkriéʃən] N recreación f, recreo m, esparcimiento m

recreational [rɛkriéʃənət] ADJ de recreo; — **vehicle** caravana f

recriminate [rɪkrímənət] vɪ/vт recriminar

recruit [rɪkrút] N recluta mf; vɪ/vт reclutar

recruitment [rɪkrútmənt] N reclutamiento m, recluta f

rectangle [rɛ́ktæŋgət] N rectángulo m

rectify [rɛ́ktəfaɪ] vт rectificar

rector [rɛ́ktɚ] N rector -ra mf

rectum [rɛ́ktəm] N recto m

recuperate [rɪkúpəret] vɪ/vт recuperar(se), recobrar(se)

recur [rɪkɚ́] vɪ volver a ocurrir, repetirse

recycle [risáɪkəł] vт reciclar

red [red] ADJ & N rojo m, colorado m; — **blood cell** glóbulo rojo m; —-**handed** *fam* in fraganti; —**headed** pelirrojo; —-**hot** candente, al rojo vivo; — **light** luz roja f; —**neck** granjero -ra blanco -ca pobre mf; — **pepper** pimienta de cayena f; — **snapper** pargo m; — **tape** trámites m pl; — **wine** vino tinto m; —**wood** secoya / secuoya f; **in the** — en números rojos; **to see** — enfurecerse

redden [rɛ́dn̩] vɪ/vт enrojecer, ruborizar(se)

reddish [rɛ́dɪʃ] ADJ rojizo, bermejo

redeem [rɪdím] vт (deliver from sin) redimir; (pay off a mortgage) cancelar; (buy back) desempeñar; (exchange) canjear; (fulfill) cumplir

redemption [rɪdɛ́mpʃən] N redención f; (of something pawned) desempeño m

redness [rɛ́dnɪs] N rojez f; (inflammation) inflamación f

redress [rídrɛs] N reparación f, desagravio m; [rɪdrɛ́s] vт reparar, desagraviar

reduce [rɪdús] vɪ/vт reducir(se); **she was —d to tears** se echó a llorar

reduction [rɪdákʃən] N reducción f

redundant [rɪdándənt] ADJ (repetitive) redundante; (superfluous) superfluo

reed [rid] N caña f, junco m, carrizo m; (of a musical instrument) lengüeta f

reef [rif] N (underwater ridge) escollo m; (of coral) arrecife m

reek [rik] vɪ heder, apestar; N hedor m

reel [riɬ] N carrete m, bobina f; vт (on a spool) bobinar; vɪ tambalearse; **to — off**

recitar; **to — in a fish** sacar un pez del agua

reelect [riɪlɛ́kt] vт reelegir

reelection [riɪlɛ́kʃən] N reelección f

reestablish [riɪstǽblɪʃ] vт restablecer

refer [rɪfɚ́] vɪ referir; (direct to a source of information) remitir; (direct to a doctor) mandar; (mention) referirse a, aludir; (look up in) consultar

referee [rɛfərí] N árbitro m; vт (a game) arbitrar; (a submission) hacer el referato

reference [rɛ́fərəns] N (mention) referencia f; — **book** libro de consulta m; **with — to** con respecto a, respecto de

referendum [rɛfəréndəm] N referéndum m

referral [rɪfɚ́ət] N **he gave me a — to a specialist** me mandó con un especialista

refill [rifíɬ] vɪ/vт rellenar; [rífɪɬ] N (for a pen) repuesto m; (for a lighter) carga f; **may I have a —?** ¿me sirve más?

refine [rɪfáɪn] vт (purify) refinar; (polish) refinar, pulir

refined [rɪfáɪnd] ADJ refinado

refinement [rɪfáɪnmənt] N (of manners) refinamiento m, pulimento m; (of oil) refinación f

refinery [rɪfáɪnəri] N refinería f; (of sugar) ingenio m

reflect [rɪflɛ́kt] vɪ/vт (mirror) reflejar; vɪ (ponder) reflexionar; **to — poorly on** desacreditar

reflection [rɪflɛ́kʃən] N (image) reflejo m; (consideration) reflexión f; (unfavorable observation) tacha f; **on —** pensándolo bien

reflector [rɪflɛ́ktɚ] N reflector m

reflex [ríflɛks] ADJ & N reflejo m

reflexive [rɪflɛ́ksɪv] ADJ reflexivo

reform [rɪfɔ́rm] vɪ/vт reformar(se); N reforma f

reformation [rɛfɚméʃən] N reforma f

reformatory [rɪfɔ́rmətəri] N reformatorio m

reformer [rɪfɔ́rmɚ] N reformador -ra mf, reformista mf

refraction [rɪfrǽkʃən] N refracción f

refractory [rɪfrǽktəri] ADJ (not malleable) refractario; (rebellious) rebelde

refrain [rɪfrén] vɪ abstenerse; N estribillo m

refresh [rɪfrɛ́ʃ] vɪ/vт refrescar(se)

refreshing [rɪfrɛ́ʃɪŋ] ADJ (drink) refrescante; (sleep) reparador; (honesty) agradable

refreshment [rɪfrɛ́ʃmənt] N (drink) refresco m; (food) refrigerio m

refrigerate [rɪfríʤəret] vт refrigerar

refrigeration [rɪfrɪʤəréʃən] N refrigeración f

refrigerator [rɪfríʤəretɚ] N *Sp* frigorífico m, nevera f; *Am* refrigerador m; *RP* heladera f

refuge [réfjudʒ] N refugio *m*

refugee [refjudʒí] N refugiado *m*

refund [rífʌnd] N reembolso *m*; [rɪfʌ́nd] VT reembolsar

refurbish [rɪfɜ́-bɪʃ] VT restaurar

refusal [rɪfjúzəł] N negativa *f*, rechazo *m*; **first —** opción *f*

refuse [rɪfjúz] VI/VT (deny a request) rehusarse (a); (decline to accept) negarse (a); VT (reject) rechazar, desechar; **to — to** rehusarse a, negarse a; [réfjus] N desechos *m pl*, desperdicios *m pl*

refute [rɪfjút] VT refutar, rebatir

regain [rɪgén] VT (recover) recobrar; (get back to) volver a

regal [rígəł] ADJ regio, real

regard [rɪgárd] VT (consider) considerar; (esteem) estimar; **as —s** en cuanto a; N (consideration) consideración *f*; (esteem) respeto *m*, estima *f*; **—s** recuerdos *m pl*, saludos *m pl*; **with — to** con respecto a

regarding [rɪgárdɪŋ] PREP con respecto a

regardless [rɪgárdlɪs] ADV LOC **— of** independientemente de

regenerate [rɪdʒénəret] VI/VT regenerar(se)

regent [rídʒənt] N regente -ta *mf*

reggae [rége] N reggae *m*

regime [rɪʒím] N régimen *m*

regiment [rédʒəmənt] N regimiento *m*

region [rídʒən] N región *f*

register [rédʒɪstɚ] N (recording, range of voice) registro *m*; (entry) asiento *m*; VI/VT (enter into a list) registrar(se); (enroll) matricular(se), inscribir(se); VT (indicate) indicar, registrar; (a letter) certificar; VI (appear) aparecer; **that didn't —** no cayó en la cuenta

registered [rédʒɪstɚd] ADJ registrado; **— mail** correo certificado *m*; **— nurse** enfermero -ra titulado -da *mf*; **— trademark** marca registrada *f*

registrar [rédʒɪstrar] N secretario -ria de admisiones *mf*

registration [redʒɪstréʃən] N registro *m*; (of a car) matrícula *f*; (of a student) inscripción *f*

regret [rɪgrét] VT (feel sorry) lamentar; (feel rueful) arrepentirse de; N arrepentimiento *m*; **to send —s** enviar sus excusas

regretful [rɪgrétfəł] ADJ lleno de remordimientos

regrettable [rɪgrédəbəł] ADJ lamentable

regroup [rigrúp] VT reagrupar; VI reorganizarse

regular [régjələ-] ADJ (symmetrical, uniform) regular; (normal) normal; (habitual) habitual; **a — fool** un verdadero necio; **a**

— guy un buen tipo; (habitual customer) parroquiano -na *mf*; (soldier) soldado de línea *m*

regularity [regjəlǽrɪɾɪ] N regularidad *f*

regulate [régjəlet] VT (control) regular; (make regular) regularizar

regulation [regjəléʃən] N regulación *f*; **—s** reglamento *m*

regulator [régjələɾɚ] N regulador *m*

regurgitate [rɪgɚ́dʒɪtet] VI/VT regurgitar

rehabilitate [rihəbílɪtet] VI/VT rehabilitar(se)

rehearsal [rɪhɜ́-səł] N ensayo *m*

rehearse [rɪhɜ́-s] VI/VT ensayar

reign [ren] N reino *m*, reinado *m*; VI reinar

reimburse [riɪmbɜ́-s] VI/VT reembolsar

reimbursement [riɪmbɜ́-smənt] N reembolso *m*

rein [ren] N rienda *f* (also control); VI **to — in** dominar, refrenar

reincarnation [riɪnkarnéʃən] N reencarnación *f*

reindeer [réndɪr] N reno *m*

reinforce [riɪnfɔ́rs] VT reforzar

reinforcement [riɪnfɔ́rsmənt] N refuerzo *m*

reiterate [riíɾəret] VT reiterar

reject [rɪdʒékt] VT rechazar; [rídʒekt] N (thing) cosa rechazada *f*, desecho *m*; (person) rechazado -da *mf*

rejoice [rɪdʒɔ́ɪs] VI regocijarse

rejoicing [rɪdʒɔ́ɪsɪŋ] N regocijo *m*

rejoin [rɪdʒɔ́ɪn] VT (come again into group) reincorporarse a; VI/VT (reunite) volver a unir(se); [rɪdʒɔ́ɪn] VI/VT replicar

rejuvenate [rɪdʒúvənet] VI/VT rejuvenecer

relapse [rɪlǽps] VI (into bad health) recaer; (into crime) reincidir; [rílæps] N (into bad health) recaída *f*; (into crime) reincidencia *f*

relate [rɪlét] VT (tell) relatar, narrar; (connect) relacionar; VI **to — to** relacionarse con

related [rɪlédɪd] ADJ (connected) relacionado; (kin) emparentado

relation [rɪléʃən] N (association) relación *f*; (act of narrating) narración *f*; (kinship) parentesco *m*; (relative) pariente -ta *mf*; **with — to** con respecto a

relationship [rɪléʃənʃɪp] N relación *f*

relative [rélədɪv] ADJ relativo; N pariente -ta *mf*, allegado -da *mf*; **— to** relativo a, referente a

relax [rɪlǽks] VI/VT relajar(se), distender(se); VT (grip) aflojar

relaxation [rilækséʃən] N (recreation) esparcimiento *m*, recreo *m*; (loosening) relajamiento *m*, relajación *f*

relay [ríle] N relevo *m*, posta *f*; (electrical) relé *m*; **— race** carrera de relevos / postas *f*;

[rɪlé] vт transmitir; **to — a broadcast** transmitir un programa

release [rɪlís] vт (let go) soltar; (free prisoners) librar, poner en libertad; (energy) liberar; (news) divulgar; (discharge from hospital) dar de alta; N (liberation) liberación f; (permission) permiso m; (of film) estreno m; (of gas) escape m; (of energy) desprendimiento m

relegate [rɛ́lɪget] vт relegar

relent [rɪlént] vɪ aplacarse

relentless [rɪléntlɪs] ADJ implacable

relevant [rɛ́ləvənt] ADJ pertinente

reliability [rɪlaɪəbílɪti] N fiabilidad f, confiabilidad f

reliable [rɪláɪəbəl] ADJ fiable, confiable; (a person) formal

reliance [rɪláɪəns] N (dependency) dependencia f; (trust) confianza f

relic [rɛ́lɪk] N reliquia f

relief [rɪlíf] N (ease) alivio m; (aid) ayuda f; (projection) relieve m; (soldier) relevo m; **in —** en relieve; **— map** mapa en relieve m

relieve [rɪlív] vт (alleviate) aliviar; (free) liberar; (replace) relevar; vɪ **to — oneself** orinar

religion [rɪlíd͡ʒən] N religión f

religious [rɪlíd͡ʒəs] ADJ religioso

relinquish [rɪlíŋkwɪʃ] vт (give up) renunciar; (let go) soltar

relish [rɛ́lɪʃ] vт (to like the taste) saborear, paladear; (enjoy) disfrutar; N (enjoyment) gusto m; (condiment) condimento de pepinillos en vinagre m

relocate [rɪlóket] vɪ/vт trasladar(se)

reluctance [rɪlʌ́ktəns] N renuencia f

reluctant [rɪlʌ́ktənt] ADJ renuente, reacio

rely [rɪláɪ] vɪ **to — on** (trust) confiar en; (depend on) depender de

REM (rapid eye movement) [ɑriém] N REM m

remain [rɪmén] vɪ (continue to be) seguir siendo; (stay) quedar(se), permanecer; (to be left) quedar, restar; (to be left over) sobrar; N **—s** restos m pl

remainder [rɪméndə-] N resto m, remanente m

remake [rɪmék] vт rehacer; (film) hacer de nuevo; [rɪ́mek] N nueva versión f

remark [rɪmɑ́rk] vт (comment) comentar, observar; (notice) notar, observar; **to — on** comentar; N observación f, comentario m

remarkable [rɪmɑ́rkəbəl] ADJ notable

remedial [rɪmídiəl] ADJ (rehabilitative) rehabilitador; (to improve skills) de

recuperación

remedy [rɛ́mɪdi] N (solution) remedio m; (cure) cura f; vт (solve) remediar, subsanar; (heal) curar

remember [rɪmémbə-] vɪ/vт recordar, acordarse (de); **— me to him** mándale saludos míos

remind [rɪmáɪnd] vт recordar

reminder [rɪmáɪndə-] N (of a date, deadline) recordatorio m; (warning) advertencia f

reminiscence [rɛmənísəns] N reminiscencia f, recuerdo m

remiss [rɪmís] ADJ negligente

remission [rɪmíʃən] N remisión f

remit [rɪmít] vɪ/vт remitir

remittance [rɪmítns] N remesa f, giro m

remnant [rɛ́mnənt] N (remainder) resto m; (of fabric) retazo m, retal m; (vestige) vestigio m

remodel [rɪmɑ́dl] vɪ/vт remodelar

remorse [rɪmɔ́rs] N remordimiento m

remote [rɪmót] ADJ (far away) remoto, recóndito; (aloof) distante; (in kinship) lejano; N **— control** control remoto m, mando a distancia m

removal [rɪmúvəl] N (dismissal) deposición f; (elimination) eliminación f; (extirpation) extirpación f

remove [rɪmúv] vт (an obstacle) remover; (take away, take off) quitar; (dismiss) deponer; (eliminate) eliminar; (extirpate) extirpar; **to — from office** separar / apartar del cargo

renaissance [rɛ́nɪsɑns] N renacimiento m

rend [rɛnd] vɪ/vт desgarrar(se), rajar(se)

render [rɛ́ndə-] vт (give) dar; (cause to become) dejar; (depict) representar; (translate) traducir; (homage, account) rendir; (services, assistance) prestar; (fat) derretir; (a verdict) pronunciar; **to — useless** inutilizar

rendition [rɛndíʃən] N (translation) traducción f; (interpretation) interpretación f, versión f

renegade [rɛ́nɪged] N renegado -da mf

renew [rɪnú] vт (vows, contract) renovar; (furniture) restaurar; (friendship, effort) reanudar; (a loan) prorrogar

renewal [rɪnúəl] N (of vows, contract) renovación f; (of furniture) restauración f; (of friendship, effort) reanudación f; (of loan) prórroga f

renounce [rɪnáuns] vт (give up) renunciar a; (repudiate) repudiar, renegar de

renovate [rɛ́nəvet] vт renovar

renown [rɪnáun] N renombre m

renowned [rɪnáund] ADJ renombrado

rent [rɛnt] N (monthly payment) alquiler *m*, arrendamiento *m*; **for —** se alquila, se arrienda; (fissure) rajadura *f*, hendidura *f*; (tear) rasgadura *f*; (schism) escisión *f*; VI/VT (lease) alquilar, arrendar

rental [rɛntl] ADJ de alquiler; N alquiler *m*, arrendamiento *m*

renter [rɛntɚ] N inquilino -na *mf*

renunciation [rɪnʌnsiéʃən] N renuncia *f*

reopen [riópən] VI/VT (doors) reabrir(se); (negotiations) reanudar(se)

reorganize [riɔ́rgənaɪz] VI/VT reorganizar(se)

repair [rɪpɛ́r] VT (fix) reparar, arreglar, componer; (shoes) remendar; **to — to** acudir a; N (fixing) reparación *f*; (of shoes) remiendo *m*, compostura *f*; **in —** en buen estado; **—man** técnico -ca en reparaciones *mf*

reparation [rɛpəréʃən] N reparación *f*, indemnización *f*

repay [rɪpé] VT (return money, favor) devolver; (pay off) pagar

repayment [rɪpémənt] N (of an object) devolución *f*; (of a sum) reembolso *m*; (of a loan) pago *m*

repeal [rɪpíł] VT derogar, revocar, abrogar; N derogación *f*, revocación *f*, abrogación *f*

repeat [rɪpít] VI/VT repetir; N repetición *f*

repeated [rɪpídɪd] ADJ repetido

repel [rɪpɛ́ł] VI/VT repeler; (an attack) rechazar

repellent [rɪpɛ́lənt] ADJ & N repelente *m*

repent [rɪpɛ́nt] VI/VT arrepentirse (de)

repentance [rɪpɛ́ntəns] N arrepentimiento *m*

repentant [rɪpɛ́ntənt] ADJ arrepentido, pesaroso

repercussion [rɛpɚkáʃən] N repercusión *f*; **to have —s** repercutir

repertoire [rɛpɚtwɑr] N repertorio *m*

repetition [rɛpɪtíʃən] N repetición *f*

replace [rɪplés] VT (place again) volver a colocar; (substitute for) reemplazar; (provide a substitute for) reponer

replaceable [rɪplésəbəl] ADJ reemplazable, sustituible

replacement [rɪplésmənt] N (substitute, substitution) reemplazo *m*; (making up for) reposición *f*

replenish [rɪplɛ́nɪʃ] VI/VT (supply) reabastecer; (fill again) rellenar

replete [rɪplít] ADJ repleto

replica [rɛ́plɪkə] N réplica *f*

replicate [rɛ́plɪket] VT reproducir

reply [rɪplái] VI replicar, contestar; N réplica *f*, contestación *f*

report [rɪpɔ́rt] VT (recount) relatar; (make a crime known, denounce) denunciar;

(make an accident known) dar parte de; VI hacer un informe, informar; **to — for duty** presentarse; **to — on** hacer un informe sobre; **to — sick** dar parte de enfermo, reportarse enfermo; **it is —ed that** se dice que; N informe *m*; (rumor) rumor *m*; (loud noise) estallido *m*; **— card** boletín de calificaciones *m*

reporter [rɪpɔ́rtɚ] N reportero -ra *mf*

repose [rɪpóz] VI/VT reposar, descansar; N reposo *m*, descanso *m*

repository [rɪpázɪtɔri] N (object) depósito *m*; (person) depositario -ria *mf*

repossess [ripəzɛ́s] VT retomar posesión de

represent [rɛprɪzɛ́nt] VT representar

representation [rɛprɪzɛntéʃən] N representación *f*

representative [rɛprɪzɛ́ntədɪv] ADJ representativo; N representante *mf*

repress [rɪprɛ́s] VI/VT reprimir

repression [rɪprɛ́ʃən] N represión *f*

reprieve [rɪprív] VT (pardon) indultar; (commute) conmutar; (delay) aplazar; N (pardon) indulto *m*; (commutation) conmutación *f*; (delay) aplazamiento *m*

reprimand [rɛ́prəmænd] N reprimenda *f*, regaño *m*; VT reprender, regañar

reprint [ríprɪnt] N reimpresión *f*; (offprint) separata *f*

reprisal [rɪpráɪzəl] N represalia *f*

reproach [rɪprótʃ] VT reprochar; N reproche *m*

reproduce [riprədús] VI/VT reproducir(se)

reproduction [riprədʌ́kʃən] N reproducción *f*

reproof [rɪprúf] N reprobación *f*

reprove [rɪprúv] VT reprobar

reptile [rɛ́ptaɪł] N reptil *m*

republic [rɪpʌ́blɪk] N república *f*

republican [rɪpʌ́blɪkən] ADJ & N republicano -na *mf*

repudiate [rɪpjúdiet] VT repudiar

repugnance [rɪpʌ́gnəns] N repugnancia *f*

repugnant [rɪpʌ́gnənt] ADJ repugnante

repulse [rɪpʌ́ls] VT repeler, rechazar; N repulsa *f*, rechazo *m*

repulsive [rɪpʌ́lsɪv] ADJ repulsivo

reputable [rɛ́pjəpəbəl] ADJ reputado

reputation [rɛpjətéʃən] N reputación *f*, fama *f*

request [rɪkwɛ́st] N solicitud *f*, petición *f*, requerimiento *m*; **at the — of** a solicitud de, a instancias de; VT solicitar, pedir

require [rɪkwáɪr] VI/VT (need) requerir; (demand) exigir

requirement [rɪkwáɪrmənt] N (demand) requisito *m*; (need) necesidad *f*

requisite [rɛ́kwɪzɪt] ADJ requerido, necesario;

N requisito *m*

requisition [rekwɪzíʃən] N (taking over) requisa *f*; (order) pedido *m*; VT (take over) requisar; (order) pedir

rerun [ríɾʌn] N refrito *m*

rescind [rɪsínd] VT rescindir

rescue [réskju] VT rescatar, salvar; N rescate *m*, salvamento *m*; **to go to the — of** acudir al socorro de, salir al quite de

research [rísɚtʃ] N investigación *f*; [rɪsɚtʃ] VI/ VT investigar

researcher [rísɚtʃɚ] N investigador -ora *mf*

resell [risél] VT revender

resemblance [rɪzémbləns] N semejanza *f*, parecido *m*

resemble [rɪzémbəl] VT semejar, asemejarse a, parecerse a

resent [rɪzént] VT resentirse de

resentful [rɪzéntfəl] ADJ resentido, rencoroso

resentment [rɪzéntmənt] N resentimiento *m*

reservation [rezɚvéʃən] N reserva *f*; *Am* reservación *f*; **to have one's —s** tener reservas

reserve [rɪzɚ́v] VT reservar; N reserva *f*; (shyness) pudor *m*

reserved [rɪzɚ́vd] ADJ reservado

reservoir [rézɚvwɑr] N (tank) depósito *m*, alberca *f*; (artificial lake) embalse *m*, represa *f*

reside [rɪzáɪd] VI residir

residence [rézɪdəns] N residencia *f*

resident [rézɪdənt] ADJ & N residente *mf*; (of a neighborhood) vecino -na *mf*

residential [rezɪdéntʃəl] ADJ residencial

residue [rézɪdu] N residuo *m*

resign [rɪzáɪn] VI/VT renunciar (a), dimitir (de); **to — oneself to** resignarse a

resignation [rezɪgnéʃən] N (act of resigning an office) renuncia *f*, dimisión *f*; (accepting attitude) resignación *f*

resilience [rɪzíljəns] N (elasticity) elasticidad *f*; (adaptability) adaptabilidad *f*

resilient [rɪzíljənt] ADJ (elastic) elástico; (adaptable) adaptable

resin [rézɪn] N resina *f*

resist [rɪzíst] VT (a temptation) resistir; VI/VT (tyranny) resistirse (a)

resistance [rɪzístəns] N resistencia *f*

resistant [rɪzístənt] ADJ resistente

resolute [rézəlut] ADJ resuelto, decidido

resolution [rezəlúʃən] N resolución *f*

resolve [rɪzálv] VT resolver(se); **to — into** convertirse en; **to — to** decidir, resolver; N resolución *f*

resonance [rézənəns] N resonancia *f*

resonate [rézənet] VI/VT resonar

resort [rɪzɔ́rt] VI **to — to** recurrir; N (seaside)

centro de veraneo *m*; (for skiing) estación de esquí *f*; **as a last —** como último recurso; **to have — to** recurrir a

resound [rɪzáʊnd] VI/VT resonar

resource [rísɔrs] N recurso *m*

resourceful [rɪzɔ́rsfəl] ADJ ingenioso

respect [rɪspékt] N (esteem) respeto *m*; (detail) aspecto *m*; **with — to** (con) respecto a, respecto de; VT respetar; **as —s** por lo que respecta a

respectable [rɪspéktəbəl] ADJ respetable

respectful [rɪspéktfəl] ADJ respetuoso

respective [rɪspéktɪv] ADJ respectivo

respiration [respɚéʃən] N respiración *f*

respite [réspɪt] N (pause) respiro *f*, tregua *m*; (postponement) prórroga *f*

resplendent [rɪspléndənt] ADJ resplandeciente, refulgente

respond [rɪspánd] VI/VT responder

response [rɪspáns] N respuesta *f*

responsibility [rɪspɑnsəbílɪdi] N responsabilidad *f*

responsible [rɪspánsəbəl] ADJ responsable

rest [rest] N (repose) descanso *m*, reposo *m*; (musical) pausa *f*; (support) apoyo *m*; (remainder) resto *m*; **an object at —** un objeto en reposo; **he's at —** descansa en paz; **— home** (for convalescents) casa de reposo *f*; (for the aged) casa de ancianos *f*; **— room** servicio *m*; *Sp* aseo *m*; VI/VT descansar, reposar; VT (one's gaze) posar; (against a wall) reclinar; VI parar; **to — on** depender de; **let it —** déjalo en paz

restaurant [réstərɑnt] N restaurante *m*; *Am* restorán *m*

restitution [restɪtúʃən] N restitución *f*

restless [réstlɪs] ADJ (worried) inquieto; (fidgety) movedizo, revuelto

restlessness [réstlɪsnɪs] N inquietud *f*, desasosiego *m*

restoration [restəréʃən] N restauración *f*

restore [rɪstɔ́r] VT restaurar

restrain [rɪstrén] VT (hold back) refrenar, contener, moderar; (bring under control) reducir

restraint [rɪstrént] N (self-control) compostura *f*, moderación *f*; (device) seguro *m*; **under —** bajo control

restrict [rɪstríkt] VT restringir; (someone's liberty) coartar

restriction [rɪstríkʃən] N restricción *f*

result [rɪzʌ́lt] VI resultar; **to — from** resultar de; **to — in** dar por resultado; N resultado *m*; **as a —** de resultas, como resultado

resume [rɪzúm] VT (take up again) reasumir, volver a asumir; (continue) reanudar

résumé [rézume] N currículum *m*, historial personal *m*

resurrection [rezərékʃən] N resurrección *f*

resuscitate [rɪsʌ́sɪtet] VI/VT resucitar

resuscitation [rɪsʌsɪtéʃən] N resucitación *f*

retail [rítel] N venta al por menor *f*; **at** — al por menor, al menudeo; — **trade** comercio minorista *m*; VI/VT vender al por menor

retailer [rítelə] N minorista *mf*, detallista *mf*

retain [rɪtén] VT (recall, confine, detain) retener; (keep) conservar, quedarse con; (hire) contratar

retainer [rɪténə] N (device that holds back) retén *m*; (payment) honorarios pagados por adelantado *m pl*

retaliate [rɪtǽliet] VI vengarse

retaliation [rɪtæliéʃən] N venganza *f*

retard [rɪtárd] VI/VT retardar

retarded [rɪtárdɪd] ADJ retrasado

retention [rɪténʃən] N retención *f*

reticence [rɛ́DɪSəns] N reserva *f*

retina [rɛ́tnə] N retina *f*

retinue [rɛ́tnu] N séquito *m*, comitiva *f*

retire [rɪtáɪr] VI/VT (stop working) retirar(se), jubilar(se); (withdraw) retirar(se); (to bed) acostarse; (money, troops, machines) retirar

retirement [rɪtáɪrmənt] N retiro *m*, jubilación *f*

retort [rɪtɔ́rt] N (reply) réplica *f*; (vessel) retorta *f*

retouch [ritʌ́tʃ] VT retocar; N retoque *m*

retrace [ritrés] VT (mental steps) repasar; (one's route) volver sobre

retract [rɪtrǽkt] VT retractar; (claws) retraer(se); VI desdecirse, retractarse

retreat [rɪtrít] N (place of refuge, period of meditation) retiro *m*, refugio *m*; (military) retirada *f*, repliegue *m*; (bugle call) retreta *f*; VI batirse en retirada, retroceder, replegarse

retrench [rɪtrɛ́ntʃ] VI economizar

retrieve [rɪtrív] VT (game) cobrar; (something lost) recuperar

retriever [rɪtrívə] N perro cobrador *m*

retroactive [rɛtroǽktɪv] ADJ retroactivo

retrospect [rɛ́trəspɛkt] ADV LOC **in** — mirando para atrás

retrovirus [rɛ́trovaɪrəs] N retrovirus *m*

return [rɪtɝ́n] VI (come back) volver, regresar; VT (put back) devolver, retornar; (a verdict) fallar; N (to a place) vuelta *f*, regreso *m*; (thing bought, of a thing) devolución *f*; (profit) ganancia *f*; (electoral) resultados *m pl*; — **address** señas del remitente *f pl*; — **game**

revancha *f*; — **ticket** billete de vuelta *m*; **bý** — **mail** a vuelta de correo; **election** —**s** resultados electorales *m pl*; **in** — a cambio; **in** — **for** a cambio de; **income tax** — *Sp* declaración de la renta *f*; *Am* declaración de impuestos *f*

reunion [rijúnjən] N reunión *f*

reunite [rijunáɪt] VI/VT reunir(se)

rev [rɛv] VI/VT acelerar en vacío

reveal [rɪvíl] VT revelar

revealing [rɪvílɪŋ] ADJ revelador; (neckline) atrevido

revel [rɛ́vəl] VI (enjoy) deleitarse, gozar; (party) parrandear; N parranda *f*

revelation [rɛvəléʃən] N revelación *f*; —**s** Apocalipsis *m sg*

revelry [rɛ́vəlri] N parranda *f*, jarana *f*

revenge [rɪvɛ́ndʒ] N venganza *f*, revancha *f*

revengeful [rɪvɛ́ndʒfəl] ADJ vengativo

revenue [rɛ́vənu] N (of a government) rentas públicas *f pl*; (of a person) ingresos *m pl*; — **stamp** sello fiscal *m*

reverberate [rɪvɝ́bəret] VI reverberar; VT hacer reverberar

revere [rɪvír] VT reverenciar

reverence [rɛ́vərəns] N reverencia *f*, veneración *f*; VT venerar

reverend [rɛ́vərənd] ADJ & N reverendo -da *mf*

reverent [rɛ́vərənt] ADJ reverente

reverie, revery [rɛ́vəri] N ensueño *m*, ensoñación *f*

reverse [rɪvɝ́s] ADJ inverso, opuesto; **the** — **side** el revés; N (opposite) lo opuesto; (back of clothing, mishap) revés *m*; (back of a coin, medal) reverso *m*; (gear) marcha atrás *f*; (back of a piece of paper) dorso *m*; VI/VT invertir(se); VT (a policy, a vehicle) dar marcha atrás; (a verdict) revocar

revert [rɪvɝ́t] VI revertir

review [rɪvjú] N (inspection of a military unit, periodical publication) revista *f*; (repetition of studied material) repaso *m*; (critique of a book, drama) reseña *f*, crítica *f*; (examination of a judicial case) revisión *f*; VI/VT (examine) repasar, revisar; VT (reexamine) revisar, examinar; (inspect troops) pasar revista a; (write a critique of) reseñar

revile [rɪváɪl] VT vilipendiar, denostar

revise [rɪváɪz] VT corregir, enmendar

revision [rɪvíʒən] N (action of revising) corrección *f*; (revised version) versión corregida *f*

revival [rɪvárvəl] N (of customs) retorno *m*; (of religious feeling) resurgimiento *m*, despertar *m*; (from unconsciousness) resucitación *f*; (of a play) reposición *f*, revisión *f*; (evangelical meeting) asamblea evangelista *f*

revive [rɪváɪv] VT (an unconscious person) reavivar, reanimar; (an apparently dead person) resucitar; (an old play) reponer; (a custom) restablecer; VI revivir, reanimarse; (be reestablished) restablecerse

revocation [rɛvəkéʃən] N revocación *f*

revoke [rɪvók] VT revocar

revolt [rɪvólt] N revuelta *f*, sublevación *f*; VI rebelarse, sublevarse; **it —s me** me da asco

revolting [rɪvóltɪŋ] ADJ repugnante, asqueroso

revolution [rɛvəlúʃən] N revolución *f*

revolutionary [rɛvəlúʃəneri] ADJ & N revolucionario -ria *mf*

revolve [rɪvɑ́lv] VI/VT girar

revolver [rɪvɑ́lvə] N révólver *m*

revue [rɪvjú] N revista *f*

revulsion [rɪvʌ́lʃən] N repugnancia *f*, asco *m*

reward [rɪwɔ́rd] N recompensa *f*; VT recompensar

rewind [riwáɪnd] VI/VT rebobinar

rewrite [rɪráɪt] VI/VT reescribir; [ríraɪt] N corrección *f*

rhea [ríə] N ñandú *m*

rhetoric [rɛ́dəɪk] N retórica *f*

rheumatism [rúmətɪzəm] N reumatismo *m*, reuma *mf*

Rh factor [ɑrɛ́tʃfæktə] N factor Rh *m*

rhinoceros [raɪnɑ́sərəs] N rinoceronte *m*

rhinovirus [ráɪnovaɪrəs] N rinovirus *m*

rhododendron [rodədéndrən] N rododendro *m*

rhubarb [rúbɑrb] N (vegetable) ruibarbo *m*; (brawl) reyerta *f*

rhyme [raɪm] N rima *f*; **without — or reason** sin ton ni son; VI/VT rimar

rhythm [ríðəm] N ritmo *m*

rhythmical [ríðmɪkəl] ADJ rítmico; (breathing) acompasado

rib [rɪb] N (of person, animal) costilla *f*; (of umbrella) varilla *f*; (in garment) canalé *m*, cordoncillo *m*; **— cage** caja torácica *f*; VT burlarse de

ribbon [ríbən] N (of cloth) cinta *f*; (of land) franja *f*, faja *f*

rice [raɪs] N arroz *m*; **— field** arrozal *m*

rich [rɪtʃ] ADJ rico; (tasty) sabroso; (buttery) mantecoso; (colorful) vivo; N **—es** riquezas *f pl*

rickety [ríkɪdi] ADJ (shaky) desvencijado; (affected with rickets) raquítico

ricochet [ríkəʃe] N rebote *m*; VI rebotar

rid [rɪd] VT librar, desembarazar; **to get — of**

librarse de, deshacerse de

riddle [rídl] N (puzzle) acertijo *m*, adivinanza *f*; (puzzling person) enigma *m*; VI hablar en enigmas; VT acribillar, perforar; **to be —d with graft** estar plagado de corrupción

ride [raɪd] VI (on a horse) cabalgar, jinetear; (on a bicycle) montar; (in a vehicle) andar, viajar / ir en; **this car —s well** este coche anda bien; **his hopes are riding on that** tiene las esperanzas puestas en eso; **just let it —** déjalo tranquilo; VT (travel on horse, bicycle) montar; (travel on bus) andar en; (harass) hostigar; **to — away** irse; **to — by** pasar; **to — out** capear; **to — up** subirse; N paseo *m*, viaje *m*; **to give someone a —** acercar en coche; **to go on a —** dar un paseo

rider [ráɪdə] N (on a horse) jinete *m*; (on a bicycle) ciclista *mf*; (on an insurance policy) cláusula añadida *f*; (law) anexo *m*

ridge [rɪdʒ] N (back of an animal) espinazo *m*, lomo *m*; (chain of hills) cadena *f*; (of a roof) caballete *m*; (of cloth) cordoncillo *m*

ridicule [rídɪkjul] N burla *f*, mofa *f*; VT ridiculizar, poner en ridículo

ridiculous [rɪdíkjələs] ADJ ridículo

riffraff [rífræf] N *pej* gentuza *f*, chusma *f*

rifle [ráɪfəl] N rifle *m*, fusil *m*; VT robar; **to — through** revolver

rift [rɪft] N (opening) grieta *f*, hendidura *f*; (disagreement) desavenencia *f*

rig [rɪg] VT (sails) aparejar, equipar; (an election) amañar; **to — up** armar; N (on a ship) aparejo *m*, equipo *m*; (apparatus) aparato *m*; (truck) camión *m*

rigging [rígɪŋ] N jarcia *f*

right [raɪt] ADJ (not left) derecho; (not wrong) correcto, acertado; (suitable) adecuado; **— angle** ángulo recto *m*; **—-hand** derecho; **—-hand man** brazo derecho *m*; **—-handed** diestro; **—-to-life** antiaborto, pro vida; **— triangle** triángulo recto *m*; **—-wing** derechista, de derecha; **at the — moment** en el momento justo; **the — people** la gente indicada; **to be —** tener razón; **to be all —** estar bien; **he's not in his — mind** no está en sus cabales; **to turn out —** salir bien; ADV (straight) derecho, directamente; (correctly) correctamente; (to the right) a la derecha; **— after** justo después de; **—-face** media vuelta a la derecha; **— now** ahora mismo; **— there** allí mismo; **it is — where you left it** está exactamente donde lo dejaste; **to hit**

— **in the eye** darle de lleno en el ojo; N (just claim) derecho *m*; (moral good) bien *m*; (direction, political persuasion) derecha *f*; — **of way** prioridad *f*, preferencia *f*; **make a — at the corner** gira / dobla a la derecha; **to the —** a la derecha; **to be in the —** tener razón; VI/VT (make upright) enderezar(se); VT (correct) corregir

righteous [ráitʃəs] ADJ recto, justo; — **rage** rabia justificada *f*

righteousness [ráitʃəsnıs] N rectitud *f*, superioridad moral *f*

rightful [ráitfəl] ADJ legítimo

rightist [ráidıst] N derechista *mf*

rightly [ráitli] ADV con razón

rigid [ríʤıd] ADJ rígido

rigidity [rıʤídıti] N rigidez *f*

rigor [ríɡəʳ] N rigor *m*

rigorous [ríɡəʳəs] ADJ riguroso

rim [rım] N (edge) borde *m*; (on a car) llanta *f*; *Am* rin *m*; (on a bicycle) aro *m*; (on a plate) filete *m*; (of glasses) montura *f*

rind [raind] N (cheese) corteza *f*; (fruit) cáscara *f*

ring [rıŋ] N (on finger, of smoke) anillo *m*; (for women only) sortija *f*; (under the eyes) ojeras *f pl*; (in the nose) argolla *f*; (circle) círculo *m*, redondel *m*, ruedo *m*; (in a circus) pista *f*; (for bullfights) plaza de toros *f*; (for boxing) cuadrilátero *m*; (for gymnastics) anillas *f pl*; (of criminals) banda *f*; (undertone) tono *m*; (sound of telephone) timbrazo *m*, telefonazo *m*; (sound of bells) retintín *m*, repique *m*; — **finger** anular *m*; —**leader** cabecilla *mf*; —**worm** tiña *f*; VT (surround) cercar; (make doorbell sound) tocar; (make bell sound) tañer; VI (of ears) zumbar; (make sound, doorbell) sonar; (make sound, bell) repicar, repiquetear; **to — the nose of an animal** ponerle una argolla en la nariz a un animal; **to — the hour** dar la hora; **to — true** parecer verdad; **to — up the sale** marcar la venta

ringlet [ríŋlıt] N (curl) rizo *m*, bucle *m*, sortija *f*; (small ring) pequeña sortija *f*

rink [rıŋk] N pista de patinaje *f*

rinkydink [ríŋkidıŋk] ADJ de pacotilla

rinse [rıns] VI/VT enjuagar, aclarar; N enjuague *m*, aclarado *m*

riot [ráiət] N (uprising) motín *m*, tumulto *m*; (excess) exceso *m*; **he's a —** es un cómico; VI amotinarse

riotous [ráiədəs] ADJ (wanton) desenfrenado; (funny) graciosísimo

rip [rıp] VI/VT rasgar(se), rajar(se); VT (something sewn) descoser; **to — away**

desprender; **to — into** asaltar; **to — off** robar; **to — out a seam** descoser una costura; N rasgadura *f*, rajadura *f*; — **cord** cordón de apertura *m*; —**off** robo *m*

ripe [raip] ADJ maduro; **to be — for** estar preparado para, listo para; — **old age** edad avanzada *f*

ripen [ráipən] VI/VT madurar(se), sazonar(se)

ripeness [ráipnıs] N madurez *f*

ripple [rípəl] VI/VT (water) rizar(se); (grass) agitar(se); N ondulación *f*, rizo *m*

rise [raiz] VI (go up) subir; (increase) aumentar; (get up, stand up) levantarse; (slope up) elevarse; (arise) surgir; (of mist) levantarse; (of the sun, moon) salir; (of dough) crecer, leudar; **to — up in rebellion** sublevarse, alzarse; **to — above** superar; **to — to the challenge** aceptar el desafío; N (of prices, volume) subida *f*, aumento *m*; (of an empire, talent) surgimiento *m*; (slope upward) elevación *f*; **to get a — out of someone** provocar a alguien; **to give — to** ocasionar

risk [rısk] N riesgo *m*; VT arriesgar, aventurar; **to — defeat** correr el riesgo de perder, exponerse a perder

risky [ríski] ADJ arriesgado, aventurado, azaroso

risqué [rıské] ADJ subido de tono, atrevido, picante

rite [rait] N rito *m*

ritual [rítʃuəl] ADJ & N ritual *m*

ritzy [rítsi] ADJ elegante

rival [ráivəl] ADJ & N rival *mf*; VT rivalizar con, competir con

rivalry [ráivəlri] N rivalidad *f*

river [rívəʳ] N río *m*; —**bank** orilla *f*, ribera *f*

rivet [rívıt] N remache *m*; VT (put rivets) remachar; (fix) fijar, clavar

RNA (ribonucleic acid) [ɑriné] N ARN *m*

roach [rotʃ] N cucaracha *f*

road [rod] N (in the country) camino *m*; (highway) carretera *f*; **on the — to recovery** en vías de recuperación; — **map** mapa carretero *m*; — **rage** ira caminera *f*; —**side** borde del camino *m*; —**way** camino *m*

roam [rom] VI/VT vagar (por), errar (por), rodar (por); VI vagabundear

roar [rɔr] VI/VT rugir, bramar; **to — with laughter** reír a carcajadas; N rugido *m*, bramido *m*; — **of laughter** risotada *f*, carcajada *f*

roast [rost] VI/VT (meat, potatoes) asar(se); (coffee, nuts) tostar, torrar; (criticize) criticar; N (meat) asado *m*; (party)

barbacoa *f;* — **beef** rosbif *m*
rob [rɑb] VI/VT robar; **to — someone of something** robarle algo a alguien
robber [rábə] N ladrón -ona *mf*
robbery [rábəri] N robo *m*
robe [rob] N manto *m*, traje talar *m*, túnica *f;* (ceremonial dress) toga *f;* (bath wrap) bata *f*
robin [rábɪn] N petirrojo *m*
robot [róbɑt] N robot *m*
robotics [robádɪks] N robótica *f*
robust [robást] ADJ (strong) robusto; (hearty) saludable; (solid) sólido
rock [rɑk] N roca *f;* (crag) peñasco *m*, peñón *m;* (diamond) diamante *m;* (music style) rock *m;* — **crystal** cristal de roca *m;* — **salt** sal de piedra *f,* sal gema / mineral *f;* **to go on the —s** tropezar en un escollo; *Am* escollar; **he hit —-bottom** tocó fondo; **—** (move to and fro) mecer(se); (stagger) sacudir, estremecer; **to — to sleep** arrullar
rocker [rákə] N mecedora *f*
rocket [rákɪt] N cohete *m*
rocketry [rákɪtri] N cohetería *f*
rocking [rákɪŋ] N — **chair** mecedora *f;* — **horse** caballito de madera *m*, caballito mecedor *m*
rocky [ráki] ADJ (with rocks) rocoso; (difficult) difícil
rod [rɑd] N vara *f,* varilla *f;* (in engine) vástago *m;* medida de longitud *f* (aproximadamente 5 metros)
rodent [ródənt] N roedor *m*
rodeo [ródio] N rodeo *m*
rogue [rog] N pícaro -ra *mf,* bribón -ona *mf;* ADJ solitario y bravo
roguish [rógɪʃ] ADJ (rascally) pícaro, bribón; (mischievous) travieso
role [rol] N papel *m,* rol *m;* — **model** modelo ejemplar *m;* **—playing** improvisación *f*
roll [rol] VI (move on wheels, rotate) rodar; (rotate one's eyes) revolear; (sway) balancearse, bambolearse; (reverberate) retumbar; (flow as waves) ondular; VT (steel) aplanar; (cigarettes) liar; (a drum) redoblar; (one's r's) pronunciar la erre; **to — over in the snow** revolcarse en la nieve; **to — up** arrollar, enrollar; **to — around** llegar; **to — back** reducir, rebajar; **to — by** pasar; **to — over** volcar, darse vuelta; **to get —ing** ponerse en marcha; N (of paper, fabric, etc.) rollo *m;* (of coins) cartucho *m;* (of a ship) balanceo *m;* (of thunder) retumbo *m;* (of a drum) redoble *m;* (catalog of members) lista *f;* (of

waves) ondulación *f;* (of a typewriter) carro *m;* (piece of bread) bollo *m,* panecillo *m;* (of dice) tiro *m;* ADJ **—-on de bolita**
roller [rólə] N (for painting, moving things) rodillo *m;* (hair) rulo *m,* rulero *m;* — **coaster** montaña rusa *f;* — **skate** patín de ruedas *m*
rolling pin [rólɪŋ pɪn] N rodillo *m,* palote *m*
roly-poly [rólipóli] ADJ rechoncho
ROM (read-only memory) [rɑm] N ROM *f*
Roman [rómən] ADJ & N romano -na *mf;* — **numeral** número romano *m*
romance [rómæns] N (love affair, story) romance *m;* (romantic atmosphere) romanticismo *m;* VT cortejar; ADJ romance, románico
romanesque [rəmənésk] ADJ románico
Romania [roméniə] N Rumania *f*
Romanian [roméniən] ADJ & N rumano -na *mf*
romantic [romántɪk] ADJ romántico
romanticism [romántəsɪzəm] N romanticismo *m*
romp [rɑmp] VI retozar, brincar; (win easily) arrasar con; N (frolic) retozo *m;* (victory) victoria fácil *f*
roof [ruf] N (ceiling) techo *m,* tejado *m;* (flat roof) azotea *f;* — **of the mouth** paladar *m;* **to hit the —** poner el grito en el cielo; VT techar
rookie [rúki] N novato -ta *mf*
room [rum] N (in building) cuarto *m;* (large) sala *f;* (in a hotel) habitación *f;* (space) lugar *m,* sitio *m;* — **and board** pensión completa *f;* — **mate** compañero -ra de cuarto *mf;* — **service** servicio a la habitación *f;* **to take up —** ocupar espacio; **the whole — laughed** todos los presentes se rieron; VI hospedarse, alojarse
roomy [rúmi] ADJ espacioso, amplio
roost [rust] N vara *f;* VI posarse (para dormir)
rooster [rústə] N gallo *m*
root [rut] N raíz *f;* **to take — (**a plant) echar raíces, prender; (an idea) arraigar(se); — **canal** tratamiento de conducto *m;* VI (grow roots) arraigar(se), echar raíces; (dig) hozar; **to — for** animar; **to — out / up** (uproot) arrancar de raíz; (eradicate) erradicar
rope [rop] N (cord) soga *f,* cuerda *f;* (lasso) reata *f,* lazo *m;* (on a ship) cabo *m;* (thick) maroma *f;* **to be at the end of one's —** no dar más; **to know the —s** conocer el paño, sabérselas todas; VT enlazar; **to — off** acordonar; **to — someone in** agarrar a alguien

rosary [rózəri] N rosario *m*
rose [roz] N rosa *f*; (color) rosa *m*; **—bud** capullo de rosa *m*, pimpollo de rosa *m*; **—bush** rosal *m*; **—-colored** de color rosa
rosemary [rózmɛri] N romero *m*
roster [rústɚ] N lista *f*
rostrum [rástrəm] N tribuna *f*
rosy [rózi] ADJ (pink) rosado, color de rosa; (of cheeks) sonrosado; **— future** porvenir halagüeño *m*
rot [rɑt] VI/VT pudrir(se); N podredumbre *f*
rotary [rótəri] ADJ rotatorio, rotativo
rotate [rótet] VI/VT rotar
rotation [rotéʃən] N rotación *f*, giro *m*
rotor [ródɚ] N rotor *m*
rotten [rátn̩] ADJ (decomposing) podrido; (stinking) hediondo; (morally corrupt) corrupto; (despicable) odioso
rotund [rotʌ́nd] ADJ rollizo
rouge [ruʒ] N colorete *m*
rough [rʌf] ADJ (coarse) áspero, rugoso; (violent) violento; (rude) tosco; (approximate) aproximado; (road) desigual, irregular; (terrain) agreste, bronco; (sea) picado, revuelto; **— diamond** diamante en bruto *m*; **— draft** borrador *m*; **— weather** mal tiempo *m*; **he had a — time** le fue mal; ADV con violencia; VI ponerse áspero; **to — it** vivir sin lujos ni comodidades
roughly [rʌ́fli] ADV (not smoothly) ásperamente; (rudely) groseramente, rudamente; (approximately) aproximadamente; **to estimate —** tantear
roughness [rʌ́fnɪs] N (lack of smoothness) aspereza *f*; (rudeness) rudeza *f*; (unevenness) desigualdad *f*; **the — of the sea** lo picado del mar
roulette [rulét] N ruleta *f*
round [raund] ADJ redondo; **— trip** viaje de ida y vuelta *m*; N (of talks, drinks, dance) ronda *f*; (of cheese) rodaja *f*; (in cards, sports) vuelta *f*; (in boxing) round *m*, asalto *m*; (of golf) partido *m*; (canon) canon *m*; **— number** número redondo *m*; **— of ammunition** carga de municiones *f*; **— of applause** aplauso *m*; **to make the —s** hacer la ronda; PREP & ADV **—about** indirecto; **—-the-clock** veinticuatro horas al día; **—up** (of cattle) rodeo *m*; (of criminals) redada *f*; **all year —** todo el año; **to come —** pasar; **to go — a corner** doblar una esquina; VT (a corner) doblar; (an edge, a number) redondear; **to — off / out** redondear; **to — up** juntar, reunir; **to — up cattle** juntar el ganado

roundness [ráundnɪs] N redondez *f*
rouse [rauz] VI/VT (wake) despertar(se); VT (instigate) incitar
rout [raut] N (defeat) derrota aplastante *f*; (flight) huida en desbandada *f*; VT (defeat) derrotar, destrozar; (cause to flee) poner en fuga
route [raut, rut] N ruta *f*, trayecto *m*; (of newspaper delivery) reparto *m*; VT dirigir
routine [rutín] N rutina *f*
rove [rov] VI/VT vagar (por), errar (por)
rover [róvɚ] N vagabundo -da *mf*
row [rau] N (fight) riña *f*, pelea *f*, bronca *f*; [ro] N (line) fila *f*, hilera *f*, ringlera *f*; **four times in a —** cuatro veces seguidas; VI/VT (propel with oars) remar, bogar; **—boat** bote de remos *m*, barca *f*, chinchorro *m*
rowdy [ráudi] ADJ (person) alborotador; (party) bullicioso; N camorrista *mf*
rower [róɚ] N remero -ra *mf*
royal [rɔ́iəl] ADJ real; **— blue** azul marino *m*; **— flush** escalera real *f*
royalty [rɔ́iəlti] N realeza *f*; (person) miembro de la realeza *m*; **royalties** derechos *m pl*, regalías *f pl*
RSVP (répondez s'il vous plaît) [ɑrɛsvipí] LOC S.R.C.
rub [rʌb] VI/VT (apply friction) frotar(se); (massage) friccionar; (spread on) aplicar frotando; (make sore) rozar; **to — off** quitar(se) frotando; **to — out** borrar; **to — shoulders with** codearse con; **to — someone the wrong way** peinar a contrapelo; **don't — it in!** ¡no me lo refriegues por la cara! VI (act of rubbing) fricción *f*; (difficulty) dificultad *f*; (abraded area) roce *m*, frote *m*
rubber [rʌ́bɚ] N caucho *m*, goma *f*; **— band** goma elástica *f*; **—s** chanclos *m pl*; **— stamp** sello de goma *m*; **— tree** gomero *m*
rubbish [rʌ́bɪʃ] N (trash) basura *f*; (nonsense) pamplinas *f pl*
rubble [rʌ́bəl] N (debris) escombros *m pl*; (stone fragments) ripios *m pl*, cascote *m*
rubric [rúbrɪk] N rúbrica *f*
ruby [rúbi] N rubí *m*
ruckus [rʌ́kəs] N barahúnda *f*, jaleo *m*
rudder [rʌ́dɚ] N timón *m*
ruddy [rʌ́di] ADJ rubicundo
rude [rud] ADJ (impolite) grosero; (uncouth, crude, simple) tosco; (harsh) rudo
rudeness [rúdnɪs] N (impoliteness) grosería *f*; (harshness) rudeza *f*; (crudeness) tosquedad *f*
rueful [rúfəl] ADJ (sad) triste; (repentant) arrepentido

ruffian [rʌfiən] N rufián m

ruffle [rʌfəł] VI/VT (gather cloth) fruncir(se); (raise feathers) erizar(se); (water) agitar(se), rizar(se); (hair) desgreñar(se); (bother) molestar(se), fastidiar(se); N (frill on clothes) volante m; (gathering in cloth) frunce m, pliegue m; (ripples in water) ondulación f, rizo m

rug [rʌg] N alfombra f; (hairpiece) peluquín m

rugby [rʌgbi] N rugby m

rugged [rʌgɪd] ADJ (terrain) escarpado, áspero, fragoso; (face) recio; (manners) tosco; (way of life) duro; (man) robusto

ruin [rúɪn] N ruina f; **to go to —** arruinarse, venirse abajo; VI/VT arruinar(se), estropear(se); (spoil) echar(se) a perder

ruinous [rúɪnəs] ADJ ruinoso

rule [ruł] N (principle) regla f; (line separating newspaper columns) filete m; (government) mando m, gobierno m; **the — of law** el imperio de la ley; **as a — of thumb** por regla general, a ojo de buen cubero; VI/VT (govern) reinar, gobernar; (decree) fallar, dictaminar, sentenciar; (put lines on paper) rayar, poner renglones; **to — out** excluir; **to — over** reinar, gobernar

ruler [rúlə] N (governor) gobernante mf; (instrument) regla f

ruling [rúlɪŋ] N (decision) fallo m, sentencia f, dictamen m; (line on paper) renglón m; ADJ (governing) gobernante

rum [rʌm] N ron m

rumble [rámbəł] VI (roar) retumbar; (of stomach) hacer ruido; (fight) pelear; N (roar) retumbo m; (of stomach) ruido m; (fight) pelea f

ruminate [rúmənet] VI rumiar

rummage [rámɪʤ] VI/VT rebuscar, hurgar; N cachivaches m pl; **— sale** venta de beneficencia f

rumor [rúmə] N rumor m; VT murmurar; **it is —ed that** se rumorea que, corre la voz que

rump [rʌmp] N (of quadruped) anca f, grupa f; (of bird) rabadilla f; (of person) trasero m

run [rʌn] VI (person, tears, water) correr; (stockings, dyes) corrserse; (function) funcionar; (travel briefly) hacer una escapadita; (circulate) circular, hacer el recorrido; (drip) chorrear; (be a candidate) presentarse como candidato; (suppurate) supurar; VT (a mile, a risk) correr; (one object through another) pasar; (a business) manejar, dirigir; (a red light) comerse; (a news story) publicar; (a sum of money)

costar; (a computer program) ejecutar; (a fever) tener; **— along now!** ¡vete! **to — across someone** encontrarse con alguien; **to — after** perseguir; **to — around with** andar con; **to — away** fugarse, escaparse; **to — down** (stop working) dejar de funcionar; (capture) aprehender; (criticize) hablar mal de; (run over) atropellar; (tire) cansar; **to — dry** secarse; **to — into** (encounter) tropezar con, encontrarse con; (collide) chocar con; **to — out** salir corriendo; **to — out of money** quedarse sin dinero; **to — over** (spill) derramarse; (run down) atropellar, arrollar; (move along a surface) deslizar por; **to — through** (stab) atravesar; (squander) despilfarrar; (repeat) repetir; **the play ran for three months** la obra estuvo en cartel durante tres meses; **it —s in the family** es un rasgo de familia; N (act of running) carrera f, corrida f; (defect in stockings) carrera f, corrida f; (routine trip) recorrido m; (of newspapers) tirada f; (of a play) temporada en cartel f; (on a bank) pánico m, corrida f; **—away** fugitivo -va mf; **—away horse** caballo desbocado m; **—down** desvencijado; **— of good luck** racha de buena suerte f; **— of performances** temporada en cartel f; **— of the mill** del montón; **—way** (for planes) pista f; (for models) pasarela f; **to be on the —** estar huyendo; **in the long — a la larga; he gave me the —around** contestó con evasivas

rung [rʌŋ] N (of a chair) barrote m; (of a ladder) peldaño m

runner [ránə] N (one who runs) corredor -ora mf; (on a table) tapete m; (on a sled) patín m; (on a skate) cuchilla f; (on a plant) estolón m; (of drugs, contraband) contrabandista mf; **—-up** segundo -da mf

running [rʌnɪŋ] N (race) corrida f, carrera f; (direction) manejo m, dirección f; (flow) flujo m; (of machines) funcionamiento m; (of a car) rodaje m; **to be out of the — estar fuera de combate; — board** estribo m; ADJ (of horses) de carrera; (of plants) trepador; (of sores) supurante; **— water** agua corriente f; **in — condition** en buen estado; **for ten days —** durante diez días seguidos

runt [rʌnt] N (animal) animal más pequeño de la camada m; (person) pej mequetrefe m

rupture [ráptʃə] N (of relations, internal organ) ruptura f; (of a tire) rotura f; (hernia) hernia f; VI/VT romper(se), reventar(se)

rural [rúrəɫ] ADJ rural

rush [rʌʃ] VI/VT (hurry) apresurar(se); Am apurar(se); VT (to dispatch) llevar con prisa, llevar rápido; (to attack) precipitarse, abalanzarse sobre; **to — by / past** pasar corriendo; **to — out** salir corriendo; N (haste) prisa f; Am apuro m; (attack) acometida f; (hurried activity) bullicio m; (plant) junco m; **— of air** ráfaga f; **— of people** tumulto m; **— of water** torrente m; **— order** pedido urgente m

Russia [rʌ́ʃə] N Rusia f

Russian [rʌ́ʃən] ADJ & N ruso -sa mf

rust [rʌst] N (oxidation) herrumbre f, orín m; (disease) tizón m; **—-colored** color herrumbre; **—-proof** inoxidable; VI/VT herrumbrar(se)

rustic [rʌ́stɪk] ADJ rústico; N campesino -na mf, paleto -ta mf

rustle [rʌ́səɫ] VI susurrar, crujir; VT hacer susurrar, hacer crujir; **to — cattle** robar ganado; N susurro m, crujido m

rusty [rʌ́sti] ADJ (oxidized) herrumbrado, oxidado; (rust-colored) color herrumbre; (out of practice) falto de práctica; **my German is —** se me ha olvidado el alemán

rut [rʌt] N (furrow) surco m; (of a wheel) rodada f; (routine) rutina f; (heat) celo m; **to be in a —** ser esclavo de la rutina; VI estar en celo

ruthless [rúθlɪs] ADJ despiadado

ruthlessness [rúθlɪsnɪs] N crueldad f

Rwanda [ruándə] N Ruanda f

Rwandan [ruándən] ADJ & N ruandés -esa mf

rye [raɪ] N centeno m; **— bread** pan de centeno m

Ss

saber [sébə-] N sable m

sabotage [sǽbətɑʒ] N sabotaje m; VT sabotear

saccharine [sǽkərɪn] ADJ empalagoso; N sacarina f

sack [sæk] N (bag) saco m, bolso m; (looting) saqueo m; **in the —** en la cama; VT (bag) embolsar, ensacar; (loot) saquear; (fire) despedir

sacrament [sǽkrəmənt] N sacramento m

sacred [sékrɪd] ADJ sagrado

sacrifice [sǽkrəfaɪs] N sacrificio m; **at a —** con pérdida; VT sacrificar

sacrilege [sǽkrəlɪdʒ] N sacrilegio m

sacrilegious [sækrəlíɟəs] ADJ sacrílego

sad [sæd] ADJ triste

sadden [sǽdn̩] VI/VT entristecer(se); VT pesar

saddle [sǽdl̩] N (for horse) silla de montar f, montura f; (for bicycle) sillín m; **—bag** alforja f; **— horse** caballo de silla m; **— pad** carona f; **— tree** arzón m; VT ensillar; **to — up** ensillar; **to — someone with responsibilities** cargar a alguien de responsabilidades

sadism [sédɪzəm] N sadismo m

sadistic [sədístɪk] ADJ sádico

sadness [sǽdnɪs] N tristeza f

safari [səfári] N safari m

safe [sef] ADJ (secure) seguro, salvo; (trustworthy) digno de confianza; (careful) precavido, prudente; **— and sound** sano y salvo; **—-conduct** salvoconducto m; **—guard** salvaguarda f; **to —guard** salvaguardar; **— in jail** confinado; **—keeping** custodia f; N caja fuerte f

safety [séfti] N seguridad f; **— belt** cinturón de seguridad m; **— device** mecanismo de seguridad m, seguro m; **— glass** vidrio inastillable m; **— net** red f; **— pin** imperdible m

saffron [sǽfrən] N (spice) azafrán m; (color) color azafrán m

sag [sæg] VI/VT (wall) combar(se), pandear(se); VI (stock market, breast) caer; (spirits) decaer; (rope) aflojarse; (pants) abolsarse; **his shoulders —** tiene las espaldas caídas; N (of a wall) pandeo m, comba f; (in prices) caída f

sage [sedʒ] ADJ sabio; N (wise person) sabio -bia mf; (plant) salvia f

sail [seɫ] N (part of a boat) vela f; (trip) viaje en barco m; **—boat** velero m; **—fish** pez vela m; **under full —** a toda vela; **to set —** zarpar; VI/VT (travel by boat) navegar; (set sail) zarpar; **to — along** deslizarse, navegar; **to — along the coast** costear; **to — through an exam** aprobar un examen con facilidad

sailor [séɫə-] N marinero -ra mf

saint [sent] N santo -ta mf; **— John** San Juan

saintly [séntli] ADJ santo, piadoso

sake [sek] N **for the — of** por; **for my —** por mí; **for pity's —** por el amor de Dios; **for brevity's —** para ser breve; **for the — of argument** por vía de argumento; **art for art's —** el arte por el arte

salad [sǽləd] N ensalada f; **— dressing** aderezo m

salamander [sǽləmændə-] N salamandra f

salary [sǽləri] N sueldo m; **— bracket** categoría salarial f

sale [seł] N (act of selling) venta f; (special sales event) liquidación f, saldo m; **—s force** personal de ventas m; **—sperson** vendedor -ora mf; (in a store) dependiente -ta mf; **—s tax** impuesto sobre las ventas m; **for —** en venta

salient [séłiənt] ADJ & N saliente m

saline [sélin] ADJ salino

saliva [səláívə] N saliva f

sally [sǽli] N (sortie) salida f; (excursion) excursión f; VI salir, hacer una salida; **to — forth** salir

salmon [sǽmən] N salmón m

salmonella [sæłmənéłə] N salmonela f

salon [səłán] N salón m; (beauty parlor) salón de belleza m, peluquería f

saloon [səłún] N salón m, taberna f, bar m

salt [sɔłt] N sal f; (for smelling) sales f pl; **the — of the earth** la sal de la tierra; **old — lobo de mar m; —cellar** salero m; **— lick** salegar m; **— mine** salina f; **—shaker** salero m; **—water** agua salada f; VT salar; **to — away** ahorrar

salty [sɔ́łti] ADJ salado, (land) salobre

salutation [sæłjətéʃən] N saludo m

salute [səłút] N saludo m; (of guns) salva f; VI/VT (greet) saludar; (acknowledge) reconocer

Salvadoran, Salvadorian [sæłvədór(i)ən] ADJ & N salvadoreño -ña mf

salvage [sǽłvɪʤ] N (recovery) salvamento m; (objects recovered) objetos salvados m pl; VT salvar

salvation [sæłvéʃən] N salvación f

salve [sæv] N ungüento m, pomada f

salvo [sǽłvo] N salva f

same [sem] ADJ (identical) mismo; (similar) igual; **it is all the — to me** me da igual, me da lo mismo; **all the —** de todos modos

Samoa [səmóə] N Samoa f

Samoan [səmóən] ADJ & N samoano -na mf

sample [sǽmpəł] N muestra f; VT (try) probar; (take samples) muestrear

sampling [sǽmplɪŋ] N muestreo m

sanctify [sǽŋktəfaɪ] VT santificar

sanction [sǽŋkʃən] N sanción f; VT sancionar

sanctity [sǽŋktɪɾi] N santidad f

sanctuary [sǽŋktʃueri] N (church auditorium, place of refuge) santuario m; (game preserve) reserva f

sand [sænd] N arena f; **—box** arenero m; **— dollar** erizo de mar plano m; **—paper** papel de lija m; **to —paper** lijar; **—stone** arenisca f; **—storm** tormenta de arena f; VT lijar, pulir

sandal [sǽndl] N sandalia f

sandwich [sǽndwɪʧ] N bocadillo m, emparedado m; VT intercalar; **to be —ed between** quedar apretado entre

sandy [sǽndi] ADJ (full of sand) arenoso, arenisco; (yellowish red) rubio

sane [sen] ADJ cuerdo

sanitarium [sænɪtériəm] N sanatorio m

sanitary [sǽnɪteri] ADJ sanitario; **— napkin** paño higiénico m

sanitation [sænɪtéʃən] N (sewers) saneamiento m; (hygiene) salubridad f

sanity [sǽnɪɾi] N cordura f

San Marinese [sænmærəníz] ADJ & N sanmarinense mf, sanmarinés -esa mf

San Marino [sænməríno] N San Marino m

Sanskrit [sǽnskrɪt] N sánscrito f

Santa Claus [sǽntəklɔz] N Papá Noel m, Santa Claus m

São Tomean [saʊtoméən] ADJ & N santotomense mf

São Tome and Principe [saʊtoméəndprínsipe] N Santo Tomé y Príncipe m

sap [sæp] N (juice) savia f; (fool) tonto -ta mf; VT (exhaust) agotar

sapling [sǽplɪŋ] N (tree) árbol joven m; (person) jovenzuelo -la mf

sapphire [sǽfaɪr] N zafiro m

sarcasm [sárkæzəm] N sarcasmo m, socarronería f

sarcastic [sɑrkǽstɪk] ADJ sarcástico, socarrón

sarcoma [sɑrkómə] N sarcoma m

sarcophagus [sɑrkáfəgəs] N sarcófago m

sardine [sɑrdín] N sardina f

sardonic [sɑrdánɪk] ADJ sardónico

sash [sæʃ] N (around waist) faja f; (around shoulder) banda f; (on window) marco m, bastidor m

sassy [sǽsi] ADJ insolente

satanic [sətǽnɪk] ADJ satánico

satchel [sǽʧəł] N cartera f

satellite [sǽdlaɪt] N satélite m; **— dish** (antenna) parabólica f

satiate [séʃiet] VT saciar, hartar

satin [sǽtn̩] N raso m, satén m

satire [sǽtaɪr] N sátira f

satirical [sətírɪkəł] ADJ satírico

satirize [sǽɾəraɪz] VT satirizar

satisfaction [sæɪ̯ɪsfǽkʃən] N satisfacción f

satisfactory [sæɪ̯ɪsfǽktəri] ADJ satisfactorio

satisfied [sǽɪ̯ɪsfaɪd] ADJ satisfecho

satisfy [sǽɪ̯ɪsfaɪ] VI/VT satisfacer

saturate [sǽʧəret] VI/VT (impregnate) saturar(se); (soak) empapar(se); **—d fat** grasa saturada f

Saturday [sǽɾə̯de] N sábado m

sauce [sɔs] N salsa f; **—pan** cacerola f; VT

aderezar con salsa

saucer [sɔ́sɚ] N platillo *m*

saucy [sɔ́si] ADJ descarado, insolente; (who talks back) respondón

Saudi Arabia [sɔ́Diərébiə] N Arabia Saudí *f*, Arabia Saudita *f*

Saudi Arabian [sɔ́Diərébiən] ADJ & N saudí *mf*, saudita *mf*

saunter [sɔ́ntɚ] VI pasearse, deambular

sausage [sɔ́sɪʤ] N (thick) chorizo *m*; (thin) salchicha *f*; (cured) longaniza *f*; **—-making** charcutería *f*

savage [sǽvɪʤ] ADJ salvaje; (furious) rabioso; (rugged) agreste; N salvaje *m*; VT hacer trizas

savagery [sǽvɪʤri] N salvajismo *m*, barbarie *f*

save [sev] VT (a sinner, a person in danger) salvar; (furniture) salvaguardar, proteger; (money, time, energy) ahorrar, economizar; (data) guardar; VI (lay up money, be economical) ahorrar; (protect) salvaguardar; **to — from** librar de; **to — one's eyes** cuidarse la vista; PREP salvo, menos

savings [sévɪŋz] N ahorros *m pl*; **— account** cuenta de ahorros *f*; **— bank** caja de ahorros *f*

savior [sévjɚ] N salvador -ora *mf*

savor [sévɚ] N (taste) sabor *m*; (trace) dejo *m*; VT saborear

savory [sévəri] ADJ sabroso

savvy [sǽvi] N astucia *f*; ADJ astuto

saw [sɔ] N sierra *f*; **—horse** caballete *m*; VI/VT aserrar(se); **—dust** aserrín *m*, serrín *m*; **—mill** aserradero *m*

saxophone [sǽksəfon] N saxofón *m*

say [se] VI/VT decir; VT (a clock) marcar; (a sign) rezar, decir; (a prayer) rezar; **—!** ¡oye! **that is to —** es decir; **— I bought it** supongamos que yo lo comprara; **it goes without —ing** huelga decirlo; **there's a lot to be said for** es muy recomendable; **when all is said and done** al fin y al cabo; **you can — that again** tú lo has dicho; N **the final —** la última palabra; **to have one's —** dar su opinión; ADV **you could earn, —, 1 million dollars** podrías ganar pongamos un millón de dólares

saying [séɪŋ] N dicho *m*, refrán *m*

scab [skæb] N (of a wound) costra *f*; (on plants) roña *f*; (strikebreaker) esquirol *m*, amarillo -lla *mf*; VI (wound) encostrarse; (break a strike) ser esquirol

scabby [skǽbi] ADJ (of wounds) costroso; (of plants) roñoso; (of scalp) tiñoso

scaffold [skǽfəld] N (in construction)

andamio *m*; (of a gallows) patíbulo *m*

scald [skɔld] VI/VT escaldar(se); N escaldadura *f*

scale [skel] N (progression) escala *f*; (for weighing) balanza *f*; (for heavy weights) báscula *f*; (on fish, reptiles, human skin) escama *f*; **pair of —s** balanza *f*; VT (climb) escalar; (remove scales) escamar; VI/VT (adjust proportionately) graduar; **to — down** rebajar proporcionalmente

scallion [skǽljən] N cebollino *m*

scallop [skǽləp] N (mollusk) vieira *f*; (of beef) escalope *m*; (of fabric) festón *m*; VT festonear

scalp [skælp] N cuero cabelludo *m*; VT (to skin) arrancar la cabellera; (to resell) revender

scalpel [skǽlpəl] N bisturí *m*

scalper [skǽlpɚ] N revendedor -ra *mf*

scam [skæm] N timo *m*, estafa *f*

scamp [skæmp] N pícaro -ra *mf*, tunante -ta *mf*, pillo -lla *mf*

scamper [skǽmpɚ] VI (run) escabullirse, escaparse; (caper) cabriolar

scan [skæn] VT (horizon) escudriñar, escrutar; (with radar) explorar; (brain) hacer una tomografía; (page) echar un vistazo a; (verse) escandir; (digitalize for computer) escanear; N tomografía *f*

scandal [skǽndḷ] N escándalo *m*

scandalize [skǽndḷaɪz] VT escandalizar

scandalous [skǽndḷəs] ADJ escandaloso

scanner [skǽnɚ] N escáner *m*

scant [skænt] ADJ escaso

scanty [skǽnti] ADJ (scant) escaso; (of a skirt) muy corto; (of a bikini) breve

scapegoat [sképgot] N chivo expiatorio *m*, cabeza de turco *m*

scar [skɑr] N cicatriz *f*, lacra *f*; VT dejar una cicatriz

scarce [skɛrs] ADJ escaso; **to be —** escasear

scarcely [skɛ́rsli] ADV (barely) apenas; **he's a genius** no es un genio ni mucho menos

scarcity [skɛ́rsɪDi] N escasez *f*, pobreza *f*, carestía *f*

scare [skɛr] VI/VT espantar(se), asustar(se); **to — away** ahuyentar; **to — up** reunir; N susto *m*, sobresalto *m*; (of war) amago *m*; **—crow** espantapájaros *m sg*

scarf [skɑrf] N (woolen) bufanda *f*; (silk, cotton) pañuelo *m*; VI **to — up** engullir

scarlet [skɑ́rlɪt] N escarlata *m*, grana *f*; **— fever** escarlatina *f*

scary [skɛ́ri] ADJ (causing fright) de miedo; (easily frightened) asustadizo

scat [skæt] INTERJ ¡fuera!

scatter [skǽɒə-] VI/VT (seeds) esparcir(se), desparramar(se), desperdigar(se); (crowd) dispersar(se); **—brain** cabeza de chorlito *mf*; **—brained** atolondrado
scavenge [skǽvɪnʤ] VT recoger, rescatar; VI hurgar
scenario [sɪnério] N guión *m*; **worst-case —** el peor de los casos
scene [sin] N escena *f*; (sphere) ambiente *m*, ámbito *m*; **to make a —** montar una escena; **behind the —s** entre bastidores
scenery [sínəri] N paisaje *m*; (on a stage) decorado *m*
scenic [sínɪk] ADJ panorámico
scent [sent] N (smell) olor *m*; (fragrance) perfume *m*; (trace) pista *f*, rastro *m*; (sense of smell) olfato *m*; VI/VT (perceive through smell) olfatear; (intuit) presentir; (give fragrance to) perfumar
schedule [skéʤuɬ] N (plan) calendario *m*; (timetable) horario *m*; (appendix) apéndice *m*; (list) lista *f*; **on —** en fecha; **ahead of —** adelantando; VT programar, fijar
scheme [skim] N (plan) plan *m*, proyecto *m*; (plot) ardid *m*, trama *f*; (of colors) combinación *f*; VI/VT maquinar, intrigar, tramar
schemer [skímə-] N maquinador -ra *mf*, intrigante *mf*
scheming [skímɪŋ] ADJ intrigante; N maquinación *f*
schizophrenia [skɪtsəfréniə] N esquizofrenia *f*
scholar [skálə-] N (student) alumno -na *mf*; (fellow) becario -ria *mf*; (erudite person) erudito -ta *mf*, estudioso -sa *mf*
scholarly [skálə-li] ADJ erudito
scholarship [skálə-ʃɪp] N (erudition) erudición *f*; (award) beca *f*
school [skuɬ] N (primary) escuela *f*, colegio *m*; (secondary) secundaria *f*; *Sp* instituto *m*; (university) universidad *f*; (of law, etc.) facultad *f*; (of language, driving) academia *f*; (of thought) escuela *f*; (of fish) banco *m*, cardumen *m*; **—boy** escolar *m*; **—girl** escolar *f*; **—house** escuela *f*; **—master** maestro -tra *mf*; **—mate** compañero -ra de escuela *mf*; **—room** aula *f*, sala de clase *f*; **—teacher** maestro -tra *mf*; **— year** año lectivo *m*; VT instruir, entrenar
schooling [skúlɪŋ] N instrucción *f*
schooner [skúnə-] N goleta *f*
sciatic nerve [saɪǽdɪknɜ-v] N nervio ciático *m*
science [sáɪəns] N ciencia *f*; **— fiction** ciencia ficción *f*

scientific [saɪəntífɪk] ADJ científico; **— method** método científico *m*
scientist [sáɪəntɪst] N científico -ca *mf*
scintillate [síntɬet] VI (diamonds) centellear, destellar; (stars) titilar
scissors [sízə-z] N tijeras *f pl*
sclerosis [sklərósɪs] N esclerosis *f*
scoff [skaf] N mofa *f*, burla *f*; VI mofarse; **to — at** mofarse de, burlarse de
scold [skoɬd] VI/VT reprender, regañar, reñir; N regañón -ona *mf*
scolding [skóɬdɪŋ] N regaño *m*, reprimenda *f*
scoliosis [skoliósɪs] N escoliosis *f*
scoop [skup] N (ladle) cucharón *m*; (spoon for ice-cream) cuchara *f*; (shovel) pala *f*; (news item) primicia *f*; VT sacar con cuchara; (report first) adelantarse a; **to — in a good profit** sacar buena ganancia; **to — out** (water) achicar; (a hole) cavar; **to — up** recoger
scoot [skut] VI (go fast) correr; (go away) largarse
scooter [skúdə-] N (with motor) scooter *m*; (toy) monopatín *m*, patinete *m*
scope [skop] N (range) alcance *m*, ámbito *m*; (sphere) esfera *f*; VT observar
scorch [skɔrtʃ] VI/VT chamuscar(se), quemar(se); N chamuscadura *f*; *Am* quemadura *f*
score [skor] N (partial result) tanteo *m*; (total result) resultado *m*; (in a test) calificación *f*; (scratch) arañazo *m*; (twenty) veintena *f*; (of music) partitura *f*; **on that —** a ese respecto; **to keep —** llevar la cuenta; **to settle old —s** ajustar cuentas; VT (a test) calificar; (to orchestrate) orquestar; (to scratch) arañar; VI/VT (points) marcar, tantear; (sexually) ligar
scorn [skɔrn] N desdén *m*, menosprecio *m*; VI/VT desdeñar, menospreciar
scornful [skɔ́rnfəɬ] ADJ desdeñoso
scorpion [skɔ́rpiən] N escorpión *m*, alacrán *m*
Scotch [skatʃ] ADJ escocés; **— whisky** whisky escocés *m*
Scotland [skátlənd] N Escocia *f*
Scotsman [skátsmən] N escocés *m*
Scotswoman [skátswumən] N escocesa *f*
Scottish [skádɪʃ] ADJ escocés
scoundrel [skáundrəɬ] N bellaco *m*, infame *m*, truhán *m*
scour [skaur] VT (clean) fregar, restregar; (search) recorrer
scourge [skɜ-ʤ] N azote *m*; VT azotar
scout [skaut] N (military) explorador -ra *mf*; (child explorer) explorador -ra *mf*, scout *mf*; (for talent) cazatalentos *mf sg*; **a good —** una buena persona; VI/VT explorar; VI

to — for buscar

scowl [skauɫ] N ceño fruncido *m*; VI fruncir el ceño

scram [skræm] VI largarse

scramble [skrǽmbəɫ] VI (climb) subir a gatas; VT (eggs) revolver; (numbers) mezclar; **to — for** pelearse por; **to — up** subir a gatas; **—d eggs** huevos revueltos *m pl*; N (difficult climb) subida difícil *f*; (struggle for possession) arrebatiña *f*

scrap [skræp] N (fragment) fragmento *m*, pedacito *m*; (of truth) ápice *m*; (fight) riña *f*, reyerta *f*; **—book** álbum de recortes *m*; **— iron** chatarra *f*; **—s** sobras *f pl*, desperdicios *m pl*; VT (break apart) desguazar; (discard) desechar; VI pelearse, reñir

scrape [skrep] VI/VT (rub) raspar; (damage) arañar; **to — along** ir tirando, ir pasándola; **to — by** arreglárselas; **to — together** reunir; **to bow and — ser muy servil;** N (act of scraping) raspado *m*; (injury) raspón *m*, raspadura *f*; (sound) chirrido *m*; (fight) pelea *f*; (difficult situation) aprieto *m*

scraper [skrépɚ] N raspador *m*

scratch [skrætʃ] VI/VT (mark) arañar, rasguñar; (relieve itching) rascar(se); (cancel from a race) retirar(se); (cause itching) picar; VI (to dig, as a hen) escarbar; **to — out** (words) tachar; (eyes) sacar; N (injury) arañazo *m*, rasguño *m*; (sound) chirrido *m*; **to start from —** empezar de cero

scrawny [skrɔ́ni] ADJ esmirriado

scream [skrim] N grito *m*, alarido *m*; **he's a — es un payaso;** VI/VT gritar

screech [skritʃ] N (of brakes) chirrido *m*; (of voice) chillido *m*; **— owl** lechuza *f*; VI (of brakes) chirriar; (of voice) chillar

screen [skrin] N (movie, computer) pantalla *f*; (divider) biombo *m*; (on window) mosquitero *m*; (sifter) tamiz *m*; **— door** puerta con mosquitero *f*; **—play** guión *m*; **—writer** guionista *mf*; VT (conceal) tapar; (sift) tamizar; (project) proyectar; (select) seleccionar

screw [skru] N tornillo *m*; (one turn) vuelta *f*; (propeller) hélice *f*; **—driver** destornillador *m* (also cocktail); VT (turn) atornillar; **to — on** enroscar; **to — up one's courage** cobrar ánimo; **to — around** perder tiempo

scribble [skríbəɫ] VI/VT garabatear, garrapatear; N garabato *m*

script [skrɪpt] N (writing) escritura *f*; (screenplay) guión *m*

scripture [skríptʃɚ] N escritura sagrada *f*

scroll [skroɫ] N (roll) rollo *m*; (adornment) voluta *f*; VI **to — down** bajar el cursor

scrub [skrʌb] VI/VT (rub) fregar, restregar; VT (cancel) cancelar; **to — up** lavarse las manos; N (cleaning) friega *f*, fregada *f*; (bushes) maleza *f*; (rough terrain) breña *f*; **— pine** pino achaparrado *m*; **— team** equipo suplente *m*; **—woman** fregona *f*

scruple [skrúpəɫ] N escrúpulo *m*

scrupulous [skrúpjələs] ADJ escrupuloso

scrutinize [skrútnaɪz] VI/VT escrutar

scrutiny [skrútni] N escrutinio *m*, examen minucioso *m*

scuba [skúbə] N escafandra *f*; VI **to —-dive** bucear

scuff [skʌf] VT (shoes) rayar; (floor) marcar; N (on shoes) raya *f*; (on floor) marca *f*

scuffle [skʌ́fəɫ] N refriega *f*, riña *f*; VI pelear, reñir; (shuffle) arrastrar los pies

sculptor [skʌ́lptɚ] N escultor -ra *mf*

sculpture [skʌ́lptʃɚ] N escultura *f*; VI/VT esculpir

scum [skʌm] N (in a glass) capa de suciedad *f*; (in a pond) verdín *m*; (people) escoria *f*; (vile person) *pej* canalla *mf*; **—bag** *pej* canalla *mf*; VI cubrirse de espuma; VT espumar

scurrilous [skɚ́-ələs] ADJ (coarse) grosero; (injurious) injurioso

scurry [skɚ́-i] VI correr; **to — away / off** escabullirse; N carrera *f*

scuttle [skʌ́dɫ] VI (run) correr; **to — away / off** escabullirse; VT (sink a ship) hundir; (abandon a plane) abandonar

scythe [saɪð] N guadaña *f*

sea [si] N mar *mf*; **at —** en el mar; **by —** por barco; **to put to —** hacerse a la mar; **on the high —s** en alta mar; ADJ marino; **— battle** batalla naval *f*; **—board** costa *f*, litoral *m*; **—coast** costa *f*, litoral *m*; **— cow** vaca marina *f*; **— current** corriente marina *f*; **—faring** marinero; **—food** frutos del mar *m pl*; **— green** verdemar *m*; **—gull** gaviota *f*; **— horse** caballito de mar *m*; **— level** nivel del mar *m*; **— lion** léon marino *m*; **—man** marino *m*, marinero *m*; **—plane** hidroavión *m*; **—port** puerto de mar *m*; **— power** potencia naval *f*; **—shore** costa *f*; **—sick** mareado; **to get —sick** marearse; **—sickness** mareo *m*; **—side** costa *f*, litoral *m*; **— turtle** tortuga marina *f*; **— urchin** erizo de mar *m*; **—weed** alga (marina) *f*; **—worthy** marinero

seal [siɫ] N (stamp) sello *m*; (on a jar) precinto *m*; (animal) foca *f*; **to set one's**

— to sellar; **—ing wax** lacre *m*; VT (put a seal on) sellar; (close with a seal) precintar; **to — one's fate** determinar el destino de uno; **to — off** acordonar; **to — in** cerrar herméticamente; **to — with sealing wax** lacrar

seam [sim] N (sewing) costura *f*; (in rock) grieta *f*; (in ore deposits) veta *f*; VT coser

seamstress [símstrɪs] N costurera *f*

seamy [símɪ] ADJ sórdido

sear [sɪr] VT chamuscar

search [sɜtʃ] VI/VT (an area) rastrear, requisar; (a suitcase) registrar; (a person) cachear; **— me!** ¡a mí que me registren! ¡yo que sé! **to — for** buscar; N (for something) búsqueda *f*; (of baggage, ships) registro *m*; (of an area) rastreo *m*; **— engine** motor de búsqueda *m*, máquina de búsqueda *f*; **—light** reflector *m*; **— warrant** orden de registro *m*; **in — of** en busca de

season [sízən] N (of the year) estación *f*; (period of time) temporada *f*, época *f*; **in —** en temporada/época; **— ticket** billete de abono *m*; **open —** temporada de caza/pèsca *f*; **out of —** fuera de temporada/época; VT (to spice) sazonar, aderezar; VI (wood) secarse; **a —ed pilot** un piloto experimentado

seasoning [sízənɪŋ] N condimento *m*, aliño *m*

seat [sit] N (furniture) asiento *m*; (of bicycle) sillín *m*; (in parliament) escaño *m*; (of government) sede *f*; (in the theater) localidad *f*; (buttocks) asentaderas *f pl*; (of clothes) fondillos *m pl*; **to take a —** sentarse, tomar asiento; **— belt** cinturón de seguridad *m*; VT (cause to sit) sentar; (accommodate with seats) tener capacidad para; (place) colocar; **to — oneself** sentarse

seclude [sɪklúd] VT aislar; **to — oneself from** recluirse de, aislarse de

secluded [sɪklúdɪd] ADJ apartado, aislado

seclusion [sɪklúʒən] N recogimiento *m*, aislamiento *m*

second [sékənd] ADJ & N segundo -da *mf*; **— fiddle** segundón -ona *mf*; **— floor** primer piso *m*; **—hand** de segunda mano; **— lieutenant** subteniente *mf*; **on — thought** pensándolo bien; **—-rate** mediocre, de segunda; N (part of a minute) segundo *m*; (helper in a duel) padrino *m*; **— child** segundón -ona *mf*; **— cousin** primo -ma segundo -da *mf*; **— nature** artículos de segunda *m pl*; **may I have —s?** ¿puedo repetir? **to —-guess** cuestionar; VT

(support) secundar, apoyar; (assist in duels) apadrinar; (support a motion) apoyar

secondary [sékənderi] ADJ secundario; **— school** escuela secundaria *f*

secondly [sékəndli] ADV en segundo lugar

secrecy [síkrɪsi] N secreto *m*

secret [síkrɪt] ADJ & N secreto *m*

secretariat [sekrɪtériət] N secretaría *f*

secretary [sékrɪteri] N (assistant) secretario -ria *mf*; (government) ministro -tra *mf*; (furniture) escritorio *m*

secrete [sɪkrít] VT (discharge) secretar, segregar; (hide) ocultar

secretion [sɪkríʃən] N secreción *f*

secretive [síkrɪdɪv] ADJ hermético

sect [sekt] N secta *f*

section [sékʃən] N sección *f*; (of a chapter) apartado *m*; (passage) trozo *m*; (of a city) sector *m*; (incision) corte *m*; (of orange) gajo *m*; VT seccionar

sector [séktɚ] N sector *m*

secular [sékjələ] ADJ secular; N seglar *mf*, lego -ga *mf*

secure [sɪkjúr] ADJ (certain, safe) seguro; (firm) firme; VT (make certain, guarantee) asegurar, afianzar; (make firm) afirmar, cimentar; (obtain) obtener; (protect) proteger; (lock) cerrar con llave; (capture) capturar; (tie) amarrar

security [sɪkjúrɪdi] N (safety, freedom from worry) seguridad *f*; (guarantee) fianza *f*, garantía *f*; (guarantor) fiador -ora *mf*; **securities** valores *m pl*

sedan [sɪdǽn] N sedán *m*

sedate [sɪdét] ADJ sosegado, tranquilo; VT sedar

sedation [sɪdéʃən] N sedación *f*

sedative [sédədɪv] ADJ & N calmante *m*, sedante *m*

sedentary [sédnteri] ADJ sedentario

sediment [sédəmənt] N sedimento *m*; (dregs) heces *f pl*

sedition [sɪdíʃən] N sedición *f*

seduce [sɪdús] VI/VT seducir (a)

seduction [sɪdʌ́kʃən] N seducción *f*

see [si] VI/VT (perceive, find out, meet, visit) ver; (understand) entender; (make sure) fijarse, asegurarse; (date) salir con; (help) ayudar; (accompany) acompañar; **to — to** encargarse de, atender; **let me — a** ver; **to — off** despedir; **to — through someone** calar a alguien; **to — about** ocuparse de; **to — out** acompañar a la puerta; N sede *f*

seed [sid] N (grains) semilla *f*; (semen) simiente *f*; **to go to —** echarse a perder;

— **bed** semillero *m*; VI/VT (sow) sembrar; VT despepitar, quitar las semillas; (player) clasificar; VI producir semillas

seedy [síDi] ADJ sórdido

seek [sik] VT (search for) buscar; (ask for) pedir; **to — after** buscar; **to — to** tratar de, esforzarse por

seem [sim] VI parecer; **they — to be here** parece que están aquí; **it —s to me** me parece

seemingly [síminli] ADV aparentemente

seep [sip] VI/VT rezumar(se)

seer [sir] N vidente *mf*

seesaw [síso] N balancín *m*, subibaja *m*; VI oscilar

seethe [sið] VI bullir, hervir; **he was seething** hervía de rabia

segment [ségmənt] N segmento *m*

segregate [ségrɪget] VI/VT segregar

seismic [sáɪzmɪk] ADJ sísmico

seize [siz] VT (grab) asir, agarrar; (take possession) apoderarse de; (take advantage of) aprovecharse de; (confiscate) embargar, incautarse de, secuestrar; **to — upon** asir; VI **to — (up)** agarrotarse; **to — upon** valerse de

seizure [síʒə] N (of power) toma *f*; (of property) confiscación *f*; (of drugs, guns) incautación *f*, secuestro *m*; (epileptic) ataque *m*

seldom [séldəm] ADV rara vez, raramente

select [sɪlékt] ADJ selecto; VI/VT elegir, seleccionar

selection [sɪlékʃən] N selección *f*, elección *f*

selective [sɪléktɪv] ADJ selectivo

self [sɛlf] N (ego) yo *m*; —**assurance** desenvoltura *f*; —**control** autocontrol *m*; —**defense** defensa propia *f*; (juridical term) legítima defensa *f*; —**denial** abnegación *f*; —**discipline** autodisciplina *f*; —**esteem** autoestima *f*; —**government** autogobierno *m*; —**help** autoayuda *f*; —**image** autoimagen *f*; —**improvement** mejora personal *f*; —**interest** interés personal *m*; —**made man** hombre que debe su éxito a sus propios esfuerzos *m*; —**pity** autocompasión *f*; —**reliance** independencia *f*; —**respect** amor propio *m*; —**sacrifice** sacrificio *m*; —**satisfaction** autosatisfacción *f*; **his better —** su lado bueno *m*; **his former —** lo que era antes *m*; ADJ —**assured** desenvuelto; —**centered** egocéntrico; —**composed** tranquilo; —**confident** con confianza de sí mismo; —**conscious** (shy) cohibido; (with complexes)

acomplejado; —**destructive** autodestructivo; —**employed** que trabaja por cuenta propia; —**evident** evidente; —**explanatory** claro, fácil de entender; —**propelled** autopropulsado; —**righteous** que afecta superioridad moral; —**satisfied** pagado de sí, satisfecho de sí; —**service** autoservicio; —**serving** interesado; —**sufficient** autosuficiente

selfish [sélfɪʃ] ADJ egoísta

selfishness [sélfɪʃnɪs] N egoísmo *m*

selfless [sélflɪs] ADJ desinteresado, generoso

sell [sɛl] VI/VT vender(se); **this book sold a thousand copies** se vendieron mil ejemplares de este libro; **to be sold on** estar entusiasmado con; **to — out** (dispose of) liquidar; (betray) traicionar, vender; (run out) agotarse; N —**off** (liquidation) liquidación *f*; (decline) baja *f*; —**out** traición *f*

seller [sélə] N vendedor -ora *mf*

semantics [sɪmǽntɪks] N semántica *f*

semblance [sémbləns] N apariencia *f*

semester [səméstə] N semestre *m*

semicircle [sémɪsəkəl] N semicírculo *m*

semicolon [sémɪkolən] N punto y coma *m*

semiconductor [sɛmɪkəndáktə] N semiconductor *m*

semifinal [sémɪfaɪnəl] ADJ & N semifinal *f*

seminar [sémənɑr] N seminario *m*

seminary [séməneri] N seminario *m*

Semitic [səmíDɪk] ADJ semítico

senate [sénɪt] N senado *m*

senator [sénəDə] N senador -ora *mf*

send [sɛnd] VT enviar, mandar; **that sent chills down my spine** me dio escalofríos; **to — away** hacer salir; **to — for** mandar buscar a; **to — in** remitir; **to — out for** encargar; **to — word** mandar decir

sender [séndə] N remitente *m*

Senegal [sénɪgɔl] N Senegal *m*

Senegalese [sɛnɪgəlíz] ADJ & N senegalés -esa *mf*

senile [sínaɪl] ADJ senil, chocho

senility [sɪnílɪDi] N senilidad *f*, chochera *f*, chochez *f*

senior [sínjə] ADJ (with more seniority) más antiguo; (in school) de cuarto año; (for the elderly) para ancianos; **John Smith — John Smith** padre; N (person of higher rank) superior *mf*; (fourth year student) estudiante de cuarto año *m*; (elderly person) persona de la tercera edad *f*; **to be somebody's —** ser mayor que alguien; —**citizen** persona de la tercera edad *f*

seniority [sinjɔ́rɪDi] N antigüedad *f*
sensation [senséʃən] N sensación *f*
sensational [senséʃənəɫ] ADJ sensacional
sense [sens] N (of humor, honor, direction)
sentido *m*; (of pain, insecurity) sensación
f; (meaning) significado *m*, sentido *m*; **to
make** — tener sentido; **to make — of
something** entender algo; **in a** — en
cierto sentido; **to take leave of one's
—s** volverse loco; **to come to one's —s**
(wake up) volver en sí; (be reasonable)
recobrar el juicio; VT (perceive) percibir,
sentir; (intuit) intuir
senseless [sénslɪs] ADJ (meaningless) sin
sentido; (unconscious) inconsciente
sensibility [sensəbíliɾi] N sensibilidad *f*
sensible [sénsəbəɫ] ADJ sensato, razonable
sensitive [sénsɪDɪv] ADJ (to emotions)
sensible; (to stimuli) sensitivo
sensitivity [sénsɪtɪvɪDi] N sensibilidad *f*
sensitize [sénsɪtaɪz] VT sensibilizar
sensor [sénsɔr] N sensor *m*
sensory [sénsəri] ADJ sensorial
sensual [sénʃuəɫ] ADJ sensual
sensuality [senʃuǽliɾi] N sensualidad *f*
sensuous [sénʃuəs] ADJ sensual
sentence [séntəns] N (to prison) sentencia *f*,
condena *f*; (phrase) oración *f*; VT
condenar, sentenciar
sentiment [séntəmənt] N sentimiento *m*
sentimental [sentəméntɫ] ADJ sentimental;
(excessively) sensiblero
sentimentality [sentəmentǽlɪDi] N
sentimentalismo *m*; (excessive) sensiblería
f
sentinel [séntənəɫ] N centinela *m*
sentry [séntri] N centinela *m*; — **box** garita *f*
separate [séprɪt] ADJ (apart) separado; [sépəret]
VI/VT separar(se)
separation [sepəréʃən] N separación *f*
Sephardi [səfúrdi] N sefardí *mf*, sefardita *mf*
September [septémbə] N septiembre *m*
sequel [síkwəɫ] N continuación *f*
sequence [síkwəns] N secuencia *f*; (of events)
serie *f*; **in** — en orden; VT secuenciar
serenade [serənéd] N serenata *f*, ronda *f*; VI/
VT dar (una) serenata (a), rondar (a)
serene [sərín] ADJ sereno
serenity [sərénɪDi] N serenidad *f*
sergeant [súrdʒənt] N sargento *m*
serial [síriəɫ] N novela por entregas *f*; ADJ
(published in installments) por entregas;
(murder) en serie
series [síriz] N serie *f*
serious [síriəs] ADJ serio; (illness) grave
seriousness [síriəsnɪs] N seriedad *f*; (of an
illness) gravedad *f*

sermon [súmən] N sermón *m*
serpent [súpənt] N sierpe *f*
serrated [sérɛDɪd] ADJ serrado
serum [sírəm] N suero *m*
servant [súvənt] N sirviente -ta *mf*, criado
-da *mf*
serve [sɝv] VI/VT (in a restaurant, in a store)
servir, atender; (in tennis) sacar; **to — a
term in prison** cumplir una condena; **to
— a warrant** entregar una orden
judicial; **to — as** servir de; **to — notice**
advertir; **to — one's purpose** resultarle
útil a alguien; **it —s me right** me lo
merezco; N saque *m*
server [súvə] N (one who serves) servidor -ra
mf; (in a restaurant) camarero -ra *mf*; (for
pie) utensilio para servir *m*; (computer)
servidor *m*
service [súvɪs] N servicio *m*; (in tennis) saque
m; (of a warrant) entrega *f*; **at your** — a
su servicio; — **entrance** entrada de
servicio *f*; —**man** (soldier) militar *m*; (for
repairs) reparador *m*; — **station** estación
de servicio *f*; VT (a car) revisar; (an
industry) atender, servir; (a debt) pagar
serviceable [súvɪsəbəɫ] ADJ (practical)
práctico; (durable) duradero
servile [súvaɪɫ] ADJ servil
servitude [súvɪtud] N servidumbre *f*
sesame [sésəmi] N sésamo *m*
session [séʃən] N sesión *f*; (semester) semestre
m; (of Congress) período de sesiones *m*
set [set] VT (place) colocar; (fix) fijar,
establecer; (sic) azuzar; (print) componer;
VI (cement) fraguar; (jelly) cuajar; (sun)
ponerse; (glue) endurecerse; **to — a bone**
reducir un hueso dislocado; **to — a
diamond** engastar un diamante; **to —
an example** dar ejemplo; **to — a poem
to music** ponerle música a un poema; **to
— a precedent** establecer un precedente;
to — a trap tender una trampa; **to — a
watch** poner el reloj en hora; **to —
about** disponerse a; **to — aside** apartar;
(money) ahorrar; (a claim) rechazar; (a
verdict) anular; **to — back** (hinder, make
earlier) atrasar; (cost) costar; (a clock)
retrasar; **to — forth** exponer; **to —
forth on a journey** ponerse en camino;
to — free librar; **to — off** (make
explode) hacer estallar; (start on a
journey) ponerse en camino; (intensify)
resaltar; **to — one's heart on** tener la
esperanza puesta en; **to — one's mind
on** resolverse a; **to — out for** partir para;
to — out to proponerse; **to — right**
rectificar; **to — the table** poner la mesa;

to — up (assemble) armar; (set a trap for) tender; (establish) establecer; **to — upon someone** acometer a alguien; ADJ (fixed) fijo; (ready) listo; (hard) duro; N (ensemble) juego *m*; (group) conjunto *m*; (TV) aparato *m*; (scenery) escenario *m*; (of tennis) set *m*; **—back** revés *m*; **— of teeth** dentadura *f*; **—up** (arrangement) arreglo *m*; (assembly) montaje *m*; (trap) tongo *m*, timo *m*

setter [sέডə·] N sétter *m*

setting [sέডɪŋ] N (act of putting down) colocación *f*; (jewel) engaste *m*; (in theater) escenario *m*; (of sun, moon) puesta *f*; **— sun** sol poniente *m*

settle [sέdl] VT (a territory) colonizar, poblar; (affairs) arreglar; (argument) zanjar; (lawsuit) arreglar; (an estate) liquidar; (a bill) saldar, solventar; (one's nerves) calmar; VI (end a dispute) llegar a un arreglo; (take up residence) establecerse; (alight) posarse; (sink to bottom) depositarse; VT **to — down** (get married) casarse; (mend one's ways) sentar cabeza; (take up residence) instalarse; (become calm) calmarse; **to — on a date** fijar / señalar una fecha; **to — for** conformarse con; **to — up** pagar

settlement [sέd|mənt] N (community) colonia *f*, población *f*; (agreement) acuerdo *m*; (of a lawsuit) arreglo *m*; (of a bill) pago *m*, finiquito *m*; (final disposition) liquidación *f*

settler [sέtlə·] N colono -na *mf*, poblador -ra *mf*

seven [sέvən] NUM siete

seventeen [sevəntín] NUM diecisiete

seventh [sέvənθ] ADJ séptimo

seventy [sέvənti] NUM setenta

sever [sέvə·] VT (an arm) cortar; (relations) romper

several [sέvə·əl] ADJ varios

severe [səvír] ADJ (criticism, standards) severo; (winter, test) duro; (storm, heat) intenso; (illness) grave

severity [səvέrɪdi] N (of criticism, standards) severidad *f*; (of water, test) dureza *f*; (of storm, heat) intensidad *f*; (of illness) gravedad *f*

sew [so] VI/VT coser

sewage [súɪʤ] N aguas negras *f pl*; **— system** alcantarillado *m*

sewer [súə·] N alcantarilla *f*, cloaca *f*, colector *m*

sewing [sóɪŋ] N costura *f*; **— machine** máquina de coser *f*

sex [sεks] N sexo *m*; **— appeal** atractivo

sexual *m*; **— symbol** símbolo sexual *m*; VT sexar

sexism [sέksɪzəm] N sexismo *m*

sexton [sέkstən] N sacristán *m*

sexual [sέkʃuəl] ADJ sexual; **— assault** violación *f*; **— harassment** acoso sexual *m*

sexuality [sεkʃuǽlɪdi] N sexualidad *f*

sexy [sέksi] ADJ sexy, morboso

Seychelles [seʃέl] N Seychelles *f pl*

shabby [ʃǽbi] ADJ (worn) gastado; (slovenly) andrajoso; (tawdry) sórdido; (mean) mezquino; **not too** — no está mal

shack [ʃæk] N casucha *f*, choza *f*

shackle [ʃǽkəl] N grillete *m*; **—s** cadenas *f pl*, grillos *m pl*; VT (put in chains) engrillar; (impede) estorbar

shad [ʃæd] N sábalo *m*

shade [ʃed] N (shadow) sombra *f*; (nuance) matiz *m*; (for windows) persiana *f*; (phantom) espectro *m*; (of a lamp) pantalla *f*; **a — longer** un poco más largo; **in the —** a la sombra; **—s** lentes negros / oscuros *m pl*; *Sp* gafas de sol *f pl*; VT (protect from sun) sombrear, dar sombra; (darken a picture) sombrear

shadow [ʃǽdo] N (dark image, shade) sombra *f*; (phantom) espectro *m*; **in the — of** a la sombra de; **without a — of doubt** sin sombra de duda; VT (darken) sombrear; (make gloomy) ensombrecer; **to — someone** seguirle la pista a alguien

shady [ʃέdi] ADJ sombreado, umbrío; **— character** sospechoso *m*; **— dealings** negocios turbios *m pl*

shaft [ʃæft] N (of a mine) pozo *m*; (of a feather) cañón *m*; (of an elevator) hueco *m*; (of an arrow) asta *f*

shaggy [ʃǽgi] ADJ peludo, lanudo

shake [ʃek] VI (tremble) temblar; VI/VT (move back and forth) sacudir(se); (in order to mix) agitar(se); (elude) deshacerse de; **to — hands** darse la mano; **to — one's head** menear la cabeza; **to — with cold** tiritar; **to — with fear** temblar de miedo; **to — off** (a cold, disappointment, etc.) deshacerse de; (depression) librarse de; **to — up** (a liquid) agitar; (a person) trastornar; VI (violent) sacudida *f*; (of milk) batido *m*; **hand—** apretón de manos *m*; **the —s** escalofríos *m pl*; **—-up** reorganización *f*

shaky [ʃέki] ADJ (hand) tembloroso; (start) vacilante

shall [ʃæl] V AUX **I — come** vendré; **— I help you?** ¿te ayudo? **thou shalt not steal** no robarás

shallow [ʃǽlo] ADJ (plate) llano; (water) poco profundo; (breathing) superficial; (explanation) superficial, somero

shallowness [ʃǽlonɪs] N (of plate) lo llano; (of water) poca profundidad *f*; (of person) superficialidad *f*

sham [ʃæm] N (hoax) farsa *f*; (trickster) farsante *mf*; **— battle** simulacro de batalla *m*

shambles [ʃǽmbəłz] N desorden *m*, caos *m*

shame [ʃem] N (embarrassment) vergüenza *f*; (dishonor) deshonra *f*; (pity) lástima *f*; **— on you!** ¡qué vergüenza! **to bring — upon** deshonrar; VT avergonzar

shameful [ʃémfəł] ADJ vergonzoso

shameless [ʃémlɪs] ADJ desvergonzado, descarado

shamelessness [ʃémlɪsnɪs] N desvergüenza *f*

shampoo [ʃæmpú] N (product) champú *m*; (wash) lavado del cabello *m*; VI/VT lavar con champú

shamrock [ʃǽmrak] N trébol *m*

shank [ʃæŋk] N (part of leg) canilla *f*, espinilla *f*; (cut of meat) pierna *f*, pata *f*

shanty [ʃǽnti] N casucha *f*; *Sp* chabola *f*; **—town** suburbio *m*

shape [ʃep] N (form) forma *f*; (condition) condición *f*; (silhouette) bulto *m*; **to be in bad —** andar mal; **to get in —** ponerse en forma; VT dar forma a; **to — up** reformarse

shapeless [ʃéplɪs] ADJ informe

share [ʃɛr] N (portion) parte *f*, porción *f*; (stock) acción *f*; **—cropper** aparcero *m*; **—holder** accionista *mf*; VI/VT compartir; **to — in** participar en

shark [ʃɑrk] N (fish) tiburón *m*; (swindler) estafador -ra *mf*

sharp [ʃɑrp] ADJ (blade) afilado, filoso; (needle) puntiagudo; (curve) cerrado; (contrast) marcado, nítido; (smell) acre; (wind) cortante; (pain) punzante; (remark) mordaz, agudo; (mind) perspicaz; (musical note) sostenido; (dresser) elegante; (cheese) picante; (ear) fino; **— eye** vista aguzada *f*; **—-tongued** mordaz; **—-witted** agudo; **—shooter** tirador -ra de primera *mf*; N sostenido *m*

sharpen [ʃárpən] VI/VT (knife) afilar(se); VT (pencil) sacar punta a; (skill) afinar

sharpness [ʃárpnɪs] N (of a blade) lo afilado; (of a needle) lo puntiagudo; (of a curve) lo cerrado; (of a contrast) nitidez *f*; (of a smell) acritud *f*; (of pain) intensidad *f*; (of a remark) mordacidad *f*; (of a mind) perspicacia *f*, agudeza *f*; (of cheese) lo picante

shatter [ʃǽɾə] VI/VT (glass) astillar(se), hacer(se) añicos; (nerves) destrozar(se); (health) quebrantar(se); (hopes) frustrar

shave [ʃev] VI/VT (beard, legs) afeitar(se), rasurar(se); VT (wood) cepillar; (graze) rozar; **to — off** rapar; N afeitado *m*, rasurado *m*; **he had a close —** se salvó por poco

shaver [ʃévə] N afeitadora *f*

shavings [ʃévɪŋz] N virutas *f pl*

shawl [ʃɔł] N mantón *m*, chal *m*

she [ʃi] PRON ella; **— who** la que, quien; N **—-bear** osa *f*

sheaf [ʃif] N (of corn) gavilla *f*; (of arrows) haz *m*; (of paper) fajo *m*

shear [ʃir] VT esquilar, trasquilar; N **—s** (for sheep) tijeras para esquilar *f pl*; (for plants) tijeras para podar *f pl*; (for metal) cizallas *f pl*; (for hair) tijeras de peluquero *f pl*

shearing [ʃírɪŋ] N esquila *f*, esquileo *m*

sheath [ʃiθ] N (of sword, peas) vaina *f*; (of knife, umbrella) funda *f*

sheathe [ʃið] VT (a sword) envainar; (a knife) enfundar

shed [ʃɛd] N cobertizo *m*, galpón *m*, tinglado *m*; VT (tears) derramar; (light) arrojar; (leaves) perder; (skin, hair) mudar, perder; VI (be waterproof) ser impermeable; (lose hair) pelechar; (lose leaves) deshojarse; (lose skin) mudar la piel

sheen [ʃin] N brillo *m*

sheep [ʃip] N oveja *f*; **—dog** perro pastor *m*, ovejero *m*; **—skin** (hide) piel de oveja *f*; (leather) badana *f*; (parchment) pergamino *m*; (diploma) diploma *m*

sheepish [ʃípɪʃ] ADJ vergonzoso, tímido

sheer [ʃir] ADJ (absolute) puro, total; (fine) fino; (vertical) vertical, acantilado

sheet [ʃit] N (bedding) sábana *f*; (of ice) capa *f*; (of paper) hoja *f*; (of glass) lámina *f*; (of rain) cortina *f*; **— metal** chapa de metal *f*; **— music** música en hojas de partitura *f*

shelf [ʃɛłf] N estante *m*, repisa *f*, anaquel *m*; (of rock) saliente *f*

shell [ʃɛł] N (turtles, snail) caparazón *f*; (of mollusk) concha *f*; (of egg, nut) cáscara *f*; (of peas) vaina *f*; (of a ship) casco *m*; (of a building) armazón *m*; (of artillery) proyectil *m*; (of a rifle) cartucho *m*; **—fish** mariscos *m pl*; VT (nuts, eggs) pelar; (peas) desgranar; (military target) bombardear

shelter [ʃɛ́łtə] N (refuge) refugio *m*, resguardo *m*, abrigo *m*; **to take —** refugiarse, guarecerse; VI/VT (take or give refuge) refugiar(se), resguardar(se), abrigar(se)

shelve [ʃɛłv] VT (place on a shelf) colocar en un estante; (defer) archivar

shepherd [ʃépəd] N pastor m; (dog) perro pastor m

sherbet [ʃɜ́·bɪt] N sorbete m

sheriff [ʃérɪf] N alguacil m

sherry [ʃéri] N jerez m

shield [ʃiːld] N escudo m; VI/VT (protect) escudar(se); VT (conceal) ocultar

shift [ʃɪft] VI/VT (gears) cambiar; **to — for oneself** arreglárselas solo; **to — the blame** echar la culpa a otro; N (of gears, of wind) cambio m; (dress) vestido suelto m; (of workers) turno m; **— key** tecla (de) mayúscula f

shiftless [ʃíftlɪs] ADJ holgazán

shimmer [ʃíməɹ] VI titilar; N titileo m

shin [ʃɪn] N espinilla f, canilla f; VI **to — up** trepar

shine [ʃaɪn] VI brillar, relucir; VT (shoes) limpiar, lustrar; (furniture) lustrar; N brillo m, resplandor m; (of shoes) lustre m

shingle [ʃíŋgəl] N (on roof) teja f; (sign) chapa f; **—s** culebrilla f, zona f; **to hang out one's —** abrir un consultorio; VT cubrir con tejas

shiny [ʃáɪni] ADJ (bright) brillante; (worn) brilloso

ship [ʃɪp] N (on water) buque m, navío m; (in air) avión m; **—builder** constructor -ra naval mf; **—mate** camarada de a bordo mf; **—wreck** naufragio m; **—yard** astillero m; ADJ **—shape** ordenado; VT transportar; **to —wreck** hacer naufragar; **to — off** sacarse de encima; VI **to —wreck** naufragar

shipment [ʃípmənt] N cargamento m, remesa f

shipper [ʃípəɹ] N (sender) expedidor -ra mf; (carrier) transportista mf

shipping [ʃípɪŋ] N envío m; **— charges** gastos de envío m pl; **— and handling** gastos de envío m pl

shirk [ʃɜ·k] VT evadir, esquivar, rehuir

shirt [ʃɜ·t] N camisa f; **in — sleeves** en mangas de camisa; **—tail** faldón m

shiver [ʃívəɹ] VI (from cold) tiritar; (from cold, fear, etc.) temblar; N temblor m; **—s** escalofríos m pl

shoal [ʃoɫ] N (sandbank) bajío m, banco de arena m; (school of fish) banco m, bandada f

shock [ʃak] N (impact, disturbance) choque m; (of electricity) sacudida f; (of wheat) hacina f; (physical convulsion) shock m, choque m; **— absorber** amortiguador m; **— of hair** guedeja f; **— troops** tropas de choque f pl; **— wave** onda expansiva f; VT (bewilder) chocar, horrorizar, azorar; (discharge electricity) dar una descarga eléctrica; (make bundles of grain) hacinar, hacer gavillas de

shocking [ʃákɪŋ] ADJ chocante, escandaloso

shoddy [ʃádi] ADJ chapucero

shoe [ʃu] N zapato m; (for brakes) zapata f; (for horses) herradura f; **—horn** calzador m; **—lace** cordón m; **—maker** zapatero -ra mf; **— polish** betún m; **— repairman** zapatero -ra remendón -ona mf; **— store** zapatería f; **—string** cordón m; **to live on a —string** vivir con poco dinero; **to tie one's —s** atarse los zapatos; VT (a person) calzar; (a horse) herrar

shoo-in [ʃúɪn] N favorito -ta f

shoot [ʃut] VT (wound with a bullet) pegar un tiro, abatir; (discharge a firearm) disparar; (film a movie) rodar; VI (discharge bullet, arrow) disparar, tirar; (be discharged) dispararse; (hunt with a gun) cazar; (germinate) brotar; (throw) lanzar; (take a photo) fotografiar; (film) filmar; (kick a ball) chutar; **to — at** disparar a, tirar·a; **to — by** pasar rápidamente; **to — down** (plane) derribar; (argument) refutar; **to — forth** brotar; **to — up** (grow) crecer rápidamente; (damage by shooting) tirotear; (inject drugs) chutar; N (new growth) yema f, retoño m, vástago m; (filming) rodaje m

shooter [ʃúɾəɹ] N (of guns) tirador -ra mf; (of balls, soccer) goleador -ra mf

shooting [ʃúɾɪŋ] N (discharge of a gun) tiro m, disparo m; (exchange of shots) tiroteo m; **— match** concurso de tiro m; **— pain** punzada f; **— star** estrella fugaz f

shop [ʃap] N (store) tienda f; (artisan's place of business, carpentry course) taller m; (business) planta f; **—keeper** tendero -ra mf; **—lifter** mechero -ra mf; **to — lift** mechar; **— window** escaparate m, vitrina f; **to talk —** hablar de negocios; VI ir de compras; **to — for** ir a comprar

shopper [ʃápəɹ] N cliente -ta mf, comprador -ra mf

shopping [ʃápɪŋ] N **to go —** ir de compras; **— center** centro comercial m

shore [ʃɔr] N costa f, ribera f; (of a lake) orilla f; VT **to — up** apuntalar

short [ʃɔrt] ADJ (not long in duration) corto, breve; (not long in length) corto; (not tall) bajo; (scanty) escaso; (curt) brusco; **— circuit** cortocircuito m; **—comings** limitaciones f pl; **—cut** atajo m, cortada f; **—fall** agujero m; **—hand** taquigrafía f; **—handed** escaso de personal; **—legged** pernicorto; **—sighted** miope, corto de vista; — **story** cuento *m*; **—wave** onda corta *f*; **in the — run (haul, term)** a corto plazo; **for** — para abreviar; **in** — en resumen, en suma; **in — order** rápidamente; **to be — on** estar escaso de, estar alcanzado de; **to be — on something** faltarle a uno algo; **to cut** — interrumpir; **I'm running — on sugar** se me está acabando el azúcar; ADV **to stop** — parar de repente, parar en seco; **to come up** — quedarse corto; N (circuit) cortocircuito *m*; **—s short** *m*, pantalón corto *m*; VI/VT (a circuit) cortocircuitar(se); (change) dar de menos; **to —change** dar de menos; **to — out** fundir

shortage [ʃɔ́rdɪʤ] N escasez *f*, penuria *f*

shorten [ʃɔ́rtn̩] VI/VT acortar(se); VT recortar

shortening [ʃɔ́rtn̩ɪŋ] N (lard) manteca *f*; (abbreviation) acortamiento *m*

shortly [ʃɔ́rtli] ADJ (soon) en breve, pronto; (curtly) bruscamente, secamente

shortness [ʃɔ́rtnɪs] N (of length, height) cortedad *f*; (of time) brevedad *f*; (of breath) falta *f*; (of a reply) brusquedad *f*

shot [ʃɑt] N (discharge) tiro *m*, disparo *m*; (photograph) foto *f*; (pellet) perdigón *m*, plomo *m*; (ball in shot-putting) bala *f*; (injection) inyección *f*; (swallow) trago *m*; (throw) tirada *f*; **—gun** escopeta *f*; **— put** lanzamiento de bala *m*; **not by a long** — ni con mucho; **he is a good** — tiene buena puntería; **to take a** — disparar; **to take a — at** intentar

should [ʃʊd] V AUX **I — think so** ya lo creo; **you — arrive before nine** deberías llegar antes de las nueve; **you — eat less** tendrías que comer menos; **you — have seen her** tendrías que haberla visto; **were he to come, I — be pleased** si viniera, me alegraría

shoulder [ʃóʊldɚ] N (of a person, coat) hombro *m*; (cut of meat) paletilla *f*; (of a road) arcén *m*; **— blade** (person) homóplato *m*; (animal) paletilla *f*; **to turn a cold — to** hacerle el vacío a; **the responsibility is on your —s** tú tienes la responsabilidad; VT (a load) cargar al hombro; (an expense) cargar con, asumir; (a door) empujar con el hombro

shout [ʃaʊt] VI/VT gritar; N grito *m*

shove [ʃʌv] VI/VT empujar; **to — aside** echar a un lado; **to — off** (go away) largarse; (push off) desatracar; N empujón *m*, empellón *m*

shovel [ʃʌvəl] N pala *f*; VT echar con la pala

show [ʃo] VT (exhibit) mostrar, manifestar; (prove) demostrar; (indicate) indicar,

marcar; (a film, a TV program) dar; VI (be visible) verse, asomar; (make an appearance) aparecerse; **— him in** hazle entrar; **to — a film** dar una película; **to — mercy** tener piedad; **to — off** hacer alarde, aparentar; **to — up** aparecer; **to — someone up** poner en evidencia; **to — the way** señalar el camino; N (exhibition) exposición *f*; (display) demostración *f*; (ostentation) ostentación *f*, alarde *m*; (performance) espectáculo *m*; (showing) función *f*; (on TV) programa *m*; (movie theater) cine *m*; **— business** farándula *f*; **—case** vitrina *f*; **to —case** presentar; **—down** confrontación *f*; **—-off** fanfarrón -ona *mf*; **to go to the** — ir al cine

shower [ʃáʊɚ] N (rain) aguacero *m*, chubasco *m*; (bath) ducha *f*; (for brides) fiesta para novias *f*; (of sparks, blows) lluvia *f*; VI (bathe) ducharse; (rain) llover; VT (with gifts) inundar; (with praise) colmar

showy [ʃóɪ] ADJ ostentoso; (attractive) vistoso

shred [ʃred] N (of paper) tira *f*; (of evidence) pizca *f*; **to be in —s** estar hecho jirones; **to tear to —s** hacer trizas; VI/VT (documents) triturar; (vegetables) rallar

shrew [ʃru] N (animal) musaraña *f*; (woman) arpía *f*

shrewd [ʃrud] ADJ astuto, sagaz

shriek [ʃrik] VI/VT chillar; N chillido *m*

shrill [ʃrɪl] ADJ chillón

shrimp [ʃrɪmp] N (animal) camarón *m*; (small person) renacuajo *m*; VI pescar camarones

shrine [ʃraɪn] N (chapel) capilla *f*; (altar) altar *m*

shrink [ʃrɪŋk] VI/VT encoger; VI (value) reducirse; **to — from** retroceder; N *fam* loquero -ra *mf*

shrinkage [ʃrɪ́ŋkɪʤ] N (of clothes) encogimiento *m*; (of value) reducción *f*

shrivel [ʃrívəl] VI/VT secar(se), marchitar(se)

shroud [ʃraʊd] N mortaja *f*; VT (to wrap for burial) amortajar; (to hide) cubrir

shrub [ʃrʌb] N arbusto *m*

shrug [ʃrʌg] VI encogerse de hombros; VT encogerse de; **to — off** minimizar, ignorar; N encogimiento de hombros *m*

shudder [ʃʌ́dɚ] VI (from cold) tiritar; (from fear) temblar, estremecerse; N temblor *m*, estremecimiento *m*

shuffle [ʃʌ́fəl] N (mix) mezclar; VI (walk) arrastrar los pies; (dance) bailar arrastrando los pies; VI/VT (cards) barajar; **to — along** ir arrastrando los pies; N (of cards) barajadura *f*; (of feet) arrastrapiés *m sg*

shun [ʃʌn] VT rehuir, evitar

shut [ʃʌt] VI/VT cerrar(se); **to — down** cerrar; **to — off** cortar; **to — out** impedir la entrada de; **to — up** (close) cerrar bien; (lock up) encerrar; (be quiet) callarse; **—down** cese de actividades *m*; **—-eye** sueño *m*; **—-in** enfermo -ma confinado -da a la casa *mf*

shutter [ʃʌɾə] N (of a window) postigo *m*, contraventana *f*; (of a camera) obturador *m*

shuttle [ʃʌɾl] N (in loom) lanzadera *f*; (spaceship) transbordador espacial *m*; (airplane) puente aéreo *m*; (bus, train) servicio regular *m*; VI ir y venir; VT llevar y traer

shy [ʃaɪ] ADJ tímido, retraído; (wary) esquivo; (lacking) escaso; VI asustarse, respingar; **to — away** (start) asustarse, respingar; (avoid) esquivar

shyness [ʃáɪnɪs] N timidez *f*, retraimiento *m*

shyster [ʃáɪstə] N *fam* picapleitos *m sg*

sic [sɪk] VT azuzar

sick [sɪk] ADJ (ill) enfermo; (deranged) enfermizo, morboso; (at heart) angustiado; **— and tired** harto; **to be — of** estar harto de; **to be — to one's stomach** tener náuseas; **to make —** (disgust) dar asco; (anger) dar rabia, enfermar; **— leave** licencia por enfermedad *f*

sicken [síkən] VI/VT (with illness) enfermar(se), poner(se) enfermo; (to disgust) dar asco; (to anger) dar rabia, enfermar

sickening [síkənɪŋ] ADJ repugnante

sickle [síkəl] N hoz *f*; **— cell anemia** anemia falciforme *f*

sickly [síkli] ADJ enfermizo, enclenque

sickness [síknɪs] N enfermedad *f*

side [saɪd] N lado *m*; (of coin, piece of paper) cara *f*; (of a person) costado *m*; (of hill) ladera *f*; (of beef) media res *f*; (of boat) banda *f*; (team) equipo *m*; (garnish) acompañamiento *m*; **— by** — uno al lado del otro; **by his —** a su lado; **by the — of** al lado de; **on all —s** por todos lados; ADJ (on the side) lateral; (secondary) secundario; **—arm** arma de mano *f*; **—board** aparador *m*; **—burns** patillas *f pl*; **—-glance** mirada de soslayo / reojo *f*; **—light** (illumination) luz lateral *f*; (detail) detalle incidental *m*; **—line** (in sports) línea de banda *f*; **to sit on the —lines** no intervenir; **to —step** evitar, esquivar; (in business) negocio suplementario *m*; **to —track** (a train) desviar; (attention) distraer; **—walk** acera *f*; *Mex* banqueta *f*; **—wall** flanco *m*; VI **to — with** ponerse

del lado de

sideways [sáɪdwez] ADV (walk) de costado; (glance) de soslayo

siege [sidʒ] N sitio *m*, asedio *m*, cerco *m*; **to lay — to** sitiar

Sierra Leone [siéɾəlión] N Sierra Leona *f*

sieve [sɪv] N tamiz *m*, cedazo *m*

sift [sɪft] VT cerner, tamizar; **to — through** revisar

sigh [saɪ] VI suspirar; N suspiro *m*

sight [saɪt] N (sense) vista *f*; (attraction) punto de interés *m*; (ridiculous thing or person) adefesio *m*, mamarracho *m*; (on a gun) mira *f*; **—seeing** turismo *m*; **in —** a la vista; **on —** en el acto; **he is out of —** ya no se ve; **at first —** a primera vista; **to catch — of** divisar; **to lose — of** perder de vista; **you're a — for sore eyes** dichosos los ojos que te ven; VT (a ship) avistar, divisar; (a gun) apuntar

sign [saɪn] N (gesture) seña *f*, señal *f*; (indication) muestra *f*, señal *f*, indicio *m*; (placard) letrero *m*; (omen) agüero *m*, presagio *m*; (astrological, mathematical) signo *m*; (on road) cartel *m*, letrero *m*; VI/VT (write name) firmar; (signal) hacer señas (de); VT (hire) contratar; (use sign language) hablar por señas; **— language** lenguaje de signos *m*; **to — over property** ceder una propiedad; **to — up** (in a club) anotarse; (in the army) alistarse

signal [sígnəl] N señal *f*; VI/VT señalar, hacer señas (a); ADJ notable

signature [sígnətʃə] N firma *f*

signer [sáɪnə] N firmante *mf*, signatario -ria *mf*

significance [sɪgnífɪkəns] N significación *f*

significant [sɪgnífɪkənt] ADJ significativo; **my — other** mi media naranja *f*

signify [sígnəfaɪ] VT significar

silence [sáɪləns] N silencio *m*; VT (child, fears) acallar; (criticism) silenciar, enmudecer

silencer [sáɪlənsə] N silenciador *m*

silent [sáɪlənt] ADJ (machine) silencioso; (person) callado, silencioso; **— agreement** acuerdo tácito *m*; **— film** película muda *f*

silhouette [sɪluét] N silueta *f*; VT **to be —d against** perfilarse contra

silicon [sílɪkən] N silicio *m*

silk [sɪlk] N seda *f*; **— industry** industria sedera *f*; **—worm** gusano de seda *m*

silken [sílkən] ADJ (of silk) de seda; (like silk) sedoso

silky [sílki] ADJ sedoso

sill [sɪl] N alféizar *m*, antepecho *m*

silly [síli] ADJ necio, bobo, lelo

silo [sáɪlo] N silo *m*

silt [sɪlt] N cieno *m*, limo *m*

silver [sɪ́lvɚ] N (metal, color) plata *f*;
(tableware) cubiertos de plata *m pl*; ADJ (of
silver) de plata; (silver-colored) plateado;
— anniversary las bodas de plata *f pl*;
—-plated bañado en plata; **—-plating**
plateado *m*; **—smith** platero -ra *mf*;
—ware cubiertos de plata *m pl*; VT
platear; (a mirror) azogar

similar [sɪ́mǝlǝ] ADJ semejante, similar

similarity [sɪmǝlǽrɪDi] N semejanza *f*,
parecido *m*

simile [sɪ́mǝli] N símil *m*

simmer [sɪ́mǝ] VI/VT hervir a fuego lento; **to
— down** calmarse

simple [sɪ́mpǝl] ADJ (uncomplicated) simple,
sencillo; (naive) simple; **—minded**
simple, simplón

simpleton [sɪ́mpǝltǝn] N simplón -ona *mf*,
mentecato -ta *mf*

simplicity [sɪmplɪ́sɪDi] N (lack of
complication) sencillez *f*, simplicidad *f*;
(naiveté) simpleza *f*

simplify [sɪ́mplǝfaɪ] VI/VT simplificar

simplistic [sɪmplɪ́stɪk] ADJ simplista

simulate [sɪ́mjǝlet] VI/VT simular

simultaneous [saɪmǝltténiǝs] ADJ simultáneo

sin [sɪn] N pecado *m*; VI pecar

since [sɪns] CONJ (continuously) desde que;
(inasmuch as) puesto que, ya que; PREP
(continuously) desde; (from a past time) a
partir de; ADV desde entonces; **ever —**
desde entonces; **he died long —** murió
hace mucho tiempo; **she has — agreed**
después de eso consintió; **we have been
here — five** estamos aquí desde las cinco

sincere [sɪnsɪ́r] ADJ sincero

sincerity [sɪnsɛ́rɪDi] N sinceridad *f*

sinew [sɪ́nju] N tendón *m*

sinewy [sɪ́njuwi] ADJ (full of tendons)
nervudo; (vigorous) membrudo; (chewy)
estropajoso

sinful [sɪ́nfǝl] ADJ (act) pecaminoso; (person)
pecador

sing [sɪŋ] VI/VT cantar; **—song** sonsonete *m*

Singapore [sɪ́ŋǝpɔr] N Singapur *m*

Singaporean [sɪŋǝpɔ́riǝn] ADJ & N
singapurense *mf*

singe [sɪnʤ] VT chamuscar, socarrar; N
chamusquina *f*, socarrina *f*

singer [sɪ́ŋǝ] N cantante *mf*

single [sɪ́ŋgǝl] ADJ (only one) solo, único;
(for one person) individual; (unmarried)
soltero; **— bed** cama de una plaza *f*; **—
entry bookkeeping** teneduría por
partida simple *f*; **— file** fila india *f*;

—-handed solo, sin ayuda; **—-minded**
resuelto; **—-spacing** sencillo *m*; **every —
one** cada uno; **not a — word** ni una
sola palabra; N (bill) billete de uno *m*;
(unmarried person) soltero -ra *mf*; (record)
disco sencillo *m*; (in tennis) **—s** single *m*;
VT **to — out** elegir

singular [sɪ́ŋgjǝlǝ] ADJ & N singular *m*

sinister [sɪ́nɪstǝ] ADJ siniestro

sink [sɪŋk] VI/VT hundir(se); VT (invest)
invertir; (dig) cavar; (put in ground)
enterrar; **it finally sank in** finalmente
nos dimos cuenta de eso; **to — one's
teeth into** clavar los dientes en; **to — to
one's knees** caer de rodillas; **sunk in
thought** absorto; **my heart sank** se me
fue el alma al piso; **the sun was —ing** se
iba poniendo el sol; N (in the kitchen)
fregadero *m*; (in bathroom) lavabo *m*;
(pond for sewage) pozo negro *m*; **—hole**
socavón *m*, sumidero *m*

sinner [sɪ́nǝ] N pecador -ora *mf*

sinuous [sɪ́njuǝs] ADJ sinuoso

sinus [sáɪnǝs] N seno *m*

sip [sɪp] VI/VT sorber; N sorbo *m*

siphon [sáɪfǝn] N sifón *m*; VI/VT (liquid) sacar
con sifón; (money) desviar

sir [sɚ] N señor *m*

siren [sáɪrǝn] N sirena *f*

sirloin [sɚ́lɔɪn] N solomillo *m*

sissy [sɪ́si] ADJ & N afeminado *m*

sister [sɪ́stǝ] N hermana *f*; **—-in-law** cuñada
f; **— Mary** Sor María *f*

sit [sɪt] VI sentar(se); (pose) posar; (be seated)
estar sentado; (be located) estar situado;
to — down sentarse; **to — in on a class**
ir de oyente a una clase; **to — on**
posponer; **to — out a dance** saltearse
una pieza; **to — still** estarse quieto; **to
— up** incorporarse; **to — up all night**
quedarse en vela; **to — well** caer bien;
—-in sentada *f*; **—-up** abdominal *m*

sitcom [sɪ́tkɑm] N comedia de situación *f*

site [saɪt] N (for construction) terreno *m*, solar
m; (on the Internet) sitio *m*

sitter [sɪ́Dǝ] N niñera *f*

sitting [sɪ́Dɪŋ] N sesión *f*; **in one —** de una
sentada, de un tirón; ADJ **— duck** blanco
fácil *m*; **— room** cuarto de estar *m*

situated [sɪtʃuéDɪd] ADJ situado, ubicado

situation [sɪtʃuéʃǝn] N situación *f*

six [sɪks] NUM seis; **—-pack** paquete de seis
m; **—-shooter** revólver de seis tiros *m*

sixteen [sɪkstín] NUM dieciséis

sixth [sɪksθ] ADV & N sexto *m*

sixty [sɪ́ksti] NUM sesenta

size [saɪz] N tamaño *m*; (clothing) talla *f*; VT clasificar según el tamaño; **to — up** juzgar

sizeable, sizable [sáɪzəbəl] ADJ de tamaño considerable

sizzle [sízəl] VI chisporrotear; N chisporroteo *m*

skate [sket] N patín *m*; VI/VT patinar; **—board** monopatín *m*

skein [sken] N madeja *f*

skeleton [skélɪtən] N esqueleto *m*, osamenta *f*; (of a building) armazón *m*; **— key** llave maestra *f*

skeptic, sceptic [sképtɪk] N escéptico -ca *mf*

skeptical [sképtɪkəl] ADJ escéptico

skepticism [sképtɪsɪzəm] N escepticismo *m*

sketch [sketʃ] N (of a drawing) boceto *m*, croquis *m*; (outline) esbozo *m*, bosquejo *m*; (skit) sketch *m*; VI/VT (outline) bosquejar; (draw) dibujar

skew [skju] VT (cloth) sesgar; (data) tergiversar

skewer [skjúə] N brocheta *f*

ski [ski] N esquí *m*; VI/VT esquiar (en); **— jump** (sport) salto con esquís *m*; (course) pista de saltos *f*; **— lift** telesquí *m*

skid [skɪd] N patinazo *m*; VI patinar

skill [skɪl] N destreza *f*, habilidad *f*, maña *f*

skilled [skɪld] ADJ diestro, habilidoso; **— worker** obrero -ra calificado -da *mf*

skillet [skílɪt] N sartén *f*

skillful, skilful [skílfəl] ADJ diestro, habilidoso

skim [skɪm] VT (milk) desnatar; (a broth) espumar; (move near surface) rozar; VI/VT (read) leer por encima, repasar; **to — over** rozar; **— milk** *Sp* leche desnatada *f*; *Am* leche descremada *f*

skimp [skɪmp] VI escatimar; **to — on** escatimar

skimpy [skímpi] ADJ (funds) escaso; (dress) corto; (bikini) pequeño

skin [skɪn] N piel *f* (also of animal, sausage, potato); (of the face) cutis *m*, tez *f*; (for carrying wine) pellejo *m*; (of boiled milk) nata *f*; (of grapes) hollejo *m*; **—deep** superficial; **—diving** natación submarina *f*; **— flint** roña *mf*; **—head** cabeza rapada *mf*; **to save one's —** salvar el pellejo; **to be saved by the — of one's teeth** salvarse por un pelo; VT (animal) despellejar, desollar; (fruit) pelar; (a person) quitarle a uno el dinero

skinny [skíni] ADJ flaco; **to —-dip** nadar desnudo

skip [skɪp] VI (jump) brincar, ir dando saltos en un pie; (omit) saltarse; (bounce) rebotar; VT (a page) saltar(se); (class) faltar

a; (a stone) hacer rebotar; **to — out** escaparse; N salto *m*, brinco *m*

skipper [skípə] N (captain) patrón -ona *mf*, capitán -ana *mf*; (jumper) saltador -ora *mf*

skirmish [skɜ́mɪʃ] N escaramuza *f*; VI escaramuzar

skirt [skɜt] N falda *f*; VT bordear; **to — an issue** evitar un tema

skit [skɪt] N sketch *m*

skull [skʌl] N cráneo *m*, calavera *f*; **— and crossbones** calavera *f*

skunk [skʌŋk] N mofeta *f*; *Am* zorrillo *m*

sky [skaɪ] N cielo *m*; **— blue** azul celeste *m*; **—diving** paracaidismo *m*; **—-high** muy alto; **—lark** alondra *f*; **—light** claraboya *f*; **—line** horizonte *m*; **—scraper** rascacielos *m sg*; **to —rocket** subir vertiginosamente

slab [slæb] N (of wood) trozo *m*; (of stone) losa *f*, laja *f*; (of meat) tajada *f*

slack [slæk] ADJ (not taut) flojo; (careless) descuidado; (sluggish) lento; **— season** temporada baja *f*; **to take up the —** llenar el vacío; **—s** pantalones *m pl*; VI holgazanear; **to — off** aflojar

slag [slæg] N escoria *f*

slalom [slálɑm] N slalom *m*

slam [slæm] VI/VT cerrar(se) de un golpe; VI (hit) chocar; VT (throw down) hacer golpear; (criticize) criticar; **to — on the brakes** dar un frenazo; **to — the door** dar un portazo; N (blow) golpazo *m*; (criticism) crítica *f*; (of a door) portazo *m*

slander [slændə] N calumnia *f*, difamación *f*; VT calumniar, difamar

slanderous [slændərəs] ADJ calumnioso, difamatorio

slang [slæŋ] N (jargon) jerga *f*; (argot) argot *m*

slant [slænt] N (orientation, bias) sesgo *m*; (of a roof) inclinación *f*; VI/VT (bias) sesgar; (slope) inclinar(se), ladear(se)

slap [slæp] N (to the body) palmada *f*; (to the face) bofetada *f*, torta *f*, cachetada *f*; (with a glove) guantada *f*; **—happy** aturdido; **—stick** de golpe y porrazo; **a — in the face** un desaire; **a — on the wrist** un tirón de orejas; **a — on the back** una palmadita en la espalda; VT abofetear; **to — down** reprimir

slash [slæʃ] VI/VT (cut) acuchillar; *Am* tajear; VT (whip) azotar; (reduce) reducir, rebajar; N (sweeping stroke, wound) cuchillada *f*, tajo *m*; (typographical sign) barra *f*

slat [slæt] N tablilla *f*

slate [slet] N (rock, roofing) pizarra *f*; (color) color pizarra *m*; (list of candidates) lista de candidatos *f*; VT empizarrar; **this**

building is —d for destruction se ha
programado la demolición de este edificio

slaughter [slɔ́Dɚ] N matanza f; **—house**
matadero m; VT (animals) matar; (people,
opponents) masacrar

slave [slev] N esclavo -va mf; **— driver**
capataz de esclavos m; **— labor** (workers)
mano de obra esclava f; (work) trabajo de
esclavos m; VI trabajar como esclavo -va

slavery [slévəri] N esclavitud f

Slavic [slávɪk] ADJ eslavo

sleazy [slízi] ADJ (squalid) sórdido;
(contemptible) despreciable

sled [slɛd] N trineo m

sledgehammer [slɛ́ɡhæmɚ] N almádena f

sleek [slik] ADJ (hair) lustroso; (sports car)
elegante

sleep [slip] VI/VT dormir; **it —s three** tiene
espacio para que duerman tres personas;
to — around ser promiscuo; **to — in**
dormir hasta tarde; **to — it off** dormir la
mona; **to — something off** dormir para
que desaparezca algo; **to — over** dormir
en casa ajena; **to — together** acostarse
juntos; **to — with** acostarse con; **to —
on it** consultarlo con la almohada; N
sueño m; **—walker** sonámbulo -la mf; **to
go to —** dormirse; **to put to —** (put to
bed) dormir a; (euthanize) sacrificar

sleeper [slípɚ] N (one who sleeps) persona
que duerme f; (beam) durmiente m; (on a
train) coche cama m; (unexpected success)
éxito inesperado m; (sofa bed) sofá-cama
m

sleepily [slípɪli] ADV con somnolencia

sleepiness [slípɪnɪs] N sueño m, somnolencia
f

sleeping [slípɪŋ] N sueño m; ADJ dormido; **—
bag** saco de dormir m; **— pill** píldora
para dormir f, somnífero m; **— sickness**
enfermedad del sueño f

sleepless [slíplɪs] ADJ (person) desvelado;
(night) en blanco

sleepy [slípi] ADJ somnoliento, adormilado;
to be — tener sueño

sleet [slit] N cellisca f; VI caer cellisca

sleeve [sliv] N manga f; **to have something
up one's —s** tener algo en la manga

sleigh [sle] N trineo m; **— bell** cascabel m; VI
pasear en trineo

sleight [slaɪt] N **— of hand** prestidigitación f

slender [slɛ́ndɚ] ADJ delgado, esbelto

sleuth [sluθ] N sabueso m

slice [slaɪs] N (of bread, cheese) rebanada f;
(of fruit) tajada f, raja f; (of meat) lonja f;
VT cortar, rebanar, tajar

slick [slɪk] ADJ (unctuous) untuoso; (sly)

astuto; (slippery) resbaladizo

slicker [slíkɚ] N impermeable m

slide [slaɪd] VI/VT deslizar(se); **to — in**
cerrar(se) deslizando; **to — out** abrirse
deslizando; **to let something —** dejar
pasar algo; N deslizamiento m;
(playground equipment) tobogán m; (of a
trombone) vara corredora f;
(photographic) diapositiva f; (for
microscopes) portaobjeto m

slight [slaɪt] N desaire m; VT (snub) desairar;
(neglect) descuidar; ADJ (slim) delgado;
(delicate) delicado, tenue; (small in
degree) leve, ligero

slim [slɪm] ADJ delgado, esbelto; **a — chance**
una posibilidad remota

slime [slaɪm] N (in rivers) limo m, fango m;
(of snails) baba f; (despicable person)
asqueroso -sa mf

slimy [slármi] ADJ (muddy) fangoso;
(slobbery) baboso, gomoso; (despicable)
asqueroso

sling [slɪŋ] N honda f; (for arm) cabestrillo m;
—shot (toy) tirachinas m sg, tirador m;
(weapon) honda f; VT lanzar; **to — a rifle
over one's shoulder** ponerse el rifle en
bandolera

slink [slɪŋk] VI (move furtively) andar
furtivamente; (move provocatively)
caminar provocativamente; **to — away**
escurrirse

slip [slɪp] VI (slide) deslizarse; (slide
accidentally) resbalar(se); (fail to engage)
patinar; (deteriorate) empeorar; VT (make
slip) hacer resbalar; (put) meter; **to —
away** escaparse, escabullirse; **to — by**
correr; **to — in** meter(se); **to — one's
dress on** ponerse el vestido; **to — out**
(leave) salir inadvertido; (say
inadvertently) escapársele a uno algo; **to
— up** meter la pata; **to let an
opportunity — by** dejar pasar una
oportunidad; **it —ped my mind** se me
olvidó; **it —ped off** se zafó; N (act of
slipping) resbalón m, traspié m; (mistake)
equivocación f; (pillow cover) funda f;
(underskirt) viso m; (piece of paper)
papeleta f, tira de papel f; (space for boats)
embarcadero m; **— of the tongue** lapsus
(linguae) m; **—knot** nudo corredizo m;
Freudian — acto fallido m

slipper [slípɚ] N zapatilla f, pantufla f

slippery [slípəri] ADJ resbaloso, resbaladizo;
(evasive) evasivo, escurridizo'

slipshod [slípʃad] ADJ chapucero

slit [slɪt] VT cortar a lo largo; **to —
someone's throat** degollar a alguien; **to**

— into strips cortar en tiras; N raja f

slither [slíðə·] VI serpentear, culebrear; N serpenteo m, culebreo m

sliver [slívə·] N astilla f; VI/VT astillar(se)

slob [slɑb] N (unkempt) dejado -da mf; (uncouth) bruto -ta mf

slobber [slábə·] N baba f; VI/VT babosear, babear(se)

slogan [slógən] N eslogan m, lema m

slop [slɑp] VT (splash) salpicar; (feed) dar de comer; N (pigswill) bazofia f; (mud) fango m

slope [slop] VI/VT inclinar(se); N vertiente f, declive m, cuesta f; (in math) pendiente f

sloppiness [slápɪnɪs] N chapucería f

sloppy [slápi] ADJ (ground) fangoso; (splashed) salpicado; (slovenly) cochino; (poorly done) chapucero

slot [slɑt] N (for coins, letters) ranura f; (place in a series) casilla f; (job) puesto m; — **machine** tragamonedas mf sg, tragaperras mf sg; VT hacer una ranura

sloth [sloθ] N (vice) pereza f; (animal) perezoso m

slouch [slaʊtʃ] N (posture) encorvamiento m; (inept person) torpe mf; (lazy person) holgazán -ana mf; VI/VT (crouch) andar agachado, encorvar(se); (shuffle) andar caído de hombros

Slovakia [slovákiə] N Eslovaquia f

Slovakian [slovákiən] ADJ & N eslovaco -ca mf

Slovene [slóvin] ADJ & N esloveno -na mf

Slovenia [slovínia] N Eslovenia f

slovenliness [slávənlɪnɪs] N (of a person) desaseo m, desaliño m; (of work) descuido m

slovenly [slávənli] ADJ (unclean) desaseado; (unkempt) desaliñado

slow [slo] ADJ (not fast) lento, tardo; (running behind) atrasado; (sluggish) lerdo, torpe, pesado; ADV lentamente, despacio; VI/VT **to — down / up** andar más despacio, frenar; **—down** (in business) disminución de actividades f; (in labor disputes) huelga de celo f; **in — motion** en cámara lenta

slowness [slónɪs] N (of speed) lentitud f; (of intelligence) torpeza f

slug [slʌg] N (bullet) bala f; (coin) moneda falsa f; (animal) babosa f; (swallow) trago m; (blow with fist) puñetazo m; VT aporrear; **to — it out** agarrarse a puñetazos

sluggard [slágə·d] N holgazán -ana mf

sluggish [slágɪʃ] ADJ (slow) lento; (torpid) aletargado, torpe

sluggishness [slágɪʃnɪs] N torpeza f

sluice [slus] N (channel with a gate) esclusa f; (channel) canal m; **— gate** compuerta f

slum [slʌm] N barrio bajo m; **—s** tugurios m pl; **—lord** propietario de tugurio m; VI visitar los barrios bajos; **to — it** divertirse en lugares de poca categoría

slumber [slámbə·] VI dormitar; N sueño ligero m; **— party** fiesta de niñas que se quedan a dormir f

slump [slʌmp] VI (a person) desplomarse; (prices, markets) bajar repentinamente; (in prices) baja repentina f; (in the economy) ralentización f; (in sports) mala racha f

slur [slɚ] VT (pronounce indistinctly) pronunciar mal; (connect notes) ligar; N (connection of notes) ligado m; (insult) insulto m

slush [slʌʃ] N (melted snow) nieve a medio derretir f; (sludge) nieve fangosa f; (mud) fango m; (refuse) desperdicios m pl; **— fund** (illicit fund) cuenta para fines ilícitos f; (petty cash) caja chica f

sly [slaɪ] ADJ astuto, taimado; **on the —** a escondidas

smack [smæk] N (taste) dejo m; Sp deje m; (kiss) beso ruidoso m; (loud eating) chasquido m; (slap) palmada f, sopapo m; (heroin) fam caballo m; VT (kiss) dar un beso ruidoso; (eat loudly) chascar, chasquear; (slap) dar una palmada; **to — of** tener un dejo de

small [smɔl] ADJ (not large) pequeño, chico; (of build) menudo; (narrow) estrecho; (lower case) minúsculo; (petty) mezquino; N (size) pequeño suelto m; **— change** cambio suelto m; **— fry** gente menuda f; **— intestine** intestino delgado m; **— of the back** baja espalda f; **—pox** viruela f; **— talk** cháchara f; **to feel —** avergonzarse

smallness [smɔlnɪs] N pequeñez f

smart [smɑrt] ADJ (intelligent) listo, inteligente; (astute) astuto; (stylish) elegante; **— alec, aleck** sabihondo -da mf; **— bomb** bomba inteligente f; **— money** inversión inteligente f; **— remark** insolencia f; N escozor m; VI picar; **I'm —ing from his rude remarks** todavía me duelen sus groserías

smash [smæʃ] VT estrellar, destrozar; (a rebellion) aplastar; **to — into** estrellarse contra; N (sound) estrépito m; (blow) choque violento m; **a — hit** un exitazo

smear [smir] VT (daub) untar; (spot, vilify) manchar; (blur) correrse; (defeat) reventar; **to — with paint** pintorrear, pintarrajear; N (stain) mancha f; (culture) frotis m; **—**

campaign campaña de difamación *f*
smell [smɛɫ] VI/VT oler; **to — of** oler a; **that —s** huele mal, apesta; **to — up** apestar; N (odor) olor *m*; (sense) olfato *m*; **— of** olor a
smelly [sméli] ADJ hediondo, apestoso
smile [smaɪɫ] VI sonreír(se); **to — approval** sonreír en aprobación; N sonrisa *f*
smiling [smáɪlɪŋ] ADJ risueño, sonriente
smirk [smɝk] N sonrisa suficiente *f*; VI sonreír con suficiencia
smith [smɪθ] N herrero -ra *mf*
smog [smɑg] N smog *m*
smoke [smok] N humo *m*; (cigarette) cigarro *m*, cigarrillo *m*; **— detector** detector de humo *m*, detector de incendios *m*; **— screen** cortina de humo *f*; **— stack** chimenea *f*; **to have a —** fumar; VI (put off smoke) echar humo; (go fast) volar; VT (tobacco) fumar; (ham, fish, glass) ahumar; **to — out** (drive out) ahuyentar con humo; (expose) poner al descubierto
smoker [smókɚ] N fumador -ora *mf*; (train car) vagón de fumar *m*
smoking [smókɪŋ] ADJ humeante; **— car** vagón de fumar *m*; **— gun** prueba irrefutable *f*; **— room** cuarto de fumar *m*; N (use of tobacco) tabaquismo *m*
smoky [smóki] ADJ humoso
smolder, smoulder [smóldɚ] VI arder
smooth [smuð] ADJ (surface) liso; (skin) suave, terso; (tire) gastado; (sea) sereno, tranquilo; (polished) agradable, fino; (ingratiating) zalamero; VT (make surface even) alisar; (make easy) allanar; **to — away** hacer desaparecer; **to — one's hair** atusarse el cabello; **to — over** limar asperezas
smoothness [smúðnɪs] N (evenness) lisura *f*; (of skin) tersura *f*, suavidad *f*; (of sea) tranquilidad *f*; (polish) fineza *f*; (suaveness) zalamería *f*
smother [smʌ́ðɚ] VT (stifle) ahogar(se), sofocar(se), asfixiar(se); (envelop) cubrir; (overprotect) sobreproteger
smudge [smʌʤ] N borrón *m*, mancha *f*; VI/VT borronear(se), manchar(se)
smug [smʌg] ADJ suficiente, petulante
smuggle [smʌ́gəɫ] VI/VT contrabandear, hacer contrabando; **to — in** entrar de contrabando; **to — out** sacar de contrabando
smuggler [smʌ́glɚ] N contrabandista *mf*
smut [smʌt] N (soot) hollín *m*; (obscenity) obscenidad *f*
snack [snæk] N tentempié *m*, bocadillo *m*; **— bar** cafetería *f*

snafu [snæfú] N relajo *m*
snag [snæg] N (a branch) gancho *m*; (in fabric) enganchón *m*; (any obstacle) pega *f*, obstáculo *m*, contrariedad *f*; **to hit a —** tropezar con un obstáculo; VI/VT enganchar(se); VT agarrar
snail [sneɫ] N caracol *m*; **— mail** correo regular *m*; **—'s pace** paso de tortuga *m*
snake [snek] N serpiente *f*; **—bite** mordedura de serpiente *f*; **— in the grass** víbora *f*; **—skin** piel de serpiente *f*; VI serpentear
snap [snæp] VI (make sound) chasquear, dar un chasquido; (lose control) estallar, perder los estribos; VT (a photograph) sacar; VI/VT (break) quebrar(se); **to — at** (try to bite) tirar un mordiscón; (speak harshly) ladrar; **to — one's fingers** chasquear los dedos, castañetear con los dedos; **to — out of** recuperarse de; **to — shut** cerrar(se) de golpe; **to — together** abrochar; **to — up** llevarse; N (sound) chasquido *m*; (fastener) broche *m*; (bite) tarascada *f*; **it's a —** es pan comido; **— judgment** decisión atolondrada *f*; **—dragon** dragón *m*; **—shot** instantánea, foto *f*
snappy [snǽpi] ADJ (that bites) mordedor; (elegant) elegante; **make it —!** ¡en seguida!
snare [snɛr] N (trap) trampa *f*; **— drum** tambor con bordón *m*; VT atrapar
snarl [snɑrɫ] VI/VT (growl) regañar; (tangle) enmarañar(se), enredar(se); N (growl) gruñido *m*; (tangle) maraña *f*, enredo *m*
snatch [snætʃ] VT (seize) arrebatar; (kidnap) secuestrar; VI **to — at** dar manotazos; N (act of snatching) arrebato *m*; (fragment) fragmento *m*
snazzy [snǽzi] ADJ llamativo
sneak [snik] VI andar furtivamente; VT (put away) meter a escondidas; **to — in** entrar a escondidas; **to — something in** meter a escondidas; **to — out** salir a hurtadillas; **to — something out** sacar a escondidas; **to — a cigarette** fumar a escondidas; N persona solapada *f*
sneakers [sníkɚz] N zapatillas (deportivas) *f pl*, tenis *m pl*
sneer [snir] VI (smile) sonreír con sorna; **to — at** mofarse de; N expresión de sorna *f*
sneeze [sniz] VI estornudar; **that's nothing to — at** no es nada desdeñable; N estornudo *m*
snicker [sníkɚ] VI reírse burlonamente; N risita burlona *f*
snide [snaɪd] ADJ malévolo
sniff [snɪf] VI/VT husmear, olfatear; **to — at**

husmear; (ridicule) menospreciar; N (act of sniffing) husmeo *m*, olfateo *m*; (smell) bocanada *f*

sniffle [snífəł] VI (with a cold) sorberse los mocos; (when crying) gimotear; N (when crying) gimoteo *m*; **the —s** un resfrío

snip [snɪp] VT tijeretear; **to — off** cortar de un tijeretazo; N (act of snipping) tijeretada *f*, tijeretazo *m*; (piece cut off) pedacito *m*, recorte *m*; **— of conversation** retazo de conversación *m*

sniper [snáɪpə-] N francotirador -ora *mf*

snitch [snɪtʃ] VI (tell on) chivar, chivatar; VT (rob) ratear; N soplón -ona *mf*, chivato -ta *mf*

snob [snɑb] N esnob *mf*

snoop [snup] VI fisgar, fisgonear; N fisgón -ona *mf*

snooze [snuz] VI dormitar; N siesta *f*; **to take a —** echar un sueñecito / sueñito

snore [snɔr] VI roncar; N ronquido *m*

snorkel [snɔ́rkəł] N esnórquel *m*

snort [snɔrt] VI resoplar, bufar; VI/VT (drugs) esnifar; N resoplido *m*, bufido *m*; (drink) trago *m*

snout [snaut] N hocico *m*, jeta *f*, morro *m*; (nose) napias *f pl*

snow [sno] N nieve *f* (also cocaine, heroin); **—ball** bola de nieve *f*; **to —ball** aumentar rápidamente; **—board** monopatín de nieve *m*; **—drift** ventisquero *m*; **—fall** nevada *f*; **—flake** copo de nieve *m*; **—man** muñeco de nieve *m*; **—mobile** motonieve *f*; **—plow** quitanieves *m sg*; **—shoe** raqueta *f*; **—storm** ventisca *f*; VI nevar; **the airport was —ed in** cerraron el aeropuerto por nieve; **to — under** (cover in snow) cubrir de nieve; (overwhelm) abrumar

snowy [snói] ADJ nevado; (white) níveo

snub [snʌb] VT volverle la cara a, desairar; (reject) despreciar; N desprecio *m*, desaire *m*; **—-nosed** chato; *Am* ñato

snuff [snʌf] VI **to — out** apagar, extinguir; N rapé *m*; **to be up to —** dar la talla

snug [snʌg] ADJ (tight-fitting) ajustado; (comfortable) cómodo

so [so] ADV (in this way) así; (to this degree) tan; (so much) tanto; **— am I** yo también; **—-and-—** fulano (de tal); **—-called** llamado; **— as to** para; **— far as I know** que yo sepa; **— many** tantos; **— much** tanto; **—-—** regular; **— much the better** tanto mejor; **— that** de modo que; **I was — a beauty queen!** ¡sí que fui reina de belleza! **— long!** ¡hasta luego! **and — forth** etcetera, y así

sucesivamente; **I believe —** creo que sí; **is that —?** ¿en serio? ¡no me digas! **ten minutes or —** unos diez minutos; INTERJ ajajá; CONJ (in order that) de modo que; (consequently) así que, entonces

soak [sok] VI/VT (immerse) remojar(se); (drench) empapar(se); **it finally —ed in on him that** por fin se dio cuenta de que; **to — through** colarse por; **to — up** absorber, embeber; **to be —ed through** estar empapado, estar calado hasta los huesos; N remojón *m*

soap [sop] N jabón *m*; (soap opera) telenovela *f*; **— bubble** pompa de jabón *f*; **— dish** jabonera *f*; VT enjabonar

soapy [sópi] ADJ jabonoso

soar [sɔr] VI/VT (airplane) elevar(se); (kite) remontar(se); (hopes) aumentar(se); (prices) disparar(se); (glider) planear(se); VI (bird) volar

sob [sab] VI sollozar, hipar; N sollozo *m*, hipo *m*

sober [sóbə-] ADJ (not drunk) sobrio; (temperate) moderado; (serious, subdued) serio, sobrio; VI **to — up** (get over drunkenness) despejarse; (become more serious) sentar cabeza

sobriety [səbráɪɪɖi] N (not being drunk) sobriedad *f*; (moderation) moderación *f*; (seriousness) seriedad *f*

soccer [sákə-] N fútbol *m*, balompié *m*

sociable [sóʃəbəł] ADJ sociable

social [sóʃəł] ADJ (of society) social; (friendly) sociable; N reunión social *f*; **— climber** arribista *mf*; **— science** ciencias sociales *f pl*; **— security** seguridad social *f*; **— welfare** asistencia social *f*; **— work** asistencia social *f*

socialism [sóʃəlɪzəm] N socialismo *m*

socialist [sóʃəlɪst] ADJ & N socialista *mf*

socialize [sóʃəlaɪz] VT socializar; VI salir, tener trato social

society [səsáɪɪɖi] N sociedad *f*; (companionship) compañía *f*

socioeconomic [sosioekənámɪk] ADJ socioeconómico

sociology [sosiáləɖi] N sociología *f*

sociopath [sósiəpæθ] N sociópata *mf*

sock [sak] N (garment) calcetín *m*; (blow) puñetazo *m*, zumbido *m*; VT pegar, zumbar; **to — away** ahorrar

socket [sákɪt] N (of eye) cuenca *f*; (electrical outlet) enchufe *m*; (for bulb) portalámparas *m sg*, casquillo *m*

sod [sad] N (lawn) césped *m*; (piece) tepe *m*; VT cubrir de césped

soda [sóɖə] N (drink) gaseosa *f*; (sodium

hydroxide) soda *f*, sosa *f*; — **fountain** bar
de bebidas sin alcohol *m*; — **pop** gaseosa
f; — **water** agua con gas *f*
sodium [sódɪəm] N sodio *m*
sodomy [sádəmi] N sodomía *f*
sofa [sófə] N sofá *m*; — **bed** sofá-cama *m*
soft [sɔft] ADJ (butter, bed, water, penalty)
blando; (life) fácil, cómodo; (hair, skin)
suave; (light) tenue; —**ball** softball *m*;
—-**boiled eggs** huevos pasados por agua
m pl; — **coal** carbón bituminoso *m*; —
drink gaseosa *f*; — **palate** velo del
paladar *m*; —**ware** software *m*
soften [sɔfən] VI/VT (butter) ablandar(se);
(skin) suavizar(se); VT (a blow) amortiguar;
(voice) bajar
softness [sɔftnɪs] N (of butter) blandura *f*; (of
hair, skin) suavidad *f*; (of light) tenuidad *f*
soggy [sági] ADJ (clothes) empapado; (day)
húmedo
soil [sɔɪl] N suelo *m*, tierra *f*; VI/VT
ensuciar(se), manchar(se)
solace [sálɪs] N consuelo *m*; VT consolar
solar [sólɚ] ADJ solar; — **eclipse** eclipse de
sol *m*; — **energy** energía solar *f*; —
plexus plexo solar *m*; — **system** sistema
solar *m*
solder [sádɚ] VI/VT soldar(se); N soldadura *f*
soldering iron [sádɚ-ɪŋaɪrn] N soldador *m*
soldier [sóldʒɚ] N (of low rank) soldado *m*;
(of any rank) militar *m*
sole [sol] ADJ solo, único; N (of a foot) planta
f; (of a shoe) suela *f*; (fish) lenguado *m*
solemn [sáləm] ADJ solemne
solemnity [salémnɪɪ] N solemnidad *f*
solenoid [sólənɔɪd] N solenoide *m*
solicit [səlísɪt] VT (aid) pedir; (a prostitute)
ofrecerse; VI (sell) vender, ofrecer
productos
solicitor [səlísɪtɚ] N abogado *m*; — **General**
Subsecretario -ria de Justicia *mf*
solicitous [səlísɪtəs] ADJ solícito
solid [sálɪd] ADJ (firm) sólido; (dense) denso;
— **blue** azul liso *m*; — **geometry**
geometría del espacio *f*; — **gold** oro puro
m; — **line** línea continua *f*; —-**state** de
estado sólido; **for one — hour** por una
hora entera; N sólido *m*
solidarity [sálɪdérɪɪ] N solidaridad *f*
solidify [səlídəfaɪ] VI/VT solidificar(se)
solidity [səlídɪɪ] N solidez *f*
solitary [sálɪteri] ADJ solitario; **to be in —
confinement** estar incomunicado
solitude [sálɪtud] N soledad *f*
solo [sólo] N solo *m*
soloist [sóloɪst] N solista *mf*
Solomon Islander [sáləmənáɪlɚndɚ] N

salomonense *mf*
Solomon Islands [sáləmənáɪləndz] N Islas
Salomón *f pl*
solstice [sólstɪs] N solsticio *m*
soluble [sáljəbəl] ADJ soluble
solution [səlúʃən] N solución *f*
solve [salv] VT resolver, solucionar
solvent [sálvənt] N solvente *m*, disolvente *m*
Somalia [somáljə] N Somalia *f*
Somalian [somáljən] ADJ & N somalí *mf*
somber [sámbɚ] ADJ sombrío
some [sʌm] ADJ alguno; **I worked for —
time** trabajé por un rato; **that is — dog!**
¡menudo perro! PRON algunos; **and then**
— y más todavía; ADV — **twenty people**
unas veinte personas; **I like it** — me
gusta un poco
somebody [sámbadi] PRON alguien
someday [sámde] ADV algún día
somehow [sámhau] ADV de alguna manera;
— **or other** de alguna manera u otra
someone [sámwʌn] PRON alguien
somersault [sámɚsɔlt] N (on ground)
voltereta *f*; (in air) salto mortal *m*; VI (on
ground) dar una voltereta; (in air) dar un
salto mortal
something [sámθɪŋ] N algo *m*; — **else** otra
cosa; **thirty**— treinta y tantos
sometime [sámtaɪm] ADV algún día, en algún
momento; —**s** a veces, de vez en cuando
somewhat [sámhwʌt] ADV algo
somewhere [sámhwer] ADV en alguna parte;
— **else** en alguna otra parte
son [sʌn] N hijo *m*; —-**in-law** yerno *m*; — **of
a gun** *fam* hijo de su madre *m*
sonar [sónar] N sonar *m*
song [sɔŋ] N canción *f*; (of a bird) canto *m*; —
and dance cuento chino *m*; —**writer**
compositor -ora *mf*; —**bird** ave canora *f*,
pájaro cantor *m*; **to buy something for
a** — comprar algo muy barato
sonic barrier [sánɪkbǽriɚ] N barrera del
sonido *f*
sonnet [sánɪt] N soneto *m*
sonorous [sánɚəs] ADJ sonoro
soon [sun] ADV pronto; — **after nine** poco
después de las nueve; **as — as** tan pronto
como, en cuanto; **see you** — hasta
pronto; **how — do you want it?** ¿para
cuándo lo necesitas? —**er or later** tarde o
temprano; **I'd** —**er stay here** prefiero
quedarme aquí
soot [sut] N hollín *m*, tizne *m*
soothe [suð] VT calmar, aliviar
soothsayer [súθseɚ] N agorero -ra *mf*
sooty [súdi] ADJ tiznado
sop [sup] VT empapar; **to — up** absorber; **to**

be —ping wet estar empapado; N sopa *f*
sophisticated [səfístıkeɪɪd] ADJ sofisticado
sophomore [sáfəmɔr] N estudiante de segundo año *mf*
soprano [səprǽno] N soprano *m*
sorcerer [sɔ́rsərə] N brujo *m*, hechicero *m*
sorceress [sɔ́rsəɪs] N hechicera *f*
sordid [sɔ́rdɪd] ADJ sórdido, escabroso
sore [sɔr] ADJ (painful) dolorido, doloroso; (grieved) dolorido; (angry) enojado; **—head** cascarrabias *mf*; **my arm is —** me duele el brazo; **to have a — throat** tener dolor de garganta; N llaga *f*, úlcera *f*
soreness [sɔ́rnɪs] N dolor *m*
sorority [sərɔ́rıdi] N asociación femenina de estudiantes *f*
sorrow [sɑ́ro] N (sadness) pena *f*, pesar *m*, pesadumbre *f*; (cause of sadness) fuente de disgustos *f*
sorrowful [sɑ́rəfəɫ] ADJ triste, pesaroso
sorry [sári] ADJ **I am —** lo siento; **I am — about that** lo lamento; **I am — for her** la compadezco; **—?** ¿Cómo? **a — SOB** *pej* un desgraciado; **you'll be —** te arrepentirás; **he was in — shape** estaba en un estado lamentable
sort [sɔrt] N clase *f*, tipo *m*; **— of tired** algo cansado; **all —s of** toda clase de; **out of —s** (depressed) de mal humor; (ill) indispuesto; VT (classify) clasificar; **to — out** separar, apartar; **to — out a problem** resolver un problema
SOS [ésoés] N SOS *m*
soul [soɫ] N alma *f*; **— music** música soul *f*; **not a —** nadie, ni un alma; **the — of tact** la imagen del tacto
sound [saʊnd] N sonido *m*; (inlet) brazo de mar *m*; **— wave** onda sonora *f*; ADJ (healthy) sano; (sane) cuerdo; (well founded) bien fundado, lógico; **— advice** buen consejo *m*; **— barrier** barrera del sonido *f*; **—proof** a prueba de sonido; **— sleep** sueño profundo *m*; **—track** banda sonora *f*; **a — beating** una buena paliza; **of — mind** en su sano juicio; **safe and — sano** y salvo; VI sonar; VT (an alarm) tocar; (a channel) sondar; (opinion) sondear; **to — out** tantear, sondear
soup [sup] N sopa *f*; **— dish** plato sopero *m*; **—spoon** cuchara sopera *f*; **— tureen** sopera *f*
sour [saʊr] ADJ (acidic) agrio, ácido; (peevish) agrio, avinagrado; **to go —** cortarse, agriarse; **— cream** *Sp* nata agria *f*; *Am* crema agria *f*; **— milk** leche cortada *f*; **—puss** cascarrabias *mf*, avinagrado -da *mf*; VI/VT agriar(se), avinagrar(se); (milk)

cortar(se)
source [sɔrs] N fuente *f*, origen *m*
sourness [sáʊrnɪs] N acidez *f*
souse [saʊs] VI/VT (plunge) zambullir(se); (soak) empapar(se); N borracho -cha *mf*, esponja *f*
south [saʊθ] N sur *m*; ADJ meridional; **— Africa** Sudáfrica *f*; **— African** sudafricano -na *mf*; **— America** América del Sur *f*, Sudamérica *f*; **— American** sudamericano -na *mf*; **—bound** con rumbo al sur; **—east** sureste, sudeste; **—eastern** sureste, sudeste; **— Korea** Corea del Sur *f*; **— Korean** surcoreano -na *mf*; **—paw** zurdo -da *mf*; **— pole** polo sur *m*; **—west** sudoeste, suroeste; **—western** sudoeste, suroeste; **to hacia el sur**
southern [sʌ́ðən] ADJ meridional, sureño
southerner [sʌ́ðənə] N sureño -ña *mf*, meridional *mf*, habitante del sur *mf*
southward [sáʊθwəd] ADV hacia el sur, rumbo al sur
souvenir [suvənír] N recuerdo *m*
sovereign [sɑ́vəɪn] ADJ & N soberano -na *mf*
sovereignty [sɑ́vəɪnti] N soberanía *f*
sow [saʊ] N puerca *f*; [so] VI/VT sembrar
soy [sɔi] N *Sp* soja *f*; *Am* soya *f*; **—bean** *Sp* semilla de soja *f*; *Am* semilla de soya *f*; **— sauce** *Sp* salsa de soja *f*; *Am* salsa de soya *f*
spa [spɑ] N balneario *m*
space [spes] N espacio *m*; **—age** de la era espacial; **—bar** barra espaciadora *f*; **—craft** nave espacial *f*; **—ship** nave espacial *f*; **— shuttle** transbordador espacial *m*; **— station** estación espacial *f*; **— suit** traje espacial *m*; VT espaciar
spacious [spéʃəs] ADJ espacioso, amplio
spade [sped] N pala *f*; (in cards) pica *f*; **to call a — a —** al pan, pan y al vino, vino
Spain [spen] N España *f*
span [spæn] N (of hand) palmo *m*; (of time) espacio *m*; (of attention) lapso *m*, período *m*; (of bridge) tramo *m*; (of wing) envergadura *f*; (of life) duración *f*; VT (time) abarcar; (a river) atravesar, salvar
Spaniard [spǽnjəd] N español -ola *mf*
Spanish [spǽnıʃ] ADJ (of Spain) español; (Spanish-speaking) hispano; N (language) español *m*
Spanish America [spǽnıʃəmérıkə] N Hispanoamérica *f*
spank [spæŋk] VT dar nalgadas; N palmada *f*, nalgada *f*
spanking [spǽŋkıŋ] N zurra en las nalgas *f*; ADJ **— new** flamante
spare [spɛr] VT (embarrassment) ahorrar,

evitar; (money) prestar; (an enemy)
perdonar la vida a; (a worker) prescindir
de; — **me!** ¡ten piedad de mí! **to — no**
expense no escatimar gastos; **to have**
time to — tener tiempo de sobra; ADJ
(austere) austero; (extra) de sobra, de más;
— **cash** dinero disponible *m*; — **parts**
repuestos *m pl*; — **time** tiempo libre *m*; N
(part) repuesto *m*; (tire) neumático de
repuesto *m*

spark [spɑrk] N chispa *f*; — **plug** bujía *f*; VI
chispear, echar chispas; VT (a riot)
desencadenar; (interest, criticism) provocar

sparkle [spɑ́rkəł] VI (diamond) centellear;
(sparkler) chispear; (eyes) brillar; N
(flashing) brillo *m*, centelleo *m*; (spirit)
viveza *f*, animación *f*

sparkling [spɑ́rklɪŋ] ADJ (diamond)
centelleante; (eyes) brillante; — **water**
agua con gas *f*; — **wine** vino espumoso *m*

sparrow [spǽro] N gorrión *m*

sparse [spɑrs] ADJ escaso; (hair) ralo

spasm [spǽzəm] N espasmo *m*

spastic [spǽstɪk] ADJ espástico

spat [spæt] N riña *f*

spatial [spéʃəł] ADJ espacial

spatter [spǽDə] VI/VT salpicar; N salpicadura
f

spatula [spǽtʃələ] N espátula *f*

spawn [spɔn] VI desovar; VT engendrar; N (of
fish) huevas *f pl*; (of frogs) huevos *m pl*

spay [spe] VT esterilizar, castrar

speak [spik] VI hablar; VT (language) hablar;
(truth, amusement) decir; (lines) recitar,
decir; **so to** — por decirlo así, valga la
expresión; **to** — **for** hablar en nombre
de / a favor de; **to** — **one's mind** hablar
sin rodeos; **to** — **out against** denunciar;
to — **out for** defender; **to** — **up** hablar
fuerte

speaker [spíkə] N orador -ra *mf*; (at a
conference) conferenciante *mf*; — **of the**
House presidente -ta de la cámara de
representantes *mf*; —**phone** teléfono con
parlante *m*

spear [spir] N lanza *f*; (for fishing) arpón *m*;
(sprout) brote *m*; VT (wound with lance)
alancear, herir con lanza; (fish with lance)
arponear

spearmint [spírmɪnt] N mentaverde *f*

special [spéʃəł] ADJ especial; — **delivery**
entrega inmediata *f*; — **education**
educación especial *f*; — **effects** efectos
especiales *m pl*; — **interest (group)**
grupo de presión *m*; N (sale item)
especialidad *f*; (TV program) especial *m*

specialist [spéʃəlɪst] N especialista *mf*

specialization [speʃəlɪzéʃən] N
especialización *f*, especialidad *f*

specialize [spéʃəlaɪz] VI/VT especializar(se)

specialty [spéʃəlti] N especialidad *f*

species [spíʃiz] N especie *f*

specific [spɪsífɪk] ADJ específico; — **gravity**
peso específico *m*; N —**s** detalles *m pl*

specify [spésəfaɪ] VI/VT especificar

specimen [spésəmən] N (representative)
espécimen *m*, ejemplar *m*; (sample)
muestra *f*

speck [spɛk] N (small dot) mota *f*, manchita *f*;
(small amount) pizca *f*

speckle [spɛ́kəł] N manchita *f*, mota *f*; VT
salpicar, motear; —**d** moteado

spectacle [spɛ́ktəkəł] N espectáculo *m*; —**s**
gafas *f pl*, anteojos *m pl*; **to make a** — **of**
oneself dar un espectáculo, ponerse en
ridículo

spectacular [spɛktǽkjəlæ] ADJ espectacular

spectator [spɛ́kteDæ] N espectador -ra *mf*

spectrum [spɛ́ktrəm] N espectro *m*

speculate [spɛ́kjələt] VI/VT especular

speculation [spɛkjəléʃən] N especulación *f*

speculator [spɛ́kjələDæ] N especulador -ora
mf

speech [spitʃ] N (faculty of speaking) habla *f*;
(formal) discurso *m*; (in a play)
parlamento *m*; **to make a** — pronunciar
un discurso; — **defect** defecto de
pronunciación *m*

speechless [spítʃlɪs] ADJ (dumb) mudo;
(astonished) estupefacto

speed [spid] N velocidad *f* (also gear), rapidez
f; (amphetamine) anfeta *f*; — **limit** límite
de velocidad *m*; **at full** — a toda
velocidad; VI (break speed limit) ir con
exceso de velocidad; **to** — **by** pasar a toda
velocidad; **to** — **off / away** irse a toda
velocidad; **to** — **up** acelerar; VT (supplies)
hacer llegar a toda velocidad; (work)
acelerar

speedometer [spɪdámɪDæ] N velocímetro *m*

speedy [spídi] ADJ veloz, rápido

spell [spɛł] N (charm) hechizo *m*, sortilegio
m, conjuro *m*; (period) temporada *f*;
(sickness) ataque *m*; —**bound** hechizado;
to put under a — hechizar; VT (spoken)
deletrear; (written) escribir; (represent)
significar, representar; **to** —-**check**
comprobar el deletreo; **I** —**ed it out for**
him se lo dije con todas las letras

spelling [spɛ́lɪŋ] N ortografía *f*; — **bee**
concurso de ortografía *m*

spend [spɛnd] VT (money) gastar; (time)
pasar; —**thrift** derrochador -ra *m*,
gastador -ra *mf*, pródigo ga *mf*

sperm [spɝm] N esperma *mf*, semen *m*; — **bank** banco de semen / esperma *m*; — **whale** cachalote *m*

sphere [sfir] N esfera *f*

spherical [sférɪkəl] ADJ esférico

spice [spaɪs] N especia *f*; VT condimentar; **to — up** dar sal

spiciness [spáɪsɪnɪs] N lo picante

spick and span [spíkənspǽn] ADJ impecable

spicy [spáɪsɪ] ADJ picante

spider [spáɪdɚ] N araña *f*; — **monkey** mono araña *m*; —'s **web** telaraña *f*

spigot [spígət] N grifo *m*, espita *f*

spike [spaɪk] N (sprout) espiga *f*; (sharp object) púa *f*, pincho *m*; (on shoes) clavo *m*; —**s** zapatillas con clavos *f pl*; VT (impale) clavar; (add alcohol to) echar alcohol a; (hit a volleyball) picar

spill [spɪɫ] VI/VT volcar(se), derramar(se), verter(se); VT (a rider) hacer caer; **to — the beans** descubrir el pastel; VI **to — over** (a liquid) desbordarse; (a conflict) extenderse; N (of water) derrame *m*; (of blood) derramamiento *m*; (fall) caída *f*

spin [spɪn] VT (wool) hilar; (a top, one's partner) hacer girar; VI dar vueltas, girar; **to — yarns** contar cuentos; N (turning) giro *m*, vuelta *f*; (of an airplane) barrena *f*; (political) sesgo *m*; **to take a —** dar una vuelta

spinach [spínɪtʃ] N espinaca *f*

spinal [spáɪnəl] ADJ espinal, vertebral; — **column** columna vertebral *f*, espina dorsal *f*; — **cord** médula espinal *f*

spindle [spíndl] N (for weaving) huso *m*; (on machines) eje *m*

spine [spaɪn] N espina *f*, espinazo *m*

spinning [spínɪŋ] N (action) hilado *m*; (art) hilandería *f*; — **machine** máquina de hilar *f*; — **mill** hilandería *f*; — **top** trompo *m*, peonza *f*; — **wheel** rueca *f*

spinster [spínstɚ] N solterona *f*

spiral [spáɪrəl] ADJ & N espiral *m*; — **notebook** cuaderno de espiral *m*; — **staircase** escalera de caracol *f*

spire [spaɪr] N aguja *f*, chapitel *m*

spirit [spírɪt] N (ghost) espíritu *m*; (animation) ánimo *m*, brío *m*; (alcohol) alcohol *m*; **low —s** abatimiento *m*; **to be in good —s** estar de buen humor; VT **to — away** llevar como por arte de magia

spirited [spírɪtɪd] ADJ fogoso, brioso

spiritual [spírɪtʃuəl] ADJ & N espiritual *m*

spit [spɪt] VI/VT escupir; N (saliva) escupitajo *m*; (for roasting) asador *m*; (of sand) banco *m*

spite [spaɪt] N despecho *m*, inquina *f*; **in —**

of a pesar de; **out of —** por despecho; VT contrariar

spiteful [spáɪtfəl] ADJ malicioso

splash [splæʃ] VI/VT salpicar; VI chapotear, chapalear; N salpicadura *f*, chapoteo *m*; **to make a —** hacer olas

splatter [splǽdɚ] VI/VT salpicar; N salpicadura *f*

spleen [splin] N bazo *m*; (ill humor) mal humor *m*

splendid [spléndɪd] ADJ espléndido

splendor [spléndɚ] N esplendor *m*

splice [splaɪs] VT (tape, genes) empalmar, unir; N empalme *m*, unión *f*

splint [splɪnt] N tablilla *f*; VT entablillar

splinter [splíntɚ] N astilla *f*; VI/VT astillar(se)

split [splɪt] VI/VT (stone, wood) hender(se), rajar(se); (candy bar) partir(se), dividir(se); **to — hairs** hilar fino; **to — one's sides with laughter** desternillarse de risa; **to — the difference** partir la diferencia; ADJ (wood) partido, hendido; (a group) dividido; —**level** en desnivel; — **personality** doble personalidad *f*; — **screen** pantalla dividida *f*; — **second** fracción de segundo *f*; N hendidura *f*, grieta *f*; (in a group) escisión *f*, división *f*

spoil [spɔɪɫ] VI (milk) cortar(se); (food) echarse a perder, averiarse; VT (vacation, performance) estropear, arruinar; (plans) desbaratar; (enjoyment) aguar; (child) malcriar, mimar demasiado; N —**s** botín *m*

spoiler [spɔ́ɪlɚ] N alerón *m*

spoke [spok] N rayo *m*

spokesperson [spókspɝsən] N portavoz *mf*, vocero -ra *mf*

sponge [spʌndʒ] N (animal, utensil) esponja *f*; (parasite) gorrón -ona *mf*; — **cake** *Am* bizcochuelo *m*; *Sp* bizcocho *m*; VI **to — off** quitar con esponja; **to — off of** gorronear; **to — up** absorber con una esponja

sponger [spʌ́ndʒɚ] N gorrón -ona *mf*, parásito *m*

spongy [spʌ́ndʒi] ADJ esponjoso, esponjado

sponsor [spʌ́nsɚ] N (of the arts) mecenas *mf*; (of sports, TV program) patrocinador -ora *mf*; (of a bill) proponente *mf*; VT (a child) apadrinar; (arts, sports, TV show) patrocinar; (bill) proponer

sponsorship [spʌ́nsɚʃɪp] N patrocinio *m*

spontaneity [spantənéɪdɪ] N espontaneidad *f*

spontaneous [spanténiəs] ADJ espontáneo

spook [spuk] N (ghost) espectro *m*; (spy) espía *mf*

spool [spuɫ] N carrete *m*, carretel *m*; VT (wool) devanar; (tape) enrollar

spoon [spun] N cuchara *f*; VT cucharear, poner con una cuchara; **to —-feed** dar de comer en la boca

spoonful [spúnfʊł] N cucharada *f*

spore [spɔr] N espora *f*

sport [spɔrt] N deporte *m*; **to be a good —** tener espíritu deportivo; VT lucir; ADJ deportivo; **— utility vehicle** vehículo utilitario deportivo *m*; **—s car** coche deportivo *m*; **—s jacket** saco de sport *m*, americana *f*; **—sman** (hunter) cazador *m*; (in sports) hombre de espíritu deportivo *m*; **—smanship** espíritu deportivo *m*, deportividad *f*; **—swriter** cronista deportivo -va *mf*

sporty [spɔ́rɾi] ADJ deportivo

spot [spɑt] N (stain) mancha *f*, mota *f*; (blemish) espinilla *f*; (insect bite) roncha *f*; (place) lugar *m*, paraje *m*; (scrape) aprieto *m*; **on the —** en el acto; **—-check** inspección al azar *f*; **—light** (in theater) foco *m*; (outdoors) reflector *m*; **to be in the —light** ser el centro de atención; **— remover** quitamanchas *m sg*; VI/VT (stain) manchar, ensuciar; VT (see in the distance) divisar; (notice) notar; (give advantage) dar como ventaja

spotless [spɑ́tlɪs] ADJ inmaculado

spotted [spɑ́tɪd] ADJ manchado, moteado

spouse [spaʊs] N cónyuge *mf*

spout [spaʊt] VT (throw) arrojar chorros de; (talk) soltar tonterías; VI (flow out) salir a chorros; (talk) perorar; N (of a fountain) caño *m*; (of a gutter) canalón *m*; (of a teapot) pico *m*

sprain [spren] VT torcerse; N torcedura *f*

sprawl [sprɔł] VI (spread limbs) despatarrarse; (extend) extenderse; (fall) tumbarse; N postura despatarrada *f*

spray [spre] N (of liquid) rociada *f*; (foam) espuma *f*; (of flowers) ramillete *m*; VI/VT rociar(se); **— can** aerosol *m*; **— paint** pintura en aerosol *f*

spread [spred] VI/VT (arms, newspaper) extender(se); (butter) untar(se); (map) desdoblar(se); (legs) abrir(se); (seeds) esparcir(se); (news) difundir(se), diseminar(se); (rumor) propalar; (panic) sembrar; VT (panic, news) sembrar; N (of ideas) difusión *f*; (of opinion) diseminación *f*; (of disease) propagación *f*; (of nuclear weapons) proliferación *f*; (for a bed) cubrecama *m*; (for bread) pasta *f*; (of food) festín *m*; (ranch) hacienda *f*; **—sheet** (paper) planilla de cálculo *f*; (program) planilla electrónica *f*

spree [spri] N parranda *f*, farra *f*; **to go on a** — ir de parranda / farra; **to go on a shopping —** gastar dinero desenfrenadamente

spring [sprɪŋ] VI saltar; **to — at** abalanzarse sobre; **to — from** nacer de; **to — to mind** venir a la mente; **to — up** surgir; VT **to — a leak** (boat) hacer agua; (pipe) comenzar a gotear; **to — news** dar una noticia de sopetón; **to — open** abrir(se) de golpe; N (season) primavera *f*; (coil) muelle *m*, resorte *m*; (elasticity) elasticidad *f*; (jump) salto *m*; (water) manantial *m*, fuente *f*; **—board** trampolín *m*; **— fever** fiebre de primavera *f*; **— mattress** colchón de muelles *m*; **—time** primavera *f*; **— water** agua de manantial *f*; **he's no — chicken** no se cuece en el primer hervor

sprinkle [sprɪ́ŋkəł] VT (with sugar) espolvorear; (with droplets) salpicar, rociar; (rain) gotear, chispear

sprint [sprɪnt] VI (run) echarse una carrera; (run a competitive race) (e)sprintar; N (run) corrida corta *f*; (race) (e)sprint *m*

sprocket [sprɑ́kɪt] N piñón *m*, rueda dentada *f*

sprout [spraʊt] VI (leaf) brotar, salir; (plants) retoñar; (seeds) germinar; (houses) surgir; VT echar; **he —ed horns** le salieron cuernos; N retoño *m*, brote *m*, renuevo *m*

spruce [sprus] N picea *f*; VI **to — up** arreglarse

spunk [spʌŋk] N agallas *f pl*

spur [spɚ] N espuela *f*; (stimulus) aguijón *m*; (of a rooster) espolón *m*; (of a mountain) estribación *f*; (of a railroad track) ramal *m*; **on the — of the moment** espontáneamente; VT espolear; **to — on** animar

spurious [spjúriəs] ADJ espurio

spurn [spɚn] VT rechazar, desdeñar

spurt [spɚt] VI salir a chorros; N (of water) chorro *m*; (of a runner) esfuerzo repentino *m*; **in —s** por rachas

sputter [spʌ́ɾɚ] VI (fire) chisporrotear; (person) refunfuñar; N (fire) chisporroteo *m*

sputum [spjúɾəm] N esputo *m*

spy [spaɪ] N espía *mf*; VI espiar; **to — on** espiar, avizorar; **—glass** catalejo *m*

squabble [skwɑ́bəł] VI reñir; N reyerta *f*

squad [skwɑd] N (of police) patrulla *f*; (for execution) pelotón *m*; (of athletes) equipo *m*; (for guarding) retén *m*; **— car** (coche) patrullero *m*

squadron [skwɑ́drən] N (in navy) escuadra *f*; (in army) escuadrón *m*

squalid [skwálɪd] ADJ escuálido

squall [skwɔl] N (rain) chubasco m, borrasca f; (sound) berrido m; VI berrear

squalor [skwálə-] N miseria f, escualidez f

squander [skwándə-] VT despilfarrar, derrochar, disipar

squanderer [skwándərə-] N derrochador -ora mf

square [skwer] N (shape) cuadrado m; (on a pattern) cuadro m; (plaza) plaza f; (tool in carpentry) escuadra f; (on chessboard) casilla f; **he is a —** es muy conservador; VT (make square) cuadrar; (draw squares on) cuadricular; (multiply by itself) elevar al cuadrado; **to — one's shoulders** erguirse; ADJ (in shape) cuadrado; (at ninety degrees) en ángulo recto; (tied) empatado; (frank) franco; **— dance** cuadrilla f; **— knot** nudo de rizo m; **— meal** comida completa f; **— root** raíz cuadrada f; **to be — with someone** estar a mano con alguien; ADV **right — between the eyes** justo entre los ojos

squash [skwɑʃ] N (gourd) calabaza f; (sport) squash m; VT aplastar, despachurrar

squat [skwɑt] VI (sit low) acuclillarse; (occupy) ocupar sin autorización; ADJ (sitting low) acuclillado; (thick set) rechoncho, achaparrado; N **in a —** en cuclillas

squawk [skwɔk] VI (of chickens) cacarear; (complain) quejarse; N (of chickens) cacareo m; (complaint) quejido m

squeak [skwik] VI (door) rechinar, chirriar; (shoe) rechinar; (mouse) chillar; N (of door) rechinamiento m, chirrido m; (of shoe) rechinamiento m; (of mouse) chillido m

squeaky [skwíki] ADJ (door) chirriante; (shoes) rechinante

squeal [skwil] VI chillar; (complain) protestar; (snitch) chivatar, delatar; N chillido m

squeamish [skwímɪʃ] ADJ delicado

squeegee [skwídʒi] N escurridor de goma m, limpiavidrios m sg

squeeze [skwiz] VT apretar; (press very hard) estrujar; (an orange) exprimir; (hug) abrazar; **to — into** meter(se) con dificultad en, encajar(se) en; **to — out** (an orange) exprimir; (a towel) escurrir; **to — through a crowd** abrirse paso entre la multitud; N (of hands) apretón m; (excessive squeeze) estrujón m; (hug) abrazo m; (lack) restricción f

squelch [skwɛltʃ] VT (revolt) aplastar, sofocar; (criticism) acallar

squid [skwɪd] N calamar m

squint [skwɪnt] VI (partially close eyes) entrecerrar los ojos; (look askance) mirar de soslayo; N (look with partially closed eyes) mirada con los ojos entrecerrados f; (side-glance) mirada de soslayo f

squirm [skwɜm] VI retorcerse; **to — out of a difficulty** zafarse de un aprieto

squirrel [skwɜ́əl] N ardilla f

squirt [skwɜt] VT echar un chisguete en; VI salir a chorritos; N chisguete m, chorrito m; **— gun** pistola lanzaagua f, pistola de agua f

Sri Lanka [srɪláŋkə] N Sri Lanka f

Sri Lankan [srɪláŋkən] ADJ & N cingalés -esa mf

stab [stæb] VI/VT apuñalar, acuchillar; **to — at** tirar puñaladas a; N (with a dagger) puñalada f; (with a knife) cuchillada f; (with a pocketknife) navajazo m; (of pain) punzada f, pinchazo m; **— wound** cuchillada f

stability [stəbílɪdi] N estabilidad f

stable [stébəl] ADJ estable; N establo m, cuadra f; (for horses) caballeriza f; VT poner en el establo

stack [stæk] N pila f, montón m; (of a chimney) chimenea f; (in a library) estantería f; VT amontonar, apilar

stadium [stédiəm] N estadio m

staff [stæf] N (stick) cayado m; (of a flag) asta f; (personnel) personal m, plantel m; (of music) pentagrama m; **— of life** pan de cada día m; **— officer** oficial de estado mayor m; **— editorial** redacción f; **— teaching** cuerpo docente m; VT contratar personal

stag [stæg] N (of deer) venado m, ciervo m; (of other animals) macho m; **— beetle** ciervo volante m; **— party** fiesta para hombres f

stage [stedʒ] N (showplace) escenario m; (for popular entertainment) tablado m; (theater) teatro m, las tablas f pl; (period) etapa f, estadio m; (distance) etapa f; **—coach** diligencia f; **— fright** miedo al escenario m, fiebre de candilejas f; **—hand** tramoyista m; **by —s** por etapas; VT (a play) poner en escena; (an attack) organizar

stagger [stǽgə-] VI (totter) tambalearse, dar tumbos; VT (hit hard) hacer tambalear; (overwhelm) dejar azorado; (alternate) escalonar; N tambaleo m

stagnant [stǽgnənt] ADJ estancado

stagnate [stǽgnet] VI estancarse

staid [sted] ADJ serio

stain [sten] VI/VT (spot) manchar(se); (color) teñir(se); **—ed-glass window** vitral *m*; N (spot) mancha *f*; (color) tinte *m*, tintura *f*

stainless [sténlɪs] ADJ sin mancha; **— steel** acero inoxidable *m*

stair [stɛr] N peldaño *m*, escalón *m*; **—case** escalera *f*; **—s** escalera *f*; **—way** escalera *f*

stake [stek] N (pole) estaca *f*; (investment) interés *m*; (bet) apuesta *f*; **at —** en juego; **to die at the —** morir en la hoguera; VT estacar; **to — out** vigilar

stalactite [stəlǽktaɪt] N estalactita *f*

stalagmite [stəlǽgmaɪt] N estalagmita *f*

stale [stel] ADJ (bread) duro; (air) viciado; (joke) viejo; **—mate** punto muerto *m*

stalk [stɔk] N tallo *m*; VT acechar

stall [stɔl] N (at a market) puesto *m*; (at a fair) caseta *f*, barraca *f*; (in a stable) compartimiento *m*; VI (airplane) entrar en pérdida; (talks) llegar a un punto muerto; (motor) pararse; **he is —ing** está arrastrando los pies; VT (airplane) hacer entrar en pérdida; (talks) paralizar; (motor) parar

stallion [stǽljən] N semental *m*

stamina [stǽmənə] N resistencia *f*, aguante *m*

stammer [stǽmɚ] VI balbucear; N balbuceo *m*

stamp [stæmp] VT (a letter) sellar; *Mex* timbrar; *Am* estampillar; (an official document) sellar, timbrar; (a coin) acuñar; VI (with foot) pisotear, patalear; (horse) piafar; **to — out** eliminar; N (on a letter) *Sp* sello *m*; *Mex* timbre *m*; *Am* estampilla *f*; (on an official document) sello *m*, timbre *m*; (instrument, character) sello *m*; (on the ground) pisotón *m*; (sound) paso *m*

stampede [stæmpíd] N estampida *f*; VI huir en estampida; VT hacer huir en estampida

stance [stæns] N posición *f*, postura *f*

stanch, staunch [stɔntʃ] VT restañar; ADJ (strong) firme; (loyal) fiel

stand [stænd] VI (take a standing position) ponerse de pie, levantarse; *Am* parar(se); (to be in a standing position) estar de pie; *Am* estar parado; (stop) detenerse; (withstand, tolerate) aguantar, tolerar, soportar; (remain valid) mantenerse; **—by** recurso viejo *m*; **—by passenger** pasajero -ra en la lista de espera *mf*; **to — aside** apartarse; **to — back** retroceder; **to — behind** respaldar; **to — by** (be uninvolved) mantenerse al margen; (be alert) estar alerta; (support) respaldar; **to — for** (mean) significar; (tolerate) tolerar; **to — one's ground** mantenerse firme; **to — out** destacarse, sobresalir; **to — up for**

defender; **it —s to reason** es razonable; **it —s one meter tall** mide un metro de alto; **to — a chance of** tener posibilidad de; **where do you — on this issue?** ¿qué opinas al respecto? N (at a market) puesto *m*; (at a fair) caseta *f*; (of trees) bosque *m*; (opinion) posición *f*; (for music) atril *m*; (for taxis) parada *f*; **—off** empate *m*; **—point** punto de vista *m*; **to come to a —still** pararse; **to be at a —still** estar parado

standard [stǽndɚd] N (of behavior) norma *f*; (of living, performance) nivel *m*; (of weights) patrón *m*; (banner) estandarte *m*; **gold —** patrón oro *m*; **to be up to —** satisfacer los requisitos; **—-bearer** portaestandarte *mf*; **— of living** nivel de vida *m*; ADJ (normal) normal; (standardized) estándar; **— deviation** desviación estándar *f*; **— time** hora oficial *f*

standardization [stændɚdɪzéʃən] N estandarización *f*

standardize [stǽndɚdaɪz] VT estandarizar, uniformar

standing [stǽndɪŋ] N (position) posición *f*; (rank) rango *m*; (reputation) reputación *f*; ADJ (not seated) derecho, en pie; (permanent) permanente; (stagnant) estancado; **— order** pedido fijo *m*; **— ovation** ovación de pie *f*

stanza [stǽnzə] N estrofa *f*

staple [stépəl] N (for paper) grapa *f*; (main product) producto principal *m*; (food) alimento básico *m*; ADJ (principal) principal; (basic) básico; VT engrapar

stapler [stéplɚ] N grapadora *f*

star [star] N estrella *f* (also actor); (asterisk) asterisco *m*; **— attraction** atracción principal *f*; **—fish** estrella de mar *f*; **—light** luz de las estrellas *f*; **—-spangled** salpicado de estrellas; **a — student** un(a) estudiante sobresaliente; VT (act in) protagonizar; (put asterisk on) marcar con asterisco; (cover with stars) estrellar

starboard [stárbɚd] N estribor *m*; ADV a estribor

starch [startʃ] N almidón *m* (also food); VT almidonar

stardom [stárdəm] N estrellato *m*

stare [stɛr] VI/VT mirar fijamente; N mirada fija *f*

stark [stark] ADJ (landscape) yermo; (truth) descarnado, desnudo; (contrast) marcado; **— naked** en cueros; **— raving mad** loco de remate

starling [stárlɪŋ] N estornino *m*

starry [stári] ADJ estrellado

start [start] VI/VT (begin) comenzar, empezar; (a car) poner(se) en marcha, arrancar; VT (a fire) provocar; VI (jump) sobresaltarse; **to — off / out / up** empezar; N (beginning) comienzo *m*, principio *m*; (of a race) salida *f*; (nervous jump) sobresalto *m*; (nervous jump of a horse) respingo *m*

starter [stárdɚ] N (on an automobile) arranque *m*; (for a race) juez de salida *m*; **for —s** para empezar

startle [stárdl] VI/VT asustar(se), sobresaltar(se)

startling [stárdlɪŋ] ADJ asombroso, sorprendente

starvation [starvéʃən] N inanición *f*

starve [starv] VI/VT hambrear; VI morirse de hambre; VT matar de hambre; (for affection) privar de cariño

starving [stárvɪŋ] ADJ hambriento, muerto de hambre

stash [stæʃ] VI **to — away** ir ahorrando; N alijo *m*

state [stet] N estado *m*; **— of the art** con los últimos avances; **—room** (on a ship) camarote *m*; (on a train) compartimiento *m*; **—sman** estadista *m*; **—swoman** estadista *f*; VT (declare) declarar, aseverar, manifestar; (describe) exponer

stately [stétli] ADJ majestuoso, imponente

statement [stétmənt] N (declaration) declaración *f*, aseveración *f*; (bill) estado de cuentas *m*

static [stǽDɪk] ADJ estático; N interferencia *f*; **— electricity** electricidad estática *f*; **don't give me any —** no me compliques la vida

station [stéʃən] N estación *f*; (of radio) emisora *f*; (of television) canal *m*; (social rank) condición *f*; **— wagon** camioneta *f*; VT (a sentry) apostar; (troops) estacionar

stationary [stéʃəneri] ADJ (not moving) estacionario; (stopped) detenido; (fixed) fijo

stationery [stéʃəneri] N (material) artículos de papelería *m pl*; (paper) papel de carta *m*

statistics [statístɪks] N (science) estadística *f*; (data) estadísticas *f pl*

statue [stǽtʃu] N estatua *f*

stature [stǽtʃɚ] N estatura *f*; (moral) talla *f*

status [stǽDəs] N (prestige, rank) status *m*; (legal, financial) situación *f*; (marital) estado *m*; **— symbol** símbolo de status *m*

statute [stǽtʃut] N (by-law) estatuto *m*; (law) ley *f*; **— of limitations** ley de prescripción *f*

statutory rape [stǽtʃətɔrirép] N estupro *m*

stave [stev] N (of a barrel) duela *f*; VI **to — off** evitar

stay [ste] VI (remain) quedarse, permanecer; **to — away** mantenerse alejado; **to — in** quedarse en casa; **to — out of trouble** no meterse en líos; **to — up** quedarse levantado; VT **to — an execution** aplazar una ejecución; N (time spent) estancia *f*, estadía *f*, permanencia *f*; (support) sostén *m*, soporte *m*

stead [sted] N **in her —** en su lugar; **to stand one in good —** ser de provecho para uno

steadfast [stédfæst] ADJ fijo, firme

steadiness [stédɪnɪs] N (firmness) firmeza *f*; (of the hand) pulso *m*; (constancy) constancia *f*; (continuity) continuidad *f*

steady [stéDi] ADJ (not shaky) firme; (constant) constante; (continuous) continuo; **— boyfriend** novio formal *m*; **— customer** cliente -ta asiduo -dua *mf*; **— income** ingreso fijo *m*; VI/VT (an object) asegurar; (nerves) calmar

steak [stek] N bistec *m*, churrasco *m*

steal [stil] VI/VT (a thing) robar, hurtar; (a girlfriend) soplar; VI **to — away / out** escabullirse, escaparse; N ganga *f*

stealth [stɛlθ] N sigilo *m*; **by —** furtivamente

stealthy [stélθi] ADJ furtivo

steam [stim] N (evaporated water) vapor *m*; (arising from an object) vaho *m*; **— engine** máquina de vapor *f*; **— roller** apisonadora *f*, aplanadora *f*; **— ship** (buque de) vapor *m*; **— shovel** excavadora *f*; VT (cook) cocer al vapor; VI (give off steam) echar vapor; **to get —ed up** (angry) indignarse; (covered with vapor) empañarse

steamer [stímɚ] N buque de vapor *m*

steed [stid] N corcel *m*

steel [stil] N acero *m*; **— blue** azul acero *m*; **— industry** siderurgia *f*; **— mill** acería *f*; **— wool** lana de acero *f*; VT acerar; **to — oneself** prepararse

steep [stip] ADJ (hill) empinado, escarpado, acantilado; (decline) marcado; (price) excesivo; VT infusionar; VI estar en infusión, infusionarse

steeple [stípəl] N (spire) aguja *f*, chapitel *m*; (bell tower) campanario *m*

steer [stir] N (young) novillo *m*; (grown) buey *m*; VI/VT (a car) conducir, manejar; (a ship) gobernar, timonear; VI (turn) girar, doblar; **to — clear of** evitar; **to — a conversation** desviar una conversación; **the car —s easily** el coche es fácil de conducir; **—ing** dirección *f*; **—ing wheel**

volante *m*

stellar [stɛ́lɚ] ADJ estelar

stem [stɛm] N (of a plant) tallo *m*; (of a leaf) pedúnculo *m*, rabo *m*; (of a glass) pie *m*; (of a pipe) cañón *m*; **— cell** célula estaminal / embrional *f*; VT detener, contener, estancar; **to — from** provenir de

stench [stɛntʃ] N hedor *m*, hediondez *f*, tufo *m*

stencil [stɛ́nsəl] N plantilla *f*, matriz *f*

stenographer [stənágrəfɚ] N taquígrafo -fa

step [stɛp] N (in walking, dancing) paso *m*; (on stairs) peldaño *m*, escalón *m*; (in music) tono *m*; **to take —s** tramitar; **— by —** paso a paso; **—ladder** escalera *f*; **in — with the music** al compás de la música; **to take —s** (walk) dar pasos; (act) tomar medidas; VI dar un paso; **— this way** pase por aquí; **to — aside** hacerse a un lado; **to — back** retroceder; **to — down** (descend) bajar; (resign) renunciar; **to — off** bajar; **to — off a distance** medir a pasos una distancia; **to — on** pisar, pisotear; **to — on the gas** pisar el acelerador; **to — out** salir; **to — up** subir

stepbrother [stɛ́pbrʌðɚ] N hermanastro *m*

stepdaughter [stɛ́pdɔðɚ] N hijastra *f*

stepfather [stɛ́pfɑðɚ] N padrastro *m*

stepmother [stɛ́pmʌðɚ] N madrastra *f*

steppe [stɛp] N estepa *f*

stepsister [stɛ́psɪstɚ] N hermanastra *f*

stepson [stɛ́psʌn] N hijastro *m*

stereo [stɛ́rio] ADJ & N estéreo *m*

stereotype [stɛ́riətaɪp] N estereotipo *m*

sterile [stɛ́rəl] ADJ estéril

sterility [stərɪ́lɪdi] N esterilidad *f*

sterilize [stɛ́rəlaɪz] VT esterilizar

stern [stɚn] ADJ austero, severo, adusto; N popa *f*

sternum [stɚ́nəm] N esternón *m*

steroid [stɛ́rɔɪd] N esteroide *m*

stethoscope [stɛ́θəskop] N estetoscopio *m*

stew [stu] VI/VT (cook) estofar(se), guisar(se); VI (worry) preocuparse; N estofado *m*, guiso *m*; **to be in a —** estar preocupado

steward [stúwɚd] N (manager) administrador *m*; (on a ship) camarero *m*; (on an airplane) auxiliar de vuelo *m*

stewardess [stúwɚDIS] N (on a ship) camarera *f*; (on an airplane) azafata *f*

stick [stɪk] N (of wood) palo *m*, vara *f*; (of firewood) raja *f*; (of dynamite) cartucho *m*; **— shift** palanca de cambios *f*; **—up** atraco *m*, asalto *m*; VI/VT (adhere) pegar(se), adherir(se); VT (place) poner,

meter; (stab) clavar, pinchar; VI (become jammed) atascarse; **— 'em up!** ¡arriba las manos! **to — out** salir, sobresalir; **to — out one's head** asomar la cabeza; **to — out one's tongue** sacar la lengua; **to — to a job** persistir en una tarea; **to — up** estar parado de punta; **to — up for** defender; **to — someone up** asaltar / atracar a alguien

sticker [stɪ́kɚ] N (thistle) abrojo *m*; (adhesive) etiqueta adhesiva *f*

sticky [stɪ́ki] ADJ pegajoso

stiff [stɪf] ADJ (leather, cardboard) tieso, duro; (drink) fuerte, cargado; (shirt) almidonado; (back) entumecido; (test) difícil; (breeze) fuerte; (personality) envarado; (climb) arduo; (price) alto; **to get —** entumecerse; N (cadaver) *fam* fiambre *m*

stiffen [stɪ́fən] VI/VT (leather) atiesar(se); (back) entumecer(se); (shirt) almidonar(se); **to — up** agarrotar(se)

stiffness [stɪ́fnɪs] N (of leather) dureza *f*, tiesura *f*; (of one's back) entumecimiento *m*; (of one's personality) envaramiento *m*; (of resistance) firmeza *f*

stifle [stáɪfəl] VI/VT ahogar(se), sofocar(se); **to — a yawn** contener un bostezo

stigma [stɪ́gmə] N estigma *m*

stigmatize [stɪ́gmətaɪz] VI/VT estigmatizar

still [stɪl] ADJ (not moving) quieto; (quiet) silencioso; **—born** nacido muerto; **— life** naturaleza muerta *f*; VT acallar; ADV todavía, aún; CONJ de todos modos; N (for distilling) alambique *m*; (quiet) silencio *m*

stillness [stɪ́lnɪs] N quietud *f*, silencio *m*

stilt [stɪlt] N (for walking) zanco *m*; (support) pilote *m*

stilted [stɪ́ltɪd] ADJ (personality) envarado; (style) afectado

stimulant [stɪ́mjələnt] ADJ & N estimulante *m*

stimulate [stɪ́mjəlet] VT estimular

stimulation [stɪmjəléʃən] N estimulación *f*

stimulus [stɪ́mjələs] N estímulo *m*

sting [stɪŋ] VI/VT (insects, thorns) picar; (insects) aguijonear; VT (shampoo) hacer picar; (rain) azotar; (cheat) timar; N (pain) picadura *f*; (stinger) aguijón *m*; (confidence game) golpe *m*; **— of remorse** punzada de remordimiento *f*; **—ray** manta raya *f*

stinger [stɪ́ŋɚ] N aguijón *m*

stinginess [stɪ́ndʒinɪs] N tacañería *f*, mezquindad *f*

stingy [stɪ́ndʒi] ADJ mezquino, tacaño

stink [stɪŋk] VI (smell bad) heder, apestar; **to — of** heder a; **to — up** dar mal olor a;

your performance stank tu actuación fue un desastre; N hedor *m*

stipend [stáɪpɪnd] N (fellowship) beca *f*; (salary) estipendio *m*

stipulate [stípjəlet] VT estipular

stipulation [stɪpjəléʃən] N estipulación *f*

stir [stɝ] VI/VT (move) bullir, rebullir; VT (mix) revolver; (move emotionally) conmover; (awake) despertar; (stoke) atizar; **to — up** (trouble) provocar, suscitar; (an old grudge) remover; N **to give something a —** revolver algo; **to cause a —** causar revuelo; **— -crazy** claustrofóbico; **to —-fry** saltear

stirring [stɝ-ɪŋ] ADJ conmovedor

stirrup [stɝ-rəp] N estribo *m*

stitch [stɪtʃ] N puntada *f*; (on a wound) punto *m*; **to be in —es** desternillarse de risa; VI/VT coser

St. Kitts and Nevis [sentkítsənnívis] N San Cristóbal y Nieves *m*

St. Lucia [sentlúʃə] N Santa Lucía *f*

St. Lucian [sentlúʃən] ADJ & N santalucense *mf*

stock [stɑk] N (selection) surtido *m*; (reserves) existencias *f pl*; (livestock) ganado *m*; (lineage) estirpe *f*; (shares) acciones *f pl*, valores *m pl*; (in grafting) patrón *m*; (broth) caldo *m*; **out of —** agotado; **in —** en existencia; ADJ (common) trillado; **—broker** corredor -ra de bolsa *mf*, bolsista *mf*; **— company** sociedad anónima *f*; **— exchange** bolsa de valores *f*; **—holder** accionista *mf*; **— market** mercado de valores *m*, bolsa de valores *f*; **— options** opciones *f pl*; **—pile** acopio *m*; **—room** depósito *m*; **— size** tamaño ordinario *m*; **—yard** corral *m*; VT (sell) vender; (fill shelves) abastecer; **to — up on** surtirse de, acumular; **to —pile** acopiar

stockade [stɑkéd] N (fence) estacada *f*, empalizada *f*; (prison) prisión militar *f*

stocking [stɑkɪŋ] N (hose) media *f*; (sock) calcetín *m*

stocky [stɑki] ADJ robusto

stoic [stóɪk] ADJ & N estoico -ca *mf*

stoke [stok] VT (fire) atizar; (engine) alimentar

stomach [stʌmək] N (organ) estómago *m*; (belly) panza *f*, barriga *f*; **he has a big —** es barrigón; **to lie on one's —** estar panza abajo; VT aguantar

stomp [stɑmp] VI pisar fuerte; VT (crush) pisotear; (defeat) aplastar

stone [ston] N (rock, gem) piedra *f*; (in fruit) hueso *m*; (in kidneys) cálculo *m*; **within**

a —'s throw a tiro de piedra; **— Age** Edad de Piedra *f*; **—-deaf** sordo como una tapia; VT (a person) lapidar; (a fruit) deshuesar

stony [stóni] ADJ (made of stone) pétreo; (driveway) pedregoso; (silence) sepulcral

stool [stuɫ] N (furniture) taburete *m*, banqueta *f*; (excrement) materia fecal *f*; **—pigeon** soplón -ona *mf*, chivato -ta *mf*

stoop [stup] VI (bend over) agacharse; (have bad posture) encorvarse; **to — to** rebajarse a; N (posture) encorvamiento *m*; (porch) entrada *f*, porche *m*; **to walk with a —** andar encorvado; **—-shouldered** encorvado, cargado de espaldas

stop [stɑp] VI (halt) parar, detenerse; (malfunction) parar(se); VT (halt) parar, detener; (cancel) cancelar; (suspend) suspender; (plug) tapar; **to — at nothing** no tener escrúpulos; **to — by / in** visitar; **to — from** impedir; **to — over at** hacer escala en; **to — short** parar en seco; **to — up** tapar, atascar; **it —ped raining** paró / dejó de llover; N parada *f*, detención *f*; (on organ) registro *m*; **—gap** arreglo provisorio *m*; **—light** semáforo *m*; **—over** escala *f*; **— sign** *Sp* stop *m*; *Am* señal de pare *f*; *Mex* alto *m*; **—watch** cronómetro *m*; **to bring to a —** parar; **to make a —** parar

stoppage [stápɪdʒ] N interrupción *f*; (strike) huelga *f*

stopper [stápɚ] N tapón *m*

storage [stɔ́rɪdʒ] N almacenaje *m*, almacenamiento *m*; **— battery** acumulador *m*; **to keep in —** almacenar

store [stɔr] N (shop) tienda *f*, almacén *m*; (supply) reserva *f*, provisión *f*; **—house** (warehouse) almacén *m*, depósito *m*; (source) mina *f*, fuente *f*; **—keeper** tendero -ra *mf*, almacenista *mf*; **—room** almacén *m*, depósito *m*; **what is in — for us?** ¿Qué nos espera? VT (commercial goods) almacenar; (personal effects) guardar; **to — up** acumular

stork [stɔrk] N cigüeña *f*

storm [stɔrm] N tormenta *f*; (at sea) tempestad *f*, temporal *m*; (of protest) ola *f*; **— troops** tropas de asalto *f pl*; VT tomar por asalto; VI **to — in / out** entrar / salir en tromba

stormy [stɔ́rmi] ADJ tormentoso, tempestuoso

story [stóri] N (tale) cuento *m*, historia *f*; (newspaper article) artículo *m*; (lie) mentira *f*; (information) información *f*; (plot) argumento *m*, trama *f*; (floor) piso *m*

stout [staʊt] ADJ (fat) corpulento; (robust)

robusto, fornido; (strong) fuerte; (courageous) valiente

stove [stov] N (for heating) estufa f; (for cooking) cocina f; *Mex* estufa f

stow [sto] VT (keep) guardar; (hide) esconder; (put in cargo hold) estibar; **to — away on a ship** viajar de polizón

stowaway [stóawe] N polizón -ona mf

straddle [strǽdl] VI/VT estar a horcajadas; VT (a fence) ponerse a horcajadas; (one's legs) abrir; (not take sides) no comprometerse

strafe [stref] VT ametrallar

straggle [strǽgəł] VI **to — along / behind** rezagarse; **to — in** entrar de a pocos

straight [stret] ADJ (not curved) recto; (not tilted) derecho; (in succession) seguido; (hair) lacio, liso; (teeth) parejo; (frank) franco; (heterosexual) heterosexual; **— A's** sobresaliente en todo; **— face** cara seria f; **— flush** escalera de color f; **—forward** campechano; **—edge** regla f; ADV **— ahead** todo derecho, todo recto; **for two hours —** dos horas seguidas; **to come — home** volver derecho a casa; **to leave — after lunch** irse justo después de comer; **to set a person —** aclararle algo a alguien; **tell me —** dímelo francamente; **he can't think —** no puede pensar con claridad; **—forward** (honest) honesto; (simple) sencillo; (clear) claro

straighten [strétn] VI/VT enderezar(se); (situation) arreglar(se); VT (hair) alisar, *RP* laciar; **to — out a child** enderezar a un niño

straightness [strétnɪs] N derechura f

strain [stren] VI (pull) tironear; (try hard) esforzarse; VT (exhaust) agotar; (hurt voice) forzar; (injure a joint) torcer; (injure a muscle) sufrir un tirón en; (hurt a relationship) crear una tirantez en; VI/VT (filter) colar(se); N (effort) esfuerzo m; (injury) torcedura f; (pressure) presión f; (trouble in a relationship) tirantez f; (lineage) cepa f; (style) veta f

strainer [strénɚ] N colador m

strait [stret] N estrecho m; **in dire —s** en aprietos; ADJ **—jacket** camisa de fuerza f, chaleco de fuerza m; **—laced** puritano

strand [strænd] VI/VT (a ship) encallar, varar; VT (a person) dejar plantado; **to be —ed** (boat) estar encallado; (person) quedar plantado; N (beach) costa f, playa f; (of rope) ramal m; (of thread) hebra f; (of hair) mechón m

strange [strendʒ] ADJ (bizarre) extraño, raro; (unknown) desconocido

strangeness [stréndʒnɪs] N (unusualness) lo

extraño, rareza f; (unexpectedness) lo inesperado

stranger [stréndʒɚ] N (unknown person) extraño -ña mf, desconocido -da mf; (outsider) forastero -ra mf; **to be no — to something** saber bien lo que es algo

strangle [strǽŋgəł] VI/VT estrangular(se); **—hold** (in wrestling) llave al cuello f; (in markets) monopolio m; VT (creativity) coartar

strap [stræp] N (leather band) correa f, tira f; (on a dress) tirante m; VT atar con correa; **to — in** amarrar(se)

stratagem [strǽtədʒəm] N estratagema f

strategic [strətídʒɪk] ADJ estratégico

strategy [strǽtədʒi] N estrategia f

stratosphere [strǽDəsfɪr] N estratosfera f

stratum [strǽDəm] N estrato m

straw [strɔ] N paja f (also for drinking); **—berry** fresa f; **—-colored** pajizo; **— man** testaferro m; **— vote** votación de prueba f

stray [stre] VI (deviate, digress) desviarse; (get lost) perderse; (wander) vagar; (morally) descarriarse, perderse; ADJ extraviado, perdido; N perro / gato mostrenco m

streak [strik] N (line) raya f; (vein) vena f; (of luck) racha f; (of light) rayo m; VI (run naked) correr desnudo; (get discolored) aclararse

stream [strim] N (jet) chorro m; (river) río m; (brook) arroyo m; VI (water) correr, fluir; (blood) derramar; **—lined** aerodinámico; **to — out** brotar, manar; **to — in** entrar a raudales

street [strit] N calle f; **—car** tranvía f; **—lamp / lamp** farol m, poste de alumbrado m; **— sweeper** barrendero -ra mf

strength [streŋθ] N fuerza f; (spiritual) firmeza f; **on the — of** en base a

strengthen [stréŋθən] VI/VT fortalecer(se), reforzar(se)

strenuous [strénjuəs] ADJ arduo

strep throat [strépθrót] N infección por estreptococo f

stress [strɛs] N (tension) tensión f; (strain) estrés m; (pressure) esfuerzo m; (emphasis) énfasis m; (accent) acento m; VT (emphasize) enfatizar; (accentuate) acentuar; (exert force) someter a un esfuerzo; (put under pressure) estresar; **to — out** estresar

stretch [strɛtʃ] VI/VT (make or become longer) estirar(se), alargar(se); (extend) extender(se); (exaggerate) exagerar; **to — oneself** estirarse, desperezarse; **to — out**

(lengthen) extender(se); (lie) tumbarse, tenderse; N (act of stretching) desperezo *m*; (length) trecho *m*, tramo *m*, tirada *f*; (period) período *m*; (exaggeration) exageración *f*; — **mark** estría *f*

stretcher [strétʃə] N camilla *f*

strew [stru]ᴺvᴛ esparcir

stricken [stríkən] ADJ (with disease) aquejado; (by a flood) afectado; (with fear) aterrado

strict [strɪkt] ADJ estricto; **in — confidence** en absoluta confianza

stride [straɪd] vɪ caminar a paso largo, dar zancadas; N (gait) paso *m*; (long step) zancada *f*, tranco *m*

strident [stráɪdənt] ADJ estridente

strife [straɪf] N conflictos *m pl*

strike [straɪk] vɪ/vᴛ (hit) golpear, pegar; (stop work) hacer huelga (contra); vᴛ (find) dar con, encontrar; (occur to) ocurrírsele a uno; (cross out) tachar; (mark by chimes) dar; (light) encender; (coin) acuñar; **to — a compromise** llegar a un acuerdo; **to — one's fancy** antojársele a uno; **to — out** (cross out) tachar; (set forth) encaminarse; (fail) fracasar; **to — up a conversation** entablar conversación; **to — up a friendship** trabar amistad; **how does she — you?** ¿qué tal te parece? N (work stoppage) huelga *f*; (attack) ataque *m*; (finding of oil) descubrimiento *m*; **—breaker** esquirol *m*, rompehuelgas *m sg*

striker [stráɪkə] N (person on strike) huelguista *mf*; (of a bell) badajo *m*

striking [stráɪkɪŋ] ADJ (unusual, conspicuous) notable; (attractive) llamativo; (on strike) en huelga

string [strɪŋ] N (cord) cuerda *f*, cordel *m*; (of pearls, ties) sarta *f*; (of questions) serie *f*; (of beans) fibra *f*; (of garlic) ristra *f*; — **bean** habichuela *f*, judía verde *f*; **—s** cuerdas *f pl*; vᴛ (beads) ensartar; (a musical instrument) encordar; **to — along** tener en ascuas; **to — out** extender(se), prolongar(se); **to — up** colgar, ahorcar; **to be strung out** estar muy tenso

stringent [stríndʒənt] ADJ (law, need) riguroso; (time limit) estrecho, ajustado

strip [strɪp] vɪ/vᴛ (make / get naked) desnudar(se); vᴛ (remove bark) descortezar; (remove leaves) deshojar; (remove sheets) deshacer; (remove varnish) quitar el barniz; (damage gears) estropear el engranaje; **to —-mine** explotar a cielo abierto; N tira *f*; (of land) faja *f*; — **mall** centro comercial *m*

stripe [straɪp] N (band) raya *f*, lista *f*, banda *f*;

(military insignia) galón *m*; (type) tipo *m*

striped [straɪpt, stráɪpɪd] ADJ listado, rayado

strive [straɪv] vɪ esforzarse por, luchar por

stroke [strok] N (in golf, tennis, of luck, of genius) golpe *m*; (cerebral hemorrhage) derrame cerebral *m*; (movement in swimming) brazada *f*; (style in swimming) estilo *m*; (of a piston) carrera *f*; (of a painter's brush) pincelada *f*; (of lightning) rayo *m*; **at the — of ten** al dar las diez; vᴛ (pet) acariciar; (praise) halagar

stroll [strol] vɪ dar un paseo, pasearse; N paseo *m*, caminata *f*

stroller [strólə] N cochecito de bebé *m*

strong [strɔŋ] ADJ fuerte; (husky) recio; (eyesight, probability) bueno; (protest) enérgico; (views, faith, support) firme; (features, resemblance) marcado; (argument) sólido; **—hold** (fortress) fortaleza *f*; (center of activity) baluarte *m*; **—-willed** (resolute) resuelto, decidido; (stubborn) terco; **to —-arm** intimidar; ADV **to be going** — seguir activo

structural [stráktʃərəl] ADJ estructural

structure [stráktʃə] N (manner of construction) estructura *f*; (thing constructed) construcción *f*

struggle [strágəl] vɪ (with difficulties) luchar, bregar; (with an assailant) forcejear; **she —s in math** le pasa mal en matemáticas; N lucha *f*; (of ideas) pugna *f*, lucha *f*; (fight) contienda *f*, forcejeo *m*; **it's a —** da mucho trabajo

strut [strʌt] vɪ pavonearse; N pavoneo *m*; (support) tirante *m*, puntal *m*; (on a car) amortiguador *m*

strychnine [stríknaɪn] N estricnina *f*

stub [stʌb] N talón *m*; vᴛ **to — one's toe** dar(se) un tropezón, reventarse el dedo

stubble [stábəl] N (of a crop) rastrojo *m*; (of a beard) barba de unos días *f*

stubborn [stábən] ADJ terco, testarudo

stubbornness [stábənnɪs] N terquedad *f*, testarudez *f*

stucco [stáko] N estuco *m*; vᴛ estucar

stuck [stʌk] ADJ atascado; **to be — on someone** estar loco por alguien; **—-up** estirado, presumido

stud [stʌd] N (knob) tachuela *f*; (earring) arete *m*; (cufflink) gemelo *m*; (on shirtfront) botón *m*; (horse, man) semental *m*, garañón *m*; vᴛ tachonar

student [stúdŋt] N alumno -na *mf*; (secondary, university) estudiante *mf*; — **body** alumnado *m*; ADJ estudiantil *m*

studio [stúdio] N estudio *m*, taller *m*; — **apartment** estudio *m*

studious [stúdiəs] ADJ estudioso

study [stʌ́di] N estudio *m;* VT estudiar

stuff [stʌf] N (material) materia *f,* material *m;* (things) trastos *m pl,* bártulos *m pl;* (cloth) paño *m,* tela *f;* (affair) cosa *f;* (junk) cachivaches *m pl;* VT (mattress) rellenar; (dead animal) embalsamar, disecar; **to — into** meter en; **I'm —ed** estoy lleno

stuffing [stʌ́fɪŋ] N relleno *m*

stuffy [stʌ́fi] ADJ (person) envarado; (air) viciado

stumble [stʌ́mbəl] VI (trip) tropezar, trastabillar, dar un traspié; (stutter) balbucear; **to — out** salir a tropezones; **to — upon** tropezar con; N tropezón *m,* tropiezo *m,* traspié *m;* **stumbling block** obstáculo *m*

stump [stʌmp] N (of a tree) tocón *m,* cepa *f;* (of a tooth) raigón *m;* (of a limb) muñón *m;* **to be on the —** hacer una campaña electoral; VT (baffle) dejar perplejo; (remove stumps) arrancar los tocones de; **to — the country** recorrer el país haciendo campaña

stun [stʌn] VT (shock, surprise) dejar atónito, pasmar; (render unconscious) dejar sin sentido; **— gun** pistola tranquilizante *f*

stunning [stʌ́nɪŋ] ADJ (shocking) pasmoso; (beautiful) elegante, bellísimo

stunt [stʌnt] VT (stop growth) atrofiar; (do acrobatic tricks) hacer acrobacia; N (feat) acrobacia *f;* (for publicity) maniobra *f;* **—man** doble *m;* **—woman** doble *f;* **to pull a —** hacerse el listo

stupefy [stúpəfaɪ] VT (make lethargic) atontar, embrutecer; (astonish) dejar estupefacto, alelar

stupendous [stupéndəs] ADJ estupendo

stupid [stúpid] ADJ tonto, estúpido, majadero

stupidity [stupídɪti] N tontería *f,* estupidez *f,* majadería *f*

stupor [stúpɚ] N estupor *m*

sturdy [stɝ́di] ADJ (person) fornido, fuerte; (construction) sólido, robusto

stutter [stʌ́dɚ] VI tartamudear, tartajear; VT decir tartamudeando; N (act of stuttering) tartamudeo *m;* (speech defect) tartamudez *f*

stutterer [stʌ́dərɚ] N tartamudo -da *mf*

stuttering [stʌ́dərɪŋ] ADJ tartamudo; N (act of stuttering) tartamudeo *m;* (speech defect) tartamudez *f*

St. Vincent and the Grenadines [sentvínsəntəndəgrénədinz] N San Vicente y las Granadinas *m*

sty [staɪ] N (for pigs) pocilga *f;* (in eye) orzuelo *m*

style [staɪl] N estilo *m;* (type) modelo *m;* **out of —** fuera de moda; **like it's going out of —** como loco; VT (a book) intitular; (hair) peinar; **he —s himself Professor Smith** se hace llamar Profesor Smith

stylish [stáɪlɪʃ] ADJ elegante, de moda

stymie, stymy [stáɪmi] VT obstaculizar

Styrofoamᵗᵐ [stáɪrəfom] N poliestireno *m*

suave [swɑv] ADJ urbano, educado

subconscious [sʌbkɑ́nʃəs] ADJ subconsciente

subcontract [sʌbkántrækt] VT subcontratar

subdivision [sʌ́bdɪvɪʒən] N subdivisión *f;* (of land) parcelación *f*

subdue [səbdú] VT (overcome, vanquish) sojuzgar, someter, rendir; (repress) reprimir; (attenuate) atenuar

subdued [səbdúd] ADJ (atmosphere) tranquilo; (mood) deprimido; (lighting, color) tenue

subject [sʌ́bdʒɪkt] N (of a king) súbdito -ta *mf;* (of a sentence, in an experiment) sujeto *m;* (in school) asignatura *f,* materia *f;* **— matter** tema *m;* ADJ **— to** (changes, laws, conditions) sujeto a; (depression, earthquakes) propenso a; [səbdʒékt] VT someter

subjection [səbdʒékʃən] N sometimiento *m*

subjective [səbdʒéktɪv] ADJ subjetivo

subjugate [sʌ́bdʒəget] VT sojuzgar, avasallar

subjunctive [səbdʒʌ́ŋktɪv] ADJ & N subjuntivo *m*

sublet [sʌblét] VI/VT subarrendar

sublime [səblɑ́ɪm] ADJ sublime

submarine [sʌbmərín] ADJ submarino; [sʌ́bmərin] N submarino *m*

submerge [səbmɝ́dʒ] VI/VT sumergir(se)

submission [səbmíʃən] N (humility) sumisión *f;* (subjugation) sometimiento *m,* sumisión *f;* (sending) entrega *f,* envío *m*

submissive [səbmísɪv] ADJ sumiso

submit [səbmít] VI/VT someter(se); (to a judge) elevar(se); **to — a report** presentar un informe

subordinate [səbɔ́rdn̩ɪt] ADJ & N subordinado -da *mf,* subalterno -na *mf;* [səbɔ́rdn̩et] VT subordinar

subpoena [səpínə] N citación *f,* orden de comparecencia *f*

subroutine [sʌ́brutin] N subrutina *f*

subscribe [səbskráɪb] VI (underwrite, sign) suscribir; (receive a magazine) abonarse, suscribirse; (agree with) adherirse a

subscriber [səbskráɪbɚ] N (to shares) suscriptor -ora *mf;* (to services) abonado -da *mf;* (to a magazine) suscriptor -ora *mf,* abonado -da *mf;* (to an idea) partidario -ria *mf*

subscription [səbskrípʃən] N suscripción f, abono m

subsequent [sábsɪkwənt] ADJ subsiguiente

subservient [səbsɚ́viənt] ADJ servil

subside [səbsáɪd] VI (sediment) hundirse; (water level) bajar; (volcano, storm, anger) calmarse, aquietarse

subsidiary [səbsídieɪɪ] ADJ subsidiario; N sucursal f

subsidize [sábsɪdaɪz] VT subvencionar

subsidy [sábsɪdi] N subvención f

substance [sábstəns] N sustancia f; — **abuse** abuso de sustancias m

substantial [səbstǽnʃəł] ADJ (changes) sustancial; (food, lecture) sustancioso; (furniture) sólido; (amount) considerable, importante; **to be in — agreement** estar básicamente de acuerdo

substantiate [səbstǽnʃiet] VT (verify) verificar; (prove) probar

substantive [sábstəntɪv] ADJ & N sustantivo m

substitute [sábstɪtut] VT **I —d water for milk** usé agua en vez de leche, sustituí/ reemplacé la leche por agua; VI **John —d for Mary** Juan sustituyó/ reemplazó a María; N (one who substitutes) sustituto m, reemplazo m; (teacher, athlete) suplente -ta mf; (thing) sucedáneo m

substitution [sʌbstɪtúʃən] N sustitución f; **the — of water for milk** la sustitución de leche por agua

subterfuge [sábtəfjudʒ] N subterfugio m

subterranean [sʌbtərénɪən] ADJ subterráneo

subtitle [sábtaɪdl] N subtítulo m

subtle [sádl] ADJ sutil

subtlety [sádlti] N sutileza f

subtract [səbtrǽkt] VT (deduct) restar; (take away) sustraer

subtraction [səbtrǽkʃən] N sustracción f, resta f

suburb [sábɚb] N barrio residencial periférico m

suburban [səbɚ́bən] ADJ (residential) residencial; (on the outskirts) periférico

subversive [səbvɚ́sɪv] ADJ subversivo

subway [sábwe] N metropolitano m, metro m, subterráneo m

succeed [səksíd] VI (be successful) tener éxito; (manage) lograr; **to — to** heredar; VT (follow) suceder a

success [səksés] N éxito m

successful [səksésfəł] ADJ exitoso; **to be —** tener éxito

succession [səkséʃən] N sucesión f

successive [səksésɪv] ADJ sucesivo

successor [səksésɚ] N sucesor -ora mf

succinct [səksíŋkt] ADJ sucinto, escueto

succor [sákɚ] N socorro m; VT socorrer

succumb [səkám] VI sucumbir

such [sʌtʃ] ADJ tal; **he's — an idiot!** ¡es tan idiota! **in — a case** en tal caso/ en semejante caso; **— as** tal como; **at — and — a place** en tal o cual lugar; **there's no — thing** eso no existe; PRON **hobbies, pastimes, and —** hobbies, pasatiempos y cosas por el estilo; **a car — as yours** un coche como el tuyo; ADV **— nice neighbors** vecinos tan simpáticos

suck [sʌk] VI/VT chupar; (suckle) mamar; (vacuum, pump) aspirar; **to be —ed into** ser arrastrado a; **to — in** (air) aspirar; (stomach) meter; (fools) timar; N chupada f

sucker [sákɚ] N (gullible person) primo -ma mf; (lollipop) Sp pirulí m; Mex paleta f; RP chupetín m

suction [sákʃən] N succión f, aspiración f

Sudan [sudǽn] N Sudán m

Sudanese [sudníz] ADJ & N sudanés -esa mf

sudden [sádn] ADJ súbito, repentino, brusco; **all of a —** de repente, de improviso

suddenness [sádnnɪs] N brusquedad f, lo repentino

suds [sʌdz] N espuma f

sue [su] VI/VT demandar, poner pleito; **to — for** pedir, suplicar; **to — for damages** demandar por daños y perjuicios

suede [swed] N gamuza f, ante m

suffer [sáfɚ] VI/VT (feel pain) sufrir, padecer; VT (tolerate) tolerar

sufferer [sáfərɚ] N paciente mf

suffering [sáfɚɪŋ] N sufrimiento m, padecimiento m

suffice [səfáɪs] VI/VT bastar, ser suficiente

sufficient [səfíʃənt] ADJ suficiente, bastante

suffix [sáfɪks] N sufijo m

suffocate [sáfəket] VI/VT ahogar(se), sofocar(se); (to die, kill) asfixiar(se)

suffocation [sʌfəkéʃən] N ahogo m, sofoco m

suffrage [sáfrɪdʒ] N sufragio m

sugar [ʃúgɚ] N azúcar mf; (endearment) cariño m; **— cane** caña de azúcar f; VT azucarar; **to — the pill** dorar la píldora

suggest [səgdʒést] VT (propose) sugerir; (hint) insinuar

suggestion [səgdʒéstʃən] N (proposal) sugerencia f; (in hypnosis) sugestión f

suggestive [səgdʒéstɪv] ADJ insinuante; **to be — of** evocar

suicide [súɪsaɪd] N (act) suicidio m; (person) suicida mf; **to commit —** suicidarse

suit [sut] N traje m; (in cards) palo m, color m; (lawsuit) demanda f, pleito m, querella *f*; **—case** maleta *f*, valija *f*; VT (adapt) adaptar, ajustar; (satisfy) satisfacer; (look good) quedarle bien a, sentarle bien a; (be convenient, appropriate) convenir, venir bien; **— yourself** haz lo te parezca

suitable [súɔbəl] ADJ (appropriate) apropiado; (apt) apto

suitably [súɔbli] ADV como corresponde

suite [swit] N (series) serie *f*; (series of rooms, musical composition) suite *f*; (furniture) juego *m*

suitor [súɔ] N pretendiente *m*, galán *m*

sulk [sʌlk] VI enfurruñarse; N **to be in a —** estar enfurruñado

sulky [sʌ́lki] ADJ malhumorado, enfurruñado

sullen [sʌ́lən] ADJ hosco, huraño

sully [sʌ́li] VT mancillar, ensuciar

sulphate, sulfate [sʌ́lfet] N sulfato *m*

sulphide, sulfide [sʌ́lfaid] N sulfuro *m*

sulphur, sulfur [sʌ́lfɚ] N azufre *m*

sulphuric, sulfuric [sʌlfjúrik] ADJ sulfúrico

sultry [sʌ́ltri] ADJ (hot) bochornoso, sofocante; (sensual) sensual

sum [sʌm] N suma *f*, adición *f*; **in —** en resumen; VI **to — up** resumir, recapitular

summarize [sʌ́mɚaiz] VI/VT resumir

summary [sʌ́mɚi] N resumen *m*; ADJ sumario

summer [sʌ́mɚ] N verano *m*, estío *m*; **— resort** balneario *m*, lugar de veraneo *m*; **— school** cursos de verano *m pl*; **—time** verano *m*; VI veranear

summit [sʌ́mit] N cumbre *f*, cima *f*

summon [sʌ́mən] VT (witness) citar; (employee, police) llamar; N **—s** citación judicial *f*

sumptuous [sʌ́mptʃuəs] ADJ suntuoso

sun [sʌn] N sol *m*; **to —bathe** tomar el sol; **—beam** rayo de sol *m*; **—block** protector solar *m*; **—burn** quemadura de sol *f*; **to —burn** quemar(se) al sol; **—dial** reloj de sol *m*; **—down** puesta de(l) sol *f*; **—flower** girasol *m*; **—glasses** gafas de sol *f pl*, anteojos de sol *m pl*; **— lamp** lámpara solar *f*; **—light** luz del sol *f*; **—rise** salida de(l) sol *f*, amanecer *m*; **—screen** protector solar *m*; **—set** puesta de(l) sol *f*; **—shine** luz (del sol) *f*; **—spot** mancha solar *f*; **—stroke** insolación *f*; **—tan** bronceado *m*; **—up** salida del sol *f*; VI **to — oneself** tomar el sol

Sunday [sʌ́nde] N domingo *m*; **— school** escuela dominical *f*

sundry [sʌ́ndri] ADJ diversos

sunny [sʌ́ni] ADJ (day, patio) soleado; (disposition) alegre

super [súpɚ] N conserje *m*; ADJ súper, bárbaro

superb [supɚ́b] ADJ excelente

supercharger [súpɚtʃɑrdʒɚ] N sobrealimentador *m*

supercomputer [súpɚkəmpjudɚ] N *Am* supercomputadora *f*; *Sp* superordenador *m*

superego [supɚígo] N superego *m*, superyó *m*

superficial [supɚfíʃəl] ADJ superficial

superfluous [supɚ́fluəs] ADJ superfluo

superhuman [supɚhjúmən] ADJ sobrehumano

superimpose [supɚimpóz] VT superponer, sobreponer

superintendent [supɚinténdənt] N (of work) superintendente *m*, supervisor -ora *mf*; (of building) portero -ra *mf*, conserje *mf*

superior [supíriɚ] ADJ & N superior *mf*

superiority [supirióɾɪDi] N superioridad *f*

superlative [supɚ́ləDɪv] ADJ & N superlativo *m*

supermarket [súpɚmɑrkɪt] N supermercado *m*

supernatural [supɚnǽtʃɚəl] ADJ sobrenatural

superpower [súpɚpauɚ] N superpotencia *f*

superscript [súpɚskrɪpt] N número volado *m*

supersede [supɚsíd] VT reemplazar

supersonic [supɚsánɪk] ADJ supersónico

superstar [súpɚstɑr] N superestrella *f*

superstition [supɚstíʃən] N superstición *f*

superstitious [supɚstíʃəs] ADJ supersticioso

supervise [súpɚvaiz] VI/VT supervisar

supervision [supɚvíʒən] N supervisión *f*

supervisor [súpɚvaizɚ] N supervisor -ra *mf*

supper [sʌ́pɚ] N cena *f*

supplant [səplǽnt] VT suplantar

supple [sʌ́pəl] ADJ (flexible) flexible, elástico; (agile) ágil, grácil

supplement [sʌ́pləmənt] N (of a newspaper) suplemento *m*; (of a book) apéndice *m*; (of one's diet) complemento *m*; [sʌ́pləmɛnt] VT complementar, suplementar

supply [səplái] VT abastecer, suministrar; N (act of supplying) abastecimiento *m*; **— and demand** oferta y demanda *f*; **supplies** suministros *m pl*, provisiones *f pl*; **office supplies** artículos de oficina *m pl*; **military supplies** pertrechos *m pl*; **in short —** escaso

support [səpórt] VT (keep from falling) sostener, soportar; (encourage) mantener, apoyar; (corroborate) corroborar; N (of a structure) sostén *m*, soporte *m*; (of a family) sustento *m*; (of a candidate, idea) apoyo *m*; (of a theory) respaldo *m*; **— group** grupo de apoyo *m*

supporter [səpórdɚ] N partidario -ria *mf*; (in sports) hincha *mf*

suppose [səpóz] VT suponer; **we are —d to go** tenemos que ir

supposition [sʌpəzíʃən] N suposición f, supuesto m

suppository [səpázɪtɔri] N supositorio m

suppress [səprés] VT (repress) reprimir; (eliminate) suprimir; (a revolt) sofocar

suppression [səpréʃən] N (repression) represión f; (elimination) supresión f

supremacy [suprémǝsi] N supremacía f

supreme [suprím] ADJ supremo

surcharge [sɝ́tʃɑrdʒ] N recargo m, prima f

sure [ʃur] ADJ seguro; (judgment) certero; (hand) firme; **to make — of** asegurarse de; ADV **he — drinks a lot** es una esponja; **may I sit here? —!** ¿me puedo sentar? ¡cómo no!

surely [ʃúrli] ADV seguramente, ciertamente; **— you jest** no hablarás en serio; **he will — come** seguramente vendrá

surf [sɝf] N (breaking waves) rompientes mf pl; (foam) espuma f; (undertow) resaca f; **—board** tabla de surf f; VI/VT (on water) hacer surfing (en), surfear; (on Internet) navegar, surfear

surface [sɝ́fɪs] N superficie f; (of a solid) cara f; VI (come to top) emerger; (turn up) salir a la luz; VT (a submarine) sacar a la superficie; (a road) revestir

surfeit [sɝ́fɪt] N (excess) exceso m; (feeling of fullness) hartazgo m; VI/VT hartar(se)

surfing [sɝ́fɪŋ] N surfing m

surge [sɝdʒ] N (of people, disgust) oleada f; (of waves) oleaje m; (of electricity) tensión f; VI (people) precipitarse; (current) subir; **— protector** protector de tensión m

surgeon [sɝ́dʒən] N cirujano -na mf

surgery [sɝ́dʒəri] N cirujía f; (room) quirófano m

surgical [sɝ́dʒɪkəl] ADJ quirúrgico

Surinam, Suriname [súrɪnɑm(ə)] N Surinam m

Surinamese [surɪnɑmíz] ADJ & N surinamés -esa mf

surly [sɝ́li] ADJ malhumorado, hosco, arisco

surmise [sɚmáɪz] VT conjeturar, suponer; N conjetura f, suposición f

surmount [sɚmáunt] VT superar

surname [sɝ́nem] N apellido m

surpass [sɚpǽs] VT superar, sobrepujar

surplus [sɝ́plʌs] N excedente m, sobrante m, sobra f; (of funds) superávit m

surprise [sɚpráiz] N sorpresa f; VT sorprender

surprising [sɚpráiziŋ] ADJ sorprendente

surrealism [sɚríəlɪzəm] N surrealismo m

surrender [sɚréndɚ] VI (accept defeat) rendir(se), darse por vencido; (give oneself up) entregarse; VT entregar; N rendición f

surreptitious [sɝ-əptíʃəs] ADJ subrepticio

surrogate [sɝ́-əgɪt] ADJ sustituto; **— mother** madre de alquiler f

surround [sɚráund] VT rodear, circundar; (a city) sitiar

surrounding [sɚráundɪŋ] ADJ circundante; **—s** alrededores m pl, inmediaciones f pl

surveillance [sɚvélans] N vigilancia f

survey [sɚvé] VT (evaluate) evaluar; (measure) medir; (contemplate) contemplar; (poll) encuestar; [sɝ́ve] N (inspection) reconocimiento m, inspección f; (measure) medición f; (overview) panorama m; (poll) encuesta f, sondeo m; **— course** curso general m

surveyor [sɚvéɚ] N agrimensor -ra mf

survival [sɚváɪvəl] N supervivencia f, sobrevivencia f; (subsistence) subsistencia f; **the — of the fittest** la supervivencia del más apto

survive [sɚváɪv] VI/VT sobrevivir (also live longer than); (subsist) subsistir

survivor [sɚváɪvɚ] N sobreviviente mf

susceptible [səséptəbəl] ADJ susceptible; **to be — of proof** poderse demostrar; **to be — to pneumonia** ser propenso a la pulmonía

suspect [sʌ́spɛkt] N sospechoso -sa mf; [səspékt] VT sospechar, barruntar, recelar

suspend [səspénd] VT suspender

suspenders [səspéndɚz] N tirantes m pl

suspense [səspéns] N (uncertainty) incertidumbre f; (in movie) suspenso m; Sp suspense m; **to keep in —** mantener en suspenso, tener en vilo

suspension [səspénʃən] N suspensión f; (of a ban) levantamiento m; **— bridge** puente colgante m

suspicion [səspíʃən] N sospecha f, barrunto m

suspicious [səspíʃəs] ADJ (causing suspicion) sospechoso; (experiencing suspicion) suspicaz, desconfiado

sustain [səstén] VT (weight) sostener, sustentar; (pretense, effort) mantener; (an injury) sufrir; (an objection) admitir; (a musical note) sostener

sustenance [sástənəns] N sustento m, alimento m

suture [sútʃɚ] N sutura f

swab [swab] N hisopo m, bola de algodón f; VT pasar un hisopo sobre

swagger [swǽgɚ] VI (walk) pavonearse, contonearse; (boast) fanfarronear; N (walk) pavoneo m, contoneo m; (bluster) fanfarronería f

swallow [swálo] N (drink) trago m; (bird)

golondrina *f*; VI/VT tragar; **to — up** consumir

swamp [swɑmp] N pantano *m*, ciénaga *f*; **—land** cenagal *m*; VI/VT (flood) inundar(se); (overwhelm) abrumar(se), agobiar(se)

swampy [swɑ́mpi] ADJ pantanoso, cenagoso

swan [swɑn] N cisne *m*; — dive salto del ángel *m*; **— song** canto de cisne *m*

swap [swɑp] VT cambiar, canjear; N cambio *m*, canje *m*

swarm [swɔrm] N enjambre *m*; VI (of bees) salir en enjambre; (of people, tourists) pulular, hormiguear; **to be —ing with** ser un hervidero de, abundar en

swarthy [swɔ́rði] ADJ trigueño, moreno

swat [swɑt] VT (a person) pegar; (flies) aplastar; **to — at** manotear; N manotazo *m*

sway [swe] VI/VT (move to and fro) balancear(se), bambolear(se); (move hips) menear(se); (influence) influir (en); N (movement) balanceo *m*, vaivén *m*, bamboleo *m*; (influence) influencia *f*; **to hold — over** dominar

Swazi [swázi] N suazi *mf*

Swaziland [swázilænd] N Suazilandia *f*

swear [swer] VI/VT (vow) jurar; (use profanity) decir palabrotas; *Sp* soltar tacos; **to — in** (give oath) juramentar; (take oath) prestar juramento; **she —s by canned peaches** para ella no hay nada como los duraznos enlatados; **to — off** renunciar a; **to — to** jurar por

sweat [swet] VI (perspire) sudar; (ooze) exudar, sudar; (worry) preocuparse; N sudor *m*; **—shirt** sudadera *f*; **—suit** equipo deportivo *m*; *Sp* chándal *m*; **no —** no hay problema

sweater [swéɾɚ] N suéter *m*, jersey *m*

sweaty [swéɾi] ADJ sudoroso, sudado

Swede [swid] N sueco -ca *mf*

Sweden [swídn] N Suecia *f*

Swedish [swídiʃ] ADJ sueco

sweep [swip] VI/VT (clean with broom, scan) barrer; (dredge) dragar; VT (touch) rozar; (search) rastrear; VI (spread) extenderse; **to — away** llevar, arrastrar; **to — down upon** caer sobre, asolar; **to — off** limpiar; **to — into** (majestically) entrar majestuoso; (quickly) entrar rápidamente; **to — up** recoger; N (cleaning) barrida *f*; (extension) extensión *f*; (movement) barrido *m*; (search) rastreo *m*

sweeping [swípiŋ] ADJ (statement) (demasiado) general; (victory) aplastante

sweet [swit] ADJ (in flavor, personality) dulce;

(in smell) bueno, fragante; **—-and-sour** agridulce; **—heart** querido -da *mf*; **— pea** *Sp* guisante de olor *m*; **— potato** batata *f*, boniato *m*; *Mex* camote *m*; **to have a — tooth** ser goloso; N dulce *m*, golosina *f*; **my —** mi vida, mi alma; **to —-talk** halagar

sweeten [swítṇ] VI/VT (a food) endulzar(se); (an experience) dulcificar(se)

sweetener [swítṇɚ] N endulzante *m*, edulcorante *m*

sweetness [swítnɪs] N (of personality) dulzura *f*; (of taste) dulzor *m*

swell [swel] VI/VT (limbs, with pride) hinchar(se), henchir(se); VI (river) crecer; (population) crecer, engrosar(se); VT (make grow) hacer crecer, hacer aumentar, engrosar; N (of ocean) oleaje *m*; ADJ estupendo, bárbaro

swelling [swéliŋ] N hinchazón *f*

swelter [swéltɚ] VI sofocarse de calor

swerve [swɜv] VI/VT (in a car) virar; (from a goal) desviar(se); N viraje *m*

swift [swift] ADJ ligero, veloz, raudo; N vencejo *m*

swiftness [swíftnɪs] N velocidad *f*, rapidez *f*

swim [swim] VI/VT nadar; (float) flotar; **to — across** atravesar nadando; **my head is —ming** me da vueltas la cabeza; N **—ming pool** piscina *f*; *Mex* alberca *f*; **—suit** traje de baño *m*; **to take a —** ir a nadar, dar una nadada

swimmer [swímɚ] N nadador -ra *mf*

swindle [swíndl] VT estafar; N estafa *f*, trapacería *f*

swine [swain] N puerco *m*, cerdo *m*; (person) *offensive* puerco -ca *mf*, sinvergüenza *mf*

swing [swiŋ] VI/VT (on a swing) columpiar(se); (move to and fro) balancear(se), bambolear(se); VI (change) virar; VT (make turn) hacer girar; (influence) influir sobre; (baseball, golf) dar un swing con; **to — a deal** concretar un negocio; **to — around** dar vueltas; **to — open** abrirse; **I can't — a new car** no me puedo dar el lujo de comprar un auto nuevo; N (playground toy) columpio *m*; (oscillation) balanceo *m*, vaivén *m*, bamboleo *m*; (in golf, baseball, music) swing *m*; (change) cambio *m*; **in full —** en su apogeo; **to get into the — of things** agarrarle la onda a algo, cogerle el tranquillo a algo

swipe [swaip] VT (steal) afanar, sisar; (slide) deslizar; N (insult) insulto *m*; **to take a — at someone** (physical) tirarle un manotazo a alguien; (verbal) insultar

swirl [swɝɫ] vɪ/vᴛ arremolinar(se); (dancers) girar; ɴ remolino *m*; (smoke) espiral *f*
Swiss [swɪs] ᴀᴅᴊ & ɴ suizo -za *mf*; **— cheese** queso suizo *m*
switch [swɪtʃ] ɴ (change) cambio *m*; (electrical) interruptor *m*, llave *f*; (stick for whipping) varilla *f*; (on railways) agujas *f pl*; **—blade** navaja automática *f*; **—board** centralita *f*; **—man** guardagujas *m sg*; vɪ/vᴛ cambiar (de); (traincars) desviar; **to — off** (current) cortar; (light, TV) apagar; **to — on** encender, prender
Switzerland [swɪtsəɫənd] ɴ Suiza *f*
swivel [swívəɫ] ɴ pivote *m*; **— chair** silla giratoria *f*
swollen [swóɫən] ᴀᴅᴊ hinchado
swoon [swun] vɪ desvanecerse, desmayarse; **to — over someone** morirse por alguien; ɴ vahído *m*
swoop [swup] vɪ **to — down upon** abalanzarse sobre; ɴ descenso súbito *m*; **at one fell —** de un tirón
sword [sɔrd] ɴ espada *f*; **—fish** pez espada *m*
sycamore [síkəmɔr] ɴ sicomoro *m*
syllable [síləbəɫ] ɴ sílaba *f*
syllabus [síləbəs] ɴ programa (de estudios) *m*
syllogism [síləʤɪzəm] ɴ silogismo *m*
symbiosis [sɪmbiósɪs] ɴ simbiosis *f*
symbol [símbəɫ] ɴ símbolo *m*
symbolic [sɪmbáɫɪk] ᴀᴅᴊ simbólico
symbolism [símbəɫɪzəm] ɴ simbolismo *m*
symmetrical [sɪmétrɪkəɫ] ᴀᴅᴊ simétrico
symmetry [símɪtri] ɴ simetría *f*
sympathetic [sɪmpəθέᴅɪk] ᴀᴅᴊ (compassionate) compasivo; (understanding) comprensivo; (favoring) favorable; (nervous system) simpático
sympathize [símpəθaɪz] vɪ (be compassionate) compadecer(se); (be understanding) comprender; **to — with** estar a favor de
sympathy [símpəθi] ɴ compasión *f*, comprensión *f*; (condolence) condolencia *f*, pésame *m*; **to extend one's —** dar el pésame
symphony [símfəni] ɴ sinfonía *f*; **— orchestra** orquesta sinfónica *f*
symposium [sɪmpóziəm] ɴ simposio *m*
symptom [símptəm] ɴ síntoma *m*
synagogue [sínəgɑg] ɴ sinagoga *f*
synchronize [síŋkrənaɪz] vɪ/vᴛ sincronizar(se)
syndicate [síndɪkɪt] ɴ sindicato *m*; [síndɪket] vɪ/vᴛ (form a syndicate) sindicar(se); vᴛ (sell rights) vender los derechos de
syndrome [síndrom] ɴ síndrome *m*
synonym [sínənɪm] ɴ sinónimo *m*

synonymous [sɪnánəməs] ᴀᴅᴊ sinónimo
synopsis [sɪnápsɪs] ɴ sinopsis *f*
syntax [síntæks] ɴ sintaxis *f*
synthesis [sínθəsɪs] ɴ síntesis *f*
synthesize [sínθəsaɪz] vɪ/vᴛ sintetizar
synthetic [sɪnθέᴅɪk] ᴀᴅᴊ sintético
syphilis [sífəlɪs] ɴ sífilis *f*
Syria [síria] ɴ Siria *f*
Syrian [síriən] ᴀᴅᴊ & ɴ sirio -ria *mf*
syringe [sərínʤ] ɴ jeringa *f*
syrup [sírəp] ɴ (food) almíbar *m*, jarabe *m*; (medicine) jarabe *m*
system [sístəm] ɴ sistema *m*
systematic [sɪstəmǽᴅɪk] ᴀᴅᴊ sistemático
systematize [sístəmətaɪz] vɪ/vᴛ sistematizar
systemic [sɪstémɪk] ᴀᴅᴊ sistémico

Tt

tab [tæb] ɴ (on typewriter) tabulador *m*; (on index cards) pestaña *f*, ceja *f*; (bill) cuenta *f*; **— key** tecla de tabulación *f*
table [tébəɫ] ɴ (furniture) mesa *f*; (list) tabla *f*; **— lamp** lámpara de mesa *f*; **— of contents** tabla de contenido *f*, índice *m*; **at —** a la mesa; vᴛ posponer indefinidamente, dar carpetazo a; **—cloth** mantel *m*; **—spoon** (spoon) cuchara grande *f*; (measurement) cucharada *f*; **—spoonful** cucharada *f*; **— tennis** tenis de mesa *m*; **—ware** vajilla *f*, servicio de mesa *m*
tablet [tǽblɪt] ɴ (pill) pastilla *f*, tableta *f*; (paper) bloc *m*; (stone) tabla *f*, lápida *f*; (portable writing surface) tablilla *f*
tabloid [tǽbloɪd] ɴ (paper size) tabloide *m*; (type of press) prensa amarilla / sensacionalista *f*
taboo [tæbú] ɴ tabú *m*
tabulate [tǽbjəlet] vᴛ tabular
tachometer [tækámɪᴅɚ] ɴ tacómetro *m*
tacit [tǽsɪt] ᴀᴅᴊ tácito
taciturn [tǽsɪtɝn] ᴀᴅᴊ taciturno
tack [tæk] ɴ (nail) tachuela *f*; (stitch) hilván *m*; (heading of a boat) rumbo *m*; (course of action) táctica *f*; (equipment for a horse) arreos *m pl*; vᴛ (to nail) clavar con tachuelas; (to stitch) hilvanar; **to — on** agregar; vɪ virar, cambiar de rumbo
tackle [tǽkəɫ] ɴ (for fishing, hoisting) aparejo *m*; (in rugby, football) placaje *m*; (person) atajador *m*; vᴛ (a problem) enfrentar, abordar; (a task) emprender; (a

horse) poner arreos; VI/VT (rugby, American football) placar, atajar; **the cowboy —d the calf** el vaquero tiró al suelo al becerro

tacky [tǽki] ADJ (in bad taste) de mal gusto, chabacano; Sp hortera *inv*; (sticky) pegajoso

tact [tækt] N tacto *m*

tactful [tǽktfəl] ADJ que tiene tacto

tactics [tǽktɪks] N táctica *f*

tactile [tǽktəl] ADJ táctil

tactless [tǽktlɪs] ADJ falto de tacto

tag [tæg] N (label) etiqueta *f*; (question) coletilla *f*; (nickname) apodo *m*; **to play — **jugar al pillapilla; VT etiquetar; (in the game of tag) pillar; **to — along** acompañar; **to — on** agregar

tail [teɫ] N cola *f*, rabo *m*; (of a shirt) faldón *m*; (pursuer) perseguidor -ra *mf*; **—bone** rabadilla *f*; **— end** (of a concert) final *m*; (of a procession) cola *f*; **to —gate** seguir demasiado de cerca (a otro coche); **—light** luz trasera *f*; **—pipe** tubo de escape *m*; **—s** (of a coin) cruz *f*; (tuxedo) frac *m*; **—spin** barrena *f*

tailor [téɫə] N sastre *m*; **— shop** sastrería *f*; VT hacer a medida; (adapt) adaptar

taint [tent] N (stain) mancha *f*; (contamination) contaminación *f*; VI/VT (stain) manchar(se); (contaminate) contaminar(se)

Taiwan [taɪwán] N Taiwán *m*

Taiwanese [taɪwaníz] ADJ & N taiwanés -esa *mf*

Tajik [taʤík] ADJ & N tayiko -ka *mf*

Tajikistan [taʤíkɪstæn] N Tayikistán *m*

take [tek] VT (carry) llevar; (conduct) conducir; (steal) robar, llevarse; (subtract) restar; (prisoner, medicine, measures, a course) tomar; (one of a set) elegir, coger; (a bribe) aceptar; (a prize) recibir; (advice) seguir; (a walk) dar; (a vacation) irse; (a trip) hacer; (a piece of news) recibir; (remove from) sacar; (a photo) sacar; **to — a bath** bañarse; **to — a chance** arriesgarse, correr un riesgo; **to — after** salir a, parecerse a; **to — a fancy to** entusiasmarse con; **to — a look at** echar un vistazo a; **to — a nap** dormir la siesta; **to — a notion to** ocurrírsele a uno; **to — an oath** prestar juramento; **to — apart** desarmar, desmontar; **to — aside** apartar; **to — away** (carry away) llevarse; (steal) sustraer; **to — back** devolver; **to — back one's words** retractarse; **to — by surprise** tomar desprevenido; **to — care of** (a person) cuidar de; (a matter) atender

a; **to — charge of** encargarse de; **to — down in writing** anotar, apuntar; **to — effect** entrar en vigencia; **to — exercise** hacer ejercicio; **to — in** (include) incluir; (comprehend) absorber; (deceive) embaucar; (orphans) albergar; (a dress) tomar, achicar; **to — leave** despedirse; **to — off** (a coat) quitar(se); (to jail) llevar; (discount) rebajar; (an airplane) despegar; **to — offense** ofenderse; **to — office** asumir un cargo; **to — on** (accept) asumir; (hire) tomar, contratar; (acquire) adquirir; **to — out** (withdraw) sacar; (carry out [food], take on a date) llevar; **to — place** tener lugar; **to — revenge** vengarse; **to — stock** hacer un balance; **to — stock in** tener confianza en; **to — the floor** tomar la palabra; **to — to heart** tomar a pecho; **to — to one's heels** poner pies en polvorosa; **to — to task** reprender, regañar; **to — up a matter** tratar un asunto; **to — up space** ocupar espacio; **I — it that** supongo que; **it —s ten minutes** lleva diez minutos; **the vaccination didn't —** la vacuna no prendió; N (profits) ingresos *m pl*; (of fish) pesca *f*, captura *f*; (of a film production) toma *f*; (opinion) opinión *f*; (approach) enfoque *m*; **—off** (of an airplane) despegue *m*; (parody) parodia *f*; **—over** (of a government) toma de poder *f*; (of a company) adquisición *f*

talcum [tǽlkəm] N talco *m*; **— powder** polvo de talco *m*

tale [teɫ] N (story) cuento *m*, relato *m*; (lie) mentira *f*

talent [tǽlənt] N talento *m*

talented [tǽləntɪd] ADJ talentoso

talk [tɔk] VI/VT hablar; (chat) charlar; VT (nonsense) decir; (French) hablar; (politics) hablar de; **to — back** contestar con impertinencia; **to — down to** hablar con arrogancia a; **to — someone into something** convencer a alguien para que haga algo; **to — out of** disuadir de; **to — over** discutir; **to — up** alabar, hacer propaganda; N (formal speech) charla *f*; (gossip) habladurías *f pl*; (lingo) habla *f*; **— of the town** la comidilla del pueblo *f*; **— show** programa de entrevistas *m*

talkative [tɔkədɪv] ADJ hablador, parlanchín, charlatán

tall [tɔɫ] ADJ alto; **— order** misión imposible *f*; **— tale** cuento chino *m*, patraña *f*; **six feet —** de seis pies de altura; **how — are you?** ¿cuánto mides?

tallow [tǽlo] N sebo *m*

tally [tǽli] N (account) cuenta *f*; VT llevar la cuenta; **to — up** sumar; **to — with** concordar con

tambourine [tæmbərín] N pandereta *f*

tame [tem] ADJ (docile) manso, dócil; (domesticated) domesticado; (dull) aburrido; VT (make docile) amansar, domar; (domesticate) domesticar

tamper [tǽmpɚ] VI **to — with** (a jury) sobornar; (a lock) intentar forzar; (a document) alterar, amañar

tampon [tǽmpɑn] N tampón *m*

tan [tæn] VI/VT (cure) curtir(se); (sunburn) broncear(se), tostar(se); VT (cure) adobar; (spank) zurrar; N color tostado *m*; (of skin) bronceado *m*; ADJ (car) color tostado; (skin) bronceado, tostado

tandem [tǽndəm] N tándem *m*; **in — with** en colaboración con

tangent [tǽndʒənt] ADJ & N tangente *f*; **to go off on a —** salirse por la tangente

tangerine [tændʒərín] N mandarina *f*; *Am* tangerina *f*

tangible [tǽndʒəbəl] ADJ tangible

tangle [tǽŋɡəl] VI/VT enredar(se), enmarañar(se); N enredo *m*, maraña *f*; (in hair) nudo *m*, enredijo *m*

tank [tæŋk] N tanque *m* (also military), depósito *m*; VT guardar en un tanque; **to — up** (with gasoline) llenar el tanque; (with alcohol) emborracharse

tannery [tǽnəri] N curtiduría *f*, tenería *f*; *Am* curtiembre *f*

tantalize [tǽntlaiz] VT atormentar con tentaciones

tantamount [tǽntəmaunt] ADJ **to be — to** equivaler a

tantrum [tǽntrəm] N berrinche *m*, perrera *f*, rabieta *f*

Tanzania [tænzǽniə] N Tanzania *f*

Tanzanian [tænzǽniən] ADJ & N tanzano -na *mf*

tap [tæp] N golpecito *m*; (repeated) golpeteo *m*; (with the hand) palmadita *f*; (faucet) llave *f*; *Sp* grifo *m*; **— dance** claqué *m*; **— water** agua de llave *f*; VI/VT (once) tocar; (repeatedly) golpetear; (with fingers) tamborilear; (utilize) explotar; (draw off liquid) extraer; **to — a tree** sangrar un árbol; **to — a telephone** intervenir un teléfono

tape [tep] N cinta *f* (also adhesive); **— measure** cinta métrica *f*; **— recorder** grabadora *f*, grabador *m*; **— recording** grabación *f*; **to —-record** grabar; **—worm** lombriz *f*, solitaria *f*; VT (tie up) atar con cinta; VI/VT (record) grabar

taper [tépɚ] N (diminished size) estrechamiento *m*; (candle) vela *f*, candela *f*; VI/VT afinar(se); **to — off** (become smaller) afinar(se); (diminish) ir disminuyendo

tapestry [tǽpɪstri] N (wall hanging) tapiz *m*; (art, industry) tapicería *f*

tapioca [tæpiókə] N tapioca *f*

tapir [tépɚ] N tapir *m*

tar [tɑr] N alquitrán *m*, brea *f*; VT alquitranar; **to — and feather** emplumar

tarantula [tərǽntʃələ] N tarántula *f*

tardy [tɑ́rdi] ADJ **to be —** llegar tarde

target [tɑ́rɡɪt] N blanco *m*; **— practice** tiro al blanco *m*

tariff [tǽrɪf] N tarifa *f*, arancel *m*

tarnish [tɑ́rnɪʃ] VI/VT (metal) deslustrar(se), empañar; (reputation) manchar(se)

tart [tɑrt] ADJ (fruit) agrio, ácido; (remark) mordaz; N (pie) tarta *f*

tartar [tɑ́rdɚ] N (in wine) tártaro *m*; (on teeth) sarro *m*; **— sauce** salsa tártara *f*

task [tæsk] N tarea *f*, labor *f*, quehacer *m*; **to take to —** reprender, regañar; **— force** fuerza de tarea *f*; **—master** tirano -na *mf*

tassel [tǽsəl] N borla *f*

taste [test] VT (perceive) sentir el gusto / sabor de; (try) probar; (try wine) catar; VI **to — of onion** saber a cebolla; **it —s sour** tiene un sabor agrio; N (sense, esthetic judgment) gusto *m*; (flavor) sabor *m*; (small amount of food) bocadito *m*; (small amount of drink) sorbo *m*; **— bud** papila gustativa *f*

tasteless [téstlɪs] ADJ (with no taste) soso, desabrido; (in bad taste) de mal gusto

tasty [tésti] ADJ sabroso

tatter [tǽdɚ] N andrajo *m*, harapo *m*, pingajo *m*

tattered [tǽdɚd] ADJ harapiento, andrajoso

tattle [tǽdl] VI acusar; **to — on** acusar a; N **—tale** alcahuete -ta *mf*, acusetas *mf sg*

tattoo [tætú] N tatuaje *m*; VI/VT tatuar(se)

taunt [tɔnt] VT provocar, burlarse de; N provocación *f*, pulla *f*

taut [tɔt] ADJ tenso, tirante

tavern [tǽvɚn] N taberna *f*, cantina *f*

tawdry [tɔ́dri] ADJ (affair) sórdido; (outfit) charro

tax [tæks] N impuesto *m*, contribución *f*, gravamen *m*; (burden) carga *f*; VT (a product) gravar; (a person) cobrarle impuestos a; (patience, resources) poner a prueba; **—-deductible** desgravable; **—-exempt** no gravable, exento de impuestos; **—payer** contribuyente *mf*; **— return** declaración de impuestos *f*; **—**

shelter refugio fiscal *m*
taxation [tækséʃən] N (result of taxing) impuestos *m pl*; (act of taxing) imposición de contribuciones *f*
taxi [tǽksi] N taxi *m*; VI ir en taxi; (an airplane) rodar por la pista; **—cab** taxi *m*
taxidermy [tǽksɪdɚmi] N taxidermia *f*
taxonomy [tæksánəmi] N taxonomía *f*
tea [ti] N té *m*; **— bag** bolsita de té *f*; **—cup** taza de té *f*; **—kettle** tetera *f*; **— party** té *m*; **—pot** tetera *f*; **—spoon** (spoon) cucharita *f*, cucharilla *f*; (measurement) cucharadita *f*; **—spoonful** cucharadita *f*; **—time** hora del té *f*
teach [titʃ] VI/VT enseñar; **to — a class** dar clase
teacher [títʃɚ] N (primary school) maestro -tra *mf*; (secondary school) profesor -ora *mf*; **—'s college** (escuela) normal *f*
teaching [títʃɪŋ] N enseñanza *f*; **—s** enseñanzas *f pl*
team [tim] N equipo *m*; (of yoked animals) yunta de bueyes *f*; (of horses) tiro *m*, enganche *m*; VI **to — up** unirse, formar un equipo
teamster [tímstɚ] N transportista *mf*, camionero -ra *mf*
tear [tir] N lágrima *f*; **—drop** lágrima *f*; **— gas** gas lacrimógeno *m*; **to burst into —s** romper a llorar; [tɛr] VI/VT rasgar(se); (rip a hole) hacer(se) un siete; VT (snatch) arrancar; (disrupt) desgarrar; **to — along** ir a toda velocidad; **to — apart** (rip up) romper, destrozar; (separate) separar; **to — away** apartar(se); **to — down** (a building) demoler, derribar; (a machine) desarmar, desmontar; (a person) denigrar; **to — one's hair** arrancarse los cabellos; N desgarrón *m*, desgarradura *f*, rasgón *m*
tearful [tírfəl] ADJ (look) lloroso; (farewell) triste
tease [tiz] VT (make fun of a person) molestar, fastidiar; (tantalize sexually) provocar; (comb wool, hair) cardar; **to — out** sacar; N provocadora *f*
teat [tit] N teta *f*
technical [tɛknɪkəl] ADJ técnico
technician [tɛkníʃən] N técnico -ca *mf*, perito -ta *mf*
technique [tɛkník] N técnica *f*
technology [tɛknáləʤi] N tecnología *f*, técnica *f*
tectonics [tɛktánɪks] N tectónica *f*
tedious [tídiəs] ADJ tedioso, aburrido
tedium [tídiəm] N hastío *m*
tee [ti] N (T-shirt) camiseta *f*; (golf ball support) tee *m*; (start of hole in golf)

punto de salida *m*
teem [tim] VI **to — with** abundar en, estar lleno de
teenager [tíneʤɚ] N adolescente *mf*
teens [tinz] N (teenage years) adolescencia *f*; (numbers 13–19) números de trece a diecinueve *m pl*
teethe [tið] VI **the baby is teething** al bebé le están saliendo los dientes
teetotaler [títódlɚ] N abstemio -mia *mf*
telecast [téləkæst] N teledifusión *f*
telecommunications [tɛlɪkəmjunɪkéʃənz] N telecomunicaciones *f pl*
teleconference [télɪkɑnfɚəns] N teleconferencia *f*
telegram [téləgræm] N telegrama *m*
telegraph [téləgræf] N telégrafo *m*; VI/VT telegrafiar
telegraphic [tɛləgrǽfɪk] ADJ telegráfico
telemarketing [tɛləmárkɪdɪŋ] N telemercadeo *m*, telemarketing *m*
telepathy [təlépəθi] N telepatía *f*
telephone [téləfon] N teléfono *m*; **— book** guía telefónica *f*; **— booth** cabina telefónica *f*; **— number** número telefónico *m*; **— operator** telefonista *mf*; **— receiver** auricular *m*, tubo de teléfono *m*; VI/VT telefonear, llamar por teléfono
telescope [téləskop] N telescopio *m*; VI plegarse
television [téləvɪʒən] N (medium) televisión *f*; (device) televisor *m*; **— viewer** televidente *mf*
tell [tɛl] VI/VT (the truth) decir; (a story) contar; **to — apart** distinguir; **to — on someone** acusar a alguien; **to — someone off** regañar a alguien; **to — time** decir la hora; **I can't — if he's old or young** no sé si es viejo o joven; **his age is beginning to —** se le comienza a notar la edad; **a —tale sign** una señal reveladora; **he is a —tale** es un acusica
teller [télɚ] N (narrator) narrador -ora *mf*; (in a bank) cajero -ra *mf*
temerity [təmérɪdi] N temeridad *f*
temper [témpɚ] N (hardness) temple *m*; (bad humor) mal genio *m*; VT templar; **to keep one's —** mantener la calma; **to lose one's —** perder los estribos, encolerizarse
temperament [témpɚəmənt] N temperamento *m*, genio *m*, talante *m*
temperance [témpɚəns] N (moderation) templanza *f*, temperancia *f*; (abstinence from alcohol) abstinencia de bebidas alcohólicas *f*
temperate [témpɚɪt] ADJ (weather) templado; (opinions, habits) moderado

temperature [témpə-ətʃur] N temperatura f; **to have a —** tener fiebre

tempest [témpɪst] N tempestad f

tempestuous [tempéstʃuəs] ADJ tempestuoso

temple [témpəł] N (church) templo m; (side of the forehead) sien f

temporal [témpə-əł] ADJ temporal

temporary [témpə-reɹi] ADJ temporal, provisional

tempt [tempt] VT tentar

temptation [temptéʃən] N tentación f

tempting [témptɪŋ] ADJ tentador

ten [ten] NUM diez

tenacious [tənéʃəs] ADJ tenaz

tenacity [tənǽsɪDi] N tenacidad f

tenant [ténənt] N inquilino -na mf, arrendatario -ria mf

tend [tend] VT (care for) cuidar; **to — to** ocuparse de; VI (lean toward) tender, inclinarse

tendency [téndənsi] N tendencia f

tender [téndə-] ADJ tierno; (painful) sensible; N (offer) oferta f; (legal currency) curso legal m; (person who tends) cuidador -ra mf, vigilante mf; VT presentar, ofrecer

tenderness [téndə-nɪs] N (of feeling) ternura f; (of meat) terneza f, ternura f; (sensitivity to pain) sensibilidad f

tendon [téndən] N tendón m

tendonitis [tendənáɪDɪs] N tendinitis f

tendril [téndrəł] N zarcillo m

tenement [ténəmənt] N casa de vecindad f

tenet [ténɪt] N principio m

tennis [ténɪs] N tenis m; **— court** cancha de tenis f, pista de tenis f; **— player** tenista mf; **— shoes** tenis m pl

tenor [ténə-] N tenor m

tense [tens] ADJ tenso; N tiempo m

tension [ténʃən] N tensión f; (tautness) tirantez f

tent [tent] N tienda de campaña f; (circus) carpa f; VI acampar

tentacle [téntəkəł] N tentáculo m

tentative [téntəDɪv] ADJ tentativo

tenth [tenθ] ADJ & N décimo m

tenuous [ténjuəs] ADJ (light, color, cloth) tenue; (peace) frágil; (rarefied) enrarecido

tenure [ténjə-] N (of professorship) titularidad f; (of an office) ocupación f

tepid [tépɪd] ADJ tibio

terabyte [térəbaɪt] N terabyte m

term [tɜ-m] N (word, mathematical expression) término m; (period) período m; (time in office) mandato m; (semester) semestre m; (trimester) trimestre m; (set date for payment) plazo m; **— paper** trabajo final m; **—s** condiciones f pl; **at —**

a término; **to be on good —s** estar en buenas relaciones; **not to be on speaking —s** no hablarse; **to come to —s** aceptar; VT denominar

terminal [tɜ-mənəł] ADJ terminal; N (of airport, computer) terminal mf; (electric) terminal m

terminate [tɜ-mənet] VI/VT terminar(se)

termination [tɜ-mənéʃən] N terminación f; (of an employee) despido m

terminology [tɜ-rmənálədʒi] N terminología f

termite [tɜ-maɪt] N termita f

terrace [térɪs] N terraza f, escalón m; VT poner terrazas en, escalonar

terrain [tərén] N terreno m

terrestrial [təréstriəł] ADJ terrestre

terrible [térəbəł] ADJ terrible, tremendo

terrier [tériə-] N terrier m

terrific [tərífɪk] ADJ estupendo

terrify [térəfaɪ] VT aterrar, aterrorizar, espeluznar

territory [térɪtɔri] N territorio m

terror [térə-] N terror m

terrorism [térə-ɪzəm] N terrorismo m

terrorist [térə-ɪst] N terrorista mf

terse [tɜ-s] ADJ lacónico

test [test] N (trial, experiment) prueba f; (of intelligence, multiple choice) test m; (examination) examen m, prueba f; **to —-drive** probar; **— pilot** piloto de pruebas m; **— tube** tubo de ensayo m, probeta f; **—-tube baby** bebé de probeta mf; **to undergo a —** someterse a una prueba; **to take a —** dar un examen; **to give a —** poner un examen; **to put to the —** poner a prueba; VT (try) probar, poner a prueba; (give an exam) poner una prueba, examinar; VI **girls — better than boys** en los exámenes salen mejor las niñas que los niños

testament [téstəmənt] N testamento m; (testimony) testimonio m

testicle [téstɪkəł] N testículo m

testify [téstəfaɪ] VI testificar; (confirm) dar fe

testimony [téstəmoni] N testimonio m

testosterone [testástəron] N testosterona f

tetanus [tétɲəs] N tétano(s) m

Teutonic [tutánɪk] ADJ teutónico

text [tekst] N texto m; **—book** libro de texto m; **— editor** editor de texto(s) m

textile [tékstaɪł] ADJ textil; N textil m, tejido m; **— mill** fábrica de tejidos f

texture [tékstʃə-] N textura f

Thai [taɪ] ADJ & N tailandés -esa mf

Thailand [táɪlænd] N Tailandia f

Thailander [táɪlændə-] ADJ & N tailandés

-esa *mf*

than [ðæn] CONJ que; **I have more — you** tengo más que tú; **more — once** más de una vez

thank [θæŋk] VT dar las gracias, agradecer; **to have oneself to — for** tener la culpa de; INTERJ **— heaven!** ¡gracias a Dios! **— you** gracias; N **—s** gracias *f pl*

thankful [θæŋkfəl] ADJ agradecido

thankfulness [θæŋkfəlnɪs] N gratitud *f*, agradecimiento *m*

thankless [θæŋklɪs] ADJ ingrato

thanksgiving [θæŋksgɪvɪŋ] N acción de gracias *f*; **— Day** día de acción de gracias *m*

that [ðæt] ADJ (something nearer the speaker) ese, esa; (something more remote from speaker) aquel, aquella; **— dog** ese/aquel perro *m*; **— one** (nearer) ese, esa; DEMON PRON (nearer to speaker) ese, esa; (more remote from speaker) aquel, aquella; (neuter) eso, aquello; **— is my daughter** esa/aquella es mi hija; **— was a nightmare** eso/aquello fue una pesadilla; REL PRON que; **the bike — disappeared** la bici que desapareció; **the pen — I was writing with** la lapicera con la que/cual escribía; **— is** es decir; CONJ que; **she said — she would come** dijo que vendría; ADV tan; **it's not — far** no queda tan lejos; **— much** tanto; **she was — tall** era así de alta

thatch [θætʃ] N paja *f*; *Am* quincha *f*; VT techar con paja; *Am* quinchar; **—ed roof** techo de paja *m*; *Am* quincha *f*

thaw [θɔ] VI/VT (food) descongelar(se); (ice and snow) derretir(se); (relations, refrigerator) deshelar(se); N deshielo *m*

the [ðə, ði] DEF ART (singular) el *m*, la *f*; **— boy** el chico *m*; (plural) los *m*, las *f*; **— girls** las chicas *f pl*; **— good thing** lo bueno; ADV **— more I work, — less I accomplish** cuanto más trabajo, menos consigo

theater [θíɑðə] N teatro *m*

theatrical [θiǽtrɪkəl] ADJ teatral

theft [θɛft] N hurto *m*, robo *m*

their [ðɛr] POSS ADJ **this is — dog** este es su perro, este es el perro de ellos

theirs [ðɛrz] PRON **this book is —** este libro es suyo, este libro es de ellos/ellas; **these things are —** estas cosas son suyas/de ellos/de ellas; **— is bigger** el suyo/la suya/el de ellos/la de ellos es más grande; **a friend of —** un amigo suyo, un amigo de ellos

them [ðɛm] PRON los *m pl*, las *f pl*; **I see —** los/las veo; **I talk to —** les hablo a ellos; **I went with —** fui con ellos/ellas

thematic [θɪmǽdɪk] ADJ temático

theme [θim] N tema *m*; (essay) ensayo *m*, redacción *f*; **— park** parque temático *m*; **— song** tema *m*

themselves [ðɛmsɛ́lvz] PRON **they — built their house** ellos mismos se construyeron la casa; **they are not — today** hoy no son los mismos de siempre; **they were sitting by —** estaban sentados solos; **they looked at — in the mirror** se miraron en el espejo; **they talk to —** hablan solos; **they bought — a yacht** se compraron un yate

then [ðɛn] ADV (at that time) entonces, en aquel tiempo; **it was cheaper —** era más barato en aquel tiempo; (after) luego, después; **from — on** a partir de entonces; **now and —** de vez en cuando; **until —** hasta entonces; **I ate, — I paid** comí, luego pagué; ADJ entonces; **the — president** el entonces presidente; CONJ entonces; **if not, — you should stay** si no, entonces deberías quedarte; **now —** ahora bien; **are you sorry —?** ¿estás arrepentido pues?

theology [θiáləʤi] N teología *f*

theoretical [θiɑrɛ́dɪkəl] ADJ teórico

theory [θíɑri] N teoría *f*

therapeutic [θɛrɑpjúdɪk] ADJ terapéutico

therapist [θɛ́rɑpɪst] N terapeuta *mf*; (psychologist) psicólogo -ga *mf*

therapy [θɛ́rɑpi] N terapia *f*

there [ðɛr] ADV ahí; *Am* allí; (more remote) allá; *Sp* allí; **—abouts** por ahí, más o menos; **—after** (after) después; (subsequently) de allí en adelante; **—by** así, de ese modo; **— ensued a war** a continuación hubo una guerra; **—fore** por consiguiente, por lo tanto; **—in** en eso, allí; **— is, — are** hay; **— goes the bus** ahí va el autobús; **— —** bueno, bueno; **—of** de eso; **—on** (on that) encima; (after) luego, después; **—upon** (after) luego, después; (for this reason) por consiguiente; (upon that) encima; **—with** (with that) con eso; (after that) luego, en seguida; **who's —?** ¿quién es? **is Mary —?** ¿está María? **we got — at 5** llegamos a las 5

thermal [θɚ́məl] ADJ termal; **— energy** energía térmica *f*

thermodynamic [θɚmodainǽmɪk] ADJ termodinámico

thermometer [θɚmámɪdɚ] N termómetro *m*

thermonuclear [θɚmonúkliɚ] ADJ termonuclear

thermos [θɝ́məs] N termo *m*

thermostat [θɝ́məstæt] N termostato *m*

thesaurus [θɪsɔ́rəs] N (synonym dictionary) diccionario de sinónimos *m*; (large dictionary) diccionario *m*

these [ðiz] ADJ & PRON estos, estas

thesis [θísɪs] N tesis *f*

they [ðe] PRON ellos, ellas

thick [θɪk] ADJ (slice) grueso; (fog, soup) espeso; (accent) marcado; (wit) torpe; **one inch —** una pulgada de espesor; **— as thieves** como carne y uña; ADV **—-headed** estúpido; **—-set** grueso; **—-skinned** insensible; N **the — of the fight** lo más reñido de la pelea; **through — and thin** pase lo que pase

thicken [θíkən] VI/VT espesar(se), trabar(se); **the plot —s** la trama se complica

thicket [θíkɪt] N soto *m*, matorral *m*, boscaje *m*

thickness [θíknɪs] N (of paper, wood) espesor *m*, grosor *m*; (of soup) lo espeso; (of lips) lo grueso; (of a beard) lo tupido; (of hair) lo abundante

thief [θif] N ladrón -ona *mf*

thieve [θiv] VI/VT hurtar, robar

thigh [θaɪ] N muslo *m*

thimble [θímbəl] N dedal *m*

thin [θɪn] ADJ (ice, wire) delgado, fino; (person) flaco; (vegetation, beard, hair) ralo; (voice) tenue, fino; (air) enrarecido; (excuse) débil; (soup) aguado; VI/VT (paint, soup, sauce) diluir; (hair) entresacar; **to — out** (hair) ralear; (crowd) dispersarse

thing [θɪŋ] N cosa *f*; **there's no such —** eso no existe; **that is the — to do** eso es lo que hay que hacer; **the — about Mary** lo que pasa con María

thingamajig [θíŋəmədʒɪg] N chisme *m*, coso *m*

think [θɪŋk] VI/VT (reason) pensar, razonar; (believe) creer, opinar; **to — about** pensar en; **to — back** recordar; **to — it over / through** pensarlo bien, reflexionar sobre; **I'm —ing of you** pienso en ti; **what do you — of Mary?** ¿qué piensas de María? **I thought of a plan** se me ocurrió un plan; **to — up an excuse** inventar / elucubrar una excusa; **I don't — so** no creo; **who does he — he is?** ¿quién se cree que es? **to — well of** tener buena opinión de; **she —s nothing of spending $1000** no le importa nada gastar $1000; **to my way of —ing** a mi parecer

thinner [θínɚ] N disolvente *m*

thinness [θínnɪs] N (of ice, person) delgadez

f, flacura *f*; (of hair) escasez *f*; (of air) enrarecimiento *m*; (of soup) fluidez *f*

third [θɝd] ADJ tercer(o); **— chapter** capítulo tercero *m*, tercer capítulo *m*; ADV tercero; N tercio *m*; (gear, musical interval) tercera *f*; **— person** tercera persona *f*; **—-rate** de poca categoría; **— World** Tercer Mundo *m*; **the — of March** el tres de marzo

thirst [θɝst] N sed *f*; VI tener sed; **to — for** tener sed de, estar sediento de

thirsty [θɝ́sti] ADJ sediento; **to be —** tener sed

thirteen [θɝtín] NUM trece

thirty [θɝ́di] NUM treinta

this [ðɪs] ADJ & PRON este *m*, esta *f*, esto (neuter); **— dog** este perro; **— is a disaster** esto es un desastre

thistle [θísəl] N cardo *m*

thong [θɔŋ] N (strip of leather) correa *f*; (garment) tanga *mf*; (shoe) chancleta *f*

thorax [θɔ́ræks] N tórax *m*

thorn [θɔrn] N (sharp growth) espina *f*; (plant) espino *m*

thorny [θɔ́rni] ADJ espinoso, escabroso

thorough [θɝ́o] ADJ (exhaustive) exhaustivo, minucioso, detenido; (conscientious) concienzudo

thoroughbred [θɝ́əbred] ADJ de pura sangre; N purasangre *m*

those [ðoz] ADJ & PRON (nearer) esos *m*, esas *f*; PRON (more remote) aquellos *m*, aquellas *f*; **— of you** los de vosotros / ustedes; **— that / who** los / las que

though [ðo] CONJ aunque; **as —** como si; ADV sin embargo

thought [θɔt] N (act, product of thinking) pensamiento *m*; (idea) idea *f*; (opinion) opinión *f*; (concern) consideración *f*; **to be lost in —** estar abstraído; **to give it no —** no darle importancia; **the very —** la mera idea; **at the — of** ante la idea de; **on second —** pensándolo bien; **my —s are with you** te acompaño en el sentimiento

thoughtful [θɔ́tfəl] ADJ (considerate) considerado, atento; (well thought out) bien pensado; (reflective) pensativo, reflexivo

thoughtfulness [θɔ́tfəlnɪs] N consideración *f*

thoughtless [θɔ́tlɪs] ADJ (inconsiderate) desconsiderado; (careless) descuidado; (not reflective) irreflexivo

thoughtlessness [θɔ́tlɪsnɪs] N (lack of consideration) desconsideración *f*; (carelessness) descuido *m*; (lack of reflection) falta de reflexión *f*

thousand [θáʊzənd] NUM mil

thrash [θræʃ] VI/VT (whip, defeat) zurrar, vapulear, apalear; (thresh) trillar, desgranar; **to — around** revolverse, agitarse; **to — out a matter** ventilar un asunto

thread [θred] N hilo m; (on a screw) rosca f; **—bare** raído; VT (a needle) enhebrar; (beads) ensartar; (a screw) enroscar; **to — one's way** abrirse paso

threat [θret] N amenaza f

threaten [θrétn] VI/VT amenazar

threatening [θrétnɪŋ] ADJ amenazador

three [θri] NUM tres; **—-dimensional** tridimensional

thresh [θreʃ] VT trillar

threshold [θréʃhoɫd] N umbral m

thrift [θrɪft] N economía f

thrifty [θrífti] ADJ económico, ahorrativo

thrill [θrɪɫ] VI/VT emocionar(se), ilusionar(se); N emoción f, ilusión f

thrive [θraɪv] VI prosperar; (plants) florecer

throat [θrot] N garganta f

throb [θrɑb] VI latir, palpitar; N latido m, palpitación f

throes [θroz] ADV LOC **in the — of war** en plena guerra; **in the — of death** agonizando

throne [θron] N trono m

throng [θrɔŋ] N muchedumbre f, turbamulta f; VI apiñarse, llegar en tropel

throttle [θrɑ́dɫ] N (of a motor) válvula reguladora/de aceleración f, regulador m; (of a motorcycle) puño giratorio del gas m; **— lever** palanca del regulador f; VT ahogar, estrangular

through [θru] PREP por, a través de; (as intermediary) por medio de; **Monday — Friday** de lunes a viernes; **all — the night** toda la noche; ADV (completely) de un lado a otro; (from beginning to end) de principio a fin, de cabo a rabo; **loyal — and —** leal a toda prueba; **an aristocrat — and —** un aristócrata de pura cepa; **to carry —** llevar a cabo; ADJ (ticket, train) directo; **to be —** (with a task) haber terminado; (in a profession) estar acabado; **we're —!** (with a boyfriend) ¡se acabó entre nosotros!

throughout [θruáʊt] PREP (all through) por todo; (during) a lo largo de, durante; ADV (duration) de principio a fin; (space) por todas partes

throw [θro] VI/VT (a ball) tirar, lanzar; (a light, voice) arrojar; (a switch) conectar; (a pot on a wheel) modelar en un torno; (a punch) lanzar; (a wrestler) tumbar; (a game for a bribe) dejarse perder; (a rider) desmontar; (a party) dar, organizar; **that really threw me** eso me confundió; **to — away** (dispose of) tirar, arrojar; (squander) malgastar; **to — down** tirar al suelo; **to — in** añadir; **to — into gear** engranar; **to — in the clutch** embragar; **to — out** (garbage) tirar, arrojar; (unruly guest) echar; **to — up** vomitar, devolver; N (act or instance of throwing) tiro m; (of dice) tirada f; (shawl) chal m; (blanket) manta f

thrush [θrʌʃ] N tordo m, zorzal m

thrust [θrʌst] VT (stab) clavar; (shove) empujar; **to — oneself upon** meterse en; **to — a task upon someone** imponerle una tarea a alguien; **to — aside** echar a un lado; **to — someone through** atravesar a alguien; VI (push) dar un empujón; (stab at) lanzar una estocada; (push through) empujar para pasar; N (stab) estocada f; (force of a jet engine) empuje m; (shove) empujón m; (military assault) arremetida f, acometida f

thud [θʌd] N golpe sordo m; VI caer con un golpe sordo

thug [θʌg] N matón m

thumb [θʌm] N pulgar m; **under the — of** bajo la bota de; VT hojear; **to give the —s up** aprobar; **—tack** chinche f, tachuela f

thump [θʌmp] N golpe sordo m; VI hacer un ruido sordo

thunder [θʌ́ndɚ] N trueno m; VI tronar; **—bolt** rayo m; **—head** nubarrón m; **—storm** tormenta eléctrica f, tronada f

thunderous [θʌ́ndɚəs] ADJ atronador, estruendoso

Thursday [θɝ́zde] N jueves m

thus [ðʌs] ADV así; **— far** (space) hasta aquí; (time) hasta ahora

thwart [θwɔrt] VT frustrar

thyme [taɪm] N tomillo m

thyroid [θáɪrɔɪd] N tiroides m sg

Tibet [tɪbét] N Tíbet m

Tibetan [tɪbétn] ADJ & N tibetano -na mf

tic [tɪk] N tic m, manía f

tick [tɪk] N (sound of a clock) tic tac m; (cover of a pillow) funda f; (check mark) marca f; (insect) garrapata f; VI hacer tic tac; **to — off** (check off) marcar; (anger) enojar

ticket [tíkɪt] N billete m; Am boleto m; (slate of candidates) candidatura f; (summons) multa f; (tag) etiqueta f; **— office** taquilla f; VT (give passage) vender billetes; (give summons) multar

tickle [tíkl] VT (poke) cosquillear, hacer cosquillas; (amuse) dar ilusión; VI picar; N picazón f, cosquilleo m

ticklish [tíklɪʃ] ADJ (prone to tickles) cosquilloso; (delicate) delicado

tidal [táɪdl] ADJ **— wave** (tsunami) maremoto m; (large wave) marejada f

tidbit [tídbɪt] N (snack) golosina f; (gossip) chisme jugoso m

tide [taɪd] N marea f; (of opinion) corriente f; **—water** (water) agua de marea f; (land) marisma f; VT **to — over** cubrir

tidy [táɪdi] ADJ (orderly) ordenado; (large) considerable; VI/VT arreglar; **to — oneself up** arreglarse

tie [taɪ] VI (fasten) atarse; (make same score) empatar; VT (fasten) atar; (make a knot) hacer un nudo; (make same score as) empatar con; **to — in** cuadrar; **to — one on** emborracharse; **to — tight** atar fuerte; **to — up** (bind) atar; (hinder) bloquear; (occupy) ocupar; (moor a ship) amarrar; N (cord) cuerda f; (relations) lazo m, vínculo m; (cravat) corbata f; (score) empate m; (railway) durmiente m, traviesa f

tier [tir] N nivel m

tiger [táɪgə] N tigre m

tight [taɪt] ADJ (knot, nut) apretado, ajustado; (clothes) ceñido, ajustado; (control) firme, estricto; (race) reñido; (stingy) tacaño, mezquino; (drunk) borracho; **—fisted** agarrado; **—rope** cuerda floja f; **—wad** tacaño -ña mf; **to be in a — spot** estar en un aprieto; **—ly** bien, herméticamente; **to hold on —** agarrarse bien

tighten [táɪtn] VI/VT (knot, nut, belt) apretar(se); (control) estrechar(se)

tightness [táɪtnɪs] N estrechez f; (stinginess) tacañería f

tile [taɪl] N (on a roof) teja f; (on a floor) baldosa f; (on a wall) azulejo m; **— roof** tejado m; VT (roof) tejar; (floor) embaldosar; (wall) azulejar

till [tɪl] PREP hasta; CONJ hasta que; VI/VT labrar, arar; N caja f

tilt [tɪlt] VI/VT ladear(se), inclinar(se); N (act or instance of tilting) ladeo m, inclinación f; (incline) declive m; (joust) justa f; **at full —** a toda velocidad

timber [tímbə] N (cut wood) madera (de construcción) f; (trees) árboles para madera m pl; (beam) viga f; **—line** límite de la vegetación arbórea m; **— wolf** lobo gris m

timbre [tímbə] N timbre m

time [taɪm] N (past, present, future) tiempo

m; (hour) hora f; (occasion) vez f; (period) período m, momento m, época f; **— bomb** bomba de tiempo f; **—keeper** cronometrador -ra mf; **— out** descanso m; **—piece** reloj m; **— signature** compás m; **—table** horario m; **— zone** huso horario m; **at —s** a veces; **at the same —** a la vez, al mismo tiempo; **at this —** en este momento; **behind —** atrasado; **lunch—** hora del almuerzo f; **from — to —** de vez en cuando; **for the — being** por el momento; **in —** a tiempo; **in no —** en seguida; **it's about —** ya era hora; **on —** puntual; **to buy on —** comprar a plazo; **— after —** una vez tras otra; **to do —** cumplir una condena; **to have a good — **divertirse; **what — is it?** ¿qué hora es? VT (a race) cronometrar; (a test) fijar la duración de; (one's arrival) fijar la hora de; **to — an attack well** atacar en el momento oportuno

timeless [táɪmlɪs] ADJ eterno

timely [táɪmli] ADJ oportuno

timer [táɪmə] N (person) cronometrador -ra mf; (device) reloj m

timid [tímɪd] ADJ tímido, apocado

timidity [tɪmídɪdi] N timidez f, apocamiento m

timing [táɪmɪŋ] N (measurement) cronometraje m; (synchronization) sincronización f; **that was good —** lo hiciste en el momento oportuno

timorous [tíməəs] ADJ timorato

tin [tɪn] N (metal) estaño m; (tin plate) hojalata f; **— can** lata f; **— foil** papel de estaño m, papel de aluminio m; VT estañar

tincture [tíŋktʃə] N tintura f

tinder [tíndə] N yesca f

tinge [tɪndʒ] VT (tint) teñir; (hint) matizar; N (of color) tinte m, matiz m; (of taste) dejo m; (of irony) matiz m

tingle [tíŋgəl] VI sentir hormigueo, hormiguear; **to — with excitement** estremecerse de entusiasmo; N hormigueo m

tinker [tíŋkə] VI ocuparse, entretenerse; **to — with** toquetear, hacer ajustes

tinkle [tíŋkəl] VT (ring lightly) tintinear; (urinate) hacer pipí; N tintineo m

tinsel [tínsəl] N (Christmas trim) espumillón m, guirnalda f; (tawdry decoration) oropel m

tint [tɪnt] N (hue) matiz m; (for hair) tinte m, tintura f; (for glass) coloreado m; VT (hair) teñir; (glasses) colorear

tiny [táɪni] ADJ diminuto, chiquito

tip [tɪp] N (point) punta f; (gratuity) propina

f; (piece of advice) consejo *m*; VI/VT (tilt) inclinar(se), ladear(se); (give a gratuity) dar propina (a); **to — a person off** advertir a alguien; **to — one's hat** sacarse / quitarse el sombrero; **to — over** volcar(se)

tipsy [típsi] ADJ alegre

tiptoe [típto] N punta del pie *f*; **on —s** de puntillas; VI andar de puntillas

tirade [táired] N diatriba *f*

tire [tair] N neumático *m*, cubierta *f*; *Mex* llanta *f*; *Am* goma *f*; VI/VT cansar(se), fatigar(se); **to — out** cansar, fatigar; ADJ **—d** cansado, fatigado; **—d out** cansado, fatigado

tireless [táirlɪs] ADJ incansable

tiresome [táirsəm] ADJ aburrido, pesado, plasta *inv*

tissue [tíʃu] N (cell aggregate) tejido *m*; (handkerchief) pañuelo de papel *m*; **— paper** papel tisú *m*

tit [tɪt] N (bird) paro *m*

titanic [taɪtǽnɪk] ADJ titánico

titanium [taɪténiəm] N titanio *m*

tithe [taɪð] N diezmo *m*; VI pagar el diezmo

titillate [tídlet] VT excitar; (interest) despertar interés

title [táidl] N título *m*; (of a picture) rótulo *m*; **— deed** título de propiedad *m*; **— page** portada *f*

TNT [tientí] N TNT *m*

to [tu] PREP **I gave it — you** te lo di a ti; **to count — ten** contar hasta diez; **I called — find out** llamé para averiguar; **— my surprise** para mi sorpresa; **a quarter — five** las cinco menos cuarto; **bills — be paid** cuentas por pagar; **things — do** cosas que hacer; **frightened — death** muerto de susto; **from house — house** de casa en casa; ADV **— and fro** de acá para allá; **to come —** volver en sí

toad [tod] N sapo *m*; **—stool** seta *f*, hongo no comestible *m*

toast [tost] VI/VT (brown) tostar(se); VT (congratulate) brindar por; (congratulation) brindis *m*

toaster [tóstɚ] N tostadora *f*; **— oven** horno tostador *m*

tobacco [təbǽko] N tabaco *m*

today [tədé] ADV hoy; (nowadays) hoy día

toddler [tádlɚ] N niño -ña pequeño -ña *mf*

toe [to] N dedo del pie *m*; (of shoe, sock) punta *f*; **—nail** uña del dedo del pie *f*; VT (touch with toe) tocar con el dedo del pie; **to — the line** hacer buena letra, entrar en vereda

together [təgéðɚ] ADV (in union) juntos; (at the same time) al mismo tiempo; **— with**

junto con; **all —** todos juntos

Togo [tógo] N Togo *m*

Togolese [togalíz] ADJ & N togolés -esa *mf*

toil [tɔɪl] N esfuerzo *m*, trabajo *m*; VI trabajar, esforzarse, bregar

toilet [tɔ́ɪlɪt] N (bowl) inodoro *m*; (lavatory) aseo *m*, lavabo *m*; **— paper** papel higiénico *m*; **—-trained** que ya no usa pañales

token [tókən] N (symbol) señal *f*; (keepsake) recuerdo *m*; (coinlike metal piece) ficha *f*; **— payment** pago nominal *m*; **as a — of friendship** en prenda de amistad

tolerance [tálərəns] N tolerancia *f*

tolerant [tálərənt] ADJ tolerante

tolerate [táləret] VT tolerar

toll [tol] N (of bells) tañido *m*; (payment) peaje *m*; (charges) tarifa *f*; (of victims) balance *m*; **— bridge** puente de peaje *m*; **— road** carretera de peaje *f*; VI/VT tañer (a muerto)

tomato [təméɖo] N tomate *m*

tomb [tum] N tumba *f*, sepulcro *m*, sepultura *f*; **—stone** lápida *f*

tomcat [támkæt] N gato macho *m*

tomorrow [təmɔ́ro] ADV & N mañana *f*; **— morning** mañana por la mañana *f*

ton [tʌn] N tonelada *f*

tone [ton] N (pitch) tono *m*; (of a speech) tono *m*, tónica *f*; VI **to — down** moderar, matizar

toner [tónɚ] N tóner *m*

Tonga [táŋgə] N Tonga *m*

Tongan [táŋgən] ADJ & N tongano -na *mf*

tongs [tɔŋz] N tenazas *f pl*

tongue [tʌŋ] N (body part, language, of a flame) lengua *f*; (of a shoe) lengüeta *f*; **to —-lash** reprender; **to be —-tied** tener trabada la lengua; **on the tip of my —** en la punta de la lengua; **to hold one's — **callarse la boca; **— in cheek** irónicamente; **— twister** trabalenguas *m sg*; VI tocar con la lengua

tonic [tánɪk] ADJ tónico; N (medicine) tónico *m*; (water, key note) tónica *f*; **— water** agua tónica *f*

tonight [tənáɪt] ADV esta noche

tonsil [tánsəl] N amígdala *f*

tonsillitis [tansəláɪdɪs] N amigdalitis *f*, anginas *f pl*

too [tu] ADV (in addition) también; (excessively) demasiado; **— bad!** ¡qué lástima! **— many** demasiados; **— much** demasiado

tool [tuɫ] N herramienta *f*; **—box** caja de herramientas *f*; **—shed** cobertizo para herramientas *m*

toot [tut] VI/VT (horn) sonar; (whistle) pitar; (trumpet) tocar; **to — one's own horn** darse autobombo; N (of horn, trumpet) toque *m*; (of horn) bocinazo *m*; (of whistle) pitido *m*

tooth [tuθ] N (front) diente *m*; (back) muela *f*; **—ache** dolor de muelas *m*; **—brush** cepillo de dientes *m*; **— decay** caries (dental) *f sg*; **— fairy** ratoncito Pérez *m*; **— mark** dentellada *f*; **—paste** pasta dental *f*, pasta dentífrica *f*; **—pick** mondadientes *m*, palillo de dientes *m*; **to fight — and nail** luchar a brazo partido; **to have a sweet —** ser goloso

toothed [tuθt] ADJ dentado

toothless [túθlɪs] ADJ desdentado

top [tɑp] N (of a mountain) cumbre *f*, cima *f*; (of a page) parte superior *f*; (of a jar) tapa *f*; (of a convertible) capota *f*; (of a table) superficie *f*; (of a tree) copa *f*; (toy) trompo *m*, peonza *f*; (blouse) blusa *f*; **he's at the — of his class** es el mejor de su clase; **at the — of one's voice** a voz en cuello; **filled up to the —** lleno hasta el tope; **from — to bottom** de arriba abajo; **on — of** encima de; ADJ (officer, floor) superior; (shelf, step) más alto; **—coat** abrigo *m*; **to be — dog** ir a la cabeza; **— dollar** precio exorbitante *m*; **— hat** sombrero de copa *m*; **—flight** de primera; **—heavy** desbalanceado; **—most** superior; **—notch** de primera; **at — speed** a velocidad máxima; VT (a tree) desmochar; (a list) encabezar; (a performance) superar; (a level) exceder; **to — off** (an action) rematar; (a tank) llenar hasta el tope; **that —s everything!** ¡eso es el colmo!

topaz [tópæz] N topacio *m*

topic [tápɪk] N tema *m*, materia *f*

topical [tápɪkəl] ADJ (of medicine) tópico; (current) de actualidad

topless [táplɪs] ADJ topless; **— swimsuit** monokini *m*

topple [tápəl] VT (knock over) derribar; (overthrow) derrocar; VI (fall) volcarse; (lose power) caer; **to — over** volcarse

topsy-turvy [tápsɪtə́·vi] ADJ & ADV patas arriba

torch [tɔrtʃ] N antorcha *f*

torment [tɔ́rment] N tormento *m*; [tɔrmént] VT atormentar, martirizar

tornado [tɔrnédo] N tornado *m*

torpedo [tɔrpído] N torpedo *m*; **— boat** torpedero *m*; VT torpedear

torpor [tɔ́rpə] N letargo *m*, torpor *m*

torque [tɔrk] N par de torsión *m*

torrent [tɔ́rənt] N torrente *m*

torrential [tɔrénʃəl] ADJ torrencial

torrid [tɔ́rɪd] ADJ tórrido

torsion [tɔ́rʃən] N torsión *f*

torso [tɔ́rso] N torso *m*, tronco *m*

tortoise [tɔ́rtɪs] N tortuga *f*

tortuous [tɔ́rtʃuəs] ADJ tortuoso

torture [tɔ́rtʃə] N tortura *f*; VT torturar

torturous [tɔ́rtʃə·əs] ADJ torturante, torturador

toss [tɔs] VT (a ball, coin) tirar; (one's head) echar; (a salad) revolver; **to — aside** echar a un lado; VI (waves) cabecear; (in bed) dar vueltas; N (of coin, ball) tiro *m*; (of head) sacudida *f*

total [tódl] ADJ & N total *m*; **— amount** importe total *m*, montante *m*

totalitarian [totælɪtériən] ADJ totalitario

totter [tádə] VI tambalear(se), titubear

touch [tʌtʃ] VI/VT tocar; (move deeply) conmover, enternecer; (compare with) compararse con, igualar; (affect) afectar; **to — down** aterrizar; **to — off** provocar; **to — up** retocar; **to — upon** mencionar; N (contact) contacto *m*, roce *m*, toque *m*; (sense) tacto *m*; (knack) mano *f*; (slight amount) poquito *m*; **—-and-go** precario; **a woman's —** un toque femenino; **—screen** pantalla táctil *f*; **—stone** piedra de toque *f*; **—-tone** de botones; **finishing —** toque final *m*; **to keep in — with** mantener(se) en contacto con

touching [tʌ́tʃɪŋ] ADJ conmovedor

touchy [tʌ́tʃi] ADJ hipersensible

tough [tʌf] ADJ (leather) fuerte, resistente; (fighter) duro, fuerte; (steak) duro, correoso; (situation) difícil; (neighborhood) bravo

toughen [tʌ́fən] VI/VT (leather) curtir(se); (meat) endurecer(se); (person) endurecerse

toughness [tʌ́fnɪs] N (of a fighter, steak) dureza *f*; (of a situation) dificultad *f*; (of a neighborhood) lo bravo

toupee [tupé] N peluquín *m*

tour [tur] N (professional, artistic) gira *f*; (touristic) tour *m*, excursión *f*; (of a building) visita *f*; VI/VT (artistic, political) hacer una gira (por); (touristic) hacer un tour

tourism [túrɪzəm] N turismo *m*

tourist [túrɪst] N turista *mf*; **— class** clase turista / turística *f*

tournament [tə́·nəmənt] N torneo *m*

tourniquet [tə́·nɪkɪt] N torniquete *m*

tow [to] VT remolcar; N (pull) remolque *m*; (fiber) estopa *f*; **—rope** cuerda de remolque *f*; — **truck** remolque *m*, grúa *f*; **in** — a cuestas

toward, towards [təwɔ́rd(z)] PREP (in the direction of) hacia; (for) para; — **four o'clock** a eso de las cuatro; **to feel angry** — estar enojado con

towel [táuəł] N toalla *f*

tower [táuə] N torre *f*; VI elevarse; **to** — **over** dominar, descollar

towering [táuə-ɪŋ] ADJ (tall) elevado, muy alto; (excessive) desmedido

town [taun] N (large) ciudad *f*; (small) pueblo *m*, localidad *f*; (downtown) centro *m*; — **hall** ayuntamiento *m*, municipio *m*; **out of** — de viaje

toxic [táksɪk] ADJ tóxico

toxin [táksɪn] N toxina *f*

toy [tɔɪ] N juguete *m*; — **poodle** caniche enano *m*; VI **to** — **with** (fiddle with) juguetear con; (consider) considerar

trace [tres] N (path, mark, footprint) huella *f*; (mark) rastro *m*, traza *f*; (vestige) vestigio *m*; (strap) tirante *m*; VT (a plan) trazar; (history) examinar; (an image) calcar; (a criminal) rastrear

trachea [trékiə] N tráquea *f*

track [træk] N (of a heel, animal) huella *f*; (of a wheel) rodada *f*; (for racing) pista *f*; (path) senda *f*, sendero *m*; (of a railroad) vía *f*; (on a record) surco *m*; (of study) orientación *f*; — **and field** atletismo *m*; — **meet** encuentro de atletismo *m*; **to be off the** — estar descarrilado; **to keep** — **of** seguir el hilo de; VI/VT (a criminal) rastrear, seguir la pista de; (an aircraft, a student, progress) seguir; VI (wheels) estar alineado; (stylus) seguir los surcos; **to** — **down** perseguir; **to** — **in mud** traer lodo en los pies

tract [trækt] N (of land) terreno *m*; (political) octavilla *f*; (digestive) tubo *m*

traction [trǽkʃən] N tracción *f*

tractor [trǽktə-] N tractor *m*; —**-trailer** tractocamión *m*

trade [tred] N (buying and selling) comercio *m*, trato *m*; (industry) industria *f*; (swap) canje *m*, cambio *m*; (manual labor) oficio *m*; (profession) profesión *f*; (people in a business) gremio *m*; —**in** entrega como parte de pago *f*; —**off** compensación *f*; —**mark** marca registrada *f*, marca de fábrica *f*; — **name** (of product) nombre comercial *m*; (of company) razón social *f*; — **school** escuela industrial *f*; — **union** sindicato *m*; VI/VT (buy and sell) comerciar, negociar; (exchange) canjear; (traffic) traficar; **to** — **in** entregar

trader [trédə-] N comerciante *mf*; (at fairs) feriante *mf*; (of slaves) tratante *mf*

tradition [trədíʃən] N tradición *f*

traditional [trədíʃənəł] ADJ tradicional

traffic [trǽfɪk] N (of drugs) tráfico *m*; (of vehicles) tránsito *m*, tráfico *m*; — **light** semáforo *m*; VI traficar

tragedy [trǽʤɪdi] N tragedia *f*

tragic [trǽʤɪk] ADJ trágico

trail [treł] VI/VT (drag) arrastrar(se); (follow in a race) ir detrás (de); (track) seguir la pista (de), rastrear; VT (leave a trace) dejar una estela / un reguero de; **to** — **off** desvanecerse, apagarse; N (trace) rastro *m*, huella *f*; (path) trocha *f*, sendero *m*, senda *f*; (of smoke) estela *f*; (of blood) reguero *m*; — **bike** motocicleta de trail *f*

trailer [trélə-] N (of a truck) remolque *m*; (house) caravana *f*; (of a film) sinopsis *f*, trailer *m*, avance *m*

train [tren] N (railroad) tren *m*; (of a dress) cola *f*; — **of thought** hilo de pensamiento *m*; VI/VT (worker) capacitar(se); (troops, athlete) adiestrar(se); *Am* entrenar(se); VT (an animal) amaestrar; (a child) educar, formar; (a cannon) apuntar; **to** — **on** (a camera, eye) enfocar

trainee [trení] N aprendiz -iza *mf*, practicante *mf*

trainer [trénə-] N (of animals) amaestrador -ora *mf*; (of workers, troops, athletes) entrenador -ora *mf*

training [trénɪŋ] N (of animals) amaestramiento *m*; (of workers, troops, athletes) adiestramiento *m*, entrenamiento *m*; (of children) educación *f*

trait [tret] N rasgo *m*, seña *f*

traitor [trétə-] N traidor -ora *mf*

trajectory [trəʤɛ́ktəri] N trayectoria *f*

tramp [træmp] VT (trample) pisar; VI andar con pasos pesados; (roam, as a hobo) vagabundear; N (hobo) vagabundo -da *mf*; (promiscuous woman) *fam* fulana *f*; *Sp fam* golfa *f*

trample [trǽmpəł] VT pisotear; **to** — **on / over** pisotear, atropellar; **to** — **out** apagar de un pisotón

trampoline [træmpəlín] N trampolín *m*, cama elástica *f*

trance [træns] N trance *m*

tranquil [trǽŋkwɪł] ADJ tranquilo

tranquility [træŋkwíłɪti] N tranquilidad *f*

tranquilizer [trǽŋkwɪlaɪzə-] N tranquilizante *m*

transact [trænzǽkt] VT hacer, llevar a cabo

transaction [trænzǽkʃən] N transacción *f*, negocio *m*; —**s** actas *f pl*

transatlantic [trænzɪtlǽntɪk] ADJ transatlántico

transcend [trænsénd] VI/VT trascender

transcendence [trænséndəns] N trascendencia *f*

transcendental [trænsendéntl] ADJ trascendental, trascendente

transcribe [trænskráɪb] VT transcribir

transcript [trænskrɪpt] N transcripción *f*

transfer [trænsfɚ] VI/VT (bus, train) trasbordar; (a prisoner, worker) trasladar(se); VT (loyalty, rights, money) transferir; (property) traspasar; N (of loyalty, rights, money) transferencia *f*; (of a prisoner, worker) traslado *m*; (of property) traspaso *m*; (on a bus, train) trasbordo *m*; **— of ownership** traspaso de propiedad *m*

transferable [trænsfɚ́əbəl] ADJ transferible

transfix [trænsfíks] VT (paralyze) paralizar; (impale) traspasar, atravesar

transform [trænsfɔ́rm] VI/VT transformar(se)

transformation [trænsfəméʃən] N transformación *f*

transformer [trænsfɔ́rmɚ] N transformador *m*

transfusion [trænsfjúʒən] N transfusión *f*

transgress [trænzgrés] VT transgredir; **to — against** pecar contra; **to — the bounds of** traspasar los límites de

transgression [trænzgréʃən] N transgresión *f*, pecado *m*

transient [trǽnziənt] ADJ transeúnte, pasajero; N transeúnte *mf*, vagabundo -da *mf*

transistor [trænzístɚ] N transistor *m*

transit [trǽnzɪt] N tránsito *m*; **in —** en tránsito, de paso

transition [trænzíʃən] N transición *f*

transitive [trǽnzɪDɪV] ADJ transitivo

transitory [trǽnzɪtɔri] ADJ transitorio, pasajero

translate [trænzlét] VI/VT traducir

translation [trænzléʃən] N (rendering in different language) traducción *f*; (movement) translación *f*

translator [trǽnzleDɚ] N traductor -ora *mf*

transmission [trænzmíʃən] N transmisión *f*

transmit [trænzmít] VI/VT transmitir

transmitter [trænzmíDɚ] N transmisor *m*

transom [trǽnsəm] N travesaño *m*, montante *m*

transparency [trænzpérənsi] N transparencia *f*

transparent [trænspérənt] ADJ transparente; **to be —** traslucirse

transpire [trænspáɪr] VI (happen) ocurrir; (become known) descubrirse; VI/VT (perspire) transpirar

transplant [trænsplǽnt] VI/VT trasplantar; [trǽnsplænt] N trasplante *m*

transport [trænspɔ́rt] VT transportar, acarrear; [trǽnsport] N (moving) transporte *m*, acarreo *m*; (airplane) avión de transporte *m*; (rapture) éxtasis *m*; (of freight) flete *m*

transportation [trænspɚtéʃən] N transporte *m*

transpose [trænspóz] VI/VT (letters) transponer; (a song) transportar

transverse [trænsvɚ́s] ADJ transversal; (flute) transverso

trap [træp] N trampa *f*; (for hunting) trampa *f*, cepo *m*; (under a sink) sifón *m*; **— door** trampilla *f*; VI/VT (to capture animals) cazar con trampa, atrapar; VT (to pinch) atrapar; (to pin) aprisionar

trapeze [træpíz] N trapecio *m*

trapezoid [trǽpəzɔɪd] N & ADJ trapezoide *m*

trash [træʃ] N basura *f*, desechos *m pl*; (people) *pej* gentuza *f*; **— can** cubo de basura *m*

trashy [trǽʃi] ADJ ordinario

trauma [trɔ́mə] N (physical) traumatismo *m*; (psychological) trauma *m*

traumatic [trəmǽDɪk] ADJ traumático

travel [trǽvəl] VI/VT viajar (por); VI (sound waves) propagarse; N (traveling) viajar *m*; **— agency** agencia de viajes *f*; **—s** viajes *m pl*

traveler [trǽvələ] N viajero -ra *mf*; **—'s check** cheque de viajero *m*

traverse [trəvɚ́s] VI/VT atravesar, cruzar; (skiing) bajar en diagonal; N (crossbar) travesaño *m*; (crossing) travesía *f*

travesty [trǽvisti] N farsa *f*

tray [tre] N bandeja *f*

treacherous [trétʃɚəs] ADJ traicionero, alevoso

treachery [trétʃəri] N traición *f*, alevosía *f*

tread [trɛd] VI/VT (trample) pisar, pisotear; VI (walk) andar, caminar; N (step) paso *m*; (on tire) banda de rodadura / rodaje *f*; (on shoe) dibujo *m*; **—mill** cinta rodante *f*

treason [trízən] N traición *f*

treasure [trɛ́ʒɚ] N tesoro *m*; **— hunt** búsqueda del tesoro *f*; VT atesorar

treasurer [trɛ́ʒɚ] N tesorero -ra *mf*

treasury [trɛ́ʒəri] N tesorería *f*, tesoro *m*; **Secretary of the —** Ministro -tra de Hacienda *mf*

treat [trit] VI/VT tratar (de); **I —ed myself to ice cream** me di un festín de helado; N (pleasure) placer *m*; (gift) regalo *m*; **my —**

yo invito
treatable [trídəbəl] ADJ tratable
treatise [trídɪs] N tratado *m*
treatment [trítmənt] N trato *m*, tratamiento
m; (artistic handling) interpretación *f*
treaty [trídi] N tratado *m*
treble [trébəl] ADJ (triple) triple; (of higher
clef) de tiple; — **clef** clave de sol *f*; N tiple
m; VI/VT triplicar
tree [tri] N árbol *m*; — **hugger** ecologista *mf*;
—**top** copa de árbol *f*; **up a** — en aprietos
treeless [trílɪs] ADJ pelado, sin árboles
trek [trɛk] N expedición *f*; VI viajar con
dificultad
tremble [trémbəl] VI temblar; N temblor *m*
tremendous [trɪméndəs] ADJ tremendo
tremor [trémə] N temblor *m*, sacudida *f*
tremulous [trémjələs] ADJ trémulo
trench [trɛntʃ] N (military) trinchera *f*; (for
pipes) zanja *f*; (on sea floor) fosa *f*; —
coat trinchera *f*, gabardina *f*
trend [trɛnd] N tendencia *f*
trendy [tréndi] ADJ de moda
trespass [tréspæs] N (illegal entry) entrada
ilegal *f*; (religious) deuda *f*; VI (enter
illegally) entrar ilegalmente; **to** —
against violar; (sin) pecar; **no** —**ing**
prohibida la entrada
triage [triáʒ] N triaje *m*, clasificación *f*
trial [tráiəl] N (testing) ensayo *m*, prueba *f*;
(attempt) tentativa *f*; (affliction) aflicción
f; (in a court of law) juicio *m*, proceso *m*;
— **balloon** globo sonda *m*; — **by fire**
prueba de fuego *f*; — **flight** vuelo de
prueba *m*; — **run** prueba *m*, prueba *f*; **by**
— **and error** por ensayo y error
triangle [tráiæŋɡəl] N triángulo *m*
triangular [traiǽŋɡjələ] ADJ triangular
tribe [traɪb] N tribu *f*
tribulation [trɪbjəléʃən] N tribulación *f*
tribunal [traɪbjúnəl] N tribunal *m*
tributary [tríbjətɛri] ADJ & N tributario *m*,
afluente *m*
tribute [tríbjut] N (tax) tributo *m*;
(testimonial) homenaje *m*
triceps [tráisɛps] N triceps *m sg*
trick [trɪk] N (ruse) treta *f*, trampa *f*,
trapisonda *f*; (magician's) truco *m*; (prank)
broma *f*; (in cards) baza *f*; **to be up to
one's old** —**s** hacer de las suyas; **to play
a** — **on someone** gastarle una broma a
alguien; VT hacer trampa, engañar; **to** —
someone into something hacer que
alguien haga algo por medio de artilugios
trickery [tríkəri] N engaños *m pl*, argucias *f
pl*
trickle [tríkəl] VI gotear; **to** — **in (out)**

llegar (irse) de a poco; N goteo *m*
trickster [tríkstə] N embustero -ra *mf*
tricky [tríki] ADJ (artful) mañoso; (difficult)
complicado
tricycle [tráisɪkəl] N triciclo *m*
trifle [tráifəl] N (worthless thing) fruslería *f*,
nadería *f*, bobada *f*; (cheap purchase)
bagatela *f*; (small sum) miseria *f*; VI **to** —
with jugar con; **to** — **away** perder
trigger [tríɡə] N gatillo *m*; VT desencadenar;
(suddenly) disparar
trill [trɪl] VI/VT (birds) trinar; (musical
instrument) tremolar; (the r sound)
pronunciar con vibración; N (of birds, etc.)
trino *m*; (of the r sound) vibración *f*
trillion [trɪljən] N billón *m*
trilogy [tríləʤi] N trilogía *f*
trim [trɪm] VT (adorn) adornar, guarnecer;
(an edge) bordear; (fingernails, hair,
threads) recortar; (hedge) podar; (airplane)
equilibrar; (a wick) despabilar; ADJ (neat)
cuidado; (slim) delgado; (fit) en buen
estado físico; N (embellishment) adorno *m*,
(of sails) orientación *f*; (cutting of hair)
recorte *m*; (cutting of hedge) poda *f*; (of
an airplane) equilibrio *m*
trimming [trímɪŋ] N (act of cutting) recorte
m; (on a uniform) orla *f*, ribete *m*; —**s**
(embellishments) adornos *m pl*; (food)
guarniciones *f pl*; (parts cut off) recortes *m
pl*
Trinidad and Tobago [trínɪdædəntəbégo] N
Trinidad y Tobago *f*
Trinidadian [trɪnɪdǽdɪən] ADJ & N trinitense
mf
trinket [tríŋkɪt] N chuchería *f*, baratija *f*
trio [trío] N trío *m*
trip [trɪp] N (journey, drug-induced
condition) viaje *m*; (experience)
experiencia *f*; (light step) paso ligero *m*;
(accidental stumble) tropezón *m*;
(throwing down) zancadilla *f*; VT (cause to
stumble) hacer una zancadilla a; (cause to
make error) confundir; (release a catch)
soltar; (blow a fuse) hacer saltar; VI
(stumble) tropezar; (skip) andar con paso
ligero; (make a mistake) equivocarse;
(hallucinate) viajar; (blow a fuse) saltar
triphthong [trípθɔŋ] N triptongo *m*
triple [trípəl] ADJ & N triple *m*; VI/VT triplicar
triplet [tríplɪt] N trillizo *m*
tripod [tráipɑd] N trípode *m*
trite [traɪt] ADJ trivial, trillado
triumph [tráiəmf] N triunfo *m*; VI triunfar
triumphant [traiámfənt] ADJ triunfante
trivial [trívɪəl] ADJ trivial, baladí, fútil
trolley [tráli] N (electric bus) trole *m*,

trolebús *m*; (on tracks) tranvía *m*

trombone [trámbon] N trombón *m*

troop [trup] N (of scouts) tropa *f*; (of soldiers) escuadrón *m*; (of tourists) horda *f*; **—s** tropas *f pl*

trophy [trófi] N trofeo *m*

tropic [trápɪk] N trópico *m*

tropical [trápɪkəł] ADJ tropical

trot [trat] VI trotar; VT hacer trotar; **to — out** sacar a relucir; N trote *m*

trouble [trʌbəł] VT (make turbid) enturbiar; (afflict) aquejar; VI/VT (bother) molestar(se); (disturb) preocupar(se); N (problem) problema *m*; (difficulty) dificultad *f*, sinsabor *m*; (disturbance) disturbio *m*; (effort) molestia *f*; (ailment) enfermedad *f*, trastorno *m*; (mechanical breakdown) avería *f*, desperfecto *m*; **to be in** — estar en un aprieto; **it is not worth the** — no vale la pena; **—maker** agitador -ra *mf*, revoltoso -sa *mf*; **—shoot** solucionar problemas; **—shooter** solucionador -ra *mf*, localizador -ra de averías *mf*; **to make** — causar problemas

trough [trɔf] N (for food) pesebre *m*, comedero *m*; (for water) abrevadero *m*, bebedero *m*; (of weather, on ocean floor) depresión *f*

trousers [tráuzɚz] N pantalones *m pl*

trousseau [trúso] N ajuar *m*

trout [traut] N trucha *f*

trowel [tráuəł] N (for mortar) llana *f*, paleta *f*; (for digging) desplantador *m*

truant [trúənt] N alumno -na que falta a clase sin permiso *mf*

truce [trus] N tregua *f*

truck [trʌk] N (vehicle) camión *m*; *Mex* troca *f*; (dealings) trato *m*; (vegetables) hortalizas *f pl*; — **driver** camionero -ra *mf*; *Mex* troquero -ra *mf*; VI/VT transportar en camión; *Mex* transportar en troca

trudge [trʌdʒ] VI andar con dificultad; N caminata difícil *f*

true [tru] ADJ verdadero; (story) verídico; (copy, translation) fiel; (well) a plomo; (wheel) alineado, centrado; —**-blue** leal; —**-false test** prueba de verdadero o falso *f*; **his dream came** — su sueño se hizo realidad

truly [trúli] ADV (surprisingly) verdaderamente; (sincerely) sinceramente; (actually) en realidad, realmente; (accurately) fielmente; **very — yours** su seguro servidor, atentamente

trumpet [trámpɪt] N trompeta *f*; VI/VT trompetear; (an elephant) barritar

trunk [trʌŋk] N (of tree, body) tronco *m*; (receptacle) baúl *m*; (of elephant) trompa *f*; (of a car) maletero *m*, *Mex* cajuela *f*; **—s** traje de baño *m*

trust [trʌst] N (responsibility) confianza *f*; (hope) esperanza *f*; (credit) crédito *m*; (charge) cargo *m*; (firm) trust *m*; (fund) fondo fideicomiso *m*; VI/VT (rely on) confiar en, fiarse de; VT (believe) creer; (hope) esperar

trustee [trʌstí] N (person holding property of another) fideicomisario -ria *mf*; (administrator) administrador -ra *mf*

trusteeship [trʌstíʃɪp] N (position of holding property) fideicomiso *m*; (administrative position) cargo de administrador *m*

trustful [trʌstfəł] ADJ confiado

trusting [trʌstɪŋ] ADJ confiado

trustworthy [trʌstwɚði] ADJ fidedigno, digno de confianza

trusty [trʌsti] ADJ leal

truth [truθ] N verdad *f*

truthful [trúθfəł] ADJ (account) verídico; (person) veraz

truthfulness [trúθfəłnɪs] N veracidad *f*

try [trai] VT (attempt) tratar de, intentar; (test, taste) probar; (strain) poner a prueba; (put on trial) procesar, enjuiciar; **to — on** probarse; **to — one's luck** probar fortuna; **to — and** tratar de; **to — out** (test) probar; (for a team) presentarse para; **—out** prueba *f*; N intento *m*, tentativa *f*

trying [tráiŋ] ADJ penoso

tryst [trɪst] N cita romántica *f*

T-shirt [tíʃɚt] N camiseta *f*

tub [tʌb] N (for bathing) bañera *f*; (for butter) envase *m*; (for washing) tina *f*

tuba [túbə] N tuba *f*

tube [tub] N tubo *m* (also electronic); (television) televisor *m*

tuberculosis [tubɚkjəlósɪs] N tuberculosis *f*

tubular [túbjələ-] ADJ tubular

tuck [tʌk] VT (stick in) meter; (make fold) alforzar; **to — in one's shirt** meter la camisa dentro del pantalón; **to — into bed** arropar; **to — something under one's arm** meterse algo bajo el brazo; N alforza *f*

Tuesday [túzde] N martes *m*

tuft [tʌft] N (of feathers) penacho *m*, copete *m*; (of hair) mechón *m*; (of plants) mata *f*

tug [tʌg] VI/VT (pull) tirar, jalar; (drag) arrastrar; **to — at** tironear; N tirón *m*; (boat) remolcador *m*

tuition [tuíʃən] N matrícula *f*

tulip [túlɪp] N tulipán *m*

tumble [támbəł] VI (fall) caer; (collapse) venirse abajo; (do handsprings, etc.) dar

volteretas; **to — down** rodar; **to — dry**
secar en la secadora; **to — over**
tropezarse; N (fall) caída f; (gymnastic
trick) voltereta f
tumbler [támblə-] N (glass) vaso m; (person)
acróbata mf
tummy [támi] N barriguita f
tumor [túmə-] N tumor m
tumult [túmʌlt] N tumulto m
tumultuous [tumʌltʃuəs] ADJ tumultuoso
tuna [túnə] N (fish) atún m, bonito m;
(prickly pear) tuna f
tune [tun] N (melody) tonada f, aire m;
(electronic adjustment) sintonía f; **to be
in —** (in pitch) estar afinado; (adjusted)
sintonizado; **to be out of —** estar
desafinado; VT (engine) afinar; (musical
instrument) afinar, templar; (radio)
sintonizar; **to — in** sintonizar; **to — out**
ignorar; **—up** afinación f
tuner [túnə-] N afinador -ra mf; (electronics)
sintonizador m
tungsten [táŋstən] N tungsteno m
tunic [túnɪk] N túnica f
Tunisia [tuníʒə] N Túnez m
Tunisian [tuníʒən] ADJ & N tunesino -na mf
tunnel [tánəl] N túnel m; (for traffic)
viaducto m; VI cavar; VT hacer un túnel
turban [tɜ́-bən] N turbante m
turbine [tɜ́-baɪn] N turbina f
turbocharger [tɜ́-botʃɑrdʒə-] N
turbocompresor m
turbojet [tɜ́-bodʒɛt] N turborreactor m
turbulent [tɜ́-bjələnt] ADJ turbulento
turf [tɜ-f] N (lawn) césped m; (peat) turba f;
(track for horseraces) pista f; (territory)
territorio m; VT cubrir con césped
Turk [tɜ-k] N turco -ca mf
turkey [tɜ́-ki] N pavo m; **— vulture** buitre
pavo m
Turkey [tɜ́-ki] N Turquía f
Turkish [tɜ́-kɪʃ] ADJ turco; **— bath** baño
turco m
Turkmen [tɜ́-kmən] ADJ & N turcomano -na
mf
Turkmenistan [tɜ-kmenɪstǽn] N
Turkmenistán m
turmoil [tɜ́-mɔɪl] N confusión f, agitación f
turn [tɜ-n] VT (corner) doblar, dar vuelta;
(wheel, key) girar, dar vuelta; (page) dar
vuelta; (soil) labrar; (stomach) revolver;
(ankle) torcerse; (a river) desviar; VI
(change color) cambiar de color; (become)
ponerse; (rotate) girar; (change direction)
girar, dar la vuelta; (be nauseated)
revolvérsele a uno; **to — against** volverse
en contra de; **to — around** dar la vuelta,

girar; **to — away** (face) volver; (eyes)
apartar; (person) rechazar; **to — back**
(return) volver; (a clock) atrasar; **to —
down** (offer) rechazar; (radio) bajar;
(request) rechazar; **to — in** (hand in /
over) entregar; (go to bed) acostarse; **to —
inside out** dar vuelta al revés; **to — into**
convertir(se) en; **to — off** (light) apagar;
(faucet) cerrar; (a road) salir de; (person in
general sense) disgustar; (person in sexual
sense) quitarle las ganas a alguien; **to —
on** (light) encender, prender; (faucet)
abrir; (person) excitar; **to — out** (light)
apagar; (people) expulsar; (product)
producir; **—out** concurrencia f; **to — out
well** salir bien; **to — over** (car)
volcar(se); (engine) arrancar; (thought,
idea, etc.) dar vueltas a; (criminal,
weapon, etc.) entregar; **—over** (of
employees) renovación f; (of merchandise)
volumen m; (pastry) empanada f, pastelito
m; (of a ball) pérdida f; **—pike** autopista f;
—stile torniquete m, molinete m; **—table**
plato giratorio m; **to — to** (have recourse
to) acudir a, recurrir a; (become)
volver(se); **to — up** aparecer; **to — up
one's nose** desdeñar; **to — up one's
sleeves** arremangarse; **to — upside
down** dar vuelta; N (rotation) vuelta f,
revolución f; (change of direction) giro m,
vuelta f; (change in condition) cambio m;
(curve) recodo m, curva f; (opportunity)
turno m; **— of mind** actitud f; **— of
phrase** giro m; **— signal** intermitente m;
at every — a cada paso; **bad —** mala
pasada f; **good —** favor m; **it's my —** me
toca a mí; **to take —s** turnarse
turnip [tɜ́-nɪp] N nabo m
turpentine [tɜ́-pəntaɪn] N trementina f,
aguarrás m
turquoise [tɜ́-kɔɪz] N turquesa f
turret [tɜ́-ɪt] N (small tower, gun tower)
torreta f; (on a ship) torre f
turtle [tɜ́-dl] N tortuga f; **—dove** tórtola f;
—neck cuello vuelto m
tusk [tʌsk] N colmillo m
tutor [túdə-] N profesor -ora particular mf; VI/
VT dar clases particulares
Tuvalu [túvəlu] N Tuvalu m
Tuvaluan [tuvəlúən] ADJ & N tuvaluano -na
mf
tuxedo [tʌksído] N esmoquin m
TV (television) [tívi] N tele f
twang [twæŋ] N (in music) tañido m; (of
speech) nasalidad f; VI (vibrate) vibrar; VT
hacer vibrar; VI/VT (speak nasally)
guanguear

twangy [twǽŋi] ADJ gangoso

tweak [twik] VT (pinch) pellizcar; (adjust) ajustar; N (pinch) pellizco *m*; (adjustment) ajuste *m*

tweed [twid] N tweed *m*

tweezers [twízɚz] N pinzas *f pl*

twelve [twɛ́lv] NUM doce

twenty [twɛ́nti] NUM veinte

twerp [twɚp] N idiota *mf*, papanatas *mf sg*

twice [twais] ADV dos veces

twig [twɪg] N ramita *f*

twilight [twáilart] N crepúsculo *m*, ocaso *m*; **— zone** zona gris *f*

twin [twɪn] ADJ & N mellizo -za *mf*, gemelo -la *mf*; **— bed** cama individual *f*

twine [twain] N cuerda *f*; VI/VT (twist) enroscar(se); (interlace) entrelazar(se)

twinge [twɪndʒ] N punzada *f*

twinkle [twɪ́ŋkəl] VI (star) titilar, parpadear; (eyes) brillar; N (of stars) titileo *m*, parpadeo *m*; (of eyes) brillo *m*

twirl [twɚl] VI/VT girar, dar vueltas (a); N giro *m*, vuelta *f*; (of ice cream) espiral *m*

twist [twist] VI/VT torcer(se); (distort) tergiversar(se); (writhe) retorcer(se); (coil) enroscar(se); N (of an ankle) torcedura *f*; (in a road, coil) vuelta *f*; (unforeseen event) vuelta de tuerca *f*; (distortion) tergiversación *f*

twister [twístɚ] N tornado *m*

twitch [twɪtʃ] VI/VT crispar(se), mover(se); N (tic) tic *m*; (pang) punzada *f*; (tug) tirón *m*

twitter [twídɚ] VI gorjear; N gorjeo *m*

two [tu] NUM dos; **—-bit** de chicha y nabo; **my — cents' worth** mi opinión *f*; **—-edged** de doble filo; **—-faced** (with two faces) de dos caras; (hypocritical) hipócrita, falso; **—-fisted** pendenciero; **—-way** de dos sentidos

tycoon [taikún] N magnate *mf*

type [taip] N tipo *m*, índole *f*; VI/VT (a letter) escribir a máquina, mecanografiar; VT (blood) determinar el grupo sanguíneo; **—script** texto escrito a máquina *m*; **to —set** componer; **to —write** escribir a máquina; **—writer** máquina de escribir *f*; **—writing** mecanografía *f*; **—written** escrito a máquina

typhoid [táifɔid] N tifoidea *f*; **— fever** fiebre tifoidea *f*, tifus *m*

typhoon [taifún] N tifón *m*

typical [típikəl] ADJ típico

typist [táipist] N mecanógrafo -fa *mf*

typographical [taipəgrǽfikəl] ADJ tipográfico; **— error** error de imprenta *m*, errata *f*

typology [taipáləd͡ʒi] N tipología *f*

tyrannical [tɪrǽnɪkəl] ADJ tiránico

tyranny [tírəni] N tiranía *f*

tyrant [táirənt] N tirano -na *mf*

Uu

ubiquitous [jubíkwɪdəs] ADJ ubicuo

U-boat [júbot] N submarino *m*

udder [ʌ́dɚ] N ubre *f*

UFO (unidentified flying object) [juɛfó] N OVNI *m*

Uganda [jugǽndə] N Uganda *f*

Ugandan [jugǽndən] ADJ & N ugandés -esa *mf*

ugliness [ʌ́glinɪs] N fealdad *f*

ugly [ʌ́gli] ADJ feo; (incident) deplorable; (mood) de perros

uh-huh [ʌhʌ́] INTERJ sí

Ukraine [jukrén] N Ucrania *f*

Ukrainian [jukrénian] ADJ & N ucraniano -na *mf*

ulcer [ʌ́lsɚ] N úlcera *f*

ulterior [ʌltíriɚ] ADJ ulterior; **— motive** segunda intención *f*

ultimate [ʌ́ltəmɪt] ADJ (destination) último, final; (authority) final, máximo; (principle) fundamental; (vacation) perfecto; N súmmum *m*

ultimatum [ʌltəmédəm] N ultimátum *m*

ultralight [ʌ́ltrəlait] ADJ & N ultraligero *m*

ultramodern [ʌ́ltrəmɑ́dɚn] ADJ ultramoderno

ultraviolet [ʌ́ltrəváiəlɪt] ADJ & N ultravioleta *m*

umbilical cord [ʌmbílikəlkɔrd] N cordón umbilical *m*

umbrella [ʌmbrélə] N paraguas *m sg*

umpire [ʌ́mpair] N árbitro *m*; VI/VT arbitrar

unable [ʌnébəl] ADJ **to be — to** no poder

unaccented [ʌnǽksɛntɪd] ADJ sin acento

unacceptable [ʌnɪksɛ́ptəbəl] ADJ inaceptable

unaccustomed [ʌnəkʌ́stəmd] ADJ (not used to) no acostumbrado; (uncommon) insólito

unadulterated [ʌnədʌ́ltəreɪd] ADJ puro

unaffected [ʌnəféktɪd] ADJ (sincere) natural, sincero; (unpretentious) sin afectación

unanimity [junəními] N unanimidad *f*

unanimous [junǽnəməs] ADJ unánime

unarmed [ʌnármd] ADJ desarmado

unassuming [ʌnəsúmɪŋ] ADJ modesto, sin pretensiones

unattached [ʌnətǽtʃt] ADJ (piece of paper)

suelto; (person) soltero

unavoidable [ʌnəvɔ́ɪdəbəl] ADJ inevitable

unaware [ʌnəwér] ADJ inconsciente; ADV **to be — of** ignorar; **—s** sin darse cuenta

unbalanced [ʌnbǽlənst] ADJ desequilibrado

unbearable [ʌnbérəbəl] ADJ inaguantable, insoportable

unbeatable [ʌnbídəbəl] ADJ imbatible

unbeaten [ʌnbítn̩] ADJ invicto

unbecoming [ʌnbikʌ́mɪŋ] ADJ (inappropriate) impropio; (unflattering) que no queda bien

unbelief [ʌnbilíf] N incredulidad f, descreimiento m

unbelievable [ʌnbɪlívəbəl] ADJ increíble

unbeliever [ʌnbɪlívə-] N descreído -da mf

unbending [ʌnbéndɪŋ] ADJ inflexible

unbiased [ʌnbáɪəst] ADJ imparcial

unbounded [ʌnbáʊndɪd] ADJ ilimitado

unbridled [ʌnbráɪdl̩d] ADJ desenfrenado

unbroken [ʌnbrókən] ADJ (intact) intacto; (not tamed) indomado; (uninterrupted) ininterrumpido

unbuckle [ʌnbʌ́kəl] VT desabrochar

unbutton [ʌnbʌ́tn̩] VI/VT desabotonar, desabrochar

uncalled-for [ʌnkɔ́ldfɔr] ADJ injustificado

uncanny [ʌnkǽni] ADJ inexplicable, misterioso

uncertain [ʌnsɚtn̩] ADJ incierto

uncertainty [ʌnsɚ́tn̩ti] N incertidumbre f

unchanged [ʌntʃéndʒd] ADJ inalterado

uncharitable [ʌntʃǽrɪdəbəl] ADJ duro, poco caritativo

uncivilized [ʌnsívəlaɪzd] ADJ incivilizado

uncle [ʌ́ŋkəl] N tío m; **to say —** darse por vencido

unclean [ʌnklín] ADJ (dirty) sucio; (impure) impuro

uncomfortable [ʌnkʌ́mfə-Dəbəl] ADJ incómodo

uncommon [ʌnkámən] ADJ (unusual) poco común; (extraordinary) extraordinario

uncompromising [ʌnkʌ́mprəmaɪzɪŋ] ADJ (intransigent) intransigente; (unfailing) incondicional

unconcerned [ʌnkənsɚ́-nd] ADJ indiferente

unconditional [ʌnkəndíʃənəl] ADJ incondicional

unconscious [ʌnkánʃəs] ADJ inconsciente

unconstitutional [ʌnkɑnstɪtúʃənəl] ADJ inconstitucional

uncontrollable [ʌnkəntróləbəl] ADJ (movement) incontrolable; (urge, laughter) incontenible

unconventional [ʌnkənvénʃənəl] ADJ poco convencional

uncouth [ʌnkúθ] ADJ tosco

uncover [ʌnkʌ́və-] VI/VT descubrir(se); VI (remove bedcovers) destaparse

unctuous [ʌ́ŋktʃuəs] ADJ untuoso, zalamero

uncultivated [ʌnkʌ́ltəvɛɪdɪd] ADJ (talent) inculto, no cultivado; (land) no cultivado

uncultured [ʌnkʌ́ltʃə-d] ADJ inculto

undaunted [ʌndɔ́ntɪd] ADJ impávido, intrépido

undecided [ʌndɪsáɪdɪd] ADJ indeciso

undeniable [ʌndɪnáɪəbəl] ADJ innegable

under [ʌ́ndə-] PREP (below) bajo, debajo de, abajo de; (in a ranking) por debajo de; (less) menos de; **— the democrats** durante el mandato de los demócratas; **— a pseudonym** bajo un seudónimo; **— cost** a menos del costo/coste, por debajo del costo/coste; ADV (below) debajo, abajo; (less than) menos; **to be —** estar inconsciente

underage [ʌndə-édʒ] ADJ menor de edad; **— drinking** consumo de alcohol por menores de edad m

underarm [ʌ́ndə-ɑrm] N axila f

underbrush [ʌ́ndə-brʌʃ] N maleza f

underclass [ʌ́ndə-klæs] N subproletariado m

undercover [ʌndə-kʌ́və-] ADJ clandestino, secreto

undercut [ʌndə-kʌ́t] VT (undermine) socavar; (sell for less) vender por menos que

underdeveloped [ʌndə-dɪvéləpt] ADJ subdesarrollado

underdog [ʌ́ndə-dɔg] N el/la de abajo

underemployed [ʌndə-ɛmplɔ́ɪd] ADJ subempleado

underestimate [ʌndə-éstəmet] VT (person) subestimar; (price) subvaluar

underfed [ʌndə-féd] ADJ desnutrido

underfoot [ʌndə-fút] ADJ (beneath the feet) bajo los pies; (in the way) estorbando

undergird [ʌndə-gɚ́d] VT reforzar

undergo [ʌndə-gó] VT (an operation) someterse a; (a change) experimentar, sufrir

undergraduate [ʌndə-grǽdʒuɪt] N estudiante de pregrado mf; **— course** programa de pregrado m

underground [ʌ́ndə-graʊnd] ADJ (under the earth) subterráneo; (secret) clandestino; N resistencia f, grupo clandestino m; ADV (under the earth) bajo tierra; (secretly) en secreto

underhanded [ʌndə-hǽndɪd] ADJ (secret) secreto, solapado; (illicit) ilícito

underlie [ʌndə-láɪ] VI/VT subyacer (a)

underline [ʌ́ndə-laɪn] VT subrayar

undermine [ʌndə-máɪn] VT minar,

menoscabar

underneath [ʌndə-níθ] PREP bajo, debajo de, abajo de; ADV debajo, abajo; N la parte inferior

underpants [ándə-pænts] N (for men) calzoncillos *m pl*; (for women) *Sp* bragas *f pl*; *Mex* pantaletas *f pl*; *RP* bombacha *f*

undersecretary [ʌndə-sékrəteri] N subsecretario -ria *mf*

undersell [ʌndə-sél] VT (to sell at a low price) malbaratar; (to sell cheaper than) vender a menos precio que

undershirt [ándə-shə-t] N camiseta *f*

underside [ándə-said] N parte inferior *f*

undersigned [ʌndə-sáind] N abajofirmante *mf*, infrascrito -ta *mf*

underskirt [ándə-skə-t] N enaguas *f pl*

understaffed [ʌndə-stǽft] ADJ falto de personal

understand [ʌndə-stǽnd] VI/VT comprender, entender; **I — you're leaving** tengo entendido que te vas; **to — about** saber de / entender de

understandable [ʌndə-stǽndəbəl] ADJ comprensible

understanding [ʌndə-stǽndɪŋ] N (comprehension) comprensión *f*, entendimiento *m*; (tolerance) comprensión mutua *f*; (agreement) acuerdo *m*; ADJ comprensivo

understate [ʌndə-stét] VT minimizar

understood [ʌndə-stúd] ADJ entendido; (implicit) sobreentendido

understudy [ándə-stʌdi] N suplente *mf*, sobresaliente *mf*; VI/VT servir de sobresaliente (para), suplir (a)

undertake [ʌndə-ték] VT emprender, acometer; **to — to** comprometerse a

undertaker [ándə-tekə] N director -ra de funeraria / pompas fúnebres *mf*, funerario -ria *mf*

undertaking [ʌndə-tékɪŋ] N empresa *f*

under-the-table [ándə-ðətébəl] ADJ ilícito, bajo cuerda

undertone [ándə-ton] N (low voice) voz baja *f*; (undercurrent) tónica *f*

undertow [ándə-to] N resaca *f*

underwater [ándə-wɔtə] ADJ submarino; [ándə-wɔtə] ADV por debajo del agua

underwear [ándə-wer] N ropa interior *f*

underweight [ándə-wet] ADJ de peso insuficiente

underworld [ándə-wə-ld] N (of criminals) hampa *f*; (netherworld) el más allá

underwrite [ándə-rait] VI/VT (finance) financiar; (sign) suscribir; (insure) asegurar

undesirable [ʌndɪzáɪrəbəl] ADJ indeseable

undisturbed [ʌndɪstə-bd] ADJ (unworried, uninterrupted) tranquilo; (unspoiled) virgen

undo [ʌndú] VT (reverse an action) deshacer; (unfasten) desabrochar, desabotonar; (destroy) destruir; (loosen hair) soltar

undoing [ʌndúɪŋ] N (reversal) deshacer *m*; (destruction) destrucción *f*, perdición *f*; (of buttons) desabrochar *m*

undone [ʌndán] ADJ (unfinished) sin terminar; (ruined) perdido; (unfastened) desabrochado; **to come —** (clothing) desabrocharse; (person) desquiciarse

undoubtedly [ʌndáʊɾɪdli] ADV indudablemente, sin duda

undress [ʌndrés] VI/VT desnudar(se), desvestir(se)

undue [ʌndú] ADJ (inappropriate) indebido; (excessive) excesivo

undulate [ándʒəlet] VI/VT ondular

undying [ʌndáɪɪŋ] ADJ imperecedero, eterno

unearth [ʌnə-θ] VT desenterrar

uneasiness [ʌnízɪnɪs] N (feeling) inquietud *f*, desasosiego *m*, desazón *f*; *Sp* grima *f*; (of peace) precariedad *f*; (of silence, situation) incomodidad *f*

uneasy [ʌnízi] ADJ (feeling) inquieto; (peace) precario; (silence) incómodo; (situation) molesto; (sleep) agitado

uneducated [ʌnédʒəkeɪɾd] ADJ inculto, ignorante

unemployed [ʌnemplɔíd] ADJ (jobless) desocupado, desempleado, parado; (unused) ocioso

unemployment [ʌnemplɔímənt] N desocupación *f*, desempleo *m*, paro *m*; **— compensation** seguro de paro *m*; *Sp* paro *m*

unending [ʌnéndɪŋ] ADJ interminable

unequal [ʌníkwəl] ADJ desigual; **to be — to a task** no ser capaz de cumplir una tarea

unequivocal [ʌnɪkwívəkəl] ADJ inequívoco, tajante

uneven [ʌnívən] ADJ (rough) irregular, accidentado; (inequitable) desigual; (not uniform) disparejo; (odd, of numbers) impar

uneventful [ʌnɪvéntfəl] ADJ sin incidente

unexpected [ʌnɪkspéktɪd] ADJ inesperado

unexpressive [ʌnɪksprésɪv] ADJ inexpresivo

unfailing [ʌnfélɪŋ] ADJ (inexhaustible) inagotable; (dependable) infalible

unfair [ʌnfér] ADJ (measure, price) injusto; (competition) injusto, desleal

unfaithful [ʌnféθfəl] ADJ infiel

unfamiliar [ʌnfəmíljə] ADJ (unknown) poco familiar, desconocido; (unacquainted) poco familiarizado

unfasten [ʌnfǽsən] VI/VT desabrochar(se), desprender(se)

unfavorable [ʌnfévə‿əbəɫ] ADJ desfavorable

unfeeling [ʌnfíliŋ] ADJ insensible

unfettered [ʌnféɖə‿d] ADJ desatado

unfinished [ʌnfíniʃt] ADJ (matter) inacabado, inconcluso; (business) pendiente; (wood) sin terminar, sin barnizar; (task) inconcluso, sin terminar

unfit [ʌnfít] ADJ (unsuitable) no apto; (incapable) incapaz

unfold [ʌnfóɫd] VT (open out) desdoblar, desplegar; VI (happen) desarrollarse; (appear) extenderse; (reveal) revelarse

unforeseen [ʌnfɔrsín] ADJ imprevisto

unforgettable [ʌnfə‿gétəbəɫ] ADJ inolvidable

unfortunate [ʌnfɔ́rtʃənɪt] ADJ desgraciado, desafortunado, desventurado

unfounded [ʌnfáundɪd] ADJ infundado

unfriendly [ʌnfréndli] ADJ (forces) hostil; (person) antipático

unfurl [ʌnfɜ́‿ɫ] VI/VT desplegar(se)

unfurnished [ʌnfɜ́‿nɪʃt] ADJ sin amueblar, desamueblado

ungainly [ʌngénli] ADJ (ungraceful) desgarbado, desmadejado; (clumsy) torpe

ungrateful [ʌngrétfəɫ] ADJ ingrato, desagradecido

unguarded [ʌngárdɪd] ADJ (incautious) descuidado, desprevenido; (unattended) sin vigilancia; (defenseless) indefenso; **an — moment** un momento de descuido

unhappiness [ʌnhǽpinɪs] N infelicidad f

unhappy [ʌnhǽpi] ADJ (sad) infeliz, desdichado, desgraciado; (dissatisfied) insatisfecho; (infelicitous) poco afortunado

unharmed [ʌnhármd] ADJ ileso

unhealthy [ʌnhéɫθi] ADJ (climate, food, lifestyle) malsano, insalubre; (complexion, obsession) enfermizo

unheard-of [ʌnhɜ́‿ɖɑv] ADJ inaudito, desconocido

unhinge [ʌnhíndʒ] VT desquiciar

unholy [ʌnhóli] ADJ (noise) infernal; (alliance) nefasto

unhook [ʌnhúk] VT (disentangle) desenganchar; (undo) desabrochar

unhurt [ʌnhɜ́‿t] ADJ ileso

uniform [júnəfɔrm] ADJ & N uniforme m

uniformity [junəfɔ́rmɪdɪ] N uniformidad f

unify [júnəfaɪ] VI/VT unificar(se)

unilateral [junəlǽɖə‿əɫ] ADJ unilateral

unimportant [ʌnɪmpɔ́rtn̩t] ADJ insignificante; sin importancia

uninhabited [ʌnɪnhǽbɪdɪd] ADJ deshabitado

uninhibited [ʌnɪnhíbɪdɪd] ADJ desinhibido,

desenfadado

uninspired [ʌnɪnspáɪrd] ADJ poco inspirado

unintelligible [ʌnɪntéliʤəbəɫ] ADJ ininteligible

union [júnjən] N unión f; (labor) sindicato m, gremio m; **— labor** mano de obra sindicalizada / agremiada f; **— leader** dirigente sindical mf

unionize [júnjənaɪz] VI/VT sindicar(se), agremiar(se)

unique [juník] ADJ único, singular; **that feature is — to the South** ese rasgo es peculiar del sur

unisex [júnəseks] ADJ unisex

unison [júnəsən] ADV LOC **in —** al unísono

unit [júnɪt] N unidad f

unite [junáɪt] VI/VT unir(se)

United Arab Emirates [junáɪdɪdǽrəbémə‿ɪts] N Emiratos Árabes Unidos m pl

United Kingdom [junáɪdɪdkíŋdəm] N Reino Unido m

United States [junáɪdɪdstéts] N Estados Unidos m pl

unity [júnɪdɪ] N unidad f; (concord) unión f

universal [junəvɜ́‿səɫ] ADJ universal; **— joint** acoplamiento universal de cardán m

universe [júnəvɜ‿s] N universo m

university [junəvɜ́‿sɪdɪ] N universidad f; **— degree** título universitario m

unjust [ʌndʒʌ́st] ADJ injusto

unjustifiable [ʌndʒʌstəfáiəbəɫ] ADJ injustificable

unkempt [ʌnkémpt] ADJ (uncombed) desgreñado, despeinado; (messy) desaliñado

unkind [ʌnkáind] ADJ antipático, poco amable

unknown [ʌnnón] ADJ desconocido; **— quantity** incógnita f; **it is —** se ignora

unlawful [ʌnlɔ́fəɫ] ADJ ilegal

unleaded [ʌnlédɪd] ADJ sin plomo

unleash [ʌnlíʃ] VT desatar

unless [ənlés] CONJ a menos que, a no ser que

unlicensed [ʌnláisənst] ADJ sin permiso, ilícito

unlike [ʌnláik] ADJ distinto, diferente; **he is — me** es diferente de mí; PREP a diferencia de; **how — you to forget!** ¡me extraña que te hayas olvidado!

unlikely [ʌnláikli] ADJ (improbable) improbable; (not realistic) inverosímil; (exotic) exótico; **I am — to come** es improbable que venga

unlimited [ʌnlímɪdɪd] ADJ ilimitado

unload [ʌnlód] VI/VT (take cargo from) descargar; VI (pour out one's feelings) desahogarse; (sell) liquidar

unlock [ʌnlák] VI/VT abrir con llave

unlucky [ʌnláki] ADJ (unfortunate)
desafortunado; (ominous) aciago, funesto;
an — number un número de mala suerte

unmanageable [ʌnmǽnɪʤəbəl] ADJ (crisis,
situation) inmanejable; (person) poco
dócil

unmanned [ʌnmǽnd] ADJ (deprived of
courage) achicado; (with no crew) no
tripulado

unmarried [ʌnmǽrid] ADJ soltero

unmask [ʌnmǽsk] VI/VT desenmascarar(se)

unmistakable [ʌnmɪstékəbəl] ADJ
inconfundible

unmitigated [ʌnmíɾɪɡeɾɪd] ADJ absoluto

unmoved [ʌnmúvd] ADJ (unflinching)
impasible; (indifferent) indiferente

unnatural [ʌnnǽʧɚəl] ADJ (contrary to
nature) no natural; (unloving)
desnaturalizado; (monstrous) monstruoso;
(affected) afectado

unnecessary [ʌnnésəseri] ADJ innecesario

unnoticed [ʌnnóɾɪst] ADJ inadvertido,
desapercibido

unobserved [ʌnəbzɚ́vd] ADJ inadvertido

unobtrusive [ʌnəbtrúsɪv] ADJ discreto

unoccupied [ʌnákjəpaɪd] ADJ (house)
desocupado; (territory) no ocupado

unofficial [ʌnəfíʃəl] ADJ extraoficial, no
oficial

unoriginal [ʌnəríʤənəl] ADJ poco original

unorthodox [ʌnɔ́rθədɑks] ADJ heterodoxo

unpack [ʌnpǽk] VT (a suitcase) deshacer,
desempacar; (a carton) desembalar

unpaid [ʌnpéd] ADJ (debt) impagado, por
pagar; (work) no remunerado

unpleasant [ʌnplézənt] ADJ desagradable

unpleasantness [ʌnplézəntnɪs] N (quality or
state of being unpleasant) lo desagradable;
(unpleasant episode) desavenencia *f*,
disgusto *m*

unplug [ʌnplág] VI/VT desenchufar

unpopular [ʌnpápjələ˞] ADJ (decision)
impopular; **she was — in school** tenía
pocos amigos en la escuela

unprecedented [ʌnprésɪdentɪd] ADJ sin
precedente, inaudito

unpredictable [ʌnprɪdíktəbəl] ADJ
impredecible, imprevisible

unpremeditated [ʌnprɪméɾɪteɾɪd] ADJ
impremeditado; (murder) sin
premeditación

unprepared [ʌnprɪpérd] ADJ (surprised)
desprevenido; (not ready) no preparado

unpretentious [ʌnprɪténʃəs] ADJ modesto,
sin pretenciones

unprincipled [ʌnprínsəpəld] ADJ sin
escrúpulos, falto de principios

unprintable [ʌnpríntəbəl] ADJ impublicable

unproductive [ʌnprədáktɪv] ADJ
improductivo

unprofessional [ʌnprəféʃənəl] ADJ poco
profesional

unprofitable [ʌnpráfɪɾəbəl] ADJ no rentable

unpublished [ʌnpáblɪʃt] ADJ inédito, sin
publicar

unqualified [ʌnkwáləfaɪd] ADJ (worker) *Sp*
no cualificado; *Am* no calificado; (support)
incondicional; (disaster) absoluto

unquestionable [ʌnkwéstʃənəbəl] ADJ
incuestionable, indiscutible

unravel [ʌnrǽvət] VI/VT (a rope)
desenredar(se); (a sweater) destejer(se);
(cloth) deshilachar(se); (a plan)
deshacer(se); VT (a mystery) desentrañar

unreal [ʌnríəl] ADJ (not real) irreal;
(unbelievable) increíble

unreasonable [ʌnrízənəbəl] ADJ (excessive)
exagerado; (irrational) irracional, poco
razonable

unrecognizable [ʌnrekəɡnáɪzəbəl] ADJ
irreconocible

unrefined [ʌnrɪfáɪnd] ADJ (oil, sugar) no
refinado; (behavior) inculto, grosero

unreliable [ʌnrɪláɪəbəl] ADJ (person)
informal; (machine, information) *Sp* poco
fiable; *Am* poco confiable

unrest [ʌnrést] N malestar *m*, agitación *f*

unroll [ʌnról] VI/VT desenrollar(se)

unruly [ʌnrúli] ADJ (students) indisciplinado,
revoltoso, díscolo; (country) ingobernable;
(hair) rebelde

unsafe [ʌnséf] ADJ (uncertain) inseguro;
(dangerous) peligroso

unsatisfactory [ʌnsædɪsfǽktəri] ADJ no
satisfactorio, insatisfactorio

unscrew [ʌnskrú] VT desatornillar,
destornillar

unscrupulous [ʌnskrúpjələs] ADJ sin
escrúpulos

unseasonable [ʌnsízənəbəl] ADJ impropio de
la estación

unseat [ʌnsít] VT derribar

unseen [ʌnsín] ADJ invisible, oculto

unselfish [ʌnséɬfɪʃ] ADJ desinteresado

unselfishness [ʌnséɬfɪʃnɪs] N desinterés *m*

unsettled [ʌnsédld] ADJ (situation)
desordenado; (life) sin domicilio fijo;
(wilderness) sin colonizar; (case)
pendiente; (weather) variable

unsightly [ʌnsáɪtli] ADJ feo, antiestético

unskilled [ʌnskíɬd] ADJ (not trained)
inexperto; (not qualified) *Sp* no

cualificado; *Am* no calificado

unsophisticated [ʌnsəfístɪkeɪtɪd] ADJ sencillo, no sofisticado

unsound [ʌnsáund] ADJ (argument) erróneo, falso; (body) enfermizo; (mind) demente; (foundation) poco sólido; (investment) poco seguro

unspeakable [ʌnspíkəbəl] ADJ indecible

unstable [ʌnstébəl] ADJ inestable

unsteady [ʌnstédɪ] ADJ (walk) inseguro, inestable; (flame) tembloroso; (pulse) irregular

unsuccessful [ʌnsəksésfəl] ADJ sin éxito, infructuoso

unsuitable [ʌnsúdəbəl] ADJ (person) no apto; (place) inadecuado, inapropiado

unsuspected [ʌnsəspéktɪd] ADJ insospechado

untenable [ʌnténəbəl] ADJ insostenible

unthinkable [ʌnθíŋkəbəl] ADJ impensable

untidy [ʌntáɪdɪ] ADJ (dress) desaliñado, desastrado; (room) desordenado

untie [ʌntáɪ] VI/VT desatar(se), destrabar(se)

until [əntíl] PREP hasta; CONJ hasta que

untimely [ʌntáɪmli] ADJ (ill-timed) inoportuno; (premature) prematuro

untiring [ʌntáɪrɪŋ] ADJ incansable, denodado

untold [ʌntóld] ADJ (riches) incalculable; (suffering) inaudito

untouched [ʌntátʃt] ADJ (not injured) ileso; (not affected) no afectado; **he left his dessert —** no tocó el postre

untrained [ʌntrénd] ADJ (worker) *Sp* no cualificado; *Am* no calificado; (animal) no amaestrado; (eye) inexperto

untried [ʌntráɪd] ADJ (untested) no probado, no ensayado; (not taken to trial) no juzgado

untrue [ʌntrú] ADJ (incorrect) falso; (unfaithful) infiel; (disloyal) desleal

untutored [ʌntúdə-d] ADJ (unschooled) sin instrucción; (unsophisticated) inculto

untwist [ʌntwíst] VT desenroscar

unused [ʌnjúzd] ADJ sin usar; (unaccustomed) no habituado

unusual [ʌnjúʒuəl] ADJ (infrequent) desacostumbrado, raro; (highly abnormal) inusitado, insólito

unvarnished [ʌnvárnɪʃt] ADJ (without varnish) sin barnizar; (straightforward) puro

unveil [ʌnvél] VT (remove a veil) quitar el velo a; (reveal) descubrir

unwarranted [ʌnwɔ́rəntɪd] ADJ injustificado

unwelcome [ʌnwélkəm] ADJ (untimely) inoportuno; (unpleasant) desagradable; (poorly received) mal recibido

unwholesome [ʌnhólsəm] ADJ malsano

unwieldy [ʌnwíldi] ADJ poco manejable, difícil de manejar

unwilling [ʌnwílɪŋ] ADJ **to be — to** no estar dispuesto a

unwise [ʌnwáíz] ADJ imprudente

unwonted [ʌnwɔ́ntɪd] ADJ inusitado, inacostumbrado

unworthy [ʌnwɔ́-ði] ADJ indigno

unwrap [ʌnrǽp] VT desenvolver

unwritten [ʌnrítn] ADJ no escrito; (agreement) de palabra

unzip [ʌnzíp] VT abrir la cremallera

up [ʌp] ADV (position) arriba; (direction) hacia arriba; ADJ levantado, derecho, erecto; (assembled) armado; (finished) terminado, concluido; **—-and-coming** prometedor; **—-to-date** actualizado; **—-front** (paid in advance) inicial; (frank) franco; **he's — for reelection** se presenta para la reelección; **I'm feeling —** me siento optimista; **I'm — for golf** tengo ganas de jugar al golf; **prices are —** los precios han subido; **that is — to you** queda en tus manos, es cosa tuya; **the children are already —** ya se levantaron los niños; **the moon is —** salió la luna; **the wheat is —** germinó el trigo; **time is —** se terminó el tiempo; **to be — on the news** estar al corriente de las noticias; **to be — to one's old tricks** hacer de las suyas; **— and down** de arriba para abajo; **— against** enfrentado con; **what's —?** ¿qué pasa? PREP **— the current** contra la corriente; **— the river** río arriba; **— the street** calle arriba; **— to now** hasta ahora; N **—s and downs** altibajos *m pl*; VI **he — and went** agarró y se fue

upbeat [ʌpbít] ADJ optimista

upbringing [ʌpbrɪŋɪŋ] N crianza *f*

update [ʌpdét] VT actualizar

upend [ʌpénd] VI/VT (stand on end) poner(se) de punta; (defeat) derrotar

upgrade [ʌpgred] VT (facilities) mejorar; (computer) actualizar; N (facilities) mejora *f*; (computer) actualización *f*

upheaval [ʌphívəl] N trastorno *m*

uphill [ʌphíl] ADV cuesta arriba; [ʌphíl] ADJ penoso, arduo

uphold [ʌphóld] VT sostener, apoyar; (legal decision) refrendar

upholster [ʌphólstə-] VT tapizar

upholstery [ʌphólstəri] N tapicería *f*

upkeep [ʌpkip] N mantenimiento *m*

uplift [ʌplíft] VT (physically) elevar; (spiritually) edificar

upload [ʌplod] VT cargar

upon [əpán] PREP sobre, encima de; **—**

arriving al llegar; **once — a time** érase una vez

upper [Ápǝ] ADJ (higher) superior; (high) alto; **to have the — hand** dominar, llevar la ventaja; N (of shoe) pala f; (of berth) litera superior f; **— class** clase alta f; **— crust** flor y nata f; **—case** mayúsculo; **—cut** gancho al mentón m; **—most** (highest) de más arriba; (most important) mayor; **—s** dentadura postiza superior f

uppity [ÁpIDi] ADJ presumido

upright [Áprait] ADJ (posture) erecto, erguido; (position) vertical; (just) íntegro, recto, cabal; **— piano** piano vertical m; N (column) montante m; (piano) piano vertical m; (post) poste m

uprightness [Ápraitnis] N rectitud f

uprising [Ápraiziŋ] N alzamiento m, levantamiento m

uproar [Áprɔr] N tumulto m, alboroto m, bulla f

uproarious [Aprórias] ADJ (tumultuous) tumultuoso; (funny) graciosísimo

uproot [Aprút] VT arrancar de raíz, desarraigar

upscale [Ápskel] ADJ de lujo

upset [Apsét] VI/VT (overturn) volcar(se), tumbar; (distress) trastornar(se), perturbar(se), alterar(se); VT (in sports) derrotar al favorito; ADJ (overturned) volcado; (ill) indispuesto; (distressed) disgustado, enojado; [Ápset] N (overturning) vuelco m; (unexpected defeat) derrota inesperada f; (emotional state) trastorno m, disgusto m; (illness) malestar m

upshot [Ápʃat] N consecuencia f

upside [Ápsaid] N (upper part) parte superior f; (positive prospect) lo bueno; **— down** al revés, patas arriba

upstage [Apstédʒ] VT eclipsar

upstairs [Apstérz] ADV (location) arriba, en el piso de arriba; (movement) (para) arriba; [Ápsterz] ADJ de arriba; N piso de arriba m

upstart [Ápstart] N advenedizo -za mf

uptake [Áptek] N **quick on the —** listo; **slow on the —** duro de entenderas

uptight [Aptáit] ADJ (nervous) nervioso; (conventional) estreñido

upturn [Áptɔrn] N (prices) aumento m, subida f; (markets) tendencia alcista f

upward [Ápwǝd] ADV (toward a higher place) hacia arriba; **— of** más de; ADJ ascendente; N **— mobility** ascenso social m

uranium [juréniǝm] N uranio m

urban [Ábǝn] ADJ urbano; **— blight** tugurización f; **— legend** leyenda urbana f; **— renewal** renovación urbana f; **— sprawl** expansión urbana f

urchin [Átʃin] N pilluelo -la mf, guaje -ja mf

urethra [juríθrǝ] N uretra f

urge [ɝdʒ] VT (exhort) exhortar, urgir; (beg) rogar; (propose) propugnar; **to — on** animar; N impulso m, gana f

urgency [ɝdʒǝnsi] N urgencia f

urgent [ɝdʒǝnt] ADJ urgente

urinal [júrinǝl] N urinario m, mingitorio m

urinary [júrǝneri] ADJ urinario

urinate [júrinet] VI/VT orinar

urine [júrin] N orina f

URL (Uniform Resource Locator) [juɑrél] N URL m

urn [ɝn] N urna f

urologist [jurálǝdʒist] N urólogo -ga mf

Uruguay [júrǝgwai] N Uruguay m

Uruguayan [jurǝgwáiǝn] ADJ & N uruguayo -ya mf

us [ʌs] PRON nos; **she saw —** nos vio; **he came with —** vino con nosotros; **he gave it to —** nos lo dio (a nosotros)

USA (United States of America) [juesé] N EEUU m sg/pl

usable [júzǝbǝl] ADJ utilizable, aprovechable

usage [júsidʒ] N uso m, costumbre f

use [juz] VT usar, utilizar (also exploit); (consume) gastar; (take advantage of) aprovecharse de; VI **I —d to smoke** antes fumaba, solía fumar; **to — up** gastar, agotar; [jus] N (application) uso m; (utilization) empleo m, utilización f, aprovechamiento m; (usefulness) utilidad f; **it is of no —** es inútil; **out of —** en desuso; **to have no — for** no soportar; **to make — of** usar, utilizar; **to put to — utilizar; what is the — of it?** ¿para qué sirve?

used [juzd] ADJ usado; [just] **to be — to** estar acostumbrado a

useful [júsfǝl] ADJ útil

usefulness [júsfǝlnis] N utilidad f

useless [júslis] ADJ inútil, inservible

uselessness [júslisnis] N inutilidad f

user [júzǝ] N usuario -ria mf; **—-friendly** fácil de utilizar

usher [ʌʃǝ] N acomodador -ra mf; VT conducir, acompañar; **to — in** (a person) acompañar; (an era) anunciar, marcar el comienzo

usual [júʒuǝl] ADJ usual, habitual; (of clothes) de todos los días; **as —** como siempre; **she wasn't her — self** no era la de siempre; **the — thing** lo normal; **more than —** más que de costumbre

usurp [jusɜ́ɹp] VI/VT usurpar
usury [júʒəri] N usura f
utensil [juténsəł] N utensilio m, útil m
uterus [júʊəəs] N útero m
utilitarian [jutɪlɪtɛ́riən] ADJ utilitario
utility [jutíłɪdi] N utilidad f; (public service)
    empresa de servicio público f; —
    furniture muebles prácticos m pl; —
    program programa utilitario m; — **room**
    lavadero m
utilization [judˌɪzéʃən] N utilización f
utilize [júdlaɪz] VT utilizar
utmost [Átmost] ADJ (extreme) sumo,
    extremo; (farthest) más distante; N
    máximo m; **he did his** — hizo cuanto
    pudo; **to the** — al máximo
utopia [jutópiə] N utopía f
utter [ʌ́dɚ] VT (emit) dar, proferir; (say) decir,
    pronunciar; (make circulate) poner en
    circulación; ADJ absoluto, completo
utterance [ʌ́dɚəns] N (of words) enunciado
    m; (of money) emisión f
uvula [júvjələ] N campanilla f, úvula f
Uzbek [Úzbɛk] ADJ & N uzbeko -ka mf
Uzbekistan [uzbɛ́kɪstæn] N Uzbekistán m

Vv

vacancy [vékənsi] N (job) vacante f; (room in
    hotel) habitación libre f; **no** — completo
vacant [vékənt] ADJ (position) vacante;
    (expression) vacío; (seat, room) libre
vacate [véket] VI/VT (a room) desalojar,
    desocupar; (a contract) anular; (a position)
    dejar vacante
vacation [vekéʃən] N vacaciones f pl
vaccinate [vǽksənet] VI/VT vacunar
vaccination [væksənéʃən] N vacunación f
vaccine [væksín] N vacuna f
vacillate [vǽsəlet] VI vacilar
vacuum [vǽkjum] N vacío m; — **cleaner**
    aspiradora f; —**-packed** envasado al
    vacío; — **tube** tubo de vacío m; VI/VT
    aspirar, pasar la aspiradora
vagabond [vǽgəbɑnd] ADJ & N vagabundo
    -da mf
vagina [vədʒáɪnə] N vagina f
vagrancy [végrənsi] N vagancia f
vagrant [végrənt] ADJ & N vagabundo -da mf
vague [veg] ADJ vago, indistinto
vain [ven] ADJ (futile) vano, hueco; (proud of
    appearance) vanidoso; **in** — en vano
valentine [vǽləntaɪn] N (card) tarjeta del día

    de San Valentín f; (person) querido -da mf;
    —**'s Day** día de San Valentín m, día de los
    enamorados m
valet [vælé] N (manservant) criado m; (in a
    hotel) mozo de habitación m; (car parker)
    aparcacoches m sg
valiant [vǽljənt] ADJ valiente
valid [vǽlɪd] ADJ válido, valedero
validity [vəlídɪti] N validez f
valise [valíz] N maleta f, valija f
valley [vǽli] N valle m
valor [vǽlɚ] N valor m, valentía f
valorous [vǽləɹəs] ADJ valeroso, valiente
valuable [vǽljəbəł] ADJ valioso, preciado; N
    —**s** objetos de valor m pl
valuation [væljuéʃən] N (value) valoración f;
    (appraisal) tasación f, valuación f
value [vǽlju] N valor m; VT valorar
valve [vǽłv] N válvula f; (on mollusks) valva
    f
vamp [væmp] N vampiresa f; VT seducir
vampire [vǽmpaɪr] N vampiro m
van [væn] N camioneta f
vandal [vǽndł] N vándalo m
vane [ven] N (for weather) veleta f; (of a fan,
    windmill) aspa f; (of propeller) paleta f
vanilla [vənílə] N vainilla f
vanish [vǽnɪʃ] VI desaparecer, esfumarse
vanity [vǽnɪdi] N vanidad f; — **table**
    tocador m
vanquish [vǽnkwɪʃ] VT vencer
vantage [vǽntɪdʒ] N — **point** mirador m
Vanuatu [vɑnuátu] N Vanuatu m
Vanuatuan [vɑnuátuən] ADJ & N
    vanuatuense mf
vapor [vépɚ] N vapor m, humo m
vaporize [vépɚaɪz] VI/VT vaporizar(se)
variable [vériəbəł] ADJ & N variable f
variance [vériəns] N discrepancia f,
    desacuerdo m; **to be at** — no concordar
variant [vériənt] N variante f
variation [veriéʃən] N variación f
varicose [vérɪkos] ADJ varicoso; — **veins** Sp
    varices f pl; Am várices f pl
varied [vérid] ADJ variado, vario
variegated [vériɪgedɪd] ADJ variopinto
variety [varáɪɪdi] N variedad f
various [vériəs] ADJ vario
varnish [vɑ́rnɪʃ] N barniz m, charol m; VT
    barnizar, charolar
varsity [vɑ́rsɪdi] N equipo universitario m
vary [véri] VI/VT variar
vascular [vǽskjələɚ] ADJ vascular
vase [ves] N jarrón m; (for flowers) florero m
vasectomy [vəsɛ́ktəmi] N vasectomía f
Vaselineᵗᵐ [vǽsəlín] N vaselina f
vast [væst] ADJ vasto, inmenso

vastly [vǽstli] ADV radicalmente

vastness [vǽstnɪs] N inmensidad f

vat [væt] N tina f, barrica f

Vatican City [vǽdɪkənsídɪ] N Ciudad del Vaticano f

vaudeville [vɔ́dvɪl] N vodevil m

vault [vɔlt] N (arched structure) bóveda f; (burial chamber) panteón m; (place for valuables) cámara acorazada f; (jump) salto m; VT (cover with a vault) abovedar; VI/VT saltar

VCR (videocassette recorder) [visiár] N video m; Sp vídeo m

veal [vil] N ternera f; — **cutlet** chuleta de ternera f

veer [vir] VI/VT virar; N virada f

vegan [vígən] ADJ & N vegan mf

vegetable [véʤtəbəl] N (food) verdura f, hortaliza f; (plant, paralyzed person) vegetal m; — **garden** huerto m; (large) huerta f; — **kingdom** reino vegetal m; — **oil** aceite vegetal m

vegetarian [veʤətériən] ADJ & N vegetariano -na mf

vegetate [véʤətet] VI vegetar

vegetation [veʤətéʃən] N vegetación f

vehemence [víəmɪns] N vehemencia f

vehement [víəmənt] ADJ vehemente

vehicle [víkəl] N vehículo m

veil [vel] N velo m; VT velar

vein [ven] N (blood vessel, style) vena f; (small deposit of ore) veta f; (large deposit of ore) filón m

veined [vend] ADJ veteado; (leaf) nervado

velocity [vəlásɪdi] N velocidad f

velvet [vélvɪt] N terciopelo m; ADJ (of velvet) de terciopelo; (like velvet) aterciopelado

velvety [vélvɪdi] ADJ aterciopelado

vendetta [vɛndédə] N vendetta f

vending machine [véndɪŋməʃɪn] N máquina expendedora f

vendor [véndɚ] N vendedor -ora mf; (in a stall) puestero -ra mf

veneer [vənír] N (layer of wood) chapa f; (outward appearance) barniz m; VT chapar, enchapar

venerable [vénəəbəl] ADJ venerable

venerate [vénəret] VT venerar

veneration [venəréʃən] N veneración f

venereal [vəníriəl] ADJ venéreo

venetian blind [vəníʃənbláind] N veneciana f

Venezuela [vɛnɪzwélə] N Venezuela f

Venezuelan [vɛnɪzwélən] ADJ & N venezolano -na mf

vengeance [vénʤəns] N venganza f; **with a** — (violently) con furia; (energetically) con ganas

vengeful [vénʤfəl] ADJ vengativo

venison [vénəsən] N carne de venado f

venom [vénəm] N veneno m

venomous [vénəməs] ADJ venenoso

vent [vent] N (outlet for air) ventilación f; (opening of a volcano) chimenea f; **to give** — **to anger** desahogar la ira; VI/VT desahogar(se), descargar(se)

ventilate [véntlet] VI/VT ventilar(se)

ventilation [ventléʃən] N ventilación f

ventilator [véntlerɚ] N ventilador m

ventricle [véntrɪkəl] N ventrículo m

venture [vénʧɚ] N (adventure) aventura f; (business enterprise) empresa f; — **capital** capital de riesgo m; VI/VT aventurar(se), arriesgar(se)

venue [vénju] N lugar m

veranda [vərǽndə] N porche m, terraza f

verb [vɚb] N verbo m

verbal [vɚbəl] ADJ (linguistic, related to verbs) verbal; (not written) oral

verbatim [vɚbédəm] ADJ textual; ADV textualmente

verbiage [vɚbiɪʤ] N palabrerío m

verbose [vɚbós] ADJ verboso

verdict [vɚdɪkt] N veredicto m

verge [vɚʤ] ADV LOC **on the** — **of** al borde de, a punto de; VI **to** — **on** rayar en, lindar con

verification [verəfɪkéʃən] N verificación f, comprobación f

verify [vérəfaɪ] VT verificar, constatar

veritable [vérɪDəbəl] ADJ verdadero

vermillion [vɚmíljən] ADJ & N bermellón m

vermin [vɚmɪn] N bichos m pl

vermouth [vəmúθ] N vermú m

vernacular [vɚnǽkjələ] ADJ vernáculo; N (plain language) lengua vernácula f

versatile [vɚsəDəl] ADJ versátil

verse [vɚs] N verso m; (stanza) estrofa f; (line of poem) verso m; (in Bible) versículo m

versed [vɚst] ADJ versado

version [vɚʒən] N versión f

versus [vɚsəs] PREP contra; (in sports) versus

vertebra [vɚDəbrə] N vértebra f

vertebrate [vɚDəbrɪt] ADJ vertebrado

vertical [vɚDɪkəl] ADJ vertical

vertigo [vɚDɪgo] N vértigo m

very [véri] ADV muy; — **many** muchísimos; — **much** muchísimo; **it is** — **cold today** hace mucho frío hoy; ADJ (same) mismo; (mere) mero

vessel [vésəl] N (container) vasija f; (duct) vaso m; (ship) nave f

vest [vest] N chaleco m; VT conferir; —**ed interests** intereses creados m pl

vestibule [véstəbjuɫ] N vestíbulo *m*, zaguán *m*

vestige [véstɪʤ] N vestigio *m*

vet [vɛt] N (veterinarian) veterinario -ria *mf*; (veteran) veterano -na militar *mf*

veteran [vɛ́Dəən] ADJ & N veterano -na *mf*

veterinarian [vɛDəənériən] N veterinario -ria *mf*

veterinary [vɛ́Dəəneri] ADJ veterinario; — **medicine** veterinaria *f*

veto [víto] N veto *m*; VT vetar

vex [vɛks] VT molestar, irritar

via [váɪə, víə] PREP (by way of) vía; (by means of) por

viable [váɪəbəɫ] ADJ viable

vial [váɪəɫ] N ampolla *f*, frasco *m*

vibrate [váɪbret] VI/VT vibrar

vibration [vaɪbréʃən] N vibración *f*

vibrator [váɪbreDə] N vibrador *m*

vicarious [vaɪkériəs] ADJ indirecto

vice [vaɪs] N vicio *m*

vice-president [váɪsprézɪdənt] N vicepresidente -ta *mf*

viceroy [váɪsrɔɪ] N virrey *m*

viceroyalty [vaɪsrɔ́ɪəɫti] ADJ virreinato

vice versa [váɪsəvə́sə] ADV viceversa

vicinity [vɪsínɪDi] N vecindad *f*, cercanías *f pl*, aledaños *m pl*

vicious [víʃəs] ADJ (having vices) vicioso; (violent) violento, sanguinario; (evil) maligno, perverso; (malicious) malicioso; — **circle** círculo vicioso *m*; — **dog** perro fiero *m*, perro bravo *m*

vicissitude [vɪsísɪtud] N vicisitud *f*, peripecia *f*

victim [víktəm] N víctima *f*

victimize [víktəmaɪz] VT (make victim) victimizar; (dupe) estafar

victor [víktə] N vencedor -ora *mf*

victorious [vɪktóriəs] ADJ victorioso

victory [víktəri] N victoria *f*

video [vídio] N *Am* video *m*; *Sp* vídeo *m*; —**cassette** *Am* video *m*; *Sp* vídeo *m*; —**cassette recorder** videocasete *m*; —**conference** videoconferencia *f*; — **game** videojuego *m*; —**tape** *Am* cinta de video *f*; *Sp* cinta de vídeo *f*

vie [vaɪ] VI competir; **to — for power** disputarse el poder

Vietnam [vietnám] N Vietnam *m*

Vietnamese [vietnəmíz] ADJ & N vietnamita *mf*

view [vju] N (field of vision) vista *f*; (opinion) opinión *f*; (panorama) visión panorámica *f*; —**point** punto de vista *m*; **in — of** en vista de; **to be within** — estar a la vista; **with a — to** con el propósito de; VT (see)

ver; (consider) enfocar

viewpoint [vjúpɔɪnt] N punto de vista *m*

vigil [víʤəɫ] N vigilia *f*, vela *f*; **to keep —** velar

vigilance [víʤələns] N vigilancia *f*

vigilant [víʤələnt] ADJ vigilante

vigor [vígə] N vigor *m*, pujanza *f*, dinamismo *m*

vigorous [vígəəs] ADJ vigoroso

vile [vaɪɫ] ADJ (evil) vil, ruin; (foul, bad) pésimo

villa [víɫə] N quinta *f*, casa de campo *f*

village [víɫɪʤ] N aldea *f*, villa *f*

villager [víɫɪʤə] N aldeano -na *mf*

villain [vílən] N villano -na *mf*

villainous [vílənəs] ADJ vil, villano

villainy [víləni] N villanía *f*, vileza *f*

vindicate [víndɪket] VT reivindicar, vindicar

vindictive [vɪndíktɪv] ADJ vengativo

vine [vaɪn] N (grapevine) vid *f*; (decorative) parra *f*; (stem) sarmiento *m*; (climbing plant) enredadera *f*

vinegar [vínɪgə] N vinagre *m*

vineyard [vínjəd] N viña *f*, viñedo *m*

vintage [víntɪʤ] N (act or season of gathering grapes) vendimia *f*; (harvest of grapes) cosecha *f*; (year) año *m*; ADJ (wine) añejo; (classic) excelente; (old) antiguo, de colección; (typical) típico

vinyl [váɪnəɫ] N vinilo *m*

viola [vióɫə] N viola *f*

violate [váɪəlet] VT violar; (a law) violar, quebrantar

violation [vaɪəléʃən] N violación *f*; (traffic) infracción *f*

violence [váɪələns] N violencia *f*

violent [váɪələnt] ADJ violento

violet [váɪəlɪt] N (flower) violeta *f*; (color) violeta *m*; ADJ violeta *inv*

violin [vaɪəlín] N violín *m*

violinist [vaɪəlínɪst] N violinista *mf*

viper [váɪpə] N víbora *f*

virgin [vɜ́ʤɪn] ADJ & N virgen *f*; (uninitiated) no iniciado -da *mf*; — **Islands** Islas Vírgenes *f pl*

virginal [vɜ́ʤɪnəɫ] ADJ virginal

virile [víɾəɫ] ADJ viril

virility [vəɾílɪDi] N virilidad *f*

virtual [vɜ́tʃuəɫ] ADJ virtual; — **reality** realidad virtual *f*

virtue [vɜ́tʃu] N virtud *f*

virtuoso [vətʃuóso] ADJ & N virtuoso -sa *mf*

virtuous [vɜ́tʃuəs] ADJ virtuoso

virulent [víɾələnt] ADJ virulento

virus [váɪɾəs] N virus *m*

visa [vízə] N *Am* visa *f*; *Sp* visado *m*

vis-à-vis [vizɑví] PREP con respecto a

visceral [vísəɾł] ADJ visceral
viscous [vískəs] ADJ viscoso
vise [vaɪs] N tornillo de banco *m*
visible [vízəbəł] ADJ visible
Visigoth [vízɪɡəθ] N visigodo -da *mf*
vision [víʒən] N (sense, apparition) visión *f*; (eyesight) vista *f*
visionary [víʒəneɾi] ADJ & N visionario -ria *mf*
visit [vízɪt] VT visitar; (afflict) infligir; VI estar de visita; **to — with** charlar con; N (stay) visita *f*; (chat) charla *f*
visitation [vɪzɪtéʃən] N (apparition) visitación *f*; (punishment) castigo *m*; (parental right) régimen de visita *m*
visitor [vízɪɾə-] N visita *f*, visitante *mf*
visor [váɪzə-] N visera *f*
vista [vístə] N (visual) vista *f*; (mental) perspectiva *f*
visual [víʒuəł] ADJ visual
visualize [víʒuəlaɪz] VT visualizar, imaginar
vital [váɪdł] ADJ vital; **— signs** signos vitales *m pl*
vitality [vaɪtǽlɪdi] N vitalidad *f*
vitamin [váɪdəmɪn] N vitamina *f*
vituperation [vaɪtupəréʃən] N vituperación *f*, vituperio *m*
vivacious [vaɪvéʃəs] ADJ vivaz, vivaracho
vivacity [vaɪvǽsɪdi] N vivacidad *f*
vivid [vívɪd] ADJ vívido, vivo
vivisection [vívɪsekʃən] N vivisección *f*
vocabulary [vokǽbjəleɾi] N vocabulario *m*
vocal [vókəł] ADJ (musical) vocal; (outspoken) vociferante; **— cords** cuerdas vocales *f pl*
vocalic [vokǽlɪk] ADJ vocálico
vocation [vokéʃən] N vocación *f*
vociferous [vosífə-əs] ADJ vociferante
vodka [vádkə] N vodka *m*
vogue [vog] N boga *f*, moda *f*; **in —** en boga, de moda
voice [vɔɪs] N voz *f*; **— mail** contestador automático *m*; VT expresar
void [vɔɪd] ADJ (devoid, empty) vacío; (not binding) nulo, inválido; **—ed check** cheque anulado *m*; **— of** desprovisto de; N vacío *m*; VT (intestines) evacuar; (a check) anular
volatile [váləɾł] ADJ (liquid) volátil; (political situation) explosivo; (stock market) voluble; (temperament) cambiante
volcanic [vɑłkǽnɪk] ADJ volcánico
volcano [vɑłkéno] N volcán *m*
volition [vəlíʃən] N volición *f*; **of one's own —** por su propia voluntad
volley [váli] N (of firearms) descarga *f*; (of protests, arrows, stones) lluvia *f*; (of balls) volea *f*; VI/VT (bullets) descargar; (balls)

volear; **—ball** voleibol *m*, balonvolea *m*
volt [vołt] N voltio *m*
voltage [vółtɪdʒ] N voltaje *m*
volume [váljəm] N volumen *m*, tomo *m*
voluminous [vəlúmɪnəs] ADJ voluminoso
voluntary [válənteɾi] ADJ voluntario
volunteer [valəntír] ADJ & N voluntario -ria *mf*; VI/VT (offer) ofrecer(se), brindar(se); RP comedir(se); VI (do volunteer work) trabajar de voluntario -ria
voluptuous [vəláptʃuəs] ADJ voluptuoso
vomit [vámɪt] N vómito *m*; VI/VT vomitar
voodoo [vúpu] N vudú *m*
voracious [vɔréʃəs] ADJ voraz
vortex [vórteks] N vórtice *m*
vote [vot] N (right, ballot) voto *m*; (act of voting) votación *f*; VI votar; VT (a bill) aprobar; (a party) votar a / por; **to — do something** votar por hacer algo
voter [vódə-] N votante *mf*
vouch [vautʃ] VI **to — for** dar fe de, salir de fiador a, fiar a; VT **to — that** dar fe de que
voucher [váutʃə-] N (receipt) comprobante *m*; (coupon) vale *m*; (person) fiador -ra *mf*, garante *mf*
vow [vaU] N voto *m*; **to take a —** prometer; VT jurar
vowel [váuəł] N vocal *f*
voyage [vɔɪɪdʒ] N viaje *m*; (by sea) travesía *f*; VI viajar
voyeur [vɔɪɚ] N mirón -ona *mf*
vulgar [váłɡə-] ADJ (rude) ordinario, grosero, soez; (popular, vernacular) vulgar
vulgarity [vʌłɡǽrɪdi] N ordinariez *f*
vulnerable [váłnə-əbəł] ADJ vulnerable
vulture [váłtʃə-] N buitre *m*

Ww

wacky [wǽki] ADJ (person) chiflado; (idea) descabellado
wad [wad] N (for artillery, for filling) taco *m*; (ball) pelota *f*, pelotón *m*; (of money) rollo *m*, fajo *m*; VI/VT (a firearm) atacar; (a piece of paper) hacer una pelota (con)
waddle [wádł] VT anadear, andar como un pato; N anadeo *m*
wade [wed] VI andar por el agua; **to — through a book** leer con dificultad un libro
wafer [wéfə-] N (cookie) oblea *f*; (in Catholic ritual) hostia *f*; (computer) lámina / oblea

de silicio *f*

waffle [wɑ́fəɫ] ADJ *Sp* gofre *m*; *Am* wafle *m*;
— **iron** *Sp* plancha para hacer gofres *f*;
Am waflera *f*

waft [wæft] VI flotar; VT llevar por el aire; N
(of air) ráfaga *f*; (of odor) ola *f*

wag [wæg] VI/VT menear(se), mover(se); **to —
the tail** colear; N (movement) meneo *m*,
movimiento *m*; (joker) bromista *mf*

wage [wedʒ] N — **earner** asalariado -da *mf*;
(paid daily) jornalero -ra *mf*; —**s** salario *m*;
(daily) jornal *m*; — **scale** escala salarial *f*;
VT (war) hacer; (battle) librar

wager [wédʒɚ] N apuesta *f*; VI/VT apostar

wagon [wǽgən] N (horsedrawn) carro *m*;
(covered) carreta *f*; (toy) carrito *m*; **to fix
someone's** — vengarse de alguien; **to be
on the** — abstenerse de las bebidas
alcohólicas

wail [weɫ] VI lamentar; N lamento *m*

waist [west] N cintura *f*; (of garment) talle *m*;
—**band** pretina *f*; —**coat** chaleco *m*;
—**line** talle *m*, cintura *f*

wait [wet] VI/VT esperar; **to — for** esperar; **to
— on** servir; **to — tables** trabajar de
camarero -ra; N espera *f*; **to lie in — for**
estar en / al acecho de

waiter [wéɾɚ] N camarero *m*, mozo *m*,
mesero *m*

waiting [wéɾɪŋ] N espera *f*; — **list** lista de
espera *f*; — **room** sala de espera *f*

waitress [wétrɪs] N camarera *f*, moza *f*,
mesera *f*

waive [wev] VT (rights) renunciar a; (rule)
hacer una excepción

waiver [wévɚ] N (of rights) renuncia *f*; (of
rules) excepción *f*

wake [wek] VI/VT despertar(se); **to — up**
despertar(se); N (at death) velatorio *m*; (of
a ship) estela *f*, surco *m*; **in the — of**
después de, detrás de; —**up call** (in a
hotel) llamada del servicio despertador *f*;
(to action) llamada de atención *f*

wakeful [wékfəɫ] ADJ (awake) despierto;
(insomniac) insomne

waken [wékən] VI/VT despertar(se)

Wales [weɫz] N Gales *m sg*

walk [wɔk] VI andar, caminar; (to a place) ir
a pie; (go away) marcharse; **to — back**
volver a pie; **to — down** bajar a pie; **to
— in** entrar caminando; **to — out** (to go
out) salir caminando; (to abandon) dejar;
(to strike) declararse en huelga; —**out**
huelga *f*; **to — up** subir a pie; VT (to cause
to walk) hacer caminar; (to trace on foot)
recorrer; **to — the streets** callejear; N
(period of walking) paseo *m*, caminata *f*;

(pace) paso *m*; (gait) andar *m*; — **of life**
condición *f*; **to take a** — pasear, dar un
paseo

walker [wɔ́kɚ] N (to aid walking) andador *m*;
(one who walks) caminante *mf*; (in sports)
marchista *mf*

walking [wɔ́kɪŋ] ADJ andante; — **papers**
despido *m*; — **stick** bastón *m*

wall [wɔɫ] N (interior) pared *f*; (garden) muro
m, tapia *f*; (fort) muralla *f*; (of silence)
barrera *f*; **to have one's back to the** —
estar entre la espada y la pared; **to drive
someone up the** — sacar a alguien de
quicio; **I was climbing the** —**s** me
moría de aburrimiento; —**to**— de pared
a pared; —**flower** alhelí *m*; **she was a
—flower** no la sacaban a bailar; —**paper**
papel de empapelar *m*; **to —paper**
empapelar

wallet [wɑ́lɪt] N cartera *f*

wallow [wɑ́lo] VI (roll) revolcarse; (indulge
oneself) regodearse

walnut [wɔ́ɫnʌt] N nuez *f*; — **tree** nogal *m*

walrus [wɔ́ɫrəs] N morsa *f*

waltz [wɔɫts] N vals *m*; VI valsar

wand [wɑnd] N (rod) vara *f*; (magic) varita *f*

wander [wɑ́ndɚ] VI/VT vagar (por), errar
(por); **to — away** perderse; **my mind
—s easily** me distraigo fácilmente

wanderer [wɑ́ndərɚ] N vagabundo -da *mf*

wane [wen] VI menguar, flaquear; N mengua
f; **to be on the** — ir menguando

wannabe [wɑ́nəbi] N imitador -ora *mf*

want [wɑnt] VI/VT (desire) querer; **he —s
judgment** le falta juicio; **he's —ed in
Texas** se lo busca en Texas; N (desire)
deseo *m*; (lack) falta *f*; (scarcity) escasez *f*;
to be in — estar necesitado; — **ad** (aviso)
clasificado *m*

wanting [wɑ́ntɪŋ] ADJ (lacking) falto;
(deficient) deficiente

wanton [wɑ́ntən] ADJ (immoderate)
desenfrenado; (immoral) lascivo;
(senseless, unprovoked) gratuito

war [wɔr] N guerra *f*; — **crime** crimen de
guerra *m*; — **games** juegos de guerra *m pl*,
simulacro de batalla *m*; —**head** ojiva *f*;
—**ship** acorazado *m*; VI guerrear, hacer la
guerra

warble [wɔ́rbəɫ] VI gorjear; N gorjeo *m*

warbler [wɔ́rblɚ] N (European) curruca *f*;
(American) arañero *m*

ward [wɔrd] N (district) distrito *m*; (of a
building) pabellón *m*; (of a tutor) pupilo
-la *mf*; VI **to — off** resguardarse de,
conjurar

warden [wɔ́rdn̩] N guardián -na *mf*; (of

prison) alcaide *m*

wardrobe [wɔ́rdrob] N (room) guardarropa *m*; (furniture) ropero *m*, armario *m*; (garments) vestuario *m*, guardarropa *m*

warehouse [wɛ́rhaʊs] N almacén *m*, depósito *m*

wares [wɛrz] N mercancías *f pl*

warfare [wɔ́rfɛr] N guerra *f*

warlike [wɔ́rlaɪk] ADJ bélico

warm [wɔrm] ADJ (bath) caliente; (clothes) abrigado; (weather) caluroso; (colors, reception) cálido; **—-blooded** de sangre caliente; **—hearted** de buen corazón; **it is — today** hace calor hoy; VI/VT calentar(se); **to — over** recalentar; **to — up** calentar(se), templar(se); **—up** precalentamiento *m*; **it —s my heart** me alegra el corazón; **she —ed to the idea** se entusiasmó con la idea

warmth [wɔrmθ] N calor *m*, tibieza *f*

warn [wɔrn] VI/VT (advise of danger) advertir; (urge to behave) amonestar

warning [wɔ́rnɪŋ] N (of danger) advertencia *f*; (of punishment) amonestación *f*

warp [wɔrp] N (yarn) urdimbre *f*; (curve) comba *f*, alabeo *m*; VI/VT (wood) combar(se), alabear(se); (character) deformar(se); **he has a —ed personality** tiene una personalidad retorcida

warrant [wɔ́rənt] N orden *f*; **a — for his arrest** una orden de arresto contra él; VT garantizar

warranty [wɔ́rənti] N garantía *f*; VT garantizar

warrior [wɔ́riɚ] N guerrero -ra *mf*

wart [wɔrt] N verruga *f*

wary [wɛ́ri] ADJ cauteloso, cauto; **to be — of** desconfiar de

wash [wɑʃ] VI/VT lavar(se); **to — down** bajar; **to — out** (clean) quitar; (demolish) destruir; **to — up** lavarse; **he was —ed away by the waves** fue arrastrado por las olas; **his excuse won't —** su excusa no va a colar; **the bottle was —ed up on the shore** la botella fue traída por el mar; **—-and-wear** de lava y pon, de no planchar; **—ed-up** fracasado; **—ed-out** desteñido; **—out** (erosion) derrubio *m*; (failure) fracaso *m*; N (act of washing) lavado *m*; (clothes to be washed) ropa para lavar *f*; (washed clothes) ropa lavada *f*; **—cloth** toallita para lavarse *f*; **—room** lavabo *m*, lavatorio *m*

washable [wɑ́ʃəbəl] ADJ lavable

washer [wɑ́ʃɚ] N (washing machine) máquina de lavar *f*; (ring) arandela *f*; **— woman** lavandera *f*

washing [wɑ́ʃɪŋ] N lavado *m*; **— machine** lavadora *f*, máquina de lavar *f*

wasp [wɑsp] N avispa *f*

WASP (white Anglo-Saxon Protestant) [wɑsp] N persona blanca, anglosajona y protestante *f*

waste [west] VI/VT (squander resources) malgastar, desperdiciar; **to — away** consumirse; VT (squander time) perder; (murder) liquidar; N (of resources) desperdicio *m*, malgasto *m*, derroche *m*; (of time) pérdida *f*; (refuse) desperdicios *m pl*, desechos *m pl*; **to go to —** desperdiciarse; **—paper basket** papelera *f*; **— products** productos de desecho *m pl*; **—land** tierra yerma *f*, páramo *m*; **to lay — to** asolar

wasted [wéstɪd] ADJ (squandered) desperdiciado; (debilitated) consumido; (drunk) borracho

wasteful [wéstfəl] ADJ despilfarrador, gastador; (method) antieconómico

watch [wɑtʃ] VI (look) mirar; (be careful) cuidarse; (be vigilant) vigilar; VT (view) mirar, ver; (observe) observar; (tend) cuidar; **— out for the cars!** ¡cuidado con los coches! **to — for** estar a la espera de; **to — over** proteger; N (timepiece) reloj *m*; (period of wakefulness) vela *f*, vigilia *f*; (vigilant guard) guardia *mf*; (duty shift) guardia *f*; (lookout) centinela *m*; **—band** pulsera *f*; **—dog** (type of dog) perro guardián *m*; (organization) organismo de control *m*; **—maker** relojero -ra *mf*; **—making** relojería *f*; **—man** vigilante *m*, sereno *m*; **—tower** atalaya *f*, torre de vigilancia *f*; **—word** (password) contraseña *f*; (motto) consigna *f*, lema *m*; **to be on the —** estar alerta; **to keep — on / over** vigilar a

watchful [wɑ́tʃfəl] ADJ alerta, atento

water [wɔ́dɚ] N agua *f*; **—bed** cama de agua *f*; **—bird** ave acuática *f*; **— buffalo** búfalo de agua *m*; **—color** acuarela *f*; **—cress** berro *m*; **—fall** (small) cascada *f*; (large) catarata *f*; **—front** muelles *m pl*; **— heater** calentador de agua *m*; **— lily** nenúfar *m*; **—logged** empapado; **—melon** sandía *f*; **— pistol** pistola de agua *f*; **— power** energía hidráulica *f*; **— proof** (fabric) impermeable; (watch) sumergible; **to —proof** impermeabilizar; **—shed** vertiente *f*; **— ski** esquí acuático *m*; **to —ski** hacer esquí acuático; **— softener** ablandador de agua *m*; **— sports** deportes acuáticos *m pl*; **—spout** (pipe) tubo de desagüe *m*; (tornado) tromba f; — **supply** abastecimiento de agua m; — **table** capa freática f; —**tight** hermético; — **vapor** vapor de agua m; —**way** vía navegable f; **my** — **broke** se me rompieron las aguas, se me rompió la fuente; VT (irrigate) regar; (dilute) aguar; VI/VT (animals) abrevar; —**ed-down** (with water) aguado; (simplified) simplificado; (softened) suavizado; **my eyes are** —**ing** me lloran los ojos; **it makes my mouth** — se me hace agua la boca

watery [wɔ́dəri] ADJ (watered-down) aguado; (like water) acuoso; (boggy) húmedo

watt [wɑt] N vatio m

wattage [wɑ́dɪʤ] N vataje m

wave [wev] N (of radio) onda f; (of water, heat, fashion) ola f; (of disgust, of people) oleada f; (with the hand) saludo m; —**length** longitud de onda f; VI/VT (flag) ondear; (hair) ondular(se); VI (greeting) saludar con la mano; **to** — **good-bye** decir adiós con la mano

waver [wévə-] VI (hesitate) vacilar, titubear; (falter) flaquear

wavy [wévi] ADJ ondeado, ondulado

wax [wæks] N cera f; (for seals) lacre m; — **paper** papel encerado m; VT encerar; (defeat) derrotar; VI crecer; **to** — **poetic** ponerse poético

way [we] N (road) camino m; (manner) modo m, manera f; — **in** entrada f; — **out** salida f; **to** —**lay** (wait in ambush) estar al acecho de; (attack) asaltar; (stop) detener; —**farer** caminante mf; —**out** estrafalario; —**s** costumbres f pl; —**side** borde del camino m; — **through** paso m, pasaje m; **a long** — **off** muy lejos; **by** — **of London** por Londres; **by** — **of comparison** a modo de comparación; **by the** — a propósito; **in no** — de ningún modo; **on the** — to rumbo a; **to get out of the** — apartarse; **to go out of one's** — desvivirse por; **to look the other** — hacer la vista gorda; **to lead the** — ir a la cabeza; **to be in a bad** — hallarse mal de salud; **to give** — (yield) ceder; (break) quebrarse; **to get one's** — salirse con la suya; **to make** — **for** abrir paso para

wayward [wéwə-d] ADJ (disobedient) desobediente; (willful) porfiado

we [wi] PRON nosotros -as mf

weak [wik] ADJ débil; (deficient) flojo; — **force** fuerza débil f; —**kneed** achicado; — **sister** (coward) cobarde mf; — **link** parte más delgada del hilo f

weaken [wíkən] VI/VT debilitar(se), quebrantar(se)

weakling [wíklɪŋ] N alfeñique m

weakness [wíknɪs] N debilidad f, flaqueza f; (deficiency) flojedad f

wealth [welθ] N riqueza f

wealthy [wélθi] ADJ rico, adinerado, pudiente

wean [win] VT destetar; **to** — **oneself of** quitarse el vicio de

weapon [wépən] N arma f

wear [wer] VT (have on) llevar, tener puesto; (dress in habitually) usar; VI/VT (waste away) desgastar(se); **to** — **away** gastar(se), desgastar(se); **to** — **down** (a person) agotar; (a pencil) desgastar; **to** — **off** perder efecto; **to** — **on** prolongarse; **to** — **out** (make unfit) gastar(se), degastar(se), sobar(se); (expend) agotar; **it** —**s well** es duradero; N (use) gasto m; (clothes) ropa f; (durability) durabilidad f; (deterioration) desgaste m; — **and tear** desgaste m

weariness [wírinɪs] N cansancio m, fatiga f

wearing [wérɪŋ] ADJ (causing wear) desgastante; (causing fatigue) cansado

wearisome [wírisəm] ADJ fastidioso

weary [wíri] ADJ cansado, fatigado; VI/VT cansar(se), fatigar(se)

weasel [wízəł] N comadreja f

weather [wéðə-] N tiempo m; (storm) tempestad f; —**beaten** desgastado/ curtido por la intemperie; — **bureau** oficina meteorológica f; — **conditions** condiciones atmosféricas f pl; —**man** meteorólogo m; —**proof** resistente a la intemperie; —**vane** veleta f; **it is fine** — hace buen tiempo; **to be under the** — estar enfermo; VI/VT gastar(se); (skin) curtir; **to** — **a storm** capear un temporal

weave [wiv] VT (cloth, basket) tejer, entretejer; (to put together) urdir, tramar; **to** — **together / into** entretejer, entrelazar; **to** — **one's way** zigzaguear; N tejido m

weaver [wívə-] N tejedor -ra mf

web [web] N (of a spider) telaraña f; (of lies) sarta f; (membrane) membrana f; —**foot** (foot) pata palmada f; (animal) palmípedo m; — **page** página web f; —**site** sitio web m

wed [wed] VI/VT casarse (con); VT casar a

wedding [wédɪŋ] N boda f, casamiento m; — **day** día de boda m; — **dress** traje de novia m; — **ring** anillo de boda m

wedge [weʤ] N cuña f; **to drive a** — **between** separar; VT acuñar, meter cuñas; **to be** —**d between** estar apretado entre

Wednesday [wénzde] N miércoles m

wee [wi] ADJ chiquito, pequeñito

weed [wid] N mala hierba f; (marijuana) hierba f; **—killer** herbicida m; VT deshierbar, escardar; **to — out** eliminar

week [wik] N semana f; **—day** día de semana m; **—end** fin de semana m; **a — from today** de aquí en una semana

weekly [wíkli] ADJ semanal; ADV semanalmente; N semanario m

weep [wip] VI llorar, lagrimear

weeping [wípıŋ] ADJ lloroso; **— willow** sauce llorón m; N llanto m

weevil [wívəl] N gorgojo m

weigh [we] VI/VT pesar; (consider) ponderar, sopesar, barajar; **to — anchor** levar anclas; **to — down** agobiar, abrumar; **to — on one's conscience** pesar en la conciencia de uno

weight [wet] N (heaviness, importance) peso m; (for clocks, scales, barbells) pesa f; **—lifting** levantamiento de pesas m, halterofilia f; **— training** levantamiento de pesas m, halterofilia f; **—watcher** persona a dieta f; **to put on —** engordar; **to lose —** adelgazar; VT (add weight) añadir peso; (in statistics) ponderar; **to — someone down** agobiarla a uno

weightless [wétlıs] ADJ ingrávido

weighty [wédi] ADJ importante

weird [wírd] ADJ (strange) extraño; (supernatural) misterioso

weirdo [wírɒo] N bicho raro m, ente m

welcome [wélkəm] N bienvenida f; ADJ bienvenido; **—!** ¡bienvenido! **— mat** alfombrilla f, felpudo m; **— rest** descanso agradable m; **you are —** no hay de qué, de nada; **you are — here** estás en tu casa; **you are — to use it** a tus órdenes; VT (friendly) dar la bienvenida, acoger; (unfriendly) recibir

weld [wɛld] VI/VT soldar(se); N soldadura f

welfare [wɛ́lfɛr] N (good fortune) bienestar m; (public assistance) asistencia social f; **— state** estado de bienestar m

well [wɛl] ADV bien; **— then** pues bien; **—-being** bienestar m; **—-bred** bien educado; **—-defined** bien definido; **—-done** (steak) bien cocido; (a task) bien hecho; **—-fed** bien alimentado; **—-fixed** adinerado; **—-founded** bien fundamentado; **—-groomed** bien arreglado, aseado; **—-heeled** adinerado; **—-informed** bien informado; **—-known** (of a fact) bien sabido; (of a person) bien conocido, notorio; **—-made** bien hecho; **—-meaning** bien intencionado; **—-nigh** casi, muy cerca de; **he is — over fifty** tiene mucho más de cincuenta años;

—-off adinerado, acomodado; **—-read** leído, educado; **—-rounded** completo; **—-spoken** bien hablado; **—-to-do** adinerado; **all is —** todo está bien; INTERJ ¡bueno! ADJ (healthy) bien de salud, sano; N (of water, oil) pozo m; (of staircase) caja f; **—spring** fuente f, manantial m; VI **tears —ed up in her eyes** se le llenaron los ojos de lágrimas

wellness [wɛ́lnıs] N (health) salud f; (health care) medicina preventiva f

welsh [wɛlʃ] VI **to — on** (a debt) no pagar; (a promise) no cumplir

Welsh [wɛlʃ] ADJ & N galés -esa mf

welt [wɛlt] N verdugón m

west [wɛst] N (cardinal point) oeste m; (hemisphere) occidente m; **— Berlin** Berlín occidental m; **— Indies** Antillas f pl; **— wind** viento del oeste m; ADV (direction) hacia el oeste; (location) al oeste

western [wɛ́stə-n] ADJ occidental, del oeste; N película del oeste f

westerner [wɛ́stə-nə-] N occidental mf

westward [wɛ́stwə-d] ADV hacia el oeste; ADJ occidental

wet [wɛt] ADJ (drenched) mojado; (damp, rainy) húmedo; **— blanket** aguafiestas mf sg; **—land** humedal m; **— nurse** nodriza f; **— paint** pintura fresca f; **— suit** traje de buzo m; VI/VT mojar(se); (dampen) humedecer(se)

wetness [wɛ́tnıs] N humedad f

whack [hwæk] VI/VT golpear, pegar; **to — off** (cut) cortar; N golpazo m; Sp hostia f; **to take a — at** hacer un intento de; **out of —** descompuesto, averiado

whale [hwel] N ballena f; VI pescar ballenas

wharf [hwɔrf] N muelle m, embarcadero m

what [hwɑt] INTERR PRON, N & ADJ qué; **— did you say?** ¿qué dijiste? **— books did you want?** ¿qué libros querías? **—'s the matter?** ¿qué pasa? **— for?** ¿para qué? **and —not** y demás; REL PRON lo que; **come — may** venga lo que venga; **take — books you need** toma los libros que necesites; **any place —soever** en cualquier lugar; ADJ qué; **— happy children!** ¡qué niños más felices! **— luck!** ¡qué buena suerte! INTERJ cómo, qué; **so —?** ¡y qué?

whatever [hwɑtévə-] PRON lo que; **— do you mean?** ¿qué demonios quieres decir? **do it, — happens** hazlo, no lo que pase; **— you may think** pienses lo que pienses; ADJ **any person —** una persona cualquiera / cualquier persona; **no money**

— nada de dinero; INTERJ ¡lo que sea!

wheat [hwit] N trigo *m*; **— germ** germen de trigo *m*

wheel [hwił] N (disc) rueda *f*; (of cheese) horma *f*; (for pottery) torno *m*; (for steering a car) volante *m*; (on a ship) timón *m*; **—barrow** carretilla *f*; **—base** batalla *f*, paso *m*; **—chair** silla de ruedas *f*; **—s** coche *m*; VT (a round object) hacer rodar; (a person, bicycle, wheelchair) empujar; VI **to — out** sacar rodando; **to — in** entrar rodando; **to — around** girar sobre los talones

wheeze [hwiz] N resuello ruidoso *m*; VI resollar

when [hwɛn] ADV & CONJ cuando; INTERJ, ADV & N cuándo

whenever [hwɛnévə] CONJ **— I see him** cada vez que lo veo; ADV **— you arrive tomorrow** cuando llegues

where [hwɛr] ADV, N & INTERR PRON dónde *m*; (direction) adónde; CONJ donde; (direction) adonde

whereabouts [hwɛrəbaʊts] N paradero *m*; INTERR ADV dónde

whereas [hwɛrǽz] CONJ mientras que; (in preambles) visto que, considerando que

whereby [hwɛrbái] ADV por lo cual

wherefore [hwɛrfɔr] ADV por lo cual

wherein [hwɛrín] ADV en donde

whereof [hwɛráv] REL PRON de que; INTERR PRON de qué

whereupon [hwɛrəpán] ADV después de lo cual

wherever [hwɛrévə] ADV dondequiera que

wherewithal [hwɛrwiðɔł] N medios *m pl*, fondos *m pl*

whet [hwɛt] VT (sharpen) afilar; (stimulate) estimular; **—stone** piedra de afilar *f*

whether [hwɛðə] CONJ **— we like it or not** nos guste o no nos guste; **I doubt — we can do it** dudo (de) que lo podamos hacer; **he asked — I was coming** me preguntó si venía

which [hwɪtʃ] INTERR PRON cuál(es); **— do you want?** ¿cuál(es) quieres? REL PRON que; **the apple — I just bought** la manzana que acabo de comprar; **the book — I was talking about** el libro del que/cual estaba hablando; **that — you don't know can hurt you** lo que no sabes puede hacerte daño; INTERR ADJ qué, cuál(es) de; **— house is it?** ¿qué casa es? ¿cuál de las casas es?

whichever [hwɪtʃévə] PRON & ADJ (no matter which) cualquiera (que); **— you choose, you'll regret it later** elijas el que elijas,

te arrepentirás después; (anyone that) el que/la que; **choose — you like** elige el que quieras

whiff [hwɪf] N (waft) soplo *m*; (odors, scandal) bocanada *f*, tufillo *m*; **to take a —** oler

while [hwaɪl] N rato *m*; **a short —** un ratito; **a short — ago** hace poco; CONJ (during) mientras; (whereas) mientras que; (even though) aunque; VT **to — away** pasar

whim [hwɪm] N capricho *m*, antojo *m*

whimper [hwímpə] VI/VT lloriquear, gimotear; N lloriqueo *m*, gimoteo *m*

whimsical [hwímzɪkəl] ADJ caprichoso, antojadizo

whine [hwaɪn] VI (whimper) gemir; (complain) quejarse; N (whimper) gemido *m*; (complaint) quejido *m*

whiner [hwáɪnə] N llorón -ona *mf*, quejica *mf*

whiny [hwáɪni] ADJ quejoso, quejica, ñoño

whip [hwɪp] N azote *m*, látigo *m*, rebenque *m*; VT (hit with a whip) azotar, fustigar; (spank) zurrar, dar una paliza; (beat to a froth) batir; (defeat) vencer; **to — out** sacar; **to — up** (prepare) preparar rápidamente; (incite) incitar

whipping [hwípɪŋ] N zurra *f*, paliza *f*; **— cream** crema para batir *f*

whir [hwɜ] VI zumbar; N zumbido *m*

whirl [hwɜł] VI girar; **to — around** arremolinarse; **my head —s** me da vueltas la cabeza; N (rotation) giro *m*; (of water) remolino *m*; **—pool** remolino *m*; **—wind** torbellino *m*, remolino de viento *m*; **—wind tour** gira relámpago *f*; **my head is in a —** me da vueltas la cabeza; **to give it a —** probarlo

whisk [hwɪsk] VT (sweep) barrer; (beat) batir; **to — away** llevarse de prisa; VI **to — by** pasar rápidamente; N (broom) escobilla *f*; (beater) batidor *m*

whisker [hwískə] N (hair of beard) pelo de la barba *m*; (sideburn) patilla *f*; (of animals) bigote *m*

whiskey, whisky [hwíski] N whisky *m*

whisper [hwíspə] VI/VT (voices) cuchichear, secretear; (leaves, water) susurrar; N (voices) cuchicheo *m*; (leaves, water) susurro *m*; **to talk in a —** cuchichear en voz baja

whistle [hwísəł] VI/VT silbar; (loud) chiflar; (in protest) rechiflar; VI (referee, train) pitar; **to — for someone** llamar a uno con un silbido; N (sound) silbido *m*; (loud sound) chiflido *m*; (of a referee) pitido *m*; (instrument) silbato *m*, pito *m*; **— blower**

acusador -ora *mf*

white [hwaɪt] ADJ (of color, ethnicity) blanco; — **blood cell** glóbulo blanco *m*; — **bread** pan blanco *m*; —**bread** soso; —**caps** cabrillas *f pl*; —**collar** administrativo, de cuello blanco; — **gold** oro blanco *m*; — **hair** cana *f*; — **lie** mentirilla *f*; — **noise** ruido blanco *m*; to —**wash** (paint) blanquear, enjalbegar; (cover up) encubrir; —**wash** (paint) lechada *f*; (cover-up) encubrimiento *m*; N blanco *m* (also ethnicity); (of egg) clara *f*

whiten [hwaɪtn̩] VI/VT blanquear(se), emblanquecer

whiteness [hwáɪtnɪs] N blancura *f*

whitish [hwáɪdɪʃ] ADJ blancuzco, blanquecino

whittle [hwíd̩l] VI/VT tallar; **to — away** ir gastando; **to — down expenses** reducir los gastos

whiz [hwɪz] VI zumbar; **to — by** pasar zumbando; N (sound) zumbido *m*; (ace) as *m*; VT hacer zumbar; — **kid** niño -ña prodigio *mf*

who [hu] REL PRON quien(es); INTERR PRON quién(es); **he** — el que

whoa [hwo] INTERJ (to express amazement) ¡jo! (to stop a horse) ¡so!

whoever [huévə] REL PRON (whatever person) quienquiera que, el que; INTERR PRON (who) quién

whole [hoɫ] ADJ (complete) completo, íntegro; (unbroken) entero; (uninjured) ileso; —**-grain** integral; —**hearted** sincero; —**heartedly** de todo corazón; — **milk** leche entera *f*; — **note** redonda *f*; —**sale** (in bulk) al por mayor; (massive) masivo; —**saler** comerciante al por mayor *mf*, mayorista *mf*, almacenista *mf*; —**sale slaughter** matanza *f*; —**-wheat** integral; **the — day** todo el día; **to go — hog** tirar la casa por la ventana; N todo *m*; (for amounts) totalidad *f*; —**sale** venta al por mayor *f*, mayoreo *m*; **as a** — en su totalidad; **on the** — en general; ADV —**sale** al por mayor; VI/VT **to** —**sale** vender al por mayor

wholesome [hóɫsəm] ADJ sano

whom [hum] REL PRON a quien(es); INTERR PRON a quién(es); **for / with** — para / con quien

whoop [hwup] N (shout) grito *m*; (gasp) respiración convulsiva *f*; VI (person) gritar; (owl) ulular; **to — it up** armar jaleo

whopper [hwápə] N (large thing) cosa enorme *f*; (lie) mentira *f*, trola *f*

whopping [hwápɪŋ] ADJ enorme

whose [huz] REL PRON cuyo; **the man — son is here** el hombre cuyo hijo está aquí; INTERR PRON de quién; — **book is this?** ¿de quién es este libro?

why [hwaɪ] ADV & CONJ por qué; **that's the reason — he left** es por eso que se fue; N porqué *m*; INTERJ —, **of course!** ¡pero, claro!

wick [wɪk] N mecha *f*, pabilo *m*

wicked [wíkɪd] ADJ malvado, perverso

wickedness [wíkɪdnɪs] N maldad *f*, perversidad *f*

wicker [wíkə] N mimbre *m*; — **chair** silla de mimbre *f*

wide [waɪd] ADJ (broad) ancho; (of great range) amplio; (spacious) vasto, extenso; — **apart** muy apartados; —**awake** muy despierto, despabilado; — **body** avión de fuselaje ancho *m*; —**-eyed** ojiabierto, con los ojos bien abiertos; — **of the mark** lejos del blanco; —**open** abierto de par en par; —**spread** (over a wide area) extendido; (among many people) generalizado; **to open** — (a door) abrir de par en par; (one's mouth) abrir bien; **two feet** — dos pies de ancho

widely [wáɪdli] ADV **it is** — **known that** es bien sabido que; **he is a** — **known artist** es un artista muy conocido; **he is** — **read** es muy leído; — **different versions** versiones muy diferentes

widen [wáɪdn̩] VI/VT ensanchar(se), ampliar(se)

widow [wído] N viuda *f*

widower [wídoə] N viudo *m*

width [wɪdθ] N ancho *m*, anchura *f*

wield [wiɫd] VT (power) ejercer; (tool) manejar; (weapon) blandir, esgrimir

wife [waɪf] N esposa *f*, mujer *f*, señora *f*

wig [wɪg] N peluca *f*

wiggle [wígəɫ] VI/VT (hips) menear(se); (toes) mover(se), N (of hips) meneo *m*; (of toes) movimiento *m*; — **room** flexibilidad *f*

wigwam [wígwɑm] N tienda indígena *f*

wild [waɪɫd] ADJ (animals, savages) salvaje, bravío, bronco; (plant) silvestre; (party) desenfrenado; (conduct) alocado; (storm, temperament) violento; (hair) desordenado; (look) extraviado, desencajado; (enthusiasm) delirante; — **boar** jabalí *m*; — **card** comodín *m*; —**cat** gato montés *m*; —**-eyed** de mirada extraviada, con los ojos desencajados; —**fire** fuego arrasador *m*; —**flower** flor silvestre *f*; — **goose chase** búsqueda inútil *f*; —**life** fauna *f*; **I'm just — about Mary** estoy loco por María; **not in your**

—est dreams ni lo pienses; **to drive someone —** volver loco a alguien; **to talk —** decir disparates; N **—s** regiones salvajes *f pl*

wilderness [wíldə‑nɪs] N (near mountains) monte *m*; (desert) desierto *m*; (jungle) jungla *f*

wile [waɪł] N artimaña *f*, treta *f*

will [wɪł] VT (use will power) conseguir a fuerza de voluntad; (bequeath) legar, dejar; V AUX **if you —** si quieres; **she — come** va a venir, vendrá; **this motorcycle — go 100 mph** esta motocicleta puede hacer 100 millas por hora; **in spite of everything, he — not stop complaining** a pesar de todo, no deja de quejarse; **she — just sit for hours doing nothing** se pasa horas sentada sin hacer nada; **that — do** basta; N (wish) voluntad *f*; (testament) testamento *m*; **—power** fuerza de voluntad *f*; **at —** a la discreción, a voluntad

willful, wilful [wíłfəł] ADJ testarudo, porfiado

willies [wíliz] N escalofríos *m pl*

willing [wílɪŋ] ADJ dispuesto, voluntarioso

willingly [wílɪŋli] ADV de buena gana, gustoso

willingness [wílɪŋnɪs] N buena voluntad *f*, buena gana *f*

willow [wílo] N sauce *m*

wilt [wɪłt] VI/VT (plant) marchitar(se); VI (person) languidecer

wily [wáili] ADJ astuto, artero

wimp [wɪmp] N pelele *m*

win [wɪn] VI/VT ganar; VT (support, fame, affection) ganarse; (victory) alcanzar, conseguir; **to — out** ganar, triunfar; **to — over** conquistar; **a —‑— situation** una situación beneficiosa para ambas partes

wince [wɪns] VI hacer una mueca; N mueca *f*

winch [wɪntʃ] N cabrestante *m*, torno *m*

wind [wɪnd] N (air) viento *m*; (gas) gases *m pl*; **—bag** charlatán ‑ana *mf*; **—breaker**ᴵᴹ cazadora *f*; **—fall** ganancia inesperada *f*; **— instrument** instrumento de viento *m*; **—mill** molino de viento *m*; **—pipe** tráquea *f*; **—shield** parabrisas *m sg*; **—shield wiper** limpiaparabrisas *m sg*; **—sock** manga de viento *f*; **—surfing** windsurf *m*; **— tunnel** túnel aerodinámico *m*; **to get — of** enterarse de; **to break —** ventosear; **to catch one's —** recobrar el aliento; ADJ **—ward** de barlovento; ADV **—ward** hacia/a barlovento; [waɪnd] VT enrollar; (watch) dar cuerda a; VI (take a bending course)

serpentear; **to — around** enrollarse; **to — down** (relax) tranquilizarse; (come to a conclusion) irse terminando; **to — up** (string) enrollar; (a clock) dar cuerda; (a project) completar; (in jail) acabar; N (turn) vuelta *f*; (bend) recodo *m*; **—up** conclusión *f*

winding [wáɪndɪŋ] ADJ sinuoso; **— staircase** escalera de caracol *f*

window [wíndo] N (in building) ventana *f*; (in car, plane) ventanilla *f*; (in a shop) escaparate *m*; *Am* vidriera *f*; **—pane** cristal *m*, vidrio *m*; **— shade** visillo *m*; **—sill** alféizar *m*

windy [wíndi] ADJ ventoso; **it is —** hace/ hay viento

wine [waɪn] N vino *m*; **— cellar** bodega *f*; **—glass** copa *f*; **—grower** viticultor ‑ora *mf*, viñatero ‑ra *mf*; **— industry** industria vinícola *f*; **—skin** odre *m*; **— tasting** cata de vinos *f*

winery [wáɪnəri] N bodega *f*

wing [wɪŋ] N ala *f* (also of building, table, army); **— nut** tuerca (de) mariposa/ palomilla *f*; **—span/—spread** envergadura *f*; **—tip** extremo del ala *m*; **in the —s** en los bastidores; **under one's —** al amparo de alguien; **to take —** levantar vuelo; VI volar; VT (transport) transportar por aire; (wound slightly) herir en el ala/brazo; **to — it** improvisar

wink [wɪŋk] VI/VT guiñar; **to — approval** guiñar en aprobación; **to — at** hacer la vista gorda; N guiño *m*, guiñada *f*; **I didn't sleep a —** no pegué un ojo

winner [wínə‑] N ganador ‑ora *mf*

winning [wínɪŋ] ADJ (successful) ganador, vencedor; (charming) atractivo; **—s** ganancias *f pl*

wino [wáɪno] N borracho ‑cha *mf*

winter [wíntə‑] N invierno *m*; **— weather** clima invernal *m*; VI invernar

wintry [wíntri] ADJ invernal

wipe [waɪp] VT (sweat, tears) enjugar; (wet surfaces) secar; (dry surface) limpiar; **to — away** enjugar; **to — off** limpiar; **to — out** aniquilar; **to — up** limpiar

wiper [wáɪpə‑] N limpiaparabrisas *m sg*

wire [waɪr] N (filament) alambre *m*; (telegram) telegrama *m*; **by —** por telégrafo; **— fence** alambrado *m*; **—tap** intervención del teléfono *f*, pinchazo *m*; **to —tap** intervenir un teléfono, pinchar un teléfono; VT (an appliance) alambrar; (a house) electrificar; VI/VT (a message) telegrafiar; (money) girar; **to — together** atar con alambre

wired [waɪrd] ADJ (installed) alambrado; (tied) atado con alambre; (electrified) electrificado; (enthusiastic) sobreexcitado

wireless [wáɪrlɪs] ADJ inalámbrico

wiring [wáɪrɪŋ] N cableado *m*

wiry [wáɪri] ADJ (skinny) nervudo; (like wire) crespo

wisdom [wízdəm] N (moral) sabiduría *f*; (scholarly) saber *m*; **— tooth** muela del juicio *f*

wise [waɪz] ADJ (discerning) sabio; (prudent) sensato, prudente; (erudite) erudito; **—crack** broma *f*, chiste *m*; **— guy** sabihondo *m*; **the Three — Men** los Tres Reyes Magos; N **in no —** de ningún modo; VI **to — up** avisparse

wish [wɪʃ] VT desear; **I — you were here** ojalá estuvieras aquí; **I — you the best** te deseo lo mejor; **to — for** pedir; **to — upon a star** pedir un deseo; N deseo *m*; **to make a —** pedir un deseo; **best —es** saludos

wishy-washy [wíʃiwaʃi] ADJ indeciso

wistful [wístfəl] ADJ (pensive) pensativo; (nostalgic) nostálgico

wit [wɪt] N (intelligence) agudeza *f*, ingenio *m*; (verbal humor) gracejo *m*, sal *f*, chispa *f*; (person) persona aguda *f*, persona ingeniosa *f*; **to be at one's —s' end** no saber qué más hacer; **to live by one's —s** vivir de su ingenio; **to lose one's —s** perder el juicio; **to use one's —s** valerse de su ingenio

witch [wɪtʃ] N bruja *f*; **—craft** brujería *f*; **—hunt** cacería de brujas *f*

with [wɪθ, wɪð] PREP con; **rice — chicken** arroz con pollo *m*; **the man — glasses** el hombre de gafas; **I left my son — Mary** dejé a mi hijo al cuidado de María; **to be — it** está al día; **— me** conmigo; **— you** contigo, con usted

withdraw [wɪðdrɔ́] VI/VT retirar(se)

withdrawal [wɪðdrɔ́əl] N (of troops) retirada *f*; (from public office) alejamiento *m*; (from a bank) *Am* retiro *m*; *Sp* retirada *f*; **— (symptoms)** síndrome de abstinencia *m*

wither [wíðə] VI/VT (of a plant) marchitar(se); (of a person) consumir(se); **she —ed him with a look** lo fulminó con la mirada

withhold [wɪθhóld] VT (approval) negar; (funds) retener; (truth) ocultar

withholding tax [wɪθhóldɪŋtæks] N impuesto deducido del salario *m*

within [wɪðín] PREP dentro de; **— five miles** a menos de cinco millas; ADV dentro, adentro

without [wɪðáʊt] PREP sin; **— my seeing him** sin que yo lo vea; ADV fuera, afuera

withstand [wɪθstǽnd] VI/VT resistir

witness [wítnɪs] N (person) testigo *mf*; (testimony) testimonio *m*; **to bear —** atestiguar; VT (see) presenciar; (sign) firmar como testigo

witticism [wítɪsɪzem] N ocurrencia *f*

witty [wídi] ADJ ocurrente, dicharachero

wizard [wízəd] N (sorcerer) mago *m*, brujo *m*, hechicero *m*; (genius) genio *m*

wobble [wábəl] N bamboleo *m*, tambaleo *m*; VI/VT tambalear(se), bombolear(se)

woe [wo] N aflicción *f*; **— is me!** ¡pobre de mí!

woeful [wófəl] ADJ lamentable

wok [wak] N wok *m*

wolf [wʊlf] N lobo *m*; **— spider** araña lobo *f*

woman [wʊmən] N mujer *f*; **a —'s touch** un toque femenino; **women's lib(eration)** movimiento de liberación femenina *m*; **women's rights** derechos de la mujer *m pl*

womanhood [wʊmənhʊd] N (condition) condición de mujer *f*; (group of women) las mujeres *f pl*

womanizer [wʊmənaɪzə] N mujeriego *m*

womankind [wʊmənkaɪnd] N las mujeres *f pl*

womanly [wʊmənli] ADJ femenino

womb [wum] N (uterus) útero *m*, matriz *f*; (insides) vientre *m*; (center) seno *m*

wonder [wándə] VI/VT preguntarse; **to — at** admirarse de, maravillarse de; **I — what time it is** ¿qué hora será? N (marvel) maravilla *f*; (surprise) asombro *m*; (miracle) milagro *m*; **it's a — that** es asombroso que; **it's no — that** no es de extrañar que

wonderful [wándəfəl] ADJ maravilloso, estupendo

woo [wu] VI/VT cortejar

wood [wʊd] N (material) madera *f*; (firewood) leña *f*; **—cutter** leñador -ora *mf*; **—louse** cochinilla *f*; **—pecker** pájaro carpintero *m*; **—s** bosque *m*; **— shaving** viruta *f*; **—shed** leñera *f*; **—sman** leñador *m*; **—winds** maderas *f pl*; **—work** carpintería *f*, maderaje *m*; **to come out of the —work** salir de la nada

wooded [wʊdɪd] ADJ arbolado

wooden [wʊdn] ADJ (of wood) de madera; (lifeless) inexpresivo

woody [wʊdi] ADJ (with trees) arbolado; (like wood) leñoso

woof [wʊf] N trama *f*; INTERJ ¡guau!

wool [wʊɫ] N lana f; — **sweater** suéter de lana m

woolen [wúlən] ADJ de lana; N —**s** (fabric) tejido de lana m; (clothes) ropa de lana f

woolly [wúli] ADJ lanudo

word [wɜ·d] N (lexical unit) vocablo m; palabra f (also promise); (news) noticia f, aviso m; (order) mandato m, orden m; **may I have a — with you?** ¿podemos hablar? — **processing** procesamiento de textos m; Sp tratamiento de texto(s) m; **by — of mouth** de palabra; —**s (of a song)** letra (de una canción) f; **to eat one's —s** tragarse / comerse las palabras; — **for —** palabra por palabra; VT (oral) expresar; (written) formular

wordy [wɜ́·ɾi] ADJ verboso, prolijo

work [wɜ·k] N (effort) trabajo m; (employment) empleo m, trabajo m; (artistic product, fortification) obra f; —**book** cuaderno / libro de trabajo m; —**day** día laborable m; —**force** mano de obra f; —**load** cantidad / carga de trabajo f; —**man** obrero m; — **of art** obra de arte f; —**place** lugar de trabajo m; —**shop** taller m; — **station** terminal de trabajo m; —**s** fábrica f; **the —s** todo; —**week** semana de trabajo f; **he's hard at** — está trabajando duro; VI (labor) trabajar; (function) funcionar; VT (change) efectuar; (metal, land) trabajar; (a crowd) manipular; (a mine) explotar; (employees) hacer trabajar; **to** — **in(to)** introducir; **to** — **loose** soltarse, aflojarse; **to** — **on** (repair) arreglar; (improve) tratar de mejorar; **to** — **one's way through college** pagarse los estudios trabajando; **to** — **one's way up** ascender a fuerza de trabajo; **to** — **out** (a plan) urdir; (a problem) resolver; **he** —**s out every day** hace ejercicio todos los días; **it all** —**ed out** al final todo salió bien; **to be all** —**ed up** estar sobreexcitado; **to get** —**ed up** agitarse

worker [wɜ́·kɚ] N trabajador -ora mf; (in a factory) obrero -ra mf; (in an office) oficinista mf

working [wɜ́·kɪŋ] N (act of someone who works, shaping of metals) trabajo m; (operation) funcionamiento m, operación f; (of a problem) cálculo m; (of a mine) explotación f; ADJ (class) obrero, trabajador; (majority) suficiente; — **class** clase obrera / trabajadora f; — **lunch** comida de trabajo f; —**man** obrero m

workmanship [wɜ́·kmənʃɪp] N (skill) habilidad f, destreza f; (quality) confección f

world [wɜ·ɫd] N mundo m; —**view** cosmovisión f; — **war** guerra mundial f; —**wide web** web f, red (mundial electrónica) f; ADJ —**class** de categoría mundial; —**shaking** trascendental; —**wide** mundial

worldly [wɜ́·ɫdli] ADJ (mundane) mundano, temporal; (sophisticated) de mundo, corrido; (material) material

worm [wɜ·m] N gusano m; ADJ —**eaten** comido por los gusanos, carcomido; VT desparasitar, quitar las lombrices; **to** — **a secret out of someone** extraerle / sonsacarle un secreto a alguien; **to** — **oneself into** insinuarse en

worn [wɔrn] ADJ desgastado, usado

worrisome [wɜ́·risəm] ADJ preocupante

worry [wɜ́·i] VI/VT preocupar(se), inquietar(se); VT (harass) atacar; VI **to** — **with** juguetear con; N preocupación f, inquietud f, zozobra f; —**wart** preocupón -ona mf

worse [wɜ·s] ADJ & ADV peor; — **and** — cada vez peor; — **than ever** peor que nunca; **from bad to** — de mal en peor; **so much the** — tanto peor; **to be** — **off** estar peor que antes; **to change for the** — empeorar(se); **to get** — empeorar(se)

worship [wɜ́·ʃɪp] N (act of worshiping) adoración f; (ceremony) culto m; VT (revere) adorar, venerar; VI (attend services) asistir al culto

worshiper [wɜ́·ʃɪpɚ] N (one who worships) adorador -ora mf; —**s** fieles mf pl

worst [wɜ·st] ADJ & ADV peor; **the** — **one** el / la peor; **the** — **thing** lo peor; —**case scenario** el peor de los casos; VT derrotar

worth [wɜ·θ] ADJ **to be** — **a dollar** valer un dólar; **to be** — **hearing** ser digno de oírse; **to be** — **while** valer la pena; **it's** — **doing** vale la pena hacerlo; N valor m, valía f; **ten cents** — **of** diez centavos de; **to get one's money's** — **out of** aprovechar al máximo

worthless [wɜ́·θlɪs] ADJ (useless) inútil; (despicable) despreciable

worthy [wɜ́·ði] ADJ digno, meritorio; (esteemed) benemérito; — **cause** causa noble f; — **of praise** digno de elogio; N notable mf

would [wʊd] V AUX **I** — **do it if I could** lo haría si pudiera; — **you please open the door?** ¿podrías abrir la puerta por favor? **he said he** — **do it** dijo que lo haría; **as a child, I** — **play all the time** de niño, jugaba todo el tiempo; — **that she were**

alive! ¡ojalá estuviera viva!

wound [wund] N herida *f*; VI/VT herir; (with an arrow) flechar

wow [waʊ] VT impresionar; INTERJ ¡huy!

wrangle [ræ̃ŋgəł] VI/VT (quarrel) discutir; (obtain) agenciarse de; VT (herd) juntar; *Am* rodear; N riña *f*, pendencia *f*

wrangler [ræ̃ŋglə] N vaquero -ra *mf*

wrap [ræp] VT envolver; **to — up** (a present) envolver; (a baby) arropar; (a task) terminar; (against the cold) abrigar(se); **to be wrapped in** estar envuelto en; **to be wrapped up in** estar absorto en; N (coat) abrigo *m*; (shawl) chal *m*; **—-up** (summary) resumen *m*; (end) final *m*

wrapper [ræpə] N envoltura *f*, envoltorio *m*

wrapping [ræpɪŋ] N envoltura *f*; **— paper** papel para envolver *m*

wrath [ræθ] N ira *f*, cólera *f*

wreak [rik] VT **to — havoc** hacer estragos

wreath [riθ] N corona *f*; **— of smoke** espiral de humo *f*

wreck [rɛk] N (building) ruina *f*; (car, plane) restos *m pl*; (a ship) pecio *m*; (shipwreck) naufragio *m*; (person) desastre *m*, ruina *f*; (accident) accidente *m*; VI tener un accidente; VT (a ship) naufragar; (a car, totally) destrozar; (a car, with minor damage) chocar; (a building) demoler

wreckage [rɛkɪʤ] N (of a car, plane) restos de un accidente *m pl*; (of a ship) pecio *m*; (of a building) escombros *m pl*

wrecker [rɛkə] N (tow truck) grúa *f*, camión de remolque *m*; (worker) obrero -ra de demolición *mf*

wrench [rɛntʃ] VT torcer, retorcer; **to — off / out** arrancar de un tirón, arrebatar; N (twist) torcedura *f*; (pull) tirón *m*; (tool) llave de tuercas *f*

wrest [rɛst] VT (pull) arrancar; (take away) arrebatar

wrestle [rɛsəł] VI/VT luchar (con / contra); N lucha *f*

wrestler [rɛslə] N luchador -ra *mf*

wrestling [rɛslɪŋ] N lucha libre *f*

wretch [rɛtʃ] N miserable *mf*, infeliz *mf*

wretched [rɛtʃɪd] ADJ (unfortunate) desdichado, infeliz; (despicable) vil, miserable, arrastrado; (inferior) pésimo

wriggle [rɪgəł] VI culebrear, serpentear; VT menear, retorcer; **to — out of** escabullirse de

wring [rɪŋ] VT (twist) torcer, retorcer; (extract) arrancar; **to — one's hands** retorcerse las manos; **to — out** escurrir

wrinkle [rɪ́ŋkəł] N arruga *f*, surco *m*; (problem) problema *m*; VI/VT arrugar(se)

wrist [rɪst] N muñeca *f*; **—watch** reloj (de) pulsera *m*

writ [rɪt] N auto *m*, mandato *m*

write [raɪt] VI/VT escribir; **to — back** contestar; **to — down** apuntar; **to — off** cancelar; **to — out** escribir en forma completa; **to — up** hacer un reportaje sobre; **it's written all over his face** se le ve en la cara; **she —s for a living** es escritora; N **—-up** reportaje *m*

writer [ráɪDə] N escritor -ora *mf*, literato -ta *mf*

writhe [raɪð] VI retorcerse

writing [ráɪDɪŋ] N (act of writing) escritura *f*; (handwriting) letra *f*, escritura *f*; (style) estilo *m*; **— desk** escritorio *m*; **— paper** papel de escribir *m*; **—s** obra *f*; **to put in —** poner por escrito

wrong [rɔŋ] ADJ (incorrect) incorrecto, equivocado; (improper) inapropiado; **what's — with you?** ¿qué te pasa? **you are —** estás equivocado; **the — side of a fabric** el revés de una tela; **— side out** con lo de adentro para afuera; **to be on the — side of the road** ir a contramano / en sentido contrario; **that is the — book** ese no es el libro; **it is in the — place** está fuera de lugar; ADV mal; **to go —** salir mal; N (evil) mal *m*; (injustice) injusticia *f*; **to be in the —** (not be right) estar equivocado; (be to blame) tener la culpa; **to do —** hacer mal; VT perjudicar

wrought [rɔt] ADJ forjado; **— iron** hierro forjado *m*

wry [raɪ] ADJ (smile) torcido; (remark, humor) irónico; **to make a — face** hacer una mala cara

Xx

xenophobia [zɛnəfóbiə] N xenofobia *f*

Xerox™ [zírɑks] N fotocopia *f*; VI/VT fotocopiar

x-rated [ɛ́ksreɪDɪd] ADJ pornográfico

x-ray [ɛ́ksre] N rayos X *m pl*, radiografía *f*; VI/VT radiografiar

xylophone [záɪləfon] N xilófono *m*, xilófono *m*

Yy

yacht [jɑt] N yate m; VI navegar en yate

y'all [jɔl] PRON ustedes mf; *Sp* vosotros -as mf

Yankee [jǽŋki] ADJ & N estadounidense del norte del país mf

yard [jɑrd] N (measure) yarda (0.9144m) f; (spar) verga f; (courtyard) patio m; (grassy area) jardín m; —**stick** (stick) vara de medida (de una yarda) f; (criterion) patrón m, norma f

yarn [jɑrn] N (material) hilo m; (story) cuento m

yawn [jɔn] VI bostezar; N bostezo m

year [jir] N año m; —**book** anuario m; —**-round** de todo el año

yearling [jírlɪŋ] N animal de un año m; (of cows) añojo -ja m

yearly [jírli] ADJ anual; ADV anualmente

yearn [jɜ·n] VI anhelar, suspirar por

yearning [jɜ·nɪŋ] N anhelo m

yeast [jist] N levadura f

yell [jeɬ] VI/VT gritar; N grito m

yellow [jélo] ADJ (color) amarillo; (coward) cobarde; — **fever** fiebre amarilla f; — **jacket** avispa f; — **pages** páginas amarillas f pl; N amarillo m; VI/VT poner(se) amarillo, amarillear

yellowish [jéloɪʃ] ADJ amarillento

yelp [jeɬp] VI gañir, aullar; N gañido m, aullido m

Yemen [jémən] N Yemen m

Yemeni [jéməni] ADJ & N yemení mf

yen [jen] N (currency of Japan) yen m; (desire) anhelo m; VI anhelar

yes [jes] ADV sí; —**-no question** pregunta de sí o no f

yesterday [jéstə·de] ADV & N ayer m; **the day before** — anteayer

yet [jet] ADV & CONJ **are they here** —? ¿ya llegaron? **they aren't here** — todavía no llegan, aún no han llegado; — **another** otro más; **ugly** — **charming** feo pero encantador; **as** — todavía, aún

yield [jiɬd] VI/VT (surrender, give in) ceder, plegar(se); (produce) rendir, redituar; **to** — **five percent** dar un cinco por ciento de interés; N (production) rendimiento m, producción f; (of stocks) rédito m

yodel [jódl] VI cantar a la tirolesa; N canto tirolés m

yoga [jógə] N yoga m

yogurt [jógə·t] N yogur m

yoke [jok] N (crossbar) yugo m; (pair of animals) yunta f; (on a shirt) canesú m; VT uncir

yolk [jok] N yema f

yonder [jándə·] ADJ aquel; ADV (location) allá; (direction) hacia allá

yore [jɔr] N **in days of** — antaño

you [ju] PRON — **came** (sg informal) tú viniste; (sg formal) usted vino; (pl informal) *Sp* vosotros vinisteis; *Am* ustedes vinieron; (formal) ustedes vinieron; **I see** — (sg informal) te veo; (sg formal) lo veo; (pl informal) *Sp* os veo; *Am* los veo; (pl formal) los veo; **I talk to** — (sg informal) te hablo; (sg formal) le hablo; (pl informal) *Sp* os hablo; *Am* les hablo; (pl formal) les hablo; **I went with** — (sg informal) fui contigo; (sg formal) fui con ústed; (pl informal) *Sp* fui con vosotros; *Am* fui con ustedes; (pl formal) fui con ustedes; **it's for** — (sg informal) es para ti; (sg formal) es para usted; (pl informal) *Sp* es para vosotros; *Am* es para ustedes; (pl formal) es para ustedes; **this is how** — **make bread** así se hace el pan

young [jʌŋ] ADJ joven; — **man** joven m; — **people** gente joven f; — **woman** joven f; N (offspring) cría f

youngster [jʌ́ŋstə·] N muchacho -cha mf, jovencito -ta mf

your [jɔr] POSS ADJ **this is** — **dog** (sg informal) este es tu perro; (sg formal) este es su perro; (pl informal) *Sp* este es vuestro perro; *Am* este es su perro; (pl formal) este es su perro

yours [jɔrz] PRON **this book is** — (sg informal) este libro es tuyo; (sg formal) este libro es suyo/de usted; (pl informal) *Sp* este libro es vuestro; *Am* este libro es suyo/de ustedes; (pl formal) este libro es suyo/de ustedes; — **is bigger** (sg informal) el tuyo/la tuya es más grande; (sg formal) el suyo/el de usted/la suya/la de usted es más grande; (pl informal) *Sp* el vuestro/la vuestra es más grande; *Am* el suyo/el de ustedes es más grande; (pl formal) el suyo/el de ustedes es más grande; **a friend of** — (sg informal) un amigo tuyo; (sg formal) un amigo suyo/de usted; (pl informal) *Sp* un amigo vuestro; *Am* un amigo suyo/de ustedes; — **truly** atentamente

yourself [jɔrséɬf] PRON **you** — **wrote the letter** (sg informal) tú mismo escribiste la carta; (sg formal) usted mismo escribió la carta; **you yourselves wrote the letter** (pl informal) *Sp* vosotros mismos escribisteis la carta; *Am* ustedes mismos escribieron la carta; (pl formal) ustedes mismos escribieron la carta; **you are not — today** (sg informal) hoy no eres el mismo de siempre; (sg formal) hoy no es el mismo de siempre; **you are not yourselves today** *Sp* hoy no sois los mismos de siempre; *Am* hoy no son los mismos de siempre; (pl formal) hoy no son los mismos de siempre; **you were sitting by —** (sg informal) tú estabas sentado solo; (sg formal) usted estaba sentado solo; **you were sitting by yourselves** (informal) *Sp* vosotros estabais sentados solos; *Am* ustedes estaban sentados solos; (pl formal) ustedes estaban sentados solos; **you look at — at the mirror** (sg informal) tú te miras en el espejo; (sg formal) usted se mira en el espejo; **you look at yourselves at the mirror** (pl informal) *Sp* vosotros os mirais en el espejo; *Am* ustedes se miran en el espejo; (pl formal) ustedes se miran en el espejo; **you bought — a house** (sg informal) te compraste una casa; (sg formal) usted se compró una casa; **you bought yourselves a house** (pl informal) *Sp* os comprasteis una casa; *Am* se compraron una casa; (pl formal) se compraron una casa

youth [juθ] N (person) joven *m*; (young age) juventud *m*

youthful [júθfəł] ADJ juvenil

yo-yo [jójo] N yo-yo *m*

yucca [jákə] N yuca *f*

yuck [jʌk] INTERJ puaj, puaf

Yugoslavia [jugosláviə] N Yugoslavia *f*

Yugoslavian [jugoslávian] ADJ & N yugoslavo -va *mf*

Yuletide [júłtaɪd] N Navidad *f*

yummy [jámi] ADJ delicioso; INTERJ ¡qué rico!

yuppie [jápi] N yuppie *mf*

Zz

Zambia [zǽmbiə] N Zambia *f*

Zambian [zǽmbiən] ADJ & N zambiano -na *mf*

zany [zéni] ADJ absurdo

zap [zæp] VT liquidar

zeal [ził] N celo *m*, fervor *m*

zealot [zélət] N fanático -ca *mf*

zealous [zéləs] ADJ celoso, fervoroso

zebra [zíbrə] N cebra *f*

zenith [zíniθ] N cenit *m*

zephyr [zéfə-] N céfiro *m*

zeppelin [zépəlɪn] N zepelín *m*, dirigible *m*

zero [ziro] N cero *m*; **there's — possibility that he'll come** las posibilidades de que venga son nulas

zest [zɛst] N entusiasmo *m*

zigzag [zígzæg] N zigzag *m*; ADJ & ADV en zigzag; VI zigzaguear, andar en zigzag; VT hacer zigzaguear

Zimbabwe [zɪmbábwe] N Zimbabue *m*

Zimbabwean [zɪmbábwean] ADJ & N zimbabuo -a *mf*

zinc [zɪŋk] N cinc *m*, zinc *m*

zip [zɪp] VI/VT cerrar/abrir con cremallera; **to — by** pasar volando; **to — over** ir corriendo; N cero *m*; **— code** código postal *m*

zipper [zípə-] N cremallera *f*, cierre (relámpago) *m*

zirconium [zɚkóniəm] N circonio *m*

zodiac [zódiæk] N zodíaco *m*

zombie [zámbi] N zombi *mf*

zone [zon] N zona *f*; VT dividir en zonas

zoo [zu] N zoológico *m*; *Sp* zoo *m*; **—keeper** guardián -ana del zoológico *mf*

zoological [zoolǽʤɪkəł] ADJ zoológico

zoology [zoáləʤi] N zoología *f*

zoom [zum] VI zumbar; **to — off** salir zumbando; N zumbido *m*; **— lens** teleobjetivo *m*, zoom *m*

zucchini [zukíni] N calabacín *m*

zygote [záɪgot] N cigoto *m*, zigoto *m*